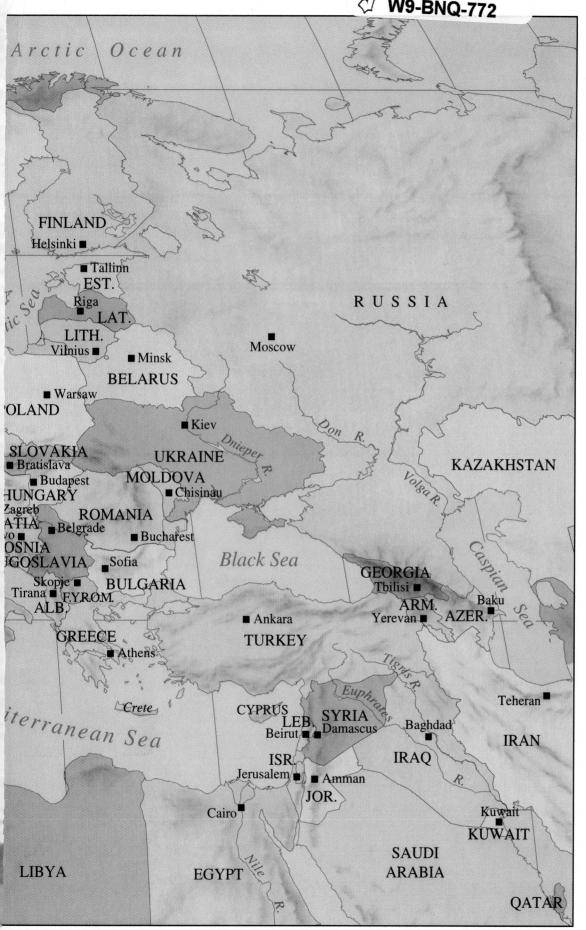

Arctic Ocean

FINLAND
Helsinki ■

■ Tallinn
EST.
Riga
■ LAT.
LITH.
Vilnius ■   ■ Minsk
BELARUS

RUSSIA

■ Warsaw
POLAND

Moscow ■

SLOVAKIA
■ Bratislava
■ Budapest
HUNGARY
Zagreb
ATIA
vo ■
OSNIA
GOSLAVIA

Kiev ■
Dnieper R.

UKRAINE
MOLDOVA
■ Chisinau

Don R.

Volga R.

KAZAKHSTAN

ROMANIA
■ Belgrade
■ Bucharest

Sofia
■ Sofia

Black Sea

Caspian Sea

GEORGIA
Tbilisi ■
ARM.
Yerevan ■   Baku
AZER. ■

Skopje ■
Tirana ■ F.Y.R.O.M.
ALB.

BULGARIA

■ Ankara

TURKEY

GREECE
■ Athens

Crete

Tigris R.

Euphrates

Teheran ■

iterranean Sea

CYPRUS
LEB. SYRIA
Beirut ■ Damascus ■   Baghdad ■

IRAN

ISR.
Jerusalem ■ ■ Amman
JOR.

IRAQ

R.

Cairo ■

Kuwait ■
KUWAIT

LIBYA

EGYPT

Nile R.

SAUDI
ARABIA

QATAR

www.wadsworth.com

wadsworth.com is the World Wide Web site for Wadsworth Publishing Company and is your direct source to dozens of online resources.

At *wadsworth.com* you can find out about supplements, demonstration software, and student resources. You can also send e-mail to many of our authors and preview new publications and exciting new technologies.

wadsworth.com
Changing the way the world learns®

FOURTH

EDITION

Western Civilization

Since 1300

Jackson J. Spielvogel

The Pennsylvania State University

Australia • Canada • Denmark • Japan • Mexico • New Zealand
Philippines • Puerto Rico • Singapore • South Africa • Spain
United Kingdom • United States

History Publisher: *Clark Baxter*
Senior Development Editor: *Sharon Adams Poore*
Assistant Editor: *Cherie Hackelberg*
Editorial Assistant: *Melissa Gleason*
Marketing Manager: *Jay Hu*
Print Buyer: *Barbara Britton*
Permissions Editor: *Susan Walters*
Interior and Cover Designer: *Norman Baugher*
Production Service: *Jon Peck, Dovetail Publishing Services*
Copy Editor: *Patricia Lewis*

Photo Researcher: *Sarah Evertson, Image Quest*
Maps: *MapQuest.com, Inc.*
Compositor: *New England Typographic Service*
Printer/Binder: *World Color, Versailles*
Cover Printer: *Phoenix Color Corp.*
Cover and page iv image: *Lesueur, Jean Baptiste and Pierre Antoine Lesueur,* Patriotic Women's Club. *Gouache. Musee de la Ville de Paris, Musee Carnavalet, Paris, France. Giraudon/Art Resource. NY*
Photo Credits begin on page xxv

Wadsworth/Thomson Learning
10 Davis Drive
Belmont, CA 94002-3098
USA
www.wadsworth.com

International Headquarters
Thomson Learning
290 Harbor Drive, 2nd Floor
Stamford, CT 06902-7477
USA

UK/Europe/Middle East
Thomson Learning
Berkshire House
168-173 High Holborn
London WC1V 7AA
United Kingdom

Asia
Thomson Learning
60 Albert Street #15-01
Albert Complex
Singapore 189969

Canada
Nelson/Thomson Learning
1120 Birchmount Road
Scarborough, Ontario M1K 5G4
Canada

Printed in the United States of America
1 2 3 4 5 6 7 03 02 01 00 99

ISBN: 0-534-56841-6

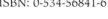

About the Author

*J*ackson J. Spielvogel is associate professor of history at
*The Pennsylvania State University. He received his Ph.D. from
The Ohio State University, where he specialized in Reformation*
history under Harold J. Grimm. *His articles and reviews have appeared
in such journals as* Moreana, Journal of General Education, Catholic
Historical Review, Archiv für Reformationsgeschichte, *and* American
Historical Review. *He has also contributed chapters or articles to* The
Social History of the Reformation, The Holy Roman Empire: A
Dictionary Handbook, Simon Wiesenthal Center Annual of Holocaust
Studies, *and* Utopian Studies. *His work has been supported by fellow-
ships from the Fulbright Foundation and the Foundation for Reformation
Research. At Penn State, he helped inaugurate the Western civilization
courses as well as a popular course on Nazi Germany. His book* Hitler
and Nazi Germany *was published in 1987 (third edition, 1996). He is
the co-author (with William Duiker) of* World History, *published in
January 1994 (second edition, 1998). Professor Spielvogel has won five
major university-wide teaching awards. During the year 1988–1989, he
held the Penn State Teaching Fellowship, the university's most prestigious teaching award. In 1996, he won the Dean Arthur Ray Warnock
Award for Outstanding Faculty Member. In 1997, he became the first
winner of the Schreyer Institute's Student Choice Award for innovative
and inspiring teaching.*

*To Diane,
whose love and support
made it all possible*

Brief Contents

Detailed Contents

❊ C H A P T E R 2 7
The Deepening of the European Crisis: World War II 815

❊ C H A P T E R 2 8
Cold War and a New Western World, 1945–1970 847

❊ C H A P T E R 2 9
The Contemporary Western World (since 1970) 879

Documents

Maps

Chronologies

Photo Credits

Art, New York, Acquired through the Lillie P. Bliss Bequest; **722** (top) Pablo Picasso, *Les Demoiselles d'Avignon*, Paris (Begun May reworked July 1907), Oil on canvas, 96 x 92″, Collection, The Museum of Modern Art, New York, Acquired through the Lillie P. Bliss Bequest, © 2000 Estate of Pablo Picasso/Artist Right's Society (ARS), New York; **722** (bottom) Vasily Kandinsky, *Painting with White Border*, May 1913, The Solomon R. Guggenheim Museum, New York; **723** Corbis; **726** Courtesy of Central Zionist Archives, Jerusalem; **729** David King Collection, London; **732** North Wind Picture Archives; **744** E.T. Archive, London

✳ C H A P T E R 2 5
747 Librarie Larousse, Paris; **750** Corbis; **754** Librarie Larousse, Paris; **755** Roger-Viollet/The Liaison Agency; **758** (bottom) Archive Photos; **758** (top) Librarie Larousse, Paris; **759** Bilderdienst Suddeutscher Verlag, Munich; **762** Corbis; **763** E.T. Archive, London; **765** © Ullstein Bilderdienst; **768** Sovfoto; **769** Brown Brothers; **776** Hulton-Getty/The Liaison Agency

✳ C H A P T E R 2 6
781 Hugo Jaeger, Life Magazine, © Time Warner, Inc.; **783** Corbis; **784** Roger-Viollet/The Liaison Agency; **791** Wide World Photos; **797** Hugo Jaeger, Life Magazine, © Time Warner, Inc.; **799** Hugo Jaeger, Life Magazine, © Time Warner, Inc.; **801** Paulman, 10 November, 1938, Photo © Bildarchiv Preussischer Kulturbesitz, Berlin; **804** David King Collection, London; **807** Courtesy of the Ford Motor Company; **809** Erich Lessing/Art Resource, NY Höch, Hannah. *Cut With the Kitchen Knife*, Photomontage. 1919. © 2000 Copyright Artist's Rights Society, (ARS), NY, VG Bild-Kunst, Bonn; **810** Salvador Dali, *The Persistence of Memory*, 1931, Oil on canvas, 9 1/2 x 13″, Collection the Museum of Modern Art, New York, Given Anonymously, © 2000 Artist Right's Society, (ARS), New York; **811** Gian Berto Vanni/Art Resource, NY

✳ C H A P T E R 2 7
815 Hugo Jaeger, Life Magazine, © Time Warner, Inc.; **820** Hugo Jaeger, Life Magazine, © Time Warner, Inc.; **823** National Archives, (#306-NT-1222E); **824** Hulton Getty/ The Liaison Agency; **826** Topham/The Image Works; **829** National Archives, (#111-C-273); **832** YIVO Institute for Jewish Research, Courtesy of the USHMM Photo Archives; **833** Courtesy of the U.S. Holocaust Museum, Washington D.C.; **836** Imperial War Museum, London; **839** The Herald and Evening Times Picture Library, © Caledonian Newspapers, Ltd.; **840** J.R. Eyerman, Life Magazine, © Time Warner, Inc.; **842** E.T. Archive

✳ C H A P T E R 2 8
847 © Prache-Lewin/Sygma; **849** School of Slavonic and Eastern European Studies, University of London; **850** Corbis; **854** Corbis; **857** © Marc Riboud/Magnum Photos; **861** Camera Press, (Jugo) London; **863** © Prache-Lewin/Sygma; **864** © Pierre Boulat-Cosmos/Woodfin Camp & Associates; **869** © Bob Adelman/Magnum Photos; **870** © Hulton Getty/The Liaison Agency; **872** Wide World Photos; **874** Archive Photos; **876** © C. Raimond-Dityvon/ Woodfin Camp & Associates

✳ C H A P T E R 2 9
879 Wide World Photos; **881** Wide World Photos; **885** Wide World Photos; **889** (top) Geroges Merillon/The Liaison Agency; **889** (bottom) Alexandra Avakian/Woodfin Camp & Associates; **890** Corbis; **891** Wide World Photos; **896** Mark Stewart/Camera Press, London; **899** Wide World Photos; **901** Wide World Photos; **903** Hans Namuth/Photo Researchers, Inc.; **904** Courtesy of The Museum of Contemporary Art, Los Angeles, CA; **905** Bruno Barbey/ Magnum Photos; **908** Courtesy of NASA; **911** Wide World Photos; **913** Courtesy of NASA

Preface

We are often reminded how important it is to understand today's world if we are to deal with our growing number of challenges. And yet that understanding will be incomplete if we in the Western world do not comprehend the meaning of Western civilization and the role Western civilization has played in the world. For all of our modern progress, we still greatly reflect our religious traditions, our political systems and theories, our economic and social structures, and our cultural heritage. I have written this history of Western civilization to assist a new generation of students in learning more about the past that has helped create them and the world in which they live.

As a teacher of Western civilization courses at a major university, I have become aware of the tendency of many textbooks to simplify the content of Western civilization courses by emphasizing an intellectual perspective or political perspective or, most recently, a social perspective, often at the expense of sufficient details in a chronological framework. This approach is confusing to students whose high school social studies programs have often neglected a systematic study of Western civilization. I have attempted to write a well-balanced work in which the political, economic, social, religious, intellectual, cultural, and military aspects of Western civilization have been integrated into a chronologically ordered synthesis. I have been especially aware of the need to integrate the latest research on social history and women's history into each chapter of the book rather than isolating it either in lengthy topical chapters, which confuse the student by interrupting the chronological narrative, or in separate sections that appear at periodic intervals between chapters. If the results of the new social and women's history are to be taken seriously, they must be fully integrated into the basic narrative itself.

Another purpose in writing this history of Western civilization has been to put the story back in history. That story is an exciting one; yet many textbooks, often the product of several authors with different writing styles, fail to capture the imagination of their readers. Narrative history effectively transmits the knowledge of the past and is the form that best aids remembrance. At the same time, I have not overlooked the need for the kind of historical analysis that makes students aware that historians often disagree in their interpretations of the past.

To enliven the past and let readers see for themselves the materials that historians use to create their pictures of the past, I have included in each chapter primary sources (boxed documents) that are keyed to the discussion in the text. The documents include examples of the religious, artistic, intellectual, social, economic, and political aspects of Western life. Such varied sources as a Roman banquet menu, a student fight song in twentieth-century Britain, letters exchanged between a husband on the battle front and his wife in World War I, the Declaration of the Rights of Woman and the Citizen in the French Revolution, and a debate in the Reformation era all reveal in a vivid fashion what Western civilization meant to the individual men and women who shaped it by their activities.

Each chapter has a lengthy introduction and conclusion to help maintain the continuity of the narrative and to provide a synthesis of important themes. Anecdotes in the chapter introductions convey more dramatically the major theme or themes of each chapter. Detailed chronologies reinforce the events discussed in the text while timelines at the end of each chapter enable students to review at a glance the major developments of an era. An annotated bibliography at the end of each chapter reviews the most recent literature on each period and also gives references to some of the older, "classic" works in each field. Extensive maps and illustrations serve to deepen the reader's understanding of the text. To facilitate understanding of cultural movements, illustrations of artistic works discussed in the text are placed next to the discussions. New to the fourth edition are chapter outlines and focus questions at the beginning of each chapter, which will help students with an overview and guide them to the main subjects of each chapter. Also new to the fourth edition are a glossary of important terms and a pronunciation guide.

As preparation for the revision of *Western Civilization*, I reexamined the entire book and analyzed the comments and reviews of many colleagues who have found the book to be a useful instrument for introducing their students to the history of Western civilization. In making revisions for the fourth edition, I sought to build upon the strengths of the first, second, and third editions and, above all, to maintain the balance, synthesis, and narrative qualities that characterized those editions. To keep up with the ever-growing body of historical scholarship, new or revised material has been added throughout the book on many topics, including, for example, civilization in Mesopotamia and Egypt; ancient Israel; Corinth, Sparta, and tyranny in ancient Greece; literature in the late Roman Republic; the late Roman Empire; women in early Christianity and the new Germanic kingdoms; the rise and spread of Islam; the Black Death; Catherine of Siena; Christine de Pizan; European discovery and expansion in the sixteenth and seventeenth centuries; the French Wars of Religion; Artemisia Gentileschi; Judith Leyster and Dutch realism; Louis XIV; nobility in the eighteenth century; female utopian socialists; women and work in the nineteenth century; women and the Paris commune; Impressionism; women reformers and the "new woman" in the nineteenth century; the history of Canada; the Great Depression; movies in the 1920s and 1930s; new attitudes toward sexuality in the 1920s; women in World War II resistance movements; history of the United States and Canada since 1945; gender issues in the welfare state; the women's liberation movement; and the war in Kosovo. Throughout the revising process I also worked to craft a book that I hope students will continue to find very readable. New subheadings were added in many chapters of the fourth edition in order to facilitate the reader's comprehension of the content of the chapters.

To provide a more logical arrangement of the material, I also made organizational changes in Chapters 1, 6, 14, 28, and 29. Chapters 9, 10, and 11 on the High Middle Ages were reorganized and condensed to form two new chapters entitled "The Recovery and Growth of European Society in the High Middle Ages" and "A New World of Cities and Kingdoms." Moreover, all "Suggestions for Further Reading" at the end of each chapter were updated, and new illustrations were added to every chapter.

The enthusiastic response to the primary sources (boxed documents) led me to evaluate the content of each document carefully and add new documents throughout the text, including "The Legal Rights of Women," "A Leader of the Paris Commune," "Hesse and the Unconcious," and "Margaret Thatcher: Entering a Man's World." For the fourth edition, the maps have been revised where needed and, as in previous editions, are carefully keyed to all text references. New maps have also been added, including "Religious Groups in the Eighteenth Century," "The Columbian Exchange," and "The Holocaust."

Because courses in Western civilization at American and Canadian colleges and universities follow different chronological divisions, a one-volume edition, two two-volume editions, and a three-volume edition of this text are being made available to fit the needs of instructors. Teaching and learning ancillaries include the following:

✳ *For the Instructor*

Instructor's Manual with Test Bank Prepared by Kevin Robbins, Indiana University Purdue University Indianapolis. This new Instructor's Manual contains chapter outlines, suggested lecture topics, and discussion questions for the maps and artwork as well as the primary source documents located in the text. Worldwide Web sites and resources, video collections, suggested student activities, and secondary sources for lecture preparation are also included. Exam questions include essays, identifications, and multiple-choice questions. Available in two volumes.

Thomson World Class Learning Testing Tools This fully integrated suite of test creation, delivery, and classroom management tools includes Thomson World Class Test, Test Online, and World Class Management software. Available for Windows and Macintosh.

Full Color Map Acetate Package This package includes maps from the text and from other sources. More than 100 four color images are provided in a handy three-ring binder. Map commentary is provided by James Harrison, Siena College.

Map Slides 100 full color map slides.

Lecture Enrichment Slides Prepared by Dale Hoak and George Strong, College of William and Mary. These 100 slides contain images of famous paintings, statues, architectural achievements, and interesting photos. The authors supply commentary for each slide.

History Video Library A completely new selection of videos to go with the fourth edition. Over 50 titles to choose from, with coverage spanning from "Egypt: A Gift to Civilization" to "Children of the Holocaust."

CNN Today Videos For *Western Civilization*, the perfect lecture launchers contain video clips ranging from one to five minutes long.

Sights and Sounds of History Videodisc and Video Short Uses focused video clips, photos, artwork, animations, music, and dramatic readings to bring history to life. The video segments average four minutes long and are available on VHS. These make excellent lecture launchers.

PowerPoint Features acetate map images in PowerPoint format. Available for Windows and Macintosh.

✳ *For the Student*

Study Guide Prepared by James Baker, Western Kentucky University. Includes chapter outlines, chapter summaries, and seven different types of questions for each chapter. Available in two volumes.

Study Tips Prepared by James Baker, Western Kentucky University. Provides a brief study guide for students containing chapter outlines, study questions, and pronunciations. Available in two volumes.

Map Exercise Workbook   This workbook, prepared by Cynthia Kosso, Northern Arizona University, has been thoroughly revised including new easier to read maps. Over 20 maps and exercises ask students to identify important cities and countries and answer critical thinking questions. Available in two volumes.

MapTutor CD ROM   This interactive map tutorial helps students learn geography by having them locate geographical features, regions, cities, and sociopolitical movements. Each map exercise is accompanied by questions that test their knowledge and promote critical thinking. Animations vividly show movements such as the conquests of the Romans, the spread of Christianity, invasions, medieval trade routes, the spread of the Black Death, and more.

Document Exercise Workbook   Prepared by Donna Van Raaphorst, Cuyahoga Community College. A collection of exercises based on primary sources. Revised for this edition, it now contains a web component that points students to museums and other useful sites. Available in two volumes.

Journey of Civilizations CD ROM   This CD-Rom takes the student on 18 interactive journeys through history. Enhanced with QuickTime movies, animations, sound clips, maps, and more, the journeys allow students to engage in history as active participants rather than as readers of past events. Available for Windows.

WebTutor   This customized online study supplement helps students succeed by taking the course beyond the classroom boundaries to a virtual environment. Professors can use *WebTutor* to provide virtual office hours, post their syllabi, set up threaded discussions, and track student progress with the quizzing material. For Students, *WebTutor* offers real-time access to a full array of study tools, including flashcards, practice quizzes and tests, online tutorials, exercises, discussion questions, web links, and a full glossary. Visit www.itped.com for a demonstration.

Hammond Historical Atlas of the World   This atlas helps integrate dozens of maps into the course.

Internet Guide for History, 2/e   Prepared by John Soares. Provides newly revised and up-to-date internet exercises by topic.

Western Civilization, Canadian Supplement   Prepared by Maryann Farkus, Dawson College. Discusses Canadian history and culture in the context of Western Civilization.

Archer, Documents of Western Civilization   Contains a broad selection of carefully chosen documents. Available in two volumes.

InfoTrac® College Edition   Create your own collection of secondary readings from more than 900 popular and scholarly periodicals such as *Smithsonian*, *Historian*, and *Harper's* for four months. Students can browse, choose, and print any articles they want 24 hours a day.

Historic Times: The Wadsworth History Resource Center   A web site just for history students. Features links to museums, documents, and other Web sites. http://history.wadsworth.com

✺ *Acknowledgements*

I began to teach at age five in my family's grape arbor. By the age of ten, I wanted to know and understand everything in the world so I set out to memorize our entire set of encyclopedia volumes. At seventeen, as editor of the high school yearbook, I chose "Patterns" as its theme. With that as my early history, followed by twenty rich years of teaching, writing, and family nurturing, it seemed quite natural to accept the challenge of writing a history of Western civilization as I approached that period in life often described as the age of wisdom. Although I see this writing adventure as part of the natural unfolding of my life, I gratefully acknowledge that without the generosity of many others, it would not have been possible.

David Redles gave generously of his time and ideas, especially for Chapters 28 and 29. Chris Colin provided research on the history of music, while Laurie Batitto, Alex Spencer, Stephen Maloney, Shaun Mason, Peter Angelos, and Fred Schooley offered valuable editorial assistance. I deeply appreciate the valuable technical assistance provided by Dayton Coles. I am also thankful to the thousands of students whose questions and responses have caused me to see many aspects of Western civilization in new ways.

My ability to undertake a project of this magnitude was in part due to the outstanding European history teachers that I had as both an undergraduate and a graduate student. These included Kent Forster (modern Europe) and Robert W. Green (early modern Europe) at The Pennsylvania State University; and Franklin Pegues (medieval), Andreas Dorpalen (modern Germany), William MacDonald (ancient), and Harold J. Grimm (Renaissance and Reformation) at The Ohio State University. These teachers provided me with profound insights into Western civilization and also taught me by their examples that learning only becomes true understanding when it is accompanied by compassion, humility, and open-mindedness.

I would like to thank the many teachers and students who have used the first three editions of my *Western Civilization*. Their enthusiastic response to a textbook that was intended to put the story back in history and capture the imagination of the reader has been very gratifying. I especially thank the many teachers and students who made the effort to contact me personally to share their enthusiasm. I also want to thank Charmarie Blaisdell of Northeastern University for her detailed analysis of women's history in the third edition. Her suggestions were very valuable in preparing the fourth edition. Thanks to West/Wadsworth's comprehensive review process, many historians were asked to evaluate my manuscript and review the first, second, and third editions. I am grateful to the following for the innumerable suggestions that have greatly improved my work:

Paul Allen
  University of Utah
Gerald Anderson
  North Dakota State University
Letizia Argenteri
  University of San Diego
Roy A. Austensen
  Illinois State University
James A. Baer
  Northern Virginia Community College—Alexandria
James T. Baker
  Western Kentucky University
Patrick Bass
  Morningside College
John F. Battick
  University of Maine
Frederic J. Baumgartner
  Virginia Polytechnic Institute
Phillip N. Bebb
  Ohio University
Anthony Bedford
  Modesto Junior College
F. E. Beemon
  Middle Tennessee State University
Leonard R. Berlanstein
  University of Virginia
Douglas T. Bisson
  Belmont University
Charmarie Blaisdell
  Northeastern University
Stephen H. Blumm
  Montgomery County Community College
Hugh S. Bonar
  California State University
Werner Braatz
  University of Wisconsin—Oshkosh
Alfred S. Bradford
  University of Missouri
Maryann E. Brink
  College of William & Mary
Blaine T. Browne
  Broward Community College
J. Holden Camp, Jr.,
  Hillyer College, University of Hartford
Martha Carlin
  University of Wisconsin—Milwaukee
Jack Cargill
  Rutgers University
Elizabeth Carney
  Clemson University
Eric H. Cline
  Xavier University
Robert Cole
  Utah State University

William J. Connell
  Rutgers University
Nancy Conradt
  College of DuPage
Marc Cooper
  Southwest Missouri State
Richard A. Cosgrove
  University of Arizona
David A. Crain
  South Dakota State University
Michael F. Doyle
  Ocean County College
James W. Ermatinger
  University of Nebraska—Kearney
Porter Ewing
  Los Angeles City College
Carla Falkner
  Northeast Mississippi Community College
Steven Fanning
  University of Illinois—Chicago
Ellsworth Faris
  California State University—Chico
Gary B. Ferngren
  Oregon State University
Mary Helen Finnerty
  Westchester Community College
A. Z. Freeman
  Robinson College
Marsha Frey
  Kansas State University
Frank J. Frost
  University of California—Santa Barbara
Frank Garosi
  California State University—Sacramento
Richard M. Golden
  University of North Texas
Manuel G. Gonzales
  Diablo Valley College
Amy G. Gordon
  Denison University
Richard J. Grace
  Providence College
Hanns Gross
  Loyola University
John F. Guilmartin
  Ohio State University
Jeffrey S. Hamilton
  Gustavus Adolphus College
J. Drew Harrington
  Western Kentucky University
James Harrison
  Siena College
A. J. Heisserer
  University of Oklahoma

Betsey Hertzler
  Mesa Community College
Robert Herzstein
  University of South Carolina
Shirley Hickson
  North Greenville College
Martha L. Hildreth
  University of Nevada
Boyd H. Hill, Jr.
  University of Colorado—Boulder
Michael Hofstetter
  Bethany College
Donald C. Holsinger
  Seattle Pacific University
Frank L. Holt
  University of Houston
W. Robert Houston
  University of South Alabama
Paul Hughes
  Sussex County Community College
Richard A. Jackson
  University of Houston
Fred Jewell
  Harding University
Jenny M. Jochens
  Towson State University
William M. Johnston
  University of Massachusetts
Jeffrey A. Kaufmann
  Muscatine Community College
David O. Kieft
  University of Minnesota
Patricia Killen
  Pacific Lutheran University
William E. Kinsella, Jr.
  Northern Virginia Community College—Annandale
James M. Kittelson
  Ohio State University
Doug Klepper
  Santa Fe Community College
Cynthia Kosso
  Northern Arizona University
Clayton Miles Lehmann
  University of South Dakota
Diana Chen Lin
  Indiana University, Northwest
Ursula W. MacAffer
  Hudson Valley Community College
Harold Marcuse
  University of California—Santa Barbara
Mavis Mate
  University of Oregon
T. Ronald Melton
  Brewton Parker College
Jack Allen Meyer
  University of South Carolina

Eugene W. Miller, Jr.
The Pennsylvania State University—Hazleton

Thomas M. Mulhern
University of North Dakota

John Patrick Montano
University of Delaware

Rex Morrow
Trident Technical College

Pierce Mullen
Montana State University

Frederick I. Murphy
Western Kentucky University

William M. Murray
University of South Florida

Otto M. Nelson
Texas Tech University

Sam Nelson
Willmar Community College

John A. Nichols
Slippery Rock University

Lisa Nofzinger
Albuquerque Technical Vocational Institute

Chris Oldstone-Moore
Augustana College

Donald Ostrowski
Harvard University

James O. Overfield
University of Vermont

Matthew L. Panczyk
Bergen Community College

Kathleen Parrow
Black Hills State University

Carla Rahn Phillips
University of Minnesota

Keith Pickus
Wichita State University

Linda J. Piper
University of Georgia

Janet Polasky
University of New Hampshire

Charles A. Povlovich
California State University — Fullerton

Nancy Rachels
Hillsborough Community College

Charles Rearick
University of Massachusetts —Amherst

Jerome V. Reel, Jr.
Clemson University

Joseph Robertson
Gadsden State Community College

Jonathan Roth
San Jose State University

Constance M. Rousseau
Providence College

Julius R. Ruff
Marquette University

Richard Saller
University of Chicago

Magdalena Sanchez
Texas Christian University

Jack Schanfield
Suffolk County Community College

Roger Schlesinger
Washington State University

Joanne Schneider
Rhode Island College

Thomas C. Schunk
University of Wisconsin—Oshkosh

Kyle C. Sessions
Illinois State University

Linda Simmons
Northern Virginia Community College—Manassas

Donald V. Sippel
Rhode Island College

Glen Spann
Asbury College

John W. Steinberg
Georgia Southern University

Paul W. Strait
Florida State University

James E. Straukamp
California State University —Sacramento

Brian E. Strayer
Andrews University

Fred Suppe
Ball State University

Roger Tate
Somerset Community College

Tom Taylor
Seattle University

Jack W. Thacker
Western Kentucky University

Thomas Turley
Santa Clara University

John G. Tuthill
University of Guam

Maarten Ultee
University of Alabama

Donna L. Van Raaphorst
Cuyahoga Community College

Allen M. Ward
University of Connecticut

Richard D. Weigel
Western Kentucky University

Michael Weiss
Linn-Benton Community College

Arthur H. Williamson
California State University —Sacramento

Katherine Workman
Wright State University

Judith T. Wozniak
Cleveland State University

Walter J. Wussow
University of Wisconsin —Eau Claire

Edwin M. Yamauchi
Miami University

The editors at Wadsworth Publishing Company have been both helpful and congenial at all times. Hal Humphrey guided the overall production of the book with much insight. I especially wish to thank Clark Baxter, whose clever wit, wisdom, gentle prodding, and good friendship have added much depth to our working relationship. Sharon Adams Poore thoughtfully guided the preparation of outstanding teaching and learning ancillaries. Jon Peck, of Dovetail Publishing Services, was extremely cooperative and competent in the production of the book. Pat Lewis, an outstanding copyeditor, taught me much about the fine points of the English language. Sarah Evertson provided valuable assistance in obtaining new illustrations for the fourth edition.

We are grateful to the authors and publishers acknowledged here for their permission to reprint copyrighted material. We have made every reasonable effort to identify copyright owners of materials in the boxed documents. If any information is found to be incomplete, we will gladly make whatever additional acknowledgements might be necessary.

Above all, I thank my family for their support. The gifts of love, laughter, and patience from my daughters, Jennifer and Kathryn, my sons, Eric and Christian, and my daughter-in-law, Liz, were invaluable. My wife and best friend, Diane, contributed editorial assistance, wise counsel, and the loving support that made it possible for me to complete a project of this magnitude. I could not have written the book without her.

Introduction to Students of Western Civilization

Civilization, as historians define it, first emerged between 5,000 and 6,000 years ago when people began to live in organized communities with distinct political, military, economic, and social structures. Religious, intellectual, and artistic activities also assumed important roles in these early societies. The focus of this book is on Western civilization, a civilization that for most of its history has been identified with the continent of Europe. Its origins, however, go back to the Mediterranean basin, including lands in North Africa, and the Near East as well as Europe itself. Moreover, the spread of Europeans abroad led to the development of offshoots of Western civilization in other parts of the world.

Because civilized life includes all the deeds and experiences of people organized in communities, the history of a civilization must encompass a series of studies. An examination of Western civilization requires us to study the political, economic, social, military, cultural, intellectual, and religious aspects that make up the life of that civilization and show how they are interrelated. In so doing, we need also at times to focus on some of the unique features of Western civilization. Certainly, science played a crucial role in the development of modern Western civilization. Although such societies as those of the Greeks, the Romans, and medieval Europeans were based largely on a belief in the existence of a spiritual order, Western civilization experienced a dramatic departure to a natural or material view of the universe in the seventeenth-century Scientific Revolution. Science and technology have been important in the growth of a modern and largely secular Western civilization, although antecedents to scientific development also existed in Greek, Islamic, and medieval thought and practice.

Many historians have also viewed the concept of political liberty, the fundamental value of every individual, and the creation of a rational outlook, based on a system of logical, analytical thought, as unique aspects of Western civilization. Of course, Western civilization has also witnessed the frightening negation of liberty, individualism, and reason. Racism, violence, world wars, totalitarianism—these, too, must form part of the story. Finally, regardless of our concentration on Western civilization and its characteristics, we need to take into account that other civilizations have influenced Western civilization and it, in turn, has affected the development of other civilizations.

In our examination of Western civilization, we need also to be aware of the dating of time. In recording the past, historians try to determine the exact time when events occurred. World War II in Europe, for example, began on September 1, 1939, when Hitler sent German troops into Poland, and ended on May 7, 1945, when Germany surrendered. By using dates, historians can place events in order and try to determine the development of patterns over periods of time.

If someone asked you when you were born, you would reply with a number, such as 1980. In the United States, we would all accept that number without question because it is part of the dating system followed in the Western world (Europe and the Western Hemisphere). In this system, events are dated by counting backward or forward from the birth of Christ (assumed to be the year 1). An event that took place 400 years before the birth of Christ would be dated 400 B.C. (before Christ). Dates after the birth of Christ are labeled A.D. These letters stand for the Latin words anno Domini, which mean "in the year of the lord." Thus, an event that took place 250 years after the birth of Christ is written A.D. 250, or in the year of the lord 250. It can also be written as 250, just as you would not give your birth year as A.D. 1980, but simply 1980. Historians also make use of other terms to refer to time. A decade is 10 years; a century is 100 years; and a millennium is 1,000 years. The phrase fourth century B.C. refers to the fourth period of 100 years counting backward from 1, the assumed date of the birth of Christ. Since the first century B.C. would be the years 100 B.C. to 1 B.C., the fourth century B.C. would be the years 400 B.C. to 301 B.C. We could say, then, that an event in 350 B.C. took place in the fourth century B.C.

The phrase fourth century A.D. refers to the fourth period of 100 years after the birth of Christ. Since the first period of 100 years would be the years 1 to 100, the fourth period or fourth century would be the years 301 to 400. We could say, then, for example, that an event in 350 took place in the fourth century. Likewise, the first millennium B.C. refers to the years 1000 B.C. to 1 B.C.; the second millennium A.D. refers to the years 1001 to 2000. Some historians now prefer to use the abbreviations B.C.E. ("before the common era") and C.E. ("common era") instead of B.C. and A.D. This is espe-

cially true of world historians who prefer to use symbols that are not so Western or Christian oriented. The dates, of course, remain the same. Thus, 1950 B.C.E. and 1950 B.C. would be the same year. In keeping with current usage by many historians of Western civilization, this book will use the terms B.C. and A.D.

The dating of events can also vary from people to people. Most people in the Western world use the Western calendar, also known as the Gregorian calendar after Pope Gregory XIII who refined it in 1582. The Hebrew calendar, on the other hand, uses a different system in which the year 1 is the equivalent of the Western year 3760 B.C., considered by Jews to be the date of the creation of the world. Thus, the Western year 2000 will be the year 5760 on the Jewish calendar. The Islamic calendar begins year 1 on the day Muhammad fled Mecca, which is the year 622 on the Western calendar.

Western Civilization to 1300

The beginnings of Western civilization can be traced back to the ancient Near East, where people in Mesopotamia and Egypt developed organized societies and created the ideas and institutions that we associate with civilization. The later Greeks and Romans, who played such a crucial role in the development of Western civilization, were themselves nourished and influenced by these older societies in the Near East. Around 3000 B.C., people in Mesopotamia and Egypt began to develop cities and wrestle with the problems of organized states. They developed writing to keep records and created literature. They constructed monumental architecture to please their gods, symbol-

ize their power, and preserve their culture for all time. They developed new political, military, social, and religious structures to deal with the basic problems of human existence and organization. These first literate civilizations left detailed records that allow us to view how they grappled with three of the fundamental problems that humans have pondered: the nature of human relationships, the nature of the universe, and the role of divine forces in that cosmos. Although later peoples in Western civilization would provide different answers from those of the Mesopotamians and Egyptians, it was they who first posed the questions, gave answers, and wrote them down. Human memory begins with these two civilizations.

By 1500 B.C., much of the creative impulse of the Mesopotamian and Egyptian civilizations was beginning to wane. The entry of new peoples known as Indo-Europeans who moved into Asia Minor and Anatolia (modern Turkey) led to the creation of a Hittite kingdom that entered into conflict with the Egyptians. The invasion of the Sea Peoples around 1200 B.C., however, destroyed the Hittites, severely weakened the Egyptians, and created a power vacuum that allowed a patchwork of petty kingdoms and city-states to emerge, especially in the area of Syria and Palestine. These small states did not last, however. Ever since the first city-states had arisen in the Near East around 3000 B.C., there had been an ongoing movement toward the creation of larger territorial states with more sophisticated systems of control. This process reached a high point in the first millennium B.C. with the appearance of empires that embraced the entire Near East. Between 1000 and 500 B.C., the Assyrians, Chaldeans, and Persians all created empires that encompassed either large areas or all of the ancient Near East. The Assyrian Empire was the first to unite almost all of the ancient Near East. Even larger, however, was the empire of the Great Kings of Persia. Although it owed much to the administrative organization created by the Assyrians, the Persian Empire had its own peculiar strengths. Persian rule was tolerant as well as efficient. Conquered peoples were allowed to keep their own religions, customs, and methods of doing business. The many years of peace that the Persian Empire brought to the Near East facilitated trade and the general well-being of its peoples. It is no wonder that many Near Eastern peoples expressed their gratitude for being subjects of the Great Kings of Persia.

The Hebrews were one of these peoples. They created no empire and were dominated by the Assyrians, Chaldeans, and Persians in turn. Nevertheless, they left a spiritual legacy that influenced much of the later development of Western

civilization. The evolution of Hebrew monotheism (belief in a single god) created in Judaism one of the world's greatest religions; it influenced the development of both Christianity and Islam. When we speak of the Judaeo-Christian heritage of Western civilization, we refer not only to the concept of monotheism, but also to ideas of law, morality, and social justice that have become important parts of Western culture.

On the western fringes of the Persian Empire, another relatively small group of people, the Greeks, were creating cultural and political ideals that would also have an important impact on Western civilization. The first Greek civilization, known as Mycenaean civilization, took shape around 1600 B.C. and fell to new Greek-speaking invaders around 1100 B.C. The ensuing so-called Dark Age (c. 1100–c. 750 B.C.) did witness the creation of a system of writing and the work of Homer, whose ideals formed the basis of Greek education for hundreds of years. By the eighth century B.C., the polis or city-state had become the chief focus of Greek life. Loyalty to the polis created a close-knit community, but also divided Greece into a host of independent states. Two of them, Sparta and Athens, became the most important. They were very different, however. Sparta created a closed, highly disciplined society while Athens moved toward an open, democratic civilization.

The classical age in Greece (c. 500–338 B.C.) began with a mighty confrontation between the Greeks and the Persian Empire. After their victory over the Persians, the Greeks began to divide into two large

alliances, one headed by Sparta and the other by Athens. Athens created a naval empire and flourished during the age of Pericles, but fear of Athens led to the Great

Peloponnesian War between Sparta and Athens and their allies. For all of their brilliant accomplishments, the Greeks were unable to rise above the divisions and rivalries that caused them to fight each other and undermine their own civilization.

The accomplishments of the Greeks formed the fountainhead of Western culture. Socrates, Plato, and Aristotle established the foundations of Western philosophy. Herodotus and Thucydides created the discipline of history. Our literary forms are largely derived from Greek poetry and drama. Greek notions of harmony, proportion, and beauty have remained the touchstones for all subsequent Western art. A rational method of inquiry, so important to modern science, was conceived in ancient Greece. Many of our political terms are Greek in origin, and so too are our concepts of the rights and duties of citizenship, especially as they were conceived in Athens, the first great democracy the world had seen. Especially during their classical period, the Greeks raised and debated the fundamental questions about the purpose of human existence, the structure of human society, and the nature of the universe that have concerned Western thinkers ever since.

While the Greek city-states were continuing to fight each other, to their north a new and powerful kingdom—Macedonia—emerged in its own right. Under King Philip II, the Macedonians defeated a Greek allied army in 338 B.C. and then consolidated

their control over the Greek peninsula. Although the independent Greek city-states lost their freedom when they were conquered by the Macedonians, Greek culture did not die. Under the leadership of Alexander the Great, son of Philip II, both Macedonians and Greeks invaded and conquered the Persian Empire. In the conquered lands, Greeks and non-Greeks established a series of kingdoms (known as the Hellenistic kingdoms) and inaugurated the Hellenistic era.

The Hellenistic period was, in its own way, a vibrant one. New cities arose and flourished. New philosophical ideas captured the minds of many. Significant achievements occurred in art, literature, and science. Greek culture spread throughout the Near East and made an impact wherever it was carried. In some areas of the Hellenistic world, queens played an active role in political life, and many upper-class women found new avenues for expressing themselves.

But serious problems remained. Hellenistic kings continued to engage in inconclusive wars. The gulf between rich and poor was indeed great. Much of the formal culture was the special preserve of the Greek conquerors whose attitude of superiority kept them largely separated from the native masses of the Hellenistic kingdoms. Although the Hellenistic world achieved a degree of political stability, by the late third century B.C., signs of decline were beginning to multiply. Some of the more farsighted perhaps realized the danger presented to the Hellenistic world by the growing power of Rome.

Sometime in the eighth century B.C., a group of Latin-speaking people built a small community called Rome on the Tiber River in Italy. Between 509 and 264 B.C., this city expanded and united almost all of Italy under its control. Even more dramatically, between 264 and 133 B.C., Rome expanded to the west and east and became master of the Mediterranean Sea.

After 133 B.C., however, Rome's republican institutions proved inadequate for the task of ruling an empire. In the breakdown that ensued, ambitious individuals saw opportunities for power unparalleled in Roman history and succumbed to the temptations. After a series of bloody civil wars, peace was finally achieved when Octavian defeated Antony and Cleopatra. Octavian's real task was at hand: to create a new system of government that seemed to preserve the Republic while establishing the basis for a new system that would rule the empire in an orderly fashion. Octavian, who came to be known by the title of Augustus, proved equal to the task.

After a century of internal upheaval, Augustus established a new order that began the Roman Empire, which experienced a lengthy period of peace and prosperity between 14 and 180. During this era, trade flourished and the provinces were governed efficiently. In the course of the third century, however, the Roman Empire came near to collapse due to invasions, civil wars, and economic decline. Although the emperors Diocletian and Constantine brought new life to the so-called Late Empire at the beginning of the fourth century, their efforts only shored up the empire temporarily. In the course of the fifth century, the empire divided into western and eastern parts, and in 476, the Roman Empire in the west came to an end with the ouster of Emperor Romulus Augustulus.

The Roman Empire was the largest empire in antiquity. Using their practical skills, the Romans made achievements in language, law, engineering, and government that were bequeathed to the future. The Romance languages of today (French, Italian, Spanish, Portuguese, and Romanian) are based on Latin. Western practices of impartial justice and trial by jury owe much to Roman law. As great builders, the Romans left monuments to their skills throughout Europe, some of which, such as aqueducts and roads, are still in use today. Aspects of Roman administrative practices survived in the Western world for centuries. The Romans also preserved the intellectual heritage of the ancient world.

During its last two hundred years, a slow transformation of the Roman world took place with the spread of Christianity. The rise of Christianity marked an important break with the dominant values of the Roman world. Christianity began as a small Jewish sect, but under the guidance of Paul of Tarsus it became a world religion that appealed to both Jews and non-Jews. Despite persecution by Roman authorities, Christianity grew and became widely accepted by the fourth century. At the end of that century, it was made the official state religion of the Roman Empire.

The period that saw the disintegration of the western part of the Roman Empire also witnessed the emer-

gence of a new European civilization in the Early Middle Ages. The early medieval civilization that arose out of the collapse of the Western Roman Empire was formed by the coalescence of three major elements: the Germanic peoples who moved into the western part of the empire and established new kingdoms; the continuing attraction of the Greco-Roman cultural legacy; and the Christian church. Politically, a new series of Germanic kingdoms emerged in western Europe. Each fused Roman and Germanic elements to create a new society. The Christian church (or Roman Catholic church as it came to be called in the west) played a crucial role in the growth of the new European civilization. The church developed an organized government under the leadership of the pope. It also assimilated the classical tradition and through its clergy brought Christianized civilization to the Germanic tribes. Especially important were the monks and nuns who led the way in converting the Germanic peoples in Europe to Christianity.

At the end of the eighth century, a new kingdom—the Carolingian Empire—came to control much of western and central Europe, especially during the reign of Charlemagne. The pope's coronation of Charlemagne, descendant of a Germanic tribe that had converted to Christianity, as Roman emperor in 800 symbolized the fusion of the three chief components of the new European civilization: the German tribes, the classical tradition, and Christianity. In the long run, the creation of a western empire fostered the idea of a distinct European identity and marked the shift of power from the south to the north. Italy and the Mediterranean had been the center of the Roman Empire. The lands north of the Alps now became the political center of Europe, and increasingly, Europe emerged as the focus and center of Western civilization.

Building upon a fusion of Germanic, classical, and Christian elements, the medieval European world first became visible in the Carolingian Empire of Charlemagne. His empire was well governed, but was ultimately held together by personal loyalty to a strong king. The economy of the eighth and ninth centuries was based almost entirely on farming, however, and this proved inadequate to maintain a large monarchical system. As a result, a new political and military order—known as feudalism—subsequently evolved to become an integral part of the political world of the

Middle Ages. The feudal order was characterized by a decentralization of political power, in which lords exercised legal, administrative, and military power. The practice of feudalism transferred public power into many private hands and seemed to provide the security sorely lacking in a time of weak central government.

European civilization began on a shaky and uncertain foundation, however. In the ninth century, Vikings, Magyars, and Muslims posed threats that could easily have stifled the new society, but the new European civilization managed to meet these challenges. The Vikings and Magyars were assimilated, and recovery slowly began to set in. By 1000, European civilization was ready to embark upon a period of dazzling vitality and expansion.

The new European civilization that had emerged in the ninth and tenth centuries began to come into its own in the eleventh and twelfth centuries as Europeans established new patterns that reached their high point in the thirteenth century. The High Middle Ages (1000–1300) was a period of recovery and growth for Western civilization, characterized by a greater sense of security and a burst of energy and enthusiasm. Climatic improvements that produced better growing conditions, an expansion of cultivated land, and technological changes combined to enable Europe's food supply to increase significantly after

1000. This increase in agricultural production helped sustain a dramatic rise in population that was physically apparent in the expansion of towns and cities.

The development of trade and the rise of cities added a dynamic new element to the civilization of the High Middle Ages. Trading activities flourished first in northern Italy and Flanders and then spread outward from these centers. In the late tenth and eleventh centuries, this renewal of commercial life led to a revival of  cities. Old Roman sites came back to life while new towns arose at major crossroads or natural harbors favorable to trading activities. By the twelfth and thirteenth centuries, both the urban centers and the urban population of Europe were experiencing a dramatic expansion. The revival of trade, the expansion of towns and cities, and the development of a money economy did not mean the end of a predominantly rural European society, but they did open the door to new ways to make a living and new opportunities for people to expand and enrich their lives. Eventually, they created the foundations for the development of a predominantly urban industrial society. Commerce, cities, and a money economy also helped to undermine feudal institutions while strengthening monarchical authority.

During the High Middle Ages, European society was dominated by a landed aristocracy whose primary function was to fight. These nobles built innumerable castles that gave a distinctive look to the countryside. Although lords and vassals seemed forever mired in endless petty conflicts, over time medieval kings began to exert a centralizing authority and inaugurated the process of developing new kinds of monarchical states. By the thirteenth century, European monarchs were solidifying their governmental institutions in pursuit of greater power. The nobles, whose warlike attitudes were rationalized by labeling them the defenders of Christian society, continued to dominate the medieval world politically, economically, and socially. But quietly and surely, within this world of castles and private power, kings gradually began to extend their public powers and developed the machinery of government that would enable them to become the centers of political authority in Europe. Although they could not know it then, the actions of these medieval monarchs laid the foundation for the European kingdoms that in one form or another have dominated the European political scene ever since.

During the High Middle Ages, the power of both nobles and kings was often overshadowed by the authority of the Catholic church, perhaps the dominant institution of the High Middle Ages. In the Early Middle Ages, the Catholic church had shared in the challenge of new growth by reforming itself and striking out on a path toward greater papal power, both within the church and over European society. The High Middle Ages witnessed a spiritual renewal that led to numerous and even divergent paths: revived papal leadership, the development of centralized administrative machinery that buttressed papal authority, and new dimensions to the religious life of the clergy and laity. A wave of religious enthusiasm in the twelfth and thirteenth centuries led to the formation of new religious orders that worked to provide for the needs of the people, especially their concern for achieving salvation.

The economic, political, and religious growth of the High Middle Ages also gave European society a new confidence that enabled it to look beyond its borders to the lands and empires of the east. Only a confident Europe could have undertaken the crusades, the military effort to recover the Holy Land of the Near East from the Muslims. The crusades gave the revived papacy of the High Middle Ages yet another opportunity to demonstrate its influence over European society.

Western assurance and energy, so crucial to the crusades, were also evident in a burst of intellectual and artistic activity. New educational institutions known as universities came into being in the twelfth century. New literature, written in the vernacular language, appealed to the growing number of people in cities or at courts who could read. The study of theology, "queen of the sciences," reached a high point in the work of Thomas Aquinas. At the same time, a religious building spree—especially evident in the great Romanesque and Gothic cathedrals of the age—left the landscape bedecked with churches that were the visible symbols of Christian Europe's vitality.

Growth and optimism seemed to characterize the High Middle Ages, but underneath the calm exterior lay seeds of discontent and change. Dissent from church teaching and practices grew in the thirteenth century, leading to a climate of fear and intolerance as the church responded with inquisitorial instruments to enforce conformity to its teachings. Minorities of all kinds suffered intolerance and, worse still, persecution at the hands of people who worked to maintain the image of an ideal Christian society. The breakdown of the old agricultural system and the creation of new relationships between lords and peasants led to local peasant uprisings in the late thirteenth century. The crusades ended ignominiously with the fall of the last crusading foothold in the east in 1291. By that time, more and more signs of ominous troubles were appearing. The fourteenth century would prove to be a time of crisis for European civilization.

FOURTH
EDITION

Western
Civilization

Since 1300

CHAPTER 11

The Late Middle Ages: Crisis and Disintegration in the Fourteenth Century

CHAPTER OUTLINE

- A Time of Troubles: Black Death and Social Crisis
- War and Political Instability
- The Decline of the Church
- The Cultural World of the Fourteenth Century
- Society in an Age of Adversity
- Conclusion

FOCUS QUESTIONS

- What was the Black Death, and what was its impact on European society?
- What major problems did European states face in the fourteenth century?
- How and why did the authority and prestige of the papacy decline in the fourteenth century?
- What were the major developments in art and literature in the fourteenth century?
- How did the adversities of the fourteenth century affect urban life and medical practices?

*T*HE HIGH MIDDLE AGES *of the eleventh, twelfth, and thirteenth centuries had been a period of great innovation, evident in significant economic, social, political, religious, intellectual, and cultural changes. And yet, by the end of the thirteenth century, certain tensions had begun to creep into European society. In the course of the next century, these tensions became a torrent of troubles. At mid-century, one of the most destructive natural disasters in history erupted—the Black Death. One contemporary observer named Henry Knighton, a canon of Saint Mary-of-the-Meadow Abbey in Leicester, England, was simply overwhelmed by the magnitude of the catastrophe. Knighton began his account of the great plague with these words: "In this year [1348] and in the following one there was a general mortality of people throughout the whole world." Few were left untouched; the plague struck even isolated monasteries: "At Montpellier, there remained out of a hundred and forty friars only seven." Animals, too, were devastated: "During this same year, there was a great mortality of sheep* *everywhere in the kingdom; in one place and in one pasture, more than five thousand sheep died and became so putrefied that neither beast nor bird wanted to touch them." Knighton was also stunned by the economic and social consequences of the Black Death. Prices dropped: "And the price of everything was cheap, because of the fear of death; there were very few who took any care for their wealth, or for anything else." Meanwhile laborers were scarce, so their wages increased: "In the following autumn, one could not hire a reaper at a lower wage than eight pence with food, or a mower at less than twelve pence with food. Because of this, much grain rotted in the fields for lack of harvesting." So many people died that some towns were deserted and some villages disappeared altogether: "Many small villages and hamlets were completely deserted; there was not one house left in them, but all those who had lived in them were dead." Some people thought the end of the world was at hand.*

Plague was not the only disaster in the fourteenth century. Signs of disintegration were everywhere: famine, economic depression, war, social upheaval, a rise in crime and violence, and a decline in the power of the universal Catholic church. Periods of disintegration, however, are often fertile grounds for change and new developments. Out of the dissolution of medieval civilization came a rebirth of culture that many historians have labeled the Renaissance.

◆ A Time of Troubles: Black Death and Social Crisis

Well into the thirteenth century, Europe had experienced good harvests and an expanding population. By the end of the thirteenth century, however, a period of disastrous changes had begun.

✷ *Famine and Population*

By the end of the thirteenth and beginning of the fourteenth century, there were noticeable changes in weather patterns as Europe entered a period that has been called a "little ice age." A small shift in overall temperature patterns resulted in shortened growing seasons and disastrous weather conditions, including heavy storms and constant rain. Between 1315 and 1317, northern Europe experienced heavy rains that destroyed harvests and caused serious food shortages, resulting in extreme hunger and starvation. The great famine of 1315–1317 in northern Europe became an all-too-familiar pattern. Southern Europe, for example, seems to have been struck by similar conditions, especially in the 1330s and 1340s. Hunger

became widespread, and the scene described by this chronicler became common:

> We saw a larger number of both sexes, not only from nearby places but from as much as five leagues away, barefooted and maybe even, except for women, in a completely nude state, together with their priests coming in procession at the Church of the Holy Martyrs, their bones bulging out, devoutly carrying bodies of saints and other relics to be adorned hoping to get relief.[1]

Some historians estimate that famine killed 10 percent of the European population in the first half of the fourteenth century.

Europe had experienced a great increase in population in the High Middle Ages. By 1300, however, indications are that Europe had reached the upper limit of its population, not in an absolute sense, but in the number of people who could be supported by existing agricultural production and technology. Virtually all productive land was being farmed, including many marginal lands that needed intensive cultivation and proved easily susceptible to changing weather patterns. We know that there was also a movement from overpopulated rural areas to urban locations. Eighteen percent of the people in the village of Broughton in England, for example, migrated between 1288 and 1340. There is no certainty that these migrants found better economic opportunities in urban areas. We might, in fact, conclude the opposite based on the reports of increasing numbers of poor people in the cities. In 1330, for example, one chronicler estimated that of the 100,000 inhabitants of Florence, 17,000 were paupers. Moreover, evidence suggests that because of the increase in population, individual peasant holdings by 1300 were shrinking in size to an acreage that could no longer support a peasant family. Europe seemed to have reached an upper limit to population growth, and the number of poor appeared to have increased noticeably.

Although the extent to which famine contributed to the decline of population in the early fourteenth century is unclear, some historians have pointed out that it could have had other effects on the surviving population. Famine may have led to chronic malnutrition, which in turn contributed to increased infant mortality, lower birthrates, and higher susceptibility to disease since malnourished people are less able to resist infection. This, they argue, helps to explain the high mortality of the great plague known as the Black Death.

✷ *The Black Death*

The Black Death of the mid-fourteenth century was the most devastating natural disaster in European history. It ravaged Europe, wiping out 25 to 50 percent of the population and causing economic, social, political, and cultural upheaval. Contemporary chroniclers lamented that parents abandoned their children; one related the words: "Oh father, why have you abandoned me? . . . Mother, where have you gone?"[2] People were horrified by an evil

MASS BURIAL OF PLAGUE VICTIMS. The Black Death spread to northern Europe by the end of 1348. Shown here is a mass burial of victims of the plague in Tournai, located in modern Belgium. As is evident in the illustration, at this stage of the plague, there was still time to make coffins for the victims' burial. Later, as the plague intensified, the dead were thrown into open pits.

force they could not understand and by the subsequent breakdown of all normal human relations.

The Black Death was all the more horrible because it was the first major epidemic disease to strike Europe since the seventh century, an absence that helps explain medieval Europe's remarkable population growth. This great plague originated in central Asia. It was spread, it is believed, both by the Mongols as they expanded across Asia and by central Asian rodents that moved westward when ecological changes made their homeland inhospitable.

Bubonic plague, which was the most common and most important form of plague in the diffusion of the Black Death, was spread by black rats infested with fleas who were host to the deadly bacterium *Yersinia pestis*. Symptoms of bubonic plague included high fever, aching joints, swelling of the lymph nodes, and dark blotches caused by bleeding beneath the skin. Bubonic plague was actually the least toxic form of plague, but nevertheless killed 50 to 60 percent of its victims. In pneumonic plague, the bacterial infection spread to the lungs, resulting in severe coughing, bloody sputum, and the relatively easy spread of the bacillus from human to human by coughing. Fortunately, this more deadly form of the plague occurred less frequently than bubonic plague. Very rare was septicemic plague, which was carried by insects. It was extremely lethal—a victim usually died within one day of the initial infection.

The plague reached Europe in October of 1347 when Genoese merchants brought it from the Black Sea to the island of Sicily off the coast of southern Italy. It spread quickly, reaching southern Italy and southern France and Spain by the end of 1347. Usually, the diffusion of the Black Death followed commercial trade routes. In 1348, the plague spread through France and the Low Countries and into Germany. By the end of that year, it had reached England, which it ravaged in 1349. By the end of 1349, it had expanded to northern Europe and Scandinavia. East-

ern Europe and Russia were affected by 1351, although mortality rates were never as high in eastern Europe as they were in western and central Europe.

Mortality figures for the Black Death were incredibly high. Italy was especially hard hit. As the commercial center of the Mediterranean, Italy possessed scores of ports where the plague could be introduced. Italy's crowded cities, whether large, such as Florence, Genoa, and Venice with populations near 100,000, or small, such as Orvieto and Pistoia, suffered losses of 50 to 60 percent (see the box on p. 300). France and England were also particularly devastated. In northern France, farming villages suffered mortality rates of 30 percent, while cities such as Rouen were more severely affected and experienced losses of 30 to 40 percent. In England and Germany, entire villages simply disappeared from history. In Germany, of approximately 170,000 inhabited locations, only 130,000 were left by the end of the fourteenth century. Overall, however, Germany suffered less than France and England.

It has been estimated that the European population declined by 25 to 50 percent between 1347 and 1351. If we accept the recent scholarly assessment of a European population of 75 million in the early fourteenth century, this means a death toll of 19 to 38 million people in four years. Moreover, the plague did not end in 1351. There were major outbreaks again in 1361–1362 and 1369 and then recurrences every five or six to ten or twelve years depending on climatic and ecological conditions during the remainder of the fourteenth century and all of the fifteenth century. Recent estimates are that the European population declined between 60 and 75 percent between 1347 and 1450 and did not begin to recover until the end of the fifteenth century; not until the mid-sixteenth century did Europe begin to regain its thirteenth-century population levels. Even then, recurrences of the plague did not end until the beginning of the eighteenth century.

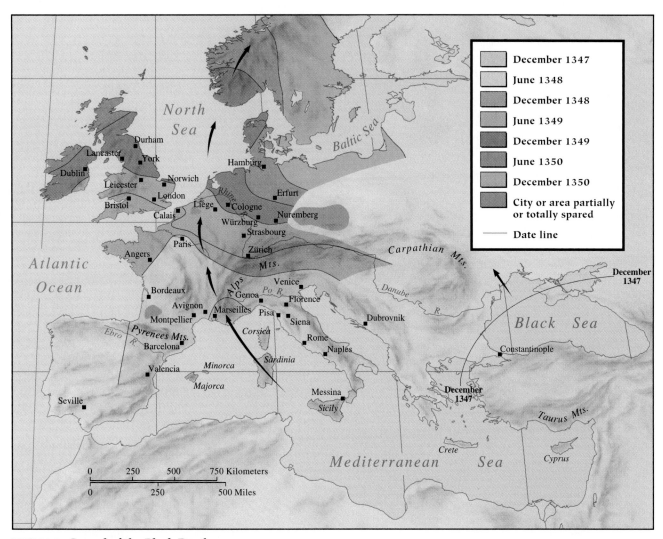

MAP 11.1 Spread of the Black Death.

LIFE AND DEATH: REACTIONS TO THE PLAGUE

Natural disasters of the magnitude of the great plague produce extreme psychological reactions. There were acts of heroism and great courage. Stories abound of priests and nuns who stayed with the suffering until they themselves died of the plague. Many other clergymen fled for their lives as fast as they could. Living for the moment, some people threw themselves with abandon into sexual and alcoholic orgies. The fourteenth-century Italian writer Giovanni Boccaccio gave a classic description of this kind of reaction to the plague in Florence in the preface to his famous work *The Decameron*:

> Others, arriving at a contrary conclusion, held that plenty of drinking and enjoyment, singing and free living and the gratification of the appetite in every possible way, letting the devil take the hindmost, was the best preventative of such a malady; and as far as they could, they suited the action to the word. Day and night they went from one tavern to another drinking and carousing unrestrainedly. At the least inkling of something that suited them, they ran wild in other people's houses, and there was no one to prevent them, for everyone had abandoned all responsibility for his belongings as well as for himself, considering his days numbered.[3]

Wealthy and powerful people fled to their country estates, as Boccaccio recounted: "Still others . . . maintained that no remedy against plagues was better than to leave them miles behind. Men and women without number . . . caring for nobody but themselves, abandoned the city, their houses and estates, their own flesh and blood even, and their effects, in search of a country place."[4]

The attempt to explain the Black Death and mitigate its harshness led to extreme sorts of behavior. To many, the plague had either been sent by God as a punishment for humans' sins or caused by the devil. Some resorted to extreme asceticism to cleanse themselves of sin and gain God's forgiveness. Such were the flagellants who became a popular movement in 1348, especially in Germany. Groups of flagellants, both men and women, wandered from town to town, flogging themselves with whips to win the forgiveness of a God whom they felt had

The Black Death

The Black Death was the most terrifying natural calamity of the entire Middle Ages. It has been estimated that 25 to 50 percent of the population died as the plague spread throughout Europe between 1347 and 1351. This contemporary description of the great plague in Florence is taken from the preface to The Decameron *by the fourteenth-century Italian writer Giovanni Boccaccio.*

❉ Giovanni Boccaccio, *The Decameron*

In the year of Our Lord 1348 the deadly plague broke out in the great city of Florence, most beautiful of Italian cities. Whether through the operation of the heavenly bodies or because of our own iniquities which the just wrath of God sought to correct, the plague had arisen in the East some years before, causing the death of countless human beings. It spread without stop from one place to another, until, unfortunately, it swept over the West. Neither knowledge nor human foresight availed against it, though the city was cleansed of much filth by chosen officers in charge and sick persons were forbidden to enter it, while advice was broadcast for the preservation of health. Nor did humble supplications serve. Not once but many times they were ordained in the form of processions and other ways for the propitiation of God by the faithful, but, in spite of everything, toward the spring of the year the plague began to show its ravages. . . .

It did not manifest itself as in the East, where if a man bled at the nose he had certain warning of inevitable death. At the onset of the disease both men and women were afflicted by a sort of swelling in the groin or under the armpits which sometimes attained the size of a common apple or egg. Some of these swellings were larger and some smaller, and were commonly called boils. From these two starting points the boils began in a little while to spread and appear generally all over the body. Afterwards, the manifestation of the disease changed into black or livid spots on the arms, thighs, and the whole person. In many these blotches were large and far apart, in others small and closely clustered. Like the boils, which had been and continued to be a certain indication of coming death, these blotches had the same meaning for everyone on whom they appeared.

Neither the advice of physicians nor the virtue of any medicine seemed to help or avail in the cure of these diseases. Indeed, . . . not only did few recover, but on the contrary almost everyone died within three days of the appearance of the signs—some sooner, some later. . . . The virulence of the plague was all the greater in that it was communicated by the sick to the well by contact, not unlike fire when dry or fatty things are brought near it. But the evil was still worse. Not only did conversation and familiarity with the diseased spread the malady and even cause death, but the mere touch of the clothes or any other object the sick had touched or used, seemed to spread the pestilence. . . .

More wretched still were the circumstances of the common people and, for a great part, of the middle class, for, confined to their homes either by hope of safety or by poverty, and restricted to their own sections, they fell sick daily by thousands. There, devoid of help or care, they died almost without redemption. A great many breathed their last in the public streets, day and night; a large number perished in their homes, and it was only by the stench of their decaying bodies that they proclaimed their death to their neighbors. Everywhere the city was teeming with corpses. . . .

So many bodies were brought to the churches every day that the consecrated ground did not suffice to hold them, particularly according to the ancient custom of giving each corpse its individual place. Huge trenches were dug in the crowded churchyards and the new dead were piled in them, layer upon layer, like merchandise in the hold of a ship. A little earth covered the corpses of each row, and the procedure continued until the trench was filled to the top.

---

sent the plague to punish humans for their sinful ways. One contemporary chronicler described a flagellant procession:

> The penitents went about, coming first out of Germany. They were men who did public penance and scourged themselves with whips of hard knotted leather with little iron spikes. Some made themselves bleed very badly between the shoulder blades and some foolish women had cloths ready to catch the blood and smear it on their eyes, saying it was miraculous blood. While they were doing penance, they sang very mournful songs about the nativity and the passion of Our Lord. The object of this penance was to put a stop to the mortality, for in that time . . . at least a third of all the people in the world died.[5]

The flagellants attracted attention and created mass hysteria wherever they went. The Catholic church, however, became alarmed when flagellant groups began to kill Jews and attack the clergy who opposed them. Some groups also developed a millenarian aspect, placing their emphasis on the coming end of the world, the return of Jesus, and the establishment of a thousand-year kingdom under his governance. Pope Clement VI condemned the flagellants in October 1349 and urged the public authorities to crush them. By the end of 1350, most of the flagellant movements had been destroyed.

An outbreak of virulent anti-Semitism also accompanied the Black Death. Jews were accused of causing the

THE FLAGELLANTS. Reactions to the plague were extreme at times. Believing that asceticism could atone for humankind's sins and win God's forgiveness, flagellants wandered from town to town flogging themselves with whips, as in this illustration.

plague by poisoning town wells. Although Jews were persecuted in Spain, the worst pogroms against this helpless minority were carried out in Germany; more than sixty major Jewish communities in Germany had been exterminated by 1351 (see the box on p. 302). Many Jews fled eastward to Russia and especially to Poland where the king offered them protection. Eastern Europe became home to large Jewish communities.

The prevalence of death because of the plague and its recurrences affected people in profound ways. Some survivors apparently came to treat life as something cheap and passing. Violence and violent death appeared to be more common after the plague than before. Postplague Europe also demonstrated a morbid preoccupation with death. In their sermons, priests reminded parishioners that each night's sleep might be their last. Tombstones were decorated with macabre scenes of naked corpses in various stages of decomposition with snakes entwined in their bones and their innards filled with worms.

✸ Economic Dislocation and Social Upheaval

The population collapse of the fourteenth century had dire economic and social consequences. Economic dislocation was accompanied by social upheaval. Between 1000 and 1300, Europe had been relatively stable. The tripartite division of society into the three estates of clergy (those who pray), nobility (those who fight), and laborers (those who work) had already begun to disintegrate in the thirteenth century, however. In the fourteenth century, a series of urban and rural revolts rocked European society.

✍ NOBLE LANDLORDS AND PEASANTS

Both peasants and landlords were affected by the demographic crisis of the fourteenth century. Most noticeably, Europe experienced a serious labor shortage that caused a dramatic rise in the price of labor. At Cuxham manor in England, for example, a farm laborer who had received two shillings a week in 1347 was paid seven in 1349 and almost

eleven by 1350. At the same time, the decline in population depressed or held stable the demand for agricultural produce, resulting in stable or falling prices for output (although in England prices remained high until the 1380s). The chronicler Henry Knighton observed: "And the price of everything was cheap. . . . For a man could buy a horse for half a mark [six shillings], which before was worth forty shillings."[6] Since landlords were having to pay more for labor at the same time that their rents or income were declining, they began to experience considerable adversity and lower standards of living. In England, aristocratic incomes dropped more than 20 percent between 1347 and 1353. The wealthiest aristocrats could still afford their privileged lifestyle, but lesser lords faced impoverishment.

Aristocrats responded to adversity by seeking to lower the wage rate. The English Parliament passed the Statute of Laborers (1351), which attempted to limit wages to preplague levels and to forbid the mobility of peasants as well. Although such laws proved largely unenforceable, they did keep wages from rising as high as they might have in a free market. Overall, the position of landlords continued to deteriorate during the late fourteenth and early fifteenth centuries. At the same time, the position of peasants improved, though not uniformly throughout Europe.

The decline in the number of peasants after the Black Death accelerated the process of converting labor services to rents, freeing peasants from the obligations of servile tenure and weakening the system of manorialism. But there were limits to how much the peasants could advance. They faced the same economic hurdles as the lords. Moreover, peasants were faced with the attempts of lords to impose wage restrictions, reinstate old forms of labor service, and create new obligations. New governmental taxes also hurt. Peasant complaints became widespread and soon gave rise to rural revolts.

✍ PEASANT REVOLTS

In 1358, a peasant revolt, known as the *Jacquerie*, broke out in northern France. The destruction of normal order by the Black Death and the subsequent economic dislocation

A Medieval Holocaust: The Cremation of the Strasbourg Jews

In their attempt to explain the widespread horrors of the Black Death, medieval Christian communities looked for scapegoats. As at the time of the crusades, the Jews were blamed for poisoning wells and hence spreading the plague. This selection by a contemporary chronicler, written in 1349, gives an account of how Christians in the town of Strasbourg in the Holy Roman Empire dealt with their Jewish community. It is apparent that financial gain was also an important motive in killing the Jews.

❋ Jacob von Königshofen, "The Cremation of the Strasbourg Jews"

In the year 1349 there occurred the greatest epidemic that ever happened. Death went from one end of the earth to the other. . . . And from what this epidemic came, all wise teachers and physicians could only say that it was God's will. . . . This epidemic also came to Strasbourg in the summer of the above-mentioned year, and it is estimated that about sixteen thousand people died.

In the matter of this plague the Jews throughout the world were reviled and accused in all lands of having caused it through the poison which they are said to have put into the water and the wells—that is what they were accused of—and for this reason the Jews were burnt all the way from the Mediterranean into Germany. . . .

[The account then goes on to discuss the situation of the Jews in the city of Strasbourg.]

On Saturday . . . they burnt the Jews on a wooden platform in their cemetery. There were about two thousand people of them. Those who wanted to baptise themselves were spared. [About 1,000 accepted baptism.] Many small children were taken out of the fire and baptized against the will of their fathers and mothers. And everything that was owed to the Jews was canceled, and the Jews had to surrender all pledges and notes that they had taken for debts. The council, however, took the cash that the Jews possessed and divided it among the working-men proportionately. The money was indeed the thing that killed the Jews. If they had been poor and if the feudal lords had not been in debt to them, they would not have been burnt. . . .

Thus were the Jews burnt at Strasbourg, and in the same year in all the cities of the Rhine, whether Free Cities or Imperial Cities or cities belonging to the lords. In some towns they burnt the Jews after a trial, in others, without a trial. In some cities the Jews themselves set fire to their houses and cremated themselves.

It was decided in Strasbourg that no Jew should enter the city for 100 years, but before 20 years had passed, the council and magistrates agreed that they ought to admit the Jews again into the city for 20 years. And so the Jews came back again to Strasbourg in the year 1368 after the birth of our Lord.

---

were important factors in causing the revolt, but the ravages created by the Hundred Years' War also affected the French peasantry (see War and Political Instability later in this chapter). Both the French and English forces followed a deliberate policy of laying waste to peasants' lands while bands of mercenaries lived off the land by taking peasants' produce as well. Thus, the *Jacquerie* was a revolt of desperation; it was linked to the political ambitions of townspeople in Paris who were also upset with the conduct of the war and wished to limit monarchical power. The leader of the peasants was actually a bourgeois draper, Etienne Marcel.

Peasant anger was also exacerbated by growing class tensions. Landed nobles were eager to hold onto their politically privileged position and felt increasingly threatened in the new postplague world of higher wages and lower prices. Aristocrats looked upon peasants with utter contempt. A French tale told to upper-class audiences contained this remarkable passage:

> Tell me, Lord, if you please, by what right or title does a villein [peasant] eat beef? . . . Should they eat fish? Rather let them eat thistles and briars, thorns and straw and hay on Sunday and peapods on weekdays. They should keep watch without sleep and have trouble always; that is how villeins should live. Yet each day they are full and drunk on the best wines, and in fine clothes. The great expenditures of villeins come as a high cost, for it is this that destroys and ruins the world. It is they who spoil the common welfare. From the villein comes all unhappiness. Should they eat meat? Rather should they chew grass on the heath with the horned cattle and go naked on all fours.[7]

The peasants reciprocated this contempt for their so-called social superiors.

The outburst of peasant anger led to savage confrontations. Castles were burned and nobles murdered (see the box on p. 303). Such atrocities did not go unanswered, however. The *Jacquerie* soon failed as the privileged classes closed ranks, savagely massacred the rebels, and ended the revolt.

The English Peasants' Revolt of 1381 was the most famous of all. It was a product not of desperation but of rising expectations. After the Black Death, the condition of the English peasants had improved as they enjoyed greater freedom and higher wages or lower rents. Aristocratic landlords had fought back with legislation to depress wages and attempted to reimpose old feudal dues. The most immediate cause of the revolt, however, was the monarchy's attempt to raise revenues by imposing a poll tax or a flat charge on each adult member of the popula-

A Revolt of French Peasants

In 1358, French peasants rose up in a revolt known as the Jacquerie. The relationship between aristocrats and peasants had degenerated as a result of the social upheavals and privations caused by the Black Death and the Hundred Years' War. This excerpt from the chronicle of an aristocrat paints a horrifying picture of the barbarities that occurred during the revolt.

❊ Jean Froissart, *Chronicles*

There were very strange and terrible happenings in several parts of the kingdom of France. . . . They began when some of the men from the country towns came together in the Beauvais region. They had no leaders and at first they numbered scarcely 100. One of them got up and said that the nobility of France, knights and squires, were disgracing and betraying the realm, and that it would be a good thing if they were all destroyed. At this they all shouted: "He's right! He's right! Shame on any man who saves the gentry from being wiped out!"

They banded together and went off, without further deliberation and unarmed except for pikes and knives, to the house of a knight who lived nearby. They broke in and killed the knight, with his lady and his children, big and small, and set fire to the house. Next they went to another castle and did much worse; for, having seized the knight and bound him securely to a post, several of them violated his wife and daughter before his eyes.

Then they killed the wife, who was pregnant, and the daughter and all the other children, and finally put the knight to death with great cruelty and burned and razed the castle.

They did similar things in a number of castles and big houses, and their ranks swelled until there were a good 6,000 of them. Wherever they went their numbers grew, for all the men of the same sort joined them. The knights and squires fled before them with their families. They took their wives and daughters many miles away to put them in safety, leaving their houses open with their possessions inside. And those evil men, who had come together without leaders or arms, pillaged and burned everything and violated and killed all the ladies and girls without mercy, like mad dogs. Their barbarous acts were worse than anything that ever took place between Christians and Saracens. Never did men commit such vile deeds. They were such that no living creature ought to see, or even imagine or think of, and the men who committed the most were admired and had the highest places among them. I could never bring myself to write down the horrible and shameful things which they did to the ladies. But, among other brutal excesses, they killed a knight, put him on a spit, and turned him at the fire and roasted him before the lady and her children. After about a dozen of them had violated the lady, they tried to force her and the children to eat the knight's flesh before putting them cruelly to death.

---

tion. Peasants in eastern England, the wealthiest part of the country, refused to pay the tax and expelled the collectors forcibly from their villages.

This action sparked a widespread rebellion of both peasants and townspeople led by a well-to-do peasant called Wat Tyler and a preacher named John Ball. The latter preached an effective message against the noble class, as recounted by the French chronicler Froissart:

> Good people, things cannot go right in England and never will, until goods are held in common and there are no more villeins and gentlefolk, but we are all one and the same. In what way are those whom we call lords greater masters than ourselves? How have they deserved it? Why do they hold us in bondage? If we all spring from a single father and mother, Adam and Eve, how can they claim or prove that they are lords more than us, except by making us produce and grow the wealth which they spend?[8]

The movement developed a famous jingle based on Ball's preaching: "When Adam delved and Eve span, who was then a gentleman?"

The revolt was initially successful as the rebels burned down the manor houses of aristocrats, lawyers, and government officials and murdered several important

PEASANT REBELLION. The fourteenth century witnessed a number of revolts of the peasantry against noble landowners. Although the revolts were initially successful, they were soon crushed. This fifteenth-century illustration shows nobles massacring the rebels in the French *Jacquerie* of 1358.

HARBOR SCENE AT HAMBURG. This illustration from a fifteenth-century treatise on the laws of Hamburg shows a busy port with ships of all sizes. At the left, a crane is used to unload barrels. In the building at the right, customs officials collect their dues. Merchants and townspeople are shown talking at dockside.

officials, including the archbishop of Canterbury. Peasants from Kent and Essex marched on London, demanding an end to serfdom and immunity from prosecution for acts undertaken during the rebellion. The young king Richard II, aged fifteen, promised to accept the rebels' demands if they returned to their homes. They accepted the king's word and dispersed, but the king reneged and with the assistance of the aristocrats arrested hundreds of the rebels. The poll tax was eliminated, however, and in the end most of the rebels were pardoned.

REVOLTS IN THE CITIES

Revolts also erupted in the cities. Commercial and industrial activity suffered almost immediately from the Black Death. An oversupply of goods and an immediate drop in demand led to a decline in trade after 1350. Some industries suffered greatly. Florence's woolen industry, one of the giants, produced 70,000 to 80,000 pieces of cloth in 1338; in 1378, it was yielding only 24,000 pieces. In Ypres, Flanders, cloth production fell an incredible 85 percent.

Bordeaux wine exports fell by 50 percent. Bourgeois merchants and manufacturers responded to the decline in trade and production by attempting to restrict competition and resist the demands of the lower classes.

In urban areas where capitalist industrialists paid low wages and managed to prevent workers from forming organizations to help themselves, industrial revolts broke out throughout Europe. Ghent experienced one in 1381, Rouen in 1382. Most famous, however, was the revolt of the *ciompi* in Florence in 1378. The *ciompi* were wool workers in Florence's most prominent industry. In the 1370s, not only was the woolen industry depressed, but the wool workers saw their real wages decline when the coinage in which they were paid was debased. Their revolt won them some concessions from the municipal government, including the right to form guilds and be represented in the government. But their newly won rights were short-lived. Government authorities brought an end to *ciompi* participation in the government by 1382.

The urban and rural revolts of the fourteenth century contained some common elements. As a result of the Black Death, both workers and peasants had sustained some basic improvements in wages and living conditions. The privileged classes, whether noble landlords or wealthy bourgeoisie, wished to retain their old advantages and deny workers and peasants their newfound gains. Peasants and workers fought back. They did so at a time when normal law and order were breaking down anyway as a result of the upheaval fostered by the Black Death and the war in France.

Although the revolts sometimes resulted in short-term gains for the participants, it is also true that the uprisings were quickly crushed and their gains lost. Geographically dispersed, rural and urban revolters were not united and had no long-range goals. Immediate gains were uppermost in their minds. Accustomed to ruling, the established classes easily combined and crushed dissent when faced with social uprisings. But after the fourteenth century, the harmony theoretically implicit in the medieval hierarchy of the classes was never the same again. The rural and urban revolts of the fourteenth century ushered in an age of social conflict that characterized much of later European history.

◆ War and Political Instability

Famine, plague, economic turmoil, social upheaval, and violence were not the only problems of the fourteenth century. War and political instability must also be added to the list. Of all the struggles that ensued in the fourteenth century, the Hundred Years' War was the most famous and the most violent.

Causes of the Hundred Years' War

In 1259, the English king, Henry III, had relinquished his claims to all the French territories previously held by the English monarchy except for one relatively small possession known as the duchy of Gascony. As duke of Gascony, the English king pledged loyalty as a vassal to the French king. But this territory gave rise to numerous disputes between the kings of England and France. By the thirteenth century, the Capetian monarchs had greatly increased their power over their more important vassals, the great lords of France. Royal officials interfered regularly in the affairs of the vassals' fiefs, especially in matters of justice. Although this policy irritated all the vassals, it especially annoyed the king of England who considered himself the peer of the French king.

An economic problem involving the county of Flanders was a second factor contributing to the Hundred Years' War. Urban revolts in Flanders pitted artisans against wealthy merchants and threatened to disrupt the lucrative shipments of English wool to Flanders. Flanders was England's chief market for raw wool, and the English king received huge revenues from export duties on wool. When the French monarchy began to intervene in Flanders on the side of the merchants, the English felt threatened. If the French were to gain control of Flanders, they could play havoc with the wool trade. Accordingly, the English king began to support the Flemish artisans.

A dispute over the right of succession to the French throne also complicated the struggle between the French and the English. In the fourteenth century, the Capetian dynasty failed to produce a male heir for the first time in almost 400 years. In 1328, the senior branch of the Capetian dynasty became extinct in the male line with the death of Charles IV. As the son of the daughter of King Philip IV, King Edward III of England (1327–1377) had a claim to the French throne as a close male relative. French practice, however, emphasized descent through the male line, and a cousin of the Capetians, Philip, duke of Valois, became king as Philip VI (1328–1350).

The immediate cause of the war between France and England was yet another quarrel over Gascony. In 1337, when Edward III, the king of England and duke of Gascony, refused to do homage to Philip VI for Gascony, the French king seized the duchy. Edward responded by declaring war on Philip, the "so-called King of France." There is no doubt that the personalities of the two monarchs also had much to do with the outbreak of the Hundred Years' War. Both Edward and Philip loved luxury and shared a desire for the glory and prestige that came from military engagements. Both were only too willing to use their respective nation's resources to satisfy their own desires. Moreover, for many nobles, the promise of plunder and territorial gain was an incentive to follow the disruptive path of their rulers.

❈ Conduct and Course of the War

The Hundred Years' War began in a burst of knightly enthusiasm. Knights were trained to be warriors; they viewed the clash of battle as the ultimate opportunity to demonstrate their chivalric qualities. The Hundred Years' War proved to be an important watershed, however, for the feudal way of life was on the decline. This would

CHRONOLOGY

The Hundred Years' War

Outbreak of hostilities	1337
Battle of Crécy	1346
Battle of Poitiers	1356
Peace of Brétigny	1359
Death of Edward III	1377
Twenty-year truce	1396
Henry V (1413–1422) renews the war	1415
Battle of Agincourt	1415
French recovery under Joan of Arc	1429–1431
End of the war	1453

become most evident when peasant foot soldiers instead of knights determined the outcomes of the chief battles of the Hundred Years' War.

It was the English, more than the French, who moved beyond the traditional feudal levy. The French army of 1337 with its heavily armed noble cavalry resembled its twelfth- and thirteenth-century forebears. The noble cavalry considered themselves the fighting elite and looked with contempt upon the foot soldiers and crossbowmen because they were peasants or other social inferiors. Such attitudes cost the French dearly in the early battles.

The English army, however, had evolved differently and had included peasants as paid foot soldiers since at least Anglo-Saxon times. Armed with pikes, many of these foot soldiers had also adopted the longbow, invented by the Welsh. The longbow had a more rapid speed of fire than the more powerful crossbow. Although the English made use of heavily armed cavalry, they relied even more on large numbers of foot soldiers.

Edward III's early campaigns in France achieved little. When Edward renewed his efforts in 1346 with an invasion of Normandy, Philip responded by raising a large force to crush the English army and met Edward's forces at Crécy, just south of Flanders. Although historians disagree on the numbers involved, the undoubtedly larger French army followed no battle plan but simply attacked the English lines in a disorderly fashion. The arrows of the English archers devastated the French cavalry. As the chronicler Froissart described it, "[with their longbows] the English continued to shoot into the thickest part of the crowd, wasting none of their arrows. They impaled or wounded horses and riders, who fell to the ground in great distress, unable to get up again [because of their heavy armor] without the help of several men."[9] It was a stunning victory for the English. Edward followed up his victory by capturing the French port of Calais to serve as a staging ground for future invasions.

The Battle of Crécy was not decisive, however. The English simply did not possess the resources to subjugate all of France. Truces, small-scale hostilities, and some

The Hundred Years' War

In his account of the Hundred Years' War, the fourteenth-century French chronicler Jean Froissart described the sack of the fortified French town of Limoges by the Black Prince, Edward, the prince of Wales. It provides a vivid example of how noncombatants fared during the war.

❋ Jean Froissart, *Chronicles*

For about a month, certainly not longer, the Prince of Wales remained before Limoges. During that time he allowed no assaults or skirmishes, but pushed on steadily with the mining. The knights inside and the townspeople, who knew what was going on, started a countermine in the hope of killing the English miners, but it was a failure. When the Prince's miners who, as they dug, were continually shoring up their tunnel, had completed their work, they said to the Prince: "My lord, whenever you like now we can bring a big piece of wall down into the moat, so that you can get into the city quite easily and safely."

The Prince was very pleased to hear this. "Excellent," he said. "At six o'clock tomorrow morning show me what you can do."

When they knew it was the right time for it, the miners started a fire in their mine. In the morning, just as the Prince had specified, a great section of the wall collapsed, filling the moat at the place where it fell. For the English, who were armed and ready waiting, it was a welcome sight. Those on foot could enter as they liked, and did so. They rushed to the gate, cut through the bars holding it and knocked it down. They did the same with the barriers outside, meeting with no resistance. It was all done so quickly that the people in the town were taken unawares. Then the Prince, the Duke of Lancaster, the Earl of Cambridge, Sir Guichard d'Angle, with all the others and their men burst into the city, followed by pillagers on foot, all in a mood to wreak havoc and do murder, killing indiscriminately, for those were their orders. There were pitiful scenes. Men, women, and children flung themselves on their knees before the Prince, crying: "Have mercy on us, gentle sir!" But he was so inflamed with anger that he would not listen. Neither man nor woman was heeded, but all who could be found were put to the sword, including many who were in no way to blame. I do not understand how they could have failed to take pity on people who were too unimportant to have committed treason. Yet they paid for it, and paid more dearly than the leaders who had committed it.

There is no man so hard-hearted that, if he had been in Limoges on that day, and had remembered God, he would not have wept bitterly at the fearful slaughter which took place. More than 3,000 persons, men, women, and children, were dragged out to have their throats cut. May God receive their souls, for they were true martyrs.

BATTLE OF CRÉCY. This fifteenth-century manuscript illustration depicts the Battle of Crécy, the first of several military disasters suffered by the French in the Hundred Years' War, and shows why the English preferred the longbow to the crossbow. At the left, the French crossbowmen stop firing and prime their weapons by cranking the handle, while English archers continue to fire their longbows (a skilled archer could fire ten arrows a minute).

major operations were combined in an orgy of seemingly incessant struggle. The English campaigns were waged by Edward III and his son Edward, the prince of Wales, known as the Black Prince. The Black Prince's campaigns in France were devastating (see the box above). Avoiding pitched battles, his forces deliberately ravaged the land, burning crops and entire unfortified villages and towns and stealing anything of value. For the English, such campaigns were profitable; for the French people, they meant hunger, deprivation, and death. When the army of the Black Prince was finally forced to do battle, the French, under their king John II (1350–1364), were once again defeated. This time even the king was captured. This Battle of Poitiers (1356) ended the first phase of the Hundred Years' War. Under the Peace of Brétigny (1359), the French agreed to pay a large ransom for King John, the English territories in Gascony were enlarged, and Edward renounced his claims to the throne of France in return for John's promise to give up any feudal control over English lands in France. This first phase of the war made it clear that, despite their victories, the English were not really strong enough to subdue all of France and make Edward III's claim to the French monarchy a reality.

Monarchs, however, could be slow learners. The Treaty of Brétigny was never really enforced. In the next

THE VISION OF CHRISTINE DE PIZAN. Christine de Pizan is one of the extraordinary vernacular writers of the late fourteenth and early fifteenth centuries. She is pictured here in a cover illustration from her *Book of the City of Ladies*. Reason, Righteousness, and Justice are shown appearing to Christine in a dream.

in them is less than decent and opposed to modesty, how much stimulation to wanton lust, how many things that drive to lust even those most fortified against it."[17]

Another leading vernacular author was Geoffrey Chaucer (c. 1340–1400), who brought a new level of sophistication to the English vernacular language in his famous work *The Canterbury Tales*. His beauty of expression and clear, forceful language were important in transforming his East Midland dialect into the chief ancestor of the modern English language. *The Canterbury Tales* constitute a group of stories told by twenty-nine pilgrims journeying from the London suburb of Southwark to the tomb of Saint Thomas Becket at Canterbury. This format gave Chaucer the chance to portray an entire range of English society, both high and low born. Among others, he presented the Knight, the Yeoman, the Prioress, the Monk, the Merchant, the Student, the Lawyer, the Carpenter, the Cook, the Doctor, the Plowman, and, of course, "A Good Wife was there from beside the city of Bath—a little deaf, which was a pity." The stories these pilgrims told to while away the time on the journey were just as varied as the storytellers themselves: knightly romances, fairy tales, saints' lives, sophisticated satires, and crude anecdotes.

Chaucer also used some of his characters to criticize the corruption of the church in the late medieval period. His portrayal of the Friar leaves no doubt of Chaucer's disdain for the corrupt practices of clerics. Of the Friar, he says:

> He knew the taverns well in every town.
> The barmaids and innkeepers pleased his mind
> Better than beggars and lepers and their kind.

And yet, Chaucer was still a pious Christian, never doubting basic Christian doctrines and remaining optimistic that the church could be reformed. The Parson was his model for what others should imitate:

> I doubt there was a priest in any place
> His better. He did not stand on dignity
> Nor affect in conscience too much nicety,
> But Christ's and his disciples' word he sought
> To teach, and first he followed what he taught.[18]

One of the extraordinary vernacular writers of the age was Christine de Pizan (c. 1364–1430). Because of her father's position at the court of Charles V of France, she received a good education. Her husband died when she was only twenty-five (they had been married for ten years), leaving her with little income and three small children and her mother to support. Christine took the unusual step of becoming a writer in order to earn her living. Her poems were soon in demand, and by 1400 she had achieved financial security.

Christine de Pizan is best known, however, for her French prose works written in defense of women. In *The Book of the City of Ladies*, written in 1404, she denounced the many male writers who had argued that women needed to be controlled by men because women by their very nature were prone to evil, unable to learn, and easily swayed. With the help of Reason, Righteousness, and

house in Naples, he fell in love with a noble lady whom he called his Fiammetta, his Little Flame. Under her inspiration, Boccaccio began to write prose romances. His best-known work, *The Decameron*, however, was not written until after he had returned to Florence. *The Decameron* is set at the time of the Black Death. Ten young people flee to a villa outside Florence to escape the plague and decide to while away the time by telling stories. Although the stories are not new and still reflect the acceptance of basic Christian values, Boccaccio does present the society of his time from a secular point of view. Boccaccio stresses cleverness and wit rather than piety and devotion. It is the seducer of women, not the knight or philosopher or pious monk, who is the real hero. Perhaps, as some historians have argued, *The Decameron* reflects the immediate easygoing, cynical postplague values. Boccaccio's later work certainly became gloomier and more pessimistic; as he grew older, he even rejected his earlier work as irrelevant. He commented in a 1373 letter that "I am certainly not pleased that you have allowed the illustrious women in your house to read my trifles. . . . You know how much

GIOTTO, *PIETÀ*. The work of Giotto marked the first clear innovation in fourteenth-century painting, making him a forerunner of the early Renaissance. In this fresco, which was part of an elaborate series in the Arena chapel in Padua begun in 1305, the solidity of Giotto's human figures gives them a three-dimensional sense.

Justice, who appear to her in a vision, Christine refutes these antifeminist attacks. Women, she argues, are not evil by nature, and they, too, could learn as well as men if they could attend the same schools: "Should I also tell you whether a woman's nature is clever and quick enough to learn speculative sciences as well as to discover them, and likewise the manual arts. I assure you that women are equally well-suited and skilled to carry them out and to put them to sophisticated use once they have learned them."[19] Much of the book includes a detailed discussion of women from the past and present who have distinguished themselves as leaders, warriors, wives, mothers, and martyrs for their religious faith. She ends by encouraging women to defend themselves against the attacks of men who are unable to understand them.

❋ Art and the Black Death

The fourteenth century produced an artistic outburst in new directions as well as a large body of morbid work influenced by the Black Death and the recurrence of the plague. The city of Florence witnessed the first dramatic break with medieval tradition in the work of Giotto (1266–1337), often considered a forerunner of Italian Renaissance painting. Born into a peasant family, Giotto acquired his painting skills in a workshop in Florence. Although he worked throughout Italy, his most famous works were done in Padua and Florence. Coming out of

the formal Byzantine school, Giotto transcended it with a new kind of realism, a desire to imitate nature that Renaissance artists later identified as the basic component of classical art. Giotto's figures were solid and rounded and, placed realistically in relationship to each other and their background, provided a sense of three-dimensional depth. The expressive faces and physically realistic bodies gave his sacred figures human qualities with which spectators could identify. Although Giotto had no immediate successors, Florentine painting in the early fifteenth century pursued even more dramatically the new direction his work represents.

The Black Death made a visible impact on art. For one thing, it wiped out entire guilds of artists. At the same time, survivors, including the newly rich who patronized artists, were no longer so optimistic. Some were more guilty about enjoying life and more concerned about gaining salvation. Postplague art began to concentrate on pain and death. A fairly large number of artistic works came to exhibit a morbid concern with death, depicting coffins, decomposing bodies, and grim figures of Death, sometimes in the form of a witch flying through the air swinging a large scythe.

◆ Society in an Age of Adversity

In the midst of disaster, the fourteenth century proved creative in its own way. New inventions made an impact on daily life at the same time that the effects of plague were felt in many areas of medieval urban life.

❋ Changes in Urban Life

One immediate by-product of the Black Death was a greater regulation of urban activities. Authorities tried to keep cities cleaner by enacting new sanitary ordinances. Viewed as unhealthy places, bathhouses were closed down, leading to a noticeable decline in cleanliness. Efforts at regulation also affected the practice of female prostitution.

Medieval society had tolerated prostitution as a lesser evil; it was better for males to frequent prostitutes than to seduce virgins or have sex with married women. Since many males in medieval towns married late, the demand for prostitutes was high and was met by a regular supply, derived no doubt from the need of many poor girls and women to survive. The recession of the fourteenth century probably increased the supply of prostitutes while the new hedonism prevalent after the Black Death also increased demand. As a result, in the later fourteenth century, cities intensified their regulation of prostitution.

By organizing brothels, city authorities could supervise as well as tax prostitutes. Officials granted charters to citizens who were allowed to set up brothels, provided they were located only in certain areas of town. Prostitutes were also expected to wear special items of clothing—such as red hats—to distinguish them from other women. In some towns, church officials forced prostitutes to sit in special areas if they wished to attend church services.

The Legal Rights of Women

During the High and Late Middle Ages, as women were increasingly viewed as weak beings who were unable to play independent roles, legal systems also began to limit the rights of women. These excerpts are taken from a variety of legal opinions in France, England, and a number of Italian cities.

❈ Excerpts from Legal Opinions

France, 1270: No married woman can go to court . . . unless someone has abused or beaten her, in which case she may go to court without her husband. If she is a tradeswoman, she can sue and defend herself in matters connected with her business, but not otherwise.

England [probably fifteenth century]: Every Feme Covert [married woman] is a sort of infant. . . . It is seldom, almost never that a married woman can have any action to use her wit only in her own name: her husband is her stern, her prime mover, without whom she cannot do much at home, and less abroad. . . . It is a miracle that a wife should commit any suit without her husband.

England [probably fifteenth century]: The very goods which a man gives to his wife, are still his own, her chain, her bracelets, her apparel, are all the goodman's goods. . . . A wife however gallant she be, glitters but in the riches of her husband, as the moon has no light but it is the sun's. . . . For thus it is, if before marriage the woman was possessed of horses . . . sheep, corn, wool, money, plate and jewels, all manner of movable substance is presently . . . the husband's to sell, keep or bequeath if she die.

Pesaro, Italy [exact date unknown]: No wife can make a contract without the consent of her husband.

Florence, Italy, 1415: A married woman with children cannot draw up a last will in her own right, nor dispose of her dowry among the living to the detriment of husband and children.

Lucca, Italy [exact date unknown]: No married woman . . . can seal or give away [anything] unless she has the agreement of her husband and nearest [male] relative.

✖ FAMILY LIFE AND GENDER ROLES IN LATE MEDIEVAL CITIES

The basic unit of the late medieval town was the nuclear family of husband, wife, and children. Especially in wealthier families, there might also be servants, apprentices, and other relatives, including widowed mothers and the husband's illegitimate children.

Before the Black Death, late marriages were common for urban couples. It was not unusual for husbands to be in their late thirties or forties and wives in their early twenties. The expense of setting up a household probably necessitated the delay in marriage. But the situation changed dramatically after the plague, reflecting new economic opportunities for the survivors and a new reluctance to postpone living in the presence of so much death.

The economic difficulties of the fourteenth century also had a tendency to strengthen the development of gender roles created by thirteenth-century scholastic theologians and to set new limits on employment opportunities for women. Thomas Aquinas and others had offered rigid conceptions of men and women that were unthinkable in earlier centuries when some women had played important roles. Based on the authority of Aristotle, Aquinas had advanced the belief that according to the natural order, men were active and domineering while women were passive and submissive. As more and more lawyers, doctors, and priests, who had been trained in universities where these notions were taught, entered society, these ideas about the different natures of men and women became widely accepted. This was evident in legal systems, many of which limited the legal capacity of women (see the box above). Increasingly, women were expected to give up any active functions in society and remain subject to direction from males. A fourteenth-century Parisian provost commented that among glass cutters "no master's widow who keeps working at his craft after her husband's death may take on apprentices, for the men of the craft do not believe that a woman can master it well enough to teach a child to master it, for the craft is a very delicate one."[20] Although this statement suggests that some women were, in fact, running businesses, it also reveals that they were viewed as incapable of undertaking all of men's activities. Based on a pattern of gender, Europeans created a division of labor roles between men and women that continued until the Industrial Revolution of the eighteenth and nineteenth centuries.

✖ MEDIEVAL CHILDREN

Medieval parents of both the High and Later Middle Ages invested considerable resources and affection in rearing their children. The dramatic increase in specialized roles that accompanied the spread of commerce and the growth of cities demanded a commitment to educating children in the marketable skills needed for the new occupations. Philip of Navarre noted in the twelfth century that boys ought to be taught a trade "as soon as possible. Those who early become and long remain apprentices ought to be the best masters."[21] Some cities provided schools to educate the young. A Florentine chronicler related that between 8,000 and 10,000 boys and girls between the ages of six and

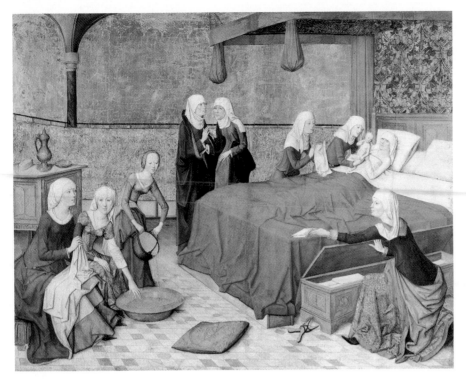

BIRTH OF A CHILD. This scene from the *Birth of the Virgin* by an unknown German artist is actually a painting of a wealthy fourteenth-century mother who has just given birth to a child. Female attendants prepare the water for the child's first bath while the mother holds her newborn in her canopied bed.

twelve attended the city's grammar schools, a figure that probably represented half of school-aged children. Although grammar school completed education for girls, around 1,100 boys went on to six secondary schools that prepared them for business careers while another 600 studied Latin and logic in four other schools that readied them for university training and a career in medicine, law, or the church. In the High Middle Ages, then, urban communities demonstrated a commitment to the training of the young.

As a result of the devastating effects of the plague and its recurrences, these same communities became concerned about investing in the survival and health of children. Although a number of hospitals existed in both Florence and Rome in the fourteenth century, it was not until the 1420s and 1430s that hospitals were established that catered only to the needs of foundlings, supporting them until boys could be taught a trade and girls could marry.

❁ New Directions in Medicine

The medical community comprised a number of different functionaries. At the top of the medical hierarchy were the physicians, usually clergymen, who received their education in the medieval universities where they studied ancient authorities, such as Hippocrates and Galen. As a result, physicians were highly trained in theory, but had little or no clinical practice. By the fourteenth century, they were educated in six chief medical schools—Salerno, Montpellier, Bologna, Oxford, Padua, and Paris. The latter was regarded as the most prestigious by the time of the Black Death.

The preplague medicine of university-trained physicians was theoretically grounded in the classical Greek theory of the "four humors," each connected to a particular organ: blood (from the heart), phlegm (from the brain), yellow bile (from the liver), and black bile (from the spleen). The four humors, in turn, corresponded to the four elemental qualities of the universe, earth (black bile), air (blood), fire (yellow bile), and water (phlegm), making a human being a microcosm of the cosmos. Good health resulted from a perfect balance of the four humors; sickness meant that the humors were out of balance. The task of the medieval physician was to restore proper order by a number of cures, such as rest, diet, herbal medicines, or bloodletting.

Beneath the physicians in the hierarchy of the medical profession stood the surgeons, whose activities included performing operations, setting broken bones, and bleeding patients. Their knowledge was largely based on practical experience. Below surgeons were midwives and the barber-surgeons, who were less trained and performed menial tasks such as bloodletting and setting simple bone fractures. Barber-surgeons supplemented their incomes by shaving and cutting hair and pulling teeth. Apothecaries also constituted part of the medical establishment. They filled herbal prescriptions recommended by physicians and also prescribed drugs on their own authority.

All of these medical practitioners proved unable to deal with the plague. When King Philip VI of France requested the opinion of the medical faculty of the University of Paris on the plague, their advice proved worthless. This failure to understand the Black Death, however,

A MEDICAL TEXTBOOK.   This illustration is taken from a fourteenth-century surgical textbook that stressed a "how-to" approach to surgical problems. *Top left*, a surgeon shows how to remove an arrow from a patient; *top right*, how to open a patient's chest; *bottom left*, how to deal with an injury to the intestines; *bottom right*, how to diagnose an abscess.

Inventions and New Patterns

Despite its problems, the fourteenth century witnessed a continuation of the technological innovations that had characterized the High Middle Ages. The most extraordinary of these inventions, and one that made a visible impact on European cities, was the clock. There had been earlier experiments with waterpowered clocks, but they had obvious limitations, particularly in northern Europe where they froze in winter. The mechanical clock was invented at the end of the thirteenth century, but not perfected until the fourteenth. The time-telling clock was actually a by-product of a larger astronomical clock. The best-designed one was constructed by Giovanni di Dondi in the mid-fourteenth century. Dondi's clock contained the signs of the zodiac, but also struck on the hour. Since clocks were expensive, they were usually installed only in the towers of churches or municipal buildings. The first clock striking equal hours was in a church in Milan; in 1335, a chronicler described it as "a wonderful clock, with a very large clapper which strikes a bell twenty-four times according to the twenty-four hours of the day and night and thus at the first hour of the night gives one sound, at the second two strikes . . . and so distinguishes one hour from another, which is of greatest use to men of every degree."[22]

Clocks introduced a wholly new conception of time into the lives of Europeans; they revolutionized how people thought about and used time. Throughout most of the Middle Ages, time was determined by natural rhythms (daybreak and nightfall) or church bells that were rung at more or less regular three-hour intervals, corresponding to the ecclesiastical offices of the church. Clocks made it possible to plan one's day and organize one's activities around the regular striking of bells. This brought a new regularity into the life of workers and merchants, defining urban existence and enabling merchants and bankers to see the value of time in a new way. Indeed, it was a conception that ultimately led them to believe that "time is money."

Like clocks, eyeglasses were introduced in the thirteenth century, but not refined until the fourteenth. Even then they were not overly effective by modern standards and were still extremely expensive. The high cost of parchment forced people to write in extremely small script; doubtlessly, eyeglasses made it more readable. At the same time, a significant change in writing materials occurred in the fourteenth century when parchment was supplemented by much cheaper paper made from cotton rags. Although it was more subject to insect and water damage than parchment, medieval paper was actually superior to modern papers made of high-acid wood pulp.

Invented earlier by the Chinese, gunpowder also made its appearance in the west in the fourteenth century. The use of gunpowder eventually brought drastic changes to European warfare. Its primary use was in cannons, although early cannons were prone to blow up, making them as dangerous to those firing them as to the enemy.

produced a crisis in medieval medicine that resulted in some new approaches to health care.

One result was the rise of surgeons to greater prominence because of their practical knowledge. Surgeons were now recruited by universities, which placed them on an equal level with physicians and introduced a greater emphasis on practical anatomy into the university curriculum. Connected to this was a rise in medical textbooks, often written in the vernacular and stressing practical, "how to" approaches to medical and surgical problems.

Finally, as a result of the plague, cities, especially in Italy, gave increased attention to public health and sanitation. Public health laws were instituted, and municipal boards of health came into being. The primary concern of the latter was to prevent plague, but gradually they came to control almost every aspect of health and sanitation. Boards of public health, consisting of medical practitioners and public officials, were empowered to enforce sanitary conditions, report on and attempt to isolate epidemics by quarantine (rarely successful), and regulate the activities of doctors. Some communities even began to hire "plague doctors," or municipal physicians and surgeons who were paid to treat victims.

Even as late as 1460, an attack on a castle using the "Lion," an enormous Flemish cannon, proved disastrous for the Scottish king James II when the "Lion" blew up, killing the king and a number of his retainers. Continued improvement in the construction of cannons, however, soon made them extremely valuable in reducing both castles and city walls. Gunpowder made castles, city walls, and armored knights obsolete.

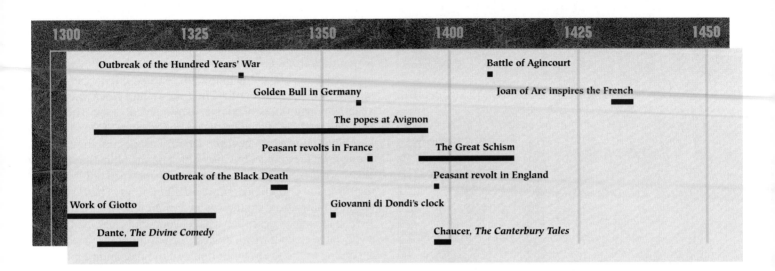

| 1300 | 1325 | 1350 | 1400 | 1425 | 1450 |

Outbreak of the Hundred Years' War

Battle of Agincourt

Golden Bull in Germany

Joan of Arc inspires the French

The popes at Avignon

Peasant revolts in France

The Great Schism

Outbreak of the Black Death

Peasant revolt in England

Work of Giotto

Giovanni di Dondi's clock

Dante, *The Divine Comedy*

Chaucer, *The Canterbury Tales*

CONCLUSION

In the eleventh, twelfth, and thirteenth centuries, European civilization developed many of its fundamental features. Territorial states, parliaments, capitalist trade and industry, banks, cities, and vernacular literatures were all products of that fertile period. During the same time, the Catholic church under the direction of the papacy reached its apogee. Fourteenth-century European society, however, was challenged by an overwhelming number of crises. Devastating plague, decline in trade and industry, bank failures, peasant revolts pitting lower classes against the upper classes, seemingly constant warfare, aristocratic factional conflict that undermined political stability, the absence of the popes from Rome, and even the spectacle of two popes condemning each other as the Antichrist all seemed to overpower Europeans in this "calamitous century." Not surprisingly, much of the art of the period depicted the Four Horsemen of the Apocalypse described in the New Testament book of Revelation: Death, Famine, Pestilence, and War. No doubt, to some people the last days of the world appeared to be at hand.

The new European society, however, proved remarkably resilient. Periods of crisis are usually paralleled by the emergence of new ideas and new practices. Intellectuals of the period saw themselves as standing on the threshold of a new age or rebirth of the best features of classical civilization. It is their perspective that led historians to speak of a Renaissance in the fifteenth century.

NOTES

1. Quoted in H. S. Lucas, "The Great European Famine of 1315, 1316, and 1317," *Speculum* 5 (1930): 359.
2. Quoted in David Herlihy, *The Black Death and the Transformation of the West*, ed. Samuel K. Cohn, Jr. (Cambridge, Mass., 1997), p. 9.
3. Giovanni Boccaccio, *The Decameron*, trans. Frances Winwar (New York, 1955), p. xxv.
4. Ibid., p. xxvi.
5. Jean Froissart, *Chronicles*, ed. and trans. Geoffrey Brereton (Harmondsworth, 1968), p. 111.
6. Quoted in James B. Ross and Mary M. McLaughlin, *The Portable Medieval Reader* (New York, 1949), pp. 218–219.
7. Quoted in Barbara W. Tuchman, *A Distant Mirror* (New York, 1978), p. 175.
8. Froissart, Chronicles, p. 212.
9. Ibid., p. 89.
10. Oliver J. Thatcher and Edgar H. McNeal, eds., *A Source Book for Medieval History* (New York, 1905), p. 288.
11. Quoted in D. S. Chambers, *The Imperial Age of Venice, 1380–1580* (London, 1970), p. 30.
12. Quoted in Robert Coogan, *Babylon on the Rhône: A Translation of Letters by Dante, Petrarch, and Catherine of Siena* (Washington, D.C., 1983), p. 115.
13. Marsiglio of Padua, *The Defender of the Peace*, trans. Alan Gewirth (New York, 1956), 2:426.
14. Quoted in Caroline Walker Bynum, *Holy Feast and Holy Fast: The Religious Significance of Food to Medieval Women* (Berkeley, 1987), p. 180.
15. Dante Alighieri, *The Divine Comedy*, trans. Dorothy Sayers (New York, 1962), "Paradise," Canto XXXIII, line 145.
16. Petrarch, *Sonnets and Songs*, trans. Anna Maria Armi (New York, 1968), No. LXXIV, p. 127.

17. Quoted in Millard Meiss, *Painting in Florence and Siena after the Black Death* (Princeton, N.J., 1951), p. 161.
18. Geoffrey Chaucer, *The Canterbury Tales*, in *The Portable Chaucer*, ed. Theodore Morrisoon (New York, 1949), pp. 67, 75.
19. Christine de Pizan, *The Book of the City of Ladies*, trans. E. Jeffrey Richards (New York, 1982), pp. 83–84.
20. Quoted in Susan Mosher Stuard, "The Dominion of Gender or How Women Fared in the High Middle Ages," in Renate Bridenthal, Claudia Koonz, and Susan Stuard, eds., *Becoming Visible: Women in European History*, 3d ed. (Boston, 1998), p. 147.
21. Quoted in David Herlihy, "Medieval Children," in Bede K. Lackner and Kenneth R. Philp, eds., *Essays on Medieval Civilization* (Austin, 1978), p. 121.
22. Quoted in Jean Gimpel, *The Medieval Machine* (New York, 1976), p. 168.

SUGGESTIONS FOR FURTHER READING ✄ ✄ ✄ ✄

For a general introduction to the fourteenth century, see D. P. Waley, *Later Medieval Europe*, 2d ed. (London, 1985); G. Holmes, *Europe: Hierarchy and Revolt, 1320–1450* (New York, 1975); and the well-written popular history by B. Tuchman, *A Distant Mirror* (New York, 1978).

On famine in the early fourteenth century, see W. C. Jordan, *The Great Famine: Northern Europe in the Early Fourteenth Century* (Princeton, N.J., 1996). On the Black Death, see P. Ziegler, *The Black Death* (New York, 1969); W. H. McNeill, *Plagues and People* (New York, 1976); and D. Herlihy, *The Black Death and the Transformation of the West*, ed. S. K. Cohn, Jr. (Cambridge, Mass., 1997). There is a good collection of sources in R. Horrox, ed., *The Black Death* (New York, 1994). On the peasant and urban revolts of the fourteenth century, see M. Mollat and P. Wolff, *The Popular Revolutions of the Late Middle Ages* (Winchester, Mass., 1973).

Recent accounts of the Hundred Years' War include A. Curry, *The Hundred Years War* (New York, 1993); and R. H. Neillands, *The Hundred Years War* (New York, 1990). On Joan of Arc, see M. Warner, *Joan of Arc: The Image of Female Heroism* (New York, 1981). On the political history of the period, see B. Guenée, *States and Rulers in Later Medieval Europe*, trans. J. Vale (Oxford, 1985). Works on individual countries include P. S. Lewis, *Later Medieval France: The Polity* (London, 1968); A. R. Myers, *England in the Late Middle Ages* (Harmondsworth, 1952); and F. R. H. Du Boulay, *Germany in the Later Middle Ages* (London, 1983). On the Italian political scene, see D. P. Waley, *The Italian City-Republics* (London, 1978); and J. Larner, *Italy in the Age of Dante and Petrarch, 1216–1380* (London, 1980).

A good general study of the church in the fourteenth century can be found in F. P. Oakley, *The Western Church in the Later Middle Ages* (Ithaca, N.Y., 1980). A good, readable biography is T. S. R. Boase, *Boniface VIII* (London, 1933). On the Avignonese papacy, see Y. Renouard, *The Avignon Papacy, 1305–1403* (London, 1970); and G. Mollat, *The Popes at Avignon* (New York, 1965). Other facets of the religious scene are examined in L. E. Boyle, *Pastoral Care, Clerical Education and Canon Law, 1200–1400* (London, 1981); and A. Hyma, *The Christian Renaissance: A History of the Devotio Moderna* (Hamden, Conn., 1965). On the role of food in the spiritual practices of medieval women, see C. W. Bynum, *Holy Feast and Holy Fast: The Religious Significance of Food to Medieval Women* (Berkeley, 1987).

A classic work on the life and thought of the Later Middle Ages is J. Huizinga, *The Autumn of the Middle Ages*, trans. R. J. Payton and U. Mammitzsch (Chicago, 1996). On the impact of the plague on culture, see the brilliant study by M. Meiss, *Painting in Florence and Siena after the Black Death* (New York, 1964). On Dante, see J. Freccero, *Dante and the Poetics of Conversion* (Cambridge, Mass., 1986). On Chaucer, see G. Kane, *Chaucer* (New York, 1984). The best work on Christine de Pizan is by C. C. Willard, *Christine de Pizan: Her Life and Works* (New York, 1984).

A wealth of material on everyday life is provided in the second volume of *A History of Private Life* edited by G. Duby, *Revelations of the Medieval World* (Cambridge, Mass., 1988). On women in the Late Middle Ages, see S. Shahar, *The Fourth Estate: A History of Women in the Middle Ages*, trans. C. Galai (London, 1983); and D. Herlihy, *Women, Family and Society: Historical Essays, 1978–1991* (Providence, R.I., 1995). On childhood, see the article by D. Herlihy cited in the notes; and B. Hanawalt, *Growing Up in Medieval London* (New York, 1993). The subject of medieval prostitution is examined in L. L. Otis, *Prostitution in Medieval Society* (Chicago, 1984). For late medieval townspeople, see J. F. C. Harrison, *The Common People of Great Britain* (Bloomington, Ind., 1985). Poor people are discussed in M. Mollat, *The Poor in the Middle Ages* (New Haven, Conn., 1986). For a general introduction to the changes in medicine, see T. McKeown, *The Role of Medicine* (Princeton, N.J., 1979). The importance of inventions is discussed in J. Gimpel, *The Medieval Machine* (New York, 1976). Another valuable discussion of medieval technology can be found in J. Le Goff, *Time, Work and Culture in the Middle Ages* (Chicago, 1980).

For additional reading, go to InfoTrac College Edition, your online research library at http://web1.infotrac-college.com

Enter the search terms *Middle Ages* using the Subject Guide.

Enter the search terms *Black Death* using Key Terms.

Enter the search terms *Edward III* using Key Terms.

Enter the search terms *Hundred Years War* using Key Terms.

CHAPTER OUTLINE

- Meaning and Characteristics of the Italian Renaissance
- The Making of Renaissance Society
- The Italian States in the Renaissance
- The Intellectual Renaissance in Italy
- The Artistic Renaissance
- The European State in the Renaissance
- The Church in the Renaissance
- Conclusion

FOCUS QUESTIONS

- What characteristics distinguish the Renaissance from the Middle Ages?
- How did Machiavelli's works reflect the political realities of Renaissance Italy?
- What was humanism, and what effect did it have on philosophy, education, attitudes toward politics, and the writing of history?
- What were the chief characteristics of Renaissance art, and how did it differ in Italy and northern Europe?
- Why do historians sometimes refer to the monarchies of the late fifteenth century as "new monarchies" or "Renaissance states"?

*M*EDIEVAL AND RENAISSANCE HISTORIANS *have argued interminably over the significance of the fourteenth and fifteenth centuries. Did they witness a continuation of the Middle Ages or the beginning of a new era? Obviously, both positions contain a modicum of truth. Although the disintegrative patterns of the fourteenth century continued into the fifteenth, at the same time there were elements of recovery that made the fifteenth century a period of significant political, economic, artistic, and intellectual change. The humanists or intellectuals of the age called their period (from the mid-fourteenth to the mid-sixteenth century) an age of rebirth, believing that they had restored arts and letters to new glory after they had been "neglected" or "dead" for centuries. The humanists also saw their age as one of great individuals who dominated the landscape of their time. Michelangelo, the great Italian artist of the early sixteenth century, and Pope Julius II, the "warrior pope," were two such titans. The artist's* temperament and the pope's temper led to many lengthy and often loud quarrels between the two. Among other commissions, the pope had hired Michelangelo to paint the ceiling of the Sistine Chapel in Rome, a difficult task for a man long accustomed to being a sculptor. Michelangelo undertook the project but refused for a long time to allow anyone, including the pope, to see his work. Julius grew anxious, pestering Michelangelo on a regular basis about when the ceiling would be finished. Exasperated by the pope's requests, Michelangelo once replied, according to Giorgio Vasari, his contemporary biographer, that the ceiling would be completed "when it satisfies me as an artist." The pope responded, "and we want you to satisfy us and finish it soon," and then threatened that if Michelangelo did not "finish the ceiling quickly he would have him thrown down from the scaffolding." Fearing the pope's anger, Michelangelo "lost no time in doing all that was wanted" and quickly completed the ceiling, one of the great masterpieces in the history of Western art.

The humanists' view of their age as a rebirth of the classical civilization of the Greeks and Romans ultimately led historians to use the word Renaissance to identify this age. Although recent historians have emphasized the many elements of continuity between the Middle Ages and the Renaissance, the latter age was also distinguished by its own unique characteristics.

◆ Meaning and Characteristics of the Italian Renaissance

The word *Renaissance* means "rebirth." A number of people who lived in Italy between c. 1350 and c. 1550 believed that they had witnessed a rebirth of antiquity or Greco-Roman civilization, which marked a new age. To them, the approximately 1,000 years between the end of the Roman Empire and their own era was a middle period (hence the "Middle Ages"), characterized by darkness because of its lack of classical culture. Historians of the nineteenth century later used similar terminology to describe this period in Italy. The Swiss historian and art critic Jacob Burckhardt created the modern concept of the Renaissance in his celebrated work, *Civilization of the Renaissance in Italy*, published in 1860. He portrayed Italy in the fourteenth and fifteenth centuries as the birthplace of the modern world (the Italians were "the firstborn among the sons of modern Europe") and saw the revival of antiquity, the "perfecting of the individual," and secularism ("worldliness of the Italians") as its distinguishing features. No doubt, Burckhardt exaggerated the individuality and secularism of the Renaissance and failed to recognize the depths of its religious sentiment. Nevertheless, he established the framework for all modern interpretations of the Renaissance. Although contemporary scholars do not believe that the Renaissance represents a sudden or dramatic cultural break with the Middle Ages (as Burckhardt argued)—there was after all much continuity in economic, political, and social life between the two periods—the Renaissance can still be viewed as a distinct period of European history that manifested itself first in Italy and then spread to the rest of Europe. What, then, are the characteristics of the Italian Renaissance?

Renaissance Italy was largely an urban society. As a result of its commercial preeminence and political evolution, northern Italy by the mid-fourteenth century was mostly a land of independent cities that dominated the country districts around them. These city-states became the centers of Italian political, economic, and social life. Within this new urban society, a secular spirit emerged as increasing wealth created new possibilities for the enjoyment of worldly things.

Above all, the Renaissance was an age of recovery from the "calamitous fourteenth century." Italy and Europe began a slow process of recuperation from the effects of the Black Death, political disorder, and economic recession. By the end of the fourteenth and beginning of the fifteenth centuries, Italians were using the words *recovery* and *revival* and were actively involved in a rebuilding process.

Recovery was accompanied by rebirth, specifically, a rebirth of the culture of classical antiquity. Increasingly aware of their own historical past, Italian intellectuals became intensely interested in the Greco-Roman culture of the ancient Mediterranean world. This new revival of classical antiquity (the Middle Ages, after all, had preserved much of ancient Latin culture) affected activities as diverse as politics and art and led to new attempts to reconcile the pagan philosophy of the Greco-Roman world with Christian thought, as well as new ways of viewing human beings.

Though not entirely new, a revived emphasis on individual ability became characteristic of the Italian Renaissance. As the fifteenth-century Florentine architect Leon Battista Alberti expressed it: "Men can do all things if they will."[1] A high regard for human dignity and worth and a realization of individual potentiality created a new social ideal of the well-rounded personality or universal person (*l'uomo universale*) who was capable of achievements in many areas of life.

These general features of the Italian Renaissance were not characteristic of all Italians, but were primarily the preserve of the wealthy upper classes who constituted a small percentage of the total population. The achievements of the Italian Renaissance were the product of an elite, rather than a mass, movement. Nevertheless, indirectly it did have some impact on ordinary people, especially in the cities where so many of the intellectual and artistic accomplishments of the period were most apparent and visible.

◆ The Making of Renaissance Society

The cultural flowering that we associate with the Italian Renaissance actually began in an era of severe economic difficulties. The commercial revolution of the twelfth, thirteenth, and early fourteenth centuries had produced great wealth and given rise to a money economy and the development of a capitalist system. Under this system, the capital or liquid wealth accumulated by private entrepreneurs was used to make further profits in trade, industry, and banking. After three centuries of economic expansion, in the second half of the fourteenth century, Europeans experienced severe economic reversals and social upheavals (see Chapter 11). By the middle of the fifteenth century, a gradual economic recovery had begun with an increase in the volume of manufacturing and trade. Economic growth varied from area to area, however, and despite the recovery Europe did not experience the economic boom of the High Middle Ages.

�֎ Economic Recovery

By the fourteenth century, Italian merchants were carrying on a flourishing commerce throughout the Mediterranean and had also expanded their lines of trade north along the Atlantic seaboard. The great galleys of the Venetian Flanders Fleet maintained a direct sea route from Venice to England and the Netherlands, where Italian merchants came into contact with the increasingly powerful Hanseatic League of merchants. Hard hit by the plague, the Italians lost their commercial preeminence while the Hanseatic League continued to prosper.

The Hanseatic League or Hansa had been formed as early as the thirteenth century, when some north German coastal towns, such as Lübeck, Hamburg, and Bremen, began to cooperate to gain favorable trading rights in Flemish cities. To protect themselves from pirates and competition from Scandinavian merchants, these and other northern towns formed a commercial and military league. By 1500, more than eighty cities belonged to the league, which had established settlements and commercial bases in many cities in England and northern Europe, including the chief towns of Denmark, Norway, and Sweden. For almost 200 years, the Hansa had a monopoly on northern European trade in timber, fish, grain, metals, honey, and wines. Its southern outlet in Flanders, the city of Bruges, became the economic crossroads of Europe in the fourteenth century since it served as the meeting place between Hanseatic merchants and the Flanders Fleet of Venice. In the fifteenth century, however, Bruges slowly began to decline. So, too, did the Hanseatic League as it proved increasingly unable to compete with the developing larger territorial states.

Overall, trade recovered dramatically from the economic contraction of the fourteenth century. The Italians and especially the Venetians, despite new restrictive pressures on their eastern Mediterranean trade from the Ottoman Turks (see The Ottoman Turks and the End of Byzantium later in this chapter), continued to maintain a wealthy commercial empire. Not until the sixteenth century, when the overseas discoveries gave new importance to the states facing the Atlantic, did the petty Italian city-states begin to suffer from the competitive advantages of the ever-growing and more powerful national territorial states.

The economic depression of the fourteenth century also affected patterns of manufacturing. The woolen industries of Flanders and the northern Italian cities had been particularly devastated. By the beginning of the fifteenth century, however, the Florentine woolen industry was experiencing a recovery. At the same time, the Italian cities began to develop and expand luxury industries, especially silk, glassware, and handworked items in metal and precious stones. Unfortunately, these luxury industries employed fewer people than the woolen industry and contributed less to overall prosperity.

Other new industries, especially printing, mining, and metallurgy, began to rival the textile industry in importance in the fifteenth century. New machinery and techniques for digging deeper mines and for separating metals from ore and purifying them were put into operation. When rulers began to transfer their rights to underground minerals to financiers as collateral for loans, these entrepreneurs quickly developed large mining operations to produce copper, iron, and silver. Especially valuable were the rich mineral deposits in central Europe, Hungary, the Tyrol, Bohemia, and Saxony. Expanding iron production and new skills in metalworking, in turn, contributed to the development of firearms that were more effective than the crude weapons of the fourteenth century.

The city of Florence regained its preeminence in banking in the fifteenth century, primarily due to the Medici family (see the box on p. 329). The Medici had expanded from cloth production into commerce, real estate, and banking. In its best days (in the fifteenth century), the House of Medici was the greatest banking house in Europe, with branches in Venice, Milan, Rome, Avignon, Bruges, London, and Lyons. Moreover, the family had controlling interests in industrial enterprises for wool, silk, and the mining of alum, used in the dyeing of textiles. Except for a brief interruption, the Medici were also the principal bankers for the papacy, a position that produced big profits and influence at the papal court. Despite its great success in the early and middle part of the fifteenth century, the Medici bank suffered a rather sudden decline at the end of the century due to poor leadership and a series of bad loans, especially uncollectible loans to rulers. In 1494, when the French expelled the Medici from Florence and confiscated their property, the Medicean financial edifice collapsed.

✖ Social Changes in the Renaissance

The Renaissance inherited a tripartite division of society from the Middle Ages. Society was fundamentally divided into three estates: the clergy, whose preeminence was grounded in the belief that people should be guided to spir-

Florence: "Queen City of the Renaissance"

Florence has long been regarded by many historians as the "queen city of the Renaissance." It was the intellectual and cultural center of Italy in the fifteenth century. In a letter written to a Venetian in 1472, Benedetto Dei, a Florentine merchant, gave a proud and boastful description of Florence's economy under the guidance of Lorenzo de' Medici.

✤ Benedetto Dei, Florence

Florence is more beautiful and five hundred years older than your Venice. We spring from triply noble blood. We are one-third Roman, one-third Frankish, and one-third Fiesolan [an ancient Etruscan town three miles northeast of Florence]. . . . We have round about us thirty thousand estates, owned by noblemen and merchants, citizens and craftsmen, yielding us yearly bread and meat, wine and oil, vegetables and cheese, hay and wood, to the value of nine hundred thousand ducats in cash, as you Venetians, Genoese, Chians, and Rhoadians who come to buy them know well enough. We have two trades greater than any four of yours in Venice put together—the trades of wool and silk. . . .

Our beautiful Florence contains within the city in this present year two hundred seventy shops belonging to the wool merchants' guild, from whence their wares are sent to Rome and the Marches, Naples and Sicily, Constantinople and Pera, Adrianople, . . . and the whole of Turkey. It contains also eighty-three rich and splendid warehouses of the silk merchants' guild, and furnishes gold and silver stuffs, velvet, brocade, damask, taffeta, and satin to Rome, Naples, Catalonia, and the whole of Spain, especially Seville, and to Turkey and Barbary. The principal fairs to which these wares go are those of Genoa, the Marches, Ferrara, Mantua, and the whole of Italy; Lyons, Avignon, Montpellier, Antwerp, and London. The number of banks amount to thirty-three; the shops of the cabinetmakers, whose business is carving and inlaid work, to eighty-four; and the workshops of the stonecutters and marble workers in the city and its immediate neighborhood, to fifty-four. There are forty-four goldsmiths' and jewelers' shops, thirty gold-beaters, silver wire-drawers, and a wax-figure maker [wax images were used in all churches]. . . . Go through all the cities of the world, nowhere will you ever be able to find artists in wax equal to those we now have in Florence. . . . Another flourishing industry is the making of light and elegant gold and silver wreaths and garlands, which are worn by young maidens of high degree, and which have given their names to the artist family of Ghirlandaio. Sixty-six is the number of the apothecaries' and grocer shops; seventy that of the butchers, besides eight large shops in which are sold fowls of all kinds, as well as game and also the native wine called Trebbiano, from San Giovanni in the upper Arno Valley; it would awaken the dead in its praise.

---

itual ends; the nobility, whose privileges were based on the principle that the nobles provided security and justice for society; and the third estate, which consisted of the peasants and inhabitants of the towns and cities. This social order experienced certain adaptations in the Renaissance, which we can see by examining the second and third estates (the clergy will be examined in Chapter 13).

☙ THE SOCIAL CLASSES: THE NOBILITY

Throughout much of Europe, the landholding nobles were faced with declining real incomes during the greater part of the fourteenth and fifteenth centuries, while the expense of maintaining noble status was rising. Nevertheless, members of the old nobility survived and new blood infused its ranks. A reconstruction of the aristocracy was well under way by 1500.

As a result of this reconstruction, the nobles, old and new, who constituted between 2 and 3 percent of the population in most countries, managed to dominate society as they had done in the Middle Ages, serving as military officers and holding important political posts as well as advising the king. Increasingly in the sixteenth century, members of the aristocracy pursued education as the means to maintain their role in government. One noble in the Low Countries, in a letter outlining how his son should be formally educated, stated that, due to his own lack of learning, he dared not express his opinions in the king's council and often "felt deep shame and humiliation" at his ignorance.

In northern Europe, the fifteenth century also saw the final flourishing of chivalry. Nobles played at being great warriors, but their tournaments were now characterized less by bloodshed than by flamboyance and a display of brilliant costumes that showed off an individual's social status.

☙ THE DEVELOPMENT OF A COURTLY SOCIETY IN ITALY

One of the more interesting social developments during the Renaissance was the change that occurred in Italian society. In the Early Renaissance, old noble families had moved into the cities and generally merged with the merchant middle classes to form the upper classes in these new urban societies. Consequently, Italy seemed to lose the notion of nobility or aristocracy. In the fifteenth century, this began to change as the tenor of Italian upperclass urban society became more aristocratic. Although this was especially evident in the princely states, such as

A Renaissance Banquet

As in Greek and Roman society, the Renaissance banquet was an occasion for good food, interesting conversation, music, and dancing. In Renaissance society, it was also a symbol of status and an opportunity to impress people with the power and wealth of one's family. Banquets were held to celebrate public and religious festivals, official visits, anniversaries, and weddings. The following menu lists the foods served at a grand banquet given by Pope Pius V in the sixteenth century.

A Sixteenth-Century Banquet

First Course:
Cold Delicacies from the Sideboard

Pieces of marzipan and marzipan balls
Neapolitan spice cakes
Malaga wine and Pisan biscuits
Fresh grapes
Prosciutto cooked in wine, served with capers
and grape pulp
Salted pork tongues cooked in wine, sliced
Spit-roasted songbirds, cold, with their
tongues sliced over them
Sweet mustard

Second Course:
Hot Foods from the Kitchen, Roasts

Fried veal sweetbreads and liver
Spit-roasted skylarks with lemon sauce
Spit-roasted quails with sliced eggplants
Stuffed spit-roasted pigeons with capers
sprinkled over them
Spit-roasted rabbits, with sauce and crushed pine nuts
Partridges larded and spit-roasted, served with lemon
Heavily seasoned poultry with lemon slices
Slices of veal, spit-roasted, with a sauce made
from the juices
Leg of goat, spit-roasted with a sauce made
from the juices
Soup of almond paste, with the flesh of three
pigeons to each serving

Third Course:
Hot Foods from the Kitchen,
Boiled Meats and Stews

Stuffed fat geese, boiled Lombard style and covered with
sliced almonds
Stuffed breast of veal, boiled, garnished with flowers
Very young calf, boiled, garnished with parsley
Almonds in garlic sauce
Turkish-style rice with milk, sprinkled with cinnamon
Stewed pigeons with mortadella sausage and
whole onions
Cabbage soup with sausages
Poultry pie, two chickens to each pie
Fricasseed breast of goat dressed with fried onions
Pies filled with custard cream
Boiled calves' feet with cheese and egg

Fourth Course:
Delicacies from the Sideboard

Bean tarts
Quince pastries
Pear tarts, the pears wrapped in marzipan
Parmesan cheese and Riviera cheese
Fresh almonds on vine leaves
Chestnuts roasted over the coals and served
with salt and pepper
Milk curds
Ring-shaped cakes
Wafers made from ground grain

---

the duchy of Milan where a courtly society emerged around the duke, even in the Italian republics the behavior of the upper class took on an aristocratic appearance (see the box above).

By 1500, certain ideals came to be expected of the noble or aristocrat. These were best expressed in *The Book of the Courtier* by the Italian Baldassare Castiglione (1478–1529). First published in 1528, Castiglione's work soon was popular throughout Europe and became a fundamental handbook for European aristocrats.

In *The Book of the Courtier*, Castiglione described the three basic attributes of the perfect courtier. First, nobles should possess fundamental native endowments, such as impeccable character, grace, talents, and noble birth. The perfect courtier must also cultivate certain achievements. Primarily, he should participate in military and bodily exercises since the principal profession of a courtier was arms. But unlike the medieval knight who had only been required to have military skill, the Renaissance courtier was also expected to have a classical education and to adorn his life with the arts by playing a musical instrument, drawing, and painting. In Castiglione's hands, the Renaissance ideal of the well-developed personality became a social ideal of the aristocracy. Finally, the aristocrat was expected to follow a certain standard of conduct. Nobles were expected to make good impressions; while being modest, they should not hide their accomplishments, but show them with grace.

But what was the purpose of these courtly standards? Castiglione said:

> Therefore, I think that the aim of the perfect Courtier, which we have not spoken of up to now, is so to win for himself, by means of the accomplishments ascribed to him by these gentlemen, the favor and mind of the prince whom he serves that he may be able to tell him, and always will tell him, the truth about everything he needs to know, without fear or risk of displeasing him; and that when he sees the mind of his prince inclined to a wrong action, he may dare to oppose him . . . so as to dissuade him of every evil intent and bring him to the path of virtue.[2]

This ideal of service to the prince reflected the secular ethic of the active life espoused by the earlier civic humanists (see Italian Renaissance Humanism later in this chapter). Castiglione put the new moral values of the Renaissance into a courtly, aristocratic form that was now acceptable to the nobility throughout Europe. Nobles would adhere to his principles for hundreds of years as they continued to dominate European life socially and politically.

❧ THE SOCIAL CLASSES: THE THIRD ESTATE OF PEASANTS AND TOWNSPEOPLE

Traditionally, peasants made up the overwhelming mass of the third estate and indeed continued to constitute as much as 85 to 90 percent of the total European population, except in the highly urbanized areas of northern Italy and Flanders. The most noticeable trend produced by the economic crisis of the fourteenth century was the decline of the manorial system and the continuing elimination of serfdom. This process had already begun in the twelfth century when the introduction of a money economy made possible the conversion of servile labor dues into rents paid in money, although they also continued to be paid in kind or labor. The contraction of the peasantry after the Black Death simply accelerated this process since lords found it convenient to deal with the peasants by granting freedom and accepting rents. The lord's lands were then tilled by hired workers or rented out. By the end of the fifteenth century, serfdom was declining, and more and more peasants were becoming legally free, although in many places lords were able to retain many of the fees they charged their peasants. Lords, then, became rentiers, and the old manorial system was replaced by a new arrangement based on cash. It is interesting to note that while serfdom was declining in western Europe, eastern Europe experienced a reverse trend. The weakness of eastern rulers enabled nobles to tie their peasants to the land and use servile labor in the large-scale production of grain for an ever-growing export market.

The remainder of the third estate centered around the inhabitants of towns and cities, originally the merchants and artisans who formed the burghers. The Renaissance town or city of the fifteenth century actually possessed a multitude of townspeople widely separated socially and economically.

At the top of urban society were the patricians, whose wealth from capitalistic enterprises in trade, industry, and banking enabled them to dominate their urban communities economically, socially, and politically. Below them were the petty burghers, the shopkeepers, artisans, guildmasters, and guild members who were largely concerned with providing goods and services for local consumption. Below these two groups were the propertyless workers earning pitiful wages and the unemployed, living squalid and miserable lives. These people constituted as much as 30 or 40 percent of the urban population. In many places in Europe in the late fourteenth and fifteenth centuries, urban poverty had increased dramatically. One rich merchant of Florence wrote:

> Those that are lazy and indolent in a way that does harm to the city, and who can offer no just reason for their condition, should either be forced to work or expelled from the Commune. The city would thus rid itself of that most harmful part of the poorest class. . . . If the lowest order of society earn enough food to keep them going from day to day, then they have enough.[3]

But even this large group was not at the bottom of the social scale; beneath them were the slaves, especially in the Italian cities.

❧ SLAVERY IN THE RENAISSANCE

Agricultural slavery had continued to exist in the Early Middle Ages, but had declined for economic reasons and been replaced by serfdom by the ninth century. Although some domestic slaves remained, slavery in European society had largely disappeared by the eleventh century. It reappeared first in Spain, where both Christians and Muslims used captured prisoners as slaves during the lengthy *reconquista*. In the second half of the fourteenth century, the shortage of workers after the Black Death led Italians to introduce slavery on a fairly large scale. In 1363, for example, the government of Florence authorized the unlimited importation of foreign slaves.

In the Italian cities, slaves were used as skilled workers, making handcrafted goods for their masters, or as household workers. Girls served as nursemaids and boys as playmates. Fiammetta Adimari wrote to her husband in 1469: "I must remind you that when Alfonso is weaned we ought to get a little slave-girl to look after him, or else one of the black boys to keep him company."[4] In Florence, wealthy merchants might possess two or three slaves. Often, men of the household took slaves as concubines, which sometimes led to the birth of illegitimate children. In 1392, the wealthy merchant Francesco Datini fathered an illegitimate daughter by Lucia, his twenty-year-old slave. His wife Margherita, who was unable to bear any children, reluctantly agreed to raise the girl as their own daughter. Many illegitimate children were not as fortunate.

Slaves for the Italian market were obtained primarily from the eastern Mediterranean and the Black Sea region and included Tartars, Russians, Albanians, and Dalmatians. There were also slaves from Africa, either Moors or Ethiopians, and Muslims from Spain. Because of the lucrative nature of the slave trade, Italian merchants became

WEDDING BANQUET. Parents arranged marriages in Renaissance Italy to strengthen business or family ties. A legally binding marriage contract was considered a necessary part of the marital arrangements. So, too, was a wedding feast. This painting by Botticelli shows the wedding banquet in Florence that celebrated the marriage of Nastagio degli Onesti and the daughter of Paulo Traversaro.

involved in the transportation of slaves. Between 1414 and 1423, 10,000 slaves were sold on the Venetian market. Most slaves were females, many of them young girls.

By the end of the fifteenth century, slavery had declined dramatically in the Italian cities. Many slaves had been freed by their owners for humanitarian reasons, and the major source of slaves dried up as the Black Sea slave markets were closed to Italian traders after the Turks conquered the Byzantine Empire. Although some other sources remained, prices rose dramatically, further cutting demand. Moreover, a general feeling had arisen that slaves—the "domestic enemy" as they were called—were dangerous and not worth the effort. By the sixteenth century, slaves were in evidence only at princely courts where they were kept as curiosities; this was especially true of black slaves.

In the fifteenth century, the Portuguese had imported increasing numbers of African slaves for southern European markets. It has been estimated that between 1444 and 1505, 140,000 slaves were shipped from Africa. The presence of blacks in European society was not entirely new. Saint Maurice, a Christian martyr of the fourth century, was portrayed by medieval artists as a black knight and became the center of a popular cult in the twelfth and thirteenth centuries. The number of blacks in Europe was small, however, until their importation as slaves.

THE FAMILY IN RENAISSANCE ITALY

The family played an important role in Renaissance Italy. Family meant, first of all, the extended household of parents, children, and servants (if the family was wealthy) and could also include grandparents, widowed mothers, and even unmarried sisters. Families that were related and bore the same surname often lived near each other and might dominate an entire urban district. Old family names, such as the Strozzi, Rucellai, and Medici, conferred great status and prestige. The family bond was a source of great security in a dangerous and violent world, and its importance helps explain the vendetta in the Italian Renaissance. A crime committed by one family member fell on the entire family, ensuring that retali-

ation by the offended family would be a bloody affair involving large numbers of people.

To maintain the family, careful attention was given to marriages, which were arranged by parents, often to strengthen business or family ties. Details were worked out well in advance, sometimes when children were only two or three, and reinforced by a legally binding marriage contract (see the box on p. 333). The important aspect of the contract was the size of the dowry, a sum of money presented by the wife's family to the husband upon marriage. The dowry could involve large sums of money and was expected of all families. The size of the dowry was an indication of whether the bride was moving upward or downward in society. With a large dowry, a daughter could marry a man of higher social status, thereby enabling her family to move up in society; if the daughter married a man of lower social status, however, then her dowry would be smaller since the reputation of her family would raise the status of the husband's family. Since poor families often had difficulty providing a dowry, wealthy families established societies to provide dowries for poor girls.

The father-husband was the center of the Italian family. He gave it his name, was responsible for it in all legal matters, managed all finances (his wife had no share in his wealth), and made the crucial decisions that determined his children's lives. A father's authority over his children was absolute until he died or formally freed his children. In Renaissance Italy, children did not become adults on reaching a certain age; instead adulthood came only when the father went before a judge and formally emancipated them. The age of emancipation varied from early teens to late twenties.

The wife managed the household, a position that gave women a certain degree of autonomy in their daily lives. Most wives, however, also knew that their primary function was to bear children. Upper-class wives were frequently pregnant; Alessandra Strozzi of Florence, for example, who had been married at the age of sixteen, bore eight children in ten years. Poor women did not conceive at the same rate because they nursed their own babies.

Marriage Negotiations

Marriages were so important in maintaining families in Renaissance Italy that much energy was put into arranging them. Parents made the choices for their children, most often for considerations that had little to do with the modern notion of love. This selection is taken from the letters of a Florentine matron of the illustrious Strozzi family to her son Filippo in Naples. The family's considerations were complicated by the fact that the son was in exile.

❁ Alessandra Strozzi to Her Son Filippo in Naples

[April 20, 1464] . . . Concerning the matter of a wife [for Filippo], it appears to me that if Francesco di Messer Tanagli wishes to give his daughter, that it would be a fine marriage. . . . Now I will speak with Marco [Parenti, Alessandra's son-in-law], to see if there are other prospects that would be better, and if there are none, then we will learn if he wishes to give her [in marriage]. . . . Francesco Tanagli has a good reputation, and he has held office, not the highest, but still he has been in office. You may ask: "Why should he give her to someone in exile?" There are three reasons. First, there aren't many young men of good family who have both virtue and property. Secondly, she has only a small dowry, 1,000 florins, which is the dowry of an artisan [although not a small sum, either—senior officials in the government bureaucracy earned 300 florins a year]. . . . Third, I believe that he will give her away, because he has a large family and he will need help to settle them. . . .

[July 26, 1465] . . . Francesco is a good friend of Marco and he trusts him. On S. Jacopo's day, he spoke to him discreetly and persuasively, saying that for several months he had heard that we were interested in the girl and . . . that when we had made up our minds, she will come to us willingly. [He said that] you were a worthy man, and that his family had always made good marriages, but that he had only a small dowry to give her, and so he would prefer to send her out of Florence to someone of worth, rather than to give her to someone here, from among those who were available, with little money. . . . We have information that she is affable and competent. She is responsible for a large family (there are twelve children, six boys and six girls), and the mother is always pregnant and isn't very competent. . . .

[August 31, 1465] . . . I have recently received some very favorable information [about the Tanagli girl] from two individuals. . . . They are in agreement that whoever gets her will be content. . . . Concerning her beauty, they told me what I had already seen, that she is attractive and well-proportioned. Her face is long, but I couldn't look directly into her face, since she appeared to be aware that I was examining her . . . and so she turned away from me like the wind. . . . She reads quite well . . . and she can dance and sing. . . .

So yesterday I sent for Marco and told him what I had learned. And we talked about the matter for a while, and decided that he should say something to the father and give him a little hope, but not so much that we couldn't withdraw, and find out from him the amount of the dowry. . . . May God help us to choose what will contribute to our tranquility and to the consolation of us all.

[September 13, 1465] . . . Marco came to me and said that he had met with Francesco Tanagli, who had spoken very coldly, so that I understand that he had changed his mind. . . .

[Filippo Strozzi eventually married Fiametta di Donato Adimari in 1466.]

Wealthy women gave their infants out to wet nurses, which enabled them to become pregnant more quickly after the birth of a child.

For women in the Renaissance, childbirth was a fearful occasion. Not only was it painful, but it could be deadly; as many as 10 percent of mothers died in childbirth. In his memoirs, the Florentine merchant Gregorio Dati recalled that three of his four wives had died in childbirth. His third wife, after bearing eleven children in fifteen years, "died in childbirth after lengthy suffering, which she bore with remarkable strength and patience."[5] Nor did the tragedies end with childbirth. Surviving mothers often faced the death of their children as well. In Florence in the fifteenth century, for example, almost 50 percent of the children born to merchant families died before the age of twenty. Given these mortality rates, many upper-class families sought to have as many children as possible to ensure that there would be a surviving male heir to the family fortune. This concern is evident in the Florentine humanist Leon Battista Alberti's treatise *On the Family*, where one of the characters remarks, "How many families do we see today in decadence and ruin! . . . Of all these families not only the magnificence and greatness but the very men, not only the men but the very names are shrunk away and gone. Their memory . . . is wiped out and obliterated."[6]

Considering that marriages had been arranged, marital relationships ran the gamut from deep emotional attachments to purely formal ties. The lack of emotional attachment from arranged marriages did encourage extramarital relationships, especially for those groups whose lifestyle offered special temptations. Although sexual license for males was the norm for princes and their courts, women were supposed to follow different guidelines. The first wife of Duke Filippo Maria Visconti of Milan had an affair with the court musician and was executed for it.

The great age difference between husbands and wives that was noticeable in Italian Renaissance marriage patterns also heightened the need for sexual outlets outside marriage. In Florence in 1427–1428, the average difference was thirteen years. Though females married between the ages of sixteen and eighteen, factors of environment, wealth, and demographic trends favored relatively late ages for the first marriages of males, who were usually in their thirties or even early forties. The existence of large numbers of young, unmarried males encouraged extramarital sex as well as prostitution. Prostitution was viewed as a necessary vice; since it could not be eliminated, it should be regulated. In Florence in 1415, the city fathers established communal brothels:

> Desiring to eliminate a worse evil by means of a lesser one, the lord priors . . . have decreed that the priors . . . may authorize the establishment of two public brothels in the city of Florence, in addition to the one which already exists. . . . [They are to be located] in suitable places or in places where the exercise of such scandalous activity can best be concealed, for the honor of the city and of those who live in the neighborhood in which these prostitutes must stay to hire their bodies for lucre.[7]

A prostitute in Florence was required to wear a traditional garb of "gloves on her hands and a bell on her head."

◆ The Italian States in the Renaissance

By the fifteenth century, five major powers dominated the Italian peninsula—the duchy of Milan, Venice, Florence, the Papal States, and the kingdom of Naples. Northern Italy was divided between the duchy of Milan and Venice. After the death of the last Visconti ruler of Milan in 1447, Francesco Sforza, one of the leading *condottieri* (see Chapter 11) of the time, turned on his Milanese employers, conquered the city, and became its new duke. Both the Visconti and the Sforza rulers worked to create a highly centralized territorial state. They were especially successful in devising systems of taxation that generated enormous revenues for the government. The maritime republic of Venice remained an extremely stable political entity governed by a small oligarchy of merchant-aristocrats. Its commercial empire brought in enormous revenues and gave it the status of an international power. At the end of the fourteenth century, Venice embarked upon the conquest of a territorial state in northern Italy to protect its food supply and its overland trade routes. Although expansion on the mainland made sense to the Venetians, it frightened Milan and Florence, which worked to curb what they perceived as the expansionary designs of the Venetians.

The republic of Florence dominated the region of Tuscany. By the beginning of the fifteenth century, Flor-

ence was governed by a small merchant oligarchy that manipulated the apparently republican government. In 1434, Cosimo de' Medici took control of this oligarchy. Although the wealthy Medici family maintained republican forms of government for appearance' sake, it ran the government from behind the scenes. Through their lavish patronage and careful courting of political allies, Cosimo (1434–1464), and later his grandson Lorenzo the Magnificent (1469–1492), were successful in dominating the city at a time when Florence was the center of the cultural Renaissance.

The Papal States lay in central Italy. Nominally under the political control of the popes, papal residence in Avignon and the Great Schism had enabled individual cities and territories, such as Urbino, Bologna, and Ferrara, to become independent of papal authority. The Renaissance popes of the fifteenth century directed much of their energy toward reestablishing their control over the Papal States (see The Renaissance Papacy later in this chapter).

The kingdom of Naples, which encompassed most of southern Italy and usually the island of Sicily, was fought over by the French and the Aragonese until the latter established their domination in the mid-fifteenth century. Throughout the Renaissance, the kingdom of Naples remained a largely feudal monarchy with a population consisting largely of poverty-stricken peasants dominated by unruly barons. It shared little in the cultural glories of the Renaissance.

Besides the five major states, there were a number of independent city-states under the control of powerful ruling families that became brilliant centers of Renaissance culture in the fifteenth century. These included Mantua under the enlightened rule of the Gonzaga lords, Ferrara governed by the flamboyant d'Este family, and perhaps the most famous, Urbino, ruled by the Montefeltro dynasty.

Federigo da Montefeltro, who ruled Urbino from 1444 to 1482, received a classical education typical of the famous humanist school in Mantua run by Vittorino da Feltre. He had also learned the skills of fighting, since the

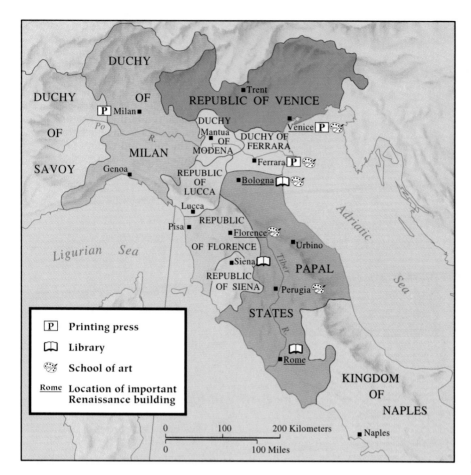

MAP 12.1 Renaissance Italy.

Montefeltro family compensated for the poverty of Urbino by hiring themselves out as *condottiere*. Federigo was not only a good ruler, but a rather unusual *condottiere* by fifteenth-century standards. Although not a brilliant general, he was reliable and honest. He did not break his promises, even when urged to do so by a papal legate. His employers included two kings of Naples, three popes, and two dukes of Milan. At the same time, Duke Federigo was one of the greatest patrons of Renaissance culture. Under his direction, Urbino became a well-known cultural and intellectual center. Though a despot, he was also benevolent. It was said of him that he could walk safely through the streets of Urbino unaccompanied by a bodyguard, a feat few Renaissance rulers dared to emulate.

A noticeable feature of these smaller Renaissance courts was the important role played by women. Battista Sforza, niece of the ruler of Milan, was the wife of Federigo da Montefeltro. The duke called his wife "the delight of both my public and my private hours." An intelligent woman, she was well versed in both Greek and Latin and did much to foster art and letters in Urbino. As a prominent *condottiere*, Federigo was frequently absent, and like earlier feudal wives, Battista Sforza was respected for governing the state "with firmness and good sense."

Perhaps the most famous of the Renaissance ruling women was Isabella d'Este (1474–1539), daughter of the duke of Ferrara, who married Francesco Gonzaga, marquis of Mantua. Their court was another important center of art and learning in the Renaissance. Educated at the brilliant court of Ferrara, Isabella was known for her intelligence and political wisdom. Called the "first lady of the world," she attracted artists and intellectuals to the Mantuan court and was responsible for amassing one of the finest libraries in all of Italy. Her numerous letters to friends, family, princes, and artists all over Europe disclose her political acumen as well as a good sense of humor (see the box on p. 337). Both before and after the death of her husband Francesco, she effectively ruled Mantua and won a reputation as a clever negotiator.

The frenzied world of the Italian territorial states gave rise to a political practice that was later used on a larger scale by competing European states. This was the concept of a balance of power, designed to prevent the aggrandizement of any one state at the expense of the others. This system was especially evident after 1454 when the Italian states signed the Peace of Lodi, which ended almost a half-century of war and inaugurated a relatively peaceful era in Italy until 1494. An alliance system (Milan, Florence, and Naples versus Venice and the papacy) was then created that led to a workable balance of power within Italy. It failed, however, to establish lasting cooperation among the major powers or a common foreign policy.

PIERO DELLA FRANCESCA,
DUKE AND DUCHESS OF URBINO.
Federigo da Montefeltro and his
wife, Battista Sforza, ruled the
small central Italian principality
of Urbino. These profile portraits
by Piero della Francesca gave a
realistic rendering of the two figures. Visible in the background
are the hills and valleys of
Urbino.

The growth of powerful monarchical states (see The "New Monarchies" later in this chapter) led to trouble for the Italians. Italy soon became a battlefield for the great power struggle between the French and Spanish monarchies. Italian wealth and splendor would probably have been inviting to its northern neighbors under any circumstances, but it was actually the breakdown of the Italian balance of power that encouraged the invasions and began the Italian wars. Feeling isolated, Ludovico Sforza, the duke of Milan, foolishly invited the French to intervene in Italian politics. The French king Charles VIII (1483–1498) was eager to do so and in 1494, with an army of 30,000 men, advanced through Italy and occupied the kingdom of Naples. Other Italian states turned to the Spanish for help, and Ferdinand of Aragon indicated his willingness to intervene. For the next fifteen years, the French and Spanish competed to dominate Italy. Beginning in the decade of the 1510s, the war was continued by a new generation of rulers, Francis I of France and Charles I of Spain (see Chapter 13). This war was part of a long struggle for power throughout Europe between the Valois and Habsburg dynasties. Italy was only a pawn for the two great powers, a convenient arena for fighting battles. The terrible sack of Rome in 1527 by the armies of the Spanish king Charles I brought a temporary end to the Italian wars. Hereafter, the Spaniards dominated Italy.

Although some Italians had developed a sense of national consciousness and differentiated between Italians and "barbarians" (all foreigners), few Italians conceived of creating an alliance or confederation of states that could repel foreign invaders. Italians remained fiercely loyal to their own petty states, making invasion a fact of life in Italian history for all too long. Italy would not achieve unification and nationhood until 1870.

❊ *The Birth of Modern Diplomacy*

The modern diplomatic system was a product of the Italian Renaissance. There were ambassadors in the Middle Ages, but they were used only on a temporary basis. Moreover, an ambassador, regardless of whose subject he was, regarded himself as the servant of all Christendom, not just of his particular employer. As a treatise on diplomacy stated: "An ambassador is sacred because he acts for the general welfare." Since he was the servant of all Christendom, "the business of an ambassador is peace."[8]

This concept of an ambassador changed during the Italian Renaissance because of the political situation in Italy. A large number of states existed, many so small that their security was easily threatened by their neighbors. To survive, the Italian states began to send resident diplomatic agents to each other to ferret out useful information. During the Italian wars, the practice of resident diplomats spread to the rest of Europe, and in the course of the sixteenth and seventeenth centuries, Europeans developed the diplomatic machinery still in use today, such as the rights of ambassadors in host countries and the proper procedures for conducting diplomatic business.

With the use of permanent resident agents or ambassadors, the conception of the purpose of the ambassador also changed. A Venetian diplomat attempted to define the function of an ambassador in a treatise written at the end of the fifteenth century. He wrote: "The first duty of an ambassador is exactly the same as that of any other servant of a government, that is, to do, say, advise, and think whatever may best serve the preservation and aggrandizement of his own state."[9] An ambassador was now simply an agent of the territorial state that sent him, not the larger body of Christendom. He could

The Letters of Isabella d'Este

Many Italian and European rulers at the beginning of the sixteenth century regarded Isabella d'Este as an important political figure. These excerpts from her letters reveal Isabella's political skills and her fierce determination. After her husband was taken prisoner by the Venetians in 1509, she refused to accept the condition for his release— namely, that her son Federico be kept as a hostage by the Venetians or the Holy Roman Emperor. She wrote to both the emperor and her husband, refusing to do as they asked.

✷ Letter of Isabella d'Este to the Imperial Envoy

As to the demand for our dearest first-born son Federico, besides being a cruel and almost inhuman thing for any one who knows the meaning of a mother's love, there are many reasons which render it difficult and impossible. Although we are quite sure that his person would be well cared for and protected by His Majesty [the Holy Roman Emperor], how could we wish him to run the risk of this long and difficult journey, considering the child's tender and delicate age? And you must know what comfort and solace, in his father's present unhappy condition, we find in the presence of this dear son, the hope and joy of all our people and subjects. To deprive us of him, would be to deprive us of life itself, and of all we count good and precious. If you take Federico away you might as well take away our life and state. . . . Once for all, we will suffer any loss rather than part from our son, and this you may take to be our deliberate and unchanging resolution.

✷ Letter of Isabella d'Este to her Husband [who had ordered her to send the boy to Venice]

If in this matter Your Excellency were to despise me and deprive me of your love and grace, I would rather endure such harsh treatment, I would rather lose our State, than deprive us of our children. I am hoping that in time your own prudence and kindness will make you understand that I have acted more lovingly toward you than you have to yourself.

Have patience! You can be sure that I think continuously of your liberation and when the time comes I will not fail you, as I have not relaxed my efforts. As witness I cite the Pope, the Emperor, the King of France, and all the other reigning heads and potentates of Christendom. Yes, and the infidels as well [she had written to the Turkish sultan for help]. If it were *really* the only means of setting you free, I would not only send Federico but all the other children as well. I will do everything imaginable. Some day I hope I can make you understand. . . .

Pardon me if this letter is badly written and worse composed, but I do not know if I am dead or alive.

> *Isabella, who desires the*
> *best for Your Excellency,*
> *written with her own hand*

[Isabella's husband was not pleased with her response and exclaimed angrily: "That whore of my wife is the cause of it all. Send me into battle alone, do what you like with me. I have lost in one blow my state, my honor and my freedom. If she does not obey, I'll cut her vocal cords."]

---

use any methods that were beneficial to the political interests of his own state. We are at the beginning of modern politics when the interests of the state supersede all other considerations.

✷ *Machiavelli and the New Statecraft*

No one gave better expression to the Renaissance preoccupation with political power than Niccolò Machiavelli (1469–1527). He entered the service of the Florentine republic in 1498, four years after the Medici family had been expelled from the city. As a secretary to the Florentine Council of Ten, he made numerous diplomatic missions, including trips to France and Germany, and saw the workings of statecraft firsthand. Since Italy had been invaded in 1494, Machiavelli was active during a period of Italian tribulation and devastation. In 1512, French defeat and Spanish victory led to the reestablishment of Medici power in Florence. Staunch republicans, including Machiavelli, were sent into exile. Forced to give up politics, the great love of his life, Machiavelli now reflected on political power and wrote books, including *The Prince* (1513), one of the most famous treatises on political power in the Western world.

Machiavelli's ideas on politics stemmed from two major sources, his preoccupation with Italy's political problems and his knowledge of ancient Rome. His major concerns in *The Prince* were the acquisition and expansion of political power as the means to restore and maintain order in his time. Machiavelli was aware that his own approach to political power was different from previous political theorists. Late medieval political theorists believed that a ruler was justified in exercising political power only if it contributed to the common good of the people he served. The ethical side of a prince's activity—how a ruler ought to behave based on Christian moral principles—was the focus of many late medieval treatises on politics. Machiavelli bluntly contradicted this approach:

> But my hope is to write a book that will be useful, at least to those who read it intelligently, and so I thought it sensible

MACHIAVELLI. In *The Prince*, Machiavelli gave concrete expression to the Renaissance preoccupation with political power. This slender volume remains one of the most famous Western treatises on politics. Machiavelli is seen here in a portrait by Santi di Tito.

Machiavelli found a good example of the new Italian ruler in Cesare Borgia, the son of Pope Alexander VI, who used ruthless measures to achieve his goal of carving out a new state in central Italy. As Machiavelli said: "So anyone who decides that the policy to follow when one has newly acquired power is to destroy one's enemies, to secure some allies, to win wars, whether by force or by fraud, to make oneself both loved and feared by one's subjects, . . . cannot hope to find, in the recent past, a better model to imitate than Cesare Borgia." Machiavelli was among the first to abandon morality as the basis for the analysis of political activity (see the box on p. 339).

Because of the ideas in *The Prince*, Machiavelli is often considered the founder of modern, secular power politics, but we should note that Machiavelli himself was primarily concerned with Italy's tragic political condition. If it hoped to free itself from the "barbarous cruelties and outrages" perpetrated by the monarchical territorial states to the north, Italy needed "someone who could bind her wounds and . . . heal her sores which long ago became infected." If any person undertook the task, "What Italian would refuse to pledge him allegiance?"[12] If he followed the principles enunciated in *The Prince*, he would succeed. Machiavelli's own sympathies for a republican form of government were clearly evident in *The Discourses*, a political treatise written a few years after *The Prince*. In this work, Machiavelli reflected on the many lessons people of his age could learn from examining the institutions of the Roman Republic. And yet, Machiavelli doubted whether it was possible, in the turbulent politics of his age, to establish a republic. He said in *The Discourses*: "If any one wanted to establish a republic at the present time, he would find it much easier with the simple mountaineers, who are almost without any civilization, than with such as are accustomed to live in cities, where civilization is already corrupt."[13]

to go straight to a discussion of how things are in real life and not waste time with a discussion of an imaginary world. . . . for the gap between how people actually behave and how they ought to behave is so great that anyone who ignores everyday reality in order to live up to an ideal will soon discover he had been taught how to destroy himself, not how to preserve himself.[10]

Machiavelli considered his approach far more realistic than that of his medieval forebears.

From Machiavelli's point of view, a prince's attitude toward power must be based on an understanding of human nature, which he perceived as basically self-centered: "For of men one can, in general, say this: They are ungrateful, fickle, deceptive and deceiving, avoiders of danger, eager to gain." Political activity, therefore, could not be restricted by moral considerations. The prince acts on behalf of the state and for the sake of the state must be willing to let his conscience sleep. As Machiavelli put it:

You need to understand this: A ruler, and particularly a ruler who is new to power, cannot conform to all those rules that men who are thought good are expected to respect, for he is often obliged, in order to hold on to power, to break his word, to be uncharitable, inhumane, and irreligious. So he must be mentally prepared to act as circumstances and changes in fortune require. As I have said, he should do what is right if he can; but he must be prepared to do wrong if necessary.[11]

◆ The Intellectual Renaissance in Italy

The emergence and growth of individualism and secularism as characteristics of the Italian Renaissance are most noticeable in the intellectual and artistic realms. Italian culture had matured by the fourteenth century. For the next two centuries, Italy was the cultural leader of Europe. This new Italian culture was primarily the product of a relatively wealthy, urban lay society. The most important literary movement we associate with the Renaissance is humanism.

✻ *Italian Renaissance Humanism*

Renaissance humanism was a form of education and culture based on the study of the classics. Humanism was not so much a philosophy of life as an educational program

Machiavelli: "Is it Better to be Loved than Feared?"

In 1513, Niccolò Machiavelli wrote a short treatise on political power that, justly or unjustly, has given him a reputation as a political opportunist. In this passage from Chapter 17 of The Prince, *Machiavelli analyzes whether it is better for a ruler to be loved than feared.*

✻ Machiavelli, *The Prince*

This leads us to a question that is in dispute: Is it better to be loved than feared, or vice versa? My reply is one ought to be both loved and feared; but, since it is difficult to accomplish both at the same time, I maintain it is much safer to be feared than loved, if you have to do without one of the two. For of men one can, in general, say this: They are ungrateful, fickle, deceptive and deceiving, avoiders of danger, eager to gain. As long as you serve their interests, they are devoted to you. They promise you their blood, their possessions, their lives, and their children, as I said before, so long as you seem to have no need of them. But as soon as you need help, they turn against you. Any ruler who relies simply on their promises and makes no other preparations, will be destroyed. For you will find that those whose support you buy, who do not rally to you because they admire your strength of character and nobility of soul, these are people you pay for, but they are never yours, and in the end you cannot get the benefit of your investment. Men are less nervous of offending someone who makes himself lovable, than someone who makes himself frightening. For love attaches men by ties of obligation, which, since men are wicked, they break whenever their interests are at stake. But fear restrains men because they are afraid of punishment, and this fear never leaves them. Still, a ruler should make himself feared in such a way that, if he does not inspire love, at least he does not provoke hatred. For it is perfectly possible to be feared and not hated. You will only be hated if you seize the property or the women of your subjects and citizens. Whenever you have to kill someone, make sure that you have a suitable excuse and an obvious reason; but, above all else, keep your hands off other people's property; for men are quicker to forget the death of their father than the loss of their inheritance. Moreover, there are always reasons why you might want to seize people's property; and he who begins to live by plundering others will always find an excuse for seizing other people's possessions; but there are fewer reasons for killing people, and one killing need not lead to another.

When a ruler is at the head of his army and has a vast number of soldiers under his command, then it is absolutely essential to be prepared to be thought cruel; for it is impossible to keep an army united and ready for action without acquiring a reputation for cruelty.

---

that revolved around a clearly defined group of intellectual disciplines or "liberal arts"—grammar, rhetoric, poetry, moral philosophy or ethics, and history—all based on an examination of classical authors.

The central importance of literary preoccupations in Renaissance humanism is evident in the professional status or occupations of the humanists. Some of them were teachers of the humanities in secondary schools and universities, where they either gave occasional lectures or held permanent positions, often as professors of rhetoric. Others served as secretaries in the chancelleries of Italian city-states or at the courts of princes or popes. All of these occupations were largely secular, and most humanists were laymen rather than members of the clergy.

✒ THE EMERGENCE OF HUMANISM

Petrarch (1304–1374) has often been called the father of Italian Renaissance humanism (see Chapter 11 on Petrarch's use of the Italian vernacular). Petrarch had rejected his father's desire that he become a lawyer and took up a literary career instead. Although he lived in Avignon for a time, most of his last decades were spent in Italy as the guest of various princes and city governments. With his usual lack of modesty, Petrarch once exclaimed, "Some of the greatest kings of our time have loved me and cultivated my friendship. . . . When I was their guest it was more as if they were mine."[14]

Petrarch did more than any other individual in the fourteenth century to foster the development of Renaissance humanism. He was the first intellectual to characterize the Middle Ages as a period of darkness, promoting the mistaken belief that medieval culture was ignorant of classical antiquity. Petrarch condemned the scholastic philosophy of the Middle Ages for its "barbarous" Latin and use of logic, rather than rhetoric, to harmonize faith and reason. Philosophy, he argued, should be the "art of virtuous living," not a science of logic chopping. Petrarch's interest in the classics led him on a quest for forgotten Latin manuscripts and set in motion a ransacking of monastic libraries throughout Europe. In his preoccupation with the classics and their secular content, Petrarch worried at times whether he was sufficiently attentive to spiritual ideals (see the box on p. 340). His qualms, however, did not prevent him from inaugurating the humanist emphasis on the use of pure classical Latin, making it fashionable for humanists to use Cicero as a model for prose and Virgil for poetry.

Petrarch: Mountain Climbing and the Search for Spiritual Contentment

Petrarch has long been regarded as the father of Italian Renaissance humanism. One of his literary masterpieces was The Ascent of Mt. Ventoux. Its colorful description of an attempt to climb a mountain in Provence in southern France and survey the world from its top has unwisely led some to see it as a vivid example of the humanists' rediscovery of nature after the medieval period's concentration on the afterlife. Of course, medieval people had been aware of the natural world. Moreover, Petrarch's primary interest is in presenting an allegory of his own soul's struggle to achieve a higher spiritual state. The work is addressed to a professor of theology in Paris who had initially led Petrarch to read Augustine. The latter had experienced a vivid conversion to Christianity almost 1,000 years earlier.

❋ Petrarch, *The Ascent of Mt. Ventoux*

Today I ascended the highest mountain in this region, which, not without cause, they call the Windy Peak. Nothing but the desire to see its conspicuous height was the reason for this undertaking. For many years I have been intending to make this expedition. You know that since my early childhood, as fate tossed around human affairs, I have been tossed around in these parts, and this mountain, visible far and wide from everywhere, is always in your view. So I was at last seized by the impulse to accomplish what I had always wanted to do. . . .

[After some false starts, Petrarch finally achieves his goal and arrives at the top of Mt. Ventoux.]

I was glad of the progress I had made, but I wept over my imperfection and was grieved by the fickleness of all that men do. In this manner I seemed to have somehow forgotten the place I had come to and why, until I was warned to throw off such sorrows, for which another place would be more appropriate. I had better look around and see what I had intended to see in coming here. The time to leave was approaching, they said. . . . Like a man aroused from sleep, I turned back and looked toward the west. . . . one could see most distinctly the mountains of the province of Lyons to the right and, to the left, the sea near Marseilles as well as the waves that break against Aigues Mortes. . . . The Rhône River was directly under our eyes.

I admired every detail, now relishing earthly enjoyment, now lifting up my mind to higher spheres after the example of my body, and I thought it fit to look in the volume of Augustine's *Confessions* which I owe to your loving kindness and preserve carefully, keeping it always in my hands, in remembrance of the author as well as the donor. It is a little book of smallest size but full of infinite sweetness. I opened it with the intention of reading whatever might occur to me first: nothing, indeed, but pious and devout sentences could come to hand. I happened to hit upon the tenth book of the work. . . . Where I fixed my eyes first, it was written: "And men go to admire the high mountains, the vast floods of the sea, the huge streams of the rivers, the circumference of the ocean, and the revolutions of the stars—and desert themselves." I was stunned, I confess. I bade my brother [who had accompanied him], who wanted to hear more, not to molest me, and closed the book, angry with myself that I still admired earthly things. Long since I ought to have learned, even from pagan philosophers, that "nothing is admirable besides the soul; compared to its greatness nothing is great."

I was completely satisfied with what I had seen of the mountain and turned my inner eye toward myself. From this hour nobody heard me say a word until we arrived at the bottom. These words occupied me sufficiently. I could not imagine that this had happened to me by chance: I was convinced that whatever I had read there was said to me and to nobody else. I remembered that Augustine once suspected the same regarding himself, when, while he was reading the Apostolic Epistles, the first passage that occurred to him was, as he himself relates: "Not in banqueting and drunkenness, not in chambering and wantonness, not in strife and envying; but put you on the Lord Jesus Christ, and make no provision for the flesh to fulfill your lusts."

As Petrarch said, "Christ is my God; Cicero is the prince of the language."

✒ HUMANISM IN FIFTEENTH-CENTURY ITALY

In Florence, the humanist movement took a new direction at the beginning of the fifteenth century when it became closely tied to Florentine civic spirit and pride, giving rise to what one modern scholar has labeled "civic humanism." Fourteenth-century humanists such as Petrarch had described the intellectual life as one of solitude. They rejected family and a life of action in the community. In the busy civic world of Florence, however, intellectuals began to take a new view of their role as intellectuals. The classical Roman Cicero, who was both a statesman and an intellectual, became their model. Leonardo Bruni (1370–1444), a humanist, Florentine patriot, and chancellor of the city, wrote a biography of Cicero entitled the *New Cicero*, in which he waxed enthusiastically about the fusion of political action and literary creation in Cicero's life. From Bruni's time on, Cicero

A Humanist's Enthusiasm for Greek

One of the first humanists to have a thorough knowledge of both Latin and Greek was the Florentine chancellor Leonardo Bruni. Bruni was fortunate to be instructed by the Greek scholar Manuel Chrysoloras, who was persuaded by the Florentines to come to Florence to teach Greek. As this selection illustrates, Bruni seized the opportunity to pursue his passion for Greek letters.

❋ Leonardo Bruni, *History of His Own Times in Italy*

Then first came the knowledge of Greek letters, which for 700 years had been lost among us. It was the Byzantine, Chrysoloras, a nobleman in his own country and most skilled in literature, who brought Greek learning back to us. Because his country was invaded by the Turks, he came by sea to Venice; but as soon as his fame went abroad, he was cordially invited and eagerly besought to come to Florence on a public salary to spread his abundant riches before the youth of the city [1396]. At that time I was studying Civil Law. But my nature was afire with the love of learning and I had already given no little time to dialectic and rhetoric. Therefore at the coming of Chrysoloras I was divided in my mind, feeling that it was a shame to desert the Law and no less wrong to let slip such an occasion for learning Greek. And often with youthful impulsiveness I addressed myself thus: "When you are privileged to gaze upon and have converse with Homer, Plato, and Demosthenes as well as the other poets, philosophers, and orators of whom such wonderful things are reported, and when you might saturate yourself with their admirable teachings, will you turn your back and flee? Will you permit this opportunity, divinely offered you, to slip by? For 700 years now no one in Italy has been in possession of Greek and yet we agree that all knowledge comes from that source. What great advancement of knowledge, enlargement of fame, and increase of pleasure will come to you from an acquaintance with this tongue! There are everywhere quantities of doctors of the Civil Law and the opportunity of completing your study in this field will not fail you. However, should the one and only doctor of Greek letters disappear, there will be no one from whom to acquire them."

Overcome at last by these arguments, I gave myself to Chrysoloras and developed such ardor that whatever I learned by day, I revolved with myself in the night while asleep.

served as the inspiration for the Renaissance ideal that it was the duty of an intellectual to live an active life for one's state. An individual only "grows to maturity—both intellectually and morally—through participation" in the life of the state. Civic humanism reflected the values of the urban society of the Italian Renaissance. Humanists came to believe that their study of the humanities should be put to the service of the state. It is no accident that humanists served the state as chancellors, councillors, and advisers.

Also evident in the humanism of the first half of the fifteenth century was a growing interest in Greek. One of the first Italian humanists to gain a thorough knowledge of Greek was Leonardo Bruni, who became an enthusiastic pupil of the Byzantine scholar Manuel Chrysoloras, who taught in Florence from 1396 to 1400 (see the box above). Humanists eagerly perused the works of Plato as well as Greek poets, dramatists, historians, and orators, such as Thucydides, Euripides, and Sophocles, all of whom had been ignored by the scholastics of the High Middle Ages as irrelevant to the theological questions they were examining.

By the fifteenth century, a consciousness of being humanists had emerged. This was especially evident in the career of Lorenzo Valla (1407–1457). Valla was brought up in Rome and educated in both Latin and Greek. Even-tually, during the pontificate of Nicholas V (1447–1455), he achieved his chief ambition of becoming a papal secretary. It was Valla, above all others, who turned his attention to the literary criticism of ancient texts. His most famous work was his demonstration that the Donation of Constantine, a document used by the popes, especially in the ninth and tenth centuries (see Chapter 8), to claim temporal sovereignty over all the west, was a forgery written in the eighth century. Valla's other major work, *The Elegances of the Latin Language*, was an effort to purify medieval Latin and restore Latin to its proper position over the vernacular. The treatise examined the proper use of classical Latin and created a new literary standard. Early humanists had tended to take as classical models any author (including Christians) who had written before the seventh century A.D. Valla identified different stages in the growth of the Latin language and accepted only the Latin of the last century of the Roman Republic and the first century of the empire.

Another significant humanist of this period was Poggio Bracciolini (1380–1459), who reflected the cult of humanism at its best. Born and educated in Florence, he went on to serve as a papal secretary for fifty years, a position that enabled him to become an avid collector of classical manuscripts. He was responsible for finding all of the writings of fifteen different authors. Poggio's best-known literary work was the *Facetiae,* a lighthearted collection of jokes, which included a rather cynical criticism of the clergy:

> A friar of Tivoli, who was not very considerate of the people, was once thundering away with many words about the detestability of adultery. Among other things, he declared that this sin was so grave that he would prefer to lie with ten virgins than with one married woman. And many of those present shared his opinion.[15]

Poggio and other Italian humanists were very critical of the Catholic church at times, but fundamentally they accepted the church and above all wished only to restore a simpler, purer, and more ethical Christianity. To the humanists, the study of the classics was perfectly compatible with Christianity.

HUMANISM AND PHILOSOPHY

In the second half of the fifteenth century, a dramatic upsurge of interest in the works of Plato occurred, especially evident among the members of the Florentine Platonic Academy. This academy was not a formal school, but rather an informal discussion group. Cosimo de' Medici, the de facto ruler of Florence, became its patron and commissioned a translation of Plato's dialogues by Marsilio Ficino (1433–1499), one of the academy's leaders. Ficino dedicated his life to the translation of Plato and the exposition of the Platonic philosophy known as Neoplatonism.

In two major works, Ficino undertook the synthesis of Christianity and Platonism into a single system. His Neoplatonism was based upon two primary ideas, the Neoplatonic hierarchy of substances and a theory of spiritual love. Drawing upon the Neoplatonists of the ancient world, Ficino restated the idea of a hierarchy of substances, or great chain of being, from the lowest form of physical matter (plants) to the purest spirit (God), in which humans occupied a central or middle position. They were the link between the material world (through the body) and the spiritual world (through the soul), and their highest duty was to ascend toward that union with God that was the true end of human existence. Ficino's theory of spiritual or Platonic love maintained that just as all people are bound together in their common humanity by love, so too are all parts of the universe held together by bonds of sympathetic love.

Renaissance Hermeticism was another product of the Florentine intellectual environment of the late fifteenth century. Upon the request of Cosimo de' Medici, Ficino translated into Latin a Greek work entitled the *Corpus Hermeticum.* The Hermetic manuscripts contained two kinds of writings. One type stressed the occult sciences with emphasis on astrology, alchemy, and magic. The other focused on theological and philosophical beliefs and speculations. Some parts of the Hermetic writings were distinctly pantheistic, seeing divinity embodied in all aspects of nature, in the heavenly bodies as well as in earthly objects. As Giordano Bruno, one of the most prominent of

the sixteenth-century Hermeticists stated: "God as a whole is in all things."[16] For Renaissance intellectuals, the Hermetic revival offered a new view of humankind. They believed that human beings had been created as divine beings endowed with divine creative power, but had freely chosen to enter the material world (nature). Humans could recover their divinity, however, through a regenerative experience or purification of the soul. Thus regenerated, they became true sages or magi, as the Renaissance called them, who had knowledge of God and of truth. In regaining their original divinity, they reacquired an intimate knowledge of nature and the ability to employ the powers of nature for beneficial purposes.

In Italy, the most prominent magi in the late fifteenth century were Ficino and his friend and pupil, Giovanni Pico della Mirandola (1463–1494). Pico produced one of the most famous writings of the Renaissance, the *Oration on the Dignity of Man,* a preface to his *900 Conclusions,* which were meant to be a summation of all learning and were offered as theses for a public debate. Pico combed diligently through the writings of many philosophers of different backgrounds for the common "nuggets of universal truth" that he believed were all part of God's revelation to humanity. In the *Oration* (see the box on p. 343), Pico offered a ringing statement of unlimited human potential: "To him it is granted to have whatever he chooses, to be whatever he wills."[17] Like Ficino, Pico took an avid interest in Hermetic philosophy, accepting it as the "science of the Divine," which "embraces the deepest contemplation of the most secret things, and at last the knowledge of all nature."[18]

Education in the Renaissance

The humanist movement had a profound effect on education. Renaissance humanists believed that human beings could be dramatically changed by education. They wrote books on education and developed secondary schools based on their ideas. Most famous was the one founded in 1423 by Vittorino da Feltre (1378–1446) at Mantua, where the ruler of that small Italian state, Gian Francesco I Gonzaga, wished to provide a humanist school for his children. Vittorino based much of his educational system on the ideas of classical authors, particularly Cicero and Quintilian.

At the core of the academic training Vittorino offered were the "liberal studies." The Renaissance view of the value of the liberal arts was most strongly influenced by a treatise on education called *Concerning Character* by Pietro Paolo Vergerio (1370–1444). This work stressed the importance of the liberal arts as the key to true freedom, enabling individuals to reach their full potential. According to Vergerio, "we call those studies liberal which are worthy of a free man; those studies by which we attain and practice virtue and wisdom; that education which calls forth, trains, and develops those highest gifts of body and mind which ennoble men, and which are rightly judged to

Pico della Mirandola and the Dignity of Man

Giovanni Pico della Mirandola was one of the foremost intellects of the Italian Renaissance. Pico boasted that he had studied all schools of philosophy, whch he tried to demonstrate by drawing up 900 theses for public disputation at the age of twenty-four. As a preface to his theses, he wrote his famous oration, On the Dignity of Man, *in which he proclaimed the unlimited potentiality of human beings.*

❈ Pico della Mirandola, *Oration on the Dignity of Man*

At last the best of artisans [God] ordained that that creature to whom He had been able to give nothing proper to himself should have joint possession of whatever had been peculiar to each of the different kinds of being. He therefore took man as a creature of indeterminate nature, and assigning him a place in the middle of the world, addressed him thus: "Neither a fixed abode nor a form that is yours alone nor any function peculiar to yourself have we given you, Adam, to the end that according to your longing and according to your judgment you may have and possess what abode, what form, and what functions you yourself desire. The nature of all other beings is limited and constrained within the bounds of laws prescribed by Us. You, constrained by no limits, in accordance with your own free will, in whose hand We have placed you, shall ordain for yourself the limits of your nature. We have set you at the world's center that you may from there more easily observe whatever is in the world. We have made you neither of heaven nor of earth, neither mortal nor immortal, so that with freedom of choice and with honor, as though the maker and molder of yourself, you may fashion yourself in whatever shape you shall prefer. You shall have the power to degenerate into the lower forms of life, which are brutish. You shalt have the power, out of your soul's judgment, to be reborn into the higher forms, which are divine."

O supreme generosity of God the Father, O highest and most marvelous felicity of man! To him it is granted to have whatever he chooses, to be whatever he wills. Beasts as soon as they are born bring with them from their mother's womb all they will ever possess. Spiritual beings, either from the beginning or soon thereafter, become what they are to be for ever and ever. On man when he came into life the Father conferred the seeds of all kinds and the germs of every way of life. Whatever seeds each man cultivates will grow to maturity and bear in him their own fruit. If they be vegetative, he will be like a plant. If sensitive, he will become brutish. If rational, he will grow into a heavenly being. If intellectual, he will be an angel and the son of God.

---

rank next in dignity to virtue only."[19] What, then, are the "liberal studies"?

> Amongst these I accord the first place to History, on grounds both of its attractiveness and of its utility, qualities which appeal equally to the scholar and to the statesman. Next in importance ranks Moral Philosophy, which indeed is, in a peculiar sense, a "Liberal Art," in that its purpose is to teach men the secret of true freedom. History, then, gives us the concrete examples of the precepts inculcated by Philosophy. The one shows what men should do, the other what men have said and done in the past, and what practical lessons we may draw therefrom for the present day. I would indicate as the third main branch of study, Eloquence. . . . By philosophy we learn the essential truth of things, which by eloquence we so exhibit in orderly adornment as to bring conviction to differing minds.[20]

The remaining liberal studies included letters (grammar and logic), poetry, mathematics, astronomy, and music ("as to Music," said Vergerio, "the Greeks refused the title of 'Educated' to anyone who could not sing or play"). Crucial to all liberal studies was the mastery of Greek and Latin since it enabled students to read the great classical authors who were the foundation stones of the liberal arts. In short, the purpose of a liberal education was to produce individuals who followed a path of virtue and wisdom and possessed the rhetorical skills to persuade others to take it.

Following the Greek precept of a sound mind in a sound body, Vittorino's school at Mantua stressed the need for physical education. Pupils were taught the arts of javelin throwing, archery, and dancing and encouraged to run, wrestle, hunt, and swim frequently. Nor was Christianity excluded from Vittorino's school. His students were taught the Scriptures and the works of the church fathers, especially Augustine. A devout Christian, Vittorino required his pupils to attend mass daily and be reverent in word and deed.

Although a small number of children from the lower classes were provided free educations, humanist schools such as Vittorino's were primarily geared for the education of an elite, the ruling classes of their communities. Also largely absent from such schools were females. Vittorino's only female pupils were the two daughters of the Gonzaga ruler of Mantua. Though these few female students studied the classics and were encouraged to know some history and to ride, dance, sing, play the lute, and appreciate poetry, they were discouraged from learning mathematics and rhetoric. In the educational treatises of the time, religion and morals were thought to "hold the first place in the education of a Christian lady."

Nevertheless, some women in Italy who were educated in the humanist fashion went on to establish their own literary careers. Isotta Nogarola, born to a noble family in Verona, mastered Latin and wrote numerous letters and treatises that brought her praise from male Italian intellectuals. Cassandra Fedele of Venice, who learned both Latin and Greek from humanist tutors hired by her family, became prominent in Venice for her public recitations of orations. In one of her writings, Cassandra defended the unusual practice of women studying the liberal arts.

The humanist schools of the Renaissance aimed to develop the human personality to the fullest extent and underscored the new social ideal of the Renaissance, the creation of the universal being known to us as the "Renaissance man." We should also note that Vittorino and other humanist educators considered a humanist education to be a practical preparation for life. The aim of humanist education was not to create great scholars but rather to produce complete citizens who could participate in the civic life of their communities. As Vittorino said: "Not everyone is obliged to excel in philosophy, medicine, or the law, nor are all equally favored by nature; but all are destined to live in society and to practice virtue."[21] Humanist schools, combining the classics and Christianity, provided the model for the basic education of the European ruling classes until the twentieth century.

Humanism and History

Humanism had a strong impact on the writing of history. Influenced by Roman and Greek historians, the humanists approached the writing of history differently from the chroniclers of the Middle Ages. The humanists' belief that classical civilization had been followed by an age of barbarism (the Middle Ages), which, in turn, had been succeeded by their own age with its rebirth of the study of the classics, enabled them to think in terms of the passage of time, of the past as past. Their division of the past into ancient world, dark ages, and their own age provided a new sense of chronology or periodization in history.

The humanists were also responsible for secularizing the writing of history. Humanist historians reduced or eliminated the role of miracles in historical interpretation, not because they were anti-Christian, but because they took a new approach to sources. They wanted to use documents and exercised their newly developed critical skills in examining them. Greater attention was paid to the political events and forces that affected their city-states or larger territorial units. Thus, Leonardo Bruni wrote a *History of the Florentine People;* the German scholar Jacob Wimpheling penned *On the Excellence and Magnificence of the Germans.* The new emphasis on secularization was also evident in the humanists' conception of causation in history. In much medieval historical literature, historical events were often portrayed as being caused by God's active involvement in human affairs. Humanists deemphasized divine intervention in favor of human motives, stressing political forces or the role of individuals in history.

The high point of Renaissance historiography was achieved at the beginning of the sixteenth century in the works of Francesco Guicciardini (1483–1540). He has been called by some Renaissance scholars the greatest historian between Tacitus in the first century A.D. (see Chapter 6) and Voltaire and Gibbon in the eighteenth century (see Chapter 17). His *History of Italy* and *History of Florence* represent the beginning of "modern analytical historiography." To Guicciardini, the purpose of writing history was to teach lessons, but he was so impressed by the complexity of historical events that he felt those lessons were not always obvious. From his extensive background in government and diplomatic affairs, he developed the political skills that enabled him to analyze political situations precisely and critically. Emphasizing political and military history, his works relied heavily on personal examples and documentary sources.

The Impact of Printing

The period of the Renaissance witnessed the invention of printing, one of the most important technological innovations of Western civilization. The art of printing made an immediate impact on European intellectual life and thought.

Printing from hand-carved wooden blocks had been present in the west since the twelfth century. What was new in the fifteenth century was multiple printing with movable metal type. The development of printing from movable type was a gradual process that culminated some time between 1445 and 1450; Johannes Gutenberg of Mainz played an important role in bringing the process to completion. Gutenberg's Bible, completed in 1455 or 1456, was the first real book produced from movable type.

The new printing spread rapidly throughout Europe in the last half of the fifteenth century. Printing presses were established throughout the Holy Roman Empire in the 1460s and within ten years had spread to Italy, England, France, the Low Countries, Spain, and eastern Europe. Especially well known as a printing center was Venice, home by 1500 to almost 100 printers who had produced almost two million volumes.

By 1500, there were more than 1,000 printers in Europe who had published almost 40,000 titles (between 8 and 10 million copies). Probably 50 percent of these books were religious in character—Bibles and biblical commentaries, books of devotion, and sermons. Next in importance were the Latin and Greek classics, medieval grammars, legal handbooks, works on philosophy, and an ever-growing number of popular romances.

Printing became one of the largest industries in Europe, and its effects were soon felt in many areas of European life. Although some humanists condemned printing because they believed that it vulgarized learn-

MASACCIO, *TRIBUTE MONEY*. With the frescoes of Masaccio, regarded by many as the first great works of Early Renaissance art, a new realistic style of painting was born. The *Tribute Money* was one of a series of frescoes that Masaccio painted in the Brancacci Chapel in the Church of Santa Maria del Carmine in Florence. In illustrating a story from the Bible, Masaccio used a rational system of perspective to create a realistic relationship between the figures and their background.

ing, the printing of books actually encouraged the development of scholarly research and the desire to attain knowledge. Moreover, printing facilitated cooperation among scholars and helped produce standardized and definitive texts. Printing also stimulated the development of an ever-expanding lay reading public, a development that had an enormous impact on European society. Indeed, without the printing press, the new religious ideas of the Reformation would never have spread as rapidly as they did in the sixteenth century.

◆ The Artistic Renaissance

Leonardo da Vinci, one of the great Italian Renaissance artists, once explained: "Hence the painter will produce pictures of small merit if he takes for his standard the pictures of others, but if he will study from natural objects he will bear good fruit . . . those who take for their standard any one but nature . . . weary themselves in vain."[22] Renaissance artists considered the imitation of nature to be their primary goal. Their search for naturalism became an end in itself: to persuade onlookers of the reality of the object or event they were portraying. At the same time, the new artistic standards reflected a new attitude of mind as well, one in which human beings became the focus of attention, the "center and measure of all things," as one artist proclaimed.

Leonardo and other Italians maintained that it was Giotto in the fourteenth century (see Chapter 11) who began the imitation of nature. But what Giotto had begun was not taken up again until the work of Masaccio (1401–1428) in Florence. Masaccio's cycle of frescoes in the Brancacci Chapel has long been regarded as the first masterpiece of Early Renaissance art. With his use of monumental figures, demonstration of a more realistic relationship between figures and landscape, and visual representation of the laws of perspective, a new realistic style of painting was born. Onlookers become aware of a world of reality that appears to be a continuation of their own world. Masaccio's massive, three-dimensional human figures provided a model for later generations of Florentine artists.

This new or Renaissance style was absorbed and modified by other Florentine painters in the fifteenth century. Especially important was the development of an experimental trend that took two directions. One emphasized the mathematical side of painting, the working out of the laws of perspective and the organization of outdoor space and light by geometry and perspective. In the work of Paolo Uccello (1397–1475), figures became mere stage props to show off his mastery of the laws of perspective. The other aspect of the experimental trend involved the investigation of movement and anatomical structure. *The Martyrdom of St. Sebastian* by Antonio Pollaiuolo (c. 1432–1498) revels in classical motifs and attempts to portray the human body under stress. Indeed, the realistic portrayal of the human nude became one of the foremost preoccupations of Italian Renaissance art. The fifteenth century, then, was a period of experimentation and technical mastery.

During the last decades of the fifteenth century, a new sense of invention emerged in Florence, especially in the circle of artists and scholars who formed part of the court of the city's leading citizen, Lorenzo the Magnificent. One of this group's prominent members was Sandro Botticelli (1445–1510), whose interest in Greek and Roman mythology was well reflected in one of his most famous works, *Primavera* or *Spring*. The painting is set in the garden of Venus, a garden of eternal spring. Though Botticelli's figures are well defined, they also possess an otherworldly quality that is far removed from the realism that characterized the painting of the Early Renaissance.

The revolutionary achievements of Florentine painters in the fifteenth century were matched by equally

BOTTICELLI, *PRIMAVERA*.   This work reflects Botticelli's strong interest in classical antiquity. At the center of the painting is Venus, the goddess of love. At the right stands Flora, a Roman goddess of flowers and fertility, while the Three Graces dance playfully at the left. Cupid, the son of Venus, aims his arrow at the Three Graces. At the far left of the picture is Mercury, the messenger of the gods. Later in his life, Botticelli experienced a profound religious crisis, leading him to reject his earlier preoccupation with pagan gods and goddesses. He burned many of his early paintings and then produced only religious works.

stunning advances in sculpture and architecture. Donato di Donatello (1386–1466) spent time in Rome, studying and copying the statues of antiquity. His subsequent work in Florence reveals how well he had mastered the essence of what he saw. Among his numerous works was a statue of David, which is the first known "lifesize freestanding bronze nude in European art since antiquity." With the severed head of the giant Goliath beneath David's feet, Donatello's statue celebrated Florentine heroism in the triumph of the Florentines over the Milanese in 1428. Like Donatello's other statues, *David* also radiated a simplicity and strength that reflected the dignity of humanity.

Filippo Brunelleschi (1377–1446) was a friend of Donatello and accompanied him to Rome. Brunelleschi drew much inspiration from the architectural monuments of Roman antiquity, and when he returned to Florence, he poured his new insights into the creation of a new architecture. When the Medici commissioned him to design the Church of San Lorenzo, Brunelleschi, inspired by Roman models, created a church interior very different from that of the great medieval cathedrals. San Lorenzo's classical columns, rounded arches, and coffered ceiling created an environment that did not overwhelm the worshiper

FILIPPO BRUNELLESCHI, INTERIOR OF SAN LORENZO. Cosimo de' Medici contributed massive amounts of money to the rebuilding of the Church of San Lorenzo. As seen in this view of the nave and choir of the church, Brunelleschi's architectural designs were based on the basilica plan borrowed by early Christians from pagan Rome. San Lorenzo's simplicity, evident in its rows of slender Corinthian columns, created a human-centered space.

DONATELLO, DAVID. Donatello's *David* first stood in the courtyard of the Medici Palace. On its base was an inscription praising Florentine heroism and virtue, leading art historians to assume that the statue was meant to commemorate the victory of Florence over Milan in 1428.

materially and psychologically as Gothic cathedrals did, but comforted as a space created to fit human, not divine, measurements. Like painters and sculptors, Renaissance architects sought to reflect a human-centered world.

The new assertion of human individuality, evident in Early Renaissance art, was also reflected in the new emphasis on portraiture. Patrons appeared in the corners of sacred pictures, and monumental tombs and portrait statues honored many of Florence's prominent citizens. By the mid-fifteenth century, artists were giving an accurate rendering of their subjects' facial features while revealing the inner qualities of their personalities. The portraits of the duke and duchess of Urbino by Piero della Francesca (c. 1410–1492) provide accurate representations as well as a sense of both the power and the wealth of the rulers of Urbino.

By the end of the fifteenth century, Italian painters, sculptors, and architects had created a new artistic envi-

ronment. Many artists had mastered the new techniques for a scientific observation of the world around them and were now ready to move into individualistic forms of creative expression. This final stage of Renaissance art, which flourished between 1480 and 1520, is called the High Renaissance. The shift to the High Renaissance was marked by the increasing importance of Rome as a new cultural center of the Italian Renaissance.

The High Renaissance was dominated by the work of three artistic giants, Leonardo da Vinci (1452–1519), Raphael (1483–1520), and Michelangelo (1475–1564). Leonardo represents a transitional figure in the shift to High Renaissance principles. He carried on the fifteenth-century experimental tradition by studying everything and even dissecting human bodies to better see how nature worked. But Leonardo stressed the need to advance beyond such realism and initiated the High Renaissance's preoccupation with the idealization of nature, or the attempt to generalize from realistic portrayal to an ideal form. Leonardo's *Last Supper*, painted in Milan, is a brilliant summary of fifteenth-century trends in its organization of space and use of perspective to depict subjects three-dimensionally in a two-dimensional medium. But it is also more. The figure of Philip is idealized, and there are profound psychological dimensions to the work. The words of

LEONARDO DA VINCI, *THE LAST SUPPER*. Leonardo da Vinci was the impetus behind the High Renaissance concern for the idealization of nature, moving from a realistic portrayal of the human figure to an idealized form. Evident in Leonardo's *Last Supper* is his effort to depict a person's character and inner nature by the use of gesture and movement. Unfortunately, Leonardo used an experimental technique in this fresco, which soon led to its physical deterioration.

RAPHAEL, *SCHOOL OF ATHENS*. Raphael arrived in Rome in 1508 and began to paint a series of frescoes commissioned by Pope Julius II for the papal apartments at the Vatican. In the *School of Athens*, painted about 1510–1511, Raphael created an imaginary gathering of ancient philosophers. In the center stand Plato and Aristotle. At the left is Pythagoras, showing his system of proportions on a slate. At the right is Ptolemy, holding a celestial globe.

Jesus that "one of you shall betray me" are experienced directly as each of the apostles reveals his personality and his relationship to Jesus. Through gestures and movement, Leonardo hoped to reveal a person's inner life.

Raphael blossomed as a painter at an early age; at twenty-five, he was already regarded as one of Italy's best painters. Raphael was acclaimed for his numerous madonnas, in which he attempted to achieve an ideal of beauty far surpassing human standards. He is well known for his frescoes in the Vatican Palace; his *School of Athens* reveals a world of balance, harmony, and order—the underlying principles of the art of the classical world of Greece and Rome.

Michelangelo, an accomplished painter, sculptor, and architect, was another giant of the High Renaissance. Fiercely driven by his desire to create, he worked with great passion and energy on a remarkable number of projects. Michelangelo was influenced by Neoplatonism, especially evident in his figures on the ceiling of the Sistine Chapel in Rome. These muscular figures reveal an ideal type of human being with perfect proportions. In good Neoplatonic fashion, their beauty is meant to be a reflection of divine beauty; the more beautiful the body, the more Godlike the figure.

Another manifestation of Michelangelo's search for ideal beauty was his *David*, a colossal marble statue commissioned by the Florentine government in 1501 and completed in 1504. Michelangelo maintained that the form of a statue already resided in the uncarved piece of stone: "I only take away the surplus, the statue is already there."[23] Out of a piece of marble that had remained unused for fifty years, Michelangelo created a fourteen-foot-high figure, the largest piece of sculpture in Italy since the time of Rome. An awe-inspiring hero, Michelangelo's *David* proudly proclaims the beauty of the human body and the glory of human beings.

A High Renaissance in architecture was also evident, especially in the work of Donato Bramante (1444–1514). He came from Urbino but took up residence in Rome, where he designed a small temple on the supposed site of Saint Peter's martyrdom. The Tempietto—or little temple—with its Doric columns surrounding a sanctuary enclosed by a dome, summarized the architectural ideals of the

MICHELANGELO, *CREATION OF ADAM*. In 1508, Pope Julius II recalled Michelangelo to Rome and commissioned him to decorate the ceiling of the Sistine Chapel. This colossal project was not completed until 1512. Michelangelo attempted to tell the story of the Fall of Man by depicting nine scenes from the biblical Book of Genesis. In this scene, the well-proportioned figure of Adam, meant by Michelangelo to be a reflection of divine beauty, awaits the divine spark.

High Renaissance. Columns, dome, and sanctuary form a monumental and harmonious whole. Inspired by antiquity, Bramante had recaptured the grandeur of ancient Rome. His achievement led Pope Julius II to commission him to design a new basilica for Rome, which eventually became the great St. Peter's.

✣ The Artist and Social Status

Early Renaissance artists began their careers as apprentices to masters in craft guilds. Apprentices with unusual talent might eventually become masters and run their own workshops. As in the Middle Ages, artists were still largely viewed as artisans. Since guilds depended on commissions for their projects, patrons played an important role in the art of the Early Renaissance. The wealthy upper classes determined both the content and purpose of the paintings and pieces of sculpture they commissioned.

By the end of the fifteenth century, a transformation in the position of the artist had occurred. Especially talented individuals, such as Leonardo, Raphael, and Michelangelo, were no longer seen as artisans, but as artistic geniuses with creative energies akin to the divine (see the box on p. 350). Artists were heroes, individuals who were praised more for their creativity than for their competence as craftspeople. Michelangelo, for example, was frequently addressed as "Il Divino"—the Divine One. As society excused their eccentricities and valued their creative genius, the artists of the High Renaissance became the first to embody the modern concept of the artist.

As respect for artists grew, so too did their ability to profit economically from their work and to rise on the social scale. Now welcomed as equals into the circles of the upper classes, they mingled with the political and intellectual elite of their society and became more aware of new intellectual theories, which they then embodied in their art. The Platonic Academy and Renaissance Neoplatonism had an especially important impact on Florentine painters.

MICHELANGELO, *DAVID*. This statue of David, cut from an eighteen-foot-high piece of marble, exalts the beauty of the human body and is a fitting symbol of the Italian Renaissance's affirmation of human power. Completed in 1504, the *David* was moved by Florentine authorities to a special location in front of the Palazzo Vecchio, the seat of the Florentine government.

The Genius of Leonardo da Vinci

During the Renaissance, artists came to be viewed as creative geniuses with almost divine qualities. One individual who helped to create this image of the Renaissance artist was himself a painter. Giorgio Vasari was an avid admirer of Italy's great artists and wrote a series of brief biographies of them. This excerpt is taken from his account of Leonardo da Vinci.

❋ Giorgio Vasari, *Lives of the Artists*

In the normal course of events many men and women are born with various remarkable qualities and talents; but occasionally, in a way that transcends nature, a single person is marvelously endowed by heaven with beauty, grace, and talent in such abundance that he leaves other men far behind, all his actions seem inspired, and indeed everything he does clearly comes from God rather than from human art.

Everyone acknowledged that this was true of Leonardo da Vinci, an artist of outstanding physical beauty who displayed infinite grace in everything he did and who cultivated his genius so brilliantly that all problems he studied he solved with ease. He possessed great strength and dexterity; he was a man of regal spirit and tremendous breadth of mind; and his name became so famous that not only was he esteemed during his lifetime but his reputation endured and became even greater after his death. . . .

He was marvelously gifted, and he proved himself to be a first-class geometrician in his work as a sculptor and architect. In his youth Leonardo made in clay several heads of women, with smiling faces, of which plaster casts are still being made, as well as some children's heads executed as if by a mature artist. He also did many architectural drawings both of ground plans and of other elevations, and, while still young, he was the first to propose reducing the Arno River to a navigable canal between Pisa and Florence. He made designs for mills, fulling machines, and engines that could be driven by waterpower; and as he intended to be a painter by profession he carefully studied drawing from life. . . . Altogether, his genius was so wonderfully inspired by the grace of God, his powers of expression were so powerfully fed by a willing memory and intellect, and his writing conveyed his ideas so precisely, that his arguments and reasonings confounded the most formidable critics. In addition, he used to make models and plans showing how to excavate and tunnel through mountains without difficulty, so as to pass from one level to another; and he demonstrated how to lift and draw great weights by means of levers and hoists and ways of cleaning harbors and using pumps to suck up water from great depths.

❋ *The Northern Artistic Renaissance*

In trying to provide an exact portrayal of their world, the artists of the north (especially the Low Countries) and Italy took different approaches. In Italy, the human form became the primary vehicle of expression as Italian artists sought to master the technical skills that allowed them to portray humans in realistic settings. The large wall spaces of Italian churches had given rise to the art of fresco painting, but in the north, the prevalence of Gothic cathedrals with their stained glass windows resulted in more emphasis on illuminated manuscripts and wooden panel painting for altarpieces. The space available in these works was limited, and great care was required to depict each object, leading northern painters to become masters at rendering details.

BRAMANTE, TEMPIETTO. Ferdinand and Isabella of Spain commissioned Donato Bramante to design a small building in Rome that would commemorate the place where Saint Peter supposedly was crucified. Completed in 1502, the temple reflected Bramante's increasing understanding of ancient Roman remains.

JAN VAN EYCK, *GIOVANNI ARNOLFINI AND HIS BRIDE*.
Northern painters took great care in depicting each object
and became masters at rendering details. This emphasis
on a realistic portrayal is clearly evident in this oil painting, supposedly a portrait of Giovanni Arnolfini, an
Italian merchant who had settled in Bruges, and his
wife, Giovanna Cenami.

ALBRECHT DÜRER, *ADORATION OF THE MAGI*. By the end
of the fifteenth century, northern artists had begun to study
in Italy and to adopt many of the techniques used by Italian painters. As is evident in this painting, which was the
central panel for an altarpiece done for Frederick the Wise
in 1504, Albrecht Dürer masterfully incorporated the laws
of perspective and the ideals of proportion into his works.
At the same time, he did not abandon the preoccupation
with detail typical of northern artists.

The most influential northern school of art in the fifteenth century was centered in Flanders. Jan van Eyck
(1390?–1441) was among the first to use oil paint, a
medium that enabled the artist to use a varied range of colors and make changes to create fine details. In the famous
Giovanni Arnolfini and His Bride, van Eyck's attention to
detail is staggering: precise portraits, a glittering chande-
lier, and a mirror reflecting the objects in the room.
Although each detail was rendered as observed, it is evident that van Eyck's comprehension of perspective was
still uncertain. His work is truly indicative of northern
Renaissance painters, who, in their effort to imitate nature,
did so not by mastery of the laws of perspective and proportion, but by empirical observation of visual reality and
the accurate portrayal of details. Moreover, northern
painters placed great emphasis on the emotional intensity
of religious feeling and created great works of devotional
art, especially in their altarpieces. Michelangelo summarized the difference between northern and Italian Renaissance painting in these words:

> In Flanders, they paint, before all things, to render exactly
> and deceptively the outward appearance of things. The
> painters choose, by preference, subjects provoking transports
> of piety, like the figures of saints or of prophets. But most of
> the time they paint what are called landscapes with plenty of
> figures. Though the eye is agreeably impressed, these pictures
> have neither choice of values nor grandeur. In short, this art
> is without power and without distinction; it aims at rendering
> minutely many things at the same time, of which a single one
> would have sufficed to call forth a man's whole application.[24]

By the end of the fifteenth century, however, artists from
the north began to study in Italy and were visually influenced by what artists were doing there.

One northern artist of this later period who was
greatly affected by the Italians was Albrecht Dürer
(1471–1528) from Nuremberg. Dürer made two trips to

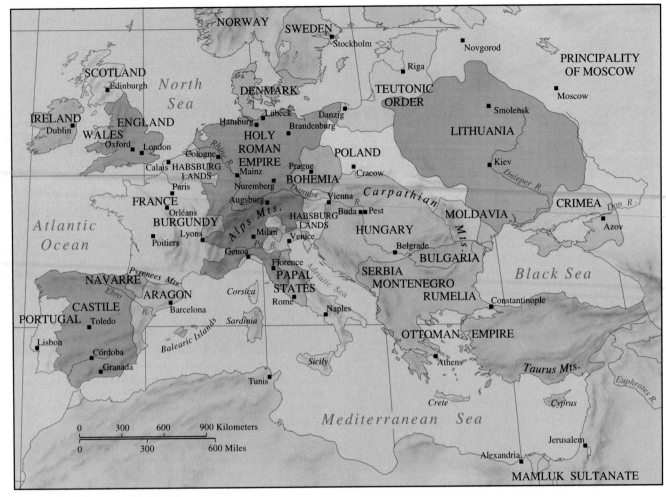

MAP 12.2 Europe in the Renaissance.

Italy and absorbed most of what the Italians could teach, as is evident in his mastery of the laws of perspective and Renaissance theories of proportion. He wrote detailed treatises on both subjects. At the same time, as in his famous *Adoration of the Magi,* Dürer did not reject the use of minute details characteristic of northern artists. He did try, however, to integrate those details more harmoniously into his works and, like the Italian artists of the High Renaissance, tried to achieve a standard of ideal beauty by a careful examination of the human form.

❋ *Music in the Renaissance*

For much of the fifteenth century, an extraordinary cultural environment was fostered in the domains of the dukes of Burgundy in northern Europe. The court of the dukes attracted some of the best artists and musicians of the time. Among them was Guillaume Dufay (c. 1400–1474), perhaps the most important composer of his time. Born in northern France, Dufay lived for a few years in Italy and was thus well suited to combine the late medieval style of France with the early Renaissance style of Italy. One

of Dufay's greatest contributions was a change in the composition of the mass. He was the first to use secular tunes to replace Gregorian chants as the fixed melody that served as the basis for the mass. Dufay also composed a number of secular songs, an important reminder that during the Renaissance music ceased to be used chiefly in the service of God and moved into the secular world of courts and cities. In Italy and France, the chief form of secular music was the madrigal.

The Renaissance madrigal was a poem set to music, and its origins were in the fourteenth-century Italian courts. The texts were usually twelve-line poems written in the vernacular, and their theme was emotional or erotic love. By the mid-sixteenth century, most madrigals were written for five or six voices and employed a technique called text painting, in which the music tried to portray the literal meaning of the text. Thus, the melody would rise for the word "heaven" or use a wavelike motion to represent the word "water." By the mid-sixteenth century, the madrigal had also spread to England, where the most popular form was characterized by the fa-la-la refrain like that found in the English carol "Deck the Halls."

◆ The European State in the Renaissance

The High Middle Ages had witnessed the emergence of territorial states that began to develop the administrative machinery of centralized government. Professional bureaucracies, royal courts, and parliamentary assemblies were all products of the twelfth and thirteenth centuries. Strong monarchy had provided the organizing power for the development of these states, but in the fourteenth century, the internal stability of European governments had been threatened by financial and dynastic problems as well as challenges from their nobilities. By the fifteenth century, rulers began to rebuild their states by checking the violent activities of their nobles and maintaining internal order. Some territorial units, such as the Holy Roman Empire and Italy, failed to develop strong national monarchies, but even in these areas, strong princes and city councils managed to centralize their authority within their smaller territorial states. In Italy, Milan, Venice, and Florence managed to become fairly well centralized territorial states. Some historians believe that the Italian Renaissance states, with their preoccupation with political power, were the first true examples of the modern secular state.

✸ The "New Monarchies"

In the first half of the fifteenth century, European states continued the disintegrative patterns of the previous century. In the second half of the fifteenth century, however, recovery set in, and attempts were made to reestablish the centralized power of monarchical governments. To characterize the results, some historians have used the label "Renaissance states"; others have spoken of the "new monarchies," especially those of France, England, and Spain at the end of the fifteenth century. Although appropriate, the term "new monarch" can also be misleading. These Renaissance monarchs were new in their concentration of royal authority, their attempts to suppress the nobility, their efforts to control the church in their lands, and their insistence upon having the loyalty of people living within definite territorial boundaries. Like the rulers of fifteenth-century Italian states, the "new monarchs" were often crafty men obsessed with the acquisition and expansion of political power. Of course, none of these characteristics was entirely new in that a number of medieval monarchs, especially in the thirteenth century, had also exhibited them. Nevertheless, the Renaissance period does mark the further extension of centralized royal authority. Of course, the degree to which monarchs were successful in extending their political authority varied from area to area. In central and eastern Europe, decentralization rather than centralization of political authority remained a fact of life.

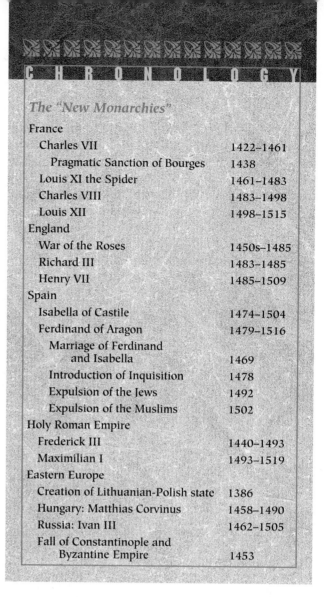

C H R O N O L O G Y

The "New Monarchies"

France	
Charles VII	1422–1461
Pragmatic Sanction of Bourges	1438
Louis XI the Spider	1461–1483
Charles VIII	1483–1498
Louis XII	1498–1515
England	
War of the Roses	1450s–1485
Richard III	1483–1485
Henry VII	1485–1509
Spain	
Isabella of Castile	1474–1504
Ferdinand of Aragon	1479–1516
Marriage of Ferdinand and Isabella	1469
Introduction of Inquisition	1478
Expulsion of the Jews	1492
Expulsion of the Muslims	1502
Holy Roman Empire	
Frederick III	1440–1493
Maximilian I	1493–1519
Eastern Europe	
Creation of Lithuanian-Polish state	1386
Hungary: Matthias Corvinus	1458–1490
Russia: Ivan III	1462–1505
Fall of Constantinople and Byzantine Empire	1453

✍ THE GROWTH OF THE FRENCH MONARCHY

The Hundred Years' War had left France prostrate. Depopulation, desolate farmlands, ruined commerce, and independent and unruly nobles had made it difficult for the kings to assert their authority. But the war had also developed a strong degree of French national feeling toward a common enemy that the kings could use to reestablish monarchical power. The need to prosecute the war provided an excuse to strengthen the authority of the king, already evident in the policies of Charles VII (1422–1461) after he was crowned king at Reims. With the consent of the Estates-General, Charles established a royal army composed of cavalry and archers. He received from the Estates-General the right to levy the *taille*, an annual direct tax usually on land or property, without any need for further approval from the Estates-General. Losing control of the purse meant less power for this parliamentary body. Charles VII also secured the Pragmatic Sanction of Bourges (1438), an agreement with the papacy that strengthened the liberties of the French church administratively at the expense of the papacy and enabled the king to begin to assume control over the church in France.

The process of developing a French territorial state was greatly advanced by King Louis XI (1461–1483), known as the Spider because of his wily and devious ways. Some historians have called this "new monarch" the founder of the French national state. By retaining the *taille* as a permanent tax imposed by royal authority, Louis secured a sound, regular source of income. Louis was not, however, completely successful in repressing the French nobility whose independence posed a threat to his own state building. A major problem was his supposed vassal, Charles the Bold, duke of Burgundy (1467–1477). Charles attempted to create a middle kingdom between France and Germany, stretching from the Low Countries in the north to Switzerland. Louis opposed his action, and when Charles was killed in 1477 fighting the Swiss, Louis added part of Charles's possessions, the duchy of Burgundy, to his own lands. Three years later, the provinces of Anjou, Maine, Bar, and Provence were brought under royal control. Louis the Spider also encouraged the growth of industry and commerce in an attempt to bolster the French economy. For example, he introduced new industries, such as the silk industry to Lyons.

Many historians believe that Louis created a base for the later development of a strong French monarchy. In any case, the monarchy was at least well enough established to weather the policies of the next two monarchs, Charles VIII (1483–1498) and Louis XII (1498–1515), whose attempts to subdue parts of Italy initiated a series of Italian wars. Internally, France survived these wars without too much difficulty.

ENGLAND: CIVIL WAR AND A NEW MONARCHY

The Hundred Years' War had also strongly affected the other protagonist in that conflict. The cost of the war in its final years and the losses in manpower strained the English economy. Moreover, the end of the war brought even greater domestic turmoil to England when the War of the Roses broke out in the 1450s. This civil war pitted the ducal house of Lancaster, whose symbol was a red rose, against the ducal house of York, whose symbol was a white rose. Many aristocratic families of England were drawn into the conflict. Finally, in 1485, Henry Tudor, duke of Richmond, defeated the last Yorkist king, Richard III (1483–1485), at Bosworth Field and established the new Tudor dynasty.

As the first Tudor king, Henry VII (1485–1509) worked to reduce internal dissension and establish a strong monarchical government. The English aristocracy had been much weakened by the War of the Roses because many nobles had been killed. Henry eliminated the private wars of the nobility by abolishing "livery and maintenance," the practice by which wealthy aristocrats maintained private armies of followers dedicated to the service of their lord. Since England, unlike France and Spain, did not possess a standing army, the king relied on special commissions to trusted nobles to raise troops

for a specific campaign, after which the troops were disbanded. Henry also controlled the irresponsible activity of the nobles by establishing the Court of Star Chamber, which did not use juries and allowed torture to be used to extract confessions.

Henry VII was particularly successful in extracting income from the traditional financial resources of the English monarch, such as the crown lands, judicial fees and fines, and customs duties. By using diplomacy to avoid wars, which are always expensive, the king avoided having to call Parliament on any regular basis to grant him funds. By not overburdening the landed gentry and middle class with taxes, Henry won their favor, and they provided much support for his monarchy.

Henry also encouraged commercial activity. By increasing wool exports, royal export taxes on wool rose. Henry's thriftiness as well as his domestic and foreign policies enabled him to leave England with a stable and prosperous government and an enhanced status for the monarchy itself.

THE UNIFICATION OF SPAIN

During the Middle Ages, several independent Christian kingdoms had emerged in the course of the long reconquest of the Iberian peninsula from the Muslims. Aragon and Castile were the strongest Spanish kingdoms; in the west was the independent monarchy of Portugal; in the north, the small kingdom of Navarre, oriented toward France; and in the south, the Muslim kingdom of Granada. Few people at the beginning of the fifteenth century could have predicted the unification of the Iberian kingdoms.

A major step in that direction was taken with the marriage of Isabella of Castile (1474–1504) and Ferdinand of Aragon (1479–1516) in 1469. This marriage was a dynastic union of two rulers, not a political union. Both kingdoms maintained their own parliaments (Cortes), courts, laws, coinage, speech, customs, and political organs. Nevertheless, the two rulers worked to strengthen royal control of government, especially in Castile. The royal council, which was supposed to supervise local administration and oversee the implementation of government policies, was stripped of aristocrats and filled primarily with middle-class lawyers. Trained in the principles of Roman law, these officials operated on the belief that the monarchy embodied the power of the state.

The towns were also enlisted in the policy of state building. Medieval town organizations known as *hermandades* ("brotherhoods"), which had been organized to maintain law and order, were revived. Ferdinand and Isabella transformed them into a kind of national militia whose primary goal was to stop the wealthy landed aristocrats from disturbing the peace, a goal also favored by the middle class. The *hermandades* were disbanded by 1498 when the royal administration became strong enough to deal with lawlessness. The appointment of *corregidores* by the crown to replace corrupt municipal officials enabled the monarchs to extend the central authority of royal government into the towns.

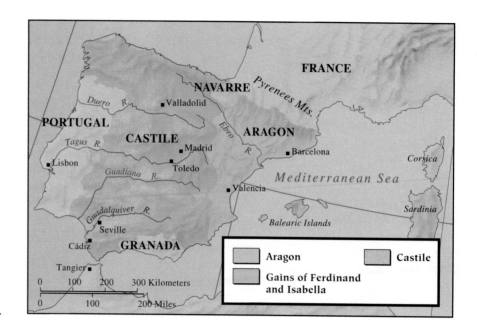

MAP 12.3 **The Iberian Peninsula.**

Seeking to replace the undisciplined feudal levies they had inherited with a more professional royal army, Ferdinand and Isabella reorganized the military forces of Spain. The development of a strong infantry force as the heart of the new Spanish army made it the best in Europe by the sixteenth century.

Ferdinand and Isabella recognized the importance of controlling the Catholic church with its vast power and wealth. They secured from the pope the right to select the most important church officials in Spain, virtually guaranteeing the foundation of a Spanish Catholic church in which the clergy became an instrument for the extension of royal power. The monarchs, who were sincere Catholics, also used their authority over the church to institute reform. Isabella's chief minister, the able and astute Cardinal Ximenes, restored discipline and eliminated immorality among the monks and secular clergy.

The religious zeal exhibited in Cardinal Ximenes's reform program was also evident in the policy of strict religious uniformity pursued by Ferdinand and Isabella. Of course, it served a political purpose as well: to create unity and further bolster royal power. Spain possessed two large religious minorities, the Jews and Muslims, both of whom had been largely tolerated in medieval Spain. In some areas of Spain, Jews exercised much influence in economic and intellectual affairs. Increased persecution in the fourteenth century, however, led the majority of Spanish Jews to convert to Christianity. Although many of these *conversos* came to play important roles in Spanish society, complaints that they were secretly reverting to Judaism prompted Ferdinand and Isabella to ask the pope to introduce the Inquisition into Spain in 1478. Under royal control, the Inquisition worked with cruel efficiency to guarantee the orthodoxy of the *conversos*, but had no authority over practicing Jews. Consequently, in 1492, flush with the success of the conquest of Muslim Granada,

Ferdinand and Isabella took the drastic step of expelling all professed Jews from Spain. It is estimated that 150,000 out of possibly 200,000 Jews fled.

Muslims, too, were "encouraged" to convert to Christianity after the conquest of Granada. In 1502, Isabella issued a decree expelling all professed Muslims from her kingdom. To a very large degree, the "Most Catholic" monarchs had achieved their goal of absolute religious orthodoxy as a basic ingredient of the Spanish state. To be Spanish was to be Catholic, a policy of uniformity enforced by the Inquisition.

During the reigns of Ferdinand and Isabella, Spain (or the union of Castile and Aragon) began to emerge as an important power in European affairs. Both Granada and Navarre had been conquered and incorporated into the royal realms. Nevertheless, Spain remained divided in many ways. Only the royal dynasty provided the centralizing force, and when a single individual, the grandson of Ferdinand and Isabella, succeeded both rulers as Charles I in 1516, he inherited lands that made him the most powerful monarch of his age.

THE HOLY ROMAN EMPIRE: THE SUCCESS OF THE HABSBURGS

Unlike France, England, and Spain, the Holy Roman Empire failed to develop a strong monarchical authority. After 1438, the position of Holy Roman Emperor remained in the hands of the Habsburg dynasty. Having gradually acquired a number of possessions along the Danube, known collectively as Austria, the house of Habsburg had become one of the wealthiest landholders in the empire and by the mid-fifteenth century began to play an important role in European affairs.

Much of the Habsburg success in the fifteenth century was due not to military success, but to a well-executed

EMPEROR MAXIMILIAN I. Although the Holy Roman Emperor possessed little power in Germany, the Habsburg dynasty, which held the position of emperor after 1438, steadily increased its wealth and landholdings through dynastic marriages. This portrait of Emperor Maximilian I reflects well the description by a Venetian ambassador: "He is not very fair of face, but well proportioned, exceedingly robust, of sanguine and choleric complexion and very healthy for his age."

policy of dynastic marriages. As the old Habsburg motto said: "Leave the waging of wars to others! But you, happy Austria, marry; for the realms which Mars [god of war] awards to others, Venus [goddess of love] transfers to you." Although Frederick III (1440–1493) lost the traditional Habsburg possessions of Bohemia and Hungary, he gained Franche-Comté in east-central France, Luxembourg, and a large part of the Low Countries by marrying his son Maximilian to Mary, the daughter of Duke Charles the Bold of Burgundy. The addition of these territories made the Habsburg dynasty an international power and brought them the undying opposition of the French monarchy because the rulers of France feared they would be surrounded by the Habsburgs.

Much was expected of the flamboyant Maximilian I (1493–1519) when he became emperor. Through the Reichstag, the imperial diet or parliament, Maximilian attempted to centralize the administration by creating new institutions common to the entire empire. Opposition from the German princes doomed these efforts, however. Maximilian's only real success lay in his marriage alliances. Philip of Burgundy, the son of Maximilian's marriage to Mary, was married to Joanna, the daughter of Ferdinand and Isabella. Philip and Joanna produced a son, Charles,

who, through a series of unexpected deaths, became heir to all three lines, the Habsburg, Burgundian, and Spanish, making him the leading monarch of his age (see Chapter 13).

Although the Holy Roman Empire did not develop along the lines of a centralized monarchical state, within the empire the power of the independent princes and electors increased steadily. In numerous German states, such as Bavaria, Hesse, Brandenburg, and the Palatinate, princes built up bureaucracies, developed standing armies, created fiscal systems, and introduced Roman law, just like the national monarchs of France, England, and Spain. They posed a real threat to the church, the emperor, and other smaller independent bodies in the Holy Roman Empire, especially the free imperial cities.

THE STRUGGLE FOR STRONG MONARCHY IN EASTERN EUROPE

In eastern Europe, rulers struggled to achieve the centralization of their territorial states but faced serious obstacles. Although the population was mostly Slavic, there were islands of other ethnic groups that caused untold difficulties. Religious differences also troubled the area, as Roman Catholics, Greek Orthodox Christians, and pagans confronted each other.

Much of Polish history revolved around the bitter struggle between the crown and the landed nobility. The dynastic union of Jagiello, grand prince of Lithuania, with the Polish queen Jadwiga resulted in a large Lithuanian-Polish state in 1386. Jagiello and his immediate successors were able to control the landed magnates, but by the end of the fifteenth century, the preoccupation of Poland's rulers with problems in Bohemia and Hungary as well as war with the Russians and Turks enabled the aristocrats to reestablish their power. Through their control of the *Sejm* or national diet, the magnates reduced the peasantry to serfdom by 1511 and established the right to elect their kings. The Polish kings proved unable to establish a strong royal authority.

Bohemia, Poland's neighbor, was part of the Holy Roman Empire, but distrust of the Germans and close ethnic ties to the Poles and Slovaks encouraged the Czechs to associate with their northeastern Slavic neighbors. The Hussite wars (see The Problems of Heresy and Reform later in this chapter) led to further dissension and civil war. Because of a weak monarchy, the Bohemian nobles increased their authority and wealth at the expense of both crown and church.

The history of Hungary had been closely tied to that of central and western Europe by its conversion to Roman Catholicism by German missionaries. The church became a large and prosperous institution. Wealthy bishops, along with the great territorial lords, became powerful, independent political figures. For a brief while, Hungary developed into an important European state, the dominant power in eastern Europe. King Matthias Corvinus (1458–1490) broke the power of the wealthy lords and created a well-organized bureaucracy. Like a typical Renais-

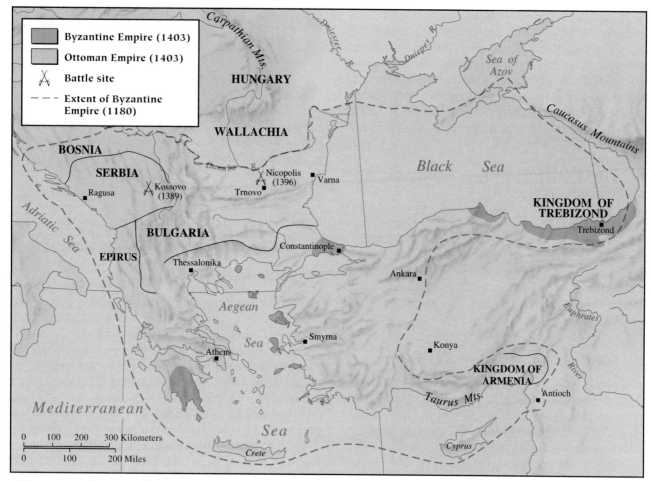

MAP 12.4 Southeastern Europe.

sance prince, he patronized the new humanist culture, brought Italian scholars and artists to his capital at Buda, and made his court one of the most brilliant outside Italy. After his death, Hungary returned to weak rule, and the work of Corvinus was largely undone.

Since the thirteenth century, Russia had been under the domination of the Mongols. Gradually, the princes of Moscow rose to prominence by using their close relationship to the Mongol khans to increase their wealth and expand their possessions. In the reign of the great prince Ivan III (1462–1505), a new Russian state was born. Ivan III annexed other Russian principalities and took advantage of dissension among the Mongols to throw off their yoke by 1480. He invaded the lands of the Lithuanian-Polish dynasty and added the territories around Kiev, Smolensk, and Chernigov to his new Muscovite state.

❧ THE OTTOMAN TURKS AND THE END OF BYZANTIUM

Eastern Europe was increasingly threatened by the steadily advancing Ottoman Turks. The Byzantine Empire had, of course, served as a buffer between the Muslim Middle East and the Latin West for centuries. It was severely weakened by the sack of Constantinople in 1204 and its occupation by the west. Although the Palaeolo-

gus dynasty (1260–1453) had tried to reestablish Byzantine power in the Balkans after the overthrow of the Latin Empire, the threat from the Turks finally doomed the long-lasting empire.

Beginning in northeastern Asia Minor in the thirteenth century, the Ottoman Turks spread rapidly, seizing the lands of the Seljuk Turks and the Byzantine Empire. In 1345, they bypassed Constantinople and moved into the Balkans, which they conquered by the end of the century. Finally, in 1453, the great city of Constantinople fell to the Turks after a siege of several months. After consolidating their power, the Turks prepared to exert renewed pressure on the west, both in the Mediterranean and up the Danube valley toward Vienna. By the end of the fifteenth century, they were threatening Hungary, Austria, Bohemia, and Poland. The Holy Roman Emperor, Charles V, became their bitter enemy in the sixteenth century.

Our survey of European political developments makes it clear that, although individual German or especially Italian princes had developed culturally brilliant states, the future belonged to territorial states organized by national monarchies. They possessed superior resources and were developing institutions that represented the interests of much of the population. Nevertheless, the Renaissance states were still only dynastic states, not nation-states. The interests of a state were the interests of its ruling dynasty. Loyalty was owed to the ruler, not the state. Residents of France considered themselves subjects of the French king, not citizens of France. Moreover, although Renaissance monarchs were strong rulers centralizing their authority, they were by no means absolute monarchs. Some chance of representative government still remained in the form of Parliament, Estates-General, Cortes, or Reichstag. Monarchs were strongest in the west and, with the exception of the Russian rulers, weakest in the east.

◆ The Church in the Renaissance

As a result of the efforts of the Council of Constance, the Great Schism had finally been brought to an end in 1417 (see Chapter 11). The council had had three major objectives: to end the schism, to eradicate heresy, and to reform the church in "head and members." The ending of the schism proved to be the council's easiest task; it was much less successful in dealing with the problems of heresy and reform.

※ The Problems of Heresy and Reform

Heresy was, of course, not a new problem, and in the thirteenth century, the church had developed inquisitorial machinery to deal with it. But two widespread movements in the fourteenth and early fifteenth centuries—Lollardy and Hussitism—posed new threats to the church.

English Lollardy was a product of the Oxford theologian John Wyclif (c. 1328–1384), whose disgust with clerical corruption led him to a far-ranging attack on papal authority and medieval Christian beliefs and practices. Wyclif alleged that there was no basis in Scripture for papal claims of temporal authority and advocated that the popes be stripped of both their authority and property. At one point, he even denounced the pope as the Antichrist. Believing that the Bible should be a Christian's sole authority, Wyclif urged that it be made available in the vernacular languages so that every Christian could read it. Rejecting all practices not mentioned in Scripture, Wyclif condemned pilgrimages, the veneration of saints, and a whole series of rituals and rites that had developed in the medieval church.

Wyclif has sometimes been viewed as a forerunner of the Reformation of the sixteenth century because his arguments attacked the foundations of the medieval Catholic church's organization and practices. His attacks on church property were especially popular, and he attracted a number of followers who came to be known as Lollards. Persecution by royal and church authorities who feared the socioeconomic consequences of Wyclif's ideas forced the Lollards to go underground after 1400.

A marriage between the royal families of England and Bohemia enabled Lollard ideas to spread to Bohemia, where they reinforced the ideas of a group of Czech reformers led by the chancellor of the university at Prague, John Hus (1374–1415). In his call for reform, Hus urged the elimination of the worldliness and corruption of the clergy

CHRONOLOGY

The Church in the Renaissance

Council of Constance	1414–1418
Burning of John Hus	1415
End of the Great Schism	1417
Pius II issues the papal bull *Execrabilis*	1460
The Renaissance papacy	
Sixtus IV	1471–1484
Alexander VI	1492–1503
Julius II	1503–1513
Leo X	1513–1521

and attacked the excessive power of the papacy within the Catholic church. Hus's objections fell on receptive ears, since the Catholic church as one of the largest landowners in Bohemia was already widely criticized. Moreover, many clergymen were German, and the native Czechs' strong resentment of the Germans who dominated Bohemia also contributed to Hus's movement.

The Council of Constance attempted to deal with the growing problem of heresy by summoning John Hus to the council. Granted a safe conduct by Emperor Sigismund, Hus went in the hope of a free hearing of his ideas. Instead he was arrested, condemned as a heretic (by a narrow vote), and burned at the stake in 1415. This action turned the unrest in Bohemia into revolutionary upheaval. The resulting Hussite wars combined religious, social, and national issues and wracked the Holy Roman Empire until a truce was arranged in 1436.

The reform of the church in "head and members" was even less successful than the attempt to eradicate heresy. Two reform decrees were passed by the Council of Constance. *Sacrosancta* stated that a general council of the church received its authority from God; hence, every Christian, including the pope, was subject to its authority. The decree *Frequens* provided for the regular holding of general councils to ensure that church reform would continue. Taken together, *Sacrosancta* and *Frequens* provided for an ecclesiastical legislative system within the church superior to the popes.

Decrees alone, however, proved insufficient to reform the church. Councils could issue decrees, but popes had to execute them and popes would not cooperate with councils that diminished their authority. Beginning as early as Martin V in 1417, successive popes worked steadfastly for the next thirty years to defeat the conciliar movement. The victory of the popes and the final blow to the conciliar movement came in 1460, when Pope Pius II issued the papal bull *Execrabilis*, condemning appeals to a council over the head of a pope as heretical.

By the mid-fifteenth century, the popes had reasserted their supremacy over the Catholic church. No longer, however, did they have any possibility of asserting supremacy over temporal governments as the medieval papacy had. Although the papal monarchy had been maintained, it had lost much moral prestige. In the fifteenth century, the Renaissance papacy contributed to an even further decline in the moral leadership of the popes.

✳ *The Renaissance Papacy*

Historians use the phrase "Renaissance papacy" to refer to the line of popes from the end of the Great Schism (1417) to the beginnings of the Reformation in the early sixteenth century. The primary concern of the papacy is governing the Catholic church as its spiritual leader. But as heads of the church, popes had temporal preoccupations as well, and the story of the Renaissance papacy is really an account of how the latter came to overshadow the popes' spiritual functions. In the process, the Renaissance papacy and the Catholic church became noticeably secularized.

The preoccupation of the popes with the territory of the Papal States and Italian politics was not new to the Renaissance. Popes had been temporal as well as spiritual rulers for centuries. The manner in which Renaissance popes pursued their temporal interests, however, especially their use of intrigue, deceit, and open bloodshed, was shocking. Of all the Renaissance popes, Julius II (1503–1513) was most involved in war and politics. The fiery "warrior-pope" personally led armies against his enemies, much to the disgust of pious Christians who viewed the pope as a spiritual leader. The great humanist Erasmus (see Chapter 13) witnessed the triumphant entry of Julius II into Bologna at the head of his troops and later wrote scathing indictments of the papal proclivity for warfare. With Julius II in mind, he proclaimed in *The Complaint of Peace*: "How, O bishop standing in the room of the Apostles, dare you teach the people the things that pertain to war?"

To further their territorial aims in the Papal States, the popes needed financial resources and loyal servants. Preoccupation with finances was not new, but its grossness received considerable comment: "Whenever I entered the chambers of the ecclesiastics of the Papal court, I found brokers and clergy engaged and reckoning money which lay in heaps before them."[25] Since they were not hereditary monarchs, popes could not build dynasties over several generations and came to rely on the practice of nepotism to promote their families' interests. Pope Sixtus IV (1471–1484), for example, made five of his nephews cardinals and gave them an abundance of church offices to build up their finances (the word *nepotism* is, in fact, derived from *nepos*, meaning nephew). Alexander VI (1492–1503), a member of the Borgia family who was known for his debauchery and sensuality, raised one son, one nephew, and the brother of one mistress to the cardinalate. A Venetian envoy stated that Alexander, "joyous by nature, thought of nothing but the aggrandizement of his children." Alexander scandalized the church by encouraging his son Cesare to carve a ter-

A RENAISSANCE POPE: SIXTUS IV. The Renaissance popes allowed secular concerns to overshadow their spiritual duties. They became concerned with territorial expansion, finances, and Renaissance culture. Pope Sixtus IV built the Sistine Chapel and later had it decorated by some of the leading artists of his day. This fresco by Melozzo da Forlì shows the pope on his throne receiving the humanist Platina (kneeling), who was keeper of the Vatican Library.

ritorial state in central Italy out of the territories of the Papal States.

The Renaissance popes were great patrons of Renaissance culture, and their efforts made Rome the focal point of the High Renaissance at the beginning of the sixteenth century. For the warrior-pope Julius II, the patronage of Renaissance culture was mostly a matter of policy as he endeavored to add to the splendor of his pontificate by tearing down the Basilica of Saint Peter, which had been built by the emperor Constantine, and beginning construction of the greatest building in Christendom, the present Saint Peter's Basilica. Julius's successor, Leo X (1513–1521), was also a patron of Renaissance culture, not as a matter of policy, but as a deeply involved participant. Such might be expected of the son of Lorenzo de' Medici. Made an archbishop at the age of eight and a cardinal at thirteen, he acquired a refined taste in art, manners, and social life among the Florentine Renaissance elite. He became pope at the age of thirty-seven, supposedly remarking to the Venetian ambassador, "Let us enjoy the papacy, since God has given it to us." Humanists were made papal secretaries, Raphael was commissioned to do paintings, and the construction of Saint Peter's was accelerated as Rome became the literary and artistic center of the Renaissance.

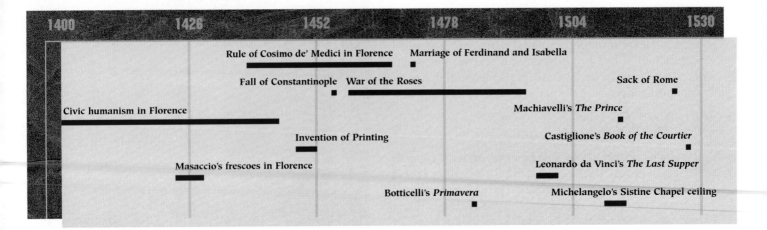

| 1400 | 1426 | 1452 | 1478 | 1504 | 1530 |

Rule of Cosimo de' Medici in Florence   Marriage of Ferdinand and Isabella

Fall of Constantinople   War of the Roses   Sack of Rome

Civic humanism in Florence   Machiavelli's *The Prince*

Invention of Printing   Castiglione's *Book of the Courtier*

Masaccio's frescoes in Florence   Leonardo da Vinci's *The Last Supper*

Botticelli's *Primavera*   Michelangelo's Sistine Chapel ceiling

CONCLUSION

Whether the Renaissance represents the end of the Middle Ages or the beginning of a new era, a frequently debated topic among medieval and Renaissance historians, is perhaps an irrelevant question. The Renaissance was a period of transition that witnessed a continuation of the economic, political, and social trends that had begun in the High Middle Ages. It was also a movement in which intellectuals and artists proclaimed a new vision of humankind and raised fundamental questions about the value and importance of the individual. Of course, intellectuals and artists wrote and painted for the upper classes, and the brilliant intellectual, cultural, and artistic accomplishments of the Renaissance were products of and for the elite. The ideas of the Renaissance did not have a broad base among the masses of the people. As Lorenzo the Magnificent, ruler of Florence, once commented: "Only men of noble birth can obtain perfection. The poor, who work with their hands and have no time to cultivate their minds, are incapable of it."

The Renaissance did, however, raise new questions about medieval traditions. In advocating a return to the early sources of Christianity and criticizing current religious practices, the humanists raised fundamental issues about the Catholic church, which was still an important institution. In the sixteenth century, the intellectual revolution of the fifteenth century gave way to a religious renaissance that touched the lives of people, including the masses, in new and profound ways. After the Reformation, Europe would never again be the unified Christian commonwealth it once believed it was.

NOTES

1. Quoted in Jacob Burckhardt, *The Civilization of the Renaissance in Italy,* trans. S. G. C. Middlemore (London, 1960), p. 81.

2. Baldassare Castiglione, *The Book of the Courtier,* trans. Charles S. Singleton (Garden City, N.Y., 1959), pp. 288–289.

3. Quoted in De Lamar Jensen, *Renaissance Europe* (Lexington, Mass., 1981), p. 94.

4. Quoted in Iris Origo, "The Domestic Enemy: The Eastern Slaves in Tuscany in the Fourteenth and Fifteenth Centuries," *Speculum* 30 (1955): 333.

5. Gene Brucker, ed., *Two Memoirs of Renaissance Florence* (New York, 1967), p. 132.

6. Quoted in Margaret L. King, *Women of the Renaissance* (Chicago, 1991), p. 3.

7. Gene Brucker, ed., *The Society of Renaissance Florence* (New York, 1971), p. 190.

8. Quoted in Garrett Mattingly, *Renaissance Diplomacy* (Baltimore, 1964), p. 42.

9. Ibid., p. 95.

10. Niccolò Machiavelli, *The Prince,* trans. David Wootton (Indianapolis, 1995), p. 48.

11. Ibid., p. 55.

12. Ibid., pp. 27, 77, 80.

13. Niccolò Machiavelli, *The Discourses,* trans. Christian Detmold (New York, 1950), p. 148.

14. Petrarch, "Epistle to Posterity," *Letters from Petrarch,* trans. Morris Bishop (Bloomington, Ind., 1966), pp. 6–7.

15. Bernhardt J. Hurwood, trans., *The Facetiae of Giovanni Francesco Poggio Bracciolini* (New York, 1968), p. 57.

16. Quoted in Frances Yates, *Giordano Bruno and the Hermetic Tradition* (Chicago, 1964), p. 211.

17. Giovanni Pico della Mirandola, *Oration on the Dignity of Man,* in E. Cassirer, P. O. Kristeller, J. H. Randall, Jr., eds., *The Renaissance Philosophy of Man* (Chicago, 1948), p. 225.

18. Ibid., pp. 247–249.

19. W. H. Woodward, *Vittorino da Feltre and Other Humanist Educators* (Cambridge, 1897), p. 102.

20. Ibid., pp. 106–107.

21. Quoted in Iris Origo, "The Education of Renaissance Man," *The Light of the Past* (New York, 1959), p. 136.

22. Quoted in Elizabeth G. Holt, ed., *A Documentary History of Art* (Garden City, N.Y., 1957), 1:286.

23. Quoted in Rosa M. Letts, *The Cambridge Introduction to Art: The Renaissance* (Cambridge, 1981), p. 86.

24. Quoted in Johan Huizinga, *The Waning of the Middle Ages* (Garden City, N.Y., 1956), p. 265.

25. Quoted in Alexander C. Flick, *The Decline of the Medieval Church* (London, 1930), 1:180.

SUGGESTIONS FOR FURTHER READING

The classic study of the Italian Renaissance is J. Burckhardt, *The Civilization of the Renaissance in Italy*, trans. S. G. C. Middlemore (London, 1960), first published in 1860. General works on the Renaissance in Europe include D. L. Jensen, *Renaissance Europe* (Lexington, Mass., 1981); P. Burke, *The European Renaissance: Centres and Peripheries* (Oxford, 1998); E. Breisach, *Renaissance Europe, 1300–1517* (New York, 1973); J. Hale, *The Civilization of Europe in the Renaissance* (New York, 1994); and the classic work by M. P. Gilmore, *The World of Humanism, 1453–1517* (New York, 1962). Although many of its interpretations are outdated, W. Ferguson's *Europe in Transition, 1300–1520* (Boston, 1962), contains a wealth of information. The brief study by P. Burke, *The Renaissance*, 2d ed. (New York, 1997), is a good summary of recent literature on the Renaissance. For beautifully illustrated introductions to the Renaissance, see G. Holmes, *Renaissance* (New York, 1996); and M. Aston, ed., *The Panorama of the Renaissance* (New York, 1996).

Brief, but basic works on Renaissance economic matters are H. A. Miskimin, *The Economy of Early Renaissance Europe, 1300–1460* (New York, 1975) and *The Economy of Later Renaissance Europe, 1460–1600* (New York, 1978). For a new interpretation of economic matters, see L. Jardine, *Worldly Goods* (New York, 1996). Numerous facets of social life in the Renaissance are examined in J. R. Hale, *Renaissance Europe: The Individual and Society* (London, 1971); B. Pullan, *Rich and Poor in Renaissance Venice* (Cambridge, Mass., 1971); J. H. Langbein, *Prosecuting Crime in the Renaissance* (Cambridge, Mass., 1974); and G. Ruggiero, *The Boundaries of Eros: Sex Crime and Sexuality in Renaissance Venice* (Oxford, 1985). On family and marriage, see D. Herlihy, *The Family in Renaissance Italy* (St. Louis, 1974); C. Klapisch-Zuber, *Women, Family, and Ritual in Renaissance Italy* (Chicago, 1985); and the well-told story by G. Brucker, *Giovanni and Lusanna: Love and Marriage in Renaissance Florence* (Berkeley, 1986). On women, see M. L. King, *Women of the Renaissance* (Chicago, 1991); and N. Z. Davis and A. Farge, eds., *A History of Women: Renaissance and Enlightenment Paradoxes* (Cambridge, Mass., 1993).

The best overall study of the Italian city-states is L. Martines, *Power and Imagination: City-States in Renaissance Italy* (New York, 1979), although D. Hay and J. Law, *Italy in the Age of the Renaissance* (London, 1989), is also a good survey. There is an enormous literature on Renaissance Florence. The best introduction is G. A. Brucker, *Renaissance Florence*, rev. ed. (Berkeley and Los Angeles, 1983). A popular biography of Isabella d'Este is G. Marek, *The Bed and the Throne* (New York, 1976). On the *condottieri*, see M. Mallett, *Mercenaries and Their Masters: Warfare in Renaissance Italy* (Totowa, 1974). The work by G. Mattingly, *Renaissance Diplomacy* (Boston, 1955) remains the basic one on the subject. Machiavelli's life can be examined in Q. Skinner, *Machiavelli* (Oxford, 1981).

Brief introductions to Renaissance humanism can be found in D. R. Kelley, *Renaissance Humanism* (Boston, 1991); C. G. Nauert, Jr., *Humanism and the Culture of Renaissance Europe* (Cambridge, 1995); and F. B. Artz, *Renaissance Humanism, 1300–1550* (Oberlin, Ohio, 1966). For a good collection of essays, see J. Kraye, ed., *The Cambridge Companion to Renaissance Humanism* (Cambridge, 1996). The fundamental work on fifteenth-century civic humanism is H. Baron, *The Crisis of the Early Italian Renaissance*, 2d ed. (Princeton, N.J., 1966). The classic work on humanist education is W. H. Woodward, *Vittorino da Feltre and Other Humanist Educators* (New York, 1963), first published in 1897. A basic work on the writing of history in the Italian Renaissance is E. Cochrane, *Historians and Historiography in the Italian Renaissance* (Chicago, 1981). The impact of printing is exhaustively examined in E. Eisenstein, *The Printing Press as an Agent of Change*, 2 vols. (New York, 1978).

For brief introductions to Renaissance art, see R. M. Letts, *The Cambridge Introduction to Art: The Renaissance* (Cambridge, 1981); and B. Cole and A. Gealt, *Art of the Western World* (New York, 1989), Chapters 6–8. Good surveys of Renaissance art include F. Hartt, *History of Italian Renaissance Art*, 4th ed. (Englewood Cliffs, N.J., 1994); S. Elliott, *Italian Renaissance Painting*, 2d ed. (London, 1993); R. Turner, *Renaissance Florence: The Invention of a New Art* (New York, 1997); and L. Murray, *The High Renaissance* (New York, 1967). For studies of individual artists, see J. H. Beck, *Raphael* (New York, 1994); M. Kemp, *Leonardo da Vinci: The Marvellous Works of Nature and of Man* (London, 1981); and A. Hughes, *Michelangelo* (London, 1997). On music, see the specialized work by H. M. Brown, *Music in the Renaissance*, 2d ed. (Englewood Cliffs, N.J., 1999).

For a general work on the political development of Europe in the Renaissance, see J. H. Shennan, *The Origins of the Modern European State, 1450–1725* (London, 1974). On France, see D. Potter, *A History of France, 1460–1560* (London, 1995). Early Renaissance England is examined in J. R. Lander, *Crown and Nobility, 1450–1509* (London, 1976). On the first Tudor king, see S. B. Chrimes, *Henry VII* (Berkeley, 1972). Good coverage of Renaissance Spain can be found in J. N. Hillgarth, *The Spanish Kingdoms, 1250–1516*, vol. 2, *Castilian Hegemony, 1410–1516* (New York, 1978). Some good works on eastern Europe include P. W. Knoll, *The Rise of the Polish Monarchy* (Chicago, 1972); and C. A. Macartney, *Hungary: A Short History* (Edinburgh, 1962). On the Ottomans and their expansion, see H. Inalcik, *The Ottoman Empire: The Classical Age, 1300–1600* (London, 1973); and the classic work by S. Runciman, *The Fall of Constantinople, 1453* (Cambridge, 1965).

On problems of heresy and reform, see C. Crowder, *Unity, Heresy and Reform, 1378–1460* (London, 1977). Aspects of the Renaissance papacy can be examined in E. Lee, *Sixtus IV and Men of Letters* (Rome, 1978); and M. Mallett, *The Borgias* (New York, 1969). On Rome, see especially P. Partner, *Renaissance Rome, 1500–1559: A Portrait of a Society* (Berkeley, 1976).

For additional reading, go to InfoTrac College Edition, your online research library at http://web1.infotrac-college.com

Enter the search term *Renaissance* using the Subject Guide.

Enter the search term *Machiavelli* using Key Terms.

Enter the search term *humanism* using Subject Guide.

Enter the search terms *Leonardo da Vinci* using Key Terms.

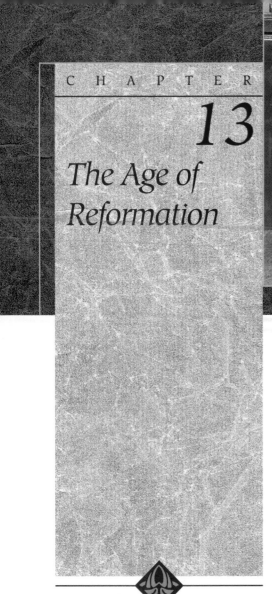

CHAPTER OUTLINE

- Prelude to Reformation: The Northern Renaissance
- Prelude to Reformation: Church and Religion on the Eve of the Reformation
- Martin Luther and the Reformation in Germany
- Germany and the Reformation: Religion and Politics
- The Spread of the Protestant Reformation
- The Social Impact of the Protestant Reformation
- The Catholic Reformation
- Conclusion

FOCUS QUESTIONS

- Who were the Christian humanists, and how did they differ from the Protestant reformers?
- What were Martin Luther's main disagreements with the Roman Catholic church, and why did the movement he began spread so quickly across Europe?
- What were the main tenets of Lutheranism, Zwinglianism, Calvinism, and Anabaptism, and how did they differ from each other and from Catholicism?
- What impact did the Protestant Reformation have on the society of the sixteenth century?
- What measures did the Roman Catholic church take to reform itself and to combat Protestantism in the sixteenth century?

O N APRIL 18, 1520, *a lowly monk stood before the emperor and princes of Germany in the city of Worms. He had been called before this august gathering to answer charges of heresy, charges that could threaten his very life. The monk was confronted with a pile of his books and asked if he wished to defend them all or reject a part. Courageously, Martin Luther defended them all and asked to be shown where any part was in error on the basis of "Scripture and plain reason." The emperor was outraged by Luther's response and made his own position clear the next day: "Not only I, but you of this noble German nation, would be forever disgraced if by our negligence not only heresy but the very suspicion of heresy were to survive. After having heard yesterday the obstinate defense of Luther, I regret that I have so long delayed in proceeding against him and his false teaching. I will have no more to do with him." Luther's appearance at Worms set the stage for a serious challenge to the authority of the Catholic church. This was by no means the first crisis in the church's 1,500-year history, but its consequences were more far-reaching than anyone at Worms in 1520 could have imagined.*

Throughout the Middle Ages, the Catholic church continued to assert its primacy of position. It had overcome defiance of its temporal authority by emperors, and challenges to its doctrines had been crushed by the Inquisition and combated by new religious orders that carried its message of salvation to all the towns and villages of medieval Europe. The growth of the papacy had paralleled the growth of the church, but by the end of the Middle Ages challenges to papal authority from the rising power of monarchical states had resulted in a loss of papal temporal authority. An even greater threat to papal authority and church unity arose in the sixteenth century when the unity of Christendom was shattered by the Reformation.

The movement begun by Martin Luther when he made his dramatic stand quickly spread across Europe, a clear indication of dissatisfaction with Catholic practices. Within a short time, new forms of religious practices, doctrines, and organizations, including Zwinglianism, Calvinism, Anabaptism, and Anglicanism, were attracting adherents all over Europe. Although seemingly helpless to stop the new Protestant churches, the Catholic church also underwent a religious renaissance and managed by the mid-sixteenth century to revive its fortunes. Those historians who speak of the Reformation as the beginning of the modern world exaggerate its importance, but there is no doubt that the splintering of Christendom had consequences that ushered in new ways of thinking and at least prepared the ground for modern avenues of growth.

◆ Prelude to Reformation: The Northern Renaissance

Martin Luther's reform movement was not the first in sixteenth-century Europe. Christian or northern Renaissance humanism, which evolved as Italian Renaissance humanism spread to northern Europe, had as one of its major goals the reform of Christendom. The new classical learning of the Italian Renaissance did not spread to the European countries north of the Alps until the second half of the fifteenth century. Northern Europe had

fewer ties to the classical past than Italy and was initially less interested in recovering Greco-Roman culture. Gradually, however, a number of intellectuals and artists from the cities north of the Alps went to Italy and returned home enthusiastic about the new education and the recovery of ancient thought and literature that we associate with Italian Renaissance humanism. In this manner, Italian humanism spread to the north, but with some noticeable differences. What, then, are the distinguishing characteristics of northern Renaissance humanism, a movement that flourished from the late fifteenth century until it was overwhelmed by the Reformation in the 1520s?

※ *Christian or Northern Renaissance Humanism*

Like their Italian counterparts, northern humanists cultivated a knowledge of the classics, the one common bond that united all humanists into a kind of international fellowship. The northern humanists brought out translations or scholarly editions of the classics for the printing press and sought to reconcile the ethical content of those works with Christian ethics. In the classics, northern humanists felt they had found a morality more humane than the theological arguments of the medieval scholastics.

In returning to the writings of antiquity, northern humanists (who have been called Christian humanists by historians because of their profound preoccupation with religion) also focused on the sources of early Christianity, the Holy Scriptures and the writings of such church fathers as Augustine, Ambrose, and Jerome. In these early Christian writings, they discovered a simple religion that they came to feel had been distorted by the complicated theological arguments of the Middle Ages. Their interest in Christian writings also led them to master Greek for the express purpose of reading the Greek New Testament and such early Greek church fathers as John Chrysostom. Some northern humanists even mastered Hebrew to study the Old Testament in its original language.

Although Christian humanists sought positions as teachers and scholars, the influence of scholastic theologians in the universities often made it difficult for them to do so. So long as they stuck to the classics, Christian humanists coexisted amicably with the scholastic theologians, but when they began to call for radical change in the methods and aims of theological study, they ran into bitter opposition. On the other hand, northern Renaissance humanists had opportunities to serve as secretaries to kings, princes, and cities, where their ability to write good prose and deliver orations made them useful. Support for humanism came from other directions as well, notably from patricians, lawyers, and civic officials, especially in the south German cities.

The most important characteristic of northern humanism was its reform program. With their belief in the ability of human beings to reason and improve themselves, the northern humanists felt that through education in the sources of classical, and especially Christian, antiquity, they could instill a true inner piety or an inward religious feeling that would bring about a reform of the church and society. For this reason, Christian humanists supported schools, brought out new editions of the classics, and prepared new editions of the Bible and writings of the church fathers. In the preface to his edition of the Greek New Testament, the famous humanist Erasmus wrote:

> Indeed, I disagree very much with those who are unwilling that Holy Scripture, translated into the vulgar tongue, be read by the uneducated, as if Christ taught such intricate doctrines that they could scarcely be understood by very few theologians, or as if the strength of the Christian religion consisted in men's ignorance of it . . . I would that even the lowliest women read the Gospels and the Pauline Epistles. And I would that they were translated into all languages so that they could be read and understood not only by Scots and Irish but also by Turks and Saracens. . . . Would that, as a result, the farmer sing some portion of them at the plow, the weaver hum some parts of them to the movement of his shuttle, the traveler lighten the weariness of the journey with stories of this kind![1]

This belief in the power of education would remain an important characteristic of European civilization. Like later intellectuals, Christian humanists believed that to change society they must first change the human beings who compose it. Although some have viewed the Christian humanists as naive, they themselves were very optimistic. Erasmus proclaimed in a letter to Pope Leo X: "I congratulate this our age—which bids fair to be an age of gold, if ever such there was—wherein I see . . . three of the chief blessings of humanity are about to be restored to her. I mean, first, that truly Christian piety, . . . secondly, learning of the best sort, . . . and thirdly, the public and lasting concord of Christendom."[2] This belief that a golden age could be achieved by applying the new learning to the reform of church and society proved to be a common bond among the Christian humanists. The turmoil of the Reformation shattered much of this intellectual optimism, as the lives and careers of two of the most prominent Christian humanists, Desiderius Erasmus and Thomas More, illustrate.

✣ ERASMUS

The most influential of all the Christian humanists, and in a way the symbol of the movement itself, was Desiderius Erasmus (1466–1536), who formulated and popularized the reform program of Christian humanism. Born in Holland, Erasmus was educated at one of the schools of the Brothers of the Common Life. He wandered to France, England, Italy, Germany, and Switzerland, conversing everywhere in the classical Latin that might be called his mother tongue. By 1500, he had turned seriously toward religious studies where he concentrated on

ERASMUS. Desiderius Erasmus was the most influential of the northern Renaissance humanists. He sought to restore Christianity to the early simplicity found in the teachings of Jesus. This portrait of Erasmus was painted in 1523 by Hans Holbein the Younger, who had formed a friendship with the great humanist while they were both in Basel.

reconciling the classics and Christianity through their common ethical focus.

In 1500, Erasmus published the *Adages,* an anthology of proverbs from ancient authors that showed his ability in the classics. The *Handbook of the Christian Knight,* printed in 1503, reflected his preoccupation with religion. He called his conception of religion "the philosophy of Christ," by which he meant that Christianity should be a guiding philosophy for the direction of daily life rather than the system of dogmatic beliefs and practices that the medieval church seemed to stress. In other words, he emphasized inner piety and deemphasized the external forms of religion (such as the sacraments, pilgrimages, fasts, veneration of saints, and relics). To return to the simplicity of the early church, people needed to understand the original meaning of the Scriptures and early church fathers. Believing that the standard Latin edition of the Bible, known as the Vulgate, contained errors, Erasmus edited the Greek text of the New Testament from the earliest available manuscripts and published it, along with a new Latin translation, in 1516.

Erasmus: In Praise of Folly

The Praise of Folly is one of the most famous pieces of literature of the sixteenth century. Erasmus, who wrote it in a short period of time during a visit to the home of Thomas More, considered it a "little diversion" from his "serious work." Yet both contemporaries and later generations have appreciated "this laughing parody of every form and rank of human life." In this selection, Erasmus belittles one of his favorite objects of scorn—the monks.

❋ Erasmus, *The Praise of Folly*

Those who are the closest to these [the theologians] in happiness are generally called "the religious" or "monks," both of which are deceiving names, since for the most part they stay as far away from religion as possible and frequent every sort of place. I cannot, however, see how any life could be more gloomy than the life of these monks if I [Folly] did not assist them in many ways. Though most people detest these men so much that accidentally meeting one is considered to be bad luck, the monks themselves believe that they are magnificent creatures. One of their chief beliefs is that to be illiterate is to be of a high state of sanctity, and so they make sure that they are not able to read. Another is that when braying out their gospels in church they are making themselves very pleasing and satisfying to God, when in fact they are uttering these psalms as a matter of repetition rather than from their hearts. . . .

Moreover, it is amusing to find that they insist that everything be done in fastidious detail, as if employing the orderliness of mathematics, a small mistake in which would be a great crime. Just so many knots must be on each shoe and the shoelace may be of only one specified color; just so much lace is allowed on each habit; the girdle must be of just the right material and width; the hood of a certain shape and capacity; their hair of just so many fingers' length; and finally they can sleep only the specified number of hours per day. Can they not understand that, because of a variety of bodies and temperaments, all this equality of restrictions is in fact very unequal? Nevertheless, because of all this detail that they employ they think that they are superior to all other people. And what is more, amid all their pretense of Apostolic charity, the members of one order will denounce the members of another order clamorously because of the way in which the habit has been belted or the slightly darker color of it. . . .

Many of them work so hard at protocol and at traditional fastidiousness that they think one heaven hardly a suitable reward for their labors; never recalling, however, that the time will come when Christ will demand a reckoning of that which he had prescribed, namely charity, and that he will hold their deeds of little account. One monk will then exhibit his belly filled with every kind of fish; another will profess a knowledge of over a hundred hymns. Still another will reveal a countless number of fasts that he has made, and will account for his large belly by explaining that his fasts have always been broken by a single large meal. Another will show a list of church ceremonies over which he has officiated so large that it would fill seven ships.

To Erasmus, the reform of the church meant spreading an understanding of the philosophy of Jesus, providing enlightened education in the sources of early Christianity, and making commonsense criticism of the abuses in the church. The latter is especially evident in his work, *The Praise of Folly*, written in 1509. It is a satirical view of his contemporary society in which folly, personified as a woman, shows how she dominates the affairs of humankind. Through this scheme, Erasmus was able to engage in a humorous, yet effective criticism of the most corrupt practices of his own society. He was especially harsh on the abuses within the ranks of the clergy (see the box above).

Erasmus's reform program was not destined to effect the reform of the church that he so desired. His moderation and his emphasis on education were quickly overwhelmed by the violence unleashed by the passions of the Reformation. Undoubtedly, though, his work helped to prepare the way for the Reformation; as contemporaries proclaimed, "Erasmus laid the egg that Luther hatched." Yet Erasmus eventually disapproved of Luther and the Protestant reformers. He had no intention of destroying the unity of the medieval Christian church, for his whole program was based on reform within the church.

✍ THOMAS MORE

Born the son of a London lawyer, Thomas More (1478–1535) received the benefits of a good education. Although trained in the law, he took an avid interest in the new classical learning and became proficient in both Latin and Greek. Like the Italian humanists who believed in putting their learning at the service of the state, More embarked on a public career that ultimately took him to the highest reaches of power as lord chancellor of England.

His career in government service, however, did not keep More from the intellectual and spiritual interests that were so dear to him. He was well acquainted with other English humanists and became an intimate friend of Erasmus. He made translations from Greek authors and wrote both prose and poetry in Latin. A deeply devout man, he spent many hours in prayer and private devotions. Many praised his household as a shining model of Christian family life.

More's most famous work, and one of the most controversial of his age, was *Utopia*, written in 1516. This literary masterpiece is an account of the idealistic life and institutions of the community of Utopia (literally "nowhere"), an imaginary island in the vicinity of the New World. It reflects More's own concerns with the economic, social, and political problems of his day. He presented a new social system in which cooperation and reason replaced power and fame as the proper motivating agents for human society. Utopian society, therefore, is based on communal ownership rather than private property. All persons work but six hours a day, regardless of occupation, and are rewarded according to their needs. Possessing abundant leisure time and relieved of competition and greed, Utopians were free to do wholesome and enriching things. As More stated in Book II: "All the rest of the twenty-four [hours] they're free to do what they like—not to waste their time in idleness or self-indulgence, but to make good use of it in some congenial activity."[3] More envisioned Utopia as an orderly world where social relations, recreation, and even travel were carefully controlled for the moral welfare of society and its members.

In serving King Henry VIII, More came face to face with the abuses and corruption he had criticized in *Utopia*. But he did not allow the idealism of Utopia to outweigh his own ultimate realism, and in *Utopia* itself he justified his service to the king:

> If you can't completely eradicate wrong ideas, or deal with inveterate vices as effectively as you could wish, that's no reason for turning your back on public life altogether. You wouldn't abandon ship in a storm just because you couldn't control the winds. On the other hand, it's no use attempting to put across entirely new ideas, which will obviously carry no weight with people who are prejudiced against them. You must go to work indirectly. You must handle everything as tactfully as you can, and what you can't put right you must try to make as little wrong as possible. For things will never be perfect, until human beings are perfect—which I don't expect them to be for quite a number of years.[4]

More's religious devotion and belief in the universal Catholic church proved even more important than his service to the king, however. Always the man of conscience, More willingly gave up his life opposing England's break with the Roman Catholic church over the divorce of King Henry VIII.

◆ Prelude to Reformation: Church and Religion on the Eve of the Reformation

The institutional problems of the Catholic church in the fourteenth and fifteenth centuries, especially the failure of the Renaissance popes to provide spiritual leadership, were bound to affect the spiritual life of all Christendom. The general impression of the tenor of religious life on the eve of the Reformation is one of much deterioration, coupled with evidence of a continuing desire for meaningful religious experience from millions of devout laypeople.

❖ The Clergy

The economic changes of the Late Middle Ages and Renaissance and the continuing preoccupation of the papal court with finances had an especially strong impact upon the clergy. One need only read the names of the cardinals in the fifteenth century to realize that the highest positions of the clergy were increasingly held by either the nobility or the wealthier members of the bourgeoisie. At the same time, to enhance their revenues, high church officials accumulated church offices in ever-larger numbers. This practice of pluralism (the holding of many church offices) led, in turn, to the problem of absenteeism, as church officeholders neglected their episcopal duties and delegated the entire administration of their dioceses to priests, who were often underpaid and little interested in performing their duties.

At the same time, these same economic forces led to a growing division between the higher and lower clergy. While cardinals, archbishops, bishops, and abbots vied for church offices and accumulated great wealth, many members of the lower clergy—the parish priests—tended to exist at the same economic level as their parishioners. Social discontent grew, especially among those able and conscientious priests whose path to advancement was blocked by the nobles' domination of higher church offices. By the same token, pluralism on the lower levels left many parishes without episcopal direction of any kind. Such a lack of leadership often resulted in lower clergy of poor quality. The fifteenth century was rife with complaints about the ignorance and incapacity of parish priests, as well as their greed and sexual offenses.

❖ Popular Religion

The atmosphere of the Late Middle Ages and Renaissance, with its uncertainty of life and immediacy of death, brought a craving for meaningful religious expression and certainty of salvation. This impulse, especially strong in Germany, expressed itself in two ways that often seemed contradictory.

One manifestation of religious piety in the fifteenth century was the almost mechanical view of the process of salvation. Collections of relics grew as more and more people sought certainty of salvation through their veneration. By 1509, Frederick the Wise, elector of Saxony and Luther's prince, had amassed over 5,000 relics to which were attached indulgences that could officially reduce one's time in purgatory by 1,443 years (an indulgence is a remission of all or part of the temporal punishment due to sin). Despite the physical dangers, increasing numbers of Christians made pilgrimages to such holy centers as Rome and Jerusalem to gain spiritual benefits.

Another form of religious piety, the quest for a tranquil spirituality, was evident in the popular mystical movement known as the Modern Devotion (see Chapter 11), which spawned the lay religious order, the Brothers and Sisters of the Common Life, and a reform of monastic life in Germany and the Low Countries. The best-known member of the Brothers of the Common Life in the fifteenth century was Thomas à Kempis (1380–1471), to whom most scholars ascribe the writing of the great mystical classic of the Modern Devotion, *The Imitation of Christ*.

One notable feature of *The Imitation of Christ* was its de-emphasis of religious dogma. A life of inner piety, totally dedicated to the moral and ethical precepts of Jesus, was preferable to dogma and intellectual speculation. As Thomas à Kempis stated, "Truly, at the day of judgment we shall not be examined by what we have read, but what we have done; not how well we have spoken, but how religiously we have lived." This portrayal of formal theology as secondary to living a good life had deep roots in an emphasis on the Bible as a Christian's primary guide to the true Christian life. In the New Testament, one could find models for the imitation of Jesus that even the uneducated could understand. The copying and dissemination of the Bible, as well as its exposition, played an important role in the work of the Brothers of the Common Life.

Popular mysticism, then, as seen in the Modern Devotion, bears an important relationship to the Reformation. Although adherents of the Modern Devotion did not question the traditional beliefs or practices of the church, their de-emphasis of them in favor of the inner life of the spirit and direct communion with God minimized the importance of the formal church and undermined the position of the church and its clergy in Christians' lives. At the same time, the movement gained its strength through its appeal to laypeople, especially townspeople who liked its direct personal approach to religion.

What is striking about the revival of religious piety in the fifteenth century—whether expressed through such external forces as the veneration of relics and the buying of indulgences or the mystical path—was its adherence to the orthodox beliefs and practices of the Catholic church. The agitation for certainty of salvation and spiritual peace occurred within the framework of the "holy mother Church." But disillusionment grew as the devout experienced the clergy's inability to live up to their expectations. The deepening of religious life, especially in the second half of the fifteenth century, found little echo among the worldly-wise clergy, and it is this environment that helps to explain the tremendous and immediate impact of Luther's ideas.

◆ Martin Luther and the Reformation in Germany

The Protestant Reformation had its beginning in a typical medieval question—what must I do to be saved? Martin Luther, a deeply religious man, found an answer that did not fit within the traditional teachings of the late medieval church. Ultimately, he split with that church, destroying the religious unity of western Christendom. That other people were concerned with the same question is evident in the rapid spread of the Reformation. But religion was so entangled in the social, economic, and political forces of the period that the Protestant reformers' hope of transforming the church quickly proved illusory.

※ *The Early Luther*

Martin Luther was born on November 10, 1483, into a peasant family, although his father raised himself into the ranks of the lower bourgeoisie by going into mining. His father wanted him to become a lawyer, so Luther enrolled at the University of Erfurt where he received his bachelor's degree in 1502. In 1505, after becoming a master in the liberal arts, the young Martin began to study law. Luther was not content with the study of law and all along had shown religious inclinations. In the summer of 1505, en route back to Erfurt after a brief visit home, he was caught in a ferocious thunderstorm and vowed that, if he were spared, he would become a monk. He then entered the monastic order of the Augustinian Hermits in Erfurt, much to his father's disgust. While in the monastery, Luther focused on his major concern, the assurance of salvation. The traditional beliefs and practices of the church seemed unable to relieve his obsession with this question, especially evident in his struggle with the sacrament of penance or confession. The sacraments were a Catholic's chief means of receiving God's grace; that of confession offered the opportunity to have one's sins forgiven. Luther spent hours confessing his sins, but he was always doubtful. Had he remembered all of his sins? Even more, how could a hopeless sinner be acceptable to a totally just and all-powerful God? Luther threw himself into his monastic routine with a vengeance:

> I was indeed a good monk and kept my order so strictly that I could say that if ever a monk could get to heaven through monastic discipline, I was that monk. . . . And yet my conscience would not give me certainty, but I always doubted and said, "You didn't do that right. You weren't contrite enough. You left that out of your confession." The more I tried to remedy an uncertain, weak and troubled conscience with human traditions, the more I daily found it more uncertain, weaker and more troubled.[5]

Despite his herculean efforts, Luther achieved no certainty and even came, as he once expressed it, to hate "this just God who punishes sinners."

To help overcome his difficulties, his superiors recommended that the intelligent, yet disturbed monk study theology. He received his doctorate in 1512 and then became a professor in the theological faculty at the University of Wittenberg, lecturing on the Bible. Probably sometime between 1513 and 1516, through his study of the Bible, he arrived at an answer to his problem.

Luther's dilemma had derived from his concept of the "justice of God," which he interpreted as a punitive justice in which God weighs the merits or good works

MARTIN LUTHER. This painting by Lucas Cranach the Elder in 1533 shows Luther at the age of 50. By this time, Luther's reforms had taken hold in many parts of Germany, and Luther himself was a happily married man with five children.

performed by humans as a necessary precondition for salvation. To Luther it appeared that the church was saying that one must earn salvation by good works. In Luther's eye, human beings, weak and powerless in the sight of an almighty God, could never do enough to justify salvation in these terms. Through his study of the Bible, especially his work on Paul's Epistle to the Romans, Luther rediscovered another way of viewing the justice of God:

> Night and day I pondered until I saw the connection between the justice of God and the statement that "the just shall live by his faith." Then I grasped that the justice of God is that righteousness by which through grace and sheer mercy God justifies us through faith. Thereupon I felt myself to be reborn and to have gone through open doors into paradise.[6]

To Luther, the "justice of God" was now not a punitive justice but the grace of God that bestows salvation freely to humans, not through their good works, but through the sacrifice of Jesus on the cross. Even faith or the power of belief is a product of divine grace or a gift of God. Humans do nothing to merit grace; it is purely God's decision. The doctrine of justification by grace through faith alone became the primary doctrine of the Protestant Reformation (justification is the act by which a person is made deserving of salvation). Since Luther had arrived at this doctrine from his study of Scripture, the Bible became for Luther as for all other Protestants the chief guide to reli-

gious truth. Justification by faith and the Bible as the sole authority in religious affairs were the twin pillars of the Protestant Reformation.

The event that propelled Luther into an open confrontation with church officials and forced him to see the theological implications of justification by faith alone was the indulgence controversy. In 1517, Pope Leo X had issued a special jubilee indulgence to finance the ongoing construction of the new Saint Peter's Basilica (see Chapter 12). This special indulgence was connected to political and ecclesiastical affairs in Germany through one Albrecht of Brandenburg. Though he was already both bishop of Halberstadt and archbishop of Magdeburg, Albrecht purchased a special dispensation from Pope Leo X to obtain yet another church office, the archbishopric of Mainz. To get the money, Albrecht borrowed from the Fugger banking firm in Augsburg, which paid the pope. Albrecht was then given the rights to sell the special jubilee indulgence in Germany for ten years, with half of the proceeds going to the Fuggers to pay off his debt and the other half to Rome to rebuild Saint Peter's. Johann Tetzel, a rambunctious Dominican, hawked the indulgences with the slogan, "As soon as the coin in the coffer rings, the soul from purgatory springs."

Luther was greatly distressed by the sale of indulgences, certain that people were simply guaranteeing their eternal damnation by relying on these pieces of paper to assure themselves of salvation. In response, he issued his Ninety-Five Theses, although scholars are unsure whether he nailed them to a church door in Wittenberg, as is traditionally alleged, or mailed them to his ecclesiastical superior. In either case, his theses were a stunning indictment of the abuses in the sale of indulgences (see the box on p. 369). If the pope had the power to grant indulgences, "Why does not the Pope empty purgatory for the sake of most holy love and the supreme need of souls?" It is doubtful that Luther intended any break with the church over the issue of indulgences. If the pope had clarified the use of indulgences, as Luther wished, then he would probably have been satisfied and the controversy closed. But the Renaissance pope Leo X did not take the issue seriously and is even reported to have said that Luther was simply "some drunken German who will amend his ways when he sobers up." But the development of printing prevented such a speedy resolution. A German translation of the Ninety-Five Theses was quickly printed in thousands of copies and received sympathetically in a Germany that had a long tradition of dissatisfaction with papal policies and power.

The controversy reached an important turning point with the Leipzig Debate in July 1519. There Luther's opponent, the capable Catholic theologian Johann Eck, forced Luther to move beyond indulgences and deny the authority of popes and councils. In effect, Luther was compelled to see the consequences of his new theology. At the beginning of 1520, he proclaimed: "Farewell, unhappy, hopeless, blasphemous Rome! The Wrath of God has come upon you, as you deserve. We have cared for Babylon, and

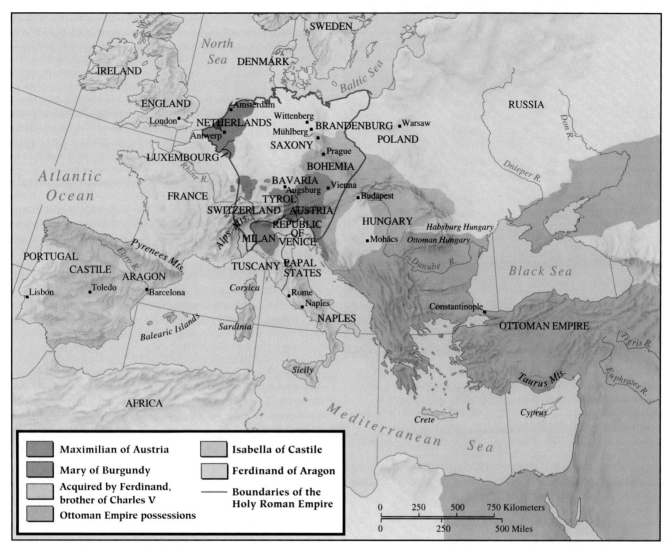

MAP 13.1 The Empire of Charles V.

◆ The Spread of the Protestant Reformation

To Catholic critics, Luther's heresy had opened the door to more extreme forms of religious and social upheaval. For both Catholics and Protestant reformers, it also raised the question of how to determine what constituted the correct interpretation of the Bible. The inability to agree on this issue led not only to theological confrontations but also to bloody warfare as each Christian group was unwilling to admit that it could be wrong.

❋ Lutheranism in Scandinavia

In 1397, the Union of Kalmar had brought about the unification of Denmark, Norway, and Sweden under the rule of one monarch, the king of Denmark. This union, however, failed to achieve any real social or political unification of the three states, particularly since the independent-minded, landed nobles worked to frustrate any increase in monarchical centralization. By the beginning of the six-

teenth century, the union was on the brink of disintegration. In 1520, Christian II (1513–1523) of Denmark, ruler of the three Scandinavian kingdoms, was overthrown by Swedish barons led by Gustavus Vasa. Three years later, Vasa became king of an independent Sweden (1523–1560) and took the lead in establishing a Lutheran Reformation in his country. Swedish nobles supported his efforts, while Olavus Petri, who had studied at Wittenberg, wrote treatises based on Luther's writings and published the first Swedish New Testament in 1526. By the 1530s, a Swedish Lutheran National Church had been created.

Meanwhile, Christian II had also been deposed as the king of Denmark by the Danish nobility; he was succeeded by his uncle, who became Frederick I (1523–1533). Frederick encouraged Lutheran preachers to spread their evangelical doctrines and to introduce a Lutheran liturgy into the Danish church service. In the 1530s, under Frederick's successor, Christian III (1534–1559), a Lutheran state church was installed with the king as the supreme authority in all ecclesiastical affairs. Christian was also instrumental in spreading Lutheranism to Norway. By the 1540s, Scandinavia had become a Lutheran stronghold.

ZWINGLI. Ulrich Zwingli began the Reformation in Switzerland through his preaching in Zürich. Zwingli's theology was accepted in Zürich and soon spread to other Swiss cities. This portrait of Zwingli was done by Hans Asper, probably in 1531.

Like the German princes, the Scandinavian monarchs had been the dominant force in establishing state-run churches.

❊ *The Zwinglian Reformation*

Switzerland, which has played little role in our history to date, was home to two major Reformation movements, Zwinglianism and Calvinism. In the sixteenth century, the Swiss Confederation was a loose association of thirteen self-governing states called cantons. Theoretically part of the Holy Roman Empire, they had become virtually independent after the Swiss defeated the forces of Emperor Maximilian in 1499. The six forest cantons were democratic republics; the seven urban cantons, which included Zürich, Bern, and Basel, were mostly governed by city councils controlled by narrow oligarchies of wealthy citizens. Perennially troubled by a weak economy, the Swiss had grown accustomed to selling their warriors as mercenary soldiers and had become the principal exporters of mercenaries in the sixteenth century. All in all, the Swiss Confederation was a loose conglomeration of states that possessed no common institutions and worked together only for survival and gain.

Ulrich Zwingli (1484–1531) was a product of the Swiss rural cantons. The precocious son of a relatively prosperous peasant, the young Zwingli eventually obtained both the bachelor of arts and master of arts degrees. During his university education at Vienna and Basel, Zwingli was strongly influenced by Christian humanism. Ordained a priest in 1506, he accepted a parish post in rural Switzerland until his appointment as a cathedral priest in the Great Minster of Zürich in 1518. Through his preaching there, Zwingli began the Reformation in Switzerland.

Zwingli always maintained that he came to his evangelical theology independently of Luther: "I began to preach the Gospel of Christ in 1516, long before anyone in our region had ever heard of Luther. . . . Why don't you call me a Paulinian since I am preaching as St. Paul preached. . . . If Luther preaches Christ, he does just what I do." Modern scholars doubt Zwingli's protestation, believing that he was influenced by Luther's writings, beginning at least in 1519. In any case, Zwingli's evangelical preaching caused such unrest that in 1523 the city council held a public disputation or debate in the town hall. The disputation became a standard method of spreading the Reformation to many cities. It gave an advantage to reformers since they had the power of new ideas and Catholics were not used to defending their teachings. Zwingli's party was accorded the victory, and the council declared that "Mayor, Council and Great Council of Zürich, in order to do away with disturbance and discord, have upon due deliberation and consultation decided and resolved that Master Zwingli should continue as heretofore to proclaim the Gospel and the pure sacred Scripture."[11] City magistrates were not always motivated solely by religious considerations. By removing the Catholic church—a rival for authority in their town—the secular authorities enhanced their own power.

Over the next two years, evangelical reforms were promulgated in Zürich by a city council strongly influenced by Zwingli. Zwingli looked to the state to supervise the church. "A church without the magistrate is mutilated and incomplete," he declared. Relics and images were abolished; all paintings and decorations were removed from the churches and replaced by whitewashed walls. The mass was replaced by a new liturgy consisting of Scripture reading, prayer, and sermons. Music was eliminated from the service as a distraction from the pure word of God. Monasticism, pilgrimages, the veneration of saints, clerical celibacy, and the pope's authority were all abolished as remnants of papal Christianity. Zwingli's movement soon spread to other cities in Switzerland, including Bern in 1528 and Basel in 1529.

By 1528, Zwingli's reform movement faced a serious political problem as the forest cantons remained staunchly Catholic. Zürich feared an alliance between them and the Habsburgs. To counteract this danger, Zwingli attempted to build a league of evangelical cities by seeking an agreement with Luther and the German reformers. An alliance between them seemed possible, since the Reformation had spread to the south German cities, especially Strasbourg, where a moderate reform movement containing characteristics of both Luther's and Zwingli's movements had been instituted by Martin Bucer (1491–1551). Both the German and the Swiss reformers realized the need for unity to defend against imperial and conservative opposition. Protestant political leaders, especially Landgrave

A Reformation Debate: The Marburg Colloquy

Debates played a crucial role in the Reformation period. They were a primary instrument in introducing the Reformation into innumerable cities as well as a means of resolving differences among like-minded Protestant groups. This selection contains an excerpt from the vivacious and often brutal debate between Luther and Zwingli over the sacrament of the Lord's Supper at Marburg in 1529. The two protagonists failed to reach agreement.

❈ The Marburg Colloquy, 1529

THE HESSIAN CHANCELLOR FEIGE: My gracious prince and lord [Landgrave Philip of Hesse] has summoned you for the express and urgent purpose of settling the dispute over the sacrament of the Lord's Supper. . . . And let everyone on both sides present his arguments in a spirit of moderation, as becomes such matters. . . . Now then, Doctor Luther, you may proceed.

LUTHER: Noble prince, gracious lord! Undoubtedly the colloquy is well intentioned. . . . Although I have no intention of changing my mind, which is firmly made up, I will nevertheless present the grounds of my belief and show where the others are in error. . . . Your basic contentions are these: In the last analysis you wish to prove that a body cannot be in two places at once, and you produce arguments about the unlimited body which are based on natural reason. I do not question how Christ can be God and man and how the two natures can be joined. For God is more powerful than all our ideas, and we must submit to his word.

Prove that Christ's body is not there where the Scripture says, "This is my body!" Rational proofs I will not listen to. . . . God is beyond all mathematics and the words of God are to be revered and carried out in awe. It is God who commands, "Take, eat, this is my body." I request, therefore, valid scriptural proof to the contrary.

Luther writes on the table in chalk, "This is my body," and covers the words with a velvet cloth.

OECOLAMPADIUS [leader of the reform movement in Basel and a Zwinglian partisan]: The sixth chapter of John clarifies the other scriptural passages. Christ is not speaking there about a local presence. "The flesh is of no avail," he says [John 6:63]. It is not my intention to employ rational, or geometrical, arguments—neither am I denying the power of God—but as long as I have the complete faith I will speak from that. For Christ is risen; he sits at the right hand of God; and so he cannot be present in the bread. Our view is neither new nor sacrilegious, but is based on faith and Scripture. . . .

ZWINGLI: I insist that the words of the Lord's Supper must be figurative. This is ever apparent, and even required by the article of faith: "taken up into heaven, seated at the right hand of the Father." Otherwise, it would be absurd to look for him in the Lord's Supper at the same time that Christ is telling us that he is in heaven. One and the same body cannot possibly be in different places. . . .

LUTHER: I call upon you as before: your basic contentions are shaky. Give way, and give glory to God!

ZWINGLI: And we call upon you to give glory to God and to quit begging the question! The issue at stake is this: Where is the proof of your position? I am willing to consider your words carefully—no harm meant! You're trying to outwit me. I stand by this passage in the sixth chapter of John, verse 63 and shall not be shaken from it. You'll have to sing another tune.

LUTHER: You're being obnoxious.

ZWINGLI: (*excitedly*) Don't you believe that Christ was attempting in John 6 to help those who did not understand?

LUTHER: You're trying to dominate things! You insist on passing judgment! Leave that to someone else! . . . It is your point that must be proved, not mine. But let us stop this sort of thing. It serves no purpose.

ZWINGLI: It certainly does! It is for you to prove that the passage in John 6 speaks of a physical repast.

LUTHER: You express yourself poorly and make about as much progress as a cane standing in a corner. You're going nowhere.

ZWINGLI: No, no, no! This is the passage that will break your neck!

LUTHER: Don't be so sure of yourself. Necks don't break this way. You're in Hesse, not Switzerland.

Philip of Hesse, fearful of Charles V's ability to take advantage of the division between the reformers, attempted to promote an alliance of the Swiss and German reformed churches by persuading the leaders of both groups to attend a colloquy (or conference) at Marburg to resolve their differences. Able to agree on virtually everything else, the gathering splintered over the interpretation of the Lord's Supper (see the box above). Zwingli believed that the scriptural words "This is my Body, This is my blood" should be taken figuratively, not literally, and refused to accept Luther's insistence on the real presence of the body and blood of Jesus "in, with, and under the bread and wine." The Marburg Colloquy of 1529 produced no agreement and no evangelical alliance. Although this failure to reach an accord was a setback for Lutheranism and Philip of Hesse, it proved even more harmful to Zwingli.

In October 1531, war erupted between the Swiss Protestant and Catholic cantons. Zürich's army was

AN ANABAPTIST EXECUTION IN THE NETHERLANDS. The Anabaptists were the radicals of the Reformation. They advocated adult baptism and believed that the true Christian should not actively participate in or be governed by the secular state. Due to their radical ideas, the Anabaptists were persecuted and put to death by Catholics and Protestants alike. This sixteenth-century woodcut depicts the execution of Anabaptist reformers.

routed, and Zwingli was found wounded on the battlefield. His enemies killed him, cut up his body, and burned the pieces, scattering the ashes. Although Zwingli was succeeded by the able Heinrich Büllinger, the momentum of the Zwinglian reform movement was slowed. This Swiss civil war of 1531 provided an early indication of what religious passions would lead to in the sixteenth century. Unable to find peaceful ways to agree on the meaning of the Gospel, the disciples of Christianity resorted to violence and decision by force. When he heard of Zwingli's death, Martin Luther, who had not forgotten the confrontation at Marburg, is supposed to have remarked that Zwingli got what he deserved.

✳ *The Radical Reformation: The Anabaptists*

Since the Reformation had broken down traditional standards and relationships, reformers such as Luther sought a new authority by allowing the state to play an important, if not dominant, role in church affairs. But some people favored a far more radical approach. Collectively called the Anabaptists, these radicals actually formed a large variety of different groups who, nevertheless, shared some common characteristics. Although some middle-class intellectuals participated in this movement, Anabaptism was especially attractive to those peasants, weavers, miners, and artisans who had been adversely affected by the economic changes of the age. The upper classes were aware of the obvious link between social dissatisfaction and religious radicalism, which was particularly evident in commercial and industrial cities like Zürich, Strasbourg, Nuremberg, and Augsburg. All of these cities initiated a Lutheran or Zwinglian Reformation early on but, thanks to

their relatively large lower classes affected by economic upheavals, also became centers for radical religious groups.

Anabaptists everywhere shared some common ideas. To them, the true Christian church was a voluntary association of believers who had undergone spiritual rebirth and had then been baptized into the church. Anabaptists advocated adult rather than infant baptism. They also tried to return literally to the practices and spirit of early Christianity. Adhering to the accounts of early Christian communities in the New Testament, they followed a strict sort of democracy in which all believers were considered equal. Each church chose its own minister, who might be any member of the community since all Christians were considered priests (though women were often excluded). Those chosen as ministers had the duty to lead services, which were very simple and contained nothing not found in the early church. Anabaptists rejected theological speculation in favor of simple Christian living according to what they believed was the pure word of God. The Lord's Supper was interpreted as a remembrance, a meal of fellowship celebrated in the evening in private houses according to Jesus' example. Finally, unlike the Catholics and other Protestants, most Anabaptists believed in the complete separation of church and state. Not only was government to be excluded from the realm of religion, it was not even supposed to exercise political jurisdiction over real Christians. Anabaptists refused to hold political office or bear arms because many took literally the commandment "Thou shall not kill," although some Anabaptist groups did become quite violent. Their political beliefs as much as their religious beliefs caused the Anabaptists to be regarded as dangerous radicals who threatened the very fabric of sixteenth-century society. Indeed, the chief thing Protestants and Catholics could agree on was the need to persecute Anabaptists.

One early group of Anabaptists known as the Swiss Brethren arose in Zürich. Their ideas frightened Zwingli, and they were soon expelled from the city. As their teachings spread through southern Germany, the Austrian Habsburg lands, and Switzerland, Anabaptists suffered ruthless persecution, especially after the Peasants' War of 1524–1525, when the upper classes resorted to repression. To Catholics and Lutherans alike, the Anabaptists threatened not only religious peace but also secular authority

The Trial of Michael Sattler

Michael Sattler had been prior of a Benedictine monastery before abandoning Catholicism for Lutheranism and then Anabaptism. He was responsible for drawing up a set of seven articles (the Schleitheim Articles) in 1527, which constituted the "first formal Anabaptist confession of faith." Both Catholics and other Protestant sects viewed Anabaptists as dangerous radicals, subversive of both church and state. This excerpt, taken from a contemporary account of Sattler's trial for heresy by Austrian authorities, begins after Sattler has given a speech detailing his beliefs. As his sentence indicates, Anabaptists were subjected to cruel and unusual punishments.

❀ The Trial of Michael Sattler

Upon this speech the judges laughed and put their heads together, and the town clerk of Ensisheim said, "Yes, you infamous, desperate rascal of a monk, should we dispute with you? The hangman will dispute with you, I assure you!"

Michael said: "God's will be done."

The town clerk said: "It were well if you had never been born."

Michael replied: "God knows what is good."

The town clerk: "You archheretic, you have seduced pious people. If they would only now forsake their error and commit themselves to grace!"

Michael: "Grace is with God alone."

The town clerk: "Yes, you desperate villain, you archheretic, I say, if there were no hangman here, I would hang you myself and be doing God a good service thereby."

Michael: "God will judge aright."

The town clerk then admonished the judges and said: "He will not cease from this chatter anyway. Therefore, my Lord Judge, you may proceed with the sentence. I call for a decision of the court."

The judge asked Michael Sattler whether he too committed it to the court. He replied: "Ministers of God, I am not sent to judge the Word of God. We are sent to testify and hence cannot consent to any adjudication, since we have no command from God concerning it. But we are not for that reason removed from being judged and we are ready to suffer and to await what God is planning to do with us. We will continue in our faith in Christ so long as we have breath in us, unless we be dissuaded from it by the Scriptures."

The town clerk, said: "The hangman will instruct you, he will dispute with you, archheretic."

Michael: "I appeal to the Scriptures."

Then the judges arose and went into another room where they . . . determined on the sentence. . . .

The judges having returned to the room, the sentence was read. It was as follows: "In the case of the attorney of His Imperial Majesty [Holy Roman Emperor] vs. Michael Sattler, judgment is passed that Michael Sattler shall be delivered to the executioner, who shall lead him to the place of execution and cut out his tongue, then forge him fast to a wagon and thereon with red-hot tongs twice tear pieces from his body; and after he has been brought outside the gate, he shall be plied five times more in the same manner."

---

because of their political ideas (see the box above). After the movement was virtually stamped out in Germany, Anabaptist survivors emerged in Moravia, Poland, and the Netherlands. In the latter, Anabaptism took on a strange form.

In the 1530s, the city of Münster in Westphalia in northwestern Germany near the Dutch border was the site of an Anabaptist uprising that determined the fate of Dutch Anabaptism. Seat of a powerful Catholic prince-bishop, Münster had experienced severe economic disasters, including crop failure and plague. Although converted to Lutheranism in 1532, Münster experienced a more radical mass religious hysteria that led to legal recognition for the Anabaptists. Soon Münster became a haven for Anabaptists from the surrounding neighborhood, especially the more wild-eyed variety known as Melchiorites who adhered to a vivid millenarianism. They believed that the end of the world was at hand and that they would usher in the Kingdom of God with Münster as the New Jerusalem. By the end of February 1534, these millenarian Anabaptists had taken control of the city, driven out those they considered godless or unbelievers, burned all books except the Bible, and proclaimed communal ownership of all property. Eventually, the leadership of this New Jerusalem fell into the hands of one man, John of Leiden, who proclaimed himself king of the New Jerusalem. As king, he would lead out the elect from Münster to cover the entire world and purify it of evil by the sword in preparation for Jesus' Second Coming and the creation of a New Age. In this new kingdom, John of Leiden believed, all goods would be held in common and the saints would live without suffering.

But it was not to be. As the Catholic prince-bishop of Münster gathered a large force and laid siege to the city, the new king repeatedly had to postpone the ushering forth from Münster. Finally, after many inhabitants had starved, a joint army of Catholics and Lutherans recaptured the city in June 1535 and executed the radical Anabaptist leaders in a gruesome fashion. The New Jerusalem had ceased to exist.

Purged of its fantasies and more extreme elements, Dutch Anabaptism reverted to its pacifist tendencies, especially evident in the work of Menno Simons (1496–1561), the man most responsible for rejuvenating Dutch Anabaptism. A popular leader, Menno dedicated his life to the spread of a peaceful, evangelical Anabaptism that stressed separation from the world in order to truly emulate the life of Jesus. Simons imposed strict discipline on his followers and banned those who refused to conform to the rules. The Mennonites, as his followers were called, spread from the Netherlands into northwestern Germany and eventually into Poland and Lithuania as well as the New World. Both the Mennonites and the Amish, who are also descended from the Anabaptists, can be found in the United States today.

✻ The Reformation in England

At one time, a Reformation in England would have been unthinkable. Had not Henry VIII penned an attack against Martin Luther in 1521, the *Defense of the Seven Sacraments,* and been rewarded for it by the pope with the title "Defender of the Faith"? Nevertheless, there were elements of discontent in England. Antipapal feeling ran high as many of the English resented papal influence in English affairs, especially in matters of taxation and justice. There was also criticism of the activities of the clergy as people denounced greedy clerics who flaunted their great wealth. One layman charged that "These [the clergy] are not the shepherds, but the ravenous wolves going in shepherds' clothing, devouring the flock."

Anticlericalism and antipapal feelings were not the only manifestations of religious sentiment in early sixteenth-century England. A craving for spiritual expression fostered the spread of Lutheran ideas, encouraged in part by two different traditions of dissent. Heretical Lollardy, stressing the use of the Bible in the vernacular and the rejection of papal supremacy, continued to exert influence among the lower classes, while Christian humanism, with its calls for reform, influenced the English middle and upper classes. People influenced by Lollardy and Christian humanism were among the first to embrace Lutheran writings when they began to arrive in England in the 1520s.

Despite these factors, there might not have been a Reformation in England had it not been for the king's desire to divorce his first wife, Catherine of Aragon. Henry VIII's reasons were twofold. Catherine had produced no male heir, an absolute essential if his Tudor dynasty were to flourish. At the same time, Henry had fallen in love with Anne Boleyn, a lady-in-waiting to Queen Catherine. Her unwillingness to be only the king's mistress, as well as the king's desire to have a legitimate male heir, made a new marriage imperative. The king's first marriage stood in the way, however.

Henry relied upon Cardinal Wolsey, the highest ranking English church official and lord chancellor to the king, to obtain an annulment of his marriage from Pope Clement VII. Normally, the pope might have been willing to oblige, but the sack of Rome in 1527 had made the pope dependent upon the Holy Roman Emperor Charles V, who happened to be the nephew of Queen Catherine. Discretion dictated delay in granting the English king's

HENRY VIII, HIS WIFE, AND CHILDREN. The desire of Henry VIII for a male heir played a significant role in his break with the Catholic church. Pictured here in the central panel of this 1545 portrait by an unknown artist are Henry VIII, Jane Seymour, his third wife, and Prince Edward, who became King Edward VI in 1547. On the far left is Princess Mary and on the far right is Princess Elizabeth.

request. Impatient with the process, Henry dismissed Wolsey in 1529.

Two new advisers now became the king's agents in fulfilling his wishes. These were Thomas Cranmer (1489–1556), who became archbishop of Canterbury in 1532, and Thomas Cromwell (1485–1540), the king's principal secretary after the fall of Wolsey. They advised the king to obtain an annulment of his marriage in England's own ecclesiastical courts. The most important step toward this goal was the promulgation by Parliament of an act cutting off all appeals from English church courts to Rome, a piece of legislation that essentially abolished papal authority in England. Henry no longer needed the pope to attain his annulment. He was now in a hurry because Anne Boleyn had become pregnant and he had secretly married her in January 1533 to legitimize the expected heir. In May, as archbishop of Canterbury and head of the highest ecclesiastical court in England, Thomas Cranmer ruled that the king's marriage to Catherine was "null and absolutely void," and then validated Henry's marriage to Anne. At the beginning of June, Anne was crowned queen. Three months later a child was born. Much to the king's disappointment, the baby was a girl, the future Queen Elizabeth I.

In 1534, Parliament completed the break of the Church of England with Rome by passing the Act of Supremacy, which declared that the king was "taken, accepted, and reputed the only supreme head on earth of the Church of England." This meant that the English monarch now controlled the church in all matters of doctrine, clerical appointments, and discipline. In addition, Parliament passed a Treason Act making it punishable by death to deny that the king was the supreme head of the church. The Act of Supremacy and the Treason Act went beyond religious issues in their implications, for they asserted that there could be no higher authority over England than laws made by the king and Parliament.

Few challenged the new order. One who did was Thomas More, the humanist and former lord chancellor, who saw clearly to the heart of the issue: loyalty to the pope in Rome was now treason in England. More refused to publicly support the new laws and was duly tried for treason. At his trial, he asked, rhetorically, what the effect of the actions of the king and Parliament would be: "Therefore am I not bound . . . to conform my conscience to the Council of one realm [England] against the general Council of Christendom?"[12] Because his conscience could not accept the victory of the national state over the church, nor would he, as a Christian, bow his head to a secular ruler in matters of faith, More was beheaded in London on July 6, 1535.

Thomas Cromwell worked out the details of the Tudor government's new role in church affairs based on the centralized power exercised by the king and Parliament. Cromwell also came to his extravagant king's financial rescue with a daring plan for the dissolution of the monasteries. About 400 religious houses were closed in 1536, and their land and possessions confiscated by the king. Many were sold to nobles, gentry, and some merchants. The king received a great boost to his treasury, as well as creating a group of supporters who now had a stake in the new Tudor order.

Although Henry VIII had broken with the papacy, little change occurred in matters of doctrine, theology, and ceremony. Some of his supporters, such as Archbishop Thomas Cranmer, wished to have a religious reformation as well as an administrative one, but Henry was unyielding. To counteract a growing Protestant sentiment, the king had Parliament pass the Six Articles Act of 1539, which reaffirmed transubstantiation, clerical celibacy, and other aspects of Catholic doctrine. No doubt, Henry's conservatism helped the English accept the basic changes he had made; since religious doctrine and worship had changed very little, most people were indifferent to the transformation that had occurred. Popular acceptance was also furthered by Henry's strategy of involving Parliament in all the changes.

The last decade of Henry's reign was preoccupied with foreign affairs, factional intrigue, and a continued effort to find the perfect wife. Henry soon tired of Anne Boleyn and had her beheaded in 1536 on a charge of adultery. His third wife, Jane Seymour, produced the long-awaited male heir but died during childbirth. His fourth marriage to Anne of Cleves, a German princess, was arranged for political reasons and on the basis of a painted portrait. Henry was shocked at her physical appearance when he first saw her in person and soon divorced her. His fifth wife, Catherine Howard, was more attractive but less moral. When she committed adultery, Henry had her beheaded. His last wife was Catherine Parr, who married the king in 1543 and outlived him. Henry was succeeded by the underage and sickly Edward VI (1547–1553), the son of his third wife.

Since the new king was only nine years old at the time of his accession to the throne, real control of England passed to a council of regency. During Edward's reign, Archbishop Cranmer and others inclined toward Protestant doctrines were able to move the Church of England in a more Protestant direction. New acts of Parliament instituted the right of the clergy to marry, the elimination of images, and the creation of a revised Protestant liturgy that was elaborated in a new prayer book and liturgical guide known as the Book of Common Prayer. These rapid changes in doctrine and liturgy aroused much opposition and prepared the way for the reaction that occurred when Mary, Henry's first daughter by Catherine of Aragon, came to the throne.

There was no doubt that Mary (1553–1558) was a Catholic who intended to restore England to Roman Catholicism. But she understood little about the practical nature of politics and even less about the changes that had swept over England in the past thirty years.

Mary's restoration of Catholicism, achieved by joint action of the monarch and Parliament, aroused much opposition. Although the new owners of monastic lands were assured otherwise, many feared that the lands confiscated by Henry would be restored to the church. Moreover, there was widespread antipathy to Mary's unfortunate marriage to Philip II, the son of Charles V and the future king of Spain. Philip was strongly disliked in England, and Mary's foreign policy of alliance with Spain aroused further hostility, especially when her forces lost Calais, the last English possession from the Hundred Years' War. The burning of more than 300 Protestant heretics roused further ire against "bloody Mary." As a result of her policies, Mary managed to achieve the opposite of what she had intended: England was more Protestant by the end of her reign than it had been at the beginning. When she came to power, Protestantism had become identified with church destruction and religious anarchy. Now people identified it with English resistance to Spanish interference. The death of Mary in 1558 ended the restoration of Catholicism in England.

✳ *John Calvin and the Development of Calvinism*

Of the second generation of Protestant reformers, one stands out as the systematic theologian and organizer of the Protestant movement—John Calvin (1509–1564). Born a generation later than Luther, Calvin reached manhood when Christian unity had for all intents and purposes already disappeared.

John Calvin began his academic training in humanistic studies in 1523 at the University of Paris, but switched to the study of law at Orléans and Bourges from 1528 to 1531, while simultaneously studying Greek. In 1531, he returned to Paris to concentrate on his humanistic pursuits. In his early development, Calvin was also influenced by Luther's writings, which were being circulated and read by French intellectuals as early as 1523. By 1533, Calvin had received a remarkably diverse education. In that same year, he experienced a religious crisis that determined the rest of his life's work. He described it in these words:

> God, by a sudden conversion, subdued and brought my mind to a teachable frame, which was more hardened in such matters than might have been expected from one at my early period of life. Having thus received some taste and knowledge of true godliness, I was immediately inflamed with so intense a desire to make progress therein, although I did not leave off other studies, I yet pursued them with less ardor.[13]

Calvin's conversion was solemn and straightforward. He was so convinced of the inner guidance of God that he became the most determined of all the Protestant reformers.

After his conversion and newfound conviction, Calvin was no longer safe in Paris, since King Francis I periodically persecuted Protestants. Eventually, Calvin made his way to Basel, where in 1536 he published the first edition of the *Institutes of the Christian Religion*, a masterful synthesis of Protestant thought, a manual for ecclesiastical organization, and a work that immediately secured his reputation as one of the new leaders of Protestantism. Although the *Institutes* were originally

JOHN CALVIN. After a conversion experience, John Calvin abandoned his life as a humanist and became a reformer. In 1536, Calvin began working to reform the city of Geneva, where he remained until his death in 1564. This sixteenth-century portrait of Calvin pictures him near the end of his life.

written in Latin, Calvin published a French edition in 1541, facilitating the spread of his ideas in French-speaking lands.

On most important doctrines, Calvin stood very close to Luther. He adhered to the doctrine of justification by faith alone to explain how humans achieved salvation. But Calvin also placed much emphasis on the absolute sovereignty of God or the "power, grace, and glory of God." Thus, "God asserts his possession of omnipotence, and claims our acknowledgment of this attribute; not such as is imagined by sophists, vain, idle, and almost asleep, but vigilant, efficacious, operative and engaged in continual action."[14]

One of the ideas derived from his emphasis on the absolute sovereignty of God—predestination—gave a unique cast to Calvin's teachings. Although it was but one aspect of his doctrine of salvation, predestination became the central focus of succeeding generations of Calvinists. This "eternal decree," as Calvin called it, meant that God had predestined some people to be saved (the elect) and others to be damned (the reprobate). According to Calvin, "He has once for all determined, both whom he would admit to salvation, and whom he would condemn to

The Role of Discipline in the "Most Perfect School of Christ on Earth"

To John Calvin's followers, the church that the French reformer had created in Geneva was, in the words of John Knox, "the most perfect school of Christ on earth." Calvin had emphasized in his reform movement that the church should have the ability to enforce proper behavior. Consequently, the Ecclesiastical Ordinances of 1541, the constitution of the church in Geneva, provided for an order of elders whose function was to cooperate with the pastors in maintaining discipline, "to have oversight of the life of everyone," as Calvin expressed it. These selections from the official records of the Consistory show the nature of its work.

✳ Reports of the Genevan Consistory

Donna Jane Peterman is questioned concerning her faith and why she does not receive communion and attend worship. She confesses her faith and believes in one God and wants to come to God and the holy Church and has no other faith. She recited the Lord's Prayer in the vernacular. She said that she believes what the Church believes. Is questioned why she never participates in communion when it is celebrated in this town, but goes to other places. She answers that she goes where it seems good to her. Is placed outside the faith.

The sister of Sr. Curtet, Lucresse, to whom remonstrances have been made on account of her going with certain monies to have masses said at Nessy by the monks of St. Claire. Questioned whether she has no scruples as to what she says. Replied that her father and mother have brought her up to obey a different law from the one now in force here. However, she does not desire the present law. Asked as to when was the festival of St. Felix, she replied that it was yesterday. Asked if she had not fasted, she replied that she fasted when it pleased her. Asked if she did not desire to pray to a single God; said that she did. Asked if she did not pray to St. Felix; said that she prayed to St. Felix and other saints who interceded for her. She is very obstinate. Decision that she be sent to some minister of her choice every sermon day and that the Lord's Supper be withheld from her.

At about this time, by resolution of the Consistory . . . the marriage contracted between the widow of Jean Archard, aged more than 70, and a servant of hers, aged about 27 or 28, was dissolved because of the too great inequality of age. The Consistory resolved further that Messieurs should be requested to make a ruling on this matter for the future.

---

destruction."[15] Calvin identified three tests that might indicate possible salvation: an open profession of faith, a "decent and godly life," and participation in the sacraments of baptism and communion. In no instance did Calvin ever suggest that worldly success or material wealth was a sign of election. Most importantly, although Calvin stressed that there could be no absolute certainty of salvation, some of his followers did not always make this distinction. The practical psychological effect of predestination was to give some later Calvinists an unshakable conviction that they were doing God's work on earth. Thus, Calvinism became a dynamic and activist faith. It is no accident that Calvinism became the militant international form of Protestantism.

To Calvin, the church was a divine institution responsible for preaching the word of God and administering the sacraments. Calvin kept only two sacraments, baptism and the Lord's Supper. Baptism was a sign of the remission of sins. Calvin believed in the real presence of Jesus in the sacrament of the Lord's Supper, but only in a spiritual sense. Jesus' body is at the right hand of God and thus cannot be in the sacrament, but to the believer, Jesus is spiritually present in the Lord's Supper. Finally, Calvin agreed with other reformers that the church had the power to discipline its members. This element of his thought was apparent when Calvin finally had the opportunity to establish his church in Geneva.

Up to 1536, John Calvin had essentially been a scholar. But in that year, he took up a ministry in Geneva that lasted until his death in 1564. Calvin achieved a major success in 1541 when the city council accepted his new church constitution known as the Ecclesiastical Ordinances. This document established four orders or offices: pastors, teachers (or doctors), elders, and deacons. The duties of the pastors or ministers were to preach the Gospel, administer the sacraments, and correct un-Christian behavior. To the teachers was given the responsibility to "instruct the faithful in sound doctrine, in order that the purity of the Gospel may not be corrupted." The elders or presbyters were laymen, chosen from and by the city magistrates; their function was to maintain discipline: "to have oversight of the life of everyone, to admonish amicably those whom they see to be erring or to be living a disordered life, and . . . to enjoin fraternal corrections." The deacons were also laymen who were responsible for the care of the poor, widows, and orphans and the administration of the city's hospitals.

The Ecclesiastical Ordinances created a special body for enforcing moral discipline. Consisting of five pastors and twelve elders, the Consistory functioned as a court to oversee the moral life, daily behavior, and doctrinal orthodoxy of Genevans and to admonish and correct deviants (see the box above). As its power increased, the Consistory went from "fraternal corrections" to the use of public penance and excommunication. More serious cases could be turned over to the city council for punishments greater than excommunication. During Calvin's last years, stricter laws against blasphemy were enacted and enforced with banishment and public whippings. Although Calvin's detractors felt that Geneva was an example of religious fanaticism, to visitors of similar inclination, it presented a glorious sight. John Knox, the Calvinist reformer of Scotland, called it "the most perfect school of Christ on earth."

Calvin's success in Geneva enabled the city to become a vibrant center of Protestantism. Following Calvin's lead, missionaries trained in Geneva were sent to all parts of Europe. Calvinism became established in France, the Netherlands, Scotland, and central and eastern Europe. By the mid-sixteenth century, Calvinism had replaced Lutheranism as the international form of Protestantism while Calvin's Geneva stood as the fortress of the Reformation.

◆ The Social Impact of the Protestant Reformation

Christianity was such an integral part of European life that it was inevitable that the Reformation would have an impact on the family, education, and popular religious practices.

❋ The Family

For centuries, Catholicism had praised the family and sanctified its existence by making marriage a sacrament. But the Catholic church's high regard for abstinence from sex as the surest way to holiness made the celibate state of the clergy preferable to marriage. Nevertheless, since not all men could remain chaste, marriage offered the best means to control sexual intercourse and give it a purpose, the procreation of children. To some extent, this attitude persisted among the Protestant reformers; Luther, for example, argued that sex in marriage allowed one to "make use of this sex in order to avoid sin," and Calvin advised that every man should "abstain from marriage only so long as he is fit to observe celibacy." If "his power to tame lust fails him," then he must marry.

But the Reformation did bring some change to the conception of the family. Both Catholic and Protestant clergy preached sermons advocating a positive view of family relationships. The Protestants were especially important in developing this new idea of the family. Since Protestantism had eliminated any idea of special holiness for celibacy, abolishing both monasticism and a celibate clergy, the family could be placed at the center of human life, and a new stress on "mutual love between man and wife" could be extolled. But were doctrine and reality the same? For more radical religious groups, at times they were (see the box on p. 385). One Anabaptist wrote to his wife before his execution: "My faithful helper, my loyal friend. I praise God that he gave you to me, you who have sustained me in all my trial."[16] But more often reality reflected the traditional roles of husband as the ruler and wife as the obedient servant whose chief duty was to please her husband. Luther stated it clearly:

> The rule remains with the husband, and the wife is compelled to obey him by God's command. He rules the home and the state, wages war, defends his possessions, tills the soil, builds, plants, etc. The woman on the other hand is like a nail driven into the wall . . . so the wife should stay at home and look after the affairs of the household, as one who has been deprived of the ability of administering those affairs that are outside and that concern the state. She does not go beyond her most personal duties.[17]

But obedience to her husband was not a wife's only role; her other important duty was to bear children. To Calvin and Luther, this function of women was part of the divine plan. God punishes women for the sins of Eve by the burdens of procreation and feeding and nurturing their children, but, said Luther, "it is a gladsome punishment if you consider the hope of eternal life and the honor of motherhood which had been left to her."[18] Although the Protestant reformers sanctified this role of woman as mother and wife, viewing it as a holy vocation, Protestantism also left few alternatives for women. Since monasticism had been destroyed, that career avenue was no longer available; for most Protestant women, family life was their only destiny. At the same time, by emphasizing the father as "ruler" and hence the center of household religion, Protestantism even removed the woman from her traditional role as controller of religion in the home.

Protestant reformers called upon men and women to read the Bible and participate in religious services together. In this way, the reformers provided a stimulus for the education of girls so they could read the Bible and other religious literature. The city council of Zwickau, for example, established a girls' school in 1525. But these schools were designed to encourage proper moral values rather than intellectual development and really did little to improve the position of women in society. Likewise, when women attempted to take more active roles in religious life, reformers—Lutheran and Calvinist alike—shrank back in horror. To them, the equality of the Gospel did not mean overthrowing the inequality of social classes or the sexes. Overall, the Protestant Reformation did not noticeably transform women's subordinate place in society.

❋ Education in the Reformation

The Reformation had an important effect upon the development of education in Europe. Renaissance humanism had significantly altered the content of education (see Chapter 12), and Protestant educators were very successful in implementing and using humanist methods in Protestant secondary schools and universities. Unlike the humanist schools, however, which had been mostly for an elite, the sons and a few daughters of the nobility and wealthier bourgeoisie, Protestant schools were aimed at a much wider audience. Protestantism created an increased

A Protestant Woman

In the initial zeal of the Protestant Reformation, women were frequently allowed to play unusual roles. Katherine Zell of Germany (c. 1497–1562) first preached beside her husband in 1527. After the death of her two children, she devoted the rest of her life to helping her husband and their Anabaptist faith. This selection is taken from one of her letters to a young Lutheran minister who had criticized her activities.

❋ Katherine Zell to Ludwig Rabus of Memmingen

I, Katherine Zell, wife of the late lamented Mathew Zell, who served in Strasbourg, where I was born and reared and still live, wish you peace and enhancement in God's grace. . . .

From my earliest years I turned to the Lord, who taught and guided me, and I have at all times, in accordance with my understanding and His grace, embraced the interests of His church and earnestly sought Jesus. Even in youth this brought me the regard and affection of clergymen and others much concerned with the church, which is why the pious Mathew Zell wanted me as a companion in marriage; and I, in turn, to serve the glory of Christ, gave devotion and help to my husband, both in his ministry and in keeping his house. . . . Ever since I was ten years old I have been a student and a sort of church mother, much given to attending sermons. I have loved and frequented the company of learned men, and I conversed much with them, not about dancing, masquerades, and worldly pleasures but about the kingdom of God. . . .

Consider the poor Anabaptists, who are so furiously and ferociously persecuted. Must the authorities everywhere be incited against them, as the hunter drives his dog against wild animals? Against those who acknowledge Christ the Lord in very much the same way we do and over which we broke with the papacy? Just because they cannot agree with us on lesser things, is this any reason to persecute them and in them Christ, in whom they fervently believe and have often professed in misery, in prison, and under the torments of fire and water?

Governments may punish criminals, but they should not force and govern belief, which is a matter for the heart and conscience not for temporal authorities. . . . When the authorities pursue one, they soon bring forth tears, and towns and villages are emptied.

---

need for at least a semiliterate body of believers who could read the Bible for themselves.

While adopting the classical emphasis of humanist schools, Protestant reformers broadened the base of those being educated. Convinced of the need to provide the church with good Christians and good pastors as well as the state with good administrators and citizens, Martin Luther advocated that all children should have the opportunity of an education provided by the state. To that end, he urged the cities and villages of Saxony to establish schools paid for by the public. Luther's ideas were shared by his Wittenberg co-worker, Philip Melanchthon, whose educational efforts earned him the title of *Praecepter Germaniae*, the Teacher of Germany. In his scheme for education in Saxony, Melanchthon divided students into three classes or divisions based on their age or capabilities.

Following Melanchthon's example, the Protestants in Germany were responsible for introducing the gymnasium,

A SIXTEENTH-CENTURY CLASSROOM. Protestants in Germany developed secondary schools that combined instruction in the liberal arts with religious education.

This scene from a painting by Hans Holbein shows a schoolmaster instructing a pupil in the alphabet while his wife helps a little girl.

or secondary school, where the humanist emphasis on the liberal arts based on instruction in Greek and Latin was combined with religious instruction. Most famous was the school in Strasbourg founded by Johannes Sturm in 1538, which served as a model for other Protestant schools. John Calvin's Genevan Academy, founded in 1559, was organized in two distinct parts. The "private school" or gymnasium was divided into seven classes for young people who were taught Latin and Greek grammar and literature as well as logic. In the "public school," students were taught philosophy, Hebrew, Greek, and, most importantly, theology. The Genevan Academy, which eventually became a university, came to concentrate on preparing ministers to spread the Calvinist view of the Gospel.

Catholics also perceived the importance of secondary schools and universities in educating people to Catholic perspectives. The Jesuits (see The Society of Jesus later in the next section) were especially proficient in combining humanist educational methods with religious instruction. Although both Catholic and Protestant secondary schools and universities were influenced by humanism, some humanists attacked them for misusing humanist methods. No doubt, as the Reformation progressed, confessional struggles made education increasingly serve the religious goal of producing zealous Protestants or Catholics. Virtually everywhere, teachers and professors were expected to follow the creeds of their ruling authorities.

✸ *Religious Practices and Popular Culture*

Although Protestant reformers were conservative in their political and social attitudes, their attacks on the Catholic church led to radical changes in religious practices. The Protestant Reformation abolished or severely curtailed such customary practices as indulgences, the veneration of relics and saints, pilgrimages, monasticism, and clerical celibacy. In Protestant cities, attacks on the veneration of saints brought an end to popular religious processions that had been an important focus of religious devotion and often served as rituals to placate nature. The elimination of saints put an end to the numerous celebrations of religious holy days and changed a community's sense of time. Thus, in Protestant communities, religious ceremonies and imagery, such as processions and statues, tended to be replaced with individual private prayer, family worship, and collective prayer and worship at the same time each week on Sunday.

Many religious practices that had played an important role in popular culture were criticized by Protestant reformers as superstitious or remnants of pagan culture. Smarting under pressure from these Protestant attacks, even Catholic leaders sought to eliminate the more frivolous aspects of popular practices, although they never went as far as the Protestants. In addition to abolishing saints' days and religious carnivals, some Protestant reformers even tried to eliminate customary forms of entertainment. English Puritans (as English Calvinists were called), for example, attempted to ban drinking in taverns, dramatic performances, and dancing. Dutch Calvinists denounced the

tradition of giving small presents to children on the feast of Saint Nicholas, near Christmas. Many of these Protestant attacks on popular culture were unsuccessful, however. The importance of taverns in English social life made it impossible to eradicate them, and celebrating at Christmas time persisted in the Dutch Netherlands.

◆ The Catholic Reformation

By the mid-sixteenth century, Lutheranism had become established in parts of Germany and Scandinavia, and Calvinism in parts of Switzerland, France, the Netherlands, and eastern Europe. In England, the split from Rome had resulted in the creation of a national church. The situation in Europe did not look particularly favorable for the Roman Catholic church. But even at the beginning of the sixteenth century, constructive, positive forces were at work for reform within the Catholic church, and by the mid-sixteenth century, they came to be directed by a revived and reformed papacy, giving the Catholic church new strength. By the second half of the sixteenth century, Catholicism had regained much that it had lost, especially in Germany and eastern Europe, and was able to make new conversions as well, particularly in the New World. We call the story of the revival of Roman Catholicism the Catholic Reformation, although some historians prefer to use the term Counter-Reformation, especially for those elements of the Catholic Reformation that were directly aimed at stopping the spread of the Protestant Reformation.

The Catholic Reformation was a mixture of old and new elements. The best features of medieval Catholicism were revived and then adjusted to meet new conditions, a situation most apparent in the revival of mysticism and monasticism. The emergence of a new mysticism, closely tied to the traditions of Catholic piety, was especially evident in the life of the Spanish mystic, Saint Teresa of Avila (1515–1582). A nun of the Carmelite order, Teresa experienced a variety of mystical visions that she claimed resulted in the ecstatic union of her soul with God. But Teresa also believed that mystical experience should lead to an active life of service on behalf of her Catholic faith. Consequently, she founded a new order of barefoot Carmelite nuns and worked to foster their mystical experiences.

The regeneration of religious orders also proved invaluable to the reform of Catholicism. Old orders, such as the Benedictines and Dominicans, were reformed and renewed. The Capuchins emerged when a group of Franciscans decided to return to the simplicity and poverty of Saint Francis of Assisi, the medieval founder of the Franciscan order. In addition to caring for the sick and the poor, the Capuchins focused on preaching the Gospel directly to the people and emerged as an effective force against Protestantism.

New religious orders and brotherhoods were also created. The Theatines, founded in 1524, placed their emphasis on reforming the secular clergy and encouraging those

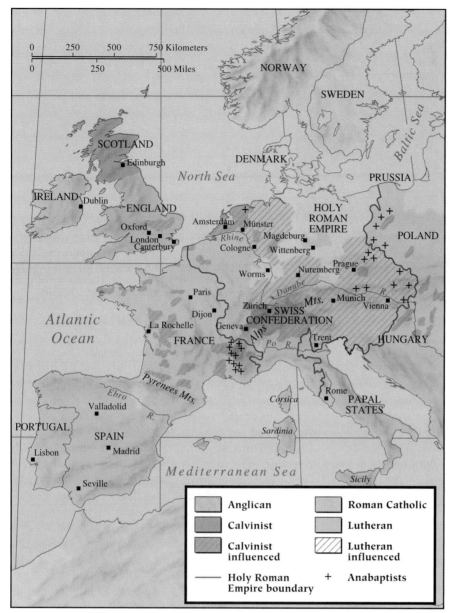

MAP 13.2 Catholics and Protestants in Europe by 1560.

clerics to fulfill their duties among the laity. The Theatines also founded orphanages and hospitals to care for the victims of war and plague. The Ursulines, a new order of nuns founded in Italy in 1535, focused their attention on establishing schools for the education of girls.

The Oratory of Divine Love, first organized in Italy in 1497, was not a new religious order but an informal group of clergy and laymen who worked to foster reform by emphasizing personal spiritual development and outward acts of charity. The "philosophy of Christ," advocated by the Christian humanist Erasmus, was especially appealing to many of them. The Oratory's members included a number of cardinals who favored the reform of the Catholic church.

✸ The Society of Jesus

Of all the new religious orders, the most important was the Society of Jesus, known as the Jesuits, who became the chief instrument of the Catholic Reformation. The Society

of Jesus was founded by a Spanish nobleman, Ignatius of Loyola (1491–1556), whose injuries in battle cut short his military career. Loyola experienced a spiritual torment similar to Luther's but, unlike Luther, resolved his problems not by a new doctrine, but by a decision to submit his will to the will of the church. Unable to be a real soldier, he vowed to be a soldier of God. Over a period of twelve years, Loyola prepared for his lifework by mortification, prayer, pilgrimages, going to school, and working out a spiritual program in his brief, but powerful book, *The Spiritual Exercises*. This was a training manual for spiritual development emphasizing exercises by which the human will could be strengthened and made to follow the will of God as manifested through his instrument, the Catholic church (see the box on p. 389).

Gradually, Loyola gathered together a small group of individuals who shared his single-minded devotion and were eventually recognized as a religious order, the Society of Jesus, by a papal bull in 1540. The new order was grounded on the principles of absolute obedience to the papacy, a strict hierarchical order for the society, the use of education to achieve its goals, and a dedication to engage in "conflict for God." Jesuit organization came to resemble the structure of a military command. A two-year novitiate weeded out all but the most dedicated. Executive leadership was put in the hands of a general, who nominated all important positions in the order and was to be revered as the absolute head of the order. Loyola served as the first general of the order until his death in 1556. A special vow of absolute obedience to the pope made the Jesuits an important instrument for papal policy.

The Jesuits pursued three major activities. They established highly disciplined schools, borrowing freely from humanist schools for their educational methods. To the Jesuits, the thorough education of young people was crucial to combat the advance of Protestantism. In the course of the sixteenth century, the Jesuits took over the premier academic posts in Catholic universities, and by 1600, they were the most famous educators in Europe. Another prominent Jesuit activity was the propagation of the Catholic faith among non-Christians. Francis Xavier (1506–1552), one of the original members of the Society of Jesus, carried the message of Catholic Christianity to the East, ministering to

IGNATIUS LOYOLA. The Jesuits became the most important new religious order of the Catholic Reformation. Shown here in a sixteenth-century painting by an unknown artist is Ignatius Loyola, founder of the Society of Jesus. Loyola is seen kneeling before Pope Paul III, who officially recognized the Jesuits in 1540.

India and Japan before dying of fever. Although conversion efforts in Japan proved short-lived, Jesuit activity in China, especially that of the Italian Matteo Ricci, was more long lasting. Finally, the Jesuits were determined to carry the Catholic banner and fight Protestantism. Jesuit missionaries proved singularly successful in restoring Catholicism to parts of Germany and eastern Europe. Poland was, in fact, largely won back for the Catholic church through Jesuit efforts. As the "shock troops of the papacy," the Jesuits proved invaluable allies of papal policies.

❧ A Revived Papacy

The involvement of the Renaissance papacy in dubious finances and Italian political and military affairs had created numerous sources of corruption. The meager steps taken to control corruption left the papacy still in need of serious reform, and it took the jolt of the Protestant Reformation to bring it about. Indeed, the change in the papacy in the course of the sixteenth century was one of the more remarkable aspects of the Catholic Reformation.

The pontificate of Pope Paul III (1534–1549) proved to be a turning point in the reform of the papacy. Raised in the lap of Renaissance luxury, Paul III continued Renaissance papal practices by appointing his nephews as cardinals, involving himself in politics, and patronizing arts and letters on a lavish scale. Nevertheless, he perceived the need for change and expressed it decisively. Advocates of reform, such as Gasparo Contarini and Gian Pietro Caraffa, were made cardinals. In 1535, Paul took the audacious step of appointing a Reform Commission to study the church's condition. The commission's report in 1537, which blamed the church's problems on the corrupt policies of popes and cardinals, was used even by Protestants to demonstrate that their criticisms of Catholic corruption had been justified. Paul III also formally recognized the Jesuits and summoned the Council of Trent.

A decisive turning point in the direction of the Catholic Reformation and the nature of papal reform came in the 1540s. In 1541, a colloquy had been held at Regensburg in a final attempt to settle the religious division peacefully. Here Catholic moderates, such as Cardinal Contarini, who favored concessions to Protestants in the hope of restoring Christian unity, reached a compromise with Protestant moderates on a number of doctrinal issues. When Contarini returned to Rome with these proposals, Cardinal Caraffa and other hard-liners, who regarded all compromise with Protestant innovations as heresy, accused him of selling out to the heretics. It soon became apparent that the conservative reformers were in the ascendancy when Caraffa was able to persuade Paul III to establish a Roman Inquisition or Holy Office in 1542 to ferret out doctrinal errors. There was to be no compromise with Protestantism.

When Cardinal Caraffa was chosen pope as Paul IV (1555–1559), he so increased the power of the Inquisition that even liberal cardinals were silenced. This "first true pope of the Catholic Counter-Reformation," as he has been called, also created an Index of Forbidden Books, a list of books that Catholics were not allowed to read. It included all the works of Protestant theologians as well as authors considered "unwholesome," a category general enough to include the works of Erasmus. Rome, the capital of Catholic Christianity, was rapidly becoming fortress Rome; any hope of restoring Christian unity by compromise was fast fading. The activities of the Council of Trent made compromise virtually impossible.

❧ The Council of Trent

In 1542, Pope Paul III took the decisive step of calling for a general council of Christendom to resolve the religious differences created by the Protestant revolt. It was not until March 1545, however, that a group of cardinals,

Loyola and Obedience to "Our Holy Mother, the Hierarchical Church"

In his Spiritual Exercises, Ignatius Loyola developed a systematic program for "the conquest of self and the regulation of one's life" for service to the hierarchical Catholic church. Ignatius's supreme goal was the commitment of the Christian to active service under Jesus' banner in the Church of Christ (the Catholic church). In the final section of the Spiritual Exercises, Loyola explained the nature of that commitment in a series of "Rules for Thinking with the Church."

❀ Ignatius Loyola, "Rules for Thinking with the Church"

The following rules should be observed to foster the true attitude of mind we ought to have in the Church militant.

1. We must put aside all judgment of our own, and keep the mind ever ready and prompt to obey in all things the true Spouse of Jesus Christ, our holy Mother, the hierarchical Church.

2. We should praise sacramental confession, the yearly reception of the Most Blessed Sacrament [the Lord's Supper], and praise more highly monthly reception, and still more weekly Communion. . . .

3. We ought to praise the frequent hearing of Mass, the singing of hymns, psalmody, and long prayers whether in the church or outside. . . .

4. We must praise highly religious life, virginity, and continency; and matrimony ought not be praised as much as any of these.

5. We should praise vows of religion, obedience, poverty, chastity, and vows to perform other works of supererogation conducive to perfection. . . .

6. We should show our esteem for the relics of the saints by venerating them and praying to the saints. We should praise visits to the Station Churches, pilgrimages, indulgences, jubilees, the lighting of candles in churches.

7. We must praise the regulations of the Church, with regard to fast and abstinence, for example, in Lent, on Ember Days, Vigils, Fridays, and Saturdays.

8. We ought to praise not only the building and adornment of churches, but also images and veneration of them according to the subject they represent.

9. Finally, we must praise all the commandments of the Church, and be on the alert to find reasons to defend them, and by no means in order to criticize them.

10. We should be more ready to approve and praise the orders, recommendations, and way of acting of our superiors than to find fault with them. Though some of the orders, etc., may not have been praiseworthy, yet to speak against them, either when preaching in public or in speaking before the people, would rather be the cause of murmuring and scandal than of profit. As a consequence, the people would become angry with their superiors, whether secular or spiritual. But while it does harm in the absence of our superiors to speak evil of them before the people, it may be profitable to discuss their bad conduct with those who can apply a remedy.

13. If we wish to proceed securely in all things, we must hold fast to the following principle: What seems to me white, I will believe black if the hierarchical Church so defines. For I must be convinced that in Christ our Lord, the bridegroom, and in His spouse the Church, only one Spirit holds sway, which governs and rules for the salvation of souls.

---

archbishops, bishops, abbots, and theologians met in the city of Trent on the border between Germany and Italy. This Council of Trent met intermittently from 1545 to 1563 in three major sessions. Two fundamental struggles determined its outcome. Whereas the pope hoped to focus on doctrinal issues, the Holy Roman Emperor Charles V wanted church reform to be the chief order of business, since he realized that defining doctrine first would only make the split in the church permanent. A second conflict focused on the division between Catholic moderates and conservatives. The former believed that compromises would have to be made in formulating doctrinal definitions, whereas the latter favored an uncompromising restatement of Catholic doctrines in strict opposition to Protestant positions. The latter group won, although not without a struggle. The Protestants were invited to attend the council, but since they were not permitted to partici-

pate, they refused the meaningless invitation. By and large, the popes controlled the council.

The final doctrinal decrees of the Council of Trent reaffirmed traditional Catholic teachings in opposition to Protestant beliefs. Scripture and tradition were affirmed as equal authorities in religious matters; only the church could interpret Scripture. Both faith and good works were declared necessary for salvation. The seven sacraments, the Catholic doctrine of transubstantiation, and clerical celibacy were all upheld. Belief in purgatory and in the efficacy of indulgences was affirmed, although the hawking of indulgences was prohibited. Of the reforming decrees that were passed, the most important established theological seminaries in every diocese for the training of priests.

After the Council of Trent, the Roman Catholic church possessed a clear body of doctrine and a unified church under the acknowledged supremacy of the popes who had triumphed over bishops and councils. The Roman Catholic church had become one Christian denomination among many with an organizational framework and doctrinal pattern that would not be significantly altered until Vatican Council II 400 years later. With a new spirit of confidence, the Catholic church entered a militant phase, as well prepared as the Calvinists to do battle for the Lord. An era of religious warfare was about to unfold.

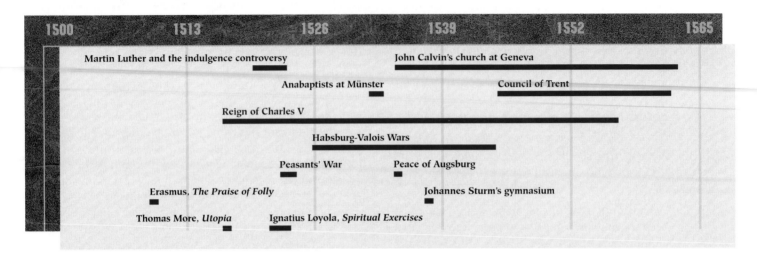

| 1500 | 1513 | 1526 | 1539 | 1552 | 1565 |

Martin Luther and the indulgence controversy

John Calvin's church at Geneva

Anabaptists at Münster

Council of Trent

Reign of Charles V

Habsburg-Valois Wars

Peasants' War

Peace of Augsburg

Erasmus, *The Praise of Folly*

Johannes Sturm's gymnasium

Thomas More, *Utopia*

Ignatius Loyola, *Spiritual Exercises*

CONCLUSION

When the Augustinian monk Martin Luther entered the public scene with a series of theses on indulgences, few people in Europe, or Germany for that matter, suspected that these theses would eventually produce a division of Europe along religious lines. But the yearning for reform of the church and meaningful religious experience caused a seemingly simple dispute to escalate into a powerful movement. Clearly, the papacy and other elements in the Catholic church underestimated the strength of Martin Luther and the desire for religious change.

Although Luther felt that his revival of Christianity based on his interpretation of the Bible should be acceptable to all, others soon appeared who also read the Bible but interpreted it in different ways. Protestantism split into different sects, which, though united in their dislike of Catholicism, were themselves divided over the interpretation of the sacraments and religious practices. As reform ideas spread, religion and politics became ever more intertwined. Political support played a crucial role in the spread of the Reformation.

Although Lutheranism was legally acknowledged in the Holy Roman Empire by the Peace of Augsburg in 1555, it had lost much of its momentum and apart from Scandinavia had scant ability to attract new supporters. Its energy was largely replaced by the new Protestant form of Calvinism, which had a clarity of doctrine and a fervor that made it attractive to a whole new generation of Europeans. Although Calvinism's militancy enabled it to expand across Europe, Catholicism was also experiencing its own revival and emerged as a militant faith, *prepared to do combat for the souls of the faithful. An age of religious passion would tragically be followed by an age of religious warfare.*

NOTES

1. Erasmus, *The Paraclesis*, in John Olin, ed., *Christian Humanism and the Reformation: Selected Writings of Erasmus*, 3d ed. (New York, 1987), p. 101.
2. Quoted in James B. Ross and Mary M. McLaughlin, eds., *The Portable Renaissance Reader* (New York, 1953), p. 83.
3. Thomas More, *Utopia*, trans. Paul Turner (Harmondsworth, 1965), p. 76.
4. Ibid., pp. 63–64.
5. Quoted in Alister E. McGrath, *Reformation Thought: An Introduction* (Oxford, 1988), p. 72.
6. Quoted in Roland Bainton, *Here I Stand: A Life of Martin Luther* (New York, 1950), pp. 49–50.
7. Quoted in Gordon Rupp, *Luther's Progress to the Diet of Worms* (New York, 1964), p. 82.
8. Quoted in ibid., p. 81.
9. *On the Freedom of a Christian Man*, quoted in E. G. Rupp and Benjamin Drewery, eds., *Martin Luther* (New York, 1970), p. 50.
10. Quoted in Bainton, *Here I Stand*, p. 144.
11. Quoted in De Lamar Jensen, *Reformation Europe* (Lexington, Mass., 1981), p. 83.
12. Quoted in A. G. Dickens and Dorothy Carr, eds., *The Reformation in England to the Accession of Elizabeth I* (New York, 1968), p. 72.
13. Quoted in Lewis W. Spitz, *The Renaissance and Reformation Movements* (Chicago, 1971), p. 414.
14. John Calvin, *Institutes of the Christian Religion*, trans. John Allen (Philadelphia, 1936), 1:220.
15. Ibid., 1:228; 2:181.
16. Quoted in Roland Bainton, *Women of the Reformation in Germany and Italy* (Minneapolis, 1971), p. 154.

17. Quoted in Bonnie S. Anderson and Judith P. Zinsser, *A History of Their Own: Women in Europe from Prehistory to the Present* (New York, 1988), 1:259.
18. Quoted in John A. Phillips, *Eve: The History of an Idea* (New York, 1984), p. 105.

SUGGESTIONS FOR FURTHER READING

Basic surveys of the Reformation period include H. J. Grimm, *The Reformation Era, 1500–1650*, 2d ed. (New York, 1973); C. Lindberg, *The European Reformations* (Cambridge, Mass., 1996); D. L. Jensen, *Reformation Europe* (Lexington, Mass., 1981); G. R. Elton, *Reformation Europe, 1517–1559* (Cleveland, 1963); and E. Cameron, *The European Reformation* (New York, 1991). L. W. Spitz, *The Protestant Reformation, 1517–1559* (New York, 1985), is a sound and up-to-date history. The significance of the Protestant Reformation is examined in S. Ozment, *Protestants: The Birth of a Revolution* (New York, 1992). A brief but very useful introduction to the theology of the Reformation can be found in A. McGrath, *Reformation Thought: An Introduction*, 2d ed. (Oxford, 1993). For an overview of how European religious life in the Late Middle Ages affected the Reformation, see J. Bossy, *Christianity in the West: 1400–1700* (Oxford, 1987). There are good collections of essays in A. Pettegree, *The Early Reformation in Europe* (Cambridge, 1992); and B. Scribner, R. Porter, and M. Teich, eds., *The Reformation in National Context* (Cambridge, 1994).

The development of humanism outside Italy is examined in C. G. Nauert, Jr., *Humanism and the Culture of Renaissance Europe* (Cambridge, 1995). On Thomas More, see R. Marius, *Thomas More: A Biography* (New York, 1984). The best general biography of Erasmus is still R. Bainton, *Erasmus of Christendom* (New York, 1969), although the shorter works by J. K. Sowards, *Desiderius Erasmus* (Boston, 1975), and J. McConica, *Erasmus* (Oxford, 1991), are also good.

The Reformation in Germany can be examined in H. Holborn, *A History of Modern Germany: The Reformation* (New York, 1959), still an outstanding survey of the entire Reformation period in Germany; and J. Lortz, *The Reformation in Germany*, trans. R. Walls, 2 vols. (New York, 1968), a detailed Catholic account. The classic account of Martin Luther's life is R. Bainton, *Here I Stand: A Life of Martin Luther* (New York and Nashville, 1950). More recent works include H. A. Oberman, *Luther* (New York, 1992); W. von Loewenich, *Martin Luther: The Man and His Work* (Minneapolis, 1986); and J. M. Kittelson, *Luther the Reformer: The Story of the Man and His Career* (Minneapolis, 1986). Luther's relations with early Protestant dissenters from his ideas can be examined in M. Edwards, Jr., *Luther and the False Brethren* (Stanford, 1975). On the Peasants' War, see especially P. Blickle, *The Revolution of 1525: The German Peasants' War from a New Perspective* (Baltimore, 1981). The spread of Luther's ideas in Germany can be examined in M. Hannemann, *The Diffusion of the Reformation in Southwestern Germany, 1518–1534* (Chicago, 1975); B. Moeller, *Imperial Cities and the Reformation* (Durham, N.C., 1982); S. Ozment, *The Reformation in the Cities* (New Haven, Conn., 1975); and R. Po-Chia Hsia, ed., *The German People and the Reformation* (Ithaca, N.Y., 1988).

The best account of Ulrich Zwingli is G. R. Potter, *Zwingli* (Cambridge, 1976), although W. P. Stephens, *Zwingli* (Oxford, 1994) is an important study of Zwingli's ideas. One aspect of the spread of the Reformation in Switzerland is exam-

ined in J. M. Kittelson, *Wolfgang Capito: From Humanist to Reformer* (Leiden, 1975).

The most comprehensive account of the various groups and individuals who are called Anabaptists is G. H. Williams, *The Radical Reformation*, 2d ed. (Kirsville, M.O., 1992). Other valuable studies include C.-P. Clasen, *Anabaptism: A Social History, 1525–1618* (Ithaca, N.Y., 1972); and M. Mullett, *Radical Religious Movements in Early Modern Europe* (London, 1980). Also see R. Po-Chia Hsia, *Society and Reformation in Münster, 1535–1618* (New Haven, Conn., 1984).

Two worthwhile surveys of the English Reformation are A. G. Dickens, *The English Reformation*, 2d ed. (New York, 1989); and G. R. Elton, *Reform and Reformation: England, 1509–1558* (Cambridge, Mass., 1977). Good biographies of the leading personalities of the age include J. J. Scarisbrick, *Henry VIII* (Berkeley, 1968); B. W. Beckensgale, *Thomas Cromwell, Tudor Minister* (Totowa, N.J., 1978); J. Ridley, *Thomas Cranmer* (Oxford, 1962); and D. M. Loades, *The Reign of Mary Tudor* (London, 1979). Other specialized works on the period include the controversial classic by G. R. Elton, *The Tudor Revolution in Government*, 2d ed. (Cambridge, 1973); and D. Knowles, *Bare Ruined Choirs: The Dissolution of the English Monasteries* (New York, 1976).

On John Calvin, see A. McGrath, *A Life of John Calvin: A Study in the Shaping of Western Culture* (Cambridge, Mass., 1990); and W. J. Bouwsma, *John Calvin* (New York, 1988). The best account of Calvin's work in the city of Geneva is W. Monter, *Calvin's Geneva* (New York, 1967).

On the impact of the Reformation on the family, see J. F. Harrington, *Reordering Marriage and Society in Reformation Germany* (New York, 1995). M. E. Wiesner's *Working Women in Renaissance Germany* (New Brunswick, N.J., 1986), covers primarily the sixteenth century. There is also a good collection of essays in S. Marshall, ed., *Women in Reformation and Counter-Reformation Europe: Public and Private Worlds* (Bloomington, Ind., 1989). On education, see G. Strauss, *Luther's House of Learning* (Baltimore, 1978). R. W. Scribner's *For the Sake of Simple Folk* (Cambridge, 1981) deals with a number of issues on the popular culture of the German Reformation.

A good introduction to the Catholic Reformation can be found in the beautifully illustrated brief study by A. G. Dickens, *The Counter Reformation* (New York, 1969). Also valuable is M. R. O'Connell, *The Counter Reformation, 1559–1610* (New York, 1974). On Loyola, see P. Caravan, *Ignatius Loyola, A Biography of the Founder of the Jesuits* (San Francisco, 1990); and W. W. Meissner, *Ignatius of Loyola: The Psychology of a Saint* (New Haven, Conn., 1994). The work by J. O'Malley, *The First Jesuits* (Cambridge, Mass., 1995), offers a clear discussion of the founding of the Jesuits. On the new religious orders, see R. L. Demolen, ed., *Religious Orders of the Catholic Reformation* (New York, 1996).

For additional reading, go to InfoTrac College Edition, your online research library at http://web1.infotrac-college.com

Enter the search term *Reformation* using the Subject Guide.

Enter the search terms *Counter-Reformation* using the Subject Guide.

Enter the search terms *Martin and Luther not King* using Key Terms.

Enter the search terms *John Calvin* using the Subject Guide.

CHAPTER

14

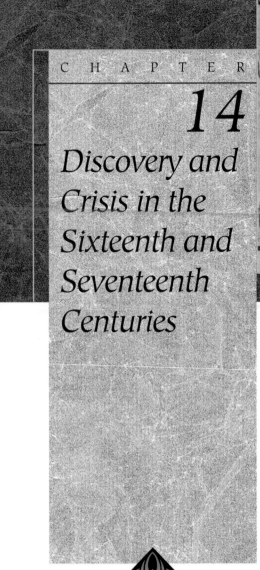

Discovery and Crisis in the Sixteenth and Seventeenth Centuries

CHAPTER OUTLINE

- An Age of Discovery and Expansion
- Politics and the Wars of Religion in the Sixteenth Century
- Economic and Social Crises
- Seventeenth-Century Crises: War and Rebellions
- The Witchcraft Craze
- Culture in a Turbulent World
- Conclusion

FOCUS QUESTIONS

- Why did Europeans begin to amass overseas empires during the sixteenth century, and what effects did this experience have on both the Europeans and conquered peoples?
- What role did religion play in the European wars of the sixteenth century and the Thirty Years' War of the seventeenth century?
- How did the religious policy, the foreign policy, and the governments of Philip II of Spain and Elizabeth I of England differ?
- What economic and social crises did Europe experience between 1560 and 1650?
- How did the turmoil in Europe between 1560 and 1650 contribute to the witchcraft craze and to the artistic and intellectual developments of the period?

B Y THE MIDDLE *of the sixteenth century, it was apparent that the religious passions of the Reformation era had brought an end to the religious unity of medieval Europe. The religious division (Catholics versus Protestants) was instrumental in beginning a series of wars that dominated much of European history between 1560 and 1650. The struggles fought in Germany at the beginning of the seventeenth century (known as the Thirty Years' War) were especially brutal and devastating. When the Catholic general Johann Tilly captured Neubrandenburg, his forces massacred the 3,000 defenders. A month later, the army of the Protestant leader Gustavus Adolphus retaliated by slaughtering the entire garrison of 2,000 men at Frankfurt-an-der-Oder. Noncombatants suffered as well, as is evident from the contemporary description by Otto von Guericke of the sack of Magdeburg. Once the* city had been captured, Tilly's forces were let loose: "Then there was nothing but beating and burning, plundering, torture, and murder." All the buildings were looted of anything valuable, and then the city was "given over to the flames, and thousands of innocent men, women, and children, in the midst of a horrible noise of heartrending shrieks and cries, were tortured and put to death in so cruel and shameful a manner that no words would suffice to describe." Thus, "in a single day this noble and famous city, the pride of the whole country, went up in fire and smoke, and the remnant of its citizens, with their wives and children, were taken prisoners and driven away by the enemy."

The wars, in turn, worsened the economic and social crises that were besetting Europe. Wars, rebellions and constitutional crises, economic depression, social disintegration, a witchcraft craze, and a demographic crisis all afflicted Europe and have led some historians to speak of the ninety years between 1560 and 1650 as an age of crisis in European life.

Periods of crisis, however, are frequently ages of opportunities, nowhere more apparent than in the geographical discoveries that made this an era of European expansion into new worlds. Although the discovery of new territories began before the sixteenth century, it was not until the sixteenth and seventeenth centuries that Europeans began to comprehend the significance of their discoveries and to exploit them for their material gain.

◆ An Age of Discovery and Expansion

Nowhere has the dynamic and even ruthless energy of Western civilization been more apparent than in its expansion into the rest of the world. By the sixteenth century, the Atlantic seaboard had become the center of a commercial activity that raised Portugal and Spain and later the Dutch Republic, England, and France to prominence. The age of expansion was a crucial factor in the European transition from the agrarian economy of the Middle Ages to a commercial and industrial capitalistic system. Expansion also led Europeans into new and lasting contacts with non-European peoples that inaugurated a new age of world history in the sixteenth century.

❀ The Motives

For almost a millennium, Catholic Europe had been confined to one geographical area. Its one major attempt to expand beyond those frontiers, the crusades, had largely failed. Of course, Europe had never completely lost touch with the outside world: the goods of Asia and Africa made their way into medieval castles; the works of Muslim philosophers were read in medieval universities; and in the ninth and tenth centuries the Vikings had even made their way to the eastern fringes of North America. But in all cases, contacts with non-European civilizations remained limited until the end of the fifteenth century, when Europeans embarked upon a remarkable series of overseas journeys. What caused Europeans to undertake such dangerous voyages to the ends of the earth?

Europeans had long been attracted to lands outside Europe. Indeed, a large body of fantasy literature about "other worlds" blossomed in the Middle Ages. In the fourteenth century, the author of *The Travels of John Mandeville* spoke of realms (which he had never seen) filled with precious stones and gold. Other lands were more frightening. In one country, "the folk be great giants of twenty-eight foot long, or thirty foot long. . . . And they eat more gladly man's flesh than any other flesh." Further north was a land inhabited by "full cruel and evil women. And they have precious stones in their eyes. And they be of that kind that if they behold any man with wrath they slay him at once with the beholding."[1] Other writers spoke of mysterious Christian kingdoms: the magical kingdom of Prester John in Africa and a Christian community in southern India that was supposedly founded by Thomas, the apostle of Jesus.

Although Muslim control of central Asia cut Europe off from the countries further east, the Mongol conquests in the thirteenth century had reopened the doors. The most famous medieval travelers to the East were the Polos of Venice. Niccolò and Maffeo, merchants from Venice, accompanied by Niccolò's son Marco, undertook the lengthy journey to the court of the great Mongol ruler Khubilai Khan (1259–1294) in 1271. As one of the Great Khan's ambassadors, Marco went on missions as well and did not return to Italy until 1295. An account of his experiences, the *Travels*, proved to be the most informative of all the descriptions of Asia by medieval European travelers. Others followed the Polos, but in the fourteenth century, the conquests of the Ottoman Turks and then the breakup of the Mongol Empire reduced Western traffic to the East. With the closing of the overland routes, a number of people in Europe became interested in the possibility of reaching Asia by sea to gain access to the spices and other precious items of the region. Christopher Columbus had a copy of Marco Polo's *Travels* in his possession when he began to envision his epoch-making voyage across the Atlantic Ocean.

An economic motive thus looms large in Renaissance European expansion. Merchants, adventurers, and government officials had high hopes of finding precious metals and new areas of trade, in particular, more direct sources for the spices of the East. The latter continued to come to Europe via Arab intermediaries but were outrageously expensive. Many European explorers and conquerors did not hesitate to express their desire for material gain. One Spanish conquistador explained that he and his kind went to the New World to "serve God and His

Majesty, to give light to those who were in darkness, and to grow rich, as all men desire to do."[2]

This statement expresses another major reason for the overseas voyages—religious zeal. A crusading mentality was particularly strong in Portugal and Spain where the Muslims had largely been driven out in the Middle Ages. Contemporaries of Prince Henry the Navigator of Portugal (see the next section) said that he was motivated by "his great desire to make increase in the faith of our Lord Jesus Christ and to bring him all the souls that should be saved." Although most scholars believe that the religious motive was secondary to economic considerations, it would be foolish to overlook the genuine desire on the part of both explorers and conquistadors, let alone missionaries, to convert the heathen to Christianity. Hernán Cortés, the conqueror of Mexico, asked his Spanish rulers if it was not their duty to ensure that the native Mexicans "are introduced into and instructed in the holy Catholic faith," and predicted that if "the devotion, trust and hope which they now have in their idols turned so as to repose with the divine power of the true God . . . they would work many miracles."[3] Spiritual and secular affairs were closely intertwined in the sixteenth century. No doubt, grandeur and glory as well as plain intellectual curiosity and spirit of adventure also played some role in European expansion.

If "God, glory, and gold" were the primary motives, what made the voyages possible? First of all, the expansion of Europe was connected to the growth of centralized monarchies during the Renaissance. Although historians still debate the degree of that centralization, the reality is that Renaissance expansion was a state enterprise. By the second half of the fifteenth century, European monarchies had increased both their authority and their resources and were in a position to turn their energies beyond their borders. For France, that meant the invasion of Italy, but for Portugal, a state not strong enough to pursue power in Europe, it meant going abroad. The Spanish scene was more complex because the Spanish monarchy was strong enough by the sixteenth century to pursue power both in Europe and beyond.

At the same time, by the end of the fifteenth century, Europeans had achieved a level of wealth and technology that enabled them to make a regular series of voyages beyond Europe. Although the highly schematic and symbolic medieval maps were of little help to sailors, the *portolani*, or detailed charts made by medieval navigators and mathematicians in the thirteenth and fourteenth centuries, were more useful. With details on coastal contours, distances between ports, and compass readings, they proved of great value for voyages in European waters. But because the *portolani* were drawn on a flat scale and took no account of the curvature of the earth, they were of little use for longer overseas voyages. Only when seafarers began to venture beyond the coast of Europe did they begin to accumulate information about the actual shape of the earth. By the end of the fifteenth century, cartography had developed to the point that Europeans possessed fairly accurate maps of the known world.

In addition, Europeans had developed remarkably seaworthy ships as well as new navigational techniques. European shipmakers had mastered the use of the axial rudder (an import from China) and had learned to combine the use of lateen sails with a square rig. With these innovations, they could construct ships mobile enough to sail against the wind and engage in naval warfare and also large enough to mount heavy cannon and carry a substantial amount of goods over long distances. Previously, sailors had used a quadrant and their knowledge of the position of the Pole Star to ascertain their latitude. Below the equator, however, this technique was useless. Only

THE CARAVEL SANTA MARIA, IN WHICH COLUMBUS FIRST SAILED ACROSS THE ATLANTIC.

THE CARAVEL, WORKHORSE OF THE AGE OF EXPLORATION. Prior to the fifteenth century, most European ships were either small craft with lateen sails used in the Mediterranean or slow, unwieldly square-rigged vessels operating in the North Atlantic. By the sixteenth century, European naval architects began to build ships that combined the maneuverability and speed offered by lateen sails with the carrying capacity and seaworthiness of the square-riggers. Shown here is a representation of Christopher Columbus's flagship *Santa Maria*, which took part in the first Spanish voyage across the Atlantic Ocean.

with the assistance of new navigational aids such as the compass and the astrolabe were they able to explore the high seas with confidence.

A final spur to exploration was the growing knowledge of the wind patterns in the Atlantic Ocean. The first European fleets sailing southward along the coast of West Africa had found their efforts to return hindered by the strong winds that blew steadily from the north along the coast. By the late fifteenth century, however, sailors had learned to tack out into the ocean, where they were able to catch westerly winds in the vicinity of the Azores islands that brought them back to the coast of western Europe. Christopher Columbus used this technique in his voyages to the Americas, and others relied on their new knowledge of the winds to round the continent of Africa in search of the Spice Islands.

✳ *The Development of a Portuguese Maritime Empire*

Portugal took the lead in exploring the coast of Africa under the sponsorship of Prince Henry the "Navigator" (1394–1460), whose motives were a blend of seeking a Christian kingdom as an ally against the Muslims, acquiring trade opportunities for Portugal, and extending Christianity. In 1419, Prince Henry founded a school for navigators on the southwestern coast of Portugal. Shortly thereafter, Portuguese fleets began probing southward along the western coast of Africa in search of gold, which had been carried northward from south of the Atlas Mountain in central Morocco for centuries. In 1441, Portuguese ships reached the Senegal River, just north of Cape Verde, and brought home a cargo of black Africans, most of whom were then sold as slaves to wealthy buyers elsewhere in Europe. Within a few years, an estimated 1,000 slaves were shipped annually from the area back to Lisbon.

Through regular expeditions, the Portuguese gradually crept down the African coast, and in 1471, they discovered a new source of gold along the southern coast of the hump of West Africa (an area that would henceforth be known to Europeans as the Gold Coast). A few years later, they established contact with the state of Bakongo, near the mouth of the Zaire (Congo) River in central Africa. To facilitate trade in gold, ivory, and slaves (some of the latter were brought back to Lisbon while others were bartered to local merchants for gold), the Portuguese leased land from local rulers and built stone forts along the coast.

Hearing reports of a route to India around the southern tip of Africa, Portuguese sea captains continued their probing. In 1488, Bartholomeu Dias (c. 1450–1500) took advantage of westerly winds in the South Atlantic to round the Cape of Good Hope, but he feared a mutiny from his crew and returned home without continuing onward. Ten years later, a fleet under the command of Vasco da Gama (c. 1460–1524) rounded the cape and stopped at several ports controlled by Muslim merchants along the coast of East Africa. Then, da Gama's fleet crossed the Arabian Sea and reached the port of Calicut, on the southwestern coast of India, on May 18, 1498. On arriving in Calicut, da Gama announced to his surprised hosts that he had arrived in search of "Christians and spices." He found no Christians, but he did find the spices he sought. Although he lost two ships en route, da Gama's remaining vessels returned to Europe with their holds filled with ginger and cinnamon, a cargo that earned the investors a profit of several thousand percent.

For the next several years, Portuguese fleets returned annually to the area, seeking to destroy Arabic shipping and establish a monopoly in the spice trade. In 1509, a Portuguese armada defeated a combined fleet of Turkish and Indian ships off the coast of India and began to impose a blockade on the entrance to the Red Sea to cut off the flow of spices to Muslim rulers in Egypt and the Ottoman Empire. The following year, seeing the need for a land base in the area, Admiral Alfonso de Albuquerque (c. 1462–1515) set up port facilities at Goa, on the western coast of India south of present-day Bombay. Goa henceforth became the headquarters for Portuguese operations throughout the entire region. Although Indian merchants were permitted to continue their trading activities, the Portuguese conducted raids against Arab shippers, provoking the following brief report from an Arab source: "In this year the vessels of the Portuguese appeared at sea en route for India and those parts. They took about seven vessels, killing those on board and making some prisoner. This was their first action, may God curse them."[4]

The Portuguese now began to range more widely in search of the source of the spice trade. In 1511, Albuquerque sailed into the harbor of Malacca on the Malay peninsula. Malacca had been transformed by its Muslim rulers into a thriving port and a major stopping point for the spice trade. For Albuquerque, control of Malacca would serve two purposes. It could help to destroy the Arab spice trade and also provide the Portuguese with a way station on the route to the Moluccas, then known as the Spice Islands. After a short but bloody battle, the Portuguese seized the city and massacred the local Arab population. This slaughter initiated a fierce and brutal struggle between the Portuguese and the Arabs. According to one account, "to enhance the terror of his name he [Albuquerque] always separated Arabs from the other inhabitants of a captured city, and cut off the right hand of the men, and the noses and ears of the women."[5]

From Malacca, the Portuguese launched expeditions further east, to China and the Spice Islands. There they signed a treaty with a local ruler for the purchase and export of cloves to the European market. The Portuguese trading empire was now complete. Within a few years, they had managed to seize control of the spice trade from Muslim traders and had garnered substantial profits for the Portuguese monarchy. Nevertheless, the Portuguese Empire remained limited, consisting only of trading posts on the coasts of India and China. The Portuguese lacked the power, the population, and the desire to colonize the Asian regions.

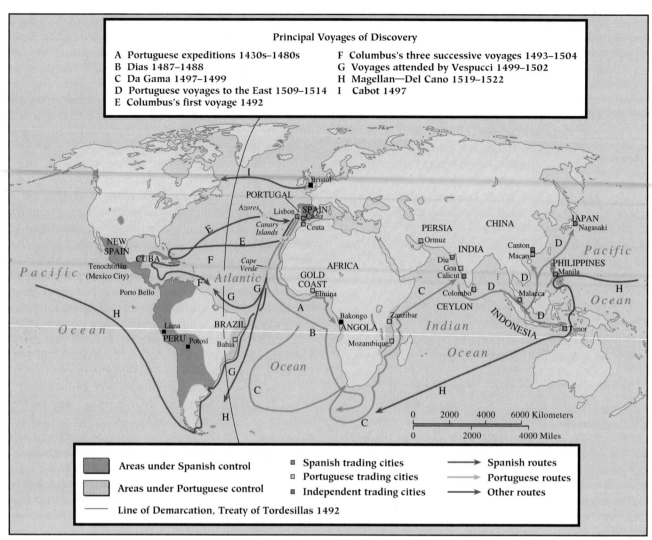

Principal Voyages of Discovery

A Portuguese expeditions 1430s–1480s   F Columbus's three successive voyages 1493–1504
B Dias 1487–1488   G Voyages attended by Vespucci 1499–1502
C Da Gama 1497–1499   H Magellan—Del Cano 1519–1522
D Portuguese voyages to the East 1509–1514   I Cabot 1497
E Columbus's first voyage 1492

Areas under Spanish control   ▪ Spanish trading cities   → Spanish routes
Areas under Portuguese control   ▫ Portuguese trading cities   → Portuguese routes
   ▪ Independent trading cities   → Other routes
— Line of Demarcation, Treaty of Tordesillas 1492

MAP 14.1   **Discoveries and Possessions in the Fifteenth and Sixteenth Centuries.**

Why were the Portuguese so successful? Basically, their success was a matter of guns and seamanship. The first Portuguese fleet to arrive in Indian waters was relatively modest in size, consisting of three ships and twenty guns, a force sufficient for self-defense and intimidation, but not for serious military operations. Later Portuguese fleets, which began to arrive with regularity early in the sixteenth century, were more heavily armed and were able not only to intimidate but also to inflict severe defeats if necessary on local naval and land forces. The Portuguese by no means possessed a monopoly on the use of firearms and explosives, but their effective use of naval technology, their heavy guns that could be mounted in the hulls of their sturdy vessels, and their tactics gave them a military superiority over lightly armed rivals that they were able to exploit until the arrival of other European forces several decades later.

✳ *Voyages to the New World*

While the Portuguese were seeking access to the spice trade of the Indies by sailing eastward through the Indian

Ocean, the Spanish were attempting to reach the same destination by sailing westward across the Atlantic. Although the Spanish came to overseas discovery and exploration after the initial efforts of Henry the Navigator, their greater resources enabled them to establish a far grander overseas empire of a quite different nature than the Portuguese Empire.

An important figure in the history of Spanish exploration was an Italian known as Christopher Columbus (1451–1506). Knowledgeable Europeans were aware that the world was round, but had little understanding of its circumference or the extent of the continent of Asia. Convinced that the circumference of the earth was less than contemporaries believed and that Asia was larger than people thought, Columbus felt that Asia could be reached by sailing west instead of around Africa. After being rejected by the Portuguese, he persuaded Queen Isabella of Spain to finance his exploratory expedition.

With three ships, the *Santa María*, *Niña*, and *Pinta*, manned by ninety men, Columbus set sail on August 3, 1492. On October 12, he reached the Bahamas and then went on to explore the coastline of Cuba and the northern

In three subsequent voyages (1493, 1498, 1502), Columbus sought in vain to find a route through the outer lands to the Asian mainland. In his four voyages, Columbus reached all the major islands of the Caribbean and the mainland of Central America.

Although Columbus clung to his belief until his death, other explorers soon realized that he had discovered a new frontier altogether. State-sponsored explorers joined the race to the New World. A Venetian seaman, John Cabot, explored the New England coastline of the Americas under a license from King Henry VII of England. The continent of South America was discovered accidentally by the Portuguese sea captain Pedro Cabral in 1500. Amerigo Vespucci, a Florentine, accompanied several voyages and wrote a series of letters describing the geography of the New World. The publication of these letters led to the use of the name "America" (after Amerigo) for the new lands.

The first two decades of the sixteenth century witnessed numerous overseas voyages that explored the eastern coasts of both North and South America. Vasco Nuñez de Balboa, a Spanish explorer, led an expedition across the Isthmus of Panama and reached the Pacific Ocean in 1513. Perhaps the most dramatic of all these expeditions was the journey of Ferdinand Magellan (1480–1521) in 1519. After passing through the straits named after him at the southern tip of South America, he sailed across the Pacific Ocean and reached the Philippines (named after King Philip of Spain by Magellan's crew) where he met his death at the hands of the natives. Although only one of his original fleet of five ships survived and returned to Spain, Magellan's name is still associated with the first known circumnavigation of the earth.

The newly discovered territories were called the New World, although they possessed flourishing civilizations populated by millions of people when the Europeans arrived. The Americas were, of course, new to the Europeans who quickly saw opportunities for conquest and exploitation. The Spanish, in particular, were interested because in 1494 the Treaty of Tordesillas had divided up the newly discovered world into separate Portuguese and Spanish spheres of influence. Hereafter the route east around the Cape of Good Hope was to be reserved for the Portuguese while the route across the Atlantic (except for the eastern hump of South America) was assigned to Spain.

✸ *The Spanish Empire in the New World*

The Spanish conquistadors were hardy individuals motivated by a typical sixteenth-century blend of glory, greed, and religious crusading zeal. Although sanctioned by the Castilian crown, these groups were financed and outfitted privately, not by the government. Their superior weapons, organizational skills, and determination brought the conquistadors incredible success. They also benefited from rivalries among the native peoples.

In 1519, a Spanish expedition under the command of Hernán Cortés (1485–1547) landed at Veracruz, on the Gulf of Mexico. He marched to the city of Tenochtitlán (see

CHRISTOPHER COLUMBUS. **Columbus was an Italian explorer who worked for the queen of Spain. He has become a symbol for two entirely different perspectives. To some, he was a great and heroic explorer who discovered the New World; to others, especially in Latin America, he was responsible for beginning a process of invasion that led to the destruction of an entire way of life. This painting by the Italian Sebastiano del Piombo in 1519 is the earliest known portrait of Columbus, but it was done thirteen years after his death and reveals as much about the painter's conception of Columbus as it does about the explorer himself.**

shores of Hispaniola (present-day Haiti and the Dominican Republic). Columbus believed that he had reached Asia, and in his reports to Queen Isabella and King Ferdinand, he assured them not only that he would eventually find gold but that they had a golden opportunity to convert the natives to Christianity:

> These islands are very green and fertile and the breezes are very soft, and it is possible that there are in them many things, of which I do not know, because I did not wish to delay in finding gold, by discovering and going about many islands. And since these men give these signs that they wear it on their arms and legs, and it is gold because I showed them some pieces of gold which I have, I cannot fail, with the aid of Our Lord, to find the place whence it comes.
> . . . So your Highnesses should resolve to make them Christians, for I believe that, if you begin, in a little while you will achieve the conversion of a great number of peoples to our holy faith, with the acquisition of great lordships and riches and all their inhabitants for Spain. For without a doubt there is a very great amount of gold in these lands.[6]

The Spanish Conquistador: Cortés and the Conquest of Mexico

Hernán Cortés was a minor Spanish nobleman who came to the New World in 1504 to seek his fortune. Contrary to his superior's orders, Cortés waged an independent campaign of conquest and overthrew the Aztec Empire in Mexico (1519–1521). Cortés wrote a series of five reports to Emperor Charles V to justify his action. The second report includes a description of Tenochtitlán, the capital of the Aztec Empire. The Spanish conquistador and his men were obviously impressed by this city, awesome in its architecture yet built by people who lacked European technology, such as wheeled vehicles and tools of hard metal.

❋ Cortés's Description of an Aztec City

The great city Tenochtitlán is built in the midst of this salt lake, and it is two leagues from the heart of the city to any point on the mainland. Four causeways lead to it, all made by hand and some twelve feet wide. The city itself is as large as Seville or Córdoba. The principal streets are very broad and straight, the majority of them being of beaten earth, but a few and at least half of the smaller thoroughfares are waterways along which they pass in their canoes. Moreover, even the principal streets have openings at regular distances so that the water can freely pass from one to another, and these openings which are very broad are spanned by great bridges of huge beams, very stoutly put together, so firm indeed that over many of them ten horsemen can ride at once. Seeing that if the natives intended any treachery against us they would have every opportunity from the way in which the city is built, for by removing the bridges from the entrances and exits they could leave us to die of hunger with no possibility of getting to the mainland, I immediately set to work as soon as we entered the city on the building of four brigs, and in a short space of time had them finished so that we could ship 300 men and the horses to the mainland whenever we so desired.

The city has many open squares in which markets are continuously held and the general business of buying and selling proceeds. One square in particular is twice as big as that of Salamanca and completely surrounded by arcades where there are daily more than 60,000 folk buying and selling. Every kind of merchandise such as may be met with in every land is for sale there, whether of food and victuals, or ornaments of gold and silver, or lead, brass, copper, tin, precious stones, bones, shells, snails and feathers; limestone for building is likewise sold there, stone both rough and polished, bricks burnt and unburnt, wood of all kinds and in all stages of preparation. . . . There is a street of herb-sellers where there are all manner of roots and medicinal plants that are found in the land. There are houses as it were of apothecaries where they sell medicines made from these herbs, both for drinking and for use as ointments and salves. There are barbers' shops where you may have your hair washed and cut. There are other shops where you may obtain food and drink. . . .

Finally, to avoid being wordy in telling all the wonders of this city, I will simply say that the manner of living among the people is very similar to that in Spain, and considering that this is a barbarous nation shut off from a knowledge of the true God or communication with enlightened nations, one may well marvel at the orderliness and good government which is everywhere maintained.

The actual service of Moctezuma and those things which call for admiration by their greatness and state would take so long to describe that I assure your Majesty I do not know where to begin with any hope of ending. For as I have already said, what could there be more astonishing than that a barbarous monarch such as he should have reproductions made in gold, silver, precious stones, and feathers of all things to be found in his land, and so perfectly reproduced that there is no goldsmith or silversmith in the world who could better them, nor can one understand what instrument could have been used for fashioning the jewels; as for the featherwork its like is not to be seen in either wax or embroidery; it is so marvelously delicate.

---

the box above) at the head of a small contingent of troops (550 soldiers and 16 horses); as he went, he made alliances with city-states that had tired of the oppressive rule of the Aztecs. Especially important was Tlaxcala, a state that the Aztecs had not been able to conquer. In November Cortés arrived at Tenochtitlán, where he received a friendly welcome from the Aztec monarch Moctezuma (often called Montezuma). At first, Moctezuma believed that his visitor was a representative of Quetzalcoatl, the god who had departed from his homeland centuries before and had promised that he would return. Riddled with fears, Moctezuma offered gifts of gold to the foreigners and gave them a palace to use while they were in the city.

But trouble eventually erupted between the Spaniards and the Aztecs. The Spaniards took Moctezuma hostage and began to pillage the city. In the fall of 1520, one year after Cortés had first arrived, the local population revolted and drove the invaders from the city. Many of the Spaniards were killed, but the Aztecs soon experienced new disasters. As one Aztec related: "But at about the time that the Spaniards had fled from Mexico, there came a great sickness, a pestilence, the smallpox." With no natural immunity to the diseases of Europeans, many Aztecs fell sick and died. Meanwhile, Cortés received fresh soldiers from his new allies; the state of Tlaxcala alone provided 50,000 warriors. After four months, the city capitu-

THE SLAUGHTER OF THE AZTECS.   Fearful of growing Aztec resistance, the Spaniards responded by slaughtering many Aztecs. This sixteenth-century watercolor shows **the massacre of Aztecs at Cholula, carried out on the orders of Cortés.**

lated. And then the destruction began. The pyramids, temples, and palaces were leveled, and the stones used to build Spanish government buildings and churches. The rivers and canals were filled in. The mighty Aztec Empire on mainland Mexico was no more. Between 1531 and 1550, the Spanish gained control of northern Mexico.

The Inca Empire high in the Peruvian Andes was still flourishing when the first Spanish expeditions arrived in the area. In December 1530, Francisco Pizarro (c. 1475–1541) landed on the Pacific coast of South America with only a small band of about 180 men, but like Cortés, he had steel weapons, gunpowder, and horses, none of which were familiar to his hosts. Pizarro was also lucky because the Inca Empire had already succumbed to an epidemic of smallpox. Like the Aztecs, the Inca had no immunities to European diseases, and all too soon, smallpox was devastating entire villages. In another stroke of good fortune for Pizarro, even the Inca emperor was a victim. Upon the emperor's death, two sons claimed the throne, leading to a civil war. Pizarro took advantage of the situation by seizing Atahualpa, whose forces had just defeated his brother's. Armed only with stones, arrows, and light spears, Incan soldiers provided little challenge to the charging horses of the Spanish, let alone their guns and cannons. After executing Atahualpa, Pizarro and his soldiers, aided by their Incan allies, marched on Cuzco and captured the Incan capital. By 1535, Pizarro had established a capital at Lima for a new colony of the Spanish Empire.

ADMINISTRATION OF THE SPANISH EMPIRE

Spanish policy toward the Indians of the New World was a combination of confusion, misguided paternalism, and cruel exploitation. Whereas the conquistadors made decisions based on expediency and their own interests, Queen Isabella declared the natives to be subjects of Castile and instituted the Spanish *encomienda*, a system that permitted the conquering Spaniards to collect tribute from the natives and use them as laborers. In return, the holders of an *encomienda* were supposed to protect the Indians, pay them wages, and supervise their spiritual needs. In practice, this meant that the settlers were free to implement the paternalistic system of the government as they pleased. Three thousand miles from Spain, Spanish settlers largely ignored their government and brutally used the Indians to pursue their own economic interests. Indians were put to work on plantations and in the lucrative gold and silver mines. Forced labor, starvation, and especially disease took a fearful toll of Indian lives. With little or no natural resistance to European diseases, the Indians of America were ravaged by the smallpox, measles, and typhus that came with the explorers and the conquistadors. Although

Las Casas and the Spanish Treatment of the American Natives

Bartolomé de Las Casas (1474–1566) participated in the conquest of Cuba and received land and Indians in return for his efforts. But in 1514 he underwent a radical transformation and came to believe that the Indians had been cruelly mistreated by his fellow Spaniards. He became a Dominican friar and spent the remaining years of his life (he lived to the age of ninety-two) fighting for the Indians. This selection is taken from his most influential work, which is known to English readers as The Tears of the Indians. *This work was largely responsible for the "black legend" of the Spanish as inherently "cruel and murderous fanatics." Most scholars feel that Las Casas may have exaggerated his account in order to shock his contemporaries into action.*

❋ Bartolomé de Las Casas, *The Tears of the Indians*

There is nothing more detestable or more cruel, than the tyranny which the Spaniards use toward the Indians for the getting of pearl. Surely the infernal torments cannot much exceed the anguish that they endure, by reason of that way of cruelty; for they put them under water some four or five ells [fifteen to eighteen feet] deep, where they are forced without any liberty of respiration, to gather up the shells wherein the pearls are; sometimes they come up again with nets full of shells to take breath, but if they stay any while to rest themselves, immediately comes a hangman row'd in a little boat, who as soon as he has well beaten them, drags them again to their labor. Their food is nothing but filth, and the very same that contains the pearl, with a small portion of that bread which that country affords; in the first whereof there is little nourishment; and as for the latter, it is made with great difficulty, besides that they have not enough of that neither for sustenance; they lie upon the ground in fetters, lest they should run away; and many times they are drown'd in this labor, and are never seen again till they swim upon the top of the waves: oftentimes they also are devoured by certain sea monsters, that are frequent in those seas. Consider whether this hard usage of the poor creatures be consistent with the precepts which God commands concerning charity to our neighbor, by those that cast them so undeservedly into the dangers of a cruel death, causing them to perish without any remorse or pity, or allowing them the benefit of the sacraments, or the knowledge of religion; it being impossible for them to live any time under the water; and this death is so much the more painful, by reason that by the constricting of the breast, while the lungs strive to do their office, the vital parts are so afflicted that they die vomiting the blood out of their mouths. Their hair also, which is by nature black, is hereby changed and made of the same color with that of the sea wolves; their bodies are also so besprinkled with the froth of the sea, that they appear rather like monsters than men.

scholarly estimates of native populations vary drastically, a reasonable guess is that 30 to 40 percent of the natives died. On Hispaniola alone, out of an initial population of 100,000 natives when Columbus arrived in 1493, only 300 Indians survived by 1570. In 1542, largely in response to the publications of Bartolomé de Las Casas, a Dominican friar who championed the Indians (see the box above), the government abolished the *encomienda* system and provided more protection for the natives.

In the New World, the Spanish developed an administrative system based on viceroys. Spanish possessions were initially divided into two major administrative units: New Spain (Mexico, Central America, and the Caribbean islands) with its center in Mexico City, and Peru (western South America), governed by a viceroy in Lima. Each viceroy served as the king's chief civil and military officer and was aided by advisory groups called *audiencias*, which also functioned as supreme judicial bodies.

By papal agreement, the Catholic monarchs of Spain were given extensive rights over ecclesiastical affairs in the New World. They could appoint all bishops and clergy, build churches, collect fees, and supervise the affairs of the various religious orders that sought to Christianize the heathen. Catholic missionaries—especially the Dominicans, Franciscans, and Jesuits—fanned out across the Spanish Empire where they converted and baptized hundreds of thousands of Indians in the early years of the conquest. To facilitate their efforts, the missionaries brought Indians together into villages where they could be converted, taught trades, and encouraged to grow crops. Removing the Indians from their homes to these villages helped the missionaries not only to gain control over the Indians' lives but also to ensure that they would be docile subjects of the empire.

The mass conversion of the Indians brought the organizational and institutional structures of Catholicism to the New World. Dioceses, parishes, cathedrals, schools, and hospitals—all the trappings of civilized European society—soon appeared in the Spanish Empire. So, too, did the Spanish Inquisition, established first in Peru in 1570 and then in Mexico in 1571.

❋ The Impact of Expansion

European expansion made an enormous impact on both the conquerors and the conquered. The native American civilizations, which had their own unique qualities and a degree of sophistication not much appreciated by Euro-

seven northern provinces were largely Germanic in culture and Dutch speaking, while the French- and Flemish-speaking southern provinces were closely tied to France. Situated at the commercial crossroads of northwestern Europe, the Netherlands had become prosperous through commerce and a flourishing textile industry. Because of its location, the Netherlands was open to the religious influences of the age. Though some inhabitants had adopted

Lutheranism or Anabaptism, by the time of Philip II, Calvinism was also making inroads. These provinces had no real political bond holding them together except their common ruler, and that ruler was Philip II, a foreigner who was out of touch with the situation in the Netherlands.

Philip II hoped to strengthen his control in the Netherlands, regardless of the traditional privileges of the separate provinces. This was strongly opposed by the nobles, towns, and provincial states, which stood to lose politically if their jealously guarded privileges and freedoms were weakened. Resentment against Philip was also aroused when the residents of the Netherlands realized that the taxes they paid were being used for Spanish interests. Finally, religion became a major catalyst for rebellion when Philip attempted both to reorganize the ecclesiastical structure of the Dutch Catholic church and to crush heresy. Calvinism continued to spread, especially among the nobility and artisans in the towns. Philip's policy of repression alienated the Calvinists without halting the spread of the movement. Resistance against the king's policies increased, especially from the aristocrats led by William of Nassau, the prince of Orange, also known as William the Silent. Violence erupted in 1566 when Calvinists—especially nobles—began to destroy statues and stained glass windows in Catholic churches. Philip responded by sending the duke of Alva with 10,000 veteran Spanish and Italian troops to crush the rebellion.

The repressive policies of the duke proved counterproductive. The levying of a permanent sales tax alienated many merchants and commoners who now joined the nobles and Calvinists in the struggle against Spanish rule. A special tribunal, known as the Council of Troubles (nicknamed by the Dutch the Council of Blood), inaugurated a reign of terror in which even powerful aristocrats were executed. As a result, the revolt now became organized, especially in the northern provinces where William of Orange and Dutch pirates known as the "Sea Beggars" mounted growing resistance. In 1573, Philip removed the duke of Alva and shifted to a more conciliatory policy to bring an end to the costly revolt.

William of Orange wished to unify all seventeen provinces, a goal seemingly realized in 1576 with the Pacification of Ghent. This agreement stipulated that all the provinces would stand together under William's leadership, respect religious differences, and demand that Spanish troops be withdrawn. But religious

PHILIP II OF SPAIN. This portrait depicts Philip II of Spain at the age of fifty-two. The king's attempts to make Spain a great power led to large debts and crushing taxes, and his military actions in defense of Catholicism ended in failure and misfortune in both France and the Netherlands.

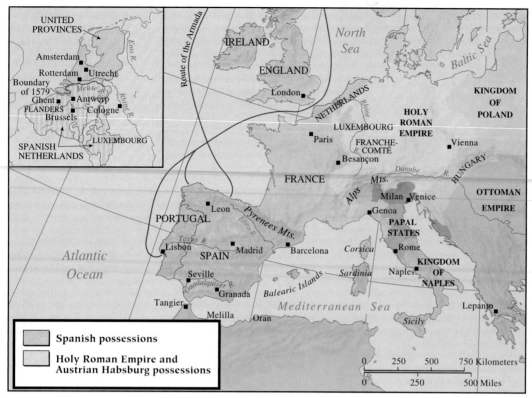

MAP 14.2 Philip II and the Height of Spanish Power.

differences proved too strong for any lasting union. When the duke of Parma, the next Spanish leader, arrived in the Netherlands, he astutely played upon the religious differences of the provinces and split their united front. The southern provinces formed a Catholic union—the Union of Arras—in 1579 and accepted Spanish control. To counter this, William of Orange organized the northern, Dutch-speaking states into a Protestant union—the Union of Utrecht—determined to oppose Spanish rule. The Netherlands was now divided along religious, geographical, and political lines into two hostile camps. Unwilling to rule themselves, the northern provinces sought to place themselves under the French king and then the English queen Elizabeth. Both refused, although Elizabeth further antagonized Philip II by continuing military assistance. The struggle went on for several years after both Philip and Elizabeth had died; finally, in 1609, the war ended with a twelve-year truce that virtually recognized the independence of the northern provinces. These "United Provinces" soon emerged as the Dutch Republic, although the Spanish did not formally recognize them as independent until 1648. The southern provinces remained a Spanish possession.

❋ The England of Elizabeth

After the death of Queen Mary in 1558, her half-sister Elizabeth ascended the throne of England. During Elizabeth's reign, England rose to prominence as the relatively small island kingdom became the leader of the Protestant nations of Europe, laid the foundations for a world empire, and experienced a cultural renaissance.

The daughter of King Henry VIII and Anne Boleyn, Elizabeth had had a difficult early life. During Mary's reign, she had even been imprisoned for a while and had learned early to hide her true feelings from both private and public sight. Though appearing irresolute in avoiding confrontation as long as possible, she was capable of decisive action when it was finally forced upon her. Intelligent and self-confident, she moved quickly to solve the difficult religious problem she had inherited from Mary, who had become extremely unpopular when she tried to return England to the Catholic fold.

Elizabeth's religious policy was based on moderation and compromise. Although she had some deep religious feelings, the changes she had experienced had taught her caution and tolerance. As a ruler, she wished to prevent England from being torn apart over matters of religion. Interests of state and personal choice combined to favor a temperate approach to religious affairs. As the Scottish Calvinist reformer John Knox remarked, "Elizabeth was neither a good Protestant nor yet a resolute Papist." Nor did she care what her subjects believed privately as long as they did not threaten the state's power.

Parliament cooperated with the queen in initiating the Elizabethan religious settlement in 1559. The Catholic legislation of Mary's reign was repealed, and a new Act of Supremacy designated Elizabeth as "the only supreme governor of this realm, as well in all spiritual or ecclesiastical things or causes, as temporal." An Act of Unifor-

PROCESSION OF QUEEN ELIZABETH I. Intelligent and learned, Elizabeth Tudor was familiar with Latin and Greek and spoke several European languages. Served by able administrators, Elizabeth ruled for nearly forty-five years and generally avoided open military action against any major power. Her participation in the revolt of the Netherlands, however, brought England into conflict with Spain. This picture painted near the end of her reign shows the queen on a ceremonial procession.

mity restored the church service of the Book of Common Prayer from the reign of Edward VI with some revisions to make it more acceptable to Catholics. Elizabeth's religious settlement was basically Protestant, but it was a moderate Protestantism that avoided overly subtle distinctions and extremes.

The new religious settlement worked, at least to the extent that it smothered religious differences in England in the second half of the sixteenth century. Two groups, however, the Catholics and Puritans, continued to oppose the new religious settlement. By the end of Elizabeth's reign, the Catholics had dwindled to a tiny minority, a process aided by the identification of Catholicism in English minds with the Spanish King Philip II, but earlier they appeared to pose a significant threat. One of Elizabeth's greatest challenges came from her Catholic cousin, Mary, queen of Scots, who was next in line to the English throne. Mary was ousted from Scotland by rebellious Calvinist nobles in 1568 and fled for her life to England. There Elizabeth placed her under house arrest and for fourteen years tolerated her involvement in a number of ill-planned Catholic plots designed to kill Elizabeth and replace her on the throne with the Catholic Mary. Finally, in 1587, after Mary became embroiled in a far more serious plot, Elizabeth had her cousin beheaded to end the threats to her regime.

Potentially more dangerous to Anglicanism in the long run were the Puritans. The word *Puritanism* first appeared in 1564 when it was used to refer to those Protestants within the Anglican church who, inspired by Calvinist theology, wanted to remove any trace of Catholicism from the Church of England. Elizabeth managed to contain the Puritans during her reign, but the indefatigable Puritans would dominate the English scene in the middle part of the seventeenth century.

Elizabeth proved as adept in government and foreign policy as in religious affairs. She was well served administratively by the principal secretary of state, an office created by Thomas Cromwell during the reign of Henry VIII. The talents of Sir William Cecil and Sir Francis Walsing-

ham, who together held the office for thirty-two years, ensured much of Elizabeth's success in foreign and domestic affairs. Elizabeth also handled Parliament with much skill; it met only thirteen times during her entire reign (see the box on p. 408).

Caution, moderation, and expediency also dictated Elizabeth's foreign policy. Fearful of other countries' motives, Elizabeth realized that war could be disastrous for her island kingdom and her own rule. Unofficially, however, she encouraged English seamen to raid Spanish ships and colonies. Francis Drake was especially adept at plundering Spanish fleets loaded with gold and silver from Spain's New World empire. While encouraging English piracy and providing clandestine aid to French Huguenots and Dutch Calvinists to weaken France and Spain, Elizabeth pretended complete aloofness and avoided alliances that would force her into war with any major power.

Gradually, however, Elizabeth was drawn into more active involvement in the Netherlands and by 1585 had reluctantly settled upon a policy of active military intervention there. This move accelerated the already mounting friction between Spain and England. After years of resisting the idea of invading England as too impractical, Philip II of Spain was finally persuaded to do so by advisers who assured him that the people of England would rise against their queen when the Spaniards arrived. Moreover, Philip was easily convinced that the revolt in the Netherlands would never be crushed as long as England provided support for it. In any case, a successful invasion of England would mean the overthrow of heresy and the return of England to Catholicism, surely an act in accordance with the will of God. The execution of Mary, queen of Scots, in 1587 reinforced the king's decision, especially when the pope, angered by Mary's beheading, offered to provide financial support for the undertaking. Accordingly, Philip ordered preparations for an Armada that would rendezvous with the army of the duke of Parma in Flanders and escort his troops across the English Channel for the invasion.

Queen Elizabeth Addresses Parliament (1601)

Queen Elizabeth I ruled England from 1558 to 1603 with a consummate skill that contemporaries considered unusual in a woman. Though shrewd and paternalistic, Elizabeth, like other sixteenth-century monarchs, depended for her power upon the favor of her people. This selection is taken from her speech to Parliament in 1601, when she had been forced to retreat on the issue of monopolies after vehement protests by members of Parliament. Although the speech was designed to make peace with Parliament, some historians also feel that it was a sincere expression of the rapport that existed between the queen and her subjects.

❋ Queen Elizabeth I, "The Golden Speech"

I do assure you there is no prince that loves his subjects better, or whose love can countervail our love. There is no jewel, be it of never so rich a price, which I set before this jewel: I mean your love. For I do esteem it more than any treasure or riches. . . . And, though God has raised me high, yet this I count the glory of my crown, that I have reigned with your loves. This makes me that I do not so much rejoice that God has made me to be a Queen, as to be a Queen over so thankful a people. . . .

Of myself I must say this: I never was any greedy, scraping grasper, nor a strait, fast-holding Prince, nor yet a waster. My heart was never set on any worldly goods, but only for my subjects' good. What you bestow on me, I will not hoard it up, but receive it to bestow on you again. Yea, mine own properties I account yours, to be expended for your good. . . .

I have ever used to set the Last-Judgement Day before mine eyes, and so to rule as I shall be judged to answer before a higher Judge, to whose judgement seat I do appeal, that never thought was cherished in my heart that tended not unto my people's good. And now, if my kingly bounties have been abused, and my grants turned to the hurt of my people, contrary to my will and meaning, and if any in authority under me neglected or perverted what I have committed to them, I hope God will not lay their culps [crimes] and offenses to my charge; who, though there were danger in repealing our grants, yet what danger would I not rather incur for your good, than I would suffer them still to continue?

There will never Queen sit in my seat with more zeal to my country, care for my subjects, and that will sooner with willingness venture her life for your good and safety, than myself. For it is my desire to live nor reign no longer than my life and reign shall be for your good. And though you have had and may have many princes more mighty and wise sitting in this seat, yet you never had nor shall have any that will be more careful and loving.

The Armada proved to be a disaster. The Spanish fleet that finally set sail had neither the ships nor the manpower that Philip had planned to send. A conversation between a papal emissary and an officer of the Spanish fleet before the Armada departed reveals the fundamental flaw:

> "And if you meet the English armada in the Channel, do you expect to win the battle?" "Of course," replied the Spaniard.
> "How can you be sure?" [asked the emissary]
> "It's very simple. It is well known that we fight in God's cause. So, when we meet the English, God will surely arrange matters so that we can grapple and board them, either by sending some strange freak of weather or, more likely, just by depriving the English of their wits. If we can come to close quarters, Spanish valor and Spanish steel (and the great masses of soldiers we shall have on board) will make our victory certain. But unless God helps us by a miracle the English, who have faster and handier ships than ours, and many more long-range guns, and who know their advantage just as well as we do, will never close with us at all, but stand aloof and knock us to pieces with their culverins, without our being able to do them any serious hurt. So," concluded the captain, and one fancies a grim smile, "we are sailing against England in the confident hope of a miracle."[11]

The hoped-for miracle never materialized. The Spanish fleet, battered by a number of encounters with the English, sailed back to Spain by a northward route around Scotland and Ireland where it was further battered by storms. Although the English and Spanish would continue their war for another sixteen years, the defeat of the Armada guaranteed for the time being that England would remain a Protestant country. Although Spain made up for its losses within a year and a half, the defeat was a psychological blow to the Spaniards.

◆ Economic and Social Crises

The period of European history from 1560 to 1650 witnessed severe economic and social crises as well as political upheaval. Economic uncertainties, intensified by wildly fluctuating boom and bust cycles, were accompanied by social uncertainties and stark contrasts between the living standards of the rich and the poor. Although historians commonly refer to a sixteenth-century price revolution and a seventeenth-century economic crisis, the lack of concrete data has made it difficult to be precise in these areas, leading to numerous historical controversies.

✤ Inflation and Economic Stagnation

Inflation was a major economic problem in the sixteenth and early seventeenth centuries. This so-called price revolution was a Europeanwide phenomenon, although different areas were affected at different times. Though the inflation rate was probably a relatively low 2 to 3 percent a year, it was noticeable in a Europe accustomed to stable prices. Foodstuffs were most subject to price increases, especially evident in the price of wheat. An upward surge in wheat prices was first noticed in the Mediterranean area—in Spain, southern France, and Italy—and reached its peak there in the 1590s. By the 1620s and 1630s, wheat prices in northern Europe had undergone similar increases.

Although precise data are lacking, economic historians believe that as a result of the price revolution, wages failed to keep up with price increases. Wage earners, especially agricultural laborers and salaried workers in urban areas, began to experience a lower standard of living. At the same time, landed aristocrats who could raise rents managed to prosper. Commercial and industrial entrepreneurs also benefited from the price revolution because of rising prices, expanding markets, and relatively cheaper labor costs. Some historians regard this profit inflation as a valuable stimulus to investment and the growth of capitalism, helping to explain the economic expansion and prosperity of the sixteenth century. Governments were likewise affected by inflation. They borrowed heavily from bankers and imposed new tax burdens on their subjects, often creating additional discontent.

The causes of the price revolution are a subject of much historical debate. Already in the 1560s European intellectuals had associated the rise in prices with the great influx of precious metals from the New World. Although this view was accepted for a long time, many economic historians now believe that the increase in population in the sixteenth century played an important role in creating inflationary pressures. A growing population increased the demand for land and food and drove up prices for both.

But the inflation-fueled prosperity of the sixteenth century showed signs of slackening by the beginning of the seventeenth century. Economic contraction began to be evident in some parts of Europe by the 1620s. In the 1630s and 1640s, as imports of silver declined, economic recession intensified, especially in the Mediterranean area. The industrial and financial center of Europe in the age of the Renaissance, Italy was now becoming an economic backwater. Spain's economy was also seriously failing by the decade of the 1640s.

✤ Trade, Industry, Banking, and Agriculture

The flourishing European trade of the sixteenth century revolved around three major areas: the Mediterranean in the south, the Low Countries and the Baltic region in the north, and central Europe, whose inland trade depended on the Rhine and Danube Rivers. As overseas trade expanded, however, the Atlantic seaboard began to play a more important role, linking the Mediterranean, Baltic, and central European trading areas together and making the whole of Europe into a more integrated market that was all the more vulnerable to price shifts. With their cheaper and faster ships, the Dutch came to monopolize both European and world trade, although they were increasingly challenged by the English and French in the seventeenth century.

The commercial expansion of the sixteenth and seventeenth centuries was made easier by new forms of commercial organization, especially the joint-stock trading company. Individuals bought shares in a company and received dividends on their investment while a board of directors ran the company and made the important business decisions. The return on investments could be spectacular. During its first ten years, investors received 30 percent on their money from the Dutch East India Company, which opened the Spice Islands and Southeast Asia to Dutch activity. The joint-stock company made it easier to raise large amounts of capital for world trading ventures.

Enormous profits were also being made in shipbuilding and in mining and metallurgy, where technological innovations, such as the use of pumps and new methods of extracting metals from ores, proved highly successful. The mining industry was closely tied to sixteenth-century family banking firms. In exchange for arranging large loans to Charles V, Jacob Fugger was given a monopoly over silver, copper, and mercury mines in the Habsburg possessions of central Europe that produced profits in excess of 50 percent per year. Though these close relationships between governments and entrepreneurs could lead to stunning successes, they could also be precarious. The House of Fugger went bankrupt at the end of the sixteenth century when the Habsburgs defaulted on their loans.

By the seventeenth century, the traditional family banking firms were no longer able to supply the numerous services needed for the commercial capitalism of the seventeenth century. New institutions arose to take their place. The city of Amsterdam created the Bank of Amsterdam in 1609 as both a deposit and a transfer institution and the Amsterdam Bourse or Exchange where the trading of stocks replaced the exchange of goods. By the first half of the seventeenth century, the Amsterdam Exchange had emerged as the hub of the European business world, just as Amsterdam itself had replaced Antwerp as the greatest commercial and banking center of Europe.

Despite the growth of commercial capitalism, most of the European economy still depended on an agricultural system that had experienced few changes since the thirteenth century. At least 80 to 90 percent of Europeans till worked on the land. Almost all of the peasants of western Europe were free of serfdom, although many still owed a variety of feudal dues to the nobility. Despite the

JACOB FUGGER THE RICH. Jacob Fugger, head of one of the wealthiest banking firms of the sixteenth century, is pictured here with his faithful secretary, Matthaus Schwartz, who painted this scene in 1516. The cabinet in the background lists the names of the cities where Fugger's firm had branch offices, including Milan, Innsbruck, Nuremberg, and Lisbon.

expanding markets and rising prices, European peasants saw little or no improvement in their lot as they faced increased rents and fees and higher taxes imposed by the state. In eastern Europe, the peasants' position even worsened as they were increasingly tied to the land in a new serfdom enforced by powerful landowners (see Chapter 15).

❈ Population and the Growth of Cities

The sixteenth century was a period of expanding population, possibly related to a warmer climate and increased food supplies. It has been estimated that the population of Europe increased from 60 million in 1500 to 85 million by 1600, the first major recovery of the European population since the devastation of the Black Death in the mid-fourteenth century. However, records also indicate that the population had leveled off by 1620 and even begun to decline by 1650, especially in central and southern Europe. Only the Dutch, English, and, to a lesser degree, the French grew in number in the first half of the seventeenth century. Europe's longtime adversaries, war, famine, and plague, continued to affect population levels. In 1630, for example, northern Italy was hit by a devastating recurrence of bubonic plague; Verona and Mantua lost 60 to 70 percent of their populations. Europe's entry into another "little ice age" after the middle of the sixteenth century, when average temperatures fell and glaciers even engulfed small Alpine villages, affected harvests and gave rise to famines. Historians have noted the parallels between population increase and economic prosperity in the sixteenth century and population decline and economic recession in the seventeenth century.

The rise in population was reflected in the growth of cities. In 1500, Paris, Constantinople, and four cities in Italy (Naples, Venice, Milan, Genoa) had populations above 100,000 people. By 1600, Naples had grown to 300,000, while Rome, Palermo, and Messina reached 100,000. Cities along coasts and well-traveled trade routes grew the most, reflecting the close ties between commerce and urban growth. Naples became the largest port in Italy while Seville in Spain, the port of entry for the wealth of the New World, and Lisbon in Portugal had populations over 100,000 by 1600. Across the English Channel, London's domination of the commercial and financial life of England pushed its population to 250,000 by 1600. By that year, Europe's greatest and most populous city was Paris with its 500,000 people.

Seventeenth-century cities visibly reflected the remarkable disparity in wealth during the seventeenth century. The beautiful houses and palaces of rich nobles and wealthy merchants contrasted sharply with the crowded tenements and dirty hovels of the lower classes. Crime, pollution, filth, and lack of sanitation, fresh water, and food were accompanied by social tensions between landed nobles who moved into the cities and the wealthy merchants who resented their presence.

◆ Seventeenth-Century Crises: War and Rebellions

Although many Europeans responded to the upheavals of the second half of the sixteenth century with a desire for peace and order, the first fifty years of the seventeenth century continued to be a period of crisis. A devastating war that affected much of Europe and rebellions seemingly everywhere protracted an atmosphere of disorder and violence.

❈ The Thirty Years' War

Religion, especially the struggle between a militant Catholicism and a militant Calvinism, certainly played an important role in the outbreak of the Thirty Years' War, often called the "last of the religious wars." As the war progressed, however, it became increasingly clear that secular, dynastic-nationalist considerations were far more important.

Although much of the fighting in the Thirty Years' War (1618–1648) took place in the Germanic lands of the Holy Roman Empire, the war became a Europeanwide struggle. In fact, some historians view it as part of a larger conflict between the Bourbon dynasty of France and the Habsburg dynasties of Spain and the Holy Roman Empire for European leadership and date it from 1609 to 1659. A brief look at the motives of the European states and the situation in the Holy Roman Empire provides the background necessary to understand the war.

Since the beginning of the sixteenth century, France had worked to break out of what it perceived as its encirclement by the house of Habsburg. The situation had eased in 1556 when Charles V abdicated and divided his empire. His son Philip inherited Spain, the Netherlands, Italy, and the New World while his brother Ferdinand became Holy Roman Emperor and received the Habsburg possessions in Austria and eastern Europe. France felt threatened by the Spanish Habsburgs and feared the consolidation of the Holy Roman Empire by the Habsburg emperor.

Spain, which viewed the twelve-year truce negotiated with the Dutch in 1609 as only temporary, was determined to regain control of the Netherlands, specifically, the northern Dutch provinces. English and Dutch control of the seas, however, forced the Spanish to seek an alternative route for shipping supplies and men to the Dutch provinces by way of Italy and western Germany.

The Austrian Habsburgs wished to consolidate their holdings in Austria and Bohemia by eliminating Protestantism and establishing stronger central authority. At the same time, as Holy Roman Emperors, they remained frustrated by their lack of real authority over the lands of Germany where hundreds of individual states still provided the real basis of political power. It was among these German states that the Thirty Years' War had its immediate beginnings.

The Peace of Augsburg in 1555 had brought an end to the religious warfare between German Catholics and Lutherans. Religion, however, continued to play a divisive role in German life as Lutherans and Catholics persisted in vying for control of various principalities. In addition,

MAP 14.3 The Thirty Years' War.

although the treaty had not recognized the rights of Calvinists, a number of German states had adopted Calvinism as their state church. At the beginning of the seventeenth century, the Calvinist ruler of the Palatinate, the Elector Palatine Frederick IV, assumed the leadership in forming a league of German Protestant states called the Protestant Union. To counteract it, a Catholic League of German states was organized by Duke Maximilian of the south German state of Bavaria. This division of Germany into two armed camps was made even more dangerous by the involvement of foreign states. The Protestant Union gained the support of the Dutch, English, and French, while Spain and the Holy Roman Emperor aided the Catholic League. By 1609, then, Germany was dividing into two armed camps in anticipation of religious war.

The religious division was exacerbated by a constitutional issue. The desire of the Habsburg emperors to consolidate their authority in the Holy Roman Empire was resisted by the princes who fought for their "German liberties," their constitutional rights and prerogatives as individual rulers. To pursue their policies, the Habsburg emperors looked to Spain for assistance while the princes turned to the enemies of Spain, especially France, for help against the emperor. The divisions in the Holy Roman Empire and Europe made it almost inevitable that if war did erupt, it would be widespread and difficult to stop. Events in Bohemia in 1617 and 1618 finally brought the outbreak of the war everyone dreaded.

Historians have traditionally divided the Thirty Years' War into four major phases. The Bohemian phase (1618–1625) began in one of the Habsburgs' own territories. In 1617, the Bohemian Estates (primarily the nobles) accepted the Habsburg Archduke Ferdinand as their king but soon found themselves unhappy with their choice. Though many of the nobles were Calvinists, Ferdinand was a devout Catholic who began a process of re-Catholicizing Bohemia and strengthening royal power. The Protestant nobles rebelled against Ferdinand in May 1618 and proclaimed their resistance by throwing two of the Habsburg governors and a secretary out of the window of the royal castle in Prague, the seat of Bohemian government. The Catholic side claimed that their seemingly miraculous escape from death in the seventy-foot fall from the castle was due to the intercession of the Virgin Mary, while Protestants pointed out that they fell into a manure pile. The Bohemian rebels now seized control of Bohemia, deposed Ferdinand, and elected as his replacement the Protestant ruler of the Palatinate, Elector Frederick V, who was also head of the Protestant Union.

Ferdinand, who in the meantime had been elected as Holy Roman Emperor, refused to accept his deposition. Aided by the imposing forces of Maximilian of Bavaria and the Catholic League, the imperial forces defeated Frederick and the Bohemian nobles at the Battle of White Mountain outside Prague on November 8, 1620. Spanish troops meanwhile took advantage of Frederick's predicament by invading the Palatinate and conquering it by the end of 1622. The unfortunate Frederick who had lost two

CHRONOLOGY

The Thirty Years' War

The Protestant Union	1608
The Catholic League	1609
Election of Habsburg Archduke Ferdinand as king of Bohemia	1617
Bohemian revolt against Ferdinand	1618
The Bohemian Phase	1618–1625
Battle of White Mountain	1620
Spanish conquest of Palatinate	1622
The Danish phase	1625–1629
Edict of Restitution	1629
The Swedish phase	1630–1635
Battle of Lützen	1632
Battle of Nördlingen	1634
The Franco-Swedish phase	1635–1648
Battle of Rocroi	1643
Peace of Westphalia	1648
Peace of the Pyrenees	1659

crowns—Bohemia and the Palatinate—fled into exile in Holland. The Spanish took control of the western part of the Palatinate (to gain the access route from Italy to the Netherlands that they had wanted), and Duke Maximilian of Bavaria took the rest of the territory. Reestablished as king of Bohemia, Emperor Ferdinand declared Bohemia a hereditary Habsburg possession, confiscated the land of the Protestant nobles, and established Catholicism as the sole religion. Some 30,000 Protestant families emigrated to Saxony and Hungary. The Spanish renewed their attack on the Dutch, and the forces of Catholicism seemed on the road to victory. But the war was far from over.

The second phase of the war, the Danish phase (1625–1629), began when King Christian IV of Denmark (1588–1648), a Lutheran, intervened on behalf of the Protestant cause by leading an army into northern Germany. Most likely, he also wished to annex territories in northern Germany that would give him control of the southern Baltic. His campaign turned out to be a complete fiasco.

The imperial forces were now led by a brilliant and enigmatic commander, Albrecht von Wallenstein, a Bohemian nobleman who had taken advantage of Ferdinand's victory to become the country's wealthiest landowner. Wallenstein marched the imperial army north, utterly defeated the Danes, and occupied parts of northern Germany, including the Baltic ports of Hamburg, Lübeck, and Bremen. Christian IV's total defeat ended Danish involvement in the Thirty Years' War and even meant the end of Danish supremacy in the Baltic.

After the success of the imperial armies, the emperor Ferdinand II was at the height of his power and took this opportunity to issue the Edict of Restitution in March 1629. His proclamation prohibited Calvinist worship and

SOLDIERS PILLAGING A FARM. This painting shows a group of soldiers running amok on a French peasant's farm. This scene was typical of many that occurred during the Thirty Years' War, especially in Germany where the war caused enormous destruction.

restored to the Catholic church all property taken by Protestant princes or cities during the past seventy-five years. But this sudden growth in the power of the Habsburg emperor frightened many German princes who feared for their independent status and reacted by forcing the emperor to dismiss Wallenstein. At the same time, Ferdinand was faced with another intervention by foreign powers as the war entered its third phase.

The Swedish phase (1630–1635) marked the entry of Gustavus Adolphus, king of Sweden (1611–1635), into the war. Gustavus Adolphus was responsible for reviving Sweden and making it into a great Baltic power. The French, disturbed by the Habsburg consolidation of power, provided financial support to Gustavus, a military genius who brought a disciplined and well-equipped Swedish army to northern Germany. Gustavus had no desire to see the Habsburgs in northern Germany since he wanted the Baltic Sea to be a Swedish lake. At the same time, Gustavus Adolphus was a devout Lutheran who felt compelled to aid his coreligionists in Germany.

Gustavus's army swept the imperial forces out of the north and moved into the heart of Germany. In desperation, the imperial side recalled Wallenstein, who was given command of the imperial army that met Gustavus Adolphus's troops near Leipzig. At the Battle of Lützen (1632), the Swedish forces prevailed but paid a high price for the victory when the Swedish king was killed in the battle. Although the Swedish forces remained in Germany, they proved much less effective. Despite the loss of Wallenstein, who was assassinated in 1634 by one of his own captains, the imperial army decisively defeated the Swedes at the Battle of Nördlingen at the end of 1634 and drove them out of southern Germany. This imperial victory guaranteed that southern Germany would remain Catholic. The emperor used this opportunity to make peace with the German princes by agreeing to annul the Edict of Restitution of 1629. But peace failed to come to war-weary Ger-

many. The Swedes wished to continue while the French, under the direction of Cardinal Richelieu, the chief minister of King Louis XIII (see Chapter 15), entered the war directly, beginning the fourth and final phase of the war, the Franco-Swedish phase (1635–1648).

By this time, religious issues were losing their significance as dynastic power politics came to the fore. The Catholic French, after all, were now supporting the Protestant Swedes against the Catholic Habsburgs of Germany and Spain. This phase of the war was fought by Sweden in northern Germany and by France in the Netherlands and along the Rhine in western Germany. The Battle of Rocroi in 1643 proved decisive as the French beat the Spanish and brought an end to Spanish military greatness. The French then moved on to victories over the imperialist-Bavarian armies in southern Germany. By this time all parties were ready for peace, and after five years of protracted negotiations, the war in Germany was officially ended by the Peace of Westphalia in 1648. The war between France and Spain, however, continued until the Peace of the Pyrenees in 1659. By that time, Spain had become a second-class power, and France had emerged as the dominant nation in Europe.

What were the results of this "basically meaningless conflict," as one historian has called it? The Peace of Westphalia ensured that all German states, including the Calvinist ones, were free to determine their own religion. Territorially, France gained parts of western Germany, part of Alsace and the three cities of Metz, Toul, and Verdun, giving the French control of the Franco-German border area and excellent bases for future military operations in Germany. While Sweden and the German states of Brandenburg and Bavaria gained some territory in Germany, the Austrian Habsburgs did not really lose any, but did see their authority as rulers of Germany further diminished. The more than 300 states that made up the Holy Roman Empire were virtually recognized as independent states, since each received the power to conduct its own foreign

The Face of War in the Seventeenth Century

The Thirty Years' War was the most devastating war Europeans had experienced since the Hundred Years' War. Destruction was especially severe in Germany. We have a firsthand account of the face of war in Germany from a picaresque novel called Simplicius Simplicissimus, *written by Jakob von Grimmelshausen. The author's experiences as a soldier in the Thirty Years' War give his descriptions of the effect of the war on ordinary people a certain vividness and reality. This selection describes the fate of a peasant farm, an experience all too familiar to thousands of German peasants between 1618 and 1648.*

❈ Jakob von Grimmelshausen, *Simplicius Simplicissimus*

The first thing these horsemen did in the nice back rooms of the house was to put in their horses. Then everyone took up a special job, one having to do with death and destruction. Although some began butchering, heating water, and rendering lard, as if to prepare for a banquet, others raced through the house, ransacking upstairs and down; not even the privy chamber was safe, as if the golden fleece of Jason might be hidden there. Still others bundled up big packs of cloth, household goods, and clothes, as if they wanted to hold a rummage sale somewhere. What they did not intend to take along they broke and spoiled. Some ran their swords into the hay and straw, as if there hadn't been hogs enough to stick. Some shook the feathers out of beds and put bacon slabs, hams, and other stuff in the ticking, as if they might sleep better on these. Others knocked down the hearth and broke the windows, as if announcing an everlasting summer. They flattened out copper and pewter dishes and baled the ruined goods. They burned up bedsteads, tables, chairs, and benches, though there were yards and yards of dry firewood outside the kitchen. Jars and crocks, pots and casseroles all were broken, either because they preferred their meat broiled or because they thought they'd eat only one meal with us. In the barn, the hired girl was handled so

roughly that she was unable to walk away, I am ashamed to report. They stretched the hired man out flat on the ground, stuck a wooden wedge in his mouth to keep it open, and emptied a milk bucket full of stinking manure drippings down his throat; they called it a Swedish cocktail. He didn't relish it and made a very wry face. By this means they forced him to take a raiding party to some other place where they carried off men and cattle and brought them to our farm. Among those were my father, mother, and Ursula [sister].

Then they used thumbscrews, which they cleverly made out of their pistols, to torture the peasants, as if they wanted to burn witches. Though he had confessed to nothing as yet, they put one of the captured hayseeds in the bake-oven and lighted a fire in it. They put a rope around someone else's head and tightened it like a tourniquet until blood came out of his mouth, nose, and ears. In short, every soldier had his favorite method of making life miserable for peasants, and every peasant had his own misery. My father was, as I thought, particularly lucky because he confessed with a laugh what others were forced to say in pain and martyrdom. No doubt because he was the head of the household, he was shown special consideration; they put him close to a fire, tied him by his hands and legs, and rubbed damp salt on the bottoms of his feet. Our old nanny goat had to lick it off and this so tickled my father that he could have burst laughing. This seemed so clever and entertaining to me—I had never seen or heard my father laugh so long—that I joined him in laughter, to keep him company or perhaps to cover up my ignorance. In the midst of such glee he told them the whereabouts of hidden treasure much richer in gold, pearls, and jewelry than might have been expected on a farm.

I can't say much about the captured wives, hired girls, and daughters because the soldiers didn't let me watch their doings. But I do remember hearing pitiful screams from various dark corners and I guess that my mother and our Ursula had it no better than the rest.

---

policy; this brought an end to the Holy Roman Empire as a political entity and ensured German disunity for another 200 years. The Peace of Westphalia also made it clear that religion and politics were now separate worlds. The pope was completely ignored in all decisions at Westphalia, and political motives became the guiding forces in public affairs as religion moved closer to becoming primarily a matter of personal conviction and individual choice.

The economic and social effects of the Thirty Years' War on Germany are still debated. The most recent work pictures a ruined German economy and a decline in German population from 21 to 16 million between 1618 and 1650. Some areas of Germany were completely devas-

tated, but others remained relatively untouched and even experienced economic growth. In any case, the Thirty Years' War was undoubtedly the most destructive conflict Europeans had yet experienced (see the box above). Unfortunately, it was not the last.

❈ A Military Revolution?

By the seventeenth century, war played an increasingly important role in European affairs. One historian has calculated that between 1562 and 1721 there were only four years in which all Europe was at peace. Military power was considered essential to a ruler's reputation and power;

thus, the pressure to build an effective military machine was intense. Although some would disagree, some historians believe that the changes that occurred in the science of warfare between 1560 and 1650 warrant the title of military revolution.

Medieval warfare, with its mounted knights and supplementary archers, had been transformed in the Renaissance by the employment of infantry armed with pikes and halberds and arranged in massed rectangles, known as squadrons or battalions. The squadron of pikemen became a crucial element in sixteenth-century armies and helps to explain the success of the Spanish who perfected its use. The utilization of firearms required adjustments to the size and shape of the massed infantry and made the cavalry less effective.

It was Gustavus Adolphus, the king of Sweden, who developed the first standing army of conscripts, notable for the flexibility of its tactics. The infantry brigades of Gustavus's army were composed of equal numbers of musketeers and pikemen, standing six men deep. They employed the salvo in which all rows of the infantry fired at once instead of row by row. These salvos of fire, which cut up the massed ranks of the opposing infantry squadrons, were followed by a pike charge, giving the infantry a primarily offensive deployment. Gustavus also used the cavalry in a more mobile fashion. After shooting a pistol volley, they charged the enemy with their swords. Additional flexibility was obtained by utilizing lighter artillery pieces that were more easily moved during battle. All of these changes required coordination, careful training, and better discipline, forcing rulers to move away from undisciplined mercenary forces. Naturally, the success of Gustavus Adolphus led to imitation. Perhaps the best example was the New Model Army of Oliver Cromwell (see Chapter 15). His army consisted of infantry (two-thirds musketeers and one-third pikemen), cavalry, mounted infantry known as dragoons, and artillery units. A well-integrated and disciplined army, it was known for its mobility and flexibility.

The military changes between 1560 and 1650 included an increased use of firearms and cannon, greater flexibility and mobility in tactics, and better disciplined and trained armies. These innovations necessitated standing armies, based partly on conscription, which grew ever larger and more expensive as the seventeenth century progressed. Such armies could only be maintained by levying heavier taxes, making war an economic burden and an ever more important part of the early modern European state. To some historians, the creation of large bureaucracies to supervise the military resources of the state was the real reason for the rise of royal absolutism in the seventeenth century (see Chapter 15).

�» *Rebellions*

Before, during, and after the Thirty Years' War, a series of rebellions and civil wars stemming from the discontent of both nobles and commoners rocked the domestic stability of many European governments. To strengthen their power, monarchs attempted to extend their authority at the expense of traditional powerful elements who resisted the rulers' efforts. At the same time, to fight their battles, governments increased taxes and created such hardships that common people also rose in opposition.

Between 1590 and 1640, peasant and lower-class revolts erupted in central and southern France, Austria, and Hungary. In the decades of the 1640s and 1650s, even greater unrest occurred. Portugal and Catalonia rebelled against the Spanish government in 1640. The common people in Naples and Sicily revolted against both the government and the landed nobility in 1647. Russia, too, was rocked by urban uprisings in 1641, 1645, and 1648. Nobles rebelled in France from 1648 to 1652 to halt the growth of royal power (see Chapter 15). The northern states of Sweden, Denmark, and Holland were also not immune from upheavals involving clergy, nobles, and mercantile groups. Even relatively stable Switzerland had a peasant rebellion in 1656. By far the most famous and wide-ranging struggle, however, was the civil war and rebellion in England, commonly known as the English Revolution (see Chapter 15).

◆ The Witchcraft Craze

In the midst of the turmoil created by wars, rebellions, and economic and social uncertainties, yet another source of disorder arose as hysteria over witchcraft came to affect the lives of many Europeans in the sixteenth and seventeenth centuries. Witchcraft trials were prevalent in England, Scotland, Switzerland, Germany, some parts of France and the Low Countries, and even New England in America. As is evident from this list, the witchcraft craze affected both Catholic and Protestant countries.

Witchcraft was not a new phenomenon in the sixteenth and seventeenth centuries. Its practice had been part of traditional village culture for centuries, but it came to be viewed as both sinister and dangerous when the medieval church began to connect witches to the activities of the devil, thereby transforming witchcraft into a heresy that had to be wiped out. After the creation of the Inquisition in the thirteenth century, some people were accused of a variety of witchcraft practices and, following the biblical injunction, "Thou shalt not suffer a witch to live," were turned over to secular authorities for burning at the stake or hanging (in England).

The search for scapegoats to explain the disaster of the Black Death in the fourteenth century led to a rise in the persecution of people accused of sorcery. In a papal bull of 1484, Pope Innocent VIII made official the belief of the Catholic church in such pernicious practices:

> It has recently come to our ears, not without great pain to us, that in some parts of upper Germany, . . . many persons of both sexes, heedless of their own salvation and forsaking the catholic faith, give themselves over to devils male and

THE ACTIVITIES OF WITCHES. Hysteria over witchcraft affected the daily lives of many Europeans in the sixteenth and seventeenth centuries. This picture by Frans Francken the Young, painted in 1607, shows a number of activities commonly attributed to witches. In the center, several witches are casting spells with their magic books and instruments, and at the top, a witch on a post prepares to fly off on her broomstick.

female, and by their incantations, charms, and conjurings, . . . ruin and cause to perish the offspring of women, the foal of animals, the products of the earth, the grapes of vines, and the fruits of trees, as well as men and women, cattle and flocks and herds and animals of every kind . . . ; that they afflict and torture with dire pains and anguish, both internal and external, these men, women, cattle, flocks, herds, and animals, and hinder men from begetting and women from conceiving, and prevent all consummation of marriage; . . . that, moreover, at the instigation of the enemy of mankind [Satan], they do not fear to commit and perpetrate many other abominable offenses and crimes.[12]

To combat these dangers, Innocent sent two Dominican friars, Jacob Sprenger and Heinrich Krämer, to Germany to investigate and root out the witches. In 1486, based on their findings, they wrote the *Malleus Maleficarum (The Hammer of the Witches)*, which until the eighteenth century remained one of the standard handbooks on the practices of witchcraft and the methods that could be used to discover and try witches.

What distinguished witchcraft in the sixteenth and seventeenth centuries from these previous developments was the increased number of trials and executions of presumed witches. Although estimates have varied widely, the most recent figures indicate that more than 100,000 people were prosecuted throughout Europe on charges of witchcraft. As more and more people were brought to trial, the fear of witches as well as the fear of being accused of witchcraft escalated to frightening proportions. Approximately 25 percent of the villages in the English county of Essex, for example, had at least one witchcraft trial in the sixteenth and seventeenth centuries. Although larger cities were affected first, the trials also spread to smaller towns and rural areas as the hysteria persisted well into the seventeenth century (see the box on p. 417).

From an account of witch persecution in the German city of Trier, we get some glimpse of who the accused were: "Scarcely any of those who were accused escaped punishment. Nor were there spared even the leading men in the city of Trier." Although this statement makes it clear that the witchcraft trials had gone so far that even city officeholders were not immune from persecution, it also implies what is borne out in most witchcraft trials—that women of the lower classes were more likely to be accused of witchcraft. Indeed, where lists are given, those mentioned most often are milkmaids, peasant women, and servant girls. In the witchcraft trials of the sixteenth and seventeenth centuries, 80 percent of those accused were women, most of them single or widowed and many over fifty years old. Moreover, almost all victims belonged to the lower classes, the poor and propertyless.

The accused witches usually confessed to a number of practices. Many of their confessions were extracted by torture, greatly adding to the number and intensity of activities mentioned. But even when people confessed voluntarily, certain practices stand out. Many said that they had sworn allegiance to the devil and attended sabbats or nocturnal gatherings where they feasted, danced, and even copulated with the devil in sexual orgies. More common, however, were admissions of using evil incantations and special ointments and powders to wreak havoc on neigh-

A Witchcraft Trial in France

Persecutions for witchcraft reached their high point in the sixteenth and seventeenth centuries when tens of thousands of people were brought to trial. In this excerpt from the minutes of a trial in France in 1652, we can see why the accused witch stood little chance of exonerating herself.

The Trial of Suzanne Gaudry

28 May, 1652. . . . Interrogation of Suzanne Gaudry, prisoner at the court of Rieux. . . . [During interrogations on May 28 and May 29, the prisoner confessed to a number of activities involving the devil.]

❈ Deliberation of the Court—June 3, 1652

The undersigned advocates of the Court have seen these interrogations and answers. They say that the aforementioned Suzanne Gaudry confesses that she is a witch, that she had given herself to the devil, that she had renounced God, Lent, and baptism, that she has been marked on the shoulder, that she has cohabited with the devil and that she has been to the dances, confessing only to have cast a spell upon and caused to die a beast of Philippe Cornié. . . .

❈ Third Interrogation—June 27

This prisoner being led into the chamber, she was examined to know if things were not as she had said and confessed at the beginning of her imprisonment.

—Answers no, and that what she has said was done so by force.

Pressed to say the truth, that otherwise she would be subjected to torture, having pointed out to her that her aunt was burned for this same subject.

—Answers that she is not a witch. . . .

She was placed in the hands of the officer in charge of torture, throwing herself on her knees, struggling to cry, uttering several exclamations, without being able, nevertheless, to shed a tear. Saying at every moment that she is not a witch.

❈ The Torture

On this same day, being at the place of torture.

This prisoner, before being strapped down, was admonished to maintain herself in her first confessions and to renounce her lover.

—Says that she denies everything she has said, and that she has no lover. Feeling herself being strapped down, says that she is not a witch, while struggling to cry. . . . and upon being asked why she confessed to being one, said that she was forced to say it.

Told that she was not forced, that on the contrary she declared herself to be a witch without any threat.

—Says that she confessed it and that she is not a witch, and being a little stretched [on the rack] screams ceaselessly that she is not a witch. . . .

Asked if she did not confess that she had been a witch for twenty-six years.

—Says that she said it, that she retracts it, crying that she is not a witch.

Asked if she did not make Philippe Cornié's horse die, as she confessed.

—Answers no, crying Jesus-Maria, that she is not a witch.

The mark having been probed by the officer, in the presence of Doctor Bouchain, it was adjudged by the aforesaid doctor and officer truly to be the mark of the devil.

Being more tightly stretched upon the torture-rack, urged to maintain her confessions.

—Said that it was true that she is a witch and that she would maintain what she had said.

Asked how long she has been in subjugation to the devil.

—Answers that it was twenty years ago that the devil appeared to her, being in her lodgings in the form of a man dressed in a little cow-hide and black breeches. . . .

❈ Verdict

July 9, 1652. In the light of the interrogations, answers and investigations made into the charge against Suzanne Gaudry, . . . seeing by her own confessions that she is said to have made a pact with the devil, received the mark from him, . . . and that following this, she had renounced God, Lent, and baptism and had let herself be known carnally by him, in which she received satisfaction. Also, seeing that she is said to have been a part of nocturnal carols and dances.

For expiation of which the advice of the undersigned is that the office of Rieux can legitimately condemn the aforesaid Suzanne Gaudry to death, tying her to a gallows, and strangling her to death, then burning her body and burying it here in the environs of the woods.

bors by killing their livestock, injuring their children, or raising storms to destroy their crops.

A number of contributing factors have been suggested to explain why the witchcraft craze became so widespread in the sixteenth and seventeenth centuries. Religious uncertainties clearly played some part. Many witchcraft trials occurred in areas where Protestantism had been recently victorious or in regions, such as southwestern Germany, where Protestant-Catholic controversies still raged. As religious passions became inflamed, accusations of being in league with the devil became common on both sides.

Recently, however, historians have emphasized the importance of social conditions, especially the problems of a society in turmoil, in explaining the witchcraft hysteria. At a time when the old communal values that stressed working together for the good of the community were disintegrating before the onslaught of a new economic ethic that emphasized that each person should look out for himself or herself, property owners became more fearful of the growing numbers of poor in their midst and transformed them psychologically into agents of the devil. Old women were particularly susceptible to suspicion. Many of them, no longer the recipients of the local charity available in traditional society, may even have tried to survive by selling herbs, potions, or secret remedies for healing. When problems arose—and there were many in this crisis-laden period—these same women were the most likely scapegoats at hand.

That women should be the chief victims of witchcraft trials was hardly accidental. Indeed, the authors of the *Malleus Maleficarum* had argued that there was a direct link between witchcraft and women. According to them, women were inferior to men both mentally and morally. Women's moral weaknesses made them especially open to temptation and hence especially vulnerable to the allures of Satan. The strong beliefs of the authors of the *Malleus Maleficarum* were repeated in virtually all of the new witchcraft treatises written in the sixteenth and seventeenth centuries. Nicholas Rémy, a witchcraft judge in France in the 1590s, found it "not unreasonable that this scum of humanity (i.e., witches) should be drawn chiefly from the feminine sex." To another judge, it came as no surprise that witches would confess to sexual experiences with Satan: "The Devil uses them so, because he knows that women love carnal pleasures, and he means to bind them to his allegiance by such agreeable provocations."[13] Of course, not only witch hunters held such low estimates of women. Most theologians, lawyers, and philosophers in early modern Europe believed in the natural inferiority of women and thus would have found it plausible that women would be more susceptible to witchcraft.

By the mid-seventeenth century, the witchcraft hysteria began to subside. The destruction of the religious wars had at least forced people to accept a grudging toleration, causing religious passions to subside. Moreover, as governments began to stabilize after the period of crisis, fewer magistrates were willing to accept the unsettling and divisive conditions generated by the trials of witches. Finally, by the end of the seventeenth and beginning of the eighteenth centuries, more and more educated people were questioning altogether their old attitudes toward religion and finding it especially contrary to reason to believe in the old view of a world haunted by evil spirits.

◆ Culture in a Turbulent World

Art and literature passed through two major stylistic stages between the Renaissance and 1650. These changes were closely linked to the religious, political, and intellectual developments of the period.

❋ *Art: Mannerism and the Baroque*

The artistic Renaissance came to an end when a new movement called Mannerism emerged in Italy in the decades of the 1520s and 1530s. The age of the Reformation had brought a revival of religious values accompanied by much political turmoil. Especially in Italy, the worldly enthusiasm of the Renaissance gave way to anxiety, uncertainty, suffering, and a yearning for spiritual experience. Mannerism reflected this environment in its deliberate attempt to break down the High Renaissance principles of balance, harmony, and moderation (the term *Mannerism* derives from critics who considered their contemporary artists to be second-rate imitators, painting in the "manner" of Michelangelo's late style). Italian Mannerist painters deliberately distorted the rules of proportion by portraying elongated figures that conveyed a sense of suffering and a strong emotional atmosphere filled with anxiety and confusion.

Mannerism spread from Italy to other parts of Europe and perhaps reached its apogee in the work of El Greco (1541–1614). Doménikos Theotocópoulos (called "the Greek"—El Greco) was from Crete, but after studying in Venice and Rome, he moved to Spain in the 1570s where he became a church painter in Toledo. El Greco's elongated and contorted figures, portrayed in unusual shades of yellow and green against an eerie background of turbulent grays, reflect well the artist's desire to create a world of intense emotion.

Mannerism was eventually replaced by a new movement—the Baroque—that dominated the artistic world for another century and a half. The Baroque began in Italy in the last quarter of the sixteenth century and spread to the rest of Europe. Baroque artists sought to harmonize the classical traditions of Renaissance art with the intense religious feelings fostered by the revival of religion in the Reformation. The Baroque first appeared in Rome in the Jesuit church of Il Gesù, whose facade was completed in 1575. Although Protestants were also affected, the Baroque was most wholeheartedly embraced by the Catholic reform movement, as is evident at the Catholic courts, especially those of the Habsburgs in Madrid, Prague, Vienna, and Brussels. Although it was resisted in France, England, and Holland, eventually the Baroque style spread to all of Europe and to Latin America.

In large part, Baroque art and architecture reflected the search for power that was characteristic of much of the seventeenth century. Baroque churches and palaces featured richly ornamented facades, sweeping staircases, and an overall splendor that were meant to impress people. Kings and princes wanted other kings and princes as well

EL GRECO, *LAOCÖON*.   Mannerism reached one of its highest expressions in the work of El Greco. Born in Crete, trained in Venice and Rome, and settling finally in Spain, El Greco worked as a church painter in Toledo. Pictured here is his version of the *Laocöon*, a famous piece of Hellenistic sculpture that had been discovered in Rome in 1506. The elongated, contorted bodies project a world of suffering while the somber background scene of the city of Toledo adds a sense of terror and doom.

as their subjects to be in awe of their power. The Catholic church, which commissioned many new churches, wanted people to see clearly the triumphant power of the Catholic faith.

Baroque painting was known for its use of dramatic effects to heighten emotional intensity. This style was especially evident in the works of Peter Paul Rubens (1577–1640), a prolific artist and an important figure in the spread of the Baroque from Italy to other parts of Europe. In his artistic masterpieces, bodies in violent motion, heavily fleshed

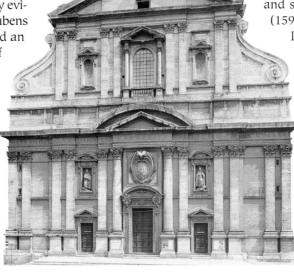

IL GESÙ.   The Jesuit church of Il Gesù in Rome was the first example of Baroque. Its facade, seen here, was completed in 1575. With its use of classical columns, entablatures, and pediments, it served as a model for later church designs done in the Baroque style.

nudes, a dramatic use of light and shadow, and rich sensuous pigments converge to show intense emotions. The restless forms and constant movement blend together into a dynamic unity.

Perhaps the greatest figure of the Baroque was the Italian architect and sculptor Gian Lorenzo Bernini (1598–1680), who completed Saint Peter's Basilica and designed the vast colonnade enclosing the piazza in front of it. Action, exuberance, profusion, and dramatic effects mark the work of Bernini in the interior of Saint Peter's, where his *Throne of Saint Peter* hovers in mid-air, held by the hands of the four great doctors of the Catholic church. Above the chair, rays of golden light drive a mass of clouds and angels toward the spectator. In his most

PETER PAUL RUBENS, *THE LANDING OF MARIE DE' MEDICI AT MARSEILLES*.   Peter Paul Rubens played a key role in spreading the Baroque style from Italy to other parts of Europe. In *The Landing of Marie de' Medici at Marseilles*, Rubens made a dramatic use of light and color, bodies in motion, and luxurious nudes to heighten the emotional intensity of the scene. This was one of a cycle of twenty-one paintings dedicated to the queen mother of France.

striking sculptural work, the *Ecstasy of Saint Theresa*, Bernini depicts a moment of mystical experience in the life of the sixteenth-century Spanish saint. The elegant draperies and the expression on her face create a sensuously real portrayal of physical ecstasy.

Less well-known than the male artists who dominated the art world of seventeenth-century Italy but prominent in her own right was Artemisia Gentileschi (1593–1653). Born in Rome, she studied painting under her father's direction. In 1616, she moved to Florence and began a successful career as a painter. At the age of twenty-three, she became the first woman to be elected to the Florentine Academy of Design. Although she was known internationally in her day as a portrait painter, her fame now rests on a series of pictures of heroines from the Old Testament, including Judith, Esther, and Bathsheba. Most famous is her *Judith Beheading Holofernes*, a dramatic rendering of the biblical scene in which Judith slays the Assyrian general Holofernes to save her besieged town from the Assyrian army.

❊ *Thought: The World of Montaigne*

The crises between 1550 and 1650 produced challenges to the optimistic moral and intellectual premises of the Renaissance. The humanist emphasis on the dignity of man and the role of education in producing moral virtue seemed questionable in view of the often violent passions of dynas-

tic and religious warfare. Intellectuals and writers began to adopt new approaches in criticizing tradition and authority. The concept of a positive skepticism is closely associated with the work of Michel de Montaigne (1533–1592).

Son of a prosperous French merchant, Montaigne received the kind of classical education advocated by Renaissance humanists. Montaigne served as a lawyer and magistrate in the Parlement of Bordeaux, but the religious wars so disgusted him that he withdrew to his country estate to think and write his *Essays*, the first two books of which were published in 1580. His aim was to "disclose himself," or to use self-knowledge as an instrument to understand the world. Montaigne questioned tradition and authority and attacked moral absolutists. He was especially critical of the Huguenot and ultra-Catholic fanatics of the French Wars of Religion who deluded themselves and took the easy way out of life's complexities by trying to kill each other: "instead of transforming themselves into angels, they transform themselves into beasts."

To counteract fanaticism, Montaigne preached moderation and toleration or the "middle way." In his *Essay on Experience*, he wrote: "It is much easier to go along the sides, where the outer edge serves as a limit and a guide, than by the middle way, wide and open, and to go by art than by nature; but it is also much less noble and less commendable. Greatness of soul is not so much pressing upward and forward as knowing how to set oneself in order."[14] Montaigne also brought his middle way and skep-

GIAN LORENZO BERNINI, *ECSTASY OF SAINT THERESA*.
One of the greatest figures of the Baroque period was the
Italian sculptor and architect Gian Lorenzo Bernini. *The
Ecstasy of Saint Theresa*, created for the Cornaro Chapel
in the Church of Santa Maria della Vittoria in Rome, was
one of Bernini's most famous pieces of sculpture. Bernini
sought to convey visually Theresa's own description of
her mystical experience when an angel supposedly
pierced her heart repeatedly with a golden arrow.

**ARTEMISIA GENTILESCHI, *JUDITH BEHEADING
HOLOFERNES*.** Artemisia Gentileschi painted a series of
pictures portraying scenes from the lives of courageous
Old Testament women. In this painting, a determined
Judith, armed with her victim's sword, struggles to saw
off the head of Holofernes. Gentileschi realistically and
dramatically shows the bloody nature of Judith's act.

tical mind to bear on other subjects of the day. He wondered, for example, whether "civilized" Europeans were
superior to the "savages" of the New World.

Montaigne was secular minded and discussed moral
issues without reference to Christian truths. He was, in
many ways, out of step with his own age of passionate religious truths and hatreds, but his ideas would be welcomed
by many Europeans once Europe passed through this
stage of intense intolerance. His maturity, experience, gen-
tleness, and openness all made Montaigne one of the timeless writers of Western civilization.

✳ *A Golden Age of Literature:
England and Spain*

Periods of crisis often produce great writing, and so it was
of this age, which was characterized by epic poetry, experimental verse, the first great chivalric novel, and, above all,
a golden age of theater. In both England and Spain, writing for the stage reached new heights between 1580 and
1640. All of this impressive literature was written in the

vernacular. Except for academic fields, such as theology,
philosophy, jurisprudence, and the sciences, Latin was no
longer a universal literary language.

The golden age of English literature is often called
the Elizabethan era because much of the English cultural
flowering of the late sixteenth and early seventeenth
centuries occurred during her reign. Elizabethan literature
exhibits the exuberance and pride associated with English
exploits under Queen Elizabeth (see the box on p. 423).
Of all the forms of Elizabethan literature, none expressed
the energy and intellectual versatility of the era better than
drama. Of all the dramatists, none is more famous than
William Shakespeare (1564–1616).

Shakespeare was the son of a prosperous glove-
maker from Stratford-upon-Avon. When he appeared in
London in 1592, Elizabethans were already addicted to
the stage. By 1576, two professional theaters run by actors'
companies were in existence. Elizabethan theater became
a tremendously successful business. In or near London, at
least four to six theaters were open six afternoons a week.
London theaters ranged from the Globe, which was a

WILLIAM SHAKESPEARE. The golden age of English literature is identified with the Elizabethan era. Drama flourished during the period, and the greatest dramatist of the age was William Shakespeare. An actor and shareholder in a theatrical company as well as a playwright, Shakespeare wrote a number of tragedies, comedies, romances, and histories.

circular unroofed structure holding 3,000, to the Black-friars, which was roofed and held only 500. In the former, an admission charge of one or two pennies enabled even the lower classes to attend; the higher prices in the latter ensured an audience of the well-to-do. Elizabethan audiences varied greatly, putting pressure on playwrights to write works that pleased nobles, lawyers, merchants, and even vagabonds.

William Shakespeare was a "complete man of the theater." Although best known for writing plays, he was also an actor and shareholder in the chief company of the time, the Lord Chamberlain's Company, which played in theaters as diverse as the Globe and the Blackfriars. Shakespeare has long been recognized as a universal genius. A master of the English language, he was instrumental in transforming a language that was still in a period of transition. His technical proficiency, however, was matched by an incredible insight into human psychology. Whether in his tragedies or comedies, Shakespeare exhibited a remarkable understanding of the human condition.

The theater was also one of the most creative forms of expression during Spain's golden century. The first professional theaters established in Seville and Madrid in the 1570s were run by actors' companies as in England. Soon a public playhouse could be found in every large town, including Mexico City in the New World. Touring companies brought the latest Spanish plays to all parts of the Spanish Empire.

Beginning in the 1580s, the agenda for playwrights was set by Lope de Vega (1562–1635). Like Shakespeare, he was from a middle-class background. He was an incred-ibly prolific writer; almost 500 of his 1,500 plays survive. They have been characterized as witty, charming, action-packed, and realistic. Lope de Vega made no apologies for the fact that he wrote his plays to please his audiences. In a treatise on drama written in 1609, he stated that the foremost duty of the playwright was to satisfy public demand. Shakespeare undoubtedly believed the same thing since his livelihood depended on public approval, but Lope de Vega was considerably more cynical about it: he remarked that if anyone thought he had written his plays for fame, "undeceive him and tell him that I wrote them for money."

One of the crowning achievements of the golden age of Spanish literature was the work of Miguel de Cervantes (1547–1616), whose *Don Quixote* has been acclaimed as one of the greatest literary works of all time. While satirizing medieval chivalric literature, Cervantes also perfected the chivalric novel and reconciled it with literary realism. The two main figures of his famous work represented the dual nature of the Spanish character. The knight Don Quixote from La Mancha is the visionary who is so involved in his lofty ideals that he is oblivious to the hard realities around him. To him, for example, windmills appear as four-armed giants. In contrast, the knight's fat and earthy squire, Sancho Panza, is the realist who cannot get his master to see the realities in front of him. But after adventures that took them to all parts of Spain, each came to see the value of the other's perspective. We are left with Cervantes's conviction that idealism and realism, visionary dreams and the hard work of reality, are both necessary to the human condition.

William Shakespeare: In Praise of England

William Shakespeare is one of the most famous playwrights of the Western world. He was a universal genius, outclassing all others in his psychological insights, depth of characterization, imaginative skills, and versatility. His historical plays reflected the patriotic enthusiasm of the English in the Elizabethan era, as this excerpt from Richard II illustrates.

❋ William Shakespeare, *Richard II*

This royal throne of kings, this sceptered isle,
This earth of majesty, this seat of Mars,
This other Eden, demi-Paradise,
This fortress built by Nature for herself
Against infection and the hand of war,
This happy breed of men, this little world,
This precious stone set in the silver sea,
Which serves it in the office of a wall
Or as a moat defensive to a house
Against the envy of less happier lands—

This blessed plot, this earth, this realm, this England,
This nurse, this teeming womb of royal kings,
Feared by their breed and famous by their birth,
Renowned for their deeds as far from home,
For Christian service and true chivalry,
As is the sepulcher in stubborn Jewry [the Holy
    Sepulcher in Jerusalem]
Of the world's ransom, blessed Mary's Son—
This land of such dear souls, this dear dear land,
Dear for her reputation through the world,
Is now leased out, I die pronouncing it,
Like a tenement or pelting farm.
England, bound in with the triumphant sea,
Whose rocky shore beats back the envious siege
Of watery Neptune, is now bound in with shame,
With inky blots and rotten parchment bonds.
That England, what was wont to conquer others,
Hath made a shamful conquest of itself.
Ah, would the scandal vanish with my life,
How happy then were my ensuing death!

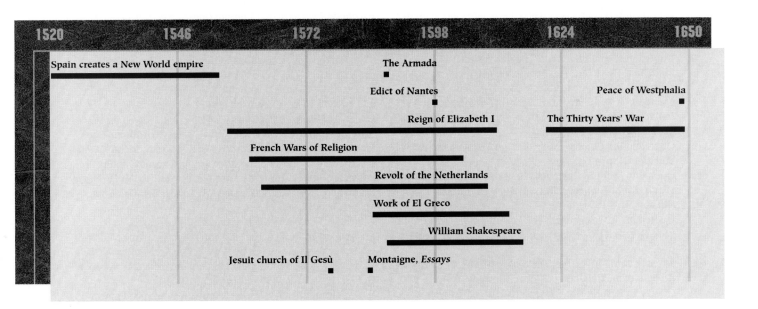

CONCLUSION ❈ ❈ ❈ ❈ ❈ ❈ ❈ ❈ ❈ ❈ ❈

The period from 1560 to 1650 witnessed Europe's attempt to adjust to a whole range of change-laden forces. Population contracted as economic expansion gave way to economic recession. The discovery of new trade routes to the East and the "accidental" discovery of the Americas led Europeans to plunge outside the medieval world in which they had been enclosed for virtually 1,000 years. The conquest of the Americas brought out the worst and some of the best of European civilization. The greedy plundering of resources and the brutal repression, enslavement, and virtual annihilation of millions of Indians were hardly balanced by attempts to create new institutions, convert the natives to Christianity, and foster the rights of the indigenous peoples.

In the sixteenth century, the discoveries made little impact on Europeans preoccupied with the problems of dynastic expansion and, above all, religious division. It took 100 years of religious warfare complicated by serious political, economic and social issues—the worst series of wars and civil wars since the collapse of the Roman Empire in the west—before Europeans finally admitted that they would have to tolerate different ways of worshiping God. That men who were disciples of the Apostle of Peace would kill each other—often in brutal and painful fashion—aroused skepticism about Christianity itself. As one German writer put it in 1650: "Lutheran, popish, and Calvinistic, we've got all these beliefs here; but there is some doubt about where Christianity has got to."[15] It is surely no accident that the search for a stable, secular order of politics and for order in the universe through natural laws played such important roles in the seventeenth century. The religious wars of the sixteenth and seventeenth centuries opened the door to the secular perspectives that have characterized modern Western civilization.

NOTES

1. Quoted in J. R. Hale, *Renaissance Exploration* (New York, 1968), p. 32.
2. Quoted in J. H. Parry, *The Age of Reconnaissance: Discovery, Exploration and Settlement, 1450 to 1650* (New York, 1963), p. 33.
3. Quoted in Richard B. Reed, "The Expansion of Europe," in Richard DeMolen, ed., *The Meaning of the Renaissance and Reformation* (Boston, 1974), p. 308.
4. Quoted in K. N. Chaudhuri, *Trade and Civilization in the Indian Ocean: An Economic History from the Rise of Islam to 1750* (Cambridge, 1985), p. 65.
5. Quoted in Ian Cameron, *Explorers and Exploration* (New York, 1991), p. 42.
6. Quoted in Mary B. Campbell, *The Witness and the Other World: Exotic European Travel Writing, 400–1600* (Ithaca, N.Y., 1991), p. 197.
7. Quoted in G. V. Scammell, *The First Imperial Age: European Overseas Expansion, c. 1400–1715* (London, 1989), p. 62.
8. Miguel Leon-Portilla, ed., *The Broken Spears: The Aztec Account of the Conquest of Mexico* (Boston, 1969), p. 51.
9. Quoted in R. J. Knecht, *The French Wars of Religion, 1559–1598*, 2d ed. (New York, 1996), p. 47.
10. Quoted in Mack P. Holt, *The French Wars of Religion, 1562–1629* (Cambridge, 1995), p. 86.
11. Quoted in Garrett Mattingly, *The Armada* (Boston, 1959), pp. 216–217.
12. Quoted in Alan Kors and Edward Peters, eds., *Witchcraft in Europe, 1100–1700* (Philadelphia, 1972), p. 112.
13. Quoted in Joseph Klaits, *Servants of Satan: The Age of the Witch Hunts* (Bloomington, Ind., 1985), p. 68.
14. *The Complete Essays of Montaigne*, trans. Donald Frame (Stanford, 1958), p. 852.
15. Quoted in Theodore Schieder, *Handbuch der Europäischen Geschichte* (Stuttgart, 1979), 3:579.

SUGGESTIONS FOR FURTHER READING

General works on the period from 1560 to 1650 include C. Wilson, *The Transformation of Europe, 1558–1648* (Berkeley, 1976); and R. Bonney, *The European Dynastic States, 1494–1660* (Oxford, 1991). For an extremely detailed account of all aspects of life in the Mediterranean basin in the second half of the sixteenth century, see F. Braudel, *The Mediterranean and the Mediterranean World in the Age of Philip II*, trans. S. Reynolds, 2 vols. (New York, 1972–73).

The best general accounts of European discovery and expansion are G. V. Scammell, *The First Imperial Age: European Overseas Expansion, c. 1400–1715* (London, 1989); J. H. Parry, *The Age of Reconnaissance: Discovery, Exploration and Settlement, 1450 to 1650* (New York, 1963); and B. Penrose, *Travel and Discovery in the Renaissance, 1420–1620* (New York, 1962). On the medieval background to European expansion, see J. R. S. Phillips, *The Medieval Expansion of Europe* (New York, 1988). On European perceptions of the world outside Europe, see M. Campbell, *The Witness and the Other World: Exotic European Travel Writing, 400–1600* (Ithaca, N.Y., 1991). On Columbus, see the brief biography by J. S. Collis, *Christopher Columbus* (London, 1976); and F. Fernandez-Armesto, *Columbus* (New York, 1991). The impact of expansion on European consciousness is explored in J. H. Elliott, *The Old World and the New, 1492–1650* (Cambridge, 1970). The human and ecological effects of the interaction of New World and Old World cultures are examined thoughtfully in A. W. Crosby, *The Columbian Exchange, Biological and Cultural Consequences of 1492* (Westport, Conn., 1972); and *Ecological Imperialism: The Biological Expansion of Europe* (New York, 1986).

For good introductions to the French Wars of Religion, see M. P. Holt, *The French Wars of Religion, 1562–1629* (Cambridge, 1995); and R. J. Knecht, *The French Wars of Religion, 1559–1598*, 2d ed. (New York, 1996). Also valuable is B. B. Diefendorf, *Beneath the Cross: Catholics and Huguenots in Sixteenth-Century Paris* (New York, 1991). On Catherine de' Medici, see R. J. Knecht, *Catherine de' Medici* (London, 1998).

Two good histories of Spain in the sixteenth century are J. Lynch, *Spain, 1516–1598: From Nation-State to World Empire* (Cambridge, Mass., 1994); and A. W. Lovett, *Early Habsburg Spain* (Oxford, 1986). The best biographies of Philip II are P. Pierson, *Philip II of Spain* (London, 1975); and G. Parker, *Philip II*, 3d ed. (Chicago, 1995). On the revolt of the Netherlands, see the classic work by P. Geyl, *The Revolt of the Netherlands, 1555–1609* (London, 1962); and the more recent work of G. Parker, *The Dutch Revolt* (London, 1977).

Elizabeth's reign can be examined in two good biographies, C. Haigh, *Elizabeth I*, 2d ed. (New York, 1998); and W. T. MacCaffrey, *Elizabeth I* (London, 1993). The classic work on the Armada is the beautifully written *The Armada* by G. Mattingly (Boston, 1959).

The classic study on the Thirty Years' War is C. V. Wedgwood, *The Thirty Years' War* (Garden City, N.Y., 1961), but it needs to be supplemented by the more recent works by G. Parker, ed, *The Thirty Years' War*, 2d ed. (London, 1997); R. G. Asch, *The Thirty Years' War: The Holy Roman Empire and Europe, 1618–1648* (New York, 1997); and the brief study by S. J. Lee, *The Thirty Years' War* (London, 1991). On Gustavus Adolphus, see M. Roberts, *Gustavus Adolphus and the Rise of Sweden* (London, 1973).

The story of the witchcraft craze can be examined in three recent works, J. Klaits, *Servants of Satan: The Age of the Witch Hunts* (Bloomington, Ind., 1985); J. B. Russell, *A History of Witchcraft* (London, 1980); and B. P. Levack, *The Witch-Hunt in Early Modern Europe* (London, 1987).

For a brief, readable guide to Mannerism, see L. Murray, *The Late Renaissance and Mannerism* (New York, 1967). For a general survey of Baroque culture, see M. and L. Mainstone, *The Cambridge Introduction to Art: The Seventeenth Century* (Cambridge, 1981); and J. S. Held, *Seventeenth and Eighteenth Century Art: Baroque Painting, Sculpture, Architecture* (New York, 1971). The best biography of Montaigne remains D. M. Frame, *Montaigne: A Biography* (New York, 1965). On the Spanish golden century of literature, see R. O. Jones, *The Golden Age: Prose and Poetry*, which is volume 2 of *The Literary History of Spain* (London, 1971). The literature on Shakespeare is enormous. For a biography, see A. L. Rowse, *The Life of Shakespeare* (New York, 1963).

For additional reading, go to InfoTrac College Edition, your online research library at http://web1.infotrac-college.com

Enter the search terms *Vasco da Gama* using Key Terms.

Enter the search terms *Christopher Columbus* using the Subject Guide.

Enter the search terms *Thirty Years' War* using Key Terms.

Enter the search terms *Elizabeth I* using Key Terms.

CHAPTER

15

Response to Crisis: State Building and the Search for Order in the Seventeenth Century

FOCUS QUESTIONS

- What theories of government were proposed by Jacques Bossuet, Thomas Hobbes, and John Locke, and how did their respective theories reflect concerns and problems of the seventeenth century?
- What was absolutism in theory, and how did its actual practice in France reflect or differ from the theory?
- What developments enabled Brandenburg-Prussia, Austria, and Russia to emerge as major powers in the seventeenth century?
- What were the main issues in the struggle between king and Parliament in seventeenth-century England, and how were they resolved?
- What role did the Netherlands play in the political, economic, and artistic life of the seventeenth century?

*T*HE AGE OF CRISIS *from 1560 to 1650 was accompanied by a decline in religious orientation and a growing secularization that affected both the political and the intellectual worlds of Europe (on the intellectual effect, see the Scientific Revolution in Chapter 16). Some historians like to speak of the seventeenth century as a turning point in the evolution of a modern state system in Europe. The idea of a united Christian Europe (the practice of a united Christendom had actually been moribund for some time) gave way to the practical realities of a system of secular states in which reason of state took precedence over the salvation of subjects' souls. Of course, these states had emerged and begun their development during the Middle Ages, but medieval ideas about statehood had still been couched in religious terms. By the seventeenth century, the credibility of Christianity had been so weakened in* the religious wars that more and more Europeans could think of politics in secular terms.

One of the responses to the crises of the seventeenth century was a search for order. As the internal social and political rebellions and revolts died down, it became apparent that the privileged classes of society—the aristocrats—remained in control, although the various states exhibited important differences in political forms. The most general trend saw an extension of monarchical power as a stabilizing force. This development, which historians have called absolutism or absolute monarchy, was most evident in France during the flamboyant reign of Louis XIV, regarded by some as the perfect embodiment of an absolute monarch. In his memoirs, the duc de Saint-Simon, who had firsthand experience of French court life, said that Louis was "the very figure of a hero, so imbued with a natural but most imposing majesty that it appeared even in his most insignificant gestures and movements." The king's natural grace gave him a special charm as well: "He was as dignified and majestic in his dressing gown as when dressed in robes of state, or on horseback at the head of his troops." He spoke well and learned quickly. He was naturally kind and "he loved truth, justice, order, and reason." His life was orderly: "Nothing could be regulated with greater exactitude than were his days and hours." His self-control was impeccable: "He did not lose control of himself ten times in his whole life, and then only with inferior persons." But even absolute monarchs had imperfections, and Saint-Simon had the courage to point them out: "Louis XIV's vanity was without limit or restraint," which led to his "distaste for all merit, intelligence, education, and, most of all, for all independence of character and sentiment in others," as well as "to mistakes of judgment in matters of importance."

But absolutism was not the only response to crisis in the seventeenth century. Other states, such as England, reacted differently to domestic crisis, and another very different system emerged where monarchs were limited by the power of their representative assemblies. Absolute and limited monarchy were the two poles of seventeenth-century state building.

◆ The Theory of Absolutism

Absolute monarchy or absolutism meant that the sovereign power or ultimate authority in the state rested in the hands of a king who claimed to rule by divine right. But what did sovereignty mean? The late sixteenth-century political theorist Jean Bodin believed that sovereign power consisted of the authority to make laws, tax, administer justice, control the state's administrative system, and determine foreign policy. These powers made a ruler sovereign.

One of the chief theorists of divine-right monarchy in the seventeenth century was the French theologian and court preacher Bishop Jacques Bossuet (1627–1704), who expressed his ideas in a book entitled *Politics Drawn from the Very Words of Holy Scripture*. Bossuet argued first that government was divinely ordained so that humans could live in an organized society. God established kings and through them reigned over all the peoples of the world. Since kings received their power from God, their authority was absolute. They were responsible to no one (including parliaments) except God. Nevertheless, Bossuet cautioned, although a king's authority was absolute, his power was not since he was limited by the law of God. Bossuet believed there was a difference between absolute monarchy and arbitrary monarchy. The latter contradicted the rule of law and the sanctity of property and was simply lawless tyranny. Bossuet's distinction between absolute and arbitrary government was not always easy to maintain. There was also a large gulf between the theory of absolutism as expressed by Bossuet and the practice of absolutism. As we shall see in our survey of seventeenth-century states, a monarch's absolute power was often limited greatly by practical realities.

◆ Absolutism in Western Europe

An examination of seventeenth-century absolutism must begin with western Europe since France during the reign of Louis XIV (1643–1715) has traditionally been regarded as the best example of the practice of absolute monarchy in the seventeenth century.

❊ *France and Absolute Monarchy*

By the end of the seventeenth century, France had come to play a dominant role in European affairs. French culture, language, and manners influenced all levels of European society. French diplomacy and wars shaped the political affairs of western and central Europe. The court of Louis XIV seemed to be imitated everywhere in Europe. Of course, the stability of Louis's reign was magnified by the instability that had preceded it.

❦ FOUNDATIONS OF FRENCH ABSOLUTISM
The history of France before the reign of Louis XIV was hardly the story of steady, unbroken progress toward the ideal of absolute monarchy that many historians have tended to portray. During the fifty years or so before Louis, royal and ministerial governments had to struggle to avoid the breakdown of the state. The line between order and anarchy was often a narrow one. The situation was especially complicated by the fact that both Louis XIII (1610–1643) and Louis XIV were only boys when they succeeded to the throne in 1610 and 1643, respectively,

CARDINAL RICHELIEU. A key figure in the emergence of a strong monarchy in France was Cardinal Richelieu, pictured here in a portrait by Philippe de Champagne. Chief minister to Louis XIII, Richelieu strengthened royal authority by eliminating the private armies and fortified cities of the Huguenots and by crushing aristocratic conspiracies.

leaving the government dependent on royal ministers. Two especially competent ministers played crucial roles in maintaining monarchical authority.

Cardinal Richelieu, Louis XIII's chief minister from 1624 to 1642, initiated policies that eventually strengthened the power of the monarchy. By eliminating the political and military rights of the Huguenots while preserving their religious ones, Richelieu transformed the Huguenots into more reliable subjects. Richelieu acted more cautiously in "humbling the pride of the great men," the important French nobility. He understood the influential role played by the nobles in the French state. The dangerous ones were those who asserted their territorial independence when they were excluded from participating in the central government. Proceeding slowly but determinedly, Richelieu developed an efficient network of spies to uncover noble plots and then crushed the conspiracies and executed the conspirators, thereby eliminating a major threat to royal authority.

To reform and strengthen the central administration, initially for financial reasons, Richelieu sent out royal officials called intendants to the provinces to execute the orders of the central government. As the functions of the intendants grew, they came into conflict with provincial governors. Since the intendants were victorious in most of these disputes, they further strengthened the power of the crown. Richelieu proved less capable in financial matters, however. Not only was the basic system of state finances corrupt, but so many people benefited from the system's inefficiency and injustice that the government faced strong resistance when it tried to reform it. The *taille* (an annual direct tax usually levied on land or property) was increased—in 1643 it was two and a half times what it had been in 1610—and crown lands were mortgaged again. Expenditures, especially the cost of war preparations, soon outstripped the additional revenues, however, and French debt continued its upward spiral under Richelieu.

The general success of Richelieu's domestic policy in strengthening the central role of the monarchy was mirrored by a successful foreign policy. That policy was dictated, first of all, by opposition to Spain, which led in turn to further anti-Habsburg activity in the Holy Roman Empire to France's east. Eventually, the Catholic cardinal of France came to subsidize Protestant Sweden and then in 1635 to intervene directly with French troops to support the Protestant cause against the Habsburgs (see Chapter 14). Although both Richelieu and Louis XIII died before the Thirty Years' War ended, French policy had proved successful at one level as France emerged as Europe's leading power by 1648.

Richelieu died in 1642, followed five months later by King Louis XIII, who was succeeded by his son Louis XIV, then but four years old. This necessitated a regency under Anne of Austria, wife of the dead king. But she allowed Cardinal Mazarin, Richelieu's trained successor, to dominate the government. An Italian who had come to France as a papal legate and then become naturalized, Mazarin attempted to carry on Richelieu's policies until his death in 1661.

The most important event during Mazarin's rule was a revolt known as the Fronde, which can be viewed as the last serious attempt to limit the growing power of the crown until the French Revolution. As a foreigner, Mazarin was greatly disliked by all elements of the French population. The nobles, who particularly resented the centralized administrative power being built up at the expense of the provincial nobility, temporarily allied with the members of the Parlement of Paris, who opposed the new taxes levied by the government to pay the costs of the Thirty Years' War, and with the masses of Paris, who were also angry at the additional taxes. The Parlement of Paris was the most important court in France with jurisdiction over half of the kingdom, and its members formed the nobles of the robe, the service nobility of lawyers and administrators. These nobles of the robe led the first Fronde (1648–1649), which broke out in Paris and was ended by compromise. The second Fronde, begun in 1650, was led by the nobles of the sword, whose ancestors were medieval nobles. They were interested in overthrowing Mazarin for their own purposes: to secure their positions and increase their own

Louis XIV: Kingly Advice

Throughout his reign, Louis XIV was always on stage, acting the role of the wise "Grand Monarch." In 1661, after he became a father, Louis began his Memoirs for the Dauphin, *a frank collection of precepts for the education of his oldest son and heir to the throne. He continued to add to these* Memoirs *over the next twenty years.*

✸ Louis XIV, *Memoirs for the Dauphin*

Kings are often obliged to do things which go against their inclinations and offend their natural goodness. They should love to give pleasure and yet they must often punish and destroy persons on whom by nature they wish to confer benefits. The interest of the state must come first. One must constrain one's inclinations and not put oneself in the position of berating oneself because one could have done better in some important affair but did not because of some private interest, because one was distracted from the attention one should have for the greatness, the good and the power of the state. Often there are troublesome places where it is difficult to make out what one should do. One's ideas are confused. As long as this lasts, one can refrain from making a decision. But as soon as one has fixed one's mind upon something which seems best to do, it must be acted upon. This is what enabled me to succeed so often in what I have done. The mistakes which I made, and which gave me infinite trouble, were the result of the desire to please or of allowing myself to accept too carelessly the opinions of others. Nothing is more dan-gerous than weakness of any kind whatsoever. In order to command others, one must raise oneself above them and once one has heard the reports from every side one must come to a decision upon the basis of one's own judgment, without anxiety but always with the concern not to command anything which is of itself unworthy either of one's place in the world or of the greatness of the state. Princes with good intentions and some knowledge of their affairs, either from experience or from study and great diligence in making themselves capable, find numerous cases which instruct them that they must give special care and total application to everything. One must be on guard against oneself, resist one's own tendencies, and always be on guard against one's own natural bent. The craft of a king is great, noble and delightful when one feels worthy of doing well whatever one promises to do. But it is not exempt from troubles, weariness and worries. Sometimes uncertainty causes despair, and when one has spent a reasonable time in examining an affair, one must make a decision and take the step which one believes to be best. When one has the state in view, one works for one's self. The good of the one constitutes the glory of the other. When the former is fortunate, eminent and powerful, he who is the cause thereof becomes glorious and consequently should find more enjoyment than his subjects in all the pleasant things of life for himself and for them. When one has made a mistake, it must be corrected as soon as possible, and no other consideration must stand in the way, not even kindness.

---

power. The second Fronde was crushed by 1652, a task made easier when the nobles began fighting each other instead of Mazarin. With the end of the Fronde, the vast majority of the French concluded that the best hope for stability in France lay in the crown. When Mazarin died in 1661, the greatest of the seventeenth-century monarchs, Louis XIV, took over supreme power.

⚜ THE REIGN OF LOUIS XIV (1643–1715)

The day after Cardinal Mazarin's death, Louis XIV, at the age of twenty-three, expressed his determination to be a real king and the sole ruler of France:

> Up to this moment I have been pleased to entrust the government of my affairs to the late Cardinal. It is now time that I govern them myself. You [secretaries and ministers of state] will assist me with your counsels when I ask for them. I request and order you to seal no orders except by my command, . . . I order you not to sign anything, not even a passport . . . without my command; to render account to me personally each day and to favor no one.[1]

His mother, who was well aware of Louis's proclivity for fun and games and getting into the beds of the maids in the royal palace, laughed aloud at these words. But Louis was quite serious.

Louis proved willing to pay the price of being a strong ruler (see the box above). He established a conscientious routine from which he seldom deviated, but he did not look upon his duties as drudgery since he judged his royal profession to be "grand, noble, and delightful." Eager for glory (in the French sense of achieving what was expected of one in an important position), Louis created a grand and majestic spectacle at the court of Versailles (see Daily Life at the Court of Versailles later in this chapter). Consequently, Louis and his court came to set the standard for monarchies and aristocracies all over Europe. Less than fifty years after his death, the great French writer Voltaire selected the title "Age of Louis XIV" for his history of Europe from 1661 to 1715. Historians have tended to use it ever since.

Although Louis may have believed in the theory of absolute monarchy and consciously fostered the myth of himself as the Sun King, the source of light for all of his people, historians are quick to point out that the realities fell far short of the aspirations. Despite the centralizing

---

LOUIS XIV. Louis XIV was determined to be the sole ruler of France. Louis eliminated the threat of the high nobility by removing them from the royal council and replacing them with relatively new aristocrats whom he could dominate. This portrait by Hyacinth Rigaud captures the king's sense of royal dignity and grandeur.

jostled for power. The greatest danger to Louis's personal rule came from the very high nobles and princes of the blood (the royal princes) who considered it their natural function to assert the policy-making role of royal ministers. Louis eliminated this threat by removing them from the royal council, the chief administrative body of the king and overseer of the central machinery of government, and enticing them to his court where he could keep them preoccupied with court life and out of politics.

Instead of the high nobility and royal princes, Louis relied for his ministers on nobles who came from relatively new aristocratic families. Such were François Michel Le Tellier, secretary of state for war; Hugues de Lionne, secretary for foreign affairs; and Nicholas Fouquet, superintendent of finances. His ministers were expected to be subservient; said Louis, "I had no intention of sharing my authority with them." When Fouquet began to flaunt the enormous wealth and power he had amassed in the king's service, Louis ordered his arrest and imprisoned him for life. Fouquet was replaced in the king's council by Jean-Baptiste Colbert (1619–1683), another noble of bourgeois origin. Louis's domination of his ministers and secretaries gave him control of the central policy-making machinery of government and thus authority over the traditional areas of monarchical power: the formulation of foreign policy, the making of war and peace, the assertion of the secular power of crown against any religious authority, and the ability to levy taxes to fulfill these functions.

Louis had considerably less success with the internal administration of the kingdom. The traditional groups and institutions of French society—the nobles, officials, town councils, guilds, and representative Estates in some provinces—were simply too powerful for the king to have direct control over the lives of his subjects. Louis had three ways of ruling the provinces. Officially, he worked through hereditary officeholders, usually aristocrats, who were untrustworthy since they were always inclined to balance the king's wishes against their own interests. The king also had his intendants as direct royal agents, but they, too, proved unreliable and their actions often provoked disturbances in the provinces. The intendants were not so much the instruments by which the central government carried out decisions, but simply the "eyes and ears of the ministers" in the provinces. Finally, the king had an informal system of royal patronage, which Louis used successfully. The king and his ministers enlisted the aid of nobles and senior churchmen and their clients by granting them offices and pensions. Thus, the central government exercised its control over the provinces and the people by carefully bribing the important people to ensure that the king's policies were executed. Nevertheless, local officials could still obstruct the execution of policies they disliked, indicating clearly that a so-called absolute monarch was not always that absolute.

The maintenance of religious harmony had long been considered an area of monarchical power. The desire to keep it led Louis into conflict with the French Huguenots. Louis XIV did not want to allow Protestants

efforts of Cardinals Richelieu and Mazarin, seventeenth-century France still possessed a bewildering system of overlapping authorities. Provinces had their own regional parlements, their own local Estates, their own sets of laws. Members of the high nobility with their huge estates and clients among the lesser nobility still exercised much authority. Both towns and provinces possessed privileges and powers seemingly from time immemorial that they would not easily relinquish. Much of Louis's success rested less on the modernization of administrative machinery, as is frequently claimed, than on his clever and adroit manipulation of the traditional priorities and values of French society.

One of the keys to Louis's power was that he was able to restructure the central policy-making machinery of government because it was part of his own court and household. The royal court was an elaborate structure that served three purposes simultaneously: it was the personal household of the king, the location of central governmental machinery, and the place where powerful subjects came to find favors and offices for themselves and their clients as well as the main arena where rival aristocratic factions

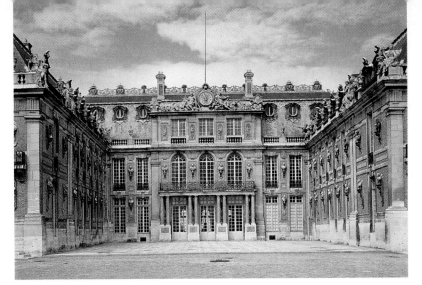

PALACE OF VERSAILLES. Louis XIV spent untold sums of money in the construction of a new royal residence at Versailles. The enormous palace of Versailles also housed the members of the king's government and served as home for thousands of French nobles. As the largest royal residence in Europe, Versailles impressed foreigners and became a source of envy for other rulers.

to practice their faith in largely Catholic France. Perhaps he was motivated by religion, but it is more likely that Louis, who believed in the motto, "one king, one law, one faith," felt that the existence of this minority undermined his own political authority. His anti-Protestant policy, aimed at converting the Huguenots to Catholicism, began mildly by offering rewards, but escalated by 1681 to a policy of forced conversions. The most favored method was to quarter French soldiers in Huguenot communities and homes with the freedom to misbehave so that their hosts would "see the light quickly." This approach did produce thousands of immediate conversions. In October 1685, Louis issued the Edict of Fontainebleau. In addition to revoking the Edict of Nantes, the new edict provided for the destruction of Huguenot churches and the closing of their schools. Although they were forbidden to leave France, it is estimated that 200,000 Huguenots left for shelter in England, the United Provinces, and the German states. Through their exodus, France lost people who had commercial and industrial skills, although some modern scholars have argued that their departure had only a minor impact on the French economy.

The cost of building Versailles and other palaces, maintaining his court, and pursuing his wars made finances a crucial issue for Louis XIV. He was most fortunate in having the services of Colbert as controller-general of finances. Colbert sought to increase the wealth and power of France through general adherence to that loose collection of economic policies called mercantilism, which stressed government regulation of economic activities to benefit the state (see Mercantilism later in this chapter). To decrease the need for imports and increase exports, Colbert attempted to expand the quantity and improve the quality of French manufactured goods. He founded new luxury industries, such as the royal tapestry works at Beauvais; invited Venetian glassmakers and Flemish clothmakers to France; drew up instructions regulating the quality of goods produced; oversaw the training of workers; and granted special privileges, including tax exemptions, loans, and subsidies, to those who established new industries. To improve communications and the transportation of goods internally, he built roads and canals. To decrease imports directly, he raised tariffs on foreign manufactured goods, especially English and Dutch cloth, and created a merchant marine to facilitate the conveyance of French goods.

Although Colbert's policies are given much credit for fostering the development of manufacturing, some historians are dubious about the usefulness of many of his mercantilistic policies. Regulations were often evaded, and the imposition of high tariffs brought foreign retaliation. French trading companies entered the scene too late to be really competitive with the English and the Dutch. And above all, Colbert's economic policies, which were geared to making his king more powerful, were ultimately self-defeating. The more revenue Colbert collected to enable the king to make war, the faster Louis depleted the treasury. At the same time, the burden of taxes fell increasingly upon the peasants who still constituted the overwhelming majority of the French population.

DAILY LIFE AT THE COURT OF VERSAILLES

The court of Louis XIV at Versailles set a standard that was soon followed by other European rulers. In 1660, Louis, who disliked Paris as a result of his humiliating experiences at the hands of Parisian mobs during the Fronde, decided to convert a hunting lodge at Versailles, located near Paris, into a chateau. Not until 1688, after untold sums of money had been spent and tens of thousands of workers had labored incessantly, was most of the construction completed on the enormous palace that housed thousands of people.

Versailles served many purposes. It was the residence of the king, a reception hall for state affairs, an office building for the members of the king's government, and the home of thousands of royal officials and aristocratic courtiers. Versailles became a symbol for the French absolutist state and the power of the Sun King, Louis XIV. As a visible manifestation of France's superiority and wealth, this lavish court was intended to overawe subjects and impress foreign powers. If an age's largest buildings reflect its values, then Versailles is a reminder of the seventeenth-century preoccupation with monarchical authority and magnificence.

Travels with the King

The duc de Saint-Simon was one of many noble courtiers who lived at Versailles and had firsthand experience of court life there. In this Memoirs, he left a controversial and critical account of Louis XIV and his court. In this selection, Saint-Simon describes the price court ladies paid for the "privilege" of riding with the great king.

❈ Duc de Saint-Simon, *Memoirs*

The King always traveled with his carriage full of women: His mistresses, his bastard daughters, his daughters-in-law, sometimes Madame [the wife of the king's brother], and the other ladies of the court when there was room. This was the case for hunts, and trips to Fontainebleau, Chantilly, Compiégne, and the like. . . . In his carriage during these trips there was always an abundance and variety of things to eat: meats, pastries, and fruit. Before the carriage had gone a quarter league the King would ask who was hungry. He never ate between meals, not even a fruit, but he enjoyed watching others stuff themselves. It was mandatory to eat, with appetite and good grace, and to be gay; otherwise; he showed his displea-sure by telling the guilty party she was putting on airs and trying to be coy. The same ladies or princesses who had eaten that day at the King's table were obliged to eat again as though they were weak from hunger. What is more, the women were forbidden to mention their personal needs, which in any case they could not have relieved without embarrassment, since there were guards and members of the King's household in front and in back of the carriage, and officers and equerries riding alongside the doors. The dust they kicked up choked everyone in the carriage, but the King, who loved fresh air, insisted that all the windows remain open. He would have been extremely displeased if one of the ladies had pulled a curtain to protect herself from the sun, the wind, or the cold.

He pretended not to notice his passengers' discomfort, and always traveled very fast, with the usual number of relays. Sickness in the carriage was a demerit which ruled out further invitations. . . . When the king had to relieve himself he did not hesitate to stop the carriage and get out; but the ladies were not allowed to budge.

Versailles also served a practical political purpose. It became home to the high nobility and princes of the blood (the royal princes), those powerful figures who had aspired to hold the policy-making role of royal ministers. By keeping them involved in the myriad activities that made up daily life at the court of Versailles, Louis excluded them from real power while allowing them to share in the mystique of power as companions of the king.

Life at Versailles became a court ceremony with Louis XIV at the center of it all. The king had little privacy; only when he visited his wife or mother or mistress or met with ministers was he free of the noble courtiers who swarmed about the palace. Most daily ceremonies were carefully staged, such as those attending Louis's rising from bed, dining, praying, attending mass, and going to bed. A mob of nobles aspired to assist the king in carrying out these solemn activities. It was considered a great honor for a noble to be chosen to hand the king his shirt while dressing. But why did nobles participate in so many ceremonies, some of which were so obviously demeaning? Active involvement in the activities at Versailles was the king's prerequisite for obtaining the offices, titles, and pensions that only he could grant. This policy reduced great nobles and ecclesiastics, the "people of quality," to a plane of equality, allowing Louis to exercise control over them and prevent them from interfering in the real lines of power. To maintain their social prestige, the "people of quality" were expected to adhere to rigid standards of court etiquette appropriate to their rank.

Indeed, court etiquette became a complex matter. Nobles and royal princes were arranged in an elaborate order of seniority and expected to follow certain rules of precedence. Who could sit down and on what kind of chair was a subject of much debate. When Philip of Orleans, the king's brother, and his wife Charlotte sought to visit their daughter, the duchess of Lorraine, they encountered problems with Louis. Charlotte told why in one of her letters:

> The difficulty is that the Duke of Lorraine claims that he is entitled to sit in an armchair in the presence of Philip and myself because the Emperor gives him an armchair. To this the King [Louis] replied that the Emperor's ceremonial is one thing and the King's another, and that, for example, the Emperor gives the cardinals armchairs, whereas here they may never sit at all in the King's presence.[2]

Louis refused to compromise; the Duke of Lorraine was only entitled to a stool. The duke refused, and Philip and Charlotte canceled their visit.

Who could sit where at meals with the king was also carefully regulated. On one occasion, when the wife of a minister sat closer to the king than a duchess at dinner, Louis XIV became so angry that he did not eat for the rest of the evening. Another time, Louis reproached his talkative brother for the sin of helping himself to a dish before Louis had touched it with the biting words: "I perceive that you are no better able to control your hands than your tongue."[3]

Besides the daily and occasional ceremonies that made up the regular side of court life at Versailles and the many hours a day Louis spent with his ministers on affairs of state, daily life at Versailles included numerous forms of entertainment. While he was healthy, Louis and his courtiers hunted at least once a week; members of the royal family nearly every day. Walks through the Versailles gardens, boating trips, performances of tragedies and comedies, ballets, and concerts all provided sources of pleasure (see the box on p. 432). Three evenings a week, from seven to ten, Louis also held an *appartement* where he was at "home" to his court. The *appartement* was characterized by a formal informality. Relaxed rules of etiquette even allowed people to sit down in the presence of their superiors. The evening's entertainment began with a concert, followed by games of billiards or cards, and ended with a sumptuous buffet.

One form of entertainment—gambling—became an obsession at Versailles. Although a few of the courtiers made a living by their gambling skill, many others were simply amateurs. This did not stop them from playing regularly and losing enormous sums of money. One princess described the scene: "Here in France as soon as people get together they do nothing but play [cards]; they play for frightful sums, and the players seem bereft of their senses. . . . One shouts at the top of his voice, another strikes the table with his fist, a third blasphemes. . . . it is horrible to watch them."[4] Louis did not share the princess's sensibilities; he was not horrified by an activity that kept the Versailles nobles busy and out of mischief.

THE WARS OF LOUIS XIV

The increase in royal power that Louis pursued as well as his desire for military glory led the king to develop a standing army subject to the monarch's command. In itself, the standing army was neither new nor a product of absolute monarchy—the first real standing armies had been organized earlier by Venice and the United Provinces. But French resources enabled Louis to develop the largest standing army that Europe had yet seen.

Under the secretary of war, François Michel Le Tellier, the marquis of Louvois, France developed a professional army numbering 100,000 men in peacetime and 400,000 in time of war. Unable to fill the ranks with volunteers, the French resorted to conscription, a practice that led to other problems as unwilling soldiers were eager to desert. But the new standing armies did not exist to be admired. Louis and other monarchs used them to make war an almost incessant activity of the seventeenth and eighteenth centuries.

Louis XIV had a great proclivity for war. Historians have debated the assertion that Louis pursued war to expand his kingdom to its "natural frontiers"—the Alps, Pyrenees, and Rhine River. But few doubt his desire to achieve the prestige and military glory befitting a Sun King as well as his dynastic ambition, his desire to ensure the domination of his Bourbon dynasty over European affairs. His ends soon outstripped his means, however, as his ambitions roused much of Europe to form coalitions that even he could not overcome.

In 1667, Louis began his first war by invading the Spanish Netherlands to his north and Franche-Comté to the east. But a Triple Alliance of the Dutch, English, and

INTERIOR OF VERSAILLES: HALL OF MIRRORS. Pictured here is the exquisite Hall of Mirrors at Versailles. A number of daily and occasional ceremonies dominated the lives of the residents of Versailles. Rules of etiquette became so complex that they guided virtually every aspect of behavior.

Swedes forced Louis to sue for peace in 1668 and accept a few towns in the Spanish Netherlands for his efforts. He never forgave the Dutch for arranging the Triple Alliance, and in 1672, after isolating the Dutch, France invaded the United Provinces with some initial success. But the French victories led Brandenburg, Spain, and the Holy Roman Emperor to form a new coalition that forced Louis to end the Dutch War by making peace at Nimwegen in 1678. While Dutch territory remained intact, France received Franche-Comté from Spain, which served merely to stimulate Louis's appetite for even more land.

This time, Louis moved eastward against the Holy Roman Empire, which he perceived from his previous war as feeble and unable to resist. The gradual annexation of the provinces of Alsace and Lorraine was followed by the occupation of the city of Strasbourg, a move that led to widespread protest and the formation of a new coalition. The creation of this League of Augsburg, consisting of Spain, the Holy Roman Emperor, the United Provinces, Sweden, and England, led to Louis's third war, the War of the League of Augsburg (1689–1697). This bitterly contested eight-year struggle brought economic depression and famine to France. The Treaty of Ryswick ending the war forced Louis to give up most of his conquests in the empire, although he was allowed to keep Strasbourg and part of Alsace. The gains were hardly worth the bloodshed and misery he had caused the French people.

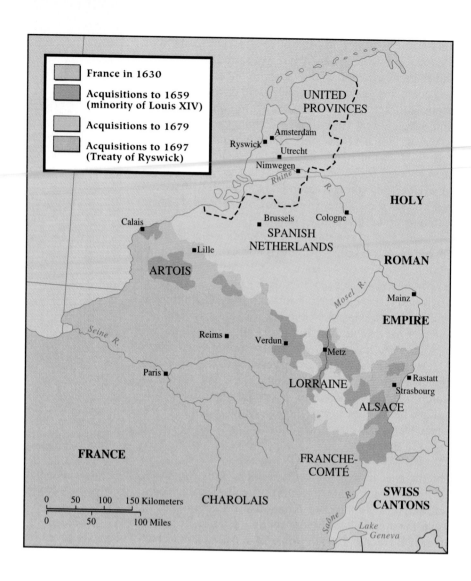

France in 1630

Acquisitions to 1659 (minority of Louis XIV)

Acquisitions to 1679

Acquisitions to 1697 (Treaty of Ryswick)

MAP 15.1 **The Wars of Louis XIV.**

Louis's fourth war, the War of the Spanish Succession (1702–1713), was over bigger stakes, the succession to the Spanish throne. Charles II, the sickly and childless Habsburg ruler, left the throne of Spain in his will to a grandson of Louis XIV. When the latter became King Philip V of Spain after Charles's death, the suspicion that Spain and France would eventually be united in the same dynastic family caused the formation of a new coalition, determined to prevent a Bourbon hegemony that would mean the certain destruction of the European balance of power. This coalition of England, Holland, Habsburg Austria, and German states opposed France and Spain in a war that dragged on in Europe and the colonial empires in North America from 1702 to 1713. In a number of battles, including the memorable defeat of the French forces at Blenheim in 1704 by allied troops led by the English commander, John Churchill, duke of Marlborough, the coalition wore down Louis's forces. An end to the war finally came with the Peaces of Utrecht in 1713 and Rastatt in 1714. Although these peace treaties confirmed Philip V as the Spanish ruler, initiating a Spanish Bourbon dynasty that would last into the twentieth century, they also affirmed that the thrones of Spain and France were to remain separated. The Span-

ish Netherlands, Milan, and Naples were given to Austria, and the newly emerging Brandenburg-Prussia gained additional territories. The real winner at Utrecht, however, was England, which received Gibraltar as well as the French possessions in America of Newfoundland, Hudson's Bay Territory, and Nova Scotia. Though France, by its sheer size and position, remained a great power, England had emerged as a formidable naval power.

Only two years after the treaty, the Sun King was dead, leaving France impoverished and surrounded by enemies. On his deathbed, the seventy-six-year-old monarch seemed remorseful when he told his successor:

> Soon you will be King of a great kingdom. I urge you not to forget your duty to God; remember that you owe everything to Him. Try to remain at peace with your neighbors. I loved war too much. Do not follow me in that or in overspending. Take advice in everything; try to find the best course and follow it. Lighten your people's burden as soon as possible, and do what I have had the misfortune not to do myself.[5]

Did Louis mean it? Did Louis ever realize how tarnished the glory he had sought had become? One of his subjects wrote ten years before the end of his reign: "Even the people . . . who have so much loved you, and have placed such trust in you, begin to lose their love, their trust, and even their respect. . . . They believe you have no pity for their sorrows, that you are devoted only to your power and your glory."[6] In any event, the advice to his successor was probably not remembered; his great-grandson was only five years old.

❋ The Decline of Spain

At the beginning of the seventeenth century, Spain possessed the most populous empire in the world, controlling almost all of South America and a number of settlements in Asia and Africa. To most Europeans, Spain still seemed the greatest power of the age, but the reality was quite different. The rich provinces of the Netherlands were lost. The treasury was empty; Philip II went bankrupt in 1596 from excessive expenditures on the Armada while his successor Philip III did the same in 1607 by spending a fortune on his court. The armed forces were out-of-date; the government inefficient; and the commercial class weak in the midst of a suppressed peasantry, a luxury-loving class of nobles, and an oversupply of priests and monks. Spain continued to play the role of a great power, but appearances were deceiving.

During the reign of Philip III (1598–1621), many of Spain's weaknesses became only too apparent. Interested only in court luxury or miracle-working relics, Philip III allowed his first minister, the greedy duke of Lerma, to run the country. The aristocratic Lerma's primary interest was accumulating power and wealth for himself and his family. While important offices were filled with his relatives, crucial problems went unsolved. His most drastic decision was to expel all remaining Moriscos (see Chapter 12) from Spain, a spectacular blunder in view of their importance to Spain's economy. During Lerma's misrule, the gap between privileged and unprivileged grew wider. Notably absent was a prosperous urban middle class, as an astute public official observed in 1600. Spain, he said, had come "to be an extreme contrast of rich and poor, . . . we have rich who loll at ease, or poor who beg, and we lack people of the middling sort, whom neither wealth nor poverty prevents from pursuing the rightful kind of business enjoined by natural law."[7] An apparent factor in this imbalance was the dominant role played by the Catholic church. While maintaining strict orthodoxy by efficient inquisitorial courts, the church prospered and attracted ever-larger numbers of clerics to its ranks. The Castilian Cortes (parliament) was informed in 1626 that Castile alone possessed 9,000 monasteries for men. The existence of so many official celibates offered little help to Spain's declining economy or its declining population.

At first, the reign of Philip IV (1621–1665) seemed to offer hope for a revival of Spain's energies, especially in the capable hands of his chief minister, Gaspar de Guzman, the count of Olivares. This clever, hard-working, and power-hungry statesman dominated the king's every move and worked to revive the interests of the monarchy. A flurry of domestic reform decrees, aimed at curtailing the power of

CHRONOLOGY

Absolutism in Western Europe

France	
Henry IV	1589–1610
Louis XIII	1610–1643
Cardinal Richelieu as chief minister	1624–1642
Ministry of Cardinal Mazarin	1642–1661
First Fronde	1648–1649
Second Fronde	1650–1652
Louis XIV	1643–1715
First war (vs. Triple Alliance)	1667–1668
Dutch War	1672–1678
Edict of Fontainebleau	1685
War of the League of Augsburg	1689–1697
War of the Spanish Succession	1702–1713
Spain	
Philip III	1598–1621
Philip IV	1621–1665
Revolts in Catalonia and Portugal	1640
Revolt in Naples	1647
Charles II	1665–1700

the church and the landed aristocracy, was soon followed by a political reform program whose purpose was to further centralize the government of all Spain and its possessions in monarchical hands. All of these efforts met with little real success, however, since both the number (estimated at one-fifth of the population) and power of the Spanish aristocrats made them too strong to curtail in any significant fashion. At the same time, most of the efforts of Olivares and Philip were undermined by their desire to pursue Spain's imperial glory and by a series of internal revolts.

During the 1620s, 1630s, and 1640s, Spain's involvement in the Thirty Years' War led to a series of frightfully expensive military campaigns that intensified the economic misery of the overtaxed Spanish subjects. Unfortunately for Spain, the campaigns also failed to produce victory. As Olivares wrote to King Philip IV, "God wants us to make peace; for He is depriving us visibly and absolutely of all the means of war."[8] At the same time, increasingly heavy financial exactions to fight the wars led to internal revolts, first in Catalonia, the northeastern province, in 1640, then in the same year in Portugal, which had been joined to Spain in 1580 by Philip II, and finally in the Italian dependency of Naples in 1647. After years of civil war, the Spanish government regained control of all these territories except for Portugal, which successfully reestablished the monarchy of the old ruling house of Braganza when Duke John was made King John IV in 1640.

The defeats in Europe and the internal revolts of the 1640s ended any illusions about Spain's greatness. The actual extent of Spain's economic difficulties is still a much

MAP 15.2   **The Growth of Brandenburg-Prussia.**

Legend:
- Brandenburg (1415)
- Prussian acquisitions to 1740
- Conquest of Silesia by 1748
- From Poland as result of first partition (1792)

debated historical topic, but there is no question about Spain's foreign losses. Dutch independence was formally recognized by the Peace of Westphalia in 1648, and the Peace of the Pyrenees with France in 1659 meant the surrender of Artois and the outlying defenses of the Spanish Netherlands as well as certain border regions that went to France. It did not augur well for the future of Spain that the king who followed Philip IV, Charles II (1665–1700), perhaps unfairly characterized by historians as a "moribund half-wit," was only of interest to the rest of Europe because he had no heirs. The French and Austrians anxiously awaited his death in the hope of placing a member of their royal houses on the Spanish throne. When he died in 1700, the War of the Spanish Succession soon followed.

◆ Absolutism in Central, Eastern, and Northern Europe

During the seventeenth century, a development of great importance for the modern Western world took place in central and eastern Europe, the appearance of three new powers: Prussia, Austria, and Russia.

✺ The German States

The Peace of Westphalia, which officially ended the Thirty Years' War in 1648, left each of the 300 or more German states comprising the Holy Roman Empire virtually autonomous and sovereign. After 1648, the Holy Roman Empire was largely a diplomatic fiction; as the French intellectual Voltaire said in the eighteenth century, the Holy Roman Empire was neither holy, nor Roman, nor an empire. Properly speaking, there was no German state, but more than 300 "Germanies." Of these states, two emerged as great European powers in the seventeenth and eighteenth centuries.

✺ THE RISE OF BRANDENBURG-PRUSSIA

The development of Brandenburg as a state was largely the story of the Hohenzollern dynasty, which in 1415 had come to rule the rather insignificant principality in northeastern Germany. In 1609, the Hohenzollerns inherited some lands in the Rhine valley in western Germany; nine years later, they received the duchy of Prussia (or East Prussia). By the seventeenth century, then, the dominions of the house of Hohenzollern, now called Brandenburg-Prussia, consisted of three disconnected masses in western, central, and eastern Germany. Each had its own privileges, customs, and loyalties; only the person of the Hohenzollern ruler connected them. Unlike France, an old kingdom possessing a reasonably common culture based on almost 1,000 years of history, Brandenburg-Prussia was an artificial creation, highly vulnerable and dependent upon its ruling dynasty to create a state where none existed.

The first important Hohenzollern ruler and the one who laid the foundation for the Prussian state was Frederick William the Great Elector (1640–1688), who came to power in the midst of the Thirty Years' War. Realizing that Brandenburg-Prussia was a small, open territory with no natural frontiers for defense, Frederick William built a competent and efficient standing army. By 1678, he possessed a force of 40,000 men that absorbed more than 50 percent of the state's revenues. To sustain the army and his own power, Frederick William established the General War Commissariat to levy taxes for the army and oversee its growth and training. The Commissariat soon evolved into an agency for civil government as well, collecting the new excise tax in the towns and overseeing the foundation of new industrial and commercial enterprises. Directly responsible to the elector, the new bureaucratic machine became his chief instrument for governing the state. Many of its officials were members of the Prussian landed aristocracy, the Junkers, who also served as officers in the all-important army.

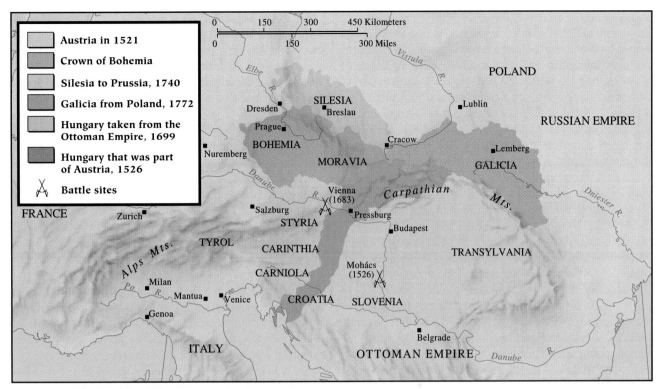

MAP 15.3 **The Growth of the Austrian Empire.**

The nobles' support for Frederick William's policies derived from the tacit agreement that he made with them. In order to eliminate the power that the members of the nobility could exercise in their provincial Estates-General, Frederick William made a deal with the nobles. In return for a free hand in running the government (in other words, for depriving the provincial Estates of their power), he gave the nobles almost unlimited power over their peasants, exempted them from taxation, and awarded them the highest ranks in the army and the Commissariat with the understanding that they would not challenge his political control. As for the peasants, the nobles were allowed to appropriate their land and bind them to the soil as serfs.

To build Brandenburg-Prussia's economy, Frederick William followed the fashionable mercantilist policies, using high tariffs, subsidies, and monopolies for manufacturers to stimulate domestic industry and the construction of roads and canals. Wisely, Frederick William invited people from other countries to settle in Brandenburg-Prussia and, in 1685, issued an edict encouraging the dispossessed Huguenots from Louis XIV's France to come to Prussia. Almost 20,000 did. At the same time, however, Frederick William continued to favor the interests of the nobility at the expense of the commercial and industrial middle classes in the towns.

In these ways, Frederick William the Great Elector laid the foundations for the Prussian state, although it would be misleading to think that he had a modern conception of that state. He thought nothing of amending his will to give pieces of his supposedly unified state as independent principalities to his younger sons. He was succeeded by his son Frederick III (1688–1713), who, less rigid and militaristic than his father, spent much of the treasury building palaces, establishing a university, and imitating the splendors of the court of Louis XIV. He did make one significant contribution to the development of Prussia. In return for aiding the Holy Roman Emperor in the War of the Spanish Succession, he received officially the title of king in Prussia. Elector Frederick III was transformed into King Frederick I, and Brandenburg-Prussia became simply Prussia. In the eighteenth century, Prussia emerged as a great power on the European stage.

THE EMERGENCE OF AUSTRIA

The Austrian Habsburgs had long played a significant role in European politics as Holy Roman Emperors, but by the end of the Thirty Years' War, the Habsburg hopes of creating an empire in Germany had been dashed. In the seventeenth century, then, the house of Austria made an important transition; the German empire was lost, but a new empire was created in eastern and southeastern Europe.

The nucleus of the new Austrian Empire remained the traditional Austrian hereditary possessions: Lower and Upper Austria, Carinthia, Carniola, Styria, and Tyrol. To these had been added the kingdom of Bohemia, which had been reclaimed by the Habsburgs during the Thirty Years' War. Since 1526, the Habsburg ruler had also been king of Hungary, although he exercised little real power except in northwestern Hungary. The eastern Hungarian principality of Transylvania remained independent while the central parts of Hungary were controlled by the Ottoman Turks.

Leopold I (1658–1705) encouraged the eastward movement of the Austrian Empire, but he was sorely challenged by the revival of Turkish power in the seventeenth century. Having moved into Transylvania, the Turks eventually pushed westward and laid siege to Vienna in 1683. Only a dramatic rescue by a combined army of Austrians, Saxons, Bavarians, and Poles saved the Austrian city. A European army, led by the Austrians, counterattacked and decisively defeated the Turks in 1687. By the Treaty of Karlowitz in 1699, Austria took control of Hungary, Transylvania, Croatia, and Slovenia, thus establishing an Austrian Empire in southeastern Europe. At the end of the War of the Spanish Succession, Austria gained possession of the Spanish Netherlands and received formal recognition of its occupation of the Spanish possessions in Italy, namely, Milan, Mantua, Sardinia, and Naples. By the beginning of the eighteenth century, the house of Austria had acquired a new empire of considerable size.

The Austrian monarchy, however, never became a highly centralized, absolutist state, primarily because it included so many different national groups. The Austrian Empire remained a collection of territories held together by a personal union. The Habsburg emperor was archduke of Austria, king of Bohemia, and king of Hungary. Each of these areas had its own laws, Estates-General, and political life. The landed aristocrats throughout the empire were connected by a common bond of service to the house of Habsburg, whether as military officers or government bureaucrats, but no other common sentiment tied the regions together. The nobles in the Austrian Empire remained quite strong and were also allowed to impose serfdom on their peasants. By the beginning of the eighteenth century, Austria was a populous empire in central Europe of great potential military strength.

Italy: From Spanish to Austrian Rule

By 1530, Emperor Charles V had managed to defeat the French armies in Italy and become the arbiter of Italy (see Chapter 13). Initially, he was content to establish close ties with many native Italian rulers and allow them to rule, provided that they recognize his dominant role. But in 1540, he gave the duchy of Milan to his son Philip II and transferred all imperial rights over Italy to the Spanish monarchy.

From the beginning of Philip II's reign in 1559 to 1713, the Spanish presence was felt everywhere in Italy. Only the major states of Florence, the Papal States, and Venice managed to maintain relatively independent policies. At the same time, the influence of the papacy became oppressive in Italy as the machinery of the Catholic Counter-Reformation—the Inquisition, Index, and the Jesuits—was used to stifle any resistance to the Catholic orthodoxy created by the Council of Trent (see Chapter 13). Though artistic and intellectual activity continued in post-Renaissance Italy, it often exacted a grievous cost. Some intellectuals, such as Galilei Galileo and Giordano Bruno (see Chapter 16), found themselves imprisoned or executed by the Inquisition.

At the beginning of the eighteenth century, Italy suffered further from the struggles between France and Spain. But it was Austria, not France, that benefited the most from the War of the Spanish Succession. By gaining Milan, Mantua, Sardinia, and Naples, Austria supplanted Spain as the dominant power in Italy.

From Muscovy to Russia

Since its origins in the Middle Ages, Russia had existed only on the fringes of European society, remote and isolated from the Western mainstream. But in the seventeenth century, the energetic Peter the Great (1689–1725) pushed Russia westward and raised it to the status of a great power.

A new Russian state had emerged in the fifteenth century under the leadership of the principality of Muscovy and its grand dukes (see Chapter 12). In the sixteenth century, Ivan IV the Terrible (1533–1584), who was the first ruler to take the title of tsar, expanded the territories of Russia eastward, after finding westward expansion blocked by the powerful Swedish and Polish states. Ivan also extended the autocracy of the tsar by crushing the power of the Russian nobility, known as the boyars.

Ivan's dynasty came to an end in 1598 and was followed by a resurgence of aristocratic power in a period of anarchy known as the Time of Troubles. It did not end until the Zemsky Sobor, or national assembly, chose Michael Romanov (1613–1645) as the new tsar, beginning a dynasty that lasted until 1917.

In the seventeenth century, Muscovite society was highly stratified. At the top was the tsar, who claimed to be a divinely ordained autocratic ruler, assisted by two consultative bodies, a Duma, or council of boyars, and the Zemsky Sobor, a landed assembly begun in 1550 by Ivan IV to facilitate support for his programs. Russian society was dominated by an upper class of landed aristocrats who, in the course of the seventeenth century, managed to bind their peasants to the land. An abundance of land and a shortage of peasants made serfdom desirable to the landowners. Under a law of 1625, the penalty for killing another's serf was merely to provide a replacement. Townspeople were also stratified and controlled. Artisans were sharply separated from merchants, and many of the latter were not allowed to move from their cities without government permission or to sell their businesses to anyone outside their class. In the seventeenth century, merchant and peasant revolts as well as a schism in the Russian Orthodox church created very unsettled conditions. In the midst of these political and religious upheavals, seventeenth-century Muscovy was experiencing more frequent contacts with the West while Western ideas also began to penetrate a few Russian circles. At the end of the seventeenth century, Peter the Great noticeably accelerated this westernizing process.

THE REIGN OF PETER THE GREAT (1689–1725)

Peter the Great was an unusual character. A strong man, towering six feet, nine inches tall, Peter was coarse in his tastes and rude in his behavior. He enjoyed a low kind

Peter the Great Deals with a Rebellion

During his first visit to the West in 1697–1698, Peter received word that the streltsy, an elite military unit stationed in Moscow, had revolted against his authority. Peter hurried home and crushed the revolt in a very savage fashion. This selection is taken from an Austrian account of how Peter dealt with the rebels.

❊ Peter and the Streltsy

How sharp was the pain, how great the indignation, to which the tsar's Majesty was mightily moved, when he knew of the rebellion of the Streltsy, betraying openly a mind panting for vengeance! He was still tarrying at Vienna, quite full of the desire of setting out for Italy; but, fervid as was his curiosity of rambling abroad, it was, nevertheless, speedily extinguished on the announcement of the troubles that had broken out in the bowels of his realm. Going immediately to Lefort . . . , he thus indignantly broke out: "Tell me, Francis, how I can reach Moscow by the shortest way, in a brief space, so that I may wreak vengeance on this great perfidy of my people, with punishments worthy of their abominable crime. Not one of them shall escape with impunity. Around my royal city, which, with their impious efforts, they planned to destroy, I will have gibbets and gallows set upon the walls and ramparts, and each and every one of them will I put to a direful death." Nor did he long delay the plan for his justly excited wrath;

he took the quick post, as his ambassador suggested, and in four weeks' time he had got over about 300 miles without accident, and arrived the 4th of September, 1698—a monarch for the well deposed, but an avenger for the wicked.

His first anxiety after his arrival was about the rebellion—in what it consisted, what the insurgents meant, who dared to instigate such a crime. And as nobody could answer accurately upon all points, and some pleaded their own ignorance, others the obstinacy of the Streltsy, he began to have suspicions of everybody's loyalty. . . . No day, holy or profane, were the inquisitors idle; every day was deemed fit and lawful for torturing. There was as many scourges as there were accused, and every inquisitor was a butcher. . . . The whole month of October was spent in lacerating the backs of culprits with the knout and with flames; no day were those that were left alive exempt from scourging or scorching; or else they were broken upon the wheel, or driven to the gibbet, or slain with the ax. . . .

To prove to all people how holy and inviolable are those walls of the city which the Streltsy rashly meditated scaling in a sudden assault, beams were run out from all the embrasures in the walls near the gates, in each of which two rebels were hanged. This day beheld about two hundred and fifty die that death. There are few cities fortified with as many palisades as Moscow has given gibbets to her guardian Streltsy.

---

of humor—belching contests, crude jokes, comical funerals—and vicious punishments including floggings, impalings, roastings, and beard burnings (see the box above). Peter gained a firsthand view of the West when he made a trip there in 1697–1698 and returned home with a firm determination to westernize or Europeanize Russia. Perhaps too much has been made of Peter's desire to westernize a "backward country." Peter's policy of Europeanization was largely technical. He admired European technology and gadgets and desired to transplant these to Russia. Only this kind of modernization could give him the army and navy he needed to make Russia a great power. His only consistent purpose was to win military victories.

As could be expected, one of his first priorities was the reorganization of the army and the creation of a navy. Employing both Russians and Europeans as officers, he conscripted peasants for twenty-five-year stints of service to build a standing army of 210,000 men. Peter has also been given credit for forming the first Russian navy.

Peter reorganized the central government, partly along Western lines. What remained of the consultative bodies disappeared; neither the Duma of boyars nor the Zemsky Sobor was ever summoned. In 1711, Peter created a Senate to supervise the administrative machinery of the state while he was away on military campaigns. In time the Senate became something like a ruling council, but its ineffectiveness caused Peter to borrow the Western institution of "colleges," or boards of administrators entrusted with specific functions, such as foreign affairs, war, and justice. To impose the rule of the central government more effectively throughout the land, Peter divided Russia into eight provinces and later, in 1719, into fifty. Although he hoped to create a "police state," by which he meant a well-ordered community governed in accordance with law, few of his bureaucrats shared his concept of honest service and duty to the state. One of his highest officials even stated: "Would your Majesty like to be a ruler without any subjects? We all steal, only some do it on a bigger scale, and in a more conspicuous way, than others."[9] Peter hoped for a sense of civic duty, but his own forceful personality created an atmosphere of fear that prevented it. He wrote to one administrator, "According to these orders act, act, act. I won't write more, but you will pay with your head if you interpret orders again." But when others were understandably cautious in interpreting his written instructions, he stated: "This is as if a servant, seeing his master drowning, would not save him until he had

PETER THE GREAT. Peter the Great wished to westernize Russia, especially in the realm of technical skills. His foremost goal was the creation of a strong army and navy in order to make Russia a great power. A Dutch painter created this portrait of the armored tsar during his visit to the West in 1697.

tional burdens upon the hapless peasants who were becoming ever more oppressed in Peter's Russia.

Peter also sought to gain state control of the Russian Orthodox church. In 1721, he abolished the position of patriarch and created a body called the Holy Synod to make decisions for the church. At its head stood a procurator, a layman who represented the interests of the tsar and assured Peter of effective domination of the church.

Already after his first trip to the West in 1697–1698, Peter began to introduce Western customs, practices, and manners into Russia. He ordered the preparation of the first Russian book of etiquette to teach Western manners. Among other things, it pointed out that it was not polite to spit on the floor or scratch oneself at dinner. Since westerners did not wear beards or the traditional long-skirted coat, Russian beards had to be shaved and coats shortened, a reform Peter personally enforced at court by shaving off his nobles' beards and cutting their coats at the knees with his own hands. Outside the court, barbers and tailors planted at town gates enforced the edicts by cutting the beards and cloaks of those who entered or left. Anyone who failed to conform was to be "beaten without mercy." For the nobles, who were already partly westernized, these changes were hardly earth-shattering. But to many others who believed that shaving the beard was a "defacement of the image of God," the attack was actually blasphemous.

One group of Russians benefited greatly from Peter's cultural reforms—women. Having watched women mixing freely with men in Western courts, Peter shattered the seclusion of upper-class Russian women and demanded that they remove the traditional veils that covered their faces. Peter also decreed that social gatherings be held three times a week in the large houses of St. Petersburg where men and women could mix for conversation, card games, and dancing, which Peter had learned in the West. The tsar also now insisted that women could marry of their own free will.

The object of Peter's domestic reforms was to make Russia into a great state and military power. His primary goal was to "open a window to the west," meaning an ice-free port easily accessible to Europe. This could only be achieved on the Baltic, but at that time the Baltic coast was controlled by Sweden, the most important power in northern Europe. Desirous of these lands, Peter, with the support of Poland and Denmark, attacked Sweden in the summer of 1700, believing that the young king of Sweden, Charles XII, could easily be defeated. Charles, however, proved to be a brilliant general. He smashed the Danes, flattened the Poles, and, with a well-disciplined force of only 8,000 men, routed the Russian army of 40,000 at the Battle of Narva (1700). The Great Northern War (1701–1721) had begun.

But Peter fought back. He reorganized his army along Western lines and in 1702 overran the Swedish Baltic provinces while Charles was preoccupied elsewhere. When the Swedish king turned his attention to Peter again in 1708, he decided to invade Russia and capture Moscow, the cap-

satisfied himself as to whether it was written down in his contract that he should pull him out of the water."[10] Peter wanted his administrators to be slaves and free men at the same time, and it did not occur to him that he was asking the impossible.

To further his administrative aims, Peter demanded that all members of the landholding class serve in either military or civil offices. Moreover, in 1722, Peter instituted a Table of Ranks to create opportunities for nonnobles to serve the state and join the ranks of the nobility. All civil offices were ranked according to fourteen levels; a parallel list of fourteen grades was also created for all military offices. Every official was then required to begin at level one and work his way up the ranks. When a nonnoble reached the eighth rank, he acquired the status of nobility. This attempt by Peter to create a new nobility based on merit was not carried on by his successors.

To obtain the enormous amount of money needed for an army and navy that absorbed as much as four-fifths of the state revenue, Peter adopted Western mercantilistic policies to stimulate economic growth. He tried to increase exports and develop new industries while exploiting domestic resources like the iron mines in the Urals. But his military needs were endless, and he came to rely on the old expedient of simply raising taxes, imposing addi-

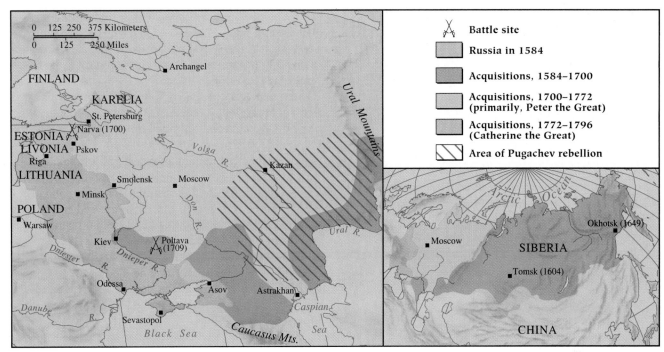

MAP 15.4 From Muscovy to Russia.

ital, but Russian weather and scorched-earth tactics devastated his army. In July 1709, at the Battle of Poltava, Peter's forces defeated Charles's army decisively. Although the war dragged on for another twelve years, the Peace of Nystadt in 1721 gave formal recognition to what Peter had already achieved: the acquisition of Estonia, Livonia, and Karelia. Sweden became a second-rate power while Russia was now the great European state Peter had wanted.

Already in 1703, in the northern marshlands along the Baltic, Peter had begun to construct a new city, St. Petersburg, his window on the west and a symbol that Russia was looking westward to Europe. Though its construction cost the lives of thousands of peasants, St. Petersburg was finished during Peter's lifetime. It remained the Russian capital until 1917.

It is difficult to assess the work of Peter the Great. He modernized and westernized Russia to the extent that it became a great military power and, by his death in 1725, an important member of the European state system. But his policies were also detrimental to Russia. Westernization was a bit of a sham, since Western culture reached only the upper classes and the real object of the reforms, the creation of a strong military, only added more burdens to the masses of the Russian people. The forceful way in which Peter the Great imposed westernization led to a distrust of Europe and Western civilization. Russia was so strained by Peter the Great that after his death an aristocratic reaction undid much of his work.

❋ The Growth of Monarchy in Scandinavia

As the economic link between the products of eastern Europe and the West, the Baltic Sea bestowed special importance on the lands surrounding it. In the sixteenth century, Sweden had broken its ties with Denmark and emerged as an independent state (see Chapter 13). Despite their common Lutheran religion, Denmark's and Sweden's territorial ambitions in northern Europe kept them in rather constant rivalry in the seventeenth century.

Under Christian IV (1588–1648), Denmark seemed the likely candidate for expansion, but it met with little success. The system of electing monarchs forced the kings to share their power with the Danish nobility who exercised strict control over the peasants who worked their lands. Danish ambitions for ruling the Baltic were severely curtailed by the losses they sustained in the Thirty Years' War and later in the so-called Northern War (1655–1660) with Sweden. Danish military losses led to a constitutional crisis in which a meeting of Denmark's Estates brought to pass a bloodless revolution in 1660. The power of the nobility was curtailed, a hereditary monarchy reestablished, and a new, absolutist constitution proclaimed in 1665. Under Christian V (1670–1699), a centralized administration was instituted with the nobility as the chief officeholders.

Compared to Denmark, Sweden seemed a relatively poor country, and historians have had difficulty explaining why it played such a large role in European affairs in the seventeenth century. Sweden's economy was weak, and the monarchy was still locked in conflict with the powerful Swedish nobility. During the reign of Gustavus Adolphus (1611–1632), his wise and dedicated chief minister, Axel Oxenstierna, persuaded the king to adopt a new policy in which the nobility formed a "first estate" occupying the bureaucratic positions of an expanded central government. This created a stable monarchy and freed the king to raise a formidable army and participate in the Thirty Years' War, only to be killed in battle in 1632.

Sweden experienced a severe political crisis after the death of Gustavus Adolphus. His daughter Christina (1633–1654) proved to be far more interested in philosophy and religion than ruling. Her tendency to favor the interests of the nobility led the other estates of the Riksdag, Sweden's parliament—the burghers, clergy, and peasants— to protest. In 1654, tired of ruling and wishing to become a Catholic, which was forbidden in Sweden, Christina abdicated in favor of her cousin, who became King Charles X (1654–1660). His accession to the throne defused a potentially explosive peasant revolt against the nobility.

Charles X reestablished domestic order, but it was his successor, Charles XI (1660–1697), who did the painstaking work of building the Swedish monarchy along the lines of an absolute monarchy. By resuming control of the crown lands and the revenues attached to them from the nobility, Charles managed to weaken the independent power of the nobility. He built up a bureaucracy, subdued both the Riksdag and the church, improved the army and navy, and left to his son, Charles XII (1697–1718), a well-organized Swedish state that dominated northern Europe. In 1693, he and his heirs were acclaimed as "absolute, sovereign kings, responsible for their actions to no man on earth."

Charles XII was primarily interested in military affairs. Energetic and regarded as a brilliant general, his grandiose plans and strategies, which involved Sweden in conflicts with Poland, Denmark, and Russia, proved to be Sweden's undoing. By the time he died in 1718, Charles XII had lost much of Sweden's northern empire to Russia, and Sweden's status as a first-class northern power had proved to be short-lived.

❈ The Ottoman Empire

After their conquest of Constantinople in 1453, the Ottoman Turks tried to complete their conquest of the Balkans, where they had been established since the fourteenth century. Although they were successful in taking the Romanian territory of Wallachia in 1476, the resistance of the Hungarians kept them from advancing up the Danube valley. From 1480 to 1520, internal problems and the need to consolidate their eastern frontiers kept the Turks from any further attacks on Europe.

The reign of Sultan Suleiman I the Magnificent (1520–1566), however, brought the Turks back to Europe's attention. Advancing up the Danube, the Turks seized Belgrade in 1521 and Hungary by 1526, although their attempts to conquer Vienna in 1529 were repulsed. At the same time, the Turks extended their power into the western Mediterranean, threatening to turn it into a Turkish lake until a large Turkish fleet was destroyed by the Spanish at Lepanto in 1571. Despite the defeat, the Turks continued to hold nominal control over the southern shores of the Mediterranean.

Although Europeans frequently spoke of new Christian crusades against the infidel Turks, by the beginning of the seventeenth century the Ottoman Empire was being treated like another European power by European rulers seeking alliances and trade concessions. The Ottoman Empire possessed a highly effective governmental system, especially when it was led by strong sultans or powerful grand viziers (prime ministers). The splendid capital Constantinople possessed a population far larger than any European city. Nevertheless, Ottoman politics periodically degenerated into bloody intrigues as factions fought each other for influence and the throne. In one particularly gruesome practice, a ruling sultan would murder his brothers to avoid challenges to his rule. Despite the periodic bouts

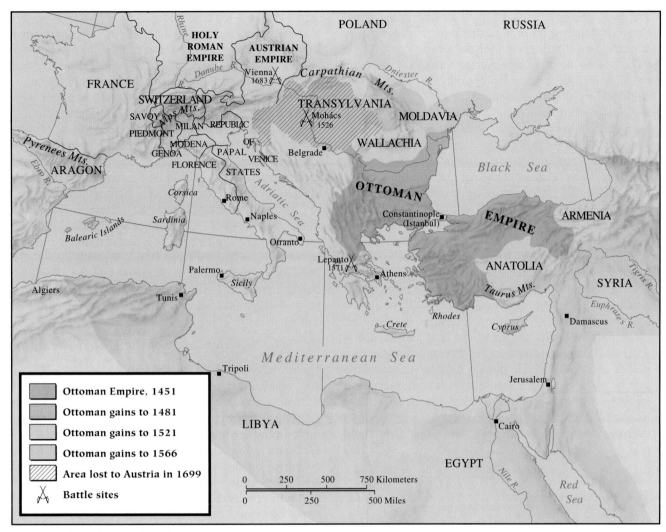

MAP 15.5 **The Ottoman Empire.**

of civil chaos, a well-trained bureaucracy of civil servants continued to administer state affairs efficiently.

A well-organized military system also added to the strength of the Ottoman Empire. Especially outstanding were the Janissaries, composed of Christian boys who had been taken from their parents, converted to the Muslim faith, and subjected to rigid military discipline to form an elite core of 8,000 troops personally loyal to the sultan. Like other praetorian guards, however, the Janissaries came to play an important role in making and unmaking sultans.

In the first half of the seventeenth century, the Ottoman Empire was a "sleeping giant." Occupied by domestic bloodletting and severely threatened by a challenge from Persia, the Ottomans were content with the status quo in eastern Europe. But under a new line of grand viziers in the second half of the seventeenth century, the Ottoman Empire again took the offensive. By mid-1683, the Ottomans had marched through the Hungarian plain and laid siege to Vienna. Repulsed by a mixed army of Austrians, Poles, Bavarians, and Saxons, the Turks retreated and were pushed out of Hungary by a new European coalition. Although they retained the core of their empire, the Ottoman Turks would never again be a threat to Europe. Although the Ottoman Empire held together for the rest of the seventeenth and eighteenth centuries, it would be faced with new challenges from the ever-growing Austrian Empire in southeastern Europe and the new Russian giant to the north.

✤ *The Limits of Absolutism*

In recent decades, historical studies of local institutions have challenged the traditional picture of absolute monarchs. Control of the administrative machinery of state did not enable rulers to dominate the everyday lives of their subjects, as was once thought. The centralization of power was an important element in the growth of the seventeenth-century state, however, and the most successful monarchs were those who managed to restructure the central policy-making machinery of government to give them a certain amount of control over the traditional areas of monarchical power: formulation of foreign policy, making of war and peace, the church, and taxation. Seventeenth-century governments also intervened in economic affairs to strengthen their war-making capacities. In all of these areas, absolute monarchy meant rulers extending their power or at least resisting challenges to their authority.

It is misleading, however, to think that so-called absolute monarchs actually controlled the lives of their subjects. In 1700, government for most people still meant the local institutions that affected their lives: local courts, local tax collectors, and local organizers of armed forces. Kings and ministers might determine policies and issue guidelines, but they still had to function through local agents and had no guarantee whatever that their wishes would be carried out. A mass of urban and provincial privileges, liberties, and exemptions (including from taxation) and a whole host of corporate bodies and interest groups—provincial and national Estates, clerical officials, officeholders who had bought or inherited their positions, and provincial nobles—limited what monarchs could achieve. The most successful rulers were not those who tried to destroy the old system, but those like Louis XIV who knew how to use the old system to their advantage. Above all other considerations stood the landholding nobility. Everywhere in the seventeenth century, the landed aristocracy played an important role in the European monarchical system. As military officers, judges, officeholders, and landowners in control of vast, untaxed estates, their power remained immense. In some places, their strength even put severe limits on how effectively monarchs could rule.

◆ Limited Monarchy and Republics

Almost everywhere in Europe in the seventeenth century, kings and their ministers were in control of central governments. But not all European states followed the pattern of absolute monarchy. In eastern Europe, the Polish aristocracy controlled a virtually powerless king. In western Europe, two great states—the Dutch Republic and England—successfully resisted the power of hereditary monarchs.

❈ The Weakness of the Polish Monarchy

Poland had played a major role in eastern Europe in the fifteenth century and had ruled over Lithuania and much of Ukraine by the end of the sixteenth. After the elective throne of Poland had been won by the Swede Sigismund III (1587–1631), Poland had a king who even thought seriously of creating a vast Polish empire that would include at least Russia and possibly Finland and Sweden. Poland not only failed to achieve this goal, but by the end of the seventeenth century, it had become a weak, decentralized state.

It was the elective nature of the Polish monarchy that reduced it to impotence. The *Sejm*, or Polish diet, was a two-chamber assembly in which landowners completely dominated the few townspeople and lawyers who were also members. To be elected to the kingship, prospective monarchs (who were mostly foreigners) had to agree to share power with the *Sejm* (in effect with the nobles) in matters of taxation, foreign and military policy, and the appointment of state officials and judges. The power of the *Sejm* had disastrous results for central monarchical authority since the real aim of most of its members was to ensure that central authority would not affect their local interests. The acceptance of the liberum veto in 1652, whereby the meetings of the *Sejm* could be stopped by a single dissenting member, reduced government to virtual chaos.

Poland, then, was basically a confederation of semi-independent estates of landed nobles. By the late seventeenth century, it also became a battleground for foreign powers who found it easy to invade, but difficult to rule. The continuation of Polish weakness into the eighteenth century eventually encouraged its more powerful neighbors—Prussia, Austria, and Russia—to dismember it.

❈ The "Golden Age" of the Dutch Republic

The seventeenth century has often been called the "golden age" of the Dutch Republic as the United Provinces held center stage as one of Europe's great powers. Like France and England, the United Provinces was an Atlantic power, underlining the importance of the shift of political and economic power from the Mediterranean basin to the countries on the Atlantic seaboard. As a result of the sixteenth-century revolt of the Netherlands, the seven northern provinces, which began to call themselves the United Provinces of the Netherlands in 1581, became the core of the modern Dutch state. The new state was officially recognized by the Peace of Westphalia in 1648.

With independence came internal dissension. There were two chief centers of political power in the new state. Each province had an official known as a stadholder who was responsible for leading the army and maintaining order. Beginning with William of Orange and his heirs, the house of Orange occupied the stadholderate in most of the seven provinces and favored the development of a centralized government with themselves as hereditary monarchs. The States General, an assembly of representatives from every province, opposed the Orangist ambitions and advocated a decentralized or republican form of government.

The political rivalry between the monarchical and republican blocs was intensified by religious division within the Calvinist church, which remained the official church of the Dutch Republic. But other religious groups were tolerated as long as they worshiped in private. Catholics, other Protestants, and even Jewish communities felt relatively free in Holland, the richest and largest province, and especially in Amsterdam. In their religious toleration, the Dutch were truly unique in the seventeenth century.

For much of the seventeenth century, the republican forces were in control. But in 1672, burdened with war against both France and England, the United Provinces

DAM SQUARE. This work by J. van der Ulft, done in 1659, shows Dam Square in Amsterdam. Merchants unloaded their cargoes here, making Dam Square one of the busiest centers of the city.

turned once again to the house of Orange and restored it to the stadholderate in the person of William III (1672–1702). From that year on, William III worked consciously to build up his pseudo-royal power. When he succeeded to the throne of England in 1688 (see England and the Emergence of Constitutional Monarchy later in the chapter), his position in the Netherlands was strengthened as well. However, his death in 1702, without direct heirs, enabled the republican forces to gain control once more. The Dutch Republic would not be seriously threatened again by the monarchical forces.

Underlying Dutch prominence in the seventeenth century was its economic prosperity, fueled by the Dutch role as carriers of European trade. But war proved disastrous to the Dutch Republic. Wars with France and England placed heavy burdens on Dutch finances and manpower. English shipping began to challenge what had been Dutch commercial supremacy, and by 1715, the Dutch were experiencing a serious economic decline.

✦ LIFE IN SEVENTEENTH-CENTURY AMSTERDAM

By the beginning of the seventeenth century, Amsterdam had replaced Antwerp as the financial and commercial capital of Europe. In 1570, Amsterdam had 30,000 inhabitants; by 1610, that number had doubled as refugees poured in, especially from the Spanish Netherlands. Intellectuals and Jews drawn by the city's reputation for toleration, as well as merchants and workers attracted by the city's prosperity, added to the number of new inhabitants. In 1613, this rapid growth caused the city government to approve an "urban expansion plan" that expanded the city's territory from 500 to 1,800 acres through the construction of three large, concentric canals. Builders prepared plots for the tall, narrow-fronted houses that were characteristic of the city by hammering wooden columns through the mud to the firm sand underneath. The canals in turn made it possible for merchants and artisans to utilize the upper stories of their houses as storerooms for their goods. Wares carried by small boats were hoisted to the top windows of these dwellings by block and tackle beams fastened to the gables of the roofs. Amsterdam's physical expansion was soon matched by its population as the city grew to 200,000 by 1660.

The exuberant expansion of Amsterdam in the seventeenth century was based upon the city's new role as the commercial and financial center of Europe (see the box on p. 446). But what had made this possible? For one thing, Amsterdam merchants possessed vast fleets of ships, many of which were used for the lucrative North Sea herring catch. Amsterdam ships were also important carriers for the products of other countries. The Dutch invention of the fluyt, a shallow-draft ship of large capacity, enabled them to transport enormous quantities of cereals, timber, and iron. The Dutch produced large ships for ocean voyages as well.

Amsterdam merchants unloaded their cargoes at Dam Square, where all goods above fifty pounds in weight were recorded and tested for quality. The quantity of goods brought to Amsterdam soon made the city a crossroads for many of Europe's chief products. Amsterdam was, of course, the chief port for the Dutch West and East Indian trading companies (see Overseas Trade and Colonies later

The Economic Superiority of the Dutch

Europeans were astonished by the apparent prosperity of the Dutch in the first half of the seventeenth century. This selection is taken from a treatise entitled Observations Touching Trade and Commerce with the Hollanders, and Other Nations. *It was written by an Englishman named John Keymer who believed that the Dutch economy could serve as a guide for the English.*

❋ John Keymer, *Observations Touching Trade and Commerce with the Hollanders, and Other Nations*

I have diligently in my travels observed how the countries herein mentioned [mainly Holland] do grow potent with abundance of all things to serve themselves and other nations, where nothing grows; and that their never dried fountains of wealth, by which they raise their estate to such an admirable height, [so] that they are . . . [now] a wonder to the world, [come] from your Majesty's seas and lands.

I thus moved, began to delve into the depth of their policies and circumventing practices, whereby they drain, and still covet to exhaust, the wealth and coin of this kingdom, and so with our own commodities to weaken us, and finally beat us quite out of trading in other countries. I found that they more fully obtained these their purposes by their convenient privileges, and settled constitutions; than England with all the laws, and superabundance of home-bred commodities which God has vouchsafed your sea and land. . . .

To bring this to pass they have many advantages of us; the one is, by their fashioned ships . . . that are made to hold great bulk of merchandise, and to sail with a few men for profit. For example . . . [Dutch ships] do serve the merchant better cheap by one hundred pounds [English money] in his freight than we can, by reason he has but nine or ten mariners, and we near thirty; thus he saves twenty men's meat and wages in a voyage; and so in all other their ships according to their burden, by which means they are freighted wheresoever they come, to great profit, while our ships lie still and decay. . . .

Thus they and others glean this wealth and strength from us to themselves; and these reasons following procure them this advantage to us.

1. The merchants . . . which make all things in abundance, by reason of their store-houses continually replenished with all kind of commodities.
2. The liberty of free traffic for strangers to buy and sell in Holland, and other countries and states, as if they were free-born, makes great intercourse.
3. The small duties levied upon merchants, draws all nations to trade with them.
4. Their fashioned ships continually freighted before ours, by reason of their few mariners and great bulk, serving the merchant cheap.
5. Their forwardness to further all manner of trading.
6. Their wonderful employment of their busses [herring boats] for fishing, and the great returns they make.
7. Their giving free custom inward and outward, for any new-erected trade, by means whereof they have gotten already almost the sole trade into their hands.

---

in this chapter). Moreover, city industries turned imported raw materials into finished goods, making Amsterdam an important producer of woolen cloth, refined sugar and tobacco products, glass, beer, paper, books, jewelry, and leather goods. Some of the city's great wealth came from war profits: by 1700, Amsterdam was the principal supplier of military goods in Europe; its gun foundries had customers throughout the continent.

A third factor in Amsterdam's prosperity was its importance as a financial center. Trading profits provided large quantities of capital for investment. Its financial role was greatly facilitated by the foundation in 1609 of the Exchange Bank of Amsterdam, long the greatest public bank in northern Europe. As an English gentleman noted, the reputation of the bank was "another invitation for People to come, and lodge here what part of their Money they could transport, and knew no way of securing at home."[11] The city also founded the Amsterdam Stock Exchange for speculating in commodities.

Amsterdam's prosperity (it possessed the highest per capita income in Europe) did not prevent it from having enormous social differences. At the bottom of the social ladder were the beggars, unskilled day laborers, and poor immigrants attracted by Amsterdam's riches. Many of these poor people were forcefully recruited as ordinary sailors, especially for dangerous overseas voyages. Above this lower class stood the artisans and manual laborers, who belonged to the guilds or worked for guild members. Since widows were allowed to take their husbands' places in the craft guilds, Amsterdam was known for its high number of businesswomen. The artisans lived in a district called the Jordaan, built outside the three new canals. Its crowded quarters and small streets crisscrossed by canals created a quaint atmosphere and sense of fellowship that appealed to many of Amsterdam's artists.

Above the craftspeople stood a professional class of lawyers, teachers, bureaucrats, and wealthier guild members, but above them were the landed nobles who intermarried with the wealthier burghers and built more elaborate town houses. At the very top of Amsterdam's society stood a select number of very prosperous manufacturers, shipyard owners, and merchants, whose wealth enabled them to control the city government of Amsterdam as well as the Dutch Republic's States General.

In the first half of the seventeenth century, the Calvinist background of the wealthy Amsterdam burghers led them to adopt a simple lifestyle. They wore dark clothes and lived in substantial, but simply furnished houses, known for their steep, narrow stairways. The oft-quoted phrase that "cleanliness is next to Godliness" was literally true for these self-confident Dutch burghers. Their houses were clean and orderly; foreigners often commented that Dutch housewives always seemed to be scrubbing. But in the second half of the seventeenth century, the wealthy burghers began to reject their Calvinist heritage, a transformation that is especially evident in their more elaborate and colorful clothes.

❊ England and the Emergence of Constitutional Monarchy

One of the most prominent examples of resistance to absolute monarchy came in seventeenth-century England where king and Parliament struggled to determine the role each should play in governing England. But the struggle over this political issue was complicated by a deep and profound religious controversy. With the victory of Parliament came the foundation for constitutional monarchy by the end of the seventeenth century.

❧ REVOLUTION AND CIVIL WAR

With the death of Queen Elizabeth in 1603, the Tudor dynasty became extinct, and the Stuart line of rulers was inaugurated with the accession to the throne of Elizabeth's cousin, King James VI of Scotland (son of Mary, queen of Scots), who became James I (1603–1625) of England. Although used to royal power as king of Scotland, James understood little about the laws, institutions, and customs of the English. He espoused the divine right of kings, the belief that kings receive their power directly from God and are responsible to no one except God. This viewpoint alienated Parliament, which had grown accustomed under the Tudors to act on the premise that monarch and Parliament together ruled England as a "balanced polity." Parliament expressed its displeasure with James's claims by refusing his requests for additional monies needed by the king to meet the increased cost of government. Parliament's power of the purse proved to be its trump card in its relationship with the king.

Some members of Parliament were also alienated by James's religious policy. The Puritans—those Protestants within the Anglican church inspired by Calvinist theology—wanted James to eliminate the episcopal system of church organization used in the Church of England (in which the bishop or *episcopos* played the major administrative role) in favor of a Presbyterian model (used in Scotland and patterned after Calvin's church organization in Geneva, where ministers and elders—also called presbyters—played an important governing role). James refused because he realized that the Anglican church, with its bishops appointed by the crown, was a major support of monarchical authority. But the Puritans were not easily cowed and added to the rising chorus of opposition to the king. Many of England's gentry, mostly well-to-do landowners below the level of the nobility, had become Puritans, and these Puritan gentry not only formed an important and substantial part of the House of Commons, the lower house of Parliament, but also held important positions locally as justices of the peace and sheriffs. It was not wise to alienate them.

The conflict that had begun during the reign of James came to a head during the reign of his son Charles I (1625–1649). In 1628, Parliament passed a Petition of Right that the king was supposed to accept before being granted any taxes. This petition prohibited taxes without Parliament's consent, arbitrary imprisonment, the quartering of soldiers in private houses, and the declaration of martial law in peacetime. Although he initially accepted it, Charles later reneged on the agreement because of its limitations on royal power. In 1629, Charles decided that since he could not work with Parliament, he would not summon it to meet. From 1629 to 1640, Charles pursued a course of "personal rule," which forced him to find ways to collect taxes without the cooperation of Parliament. One expedient was a tax called Ship Money, a levy on seacoast towns to pay for coastal defense, which was now collected annually by the king's officials throughout England and used to finance other government operations besides defense. This use of Ship Money aroused opposition from middle-class merchants and landed gentry who believed the king was attempting to tax without Parliament's consent.

The king's religious policy also proved disastrous. His marriage to Henrietta Maria, the Catholic sister of King Louis XIII of France, aroused suspicions about the king's own religious inclinations. Even more important, however, the efforts of Charles and William Laud, the archbishop of Canterbury, to introduce more ritual into the Anglican church struck the Puritans as a return to Catholic popery. Grievances mounted, yet Charles might have survived unscathed if he could have avoided calling Parliament, which alone could provide a focus for the many cries of discontent throughout the land. But when the king and Archbishop Laud attempted to impose the Anglican Book of Common Prayer upon the Scottish Presbyterian church, the Scots rose up in rebellion against the king. Financially strapped and unable to raise troops to defend against the Scots, the king was forced to call Parliament into session. Eleven years of frustration welled up to create a Parliament determined to deal with the king.

In its first session from November 1640 to September 1641, the so-called Long Parliament (because it lasted in one form or another from 1640 to 1660) took a series of steps that placed severe limitations upon royal authority.

OLIVER CROMWELL. Oliver Cromwell was a dedicated Puritan who formed the New Model Army and defeated the forces supporting King Charles I. Unable to work with Parliament, he came to rely on military force to rule England. Cromwell is pictured here in 1649, on the eve of his ruthless military campaign in Ireland.

These included the abolition of arbitrary courts, the abolition of taxes that the king had collected without Parliament's consent, such as Ship Money, and the passage of the revolutionary Triennial Act, which specified that Parliament must meet at least once every three years, with or without the king's consent. By the end of 1641, one group within Parliament was prepared to go no further, but a group of more radical parliamentarians pushed for more change, including the elimination of bishops in the Anglican church. When the king tried to take advantage of the split by arresting some members of the more radical faction in Parliament, a large group in Parliament led by John Pym and his fellow Puritans decided that the king had gone too far. England now slipped into civil war (1642).

Parliament proved victorious in the first phase of the English Civil War (1642–1646). Most important to Parliament's success was the creation of the New Model Army by Oliver Cromwell. The New Model Army was composed primarily of more extreme Puritans known as the Independents, who believed they were doing battle for the Lord. It is striking to read in Cromwell's military reports such statements as "Sir, this is none other but the hand of God; and to Him alone belongs the glory." We might also attribute some of the credit to Cromwell himself since his crusaders were well disciplined and trained in the new continental military tactics. Supported by the New Model Army, Parliament ended the first phase of the civil war with the capture of King Charles I in 1646.

A split now occurred in the parliamentary forces. A Presbyterian majority wanted to disband the army and restore Charles I with a Presbyterian state church. The army, composed mostly of the more radical Independents, who opposed an established Presbyterian church, marched on London in 1647 and began negotiations with the king. Charles took advantage of this division to flee and seek help from the Scots. Enraged by the king's treachery, Cromwell and the army engaged in a second civil war (1648) that ended with Cromwell's victory and the capture of the king. This time Cromwell was determined to achieve a victory for the army's point of view. The Presbyterian members of Parliament were purged, leaving a Rump Parliament of fifty-three members of the House of Commons who then tried and condemned the king on a charge of treason and adjudged that "he, the said Charles Stuart, as a tyrant, traitor, murderer, and public enemy to the good people of this nation, shall be put to death by the severing of his head from his body." On January 30, 1649, Charles was beheaded, a most uncommon act in the seventeenth century. The revolution had triumphed, and the monarchy in England had been destroyed, at least for the moment.

After the death of the king, the Rump Parliament abolished the monarchy and the House of Lords and proclaimed England a republic or Commonwealth (1649–1653). This was not an easy period for Cromwell. As commander-in-chief of the army, he had to crush a Catholic uprising in Ireland, which he accomplished with a brutality that earned him the eternal enmity of the Irish people, as well as an uprising in Scotland on behalf of the son of Charles I. He also faced opposition at home, especially from more radically minded groups who took advantage of the upheaval in England to push their agendas. The Levellers, for example, advocated such advanced ideas as freedom of speech, religious toleration, and a democratic republic. Cromwell, a country gentleman and defender of property and the ruling classes, smashed the radicals by force. At the same time, Cromwell found it difficult to work with the Rump Parliament and finally dispersed it by force. As the members of Parliament departed (April 1653), he shouted after them: "It's you that have forced me to do this, for I have sought the Lord night and day that He would slay me rather than put upon me the doing of this work." With the certainty of one who is convinced he is right, Cromwell had destroyed both king and Parliament.

The army provided a new government when it drew up the Instrument of Government, England's first and last written constitution. Executive power was vested in the Lord Protector (a position held by Cromwell) and legislative power in a Parliament. But the new system also failed to work. Cromwell found it difficult to work with the Parliament, especially when its members debated his authority and advocated once again the creation of a Presbyterian state church. In 1655, Cromwell dissolved Parliament and divided the country into eleven regions, each ruled by a major general who served virtually as a military governor. To meet the cost of military government, Cromwell levied a 10 percent land tax on all former Royalists. Unable to establish a constitutional basis for a working government, Cromwell had resorted to military force to maintain the rule of the Independents, ironically using even more arbitrary policies than those of Charles I.

Oliver Cromwell died in 1658. After floundering for eighteen months, the military establishment decided that arbitrary rule by the army was no longer feasible and reestablished the monarchy in the person of Charles II, the son of Charles I. The restoration of the Stuart monarchy ended England's time of troubles, but it was not long before England experienced yet another constitutional crisis.

✵ RESTORATION AND A GLORIOUS REVOLUTION

After eleven years of exile, Charles II (1660–1685) returned to England. As he entered London amid the acclaim of the people, he remarked sardonically, "I never knew that I was so popular in England." The restoration of the monarchy and the House of Lords did not mean, however, that the work of the English Revolution was undone. Parliament kept much of the power it had won: its role in government was acknowledged; the necessity for its consent to taxation was accepted; and arbitrary courts were still abolished. Yet Charles continued to push his own ideas, some of which were clearly out of step with many of the English people.

A serious religious problem disturbed the tranquillity of Charles II's reign. After the restoration of the monarchy, a new Parliament (the Cavalier Parliament) met in 1661 and restored the Anglican church as the official church of England. In addition, laws were passed to force everyone, particularly Catholics and Puritan Dissenters, to conform to the Anglican church. Charles, however, was sympathetic to and perhaps even inclined to Catholicism. Moreover, Charles's brother James, heir to the throne, did not hide the fact that he was a Catholic. Parliament's suspicions were therefore aroused in 1672 when Charles took the audacious step of issuing a Declaration of Indulgence that suspended the laws that Parliament had passed against Catholics and Puritans. Parliament would have none of it and induced the king to suspend the declaration. Propelled by a strong anti-Catholic sentiment, Parliament then passed a Test Act in 1673, specifying that only Anglicans could hold military and civil offices.

A supposed Catholic plot to assassinate King Charles and place his brother James on the throne, although shown to be imaginary, inflamed Parliament to attempt to pass an Exclusion Bill between 1678 and 1681 that would have barred James from the throne as a professed Catholic. Although these attempts failed, the debate over the bill created two political groupings: the Whigs, who wanted to exclude James and establish a Protestant king with toleration of Dissenters, and the Tories, who supported the king, despite their dislike of James as a Catholic, because they did not believe Parliament should tamper with the lawful succession to the throne. To foil these efforts, Charles dismissed Parliament in 1681, relying on French

Limited Monarchy and Republics	
Poland	
Sigismund III	1587–1631
Beginning of liberum veto	1652
The United Provinces	
Official recognition of United Provinces	1648
House of Orange	
William III	1672–1702
England	
James I	1603–1625
Charles I	1625–1649
Petition of Right	1628
First Civil War	1642–1646
Second Civil War	1648
Execution of Charles I	1649
Commonwealth	1649–1653
Death of Cromwell	1658
Restoration of monarchy—Charles II	1660
Charles II	1660–1685
Cavalier Parliament	1661
Declaration of Indulgence	1672
Test Act	1673
James II	1685–1688
Declaration of Indulgence	1687
Glorious Revolution	1688
Bill of Rights	1689

subsidies to rule alone. When he died in 1685, his Catholic brother came to the throne.

The accession of James II (1685–1688) to the crown virtually guaranteed a new constitutional crisis for England. An open and devout Catholic, his attempt to further Catholic interests made religion once more a primary cause of conflict between king and Parliament. Contrary to the Test Act, James named Catholics to high positions in the government, army, navy, and universities. In 1687, he issued a Declaration of Indulgence, which suspended all laws barring Catholics and Dissenters from office. Parliamentary outcries against James's policies stopped short of rebellion because members knew that he was an old man and his successors were his Protestant daughters Mary and Anne, born to his first wife. But on June 10, 1688, a son was born to James II's second wife, also a Catholic. Suddenly the specter of a Catholic hereditary monarchy loomed large. A group of seven prominent English noblemen invited William of Orange, husband of James's daughter Mary, to invade England. An inveterate foe of Louis XIV, William welcomed this opportunity to fight France with England's resources. William and Mary raised an army and invaded England while James, his wife, and infant son fled to France. With almost no

The Bill of Rights

In 1688, the English experienced yet another revolution, a rather bloodless one in which the Stuart king James II was replaced by Mary, James's daughter, and her husband, William of Orange. After William and Mary had assumed power, Parliament passed a Bill of Rights that specified the rights of Parliament and laid the foundation for a constitutional monarchy.

❋ The Bill of Rights

Whereas the said late King James II having abdicated the government, and the throne being thereby vacant, his Highness the prince of Orange (whom it has pleased Almighty God to make the glorious instrument of delivering this kingdom from popery and arbitrary power) did (by the device of the lords spiritual and temporal, and diverse principal persons of the Commons) cause letters to be written to the lords spiritual and temporal, being Protestants, and other letters to the several counties, cities, universities, boroughs, and Cinque Ports, for the choosing of such persons to represent them, as were of right to be sent to parliament, to meet and sit at Westminster upon the two and twentieth day of January, in this year 1689, in order to such an establishment as that their religion, laws, and liberties might not again be in danger of being subverted; upon which letters elections have been accordingly made.

And thereupon the said lords spiritual and temporal and Commons, pursuant to their respective letters and elections, being now assembled in a full and free representation of this nation, taking into their most serious consideration the best means for attaining the ends aforesaid, do in the first place (as their ancestors in like case have usually done), for the vindication and assertion of their ancient rights and liberties, declare:

1. That the pretended power of suspending laws, or the execution of laws, by regal authority, without consent of parliament is illegal.

2. That the pretended power of dispensing with the laws, or the execution of law by regal authority, as it has been assumed and exercised of late, is illegal.

3. That the commission for erecting the late court of commissioners for ecclesiastical causes, and all other commissions and courts of like nature, are illegal and pernicious.

4. That levying money for or to the use of the crown by pretense of prerogative, without grant of parliament, for longer time or in other manner than the same is or shall be granted, is illegal.

5. That it is the right of the subjects to petition the king, and all commitments and prosecutions for such petitioning are illegal.

6. That the raising or keeping a standing army within the kingdom in time of peace, unless it be with consent of parliament, is against law.

7. That the subjects which are Protestants may have arms for their defense suitable to their conditions, and as allowed by law.

8. That election of members of parliament ought to be free.

9. That the freedom of speech, and debates or proceedings in parliament, ought not to be impeached or questioned in any court or place out of parliament.

10. That excessive bail ought not to be required, nor excessive fines imposed, nor cruel and unusual punishments inflicted.

11. That jurors ought to be duly impaneled and returned, and jurors which pass upon men in trials for high treason ought to be freeholders.

12. That all grants and promises of fines and forfeitures of particular persons before conviction are illegal and void.

13. And that for redress of all grievances, and for the amending, strengthening, and preserving of the laws, parliament ought to be held frequently.

---

bloodshed, England had undergone a "Glorious Revolution," not over the issue of whether there would be a monarchy, but rather over who would be monarch.

The events of late 1688 constituted only the initial stage of the Glorious Revolution. The second, and far more important part, was the Revolution Settlement that confirmed William and Mary as monarchs. In January 1689, a Convention Parliament asserted that James had tried to subvert the constitution "by breaking the original contract between king and people," and declared the throne of England vacant. It then offered the throne to William and Mary, who accepted it along with the provisions of a Declaration of Rights, later enacted into law as a Bill of Rights in 1689 (see the box above). The Bill of Rights affirmed Parliament's right to make laws and levy taxes and made it impossible for kings to oppose or do without Parliament by stipulating that standing armies could be raised only with the consent of Parliament. Both elections and debates of Parliament had to be free, meaning that the king could not interfere. The rights of citizens to petition the sovereign, keep arms, have a jury trial, and not be subject to excessive bail were also confirmed. The Bill of Rights helped to fashion a system of government based on the rule of law and a freely elected Parliament, thus laying the foundation for a constitutional monarchy.

The Bill of Rights did not settle the religious questions that had played such a large role in England's troubles in the seventeenth century. The Toleration Act of 1689

Hobbes and Locke: Two Views of Political Authority

The seventeenth-century obsession with order and power was well reflected in the political thought of the Englishmen Thomas Hobbes and John Locke. In his Leviathan, *Hobbes presented the case for the state's claim to absolute authority over its subjects. John Locke, on the other hand, argued for limiting government power in his* Two Treatises of Government.

✳ Thomas Hobbes, *Leviathan*

The only way to erect a Common Power, as may be able to defend them from the invasion of foreigners and the injuries of one another, and thereby to secure them in such sort, as that by their own industry, and by the fruits of the Earth, they may nourish themselves and live contentedly; is, to confer all their power and strength upon one Man, or upon one Assembly of men, that may reduce all their Wills, by plurality of voices, unto one Will . . . and therein to submit their Wills, every one to his Will, and their Judgments, to his Judgment. This is more than Consent, or Concord; it is a real Unity of them all, in one and the same Person, made by Covenant of every man with every man. . . . This done, the Multitude so united in one Person, is called a COMMONWEALTH. . . .

They that have already instituted a Commonwealth, being thereby bound by Covenant cannot lawfully make a new Covenant, among themselves, to be obedience to any other, in any thing whatsoever, without his permission. And therefore, they that are subjects to a Monarch, cannot without his leave cast off Monarchy, and return to the confusion of a disunited Multitude; nor transfer their Person from him that bears it, to another Man, or other Assembly of men: for they . . . are bound, every man to every man, to acknowledge that he that already is their Sovereign, shall do, and judge fit to be done; so

that those who do not obey break their Covenant made to that man, which is injustice. . . . Consequently, none of the sovereign's Subjects, by any pretense of forfeiture, can be free from his Subjection.

✳ John Locke, *The Second Treatise of Government*

There is, therefore, another way whereby governments are dissolved, and that is when the legislative or the prince, either of them, act contrary to their trust. . . . Whenever the legislators endeavor to take away and destroy the property of the people, or to reduce them to slavery under arbitrary power, they put themselves into a state of war with the people who are thereupon absolved from any further obedience, and are left to the common refuge which God has provided for all men against force and violence. Whensoever, therefore, the legislative shall transgress this fundamental rule of society, and either by ambition, fear, folly, or corruption, endeavor to grasp themselves, or put into the hands of any other, an absolute power over the lives, liberties, and estates of the people, by this breach of trust they forfeit the power the people had put into their hands for quite contrary ends, and it devolves to the people, who have a right to resume their original liberty and, by the establishment of a new legislative, such as they shall think fit, provide for their own safety and security, which is the end for which they are in society. What I have said here concerning the legislative in general holds true also concerning the supreme executor, who having a double trust put in him—both to have a part in the legislative and the supreme execution of the law—acts against both when he goes about to set up his own arbitrary will as the law of the society.

---

granted Puritan Dissenters the right of free public worship (Catholics were still excluded), although they did not yet have full civil and political equality since the Test Act was not repealed. Although the Toleration Act did not mean complete religious freedom and equality, it marked a departure in English history: few people would ever again be persecuted for religious reasons.

Many historians have viewed the Glorious Revolution as the end of the seventeenth-century struggle between king and Parliament. By deposing one king and establishing another, Parliament had destroyed the divine-right theory of kingship (William was, after all, king by grace of Parliament, not God) and confirmed its right to participate in the government. Parliament did not have complete control of the government, but it now had an unquestioned right to participate in affairs of state. Over the next century,

it would gradually prove to be the real authority in the English system of constitutional monarchy.

✷ RESPONSES TO REVOLUTION

The English revolutions of the seventeenth century prompted very different responses from two English political thinkers—Thomas Hobbes and John Locke (see the box above). Thomas Hobbes (1588–1679), who lived during the English Civil War, was alarmed by the revolutionary upheavals in his contemporary England. Hobbes's name has since been associated with the state's claim to absolute authority over its subjects, a topic that he elaborated in his major treatise on political thought known as the *Leviathan,* published in 1651.

Hobbes claimed that in the state of nature, before society was organized, human life was "solitary, poor, nasty, brutish, and short." Humans were guided not by reason and moral ideals, but by animalistic instincts and a ruthless struggle for self-preservation. To save themselves from destroying each other (the "war of every man against every man"), people contracted to form a commonwealth, which Hobbes called "that great Leviathan (or rather, to speak more reverently, that mortal god) to which we owe our peace and defense." This commonwealth placed its collective power into the hands of a sovereign authority, preferably a single ruler, who served as executor, legislator, and judge. This absolute ruler possessed unlimited power. In Hobbes's view, subjects may not rebel; if they do, they must be suppressed.

John Locke (1632–1704) viewed the exercise of political power quite differently from Hobbes and argued against the absolute rule of one man. Locke's experience of English politics during the Glorious Revolution was incorporated into a political work called *Two Treatises of Government*. Like Hobbes, Locke began with the state of nature before human existence became organized socially. But, unlike Hobbes, Locke believed humans lived then in a state of equality and freedom rather than a state of war. In this state of nature, humans had certain inalienable natural rights—to life, liberty, and property. Like Hobbes, Locke did not believe all was well in the state of nature. Since there was no impartial judge in the state of nature, people found it difficult to protect these natural rights. So they mutually agreed to establish a government to ensure the protection of their rights. This agreement established mutual obligations: government would protect the rights of the people while the people would act reasonably toward government. But if a government broke this agreement—if a monarch, for example, failed to live up to his obligation to protect the natural rights or claimed absolute authority and made laws without the consent of the community—the people might form a new government. "The community perpetually retains a supreme power," Locke claimed. For Locke, however, the community of people was primarily the landholding aristocracy who were represented in Parliament, not the landless masses. Locke was hardly an advocate of political democracy, but his ideas proved important to both Americans and French in the eighteenth century and were used to support demands for constitutional government, the rule of law, and the protection of rights.

◆ Economic Trends: Mercantilism and European Colonies in the Seventeenth Century

The seventeenth century was marked by economic contraction, although variations existed depending on the country or region. Trade, industry, and agriculture all felt the pinch of a depression, which some historians believe

bottomed out between 1640 and 1680, while others argue that the decade of the 1690s was still bad, especially in France. Translated into everyday life, for many people the economic contraction of the seventeenth century meant scarce food, uncertain employment, and high rates of taxation.

Climate, too, played a factor in this economic reversal as Europeans experienced worsening weather patterns. In this "little ice age," extending from the sixteenth well into the eighteenth century, average temperatures fell, winters were colder, summers were wetter, and devastating storms seemed more frequent. Although the exact impact of climatic changes is uncertain, there were numerous reports of crop failures, the worst in 1649, 1660–1661, and the 1690s.

Population was also affected. Based on the birthrate of the seventeenth century, demographers would expect the European population to have doubled every twenty-five years. In reality, the population either declined or increased only intermittently as a result of a variety of factors. Infant mortality rates were high, 30 percent in the first year of life and 50 percent before the age of ten. Epidemics and famines were again common experiences in European life. The last great epidemic of bubonic plague spread across Europe in the middle and late years of the seventeenth century. The Mediterranean region suffered from 1646 to 1657, when the plague killed off 130,000 persons in Naples alone. In 1665, it struck England and devastated London, killing 20 percent of its population.

❋ *Mercantilism*

Mercantilism is the name historians use to identify a set of economic principles that dominated economic thought in the seventeenth century. Fundamental to mercantilism was the belief that the total volume of trade was unchangeable. Therefore, as Colbert, the French practitioner of mercantilism, stated: "Trade causes perpetual conflict, both in war and in peace, among the nations of Europe, as to who should carry off the greatest part. The Dutch, the English and the French are the actors in this conflict."[12] Since one nation could expand its trade and hence its prosperity only at the expense of others, to mercantilists, economic activity was war carried on by peaceful means.

According to the mercantilists, the prosperity of a nation depended upon a plentiful supply of bullion, or gold and silver. For this reason, it was desirable to achieve a favorable balance of trade in which goods exported were of greater value than those imported, promoting an influx of gold and silver payments that would increase the quantity of bullion. Furthermore, to encourage exports, governments should stimulate and protect export industries and trade by granting trade monopolies, encouraging investment in new industries through subsidies, importing foreign artisans, and improving transportation systems by building roads, bridges, and canals. By placing high tariffs on foreign goods, they could be kept out of the country and

THE DUTCH EAST INDIA COMPANY IN INDIA.
Pictured here is the Dutch trading post known as Hugly, founded in Bengal in 1610. This 1665 painting shows warehouses laid out in precise patterns surrounded by protective walls. Hugly was an important link in the network of bases that constituted Holland's trading empire in the East.

prevented from competing with domestic industries. Colonies were also deemed valuable as sources of raw materials and markets for finished goods.

As a system of economic principles, mercantilism focused on the role of the state, believing that state intervention in some aspects of the economy was desirable for the sake of the national good. Government regulations to ensure the superiority of export goods, the construction of roads and canals, and the granting of subsidies to create trade companies were all predicated on government involvement in economic affairs.

❈ Overseas Trade and Colonies

Mercantilist theory on the role of colonies was matched in practice by Europe's overseas expansion. With the development of colonies and trading posts in the Americas and the East, Europeans entered into an age of international commerce in the seventeenth century. Although some historians speak of a world economy, we should remember that local, regional, and intra-European trade still dominated the scene. At the end of the seventeenth century, for example, English imports totaled 360,000 tons, but only 5,000 tons came from the East Indies. About one-tenth of English and Dutch exports were shipped across the Atlantic; slightly more went to the East. What made the transoceanic trade rewarding, however, was not the volume, but the value of its goods. Dutch, English, and French merchants were bringing back products that were still consumed largely by the wealthy, but were beginning to make their way into the lives of artisans and merchants. Pepper and spices from the Indies, West Indian and Brazilian sugar, and Asian coffee and tea were becoming more readily available to European consumers. The first coffee and tea houses opened in London in the 1650s and spread rapidly to other parts of Europe.

In 1600, much overseas trade was still carried by the Spanish and Portuguese, who alone possessed colonies of any significant size. But war and steady pressure from their Dutch and English rivals eroded Portuguese trade in both the West and the East, although Portugal continued to profit from its large colonial empire in Brazil. The Spanish also maintained an enormous South American empire, but Spain's importance as a commercial power declined rapidly in the seventeenth century because of a drop in the output of the silver mines and the poverty of the Spanish monarchy.

Although the Dutch became the leading carriers of European products within Europe, they faced more severe competition when they moved into Asian and American markets. The Dutch East India Company was formed in 1602 to consolidate the gains made at the expense of the Portuguese and exploit the riches of the East. Since the wealthy oligarchy that controlled the company also dominated the Dutch government, this joint-stock company not only had a monopoly on all Asian trade but also possessed the right to make war, sign treaties, establish military and trading bases, and appoint governing officials. Gradually, the Dutch East India Company took control of most of the Portuguese bases in the East and opened trade with China and Japan. Its profits were spectacular in the first ten years.

The Dutch West India Company, created in 1621, was less successful. Its efforts were aimed against Portuguese and Spanish trade and possessions, and though it made some inroads in Portuguese Brazil and the Caribbean, they were not enough to compensate for the company's expenditures. Dutch settlements were also established on the North American continent. The mainland colony of New Netherlands stretched from the mouth of the Hudson as far north as Albany, New York. Present-day names such as Staten Island and Harlem remind us that it was the Dutch who initially settled the Hudson River valley. In the second half of the seventeenth century, competition from the English and French and years of warfare with those rivals led to the decline of the Dutch commercial empire. In 1664, the English seized the colony of

West Meets East: An Exchange of Royal Letters

Economic gain was not the only motivation of Western rulers who wished to establish a European presence in the East. In 1681, King Louis XIV of France wrote a letter to the king of Tonkin asking permission for Christian missionaries to proselytize in Vietnam. The king of Tonkin politely declined the request.

✾ A Letter to the King of Tonkin

Most high, most excellent, most mighty and most magnanimous Prince, our very dear and good friend, may it please God to increase your greatness with a happy end!

We hear from our subjects who were in your Realm what protection you accorded them. We appreciate this all the more since we have for you all the esteem that one can have for a prince as illustrious through his military valor as he is commendable for the justice which he exercises in his Realm. . . . Since the war which we have had for several years, in which all of Europe had banded together against us, prevented our vessels from going to the Indies, at the present time, when we are at peace after having gained many victories and expanded our Realm through the conquest of several important places, we have immediately given orders to the Royal Company to establish itself in your kingdom as soon as possible. . . . We have given orders to have brought to you some presents which we believe might be agreeable to you. But the one thing in the world which we desire most, both for you and for your Realm, would be to obtain for your subjects who have already embraced the law of the only true God of heaven and earth, the freedom to profess it, since this law is the highest, the noblest, the most sacred and especially the most suitable to have kings reign absolutely over the people.

We are even quite convinced that, if you knew the truths and the maxims which it teaches, you would give first of all to your subjects the glorious example of embracing it. We wish you this incomparable blessing together with a long and happy reign, and we pray God that it may please Him to augment your greatness with the happiest of endings.

Your very dear and good friend,
Louis

✾ Answers from the King of Tonkin to Louis XIV

The King of Tonkin sends to the King of France a letter to express to him his best sentiments. . . . Your communication, which comes from a country which is a thousand leagues away, and which proceeds from the heart as a testimony of your sincerity, merits repeated consideration and infinite praise. Politeness toward strangers is nothing unusual in our country. There is not a stranger who is not well received by us. How then could we refuse a man from France, which is the most celebrated among the kingdoms of the world and which for love of us wishes to frequent us and bring us merchandise? These feelings of fidelity and justice are truly worthy to be applauded. As regards your wish that we should cooperate in propagating your religion, we do not dare to permit it, for there is an ancient custom, introduced by edicts, which formally forbids it. Now, edicts are promulgated only to be carried out faithfully; without fidelity nothing is stable. How could we disdain a well-established custom to satisfy a private friendship? . . . This then is my letter. We send you herewith a modest gift which we offer you with a glad heart.

This letter was written at the beginning of winter and on a beautiful day.

New Netherlands and renamed it New York; soon afterward the Dutch West India Company went bankrupt. By the end of the seventeenth century, the Dutch golden age was beginning to tarnish.

The Dutch overseas trade and commercial empire faced two major rivals in the seventeenth century—the English and French. The English had founded their own East India Company in 1601 and proceeded to create a colonial empire in the New World along the Atlantic seaboard of North America. The failure of the Virginia Company made it evident that the colonizing of American lands was not necessarily conducive to quick profits. But the desire to practice one's own religion combined with economic interests could lead to successful colonization, as the Massachusetts Bay Company demonstrated. The Massachusetts colony had 4,000 settlers in its early years, but by 1660 had swelled to 40,000. Although the English had established control over most of the eastern seaboard by the end of the seventeenth century, the North American colonies were still of only minor significance to the English economy.

French commercial companies in the East experienced much difficulty. Though due in part to a late start, French problems also demonstrated the weakness of a commerce dependent on political rather than economic impetus (see the box above). The East India Companies set up by Henry IV and Richelieu all failed. In 1664, Colbert established a new East India Company that only barely managed to survive. The French had greater success in North America where in 1663 Canada was made the property of the crown and administered like a French province. But the French failed to provide adequate men or money, allowing their continental wars to take precedence over the conquest of the North American continent. Already in 1713, by the Treaty of Utrecht, the French began to cede some of their American possessions to their English rival.

◆ The World of Seventeenth-Century Culture

The seventeenth century was a remarkably talented one. In addition to the intellectuals responsible for the Scientific Revolution (see Chapter 16), the era was blessed with a number of prominent thinkers, artists, and writers. Some historians have even labeled it a century of genius.

❋ Art: French Classicism and Dutch Realism

In the second half of the seventeenth century, France replaced Italy as the cultural leader of Europe. Rejecting the Baroque style as overly showy and passionate, the French remained committed to the classical values of the High Renaissance. French late Classicism with its emphasis on clarity, simplicity, balance, and harmony of design was, however, a rather austere version of the High Renaissance style. Its triumph reflected the shift in seventeenth-century French society from chaos to order. Though it rejected the emotionalism and high drama of the Baroque, French Classicism continued the Baroque's conception of grandeur in the portrayal of noble subjects, especially those from classical antiquity. Nicholas Poussin (1594–1665) exemplified these principles in his paintings. His choice of scenes from classical mythology, the orderliness of his landscapes, the postures of his figures copied from the sculptures of antiquity, and his use of brown tones all reflect French Classicism of the late seventeenth century.

The supremacy of Dutch commerce in the seventeenth century was paralleled by a brilliant flowering of Dutch painting. Wealthy patricians and burghers of Dutch urban society commissioned works of art for their guild halls, town halls, and private dwellings. The interests of this burgher society were reflected in the subject matter of many Dutch paintings: portraits of themselves, group portraits of their military companies and guilds, landscapes, seascapes, genre scenes, still lifes, and the interiors of their residences. Neither classical nor Baroque, Dutch painters were primarily interested in the realistic portrayal of secular, everyday life.

This interest in painting scenes of everyday life is evident in the work of Judith Leyster (c. 1609–1660), who established her own independent painting career, a remarkable occurrence in seventeenth-century Europe. Leyster became the first female member of the painting Guild of St. Luke in Haarlem, which enabled her to set up her own workshop and take on three male pupils. Musicians playing their instruments, women sewing, children laughing while playing games, and actors performing, all form the subject matter of Leyster's portrayals of everyday Dutch life. But she was also capable of introspection, as is evident in her *Self-Portrait*.

The finest example of the golden age of Dutch painting was Rembrandt van Rijn (1606–1669). Rembrandt's early career was reminiscent of Rubens in that he painted opulent portraits and grandiose scenes in often colorful fashion. Like Rubens, he was prolific and successful; unlike Rubens, he turned away from materialistic success and public approval to follow his own artistic path. In the process, he lost public support and died bankrupt.

NICHOLAS POUSSIN, *LANDSCAPE WITH THE BURIAL OF PHOCIAN*. France became the new cultural leader of Europe in the second half of the seventeenth century. French Classicism upheld the values of High Renaissance style, but in a more static version. In Nicholas Poussin's work, we see the emphasis of French Classicism on the use of scenes from classical sources and the creation of a sense of grandeur and noble strength in both human figures and landscape.

REMBRANDT VAN RIJN, *SYNDICS OF THE CLOTH GUILD.*
The Dutch experienced a golden age of painting during
the seventeenth century. The burghers and patricians of
Dutch urban society commissioned works of art, and
these quite naturally reflected the burghers' interests, as
this painting by Rembrandt illustrates.

JUDITH LEYSTER, *SELF-PORTRAIT.* Although Judith
Leyster was a well-known artist to her Dutch contemporaries, her fame diminished soon after her death. In the
late nineteenth century, however, a Dutch art historian
rediscovered her work. In her *Self-Portrait*, painted in
1635, she is seen pausing in her work in front of one of
the scenes of daily life that made her such a popular
artist in her own day.

Although Rembrandt shared the Dutch predilection
for realistic portraits, he became more introspective as
he grew older. He refused to follow his contemporaries
whose pictures were largely secular in subject matter; half
of his paintings focused on scenes from biblical tales.
Since the Protestant tradition of hostility to religious
pictures had discouraged artistic expression, Rembrandt
stands out as the one great Protestant painter of the seventeenth century. Rembrandt's religious pictures, however,
avoided the monumental subjects, such as the Creation
and Last Judgment, that were typical of Catholic artists.
Instead, he favored pictures that focused on the individual's relationship with God and depicted people's inward
suffering in quiet, evocative scenes.

French Comedy: The Would-Be Gentleman

The comedy writer Jean-Baptiste Molière has long been regarded as one of the best playwrights of the age of Louis XIV. Molière's comedy, The Would-Be Gentleman, focuses on Monsieur Jourdain, a vain and pretentious Parisian merchant who aspires to become a gentleman (at that time, a term for a member of the nobility who possessed, among other things, a title, fine clothes, and good taste). Jourdain foolishly believes that he can buy these things and hires a number of teachers to instruct him. In this scene from Act II, Jourdain learns from his philosophy teacher that he has been speaking prose all his life.

✳ Jean-Baptiste Molière, *The Would-Be Gentleman*

PHILOSOPHY MASTER: I will explain to you all these curiosities to the bottom.

M. JOURDAIN: Pray do. But now, I must commit a secret to you. I'm in love with a person of great quality, and I should be glad you would help me to write something to her in a short *billet-doux* [love letter], which I'll drop at her feet.

PHILOSOPHY MASTER: Very well.

M. JOURDAIN: That will be very gallant, won't it?

PHILOSOPHY MASTER: Without doubt. Is it verse that you would write to her?

M. JOURDAIN: No, no, none of your verse.

PHILOSOPHY MASTER: You would only have prose?

M. JOURDAIN: No, I would neither have verse nor prose.

PHILOSOPHY MASTER: It must be one or the other.

M. JOURDAIN: Why so?

PHILOSOPHY MASTER: Because, sir, there's nothing to express one's self by, but prose, or verse.

M. JOURDAIN: Is there nothing then but prose, or verse?

PHILOSOPHY MASTER: No, sir, whatever is not prose, is verse; and whatever is not verse, is prose.

M. JOURDAIN: And when one talks, what may that be then?

PHILOSOPHY MASTER: Prose.

M. JOURDAIN: How? When I say, Nicole, bring me my slippers, and give me my nightcap, is that prose?

PHILOSOPHY MASTER: Yes, sir.

M. JOURDAIN: On my conscience, I have spoken prose above these forty years without knowing anything of the matter; and I have all the obligations in the world to you for informing me of this. I would therefore put into a letter to her: Beautiful marchioness, your fair eyes make me die with love; but I would have this placed in a gallant manner; and have a gentle turn.

PHILOSOPHY MASTER: Why, add that the fire of her eyes has reduced your heart to ashes: that you suffer for her night and day all the torments—

M. JOURDAIN: No, no, no, I won't have all that—I'll have nothing but what I told you. Beautiful marchioness, your fair eyes make me die with love.

PHILOSOPHY MASTER: You must by all means lengthen the thing out a little.

M. JOURDAIN: No, I tell you, I'll have none but those very words in the letter: but turned in a modish way, ranged handsomely as they should be. I desire you'd show me a little, that I may see the different manners in which one may place them.

PHILOSOPHY MASTER: One may place them first of all as you said: Beautiful marchioness, your fair eyes make me die for love. Or suppose: For love die me make, beautiful marchioness, your fair eyes. Or perhaps: Your eyes fair, for love me make, beautiful marchioness, die. Or suppose: Die your fair eyes, beautiful marchioness, for love me make. Or however: Me make your eyes fair die, beautiful marchioness, for love.

M. JOURDAIN: But of all these ways, which is best?

PHILOSOPHY MASTER: That which you said: Beautiful marchioness, your fair eyes make me die for love.

M. JOURDAIN: Yet at the same time, I never studied it, and I made the whole of it at the first touch. I thank you with all my heart, and desire you would come in good time tomorrow.

PHILOSOPHY MASTER: I shall not fail.

✳ *The Theater: The Triumph of French Neoclassicism*

As the great age of theater in England and Spain was drawing to a close around 1630, a new dramatic era began to dawn in France that lasted into the 1680s. Unlike Shakespeare in England and Lope de Vega in Spain, French playwrights wrote more for an elite audience and were forced to depend upon royal patronage. Louis XIV used theater as he did art and architecture—to attract attention to his monarchy.

French dramatists cultivated a classical style in which the Aristotelian rules of dramatic composition, observing the three unities of time, place, and action, were closely followed. French Neoclassicism emphasized the clever, polished, and correct over the emotional and imaginative. Many of the French works of the period derived both their themes and their plots from Greek and Roman sources, especially evident in the works of Jean-Baptiste Racine (1639–1699). In *Phédre*, which has been called his best play, Racine followed closely the plot of the Greek tragedian Euripides' *Hippolytus*. Like the ancient tragedians,

Racine, who perfected the French neoclassical tragic style, focused on conflicts, such as between love and honor or inclination and duty, that characterized and revealed the tragic dimensions of life.

Jean-Baptiste Molière (1622–1673) enjoyed the favor of the French court and benefited from the patronage of the Sun King. He wrote, produced, and acted in a series of comedies that often satirized the religious and social world of his time (see the box on p. 455). In *The Misanthrope*, he mocked the corruption of court society, while in *Tartuffe*, he ridiculed religious hypocrisy. Molière's satires, however, sometimes got him into trouble. The Paris clergy did not find *Tartuffe* funny and had it banned for five years. Only the protection of Louis XIV saved Molière from more severe harassment.

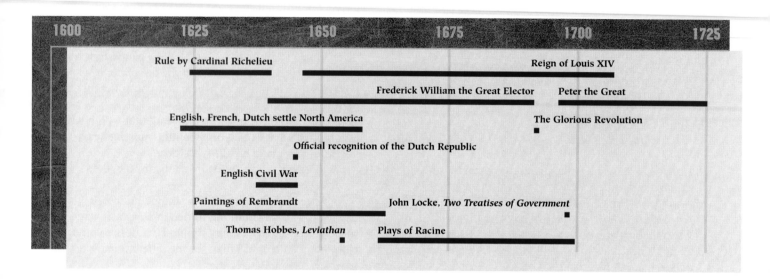

CONCLUSION

To many historians, the seventeenth century has assumed extraordinary proportions. The divisive effects of the Reformation had been assimilated and the concept of a united Christendom, held as an ideal since the Middle Ages, had been irrevocably destroyed by the religious wars, making possible the emergence of a system of nation-states in which power politics took on an increasing significance. The growth of political thought focusing on the secular origins of state power reflected the changes that were going on in seventeenth-century society.

Within those states, there slowly emerged some of the machinery that made possible a growing centralization of power. In those states called absolutist, strong monarchs with the assistance of their aristocracies took the lead in providing the leadership for greater centralization. But in England, where the landed aristocracy gained power at the expense of the monarchs, the foundations were laid for a constitutional government in which Parliament provided the focus for the institutions of centralized power. In all the major European states, a growing concern for power and dynastic expansion led to larger armies and greater conflict. War remained an endemic feature of Western civilization.

But the search for order and harmony continued, evident in art and literature. At the same time, though it would be misleading to state that Europe had become a secular world, we would have to say that religious preoccupations and values were losing ground to secular considerations. The seventeenth century was a transitional period to a more secular spirit that has characterized modern Western civilization until the present time. No stronger foundation for this spirit could be found than in the new view of the universe that was created by the Scientific Revolution of the seventeenth century, and it is to that story that we must now turn.

NOTES

1. Quoted in John B. Wolf, *Louis XIV* (New York, 1968), p. 134.
2. Quoted in James B. Collins, *The State in Early Modern France* (Cambridge, 1995), p. 130.
3. Quoted in W. H. Lewis, *The Splendid Century* (Garden City, N.Y., 1953), pp. 39–40.
4. Quoted in Wolf, *Louis XIV*, p. 284.
5. Quoted in ibid., p. 618.
6. Quoted in D. H. Pennington, *Europe in the Seventeenth Century*, 2d ed. (London and New York, 1989), p. 494.
7. Quoted in J. H. Elliott, *Imperial Spain, 1469–1716* (New York, 1963), p. 306.

8. Quoted in ibid., p. 338.
9. Quoted in Vasili Klyuchevsky, *Peter the Great*, trans. Liliana Archibald (New York, 1958), p. 244.
10. Quoted in B. H. Sumner, *Peter the Great and the Emergence of Russia* (New York, 1962), p. 122.
11. Quoted in Violet Barbour, *Capitalism in Amsterdam in the 17th Century* (Ann Arbor, Mich., 1963), p. 46.
12. Quoted in H. G. Koenigsberger, *Early Modern Europe: 1500–1798* (London, 1987), p. 172.

SUGGESTIONS FOR FURTHER READING

In addition to the general works listed in Chapter 14, see also D. H. Pennington, *Europe in the Seventeenth Century*, 2d ed. (London and New York, 1989); T. Munck, *Seventeenth Century Europe, 1598–1700* (London, 1990); and R. S. Dunn, *The Age of Religious Wars, 1559–1715*, 2d ed. (New York, 1979).

For brief accounts of seventeenth-century French history, see R. Briggs, *Early Modern France, 1560–1715* (Oxford, 1977); and J. B. Collins, *The State in Early Modern France* (Cambridge, 1995). More detailed studies on France during the periods of Cardinals Richelieu and Mazarin are R. Bonney, *Society and Government in France under Richelieu and Mazarin, 1624–1662* (London, 1985); and J. Bergin, *Cardinal Richelieu: Power and the Pursuit of Wealth* (London, 1985). A solid and very readable biography of Louis XIV is J. B. Wolf, *Louis XIV* (New York, 1968). For a brief study, see P. R. Campbell, *Louis XIV, 1661–1715* (London, 1993). Also of value are the works by O. Bernier, *Louis XIV* (New York, 1988); and P. Goubert, *Louis XIV and Twenty Million Frenchmen*, trans. A. Carter (New York, 1970). A now classic work on life in Louis XIV's France is W. H. Lewis, *The Splendid Century* (Garden City, N.Y., 1953). Well-presented summaries of revisionist views on Louis's monarchical power are R. Mettam, *Power and Faction in Louis XIV's France* (Oxford, 1988); and W. Beik, *Absolutism and Society in Seventeenth-Century France* (Cambridge, 1985). C. W. Cole, *Colbert and a Century of French Mercantilism*, 2 vols. (London, 1939), is still the fundamental study.

Good general works on seventeenth-century Spanish history include J. Lynch, *Spain under the Habsburgs*, 2d ed. (New York, 1981); and the relevant sections of J. H. Elliott, *Imperial Spain, 1469–1716* (New York, 1963; rev. ed. 1977). The important minister Olivares is examined in J. H. Elliott, *The Count-Duke of Olivares: The Statesman in an Age of Decline* (London, 1986).

An older, but still valuable survey of the German states in the seventeenth century can be found in H. Holborn, *A History of Modern Germany, 1648–1840* (London, 1965). An important recent work is M. Hughes, *Early Modern Germany, 1477–1806* (Philadelphia, 1992). On the creation of an Austrian state, see R. J. W. Evans, *The Making of the Habsburg Monarchy, 1550–1700* (Oxford, 1979); and C. Ingrao, *The Habsburg Monarchy, 1618–1815* (Cambridge, 1994). The older work by F. L. Carsten, *The Origins of Prussia* (Oxford, 1954), remains an outstanding study of early Prussian history. A good biography of the dynamic Charles XII is R. Hatton, *Charles XII of Sweden* (London, 1968). For an introduction to Polish history, see N. Davies, *God's Playground: A History of Poland*, vol. 1, *The Origins to 1795* (Oxford, 1981).

On Russian history before Peter the Great, see the classic work by V. O. Klyuchevsky, *A Course in Russian History: The Seventeenth Century* (Chicago, 1968). Works on Peter the Great include L. Hughes, *Russia in the Age of Peter the Great* (New Haven, Conn., 1998); M. S. Anderson, *Peter the Great*, 2d ed. (New York, 1995); and the massive popular biography by R. K. Massie, *Peter the Great* (New York, 1980).

Good general works on the period of the Revolution include M. A. Kishlansky, *A Monarchy Transformed* (London, 1996); G. E. Aylmer, *Rebellion or Revolution? England, 1640–1660* (New York, 1986); and A. Hughes, *The Causes of the English Civil War* (New York, 1991). On the war itself, see R. Ashton, *The English Civil War: Conservatism and Revolution, 1604–1649* (London, 1976). On Oliver Cromwell, see R. Howell, Jr., *Cromwell* (Boston, 1977); and P. Gaunt, *Oliver Cromwell* (Cambridge, Mass., 1996). For a general survey of the post-Cromwellian era, see J. R. Jones, *Country and Court: England, 1658–1714* (London, 1978). A more specialized study is W. A. Speck, *The Revolution of 1688* (Oxford, 1988). On Charles II, see the scholarly biography by R. Hutton, *Charles II* (Oxford, 1989). Locke's political ideas are examined in J. H. Franklin, *John Locke and the Theory of Sovereignty* (London, 1978). On Thomas Hobbes, see D. D. Raphael, *Hobbes* (London, 1977).

On the United Provinces, there is a valuable but very lengthy study by J. Israel, *The Dutch Republic: Its Rise, Greatness, and Fall* (New York, 1995). See also the short, but sound introduction by K. H. D. Haley, *The Dutch in the Seventeenth Century* (London, 1972). Of much value is S. Schama, *The Embarrassment of Riches: An Interpretation of Dutch Culture in the Golden Age* (New York, 1987).

On the economic side of the seventeenth century, there are the three volumes by F. Braudel, *Civilization and Capitalism in the 15th to 18th Century*, which obviously cover much more than just the seventeenth century: *The Structures of Everyday Life* (London, 1981); *The Wheels of Commerce* (London, 1982); and *The Perspective of the World* (London, 1984). Two single-volume comprehensive surveys are J. de Vries, *The Economy of Europe in an Age of Crisis* (Cambridge, 1976); and R. S. Duplessis, *Transitions to Capitalism in Early Modern Europe* (Cambridge, 1997). On overseas trade and colonial empires, see C. R. Boxer, *The Dutch Seaborne Empire, 1600–1800* (New York, 1965); and R. Davis, *English Overseas Trade, 1500–1700* (London, 1973). Although frequently criticized, the standard work on mercantilism remains E. Heckscher, *Mercantilism*, 2 vols. (London, 1935).

French theater and literature are examined in A. Adam, *Grandeur and Illusion: French Literature and Society, 1600–1715*, trans. J. Tint (New York, 1972). For an examination of French and Dutch art, see A. Merot, *French Painting in the Seventeenth Century* (New Haven, Conn., 1995); and S. Slive, *Dutch Painting, 1600–1800* (New Haven, Conn., 1993).

For additional reading, go to InfoTrac College Edition, your online research library at http://web1.infotrac-college.com

Enter the search terms *Louis XIV* using Key Terms.

Enter the search terms *Peter the Great* using Key Terms.

Enter the search terms *Oliver Cromwell* using Key Terms.

Enter the search term *mercantilism* using the Subject Guide.

Toward a New Heaven and a New Earth: The Scientific Revolution and the Emergence of Modern Science

CHAPTER OUTLINE

- Background to the Scientific Revolution
- Toward a New Heaven: A Revolution in Astronomy
- Advances in Medicine
- Women in the Origins of Modern Science
- Toward a New Earth: Descartes, Rationalism, and a New View of Humankind
- The Scientific Method
- Science and Religion in the Seventeenth Century
- The Spread of Scientific Knowledge
- Conclusion

FOCUS QUESTIONS

- What developments during the Middle Ages and Renaissance contributed to the Scientific Revolution of the seventeenth century?
- What did Copernicus, Kepler, Galileo, and Newton contribute to a new vision of the universe, and how did it differ from the Ptolemaic conception of the universe?
- What role did women play in the Scientific Revolution?
- What problems did the Scientific Revolution present for organized religion, and how did both the church and the emerging scientists attempt to solve these problems?
- How were the ideas of the Scientific Revolution disseminated, and what impact did they have on society?

I N ADDITION *to the political, economic, social, and international crises of the seventeenth century, we need to add an intellectual one. The Scientific Revolution questioned and ultimately challenged conceptions and beliefs about the nature of the external world and reality that had crystallized into a rather strict orthodoxy by the Late Middle Ages. Derived from the works of ancient Greeks and Romans and grounded in Christian thought, the medieval worldview had become a formidable one. No doubt, the breakdown of Christian unity during the Reformation and the subsequent religious wars had created an environment in which Europeans had become accustomed to challenging both*

these general concepts could then be tested and verified by precise experiments.

The scientific method, of course, was valuable in answering the question "how" something works, and its success in doing this gave others much confidence in the method. It did not attempt to deal with the question of "why" something happens or the purpose and meaning behind the world of nature. This allowed religion still to be important in the seventeenth century.

◆ Science and Religion in the Seventeenth Century

In Galileo's struggle with the inquisitorial Holy Office of the Catholic church, we see the beginning of the conflict between science and religion that has marked the history of modern Western civilization. Since time immemorial, theology had seemed to be the queen of the sciences. It was natural that the churches would continue to believe that religion was the final measure of all things. To the emerging scientists, however, it often seemed that theologians knew not of what they spoke. These "natural philosophers" then tried to draw lines between the knowledge of religion and the knowledge of "natural philosophy" or nature. Galileo had clearly felt that it was unnecessary to pit science against religion:

> In discussions of physical problems we ought to begin not from the authority of scriptural passages, but from sense-experiences and necessary demonstrations; for the holy Bible and the phenomena of nature proceed alike from the divine word, the former as the dictate of the Holy Ghost and the latter as the observant executrix of God's commands. It is necessary for the Bible, in order to be accommodated to the understanding of every man, to speak many things which appear to differ from the absolute truth so far as the bare meaning of the words is concerned. But Nature, on the other hand, is inexorable and immutable; she never transgresses the laws imposed upon her, or cares a whit whether her abstruse reasons and methods of operation are understandable to men.[22]

To Galileo it made little sense for the church to determine the nature of physical reality on the basis of biblical texts that were subject to radically divergent interpretations. The church, however, decided otherwise in Galileo's case and lent its great authority to one scientific theory, the Ptolemaic-Aristotelian cosmology, no doubt because it fit so well with its own philosophical views of reality. But the church's decision had tremendous consequences, just as the rejection of Darwin's ideas did in the nineteenth century. For educated individuals, it established a dichotomy between scientific investigations and religious beliefs. As the scientific beliefs triumphed, it became almost inevitable that religious beliefs would suffer, leading to a growing secularization in European intellectual life, precisely what the church had hoped to combat by opposing Copernicanism. Many seventeenth-century intellectuals were both religious and scientific and believed that the

implications of this split would be tragic. Some believed that the split was largely unnecessary while others felt the need to combine God, humans, and a mechanistic universe into a new philosophical synthesis. Two individuals—Spinoza and Pascal—illustrate some of the wide diversity in the response of European intellectuals to the implications of the cosmological revolution of the seventeenth century.

Benedict de Spinoza (1632–1677) was a philosopher who grew up in the relatively tolerant atmosphere of Amsterdam. He was excommunicated from the Amsterdam synagogue at the age of twenty-four for rejecting the tenets of Judaism. Ostracized by the local Jewish community and major Christian churches alike, Spinoza lived a quiet, independent life, earning a living by grinding optical lenses and refusing to accept an academic position in philosophy at the University of Heidelberg for fear of compromising his freedom of thought. Spinoza read a great deal of the new scientific literature and was influenced by Descartes.

Although he followed Descartes's rational approach to knowledge, Spinoza was unwilling to accept the implications of Descartes's ideas, especially the separation of mind and matter and the apparent separation of an infinite God from the finite world of matter. God was not simply creator of the universe, he was the universe. All that is is in God, and nothing can be apart from God. This philosophy of pantheism (others have labeled it panentheism or monism) was set out in Spinoza's book, *Ethics Demonstrated in the Geometrical Manner*, which was not published until after his death.

To Spinoza, human beings are not "situated in nature as a kingdom within a kingdom," but are as much a part of God or nature or the universal order as other natural objects. The failure to understand God had led to many misconceptions; for one, that nature exists only for one's use:

> As they find in themselves and outside themselves many means which assist them not a little in their search for what is useful, for instance, eyes for seeing, teeth for chewing, herbs and animals for yielding food, the sun for giving light, the sea for breeding fish, they come to look on the whole of nature as a means for obtaining such conveniences.[23]

Furthermore, unable to find any other cause for the existence of these things, they attributed them to a creator-God who must be worshiped to gain their ends: "Hence also it follows, that everyone thought out for himself, according to his abilities, a different way of worshiping God, so that God might love him more than his fellows, and direct the whole course of nature for the satisfaction of his blind cupidity and insatiable avarice." Then, when nature appeared unfriendly in the form of storms, earthquakes, and diseases, "they declared that such things happen, because the gods are angry at some wrong done them by men, or at some fault committed in their worship," rather than realizing "that good and evil fortunes fall to the lot of pious and impious alike."[24] Likewise, human beings made moral condemnations of others because they failed to understand that human emotions, "passions of hatred, anger, envy and so, considered in themselves, follow from the same necessity and efficacy of nature" and "nothing comes to pass in nature in contravention to her universal laws." To explain human emotions, like everything else, we need to analyze them as we would the movements of planets: "I shall, therefore, treat of the nature and strength of my emotions according to the same method as I employed heretofore in my investigations concerning God and the mind. I shall consider human actions and desires in exactly the same manner as though I were concerned with lines, planes, and solids."[25] Everything has a rational explanation and humans are capable of finding it. In using reason, people can find true happiness. Their real freedom comes when they understand the order and necessity of nature and achieve detachment from passing interests.

Spinoza's complex synthesis of God, humans, and the universe was not easily accepted by his contemporaries, and his pantheism was mistakenly condemned as "hideous atheism." Others were upset by his attitude toward morality because he viewed it as found in nature and known by reason, not revealed to people through the Bible. Even Spinoza declared that some would find strange his attempt to treat of human desires "in exactly the same manner as though I were concerned with lines, planes, and solids."

Blaise Pascal (1623–1662) was a French scientist who sought to keep science and religion united. He had a brief, but checkered career. For a short time, he was a reader of Montaigne and a companion of freethinkers. An accomplished scientist and brilliant mathematician, he excelled at both the practical, by inventing a calculating machine, and the abstract, by devising a theory of chance or probability and doing work on conic sections. After a profound mystical vision on the night of November 23, 1654, which assured him that God cared for the human soul, he devoted the rest of his life to religious matters. He planned to write an "Apology for the Christian Religion" but died before he could do so. He did leave a set of notes for the larger work, however, which in published form became known as *Pensées* or *The Thoughts*.

In *Pensées*, Pascal tried to convert rationalists to Christianity by appealing both to their reason and to their emotions. Humans were, he argued, frail creatures, often deceived by their senses, misled by reason, and battered by their emotions. And yet they were beings whose very nature involved thinking: "Man is but a reed, the weakest in nature; but he is a thinking reed. . . . Our whole dignity consists, therefore, in thought. By thought we must raise ourselves. . . . Let us endeavor, then, to think well; this is the beginning of morality."[26]

Pascal was determined to show that the Christian religion was not contrary to reason: "If we violate the principles of reason, our religion will be absurd, and it will be laughed at." Christianity, he felt, was the only religion that recognized people's true state of being as both vulnerable and great. To a Christian, a human being was both fallen and at the same time God's special creation. But it was not necessary to emphasize one at the expense of the other—to view humans as only rational or only hopeless. Thus,

PASCAL. Blaise Pascal was a brilliant scientist and mathematician who hoped to keep science and Christianity united. In the *Pensées,* he made a passionate argument on behalf of the Christian religion. He is pictured here in a posthumous portrait by Quesnel.

"knowledge of God without knowledge of man's wretchedness leads to pride. Knowledge of man's wretchedness without knowledge of God leads to despair. Knowledge of Jesus Christ is the middle course, because by it we discover both God and our wretched state." Pascal even had an answer for skeptics in his famous wager. God is a reasonable bet; it is worthwhile to assume that God exists. If he does, then we win all; if he does not, we lose nothing.

Despite his background as a scientist and mathematician, Pascal refused to rely on the scientist's world of order and rationality to attract people to God: "If we submit everything to reason, there will be no mystery and no supernatural element in our religion." In the new cosmology of the seventeenth century, "finite man," Pascal believed, was lost in the new infinite world, a realization that frightened him: "The eternal silence of those infinite spaces strikes me with terror" (see the box on p. 481). The world of nature, then, could never reveal God: "Because they have failed to contemplate these infinites, men have rashly plunged into the examination of nature, as though they bore some proportion to her. . . . Their assumption is as infinite as their object." A Christian could only rely on a God who through Jesus cared for human beings. In the final analysis, after providing reasonable arguments for Christianity, Pascal came to rest on faith. Reason, he believed, could take people only so far: "The heart has its reasons of which the reason knows nothing." As a Christian, faith was the final step: "The heart feels God, not the reason. This is what constitutes faith: God experienced by the heart, not by the reason."[27]

Pascal: "What Is a Man in the Infinite?"

Perhaps no intellectual in the seventeenth century gave greater expression to the uncertainties generated by the cosmological revolution than Blaise Pascal. Himself a scientist, Pascal's mystical vision of God's presence caused him to pursue religious truths with a passion. His work, the Pensées, consisted of notes for a larger, unfinished work justifying the Christian religion. In this selection, Pascal presents his musings on the human place in an infinite world.

❀ Blaise Pascal, *Pensées*

Let man then contemplate the whole of nature in her full and exalted majesty. Let him turn his eyes from the lowly objects which surround him. Let him gaze on that brilliant light set like an eternal lamp to illumine the Universe; let the earth seem to him a dot compared with the vast orbit described by the sun, and let him wonder at the fact that this vast orbit itself is no more than a very small dot compared with that described by the stars in their revolutions around the firmament. But if our vision stops here, let the imagination pass on; it will exhaust its powers of thinking long before nature ceases to supply it with material for thought. All this visible world is no more than an imperceptible speck in nature's ample bosom. No idea approaches it. We may extend our conceptions beyond all imaginable space; yet pro-

duce only atoms in comparison with the reality of things. It is an infinite sphere, the center of which is everywhere, the circumference nowhere. In short, it is the greatest perceptible mark of God's almighty power that our imagination should lose itself in that thought.

Returning to himself, let man consider what he is compared with all existence; let him think of himself as lost in his remote corner of nature; and from this little dungeon in which he finds himself lodged—I mean the Universe—let him learn to set a true value on the earth, its kingdoms, and cities, and upon himself. What is a man in the infinite? . . .

For, after all, what is a man in nature? A nothing in comparison with the infinite, an absolute in comparison with nothing, a central point between nothing and all. Infinitely far from understanding these extremes, the end of things and their beginning are hopelessly hidden from him in an impenetrable secret. He is equally incapable of seeing the nothingness from which he came, and the infinite in which he is engulfed. What else then will he perceive but some appearance of the middle of things, in an eternal despair of knowing either their principle or their purpose? All things emerge from nothing and are borne onward to infinity. Who can follow this marvelous process? The Author of these wonders understands them. None but He can.

In retrospect, it is obvious that Pascal failed to achieve his goal of uniting Christianity and science. Increasingly, the gap between science and traditional religion grew wider as Europe continued along its path of secularization. Of course, traditional religions were not eliminated, nor is there any evidence that churches had yet lost their numbers. That would happen later. Nevertheless, more and more of the intellectual, social, and political elites began to act on the basis of secular rather than religious assumptions.

◆ The Spread of Scientific Knowledge

In the course of the seventeenth century, scientific learning and investigation began to increase dramatically. Major universities in Europe established new chairs of science, especially in medicine. Royal and princely patronage of individual scientists became an international phenomenon. The king of Denmark constructed an astronomical observatory for Tycho Brahe; Emperor Rudolf II hired Tycho Brahe and Johannes Kepler as imperial mathematicians; the grand duke of Tuscany appointed Galileo to a similar post. Of greater importance to the work of science, how-

ever, was the emergence of new learned societies and journals that enabled the new scientists to communicate their ideas to each other and to disseminate them to a wider, literate public.

❀ *The Scientific Societies*

The first of these scientific societies appeared in Italy, but those of England and France were ultimately of more significance. The English Royal Society evolved out of informal gatherings of scientists at London and Oxford in the 1640s, although it did not receive a formal charter from King Charles II until 1662. The French Royal Academy of Sciences also arose out of informal scientific meetings in Paris during the 1650s. In 1666, urged on by his minister Colbert, Louis XIV formally recognized the group. The French Academy received abundant state support and remained under government control; its members were appointed and paid salaries by the state. In contrast, the Royal Society of England received little government encouragement, and its fellows simply co-opted new members.

Early on, both the English and French scientific societies formally emphasized the practical value of scientific research. The Royal Society established a committee to investigate technological improvements for industry while

LOUIS XIV AND COLBERT VISIT THE ACADEMY OF SCIENCES. In the seventeenth century, individual scientists received royal and princely patronage, and a number of learned societies were established. In France, Louis XIV, urged on by his minister Colbert, gave formal recognition to the French Academy in 1666. In this painting by Henri Testelin, Louis XIV is shown seated, surrounded by Colbert and members of the French Royal Academy of Sciences.

the French Academy collected tools and machines. This concern with the practical benefits of science proved short-lived, however, as both societies came to focus their primary interest on theoretical work in mechanics and astronomy. The construction of observatories at Paris in 1667 and at Greenwich, England, in 1675 greatly facilitated research in astronomy by both groups. The French Academy, however, since it was controlled by the state, was forced by the war minister of France, the marquis de Louvois, to continue its practical work to benefit both the "king and the state." The French example was especially important as a model for the scientific societies established in neighboring Germany. German princes and city governments encouraged the foundation of small-scale scientific societies of their own. Most of them, such as the Scientific Academy created in 1700 by the elector of Brandenburg, as well as the scientific academies established in most European countries in the eighteenth century, were spon-

sored by governments and were mainly devoted to the betterment of the state. Although both the English and French societies made useful contributions to scientific knowledge in the second half of the seventeenth century, their true significance arose from their example that science should proceed as a cooperative venture.

Scientific journals furthered this concept of cooperation. The French *Journal des Savants,* published weekly beginning in 1665, printed results of experiments as well as general scientific knowledge. Its format appealed to both scientists and the educated public interested in the new science. The *Philosophical Transactions* of the Royal Society, however, also initiated in 1665, published papers of its members and learned correspondence and was aimed at practicing scientists. It became a prototype for the scholarly journals of later learned and academic societies and a crucial instrument for circulating news of scientific and academic activities.

THE ROYAL OBSERVATORY AT GREENWICH. To facilitate their astronomical investigations, both the English and the French constructed observatories, such as the one pictured here, which was built at Greenwich, England, in 1675. Here the royal astronomer works at the table while his two assistants make observations.

✤ Science and Society

The importance of science in the history of modern Western civilization is usually taken for granted. No doubt the Industrial Revolution of the nineteenth century provided tangible proof of the effectiveness of science and ensured its victory over Western minds. But how did science become such an integral part of Western culture in the seventeenth and eighteenth centuries? Recent research has stressed that one cannot simply assert that people perceived that science was a rationally superior system. Two important social factors, however, might help to explain the relatively rapid acceptance of the new science.

It has been argued that the literate mercantile and propertied elites of Europe were attracted to the new science because it offered new ways to exploit resources for profit. Some of the early scientists made it easier for these groups to accept the new ideas by showing how they could be applied directly to specific industrial and technological needs. Galileo, for example, consciously sought an alliance between science and the material interests of the educated elite when he assured his listeners that the science of mechanics would be quite useful "when it becomes necessary to build bridges or other structures over water, something occurring mainly in affairs of great importance." At the same time, Galileo stressed that science was fit for the "minds of the wise" and not for "the shallow minds of the common people." This made science part of the high culture of Europe's wealthy elites at a time when that culture was being increasingly separated from the popular culture of the lower classes (see Chapter 17).

It has also been argued that political interests used the new scientific conception of the natural world to bolster social stability. One scholar has recently argued that "no single event in the history of early modern Europe more profoundly shaped the integration of the new science into Western culture than did the English Revolution (1640–1660)."[28] Fed by their millenarian expectations that the end of the world would come and usher in a 1,000-year reign of the saints, Puritan reformers felt it was important to reform and renew their society. They

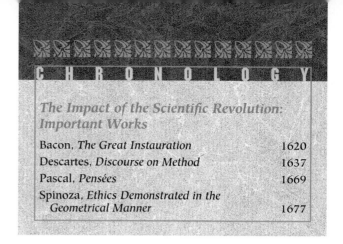

CHRONOLOGY

The Impact of the Scientific Revolution: Important Works

Bacon, *The Great Instauration*	1620
Descartes, *Discourse on Method*	1637
Pascal, *Pensées*	1669
Spinoza, *Ethics Demonstrated in the Geometrical Manner*	1677

seized on the new science as a socially useful instrument to accomplish this goal. The Puritan Revolution's role in the acceptance of science, however, stemmed even more from the reaction to the radicalism spawned by the revolutionary ferment. The upheavals of the Puritan Revolution gave rise to groups, such as the Levellers, Diggers, and Ranters, who advocated not only radical political ideas, but also a new radical science based on Paracelsus and the natural magic associated with the Hermetic tradition. The chaplain of the New Model Army said that the radicals wanted "the philosophy of Hermes, revived by the Paracelsian schools." The propertied and educated elites responded vigorously to these challenges to the established order by supporting the new mechanistic science and appealing to the material benefits of science. Hence, the founders of the Royal Society were men who wanted to pursue an experimental science that would remain detached from radical reforms of church and state. Although willing to make changes, they now viewed those changes in terms of an increase in food production and commerce. By the eighteenth century, the Newtonian world-machine had been readily accepted, and Newtonian science would soon be applied to trade and industry by a mercantile and landed elite that believed that they "could retain a social order that primarily rewarded and enriched themselves while still improving the human condition."

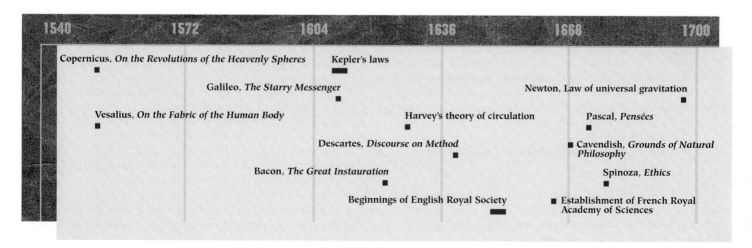

Copernicus, *On the Revolutions of the Heavenly Spheres*

Kepler's laws

Galileo, *The Starry Messenger*

Newton, Law of universal gravitation

Vesalius, *On the Fabric of the Human Body*

Harvey's theory of circulation

Pascal, *Pensées*

Descartes, *Discourse on Method*

Cavendish, *Grounds of Natural Philosophy*

Bacon, *The Great Instauration*

Spinoza, *Ethics*

Beginnings of English Royal Society

Establishment of French Royal Academy of Sciences

1540   1572   1604   1636   1668   1700

CONLUSION ⬙⬙⬙⬙⬙⬙⬙⬙⬙⬙⬙⬙

The Scientific Revolution represents a major turning point in modern Western civilization. In the Scientific Revolution, the Western world overthrew the medieval, Ptolemaic-Aristotelian worldview and arrived at a new conception of the universe: the sun at the center, the planets as material bodies revolving around the sun in elliptical orbits, and an infinite rather than finite world. With the changes in the conception of "heaven" came changes in the conception of "earth." The work of Bacon and Descartes left Europeans with the separation of mind and matter and the belief that by using only reason they could, in fact, understand and dominate the world of nature. The development of a scientific method furthered the work of scientists while the creation of scientific societies and learned journals spread its results. Although traditional churches stubbornly resisted the new ideas and a few intellectuals pointed to some inherent flaws, nothing was able to halt the replacement of the traditional ways of thinking by new ways of thinking that created a more fundamental break with the past than that represented by the breakup of Christian unity in the Reformation.

The Scientific Revolution forced Europeans to change their conception of themselves. At first, some were appalled and even frightened by its implications. Formerly, humans on earth had been at the center of the universe. Now the earth was only a tiny planet revolving around a sun that was itself only a speck in a boundless universe. Most people remained optimistic despite the apparent blow to human dignity. After all, had Newton not demonstrated that the universe was a great machine governed by natural laws? Newton had found one—the universal law of gravitation. Could others not find other laws? Were there not natural laws governing every aspect of human endeavor that could be found by the new scientific method? Thus, the Scientific Revolution leads us logically to the age of the Enlightenment of the eighteenth century.

NOTES ⬙⬙⬙⬙⬙⬙⬙⬙⬙⬙⬙⬙⬙⬙⬙⬙

1. Quoted in Alan G. R. Smith, *Science and Society in the Sixteenth and Seventeenth Centuries* (London, 1972), p. 59.
2. Edward MacCurdy, *The Notebooks of Leonardo da Vinci* (London, 1948), 1:634.
3. Ibid., p. 636.
4. Frances Yates, *Giordano Bruno and the Hermetic Tradition* (New York, 1964), p. 448.
5. Ibid., p. 450.
6. Quoted in Smith, *Science and Society in the Sixteenth and Seventeenth Centuries*, p. 97.
7. Logan P. Smith, *Life and Letters of Sir Henry Wotton* (Oxford, 1907), 1:486–487.
8. Quoted in John H. Randall, *The Making of the Modern Mind* (Boston, 1926), p. 234.
9. Quoted in Smith, *Science and Society in the Sixteenth and Seventeenth Centuries*, p. 124.
10. Quoted in Betty J. Dobbs, *The Foundations of Newton's Alchemy* (Cambridge, 1975), pp. 13–14.
11. Jolande Jacobi, ed., *Paracelsus: Selected Writings* (New York, 1965), pp. 5–6.
12. Ibid., p. 21.
13. Quoted in Londa Schiebinger, *The Mind Has No Sex? Women in the Origins of Modern Science* (Cambridge, Mass., 1989), pp. 52–53.
14. Ibid., p. 85.
15. Galen, *On the Usefulness of the Parts of the Body*, trans. Margaret May (Ithaca, N.Y., 1968), 2:628–629.
16. Quoted in Phyllis Stock, *Better Than Rubies: A History of Women's Education* (New York, 1978), p. 16.
17. René Descartes, *Philosophical Writings*, ed. and trans. Norman K. Smith (New York, 1958), p. 95.
18. Ibid., pp. 118–119.
19. Ibid., p. 120.
20. Francis Bacon, *The Great Instauration*, trans. Jerry Weinberger (Arlington Heights, Ill., 1989), pp. (in order of quotations) 2, 8, 2, 16, 21.
21. Descartes, *Discourse on Method*, in *Philosophical Writings*, p. 75.
22. Stillman Drake, ed. and trans., *Discoveries and Opinions of Galileo* (New York, 1957), p. 182.
23. Benedict de Spinoza, *Ethics*, trans. R. H. M. Elwes (New York, 1955), pp. 75–76.
24. Ibid., p. 76.
25. Benedict de Spinoza, *Letters*, quoted in Randall, *The Making of the Modern Mind*, p. 247.
26. Blaise Pascal, *The Pensées*, trans. J. M. Cohen (Harmondsworth, 1961), p. 100.
27. Ibid., pp. (in order of quotations) 31, 45, 31, 52–53, 164, 165.
28. Margaret C. Jacob, *The Cultural Meaning of the Scientific Revolution* (New York, 1988), p. 73.

SUGGESTIONS FOR FURTHER READING ⬙⬙⬙⬙

Four general surveys of the entire Scientific Revolution are A. G. R. Smith, *Science and Society in the Sixteenth and Seventeenth Centuries* (London, 1972); J. R. Jacob, *The Scientific Revolution: Aspirations and Achievements, 1500–1700* (Atlantic Highlands, N.J., 1998); S. Shapin, *The Scientific Revolution* (Chicago, 1996); and J. Henry, *The Scientific Revolution and the Origins of Modern Science* (New York, 1997). Also of much value is A. G. Debus, *Man and Nature in the Renaissance* (Cambridge, 1978), which covers the period from the mid-fifteenth through the mid-seventeenth century. On the relationship of magic to the beginnings of the Scientific Revolution, see the pioneering works by F. Yates, *Giordano Bruno and the Hermetic Tradition* (New York, 1964), and *The Rosicrucian Enlightenment* (London, 1975). Some criticism of this approach is provided in R. S. Westman and J. E. McGuire, eds., *Hermeticism and the Scientific Revolution* (Los Angeles, 1977).

A good introduction to the transformation from the late medieval to the early modern worldview is A. Koyré, *From the Closed World to the Infinite Universe* (New York, 1958). Also still of value is A. Koestler, *The Sleepwalkers: A History of Man's Changing Vision of the Universe* (New York, 1959). On the important figures of the revolution in astronomy, see E. Rosen, *Copernicus and the Scientific Revolution* (New York, 1984); M. Sharratt, *Galileo: Decisive Innovator* (Oxford, 1994); S. Drake, *Galileo, Pioneer Scientist* (Toronto, 1990); M. Casper, *Johannes Kepler*, trans. C. D. Hellman (London, 1959), the standard biography; and R. S. Westfall, *The Life of Isaac Newton* (New York, 1993). On Newton's relationship to alchemy, see the invaluable study by B. J. Dobbs, *The Foundations of Newton's Alchemy* (Cambridge, 1975); and M. White, *Isaac Newton: The Last Sorcerer* (Reading, Mass., 1997).

The worldview of Paracelsus and his followers can be examined in A. G. Debus, *The Chemical Philosophy: Paracelsian Science and Medicine in the Sixteenth and Seventeenth Centuries*, 2 vols. (New York, 1977). The standard biography of Vesalius is C. D. O'Malley, *Andreas Vesalius of Brussels, 1514–1564* (Berkeley, 1964). The work of Harvey is discussed in G. Whitteridge, *William Harvey and the Circulation of the Blood* (London, 1971). A good general account of the development of medicine can be found in W. P. D. Wightman, *The Emergence of Scientific Medicine* (Edinburgh, 1971).

The importance of Francis Bacon in the early development of science is underscored in P. Zagorin, *Francis Bacon* (Princeton, N.J., 1998). A good introduction to the work of Descartes can be found in G. Radis-Lewis, *Descartes: A Biography* (Ithaca, N.Y., 1998). The standard biography of Spinoza in English is S. Hampshire, *Spinoza* (New York, 1961).

For histories of the scientific academies, see R. Hahn, *The Anatomy of a Scientific Institution: The Paris Academy of Sciences, 1666–1803* (Berkeley, 1971); and M. Purver, *The Royal Society, Concept and Creation* (London, 1967).

On the subject of women and early modern science, see the comprehensive and highly informative work by L. Schiebinger, *The Mind Has No Sex? Women in the Origins of Modern Science* (Cambridge, Mass., 1989). See also C. Merchant, *The Death of Nature: Women, Ecology, and the Scientific Revolution* (San Francisco, 1980). There is a chapter on Maria Sibylla Merian in N. Davis, *Women on the Margins* (Cambridge, Mass., 1995). The social and political context for the triumph of science in the seventeenth and eighteenth centuries is examined in M. Jacobs, *The Cultural Meaning of the Scientific Revolution* (New York, 1988), and *The Newtonians and the English Revolution, 1689–1720* (Ithaca, N.Y., 1976).

For additional reading, go to InfoTrac College Edition, your online research library at http://web1.infotrac-college.com

Enter the search term *Copernicus* using Key Terms.

Enter the search terms *Galileo not Jupiter* using Key Terms.

Enter the search terms *Isaac Newton* using Key Terms.

Enter the search terms *Rene Descartes* using Key Terms.

CHAPTER 17

The Eighteenth Century: An Age of Enlightenment

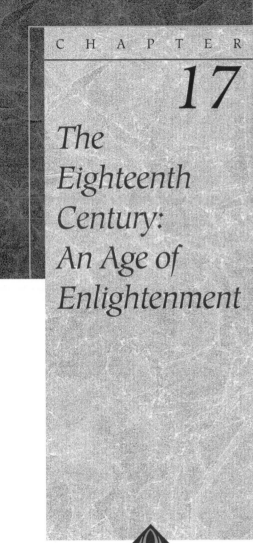

CHAPTER OUTLINE

- The Enlightenment
- Culture and Society in an Age of Enlightenment
- Religion and the Churches
- Conclusion

FOCUS QUESTIONS

- What intellectual developments led to the emergence of the Enlightenment?
- Who were the leading figures of the Enlightenment, and what were their main contributions?
- In what type of social environment did the philosophes thrive, and what role did women play in that environment?
- What innovations in art, music, and literature occurred in the eighteenth century?
- How did popular culture and popular religion differ from high culture and institutional religion in the eighteenth century?

*T*HE EARTH-SHATTERING WORK of the "natural philosophers" in the Scientific Revolution had affected only a relatively
small number of Europe's educated elite. In the eighteenth century,
this changed dramatically as a group of intellectuals known as the philosophes popularized the ideas of the Scientific Revolution and used
them to undertake a dramatic reexamination of all aspects of life. In
Paris, the cultural capital of Europe, women took the lead in bringing
together groups of men and women to discuss the new ideas of the
philosophes. At her fashionable home in the Rue St.-Honoré, Marie-
Thérèse de Geoffrin, wife of a wealthy merchant, held sway over gatherings that became the talk of France and even Europe. Distinguished
foreigners, including a future king of Sweden and a future king of
Poland, competed to receive invitations. When Madame Geoffrin made
a visit to Vienna, she was so well received that she exclaimed, "I am
better known here than a couple of yards from my own house." Madame
Geoffrin was an amiable but firm hostess who allowed wide-ranging
discussions as long as they remained in good taste. When she found

that artists and philosophers did not mix particularly well (the artists were high-strung and the philosophers talked too much), she set up separate meetings. Artists were invited only on Mondays; philosophers on Wednesdays. These gatherings were but one of many avenues for the spread of the ideas of the philosophes. And those ideas had such a widespread impact on their society that historians ever since have called the eighteenth century an age of Enlightenment.

For most of the philosophes, "enlightenment" included the rejection of traditional Christianity. The religious wars and intolerance of the sixteenth and seventeenth centuries had created an environment in which intellectuals had become so disgusted with religious fanaticism that they were open to the new ideas of the Scientific Revolution. Though the great scientists of the seventeenth century believed that their work exalted God, the intellectuals of the eighteenth century read their conclusions a different way and increasingly turned their backs on Christian orthodoxy. Consequently, European intellectual life in the eighteenth century was marked by the emergence of the secularization that has characterized the modern Western mentality. Although some historians have argued that this secularism first arose in the Renaissance, it never developed then to the same extent that it did in the eighteenth century. Ironically, at the same time that reason and materialism were beginning to replace faith and worship, a great outburst of religious sensibility manifested itself in music and art. Merely to mention the name of Johann Sebastian Bach is to remind us that the growing secularization of the eighteenth century had not yet captured the hearts and minds of all European intellectuals and artists.

◆ The Enlightenment

In 1784, the German philosopher Immanuel Kant defined the Enlightenment as "man's leaving his self-caused immaturity." Whereas earlier periods had been handicapped by the inability to "use one's intelligence without the guidance of another," Kant proclaimed as the motto of the Enlightenment: "Dare to Know!: Have the courage to use your own intelligence!" The eighteenth-century Enlightenment was a movement of intellectuals who dared to know. They were greatly impressed with the accomplishments of the Scientific Revolution, and when they used the word *reason*—one of their favorite words—they were advocating the application of the scientific method to the understanding of all life. All institutions and all systems of thought were subject to the rational, scientific way of thinking if only people would free themselves from the shackles of past, worthless tradi-

tions, especially religious ones. If Isaac Newton could discover the natural laws regulating the world of nature, they too by using reason could find the laws that governed human society. This belief in turn led them to hope that they could make progress toward a better society than the one they had inherited. Reason, natural law, hope, progress—these were common words in the heady atmosphere of the eighteenth century. But the philosophes were not naive optimists. Many of them realized that the ignorance and suffering of their society were not easily overcome and that progress would be slow and would exact a price.

✳ *The Paths to Enlightenment*

Many philosophes saw themselves as the heirs of the pagan philosophers of antiquity and the Italian humanists of the Renaissance who had revived the world of classical antiquity. To the philosophes, the Middle Ages had been a period of intellectual darkness, when a society dominated by the dogmatic Catholic church allowed faith to obscure and diminish human reason. Closer to their own period, however, the philosophes were especially influenced by the revolutionary thinkers of the seventeenth century. What were the major intellectual changes, then, that culminated in the intellectual movement of the Enlightenment?

❦ THE POPULARIZATION OF SCIENCE

Although the philosophes of the eighteenth century were much influenced by the scientific ideas of the seventeenth century, they did not always acquire this knowledge directly from the original sources. After all, Newton's *Principia* was not an easy book to read or comprehend. Scientific ideas were spread to ever-widening circles of educated Europeans not so much by scientists themselves as by popularizers. Especially important as the direct link between the Scientific Revolution of the seventeenth century and the philosophes of the eighteenth was Bernard de Fontenelle (1657–1757), secretary of the French Royal Academy of Science from 1691 to 1741.

Although Fontenelle neither performed any scientific experiments nor made any scientific discoveries, he possessed a deep knowledge of all the scientific work of earlier centuries and his own time. Moreover, he was able to communicate that body of scientific knowledge in a clear and even witty fashion that appealed to his upper-class audiences in a meaningful way. One of his most successful books, the *Plurality of Worlds*, was actually presented in the form of an intimate conversation between a lady aristocrat and her lover who are engaged in conversation under the stars. What are they discussing? "Tell me," she exclaims, "about these stars of yours." Her lover proceeds to tell her of the tremendous advances in cosmology after the foolish errors of their forebears:

> There came on the scene a certain German, one Copernicus, who made short work of all those various circles, all those solid skies, which the ancients had pictured to

The intellectual inspiration for the Enlightenment came primarily from two Englishmen, Isaac Newton and John Locke, acknowledged by the philosophes as two great minds. Newton was frequently singled out for praise as the "greatest and rarest genius that ever rose for the ornament and instruction of the species." One English poet declared: "Nature and Nature's Laws lay hid in Night; God said, 'Let Newton be,' and all was Light." Enchanted by the grand design of the Newtonian world-machine, the intellectuals of the Enlightenment were convinced that by following Newton's rules of reasoning they could discover the natural laws that governed politics, economics, justice, religion, and the arts. The world and everything in it were like a giant machine.

In the eyes of the philosophes, only the philosopher John Locke came close to Newton's genius. Although Locke's political ideas had an enormous impact on the Western world in the eighteenth century, it was his theory of knowledge that especially influenced the philosophes. In his *Essay Concerning Human Understanding*, written in 1690, Locke denied Descartes's belief in innate ideas. Instead, argued Locke, every person was born with a *tabula rasa*, a blank mind:

> Let us then suppose the mind to be, as we say, white paper, void of all characters, without any ideas. How comes it to be furnished? Whence comes it by that vast store which the busy and boundless fancy of man has painted on it with an almost endless variety? Whence has it all the materials of reason and knowledge? To this I answer, in one word, from experience. . . . Our observation, employed either about external sensible objects or about the internal operations of our minds perceived and reflected on by ourselves, is that which supplies our understanding with all the materials of thinking.[3]

Our knowledge, then, is derived from our environment, not from heredity; from reason, not from faith. Locke's philosophy implied that people were molded by their environment, by the experiences that they received through their senses from their surrounding world. By changing the environment and subjecting people to proper influences, they could be changed and a new society created. Evil was not innate in human beings, but a product of bad education, rotten institutions, and inherited prejudices. And how should the environment be changed? Newton had already paved the way by showing how reason enabled enlightened people to discover the natural laws to which all institutions should conform. No wonder the philosophes were enamored of Newton and Locke. Taken together, their ideas seemed to offer the hope of a "brave new world" built on reason.

✴ The Philosophes and Their Ideas

The intellectuals of the Enlightenment were known by the French name of philosophes although not all of them were French and few were philosophers in the literal sense of the term. They were literary people, professors, journalists, statesmen, economists, political scientists, and, above all, social reformers. They came from both the nobility and the middle class, and a few even stemmed from lower-middle-class origins. Although it was a truly international and cosmopolitan movement, the Enlightenment also enhanced the dominant role being played by French culture. Paris was the recognized capital of the Enlightenment, and most of its leaders were French. The French philosophes, in turn, affected intellectuals elsewhere and created a movement that touched the entire Western world, including the British and Spanish colonies in America.

Although the philosophes faced different political circumstances depending upon the country in which they lived, they shared common bonds as part of a truly international movement. Although they were called philosophers, what did philosophy mean to them? The role of philosophy was to change the world, not just discuss it. As one writer said, the philosophe is one who "applies himself to the study of society with the purpose of making his kind better and happier." To the philosophes, rationalism did not mean the creation of a grandiose system of thought to explain all things. Reason was scientific method, and it meant an appeal to facts and experience. A spirit of rational criticism was to be applied to everything, including religion and politics. The philosophes aggressively pursued a secular view of life since their focus was not on an afterlife, but on this world and how it could be improved and enjoyed.

The philosophes' call for freedom of expression is a reminder that their work was done in an atmosphere of censorship. The philosophes were not free to write whatever they chose. Although standards fluctuated wildly at times, state censors decided what could be published, and protests from any number of government bodies could result in the seizure of books and the imprisonment of their authors, publishers, and sellers.

The philosophes found ways to get around state censorship. Some published under pseudonyms or anonymously or abroad, especially in Holland. The use of double meanings, such as talking about the Persians when they meant the French, became standard procedure for many. Books were also published and circulated secretly or in manuscript form to avoid the censors. As frequently happens with attempted censorship, the government's announcement that a book had been burned often made the book more desirable and more popular.

Although the philosophes constituted a kind of "family circle" bound together by common intellectual bonds, they often disagreed as well. Spanning almost an entire century, the Enlightenment evolved over time with each succeeding generation becoming more radical as it built upon the contributions of the previous one. A few people, however, dominated the landscape completely, and we might best begin our survey of the ideas of the philosophes by looking at three French giants—Montesquieu, Voltaire, and Diderot.

THE POPULARIZATION OF SCIENCE: FONTENELLE AND THE *PLURALITY OF WORLDS*. The most important popularizer of the ideas of the Scientific Revolution was Bernard de Fontenelle who, though not a scientist himself, had much knowledge of scientific matters. In this frontispiece illustration to his *Plurality of Worlds*, an aristocratic lady listens while her astronomer-friend explains the details of the new cosmology.

themselves. The former he abolished; the latter, he broke in pieces. Fired with the noble zeal of a true astronomer, he took the earth and spun it very far away from the center of the universe, where it had been installed, and in that center he put the sun, which had a far better title to the honor.[1]

In the course of two evenings under the stars, the lady learned the basic fundamentals of the new mechanistic universe. So too did scores of the educated elite of Europe. What bliss it was to learn the "truth" in such lighthearted fashion.

Thanks to Fontenelle, science was no longer the monopoly of experts, but part of literature. He was especially fond of downplaying the religious backgrounds of the seventeenth-century scientists. Himself a skeptic, Fontenelle contributed to the growing skepticism toward religion at the end of the seventeenth century by portraying the churches as enemies of scientific progress.

A NEW SKEPTICISM

The great scientists of the seventeenth century, such as Kepler, Galileo, and Newton, had pursued their work in a spirit of exalting God, not undermining Christianity. But as scientific knowledge spread, more and more educated men and women began to question religious truths and values. Skepticism about religion and a growing secularization of thought were especially evident in the work of Pierre Bayle (1647–1706), who remained a Protestant while becoming a leading critic of traditional religious attitudes. Bayle attacked superstition, religious intolerance, and dogmatism. In his view, compelling people to believe a particular set of religious ideas (as Louis XIV was doing in Bayle's contemporary France) was wrong. It simply created hypocrites and in itself was contrary to what religion should be about. Individual conscience should determine one's actions. Bayle argued for complete religious toleration, maintaining that the existence of many religions would benefit rather than harm the state.

Bayle was one of a number of intellectuals who believed that the new rational principles of textual criticism should be applied to the Bible as well as secular documents. In his most famous work, *Historical and Critical Dictionary*, Bayle demonstrated the results of his own efforts with a famous article on the Israelite King David. Undermining the traditional picture of the heroic David, he portrayed the king as a sensual, treacherous, cruel, and basically evil man. Bayle's *Dictionary*, which attacked traditional religious practices and heroes, was well known to eighteenth-century philosophes. One critic regarded it as the "Bible of the eighteenth century."

THE IMPACT OF TRAVEL LITERATURE

Skepticism about both Christianity and European culture itself was nourished by travel reports. In the course of the seventeenth century, traders, missionaries, medical practitioners, and navigators began to publish an increasing number of travel books that gave accounts of many different cultures. By the end of the seventeenth century, this travel literature began to make an impact on the minds of educated Europeans. The realization that there were highly developed civilizations with different customs in other parts of the world forced Europeans to evaluate their own civilization relative to others. What had seemed to be practices grounded in reason now appeared to be matters of custom. Certainties about European practices gave way to cultural relativism.

Cultural relativism was accompanied by religious skepticism. As these travel accounts made clear, the Christian perception of God was merely one of many. Some people were devastated by this revelation: "Some complete their demoralization by extensive travel, and lose whatever shreds of religion remained to them. Every day they see a new religion, new customs, new rites."[2]

The Separation of Powers

The Enlightenment affected the "new world" of America as much as it did the "old world" of Europe. American philosophes, such as Benjamin Franklin, James Madison, and Thomas Jefferson, were well aware of the ideas of European Enlightenment thinkers. This selection from Montesquieu's The Spirit of the Laws *enunciates the "separation of powers" doctrine.*

Montesquieu, *The Spirit of the Laws*

✷ Of the Constitution of England

In every government there are three sorts of power: the legislative; the executive in respect to things dependent on the law of nations; and the executive in regard to matters that depend on the civil law.

By virtue of the first, the prince or magistrate enacts temporary or perpetual laws, and amends or abrogates those that have been already enacted. By the second, he makes peace or war, sends or receives embassies, establishes the public security, and provides against invasions. By the third, he punishes criminals, or determines the disputes that arise between individuals. The latter we shall call the judiciary power, and the other simply the executive power of the state.

The political liberty of the subject is a tranquillity of mind arising from the opinion each person has of his safety. In order to have this liberty, it is requisite the government be so constituted as one man need not be afraid of another.

When the legislative and executive powers are united in the same person, or in the same body of magistrates, there can be no liberty; because apprehensions may arise, lest the same monarch or senate should enact tyrannical laws, to execute them in a tyrannical manner.

Again, there is no liberty, if the judiciary power be not separated from the legislative and executive. Were it joined with the legislative, the life and liberty of the subject would be exposed to arbitrary control; for the judge would be then the legislator. Were it joined to the executive power, the judge might behave with violence and oppression.

There would be an end of everything, were the same man or the same body, whether of the nobles or of the people, to exercise those three powers, that of enacting laws, that of executing the public resolutions, and of trying the causes of individuals.

✷ MONTESQUIEU AND POLITICAL THOUGHT

Charles de Secondat, the baron de Montesquieu (1689–1755), came from the French nobility. He received a classical education and then studied law. His own estate, as well as his marriage to a wealthy Protestant heiress, enabled him to live a life dedicated to travel, study, and writing. In his first work, the *Persian Letters,* published in 1721, he used the format of two Persians supposedly traveling in Western Europe and sending their impressions back home, to enable him to criticize French institutions, especially the Catholic church and the French monarchy. Much of the program of the French Enlightenment is contained in this work: the attack on traditional religion, the advocacy of religious toleration, the denunciation of slavery, and the use of reason to liberate human beings from their prejudices.

Montesquieu's most famous work, *The Spirit of the Laws,* was published in 1748. This treatise was a comparative study of governments in which Montesquieu attempted to apply the scientific method to the social and political arena to ascertain the "natural laws" governing the social relationships of human beings. Montesquieu distinguished three basic kinds of governments: republics, suitable for small states and based on citizen involvement; monarchy, appropriate for middle-sized states and grounded in the ruling class's adherence to law; and despotism, apt for large empires and dependent on fear to inspire obedience. Montesquieu used England as an example of the second category, and it was his praise and analysis of England's constitution that led to his most far-reaching and lasting contribution to political thought—the importance of checks and balances created by means of a separation of powers (see the box above). He believed that England's system, with its separate executive, legislative, and judicial powers that served to limit and control each other, provided the greatest freedom and security for a state. In large part, Montesquieu misread the English situation and insisted on a separation of powers because he wanted the nobility of France (of which he was a member) to play an active role in the running of the French government. The translation of his work into English two years after publication ensured that it would be read by American philosophes, such as Benjamin Franklin, James Madison, John Adams, Alexander Hamilton, and Thomas Jefferson, who incorporated its principles into the U.S. Constitution (see Chapter 19).

✷ VOLTAIRE AND THE ENLIGHTENMENT

The greatest figure of the Enlightenment was Francois-Marie Arouet, known simply as Voltaire (1694–1778). Son of a prosperous middle-class family from Paris, Voltaire received a classical education typical of Jesuit schools. Although he studied law, he wished to be a writer and achieved his first success as a playwright. By his mid-twenties, Voltaire had been hailed as the successor to Racine (see Chapter 15) for his tragedy *Oedipe* and his epic *Henriade* on his favorite king, Henry IV. His wit made him a darling of the Parisian intellectuals but also involved him in a quarrel with a dissolute nobleman that forced him to flee France and live in England for almost two years.

Well received in English literary and social circles, the young playwright was much impressed by England. His *Philosophic Letters on the English*, written in 1733, expressed a deep admiration of English life, especially its respect for merchants, scientists, and literary figures, its freedom of the press, its political freedom, and its religious toleration. In judging the English religious situation, he made the famous remark that "if there were just one religion in England, despotism would threaten, if there were two religions, they would cut each other's throats, but there are thirty religions, and they live together peacefully and happily." Although he clearly exaggerated the freedoms England possessed, in a roundabout way Voltaire had managed to criticize many of the ills oppressing France, especially royal absolutism and the lack of religious toleration and freedom of thought. He had left France a playwright; he came back a philosophe.

Upon his return to France, Voltaire's reputation as the author of the *Philosophic Letters* made it necessary for him to retire to Cirey, near France's eastern border, where he lived in semiseclusion on the estate of his mistress, Madame de Châtelet. He eventually settled on a magnificent estate at Ferney. Located in France near the Swiss border, Ferney gave Voltaire the freedom to write what he wished. By this time, through his writings, inheritance, and clever investments, Voltaire had become wealthy and now had the leisure to write an almost endless stream of pamphlets, novels, plays, letters, and histories.

Although he touched on all of the themes of importance to the philosophes, Voltaire was especially well known for his criticism of traditional religion and his strong attachment to the ideal of religious toleration (see the box on p. 492). He lent his prestige and skills as a polemicist to fight cases of intolerance in France. The most famous incident was the Calas affair. Jean Calas was a Protestant from Toulouse who was accused of murdering his own son to stop him from becoming a Catholic. Tortured to confess his guilt, Calas died shortly thereafter. An angry and indignant Voltaire published devastating broadsides that aroused public opinion and forced a retrial in which Calas was exonerated when it was proved that his son had actually committed suicide. The family was paid an indemnity, and Voltaire's appeals for toleration appeared all the more reasonable. In 1763, he penned his *Treatise on Toleration* in which he argued that religious toleration had created no problems for England and Holland and reminded governments that "all men are brothers under God." As he grew older, Voltaire became ever more strident in his denunciations. "Crush the infamous thing," he thundered repeatedly—the infamous thing being religious fanaticism, intolerance, and superstition.

Throughout his life, Voltaire championed not only religious tolerance, but also deism, a religious outlook

VOLTAIRE. François-Marie Arouet, better known as Voltaire, achieved his first success as a playwright. A philosophe, Voltaire was well known for his criticism of traditional religion and his support of religious toleration.

shared by most other philosophes. Deism was built upon the Newtonian world-machine, which implied the existence of a mechanic (God) who had created the universe. Voltaire said: "In the opinion that there is a God, there are difficulties, but in the contrary opinion there are absurdities." To Voltaire and most other philosophes, God had no direct involvement in the world he had created and allowed to run according to its own natural laws. God did not extend grace or answer prayers as Christians liked to believe. Jesus might be a "good fellow," as Voltaire called him, but he was not divine as Christianity claimed.

✕ DIDEROT AND THE *ENCYCLOPEDIA*

Denis Diderot (1713–1784) was the son of a skilled craftsman from eastern France. He received a Jesuit education and went on to the University of Paris to fulfill his father's hopes that he would be a lawyer or pursue a career in the church. Diderot did neither. Instead he became a freelance writer so that he could be free to study and read in many subjects and languages. For the rest of his life, Diderot remained dedicated to his independence and was always in love with new ideas.

Diderot's numerous writings reflected typical Enlightened interests. One of his favorite topics was Christianity, which he condemned as fanatical and unreasonable. As he grew older, his literary attacks on Christianity grew more vicious. Of all religions, he maintained, Christianity was the worst, "the most absurd and the most atrocious

The Attack on Religious Intolerance

Although Voltaire's attacks on religion were in no way original, his lucid prose, biting satire, and clever wit caused his works to be widely read and all the more influential. These two selections present different sides of Voltaire's attack on religious intolerance. The first is from his straightforward treatise, The Ignorant Philosopher, and the second is from his only real literary masterpiece, the novel Candide, where he uses humor to make the same fundamental point about religious intolerance.

❀ Voltaire, *The Ignorant Philosopher*

The contagion of fanaticism then still subsists. . . . The author of the Treatise upon Toleration has not mentioned the shocking executions wherein so many unhappy victims perished in the valleys of Piedmont. He has passed over in silence the massacre of six hundred inhabitants of Valtelina, men, women, and children, who were murdered by the Catholics in the month of September, 1620. I will not say it was with the consent and assistance of the archbishop of Milan, Charles Borome, who was made a saint. Some passionate writers have averred this fact, which I am very far from believing; but I say, there is scarce any city or borough in Europe, where blood has not been spilt for religious quarrels; I say, that the human species has been perceptibly diminished, because women and girls were massacred as well as men; I say, that Europe would have had a third larger population, if there had been no theological disputes. In fine, I say, that so far from forgetting these abominable times, we should frequently take a view of them, to inspire an eternal horror for them; and that it is for our age to make reparation by toleration, for this long collection of crimes, which has taken place through the want of toleration, during sixteen barbarous centuries.

Let it not then be said, that there are no traces left of that shocking fanaticism, of the want of toleration; they are still everywhere to be met with, even in those countries that are esteemed the most humane. The Lutheran and Calvinist preachers, were they masters, would, perhaps, be as little inclined to pity, as obdurate, as insolent as they upbraid their antagonists with being.

❀ Voltaire, *Candide*

At last he [Candide] approached a man who had just been addressing a big audience for a whole hour on the subject of charity. The orator peered at him and said:

"What is your business here? Do you support the Good Old Cause?"

"There is not effect without a cause," replied Candide modestly. "All things are necessarily connected and arranged for the best. It was my fate to be driven from Lady Cunégonde's presence and made to run the gauntlet, and now I have to beg my bread until I can earn it. Things should not have happened otherwise."

"Do you believe that the Pope is Antichrist, my friend?" said the minister.

"I have never heard anyone say so," replied Candide; "but whether he is or he isn't, I want some food."

"You don't deserve to eat," said the other. "Be off with you, you villain, you wretch! Don't come near me again or you'll suffer for it."

The minister's wife looked out of the window at that moment, and seeing a man who was not sure that the Pope was Antichrist, emptied over his head a chamber pot, which shows to what lengths ladies are driven by religious zeal.

---

in its dogma" (see the box on p. 494). Near the end of his life, he argued for an essentially materialistic conception of life: "This world is only a mass of molecules. There is a law of necessity that works without design, without effort, without intelligence, and without progress."

Diderot's most famous contribution to the Enlightenment was the twenty-eight–volume *Encyclopedia, or Classified Dictionary of the Sciences, Arts, and Trades,* that he edited and called the "great work of his life." Its purpose, according to Diderot, was to "change the general way of thinking." It did precisely that in becoming a major weapon of the philosophes' crusade against the old French society. The contributors included many philosophes who expressed their major concerns. They attacked religious superstition and advocated toleration as well as a program for social, legal, and political improvements that would lead to a society that was more cosmopolitan, more tol-

erant, more humane, and more reasonable. In later editions, the price of the *Encyclopedia* was drastically reduced, dramatically increasing its sales and making it available to doctors, clergy, teachers, lawyers, and even military officers. The ideas of the Enlightenment were spread even further as a result.

❧ TOWARD A NEW "SCIENCE OF MAN"

The Enlightenment belief that Newton's scientific methods could be used to discover the natural laws underlying all areas of human life led to the emergence in the eighteenth century of what the philosophes called a "science of man" or what we would call the social sciences. In a number of areas, philosophes arrived at natural laws that they believed governed human actions. If these "natural laws" seem less than universal to us, it reminds us how much the philosophes were people of their times reacting to the conditions they faced. Nevertheless, their efforts did at least lay the foundations for the modern social sciences.

That a "science of man" was possible was a strong belief of the Scottish philosopher David Hume (1711–1776). An important figure in the history of philosophy, Hume has also been called "a pioneering social scientist." In his *Treatise on Human Nature,* which he subtitled "An Attempt to Introduce the Experimental Method of Reasoning into Moral Subjects," Hume argued that observation and reflection, grounded in "systematized common sense," made conceivable a "science of man." Careful examination of the experiences that constituted human life would lead to the knowledge of human nature that would make possible "a science, which will not be inferior in certainty, and will be much superior in utility, to any other of human comprehension."

The Physiocrats and Adam Smith have been viewed as founders of the modern discipline of economics. The leader of the Physiocrats was François Quesnay (1694–1774), a highly successful French court physician. Quesnay and the Physiocrats claimed they would discover the natural economic laws that governed human society because they were "susceptible of demonstration as severe and incontestable as those of geometry and algebra." Their first principle was that land constituted the only source of wealth and that wealth itself could be increased only by agriculture because all other economic activities were unproductive and sterile. To the Physiocrats, agriculture included the exploitation of natural resources, especially mining. Even the state's revenues should come from a single tax on the land rather than the hodgepodge of inequitable taxes and privileges currently in place. In stressing the economic primacy of agricultural production, the Physiocrats were rejecting the mercantilist emphasis on the significance of money—that is, gold and silver—as the primary determinants of wealth (see Chapter 15).

Their second major "natural law" of economics also represented a repudiation of mercantilism, specifically, its emphasis on a controlled economy for the benefit of the state. Instead the Physiocrats stressed that the existence of the natural economic forces of supply and demand made it imperative that individuals should be left free to pursue their own economic self-interest. In doing so, all of society would ultimately benefit. Consequently, they argued that the state should in no way interrupt the free play of natural economic forces by government regulation of the economy, but leave it alone, a doctrine that subsequently became known by its French name, *laissez-faire* (to let alone).

The best statement of laissez-faire was made in 1776 by a Scottish philosopher, Adam Smith (1723–1790), when he published his famous work, *Inquiry into the Nature and Causes of the Wealth of Nations,* known simply as *The Wealth of Nations.* In the process of enunciating three of his basic principles of economics, Smith presented a strong attack on mercantilism. First, he condemned the mercantilist use of protective tariffs to protect home industries. A

DENIS DIDEROT. Editor of the *Encyclopedia,* Diderot was a major figure in propagating the ideas of the French philosophes. He had diverse interests and penned an incredible variety of literary works. He is shown here in a portrait by Jean Honoré Fragonard.

tailor, he argued, does not try to make his own shoes, nor does a shoemaker try to make his own clothes. Following this line of reasoning, if one country can supply another country with a product cheaper than the latter can make it, it is better to purchase than to produce it. Each nation, then, should produce what it did best without the artificial barriers of tariffs. To Adam Smith, free trade was a fundamental economic principle. Smith's second principle was his labor theory of value. Like the Physiocrats, he claimed that gold and silver were not the source of a nation's true wealth, but, unlike the Physiocrats, he did not believe that soil was either. Rather labor—the labor of individual farmers, artisans, and merchants—constituted the true wealth of a nation. Finally, like the Physiocrats, Smith believed that the state should not interfere in economic matters; indeed, he gave to government only three basic functions: it should protect society from invasion (army); defend individuals from injustice and oppression (police); and keep up certain public works, such as roads and canals, that private individuals could not afford. Thus, in Smith's view the state should be a kind of "passive policeman" that stays out of the lives of individuals. In emphasizing the economic liberty of the individual, the Physiocrats and Adam Smith laid the foundation for what became known in the nineteenth century as economic liberalism.

THE LATER ENLIGHTENMENT

By the late 1760s, a new generation of philosophes who had grown up with the worldview of the Enlightenment began to move beyond their predecessors' beliefs. Baron Paul d'Holbach (1723–1789), a wealthy German aristocrat who settled in Paris, preached a doctrine of strict

DIDEROT QUESTIONS CHRISTIAN SEXUAL STANDARDS

Denis Diderot was one of the bolder thinkers of the Enlightenment. Although best remembered for the Encyclopedia, he was the author of many works that he considered too advanced and withheld from publication. In his Supplement to the Voyage of Bouganville, he constructed a dialogue between Orou, a Tahitian who symbolizes the wisdom of a philosophe, and a chaplain who defends Christian sexual mores. The dialogue gave Diderot the opportunity to criticize the practice of sexual chastity and monogamy.

✳ Denis Diderot, *Supplement to the Voyage of Bouganville*

[Orou] "You are young and healthy [speaking to the chaplain] and you have just had a good supper. He who sleeps alone sleeps badly; at night a man needs a woman at his side. Here is my wife and here are my daughters. Choose whichever one pleases you most, but if you would like to do me a favor, you will give your preference to my youngest girl, who has not yet had any children. . . ."

The chaplain replied that his religion, his holy orders, his moral standards and his sense of decency all prevented him from accepting Orou's invitation.

Orou answered: "I don't know what this thing is that you call religion, but I can only have a low opinion of it because it forbids you to partake of an innocent pleasure to which Nature, the sovereign mistress of us all, invites everybody. It seems to prevent you from bringing one of your fellow creatures into the world, from doing a favor asked of by a father, a mother and their children, from repaying the kindness of a host, and from enriching a nation by giving it an additional citizen. . . . Look at the distress you have caused to appear on the faces of these four women—they are afraid you have noticed some defect in them that arouses your distaste. . . ."

The Chaplain: "You don't understand—it's not that. They are all four of them equally beautiful. But there is my religion! My holy orders! . . . [God] spoke to our ancestors and gave them laws; he prescribed to them the way in which he wishes to be honored; he ordained that certain actions are good and others he forbade them to do as being evil."

Orou: "I see. And one of these evil actions which he has forbidden is that of a man who goes to bed with a woman or girl. But in that case, why did he make two sexes?"

The Chaplain: "In order that they might come together—but only when certain conditions are satisfied and only after certain initial ceremonies one man belongs to one woman and only to her; one woman belongs to one man and only to him." Orou: "For their whole lives?"

The Chaplain: "For their whole lives. . . ."

Orou: "I find these strange precepts contrary to nature, and contrary to reason. . . . Furthermore, your laws seem to me to be contrary to the general order of things. For in truth is there anything so senseless as a precept that forbids us to heed the changing impulses that are inherent in our being, or commands that require a degree of constancy which is not possible, that violate the liberty of both male and female by chaining them perpetually to one another? . . . I don't know what your great workman [God] is, but I am very happy that he never spoke to our forefathers, and I hope that he never speaks to our children, for if he does, he may tell them the same foolishness, and they may be foolish enough to believe it."

---

atheism and materialism. In his *System of Nature*, written in 1770, he argued that everything in the universe consisted of matter in motion. Human beings were simply machines; God was a product of the human mind and was unnecessary for leading a moral life. People needed only reason to live in this world: "Let us persuade men to be just, beneficent, moderate, sociable; not because the gods demand it, but because they must please men. Let us advise them to abstain from vice and crimes; not because they will be punished in the other world, but because they will suffer for it in this."[4] Holbach shocked almost all of his fellow philosophes with his uncompromising atheism. Most intellectuals remained more comfortable with deism and feared the effect of atheism on society.

Marie-Jean de Condorcet (1743–1794), another French philosophe, made an exaggerated claim for optimism that appears utopian in comparison with his predecessors' cautious hopes for gradual progress. Condorcet was a victim of the turmoil of the French Revolution and wrote his chief work, *The Progress of the Human Mind*, while in hiding during the Reign of Terror (see Chapter 19). His survey of human history convinced him that humans had progressed through nine stages of history. Now, with the spread of science and reason, humans were about to enter the tenth stage, one of perfection, in which they will see that "there is no limit to the perfecting of the powers of man; that human perfectibility is in reality indefinite, that the progress of this perfectibility . . . has no other limit than the duration of the globe upon which nature has placed us." Shortly after composing this work, the prophet of humankind's perfection died in a French revolutionary prison.

✳ ROUSSEAU AND THE SOCIAL CONTRACT

No one was more critical of the work of his predecessors than Jean-Jacques Rousseau (1712–1778). Born in the city of Geneva, he was abandoned by his family at an early age and spent his youth wandering about France and Italy holding various jobs. He went back to school for a while to study music and the classics (he could afford to do so after becoming the paid lover of an older woman). Eventually, he made his way to Paris where he became a friend of Diderot and was introduced into the circles of the philosophes. He never really liked the social life of the cities, however, and frequently withdrew into long periods of solitude.

Rousseau's political beliefs were presented in two major works. In his *Discourse on the Origins of the Inequality of Mankind*, Rousseau began with humans in their primitive condition (or state of nature—see Chapter 15) where they were happy. There were no laws, no judges; all people were equal. But what had gone wrong?

> The first man who, having enclosed a piece of ground, thought of saying, This is mine, and found people simple enough to believe him, was the true founder of civil society. How many crimes, wars, murders; how much misery and horror the human race would have been spared if someone had pulled up the stakes and filled in the ditch, and cried to his fellow men: "Beware of listening to this impostor. You are lost if you forget that the fruits of the earth belong to everyone and that the earth itself belongs to no one!"[5]

In order to preserve their private property, people adopted laws and governors. In so doing, they rushed headlong not to liberty, but into chains. "What then is to be done? Must societies be totally abolished? . . . Must we return again to the forest to live among bears?" No, civilized humans

JEAN-JACQUES ROUSSEAU. By the late 1760s, a new generation of philosophes arose who began to move beyond and even to question the beliefs of their predecessors. Of the philosophes of the late Enlightenment, Jean-Jacques Rousseau was perhaps the most critical of his predecessors.

CHRONOLOGY

Works of the Philosophes

Montesquieu, *Persian Letters*	1721
Voltaire, *Philosophic Letters on the English*	1733
Hume, *Treatise on Human Nature*	1739–1740
Montesquieu, *The Spirit of the Laws*	1748
Voltaire, *The Age of Louis XIV*	1751
Diderot, *The Encyclopedia*	1751–1765
Rousseau, *The Social Contract, Emile*	1762
Voltaire, *Treatise on Toleration*	1763
Beccaria, *On Crimes and Punishments*	1764
Holbach, *System of Nature*	1770
Smith, *The Wealth of Nations*	1776
Gibbon, *The Decline and Fall of the Roman Empire*	1776–1788
Wollstonecraft, *Vindication of the Rights of Woman*	1792
Condorcet, *The Progress of the Human Mind*	1794

could "no longer subsist on plants or acorns or live without laws and magistrates." Government was an evil, but a necessary one.

In his celebrated treatise *The Social Contract*, published in 1762, Rousseau tried to harmonize individual liberty with governmental authority (see the box on p. 496). The social contract was basically an agreement on the part of an entire society to be governed by its general will. If any individual wished to follow his own self-interest, then he should be compelled to abide by the general will. "This means nothing less than that he will be forced to be free," said Rousseau, because the general will represented a community's highest aspirations, that which was best for the entire community. Thus, liberty was achieved through being forced to follow what was best for all people because, he believed, what was best for all was best for each individual. True freedom is adherence to laws that one has imposed on one's self. To Rousseau, because everybody was responsible for framing the general will, the creation of laws could never be delegated to a parliamentary institution:

> Thus the people's deputies are not and could not be its representatives; they are merely its agents; and they cannot decide anything finally. Any law which the people has not ratified in person is void; it is not law at all. The English people believes itself to be free; it is gravely mistaken; it is free only during the election of Members of Parliament; as soon as the Members are elected, the people is enslaved; it is nothing.[6]

This is an extreme, idealistic statement, but it is the ultimate statement of participatory democracy. Perhaps Rousseau was thinking of his native city of Geneva, a

A Social Contract

Although Jean-Jacques Rousseau was one of the French philosophes, he has also been called "the father of Romanticism." His political ideas have proved extremely controversial. Though some have hailed him as the prophet of democracy, others have labeled him an apologist for totalitarianism. This selection is taken from one of his most famous books, The Social Contract.

Jean-Jacques Rousseau, *The Social Contract*

❊ Book 1, Chapter 6: The Social Pact

"How to find a form of association which will defend the person and goods of each member with the collective force of all, and under which each individual, while uniting himself with the others, obeys no one but himself, and remains as free as before." This is the fundamental problem to which the social contract holds the solution. . . .

❊ Chapter 7: The Sovereign

Despite their common interest, subjects will not be bound by their commitment unless means are found to guarantee their fidelity.

For every individual as a man may have a private will contrary to, or different from, the general will that he has as a citizen. His private interest may he speak with a very different voice from that of the public interest; his absolute and naturally independent existence may make him regard what he owes to the common cause as a gratuitous contribution, the loss of which would be less painful for others than the payment is onerous for him; and fancying that the artificial person which constitutes the state is a mere rational entity, he might seek to enjoy the rights of a citizen without doing the duties of a subject. The growth of this kind of injustice would bring about the ruin of the body politic.

Hence, in order that the social pact shall not be an empty formula, it is tacitly implied in that commitment—which alone can give force to all others—that whoever refused to obey the general will shall be constrained to do so by the whole body, which means nothing other than that he shall be forced to be free; for this is the condition which, by giving each citizen to the nation, secures him against all personal dependence, it is the condition which shapes both the design and the working of the political machine, and which alone bestows justice on civil contracts—without it, such contracts would be absurd, tyrannical and liable to the grossest abuse.

---

community small enough that it could conform to these strict rules of absolute democracy. But we do not really know. *The Social Contract* has evoked contradictory interpretations ever since the outbreak of the French Revolution. The more radical revolutionaries used it during the second stage of the French Revolution to justify democratic politics, but others have viewed Rousseau's emphasis on a coercive general will ("forced to be free") as leading to a totalitarian system. Rousseau himself said, "Those who boast that they understand the whole of it are cleverer than I am."

Another influential treatise by Rousseau also appeared in 1762. Entitled *Emile,* it is one of the Enlightenment's most important works on education. Written in the form of a novel, the work was really a general treatise "on the education of the natural man." During the years from five to twelve, the boy Emile was allowed to encounter nature directly and learn by experience. From twelve to sixteen, he was open to more abstract thoughts; this was the time when education in ethics would take hold. Seventeen to nineteen was the proper time for encouraging the use of reason. Rousseau's fundamental concern was that education should foster rather than restrict children's natural instincts. Life's experiences had shown Rousseau the importance of the promptings of the heart, and what he sought was a balance between heart and mind, between sentiment and reason. This emphasis on heart and sentiment made him a precursor of the intellectual movement called Romanticism that dominated Europe at the beginning of the nineteenth century.

But Rousseau did not necessarily practice what he preached. His own children were sent to foundling homes, where many children died at a young age. Rousseau also viewed women as "naturally" different from men: "To fulfill [a woman's] functions, an appropriate physical constitution is necessary to her . . . she needs a soft sedentary life to suckle her babies. How much care and tenderness does she need to hold her family together." In Rousseau's *Emile,* Sophie, who was Emile's intended wife, was educated for her role as wife and mother by learning obedience and the nurturing skills that would enable her to provide loving care for her husband and children. Not everyone in the eighteenth century agreed with Rousseau, however, making ideas of gender an important issue in the Enlightenment.

❧ THE "WOMAN'S QUESTION" IN THE ENLIGHTENMENT

For centuries, men had dominated the debate about the nature and value of women. In general, many male intellectuals had argued that the base nature of women made them inferior to men and made male domination of women

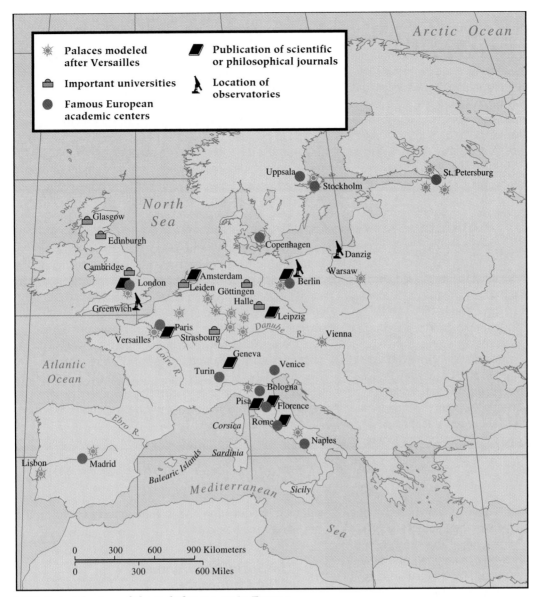

MAP 17.1   The Age of the Enlightenment in Europe.

necessary (see Chapter 16). In the seventeenth and eighteenth centuries, many male thinkers reinforced this view by arguing that it was based on "natural" biological differences between men and women. Like Rousseau, they argued that the female constitution made women mothers. Male writers, in particular, were critical of the attempts of some women in the Enlightenment to write on intellectual issues, arguing that women by nature were intellectually inferior to men. Nevertheless, some Enlightenment thinkers offered more positive views of women. Diderot, for example, maintained that men and women were not all that different, and Voltaire asserted that "women are capable of all that men are" in intellectual affairs.

It was women thinkers, however, who added new perspectives to the "woman's question" by making specific suggestions for improving the condition of women. Mary Astell (1666–1731), daughter of a wealthy English coal merchant, argued in 1697 in *A Serious Proposal to the Ladies* that women needed to become better educated.

Men, she believed, would resent her proposal, "but they must excuse me, if I be as partial to my own sex as they are to theirs, and think women as capable of learning as men are, and that it becomes them as well."[7] In a later work entitled *Some Reflections upon Marriage*, Astell argued for the equality of the sexes in marriage: "If absolute sovereignty be not necessary in a state, how comes it to be so in a family. . . . For if arbitrary power is evil in itself, and an improper method of governing rational and free agents, it ought not be practiced anywhere. . . . If all men are born free, how is it that all women are born slaves?"[8]

The strongest statement for the rights of women in the eighteenth century was advanced by the English writer Mary Wollstonecraft (1759–1797), viewed by many as the founder of modern European feminism. In *Vindication of the Rights of Woman*, written in 1792, Wollstonecraft pointed out two contradictions in the views of women held by such Enlightenment thinkers as Rousseau. To argue that women must obey men, she said, was contrary to the

The Rights of Women

Mary Wollstonecraft responded to an unhappy childhood in a large family by seeking to lead an independent life. Few occupations were available for middle-class women in her day, but she survived by working as a teacher, chaperone, and governess to aristocratic children. All the while, she wrote and developed her ideas on the rights of women. This excerpt is taken from her Vindication of the Rights of Woman, *written in 1792. This work led to her reputation as the foremost British feminist thinker of the eighteenth century.*

❀ Mary Wollstonecraft, *Vindication of the Rights of Woman*

It is a melancholy truth—yet such is the blessed effect of civilization—the most respectable women are the most oppressed; and, unless they have understandings far superior to the common run of understandings, taking in both sexes, they must, from being treated like contemptible beings, become contemptible. How many women thus waste life away the prey of discontent, who might have practiced as physicians, regulated a farm, managed a shop, and stood erect, supported by their own industry, instead of hanging their heads surcharged with the dew of sensibility, that consumes the beauty to which it at first gave luster. . . .

Proud of their weakness, however, [women] must always be protected, guarded from care, and all the rough toils that dignify the mind. If this be the fiat of fate, if they will make themselves insignificant and contemptible, sweetly to waste "life away," let them not expect to be valued when their beauty fades, for it is the fate of the fairest flowers to be admired and pulled to pieces by the careless hand that plucked them. In how many ways do I wish, from the purest benevolence, to impress this truth on my sex; yet I fear that they will not listen to a truth that dear-bought experience has brought home to many an agitated bosom, nor willingly resign the privileges of rank and sex for the privileges of humanity, to which those have no claim who do not discharge its duties. . . .

Would men but generously snap our chains, and be content with the rational fellowship instead of slavish obedience, they would find us more observant daughters, more affectionate sisters, more faithful wives, and more reasonable mothers—in a word, better citizens. We should then love them with true affection, because we should learn to respect ourselves; and the peace of mind of a worthy man would not be interrupted by the idle vanity of his wife.

---

beliefs of the same individuals that a system based on the arbitrary power of monarchs over their subjects or slave owners over their slaves was wrong. The subjection of women to men was equally wrong. In addition, she argued that the Enlightenment was based on an ideal of reason innate in all human beings. If women have reason, then they too are entitled to the same rights that men have. Women, Wollstonecraft declared, should have equal rights with men in education and in economic and political life as well (see the box above).

❀ The Social Environment of the Philosophes

The social background of the philosophes varied considerably, from the aristocratic Montesquieu to the lower-

THE SALON OF MADAME GEOFFRIN. An important factor in the development of the Enlightenment was the spread of new ideas to the literate elites of European society. Salons were an important part of this process. Madame Geoffrin, who presided over one of the best-known Parisian salons, is shown here, the third figure from the right in the front row.

The Salon: Can Men and Women Be Friends without Sex?

The salon was established in the seventeenth century by aristocratic women who sought conversation with men as intellectual equals without the demands of sexual love. These "precious women," who sought to gain moral prestige over their male suitors by their chastity, dominated the French salon in the early seventeenth century. But in the late seventeenth and eighteenth centuries, the females who organized the salons were well known for their sexual affairs and marriages with the great men invited to their salons. It was now taken for granted "that relations between women and men, however intellectual or artistic they might appear, could not remain platonic." The first two selections are from the novel The Great Cyrus *by Mlle. de Scudéry, who maintained one of the most famous literary salons. She applauded platonic love and scorned marriage. The third selection is from a nostalgic letter of Abbé Galiani to his former salon hostess, Mme. Necker, and describes an eighteenth-century salon.*

✲ Mlle. de Scudéry, *The Great Cyrus*

Among us, love is not a simple passion as it is elsewhere; it is one of the requirements for good breeding. Every man must be in love. Every lady must be loved. No one among us is indifferent. Anyone capable of such hardness of heart would be reproached as for a crime; such liberty is so shameful that those who are not in love at least pretend to be. Custom does not oblige ladies to love but merely to allow themselves to be loved, and they put their pride in making illustrious conquests and in never losing those whom they have brought under their rule; yet they are severe, for the honor of our beauties consists in keeping the slaves they have made by the sheer power of their attractions and not by according favors; so that, by this custom, to be a lover is almost necessarily to be unhappy. . . . Yet it is

not forbidden to reward a lover's perseverance by a totally pure affection . . . whatever can render them more lovable and loving is allowed, provided it does not shock that purity or modesty which, despite their gallantry, is these ladies' supreme virtue.

✲ Mlle. de Scudéry, *The Great Cyrus*

"Then, said Tisandre [to Sapho—the name under which Mlle. de Scudéry portrayed herself] "you can hardly regard marriage as desirable." "It is true," replied Sapho, "that I consider it a lengthy slavery." "So you think all men are tyrants" "I think they may all become so . . . I know of course that there are some very worthy men who deserve all my esteem and could even acquire some friendship from me; but again, as soon as I think of them as husbands, I see them as masters so likely to turn into tyrants that I cannot help hating them there and then and thank the gods for giving me an inclination totally opposed to marriage."

✲ Abbé Galiani, Letter to Mme. Necker

Not a Friday passes but I visit you in spirit. I arrive. I find you putting the finishing touches to your clothes. I sit at your feet. . . . Dinner is announced. We come out. The others eat meat. I abstain. I eat a lot of that green Scotch cod which I love. I give myself indigestion while admiring Abbé Morellet's skill at carving a young turkey. We get up from table. Coffee is served. Everyone talks at once. The Abbé Raynal agrees with me that Boston has severed its links with England forever and the same time Creutz and Marmontel agree that Grétry is the Pergolese of France. M. Necker thinks everything is perfect, bows his head, and goes away. That is how I spend my Fridays.

---

middle-class Diderot and Rousseau. The Enlightenment was not the preserve of any one class, although obviously its greatest appeal was to the aristocracy and upper middle classes of the major cities. The common people, especially the peasants, were little affected by the Enlightenment.

Of great importance to the Enlightenment was the spread of its ideas to the literate elite of European society. Although the publication and sale of books and treatises were crucial to this process, the salon was also a factor. Salons came into being in the seventeenth century but rose to new heights in the eighteenth. The salons were the elegant drawing rooms in the great urban houses of the wealthy where invited philosophes and guests gathered together and engaged in witty, sparkling conversations often centered on the new ideas of the philosophes. In France's rigid hierarchical society, the salons were important in bring-

ing together writers and artists with aristocrats, government officials, and wealthy bourgeoisie.

As hostesses of the salons, women found themselves in a position to affect the decisions of kings, sway political opinion, and influence literary and artistic taste. Salons provided havens for people and views unwelcome in the royal court. When the *Encyclopedia* was suppressed by the French authorities, Marie-Thérèse de Geoffrin (1699–1777), a wealthy bourgeois widow whose father had been a valet, welcomed the encyclopedists to her salon and offered financial assistance to complete the work in secret.

Mme. Geoffrin was not without rivals, however. The marquise du Deffand (1697–1780) had abandoned her husband in the provinces and established herself in Paris where her ornate drawing room attracted many of the Enlightenment's great figures, including Montesquieu, Hume, and

Voltaire. In 1754, after she began to go blind, she was joined as a hostess by her illegitimate niece, Julie de Lespinasse (1733–1776). For the next ten years, their salon was the most brilliant in Europe until they quarreled and separated.

Although the salons were run by women, the reputation of a salon depended upon the stature of the males a hostess was able to attract (see the box on p. 499). Despite this male domination, however, both French and foreign observers complained that females exerted undue influence in French political affairs. Though exaggerated, this perception led to the decline of salons during the French Revolution.

The salon served an important role in promoting conversation and sociability between upper-class men and women as well as spreading the ideas of the Enlightenment. But other means of spreading Enlightenment ideas were also available. Coffeehouses, cafés, reading clubs, and public lending libraries established by the state were gathering places to exchange ideas. Learned societies were formed in cities throughout Europe and America. At such gatherings as the Select Society of Edinburgh, Scotland, and the American Philosophical Society in Philadelphia, lawyers, doctors, and local officials gathered to discuss Enlightened ideas. Secret societies also developed. The most famous was the Freemasons, established in London in 1717, France and Italy in 1726, and Prussia in 1744, where Frederick II himself was a grand master. It was no secret that the Freemasons were sympathetic to the ideas of the philosophes.

◆ Culture and Society in an Age of Enlightenment

The intellectual adventure fostered by the philosophes was accompanied by both traditional practices and important changes in the eighteenth-century world of culture and society.

❋ Innovations in Art, Music, and Literature

Although the Baroque and Neoclassical styles that had dominated the seventeenth century continued into the eighteenth century, by the 1730s a new style known as Rococo had begun to affect decoration and architecture all over Europe. Though a French invention and enormously popular in Germany, Rococo became a truly international style.

Unlike the Baroque, which stressed majesty, power, and movement, Rococo emphasized grace and gentle action. Rococo rejected strict geometrical patterns and had a fondness for curves; it liked to follow the wandering lines of natural objects, such as seashells and flowers. It made much use of interlaced designs colored in gold with delicate contours and graceful curves. Highly secular, its lightness and charm spoke of the pursuit of pleasure, happiness, and love.

Some of Rococo's appeal is evident already in the work of Antoine Watteau (1684–1721), whose lyrical views of aristocratic life—refined, sensual, civilized, with gentlemen and ladies in elegant dress—revealed a world of upper-class pleasure and joy. Underneath that exterior, however, was an element of sadness as the artist revealed the fragility and transitory nature of pleasure, love, and life.

Another aspect of Rococo was the sense of enchantment and exuberance, especially evident in the work of Giovanni Battista Tiepolo (1696–1770). Much of Tiepolo's painting came to adorn the walls and ceilings of churches and palaces. His masterpiece is the ceiling of the Bishop's Palace at Würzburg, a massive scene representing the four continents. Tiepolo's work reminds us that Rococo decorative work could easily be used with Baroque architecture.

The palace of Versailles had made an enormous impact on Europe. "Keeping up with the Bourbons" became important as the Austrian emperor, the Swedish king, German princes and prince-bishops, Italian princes,

ANTOINE WATTEAU, *THE PILGRIMAGE TO CYTHERA.* Antoine Watteau was one of the most gifted painters in eighteenth-century France. His portrayal of aristocratic life reveals a world of elegance, wealth, and pleasure. In this painting, Watteau depicts a group of aristocratic pilgrims about to depart the island of Cythera, where they have paid homage to Venus, the goddess of love.

VIERZEHNHEILIGEN, INTERIOR VIEW.
Pictured here is the interior of the Vierzehnheiligen, the pilgrimage church designed by
Balthasar Neumann. As this illustration
shows, the Baroque-Rococo style of architecture created lavish buildings in which secular and spiritual elements became easily
interchangeable. Elaborate detail, blazing
light, rich colors, and opulent decoration
were blended together to create a work of
stunning beauty.

and even a Russian tsar built grandiose palaces. While
emulating Versailles's size, they were modeled less after
the French classical style of Versailles than after the
seventeenth-century Italian Baroque, as modified by a
series of brilliant German and Austrian sculptor-architects.
This Baroque-Rococo architectural style of the eighteenth
century was conceived as a total work of art in which
building, sculptural figures, and wall and ceiling paintings
were blended into a harmonious whole. This style was
used in both palaces and churches, and often the same
architects did both. This is evident in the work of one of
the greatest architects of the eighteenth century, Balthasar
Neumann (1687–1753).

Neumann's two masterpieces are the pilgrimage
church of the Vierzehnheiligen (The Fourteen Saints) in
southern Germany and the Bishop's Palace known as the
Residenz, the residential palace of the Schönborn prince-
bishop of Würzburg. Secular and spiritual become easily
interchangeable as lavish and fanciful ornament, light,
bright colors, and elaborate and rich detail greet us in both
buildings. An even more stunning example of Rococo
is evident in the pilgrimage church of the Wies in southern Bavaria, designed by Domenikus Zimmermann

VIERZEHNHEILIGEN, EXTERIOR VIEW.   Balthasar
Neumann, one of the most prominent architects of the
eighteenth century, used the Baroque-Rococo style of
architecture to design some of the most beautiful buildings of the century. Pictured here is the exterior of his
pilgrimage church of the Vierzehnheiligen (The Fourteen
Saints), located in southern Germany.

JACQUES-LOUIS DAVID, *OATH OF THE HORATII.* The Frenchman David was one of the most famous Neoclassical artists of the late eighteenth century. In order to immerse himself in the world of classical antiquity, he painted the *Oath of the Horatii* in Rome. With its emphasis on patriotic duty, the work became an instant success in both Paris and Rome.

(1685–1766). The pilgrim in search of holiness is struck by an incredible richness of detail. Persuaded by joy rather than fear, the believer is lifted toward heaven on a cloud of rapture.

Despite the popularity of the Rococo style, Neoclassicism continued to maintain a strong appeal and in the late eighteenth century emerged in France as an established movement. Neoclassical artists wanted to recapture the dignity and simplicity of the classical style of ancient Greece and Rome. Some were especially influenced by the recent excavations of the ancient Roman cities of Herculaneum and Pompeii. Classical elements are evident in the work of Jacques-Louis David (1748–1825). In the *Oath of the Horatii,* he re-created a scene from Roman history in which the three Horatii brothers swore an oath before their father, proclaiming their willingness to sacrifice their lives for their country. David's Neoclassical style, with its moral seriousness and its emphasis on honor and patriotism, made him extremely popular during the French Revolution.

✄ THE DEVELOPMENT OF MUSIC

The seventeenth and eighteenth centuries were the formative years of classical music and saw the rise of the opera and oratorio, the sonata, the concerto, and the symphony. The Italians were the first to develop these genres, but were soon followed by the Germans, Austrians, and English. As in previous centuries, most musicians depended on a patron—a prince, a well-endowed ecclesiastic, or an aristocrat. The many individual princes, archbishops, and bishops, each with his own court, provided the patronage that made Italy and Germany the musical leaders of Europe.

Many of the techniques of the Baroque musical style, which dominated Europe between 1600 and 1750, were perfected by two composers—Bach and Handel—who stand out as musical geniuses. Johann Sebastian Bach (1685–1750) came from a family of musicians. Bach held the post of organist and music director at a number of small German courts before becoming director of church music at the Church of St. Thomas in Leipzig in 1723. There Bach composed his Mass in B Minor, his St. Matthew's Passion, and the cantatas and motets that have established his reputation as one of the greatest composers of all time. Like the architect Balthasar Neumann, Bach could move with ease from the religious to the secular. In fact, his secular music reflects a boisterous spirit; his Coffee Cantata was a dialogue between father and daughter over the daughter's desire to drink the new beverage. Bach had no problem adding religious texts to the secular music he had composed in princely courts to make it church music. Above all for Bach, music was a means to worship God; in his own words, his task in life was to make "well-ordered music in the honor of God."

The other great musical giant of the early eighteenth century, George Frederick Handel (1685–1759) was, like Bach, born in Saxony in Germany and in the same year. In contrast to Bach's quiet provincial life, however, Handel experienced a stormy international career and was profoundly secular in temperament. After studying in Italy, where he began his career by writing operas in the Italian manner, in 1712 he moved to England where he spent most of his adult life attempting to run an opera company. Although patronized by the English royal court, Handel wrote music for large public audiences and was not averse to writing huge, unusual-sounding pieces. The band for his Fireworks Music, for example, was supposed

MOZART AS CHILD PRODIGY. This painting, done in Paris between 1763 and 1764, shows the seven-year-old Mozart playing at the harpsichord while his composer-father Leopold plays the violin and his sister Nannerl sings. Crowds greeted the young Mozart enthusiastically throughout the family's three-year tour of northern Europe.

to be accompanied by 101 cannon. Although he wrote more than forty operas and much other secular music, ironically the worldly Handel is probably best known for his religious music. He had no problem moving from Italian opera to religious oratorios when they proved to be more popular with his English public. An oratorio was an extended musical composition on a religious subject, usually taken from a biblical story. Only one of Handel's great oratorios, the *Messiah,* is well known today. It has been called "one of those rare works that appeal immediately to everyone, and yet is indisputably a masterpiece of the highest order."[9]

Although Bach and Handel composed many instrumental suites and concerti, orchestral music did not come to the fore until the second half of the eighteenth century, when new instruments such as the piano appeared. A new musical period, the classical era (1750–1830), also emerged, represented by two great innovators—Haydn and Mozart. Their renown caused the musical center of Europe to shift from Italy and Germany to the Austrian Empire.

Franz Joseph Haydn (1732–1809) spent most of his adult life as musical director for the wealthy Hungarian princes, the Esterhazy brothers. Haydn was incredibly prolific, composing 104 symphonies in addition to string quartets, concerti, songs, oratorios, and masses. In particular, Haydn developed new forms of instrumental music. His visits to England in 1790 and 1794 introduced him to another world where musicians wrote for public concerts rather than princely patrons. This "liberty," as he called it,

induced him to write his two great oratorios, *The Creation* and *The Seasons,* both of which were dedicated to the common people.

The concerto, symphony, and opera all witnessed a climax in the works of Wolfgang Amadeus Mozart (1756–1791), a child prodigy who gave his first harpsichord concert at six and wrote his first opera at twelve. He, too, sought a patron, but his discontent with the overly demanding archbishop of Salzburg forced him to move to Vienna where his failure to find a permanent patron made his life miserable. Nevertheless, he wrote music prolifically and passionately until he died at thirty-five, a debt-ridden pauper. Mozart carried the tradition of Italian comic opera to new heights with *The Marriage of Figaro,* based on a Parisian play of the 1780s in which a valet outwits and outsings his noble employers, and *Don Giovanni,* a "black comedy" about the havoc Don Giovanni wrought on earth before he descended into hell. *The Marriage of Figaro, The Magic Flute,* and *Don Giovanni* are three of the world's greatest operas. Mozart composed with an ease of melody and a blend of grace, precision, and emotion that arguably no one has ever excelled. Haydn remarked to Mozart's father that "your son is the greatest composer known to me either in person or by reputation."

THE DEVELOPMENT OF THE NOVEL

Literary historians credit the eighteenth century with the decisive steps in the development of the novel. The novel was not a completely new literary genre but grew out of the medieval romances and the picaresque stories of the sixteenth century, such as Cervantes's *Don Quixote*. The English are credited with establishing the "modern novel as the chief vehicle" for fiction writing. With no established rules, the novel was open to much experimentation. It also proved especially attractive to women readers and women writers.

Samuel Richardson (1689–1761) was a printer by trade who did not turn to writing until his fifties. His first novel, *Pamela: or, Virtue Rewarded,* focused on a servant girl's resistance to numerous seduction attempts by her master. Finally, by reading the girl's letters describing her feelings about his efforts, the master realizes that she has a good mind as well as body and marries her. Virtue is rewarded. *Pamela* won Richardson a large audience as he appealed to the growing cult of sensibility in the eighteenth century—the taste for the sentimental and emotional. Samuel Johnson, another great English writer of the century and an even greater wit, remarked, "If you were to read Richardson for the story . . . you would hang yourself. But you must read him for the sentiment."

Reacting against the moral seriousness of Richardson, Henry Fielding (1707–1754) wrote novels about people without scruples who survived by their wits. His best work was *The History of Tom Jones, A Foundling,* a lengthy novel about the numerous adventures of a young scoundrel. Fielding presented scenes of English life from the hovels of London to the country houses of the aristocracy. In a number of hilarious episodes, he described characters akin to real types in English society. Although he emphasized action rather than inner feeling, Fielding did his own moralizing by attacking the hypocrisy of his age.

THE WRITING OF HISTORY

The philosophes were responsible for creating a "revolution" in the writing of history. Their secular orientation caused them to eliminate the role of God in history and freed them to concentrate on events themselves and search for causal relationships within a natural world. Earlier, the humanist historians of the Renaissance had also placed their histories in purely secular settings, but not with the same intensity and complete removal of God. Whereas the humanists had de-emphasized Christian presuppositions in favor of humans, Voltaire and other philosophe-historians eliminated those presuppositions altogether.

The philosophe-historians also broadened the scope of history from the humanists' preoccupation with politics. Politics still predominated in the work of Enlightenment historians, but they also paid attention to economic, social, intellectual, and cultural developments. As Voltaire explained in his masterpiece, *The Age of Louis XIV:* "It is not merely the life of Louis XIV that we propose to write; we have a wider aim in view. We shall endeavor to depict for posterity, not the actions of a single man, but the spirit of men in the most enlightened age the world has ever seen."[10] In seeking to describe the "totality of past human experience," Voltaire initiated the modern ideal of social

history. He was also one of the first historians to include art history in his work.

The weaknesses of these philosophe-historians stemmed from their preoccupations as philosophes. Following the ideals of the classics that dominated their minds, the philosophes sought to instruct as well as entertain. Their goal was to help civilize their age, and history could play a role by revealing its lessons according to their vision. Their emphasis on science and reason and their dislike of Christianity made them less than sympathetic to the period we call the Middle Ages. This is particularly noticeable in the other great masterpiece of eighteenth-century historiography, the six-volume *Decline and Fall of the Roman Empire* by Edward Gibbon (see the box on p. 505). Although Gibbon thought that the decline of Rome had many causes, he portrayed the growth of Christianity as a major reason for Rome's eventual collapse.

The High Culture of the Eighteenth Century

Historians and cultural anthropologists have grown accustomed to distinguishing between a civilization's high culture and its popular culture. By high culture is usually meant the literary and artistic culture of the educated and wealthy ruling classes; by popular culture is meant the written and unwritten culture of the masses, most of which is passed down orally. By the eighteenth century, European high culture consisted of a learned world of theologians, scientists, philosophers, intellectuals, poets, and dramatists, for whom Latin remained a truly international language. Their work was supported by a wealthy and literate lay group, the most important of whom were the landed aristocracy and the wealthier upper classes in the cities. European high culture was noticeably cosmopolitan. In addition to Latin, French had become an international language of the cultural elites. This high culture of Europe's elite was institutionally expressed in the salons, the universities, and the academies.

Especially noticeable in the eighteenth century was an expansion of both the reading public and publishing. One study of French publishing, for example, reveals that French publishers were issuing about 1,600 titles yearly in the 1780s, up from 300 titles in 1750. Though many of these titles were still aimed at small groups of the educated elite, many were also directed to the new reading public of the middle classes, which included women and even urban artisans. The growth of publishing houses made it possible for authors to make money from their works and be less dependent on wealthy patrons. Of course, the increase in quantity does not necessarily mean that people were reading books of greater significance and quality, as the best-seller in eighteenth-century England, Bishop Sherlock's *Letter from the Lord Bishop of London to the Clergy and People of London on the Occasion of the Late Earthquakes,* would indicate.

Gibbon and the Idea of Progress

Edward Gibbon's The Decline and Fall of the Roman Empire *was one of the great historical masterpieces of the eighteenth century. Like some of the philosophes, Gibbon believed in the idea of progress and, in reflecting on the decline and fall of Rome, expressed his optimism about the future of European civilization and the ability of Europeans to avoid the fate of the Romans.*

❊ Edward Gibbon, *The Decline and Fall of the Roman Empire*

It is the duty of a patriot to prefer and promote the exclusive interest and glory of his native county; but a philosopher may be permitted to enlarge his views, and to consider Europe as one great republic, whose various inhabitants have attained almost the same level of politeness and cultivation. The balance of power will continue to fluctuate, and the prosperity of our own, or the neighboring kingdoms, may be alternately exalted or depressed; but these partial events cannot essentially injure our general state of happiness, the system of arts, and laws, and manners, which so advantageously distinguish, above the rest of mankind, the Europeans and their colonies. The savage nations of the globe are the common enemies of civilized society; and we may inquire, with anxious curiosity, whether Europe is still threatened with a repetition of those calamities, which formerly oppressed the arms and institutions of Rome. Perhaps the same reflections will illustrate the fall of the mighty empire, and explain the probable causes of our actual security. . . .

Should these speculations be found doubtful or fallacious, there still remains a more humble source of comfort and hope. The discoveries of ancient and modern navigators, and the domestic history, or tradition, of the most enlightened nations, represent the *human* savage, naked both in mind and body, and destitute of laws, of arts, of ideas, and almost of language. From this abject condition, perhaps the primitive and universal state of man, he has gradually arisen to command the animals, to fertilize the earth, to traverse the oceans, and to measure the heavens. His progress in the improvement and exercise of his mental and corporeal faculties has been irregular and various; infinitely slow in the beginning, and increasing by degree with redoubled velocity: ages of laborious ascent have been followed by a moment of rapid downfall; and the several climates of the globe have felt the vicissitudes of light and darkness. Yet the experience of four thousand years should enlarge our hopes, and diminish our apprehensions: we cannot determine to what height the human species may aspire in their advances toward perfection; but it may safely be presumed, that no people, unless the face of nature is changed, will relapse into their original barbarism. . . . Fortunately for mankind, the more useful, or, at least, more necessary arts, can be performed without superior talents, or national subordination. . . . Each village, each family, each individual must always possess both ability and inclination, to perpetuate the use of fire and of metals; the propagation and service of domestic animals; the methods of hunting and fishing; the rudiments of navigation; the imperfect cultivation of corn, or other nutritive grain; and the simple practice of the mechanic trades. Private genius and public industry may be extirpated; but these hardy plants survive the tempest, and strike an everlasting root into the most unfavorable soil. The splendid days of Augustus and Trajan were eclipsed by a cloud of ignorance: and the Barbarians subverted the laws and palaces of Rome. But the scythe . . . still continued annually to mow the harvests of Italy. . . .

Since the first discovery of the arts, war, commerce, and religious zeal have diffused, among the savages of the Old and New World, these inestimable gifts: they have been successively propagated; they can never be lost. We may therefore acquiesce in the pleasing conclusion, that every age of the world has increased, and still increases, the real wealth, the happiness, the knowledge, and perhaps the virtue of the human race.

An important aspect of the growth of publishing and reading in the eighteenth century was the development of magazines for the general public. Great Britain, an important center for the new magazines, saw 25 periodicals published in 1700, 103 in 1760, and 158 in 1780. Although short-lived, the best known was Joseph Addison's and Richard Steele's *Spectator,* begun in 1711. Its goal was "to enliven Morality with wit, and to temper Wit with Morality. . . . To bring Philosophy out of the closets and libraries, schools and colleges, to dwell in clubs and assemblies, at tea-tables and coffeehouses." In keeping with one of the chief intellectual goals of the philosophes, the *Spectator* wished to instruct and entertain at the same time. With its praise of family, marriage, and courtesy, the *Spectator* also had a strong appeal to women. Some of the new magazines were aimed specifically at women, such as *The Female Spectator* in England, which was also edited by a woman, Eliza Haywood, and featured articles by female writers.

Along with magazines came daily newspapers. The first was printed in London in 1702, but by 1780 thirty-seven other English towns had their own newspapers. Filled with news and special features, they were relatively cheap and were provided free in coffeehouses. Books, too, received wider circulation through the development of public libraries in the cities as well as private circulating libraries, which offered books for rental.

A LONDON COFFEEHOUSE. Coffeehouses first appeared in Venice and Constantinople but quickly spread throughout Europe by the beginning of the eighteenth century. In addition to drinking coffee, patrons of coffeehouses could read magazines and newspapers, exchange ideas, play chess, smoke, and even engage in business transactions. In this scene from a London coffeehouse of 1705, well-attired gentlemen make bids on commodities. Bidding went on until pins, which had been placed in lit candles, fell to the table. Thus, bidding stopped when patrons could "hear a pin drop."

EDUCATION AND UNIVERSITIES

By the eighteenth century, Europe was home to a large number of privately endowed secondary schools, such as the grammar and public school in England, the gymnasium in German-speaking lands, and the collège in France and Spain. In many countries these secondary schools were often dominated by religious orders, especially by the Jesuits who had made education an important part of their philosophy.

These schools tended to be elitist, designed to meet the needs of the children of the upper classes of society. Some scholarships were provided for poor children if they were sponsored by local clerics or nobles. But their lot was not easy, and poor students who completed their studies usually went into the ranks of the lower clergy. Basically then, European secondary schools reinforced the class hierarchy of Europe rather than creating avenues for social mobility. In fact, most of the philosophes reinforced the belief that education should function to keep people in their own social class. Baron d'Holbach said, "Education should teach princes to reign, the ruling classes to distinguish themselves by their merit and virtue, the rich to use their riches well, the poor to live by honest industry."

The curriculum of these secondary schools still largely concentrated on the Greek and Latin classics with little attention paid to mathematics, the sciences, and modern languages. Complaints from philosophe-reformers, as well as from merchants and other middle-class people who wanted their sons to have a more practical education, led to the development of new schools designed to provide a broader education. In Germany, the first *Realschule* was opened in Berlin in 1747 and offered modern languages, geography, and bookkeeping to prepare boys for careers in business. New schools of this kind were also created for upper-class girls although they placed most of their emphasis on religion and domestic skills.

The most common complaint about universities, especially from the philosophes, was the old-fashioned curriculum that focused on the classics and Aristotelian philosophy and left out training in the sciences and modern languages. Before the end of the century, this criticism led to reforms that introduced new ideas in the areas of physics, astronomy, and even mathematics into the universities. It is significant, however, that very few of the important scientific discoveries of the eighteenth century occurred in the universities. Most universities produced little intellectual growth and scholarship, although there were exceptions, such as Göttingen and Edinburgh. The University of Göttingen in Hanover, founded in 1737, emphasized the physical sciences. Although a new institution, it had the greatest university library in Europe by the end of the century. Newtonian science was introduced at the University of Edinburgh in the 1730s, and its scientists and philosophers became well known in Europe.

Crime and Punishment

By the eighteenth century, most European states had developed a hierarchy of courts to deal with crimes. Except in England, judicial torture remained an important means of obtaining evidence before a trial. Courts used the rack, thumbscrews, and other instruments to obtain confessions in criminal cases. Punishments for crimes were often cruel and even spectacular. Public executions were a basic part of traditional punishment and were regarded as a neces-

The Punishment of Crime

Torture and capital punishment remained common features of European judicial systems well into the eighteenth century. Public spectacles were especially gruesome as this excerpt from the Nocturnal Spectator of Restif de la Bretonne demonstrates.

Restif de la Bretonne, *Nocturnal Spectator*

❋ The Broken Man

I went home by way of rue Saint-Antoine and the Place de Gréve. Three murderers had been broken on the wheel there, the day before. I had not expected to see any such spectacle, one that I had never dared to witness. But as I crossed the square I caught sight of a poor wretch, pale, half dead, wracked by the pains of the interrogation inflicted on him twenty hours earlier; he

was stumbling down from the Hôtel de Ville supported by the executioner and the confessor. These two men, so completely different, inspired an inexpressible emotion in me! I watched the latter embrace a miserable man consumed by fever, filthy as the dungeons he came from, swarming with vermin! And I said to myself, "O Religion, here is your greatest glory! . . . "

I saw a horrible sight, even though the torture had been mitigated. . . . The wretch had revealed his accomplices. He was garroted before he was put to the wheel. A winch set under the scaffold tightened a noose around the victim's neck and he was strangled; for a long while the confessor and the hangman felt his heart to see whether the artery still pulsed, and the hideous blows were dealt only after it beat no longer. . . . I left, with my hair standing on end in horror.

---

sary means of deterring potential offenders in an age when a state's police arm was too weak to assure the capture of criminals. Although nobles were executed by simple beheading, lower-class criminals condemned to death were tortured, broken on the wheel, or drawn and quartered (see the box above). The death penalty was still commonly used in property as well as criminal cases. By 1800, more than 200 crimes were subject to the death penalty in England. In addition to executions, European states resorted to forced labor in mines, forts, and navies. England also sent criminals as indentured servants to colonies in the New World and, after the American Revolution, to Australia.

Appalled by the unjust laws and brutal punishments of their times, some philosophes sought to create a new approach to justice. The most notable effort was made by the Italian philosophe, Cesare Beccaria (1738–1794). In his essay, *On Crimes and Punishments*, written in 1764, Beccaria argued that punishments should serve only as deterrents, not as exercises in brutality: "Such punishments . . . ought to be chosen as will make the strongest and most lasting impressions on the minds of others, with the least torment to the body of the criminal."[11] Beccaria was also opposed to the use of capital punishment. It was spectacular, but failed to stop others from committing crimes. Imprisonment, the deprivation of freedom, made a far more lasting impression. Moreover, capital punishment was harmful to society because it set an example of barbarism: "Is it not absurd, that the laws, which detest and punish homicide, should, in order to prevent murder, publicly commit murder themselves?"

By the end of the eighteenth century, a growing sentiment against executions and torture led to a decline in both corporal and capital punishment. A new type of prison, in which criminals were placed in cells and sub-

jected to discipline and regular work to rehabilitate them, began to replace the public spectacle of barbarous punishments.

❋ The World of Medicine

In the eighteenth century, medicine was practiced by a hierarchy of practitioners. At the top stood the physicians, who were university graduates and enjoyed a high social status. Despite the scientific advances of the seventeenth and eighteenth centuries, however, university medical education was still largely conducted in Latin and was based primarily on Galen's work. New methods emphasizing clinical experience did begin to be introduced at the University of Leiden, which replaced Padua as the foremost medical school of Europe in the first half of the seventeenth century, only to be surpassed in the last half of that century by Vienna. A graduate with a doctorate in medicine from a university needed to receive a license before he could be a practicing member of the physicians' elitist corporate body. In England the Royal College of Physicians licensed only 100 physicians in the early eighteenth century. Only officially licensed physicians could hold regular medical consultations with patients and receive payments, already regarded in the eighteenth century as outrageously high.

Below the physicians were the surgeons, who were still known as barber-surgeons well into the eighteenth century from their original dual occupation. Their primary functions were to bleed patients and perform surgery; the latter was often done in a crude fashion since it was performed without painkillers and in filthy conditions because there was no understanding of bacteria and infection. Bleeding was widely believed to be efficacious as this doctor reported in 1799:

Bleeding is proper at the beginning of all inflammatory fevers, as pleurisies. . . . It is likewise proper in all topical inflammations, as those of the intestines, womb, bladder, stomach, kidneys, throat, eyes, etc. as also in the asthma, sciatic pains, coughs, head-aches, rheumatisms, the apoplexy, epilepsy, and bloody flux. After falls, blows, bruises, or any violent hurt received either externally or internally, bleeding is necessary.[12]

The surgeons underwent significant changes in the course of the eighteenth century. In the 1740s, they began to separate themselves from the barbers and organize their own guilds. At the same time, they started to undergo additional training by dissecting corpses and studying anatomy more systematically. As they became more effective, the distinction between physicians and surgeons began to break down, and surgeons were examining patients in a fashion similar to physicians by the end of the century. Moreover, surgeons also began to be licensed. In England the Royal College of Surgeons required clinical experience before granting the license.

Other medical practitioners, such as apothecaries, midwives, and faith healers, primarily served the common people in the eighteenth century. Although their primary function was to provide herbs and potions as recommended by physicians, apothecaries or pharmacists also acted independently in diagnosing illnesses and selling remedies. In the course of the eighteenth century, male doctors increasingly supplanted midwives in delivering babies. However, the tradition of faith healing, so prominent in medieval medicine, continued to be practiced, especially in the rural areas of Europe.

Hospitals in the eighteenth century seemed more a problem than an aid in dealing with disease and illness. That conditions were bad is evident in this description by the philosophe Denis Diderot, who characterized the Hôtel-Dieu in Paris, France's "biggest, roomiest, and richest" hospital, in these words:

Imagine a long series of communicating wards filled with sufferers of every kind of disease who are sometimes packed three, four, five or even six into a bed, the living alongside the dead and dying, the air polluted by this mass of unhealthy bodies, passing pestilential germs of their afflictions from one to the other, and the spectacle of suffering and agony on every hand. That is the Hôtel-Dieu.

The result is that many of these poor wretches come out with diseases they did not have when they went in, and often pass them on to the people they go back to live with. Others are half-cured and spend the rest of their days in an invalidism as hard to bear as the illness itself; and the rest perish, except for the fortunate few whose strong constitutions enable them to survive.[13]

Despite appeals, reform efforts for hospitals in the eighteenth century remained in an infantile stage.

❋ *Popular Culture*

Popular culture refers to the often unwritten and unofficial culture passed down orally that was fundamental to the lives of most people. The distinguishing characteristic of popular culture is its collective and public nature. Group activity was especially evident in the festival, a broad name used to cover a variety of celebrations: family festivals, such as weddings; community festivals in Catholic Europe that celebrated the feastday of the local patron saint; annual festivals, such as Christmas and Easter that go back to medieval Christianity; and Carnival, the most spectacular form of festival, which was celebrated in the Mediterranean world of Spain, Italy, and France as well as in Germany and Austria. All of these festivals shared common characteristics. While having a spiritual function, they were celebrated in a secular fashion. They were special occasions on which people ate, drank, and celebrated to excess. In traditional societies, festival was a time of play because much of the rest of the year was a time of unrelieved work. As the poet Thomas Gray said of Carnival in Turin in 1739: "This Carnival lasts only from Christmas to Lent; one half of the remaining part of the year is passed in remembering the last, the other in expecting the future Carnival."[14]

"The example par excellence of the festival" was Carnival, which started in January and lasted until the beginning of Lent, traditionally the forty-day period of fasting and purification leading up to Easter. Carnival was a time of great indulgence, just the reverse of Lent when people were expected to abstain from meat, sex, and most recreations. A heavy consumption of food, especially meat and other delicacies, and heavy drinking were the norm: "they drink as if they were never to drink more." Carnival was a time of intense sexual activity as well. Songs with double meanings could be sung publicly at this time of year whereas otherwise they would be considered offensive to the community. A float of Florentine "key-makers," for example, sang this ditty to the ladies: "Our tools are fine, new and useful; We always carry them with us; They are good for anything, If you want to touch them, you can."[15] Finally, it was a time of aggression, a time to release pent-up feelings. Most often this took the form of verbal aggression since people could openly insult other people and were even allowed to criticize their social superiors and authorities. But other acts of violence were also permitted. People pelted each other with apples, eggs, flour, and pig's bladders filled with water. This limited and sanctioned violence also led to unplanned violence. All contemporaries observed that Carnival was a time when the incidence of murder increased dramatically.

The same sense of community evident in festival was also present in the chief gathering places of the common people, the local taverns or cabarets. Taverns were supposedly for travelers but functioned more frequently as a regular gathering place for neighborhood men to talk, play games, conduct small business matters, and, of course, to drink. In some countries, the favorite drinks of poor people, such as gin in England and vodka in Russia, proved devastating as poor people regularly drank themselves into oblivion. Gin was cheap; the classic sign in English taverns, "Drunk for a penny, dead drunk for two pence," was literally true. In England the consumption of gin rose from two to five million gallons between 1714 and 1733 and only declined when complaints finally led to strict laws to restrict sales in the 1750s. Of course, the rich drank too. Samuel Johnson once remarked: "All the decent people in Lichfield got drunk every night and were not the worse thought of." But unlike the poor, the rich drank port and brandy, usually in large quantities.

This difference in drinking habits between rich and poor reminds us of the ever-widening separation between the elite and poor in the eighteenth century. In 1500, popular culture was for everyone; a second culture for the elite, it was the only culture for the rest of society. But between 1500 and 1800, the nobility, clergy, and bourgeoisie had abandoned popular culture to the lower classes. This was, of course, a gradual process, and in abandoning the popular festivals, the upper classes were also abandoning the popular worldview as well. The new scientific outlook had brought a new mental world for the upper classes, and they now viewed such things as witchcraft, faith healing, fortune telling, and prophecy as the beliefs of "such as are of the weakest judgment and reason, as women, children, and ignorant and superstitious persons."

Despite this growing gulf between elite and common people, there were still some forms of entertainment that occasionally brought them together. Most common were the urban fairs, a product of what some historians now call the "commercialization of leisure," or the attempt by businesses to turn leisure activities into a good investment. The three fairs in Paris provided entertainment—farcical theater, magic shows, circus performers, or freak shows—as well as food booths and popular wares for purchase. Both the privileged and unprivileged classes were still attracted to boxing matches and horse races as well as the bloodier spectacles of bullbaiting, bearbaiting, and cockfighting.

Popular culture had always included a vast array of traditional songs and stories that were passed down from generation to generation. But popular culture was not entirely based on an oral tradition; a popular literature existed as well. So-called chapbooks, printed on cheap paper, were short brochures sold by itinerant peddlers to the lower classes. They contained both spiritual and secular material; lives of saints and inspirational stories competed with crude satires and adventure stories.

It is apparent from the chapbooks that popular culture did not have to remain primarily oral. Its ability to change was dependent upon the growth of literacy. There is still considerable uncertainty about literacy in early modern Europe because of the difficulty in measuring it. Some reasonable estimates based on studies in France indicate that literacy rates for men increased from 29 percent in the late seventeenth century to 47 percent in the late eighteenth century; for women, the increase was from 14 to 27 percent during the same period. Of course, certain groups were more likely to be literate than others. Upper-class elites as well as the upper middle classes in the cities were mostly all literate. However, the figures also indicate dramatic increases for lower-middle-class artisans in urban areas. Recent research in the city of Marseilles, for example, indicates that literacy of male

artisans and workers increased from 28 percent in 1710 to 85 percent in 1789, though the rate for women remained at 15 percent. Peasants, who constituted as much as 75 percent of the French population, remained largely illiterate.

The spread of literacy was closely connected to primary education. In Catholic Europe, primary education was largely a matter of local community effort, leading to little real growth. Only in the Habsburg Austrian Empire was a system of state-supported primary schools (*Volkschulen*) established. Although attendance was supposedly compulsory, a 1781 census revealed that only one in four school-age children was actually attending.

The emphasis of the Protestant reformers on reading the Bible had led Protestant states to take greater interest in primary education. Some places, especially the Swiss cantons, Scotland, and the German states of Saxony and Prussia, witnessed the emergence of universal primary schools that provided a modicum of education for the masses. An edict of the Prussian king Frederick II (see Chapter 18) in 1763 made the schooling of children compulsory. But effective systems of primary education were hindered by the attitudes of the ruling classes, who feared the consequences of any education beyond teaching the lower classes the virtues of hard work and deference to their superiors. Hannah More, an English writer who set up a network of Sunday schools, made clear the philosophy of her charity school for poor children: "My plan of instruction is extremely simple and limited. They learn on weekdays such coarse work as may fit them for servants. I allow of no writing for the poor. My object is to train up the lower classes in habits of industry and piety."

◆ Religion and the Churches

The music of Bach and the pilgrimage and monastic churches of southern Germany and Austria make us aware of a curious fact. Though much of the great art and music of the time was religious, the thought of the time was antireligious as life became increasingly secularized and men of reason attacked the established churches. And yet most Europeans were still Christians. Even many of those most critical of the churches accepted that society could not function without religious faith.

✿ The Institutional Church

In the eighteenth century, the established Catholic and Protestant churches were basically conservative institutions that upheld society's hierarchical structure, privileged classes, and traditions. Although churches experienced change because of new state policies, they did not sustain any dramatic internal changes. Whether in Catholic or Protestant countries, the parish church run by priest or pastor remained the center of religious practice. In addition to providing religious services, the parish church kept records of births, deaths, and marriages, provided charity for the poor, supervised whatever primary education there was, and cared for orphans.

⚘ CHURCH-STATE RELATIONS

Early on, the Protestant Reformation had solved the problem of the relationship between church and state by establishing the principle of state control over the churches. In the eighteenth century, Protestant state churches flourished throughout Europe: Lutheranism in Scandinavia and the north German states; Anglicanism in England; and Calvinism (or Reformed churches) in Scotland, the United Provinces, and some of the Swiss cantons and German states. There were also Protestant minorities in other European countries.

In 1700, the Catholic church still exercised much power in Catholic European states: Spain, Portugal, France, Italy, the Habsburg Empire, Poland, and most of southern Germany. The church also continued to possess enormous wealth. In Spain, 3,000 monastic institutions housing 100,000 men and women controlled enormous landed estates.

The Catholic church remained hierarchically structured. In most Catholic countries, the highest clerics, such as bishops, archbishops, abbots, and abbesses, were members of the upper class, especially the landed nobility, and received enormous revenues from their landed estates and tithes from the faithful. A wide gulf existed between the upper and lower clergy. While the French bishop of Strasbourg, for example, received 100,000 livres a year, parish priests were paid only 500.

In the eighteenth century, the governments of many Catholic states began to seek greater authority over the churches in their countries. This "nationalization" of the

MAP 17.2   **Religious Population of Eighteenth-Century Europe.**

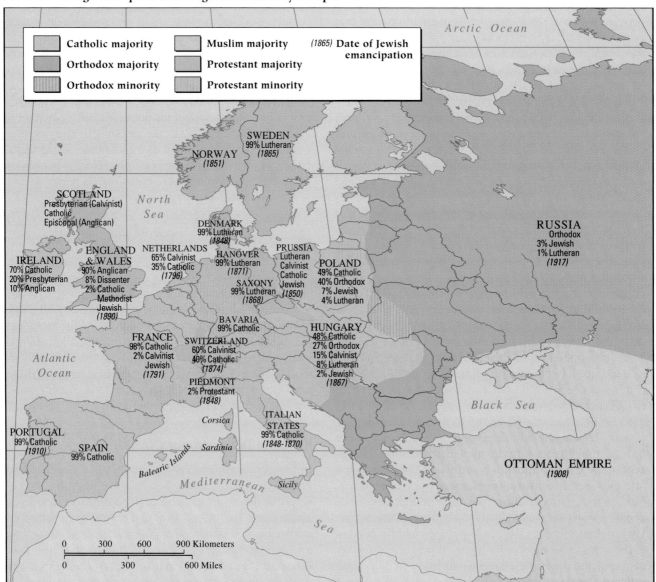

Catholic church meant controlling the papacy and in turn the chief papal agents, the Society of Jesus. The Jesuits had proved extremely successful, perhaps too successful for their own good. They had created special enclaves, virtually states-within-states, in the French, Spanish, and Portuguese colonies in the New World. Through their excellent secondary schools, they directed the education of the sons of Catholic aristocrats. As advisers to Catholic rulers, they exercised considerable political influence. But the high profile the Jesuits achieved through their successes led to a wide range of enemies, and a series of actions soon undermined Jesuit power. The Portuguese monarch destroyed the powerful Jesuit state in Paraguay and then in 1759 expelled the Jesuits from Portugal and confiscated their property. In 1764, they were expelled from France and three years later from Spain and the Spanish colonies. In 1773, when Spain and France demanded that the entire society be dissolved, Pope Clement XIV reluctantly complied. The dissolution of the Jesuit order, the pillar of Catholic fanaticism and strength, was yet another victory for Catholic governments determined to win control over their churches.

The end of the Jesuits was paralleled by a decline in papal power. Already by the mid-eighteenth century, the papacy played only a minor role in diplomacy and international affairs. The nationalization of the churches by the states meant the loss of the papacy's power to appoint high clerical officials.

Another aspect of state control over the Catholic church involved the regulation and suppression of monastic orders. The most radical program was carried out in the Austrian Empire. By the Edict on Idle Institutions in 1782, Emperor Joseph II suppressed all the contemplative monastic orders, allowing only those that provided charitable or educational services to survive. The number of monks in the Austrian Empire was cut in half, and the confiscated monastic properties were used to extend education.

TOLERATION AND RELIGIOUS MINORITIES

One of the chief battle cries of the philosophes had been a call for religious toleration. Out of political necessity, a certain level of tolerance of different creeds had occurred in the seventeenth century in such places as Germany after the Thirty Years' War and France after the divisive religious wars. But many rulers still found it difficult to accept. Louis XIV had turned back the clock in France at the end of the seventeenth century, insisting on religious uniformity and suppressing the rights of the Huguenots (see Chapter 15). Some devout rulers, such as Maria Theresa of Austria, continued to believe that there was only one path to salvation; it was the true duty of a ruler not to allow subjects to be condemned to hell by being heretics. Catholic minorities in Protestant countries and Protestant minorities in Catholic countries did not enjoy full civil or political rights. Persecution of heretics continued; the last burning of a heretic took place in 1781.

Nevertheless, some progress was made toward the principle of religious toleration. No ruler was more interested in the philosophes' call for religious toleration than Joseph II of Austria. His Toleration Patent of 1781, while recognizing Catholicism's public practice, granted Lutherans, Calvinists, and Greek Orthodox the right to worship privately. In all other ways, all subjects were now equal: "Non-Catholics are in future admitted under dispensation to buy houses and real property, to practice as master craftsmen, to take up academic appointments and posts in public service, and are not to be required to take the oath in any form contrary to their religious tenets."[16]

TOLERATION AND THE JEWS

The Jews remained the despised religious minority of Europe. The largest number of Jews (known as the Ashkenazic Jews) lived in eastern Europe. Except in relatively tolerant Poland, Jews were restricted in their movements, forbidden to own land or hold many jobs, forced to pay burdensome special taxes, and also subject to periodic outbursts of popular wrath. The resulting pogroms in which Jewish communities were looted and massacred made Jewish existence precarious and dependent upon the favor of their territorial rulers.

Another major group was the Sephardic Jews who had been expelled from Spain in the fifteenth century. Although many had migrated to Turkish lands, some of them had settled in cities, such as Amsterdam, Venice, London, and Frankfurt, where they were relatively free to participate in the banking and commercial activities that Jews had practiced since the Middle Ages. The highly successful ones came to provide valuable services to rulers, especially in central Europe where they were known as the court Jews. But even these Jews were insecure since their religion set them apart from the Christian majority and served as a catalyst to social resentment.

Some Enlightenment thinkers in the eighteenth century favored a new acceptance of Jews. They argued that Jews and Muslims were all human and deserved the full rights of citizenship despite their religion. Many philosophes denounced persecution of the Jews but made no attempt to hide their hostility and ridiculed Jewish customs. Diderot, for example, said that the Jews had "all the defects peculiar to an ignorant and superstitious nation." Many Europeans favored the assimilation of the Jews into the mainstream of society, but only by the conversion of Jews to Christianity as the basic solution to the "Jewish problem." This, of course, was not acceptable to most Jews.

The Austrian emperor Joseph II attempted to adopt a new policy toward the Jews, although it too was limited. It freed Jews from nuisance taxes and allowed them more freedom of movement and job opportunities, but they were still restricted from owning land and worshiping in public. At the same time, Joseph II encouraged Jews to learn German and work toward greater assimilation into Austrian society. Joseph's policy was but a small step in the liberation of the Jews as it took a moderate position between toleration and assimilation.

✳ *Popular Religion in the Eighteenth Century*

Despite the rise of skepticism and the intellectuals' belief in deism and natural religion, it would appear that religious devotion remained strong in the eighteenth century. Catholic popular piety continued to be strong, and within Protestantism the desire for more direct spiritual experience actually led to religious revivalism, especially in Germany and England.

✗ CATHOLIC PIETY

It is difficult to assess the religiosity of Europe's Catholics precisely. The Catholic parish church remained an important center of life for the entire community. How many people went to church regularly cannot be known exactly, but it has been established that 90 to 95 percent of Catholic populations did go to mass on Easter Sunday, one of the church's most special celebrations. Confraternities, which were organizations of laypeople dedicated to good works and acts of piety, were especially popular with townspeople. Each confraternity honored its patron saint by holy processions in which members proudly wore their special robes.

Catholic religiosity proved highly selective, however. Despite the Reformation, much popular devotion was still directed to an externalized form of worship focusing on prayers to saints, pilgrimages, and devotion to relics and images. The latter bothered many clergymen who felt that their parishioners were "more superstitious than devout," as one Catholic priest remarked. Many common people continued to fear witches and relied on the intervention of the saints and the Virgin Mary to save them from personal disasters caused by the devil.

✗ PROTESTANT REVIVALISM

After the initial century of religious fervor that created Protestantism in the sixteenth century, Protestant churches in the seventeenth century had settled down into well-established patterns controlled by state authorities and served by a well-educated clergy. Protestant churches became bureaucratized and bereft of religious enthusiasm. In Germany and England, where rationalism and deism had become influential and moved some theologians to a more "rational" Christianity, the desire of ordinary Protestant churchgoers for greater depths of religious experience led to new and dynamic religious movements.

Pietism in Germany was a response to this desire for a deeper personal devotion to God. Begun in the seventeenth century by a group of German clerics who wished their religion to be more personal and transformative of daily experience, Pietism was spread by the teachings of Count Nikolaus von Zinzendorf (1700–1760). To Zinzendorf and his Moravian Brethren, as his sect was called, it was the mysticial dimensions—the personal experience of God—in one's life that constituted true religious experience. He was utterly opposed to what he perceived as the rationalistic approach of orthodox Lutheran clergy who were being educated in new "rational" ideas. As Zinzendorf commented: "He who wishes to comprehend God with his mind becomes an atheist."

After the civil wars of the seventeenth century, England too had arrived at a respectable, uniform, and complacent state church. While local Anglican parish rectors were under the control of neighboring landholding nobles and reflected their social prejudices, higher members of the clergy—the bishops—were appointed by the crown, most often for political reasons. A pillar of the establishment, the Anglican church seemed to offer little spiritual excitement, especially to the masses of people. The dissenting Protestant groups—the Puritans, Quakers, Baptists—were relatively subdued while the growth of deism seemed to challenge Christianity itself. The desire

JOHN WESLEY. **In leading a deep spiritual revival in Britain, John Wesley founded a religious movement that came to be known as Methodism. He loved to preach to the masses, and this 1766 portrait by Nathaniel Hope shows him as he might have appeared before a crowd of people.**

The Conversion Experience in Wesley's Methodism

After his own conversion experience, John Wesley traveled extensively to bring the "glad tidings" of Jesus to other people. It has been estimated that he preached over 40,000 sermons, some of them to audiences numbering 20,000 listeners. Wesley gave his message wherever people gathered—in the streets, hospitals, private houses, and even pubs. In this selection from his journal, Wesley describes how emotional and even violent conversion experiences could be.

❋ The Works of the Reverend John Wesley

Sunday, May 20 [1759], being with Mr. B—11 at Everton, I was much fatigued, and did not rise: but Mr. B. did, and observed several fainting and crying out, while Mr. Berridge was preaching: afterwards at Church, I heard many cry out, especially children, whose agonies were amazing: one of the eldest, a girl of ten or twelve years old, was full in my view, in violent contortions of body, and weeping aloud, I think incessantly, during the whole service. . . . The Church was equally crowded in the afternoon, the windows being filled within and without, and even the outside of the pulpit to the very top; so that Mr. B. seemed almost stifled by their breath; yet feeble and sickly as he is, he was continually strengthened, and his voice, for the most part, distinguishable; in the midst of all the outcries. I believe there were present three times more men than women, a great part of whom came from far; thirty of them having set out at two in the morning, from a place thirteen miles off. The text was, *Having a form of godliness, but denying the power thereof.* When the power of religion began to be spoken of, the presence of God really filled the place: and while poor sinners felt the sentence of death in their souls, what sounds of distress did I hear! The greatest number of them who cried or fell, were men: but some women, and several children, felt the power of the same almighty Spirit, and seemed just sinking into hell. This occasioned a mixture of several sounds; some shrieking, some roaring aloud. The most general was a loud breathing, like that of people half strangled and gasping for life: and indeed almost all the cries were like those of human creatures, dying in bitter anguish. Great numbers wept without any noise: others fell down as death: some sinking in silence; some with extreme noise and violent agitation. I stood on the pew-seat, as did a young man in the opposite pew, an able-bodied, fresh, healthy countryman: but in a moment, while he seemed to think of nothing less, down he dropped with a violence inconceivable. The adjoining pews seemed to shake with his fall: I heard afterwards the stamping of his feet; ready to break the boards, as he lay in strong convulsions, at the bottom of the pew. Among several that were struck down in the next pew, was a girl, who was as violently seized as he. . . . Among the children who felt the arrows of the Almighty, I saw a sturdy boy, about eight years old, who roared above his fellows, and seemed in his agony to struggle with the strength of a grown man. His face was as red as scarlet: and almost all on whom God laid his hand, turned either very red or almost black. . . .

The violent struggling of many in the above-mentioned churches, has broken several pews and benches. Yet it is common for people to remain unaffected there, and afterwards to drop down on their way home. Some have been found lying as dead on the road: others, in Mr. B.'s garden; not being able to walk from the Church to his house, though it is not two hundred yards.

---

for deep spiritual experience seemed unmet until the advent of John Wesley (1703–1791).

An ordained Anglican minister, John Wesley took religion very seriously, experienced a deep spiritual crisis, and underwent a mystical experience: "I felt I did trust in Christ alone for salvation; and an assurance was given me, that He had taken away my sins, even mine, and saved me from the law of sin and death. I felt my heart strangely warmed." To Wesley, "the gift of God's grace" assured him of salvation and led him to become a missionary to the English people, bringing the "glad tidings" of salvation to all people, despite opposition from the Anglican church, which criticized this emotional mysticism or religious enthusiasm as superstitious nonsense. To Wesley, all could be saved by experiencing God and opening the doors to his grace.

In taking the Gospel to the people, Wesley preached to the masses in open fields, appealing especially to the lower classes neglected by the socially elitist Anglican church. He tried, he said, "to lower religion to the level of the lowest people's capacities." Wesley's charismatic preaching often provoked highly charged and even violent conversion experiences (see the box above). Afterward, converts were organized into so-called Methodist societies or chapels in which they could aid each other in doing the good works that Wesley considered a component of salvation. A Central Methodist Conference supervised new lay preachers from Methodist circles. Controlled by Wesley, it enabled him to dominate the evangelical movement he had created. Although Wesley sought to keep Methodism within the Anglican church, after his death it became a separate and independent sect. Methodism was an important revival of Christianity and proved that the need for spiritual experience had not been expunged by the eighteenth-century search for reason.

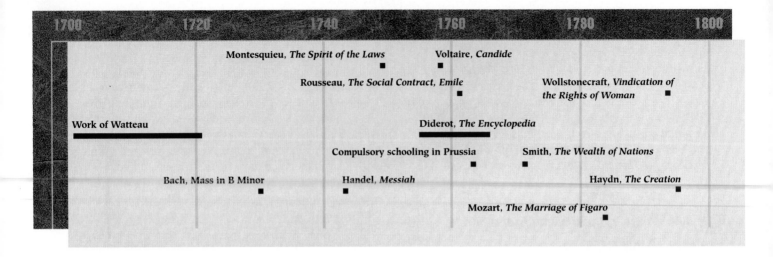

| 1700 | 1720 | 1740 | 1760 | 1780 | 1800 |

Montesquieu, *The Spirit of the Laws*

Voltaire, *Candide*

Rousseau, *The Social Contract, Emile*

Wollstonecraft, *Vindication of the Rights of Woman*

Work of Watteau

Diderot, *The Encyclopedia*

Compulsory schooling in Prussia

Smith, *The Wealth of Nations*

Bach, Mass in B Minor

Handel, *Messiah*

Haydn, *The Creation*

Mozart, *The Marriage of Figaro*

CONCLUSION

One prominent historian of the eighteenth century has appropriately characterized it as a century of change and tradition. Highly influenced by the new worldview created by the Scientific Revolution and especially the ideas of Locke and Newton, the philosophes hoped that they could create a new society by using reason to discover the natural laws that governed it. Like the Christian humanists of the fifteenth and sixteenth centuries, they believed that education could create better human beings and a better human society. By attacking traditional religion as the enemy and creating the new "sciences of man" in economics, politics, justice, and education, the philosophes laid the foundation for a modern worldview based on rationalism and secularism.

But it was also an age of tradition. Although secular thought and rational ideas began to pervade the mental world of the ruling elites, most people in eighteenth-century Europe still lived by seemingly eternal verities and practices—God, religious worship, and farming. The most brilliant architecture and music of the age were religious. And yet, the forces of secularization were too strong to stop. In the midst of intellectual change, economic, political, and social transformations of great purport were taking shape and, by the end of the eighteenth century, were to lead to both political and industrial revolutions. It is time now to examine the political, economic, and social traditions and changes of the century.

NOTES

1. Quoted in Paul Hazard, *The European Mind, 1680–1715* (New York, 1963), pp. 304–305.
2. Ibid., p. 12.
3. John Locke, *An Essay Concerning Human Understanding* (New York, 1964), pp. 89–90.
4. Baron d'Holbach, *Common Sense*, as quoted in Frank E. Manuel, ed., *The Enlightenment* (Englewood Cliffs, N.J., 1965), p. 62.
5. Jean-Jacques Rousseau, *A Discourse on Inequality*, trans. Maurice Cranston (Harmondsworth, 1984), p. 109.
6. Jean-Jacques Rousseau, *The Social Contract*, trans. Maurice Cranston (Harmondsworth, 1968), p. 141.
7. *A Serious Proposal to the Ladies*, in Moira Ferguson, ed., *First Feminists: British Women Writers, 1578–1799* (Bloomington, Ind., 1985). p. 190.
8. Ibid., p. 193.
9. Kenneth Clark, *Civilisation* (New York, 1969), p. 231.
10. Voltaire, *The Age of Louis XIV*, trans. Martyn P. Pollack (New York, 1961), p. 1.
11. Cesare Beccaria, *An Essay on Crimes and Pubishments*, trans. E. D. Ingraham (Philadelphia, 1819), pp. 59–60.
12. Quoted in Lester S. King, *The Medical World of the Eighteenth Century* (Chicago, 1958), pp. 318–319.
13. Quoted in Rene Sand, *The Advance to Social Medicine* (London, 1952), pp. 86–87.
14. Quoted in Peter Burke, *Popular Culture in Early Modern Europe* (New York, 1978), p. 179.
15. Quotations (in order of appearance) are from ibid., pp. 183, 186.
16. Quoted in C. A. Macartney, *The Habsburg and Hohenzollern Dynasties in the Seventeenth and Eighteenth Centuries* (New York, 1970), p. 157.

SUGGESTIONS FOR FURTHER READING

Two sound, comprehensive surveys of eighteenth-century Europe are I. Woloch, *Eighteenth-Century Europe* (New York, 1982); and M. S. Anderson, *Europe in the Eighteenth Century* (London, 1987). See also R. Birn, *Crisis, Absolutism, Revolution: Europe 1648–1789*, 2d ed. (Fort Worth, Tex., 1992).

Good introductions to the Enlightenment can be found in N. Hampson, *A Cultural History of the Enlightenment* (New York, 1968); U. Im Hof, *The Enlightenment* (Oxford, 1994); D. Goodman, *The Republic of Letters: A Cultural History of the French Enlightenment* (Ithaca, N.Y., 1994); and D. Outram,

The Enlightenment (Cambridge, 1995). A more detailed synthesis can be found in P. Gay, *The Enlightenment: An Interpretation*, 2 vols. (New York, 1966–69). For a short, popular survey on the French philosophes, see F. Artz, *The Enlightenment in France* (Kent, Ohio, 1968). Also of value are E. J. Wilson and P. H. Reill, *Encyclopedia of the Enlightenment* (New York, 1996); and J. W. Yolton, ed., *The Blackwell Companion to the Enlightenment* (Cambridge, Mass., 1995). Studies of the major Enlightenment intellectuals include J. Sklar, *Montesquieu* (Oxford, 1987); H. T. Mason, *Voltaire: A Biography* (Baltimore, 1981); P. N. Furbank, *Diderot: A Critical Biography* (New York, 1992); and M. Cranston, *The Noble Savage: Jean-Jacques Rousseau* (New York, 1991). Specialized studies on various aspects of the Enlightenment include M. W. Cranston, *Philosophers and Pamphleteers: Political Theorists of the Enlightenment* (London, 1986); M. C. Jacob, *The Radical Enlightenment: Pantheists, Freemasons and Republicans* (London, 1981); and J. Censer, *The French Press in the Age of Enlightenment* (New York, 1994). On women in the eighteenth century, see N. Z. Davis and A. Farge, eds., *A History of Women: Renaissance and Enlightenment Paradoxes* (Cambridge, Mass., 1993); C. Lougee, *Le Paradis des Femmes: Women, Salons, and Social Stratification* (Princeton, N.J., 1976); O. Hufton, *The Prospect before Her: A History of Women in Western Europe, 1500–1800* (New York, 1998); and B. S. Anderson and J. P. Zinsser, *A History of Their Own*, vol. 2 (New York, 1988).

Two readable general surveys on the arts and literature are M. Levy, *Rococo to Revolution* (London, 1966); and H. Honour, *Neo-classicism* (Harmondsworth, 1968). On the eighteenth-century novel, see G. J. Barker-Benfield, *The Culture of Sensibility: Sex and Society in the Eighteenth Century English Novel* (Chicago, 1992). On Gibbon, see W. B. Carnuchan, *Gibbon's Solitude: The Inward World of the Historian* (London, 1987). On the growth of literacy, see R. A. Houston, *Literacy in Early Modern Europe: Culture and Education, 1500–1800* (New York, 1988). Different facets of crime and punishment are examined in the important works by M. Foucault, *Discipline and Punish: The Birth of the Prison* (New York, 1977); and J. Langbein, *Torture and the Law of Proof* (Chicago, 1977). On the medical profession, see L. King, *The Medical World of the Eighteenth Century* (Chicago, 1958); and A. Cunningham and R. French, eds., *The Medical Enlightenment of the Eighteenth Century* (New York, 1990).

Important studies on popular culture include P. Burke, *Popular Culture in Early Modern Europe* (New York, 1978); and R. Darnton, *The Great Cat Massacre and Other Episodes in French Cultural History* (New York, 1984). Recreational activities are covered in R. Malcolmson, *Popular Recreation in English Society, 1700–1850* (Cambridge, 1973); and R. Isherwood, *Farce and Fantasy: Popular Entertainment in Eighteenth-Century Paris* (New York, 1986).

A good introduction to the religious history of the eighteenth century can be found in G. R. Cragg, *The Church and the Age of Reason, 1648–1789* (London, 1966). The problem of religious toleration is examined in J. I. Israel, *European Jewry in the Age of Mercantilism, 1550–1750*, 2d ed. (New York, 1989). On Pietism, see R. Gawthrop, *Pietism and the Making of Eighteenth-Century Prussia* (New York, 1993). On John Wesley, see H. Rack, *Reasonable Enthusiast: John Wesley and the Rise of Methodism* (New York, 1989).

For additional reading, go to InfoTrac College Edition, your online research library at http://web1.infotrac-college.com

Enter the search term *Enlightenment* using the Subject Guide.

Enter the search term *Voltaire* using Key Terms.

Enter the search term *Diderot* using Key Terms.

Enter the search term *Rousseau* using Key Terms.

CHAPTER

18

The Eighteenth Century: European States, International Wars, and Social Change

FOCUS QUESTIONS

- What do historians mean by the term *enlightened absolutism,* and to what degree did eighteenth-century Prussia, Austria, and Russia exhibit its characteristics?
- How did the concepts of "balance of power" and "reason of state" influence international relations in the eighteenth century?
- What were the causes and results of the Seven Years' War?
- What changes occurred in agriculture, finance, industry, and trade during the eighteenth century?
- Who were the main groups making up the European social order in the eighteenth century, and how did the conditions in which they lived differ both between groups and between different parts of Europe?

H ISTORIANS HAVE OFTEN DEFINED the eighteenth century chronologically as spanning the years from 1715 to 1789. Politically, this makes sense since 1715 marks the end of the age of Louis XIV and 1789 was the year in which the French Revolution erupted. This period has often been portrayed as the final phase of Europe's old order, before the violent upheaval and reordering of society associated with the French Revolution. Europe's old order, still largely agrarian, dominated by kings and landed aristocrats, and grounded in privileges for nobles, clergy, towns, and provinces, seemed to continue a basic pattern that had prevailed in Europe since medieval times. But new ideas and new practices were also beginning to emerge. Just as a new intellectual order based on rationalism and secularism was emerging from the intellectual revolution of the Scientific Revolution and Enlightenment, demographic, economic, and social patterns were beginning to change in ways that represent the emergence of a modern new order.

For some, the ideas of the Enlightenment seemed to herald the possibility of a new political age as well. Catherine the Great, who ruled Russia from 1762 to 1796, wrote to Voltaire: "Since 1746 I have been under the greatest obligations to you. Before that period I read nothing but romances, but by chance your works fell into my hands, and ever since then I have never ceased to read them, and have no desire for books less well written than yours, or less instructive." The empress of Russia also invited Diderot to Russia and, when he arrived, urged him to speak frankly "as man to man." Diderot did, offering her advice for a far-ranging program of political and financial reform. But Catherine's apparent eagerness to make enlightened reforms was tempered by skepticism. She said of Diderot: "If I had believed him everything would have been turned upside down in my kingdom; legislation, administration, finance—all would have been turned topsy-turvy to make room for impractical theories." For Catherine, enlightened reform remained more a dream than a reality, and in the end, the waging of wars to gain more power was more important.

In the eighteenth century, the process of centralization that had characterized the growth of states since the Middle Ages continued as most European states enlarged their bureaucratic machinery and consolidated their governments in order to collect the revenues and build the armies they needed to compete militarily with the other European states. International competition continued to be the favorite pastime of eighteenth-century rulers. Within the European state system, the nations that would dominate Europe until World War I—Britain, France, Austria, Prussia, and Russia—emerged as the five great powers of Europe. Their rivalries led to major wars, which some have called the first "world wars" because they were fought outside as well as inside Europe. In the midst of this state building and war making, dramatic demographic, economic, and social changes heralded the emergence of a radical transformation in the way Europeans would raise food and produce goods.

◆ The European States

Most European states in the eighteenth century were ruled by monarchs. Few people questioned either the moral or practical superiority of hereditary monarchy as the best form of government, especially in the large and successful states. As Catherine II wrote in 1764: "The Russian Empire is so large that apart from the Autocratic Sovereign every other form of government is harmful to it, because all others are slower in their execution and contain a great mul-

titude of various horrors, which lead to the disintegration of power and strength more than that of one Sovereign."[1]

Although the seventeenth-century justification for strong monarchy on the basis of divine right continued into the succeeding century, as the eighteenth century became increasingly secularized, divine-right assumptions were gradually superseded by influential utilitarian arguments. The Prussian king Frederick II expressed these well when he attempted to explain the services a monarch must provide for his people:

> These services consisted in the maintenance of the laws; a strict execution of justice; an employment of his whole powers to prevent any corruption of manners; and defending the state against its enemies. It is the duty of this magistrate to pay attention to agriculture; it should be his care that provisions for the nation should be in abundance, and that commerce and industry should be encouraged. He is a perpetual sentinel, who must watch the acts and the conduct of the enemies of the state. . . . If he be the first general, the first minister of the realm, it is not that he should remain the shadow of authority, but that he should fulfill the duties of such titles. He is only the first servant of the state.[2]

This utilitarian argument was reinforced by the praises of the philosophes.

❈ Enlightened Absolutism?

There is no doubt that Enlightenment thought had some impact on the political development of European states in the eighteenth century. Closely related to the Enlightenment idea of natural laws was the belief in natural rights, which were thought to be inalienable privileges that ought not to be withheld from any person. These natural rights included equality before the law, freedom of religious worship, freedom of speech and press, and the right to assemble, hold property, and pursue happiness. The American Declaration of Independence summarized the Enlightenment concept of natural rights in its opening paragraph: "We hold these truths to be self-evident, that all men are created equal; that they are endowed by their creator with certain unalienable rights; that among these are life, liberty and the pursuit of happiness."

But how were these natural rights to be established and preserved? In The Spirit of the Laws, Montesquieu had argued for constitutional guarantees achieved by a separation of powers. Rousseau had advocated a democratic society as the ideal path to maintain people's natural rights. Most philosophes, however, did not trust the "people." "It must please the animals," Voltaire said, "when they see how foolishly men behave." In the opinion of the philosophes, most people needed the direction provided by an enlightened ruler. What, however, made rulers enlightened? They must allow religious toleration, freedom of speech and press, and the right to hold private property. They must foster the arts, sciences, and education. Above all, they must not be arbitrary in their rule; they must obey the laws and enforce them fairly for all subjects. To

Voltaire, only strong monarchs seemed capable of overcoming vested interests and effecting the reforms society needed. Reforms then should come from above—from the rulers rather than from the people. Distrustful of the masses, the philosophes believed that absolute rulers, swayed by enlightened principles, were the best hope of reforming their societies.

The extent to which rulers actually did so is frequently discussed in political histories of the eighteenth century. Many historians once assumed that a new type of monarchy emerged in the later eighteenth century, which they called "enlightened despotism" or "enlightened absolutism." Monarchs such as Frederick II of Prussia, Catherine the Great of Russia, and Joseph II of Austria supposedly followed the advice of the philosophes and ruled by enlightened principles, establishing a path to modern nationhood. Recent scholarship, however, has questioned the usefulness of the concept of "enlightened absolutism." We can best determine the extent to which it can be applied by surveying the development of the European states in the eighteenth century and then making a judgment about the "enlightened absolutism" of the later eighteenth century.

❋ The Atlantic Seaboard States

As a result of overseas voyages in the sixteenth century, the European economic axis began to shift from the Mediterranean to the Atlantic seaboard. In the seventeenth century, the English and Dutch expanded as Spain and Portugal declined. By the eighteenth century, Dutch power had waned, and it was left to the English and French to build the commercial empires that presaged the growth of a true global economy.

FRANCE: THE LONG RULE OF LOUIS XV

In the eighteenth century, France experienced an economic revival while the movement of the Enlightenment gained strength. The French monarchy, however, was not overly influenced by the philosophes and resisted reforms as the French aristocracy grew stronger.

Louis XIV had left France with enlarged territories but also an enormous debt, an unhappy populace, and a five-year-old great-grandson as his successor. The governing of France fell into the hands first of the regent, the duke of Orléans, whose good intentions were undermined by his drunken and immoral behavior, and later of Cardinal Fleury, the king's minister. France pulled back from foreign adventures while commerce and trade expanded and the government promoted the growth of industry, especially in coal and textiles. The budget was even balanced for a while. When Fleury died in 1743, Louis XV (1715–1774) decided to rule alone. But Louis was both lazy and weak, and ministers and mistresses soon began to influence the king, control the affairs of state, and undermine the prestige of the monarchy. One mistress—probably the most famous of eighteenth-century Europe—was Madame de Pompadour. An intelligent and beautiful woman, she charmed Louis XV and gained both wealth and power, often making important government decisions and giving advice on appointments and foreign policy. The loss of an empire in the Seven Years' War, accompanied by burdensome taxes, an ever-mounting public debt, more hungry people, and a court life at Versailles that remained frivolous and carefree, forced even Louis to realize the growing disgust with his monarchy. "Things will last my time at any rate," he remarked myopically and prophetically.

Perhaps all might not have been in vain if Louis had been succeeded by a competent king. But the new king, Louis's twenty-year-old grandson who became Louis XVI (1774–1792), knew little about the operations of the French government and lacked the energy to deal decisively with state affairs (see the box on p. 519). His wife, Marie Antoinette, was a spoiled Austrian princess who devoted much of her time to court intrigues. As France's financial crises worsened, neither Louis nor his queen seemed able to fathom the depths of despair and discontent that soon led to violent revolution (see Chapter 19).

GREAT BRITAIN: KING AND PARLIAMENT

The success of the Glorious Revolution in England had prevented absolutism without clearly inaugurating constitutional monarchy. The eighteenth-century British political system was characterized by a sharing of power between king and Parliament, with Parliament gradually gaining the upper hand. (The United Kingdom of Great Britain came into existence in 1707 when the governments of England and Scotland were united; the term *British* came into use to refer to both English and Scots.) The king chose ministers responsible to himself who set policy and guided Parliament; Parliament had the power to make laws, levy taxes, pass the budget, and indirectly influence the king's ministers. The eighteenth-century British Parliament was dominated by a landed aristocracy that historians usually divide into two groups: the peers, who sat in the House of Lords and served as lord lieutenants controlling the appointment of the justices of the peace; and the landed gentry, who sat in the House of Commons and served as justices of the peace in the counties. There is much historical debate over whether it makes sense to distinguish between the aristocracies because the two groups had much in common. Both were landowners with similar economic interests, and they frequently intermarried.

Although the British monarchy was faced with a powerful aristocracy that monopolized Parliament and held most of the important governing posts locally (as justices of the peace in the counties) and nationally, it still exercised considerable power. Because the aristocracy was divided by factional struggles based on family rivalries, the kings could take advantage of the divisions to win aristocratic supporters through patronage, awarding them titles, government posts, and positions in the church and household staff.

The French King's Bedtime

Louis XIV had used court etiquette to magnify the dignity of kingship. During the reign of Louis XVI (1774–1792), however, court etiquette degenerated to ludicrous depths. This excerpt from the Memoirs *of the Comtesse de Boigne describes the king's* coucher, *the formal ceremony in which the king retired for the night.*

✽ Comtesse de Boigne, *Memoirs*

The king [Louis XVI] went to his *coucher*. The so-called *coucher* took place every evening at half past nine. The gentlemen of the court assembled in the bedroom of Louis XVI (but Louis XVI did not sleep there). I believe that all those who had been presented at court were permitted to attend.

The king came in from an adjoining room, followed by his domestic staff. His hair was in curlers, and he was not wearing his decorations. Without paying attention to anybody, he stepped behind the handrail surrounding the bed, and the chaplain on duty was given the prayer book and a tall taperstand with two candles by one of the valets. He then joined the king behind the handrail, handed him the book, and held the taperstand during the king's prayer, which was short. The king then went to the part of the room where the courtiers were, and the chaplain gave the taperstand back to the first valet who, in turn, took it over to a person indicated by the king. This person held it as long as the *coucher* lasted. This distinction was very much sought after. . . .

The king had his coat, vest and finally shirt removed. He was naked to the waist, scratching and rubbing himself as if alone, though he was in the presence of the whole court and often a number of distinguished foreigners.

The first valet handed the nightshirt to the most qualified person. . . . If it was a person with whom the king was on familiar terms, he often played little tricks before donning it, missed it, passed it, and ran away, accompanying this charming nonsense with hearty laughter, making those who were sincerely attached to him suffer. Having donned the nightshirt, he put on his robe and three valets unfastened the belt and the knee buckles of his trousers, which fell down to his feet. Thus attired, hardly able to walk so absurdly encumbered, he began to make the round of the circle.

The duration of this reception was by no means fixed; sometimes it lasted only a few minutes, sometimes almost an hour; it depended on who was there. . . . When the king had enough, he dragged himself backward to an easy chair which had been pushed to the middle of the room and fell heavily into it, raising both legs. Two pages on their knees seized his shoes, took them off, and dropped them on the floor with a thump, which was part of the etiquette. When he heard it, the doorman opened the door and said, "This way, gentlemen." Everybody left, and the ceremony was over. However, the person who held the taperstand was permitted to stay if he had anything special to say to the king. This explains the high price attached to this strange favor.

What enabled the British system of political patronage to work was the structure of parliamentary elections. The deputies to the House of Commons were chosen from the boroughs and counties but not by popular vote and hardly in any equitable fashion. Of the almost 500 deputies in the House of Commons, about 400 were chosen from the boroughs. Past history rather than population determined the number of delegates from each borough, however, so in one borough six people might choose two representatives whereas new cities like Manchester had no delegates at all despite their growing populations. Who could vote also varied wildly, enabling wealthy landed aristocrats to gain support by patronage and bribery; the result was a number of "pocket boroughs" controlled by a single person (hence "in his pocket"). The duke of Newcastle, for example, controlled the representatives from seven boroughs. It has been estimated that out of 405 borough deputies, 293 were chosen by fewer than 500 voters. This aristocratic control also extended to the county delegates, two from each of England's forty counties. Although all holders of property worth at least forty shillings a year could vote, members of the leading landed gentry families were elected over and over again. Parliament then was an institution largely dominated by the landed aristocracy, but their factional struggles enabled the monarchy still to exercise some power by its control of patronage.

Since the ministers were responsible for exercising the king's patronage, who became his chief ministers took on great political significance. In 1714, a new dynasty—the Hanoverians—was established when the last Stuart ruler, Queen Anne (1702–1714), died without an heir. The crown was offered to the Protestant rulers of the German state of Hanover. Both George I (1714–1727) and George II (1727–1760) relied on Robert Walpole as their chief or prime minister and the duke of Newcastle as their main dispenser of patronage, putting the latter at the center of British politics. Since the first Hanoverian king did not speak English and neither the first nor the second George had much familiarity with the British system, the chief ministers were allowed to handle Parliament and dispense patronage. Many historians feel that this exercise of ministerial power was an important step in the development of the modern cabinet system in British government.

Robert Walpole served as prime minister from 1721 to 1742 and pursued a peaceful foreign policy to avoid new land taxes. But new forces were emerging in eighteenth-century Britain as growing trade and industry led an ever-increasing middle class to favor expansion of trade and world empire. The exponents of empire found a spokesman in William Pitt the Elder, who became prime minister in 1757 and furthered imperial ambitions by acquiring Canada and India in the Seven Years' War (see The Seven Years' War later in this chapter).

Despite his successes, however, Pitt the Elder was dismissed by the new king George III (1760–1820) in 1761 and replaced by the king's favorite, Lord Bute. Although characterized as a rather stupid person, George III was not the tyrant he is often portrayed as being. Determined to strengthen monarchical authority, his desire to wield the power of patronage personally led to the ouster of Pitt. At the same time, however, as a growing number of newspapers spread Enlightenment ideas to an expanding reading public, the clamor for the reform of both patronage and the electoral system began to increase. The saga of John Wilkes soon intensified the public outcry.

An ambitious middle-class member of the House of Commons, John Wilkes was an outspoken journalist who publicly criticized the king's ministers. Arrested and soon released, Wilkes was expelled from his seat in Parliament. When he persevered and won another parliamentary seat from the county of Middlesex near London, he was again denied the right to take his place in Parliament. The cause of John Wilkes quickly became identified with liberty, and the slogan "Wilkes and Liberty" was frequently used by his supporters who came from two major social groups: the common people of London, who had no voting rights, and a middle element of voting freeholders, such as guild masters and small merchants in London and the surrounding counties. The cry for liberty soon spilled over into calls for the reform of Parliament and an end to parliamentary privileges. In 1780, the House of Commons affirmed that "the influence of the crown has increased, is increasing, and ought to be diminished." At the same time, criticism at home was exacerbated by criticism abroad, especially by the American colonists whose discontent with the British system had led to rebellion and separation (see Chapter 19). Although minor reforms of the patronage system were made in 1782, King George III managed to avoid more drastic change by appointing William Pitt the Younger (1759–1806), son of William Pitt the Elder, as prime minister in 1783. Supported by the merchants,

THE BRITISH HOUSE OF COMMONS. A sharing of power between king and Parliament characterized the British political system in the eighteenth century. Parliament was divided into the House of Lords and House of Commons. This painting shows the House of Commons in session in 1793 during a debate over the possibility of war with France. William Pitt is addressing the House.

MAP 18.1 Europe in 1763.

industrial classes, and the king, who used patronage to gain support for Pitt in the House of Commons, the latter managed to stay in power through the French revolutionary and Napoleonic eras. George III, however, remained an uncertain supporter because of periodic bouts of insanity (he once thought a tree in Windsor Park was the king of Prussia). With Pitt's successes, serious reform of the corrupt parliamentary system was avoided for another generation.

✒ THE DECLINE OF THE DUTCH REPUBLIC

After its century in the sun, the Dutch Republic or United Netherlands suffered a decline in economic prosperity. Both local and national political affairs were dominated by the oligarchies that governed the Dutch Republic's towns. In the eighteenth century, the struggle continued between these oligarchs (or regents as they were called from their governing positions) and the house of Orange, who as stadholders headed the executive branch of government. The regents sought to reduce the power of the Orangists but soon became divided when Dutch burghers who called themselves the Patriots (artisans, merchants, shopkeepers) began to agitate for democratic reforms that would open up the municipal councils to greater participation than that of the oligarchs. The success of the Patriots, however, led to foreign interference when the Prussian king sent troops to protect his sister, wife of the Orangist

stadholder. The Patriots were crushed, and both Orangists and regents reestablished the old system. The intervention by Prussia serves to remind us of the growing power of the central European states.

✤ *Absolutism in Central and Eastern Europe*

Of the five major European states, three were located in central and eastern Europe and came to play an increasingly important role in European international politics.

✒ PRUSSIA: THE ARMY AND THE BUREAUCRACY

Two able Prussian kings in the eighteenth century, Frederick William I and Frederick II, further developed the two major institutions—the army and the bureaucracy—that were the backbone of Prussia. Frederick William I (1713–1740) promoted the evolution of Prussia's highly efficient civil bureaucracy by establishing the General Directory. It served as the chief administrative agent of the central government, supervising military, police, economic, and financial affairs. Because Prussia's disjointed territories could hardly have been preserved without a centralized administrative machine, Frederick William strove to maintain a highly efficient bureaucracy of civil service workers. It became a special kind of organization with its own code in which the supreme values were obedience,

FREDERICK II AT SANS-SOUCI. Frederick II was one of the most cultured and well-educated European monarchs. In this painting, he is shown visiting the building site of his residential retreat of Sans-Souci at Potsdam.

honor, and service to the king as the highest duty. As Frederick William asserted: "One must serve the king with life and limb, with goods and chattels, with honor and conscience, and surrender everything except salvation. The latter is reserved for God. But everything else must be mine."[3] For his part, Frederick William personally kept a close watch over his officials to ensure that they performed their duties. As the Saxon minister at Berlin related:

> Every day His Majesty gives new proofs of his justice. Walking recently at Potsdam at six in the morning, he saw a post-coach arrive with several passengers who knocked for a long time at the post-house which was still closed. The King, seeing that no one opened the door, joined them in knocking and even knocked in some window-panes. The master of the post then opened the door and scolded the travelers, for no one recognized the King. But His Majesty let himself be known by giving the official some good blows of his cane and drove him from his house and his job after apologizing to the travelers for his laziness. Examples of this sort, of which I could relate several others, make everybody alert and exact.[4]

Close, personal supervision of the bureaucracy became a hallmark of the eighteenth-century Prussian rulers.

Under Frederick William I, the rigid class stratification that had emerged in seventeenth-century Brandenburg-Prussia persisted. The nobility or landed aristocracy known as Junkers, who owned large estates with many serfs, still played a dominating role in the Prussian state. The Junkers held a complete monopoly over the officer corps of the Prussian army, which Frederick William passionately continued to expand. By the end of his reign, the army had grown from 45,000 to 83,000 men. Though tenth in physical size and thirteenth in population among the European states, Prussia had the fourth largest army after France, Russia, and Austria.

While nobles served as officers, rank-and-file soldiers were usually peasants who served a long number of years. Discipline in the army was extremely rigid and even cruel—so cruel, in fact, that desertion was common. The king advised his generals not to take troops through a forest on maneuvers because it offered too many opportunities for running away. By using nobles as officers, Frederick William ensured a close bond between the nobility and the army and, in turn, the loyalty of the nobility to the absolute monarch.

As officers, the Junker nobility became imbued with a sense of service to the king or state. All the virtues of the Prussian nobility were, in effect, military virtues: duty, obedience, sacrifice. At the same time, because of its size and reputation as one of the best armies in Europe, the Prussian army was the most important institution in the state. "Prussian militarism" became synonymous with the extreme exaltation of military virtues. Indeed, one Prussian minister remarked around 1800 that "Prussia was not a country with an army, but an army with a country which served as headquarters and food magazine."[5]

The remaining classes in Prussia were considerably less important than the nobility. The peasants were born

Frederick the Great and His Father

As a young man, the future Frederick the Great was quite different from his strict and austere father, Frederick William I. Possessing a high regard for French culture, poetry, and flute playing, Frederick resisted his father's wishes that he immerse himself in governmental and military affairs. Eventually, Frederick capitulated to his father's will and accepted the need to master affairs of state. These letters, written when Frederick was sixteen, illustrate the difficulties in their relationship.

❈ Frederick to His Father, Frederick William I (September 11, 1728)

I have not ventured for a long time to present myself before my dear papa, partly because I was advised against it, but chiefly because I anticipated an even worse reception than usual and feared to vex my dear papa still further by the favor I have now to ask; so I have preferred to put it in writing.

I beg my dear papa that he will be kindly disposed toward me. I do assure him that after long examination of my conscience I do not find the slightest thing with which to reproach myself; but if, against my wish and will, I have vexed my dear papa, I hereby beg most humbly for forgiveness, and hope that my dear papa will give over the fearful hate which has appeared so plainly in his whole behavior and to which I cannot accustom myself. I have always thought hitherto that I had a kind father, but now I see the contrary. However, I will take courage and hope that my dear papa will think this all over and take me again into his favor. Meantime I assure him that I will never, my life long, willingly fail him, and in spite of his disfavor I am still, with most dutiful and childlike respect, my dear papa's

Most obedient and faithful servant and son,

Frederick

❈ Frederick William to His Son Frederick

A bad, obstinate boy, who does not love his father; for when one does one's best, and especially when one loves one's father, one does what he wishes not only when he is standing by but when he is not there to see. Moreover you know very well that I cannot stand an effeminate fellow who has no manly tastes, who cannot ride or shoot (to his shame be it said!), is untidy about his person, and wears his hair curled like a fool instead of cutting it; and that I have condemned all these things a thousand times, and yet there is no sign of improvement. For the rest, haughty, offish as a country lout, conversing with none but a favored few instead of being affable and popular, grimacing like a fool, and never following my wishes out of love for me but only when forced into it, caring for nothing but to have his own way, and thinking nothing else is of any importance. This is my answer.

Frederick William

---

on their lords' estates and spent most of the rest of their lives there or in the army. They had few real rights and even needed their Junker's permission to marry. For the middle class, the only opportunity for any social prestige was in the Prussian civil service where the ideal of loyal service to the state became a hallmark of the middle-class official. Frederick William allowed and even encouraged men of nonnoble birth to serve in important administrative posts. When he died in 1740, only three of his eighteen privy councillors were of noble birth.

Frederick the Great (1740–1786) was one of the best educated and most cultured monarchs in the eighteenth century. He was well versed in Enlightenment thought and even invited Voltaire to live at his court for several years. His intellectual interests were despised by his father who forced his intelligent son to prepare for a career in ruling (see the box above). A believer in the king as the "first servant of the state," Frederick the Great became a conscientious ruler who made few innovations in the administration of the state. His diligence in overseeing its operation, however, made the Prussian bureaucracy well known for both its efficiency and its honesty.

For a time, Frederick seemed quite willing to follow the philosophes' recommendations for reform. He established a single code of laws for his territories that eliminated the use of torture except in treason and murder cases. He also granted a limited freedom of speech and press as well as complete religious toleration, no difficult task since he had no strong religious convictions anyway. Although Frederick was well aware of the philosophes' condemnation of serfdom, he was too dependent on the Prussian nobility to interfere with it or with the hierarchical structure of Prussian society. In fact, Frederick II was a social conservative who made Prussian society even more aristocratic than it had been before. Frederick reversed his father's policy of allowing commoners to rise to power in the civil service and reserved the higher positions in the bureaucracy for members of the nobility. The upper ranks of the bureaucracy came close to constituting a hereditary caste over time.

Like his predecessors, Frederick the Great took a great interest in military affairs and enlarged the Prussian army (to 200,000 men). Unlike his predecessors, he had no objection to using it. Frederick did not hesitate to take advantage of a succession crisis in the Habsburg monarchy to seize the Austrian province of Silesia for Prussia. This act aroused Austria's bitter hostility and embroiled Frederick in two major wars, the War of the Austrian

MARIA THERESA AND HER FAMILY. Maria Theresa governed the vast possessions of the Austrian Empire from 1740 to 1780. Of her ten surviving children, Joseph II succeeded her; Leopold became grand-duke of Tuscany and the ruler of Austria after Joseph's death; Ferdinand was made duke of Modena; and Marie Antoinette became the bride of King Louis XVI of France.

Succession and the Seven Years' War (see Wars and Diplomacy later in this chapter). Although the latter war left his country exhausted, Frederick succeeded in keeping Silesia. After the wars, the first partition of Poland with Austria and Russia in 1772 gave him the Polish territory between Prussia and Brandenburg and created greater unity for the scattered lands of Prussia. By the end of his reign, Prussia was recognized as a great European power.

❧ THE AUSTRIAN EMPIRE OF THE HABSBURGS

The Austrian Empire had become one of the great European states by the beginning of the eighteenth century. The city of Vienna, center of the Habsburg monarchy, was filled with magnificent palaces and churches built in the Baroque style and became the music capital of Europe. And yet Austria, by its very nature as a sprawling empire composed of many different nationalities, languages, religions, and cultures, found it difficult to provide common laws and a centralized administration for its people.

Empress Maria Theresa (1740–1780), however, stunned by the loss of Austrian Silesia to Prussia in the War of the Austrian Succession, resolved to reform her empire in preparation for the seemingly inevitable next conflict with rival Prussia. Although Maria Theresa was forced to accept the privileges of the Hungarian nobility and the right of her Hungarian subjects to have their own laws, she did abolish the Austrian and Bohemian chancelleries and replaced them with departments of foreign affairs, justice, war, commerce, and internal affairs that functioned for both territories. Maria Theresa also curtailed the role of the diets or provincial assemblies in taxation and local administration. Now clergy and nobles were forced to pay property and income taxes to royal officials rather than the diets. The Austrian and Bohemian lands were divided into ten provinces and subdivided into districts, all administered by royal officials rather than representatives of the diets, making part of the Austrian Empire more centralized and more bureaucratic. But these administrative reforms were done for practical reasons—to strengthen the power of the Habsburg state—and were accompanied by an enlargement and modernization of the armed forces. Maria Theresa remained staunchly Catholic and conservative and was not open to the wider reform calls of the philosophes. But her successor was.

From 1765 to 1780, Maria Theresa had allowed her son Joseph II to share rule with her, although Joseph felt restrained by his mother's lack of interest in the reform ideas of the Enlightenment that greatly appealed to him. When he achieved sole power in 1780, he was determined to make changes; at the same time, he carried on his mother's chief goal of enhancing Habsburg power within the monarchy and Europe. Joseph II was an earnest man who believed in the need to sweep away anything standing in the path of reason. As Joseph expressed it: "I have made Philosophy the lawmaker of my empire, her logical applications are going to transform Austria."

Joseph's reform program was far-reaching. He abolished serfdom and tried to give the peasants hereditary rights to their holdings. An exponent of Physiocratic ideas (see Chapter 17), he abandoned economic restraints by eliminating internal trade barriers, ending monopolies, and removing guild restrictions. A new penal code was instituted that abrogated the death penalty and established the principle of equality of all before the law. Joseph introduced drastic religious reforms as well, including complete religious toleration and restrictions on the Catholic church. Altogether, Joseph II issued 6,000 decrees and 11,000 laws in his effort to transform Austria.

Joseph's reform program proved overwhelming for Austria, however. He alienated the nobility by freeing the

The Proposals of Catherine II for a New Law Code

Catherine II the Great of Russia appeared for a while to be an enlightened ruler. In 1767, she convened a legislative commission to prepare a new code of laws for Russia. In her famous Instruction, *she gave the delegates a detailed guide to the principles they should follow. Although the guidelines were obviously culled from the liberal ideas of the philosophes, the commission itself accomplished nothing, and Catherine's* Instruction *was soon forgotten.*

✺ Catherine II, *Proposals for a New Law Code*

13. What is the true End of Monarchy? Not to deprive People of their natural Liberty; but to correct their Actions, in order to attain the supreme good.

33. The Laws ought to be so framed, as to secure the Safety of every Citizen as much as possible.

34. The Equality of the Citizens consists in this; that they should all be subject to the same Laws.

38. A Man ought to form in his own Mind an exact and clear Idea of what Liberty is. Liberty is the Right of doing whatsoever the Laws allow: And if any one Citizen could do what the Laws forbid, there would be no more Liberty; because others would have an equal Power of doing the same.

123. The Usage of Torture is contrary to all the Dictates of Nature and Reason; even Mankind itself cries out against it, and demands loudly the total Abolition of it.

180. That Law, therefore, is highly beneficial to the Community where it is established, which ordains that every Man shall be judged by his Peers and Equals. For when the Fate of a Citizen is in Question, all Prejudices arising from the Difference of Rank or Fortune should be stifled; because they ought to have no Influence between the Judges and the Parties accused.

194. No Man ought to be looked upon as guilty, before he has received his judicial Sentence; nor can the Laws deprive him of their Protection, before it is proved that he has forfeited all Right to it. What Right therefore can Power give to any to inflict Punishment upon a Citizen at a Time, when it is yet dubious, whether he is Innocent or guilty?

270. It is highly necessary that the Law should prescribe a Rule to the Lords, for a more judicious Method of raising their Revenues; and oblige them to levy such a Tax, as tends least to separate the Peasant from His House and Family; this would be the Means by which Agriculture would become more extensive, and Population be more increased in the Empire.

---

serfs and alienated the church by his attacks on the monastic establishment. Even the serfs were unhappy, unable to comprehend the drastic changes inherent in Joseph's policies. His attempt to rationalize the administration of the empire by imposing German as the official bureaucratic language alienated the non-German nationalities. As Joseph complained, there were not enough people for the kind of bureaucracy he needed. His deep sense of failure is revealed in the epitaph he wrote for his gravestone: "Here lies Joseph II who was unfortunate in everything that he undertook." His successors undid many of his reform efforts.

❧ RUSSIA UNDER CATHERINE THE GREAT

Peter the Great was followed by a series of six successors who were made and unmade by the palace guard. The last of these six was Peter III, whose German wife Catherine learned Russian and won the favor of the palace guard. Peter was murdered by a faction of nobles, and Catherine II the Great (1762–1796) emerged as autocrat of all the Russias.

Catherine was an intelligent woman who was familiar with the works of the philosophes. Voltaire and Diderot were among her correspondents, although some historians believe she corresponded with philosophes simply to improve her image abroad. Catherine claimed that she wished to reform Russia along the lines of Enlightenment ideas, but she was always shrewd enough to realize that her success depended upon the support of the palace guard and the gentry class from which it stemmed. She could not afford to alienate the Russian nobility.

Initially, Catherine seemed eager to pursue reform. She called for the election of an assembly in 1767 to debate the details of a new law code. In her *Instruction*, written as a guide to the deliberations, Catherine questioned the institution of serfdom, torture, and capital punishment and even advocated the principle of the equality of all people in the eyes of the law (see the box above). But one and one-half years of negotiation produced little real change.

In fact, Catherine's subsequent policies had the effect of strengthening the landholding class at the expense of all others, especially the Russian serfs. In order to reorganize local government, Catherine divided Russia into fifty provinces, each of which in turn was subdivided into districts whose ruling officials were chosen by the nobles. In this way, the local nobility became responsible for the day-to-day governing of Russia. Moreover, the

CATHERINE THE GREAT. Autocrat of Russia, Catherine was an intelligent ruler who favored reform. She found it expedient, however, to retain much of the old system in order to keep the support of the landed nobility. In this portrait by Dmitry Levitsky, she is shown in legislative regalia in the Temple of Justice in 1783.

gentry were now formed into corporate groups with special legal privileges, including the right to trial by peers and exemption from personal taxation and corporal punishment. A Charter of the Nobility formalized these rights in 1785.

Catherine's policy of favoring the landed nobility led to even worse conditions for the Russian peasantry. In 1767, serfs were forbidden to appeal to the state against their masters. The attempt of the Russian government to impose restrictions upon free peasants in the border districts of the Russian Empire soon led to a full-scale revolt that spread to the Volga valley. It was intensified by the support of the Cossacks, independent tribes of fierce warriors who had at times fought for the Russians against the Turks but now resisted the government's attempt to absorb them into the empire.

An illiterate Cossack, Emelyan Pugachev, succeeded in welding the disparate elements of discontent into a mass revolt. Beginning in 1773, Pugachev's rebellion spread across southern Russia from the Urals to the Volga River. Initially successful, Pugachev won the support of many peasants when he issued a manifesto in July 1774, freeing all peasants from oppressive taxes and military

service. Encouraged to seize their landlords' estates by Pugachev, the peasants responded by killing more than 1,500 estate owners and their families. The rebellion soon faltered, however, as government forces rallied and became more effective. Betrayed by his own subordinates, Pugachev was captured, tortured, and executed. The rebellion collapsed completely, and Catherine responded with even greater repression of the peasantry. All rural reform was halted; serfdom was expanded into newer parts of the empire, and peasants on crown land were also reduced to serfdom.

Above all, Catherine proved a worthy successor to Peter the Great by expanding Russia's territory westward (into Poland) and southward (to the Black Sea). Russia spread southward by defeating the Turks. In the Treaty of Kuchuk-Kainarji in 1774, the Russians gained some land, the privilege of protecting Greek Orthodox Christians in the Ottoman Empire, and the right to sail in Turkish waters. Russian expansion westward occurred at the expense of neighboring Poland. In the three partitions of Poland, Russia gained about 50 percent of Polish territory.

THE DESTRUCTION OF POLAND

Poland was an excellent example of why a strong monarchy was needed in early modern Europe. The failure to develop the machinery of state building because of the excessive powers of the aristocracy proved disastrous. The Polish king was elected by the Polish nobles and forced to accept drastic restrictions upon his power, including limited revenues, a small bureaucracy, and a standing army of no more than 20,000 soldiers. For Polish nobles, these

age for men in northwestern Europe was between twenty-seven and twenty-eight, for women between twenty-five and twenty-seven.

Late marriages imposed limits on the birthrate; in fact, they might be viewed as a natural form of birth control. But was this limitation offset by the number of babies born illegitimately? From the low illegitimacy rate of 1 percent in some places in France and 5 percent in some English parishes, it would appear that it was not, at least in the first half of the eighteenth century. After 1750, however, illegitimacy appears to have increased. Studies in Germany, for example, show that rates of illegitimacy increased from 2 percent in 1700 to 5 percent in 1760 and to 10 percent in 1800, followed by an even more dramatic increase in the early nineteenth century.

For married couples, the first child usually appeared within one year of marriage, and additional children came at intervals of two or three years, producing an average number of five births per family. It would appear then that the birthrate had the potential of creating a significant increase in population. This possibility was restricted, however, because 40 to 60 percent of European women of childbearing age (between fifteen and forty-four) were not married at any given time. Moreover, by the end of the eighteenth century, especially among the upper classes in France and Britain, birth control techniques were being used to limit the number of children. Figures for the French aristocracy indicate that the average number of children declined from six in the period between 1650 and 1700 to three between 1700 and 1750 and to two between 1750 and 1780. These figures are even more significant when one considers that aristocrats married at younger ages than the rest of the population. Coitus interruptus remained the most commonly used form of birth control.

Among the working classes, whether peasants or urban workers, the contributions of women and children to the "family economy" were often crucial. In urban areas, both male and female children either helped in the handicraft manufacturing done in the home or were sent out to work as household servants. In rural areas, children worked on the land or helped in the activities of cottage industry. Married women grew vegetables in small plots, tended livestock, and sold eggs, vegetables, and milk. Wives of propertyless agricultural workers labored in the fields or as textile workers, spinning or knitting. In the cities, wives of artisans helped their husbands at their crafts or worked as seamstresses. The wives of unskilled workers labored as laundresses and cleaners for the rich or as peddlers of food or used clothing to the lower classes. But the family economy was often precarious.

THE PRACTICE OF INFANTICIDE. Infanticide remained one of the solutions to the problem of too many children in the eighteenth century. This engraving recounts the story of one infanticide in Germany. *Top left*: the infant is discovered, smothered under a mattress. *Bottom left*: the mother is taken from prison to be executed. *Right*: a large crowd observes the execution of the mother for her crime.

Bad harvests in the countryside or a downturn in employment in the cities often reduced people to utter poverty and a life of begging.

❋ An Agricultural Revolution?

Did improvements in agricultural practices and methods in the eighteenth century lead to an agricultural revolution? The topic is much debated. Some historians have noted the beginning of agrarian changes already in the seventeenth century, especially in the Low Countries. Others, however, have questioned the use of the term, arguing that significant changes occurred only in England and noting that even there the upward trend in agricultural production was not maintained after 1750.

Eighteenth-century agriculture was characterized by increases in food production that can be attributed to four interrelated factors: more land under cultivation, increased yields per acre, healthier and more abundant livestock, and an improved climate. Climatologists believe that the "little ice age" of the seventeenth century declined in the eighteenth, especially evident in the moderate summers that provided more ideal growing conditions.

The amount of land under cultivation was increased by abandoning the old open field system in which part of the land was left to lie fallow to renew it. New crops, such as alfalfa, turnips, and clover, which stored nitrogen in their roots and helped to restore the soil's fertility, were planted in England, parts of France, and the Low Countries. These crops not only renewed the soil but also provided winter fodder for livestock, enabling landlords to maintain an ever-larger number of animals; some enterprising landlords also engaged in scientific breeding and produced stronger and more productive strains of animals.

The more numerous livestock increased the amount of meat in the European diet and enhanced food production by making available more animal manure, which was used to fertilize fields and produce better yields per acre. Increased yields were also encouraged by landed aristocrats who shared in the scientific experimentation of the age. In England, Jethro Tull (1674–1741) discovered that using a hoe to keep the soil loose allowed air and moisture to reach plants and enabled them to grow better. He also used a drill to plant seeds in rows instead of scattering them by hand, a method that had lost much seed to the birds.

The eighteenth century witnessed greater yields of vegetables, including two important American crops, the potato and maize (Indian corn). Although they were not grown in quantity until after 1700, both had been brought to Europe from America in the sixteenth century and were part of what some historians have called the Columbian exchange—a reciprocal exchange of plants and animals between Europe and America. The potato became a staple in Germany, the Low Countries, and especially Ireland, where repression by English landlords forced large numbers of poor peasants to survive on small pieces of marginal land. The potato took relatively little effort to produce in large quantities. High in carbohydrates and calories, rich in vitamins A and C, it could be easily stored for winter use.

The new agricultural techniques were considered best suited to large-scale farms. Consequently, a change in landholding accompanied the increase in food production. Large landowners or yeomen farmers enclosed the old open fields, combining the many small holdings that made up the fields into larger units. The end of the open field system led to the demise of the cooperative farming of the village community. In England, where small landholders resisted this process, Parliament, dominated by the landed aristocracy, enacted legislation allowing agricultural lands to be legally enclosed. As a result of these enclosure acts, England gradually became a land of large estates, and many small farmers were forced to become wage laborers or tenant farmers working farms of 100–500 acres. Although some historians have emphasized the advantages of enclosures in enabling large landowners to practice new agricultural techniques and increase food production, the enclosure movement and new agricultural practices also effectively destroyed the traditional patterns of English village life.

In the eighteenth century, the English were the leaders in adopting the new techniques that have been characterized as an agricultural revolution (see the box on p. 538). This early modernization of English agriculture with its noticeable increase in productivity made possible the feeding of an expanding population about to enter a new world of industrialization and urbanization.

❋ New Methods of Finance and Industry

The decline in the available supply of gold and silver in the seventeenth century had created a chronic shortage of money that undermined the efforts of governments to meet their needs. The creation of new public and private banks and the acceptance of paper notes made possible an expansion of credit in the eighteenth century.

Perhaps the best example of this process can be observed in England where the Bank of England was founded in 1694. Unlike other banks accustomed to receiving deposits and exchanging foreign currencies, the Bank of England also made loans. In return for lending money to the government, the bank was allowed to issue paper "bank notes" backed by its credit. These soon became negotiable and provided a paper substitute for gold and silver currency. In addition, the issuance of government bonds paying regular interest, backed by the Bank of England and the London financial community, created the notion of a public or "national debt" distinct from the monarch's personal debts. This process meant that capital for financing larger armies and other government undertakings could be raised in ever-greater quantities.

These new financial institutions and methods were not risk-free, however. In both Britain and France in the early eighteenth century, speculators provided opportunities for people to invest in colonial trading companies. The French company under John Law was also tied to his

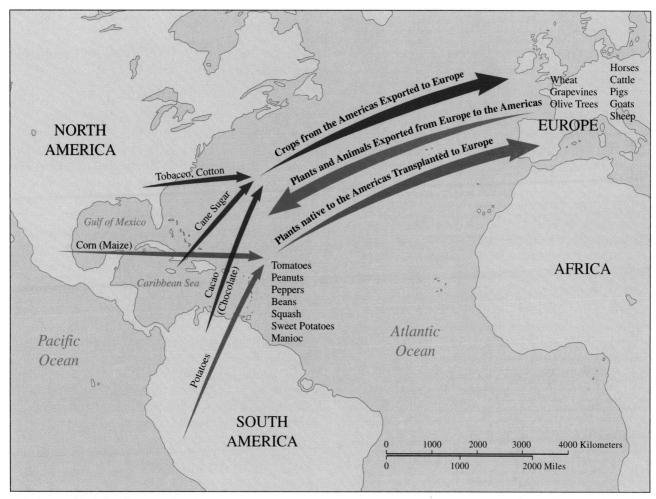

MAP 18.4 The Columbian Exchange.

attempt to create a national bank and paper currency for France. When people went overboard and drove the price of the stock to incredibly high levels, the bubble burst. Law's company and bank went bankrupt, leading to a loss of confidence in paper money that prevented the formation of a French national bank. Consequently, French public finance developed slowly in the eighteenth century.

This was not the case in Britain, however. Despite crises, public confidence in the new financial institutions enabled the British government to borrow large sums of money at relatively low rates of interest, giving it a distinct advantage in the struggle with France. According to a contemporary observer, Britain's public credit was "the permanent miracle of her policy, which has inspired both astonishment and fear in the States of Europe."[7] Despite Britain's growing importance in finance, however, the Dutch Republic remained the leader in Europe's financial life, and Amsterdam continued to be the center of international finance until London replaced it in the nineteenth century. One observer noted in 1769:

> If ten or twelve businessmen of Amsterdam of the first rank meet for a banking operation, they can in a moment send circulating throughout Europe over two hundred million florins in paper money, which is preferred to cash. There is

no Sovereign who could do as much. . . . This credit is a power which the ten or twelve businessmen will be able to exert over all the States of Europe, in complete independence of any authority.[8]

The decline of Dutch trade, industry, and power meant that Dutch capitalists were inclined to lend money abroad because they had fewer opportunities at home.

The most important product of European industry in the eighteenth century was textiles. Woolen cloth made up 75 percent of Britain's exports in the early eighteenth century. France, too, was a leader in the production of woolen cloth, and other major states emulated both France and Britain by encouraging the development of their own textile industries.

Most textiles were still produced by traditional methods. In cities that were textile centers, master artisans employed timeworn methods to turn out finished goods in their guild workshops. But by the eighteenth century textile production was beginning to shift to the countryside in parts of Europe. In the countryside, textiles were produced by the "putting-out" or "domestic" system in which a merchant-capitalist entrepreneur bought the raw materials, mostly wool and flax, and "put them out" to rural workers who spun the raw material into yarn and

Propaganda for the New Agriculture

Enthusiastic supporters of the new English agricultural practices went to the continent to examine less efficient kinds of farming. One of these Englishmen, Arthur Young, wrote an account of his travels in which he blamed the low yields of French farmers on the old system of allowing part of the land to lie fallow and the small size of the farms. The latter factor was especially important to English aristocratic landholders who wished to justify the enclosure movement. This selection is taken from Young's account.

✳ Arthur Young, *Travels during the Years, 1787, 1788, and 1789 . . . in the Kingdom of France*

The Englishman, in eleven years, gets three bushels more of wheat than the Frenchman. He gets three crops of barley, tares, or beans, which produce nearly twice as many bushels per acre, as what the three French crops of spring corn produce. And he farther gets, at the same time, three crops of turnips, and two of clover, the turnips worth 40s. the acre, and the clover 60s. That is 121 for both. What an enormous superiority. More wheat; almost double of the spring corn; and above 20s. per acre per annum in turnips and clover. But farther; the Englishman's land, by means of the manure arising from the consumption of the turnips and clover is in a constant state of improvement, while the Frenchman's farm is stationary.

The great populousness of France, I attribute very much to the division of the lands into small properties, which takes place in that country to a degree of which we have in England but little conception. . . . it has been said to me in France, "Would you leave uncultivated lands wastes, rather than let them be cultivated in small portions, through a fear of population?" I certainly would not: I would, on the contrary, encourage their culture; but I would prohibit the division of small farms, which is as mischievous to cultivation, as it is sure to be distressing to the people. . . . Go to districts where the properties are minutely divided, and you will find (at least I have done it) universally, great distress, and even misery, and probably very bad agriculture. Go to others, where such sub-division has not taken place, and you will find a better cultivation, and infinitely less misery. When you are engaged in this political tour, finish it by seeing England, and I will show you a set of peasants well clothed, well nourished, and tolerably drunken from superfluity, well-lodged, and at their ease.

---

then wove it into cloth on simple looms. Capitalist-entrepreneurs sold the finished product, made a profit, and used it to manufacture more. This system became known as the "cottage industry," because spinners and weavers did their work on spinning wheels and looms in their own cottages. Cottage industry was truly a family enterprise since women and children could spin while men wove on the looms, enabling rural people to earn incomes that supplemented their pitiful wages as agricultural laborers.

The cottage system utilized traditional methods of manufacturing and spread to many areas of rural Europe in the eighteenth century. But significant changes in industrial production also began to occur in the second half of the century, pushed along by the introduction of cotton, originally imported from India. The importation of raw cotton from slave plantations encouraged the production of cotton cloth in Europe where a profitable market developed because of the growing demand for lightweight cotton clothes that were less expensive than linens and woolens. But the traditional methods of the cottage industry proved incapable of keeping up with the growing demand, leading English cloth entrepreneurs to develop new methods and new machines. The flying shuttle sped up the process of weaving on a loom, thereby increasing the need for large quantities of yarn. In response, Richard Arkwright (1732–1792) invented a "water frame," powered by horse or water, which turned out yarn much faster than cottage spinning wheels. This abundance of yarn, in turn, led to the development of mechanized looms, invented in the 1780s but not widely adopted until the early nineteenth century. By that time Britain was in the throes of an industrial revolution, but already at the end of the eighteenth century, rural workers, perceiving that the new machines threatened their traditional livelihood, had begun to call for the machines' destruction (see the box on p. 539).

✳ *Toward a Global Economy: Mercantile Empires and Worldwide Trade*

Though bankers and industrialists came to dominate the economic life of the nineteenth century, in the eighteenth century merchants and traders still reigned supreme. Trade within Europe still dominated total trade figures as wheat, timber, and naval stores from the Baltic, wines from France, wool and fruit from Spain, and silk from Italy were exchanged along with a host of other products. But the eighteenth century witnessed only a slight increase in this trade while overseas trade boomed. From 1716 to 1789, total French exports quadrupled; intra-European trade, which constituted 75 percent of these exports in 1716, constituted only 50 percent of the total in 1789. This increase in overseas trade has led some historians to speak of the emergence of a truly global economy in the eighteenth century. By the beginning of the century, Spain, Portugal, and the Dutch Republic, which had earlier monopolized over-

The Beginnings of Mechanized Industry: The Attack on New Machines

Already by the end of the eighteenth century, mechanization was beginning to bring changes to the traditional cottage industry of textile manufacturing. Rural workers who depended on the extra wages earned in their own homes often reacted by attacking the machinery that threatened their livelihoods. This selection is a petition that English wool workers published in their local newspapers asking that machines no longer be used to prepare wool for spinning.

❋ The Leeds Woolen Workers' Petition (1786)

To the Merchants, Clothiers and all such as wish well to the Staple Manufactory of this Nation.

The Humble ADDRESS and PETITION of Thousands, who labor in the Cloth Manufactory.

The Scribbling-Machines have thrown thousands of your petitioners out of employ, whereby they are brought into great distress, and are not able to procure a maintenance for their families, and deprived them of the opportunity of bringing up their children to labor: We have therefore to request, that prejudice and self-interest may be laid aside, and that you may pay that attention to the following facts, which the nature of the case requires.

The number of Scribbling-Machines extending about seventeen miles southwest of LEEDS, exceed all belief, being no less than *one hundred and seventy!* and as each machine will do as much work in twelve hours, as ten men can in that time do by hand (speaking within bounds) and they working night and day, one machine will do as much work in one day as would otherwise employ twenty men.

As we do not mean to assert any thing but what we can prove to be true, we allow four men to be employed at each machine twelve hours, working night and day, will take eight men in twenty-four hours; so that, upon a moderate computation twelve men are thrown out of employ for every single machine used in scribbling; and as it may be supposed the number of machines in all the other quarters together, nearly equal those in the South-West, full four thousand men are left to shift for a living how they can, and must of course fall to the Parish, if not time relieved. Allowing one boy to be bound apprentice from each family out of work, eight thousand hands are deprived of the opportunity of getting a livelihood.

We therefore hope, that the feelings of humanity will lead those who have it in their power to prevent the use of those machines, to give every discouragement they can to what has a tendency so prejudicial to their fellow-creatures. . . .

We wish to propose a few queries to those who would plead for the further continuance of these machines:

How are those men, thus thrown out of employ to provide for their families; and what are they to put their children apprentice to, that the rising generation may have something to keep them at work, in order that they may not be like vagabonds strolling about in idleness? Some day, Begin and learn some other business.—Suppose we do, who will maintain our families, whilst we undertake the arduous task; and when we have learned it, how do we know we shall be any better for all our pains; for by the time we have served our second apprenticeship, another machine may arise, which may take away that business also. . . .

But what are our children to do; are they to be brought up in idleness? Indeed as things are, it is no wonder to hear of so many executions; for our parts, though we may be thought illiterate men, our conceptions are, that bringing children up to industry, and keeping them employed, is the way to keep them from falling into those crimes, which an idle habit naturally leads to.

---

seas trade, found themselves increasingly overshadowed by France and Britain. The rivalry between these two great western European powers was especially evident in the Americas and the East.

✺ COLONIAL EMPIRES

Both the French and British colonial empires in the New World included large parts of the West Indies and the North American continent. In the former, the British held Barbados, Jamaica, and Bermuda, and the French possessed Saint Dominique, Martinique, and Guadeloupe. On these tropical islands, both the British and the French had developed plantation economies, worked by African slaves, which produced tobacco, cotton, coffee, and sugar, all products increasingly in demand in Europe.

The French and British colonies on the North American continent were structured in different ways. French North America (Canada and Louisiana) was run autocratically as a vast trading area, where valuable furs, leather, fish, and timber were acquired. However, the inability of the French state to get its people to emigrate to these North American possessions left them thinly populated.

British North America had come to consist of thirteen colonies on the eastern coast of the present United States. They were thickly populated, containing about 1.5 million people by 1750, and were also prosperous. Supposedly run by the British Board of Trade, the Royal Council, and Parliament, these thirteen colonies had legislatures that tended to act independently. Merchants in such port cities as Boston, Philadelphia, New York, and Charleston resented and resisted regulation from the British government.

Both the North American and West Indian colonies of Britain and France were assigned roles in keeping with mercantilist theory. They provided raw materials for the mother country while buying the latter's manufactured goods. Navigation acts regulated what could be taken from and sold to the colonies. Theoretically, the system was supposed to provide a balance of trade favorable to the mother country.

British and French rivalry was also evident in the Spanish and Portuguese colonial empires in Latin America. The decline of Spain and Portugal had led these two states to depend even more on resources from their colonies, and they imposed strict mercantilist rules to keep others out. Spain, for example, tried to limit all trade with its colonies to Spanish ships. But the British and French were too powerful to be excluded. The British cajoled the Portuguese into allowing them into the lucrative Brazilian trade. The French, however, were the first to break into the Spanish Latin American market when the French Bourbons became kings of Spain. Britain's entry into Spanish American markets first came in 1713, when the British were granted the privilege, known as the *asiento*, of transporting 4,500 slaves a year into Spanish Latin America.

The rivalry also extended to the East where Britain and France competed for the tea, spices, cotton, hard woods, and luxury goods of India and the East Indies. The rivalry between the two countries was played out by their state-backed national trading companies. In the course of the eighteenth century, the British defeated the French, and by the mid-nineteenth century, they had assumed control of the entire Indian subcontinent.

✿ GLOBAL TRADE

To justify the term *global economy*, historians have usually pointed to the patterns of trade that interlocked Europe, Africa, the East, and the American continents. In an example of triangular trade, British merchant ships carried British manufactured goods to Africa, where they were traded for a cargo of slaves, which were then shipped to Virginia and paid for by tobacco, which in turn was shipped back to England where it was processed and then sold in Germany for cash.

Of all the goods traded in the eighteenth century, perhaps the most profitable and certainly the most infamous were African slaves. Of course, the slave trade was not new; the Spanish and Portuguese had introduced black slaves into America in the sixteenth century. But the need for slaves on the plantations where they produced the lucrative sugar, tobacco, rice, and cotton made the eighteenth century the high point of the Atlantic slave trade. It has been estimated that of the total 9.3 million slaves transported from Africa, almost two-thirds were taken in the eighteenth century. Between 75,000 and 90,000 Africans were transported annually, 50 percent

THE SALE OF SLAVES. In the eighteenth century, the slave trade was one of the more profitable commercial enterprises. This painting shows a Western slave merchant negotiating with a local African leader over slaves at Goree, Senegal, in West Africa in the late eighteenth century.

in British ships, with the rest divided among French, Dutch, Portuguese, Danish, and American ships.

Slaving ships sailed from a European port to the African coast where Europeans had established bases where merchants could trade manufactured goods, rum, and brandy for blacks captured by African intermediaries. The captives were then closely packed into cargo ships, 300 to 450 per ship, and chained in holds without sanitary facilities or enough space to stand up; there they remained during the voyage to America, which took at least 100 days (see the box on p. 541). Mortality rates averaged 10 percent except when longer journeys due to storms or adverse winds resulted in even higher death rates.

As soon as the human cargoes arrived in the New World, they entered the plantation economy. Here the "sugar factories," as the sugar plantations in the Caribbean were called, played an especially prominent role. By the last two decades of the eighteenth century, the British colony of Jamaica, one of Britain's most important, was producing 50,000 tons of sugar annually with the slave labor of 200,000 blacks. The French colony of Saint Dominique (later Haiti) had 500,000 slaves working on 3,000 plantations at the same time. This colony produced

The Atlantic Slave Trade

One of the most odious practices of early modern Western society was the Atlantic slave trade, which reached its height in the eighteenth century. Blacks were transported in densely packed cargo ships from the western coast of Africa to the Americas to work as slaves in the plantation economy. Not until late in the eighteenth century did a rising chorus of voices raise serious objections to this trade in human beings. This excerpt presents a criticism of the slave trade from an anonymous French writer.

✱ Diary of a Citizen

As soon as the ships have lowered their anchors off the coast of Guinea, the price at which the captains have decided to buy the captives is announced to the Negroes who buy prisoners from various princes and sell them to Europeans. Presents are sent to the sovereign who rules over that particular part of the coast, and permission to trade is given. Immediately the slaves are brought by inhuman brokers like so many victims dragged to a sacrifice. White men who covet that portion of the human race receive them in a little house they have erected on the shore, where they have entrenched themselves with two pieces of cannon and twenty guards. As soon as the bargain is concluded, the Negro is put in chains and led aboard the vessel, where he meets his fellow sufferers. Here sinister reflections come to his mind; everything shocks and frightens him and his uncertain destiny gives rise to the greatest anxiety. . . .

The vessel sets sail for the Antilles, and the Negroes are chained in a hold of the ship, a kind of lugubrious prison where the light of day does not penetrate, but into which the air is introduced by means of a pump. Twice a day some disgusting food is distributed to them. Their consuming sorrow and the sad state to which they are reduced would make them commit suicide if they were not deprived of all the means for an attempt upon their lives. Without any kind of clothing it would be difficult to conceal from the watchful eyes of the sailors in charge any instrument apt to alleviate their despair. The fear of a revolt, such as sometimes happens on the voyage from Guinea, is the basis of a common concern and produces as many guards as there are men in the crew. The slightest noise or a secret conversation among two Negroes is punished with utmost severity. All in all, the voyage is made in a continuous state of alarm on the part of the white men, who fear a revolt, and in a cruel state of uncertainty on the part of the Negroes, who do not know the fate awaiting them.

When the vessel arrives at a port in the Antilles, they are taken to a warehouse where they are displayed, like any merchandise, to the eyes of buyers. The plantation owner pays according to the age, strength, and health of the Negro he is buying. He has him taken to his plantation, and there he is delivered to an overseer who then and there becomes his tormentor. In order to domesticate him, the Negro is granted a few days of rest in his new place, but soon he is given a hoe and a sickle and made to join a work gang. Then he ceases to wonder about his fate; he understands that only labor is demanded of him. But he does not know yet how excessive this labor will be. As a matter of fact, his work begins at dawn and does not end before nightfall; it is interrupted for only two hours at dinnertime. The food a full-grown Negro is given each week consists of two pounds of salt beef or cod and two pots of tapioca meal. . . . A Negro of twelve or thirteen years or under is given only one pot of meal and one pound of beef or cod. In place of food some planters give their Negroes the liberty of working for themselves every Saturday; others are even less generous and grant them this liberty only on Sundays and holidays.

100,000 tons of sugar a year but at the expense of a high death rate from the brutal treatment of the slaves. It is not surprising that Saint Dominique saw the first successful slave uprising in 1793.

Despite a rising chorus of humanitarian sentiments from the philosophes, the use of black slaves remained acceptable to Western society. By and large, Europeans continued to view blacks as inferior beings fit primarily for slave labor. Not until the Society of Friends or Quakers began to criticize slavery in the 1770s and exclude from their church any member adhering to slave trafficking, did European sentiment against slavery begin to build. Even then it was not until the radical stage of the French Revolution in the 1790s that the French abolished slavery. The British followed suit in 1807. Despite the elimination of the African source, slavery continued in the newly formed United States until the Civil War of the 1860s.

◆ The Social Order of the Eighteenth Century

The pattern of Europe's social organization, first established in the Middle Ages, continued well into the eighteenth century. Social status was still largely determined not by wealth and economic standing but by the division into the traditional "orders" or "estates" determined by heredity and quality. This divinely sanctioned division of society into traditional orders was supported by Christian teaching, which emphasized the need to fulfill the responsibilities of one's estate. Although Enlightenment intellectuals attacked these traditional distinctions, they did not die easily. In the Prussian law code of 1794, marriage between noble males and middle-class females was forbidden without a government dispensation. Even without government regulation, however, different social groups remained easily distinguished everywhere in Europe by the distinctive, traditional clothes they wore.

Nevertheless, some forces of change were at work in this traditional society. The ideas of the Enlightenment made headway as reformers argued that the idea of an unchanging social order based on privilege was hostile to the progress of society. Moreover, especially in some cities, the old structures were more difficult to maintain as new economic structures, especially the growth of larger industries, brought new social contrasts that destroyed the old order. Despite these forces of change, however, it would take the revolutionary upheavals at the end of the eighteenth century before the old order would finally begin to disintegrate.

❀ *The Peasants*

Since society was still mostly rural in the eighteenth century, the peasantry constituted the largest social group, making up as much as 85 percent of Europe's population. The conditions of peasant life differed significantly from area to area, however. The most important distinction—at least legally—was between the free peasant and the serf. Peasants in Britain, northern Italy, the Low Countries, Spain, most of France, and some areas of western Germany shared freedom despite numerous regional and local differences. Legally free peasants, however, were not exempt from burdens. Some free peasants in Andalusia in Spain, southern Italy, Sicily, and Portugal lived in a poverty more desperate than that of many serfs in Russia and eastern Germany. In France, 40 percent of free peasants owned little or no land whatever by 1789.

Small peasant proprietors or tenant farmers in western Europe were also not free from compulsory services. Most owed tithes, often one-third of their crops. Although tithes were intended for parish priests, in France only 10 percent of the priests received them. Instead the tithes wound up in the hands of towns and aristocratic landowners. Moreover, peasants could still owe a variety of dues and fees. Local aristocrats claimed hunting rights on peasant land and had monopolies over the flour mills, community ovens, and wine and oil presses needed by the peasants. Hunting rights, dues, fees, and tithes were all deeply resented.

Eastern Europe continued to be dominated by large landed estates owned by powerful lords and worked by serfs. Serfdom had come late to the east, having largely been imposed in the sixteenth and seventeenth centuries. Peasants in eastern Germany were bound to the lord's estate, had to perform labor services on the lord's land, and could not marry or move without permission and payment of a tax. By the eighteenth century, landlords also possessed legal jurisdiction, giving them control over the administration of justice. Only in the Habsburg empire had a ruler attempted to improve the lot of the peasants through a series of reforms. With the exception of the clergy and a small merchant class, eighteenth-century Russia, unlike the rest of Europe, was still largely a society of landlords and serfs. Russian peasants were not attached to the land but to the landlord and thus existed in a condition approaching slavery. In 1762, landowners were given the right to transfer their serfs from one estate to another.

The local villages in which they dwelt remained the centers of peasants' social lives. Villages, especially in western Europe, maintained public order; provided poor relief, a village church, and sometimes a schoolmaster; collected taxes for the central government; maintained roads and bridges; and established common procedures for sowing, plowing, and harvesting crops. But villages were often dominated by richer peasants and proved highly resistant to innovations, such as new crops and agricultural practices.

The diet of the peasants in the eighteenth century did not vary much from that of the Middle Ages. Dark bread, made of roughly ground wheat and rye flour, remained the basic staple. It was quite nourishing and high in vitamins, minerals, and even proteins since the bran and germ were not ground out. Peasants drank water, wine, and beer and ate soups and gruel made of grains and vegetables. Especially popular were peas and beans, eaten fresh in summer but dried and used in soups and stews in winter. The new foods of the eighteenth century, potatoes and American corn, added important elements to the peasant diet. Of course, when harvests were bad, hunger and famine became the peasants' lot in life, making them even more susceptible to the ravages of disease.

❀ *The Nobility*

The nobles, who constituted about 2 or 3 percent of the European population, played a dominating role in society. Being born a noble automatically guaranteed a place at the top of the social order with all of its attendant special privileges and rights. The legal privileges of the nobility included judgment by their peers, immunity from severe punishment, exemption from many forms of taxation, and rights of jurisdiction. Especially in central and eastern Europe, the rights of landlords over their serfs were overwhelming. In Poland until 1768, the nobility even possessed the right of life or death over their serfs.

In many countries, nobles were self-conscious about their unique style of life that set them apart from the rest of society. This did not mean, however, that they were unwilling to bend the conventions of that lifestyle if there were profits to be made. For example, by convention nobles were expected to live off the yields of their estates. But although nobles almost everywhere talked about trade as being beneath their dignity, many were not averse to mercantile endeavors. Many were also only too eager to profit from industries based on the exploitation of raw materials found on their estates; as a result, many nobles were involved in mining, metallurgy, and glassmaking.

Their diet also set them off from the rest of society. Aristocrats consumed enormous quantities of meat and fish dishes accompanied by cheeses, nuts, and a variety of sweets.

Nobles also played important roles in military and government affairs. Since medieval times, landed aristocrats had functioned as military officers. Although monarchs found it impossible to exclude commoners from the ranks of officers, tradition maintained that nobles made the most natural and hence the best officers. Moreover, the eighteenth-century nobility played a significant role in the administrative machinery of state. In some countries, such as Prussia, the entire bureaucracy reflected aristocratic values. Moreover, in most of Europe, the landholding nobility controlled much of the local government in their districts.

The nobility or landowning class was not a homogeneous social group. Landlords in England leased their land to tenant farmers while those in eastern Europe used the labor services of serfs. Nobles in Russia and Prussia served the state, but those in Spain and Italy had few official functions. Differences in wealth, education, and political power also led to differences within countries as well. In France, where there were about 350,000 nobles, only 4,000 noble families had access to the court. The gap between rich and poor nobles could be enormous. According to figures for the poll tax in France, the richest nobles were assessed 2,000 livres a year while some nobles, because of their depressed economic state, paid only 6. Both groups were legally nobles. As the century progressed, poor nobles sometimes sank into the ranks of the unprivileged masses of the population. It has been estimated that the number of European nobles declined by one-third between 1750 and 1815.

Although the nobles clung to their privileged status and struggled to keep others out, almost everywhere a person with money found it possible to enter the ranks of the nobility. Rights of nobility were frequently attached to certain lands, so purchasing the lands made one a noble; the acquisition of government offices also often conferred noble status.

THE ARISTOCRATIC WAY OF LIFE: THE COUNTRY HOUSE

One aristocrat who survived the French Revolution once commented that "no one who did not live before the Revolution" could know the real sweetness of living. Of course, he spoke not for the peasants whose labor maintained the system, but for the landed aristocrats. For them the eighteenth century was a final century of "sweetness" before the Industrial Revolution and bourgeois society diminished their privileged way of life.

In so many ways, the court of Louis XIV had provided a model for other European monarchs who built palaces and encouraged the development of a court society as a center of culture. As at Versailles, these courts were peopled by members of the aristocracy whose income from rents or officeholding enabled them to participate in this lifestyle. This court society, whether in France, Spain, or Germany, manifested common characteristics: participation in intrigues for the king's or prince's favor, serene walks in formal gardens, and duels to maintain one's honor.

The majority of aristocratic landowners, however, remained on their country estates and did not participate in court society; their large houses continued to give witness to their domination of the surrounding countryside. This was especially true in England where the court of the Hanoverian kings (Georges I–III from 1714 to 1820) made little impact on the behavior of upper-class society. English landed aristocrats invested much time, energy, and money in their rural estates, giving the English country house an important role in English social life. One American observer remarked: "Scarcely any persons who hold a leading place in the circles of their society live in London. They have houses in London, in which they stay while Parliament sits, and occasionally visit at other seasons; but their homes are in the country."[9]

After the seventeenth century, the English referred to their country homes, regardless of size, not as chateaus or villas but merely houses. Although there was much variety in country houses, many in the eighteenth century were built in the Georgian style named after the Hanoverian kings. This style was greatly influenced by the classical serenity and sedateness of the sixteenth-century Venetian architect Andrea Palladio, who had specialized in the design of country villas. The Georgian country house combined elegance with domesticity, and its interior was often characterized as possessing a comfort of home that combined visual delight and usefulness.

The country house also fulfilled a new desire for greater privacy that was reflected in the growing separation between the lower and upper floors. The lower floors were devoted to public activities—dining, entertaining, and leisure. A central entrance hall provided the setting for the ceremonial arrival and departure of guests on formal occasions. From the hall, guests could proceed to a series of downstairs common rooms. The largest was the drawing room (larger houses possessed two), which contained musical instruments and was used for dances or card games, a favorite pastime. Other common rooms included a formal dining room, informal breakfast room, library, study, gallery, billiard room, and conservatory. The entrance hall also featured a large staircase that led to the upstairs rooms, which consisted of bedrooms for husbands and wives, sons, and daughters. These rooms were used not only for sleeping but also for private activities, such as playing for the children and sewing, writing, and reading for wives. This arrangement reflected the new desire for privacy. "Going upstairs" literally meant leaving the company of others in the downstairs common rooms to be alone in the privacy of one's bedroom. This eighteenth-century desire for privacy also meant keeping servants at a distance. They were now

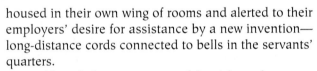

THE ARISTOCRATIC WAY OF LIFE. The eighteenth-century country house in Britain fulfilled the desire of aristocrats for both elegance and greater privacy. The painting above by Richard Wilson shows a typical English country house of the eighteenth century surrounded by a simple and serene landscape. Thomas Gainsborough's *Conversation in the Park*, shown at right, captures the relaxed life of two aristocrats in the park of their country estate.

housed in their own wing of rooms and alerted to their employers' desire for assistance by a new invention—long-distance cords connected to bells in the servants' quarters.

Although the arrangement of the eighteenth-century Georgian house originally reflected male interests, the influence of women was increasingly evident by the second half of the eighteenth century. Already in the seventeenth century, it had become customary for the sexes to separate after dinner; while the men preoccupied themselves with brandy and cigars in the dining room, women would exit to a "withdrawing room" for their own conversation. In the course of the eighteenth century, the drawing room became a larger, more feminine room with comfortable furniture grouped casually in front of fireplaces to create a cozy atmosphere.

Aristocratic landowners, especially in Britain, also sought to expand the open space around their country houses to separate themselves from the lower classes in the villages and to remove farmland from their view. Often these open spaces were then enclosed by walls to create parks (as they were called in England) to provide even more privacy. Sometimes entire villages were destroyed to create a park, causing one English poet to lament the social cost:

The man of wealth and pride
Takes up the space that many poor supplied;
Space for his lake, his park's extended bounds,
Space for his horses, equipage and hounds.[10]

Along with a sense of privacy, parks gave landed aristocrats the ability to reshape their property to meet their leisure needs.

THE ARISTOCRATIC WAY OF LIFE: THE GRAND TOUR

One characteristic of the high culture of the Enlightenment was its cosmopolitanism, reinforced by education in the Latin classics and the use of French as an international language. Travel was another manifestation of the Enlightenment's cosmopolitanism and interest in new vistas. One important aspect of eighteenth-century travel was the Grand Tour in which the sons of aristocrats completed their educations by making a tour of Europe's major cities. The English aristocracy in particular regarded the Grand Tour as crucial to their education. The great-aunt of Thomas Coke wrote to him upon his completion of school: "Sir, I understand you have left Eton and probably intend to go to one of those Schools of Vice, the Universities. If, however, you choose to travel I will give you 500 pounds [about $12,500] per annum."[11] Coke was no fool and went on the Grand Tour, along with many others. In one peak year alone, 40,000 Englishmen were traveling in Europe.

Travel was not easy in the eighteenth century. Crossing the English Channel could be difficult in rough seas and might take anywhere from three to twelve hours. The trip from France to Italy could be made by sea, where the traveler faced the danger of pirates, or overland by sedan chair

A MARKET IN TURIN. Below the wealthy patrician elites who dominated the towns and cities were a number of social groups with a wide range of incomes and occupations. This remarkable diversity is evident in this view of a market square in the Italian city of Turin.

over the Alps, where narrow passes made travel an adventure in terror. Inns, especially in Germany, were populated by thieves and the ubiquitous bed bugs. The English in particular were known for spending vast sums of money during their travels; as one observer recounted: "The French usually travel to save money, so that they sometimes leave the places where they sojourn worse off than they found them. The English, on the other hand, come over with plenty of cash, plenty of gear, and servants to wait on them. They throw their money about like lords."[12]

Since the trip's purpose was educational, young Englishmen in particular were usually accompanied by a tutor who ensured that his charges spent time looking at museum collections of natural history and antiquities. But tutors were not able to stop young men from also pursuing wine, women, and song. After crossing the Channel, English visitors went to Paris for a cram course on how to act sophisticated. They then went on to Italy, where their favorite destinations were Florence, Venice, and Rome. In Florence, the studious and ambitious studied art in the Uffizi Gallery. The less ambitious followed a less vigorous routine; according to the poet Thomas Gray, they "get up at twelve o'clock, breakfast till three, dine till five, sleep till six, drinking cooling liquors till eight, go to the bridge till ten, sup till two, and so sleep till twelve again." In Venice, where sophisticated prostitutes had flourished since Renaissance times, the chief attraction for young English males was women. As Samuel Johnson remarked: "If a young man is wild, and must run after women and bad company, it is better this should be done abroad." Rome was another "great object of our pilgrimage," where travelers visited the "modern" sights, such as Saint Peter's and, above all, the ancient ruins. To a generation raised on a classical education, souvenirs of ruins and Piranesi's

etchings of classical ruins were required purchases. The accidental rediscovery of the ancient Roman towns of Herculaneum and Pompeii made them a popular eighteenth-century tourist attraction.

❋ The Inhabitants of Towns and Cities

The social importance of towns differed significantly between eastern and western Europe. In eastern Europe, cities were generally smaller and had little real autonomy. In western Europe, they were larger and frequently were accustomed to municipal self-government and municipal privileges.

Except in the Dutch Republic, Britain, and parts of Italy, townspeople were still a distinct minority of the total population. At the end of the eighteenth century, about one-sixth of the French population lived in towns of 2,000 or more. The biggest city in Europe was London with its 1 million inhabitants while Paris numbered between 550,000 and 600,000. Altogether, Europe had at least twenty cities in twelve countries with populations over 100,000, including Naples, Lisbon, Moscow, St. Petersburg, Vienna, Amsterdam, Berlin, Rome, and Madrid.

Although urban dwellers were vastly outnumbered by rural inhabitants, towns played an important role in Western culture. The contrasts between a large city with its education, culture, and material consumption and the surrounding, often poverty-stricken countryside were striking, evident in this British traveler's account of Russia's St. Petersburg in 1741:

The country about Petersburg has full as wild and desert a look as any in the Indies; you need not go above 200 paces out of the town to find yourself in a wild wood of firs, and

Poverty in France

Unlike the British, who had a system of public-supported poor relief, the French responded to poverty with ad hoc policies when conditions became acute. This selection is taken from an intendant's report to the controller-general at Paris describing his suggestions for a program to relieve the grain shortages expected for the winter months.

❉ M. de la Bourdonnaye, Intendant of Bordeaux, to the Controller-General, September 30, 1708

Having searched for the means of helping the people of Agen in this cruel situation and having conferred with His Eminence, the Bishop, it seems to us that three things are absolutely necessary if the people are not to starve during the winter.

Most of the inhabitants do not have seed to plant their fields. However, we decided that we would be going too far if we furnished it, because those who have seed would also apply [for more]. Moreover, we are persuaded that all the inhabitants will make strenuous efforts to find some seed, since they have every reason to expect prices to remain high next year. . . .

But this project will come to nothing if the collectors of the taille continue to be as strict in the exercise of their functions as they have been of late and continue to employ troops [to force collection]. Those inhabitants who have seed grain would sell it to be freed from an oppressive garrison, while those who must buy seed, since they have none left from their harvest and have scraped together a little money for this purchase, would prefer to give up that money [for taxes] when put under police constraint. To avoid this, I feel it is absolutely necessary that you order the receivers-general to reduce their operations during this winter, at least with respect to the poor. . . .

We are planning to import wheat for this region from Languedoc and Quercy, and we are confident that there will be enough. But there are two things to be feared: one is the greed of the merchants. When they see that general misery has put them in control of prices, they will raise them to the point where the calamity is almost as great as if there were no provisions at all. The other fear is that the artisans and the lowest classes, when they find themselves at the mercy of the merchants, will cause disorders and riots. As a protective measure, it would seem wise to establish two small storehouses. . . . Ten thousand ecus [30,000 livres] would be sufficient for each. . . .

A third point demanding our attention is the support of beggars among the poor, as well as of those who have no other resources than their wages. Since there will be very little work, these people will soon be reduced to starvation. We should establish public workshops to provide work as was done in 1693 and 1694. I should choose the most useful kind of work, located where there are the greatest number of poor. In this manner, we should rid ourselves of those who do not want to work and assure the others a moderate subsistence. For these workshops, we would need about 40,000 livres, or altogether 100,000 livres. The receiver-general of the taille of Agen could advance this sum. The 60,000 livres for the storehouses he would get back very soon. I shall await your orders on all of the above.

❉ Marginal Comments by the Controller-General

Operations for the collection of the taille are to be suspended. The two storehouses are to be established; great care must be taken to put them to good use. The interest on the advances will be paid by the king. His Majesty has agreed to the establishment of the public workshops for the able-bodied poor and is willing to spend up to 40,000 livres on them this winter.

---

such a low, marshy, boggy country that you would think God when he created the rest of the world for the use of mankind had created this for an inaccessible retreat for all sorts of wild beasts.[13]

Peasants often resented the prosperity of towns and their exploitation of the countryside to serve urban interests. Palermo in Sicily used one-third of the island's food production while paying only one-tenth of the taxes. Towns lived off the countryside not by buying peasant produce, but by acquiring it through tithes, rents, and dues.

Many cities in western and even central Europe had a long tradition of patrician oligarchies that continued to control their communities by dominating town and city councils. Despite their domination, patricians constituted only a small minority of the urban population. Just below the patricians stood an upper crust of the middle classes: nonnoble officeholders, financiers and bankers, merchants, wealthy rentiers who lived off their investments, and important professionals, including lawyers. Another large urban group was the petty bourgeoisie or lower middle class made up of master artisans, shopkeepers, and small traders. Below them were the laborers or working classes. Much urban industry was still carried on in small guild workshops by masters, journeymen, and apprentices. Apprentices who acquired the proper skills became journeymen before entering the ranks of the masters, but increasingly in the eighteenth century, guilds became closed oligarchies as membership was restricted to the relatives of masters. Many skilled artisans were then often forced to become low-paid workers. Urban communities also had a large group of unskilled workers who served as servants, maids, and cooks

The Fall of the Bastille

On July 14, 1789, Parisian crowds in search of weapons attacked and captured the royal armory known as the Bastille. It had also been a state prison, and its fall marked the triumph of "liberty" over despotism. This intervention of the Parisian populace saved the Third Estate from Louis XVI's attempted counterrevolution.

❋ A Parisian Newspaper Account of the Fall of the Bastille

First, the people tried to enter this fortress by the Rue St.—Antoine, this fortress, which no one has even penetrated against the wishes of this frightful despotism and where the monster still resided. The treacherous governor had put out a flag of peace. So a confident advance was made; a detachment of French Guards, with perhaps five to six thousand armed bourgeois, penetrated the Bastille's outer courtyards, but as soon as some six hundred persons had passed over the first drawbridge, the bridge was raised and artillery fire mowed down several French Guards and some soldiers; the cannon fired on the town, and the people took fright; a large number of individuals were killed or wounded; but then they rallied and took shelter from the fire . . . meanwhile, they tried to locate some cannon; they attacked from the water's edge through the gardens of the arsenal, and from there made an orderly siege; they advanced from various directions, beneath a ceaseless round of fire. It was a terrible scene. . . . The fighting grew steadily more intense; the citizens had become hardened to the fire; from all directions they clambered onto the roofs or broke into the rooms; as soon as an enemy appeared among the turrets on the tower, he was fixed in the sights of a hundred guns and mown down in an instant; meanwhile cannon fire was hurriedly directed against the second drawbridge, which it pierced, breaking the chains; in vain did the cannon on the tower reply, for most people were sheltered from it; the fury was at its height; people bravely faced death and every danger; women, in their eagerness, helped us to the utmost; even the children, after the discharge of fire from the fortress, ran here and there picking up the bullets and shot; [and so the Bastille fell and the governor, de Launey, was captured]. . . . Serene and blessed liberty, for the first time, has at last been introduced into this abode of horrors, this frightful refuge of monstrous despotism and its crimes.

Meanwhile, they get ready to march; they leave amidst an enormous crowd; the applause, the outbursts of joy, the insults, the oaths hurled at the treacherous prisoners of war; everything is confused; cries of vengeance and of pleasure issue from every heart; the conquerors, glorious and covered in honor, carry their arms and the spoils of the conquered, the flags of victory, the militia mingling with the soldiers of the fatherland, the victory laurels offered them from every side, all this created a frightening and splendid spectacle. On arriving at the square, the people, anxious to avenge themselves, allowed neither de Launey nor the other officers to reach the place of trial; they seized them from the hands of their conquerors, and trampled them underfoot one after the other. De Launey was struck by a thousand blows, his head was cut off and hoisted on the end of a pike with blood streaming down all sides. . . . This glorious day must amaze our enemies, and finally usher in for us the triumph of justice and liberty. In the evening, there were celebrations.

---

constitution. These actions of June 17 and June 20 constitute the first step in the French Revolution since the Third Estate had no legal right to act as the National Assembly. This revolution, largely the work of the lawyers of the Third Estate, was soon in jeopardy, however, as the king sided with the First Estate and threatened to dissolve the Estates-General. Louis XVI now prepared to use force. The revolution of the lawyers appeared doomed.

✎ THE COMMON PEOPLE INTERVENE

The intervention of the common people, however, in a series of urban and rural uprisings in July and August of 1789 saved the Third Estate from the king's attempt to stop the revolution. From now on, the common people would be mobilized by both revolutionary and counterrevolutionary politicians and used to support their interests. The common people had their own interests as well and would use the name of the Third Estate to wage a war on the rich, claiming that the aristocrats were plotting to destroy the Estates-General and retain its privileges. This war was not what the deputies of the Third Estate had planned.

The most famous of the urban risings was the fall of the Bastille (see the box above). The king's attempt to take defensive measures by increasing the number of troops at the arsenals in Paris and along the roads to Versailles served not to intimidate but rather to inflame public opinion. Increased mob activity in Paris led Parisian leaders to form a Permanent Committee to keep order. Needing arms, they organized a popular force to capture the Invalides, a royal armory, and on July 14 attacked the Bastille, another royal armory. But the Bastille had also been a state prison, and though it now contained only seven prisoners (five forgers and two insane people), its fall quickly became a popular symbol of triumph over despotism. Paris was abandoned to the insurgents, and Louis XVI was soon informed that the royal troops were unreliable. Louis's acceptance of that reality signaled the collapse of royal authority; the king could no longer

STORMING OF THE BASTILLE. Louis XVI planned to use force to dissolve the Estates-General, but a number of rural and urban uprisings by the common people pre- vented this action. The fall of the Bastille, pictured here in an anonymous painting, is perhaps the most famous of the urban risings.

enforce his will. Louis then confirmed the appointment of the marquis de Lafayette as commander of a newly cre- ated citizens' militia known as the National Guard. The fall of the Bastille had saved the National Assembly.

At the same time, independently of what was going on in Paris, popular revolutions broke out in numerous cities. In Nantes, Permanent Committees and National Guards were created to maintain order after crowds had seized the chief citadels. This collapse of royal authority in the cities was paralleled by peasant revolutions in the countryside.

A growing resentment of the entire seigneurial sys- tem with its fees and obligations, greatly exacerbated by the economic and fiscal activities of the great estate holders—whether noble or bourgeois—in the difficult decade of the 1780s, created the conditions for a popu- lar uprising. The fall of the Bastille and the king's appar- ent capitulation to the demands of the Third Estate now encouraged peasants to take matters into their own hands. From July 19 to August 3, peasant rebellions

occurred in five major areas of France. Patterns varied. In some places, peasants simply forced their lay and ecclesiastical lords to renounce dues and tithes; else- where they burned charters listing their obligations. The peasants were not acting in blind fury; they knew what they were doing. Many also believed that the king sup- ported their actions. As a contemporary chronicler wrote: "For several weeks, news went from village to village. They announced that the Estates-General was going to abolish tithes, quitrents and dues, that the King agreed but that the peasants had to support the public authori- ties by going themselves to demand the destruction of titles."[5]

The agrarian revolts served as a backdrop to the Great Fear, a vast panic that spread like wildfire through France between July 20 and August 6. Fear of invasion by foreign troops, aided by a supposed aristocratic plot, encouraged the formation of more citizens' militias and permanent committees. The greatest impact of the agrar- ian revolts and Great Fear was on the National Assem-

Declaration of the Rights of Man and the Citizen

One of the important documents of the French Revolution, the Declaration of the Rights of Man and the Citizen, was adopted in August 1789 by the National Assembly. The declaration affirmed that "Men are born and remain free and equal in rights," that governments must protect these natural rights, and that political power is derived from the people.

✵ Declaration of the Rights of Man and the Citizen

The representatives of the French people, organized as a national assembly, considering that ignorance, neglect, and scorn of the rights of man are the sole causes of public misfortunes and of corruption of governments, have resolved to display in a solemn declaration the natural, inalienable, and sacred rights of man, so that this declaration, constantly in the presence of all members of society, will continually remind them of their rights and their duties. . . . Consequently, the National Assembly recognizes and declares, in the presence and under the auspices of the Supreme Being, the following rights of man and citizen:

1. Men are born and remain free and equal in rights; social distinctions can be established only for the common benefit.
2. The aim of every political association is the conservation of the natural and imprescriptible rights of man; these rights are liberty, property, security, and resistance to oppression.
3. The source of all sovereignty is located in essence in the nation; no body, no individual can exercise authority which does not emanate from it expressly.
4. Liberty consists in being able to do anything that does not harm another person. . . .
6. The law is the expression of the general will; all citizens have the right to concur personally or through their representatives in its formation; it must be the same for all, whether it protects or punishes. All citizens being equal in its eyes are equally admissible to all honors, positions, and public employments, according to their capabilities and without other distinctions than those of their virtues and talents.
7. No man can be accused, arrested, or detained except in cases determined by the law, and according to the forms which it has prescribed. . . .
10. No one may be disturbed because of his opinions, even religious, provided that their public demonstration does not disturb the public order established by law.
11. The free communication of thoughts and opinions is one of the most precious rights of man: every citizen can therefore freely speak, write, and print. . . .
12. The guaranteeing of the rights of man and citizen necessitates a public force; this force is therefore instituted for the advantage of all, and not for the private use of those to whom it is entrusted. . . .
14. Citizens have the right to determine for themselves or through their representatives the need for taxation of the public, to consent to it freely, to investigate its use, and to determine its rate, basis, collection, and duration.
15. Society has the right to demand an accounting of his administration from every public agent.
16. Any society in which guarantees of rights are not assured nor the separation of powers determined has no constitution.
17. Property being an inviolable and sacred right, no one may be deprived of it unless public necessity, legally determined, clearly requires such action, and then only on condition of a just and prior indemnity.

bly meeting in Versailles. We will now examine its attempt to reform France.

✵ The Destruction of the Old Regime

One of the first acts of the National Assembly, which was also called the Constituent Assembly because from 1789 to 1791 it was writing a new constitution, was to destroy the relics of feudalism or aristocratic privileges. To some deputies, this measure was necessary to calm the peasants and restore order in the countryside, although many urban bourgeoisie were willing to abolish feudalism as a matter of principle. On the night of August 4, 1789, the National Assembly in an astonishing session voted to abolish seigneurial rights as well as the fiscal privileges of nobles, clergy, towns, and provinces.

✵ THE DECLARATION OF THE RIGHTS OF MAN AND THE CITIZEN

On August 26, the assembly provided the ideological foundation for its actions and an educational device for the nation by adopting the Declaration of the Rights of Man and the Citizen (see the box above). This charter of basic liberties reflected the ideas of the major philosophes of the French Enlightenment and also owed much to the American Declaration of Independence and American state constitutions. The declaration began with a ringing affirmation of "the natural and imprescriptible rights of man" to "liberty, property, security and resistance to oppression." It went on to affirm the destruction of aristocratic privileges by proclaiming an end to exemptions from taxation, freedom and equal rights for all men, and access to public office based on talent. The monarchy was restricted, and all citizens were to have the right to take part in the legislative process. Freedom of speech and press were coupled with the outlawing of arbitrary arrests.

The Declaration also raised another important issue. Did the proclamation's ideal of equal rights for all men also include women? Many deputies insisted that it did, at least in terms of civil liberties, provided that, as one said, "women do not aspire to exercise political rights and functions." Olympe de Gouges, a playwright and pamphleteer, refused to accept this exclusion of women from political rights. Echoing the words of the official declaration, she penned a Declaration of the Rights of Woman and the Female Citizen, in which she insisted that women should have all the same rights as men (see the box on p. 563). The National Assembly ignored her demands.

✄ THE KING AND THE CHURCH

In the meantime, Louis XVI had remained inactive at Versailles. He did refuse, however, to promulgate the decrees on the abolition of feudalism and the Declaration of Rights, but an unexpected turn of events soon forced the king to change his mind. On October 5, after marching to the Hôtel de Ville, the city hall, to demand bread, crowds of Parisian women numbering in the thousands set off for Versailles, twelve miles away, to confront the king and the National Assembly. One eyewitness was amazed at the sight of "detachments of women coming up from every direction, armed with broomsticks, lances, pitchforks, swords, pistols and muskets." After meeting with a delegation of these women, who tearfully described how their children were starving from a lack of bread, Louis XVI promised them grain supplies for Paris, thinking that this would end the protest. But the women's action had forced

the Parisian National Guard under Lafayette to follow their lead and march to Versailles. The crowd now insisted that the royal family return to Paris. On October 6, the king complied. As a goodwill gesture, he brought along wagonloads of flour from the palace stores. All were escorted by women armed with pikes (some of which held the severed heads of the king's guards) singing, "We are bringing back the baker, the baker's wife, and the baker's boy" (the king, queen, and their son). The king now accepted the National Assembly's decrees; it was neither the first nor the last occasion when Parisian crowds would affect national politics. The king was virtually a prisoner in Paris, and the National Assembly, now meeting in Paris, would also feel the influence of Parisian insurrectionary politics.

The Catholic church was viewed as an important pillar of the old order, and it soon also felt the impact of reform. Because of the need for money, most of the lands of the church were confiscated, and assignats, a form of paper money, were issued based on the collateral of the newly nationalized church property. The church was also secularized. In July 1790, a new Civil Constitution of the Clergy was put into effect. Both bishops and priests of the Catholic church were to be elected by the people and paid by the state. All clergy were also required to swear an oath of allegiance to the Civil Constitution. Since the pope forbade it, only 54 percent of the French parish clergy took the oath, and the majority of bishops refused. This was a critical development because the Catholic church, still an important institution in the life of the French people, now became an enemy of the Revolution. The Civil Constitution has often been viewed as a serious tactical blunder on the part of the National Assembly for, by arousing the opposition of the church, it gave counterrevolution a popular base from which to operate.

✄ A NEW CONSTITUTION

By 1791, the National Assembly had finally completed a new constitution that established a limited, constitutional

Depart des Heroines de Paris pour Versailles le 5 Octobre 1789.

THE WOMEN'S MARCH TO VERSAILLES. On October 5, 1789, thousands of Parisian women marched to Versailles to confront King Louis XVI and to demand bread for their starving children. This contemporary print shows a group of dedicated marchers armed with pikes and other weapons and pulling an artillery piece.

new Paris Commune, composed of many who proudly called themselves the sans-culottes, ordinary patriots without fine clothes. Although it has become customary to equate the more radical sans-culottes with working people or the poor, many were merchants and better-off artisans who were often the elite of their neighborhoods and trades.

❋ *The Radical Revolution*

Before the National Convention met, the Paris Commune dominated the political scene. Led by the newly appointed minister of justice, Georges Danton (1759–1794), the sans-culottes sought revenge on those who had aided the king and resisted the popular will. Thousands of presumed traitors were arrested and then massacred as ordinary Parisian tradespeople and artisans solved the problem of overcrowded prisons by mass executions of their inmates. In September 1792, the newly elected National Convention began its sessions. Although it was called to draft a new constitution, it also acted as the sovereign ruling body of France.

Socially, the composition of the National Convention was similar to its predecessors. Dominated by lawyers, professionals, and property owners, it also included for the first time a handful of artisans. Two-thirds of the deputies were under age forty-five, and almost all had had political experience as a result of the Revolution. Almost all were also intensely distrustful of the king and his activities. It was therefore no surprise that the convention's first major step on September 21 was to abolish the monarchy and establish a republic. But that was about as far as members of the convention could agree, and the National Convention soon split into factions over the fate of the king. The two most important were the Girondins and the Mountain. Both were members of the Jacobin club.

Representing primarily the provinces, the Girondins came to fear the radical mobs in Paris and were disposed to keep the king alive as a hedge against future eventualities. The Mountain, on the other hand, represented the interests of the city of Paris and owed much of its strength to the radical and popular elements in the city, although the members of the Mountain themselves were middle class. The Mountain won out at the beginning of 1793 when they passed a decree condemning Louis XVI to death, although by a very narrow margin. On January 21, 1793, the king was executed and the destruction of the old regime was complete. Now there could be no turning back. But the execution of the king produced new challenges by creating new enemies for the Revolution both at home and abroad while strengthening those who were already its enemies.

Factional disputes between Girondins and the Mountain were only one aspect of France's domestic crisis in 1792 and 1793. Within Paris the local government was controlled by the Commune, which drew a number

EXECUTION OF THE KING. At the beginning of 1793, the National Convention decreed the death of the king, and on January 21 of that year, Louis XVI was executed. As seen in this engraving by Carnavalet, the execution of the king was accomplished by the new revolutionary device of the guillotine.

of its leaders from the city's artisans and shopkeepers. The Commune favored radical change and put constant pressure on the National Convention, pushing it to ever more radical positions. As one man warned his fellow deputies: "Never forget that you were sent here by the sans-culottes."[8] At the end of May and the beginning of June 1793, the Commune organized a demonstration, invaded the National Convention, and forced the arrest and execution of the leading Girondins, thus leaving the Mountain in control of the convention. The National Convention itself still did not rule all France. The authority of the convention was repudiated in western France, particularly in the department of the Vendée, by peasants who revolted against the new military draft (see A Nation in Arms later in this chapter). The Vendéan rebellion soon escalated into a full-blown counterrevolutionary appeal: "Long live the king and our good priests. We want our king, our priests and the old regime." Some of France's major provincial cities, including Lyons and Marseilles, also began to break away from the central authority. Arguing as Marseilles did that "it is time for the anarchy of a few men of blood to stop,"[9] these cities favored a decentralized republic to free themselves from the ascendancy of Paris. In no way did they favor breaking up the "indivisible Republic."

The French Revolution

The National Assembly (Constituent Assembly)	**1789–1791**
Meeting of Estates-General	May 5, 1789
Formation of National Assembly	June 17, 1789
Tennis Court Oath	June 20, 1789
Fall of the Bastille	July 14, 1789
Great Fear	Summer 1789
Abolition of feudalism	August 4, 1789
Declaration of the Rights of Man and the Citizen	August 26, 1789
Women's march to Versailles; the king's return to Paris	October 5–6, 1789
Civil Constitution of the Clergy	July 12, 1790
Flight of the king	June 20–21, 1791
Declaration of Pillnitz	August 27, 1791
The Legislative Assembly	**1791–1792**
France declares war on Austria	April 20, 1792
Attack on the royal palace	August 10, 1792
The National Convention	**1792–1795**
Abolition of the monarchy	September 21, 1792
Execution of the king	January 21, 1793
Universal mobilization of the nation	August 23, 1793
Execution of Robespierre	July 28, 1794
The Directory	**1795–1799**
Constitution of 1795 is adopted	August 22, 1795

Domestic turmoil was paralleled by a foreign crisis. By the beginning of 1793, after the king had been executed, much of Europe—an informal coalition of Austria, Prussia, Spain, Portugal, Britain, and the Dutch Republic—was pitted against France. Carried away by initial successes and their own rhetoric, the French welcomed the struggle. Danton exclaimed to the convention: "They threaten you with kings! You have thrown down your gauntlet to them, and this gauntlet is a king's head, the signal of their coming death."[10] Grossly overextended, the French armies began to experience reverses, and by late spring some members of the anti-French coalition were poised for an invasion of France. If successful, both the Revolution and the revolutionaries would be destroyed and the old regime reestablished. The Revolution had reached a decisive moment.

To meet these crises, the program of the National Convention became one of curbing anarchy and counterrevolution at home while attempting to win the war by a great national mobilization. To administer the govern-ment, the convention gave broad powers to an executive committee known as the Committee of Public Safety, which was dominated initially by Danton. Maximilien Robespierre (1758–1794) eventually became one of its most important members. For a twelve-month period, from 1793 to 1794, virtually the same twelve members were reelected and gave the country the leadership it needed to weather the domestic and foreign crises of 1793.

A NATION IN ARMS

To meet the foreign crisis and save the Republic from its foreign enemies, the Committee of Public Safety decreed a universal mobilization of the nation on August 23, 1793:

> Young men will fight, young men are called to conquer. Married men will forge arms, transport military baggage and guns and will prepare food supplies. Women, who at long last are to take their rightful place in the revolution and follow their true destiny, will forget their futile tasks: their delicate hands will work at making clothes for soldiers; they will make tents and they will extend their tender care to shelters where the defenders of the Patrie [nation] will receive the help that their wounds require. Children will make lint of old cloth. It is for them that we are fighting: children, those beings destined to gather all the fruits of the revolution, will raise their pure hands toward the skies. And old men, performing their missions again, as of yore, will be guided to the public squares of the cities where they will kindle the courage of young warriors and preach the doctrines of hate for kings and the unity of the Republic.[11]

In less than a year, the French revolutionary government had raised an army of 650,000; by September 1794, it numbered 1,169,000. The Republic's army was the largest ever seen in European history. It now pushed the allies back across the Rhine and even conquered the Austrian Netherlands. By May 1795, the anti-French coalition of 1793 was breaking up.

Historians have focused on the importance of the French revolutionary army in the creation of modern nationalism. Previously, wars had been fought between governments or ruling dynasties by relatively small armies of professional soldiers. The new French army, however, was the creation of a "people's" government; its wars were now "people's" wars. The entire nation was to be involved in the war. But when dynastic wars became people's wars, warfare increased in ferocity and lack of restraint. Although innocent civilians had suffered in the earlier struggles, now the carnage became appalling at times. The wars of the French revolutionary era opened the door to the total war of the modern world.

THE COMMITTEE OF PUBLIC SAFETY AND THE REIGN OF TERROR

To meet the domestic crisis, the National Convention and the Committee of Public Safety established the "Reign of Terror." Revolutionary courts were organized to protect the revolutionary Republic from its internal enemies, those "who either by their conduct, their contacts, their words

CITIZENS ENLIST IN THE NEW FRENCH ARMY. To save the Republic from its foreign enemies, the National Convention created a new revolutionary army of unprecedented size. In this painting, citizens joyfully hasten to sign up at the recruitment tables set up in the streets. On this occasion, officials are distributing coins to those who have enrolled.

or their writings, showed themselves to be supporters of tyranny or enemies of liberty," or those "who have not constantly manifested their attachment to the revolution."[12] Victims of the Terror ranged from royalists, such as Queen Marie Antoinette, to former revolutionary Girondins, including Olympe de Gouges, the chief advocate for political rights for women, and even included thousands of peasants. Many victims were persons who had opposed the radical activities of the sans-culottes (see the box on p. 568). In the course of nine months, 16,000 people were officially killed under the blade of the guillotine, the latter a revolutionary device for the quick and efficient separation of heads from bodies. But the true number of the Terror's victims was probably closer to 50,000. The bulk of the Terror's executions took place in the Vendée and in cities such as Lyons and Marseilles, places that had been in open rebellion against the authority of the National Convention.

Military force in the form of Revolutionary Armies was used to bring recalcitrant cities and districts back under the control of the National Convention. Marseilles fell to a Revolutionary Army in August. Starving Lyons surrendered early in October after two months of bombardment and resistance. Since Lyons was France's second city after Paris and had defied the National Convention during a time when the Republic was in peril, the Committee of Public Safety decided to make an example of it. By April 1794, 1,880 citizens of Lyons had been executed. When guillotining proved too slow, cannon fire and grape shot were used to blow condemned men into open graves. A German observed:

> . . . whole ranges of houses, always the most handsome, burnt. The churches, convents, and all the dwellings of the former patricians were in ruins. When I came to the guillotine, the blood of those who had been executed a few hours beforehand was still running in the street . . . I said to a group of sansculottes that it would be decent to clear away all this human blood. Why should it be cleared? one of them said to me. It's the blood of aristocrats and rebels. The dogs should lick it up.[13]

In the Vendée, Revolutionary Armies were also brutal in defeating the rebel armies. After destroying one army on December 12, the commander of the Revolutionary Army ordered that no quarter be given: "The road to Laval is strewn with corpses. Women, priests, monks, children, all have been put to death. I have spared nobody." The Terror was at its most destructive in the Vendée. Forty-two percent of the death sentences during the Terror were passed in territories affected by the Vendée rebellion. Perhaps the most notorious act of violence occurred in Nantes where victims were executed by sinking them in barges in the Loire River.

Contrary to popular opinion, the Terror demonstrated no class prejudice. Estimates are that the nobles constituted 8 percent of its victims; the middle classes, 25 percent; the clergy, 6; and the peasant and laboring classes, 60. To the Committee of Public Safety, this bloodletting was only a temporary expedient. Once the war and domestic emergency were over, "the republic of virtue" would ensue, and the Declaration of the Rights of Man and the Citizen would be fully established. Although theoretically a republic, the French government during the Terror was led by a group of twelve men who ordered the execution of people as enemies of the Republic. But how did they justify this? Louis Saint-Just, one of the younger members of the Committee of Public Safety, explained their rationalization in a speech to the

A Victim of the Reign of Terror

The Reign of Terror created a repressive environment in which even quite innocent people could be accused of crimes against the Republic. As seen in this letter by Anne-Félicité Guinée, wife of a wig maker, merely insulting an official could lead to arrest and imprisonment.

❋ Letter of Anne-Félicité Guinée

Citizen Anne-Félicité Guinée, twenty-four years old . . . informs you that she was arrested at the Place des Droits de l'Homme, where I had gone to get butter. I point out to you that for a long time I have had to feed the members in my household on bread and cheese and that, tired of complaints from my husband and my boys, I was compelled to go wait in line to get something to eat. For three days I had been going to the same market without being able to get anything, despite the fact that I had waited from 7 or 8 A.M. until 5 or 6 P.M. After the distribution of butter on the twenty-second, . . . a citizen came over to me and said that I was in a very delicate condition. To that I answered, "You can't be delicate and be on your legs for so long. I wouldn't have come if there were any other food." He replied that I needed to drink milk. I answered that I had men in my house who worked and that I couldn't nourish them with milk, that I was convinced that if he, the speaker, was sensitive to the difficulty of obtaining food, he would not vex me so, and that he was an imbecile and wanted to play despot, and no one had that right. Here, on the spot, I was arrested and brought to the guard house. I wanted to explain myself. I was silenced and dragged off to prison. . . . About 7 P.M., I was led to the Revolutionary Commit-

tee [of the section], where I was called a counterrevolutionary and was told I was asking for the guillotine because I told them I preferred death to being treated ignominiously the way he was treating me. . . . I was asked if I knew whom I had called a despot. I answered, "I didn't know him," and I was told that he was the commander of the post. I said that he was more [a commander] beneath his own roof than anyone, given that he was there to maintain order and not to provoke bad feelings. . . . I was told that I had done three times more than was needed to get the guillotine and that I would be explaining myself before the Revolutionary Tribunal. The next day, I was taken to the Revolutionary Committee, which, without waiting to hear me, had me taken to the Mairie, where I stayed for nine days without a bed or a chair with vermin and with women addicted to all sorts of crimes. . . .

On the ninth day I was transferred to the prison of La Force. . . . In the end I can give you only the very slightest idea of all the horrors that are committed in these terrible prisons. . . . I was thrown together not with women but with monsters who gloried in all their crimes and who gave themselves over to all the most horrible excesses. One day, two of them fought each other with knives. Day and night I lived in mortal fear. The food that was sent in to me was grabbed away immediately. That was my cruel situation for seventeen days. My whole body was swollen from . . . the poor treatment I had endured. . . . [Anne-Félicité Guinée was discharged provisionally after the authorities realized that she was pregnant.]

---

convention: "Since the French people has manifested its will, everything opposed to it is outside the sovereign. Whatever is outside the sovereign is an enemy."[14] Clearly, Saint-Just was referring to Rousseau's concept of the general will, but it is equally apparent that these twelve men, in the name of the Republic, had taken to themselves the right to ascertain the sovereign will of the French people (see the box on p. 569) and to kill their enemies as "outside the sovereign."

✎ THE "REPUBLIC OF VIRTUE"

Along with the Terror, the Committee of Public Safety took other steps both to control France and to create a new republican order and new republican citizens. By spring 1793, they were sending "representatives on mission" as agents of the central government to all departments to explain the war emergency measures and to implement the laws dealing with the wartime emergency.

The committee also attempted to provide some economic controls, especially since members of the more radical working class were advocating them. They established a system of requisitioning food supplies for the cities enforced by the forays of Revolutionary Armies into the countryside. The Law of the General Maximum established price controls on goods declared of first necessity ranging from food and drink to fuel and clothing. The controls failed to work very well because the government lacked the machinery to enforce them.

Women continued to play an active role in this radical phase of the French Revolution. As spectators at sessions of revolutionary clubs and the National Convention, women made the members and deputies aware of their demands. When on Sunday, February 25, 1793, a group of women appealed formally to the National Convention for lower bread prices, the convention reacted by adjourning until Tuesday. The women

Robespierre and Revolutionary Government

In its time of troubles, the National Convention, under the direction of the Committee of Public Safety, instituted a Reign of Terror to preserve the Revolution from its internal enemies. In this selection, Maximilien Robespierre, one of the committee's leading members, tries to justify the violence to which these believers in republican liberty resorted.

❋ Robespierre, Speech on Revolutionary Government

The theory of revolutionary government is as new as the Revolution that created it. It is as pointless to seek its origins in the books of the political theorists, who failed to foresee this revolution, as in the laws of the tyrants, who are happy enough to abuse their exercise of authority without seeking out its legal justification. And so this phrase is for the aristocracy a mere subject of terror or a term of slander, for tyrants an outrage and for many an enigma. It behooves us to explain it to all in order that we may rally good citizens, at least, in support of the principles governing the public interest.

It is the function of government to guide the moral and physical energies of the nation toward the purposes for which it was established.

The object of constitutional government is to preserve the Republic; the object of the revolutionary government is to establish it.

Revolution is the war waged by liberty against its enemies; a constitution is that which crowns the edifice of freedom once victory has been won and the nation is at peace.

The revolutionary government has to summon extraordinary activity to its aid precisely because it is at war. It is subjected to less binding and less uniform regulations, because the circumstances in which it finds itself are tempestuous and shifting above all because it is compelled to deploy, swiftly and incessantly, new resources to meet new and pressing dangers.

The principal concern of constitutional government is civil liberty; that of revolutionary government, public liberty. Under a constitutional government little more is required than to protect the individual against abuses by the state, whereas revolutionary government is obliged to defend the state itself against the factions that assail it from every quarter.

To good citizens revolutionary government owes the full protection of the state; to the enemies of the people it owes only death.

---

responded bitterly by accosting the deputies: "We are adjourned until Tuesday; but as for us, we adjourn ourselves until Monday. When our children ask us for milk, we don't adjourn them until the day after tomorrow."[15] In 1793, two women—an actress and a chocolate manufacturer—founded the Society for Revolutionary Republican Women. Composed largely of working-class women, this Parisian group viewed themselves as a "family of sisters" and vowed "to rush to the defense of the Fatherland."

Despite the importance of women to the revolutionary cause, male revolutionaries reacted disdainfully to female participation in political activity. In the radical phase of the Revolution, the Paris Commune outlawed women's clubs and forbade women to be present at its meetings. One of its members explained why:

> It is horrible, it is contrary to all laws of nature for a woman to want to make herself a man. The Council must recall that some time ago these denatured women, these viragos, wandered through the markets with the red cap to sully that badge of liberty and wanted to force all women to take off the modest headdress that is appropriate for them [the bonnet]. . . . Is it the place of women to propose motions? Is it the place of women to place themselves at the head of our armies?[16]

WOMEN PATRIOTS. Women played a variety of roles in the events of the French Revolution. This picture shows a women's patriotic club discussing the decrees of the National Convention, an indication that some women had become highly politicized by the upheavals of the Revolution.

MAP 19.2 **French Conquests during the Revolutionary Wars**.

Most men—whether radical or conservative—agreed that a woman's place was in the home and not in military or political affairs. As one man asked: "Since when is it considered normal for a woman to abandon the pious care of her home, the cradle of her children, to listen to speeches in the public forum?"[17]

In its attempt to create a new order, the National Convention also pursued a policy of dechristianization. The word "saint" was removed from street names, churches were pillaged and closed by Revolutionary Armies, and priests were encouraged to marry. In Paris, the cathedral of Notre Dame was designated a Temple of Reason. In November 1793, a public ceremony dedicated to the worship of reason was held in the former cathedral; patriotic maidens adorned in white dresses paraded before a temple of reason where the high altar once stood. At the end of the ceremony, a female figure personifying Liberty rose out of the temple. As Robespierre came to realize, dechristianization backfired because France was still overwhelmingly Catholic. In fact, dechristianization created more enemies than friends.

Yet another manifestation of dechristianization was the adoption of a new republican calendar on October 5, 1793. Years would no longer be numbered from the birth of Jesus but from September 22, 1792, the day the French Republic was proclaimed. Thus, at the time the calendar was adopted, the French were already living in year two. The calendar contained twelve months; each month consisted of three ten-day weeks (*décades*) with the tenth day of each week a rest-day (*décadi*). This eliminated Sundays and Sunday worship services and put an end to the ordering of French lives by a Christian calendar that emphasized Sundays, saints' days, and church holidays and festivals. The latter were to be replaced by revolutionary festivals. Especially important were the five days (six in leap years) left over in the calendar at the end of the year. These days were to form a half-week of festivals to celebrate the revolutionary virtues—Virtue, Intelligence, Labor, Opinion, and Rewards. The sixth extra day in a leap year would be a special festival day when French citizens would "come from all parts of the Republic to celebrate liberty and equality, to cement by their embraces the national fraternity." Of course, ending church holidays also reduced the number of nonworking holidays from fifty-six to thirty-two, a goal long recommended by eighteenth-century economic theorists.

The anti-Christian purpose of the calendar was reinforced in the naming of the months of the year. The months were given names that were supposed to evoke the seasons, the temperature, or the state of the vegetation: Vendémiaire (harvest—the first month of thirty days beginning September 22), Brumaire (mist), Frimaire (frost), Nivôse (snow), Pluviôse (rain), Ventôse (wind), Germinal (seeding), Floréal (flowering), Prairial (meadows), Messidor (wheat harvest), Thermidor (heat), and Fructidor (ripening).

The new calendar faced intense popular opposition, and the revolutionary government relied primarily on coercion to win its acceptance. Journalists, for example, were commanded to use republican dates in their newspaper articles. But many people refused to give up the old calendar, as one official reported:

> Sundays and Catholic holidays, even if there are ten in a row, have for some time been celebrated with as much pomp and splendor as before. The same cannot be said of *décadi*, which is observed by only a small handful of citizens. The first to disobey the law are the wives of public officials, who dress up on the holidays of the old calendar and abstain from work more religiously than anyone else.[18]

The government could hardly expect peasants to follow the new calendar when government officials were ignoring it. Napoleon later perceived that the revolutionary calendar was politically unpopular, and he simply abandoned it on January 1, 1806.

In addition to its anti-Christian function, the revolutionary calendar had also served to mark the Revolution as a new historical beginning, a radical break in time. Revolutionary upheavals often project millenarian expectations, the hope that a new age is dawning. The revolutionary dream of a new order presupposed the creation of a new human being freed from the old order and its symbols, a new citizen surrounded by a framework of new habits. Restructuring time itself offered the opportunity to forge new habits and create a lasting new order.

But maintaining the revolutionary ideals was not easy. By the Law of 14 Frimaire (passed on December 4, 1793), the Committee of Public Safety sought to centralize the administration of France more effectively and to exercise greater control in order to check the excesses of the Reign of Terror. The activities of both the representatives on mission and the Revolutionary Armies were scrutinized more carefully, and the campaign against Christianity was also dampened. Finally, in 1794, the Committee of Public Safety turned against its radical Parisian supporters, executed the leaders of the revolutionary Paris Commune, and turned it into a docile tool. This might have been a good idea for the sake of order, but in suppressing the people who had been its chief supporters, the National Convention alienated an important group. At the same time, the French had been successful against their foreign foes. The military successes meant that the Terror no longer served much purpose. But the Terror continued because Robespierre, now its dominant figure, had become obsessed with purifying the body politic of all the corrupt. Only then could the Republic of Virtue follow. Many deputies in the National Convention

ROBESPIERRE. Maximilien Robespierre eventually came to exercise much control over the Committee of Public Safety. Robespierre and the committee worked to centralize the administration of France and curb the excesses of the Reign of Terror. However, fear of Robespierre led many in the National Convention to condemn him, and on July 28, 1794, he was executed.

feared, however, that they were not safe while Robespierre was free to act. An anti-Robespierre coalition in the National Convention, eager now to destroy Robespierre before he destroyed them, gathered enough votes to condemn him. Robespierre was guillotined on July 28, 1794, beginning a reaction that brought an end to this radical stage of the French Revolution.

The National Convention and its Committee of Public Safety had accomplished a great deal. By creating a nation in arms, they preserved the French Revolution and prevented it from being destroyed by its foreign enemies, who, if they had been successful, would have re-established the old monarchical order. Domestically, the Revolution had also been saved from the forces of counterrevolution. The committee's tactics, however, provided an example for the use of violence in domestic politics that has continued to bedevil the Western world until this day.

❁ *Reaction and the Directory*

After the death of Robespierre on July 28, 1794, revolutionary fervor began to give way to the Thermidorean Reaction, named after the month of Thermidor. The Terror began to abate. The National Convention curtailed the power of the Committee of Public Safety, shut down the Jacobin club, and attempted to provide better protection for its deputies against the Parisian mobs. Churches were allowed to reopen for public worship, and a decree of February 21, 1795, gave freedom of worship to all cults. Economic regulation was dropped in favor of laissez-faire policies, another clear indication that moderate forces were again gaining control of the Revolution. In addition, a new constitution was created in August 1795 that reflected this more conservative republicanism or a desire for a stability that did not sacrifice the ideals of 1789.

To avoid the dangers of another single legislative assembly, the Constitution of 1795 established a national legislative assembly consisting of two chambers: a lower house, known as the Council of 500, whose function was to initiate legislation, and an upper house of 250 members, the Council of Elders, composed of married or widowed members over age forty, which accepted or rejected the proposed laws. The 750 members of the two legislative bodies were chosen by electors who had to be owners or renters of property worth between 100 and 200 days' labor, a requirement that limited their number to 30,000, an even smaller base than the Constitution of 1791 had provided. The electors were chosen by the active citizens, now defined as all male taxpayers over twenty-one. The Council of Elders elected five directors from a list presented by the Council of 500 to act as the executive authority or Directory. To ensure some continuity from the old order to the new, the members of the National Convention ruled that two-thirds of the new members of the National Assembly must be chosen from their ranks. This decision produced disturbances in Paris

and an insurrection at the beginning of October that was dispersed after fierce combat by an army contingent under the artillery general Napoleon Bonaparte. This would be the last time in the great French Revolution that the city of Paris would attempt to impose its wishes on the central government. Even more significant and ominous was this use of the army, which made it clear that the Directory from the beginning had to rely upon the military for survival.

The period of the Directory was an era of stagnation, corruption, and graft, a materialistic reaction to the sufferings and sacrifices that had been demanded in the Reign of Terror and the Republic of Virtue. Speculators made fortunes in property by taking advantage of the government's severe monetary problems. Elaborate fashions, which had gone out of style because of their identification with the nobility, were worn again. Gambling and roulette became popular once more.

The government of the Directory was faced with political enemies from both the left and the right of the political spectrum. On the right, royalists who dreamed of restoring the monarchy continued their agitation; some still toyed with violent means. On the left, Jacobin hopes of power were revived by continuing economic problems, especially the total collapse in the value of the assignats. Some radicals even went beyond earlier goals, especially Gracchus Babeuf who raised the question "What is the French Revolution? An open war between patricians and plebeians, between rich and poor." Babeuf, who was appalled at the misery of the common people, wanted to abolish private property and eliminate private enterprise. His Conspiracy of Equals was crushed in 1796, and he was executed in 1797.

New elections in 1797 created even more uncertainty and instability. Battered by the left and right, unable to find a definitive solution to the country's economic problems, and still carrying on the wars left from the Committee of Public Safety, the Directory increasingly relied on the military to maintain its power. This led to a coup d'etat in 1799 in which the successful and popular general Napoleon Bonaparte was able to seize power.

◆ The Age of Napoleon

Napoleon dominated both French and European history from 1799 to 1815. The coup d'etat that brought him to power occurred exactly ten years after the outbreak of the French Revolution. In a sense, Napoleon brought the Revolution to an end in 1799, but Napoleon was also a child of the Revolution; he called himself the son of the Revolution. The French Revolution had made possible his rise first in the military and then to supreme power in France. Even beyond this, Napoleon had once said, "I am the revolution," and he never ceased to remind the French that they owed to him the preservation of all that was beneficial in the revolutionary program.

NAPOLEON AS A YOUNG OFFICER. Napoleon had risen quickly through the military ranks, being promoted to the rank of brigadier general at the age of twenty-five. This painting of Napoleon by the Romantic painter Baron Gros presents an idealized, heroic image of the young Napoleon.

✸ The Rise of Napoleon

Napoleon was born in Corsica in 1769, only a few months after France had annexed the island. The son of a lawyer whose family stemmed from the Florentine nobility, the young Napoleon obtained a royal scholarship to study at a military school in France. His education in French military schools led to his commission in 1785 as a lieutenant, although he was not well liked by his fellow officers because he was short, spoke with an Italian accent, and had little money. For the next seven years, Napoleon spent much of his time reading the works of the philosophes and educating himself in military matters by studying the campaigns of great military leaders from the past. The French Revolution and the European war that followed broadened his sights and presented him with new opportunities.

Napoleon rose quickly through the ranks. In 1792, he became a captain and in the following year performed so well as an artillery commander that he was promoted to the rank of brigadier general in 1794, when he was only twenty-five. In October 1795, he saved the National Convention from the Parisian mob and in 1796 was made commander of the French army in Italy (see the box on p. 574). There he turned a group of ill-disciplined soldiers

into an effective fighting force and, in a series of stunning victories, defeated the Austrians and dictated peace to them in 1797. Throughout his Italian campaigns, Napoleon won the confidence of his men by his energy, charm, and ability to comprehend complex issues quickly and make decisions rapidly. These qualities, combined with his keen intelligence, ease with words, and supreme confidence in himself, enabled him throughout the rest of his life to influence people and win their firm support (see the box on p. 575).

In 1797, Napoleon returned to France as a conquering hero and was given command of an army in training to invade England. Believing that the French were unready for such an invasion, he proposed instead to strike indirectly at Britain by taking Egypt and threatening India, a major source of British wealth. But the British controlled the seas and, by 1799, had cut off supplies from Napoleon's army in Egypt. Seeing no future in certain defeat, Napoleon did not hesitate to abandon his army and return to Paris where he participated in the coup d'etat that ultimately led to his virtual dictatorship of France. He was only thirty years old at the time.

With the coup d'etat of 1799, a new form of the Republic was proclaimed with a constitution that established a bicameral legislative assembly elected indirectly

Napoleon and Psychological Warfare

In 1796, at the age of twenty-seven, Napoleon Bonaparte was given command of the French army in Italy where he won a series of stunning victories. His use of speed, deception, and surprise to overwhelm his opponents is well known. In this selection from a proclamation to his troops in Italy, Napoleon also appears as a master of psychological warfare.

✾ Napoleon Bonaparte, Proclamation to the French Troops in Italy (April 26, 1796)

Soldiers:

In a fortnight you have won six victories, taken twenty-one standards, fifty-five pieces of artillery, several strong positions, and conquered the richest part of Piedmont [in northern Italy]; you have captured 15,000 prisoners and killed or wounded more than 10,000 men. . . . You have won battles without cannon, crossed rivers without bridges, made forced marches without shoes, camped without brandy and often without bread. Soldiers of liberty, only republican troops could have endured what you have endured. Soldiers, you have our thanks! The grateful Patrie [nation] will owe its prosperity to you. . . .

The two armies which but recently attacked you with audacity are fleeing before you in terror; the wicked men who laughed at your misery and rejoiced at the thought of the triumphs of your enemies are confounded and trembling.

But, soldiers, as yet you have done nothing compared with what remains to be done. . . . Undoubtedly the greatest obstacles have been overcome; but you still have battles to fight, cities to capture, rivers to cross. Is there one among you whose courage is abating? No. . . . All of you are consumed with a desire to extend the glory of the French people; all of you long to humiliate those arrogant kings who dare to contemplate placing us in fetters; all of you desire to dictate a glorious peace, one which will indemnify the Patrie for the immense sacrifices it has made; all of you wish to be able to say with pride as you return to your villages, "I was with the victorious army of Italy!"

---

to reduce the role of elections. Executive power in the new government was vested in the hands of three consuls although as Article 42 of the constitution said, "The decision of the First Consul shall suffice." As first consul, Napoleon directly controlled the entire executive authority of government. He had overwhelming influence over the legislature, appointed members of the bureaucracy, controlled the army, and conducted foreign affairs. In 1802, Napoleon was made consul for life and in 1804 returned France to monarchy when he crowned himself as Emperor Napoleon I. This step undoubtedly satisfied his enormous ego but also stabilized the regime and provided a permanency not possible in the consulate. The revolutionary era that had begun with an attempt to limit arbitrary government had ended with a government far more autocratic than the monarchy of the old regime. As his reign progressed and the demands of war increased, Napoleon's regime became ever more dictatorial.

✾ The Domestic Policies of Emperor Napoleon

Napoleon often claimed that he had preserved the gains of the Revolution for the French people. The ideal of republican liberty had, of course, been destroyed by Napoleon's thinly disguised autocracy. But were revolutionary ideals maintained in other ways? An examination of his domestic policies will enable us to judge the truth or falsehood of Napoleon's assertion.

In 1801, Napoleon made peace with the oldest and most implacable enemy of the Revolution, the Catholic church. Napoleon himself was devoid of any personal faith; he was an eighteenth-century rationalist who regarded religion at most as a convenience. In Egypt, he called himself a Muslim; in France, a Catholic. But Napoleon saw the necessity to come to terms with the Catholic church in order to stabilize his regime. In 1800, he had declared to the clergy of Milan: "It is my firm intention that the Christian, Catholic, and Roman religion shall be preserved in its entirety. . . . No society can exist without morality; there is no good morality without religion. It is religion alone, therefore, that gives to the State a firm and durable support."[19] Soon after making this statement, Napoleon opened negotiations with Pope Pius VII to reestablish the Catholic church in France.

Both sides gained from the Concordat that Napoleon arranged with the pope in 1801. Although the pope gained the right to depose French bishops, this gave him little real control over the French Catholic church since the state retained the right to nominate bishops. The Catholic church was also permitted to hold processions again and reopen the seminaries. But Napoleon gained more than the pope. Just by signing the Concordat, the pope acknowledged the accomplishments of the Revolution. Moreover, the pope agreed not to raise the question of the church lands confiscated during the Revolution. Contrary to the pope's wishes, Catholicism was not reestablished as the state religion; Napoleon was only willing to recognize

The Man of Destiny

Napoleon possessed an overwhelming sense of his own importance. Among the images he fostered, especially as his successes multiplied and his megalomaniacal tendencies intensified, were those of the man of destiny and the great man who masters luck.

❈ Selections from Napoleon

When a deplorable weakness and ceaseless vacillations become manifest in supreme councils; when, yielding in turn to the influences of opposing parties, making shift from day to day, and marching with uncertain pace, a government has proved the full measure of its impotence; when even the most moderate citizens are forced to admit that the State is no longer governed; when, in fine, the administration adds to its nullity at home the gravest guilt it can acquire in the eyes of a proud nation—I mean its humiliation abroad—then a vague unrest spreads through the social body, the instinct of self-preservation is stirred, and the nation casts a sweeping eye over itself, as if to seek a man who can save it.

This guardian angel a great nation harbors in its bosom at all times; yet sometimes he is late in making his appearance. Indeed, it is not enough for him to exist: he also must be known. He must know himself. Until then, all endeavors are in vain, all schemes collapse. The inertia of the masses protects the nominal government, and despite its ineptitude and weakness the efforts of its enemies fail. But let that impatiently awaited savior give a sudden sign of his existence, and the people's instinct will divine him and call upon him. The obstacles are smoothed before his steps, and a whole great nation, flying to see him pass, will seem to be saying: "Here is the man!"

. . . A consecutive series of great actions never is the result of chance and luck; it always is the product of planning and genius. Great men are rarely known to fail in their most perilous enterprises. . . . Is it because they are lucky that they become great? No, but being great, they have been able to master luck.

Catholicism as the religion of a majority of the French people. The clergy would be paid by the state, but to avoid the appearance of a state church, Protestant ministers were also put on the state payroll. As a result of the Concordat, the Catholic church was no longer an enemy of the French government. At the same time, the agreement reassured those who had acquired church lands during the Revolution that they would not be stripped of them, an assurance that obviously made them supporters of the Napoleonic regime.

Before the Revolution, France did not have a single set of laws, but rather virtually 300 different legal systems. During the Revolution, efforts were made to prepare a codification of laws for the entire nation, but it remained for Napoleon to bring the work to completion in seven codes of law, of which the most important was the Civil Code (or Code Napoléon). This preserved most of the revolutionary gains by recognizing the principle of the equality of all citizens before the law, the right of individuals to choose their professions, religious toleration, and the abolition of serfdom and feudalism. Property rights continued to be carefully protected while the interests of employers were safeguarded by outlawing trade unions and strikes. The Civil Code clearly reflected the revolutionary aspirations for a uniform legal system, legal equality, and protection of property and individuals.

But the rights of some people were strictly curtailed by the Civil Code. During the radical phase of the French Revolution, new laws had made divorce an easy process for both husbands and wives, restricted the rights of fathers over their children (they could no longer have their children put in prison arbitrarily), and allowed all children (including daughters) to inherit property equally. Napoleon's Civil Code undid most of this legislation. The control of fathers over their families was restored. Divorce was still allowed, but made more difficult for women to obtain. A wife caught in adultery, for example, could be divorced by her husband and even imprisoned. A husband, on the other hand, could only be accused of adultery if he moved his mistress into his home. Women were now "less equal than men" in other ways as well. When they married, their property was brought under the control of their husbands. In lawsuits they were treated as minors, and their testimony was regarded as less reliable than that of men.

Napoleon also worked on rationalizing the bureaucratic structure of France by developing a powerful, centralized administrative machine. During the Revolution, the National Assembly had divided France into eighty-three departments and replaced the provincial estates, nobles, and intendants with self-governing assemblies. Napoleon kept the departments but eliminated the locally elected assemblies and instituted new officials, the most important of which were the prefects. As the central government's agents, appointed by the first consul (Napoleon), the prefects were responsible for supervising all aspects of local government. Yet they were not local men and their careers depended on the central government.

As part of Napoleon's overhaul of the administrative system, tax collection became systematic and efficient

THE CORONATION OF NAPOLEON. In 1804, Napoleon restored monarchy to France when he crowned himself as emperor. In the coronation scene painted by Jacques-Louis David, Napoleon is shown crowning the empress Josephine while the pope looks on. Shown seated in the box in the background is Napoleon's mother, even though she was not at the ceremony.

(which it had never been under the old regime). Taxes were now collected by professional collectors employed by the state who dealt directly with each individual taxpayer. No tax exemptions due to birth, status, or special arrangement were granted. In principle these changes had been introduced in 1789, but not until Napoleon did they actually work. In 1802, the first consul proclaimed a balanced budget.

Administrative centralization required a bureaucracy of capable officials, and Napoleon worked hard to develop one. Early on, the regime showed its preference for experts and cared little whether that expertise had been acquired in royal or revolutionary bureaucracies. Promotion, whether in civil or military offices, was to be based not on rank or birth but only on demonstrated abilities. This was, of course, what many bourgeoisie had wanted before the Revolution. Napoleon, however, also created a new aristocracy based on merit in the state service. Napoleon created 3,263 nobles between 1808 and 1814; nearly 60 percent were military officers, and the remainder came from the upper ranks of the civil service and other state and local officials. Socially, only 22 percent of Napoleon's aristocracy came from the nobility of the old regime; almost 60 percent were bourgeois in origin.

In his domestic policies, then, Napoleon both destroyed and preserved aspects of the Revolution. Although equality was preserved in the law code and the opening of careers to talent, the creation of a new aristocracy, the strong protection accorded to property rights, and the use of conscription for the military make it clear that much equality had been lost. Liberty had been replaced by an initially benevolent despotism that grew increasingly arbitrary. Napoleon shut down sixty of France's seventy-three newspapers and insisted that all manuscripts be subjected to government scrutiny before they were published. Even the mail was opened by government police. One prominent writer—Germaine de Staël—refused to accept Napoleon's growing despotism. Educated in Enlightenment ideas, Madame de Staël wrote novels and political works that denounced Napoleon's rule as tyrannical. Napoleon banned her books in France and exiled her to the German states, where she continued to write.

❋ Napoleon's Empire and the European Response

When Napoleon became consul in 1799, France was at war with a second European coalition of Russia, Great Britain, and Austria. Napoleon realized the need for a pause. He remarked to a Prussian diplomat "that the French Revolution is not finished so long as the scourge of war lasts. . . . I want peace, as much to settle the present French government, as to save the world from chaos."[20] The peace he sought was achieved at Amiens in March 1802 and left France with new frontiers and a number of client territories from the North Sea to the Adriatic. But the peace did not last because the British and French both regarded it as temporary and had little inten-

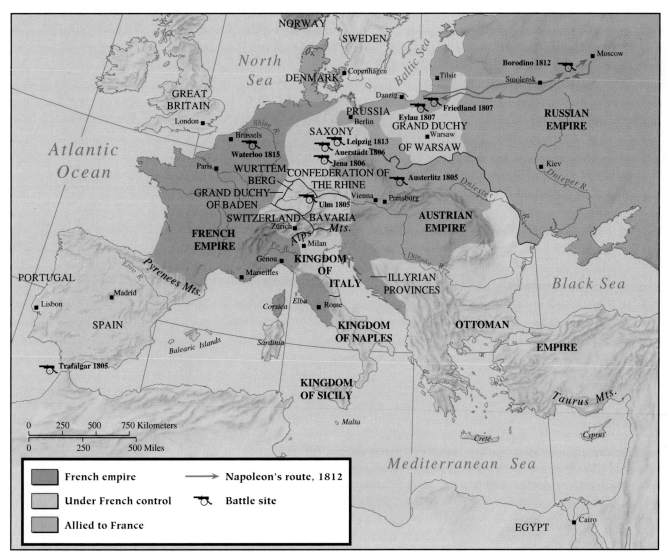

MAP 19.3 Napoleon's Grand Empire.

tion of adhering to its terms. In 1803, war was renewed with Britain, which was soon joined by Austria, Russia, and Prussia in the Third Coalition. In a series of battles at Ulm, Austerlitz, Jena, and Eylau from 1805 to 1807, Napoleon's Grand Army defeated the continental members of the coalition, giving him the opportunity to create a new European order. The Grand Empire was composed of three major parts: the French empire, a series of dependent states, and allied states. The French empire, the inner core of the Grand Empire, consisted of an enlarged France extending to the Rhine in the east and including the western half of Italy north of Rome. Dependent states included Spain, Holland, the kingdom of Italy, the Swiss Republic, the Grand Duchy of Warsaw, and the Confederation of the Rhine, the latter a union of all German states except Austria and Prussia. Allied states were those defeated by Napoleon and forced to join his struggle against Britain; they included Prussia, Austria, and Russia. Although the internal structure of the Grand

Empire varied outside its inner core, Napoleon considered himself leader of the whole: "Europe cannot be at rest except under a single head who will have kings for his officers, who will distribute his kingdom to his lieutenants."

Within his empire, Napoleon demanded obedience, in part because he needed a common front against the British and in part because his growing egotism required obedience to his will. But as a child of the Enlightenment and Revolution, Napoleon also sought acceptance everywhere of certain revolutionary principles, including legal equality, religious toleration, and economic freedom. As he explained to his brother Jerome after he had made him king of the new German state of Westphalia:

What the peoples of Germany desire most impatiently is that talented commoners should have the same right to your esteem and to public employments as the nobles, that any trace of serfdom and of an intermediate hierarchy between the sovereign and the lowest class of the people should be completely abolished. The benefits of the Code Napoléon, the publicity of judicial procedure, the creation of juries must be so many distinguishing marks of your monarchy. . . . What nation would wish to return under the arbitrary Prussian government once it had tasted the benefits of a wise and liberal administration? The peoples of Germany, the peoples of France, of Italy, of Spain all desire equality and liberal ideas. I have guided the affairs of Europe for many years now, and I have had occasion to convince myself that the buzzing of the privileged classes is contrary to the general opinion. Be a constitutional king.[21]

In the inner core and dependent states of his Grand Empire, Napoleon tried to destroy the old order. Nobility and clergy everywhere in these states lost their special privileges. He decreed equality of opportunity with offices open to talent, equality before the law, and religious toleration. This spread of French revolutionary principles was an important factor in the development of liberal traditions in these countries. These reforms have led some historians to view Napoleon as the last of the enlightened absolutists.

Like Hitler 130 years later, Napoleon hoped that his Grand Empire would last for centuries; like Hitler's empire, it collapsed almost as rapidly as it had been formed. Two major reasons help to explain this, the survival of Great Britain and the force of nationalism. Britain's survival was primarily due to its seapower. As long as Britain ruled the waves, it was almost invulnerable to military attack. Although Napoleon contemplated an invasion of England and even collected ships for it, he could not overcome the British navy's decisive defeat of a combined French-Spanish fleet at Trafalgar in 1805. Napoleon then turned to his Continental System to defeat Britain. Put into effect between 1806 and 1807, it attempted to prevent British goods from reaching the European continent in order to weaken Britain economically and destroy its capacity to wage war. But the Continental System failed. Allied states resented the ever-tightening French economic hegemony; some began to cheat and others to resist, thereby opening the door to British collaboration. New markets in the Levant and in Latin America also provided compensation for the British. Indeed, by 1809–1810 British overseas exports were at near-record highs.

A second important factor in the defeat of Napoleon was nationalism. This political creed had arisen during the French Revolution in the French people's emphasis on brotherhood (*fraternité*) and solidarity against other peoples. Nationalism involved the unique cultural identity of a people based on common language, religion, and national symbols. The spirit of French nationalism had made possible the mass armies of the revolutionary and Napoleonic eras. But Napoleon's spread of the principles of the French Revolution beyond France inadvertently brought a spread of nationalism as well. The French aroused nationalism in two ways: by making themselves

CHRONOLOGY

The Napoleonic Era, 1799–1815

Napoleon as first consul	1799–1804
Concordat with Catholic church	1801
Peace of Amiens	1802
Emperor Napoleon I	1804–1815
Battles of Austerlitz; Trafalgar; Ulm	1805
Battle of Jena	1806
Continental System established	1806
Battle of Eylau	1807
Invasion of Russia	1812
War of liberation	1813–1814
Exile to Elba	1814
Battle of Waterloo; exile to Saint Helena	1815
Death of Napoleon	1821

hated oppressors and thus arousing the patriotism of others in opposition to French nationalism, and by showing the people of Europe what nationalism was and what a nation in arms could do. The lesson was not lost on other peoples and rulers. A Spanish uprising against Napoleon's rule, aided by British support, kept a French force of 200,000 pinned down for years.

The beginning of Napoleon's downfall came in 1812 with his invasion of Russia. The latter's defection from the Continental System left Napoleon with little choice. Although aware of the risks in invading such a large country, he also knew that if the Russians were allowed to challenge the Continental System unopposed, others would soon follow suit. In June 1812, a Grand Army of more than 600,000 men entered Russia. Napoleon's hopes for victory depended on quickly meeting and defeating the Russian armies, but the Russian forces refused to give battle and retreated for hundreds of miles while torching their own villages and countryside to prevent Napoleon's army from finding food and forage. When the Russians did stop to fight at Borodino, Napoleon's forces won an indecisive and costly victory. When the remaining troops of the Grand Army arrived in Moscow, they found the city ablaze. Lacking food and supplies, Napoleon abandoned Moscow late in October and made the "Great Retreat" across Russia in terrible winter conditions. Only 40,000 out of the original army managed to straggle back to Poland in January 1813. This military disaster then led to a war of liberation all over Europe, culminating in Napoleon's defeat in April 1814.

The defeated emperor of the French was allowed to play ruler on the island of Elba, off the cost of Tuscany, while the Bourbon monarchy was restored to France in the person of Louis XVIII, brother of the executed king. But the new king had little support, and Napoleon, bored on the island of Elba, slipped back into France. The troops sent to capture him went over to his side, and Napoleon entered Paris in triumph on March 20, 1815. The powers that had defeated him pledged once more to fight this person they called the "Enemy and Disturber of the Tranquility of the World." Having decided to strike first at his enemies, Napoleon raised yet another army and moved to attack the nearest allied forces stationed in Belgium. At Waterloo on June 18, Napoleon met a combined British and Prussian army under the duke of Wellington and suffered a bloody defeat. This time the victorious allies exiled him to Saint Helena, a small and forsaken island in the South Atlantic. Only Napoleon's memory would continue to haunt French political life.

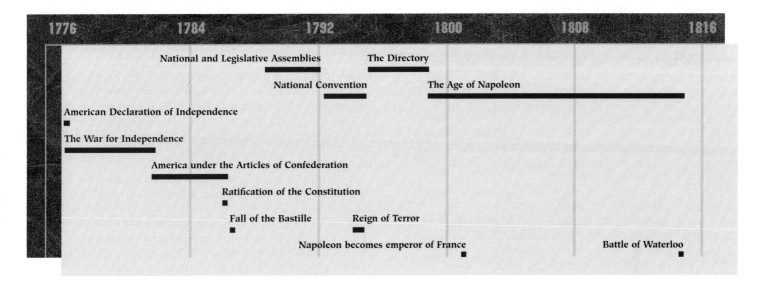

CONCLUSION

The revolutionary era of the late eighteenth century witnessed a dramatic political transformation. Revolutionary upheavals, beginning in North America and continuing in France, produced movements for political liberty and equality. The documents created by these revolutions, the Declaration of Independence and the Declaration of the Rights of Man and the Citizen, embodied the fundamental ideas of the Enlightenment and set forth a liberal political agenda based on a belief in popular sovereignty—the people are the source of political power—and the principles of liberty and equality. Liberty, frequently limited in practice, meant, in theory, freedom from arbitrary power as well as the freedom to think, write, and worship as one chose. Equality meant equality in rights and equality of opportunity based on talent rather than birth. In practice, equality remained limited; those who owned property had greater opportunities for voting and office-holding, and there was certainly no equality between men and women.

The leaders of France's liberal revolution, achieved between 1789 and 1791, were men of property, both bourgeois and noble, but they were assisted by commoners, both sans-culottes and peasants. Yet the liberal revolution, despite the hopes of the men of property, was not the end of the Revolution. The deci-

sion of the revolutionaries to go to war "revolutionized the Revolution," opening the door to a more radical, democratic, and violent stage. The excesses of the Reign of Terror, however, led to a reaction, first under the Directory and then under Napoleon, when men of property were willing to give up liberty in exchange for order, security, and economic opportunity. Napoleon, while diminishing freedom by establishing order and centralizing the government, shrewdly preserved equality of rights and the opening of careers to talent and integrated the bourgeoisie and old nobility into a new elite of property owners. For despite the anti-aristocratic revolutionary rhetoric and the loss of their privileges, nobles remained important landowners. Though the nobles lost some of their lands during the Revolution, they were still the largest proprietors in the early 1800s. The great gainers from the redistribution of clerical and noble property, however, had been the bourgeoisie, who also gained dramatically when important government and military positions were opened to men of talent. After 1800, an elite group of property owners, both noble and middle class, dominated French society.

The French Revolution created a modern revolutionary concept. No one had foreseen or consciously planned the upheaval that began in 1789, but after 1789 "revolutionaries" knew that the proper use of mass uprisings could succeed in overthrowing *unwanted governments. The French Revolution became the classical political and social model for revolution. At the same time, the liberal and national political ideals created by the Revolution and spread through Europe by Napoleon's conquests dominated the political landscape of the nineteenth and early twentieth centuries. A new European era had begun and Europe would never again be the same.*

NOTES

1. Quoted in R. R. Palmer, *The Age of the Democratic Revolutions* (Princeton, N.J., 1959), 1:239.
2. Quoted in ibid., p. 242.
3. Quoted in O. J. Hufton, "Toward an Understanding of the Poor of Eighteenth Century France," in J. F. Bosher, ed., *French Government and Society, 1500–1850* (London, 1973), p. 152.
4. Arthur Young, *Travels in France during the Years 1787, 1788 and 1789* (Cambridge, 1929), p. 23.
5. Quoted in D. M. G. Sutherland, *France 1789–1815: Revolution and Counter-Revolution* (New York, 1986), p. 74.
6. Quoted in William Doyle, *The Oxford History of the French Revolution* (Oxford, 1989), p. 156.
7. Quoted in ibid., p. 184.
8. Quoted in J. Hardman, ed., *French Revolution Documents* (Oxford, 1973), 2:23.
9. Quoted in W. Scott, *Terror and Repression in Revolutionary Marseilles* (London, 1973), p. 84.
10. Quoted in H. Morse Stephens, *The Principal Speeches of the Statesmen and Orators of the French Revolution* (Oxford, 1892), 2:189.
11. Quoted in Leo Gershoy, *The Era of the French Revolution* (Princeton, N.J., 1957), p. 157.
12. Quoted in J. M. Thompson, *French Revolution Documents* (Oxford, 1933), pp. 258–259.
13. Quoted in Doyle, *The Oxford History of the French Revolution*, p. 254.
14. Quoted in R. R. Palmer, *Twelve Who Ruled* (New York, 1965), p. 75.
15. Quoted in Darline Gay Levy, Harriet Branson Applewhite, and Mary Durham Johnson, eds., *Women in Revolutionary Paris, 1789–1795* (Urbana, Ill., 1979), p. 132.
16. Ibid., pp. 219–220.
17. Quoted in Elizabeth G. Sledziewski, "The French Revolution as the Turning Point," in Geneviève Fraisse and Michelle Perrot, eds., *A History of Women in the West* (Cambridge, 1993), 4:39.
18. Quoted in François Furet and Mona Ozouf, *A Critical Dictionary of the French Revolution*, trans. Arthur Goldhammer (Cambridge, Mass., 1989), p. 545.
19. Quoted in Felix Markham, *Napoleon* (New York, 1963), pp. 92–93.
20. Quoted in Doyle, *The Oxford History of the French Revolution*, p. 381.
21. Quoted in J. Christopher Herold, ed., *The Mind of Napoleon* (New York, 1955), pp. 74–75.

SUGGESTIONS FOR FURTHER READING

A well-written, up-to-date introduction to the French Revolution can be found in W. Doyle, *The Oxford History of the French Revolution* (Oxford, 1989). For the entire revolutionary and Napoleonic eras, see O. Connelly, *The French Revolution and Napoleonic Era*, 2d ed. (Fort Worth, 1991); and D. M. G. Sutherland, *France 1789–1815: Revolution and Counter-Revolution* (New York, 1986). Two brief works are A. Forrest, *The French Revolution* (Oxford, 1995); and J. M. Roberts, *The French Revolution*, 2d ed. (New York, 1997). A different approach to the French Revolution can be found in E. Kennedy, *A Cultural History of the French Revolution* (New Haven, Conn., 1989). Three comprehensive reference works are S. F. Scott and B. Rothaus, eds., *Historical Dictionary of the French Revolution*, 2 vols. (Westport, Conn., 1985); F. Furet and M. Ozouf, *A Critical Dictionary of the French Revolution*, trans. A. Goldhammer (Cambridge, Mass., 1989); and O. Connelly, et al., *Historical Dictionary of Napoleonic France, 1799–1815* (Westport, Conn., 1985).

The origins of the French Revolution are examined in W. Doyle, *Origins of the French Revolution* (Oxford, 1988). See also R. Chartier, *The Cultural Origins of the French Revolution* (Durham, N.C., 1991). On the early years of the Revolution, see M. Kennedy, *The Jacobin Clubs in the French Revolution: The First Years* (Princeton, N.J., 1982); N. Hampson, *Prelude to Terror* (Oxford, 1988); T. Tackett, *Becoming a Revolutionary* (Princeton, N.J., 1996), on the deputies to the National Assembly; and J. Markoff, *The Abolition of Feudalism: Peasants, Lords, and Legislators in the French Revolution* (University Park, Pa., 1996). Important works on the radical stage of the French Revolution include N. Hampson, *The Terror in the French Revolution* (London, 1981); A. Soboul, *The Sans-Culottes* (New York, 1972); R. R. Palmer, *Twelve Who Ruled* (New York, 1965); and R. Cobb, *The People's Armies* (London, 1987). For a biography of Robespierre, one of the leading figures of this period, see N. Hampson, *The Life and Opinions of Maximilien Robespierre* (London, 1974). The importance of the revolutionary wars in the radical stage of the Revolution is underscored in T. C. W. Blanning, *The French Revolutionary Wars, 1787–1802* (New York, 1996). The importance of the popular revolutionary crowds is examined in the classic work by G. Rudé, *The Crowd in the French Revolution* (Oxford, 1959); and D. Roche, *The People of Paris: An Essay in Popular Culture* (Berkeley, 1987). On the Directory, see M. Lyons, *France under the Directory* (Cambridge, 1975); and R. B. Rose, *Gracchus Babeuf* (Stanford, 1978).

The religious history of the French Revolution is covered in J. McManners, *The French Revolution and the Church* (London, 1969). On the Great Fear, there is the classic work by G. Lefebvre, *The Great Fear of 1789: Rural Panic in Revolutionary France* (London, 1973). On the role of women in revolutionary France, see O. Hufton, *Women and the Limits of Citizenship in the French Revolution* (Toronto, 1992); J. Landes, *Women and the Public Sphere in the Age of the French Revolution* (Ithaca, N.Y., 1988); and the essays in G. Fraisse and M. Perrot, eds., *A History of Women in the West*, vol. 4 (Cambridge, Mass., 1993). There is a good collection of essays in S. E. Melzer and L. Rabine, eds., *Rebel Daughters: Women and the French Revolution* (New York, 1992).

The best, brief biography of Napoleon is F. Markham, *Napoleon* (New York, 1963). Also valuable are G. J. Ellis,

Napoleon (New York, 1997); M. Lyons, *Napoleon Bonaparte and the Legacy of the French Revolution* (New York, 1994); and the recent massive biographies by F. J. McLynn, *Napoleon: A Biography* (London, 1997); and A. Schom, *Napoleon Bonaparte* (New York, 1997). On Napoleon's wars, see S. J. Woolf, *Napoleon's Integration of Europe* (New York, 1991).

A history of the revolutionary era in America can be found in R. Middlekauff, *The Glorious Cause: The American Revolution, 1763–1789* (New York, 1982); and C. Bonwick, *The American Revolution* (Charlottesville, Va., 1991). The importance of ideology is treated in G. Wood, *The Radicalism of the American Revolution* (New York, 1992). A comparative study that puts the American Revolution into a larger context is R. R. Palmer, *The Age of the Democratic Revolutions: A Political History of Europe and America, 1760–1800*, 2 vols. (Princeton, N.J., 1959–64).

For additional reading, go to InfoTrac College Edition, your online research library at http://web1.infotrac-college.com

Enter the search terms *French Revolution* using Key Terms.

Enter the search terms *American Revolution* using Key Terms.

Enter the search term *Napoleon* using Key Terms.

Enter the search terms *Napoleonic Wars* using Key Terms.

CHAPTER

20

The Industrial Revolution and Its Impact on European Society

CHAPTER OUTLINE

- The Industrial Revolution in Great Britain
- The Spread of Industrialization
- The Social Impact of the Industrial Revolution
- Conclusion

FOCUS QUESTIONS

- What conditions and developments coalesced in Great Britain to bring about the first Industrial Revolution?
- What were the basic features of the new industrial system created by the Industrial Revolution?
- How did the Industrial Revolution spread from Great Britain to the Continent and the United States, and how did industrialization in those areas differ from British industrialization?
- What effects did the Industrial Revolution have on urban life, social classes, family life, and standards of living?
- What were working conditions like in the early decades of the Industrial Revolution, and what efforts were made to improve them?

*T*HE FRENCH REVOLUTION dramatically and quickly altered the political structure of France, and the Napoleonic conquests spread many of the revolutionary principles in an equally rapid and stunning fashion to other parts of Europe. During the late eighteenth and early nineteenth centuries, another revolution—an industrial one— was transforming the economic and social structure of Europe, although in a less dramatic and rapid fashion.

The period of the Industrial Revolution witnessed a quantum leap in industrial production. New sources of energy and power, especially coal and steam, replaced wind and water to create labor-saving machines that dramatically decreased the use of human and animal labor and, at the same time, increased the level of productivity. In turn, power machinery called for new ways of organizing human labor to maximize the benefits and profits from the new machines; factories replaced shop and home workrooms. Many early factories were dreadful places with difficult working conditions. Reformers, appalled at these conditions, were especially critical of the treatment of married women.

One reported: "We have repeatedly seen married females, in the last stage of pregnancy, slaving from morning to night beside these never-tiring machines, and when . . . they were obliged to sit down to take a moment's ease, and being seen by the manager, were fined for the offense." But there were also examples of well-run factories. William Cobbett described one in Manchester in 1830: "In this room, which is lighted in the most convenient and beautiful manner, there were five hundred pairs of looms at work, and five hundred persons attending those looms; and, owing to the goodness of the masters, the whole looking healthy and well-dressed."

During the Industrial Revolution, Europe experienced a shift from a traditional, labor-intensive economy based on farming and handicrafts to a more capital-intensive economy based on manufacturing by machines, specialized labor, and industrial factories. Although the Industrial Revolution took decades to spread, it was truly revolutionary in the way it fundamentally changed Europeans, their society, and their relationship to other peoples. The development of large factories encouraged mass movements of people from the countryside to urban areas where impersonal coexistence replaced the traditional intimacy of rural life. Higher levels of productivity led to a search for new sources of raw materials, new consumption patterns, and a revolution in transportation that allowed raw materials and finished products to be moved quickly around the world. The creation of a wealthy industrial middle class and a huge industrial working class (or proletariat) substantially transformed traditional social relationships.

◆ The Industrial Revolution in Great Britain

Although the Industrial Revolution evolved out of antecedents that occurred over a long period of time, historians generally agree that it had its beginnings in Britain in the second half of the eighteenth century. By 1850, the Industrial Revolution had made Great Britain the wealthiest country in the world; by that time it had also spread to the European continent and the New World. By the end of the nineteenth century, both Germany and the United States would surpass Britain in industrial production.

✳ Origins

A number of factors or conditions coalesced in Britain to produce the first Industrial Revolution. One of these was the agricultural revolution of the eighteenth century. The changes in the methods of farming and stock breeding that characterized this agricultural transformation led to a significant increase in food production. British agriculture could now feed more people at lower prices with less labor. Unlike the rest of Europe, even ordinary British families did not have to use most of their income to buy food, giving them the potential to purchase manufactured goods. At the same time, a rapid growth of population in the second half of the eighteenth century provided a pool of surplus labor for the new factories of the emerging British industry. Rural workers in cottage industries also provided a potential labor force for industrial enterprises.

Britain had a ready supply of capital for investment in the new industrial machines and the factories that were needed to house them. In addition to profits from trade and cottage industry, Britain possessed an effective central bank and well-developed, flexible credit facilities. Nowhere in Europe were people so accustomed to using paper instruments to facilitate capital transactions. Many early factory owners were merchants and entrepreneurs who had profited from eighteenth-century cottage industry. Of 110 cotton spinning mills in operation in the area known as the Midlands between 1769 and 1800, 62 were established by hosiers, drapers, mercers, and others involved in some fashion in the cottage textile industry. But capital alone is only part of the story. Britain had a fair number of individuals who were interested in making profits if the opportunity presented itself (see the box on p. 585). The British were a people, as one historian has said, "fascinated by wealth and commerce, collectively and individually." These early industrial entrepreneurs faced considerable financial hazards, however. Fortunes were made quickly and lost just as quickly. The structure of early firms was open and fluid. An individual or family proprietorship was the usual mode of operation, but entrepreneurs also brought in friends to help them. They just as easily jettisoned them. John Marshall, who made money in flax spinning, threw out his partners: "As they could neither of them be of any further use, I released them from the firm and took the whole upon myself."[1]

Britain was richly supplied with important mineral resources, such as coal and iron ore, needed in the manufacturing process. Britain was also a small country, and the relatively short distances made transportation readily accessible. In addition to nature's provision of abundant rivers, from the mid-seventeenth century onward, both private and public investment poured into the construction of new roads, bridges, and, beginning in the 1750s and 1760s, canals. By 1780, roads, rivers, and canals linked the major industrial centers of the North, the Midlands, London, and the Atlantic. Unlike the continental countries, Britain had no internal customs barriers to hinder domestic trade.

Britain's government also played a significant role in the process of industrialization. Parliament contributed to the favorable business climate by providing a stable government and passing laws that protected private property. Moreover, Britain was remarkable for the freedom

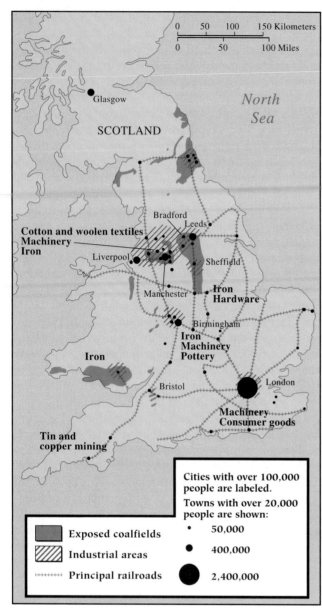

MAP 20.1 Britain in the Industrial Revolution.

it provided for private enterprise. It placed fewer restrictions on private entrepreneurs than any other European state.

Finally, a supply of markets gave British industrialists a ready outlet for their manufactured goods. British exports quadrupled from 1660 to 1760. In the course of its eighteenth-century wars and conquests, Great Britain had developed a vast colonial empire at the expense of its leading continental rivals, the Dutch Republic and France. Britain also possessed a well-developed merchant marine that was able to transport goods to any place in the world. A crucial factor in Britain's successful industrialization was the ability to produce cheaply those articles most in demand abroad. And the best markets abroad were not in Europe, where countries protected their own incipient industries, but in the Americas, Africa, and the East, where people wanted sturdy, inexpensive clothes rather than costly, highly finished, luxury items. Britain's machine-

produced textiles fulfilled that demand. Nor should we overlook the British domestic market. Britain had the highest standard of living in Europe and a rapidly growing population. As Daniel Defoe noted already in 1728:

> For the rest, we see their Houses and Lodgings tolerably furnished, at least stuff'd well with useful and necessary household Goods: Even those we call poor People, Journeymen, working and Pains-staking People do thus; they lye warm, live in Plenty, work hard, and [need] know no Want. These are the People that carry off the Gross of your Consumption; 'tis for these your Markets are kept open late on Saturday nights; because they usually receive their Week's Wages late . . . in a Word, these are the Life of our whole Commerce, and all by their Multitude: Their Numbers are not Hundreds or Thousands, or Hundreds of Thousands, but Millions; . . . by their Wages they are able to live plentifully, and it is by their expensive, generous, free way of living, that the Home Consumption is rais'd to such a Bulk, as well of our own, as of foreign Production.[2]

This demand from both domestic and foreign markets and the inability of the old system to fulfill it led entrepreneurs to seek and adopt the new methods of manufacturing that a series of inventions provided. In so doing, these individuals produced the Industrial Revolution.

❊ *Technological Changes and New Forms of Industrial Organization*

In the 1770s and 1780s, the cotton textile industry took the first major step toward the Industrial Revolution with the creation of the modern factory.

❧ THE COTTON INDUSTRY

Already in the eighteenth century, Great Britain had surged ahead in the production of cheap cotton goods using the traditional methods of cottage industry. The development of the flying shuttle had sped the process of weaving on a loom and enabled weavers to double their output. This created shortages of yarn, however, until James Hargreaves's spinning jenny, perfected by 1768, enabled spinners to produce yarn in greater quantities. Richard Arkwright's water frame spinning machine, powered by water or horse, and Samuel Crompton's so-called mule, which combined aspects of the water frame and spinning jenny, increased yarn production even more. Edmund Cartwright's power loom, invented in 1787, allowed the weaving of cloth to catch up with the spinning of yarn. Even then, early power looms were grossly inefficient, enabling cottage, hand-loom weavers to continue to prosper, at least until the mid-1820s. After that they were gradually replaced by the new machines. In 1813, there were 2,400 power looms in operation in Great Britain; they numbered 14,150 in 1820, 100,000 in 1833, and 250,000 by 1850. In the 1820s, there were still 250,000 hand-loom weavers in Britain; by 1860, only 3,000 were left.

The water frame, Crompton's mule, and power looms presented new opportunities to entrepreneurs. It was

The Traits of the British Industrial Entrepreneur

Richard Arkwright (1732–1792), inventor of a spinning frame and founder of cotton factories, was a good example of the successful entrepreneur in the early Industrial Revolution in Britain. In this selection, Edward Baines, who wrote The History of the Cotton Manufacture in Great Britain *in 1835, discusses the traits that explain the success of Arkwright and presumably other British entrepreneurs.*

Edward Baines, *The History of the Cotton Manufacture in Great Britain*

Richard Arkwright rose by the force of his natural talents from a very humble condition in society. He was born at Preston on the 23rd of December, 1732, of poor parents: being the youngest of thirteen children, his parents could only afford to give him an education of the humblest kind, and he was scarcely able to write. He was brought up to the trade of a barber at Kirkham and Preston, and established himself in that business at Bolton in the year 1760. Having become possessed of a chemical process for dyeing human hair, which in that day (when wigs were universal) was of considerable value, he traveled about collecting hair, and again disposing of it when dyed. In 1761, he married a wife from Leigh, and the connections he thus formed in that town are supposed to have afterwards brought him acquainted with Highs's experiments in making spinning machines. He himself manifested a strong bent for experiments in mathematics, which he is stated to have followed with so much devotedness as to have neglected his business and injured his circumstances. His natural disposition was ardent, enterprising, and stubbornly persevering: his mind was as coarse as it was bold and active, and his manners were rough and unpleasing. . . .

The most marked traits in the character of Arkwright were his wonderful ardor, energy, and perseverance. He commonly laboured in his multifarious concerns from five o'clock in the morning till nine at night; and when considerably more than fifty years of age,—feeling that the defects of his education placed him under great difficulty and inconvenience in conducting his correspondence, and in the general management of his business,—he encroached upon his sleep, in order to gain an hour each day to learn English grammar, and another hour to improve his writing and orthography [spelling]! He was impatient of whatever interfered with his favorite pursuits; and the fact is too strikingly characteristic not to be mentioned, that he separated from his wife not many years after their marriage, because she, convinced that he would starve his family [because of the impractical nature of his schemes], broke some of his experimental models of machinery. Arkwright was a severe economist of time; and, that he might not waste a moment, he generally traveled with four horses, and at a very rapid speed. His concerns in Derbyshire, Lancashire, and Scotland were so extensive and numerous, as to [show] at once his astonishing power of transacting business and his all grasping spirit. In many of these he had partners, but he generally managed in such a way, that, whoever lost, he himself was a gainer.

much more efficient to bring workers to the machines and organize their labor collectively in factories located next to rivers and streams, the sources of power for many of these early machines, than to leave the workers dispersed in their cottages. The concentration of labor in the new factories also brought the laborers and their families to live in the new towns that rapidly grew up around the factories.

The early devices used to speed up the processes of spinning and weaving were the products of weavers and spinners, in effect, of artisan tinkerers. But the subsequent expansion of the cotton industry and the ongoing demand for even more cotton goods created additional pressure for new and more complicated technology. The invention that pushed the cotton industry to even greater heights of productivity was the steam engine.

THE STEAM ENGINE

The invention of the steam engine played a major role in the Industrial Revolution. It revolutionized the production of cotton goods and caused the factory system to spread to other areas of production, thereby creating whole new industries. The steam engine secured the triumph of the Industrial Revolution.

As in much of the Industrial Revolution, one kind of change forced other changes. In many ways the steam engine was the result of the need for more efficient pumps to eliminate water seepage from deep mines. Deep coal mines were in turn the result of Britain's need and desire to find new sources of energy to replace wood. By the early eighteenth century, the British were acutely aware of a growing shortage of timber, which was used in heating, to build homes and ships, and in enormous quantities to produce the charcoal utilized in smelting iron ore to make pig iron. At the beginning of the eighteenth century, the discovery of new processes for smelting iron ore with coal and coke (see the next section) led to deeper and deeper mines for more intensive mining of coal. But as mines were dug below the water table, they filled with water. An early solution to the problem was the use of mechanical pumps powered by horses walking in circles. In one coal mine in Warwickshire, for example, 500 horses were used to lift the water from the mine, bucket by bucket. The need for more efficient pumps led Thomas Newcomen to develop a steam pump or, as it was called, an "atmospheric engine" that was first used in 1712. Though better than horses, it was still inefficient.

In the 1760s, a Scottish engineer, James Watt (1736–1819), was asked to repair a Newcomen engine. Instead he added a separate condenser and steam pump and transformed Newcomen's machine into a genuine steam engine. Power was derived not from air pressure as in Newcomen's atmospheric engine, but from steam itself. Much more efficient than a Newcomen engine, Watt's engine could pump water three times as quickly. Initially, it possessed one major liability, however; as a contemporary noted in 1778: "the vast consumption of fuel in these engines is an immense drawback on the profit of our mines, for every fire-engine of magnitude consumes £3000 worth of coals per annum. This heavy tax amounts almost to a prohibition."[3] As steam engines were made more efficient, however, they also became cheaper to use.

In 1782, James Watt enlarged the possibilities of the steam engine when he developed a rotary engine that could turn a shaft and thus drive machinery. Steam power could now be applied to spinning and weaving cotton, and before long cotton mills using steam engines were multiplying across Britain. By 1850, seven-eighths of the power available to the entire British cotton industry came from steam. Since steam engines were fired by coal, they did not need to be located near rivers; entrepreneurs now had greater flexibility in their choice of location.

The new boost given to cotton textile production by technological changes became readily apparent. In 1760, Britain had imported 2.5 million pounds of raw cotton, which was farmed out to cottage industries. All work was done by hand either in workers' homes or in the small shops of master weavers. In 1787, the British imported 22 million pounds of cotton; most of it was spun on machines, some powered by water in large mills. By 1840, 366 million pounds of cotton were imported annually, much of it from the American South where it was grown by plantation owners using slave labor. By this time, cotton cloth was Britain's most important product by value and was produced mainly in factories, although some hand-loom weavers still worked in their cottages. The price of yarn was but one-twentieth of what it had been. The cheapest labor in India could not compete in quality or quantity with Britain. British cotton goods sold everywhere in the world. And in Britain itself, cheap cotton cloth made it possible for millions of poor people to wear undergarments, long a preserve of the rich who alone could afford underwear made with expensive linen cloth. New work clothing that was tough, comfortable to the skin, and yet cheap and easily washable became common. Even the rich liked the colorful patterns of cotton prints and their light weight for summer use.

The steam engine proved invaluable to Britain's Industrial Revolution. In 1800, engines were generating 10,000 horsepower; by 1850, 500,000 horsepower were being generated by stationary engines and 790,000 by mobile engines, the last largely in locomotives (see the next section). Unlike horses, the steam engine was a tireless source of power and depended for fuel on a substance—namely, coal—that seemed then to be unlimited in quantity. The popular saying that "Steam is an Englishman" had real significance by 1850. The steam engine also replaced waterpower in such places as flour and sugar mills. Just as the need for more coal had helped lead to the steam engine, so the success of the steam engine increased the demand for coal and led to an expansion in coal production; between 1815 and 1850, the output of coal quadrupled. In turn, new processes using coal furthered the development of an iron industry.

✦ THE IRON INDUSTRY

The British iron industry was radically transformed during the Industrial Revolution. Britain had large resources of

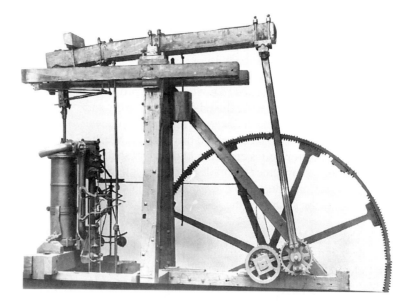

A BOULTON AND WATT STEAM ENGINE. Encouraged by his business partner, Matthew Boulton, James Watt developed the first genuine steam engine. Pictured here is a typical Boulton and Watt engine. Steam pressure in the cylinder on the left drives the beam upward and sets the flywheel in motion.

RAILROAD LINE FROM LIVERPOOL TO MANCHESTER. The railroad line from Liverpool to Manchester, first opened in 1830, relied on steam locomotives. As is evident in this illustration, carrying passengers was the railroad's main business. First-class passengers rode in covered cars; second- and third-class passengers in open cars.

iron ore, but at the beginning of the eighteenth century, the basic process of producing iron had altered little since the Middle Ages and still depended heavily on charcoal. In the early eighteenth century, new methods of smelting iron ore to produce cast iron were devised based on the use of coke derived from coal. Still, a better quality of iron was not possible until the 1780s when Henry Cort developed a system called puddling, in which coke was used to burn away impurities in pig iron to produce an iron of high quality. A boom then ensued in the British iron industry. In 1740, Britain produced 17,000 tons of iron; in the 1780s, almost 70,000 tons; by the 1840s, over two million tons; and by 1852, almost three million tons, more than the rest of the world combined.

The development of the iron industry was in many ways a response to the demand for the new machines. The high-quality wrought iron produced by the Cort process made it the most widely used metal until the production of cheaper steel in the 1860s. The growing supply of less costly metal encouraged the use of machinery in other industries, most noticeably in new means of transportation.

A REVOLUTION IN TRANSPORTATION

The eighteenth century had witnessed an expansion of transportation facilities in Britain as entrepreneurs realized the need for more efficient means of moving resources and goods. Turnpike trusts constructed new roads, and between 1760 and 1830 a network of canals was built. But both roads and canals were soon overtaken by a new form of transportation that dazzled people with its promise. To many economic historians, railroads were the "most important single factor in promoting European economic progress in the 1830s and 1840s." Again, Britain was the leader in the revolution.

The beginnings of railways can be found in mining operations in Germany as early as 1500 and in British coal mines after 1600 where small handcarts filled with coal were pushed along parallel wooden rails. The rails reduced friction, enabling horses to haul more substantial loads. By 1700, some entrepreneurs began to replace wooden rails with cast-iron rails, and by the early nineteenth century, railways—still dependent on horsepower—were common in British mining and industrial districts. The development of the steam engine led to a radical transformation of the railways.

In 1804, Richard Trevithick pioneered the first steam-powered locomotive on an industrial rail-line in south Wales. It pulled ten tons of ore and seventy people at five miles per hour. Better locomotives soon followed. The engines built by George Stephenson and his son proved superior, and it was in their workshops in Newcastle upon Tyne that the locomotives for the first modern railways in Britain were built. George Stephenson's *Rocket* was used on the first public railway line, which opened in 1830, extending thirty-two miles from Liverpool to Manchester. *Rocket* sped along at sixteen miles per hour. Within twenty years, locomotives had reached fifty miles per hour, an incredible speed to contemporary passengers. During the same period, new companies were formed to build additional railroads as the infant industry proved to be not only technically but financially successful. In 1840, Britain had almost 2,000 miles of railroads; by 1850, 6,000 miles of railroad track crisscrossed much of the country.

The railroad contributed significantly to the success and maturing of the Industrial Revolution. The railroad's demands for coal and iron furthered the growth of those industries. British supremacy in civil and mechanical engineering, so evident after 1840, was in large part based upon the skills acquired in railway building. The huge capital demands necessary for railway construction encouraged a whole new group of middle-class investors to invest their money in joint-stock companies (see Limitations to Industrialization later in this chapter). Railway construction created new job opportunities, especially for farm laborers and peasants who had long been accustomed to

OPENING OF THE ROYAL ALBERT BRIDGE. This painting by Thomas Roberts shows the ceremonies attending the official opening of the Royal Albert Bridge. I. K. Brunel, one of Britain's great engineers, designed this bridge, which carried a railroad line across the Tamar River into Cornwall. As is evident in the picture, the bridge was high enough to allow ships to pass underneath.

finding work outside their local villages. Perhaps most importantly, a cheaper and faster means of transportation had a rippling effect on the growth of an industrial economy. By reducing the price of goods, larger markets were created; increased sales necessitated more factories and more machinery, thereby reinforcing the self-sustaining nature of the Industrial Revolution, which marked a fundamental break with the traditional European economy. The great productivity of the Industrial Revolution enabled entrepreneurs to reinvest their profits in new capital equipment, further expanding the productive capacity of the economy. Continuous, even rapid, self-sustaining economic growth came to be seen as a fundamental characteristic of the new industrial economy.

The railroad was the perfect symbol of this aspect of the Industrial Revolution. The ability to transport goods and people at dramatic speeds also provided visible confirmation of a new sense of power. When railway engineers pierced mountains with tunnels and spanned chasms with breathtaking bridges, contemporaries experienced a sense of power over nature not felt before in Western civilization.

THE INDUSTRIAL FACTORY

Initially the product of the new cotton industry, the factory became the chief means of organizing labor for the new machines. As the workplace shifted from the artisan's shop and the peasant's cottage to the factory, the latter was not viewed as just a larger work unit. Employers hired workers who no longer owned the means of production but were simply paid wages to run the machines.

From its beginning, the factory system demanded a new type of discipline from its employees. Factory owners could not afford to let their expensive machinery stand idle. Workers were forced to work regular hours and in shifts to keep the machines producing at a steady pace for maximum output. This represented a massive adjustment for early factory laborers.

Preindustrial workers were not accustomed to a "timed" format. Agricultural laborers had always kept irregular hours; hectic work at harvest time might be followed by periods of inactivity. Even in the burgeoning cottage industry of the eighteenth century, weavers and spinners who worked at home might fulfill their weekly quotas by working around the clock for two or three days, followed by a leisurely pace until the next week's demands forced another work spurt.

Factory owners, therefore, faced a formidable task. They had to create a system of time-work discipline that would accustom employees to working regular, unvarying hours during which they performed a set number of tasks over and over again as efficiently as possible. One early industrialist said that his aim was "to make such machines of the men as cannot err." Such work, of course, tended to be repetitive and boring, and factory owners resorted to tough methods to accomplish their goals. Factory regulations were minute and detailed (see the box on p. 589). Adult workers were fined for a wide variety of minor infractions, such as being a few minutes late for work, and dismissed for more serious misdoings, especially drunkenness. The latter was viewed as particularly offensive because it set a bad example for younger workers and also courted disaster in the midst of dangerous machinery. Employers found that dismissals and fines worked well for adult employees; in a time when great population growth had produced large numbers of unskilled workers, dismissal could be disastrous. Children were less likely to understand the implications of dismissal so they were sometimes disciplined more directly—frequently by beating.

The efforts of factory owners in the early Industrial Revolution to impose a new set of values were frequently reinforced by the new evangelical churches. Methodism, in particular, emphasized that people reborn in Jesus must forgo immoderation and follow a disciplined path. Laziness and wasteful habits were sinful. The acceptance of

Discipline in the New Factories

Workers in the new factories of the Industrial Revolution had been accustomed to a lifestyle free of overseers. Unlike the cottages, where workers spun thread and wove cloth in their own rhythm and time, the factories demanded a new, rigorous discipline geared to the requirements of the machines. This selection is taken from a set of rules for a factory in Berlin in 1844. They were typical of company rules everywhere the factory system had been established.

❖ The Foundry and Engineering Works of the Royal Overseas Trading Company, Factory Rules

In every large works, and in the co-ordination of any large number of workmen, good order and harmony must be looked upon as the fundamentals of success, and therefore the following rules shall be strictly observed.

1. The normal working day begins at all seasons at 6 A.M. precisely and ends, after the usual break of half an hour for breakfast, an hour for dinner and half an hour for tea, at 7 P.M., and it shall be strictly observed. . . .

    Workers arriving 2 minutes late shall lose half an hour's wages; whoever is more than 2 minutes late may not start work until after the next break; or at least shall lose his wages until then. Any disputes about the correct time shall be settled by the clock mounted above the gatekeeper's lodge. . . .

3. No workman, whether employed by time or piece, may leave before the end of the working day, without having first received permission from the overseer and having given his name to the gatekeeper. Omission of these two actions shall lead to a fine of ten silver groschen [pennies] payable to the sick fund.

4. Repeated irregular arrival at work shall lead to dismissal. This shall also apply to those who are found idling by an official or overseer, and refused to obey their order to resume work. . . .

6. No worker may leave his place of work otherwise than for reasons connected with his work.

7. All conversation with fellow-workers is prohibited; if any worker requires information about his work, he must turn to the overseer, or to the particular fellow-worker designated for the purpose.

8. Smoking in the workshops or in the yard is prohibited during working hours; anyone caught smoking shall be fined five silver groschen for the sick fund for every such offense. . . .

10. Natural functions must be performed at the appropriate places, and whoever is found soiling walls, fences, squares, etc., and similarly, whoever is found washing his face and hands in the workshop and not in the places assigned for the purpose, shall be fined five silver groschen for the sick fund. . . .

12. It goes without saying that all overseers and officials of the firm shall be obeyed without question, and shall be treated with due deference. Disobedience will be punished by dismissal.

13. Immediate dismissal shall also be the fate of anyone found drunk in any of the workshops. . . .

14. Every workman is obliged to report to his superiors any acts of dishonesty or embezzlement on the part of his fellow workmen. If he omits to do so, and it is shown after subsequent discovery of a misdemeanor that he knew about it at the time, he shall be liable to be taken to court as an accessory after the fact and the wage due to him shall be retained as punishment.

hardship in this life paved the way for the joys of the next. Evangelical values paralleled the efforts of the new factory owners to instill laborers with their own middle-class values of hard work, discipline, and thrift. In one crucial sense, the early industrialists proved successful. As the nineteenth century progressed, the second and third generations of workers came to view a regular working week as a natural way of life. It was, of course, an attitude that made possible Britain's incredible economic growth in that century.

❖ The Great Exhibition: Britain in 1851

In 1851, the British organized the world's first industrial fair. It was housed at Kensington in London in the Crystal Palace, an enormous structure made entirely of glass and iron, a tribute to British engineering skills. Covering nineteen acres, the Crystal Palace contained 100,000 exhibits that showed the wide variety of products created by the Industrial Revolution. Six million people visited the fair in six months. Though most of them were Britons, who had traveled to London by train, foreign visitors were also prominent. The Great Exhibition displayed Britain's wealth to the world; it was a gigantic symbol of British success. Even trees were brought inside the Crystal Palace as a visible symbol of how the Industrial Revolution had achieved human domination over nature. Prince Albert, Queen Victoria's husband, expressed the sentiments of the age when he described the exhibition as a sign that "man is approaching a more complete

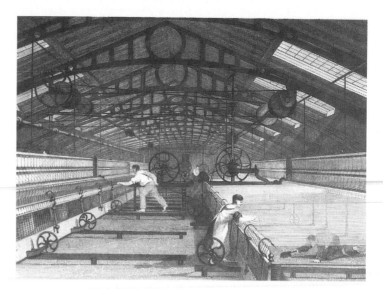

INSIDE AN EARLY COTTON FACTORY. The development of the factory changed the relationship between workers and employers as workers were encouraged to adjust to a new system of discipline that forced them to work regular hours and in shifts. This engraving depicts the interior of an early textile factory.

fulfillment of that great and sacred mission which he has to perform in this world . . . to conquer nature to his use." Not content with that, he also linked British success to divine will: "In promoting [the progress of the human race], we are accomplishing the will of the great and blessed God."[4]

By the year of the Great Exhibition, Great Britain had become the world's first and richest industrial nation. Britain was the "workshop, banker, and trader of the world." It produced one-half of the world's coal and manufactured goods; its cotton industry alone in 1851 was equal in size to the industries of all other European countries combined. The quantity of goods produced was growing at three times the growth rate in 1780. No doubt, Britain's certainty about its mission in the world in the nineteenth century was grounded in its incredible material success story.

◆ The Spread of Industrialization

Beginning first in Great Britain, industrialization spread to the continental countries of Europe and the United States at different times and speeds during the nineteenth century. First to be industrialized on the Continent were Belgium, France, and the German states and in North America, the new nation of the United States. Not until after 1850 did the Industrial Revolution spread to the rest of Europe and other parts of the world.

❋ Limitations to Industrialization

In 1815, Belgium, France, and the German states were still largely agrarian. During the eighteenth century, some of the continental countries had experienced developments similar to those of Britain. They, too, had achieved population growth, made agricultural improvements, expanded their cottage industries, and witnessed growth in foreign trade. But whereas Britain's economy began to move in new industrial directions in the 1770s and 1780s, continental countries lagged behind because they did not share some of the advantages that had made Britain's Industrial Revolution possible. Lack of good roads and problems with river transit made transportation difficult. Toll stations on important rivers and customs barriers along state boundaries increased the costs and prices of goods. Guild restrictions were also more prevalent, creating restrictions that pioneer industrialists in Britain did not have to face. Finally, continental entrepreneurs were generally less enterprising than their British counterparts and tended to adhere to traditional business attitudes, such as a dislike of competition, a high regard for family security coupled with an unwillingness to take risks in investment, and an excessive worship of thriftiness.

One additional factor also affected most of the Continent between 1790 and 1812: the upheavals associated with the wars of the French revolutionary and Napoleonic eras. Disruption of regular communications between Britain and the Continent made it difficult for continental countries to keep up with the new British technology. Moreover, the wars wreaked havoc with trade, caused much physical destruction and loss of manpower, weakened currencies, and led to political and social instability. Napoleon's Continental System helped to ruin a number of hitherto prosperous ports. The elimination of European markets for British textiles did temporarily revive the woolen industry in France and Belgium and stimulated textile manufacturing along the Rhine and in Silesia. After 1815, however, when cheap British goods again flooded European markets, the European textile industry suffered.

In the long run, the revolutionary and Napoleonic wars created an additional obstacle to rapid industrialization by widening the gap between British and continental industrial machinery. By 1815, after Napoleon had

THE CRYSTAL PALACE. The Great Exhibition, organized in 1851, was a symbol of the success of Great Britain, which had become the world's first and richest industrial nation. Over 100,000 exhibits were housed in the Crystal Palace, a giant structure of cast iron and glass. This illustration shows the front of the palace and some of its numerous visitors.

finally been defeated and normal communication between Britain and the Continent had been restored, British industrial equipment had grown larger and become more expensive. As a result, self-financed family enterprises were either unable or unwilling to raise the amount of capital necessary to modernize by investing in the latest equipment. Instead, most entrepreneurs in France, Belgium, and Germany initially chose to invest in used machines and less productive mills. Consequently, industrialization on the Continent faced numerous hurdles, and as it proceeded in earnest after 1815, it did so along lines that were somewhat different from Britain's.

Lack of technical knowledge was initially a major obstacle to industrialization. But the continental countries possessed an advantage here; they could simply borrow British techniques and practices. Of course, the British tried to prevent that. Until 1825, British artisans were prohibited from leaving the country; until 1842, the export of important machinery and machine parts, especially for textile production, was forbidden. Nevertheless, the British were not able to control this situation by legislation. Already by 1825, there were at least 2,000 skilled British mechanics on the Continent, and British equipment was also being sold abroad, whether legally or illegally.

Although many Britons who went abroad to sell their skills were simply skilled mechanics, a number of them were accomplished entrepreneurs who had managerial as well as technical skills. John Cockerill, for example, was an aggressive businessman who established a highly profitable industrial plant at Seraing near Liège in southern Belgium in 1817. Encouraged by the Belgian government, Cockerill thought nothing of pirating the innovations of other British industrialists to further his own factories. Aware of their importance, British technicians abroad were often contentious and arrogant, arousing the anger of continental industrialists. Fritz Harkort, who initiated the engineering industry in Germany, once exclaimed that he could scarcely wait for Germans to be trained "so that the Englishmen could all be whipped out: we must even now tread softly with them, for they're only too quick to speak of quitting if one does so little as not look at them in a friendly fashion."[5]

Gradually, the Continent achieved technological independence as local people learned all the skills their British teachers had to offer. By the 1840s, a new generation of skilled mechanics from Belgium and France was spreading their knowledge east and south, playing the same role that the British had earlier. More importantly, however, continental countries, especially France and the German states, began to establish a wide range of technical schools to train engineers and mechanics.

That government played an important role in this regard brings us to a second difference between British and continental industrialization. Governments in most of the continental countries were accustomed to playing a significant role in economic affairs. Furthering the development of industrialization was a logical extension of that attitude. Hence, governments provided for the costs of technical education; awarded grants to inventors and foreign entrepreneurs; exempted foreign industrial equipment from import duties; and, in some places, even financed factories. Of equal, if not greater importance in the long run, governments actively bore much of the cost of building roads and canals, deepening and widening river channels, and constructing railroads. By 1850, a network of iron rails had spread across Europe, although only Germany and Belgium had completed major parts of their systems by that time. Although European markets did not feel the real impact of the railroad until after 1850, railroad construction itself in the 1830s and 1840s gave great impetus to the metalworking and engineering industries.

Governments on the Continent also used tariffs to further industrialization. After 1815, cheap British goods flooded continental markets. The French responded with high tariffs to protect their fledgling industries. The most

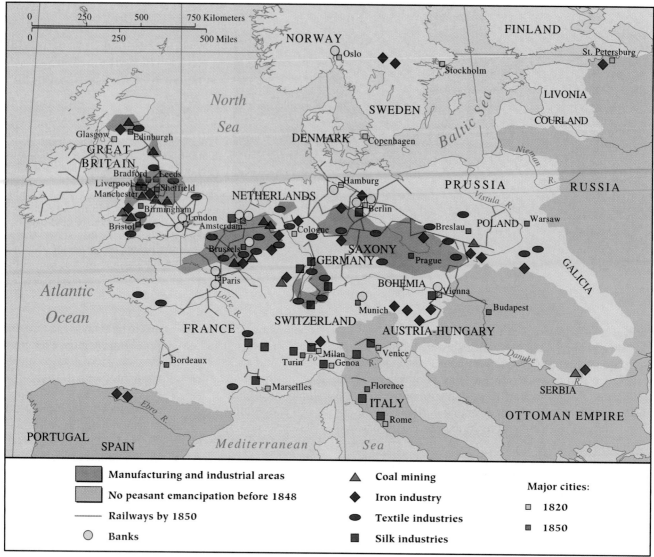

MAP 20.2 **The Industrialization of Europe by 1850.**

systematic exposition for the use of tariffs, however, was made by a German writer, Friedrich List (1789–1846), who emigrated to America and returned to Germany as a United States consul. In his *National System of Political Economy*, written in 1844, List advocated a rapid and large-scale program of industrialization as the surest path to develop a nation's strength. To assure that path to industrialization, he felt that a nation must use protective tariffs. If countries followed the British policy of free trade, then cheaper British goods would inundate national markets and destroy infant industries before they had a chance to grow. Germany, he insisted, could not compete with Britain without protective tariffs.

A third significant difference between British and continental industrialization was the role of the joint-stock investment bank on the Continent. Such banks mobilized the savings of thousands of small and large investors, creating a supply of capital that could then be plowed back into industry. Previously, continental banks had been

mostly merchant or private banks, but in the 1830s two Belgian banks, the Société Générale and the Banque de Belgique, took a new approach. By accepting savings from many depositors, they developed large capital resources that they invested on a large scale in railroads, mining, and heavy industry. These investments were especially important to the Belgian coal industry, which became the largest on the Continent in the 1840s. Shareholders in these joint-stock corporations had limited liability; they could only be held responsible for the amount of their investment.

Similar institutions emerged in France and German-speaking lands as well in the 1850s with the establishment of the Crédit Mobilier in France, the Darmstadt Bank in Germany, and the Kreditanstalt in Austria. They, too, took in savings of small investors and bought shares in the new industries. The French consul in Leipzig noted their significance: "Every town and state [in Germany]," he pointed out, "however small it may be, wants its bank and its Crédit Mobilier." These investments proved invaluable

THE SPREAD OF INDUSTRIALIZATION: FRENCH IRONWORKS.
Industrialization on the Continent lagged considerably
behind that of Great Britain. This 1800 engraving shows
the Manufacture Nationale, a small French ironworks
in Paris. Industrialization in France was a slow process
until the mid-nineteenth century.

to continental industrialization. By starting with less
expensive machines, the British had been able to indus-
trialize largely through the private capital of successful
individuals who reinvested their profits. On the Continent
advanced industrial machines necessitated large amounts
of capital; joint-stock industrial banks provided it.

✻ *Centers of Continental Industrialization*

The Industrial Revolution on the Continent occurred in
three major centers between 1815 and 1850—Belgium,
France, and the German states. Here, too, cotton played
an important role, although it was not as significant as
heavy industry. France was the continental leader in the
manufacture of cotton goods but still lagged far behind
Great Britain. In 1849, France used 64,000 tons of raw
cotton, Belgium, 11,000, and Germany, 20,000, whereas
Britain utilized 286,000 tons. Continental cotton factories were older, used less efficient machines, and had less
productive labor. In general, continental technology in
the cotton industry was a generation behind Great
Britain. But that is not the whole story. With its cheap
coal and scarce water, Belgium gravitated toward the use
of the steam engine as the major source of power and
invested in the new machines. By the mid-1840s, Belgium had the most modern cotton-manufacturing system
on the Continent.

The development of cotton manufacturing on the
Continent and in Britain differed in two significant ways.
Unlike Britain, where cotton manufacturing was mostly
centered in Lancashire (in northwestern England) and the
Glasgow area, cotton mills in France, Germany, and, to a
lesser degree, Belgium were dispersed through many
regions. Noticeable, too, was the mixture of old and new.
The old techniques of the cottage system, such as the use
of hand looms, held on much longer. In the French district
of Normandy, for example, in 1849 eighty-three mills were
still driven by hand or animal power.

As traditional methods persisted alongside the new
methods in cotton manufacturing, the new steam engine
came to be used primarily in mining and metallurgy on the
Continent rather than in textile manufacturing. At first,
almost all of the steam engines on the Continent came
from Britain; not until the 1820s was a domestic machine
industry developed.

In Britain, the Industrial Revolution had been built
upon the cotton industry; on the Continent, the iron and
coal of heavy industry led the way. As in textiles, however,
heavy industry on the Continent before 1850 was a mixture of old and new. The adoption of new techniques, such
as coke-smelted iron and puddling furnaces, coincided
with the expansion of old-type charcoal blast furnaces.
Before 1850, Germany lagged significantly behind both
Belgium and France in heavy industry, and most German
iron manufacturing remained based on old techniques.
Not until the 1840s was coke-blast iron produced in the
Rhineland. At that time, no one had yet realized the treasure of coal buried in the Ruhr valley. A German official
wrote in 1852 that "it is clearly not to be expected that Germany will ever be able to reach the level of production of
coal and iron currently attained in England. This is implicit
in our far more limited resource endowment." Little did he
realize that although the industrial development of continental Europe was about a generation behind Britain at

mid-century, after 1850 an incredibly rapid growth in continental industry would demonstrate that Britain was not, after all, destined to remain the world's greatest industrial nation.

※ *The Industrial Revolution in the United States*

In 1800, the United States was an agrarian society. There were no cities over 100,000, and six out of every seven American workers were farmers. By 1860, however, the population had grown from 5 to 30 million people, larger than Great Britain. Almost half of them lived west of the Appalachian Mountains. The number of states had more than doubled, from sixteen to thirty-four, and nine American cities had over 100,000 in population. Only 50 percent of American workers were farmers. Between 1800 and the eve of the Civil War, the United States had experienced an industrial revolution and the urbanization that accompanied it.

The initial application of machinery to production was accomplished—as in continental Europe—by borrowing from Great Britain. A British immigrant, Samuel Slater, established the first textile factory using water-powered spinning machines in Rhode Island in 1790. By 1813, factories with power looms copied from British versions were being established. Soon thereafter, however, Americans began to equal or surpass British technical inventions. The Harpers Ferry arsenal, for example, built muskets with interchangeable parts. Because all the individual parts of a musket were identical (for example, all triggers were the same), the final product could be put together quickly and easily; this enabled Americans to avoid the more costly system in which skilled workers fitted together individual parts made separately. The so-called American system reduced costs and revolutionized production by saving labor, important to a society that had few skilled artisans.

Unlike Britain, the United States was a large country. The lack of a good system of internal transportation seemed to limit American economic development by making the transport of goods prohibitively expensive. This deficiency was gradually remedied, however. Thousands of miles of roads and canals were built linking east and west. The steamboat facilitated transportation on the Great Lakes, Atlantic coastal waters, and rivers. It was especially important to the Mississippi valley; by 1860, 1,000 steamboats plied that river (see the box on p. 595). Most important of all in the development of an American transportation system was the railroad. Beginning with 100 miles in 1830, by 1860 more than 27,000 miles of railroad track covered the United States. This transportation revolution turned the United States into a single massive market for the manufactured goods of the Northeast, the early center of American industrialization.

Labor for the growing number of factories in this area came primarily from rural New England. The United States did not possess a large number of craftspeople, but it did have a rapidly expanding farm population; its size in the Northeast soon outstripped the available farmland. While some of this excess population, especially men, went west, others, mostly women, found work in the new textile and shoe factories of New England. Indeed, women made up more than 80 percent of the laboring force in the large textile factories. In Massachusetts mill towns, company boarding houses provided rooms for large numbers of young women who worked for several years before marriage. Outside Massachusetts, factory owners sought entire families including children to work in their mills; one mill owner ran this advertisement in a newspaper in Utica, New York: "Wanted: A few sober and industrious families of at least five children each, over the age of eight years, are wanted at the Cotton Factory in Whitestown. Widows with large families would do well to attend this notice." When a decline in rural births threatened to dry up this labor pool in the 1830s and 1840s, European immigrants, especially poor and unskilled Irish, English, Scottish, and Welsh, appeared in large numbers to replace American women and children in the factories.

Women, children, and these immigrants had one thing in common as employees; they were largely unskilled laborers. Unskilled labor pushed American industrialization into a capital-intensive pattern. Factory owners invested heavily in machines that could produce in quantity at the hands of untrained workers. In Britain, the pace of mechanization was never as rapid because Britain's supply of skilled artisans made it more profitable to pursue a labor-intensive economy.

By 1860, the United States was well on its way to being an industrial nation. In the Northeast, the most industrialized section of the country, per capita income was 40 percent higher than the national average. Diets, it has been argued, were better and more varied; machine-made clothing was more abundant. Industrialization did not necessarily lessen economic disparities, however. Despite a growing belief in a myth of social mobility based upon equality of economic opportunity, the reality was that the richest 10 percent of the population in the cities held 70 to 80 percent of the wealth compared to 50 percent in 1800. Nevertheless, American historians generally argue that while the rich got richer, the poor, thanks to an increase in their purchasing power, did not get poorer.

◆ The Social Impact of the Industrial Revolution

Eventually, the Industrial Revolution revolutionized the social life of Europe and the world. Although much of Europe remained bound by its traditional ways, already in the first half of the nineteenth century, the social impact

"S–т–e–a–ϣ–boaт a–coϣinɢ!"

Steamboats and railroads were crucial elements in a transportation revolution that enabled industrialists to expand markets by shipping goods cheaply and efficiently. At the same time, these marvels of technology aroused a sense of power and excitement that was an important aspect of the triumph of industrialization. The American novelist Mark Twain captured this sense of excitement in this selection from Life on the Mississippi.

❋ Mark Twain, *Life on the Mississippi*

After all these years I can picture that old time to myself now, just as it was then: the white town drowsing in the sunshine of a summer's morning; the streets empty, or pretty nearly so; one or two clerks sitting in front of the Water street stores, with their splint-bottomed chairs tilted back against the walls, chins on breasts, hats slouched over their faces, asleep; . . . two or three lonely little freight piles scattered about the "levee"; a pile of "skids" on the slope of the stone-paved wharf, and the fragrant town drunkard asleep in the shadow of them; . . . the great Mississippi, the majestic, the magnificent Mississippi, rolling its mile-wide along, shining in the sun; the dense forest away on the other side; the "point" above the town, and the "point" below, bounding the river glimpse and turning it into a sort of sea, and withal a very still and brilliant and lonely one. Presently a film of dark smoke appears above on those remote "points"; instantly a negro drayman, famous for his quick eye and prodigious voice, lifts up to cry, "S–т–e–a–m–boat a–coming!" and the scene changes! The town drunkard stirs, the clerks wake up, a furious clatter of drays follows, every house and store pours out a human contribution, and all in a twinkling the dead town [Hannibal, Missouri] is alive and moving. Drays, carts, men, boys, all go hurrying from many quarters to a common center, the wharf. Assembled there, the people fasten their eyes upon the coming boat as upon a wonder they are seeing for the first time. And the boat is rather a handsome sight, too. She is long and sharp and trim and pretty; she has two tall, fancy-topped chimneys, with a gilded device of some kind swung between them; a fanciful pilot-house, all glass and "ginger bread," perched on top of the "texas" deck behind them; the paddle-boxes are gorgeous with a picture or with gilded rays above the boat's name; the boiler deck, the hurricane deck, and the texas deck are fenced and ornamented with clean white railings; there is a flag gallantly flying from the jack-staff; the furnace doors are open and the fires glaring bravely; the upper decks are black with passengers; the captain stands by the big bell, calm, imposing, the envy of all; great volumes of the blackest smoke are rolling and tumbling out of the chimneys—a husbanded grandeur created with a bit of pitch pine just before arriving at a town; the crew are grouped on the forecastle; the broad stage is run far out over the port bow, and an envied deck-hand stands picturesquely on the end of it with a coil of rope in his hand; the pent steam is screaming through the gaugecocks; the captain lifts his hand, a bell rings, the wheels stop; then they turn back, churning the water to foam, and the steam is at rest. Then such a scramble as there is to get aboard, and to get ashore, and to take in freight and discharge freight, all at one and the same time; and such a yelling and cursing as the mates facilitate it all with! Ten minutes later the steamer is under way again, with no flag on the jack-staff and no black smoke issuing from the chimneys. After ten more minutes the town is dead again, and the town drunkard asleep by the skids once more.

---

of the Industrial Revolution was being felt, and future avenues of growth were becoming apparent. Vast changes in the number of people and where they lived were already dramatically evident.

❋ Population Growth

Population increases had already begun in the eighteenth century, but they became dramatic in the nineteenth century. They were also easier to discern because record keeping became more accurate. In the nineteenth century, governments began to take periodic censuses and systematically collect precise data on births, deaths, and marriages. In Britain, for example, the first census was taken in 1801, and a systematic registration of births, deaths, and marriages was begun in 1836. In 1750, the total European population stood at an estimated 140 million; by 1800, it had increased to 187 million and by 1850 to 266 million, almost twice its 1750 level.

This population explosion cannot be explained by a higher birthrate for birthrates were declining after 1790. Between 1790 and 1850, Germany's birthrate dropped from 40 per 1,000 to 36.1; Great Britain's from 35.4 to 32.6, and France's from 32.5 to 26.7. The key to the expansion of population was the decline in death rates evident throughout Europe. Historians now believe that two major causes explain this decline. There was a drop in the number of deaths from famines, epidemics, and war. Major epidemic diseases, in particular, such as plague and smallpox declined noticeably, although small-scale epidemics continued. The ordinary death rate also declined as a general increase in the food supply, already evident in the

---

The Great Irish Famine

The Great Irish Famine was one of the nineteenth century's worst natural catastrophes. Overly dependent on a single crop, the Irish were decimated by the potato blight. In this selection, an Irish nationalist reported what he had witnessed in Galway in 1847.

�֎ John Mitchel, *The Last Conquest of Ireland*

In the depth of winter we traveled to Galway, through the very center of that fertile island, and saw sights that will never wholly leave the eyes that beheld them—cowering wretches, almost naked in the savage weather, prowling in turnip-fields, and endeavoring to grub up roots which had been left, but running to hide as the mail-coach rolled by;—very large fields where small farms had been "consolidated," showing dark bars of fresh mold running through them where the ditches had been leveled;—groups and families, sitting or wandering on the high-road, with failing steps and dim patient eyes, gazing hopelessly into infinite darkness; before them, around them, above them, nothing but darkness and despair—parties of tall brawny men, once the flower of Meath and Galway, stalking by with a fierce but vacant scowl; as if they knew that all this ought not to be, but knew not whom to blame, saw none whom they could rend in their wrath. . . . Around those farmhouses which were still inhabited were to be seen hardly any stacks of grain; the poor-rate collector, the rent agent, the county-cess collector had carried it off; and sometimes I could see in front of the cottages little children leaning against a fence when the sun shone out—for they could not stand—their limbs fleshless, their bodies half naked, their faces bloated yet wrinkled, and of a pale greenish hue,—children who would never, it was too plain, grow up to be men and women.

---

agricultural revolution of Britain in the late eighteenth century, spread to more areas. More food enabled a greater number of people to be better fed and therefore more resistant to disease. Famine largely disappeared from western Europe, although there were dramatic exceptions in isolated areas, Ireland being the most significant.

Although industrialization itself did not cause population growth, industrialized areas did experience a change in the composition of the population. By 1850, the proportion of the active population involved in manufacturing, mining, or building had risen to 48 percent in Britain, 37 percent in Belgium, and 27 percent in France. But the actual areas of industrialization in 1850 were minimal, being concentrated in northern and central England, northern France, Belgium, and sections of western and eastern Germany. As one author has commented, "they were islands in an agricultural sea."

This minimal industrialization, in light of the growing population, meant severe congestion in the countryside where a growing population divided the same amount of land into ever-smaller plots and also created an ever-larger mass of landless peasants. Overpopulation, especially noticeable in parts of France, northern Spain, southern Germany, Sweden, and Ireland, magnified the already existing problem of rural poverty. In Ireland, it produced the century's greatest catastrophe.

✺ THE GREAT HUNGER

Ireland was one of the most oppressed areas in western Europe. The predominantly Catholic peasant population rented land from mostly absentee British Protestant landlords whose primary concern was collecting their rents. Irish peasants lived in mud hovels in desperate poverty. The cultivation of the potato, a nutritious and relatively easy food to grow that produced three times as much food per acre as grain, gave Irish peasants a basic staple that enabled them to survive and even expand in numbers. As only an acre or two of potatoes was sufficient to feed a family, Irish men and women married earlier than elsewhere and started having children earlier as well. This led to significant growth in the population. Between 1781 and 1845, the Irish population doubled from four to eight million. Probably half of this population depended on the potato for survival. In the summer of 1845, the potato crop in Ireland was struck by blight due to a fungus that turned the potatoes black. Between 1845 and 1851, the Great Famine decimated the Irish population (see the box above). Over one million died of starvation and disease, and almost two million emigrated to the United States and Britain. Of all the European nations, only Ireland had a declining population in the nineteenth century. But other countries, too, faced problems of dire poverty and declining standards of living as their populations exploded.

The flight of so many Irish to America reminds us that the traditional safety valve for overpopulation has always been emigration. Between 1821 and 1850, the number of emigrants from Europe averaged about 110,000 a year. Most of these emigrants came from places like Ireland and southern Germany, where peasant life had been reduced to marginal existence. Times of agrarian crisis resulted in great waves of emigration. Bad harvests in Europe in 1846–1847 (such as the catastrophe in Ireland) produced massive numbers of emigrants. In addition to the estimated 1.6 million from Ireland, for example, 935,000 people left Germany between 1847 and 1854. More often than emigrating, however, the rural masses sought a solution to their poverty by moving to towns and cities within their own countries to find work. It should not astonish us, then, that the first half of the nineteenth century was a period of rapid urbanization.

✸ The Growth of Cities

Although the Western world would not become a predominantly urban society until the twentieth century, cities and towns had already grown dramatically in the first half of the nineteenth century, a phenomenon related to industrialization. Cities had traditionally been centers for princely courts, government and military offices, churches, and commerce. By 1850, especially in Great Britain and Belgium, they were rapidly becoming places for manufacturing and industry. With the steam engine, entrepreneurs could locate their manufacturing plants in urban centers where they had ready access to transportation facilities and unemployed people from the country looking for work.

In 1800, Great Britain had one major city, London, with a population of 1 million, and six cities between 50,000 and 100,000. Fifty years later, London's population had swelled to 2,363,000, and there were nine cities over 100,000 and eighteen cities with populations between 50,000 and 100,000. All together, these twenty-eight cities accounted for 5.7 million or one-fifth of the total British population. When the populations of cities under 50,000 are added to this total, we realize that more than 50 percent of the British population lived in towns and cities by 1850. Britain was forced to become a food importer rather than an exporter as the number of people involved in agriculture declined to 20 percent of the population.

Urban populations also grew on the Continent, but less dramatically. Paris had 547,000 inhabitants in 1800, but only two other French cities had populations of 100,000: Lyons and Marseilles. In 1851, Paris had grown to 1 million while Lyons and Marseilles were still under 200,000. German and Austrian lands had only three cities with over 100,000 inhabitants (Vienna had 247,000) in 1800; fifty years later, there were only five, but Vienna had grown to 440,000. As these figures show, urbanization did not proceed as rapidly here as in Britain; of course, neither had industrialization. Even in Belgium, the most heavily industrialized country on the Continent, almost 50 percent of the male workforce was still engaged in agriculture by midcentury.

❧ URBAN LIVING CONDITIONS IN THE EARLY INDUSTRIAL REVOLUTION

The dramatic growth of cities in the first half of the nineteenth century produced miserable living conditions for many of the inhabitants. Of course, the quality of life had been poor for centuries for many people in European cities, but the rapid urbanization associated with the Industrial Revolution intensified the problems in the first half of the nineteenth century and made these wretched conditions all the more apparent. City authorities of whatever kind either felt little responsibility for these conditions or more frequently did not have the skills to cope with the complex, new problems associated with such rapidly growing populations. City authorities might also often be fac-

A NEW INDUSTRIAL TOWN. Cities and towns grew dramatically in Britain in the first half of the nineteenth century, largely as a result of industrialization. Pictured here is Saltaire, a model textile factory and town founded near Bradford by Titus Salt in 1851. To facilitate the transportation of goods, the town was built on the Leeds and Liverpool canals.

tory owners who possessed little or no tradition of public service or public responsibility.

Wealthy, middle-class inhabitants, as usual, insulated themselves as best they could, often living in suburbs or the outer ring of the city where they could have individual houses and gardens. In the inner ring of the city stood the small row houses, some with gardens, of the artisans and lower middle class. Finally, located in the center of most industrial towns were the row houses of the industrial workers. This report on working-class housing in the British city of Birmingham in 1843 gives an idea of the general conditions they faced:

> The courts [of working-class row houses] are extremely numerous; . . . a very large portion of the poorer classes of the inhabitants reside in them. . . . The courts vary in the number of the houses which they contain, from four to twenty, and most of these houses are three stories high, and built, as it is termed, back to back. There is a wash-house, an ash-pit, and a privy at the end, or on one side of the court, and not unfrequently one or more pigsties and heaps of manure. Generally speaking, the privies in the old courts are in a most filthy condition. Many which we have inspected were in a state which renders it impossible for us to conceive how they could be used; they were without doors and overflowing with filth.

The people who lived in such houses were actually the fortunate; the truly unfortunate were those forced to live in cellars. One reformer asked, "How can a hole underground of from 12 to 15 feet square admit of ventilation so as to fit it for a human habitation?" Rooms were not large and were frequently overcrowded, as this government report of 1838 revealed: "I entered several of the tenements. In one of them, on the ground floor, I found six persons occupying a very small room, two in bed, ill with fever. In the room above this were two more persons in one bed ill with fever." Another report said: "There were

63 families where there were at least five persons to one bed; and there were some in which even six were packed in one bed, lying at the top and bottom—children and adults."[6]

Sanitary conditions in these towns were appalling. Due to the lack of municipal direction, city streets were often used as sewers and open drains: "In the center of this street is a gutter, into which potato parings, the refuse of animal and vegetable matters of all kinds, the dirty water from the washing of clothes and of the houses, are all poured, and there they stagnate and putrefy."[7] Unable to deal with human excrement, cities in the new industrial era smelled horrible and were extraordinarily unhealthy. Towns and cities were fundamentally death traps. As deaths outnumbered births in most large cities in the first half of the nineteenth century, only a constant influx of people from the country kept them alive and growing.

Adding to the deterioration of urban life was the adulteration of food. Consumers were defrauded in a variety of ways: alum was added to make bread look white and hence more expensive; beer and milk were watered down; and red lead despite its poisonous qualities was substituted for pepper. The government refused to intervene; a parliamentary committee stated that "more benefit is likely to result from the effects of a free competition . . . than can be expected to result from any regulations." It was not until 1875 that an effective Food and Drugs Act was passed in Britain.

Our knowledge of the pathetic conditions in the early industrial cities is largely derived from an abundance of social investigations. Such investigations began in France in the 1820s. In Britain the Poor Law Commissioners produced detailed reports. The investigators were often struck by the physically and morally debilitating effects of urban industrial life on the poor. They observed, for example, that young working-class men were considerably shorter and scrawnier than the sons of middle-class families and much more subject to disease. They were especially alarmed by what they considered the moral consequences of such living conditions: prostitution, crime, and sexual immoralities, all of which they saw as the effect of such squalid lives.

To many of the well-to-do middle classes, this situation presented a clear danger to society. Were not these masses of workers, sunk in crime, disease, and immorality, a potential threat to their own well-being? Might not the masses be organized and used by unscrupulous demagogues to overthrow the established order? One of the most eloquent British reformers of the 1830s and 1840s, James Kay-Shuttleworth, described them as "volcanic elements, by whose explosive violence the structure of society may be destroyed." Another observer spoke more contemptuously in 1850:

> They live precisely like brutes, to gratify . . . the appetites of their uncultivated bodies, and then die, to go they have never thought, cared, or wondered whither. . . . Brought up in the darkness of barbarism, they have no idea that it is possible for them to attain any higher condition; they are not even sentient enough to desire to change their situation. . . . they eat, drink, breed, work and die; and . . . the richer and more intelligent classes are obliged to guard them with police.[8]

SLUMS OF INDUSTRIAL LONDON. Industrialization and rapid urban growth produced dreadful living conditions in many nineteenth-century cities. Filled with garbage and human waste, cities often smelled terrible and were extremely unhealthy. This drawing by Gustave Doré shows a London slum district overshadowed by rail viaducts.

Some observers were less arrogant, however, and wondered if the workers could be held responsible for their fate.

One of the best of a new breed of urban reformers was Edwin Chadwick (1800–1890). With a background in law, Chadwick became obsessed with eliminating the poverty and squalor of the metropolitan areas. He became a civil servant and was soon appointed to a number of government investigatory commissions. As secretary of the Poor Law Commission, he initiated a passionate search for detailed facts about the living conditions of the working classes. After three years of investigation, Chadwick summarized the results in his *Report on the Condition of the Labouring Population of Great Britain*, published in 1842. In it he concluded that "the various forms of epidemic, endemic, and other disease" were directly caused by the "atmospheric impurities produced by decomposing animal and vegetable substances, by damp and filth, and close overcrowded dwellings [prevailing] amongst the population in every part of the kingdom." Such conditions, he argued, could be eliminated. As to the means: "The primary and most important measures, and at the same time the most practicable, and within the recognized province of public administration, are drainage, the removal of all refuse of habitations, streets, and roads, and the improvement of the supplies of water."[9] In other words, Chadwick was advocating a system of modern sanitary reforms consisting of efficient sewers and a supply of piped water. Six years after his report and largely due to his efforts, Britain's first Public Health Act created a National Board of Health empowered to form local boards that would establish modern sanitary systems.

Many middle-class citizens were quite willing to support the public health reforms of men like Chadwick because of their fear of cholera. Outbreaks of this deadly disease had ravaged Europe in the early 1830s and late 1840s and were especially rampant in the overcrowded cities. As city authorities and wealthier residents became convinced that filthy conditions helped to spread the disease, they began to support the call for new public health measures.

❈ New Social Classes: The Industrial Middle Class

The rise of industrial capitalism produced a new middle-class group. The bourgeois or middle class was not new; it had existed since the emergence of cities in the Middle Ages. Originally, the bourgeois was the burgher or town dweller, whether active as a merchant, official, artisan, lawyer, or scholar, who enjoyed a special set of rights from the charter of the town. As wealthy townspeople bought land, the original meaning of the word *bourgeois* became lost, and the term came to include people involved in commerce, industry, and banking as well as professionals, such as lawyers, teachers, physicians, and government officials at various levels. At the lower end of the economic scale were master craftspeople and shopkeepers.

Lest we make the industrial middle class too much of an abstraction, we need to look at who the new industrial entrepreneurs actually were. These were the people who constructed the factories, purchased the machines, and figured out where the markets were. Their qualities included resourcefulness, single-mindedness, resolution, initiative, vision, ambition, and often, of course, greed. As Jedediah Strutt, the cotton manufacturer said, "Getting of money . . . is the main business of the life of men."

But this was not an easy task. The early industrial entrepreneurs were called upon to superintend an enormous array of functions that are handled today by teams of managers; they raised capital, determined markets, set company objectives, organized the factory and its labor, and trained supervisors who could act for them. The opportunities for making money were great, but the risks were also tremendous. The cotton trade, for example, which was so important to the early Industrial Revolution, was intensely competitive. Only through constant expansion could one feel secure, so early entrepreneurs reinvested most of their initial profits. Fear of bankruptcy was constant, especially among small firms. Furthermore, most early industrial enterprises were small. Even by the 1840s, only 10 percent of British industrial firms employed more than 5,000 workers; 43 percent had fewer than 100 workers. As entrepreneurs went bankrupt, new people could enter the race for profits, especially since the initial outlay required was not gigantic. In 1816, only one mill in five in the important industrial city of Manchester was in the hands of its original owners.

The social origins of industrial entrepreneurs were incredibly diverse. Many of the most successful came from a mercantile background. Three London merchants, for example, founded a successful ironworks in Wales that owned eight steam engines and employed 5,000 men. In Britain, land and domestic industry were often interdependent. Joshua Fielden, for example, acquired sufficient capital to establish a factory by running a family sheep farm while working looms in the farmhouse. Intelligent, clever, and ambitious apprentices who had learned their trades well could also strike it rich. William Radcliffe's family engaged in agriculture and spinning and weaving at home; he learned quickly how to succeed:

> Availing myself of the improvements that came out while I was in my teens . . . with my little savings and a practical knowledge of every process from the cotton bag to the piece of cloth . . . I was ready to commence business for myself and by the year 1789 I was well established and employed many hands both in spinning and weaving as a master manufacturer.[10]

By 1801, Radcliffe was operating a factory employing 1,000 workers.

Members of dissenting religious minorities were often prominent among the early industrial leaders of Britain. The Darbys and Lloyds who were iron manufacturers, the Barclays and Lloyds who were bankers, and the Trumans and Perkins who were brewers were all Quakers. These were expensive trades and depended upon the financial support that co-religionists in religious minorities provided for each other. Most historians believe that a major reason members of these religious minorities were so prominent in business was that they lacked other opportunities. Legally excluded from many public offices, they directed their ambitions into the new industrial capitalism.

It is interesting to note that in Britain in particular aristocrats also became entrepreneurs. The Lambtons in Northumberland, the Curwens in Cumberland, the Norfolks in Yorkshire, and the Dudleys in Staffordshire all invested in mining enterprises. This close relationship between land and industry helped Britain to assume the leadership role in the early Industrial Revolution.

By 1850, in Britain at least, the kind of traditional entrepreneurship that had created the Industrial Revolution was declining and was being replaced by a new business aristocracy. This new generation of entrepreneurs stemmed from the professional and industrial middle classes, especially as sons inherited the successful businesses established by their fathers. It must not be forgotten, however, that even after 1850 a large number of small businesses existed in Britain and some were still founded by people from humble backgrounds. Indeed, the age of large-scale corporate capitalism did not begin until the 1890s (see Chapter 23).

Increasingly, the new industrial entrepreneurs—the bankers and owners of factories and mines—came to amass much wealth and play an important role alongside the traditional landed elites of their societies. The Industrial Revolution began at a time when the pre-industrial agrarian world was still largely dominated by landed elites. As the new bourgeoisie bought great estates and acquired social respectability, they also sought political power, and in the course of the nineteenth century, their wealthiest members would merge with those old elites.

✳ New Social Classes: Workers in the Industrial Age

At the same time the members of the industrial middle class were seeking to reduce the barriers between themselves and the landed elite, they also were trying to separate themselves from the laboring classes below them. The working class was actually a mixture of different groups in the first half of the nineteenth century. In the course of the nineteenth century, factory workers would form an industrial proletariat, but in the first half of that century, they by no means constituted a majority of the working class in any major city, even in Britain. According to the 1851 census in Britain, there were 1.8 million agricultural laborers and 1 million domestic servants, but only 811,000 workers in the cotton and woolen industries. Even one-third of these were still working in small workshops or in their own homes.

Within the cities, artisans or craftspeople remained the largest group of urban workers during the first half of the nineteenth century. They worked in numerous small industries, such as shoemaking, glovemaking, bookbinding, printing, and bricklaying. Some craftspeople formed a kind of aristocracy of labor, especially those employed in such luxury trades as coachbuilding and clockmaking who earned higher wages than others. Artisans were not factory workers; they were traditionally organized in guilds where they passed on their skills to apprentices. But guilds were increasingly losing their power, especially in industrialized countries. Fearful of losing out to the new factories that could produce goods more cheaply, artisans tended to support movements against industrialization. Industrialists welcomed the decline of skilled craftspeople, as one perceptive old tailor realized in telling his life story:

> It is upwards of 30 years since I first went to work at the tailoring trade in London. . . . I continued working for the honorable trade and belonging to the Society [for tailors] for about 15 years. My weekly earnings then averaged £1 16s. a week while I was at work, and for several years I was seldom out of work . . . no one could have been happier than I was. . . . But then, with my sight defective . . . I could get no employment at the honorable trade, and that was the ruin of me entirely; for working there, of course, I got "scratched" from the trade society, and so lost all hope of being provided for by them in my helplessness. The workshop . . . was about seven feet square, and so low, that as you [sat] on the floor you could touch the ceiling with the tip of your finger. In this place seven of us worked. [The master] paid little more than half the regular wages, and employed such men as myself—only those who couldn't get anything better to do. . . . I don't think my wages there averaged above 12s. a week. . . . I am convinced I lost my eyesight by working in that cheap shop. . . . It is by the ruin of such men as me that these masters are enabled to undersell the better shops. . . . That's the way, sir, the cheap clothes is produced, by making blind beggars of the workmen, like myself, and throwing us on the parish in our old age.[11]

Servants also formed another large group of urban workers, especially in major cities like London and Paris. Many were women from the countryside who became utterly dependent upon their upper- and middle-class employers.

✍ WORKING CONDITIONS FOR THE INDUSTRIAL WORKING CLASS

Workers in the new industrial factories also faced wretched working conditions. We have already observed the psychological traumas workers experienced from their employers' efforts to break old preindustrial work patterns and create a well-disciplined labor force. But what were the physical conditions of the factories?

Unquestionably, in the early decades of the Industrial Revolution, "places of work," as early factories were called, were dreadful. Work hours ranged from twelve to sixteen hours a day, six days a week, with a half hour for lunch and dinner. There was no security of employment and no minimum wage. The worst conditions were in the cotton mills where temperatures were especially debilitating. One report noted that "in the cotton-spinning work, these creatures are kept, fourteen hours in each day, locked up, summer and winter, in a heat of from eighty to eighty-four degrees." Mills were also dirty, dusty, and unhealthy:

> Not only is there not a breath of sweet air in these truly infernal scenes, but . . . there is the abominable and pernicious stink of the gas to assist in the murderous effects of the heat. In addition to the noxious effluvia of the gas, mixed with the steam, there are the dust, and what is called cotton-flyings or fuz, which the unfortunate creatures have to inhale; and . . . the notorious fact is that well constitutioned men are rendered old and past labor at forty years of age, and that children are rendered decrepit and deformed, and thousands upon thousands of them slaughtered by consumptions, before they arrive at the age of sixteen.[12]

Thus ran a report on working conditions in the cotton industry in 1824.

Conditions in the coal mines were also harsh. The introduction of steam power meant only that steam-powered engines mechanically lifted coal to the top. Inside the mines, men still bore the burden of digging the coal out while horses, mules, women, and children hauled coal carts on rails to the lift. Dangers abounded in coal mines; cave-ins, explosions, and gas fumes (called "bad air") were a way of life. The cramped conditions—tunnels often did not exceed three or four feet in height—and constant dampness in the mines resulted in deformed bodies and ruined lungs.

Both children and women were employed in large numbers in early factories and mines. Children had been an important part of the family economy in preindustrial times, working in the fields or carding and spinning wool at home with the growth of cottage industry. In the Industrial Revolution, however, child labor was exploited more than ever and in a considerably more systematic fashion (see the boxes on pp. 602–603). The owners of cotton factories appreciated certain features of child labor. Children had an especially delicate touch as spinners of cotton. Their smaller size made it easier for them to crawl under machines to gather loose cotton. Moreover, children were more easily broken to factory work. Above all, children represented a cheap supply of labor. In 1821, 49 percent of the British people were under twenty years of age. Hence, children made up a particularly abundant supply of labor, and they were paid only about one-sixth or one-third of what a man was paid. In the cotton factories in 1838, children under eighteen made up 29 percent of the total workforce; children as young as seven worked twelve to fifteen hours per day six days a week in cotton mills.

Especially terrible in the early Industrial Revolution was the use of so-called pauper apprentices. These were orphans or children abandoned by their parents who had wound up in the care of local parishes. To save on their upkeep, parish officials found it convenient to apprentice them to factory owners looking for a cheap source of labor. These children worked long hours under strict discipline and received inadequate food and recreation; many became deformed from being kept too long in unusual positions. Although economic liberals and some industrialists were against all state intervention in economic matters, Parliament eventually remedied some of the worst ills of child abuse in factories and mines (see Efforts at Change: Reformers and Government later in this chapter). The legislation of the 1830s and 1840s, however, primarily affected child labor in textile factories and mines. It did not touch the use of children in small workshops or the nonfactory trades that were not protected. As these trades were in competition with the new factories, conditions there were often even worse. Pottery works, for example, were not investigated until the 1860s when it was found that 17 percent of the workers were under eleven years of age. One investigator reported what he found:

> The boys were kept in constant motion throughout the day, each carrying from thirty to fifty dozen of molds into the stoves, and remaining . . . long enough to take the dried earthenware away. The distance thus run by a boy in the course of a day . . . was estimated at seven miles. From the very nature of this exhausting occupation children were rendered pale, weak and unhealthy. In the depth of winter,

WOMEN IN THE MINES. Both women and children were often employed in the early factories and mines of the nineteenth century. As is evident in this illustration of a woman dragging a cart loaded with coal behind her, they often worked under very trying conditions.

Child Labor: Discipline in the Textile Mills

Child labor was certainly not new, but in the early Industrial Revolution it was exploited more systematically. These selections are taken from the Report of Sadler's Committee, which was commissioned in 1832 to inquire into the condition of child factory workers.

❋ How They Kept the Children Awake

It is a very frequent thing at Mr. Marshall's [at Shrewsbury] where the least children were employed (for there were plenty working at six years of age), for Mr. Horseman to start the mill earlier in the morning than he formerly did; and provided a child should be drowsy, the overlooker walks round the room with a stick in his hand, and he touches that child on the shoulder, and says, "Come here." In a corner of the room there is an iron cistern; it is filled with water; he takes this boy, and takes him up by the legs, and dips him over head in the cistern, and sends him to work for the remainder of the day. . . .

What means were taken to keep the children to their work?—Sometimes they would tap them over the head, or nip them over the nose, or give them a pinch of snuff, or throw water in their faces, or pull them off where they were, and job them about to keep them waking.

❋ The Sadistic Overlooker

Samuel Downe, age 29, factory worker living near Leeds; at the age of about ten began work at Mr. Marshall's mills at Shrewsbury, where the customary hours when work was brisk were generally 5 A.M. to 8 P.M., sometimes from 5:30 A.M. to 8 or 9:

What means were taken to keep the children awake and vigilant, especially at the termination of such a day's labor as you have described?—There was generally a blow or a box, or a tap with a strap, or sometimes the hand.

Have you yourself been strapped?—Yes, most severely, till I could not bear to sit upon a chair without having pillows, and through that I left. I was strapped both on my own legs, and then I was put upon a man's back, and then strapped and buckled with two straps to an iron pillar, and flogged, and all by one overlooker; after that he took a piece of tow, and twisted it in the shape of a cord, and put it in my mouth, and tied it behind my head.

He gagged you?—Yes; and then he orders me to run round a part of the machinery where he was overlooker, and he stood at one end, and every time I came there he struck me with a stick, which I believe was an ash plant, and which he generally carried in his hand, and sometimes he hit me, and sometimes he did not; and one of the men in the room came and begged me off, and that he let me go, and not beat me any more, and consequently he did.

You have been beaten with extraordinary severity?—Yes, I was beaten so that I had not power to cry at all, or hardly speak at one time. What age were you at that time?—Between 10 and 11.

---

with the thermometer in the open air sometimes below zero, boys, with little clothing but rags, might be seen running to and fro on errands or to their dinners with the perspiration on their foreheads, "after laboring for hours like little slaves." The inevitable result of such transitions of temperature were consumption, asthma, and acute inflammation.[13]

Little wonder that child labor legislation enacted in 1864 included pottery works.

By 1830, women and children made up two-thirds of the cotton industry's labor. However, as the number of children employed declined under the Factory Act of 1833, their places were taken by women, who came to dominate the labor forces of the early factories. Women made up 50 percent of the labor force in textile (cotton and woolen) factories before 1870. They were mostly unskilled labor and were paid half or less of what men received. Excessive working hours for women were outlawed in 1844, but only in textile factories and mines; not until 1867 were they outlawed in craft workshops.

The employment of children and women in large part represents a continuation of a preindustrial kinship pattern. Cottage industry had always involved the efforts of the entire family, and it seemed perfectly natural to continue this pattern. Men migrating from the countryside to industrial towns and cities took their wives and children with them into the factory or into the mines. Of 136 employees in Robert Peel's factory at Bury in 1801, 95 belonged to twenty-six families. The impetus for this family work often came from the family itself. The factory owner Jedediah Strutt was opposed to child labor under ten but was forced by parents to take children as young as seven.

The employment of large numbers of women in factories did not produce a significant transformation in female working patterns, as was once assumed. Studies of urban households in France and Britain, for example, have revealed that throughout the nineteenth century traditional types of female labor still predominated in the women's work world. In 1851, fully 40 percent of the female workforce in Britain consisted of domestic servants. In France, the largest group of female workers, 40 percent, worked in agriculture. In addition, only 20 percent of female workers in Britain labored in factories, and only 10 percent did so in France. Regional and local studies have

---

Child Labor: The Mines

After examining conditions in British coal mines, a government official commented that "the hardest labor in the worst room in the worst-conducted factory is less hard, less cruel, and less demoralizing than the labor in the best of coal-mines." Yet it was not until 1842 that legislation was passed eliminating the labor of boys under ten from the mines. This selection is taken from a government report on the mines in Lancashire.

✺ The Black Holes of Worsley

Examination of Thomas Gibson and George Bryan, witnesses from the coal mines at Worsley:

Have you worked from a boy in a coal mine?—(Both) Yes.

What had you to do then?—Thrutching the basket and drawing. It is done by little boys; one draws the basket and the other pushes it behind. Is that hard labor?—Yes, very hard labor.

For how many hours a day did you work?—Nearly nine hours regularly; sometimes twelve; I have worked about thirteen. We used to go in at six in the morning, and took a bit of bread and cheese in our pocket, and stopped two or three minutes; and some days nothing at all to eat.

How was it that sometimes you had nothing to eat?—We were over-burdened. I had only a mother, and she had nothing to give me. I was sometimes half starved. . . .

Do they work in the same way now exactly?—Yes, they do; they have nothing more than a bit of bread and cheese in their pocket, and sometimes can't eat it all, owing to the dust and damp and badness of air; and sometimes it is as hot as an oven; sometimes I have seen it so hot as to melt a candle.

What are the usual wages of a boy of eight?—They used to get 3d or 4d a day. Now a man's wages is divided into eight eighths; and when a boy is eight years old he gets one of those eighths; at eleven, two eighths; at thirteen, three eighths; at fifteen, four eighths; at twenty, man's wages.

What are the wages of a man?—About 15s if he is in full employment, but often not more than 10s, and out of that he has to get his tools and candles. He consumes about four candles in nine hours' work, in some places six; 6d per pound, and twenty-four candles to the pound.

Were you ever beaten as a child?—Yes, many a score of times; both kicks and thumps.

Are many girls employed in the pits?—Yes, a vast of those. They do the same kind of work as the boys till they get about 14 years of age, when they get the wages of half a man, and never get more, and continue at the same work for many years.

Did they ever fight together?—Yes, many days together. Both boys and girls; sometimes they are very loving with one another.

---

also found that most of the workers were single women. Few married women worked outside their homes.

The Factory Acts that limited the work hours of children and women also began to break up the traditional kinship pattern of work and led to a new pattern based on a separation of work and home. Men came to be regarded as responsible for the primary work obligations as women assumed daily control of the family and performed low-paying jobs such as laundry work that could be done in the home. Domestic industry made it possible for women to continue their contributions to family survival.

Historians have also reminded us that if the treatment of children in the mines and factories seems particularly cruel and harsh, contemporary treatment of children in general was often brutal. Beatings, for example, had long been regarded, even by dedicated churchmen and churchwomen, as the best way to discipline children.

✺ Standards of Living

One of the most heated debates on the Industrial Revolution concerns the standard of living. Most historians assume that in the long run the Industrial Revolution increased living standards dramatically in the form of higher per capita incomes and greater consumer choices. But did the first generation of industrial workers experience a decline in their living standards and suffer unnecessarily? Some historians have argued that early industrialization required huge profits to be reinvested in new and ever more expensive equipment; thus, to make the requisite profits, industrialists had to keep wages low. Others have questioned that argument, pointing out that initial investments in early machinery were not necessarily large nor did they need to be. What certainly did occur in the first half of the nineteenth century was a widening gap between rich and poor. One estimate, based on income tax returns in Britain, is that the wealthiest 1 percent of the population increased its share of the national product from 25 percent in 1801 to 35 percent in 1848.

Wages, prices, and consumption patterns are some of the criteria used for measuring the standard of living. Between 1780 and 1850, as far as we can determine from the available evidence, both wages and prices fluctuated widely. Most historians believe that during the Napoleonic wars the increase in prices outstripped wages. Between

1815 and 1830, a price fall was accompanied by a slight increase in wages. But from 1830 to the late 1840s, real wages seem to have improved although regional variations make generalizations dangerous.

When we look at consumption patterns, we find that in Britain in 1850 tea, sugar, and coffee were still semiluxuries consumed primarily by the upper and middle classes and better-off artisans. Meat consumption per capita was less in 1840 than in 1780. On the other hand, a mass market had developed in the cheap cotton goods so important to the Industrial Revolution. As a final note on the question of the standard of living, some historians who take a positive view of the early Industrial Revolution have questioned what would have happened to Britain's growing population without the Industrial Revolution. Would it have gone the way of Ireland's in the Great Hunger of the mid-nineteenth century? No one really knows.

No doubt the periodic crises of overproduction that haunted industrialization from its beginnings caused even further economic hardship. Short-term economic depressions brought high unemployment and increased social tensions. Unemployment figures could be astronomical. During one of these economic depressions in 1842, for example, 60 percent of the factory employees in Bolton were laid off. Cyclical depressions were particularly devastating in towns whose prosperity rested on one industry.

Overall we can say that some evidence exists for an increase in real wages for the working classes between 1790 and 1850, especially in the 1840s. But can standards of living be assessed only in terms of prices, wages, and consumption patterns? No doubt those meant little to people who faced dreadful housing, adulterated food, public health hazards, and the psychological traumas associated with a complete change in work habits and way of life. The real gainers in the early Industrial Revolution were members of the middle class—and some skilled workers whose jobs were not eliminated by the new machines. But industrial workers themselves would have to wait until the second half of the nineteenth century to reap the benefits of industrialization.

❋ Efforts at Change: The Workers

Before long, workers looked to the formation of labor organizations to gain decent wages and working conditions. The British government, reacting against the radicalism of the French revolutionary working classes, had passed a series of Combination Acts in 1799 and 1800 outlawing associations of workers. The legislation failed to prevent the formation of trade unions, however. Similar to the craft societies of earlier times, these new associations were formed by skilled workers in a number of new industries, including the cotton spinners, ironworkers, coal miners, and shipwrights. These unions served two purposes. One was to preserve their own workers' position by limiting entry into their trade; another was to gain benefits from the employers. These early trade unions had limited goals.

They favored a working-class struggle against employers, but only to win improvements for the members of their own trades.

Some trade unions were even willing to strike to gain their goals. Bitter strikes were carried out by hand-loom weavers in Glasgow in 1813, cotton spinners in Manchester in 1818, and miners in Northumberland and Durham in 1810. Such blatant illegal activity caused Parliament to repeal the Combination Acts in 1824, accepting the argument of some members that the acts themselves had so alienated workers that they had formed unions. Unions were now tolerated, but other legislation enabled authorities to keep close watch over their activities.

In the 1820s and 1830s, the union movement began to focus on the creation of national unions. One of the leaders in this effort was a well-known cotton

A TRADE UNION MEMBERSHIP CARD. Skilled workers in a number of new industries formed trade unions in an attempt to gain higher wages, better working conditions, and special benefits. The scenes at the bottom of this membership card for the Associated Shipwright's Society illustrate some of the medical and social benefits it provided for its members.

magnate and social reformer, Robert Owen (1771–1858). Owen came to believe in the creation of voluntary associations that would demonstrate to others the benefits of cooperative rather than competitive living (see Chapter 21 on the utopian socialists). Although Owen's program was not directed specifically to trade unionists, his ideas had great appeal to some of their leaders. Under Owen's direction, plans emerged for a Grand National Consolidated Trades Union, which was formed in February 1834. As a national federation of trade unions, its primary purpose was to coordinate a general strike for the eight-hour working day. Rhetoric, however, soon outpaced reality, and by the summer of the same year, the lack of real working-class support led to its total collapse. Afterward, the union movement reverted to trade unions for individual crafts. The largest and most successful was the Amalgamated Society of Engineers, formed in 1850. Its provision of generous unemployment benefits in return for a small weekly payment was precisely the kind of practical gains these trade unions sought. Larger goals would have to wait.

Trade unionism was not the only type of collective action by workers in the early decades of the Industrial Revolution. The Luddites were skilled craftspeople in the Midlands and northern England who in 1812 attacked the machines that they believed threatened their livelihoods. These attacks failed to stop the industrial mechanization of Britain and have been viewed as utterly naive. Some historians, however, have also seen them as an intense eruption of feeling against unrestrained industrial capitalism. The inability of 12,000 troops to find the culprits provides stunning evidence of the local support they received in their areas.

A much more meaningful expression of the attempts of British workers to improve their condition developed in the movement known as Chartism. It was the first "important political movement of working men organized during the nineteenth century." Its aim was to achieve political democracy. A People's Charter drawn up in 1838 demanded universal male suffrage, payment for members of Parliament, and annual sessions of Parliament (see the box on p. 606). Two national petitions incorporating these points, affixed with millions of signatures, were presented to Parliament in 1839 and 1842. Both were rejected by the members of Parliament who were not at all ready for political democracy. As one member said, universal suffrage would be "fatal to all the purposes for which government exists" and was "utterly incompatible with the very existence of civilization." After 1843, Chartism as a movement had largely played itself out. It had never really posed a serious threat to the British establishment, but it had not been a total failure either. Its true significance stemmed from its ability to arouse and organize millions of working-class men and women, to give them a sense of working-class consciousness that they had not really possessed before. This political education of working people was important to the ultimate acceptance of all the points of the People's Charter in the future.

✳ Efforts at Change: Reformers and Government

Efforts to improve the worst conditions of the industrial factory system also came from outside the ranks of the working classes. From its beginning, the Industrial Revolution had drawn much criticism. Romantic poets like William Wordsworth (see Chapter 21) decried the destruction of the natural world:

> I grieve, when on the darker side
> Of this great change I look; and there behold
> Such outrage done to nature as compels
> The indignant power to justify herself.

Reform-minded individuals, be they factory owners who felt twinges of conscience or social reformers in Parliament, campaigned against the evils of the industrial factory, especially condemning the abuse of children. One hoped for the day "that these little ones should once more see the rising and setting of the sun."

As it became apparent that the increase in wealth generated by the Industrial Revolution was accompanied by ever-increasing numbers of poor people, more and more efforts were made to document and deal with the problems. As reports from civic-minded citizens and parliamentary commissions intensified and demonstrated the extent of poverty, degradation, and suffering, the reform efforts began to succeed.

Their first success was a series of Factory Acts passed between 1802 and 1819 that limited labor for children between the ages of nine and sixteen to twelve hours a day; the employment of children under nine years old was forbidden. Moreover, the laws stipulated that children were to receive instruction in reading and arithmetic during working hours. But these acts applied only to cotton mills, not to factories or mines where some of the worst abuses were taking place. Just as important, no provision was made for enforcing the acts through a system of inspection.

In the reform-minded decades of the 1830s and 1840s, new legislation was passed. The Factory Act of 1833 strengthened earlier labor legislation. All textile factories were now included. Children between nine and thirteen could work only eight hours a day; those between thirteen and eighteen, twelve hours. Factory inspectors were appointed with the power to fine those who broke the law. Another piece of legislation in 1833 required that children between nine and thirteen have at least two hours of elementary education during the working day. In 1847, the Ten Hours Act reduced the work day for children between thirteen and eighteen to ten hours. Women were also now included in the ten-hour limitation. In 1842, a Coal Mines Act eliminated the employment of boys under ten and women in mines. Eventually, men too would benefit from the move to restrict factory hours.

The Political Demands of the Chartist Movement

In the late 1830s and early 1840s, working-class protest centered on achieving a clear set of political goals, particularly universal male suffrage, as the means to achieve economic and social improvements. This selection is taken from one of the national petitions presented to Parliament by the Chartist movement. Although the petition failed, Chartism helped to arouse and organize millions of workers.

❋ National Petition (1839)

To the Honorable the Commons of the United Kingdom of Great Britain and Ireland, in Parliament assembled, the Petition of the undersigned, their suffering countrymen, HUMBLY SHOWS,—

The energies of a mighty kingdom have been wasted in building up the power of selfish and ignorant men, and its resources squandered for their aggrandizement. The good of a part has been advanced at the sacrifice of the good of the nation. The few have governed for the interest of the few, while the interests of the many have been sottishly neglected, or insolently . . . trampled upon. . . . We come before your honorable house to tell you, with all humility, that this state of things must not be permitted to continue. That it cannot long continue, without very seriously endangering the stability of the throne, and the peace of the kingdom, and that if, by God's help, and all lawful and constitutional appliances, an end can be put to it, we are fully resolved that it shall speedily come to an end. . . . Required, as we are universally, to support and obey the laws, nature and reason entitle us to demand that in the making of the laws the universal voice shall be implicitly listened to. We perform the duties of freemen; we must have the privileges of freemen. Therefore, we demand universal suffrage.

The suffrage, to be exempt from the corruption of the wealthy and the violence of the powerful, must be secret. . . . To public safety, as well as public confidence, frequent elections are essential. Therefore, we demand annual parliaments. With power to choose, and freedom in choosing, the range of our choice must be unrestricted. We are compelled, by existing laws, to take for our representatives men who are incapable of appreciating our difficulties, or have little sympathy with them; merchants who have retired from trade and no longer feel its harassings; proprietors of land who are alike ignorant of its evils and its cure; lawyers by whom the notoriety of the senate is courted only as a means of obtaining notice in the courts. . . . We demand that in the future election of members of your . . . house, the approbation of the constituency shall be the sole qualification, and that to every representative so chosen, shall be assigned out of the public taxes, a fair and adequate remuneration for the time which he is called upon to devote to the public service. . . . Universal suffrage will, and it alone can, bring true and lasting peace to the nation; we firmly believe that it will also bring prosperity. May it therefore please your honorable house, to take this our petition into your most serious consideration, and to use your utmost endeavors, by all constitutional means, to have a law passed, granting to every male of lawful age, sane mind, and unconvicted of crime, the right of voting for members of parliament, and directing all future elections of members of parliament to be in the way of secret ballot, and ordaining that the duration of parliament, so chosen, shall in no case exceed one year, and abolishing all property qualifications in the members, and providing for their due remuneration while in attendance on their parliamentary duties.

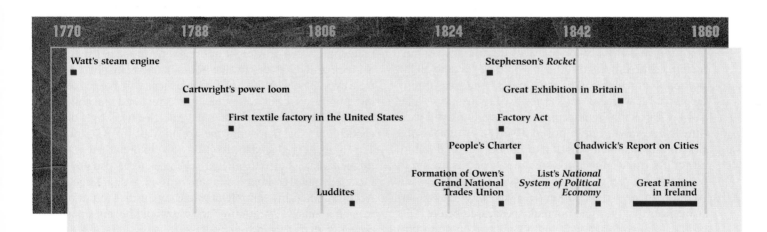

1770	1788	1806	1824	1842	1860

Watt's steam engine

Cartwright's power loom

First textile factory in the United States

Luddites

Formation of Owen's Grand National Trades Union

People's Charter

List's *National System of Political Economy*

Stephenson's *Rocket*

Factory Act

Great Exhibition in Britain

Chadwick's Report on Cities

Great Famine in Ireland

CONCLUSION ※※※※※※※※※※※

The Industrial Revolution became one of the major forces of change in the nineteenth century as it led Western civilization into the industrial era that has characterized the modern world. Beginning in Britain, its spread to the Continent and the new American nation ensured its growth and domination of the Western world.

The Industrial Revolution seemed to prove to Europeans the underlying assumption of the Scientific Revolution of the seventeenth century—that human beings were capable of dominating nature. By rationally manipulating the material environment for human benefit, people could create new levels of material prosperity and produce machines not dreamed of in their wildest imaginings. Lost in the excitement of the Industrial Revolution were the voices that pointed to the dehumanization of the workforce and the alienation from one's work, one's associates, one's self, and the natural world.

The Industrial Revolution also transformed the social world of Europe. The creation of an industrial proletariat produced a whole new force for change. The development of a wealthy industrial middle class presented a challenge to the long-term hegemony of landed wealth. Though that wealth had been threatened by the fortunes of commerce, it had never been overturned. But the new bourgeoisie was more demanding. How, in some places, this new industrial bourgeoisie came to play a larger role in the affairs of state will become evident in the next chapter.

NOTES ※※※※※※※※※※※※※※※

1. Quoted in W. Gorden Rimmer, *Marshall's of Leeds, Flax-Spinners 1788–1886* (Cambridge, 1960), p. 40.
2. Daniel Defoe, *A Plan of the English Commerce* (Oxford, 1928), pp. 76–77.
3. Quoted in David Landes, *The Unbound Prometheus: Technological Change and Industrial Development in Western Europe from 1750 to the Present* (Cambridge, 1969), pp. 99–100.
4. Quoted in Albert Tucker, *A History of English Civilization* (New York, 1972), p. 583.
5. Quoted in Landes, *The Unbound Prometheus*, pp. 149–150.
6. Quotations can be found in E. Royston Pike, *Human Documents of the Industrial Revolution in Britain* (London, 1966), pp. (in order of quotations) 320, 313, 314, 343.
7. Ibid., p. 315.
8. Quoted in A. J. Donajgrodzi, ed., *Social Control in Nineteenth Century Britain* (London, 1977), p. 141.
9. Quoted in Pike, *Human Documents of the Industrial Revolution in Britain*, pp. 343–344.
10. Quoted in Eric J. Evans, *The Forging of the Modern State: Early Industrial Britain, 1783–1870* (London, 1983), p. 113.
11. Henry Mayhew, *London Labour and the London Poor* (London, 1851), 1:342–343.
12. Quoted in Pike, *Human Documents of the Industrial Revolution in Britain*, pp. 60–61.
13. Quoted in Evans, *The Forging of the Modern State*, p. 124.

SUGGESTIONS FOR FURTHER READING ※※※※

The well-written work by D. Landes, *The Unbound Prometheus: Technological Change and Industrial Development in Western Europe from 1750 to the Present* (Cambridge, 1969), is a good introduction to the Industrial Revolution. Although more technical, also of value are C. Trebilcock, *The Industrialization of the Continental Powers, 1780–1914* (London, 1981); and S. Pollard, *Peaceful Conquest: The Industrialization of Europe, 1760–1970* (Oxford, 1981). There are good collections of essays in P. Mathias and J. A. Davis, eds., *The First Industrial Revolutions* (Oxford, 1989); and M. Teich and R. Porter, eds., *The Industrial Revolution in National Context: Europe and the USA* (Cambridge, 1996). See also D. Fisher, *The Industrial Revolution* (New York, 1992). For a broader perspective, see P. Stearns, *The Industrial Revolution in World History* (Boulder, Colo., 1993). Although older and dated, T. S. Ashton, *The Industrial Revolution, 1760–1830* (New York, 1948) still provides an interesting introduction to the Industrial Revolution in Britain. Much better, however, are P. Mathias, *The First Industrial Nation: An Economic History of Britain, 1700–1914*, 2d ed. (New York, 1983); and R. Brown, *Society and Economy in Modern Britain, 1700–1850* (London, 1991). On the spread of industrialization to the Continent, see A. Milward and S. B. Saul, *The Development of the Economies of Continental Europe* (Oxford, 1977); and T. Kemp, *Industrialization in Nineteenth-Century Europe*, 2d ed. (London, 1985).

Given the importance of Great Britain in the Industrial Revolution, a number of books are available that place the Industrial Revolution in Britain in a broader context. See E. J. Evans, *The Forging of the Modern State: Early Industrial Britain, 1783–1870* (London, 1983); S. Checkland, *British Public Policy, 1776–1939: An Economic, Social and Political Perspective* (Cambridge, 1983); and P. K. O'Brien and R. Quinault, eds., *The Industrial Revolution and British Society* (New York, 1993).

The early industrialization of the United States is examined in B. Hindle and S. Lubar, *Engines of Change: The American Industrial Revolution, 1790–1860* (Washington, D.C., 1986). On the economic ties between Great Britain and the United States, see D. Jeremy, *Transatlantic Industrial Revolution: The Diffusion of Textile Technology between Britain and America, 1790–1830* (Cambridge, Mass., 1981).

A general discussion of population growth in Europe can be found in T. McKeown, *The Modern Rise of Population* (London, 1976). For an examination of urban growth, see the older but classic work of A. F. Weber, *The Growth of Cities in the Nineteenth Century: A Study in Statistics* (Ithaca, N.Y., 1963); A. R. Sutcliffe, *Towards the Planned City: Germany, Britain, the United States and France, 1780–1914* (Oxford, 1981); and L. D. Schwarz, *London in the Age of Industrialization* (New York, 1992). C. Kinealy, *A Death-Dealing Famine: The Great Hunger* in Ireland (Chicago, 1997) is a good account of the great Irish tragedy. Many of the works cited above have much information on the social impact of the Industrial Revolution, but additional material is available in F. Crouzet, *The First Industrialists: The Problems of Origins* (Cambridge, 1985), on British entrepreneurs; J. Merriman, *The Margins of City Life* (New York, 1991), on French cities; P. Pilbeam, *The Middle Classes in Europe, 1789–1914* (Basingstoke, 1990); and T. Koditschek, *Class Formation and Urban Industrial Society* (New York, 1990). G. Himmelfarb, *The Idea of Poverty: England in the Early Industrial Age* (New York, 1984) traces the concepts of poverty and poor from the mid-eighteenth century to the mid-nineteenth century. A classic work on female labor patterns is L. A. Tilly and J. W. Scott, *Women, Work, and Family* (New York, 1978). See also J. Lown, *Women and Industrialization: Gender at Work in Nineteenth-Century England* (Minneapolis,

Minn., 1990); and L. L. Frader, "Doing Capitalism's Work: Women in the Western European Industrial Economy," in R. Bridenthal, S. M. Stuard, and M. E. Wiesner, eds., *Becoming Visible,* 3d ed. (Boston, 1998).

For additional reading, go to InfoTrac College Edition, your online research library at http://web1.infotrac-college.com

Enter the search terms *industrial revolution* using Key Terms.

Enter the search terms *industrial development* using the Subject Guide.

Enter the search term *Chartism* using the Subject Guide.

CHAPTER

21

Reaction, Revolution, and Romanticism, 1815–1850

CHAPTER OUTLINE

- The Conservative Order (1815–1830)
- The Ideologies of Change
- Revolution and Reform (1830–1850)
- The Emergence of an Ordered Society
- Culture in an Age of Reaction and Revolution: The Mood of Romanticism
- Conclusion

FOCUS QUESTIONS

- What were the goals of the Congress of Vienna and the Concert of Europe, and how successful were they in achieving those goals?
- What were the main tenets of conservatism, liberalism, nationalism, and utopian socialism, and what role did each ideology play in Europe in the first half of the nineteenth century?
- What forces for change were present in France and Great Britain between 1830 and 1848, and how did each nation respond?
- What were the causes of the revolutions of 1848, and why did the revolutions fail?
- What were the characteristics of Romanticism, and how were they reflected in literature, art, and music?

*I*N SEPTEMBER 1814, hundreds of foreigners began to converge on Vienna, the capital city of the Austrian Empire. Many were members of European royalty—kings, archdukes, princes, and their wives—accompanied by their diplomatic advisers and scores of servants. Their congenial host was the Austrian emperor Francis I, who never tired of providing Vienna's guests with concerts, glittering balls, sumptuous feasts, and an endless array of hunting parties. One participant remembered, "Eating, fireworks, public illuminations. For eight or ten days, I haven't been able to work at all. What a life!" Of course, not every waking hour was spent in pleasure during this gathering of notables, known to history as the Congress of Vienna. These people were also representatives of all the states that had fought Napoleon, and their real business was to arrange a final peace settlement after almost a decade of war. On June 8, 1815, they finally completed their task.

609

The forces of upheaval unleashed during the French revolutionary and Napoleonic wars were temporarily quieted in 1815 as rulers sought to restore stability by reestablishing much of the old order to a Europe ravaged by war. Kings, landed aristocrats, and bureaucratic elites regained their control over domestic governments, and internationally the forces of conservatism tried to maintain the new status quo; some states even used military force to intervene in the internal affairs of other countries in their desire to crush revolutions.

But the Western world had been changed, and it would not readily go back to the old system. New ideologies of change, especially liberalism and nationalism, both products of the revolutionary upheaval initiated in France, had become too powerful to be contained. Not content with the status quo, the forces of change gave rise first to the revolts and revolutions that periodically shook Europe in the 1820s and 1830s and then to the widespread revolutions of 1848. Some of the revolutions and revolutionaries were successful; most were not. Although the old order usually appeared to have prevailed, by 1850, it was apparent that its days were numbered. This perception was reinforced by the changes wrought by the Industrial Revolution. Together the forces unleashed by the dual revolutions—the French Revolution and the Industrial Revolution—made it impossible to return to prerevolutionary Europe. Nevertheless, although these two revolutions initiated what historians like to call the modern European world, it will also be apparent that much of the old still remained in the midst of the new.

Although all the powers were invited to attend the congress, important decisions were closely guarded by the representatives of the four great powers. The victorious British, who had no desire for territorial gains on the Continent but did wish to secure their control of the seas, were ably represented at the conference by Viscount Castlereagh (1769–1822), a shy but determined man. The skillful maneuvering of the French representative, the clever Prince Talleyrand, enabled the defeated power, France, to participate in some of the decisions. Above all, however, the congress was dominated by the Austrian foreign minister, Prince Klemens von Metternich (1773–1859). An experienced diplomat who was also conceited and self-assured, Metternich described himself in his memoirs in 1819: "There is a wide sweep about my mind. I am always above and beyond the preoccupation of most public men; I cover a ground much vaster than they can see. I cannot keep myself from saying about twenty times a day: 'How right I am, and how wrong they are.'"[1]

Metternich claimed that he was guided at Vienna by the principle of legitimacy. To reestablish peace and stability in Europe, he considered it necessary to restore the legitimate monarchs who would preserve traditional institutions. This had already been done in the restoration of the Bourbons in France and Spain, as well as in the return of a number of rulers to their thrones in the Italian states.

METTERNICH. Prince Klemens von Metternich, the foreign minister of Austria, played a major role at the Congress of Vienna as the chief exponent of the principle of legitimacy. To maintain the new conservative order after 1815, Metternich espoused the principle of intervention, by which he meant that the great powers had the right to intervene militarily in other countries in order to crush revolutionary movements against legitimate rulers.

◆ The Conservative Order

(1815–1830)

The immediate response to the defeat of Napoleon was the desire to contain revolution and the revolutionary forces by restoring much of the old order. But the triumphant rulers were not naive and realized that they could not return to 1789.

❈ *The Peace Settlement*

In March 1814, even before Napoleon had been defeated, his four major enemies—Great Britain, Austria, Prussia, and Russia—had agreed to remain united, not only to defeat France but to ensure peace after the war. After Napoleon's defeat, this Quadruple Alliance restored the Bourbon monarchy to France in the person of Louis XVIII and agreed to meet at a congress in Vienna in September 1814 to arrange a final peace settlement.

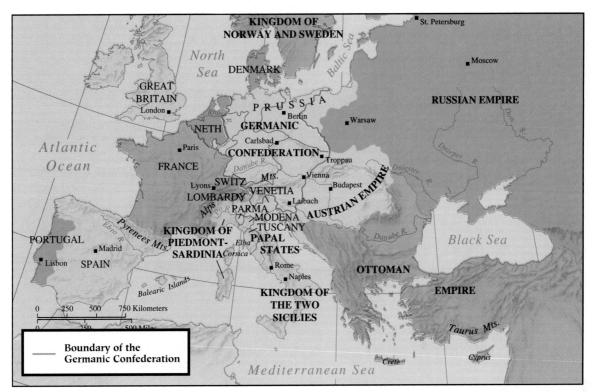

MAP 21.1 **Europe after the Congress of Vienna.**

Elsewhere, however, the principle of legitimacy was largely ignored and completely overshadowed by more practical considerations of power. The congress's treatment of Poland, to which Russia, Austria, and Prussia all had claims, illustrates this approach. Prussia and Austria were allowed to keep some Polish territory. A new, nominally independent Polish kingdom, about three-quarters of the size of the duchy of Warsaw, was established with the Romanov dynasty of Russia as its hereditary monarchs. Although the Russian tsar Alexander I (1801–1825) voluntarily granted the new kingdom a constitution guaranteeing its independence, Poland's foreign policy (and Poland) remained under Russian control. Prussia was compensated for its loss of Polish lands by receiving two-fifths of Saxony, the Napoleonic German kingdom of Westphalia, and the left bank of the Rhine. Austria in turn was compensated for its loss of the Austrian Netherlands by being given control of two northern Italian provinces, Lombardy and Venetia.

In making these territorial rearrangements, the powers at Vienna believed they were following the familiar eighteenth-century practice of maintaining a balance of power or equilibrium among the great powers. Essentially, this meant a balance of political and military forces that guaranteed the independence of the great powers by ensuring that no one country could dominate Europe. To balance Russian gains, Prussia and Austria had been strengthened. According to Metternich, this arrangement had clearly avoided a great danger: "Prussia and Austria are completing their systems of defense; united, the two monarchies form an unconquerable barrier against the enterprises of any conquering prince who might perhaps once again occupy the throne of France or that of Russia."[2]

Considerations of the balance of power also dictated the allied treatment of France. France had not been overly weakened so that it could remain a great power. Nevertheless, the fear that France might again upset the European peace remained strong enough that the great powers attempted to establish major defensive barriers against possible French expansion. To the north of France, they created a new enlarged kingdom of the Netherlands composed of the former Dutch Republic and the Austrian Netherlands (Belgium) under a new ruler, King William I of the House of Orange. To the southeast, Piedmont (officially styled the kingdom of Sardinia) was enlarged. On France's eastern frontier, Prussia was strengthened by giving it control of the territory along the east bank of the Rhine. The British at least expected Prussia to be the major bulwark against French expansion in central Europe, but the Congress of Vienna also created a new league of German states, the Germanic Confederation, to replace the Napoleonic Confederation of the Rhine.

Napoleon's escape from Elba and his One Hundred Days in the midst of the Congress of Vienna delayed the negotiations but did not significantly alter the overall agreement. It was decided, however, to punish the French people for their enthusiastic response to Napoleon's return. France's borders were returned to those of 1790, and it was forced to pay an indemnity and accept an army of occupation for five years.

The Vienna peace settlement of 1815 has sometimes been criticized for its failure to recognize the liberal and

The Voice of Conservatism: Metternich of Austria

There was no greater symbol of conservatism in the first half of the nineteenth century than Prince Klemens von Metternich of Austria. Metternich played a crucial role at the Congress of Vienna and worked tirelessly for thirty years to repress the "revolutionary seed," as he called it, that had been spread to Europe by the "military despotism of Bonaparte."

✸ Klemens von Metternich, *Memoirs*

We are convinced that society can no longer be saved without strong and vigorous resolutions on the part of the Governments still free in their opinions and actions.

We are also convinced that this may be, if the Governments face the truth, if they free themselves from all illusion, if they join their ranks and take their stand on a line of correct, unambiguous, and frankly announced principles.

By this course the monarchs will fulfill the duties imposed upon them by Him who, by entrusting them with power, has charged them to watch over the maintenance of justice, and the rights of all, to avoid the paths of error, and tread firmly in the way of truth. . . .

If the same elements of destruction which are now throwing society into convulsions have existed in all ages—for every age has seen immoral and ambitious men, hypocrites, men of heated imaginations, wrong motives, and wild projects—yet ours, by the single fact of the liberty of the press, possesses more than any preceding age the means of contact, seduction, and attraction whereby to act on these different classes of men.

We are certainly not alone in questioning if society can exist with the liberty of the press, a scourge unknown to the world before the latter half of the seventeenth century, and restrained until the end of the eighteenth, with scarcely any expectations but England—a part of Europe separated from the continent by the sea, as well as by her language and by her peculiar manners.

The first principle to be followed by the monarchs, united as they are by the coincidence of their desires and opinions, should be that of maintaining the stability of political institutions against the disorganized excitement which has taken possession of men's minds; the immutability of principles against the madness of their interpretation; and respect for laws actually in force against a desire for their destruction. . . .

The first and greatest concern for the immense majority of every nation is the stability of the laws, and their uninterrupted action—never their change. Therefore, let the Governments govern, let them maintain the groundwork of their institutions, both ancient and modern; for if it is at all times dangerous to touch them, it certainly would not now, in the general confusion, be wise to do so. . . .

Let them maintain religious principles in all their purity, and not allow the faith to be attacked and morality interpreted according to the social contract or the visions of foolish sectarians.

Let them suppress Secret Societies, that gangrene of society. . . .

To every great State determined to survive the storm there still remain many chances of salvation, and a strong union between the States on the principles we have announced will overcome the storm itself.

---

national forces unleashed by the French revolutionary and Napoleonic eras. Containing these revolutionary forces was precisely what the diplomats at Vienna hoped to achieve. Their transfers of territories and peoples to the victors to create a new balance of power, with little or no regard for the wishes of the peoples themselves, was in accord with long-standing traditions of European diplomacy. One could hardly expect Metternich, foreign minister of the Austrian Empire, a dynastic state composed of many different peoples, to espouse a principle of self-determination for European nationalities. Whatever its weaknesses, the Congress of Vienna has received credit for establishing a European order that managed to avoid a general European conflict for almost a century.

✸ *The Ideology of Conservatism*

The peace arrangements of 1815 were but the beginning of a conservative reaction determined to contain the liberal and nationalist forces unleashed by the French Revolution. Metternich and his kind were representatives of the ideology known as conservatism (see the box above). As a modern political philosophy, conservatism dates from 1790 when Edmund Burke (1729–1797) wrote his *Reflections on the Revolution in France* in reaction to the French Revolution, especially its radical republican and democratic ideas. Burke maintained that society was a contract, but "the state ought not to be considered as nothing better than a partnership agreement in a trade of pepper and coffee, to be taken up for a temporary interest and to be dissolved by the fancy of the parties." The state was a partnership but one "not only between those who are living, but between those who are living, those who are dead and those who are to be born."[3] No one generation therefore has the right to destroy this partnership; instead, each generation has the duty to preserve and transmit it to the next. Burke advised against the violent overthrow of a government by revolution, but he did not reject the possibility of change. Sudden change was unacceptable, but that did not eliminate gradual or evolutionary improvements.

Burke's conservatism, however, was not the only kind. The Frenchman Joseph de Maistre (1753–1821) was the most influential spokesman for a counterrevolutionary and authoritarian conservatism. De Maistre espoused the restoration of hereditary monarchy, which he regarded as a divinely sanctioned institution. Only absolute monarchy could guarantee "order in society" and avoid the chaos generated by movements like the French Revolution.

Despite their differences, most conservatives held to a general body of beliefs. They favored obedience to political authority, believed that organized religion was crucial to social order, hated revolutionary upheavals, and were unwilling to accept either the liberal demands for civil liberties and representative governments or the nationalistic aspirations generated by the French revolutionary era. The community took precedence over individual rights; society must be organized and ordered, and tradition remained the best guide for order. After 1815, the political philosophy of conservatism was supported by hereditary monarchs, government bureaucracies, landowning aristocracies, and revived churches, be they Protestant or Catholic. Although not unopposed, both internationally and domestically the conservative forces appeared dominant after 1815.

✳ *The Conservative Domination: The Concert of Europe*

The conservative order that European diplomats were constructing at Vienna must have seemed fragile when the French people greeted Napoleon enthusiastically after his escape from Elba. The great powers' fear of revolution and war led them to develop the Concert of Europe as a means to maintain the new status quo they had constructed. This Concert of Europe grew out of the reaffirmation of the Quadruple Alliance in November 1815. Great Britain, Russia, Prussia, and Austria renewed their commitment against any attempted restoration of Bonapartist power and agreed to meet periodically in conferences to discuss their common interests and examine measures that "will be judged most salutary for the repose and prosperity of peoples, and for the maintenance of peace in Europe."

In accordance with the agreement for periodic meetings, four congresses were held between 1818 and 1822. The first congress, held in 1818 at Aix-la-Chapelle, was by far the most congenial. "Never have I known a prettier little congress," said Metternich. The four great powers agreed to withdraw their army of occupation from France and to add France to the Concert of Europe. The Quadruple Alliance became a Quintuple Alliance.

The next congress proved far less pleasant and produced the first fissure in the ranks of the allies. This session at Troppau was called in the autumn of 1820 to deal with the outbreak of revolution in Spain and Italy. The revolt in Spain was directed against Ferdinand VII, the Bourbon king who had been restored to the throne in 1814. In southern Italy, the restoration of another Bourbon, Ferdinand I, as king of Naples and Sicily was accompanied by the return of the nobility and clergy to their privileged positions. Army officers and businessmen led a rebellion that soon spread to the northern Italian kingdom of Piedmont.

Metternich was especially disturbed by the revolts in Italy since he saw them as a threat to Austria's domination of the peninsula. At Troppau, he proposed a protocol that established the principle of intervention. It read:

> States which have undergone a change of Government due to revolution, the results of which threaten other states, *ipso facto* cease to be members of the European Alliance, and remain excluded from it until their situation gives guarantees for legal order and stability. If, owing to such situations, immediate danger threatens other states, the Powers bind themselves, by peaceful means, or if need be by arms, to bring back the guilty state into the bosom of the Great Alliance.[4]

The principle of intervention meant the great powers had the right to send armies into countries where there were revolutions to restore legitimate monarchs to their thrones. Britain refused to agree to the principle, arguing that it had never been the intention of the Quadruple Alliance to interfere in the internal affairs of other states, except in France. In Britain's eyes, only revolutionary outbursts threatening the peace of Europe necessitated armed intervention. Ignoring the British response, Austria, Prussia, and Russia met in a third congress at Laibach in January 1821 and authorized the sending of Austrian troops to Naples. These forces crushed the revolt, restored Ferdinand I to the throne, and then moved north to suppress the rebels in Sardinia. At the fourth postwar conference, held at Verona in October 1822, the same three powers authorized France to invade Spain to crush the revolt against Ferdinand VII. In the spring of 1823, French forces restored the Bourbon monarch.

The policy of intervention had succeeded in defeating revolutionary movements in Spain and Italy and in restoring legitimate (and conservative) monarchs to their thrones. It had been done at a price, however. The Concert of Europe had broken down when the British rejected Metternich's principle of intervention. And although the British had failed to thwart allied intervention in Spain and Italy, they were successful in keeping the continental powers from interfering with the revolutions in Latin America.

✒ THE REVOLT OF LATIN AMERICA

Although much of North America had been freed of European domination in the eighteenth century by the American Revolution, Latin America remained in the hands of the Spanish and Portuguese. Napoleon's continental wars at the beginning of the nineteenth century, however, soon had repercussions in Latin America. When the Bourbon monarchy of Spain was toppled by Bonaparte, Spanish authority in its colonial empire was weakened. By 1810, the disintegration of royal power in Argentina had led to that nation's independence. In Venezuela a bitter struggle for independence was led by Simón Bolívar (1783–1830), hailed as the Liberator. His forces freed Colombia in 1819 and Venezuela in 1821. A second liberator was José de San Martín (1778–1850) who liberated Chile in 1817 and then, in 1821, moved on to Lima, Peru, the center of Spanish authority. He was soon joined by Bolívar who assumed the task of crushing the last significant Spanish army in 1824. Mexico and the Central American provinces also achieved their freedom, and by 1825, after Portugal had recognized the independence of Brazil, almost all of Latin America had been freed of colonial domination.

In the early 1820s, only one major threat to the newly independent Latin American states remained. Flushed by their success in crushing rebellions in Spain and Italy, the victorious continental powers favored the use of troops to restore Spanish control in Latin America. This time British opposition to intervention prevailed. Eager to gain access to an entire continent for investment and trade, the British proposed joint action with the United States against European interference in Latin America. Distrustful of British motives, President James Monroe acted alone in 1823, guaranteeing the independence of the new Latin American nations and warning against any further European intervention in the New World in the famous Monroe Doctrine. Actually, British ships were more important to Latin American independence than American words. Britain's navy stood between Latin America and any European invasion force, and the continental powers were extremely reluctant to challenge British naval power.

THE GREEK REVOLT (1821–1832)

The principle of intervention proved to be a double-edged sword. Designed to prevent revolution, it could also be used to support revolution if the great powers found it in their interest to do so. Despite their differences in the

MAP 21.2 Latin America in the First Half of the Nineteenth Century.

congresses, Great Britain, France, and Russia found cause for cooperation.

In 1821, the Greeks revolted against their Ottoman Turkish masters. Although subject to Muslim control for 400 years, the Greeks had been allowed to maintain their language and their Greek Orthodox faith. A revival of Greek national sentiment at the beginning of the nineteenth century added to the growing desire for "the liberation of the fatherland from the terrible yoke of Turkish oppression." Initial reaction to the Greek revolt by the European powers was negative since this appeared to be simply another revolt against established authority that should be crushed. But the Greek revolt was soon transformed into a noble cause by an outpouring of European sentiment for the Greeks' struggle. Liberals rallied to the cause of Greek freedom, arguing that Greek democracy was being reborn. Romantic poets and artists (see Culture in an Age of Reaction and Revolution: The Mood of Romanticism later in this chapter) also publicized the cause of Greek independence.

Despite the public groundswell, mutual fears and other interests kept the European powers from intervening until 1827 when a combined British and French fleet went to Greece and defeated a large Ottoman fleet. In 1828, Russia declared war on the Ottoman Empire and invaded its European provinces of Moldavia and Wallachia. By the Treaty of Adrianople in 1829, which ended the Russian-Turkish war, the Russians received a protectorate over the two provinces. By the same treaty, the Ottoman Empire agreed to allow Russia, France, and Britain to decide the fate of Greece. In 1830, the three powers declared Greece an independent kingdom, and two years later a new royal dynasty was established in the hands of a son of the Bavarian king.

The Greek revolt made a deep impression on Europeans. It was the first successful revolt against the status quo and represented a victory for both the liberal and the national forces that the great powers were trying so hard to repress. But to keep this in perspective, we need to remember that the European powers did not quite see it that way. They had given the Greeks a German king, and the revolution had been successful only because the great powers themselves supported it. Until 1830 the Greek revolt had been the only successful one in Europe; the conservative domination was still largely intact.

✳ The Conservative Domination: The European States

Between 1815 and 1830, the conservative domination of Europe evident in the Concert of Europe was also apparent in domestic affairs.

✺ GREAT BRITAIN: RULE OF THE TORIES

In 1815, Great Britain was governed by the aristocratic landowning classes that dominated both houses of Parliament. Suffrage for elections to the House of Commons, controlled by the landed gentry, was restricted and un-

THE GREEK STRUGGLE FOR FREEDOM: EUGÈNE DELACROIX, *GREECE EXPIRING ON THE RUINS OF MISSOLONGHI*. The Greek revolt against the Ottoman Empire brought a massive outpouring of European sentiment for the Greeks. Romantic artists and poets were especially eager to publicize the struggle of the Greeks for independence. In this painting, the French painter Delacroix personified Greece as a majestic, defenseless woman appealing for aid against the victorious Ottoman Turk seen in the background. Delacroix's painting was done soon after the fall of the Greek fortress of Missolonghi to the Ottomans.

equal, especially in light of the changing distribution of the British population due to the Industrial Revolution. Large, new industrial cities such as Birmingham and Manchester, for example, had no representatives while landowners used pocket and rotten boroughs (see Chapter 18) to control seats in the House of Commons. Although the monarchy was not yet powerless, in practice the power of the crown was largely in the hands of the ruling party in Parliament.

Within Parliament there were two political factions, the Tories and Whigs. Although both of them were still dominated by members of the landed classes, the Whigs were beginning to receive support from the new moneyed interests generated by industrialization. Tory ministers largely dominated the government until 1830 and had little desire to change the existing political and electoral system. Tory leadership during the Napoleonic wars made them wary of radicalism and reform movements, an attitude that governed their activities after 1815.

Popular discontent grew apace after 1815 because of severe economic difficulties. The Tory government's response to falling agricultural prices was the Corn Law of 1815, a measure that placed extraordinarily high tariffs on foreign grain. Though beneficial to the landowners, subsequent high prices for bread made conditions for the working classes more difficult. Mass protest meetings took a nasty turn when a squadron of cavalry attacked a crowd of 60,000 demonstrators at St. Peter's Fields in Manchester in 1819. The death of eleven people, called the Peterloo Massacre by government detractors, led Parliament to take even more repressive measures. The government restricted large public meetings and the dissemination of pamphlets among the poor. Before further repression could lead to greater violence, the Tory ministry was broadened by the addition of men who believed that some concessions to change rather than sheer repression might best avoid revolution. By making minor reforms in the 1820s, the Tories managed to avoid meeting the demands for electoral reforms—at least until 1830 (see Reform in Great Britain later in this chapter).

❧ RESTORATION IN FRANCE

In 1814, the Bourbon family was restored to the throne of France in the person of Louis XVIII (1814–1824). Louis understood the need to accept some of the changes brought to France by the revolutionary and Napoleonic eras. Consequently, the constitutional Charter of 1814 maintained Napoleon's Concordat with the pope and accepted Napoleon's Civil Code with its recognition of the principle of equality before the law (see Chapter 19). The property rights of those who had purchased confiscated lands during the Revolution were preserved. The Charter of 1814 also established a bicameral (two-house) legislature with a Chamber of Peers chosen by the king and a Chamber of Deputies chosen by an electorate restricted to slightly fewer than 100,000 wealthy people.

Louis's grudging moderation, however, was opposed by liberals anxious to extend the revolutionary reforms and by a group of ultraroyalists who criticized the king's willingness to compromise and retain so many features of the Napoleonic era. The ultras hoped to return to a monarchical system dominated by a privileged landed aristocracy and to restore the Catholic church to its former position of influence.

The initiative passed to the ultraroyalists in 1824 when Louis XVIII died and was succeeded by his brother, the count of Artois, who became Charles X (1824–1830). Charles had been the leader of the ultraroyalists and was determined to restore the old regime as far as possible. In 1825, he granted an indemnity to aristocrats whose lands had been confiscated during the Revolution. Moreover, the king pursued a religious policy that encouraged the church to reestablish control over the French educational system. Public outrage, fed by liberal newspapers, forced the king to compromise in 1827 and even to accept the principle of ministerial responsibility—that the ministers of the king were responsible to the legislature. But in 1829 he violated his commitment. A protest by the deputies led the king to dissolve the legislature in 1830 and call for new elections. France was on the brink of another revolution.

❧ INTERVENTION IN THE ITALIAN STATES AND SPAIN

In 1815, the Italian peninsula was still divided into a number of states. The Congress of Vienna had established nine states, including Piedmont (officially Sardinia) in the north ruled by the house of Savoy; the kingdom of the Two Sicilies (Naples and Sicily); the Papal States; a handful of small duchies ruled by relatives of the Austrian emperor; and the important northern provinces of Lombardy and Venetia that were now part of the Austrian Empire. Much of Italy was under Austrian domination, and all the states had extremely reactionary governments eager to smother any liberal or nationalist sentiment. The crushing of attempts at revolt in the kingdom of the Two Sicilies and Piedmont in 1821 discouraged opposition, although secret societies motivated by nationalistic dreams and known as the Carbonari—the charcoal burners—continued to conspire and plan for revolution.

In Spain, another Bourbon dynasty had been restored in the person of Ferdinand VII in 1814. Ferdinand (1814–1833) had agreed to observe the liberal constitution of 1812, which allowed for the functioning of an elected parliamentary assembly known as the Cortes. But the king soon reneged on his promises, tore up the constitution, dissolved the Cortes, and persecuted its members, which led a combined group of army officers, upper-middle-class merchants, and liberal intellectuals to revolt. The king capitulated in March 1820 and promised once again to restore the constitution and the Cortes.

Metternich's policy of intervention came to Ferdinand's rescue. In April 1823, a French army moved into Spain and forced the revolutionary government to flee Madrid. By August of that year, the king had been restored to his throne. Ignoring French advice to adopt moderate policies, Ferdinand VII tortured to death, imprisoned, or exiled the supporters of a constitutional system. Intervention had succeeded.

REPRESSION IN CENTRAL EUROPE

After 1815, the forces of reaction were particularly successful in central Europe. The Habsburg empire and its chief agent, Prince Klemens von Metternich, played an important role. Metternich boasted: "You see in me the chief Minister of Police in Europe. I keep an eye on everything. My contacts are such that nothing escapes me."[5] Metternich's spies were everywhere, searching for evidence of liberal or nationalist plots. Metternich worried too much in 1815. Although both liberalism and nationalism emerged in the German states and the Austrian Empire, they were initially weak as central Europe tended to remain under the domination of aristocratic landowning classes and autocratic, centralized monarchies.

The Vienna settlement in 1815 recognized the existence of thirty-eight sovereign states in what had once been the Holy Roman Empire. Austria and Prussia were the two great powers although their non-German territory was not included in the confederation. The other states varied considerably in size from the large south German kingdom of Bavaria to the small principality of Schaumburg-Lippe. Together these states formed the Germanic Confederation, but the confederation had little real power. It had no real executive, and its only central organ was the federal diet, which needed the consent of all member states to take action, making it virtually powerless. The purpose of the Germanic Confederation was not to govern the German states but to provide a common defense against France or Russia. However, it also came to serve as Metternich's instrument to repress revolutionary movements within the German states.

Initially, Germans who favored liberal principles and German unity looked to Prussia for leadership. During the Napoleonic era, King Frederick William III (1797–1840), following the advice of his two chief ministers, Baron Heinrich von Stein and Baron Karl von Hardenberg, instituted political and institutional reforms in response to Prussia's defeat at the hands of Napoleon. Hardenberg told the king in 1806: "Your Majesty! We must do from above what the French have done from below." The reforms included the abolition of serfdom, municipal self-government through town councils, the expansion of primary and secondary schools, and universal military conscription to form a national army. The reforms, however, did not include the creation of a legislative assembly or representative government as Stein and Hardenberg wished. After 1815 Frederick William grew more reactionary and was content to follow Metternich's lead. Though reforms had made Prussia strong, it remained largely an absolutist state with little interest in German unity.

Liberal and national movements in the German states seemed largely limited to university professors and students. The latter began to organize *Burschenschaften* or student societies dedicated to fostering the goal of a free, united Germany (see the box on p. 618). Their ideas and their motto, "Honor, Liberty, Fatherland," were in part inspired by Friedrich Ludwig Jahn, who had organized gymnastic societies during the Napoleonic wars to promote the regeneration of German youth. Jahn was a noisy nationalist who encouraged Germans to pursue their Germanic heritage and urged his followers to disrupt the lectures of professors whose views were not nationalistic.

From 1817 to 1819, the *Burschenschaften* pursued a variety of activities that alarmed German governments. An aide wrote to Metternich that "of all the evils affecting Germany today, even including the licentiousness of the press, this student nuisance is the greatest, the most urgent and the most threatening."[6] At an assembly held at the Wartburg Castle in 1817, marking the three-hundredth anniversary of Luther's Ninety-Five Theses, the crowd burned books written by conservative authors. When a deranged student assassinated a reactionary playwright, Metternich had the diet of the Germanic Confederation draw up the Karlsbad Decrees of 1819. These closed the *Burschenschaften*, provided for censorship of the press, and placed the universities under close supervision and control. Thereafter, except for a minor flurry of activity from 1830 to 1832, Metternich and the cooperative German rulers maintained the conservative status quo.

The Austrian Empire was a multinational state, a collection of different peoples under the Habsburg emperor who provided a common bond. The empire encompassed eleven peoples of different national origin, including Germans, Czechs, Magyars (Hungarians), Slovaks, Romanians, Slovenes, Poles, Serbians, and Italians. The Germans, though only a quarter of the population, were economically the most advanced and played a leading role in governing Austria. Since Austria was predominantly agricultural, the landed nobility continued to be the most important class and held most of the important positions as army officers, diplomats, ministers, and civil servants. Essentially, the Austrian Empire was held together by the dynasty, the imperial civil service, the imperial army, and the Catholic church. But its national groups, especially the Hungarians, with their increasing desire for autonomy acted as forces to break the Austrian Empire apart.

Still Metternich managed to hold it all together after 1815. His antipathy to liberalism and nationalism was understandably grounded in the realization that these forces threatened to tear the empire apart. The growing

University Students and German Unity

In the early nineteenth century, university students and professors were the chief supporters of German nationalism. Especially important were the Burschenschaften, student societies that espoused the cause of German unity. In this selection, the liberal Heinrich von Gagern explains the purpose of the Burschenschaften to his father.

❈ Heinrich von Gagern, Letter to His Father

It is very hard to explain the spirit of the student movement to you, but I shall try, even though I can only give you a few characteristics. . . . It speaks to the better youth, the man of heart and spirit and love for all this good, and gives him nourishment and being. For the average student of the past, the university years were a time to enjoy life, and to make a sharp break with his own background in defiance of the philistine world, which seemed to him somehow to foreshadow the tomb. Their pleasures, their organizations, and their talk were determined by their *status* as students, and their university obligation was only to avoid failing the examination and scraping by adequately—bread-and-butter learning. They were satisfied with themselves if they thought they could pass the examination. There are still many of those nowadays, indeed the majority over-all. But at several universities, and especially here, another group—in my eyes a better one—has managed to get the upper hand in the sense that it sets the mood. I prefer really not to call it a mood; rather, it is something that presses hard and tried to spread its ideas. . . .

Those who share in this spirit have then quite another tendency in their student life. Love of Fatherland is their guiding principle. Their purpose is to make a better future for the Fatherland, each as best he can, to spread national consciousness, or to use the much ridiculed and maligned Germanic expression, more folkishness, and to work for better constitutions. . . .

We want more sense of community among the several states of Germany, greater unity in their policies and in their principles of government; no separate policy for each state, but the nearest possible relations with one another; above all, we want Germany to be considered *one* land and the German people *one* people. In the forms of our student comradeship we show how we want to approach this as nearly as possible in the real world. Regional fraternities are forbidden, and we live in a German comradeship, one people in spirit, as we want it for all Germany in reality. We give our selves the freest of constitutions, just as we should like Germany to have the freest possible one, insofar as that is suitable for the German people. We want a constitution for the people that fits in with the spirit of the times and with the people's own level of enlightenment, rather than what each prince gives his people according to what he likes and what serves his private interest. Above all, we want the princes to understand and to follow the principle that they exist for the country and not the country for them. In fact, the prevailing view is that the constitution should not come from the individual states at all. The main principles of the German constitution should apply to all states in common, and should be expressed by the German federal assembly. This constitution should deal not only with the absolute necessities, like fiscal administration and justice, general administration and church and military affairs and so on; this constitution ought to be extended to the education of the young, at least at the upper age levels, and to many other such things.

---

liberal belief that each national group had the right to its own system of government could only mean disaster for the multinational Austrian Empire. While the forces of liberalism and nationalism grew, the Austrian Empire largely stagnated. Metternich had not prevented an explosion in Austria; he only postponed it until 1848.

✍ RUSSIA: AUTOCRACY OF THE TSARS

At the beginning of the nineteenth century, Russia was overwhelmingly rural, agricultural, and autocratic. The Russian tsar was still regarded as a divine-right monarch with unlimited power although the extent of the Russian Empire made the claim impractical. Most of the Russian land remained in the control of a class of noble landlords who monopolized the civil service and army officer corps. The land was tilled by serfs, the most exploited lower class in Europe.

In 1801, Alexander I (1801–1825) came to the Russian throne after a group of aristocrats assassinated his detested father, Tsar Paul I (1796–1801). Alexander had been raised in the ideas of the Enlightenment and gave every appearance of being liberal minded. But his liberalism was always conditioned by the autocratic tradition of the tsars. As one adviser said: "He would have willingly agreed that every man should be free, on the condition that he should voluntarily do only what the Emperor wished."

Initially, however, Alexander seemed willing to make reforms. With the aid of his liberal adviser, Michael Speransky, he relaxed censorship, freed political prisoners, and reformed the educational system. He refused, however, to grant a constitution or free the serfs in the face of opposition from the nobility. Then, too, Alexander himself gradually moved away from his reforming tendencies, and after the defeat of Napoleon, Alexander reverted to strict and arbitrary censorship. Soon opposition to Alexander arose from a group of secret societies.

One of these societies, known as the Northern Union, was composed of young aristocrats who had served in the Napoleonic wars and had become aware of the world outside Russia as well as intellectuals alienated by the censorship and lack of academic freedom in Russian universities. The Northern Union favored the establishment of a constitutional monarchy and the abolition of serfdom. The sudden death of Alexander in 1825 offered them their opportunity.

Although Alexander's brother Constantine was the legal heir to the throne, he had renounced his claims in favor of his brother Nicholas. Constantine's abdication had not been made public, however, and during the ensuing confusion in December 1825, the military leaders of the Northern Union rebelled against the accession of Nicholas. This so-called Decembrist Revolt was soon crushed by troops loyal to Nicholas and its leaders executed.

The revolt transformed Nicholas I (1825–1855) from a conservative into a reactionary determined to avoid another rebellion. Under Nicholas both the bureaucracy and the secret police were strengthened. Constituting the Third Section of the tsar's chancellery, the political police

PORTRAIT OF NICHOLAS I. **Tsar Nicholas I was a reactionary ruler who sought to prevent rebellion in Russia by strengthening the government bureaucracy, increasing censorship, and suppressing individual freedom by the use of political police. One of his enemies remarked about his facial characteristics: "The sharply retreating forehead and the lower jaw were expressive of iron will and feeble intelligence."**

were given sweeping powers over much of Russian life. They deported suspicious or dangerous persons, maintained close surveillance of foreigners in Russia, and reported regularly to the tsar on public opinion.

Matching Nicholas's fear of revolution at home was his fear of revolution abroad. There would be no revolution in Russia during the rest of his reign; if he could help it, there would be none in Europe either. Contemporaries called him the Policeman of Europe because of his willingness to use Russian troops to crush revolutions.

◆ The Ideologies of Change

Although the conservative forces were in the ascendancy from 1815 to 1830, powerful movements for change were also at work. These depended on ideas embodied in a series of political philosophies or ideologies that came into their own in the first half of the nineteenth century.

❊ *Liberalism*

One of these ideologies was liberalism, which owed much to the Enlightenment of the eighteenth century and to the American and French Revolutions at the end of that century. In addition, liberalism became even more significant as the Industrial Revolution made rapid strides, since the developing industrial middle class largely adopted the doctrine as its own. There were divergences of opinion among people classified as liberals, but all began with a common denominator, the belief that people should be as free from restraint as possible. This idea is evident in both economic and political liberalism.

Also called classical economics, economic liberalism had as its primary tenet the concept of laissez-faire, or the belief that the state should not interrupt the free play of natural economic forces, especially supply and demand. Government should not interfere with the economic liberty of the individual and should restrict itself to only three primary functions: defense of the country, police protection of individuals, and the construction and maintenance of public works too expensive for individuals to undertake. If individuals were allowed economic liberty, ultimately they would bring about the maximum good for the maximum number and benefit the general welfare of society.

The case against government interference in economic matters was greatly enhanced by Thomas Malthus (1766–1834). In his major work, *Essay on the Principles of Population*, Malthus argued that population, when unchecked, increases in a geometric ratio while the food supply correspondingly increases only in an arithmetic ratio. The result will be severe overpopulation and ultimately starvation for the human race if this growth is not held in check. According to Malthus, nature imposes a major restraint: "Unwholesome occupations, severe labor and exposure to the seasons, extreme poverty, bad nursing of children, great towns, excesses of all kinds, the whole train of common disease, and epidemics, wars, plague and famine." Misery and poverty were simply the inevitable result of the law of nature; no government or individual should interfere with its operation.

The ideas of Thomas Malthus were further developed by David Ricardo (1772–1823). In his *Principles of Political Economy*, written in 1817, Ricardo developed his famous "iron law of wages." Following Malthus, Ricardo argued that an increase in population means more workers; more workers in turn cause wages to fall below the subsistence level. The result is misery and starvation, which then reduce the population. Consequently, the number of workers declines, and wages rise above the subsistence level again, which in turn encourages workers to have larger families as the cycle is repeated. According to Ricardo, raising wages arbitrarily would be pointless since it would accomplish little but this vicious cycle. Nature is harsh, but attempting to change the laws of nature through the charity of employers or legislation by the state would merely make the situation worse.

Like economic liberalism, political liberalism stressed that people should be free from restraint. Politically, liberals came to hold a common set of beliefs. Chief among them was the protection of civil liberties or the basic rights of all people, which included equality before the law, freedom of assembly, speech, and press, and freedom from arbitrary arrest. All of these freedoms should be guaranteed by a written document, such as the American Bill of Rights or the French Declaration of the Rights of Man and the Citizen. In addition to religious toleration for all, most liberals advocated separation of church and state. The right of peaceful opposition to the government in and out of parliament and the making of laws by a representative assembly (legislature) elected by qualified voters constituted two other liberal demands. Many liberals believed, then, in a constitutional monarchy or constitutional state with limits on the powers of government in order to prevent despotism, and in written constitutions that would also help to guarantee these rights.

Many liberals also advocated ministerial responsibility or a system in which ministers of the king were responsible to the legislature rather than to the king, giving the legislative branch a check upon the power of the executive. Liberals in the first half of the nineteenth century also believed in a limited suffrage. Although all people were entitled to equal civil rights, they should not have equal political rights. The right to vote and hold office would be open only to men who met certain property qualifications. As a political philosophy, liberalism was tied to middle-class men, especially industrial, middle-class men who favored the extension of voting rights so that they could share power with the landowning classes. They had little desire to let the lower classes share that power. Liberals were not democrats.

One of the most prominent advocates of liberalism in the nineteenth century was the English philosopher John Stuart Mill (1806–1873). *On Liberty*, his most famous work published in 1859, has long been regarded as a classic statement on the liberty of the individual (see the box on p. 621). Mill argued for an "absolute freedom of opinion and sentiment on all subjects" that needed to be protected from both government censorship and the tyranny of the majority.

Mill was also instrumental in expanding the meaning of liberalism by becoming an enthusiastic supporter of women's rights. When his attempt to include women in the voting reform bill of 1867 failed, Mill published an essay entitled *On the Subjection of Women*, which he had written earlier with his wife, Harriet Taylor. He argued that "the legal subordination of one sex to the other" was wrong. Differences between women and men, he claimed, were due not to different natures but simply to social practices. With equal education, women could achieve as much as men. *On the Subjection of Women* would become an important work in the nineteenth-century movement for women's rights.

✺ *Nationalism*

Nationalism was based on an awareness of being part of a community that has common institutions, traditions, language, and customs. This community is called a "nation," and it, rather than a dynasty, city-state, or other political unit, becomes the focus of the individual's primary political loyalty. Nationalism did not become a popular force for change until the French Revolution, and even then nationalism was not so much political as cultural with its emphasis upon the uniqueness of a particular nationality. Cultural nationalism, however, evolved into political nationalism. The latter advocated that governments should coincide with nationalities. Thus, a divided people such as the Germans wanted national unity in a German nation-state with one central government. Subject peoples, such as the Hungarians, wanted national self-determination or the right to establish their own autonomy rather than be subject to a German minority in a multinational empire.

Nationalism was fundamentally radical in that it threatened to upset the existing political order, both internationally and nationally. A united Germany or united Italy would upset the balance of power established in 1815. By the same token, an independent Hungarian state would mean the breakup of the Austrian Empire. The conservatives tried so hard to repress nationalism because they were acutely aware of its potential to bring about such dramatic change.

At the same time, in the first half of the nineteenth century, nationalism and liberalism became strong allies. Most liberals believed that liberty could only be realized by peoples who ruled themselves. One British liberal said, "it is in general a necessary condition of free institutions that the boundaries of governments should coincide in the main with those of nationalities." The combination of liberalism with nationalism also gave a cosmopolitan dimension to nationalism. Many nationalists believed that once

The Voice of Liberalism: John Stuart Mill on Liberty

John Stuart Mill (1806–1873) was one of Britain's most famous philosophers of liberalism. Mill's On Liberty is viewed as a classic statement of the liberal belief in the unfettered freedom of the individual. In this excerpt, Mill defends freedom of opinion from both government and the coercion of the majority.

✳ John Stuart Mill, *On Liberty*

The object of this Essay is to assert one very simple principle, as entitled to govern absolutely the dealings of society with the individual in the way of compulsion and control, whether the means used by physical force in the form of legal penalties, or the moral coercion of public opinion. That principle is, that the sole end for which mankind are warranted, individually or collectively, interfering with the liberty of action of any of their number, is self-protection. That the only purpose for which power can be rightfully exercised over any member of a civilized community, against his will, is to prevent harm to others. His own good, either physical or moral, is not a sufficient warrant. . . . These are good reasons for remonstrating with him, or reasoning with him, or persuading him, or entreating him, but not for compelling him, or visiting him with any evil in case he do otherwise. To justify that, the conduct from which it is desired to deter him, must be calculated to produce evil to some one else. The only part of the conduct of any one, for which he is amenable to society, is that which concerns others. In the part which merely concerns himself, his independence is, of right, absolute. Over himself, over his own body and mind, the individual is sovereign. . . .

Society can and does execute its own mandates: and if it issues wrong mandates instead of right, or any mandates at all in things with which it ought not to meddle, it practices a social tyranny more formidable than many kinds of political oppression, since, though not usually upheld by such extreme penalties, it leaves fewer means of escape, penetrating more deeply into the details of life, and enslaving the soul itself. Protection, therefore, against the tyranny of the magistrate is not enough: there needs protection also against the tyranny of prevailing opinion and feeling, against the tendency of society to impose, by other means than civil penalties, its own ideas and practices as rules of conduct on those who dissent from them. . . .

But there is a sphere of action in which society, as distinguished from the individual has, if any, only an indirect interest; comprehending all that portion of a person's life and conduct which affects only himself, or if it also affects others, only with their free, voluntary and undeceived consent and participation. . . . This then is the appropriate region of human liberty. It comprises, first, the inward domain of consciousness; demanding liberty of conscience in the most comprehensive sense; liberty of thought and feeling; absolute freedom of opinion and sentiment on all subjects, practical or speculative, scientific, moral, or theological. . . .

Let us suppose, therefore, that the government is entirely at one with the people, and never thinks of exerting any power of coercion unless in agreement with what it conceives to be their voice. But I deny the right of the people to exercise such coercion, either by themselves or by their government. The power itself is illegitimate. The best government has no more title to it than the worst. It is as noxious, or more noxious, when exerted in accordance with public opinion, than when in opposition to it. If all mankind minus one were of one opinion, and only one person were of the contrary opinion, mankind would be no more justified in silencing that one person, than he, if he had the power, would be justified in silencing mankind. . . . The peculiar evil of silencing the expression of an opinion is, that it is robbing the human race; posterity as well as the existing generation; those who dissent from the opinion, still more than those who hold it. If the opinion is right, they are deprived of the opportunity of exchanging error for truth: if wrong, they lose, what is almost as great a benefit, the clearer perception and livelier impression of truth, produced by its collision with error.

---

each people obtained their own state, all nations could be linked together into a broader community of all humanity.

❋ *Early Socialism*

In the first half of the nineteenth century, the pitiful conditions found in the slums, mines, and factories of the Industrial Revolution gave rise to another ideology for change known as socialism. The term eventually became associated with a Marxist analysis of human society (see Chapter 22), but early socialism was largely the product of political theorists or intellectuals who wanted to introduce equality into social conditions and believed that human cooperation was superior to the competition that characterized early industrial capitalism. To later Marxists, such ideas were impractical dreams, and they contemptuously labeled the theorists utopian socialists. The term has endured to this day.

The utopian socialists were against private property and the competitive spirit of early industrial capitalism. By eliminating them and creating new systems of social organization, they thought that a better environment for humanity could be achieved. Early socialists proposed a variety of ways to accomplish that task.

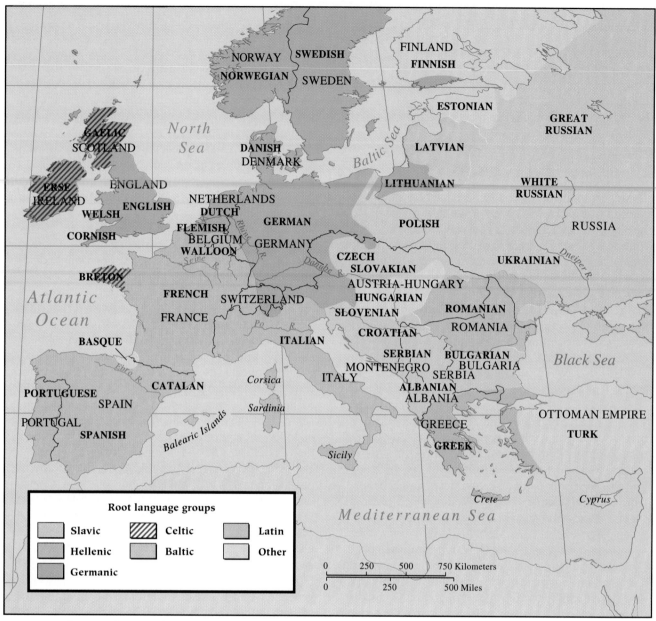

MAP 21.3 **The Distribution of Languages in Nineteenth-Century Europe.**

One approach, set out in the teachings of the Frenchman Henri de Saint-Simon (1760–1825), was the organization of all society into a cooperative community. Two elites, the intellectual leaders and the industrial managers, would use industrial and scientific technology to coordinate society for the benefit of all. In the process, government would vanish, as it would no longer be needed in the new society.

Another group of early socialists sought to create voluntary associations that would demonstrate the advantages of cooperative living. To Charles Fourier (1772–1838), the competitive industrial system was failing to satisfy human passions and actually repressed them. He proposed instead the creation of small model communities called phalansteries. These were self-contained cooperatives, each consisting ideally of 1,620 people. Communally

housed, the inhabitants of the phalanstery would live and work together for their mutual benefit. Work assignments would be rotated frequently to relieve workers of undesirable tasks. Unable to gain financial backing for his phalansteries, Fourier's plan remained untested.

Robert Owen (1771–1858), the British cotton manufacturer, also believed that humans would reveal their true natural goodness if they lived in a cooperative environment. At New Lanark in Scotland, he was successful in transforming a squalid factory town into a flourishing, healthy community. But when he attempted to create a self-contained cooperative community at New Harmony, Indiana, in the United States in the 1820s, internal bickering within the community eventually destroyed his dream. One of Owen's disciples, a wealthy woman named Frances Wright, bought slaves in order to set up a

CHILDREN AT NEW LANARK. Robert Owen created an early experiment in utopian socialism by establishing a model industrial community at New Lanark, Scotland. In this illustration, the children of factory workers are shown dancing the quadrille.

model community at Nashoba, Tennessee. The community failed, but Wright continued to work for women's rights.

The Frenchman Louis Blanc (1813–1882) offered yet another early socialist approach to a better society. In *The Organization of Work*, he maintained that social problems could be solved by government assistance. Denouncing competition as the main cause of the economic evils of his day, he called for the establishment of workshops that would manufacture goods for public sale. The state would finance these workshops, but the workers would own and operate them. Blanc believed that the gradual spread of these workshops would provide a cooperative rather than competitive foundation for the entire economic life of the nation.

With their plans for the reconstruction of society, utopian socialists attracted a number of female supporters who believed that only a reordering of society would help women. Zoé Gatti de Gamond, a Belgian follower of Fourier, established her own phalanstery, which was supposed to provide men and women with the same educational and job opportunities. As part of collective living, men and women were to share responsibilities for child care and housecleaning. The ideas of Saint-Simon proved especially attractive to a number of women who participated in the growing activism of women in politics that had been set in motion during the French Revolution. Saint-Simon's cooperative society recognized the principle of equality between men and women, and a number of working-class women, including Suzanne Voilquin, Claire Démar, and Reine Guindorf, published a newspaper dedicated to the emancipation of women.

One female utopian socialist, Flora Tristan (1803–1844), even attempted to foster a "utopian synthesis of socialism and feminism." She traveled through France preaching the need for the liberation of women. Her *Worker's Union*, published in 1843, advocated the application of Fourier's ideas to reconstruct both family and work:

Workers, be sure of it. If you have enough equity and justice to inscribe into your Charter the few points I have just outlined, this declaration of the rights of women will soon pass into custom, from custom into law, and before twenty-five years pass you will then see inscribed in front of the book of laws which will govern French society: THE ABSOLUTE EQUALITY of man and woman. Then, my brothers, and only then, will human unity be constituted.[7]

She envisioned this absolute equality as the only hope to free the working class and transform civilization.

Flora Tristan, like the other utopian socialists, was largely ignored by her contemporaries. Although criticized for their impracticality, the utopian socialists at least laid the groundwork for later attacks on capitalism that would have a far-reaching result. But further industrialization would have to occur before those changes could be realized. In the first half of the nineteenth century, socialism remained merely a fringe movement compared to liberalism and nationalism.

◆ Revolution and Reform
(1830–1850)

Beginning in 1830, the forces of change began to break through the conservative domination of Europe, more successfully in some places than in others. Finally, in 1848 a wave of revolutionary fervor moved through Europe, causing liberals and nationalists everywhere to think that they were on the verge of creating a new order.

✳ *Another French Revolution*

The new elections Charles X had called in 1830 produced another victory for the French liberals; at this point the king decided to seize the initiative. He believed that concessions had brought the downfall of Louis XVI during the first French Revolution and was determined not to go in that direction. On July 26, 1830, Charles issued a set of edicts (July Ordinances) that imposed a rigid censorship on the press, dissolved the legislative assembly, and reduced the electorate in preparation for new elections. Charles's actions produced an immediate rebellion—the July Revolution. Barricades went up in Paris as a provisional government led by a group of moderate, propertied liberals was hastily formed and appealed to Louis-Philippe, the duke of Orléans, a cousin of Charles X, to become the constitutional king of France. Charles X fled to Britain; a new monarchy had been born.

Louis-Philippe (1830–1848) was soon called the bourgeois monarch because political support for his rule came from the upper middle class. Louis-Philippe even dressed like a member of the middle class in business suits and hats. Constitutional changes that favored the interests of the upper bourgeoisie were instituted. Financial qualifications for voting were reduced, yet remained sufficiently high that the number of voters only increased from 100,000 to barely 200,000, guaranteeing that only the wealthiest people would vote.

To the upper middle class, the bourgeois monarchy represented the stopping place for political progress. To the lesser bourgeoisie and the Parisian working class, who had helped to overthrow Charles X in 1830, it was a severe disappointment because they had been completely excluded from political power. The rapid expansion of French industry in the 1830s and 1840s gave rise to an industrial working class concentrated in certain urban areas. Terrible working and living conditions and the periodic economic crises that created high levels of unemployment led to worker unrest and sporadic outbursts of violence. In 1831 and 1834, government troops were used to crush working-class disturbances in Lyons, center of the silk industry. These insurrections witnessed an emerging alliance between workers and radical advocates of a republic. The government's response—repression and strict censorship of the press—worked temporarily to curb further overt resistance.

Even in the legislature—the Chamber of Deputies—there were differences of opinion about the bourgeois monarchy and the direction in which it should grow. Two groups rapidly emerged, although both were composed of upper-middle-class representatives. The Party of Movement, which was led by Adolphe Thiers, favored ministerial responsibility, the pursuit of an active foreign policy, and limited expansion of the franchise. The Party of Resistance was led by François Guizot who believed that France had finally reached the "perfect form" of government and needed no further institutional changes. After 1840, the Party of Resistance dominated the Chamber of Deputies. Guizot cooperated with Louis-Philippe in suppressing ministerial responsibility and pursuing a policy favoring the interests of the wealthier manufacturers and tradespeople. The government's unwillingness to change led to growing frustration and revolutionary stirrings. They finally erupted in 1848.

❈ Revolutionary Outbursts in Belgium, Poland, and Italy

Supporters of liberalism played a primary role in the July Revolution in France, but nationalism was the crucial force in three other revolutionary outbursts in 1830. Rebels in all three states, however, were motivated by the success of the French revolutionaries. Nationalism was the key factor in a revolt that took place in the Netherlands. In an effort to create a stronger, larger state on France's north-

THE JULY REVOLUTION IN PARIS. In 1830, the forces of change began to undo the conservative domination of Europe. In France, the reactionary Charles X was overthrown. In this painting, students, former soldiers of the Empire, and middle-class citizens are seen joining the rebels who are marching on city hall to demand a republic. The forces of Charles X, seen firing from a building above, failed to halt the rebels.

ern border, the Congress of Vienna had added the area once known as the Austrian Netherlands to the Dutch Republic. The combination of two states with different languages, traditions, and religions was never really acceptable to the Belgians, nor did they appreciate the absolutist rule of the Dutch king, William of Orange. In 1830, the Belgians rose up against the Dutch and succeeded in convincing the major European powers to accept an independent, neutral Belgium. Leopold of Saxe-Coburg, a minor German prince, was designated to be the new king, and a Belgian national congress established a constitutional monarchy for the new state.

The revolutionary scenarios in Italy and Poland were much less successful. Metternich sent Austrian troops to crush revolts in three Italian states. Poland, too, had a nationalist uprising in 1830 when revolutionaries tried to end Russian control of their country. But the Polish insurgents failed to get hoped-for support from France and Britain, and by September 1831 the Russians had crushed the revolt and established an oppressive military dictatorship over Poland.

❈ *Reform in Great Britain*

In 1830, new parliamentary elections brought the Whigs to power in Britain. At the same time, the successful July Revolution in France served to catalyze change in Britain. The Industrial Revolution had led to an expanding group of industrial leaders who objected to the corrupt British electoral system, which excluded them from political power. The Whigs, though also members of the landed classes, realized that concessions to reform were superior to revolution; the demands of the wealthy industrial middle class could no longer be ignored. In 1830, the Whigs introduced an election reform bill that was enacted in 1832 after an intense struggle (see the box on p. 626).

The Reform Act gave explicit recognition to the changes wrought in British life by the Industrial Revolution. It disfranchised fifty-six rotten boroughs and enfranchised forty-two new towns and cities and reapportioned others. This gave the new industrial urban communities some voice in government. A property qualification (of £10 annual rent) for voting was retained, however, so the number of voters only increased from 478,000 to 814,000, a figure that still meant that only one in every thirty people was represented in Parliament. Thus, the Reform Act of 1832 primarily benefited the upper middle class; the lower middle class, artisans, and industrial workers still had no vote. Moreover, the change did not significantly alter the composition of the House of Commons. One political leader noted that the Commons chosen in the first election after the Reform Act seemed "to be very much like

MAP 21.4 **European Revolts in the 1820s and 1830s.**

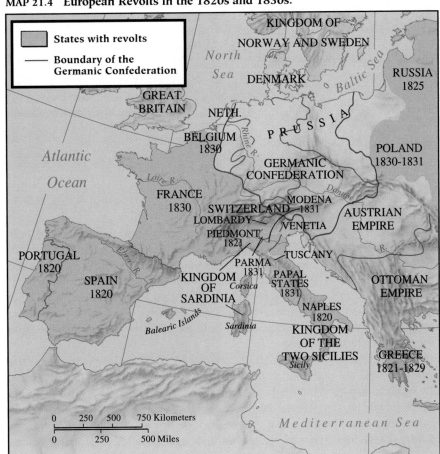

The Voice of Reform: Macaulay on the Reform Act of 1832

Thomas Babington Macaulay (1800–1859) was a historian and Whig member of Parliament. This selection is an excerpt from his speech given in Parliament in support of the Reform Act of 1832, which extended the right to vote to the industrial middle classes of Britain. His argument was very simple: it is better to reform than to have a political revolution.

❋ Thomas Babington Macaulay, Speech of March 2, 1831

My hon. friend the member of the University of Oxford tells us that, if we pass this law, England will soon be a Republic. The reformed House of Commons will, according to him, before it has sat ten years, depose the King, and expel the Lords from their House. Sir, if my hon. friend could prove this, he would have succeeded in bringing an argument for democracy infinitely stronger than any that is to be found in the works of Paine. His proposition is, in fact, this—that our monarchical and aristocratical institutions have no hold on the public mind of England; that these institutions are regarded with aversion by a decided majority of the middle class. . . . Now, sir, if I were convinced that the great body of the middle class in England look with aversion on monarchy and aristocracy, I should be forced, much against my will, to come to this conclusion, that monarchical and aristocratical institutions are unsuited to this country. Monarchy and aristocracy, valuable and useful as I think them, are still valuable and useful as means, and not as ends. The end of government is the happiness of the people; and I do not conceive that, in a country like this, the happiness of the people can be promoted by a form of government in which the middle classes place no confidence, and which exists only because the middle classes have no organ by which to make their sentiments known. But, sir, I am fully convinced that the middle classes sincerely wish to uphold the royal prerogatives, and the constitutional rights of the Peers. . . .

But let us know our interest and our duty better. Turn where we may—within, around—the voice of great events is proclaiming to us, "Reform, that you may preserve." Now, therefore, while everything at home and abroad forebodes ruin to those who persist in a hopeless struggle against the spirit of the age; now, while the crash of the proudest throne of the Continent is still resounding in our ears; . . . now, while the heart of England is still sound; now, while the old feelings and the old associations retain a power and a charm which may too soon pass away; now, in this your accepted time; now, in this your day of salvation, take counsel, not of prejudice, not of party spirit, not of the ignominious pride of a fatal consistency, but of history, of reason, of the ages which are past, of the signs of this most portentous time. Pronounce in a manner worthy of the expectation with which this great debate has been anticipated, and of the long remembrance which it will leave behind. Renew the youth of the State. Save property divided against itself. Save the multitude, endangered by their own ungovernable passions. Save the aristocracy, endangered by its own unpopular power. Save the greatest, and fairest, and most highly civilized community that ever existed, from calamities which may in a few days sweep away all the rich heritage of so many ages of wisdom and glory. The danger is terrible. The time is short. If this Bill should be rejected, I pray to God that none of those who concur in rejecting it may ever remember their votes with unavailing regret, amidst the wreck of laws, the confusion of ranks, the spoliation of property, and the dissolution of social order.

every other parliament." Nevertheless, a significant step had been taken. The "monied, manufacturing, and educated elite" had been "hitched" to the landed interests in ruling Britain.

The 1830s and 1840s witnessed considerable reform legislation. The aristocratic landowning class was usually (but not always) the driving force for legislation that halted some of the worst abuses in the industrial system by instituting government regulation of working conditions in the factories and mines. The industrialists and manufacturers now in Parliament opposed such legislation and were usually (but not always) the driving forces behind legislation that favored the principles of economic liberalism. The Poor Law of 1834 was based on the theory that giving aid to the poor and unemployed only encouraged laziness and increased the number of paupers. The Poor Law of 1834 tried to remedy this by making paupers so wretched they would choose to work. Those unable to support themselves were crowded together in workhouses where living and working conditions were intentionally miserable so that people would be encouraged to find profitable employment.

Another piece of liberal legislation involved the repeal of the Corn Laws. This was primarily the work of the manufacturers Richard Cobden and John Bright who formed the Anti-Corn Law League in 1838 to help workers by lowering bread prices. But abolishing the Corn Laws would also aid the industrial middle classes who, as economic liberals, favored the principles of free trade. Repeal came in 1846 when Robert Peel (1788–1850), leader of the Tories, persuaded some of his associates to support free trade principles and abandon the Corn Laws.

The year 1848, which witnessed revolutions in most of Europe, ended without a major crisis in Britain. On the Continent, middle-class liberals and nationalists were at the forefront of the revolutionary forces. In Britain, however, the middle class had been largely satisfied by the Reform Act of 1832 and the repeal of the Corn Laws in 1846. The British working classes were discontented, but they would have to wait until the second half of the nineteenth century to begin to achieve their goals.

✼ *The Growth of the United States*

The U.S. Constitution, ratified in 1789, committed the United States to two of the major forces of the first half of the nineteenth century, liberalism and nationalism. Initially, this constitutional commitment to national unity was challenged by divisions over the power of the federal government vis-à-vis the individual states. Bitter conflict erupted between the Federalists and the Republicans. Led by Alexander Hamilton (1757–1804), the Federalists favored a financial program that would establish a strong central government. The Republicans, guided by Thomas Jefferson (1743–1826) and James Madison (1751–1836), feared centralization and its consequences for popular liberties. These divisions were intensified by European rivalries as the Federalists were pro-British and the Republicans pro-French. The conclusion of the War of 1812 brought an end to the Federalists, who had opposed the war, while the surge of national feeling generated by the war served to heal the nation's divisions.

Another strong force for national unity came from the Supreme Court where John Marshall (1755–1835) was chief justice from 1801 to 1835. Marshall made the Supreme Court into an important national institution by asserting the right of the Court to overrule an act of Congress if the Court found it to be in violation of the Constitution. Under Marshall, the Supreme Court contributed further to establishing the supremacy of the national government by curbing the actions of state courts and legislatures.

The election of Andrew Jackson (1767–1845) as president in 1828 opened a new era in American politics. Jacksonian democracy introduced mass democratic politics. The electorate was expanded by dropping traditional property qualifications; by the 1830s suffrage had been extended to almost all adult white males. During the period from 1815 to 1850, the traditional liberal belief in the improvement of human beings was also given concrete expression. Americans developed detention schools for juvenile delinquents and new penal institutions, both motivated by the liberal belief that the right kind of environment would rehabilitate those in need of it. The abolitionist or national antislavery movement that developed

in the 1830s also stemmed from liberal convictions. The American Anti-Slavery Society, established by William Lloyd Garrison (1805–1879) in 1833, already had 250,000 members by 1838.

By 1850, Europeans had become well aware of the growth of the American republic. Between 1830 and 1850, a wide variety of European political writers visited and examined the United States. The general thrust of their collective wisdom was that the United States was emerging as a world power. The French critic Sainte-Beuve wrote in 1847 that "Russia is still barbarous, but she is great. . . . The other youthful people is America . . . the future of the world is there, between these two great worlds." Sainte-Beuve had the right idea even if he was somewhat premature.

✼ *The Revolutions of 1848*

Despite the successes of revolutions in France, Belgium, and Greece, the conservative order continued to dominate much of Europe. But the forces of liberalism and nationalism, first generated by the French Revolution, continued to grow. In 1848, these forces of change erupted once more. As usual, revolution in France provided the spark for other countries, and soon most of central and southern Europe was ablaze with revolutionary fires. Tsar Nicholas I of Russia lamented to Queen Victoria in April 1848, "What remains standing in Europe? Great Britain and Russia."

✼ YET ANOTHER FRENCH REVOLUTION

Numerous signs of trouble preceded the revolution. A severe industrial and agricultural depression beginning in 1846 brought untold hardship to the lower middle class, workers, and peasants. One-third of the workers in Paris were unemployed by the end of 1847. Scandals, graft, and corruption were rife while the government's persistent refusal to extend the suffrage angered the disfranchised members of the middle class. Even members of the upper middle class were discontented with the colorless reign of Louis-Philippe.

As Louis-Philippe's government continued to refuse to make changes, opposition grew. Radical republicans and socialists, joined by the upper middle class under the leadership of Adolphe Thiers, agitated for the dismissal of Guizot. Since they were forbidden by law to stage political rallies, they used the political banquet to call for reforms. Almost seventy such banquets were held in France during the winter of 1847–1848; a grand, culminating banquet was planned for Paris on February 22. When the government forbade it, people came anyway; students and workers threw up barricades in Paris. Although Louis-Philippe now proposed reform, he was unable to form another ministry and abdicated on February 24 and fled to Britain. A provisional government was established by a group of moderate and radical republicans; the latter even included the socialist Louis

Blanc. The provisional government ordered that representatives for a Constituent Assembly to draw up a new constitution be elected by universal manhood suffrage.

The provisional government also established national workshops under the influence of Louis Blanc. As Blanc envisioned them, the workshops were to be cooperative factories run by the workers. In fact, the workshops became unemployment compensation units or public works, except that they provided little work beyond leaf raking and ditch digging. The cost of the program became increasingly burdensome to the government.

The result was a growing split between the moderate republicans, who had the support of most of France, and the radical republicans, whose main support came from the Parisian working class. In the elections for the National Assembly, 500 seats went to moderate republicans and 300 to avowed monarchists while the radicals gained only 100. From March to June, the number of unemployed enrolled in the national workshops rose from 10,000 to almost 120,000, emptying the treasury and frightening the moderates who responded by closing the workshops on June 21. The workers refused to accept this decision and poured into the streets. Four days of bitter and bloody fighting by government forces crushed the working-class revolt, described by some as a "class struggle." Thousands were killed, and 11,000 prisoners were deported to the French colony of Algeria in North Africa. These "June days" left a legacy of hate. They had aspects of class warfare as the propertied classes became convinced that they had barely averted an attempt by the working class to destroy the social order. To many Europeans, the "June days" appeared to be a struggle of the bourgeoisie against the working class.

The new constitution, ratified on November 4, 1848, established a republic (Second Republic) with a unicameral (one-house) legislature of 750 elected by universal male suffrage for three years and a president, also elected by universal male suffrage, for four years. In the elections for the presidency held in December 1848, four republicans who had been associated with the early months of the Second Republic were resoundingly defeated by Charles Louis Napoleon Bonaparte, the nephew of Napoleon Bonaparte.

How could a virtual unknown who had been arrested twice and sent into exile once be chosen president by a landslide? The name of Bonaparte had obviously worked its magic. The Napoleonic revival had been going on for years as romanticists glorified his legend. One old veteran said: "Why shouldn't I vote for this gentleman. I, whose nose was frozen near Moscow." Perhaps just as important, the French were tired of revolution, and Louis Napoleon had posed as a defender of order. Members of the rural and urban masses who voted for Napoleon in large numbers saw him as a man of the people. Since they had been excluded from political life since 1815, what better choice did they have? Within four years President Napoleon would become Emperor Napoleon (see Chapter 22). The French had once again made a journey from republican hopes to authoritarian order, a pattern that was becoming all too common in French history.

REVOLUTION IN CENTRAL EUROPE

Like France, central Europe experienced rural and urban tensions due to an agricultural depression beginning in 1845. But the upheaval here seems to have been set off by news of the revolution in Paris in February 1848 (see the box on p. 629). By early March 1848, handicraft workers in many German states were destroying the machines and factories that they blamed for depriving them of their jobs; peasants looted and burned the manor houses of the nobility. Many German rulers promised constitutions, a free press, jury trials, and other liberal reforms. In Prussia concessions were also made to appease the revolutionaries. King Frederick William IV (1840–1861) agreed to abolish censorship, establish a new constitution, and work for a united Germany. The latter promise had its counterpart throughout all the German states as governments allowed elections by universal male suffrage for deputies to an all-German parliament to meet in Frankfurt, the seat of the German Confederation. Its purpose was to fulfill a liberal dream—the preparation of a constitution for a new united Germany.

This Frankfurt Assembly was dominated by well-educated, articulate, middle-class delegates, many of them professors, lawyers, and bureaucrats. When it came to nationalism, many were ahead of the times and certainly ahead of the governments of their respective states. From the beginning, the assembly aroused controversy by claiming to be the government for all of Germany. Then, it became embroiled in a sticky debate over the composition of the new German state. Supporters of a *Grossdeutsch* ("Big German") solution wanted to include the German province of Austria, whereas proponents of a *Kleindeutsch* ("Small German") solution favored excluding Austria and making the Prussian king the emperor of the new German state. The problem was solved when the Austrians withdrew, leaving the field to the supporters of the *Kleindeutsch* solution. Their victory was short-lived, however, as Frederick William IV gruffly refused the assembly's offer of the title of "emperor of the Germans" in March 1849 and ordered the Prussian delegates home.

The Frankfurt Assembly soon disbanded. Although some members spoke of using force, they had no real means of compelling the German rulers to accept the constitution they had drawn up. The attempt of the German liberals at Frankfurt to create a German state had failed.

The Austrian Empire also had its social, political, and nationalist grievances and needed only the news of the revolution in Paris to encourage it to erupt in flames in March 1848. The Hungarian liberal gentry under Louis Kossuth agitated for "commonwealth" status; they were willing to keep the Habsburg monarch, but wanted their own legislature. In March, demonstrations in Budapest,

Revolutionary Excitement: Carl Schurz and the Revolution of 1848 in Germany

The excitement with which German liberals and nationalists received the news of the February Revolution in France and their own expectations for Germany are well captured in this selection from the Reminiscences of Carl Schurz (1829–1906). Schurz made his way to the United States after the failure of the German revolution and eventually became a U.S. senator.

❋ Carl Schurz, *Reminiscences*

One morning, toward the end of February, 1848, I sat quietly in my attic-chamber, working hard at my tragedy of "Ulrich von Hutten," [a sixteenth-century German knight] when suddenly a friend rushed breathlessly into the room, exclaiming: "What, you sitting here! Do you not know what has happened?"

"No; what?"

"The French have driven away Louis Philippe and proclaimed the republic."

I threw down my pen—and that was the end of "Ulrich von Hutten." I never touched the manuscript again. We tore down the stairs, into the street, to the market-square, the accustomed meeting-place for all the student societies after their midday dinner. Although it was still forenoon, the market was already crowded with young men talking excitedly. There was no shouting, no noise, only agitated conversation. What did we want there? This probably no one knew. But since the French had driven away Louis Philippe and proclaimed the republic, something of course must happen here, too. . . . We were dominated by a vague feeling as if a great outbreak of elemental forces had begun, as if an earthquake was impending of which we had felt the first shock, and we instinctively crowded together. . . .

The next morning there were the usual lectures to be attended. But how profitless! The voice of the professor sounded like a monotonous drone coming from far away. What he had to say did not seem to concern us. The pen that should have taken notes remained idle. At last we closed with a sigh the notebook and went away, impelled by a feeling that now we had something more important to do—to devote ourselves to the affairs of the fatherland. And this we did by seeking as quickly as possible again the company of our friends, in order to discuss what had happened and what was to come. In these conversations, excited as they were, certain ideas and catchwords worked themselves to the surface, which expressed more or less the feelings of the people. Now had arrived in Germany the day for the establishment of "German Unity," and the founding of a great, powerful national German Empire. In the first line the convocation of a national parliament. Then the demands for civil rights and liberties, free speech, free press, the right of free assembly, equality before the law, a freely elected representation of the people with legislative power, responsibility of ministers, self-government of the communes, the right of the people to carry arms, the formation of a civic guard with elective officers, and so on—in short, that which was called a "constitutional form of government on a broad democratic basis." Republican ideas were at first only sparingly expressed. But the word democracy was soon on all tongues, and many, too, thought it a matter of course that if the princes should try to withhold from the people the rights and liberties demanded, force would take the place of mere petition. Of course the regeneration of the fatherland must, if possible, be accomplished by peaceable means. . . . Like many of my friends, I was dominated by the feeling that at last the great opportunity had arrived for giving to the German people the liberty which was their birthright and to the German fatherland its unity and greatness, and that it was now the first duty of every German to do and to sacrifice everything for this sacred object.

Prague, and Vienna led to Metternich's dismissal. The arch-symbol of the conservative order fled abroad. In Vienna, revolutionary forces, carefully guided by the educated and propertied classes, took control of the capital and insisted that a constituent assembly be summoned to draw up a liberal constitution. Hungary was granted its wish for its own legislature, a separate national army, and control over its foreign policy and budget. Allegiance to the Habsburg dynasty was now Hungary's only tie to the Austrian Empire. In Bohemia, the Czechs began to demand their own government as well.

Although Emperor Ferdinand I and Austrian officials had made concessions to appease the revolutionaries, they awaited an opportunity to reestablish their firm control. As in the German states, the conservatives were increasingly encouraged by the divisions between radical and moderate revolutionaries and played upon the middle-class fear of a working-class social revolution. Their first success came in June 1848 when a military force under General Alfred Windischgrätz ruthlessly suppressed the Czech rebels in Prague. In October the death of the minister for war at the hands of a Viennese mob gave Windischgrätz the pretext for an attack on Vienna. By the end of the month, radical rebels there had been crushed. In December the feebleminded Ferdinand I agreed to abdicate in favor of his nephew, Francis Joseph I (1848–1916), who

AUSTRIAN STUDENTS IN THE REVOLUTIONARY CIVIL GUARD. In 1848, revolutionary fervor swept through Europe and toppled governments in France, central Europe, and Italy. In the Austrian Empire, students joined the revolutionary civil guard in taking control of Vienna and forcing the Austrian emperor to call a constituent assembly to draft a liberal constitution.

worked vigorously to restore the imperial government in Hungary. The Austrian armies, however, were unable to defeat Kossuth's forces, and it was only through the intervention of Nicholas I, who sent a Russian army of 140,000 men to aid the Austrians, that the Hungarian revolution was finally crushed in 1849. The revolutions in Austria had also failed. Autocratic government was restored; emperor and propertied classes remained in control while the numerous nationalities were still subject to the Austrian government.

✖ REVOLTS IN THE ITALIAN STATES

The failure of the revolutionary uprisings in Italy in 1830–1831 had served to discredit the secret societies that had fomented them and encouraged the Italian movement for unification to take a new direction. The leadership of Italy's *risorgimento* ("Resurgence") passed into the hands of Giuseppe Mazzini (1805–1872), a dedicated Italian nationalist who founded an organization known as Young Italy in 1831 (see the box on p. 631). This group set as its goal the creation of a united Italian republic. In his work *The Duties of Man*, Mazzini urged Italians to dedicate their lives to the Italian nation: "O my Brother! love your Country. Our Country is our home." A number of Italian women also took up Mazzini's call. Especially noticeable was Cristina Belgiojoso, a wealthy aristocrat who worked to bring about Italian unification. Pursued by the Austrian authorities, she fled abroad and started a newspaper in Paris to espouse the Italian cause.

The dreams of Mazzini and Belgiojoso seemed on the verge of fulfillment when a number of Italian states rose in revolt in 1848. Beginning in Sicily, rebellions spread northward as ruler after ruler granted a constitution to his people. Citizens in Lombardy and Venetia also rebelled against their Austrian overlords. The Venetians declared a republic in Venice. The king of the northern Italian state of Piedmont, Charles Albert (1831–1849), took up the call and assumed the leadership for a war of liberation from Austrian domination. His invasion of Lombardy proved unsuccessful, however, and by 1849 the Austrians had reestablished complete control over Lombardy and Venetia. Counterrevolutionary forces also prevailed throughout Italy. French forces helped Pope Pius IX regain control of Rome. Elsewhere Italian rulers managed to recover power on their own. Only Piedmont was able to keep its liberal constitution.

✖ THE FAILURES OF 1848

Throughout Europe in 1848, popular revolts had initiated revolutionary upheavals that had led to the formation of liberal constitutions and liberal governments. But how could so many immediate successes in 1848 be followed by so many disasters only months later? Two reasons stand out. The unity of the revolutionaries had made the revolutions possible, but divisions soon shattered their ranks. Except in France, moderate liberals from the propertied classes failed to extend suffrage to the working classes who had helped to achieve the revolutions. But as radicals pushed for universal male suffrage, liberals everywhere pulled back.

The Voice of Italian Nationalism: Giuseppe Mazzini and Young Italy

After the failure of the uprisings in Italy in 1830–1831, Giuseppe Mazzini emerged as the leader of the Italian risorgimento—the movement for Italian nationhood. In 1831, he founded an organization known as Young Italy whose goal was the creation of a united Italian republic. This selection is excerpted from the oath that the members of young Italy were required to take.

❊ Giuseppe Mazzini, The Young Italy Oath

Young Italy is a brotherhood of Italians who believe in a law of Progress and Duty, and are convinced that Italy is destined to become one nation,—convinced also that she possesses sufficient strength within herself to become one, and that the ill success of her former efforts is to be attributed not to the weakness, but to the misdirection of the revolutionary elements within her,—that the secret of force lies in constancy and unity of effort. They join this association in the firm intent of consecrating both thought and action to the great aim of reconstituting Italy as one independent sovereign nation of free men and equals. . . .

Each member will, upon his initiation into the association of Young Italy, pronounce the following form of oath, in the presence of the initiator:

In the name of God and of Italy;

In the name of all the martyrs of the holy Italian cause who have fallen beneath foreign and domestic tyranny;

By the duties which bind me to the land wherein God has placed me, and to the brothers whom God has given me;

By the love—innate in all men—I bear to the country that gave my mother birth, and will be the home of my children. . . .

By the sufferings of the millions,—

I, . . . believing in the mission intrusted by God to Italy, and the duty of every Italian to strive to attempt its fulfillment; convinced that where God has ordained that a nation shall be, He has given the requisite power to create it; that the people are the depositaries of that power, and that in its right direction for the people, and by the people, lies the secret of victory; convinced that virtue consists in action and sacrifice, and strength in union and constancy of purpose: I give my name to Young Italy, an association of men holding the same faith, and swear:

To dedicate myself wholly and forever to the endeavor with them to constitute Italy one free, independent, republican nation; to promote by every means in my power—whether by written or spoken word, or by action—the education of my Italian brothers toward the aim of Young Italy; toward association, the sole means of its accomplishment, and to virtue, which alone can render the conquest lasting; to abstain from enrolling myself in any other association from this time forth; to obey all the instructions, in conformity with the spirit of Young Italy, given me by those who represent with me the union of my Italian brothers; and to keep the secret of these instructions, even at the cost of my life; to assist my brothers of the association both by action and counsel—NOW AND FOREVER.

Concerned about their property and security, they rallied to the old ruling classes for the sake of order and out of fear of social revolution by the working classes. All too soon, established governments were back in power.

In 1848, nationalities everywhere had also revolted in pursuit of self-government. But here too, frightfully little was achieved as divisions among nationalities proved utterly disastrous. Though the Hungarians demanded autonomy from the Austrians, at the same time they refused the same to their minorities—the Slovenes, Croats, and Serbs. Instead of joining together against the old empire, minorities fought each other. No wonder that one Czech could remark in April 1848: "If the Austrian state had not already existed for so long, it would have been in the interests of Europe, indeed of humanity itself, to endeavor to create it as soon as possible."[8] The Austrians' efforts to recover the Hungarian provinces met with little success until they began to play off Hungary's rebellious minority nationalities against the Hungarians.

◆ The Emergence of an Ordered Society

Everywhere in Europe, the revolutionary upheavals of the late eighteenth and early nineteenth centuries made the ruling elite nervous about social disorder and the potential dangers to their lives and property. At the same time, the influx of large numbers of people from the countryside into rapidly growing cities had led to horrible living conditions, poverty, unemployment, and great social dissatisfaction. The first half of the nineteenth century witnessed a significant increase in crime rates, especially against property, in Britain, France, and Germany. The rise in crimes of property caused a severe reaction by middle-class urban inhabitants who feared the threat the urban poor posed to their security and possessions. New police forces soon appeared to defend the propertied classes from criminals and social misfits.

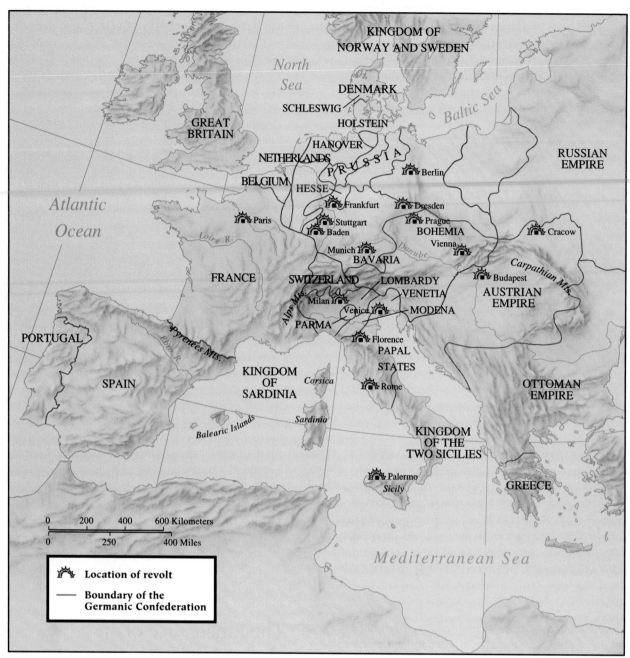

MAP 21.5 **The Revolutions of 1848–1849.**

✳ *The Development of New Police Forces*

The first major contribution of the nineteenth century to the development of a disciplined or ordered society in Europe was a regular system of police. A number of European states established civilian police forces—a group of well-trained law enforcement officers who were to preserve property and lives, maintain domestic order, investigate crime, and arrest offenders. It was hoped that their very presence would prevent crime. The new police forces were not readily welcomed, especially in countries where the memory of oppressive acts carried out by political and secret police still lingered. The function of the new police—to protect citizens—eventually made them acceptable, and

by the end of the nineteenth century, many Europeans viewed them approvingly.

This new approach to policing made its first appearance in France in 1828 when Louis-Maurice Debelleyme, the prefect of Paris, proclaimed as his goal: "The essential object of our municipal police is the safety of the inhabitants of Paris. Safety by day and night, free traffic movement, clean streets, the supervision of and precaution against accidents, the maintenance of order in public places, the seeking out of offenses and their perpetrators."[9] In March 1829, the new police, known as *serjents*, became visible on Paris streets. They were dressed in blue uniforms to make them easily recognizable by all citizens. They were also lightly armed with a white

Reform, Reaction, and Revolution: The European States, 1815–1850

Great Britain	
Corn Law	1815
Peterloo Massacre	1819
Reform Act	1832
Poor Law	1834
Formation of Anti-Corn Law League	1838
Repeal of Corn Laws	1846
France	
Louis XVIII	1814–1824
Constitutional Charter	1814
Charles X	1824–1830
July Revolution	1830
Louis-Philippe	1830–1848
Abdication of Louis-Philippe; formation of provisional government	1848 (February 22–24)
Formation of national workshops	1848 (February 26)
June days: workers' revolt in Paris	1848 (June)
Establishment of Second Republic	1848 (November)
Election of Louis Napoleon as French president	1848 (December)
Low Countries	
Union of Netherlands and Belgium	1815
Belgian revolt	1830
The German States	
Frederick William III of Prussia	1797–1840
Germanic Confederation established	1815
Burschenschaften at the Wartburg	1817
Karlsbad Decrees	1819

Frederick William IV of Prussia	1840–1861
Revolution in Germany	1848
Frankfurt Assembly	1848–1849
The Austrian Empire	
Emperor Ferdinand I	1835–1848
Revolt in Austrian Empire; Metternich dismissed	1848 (March)
Austrian forces under General Windischgrätz crush Czech rebels	1848 (June)
Viennese rebels crushed	1848 (October)
Abdication of Ferdinand I	1848 (December)
Francis Joseph I	1848–1916
Defeat of Hungarians with help of Russian troops	1849
The Italian States	
Revolts in southern Italy and Sardinia crushed	1821
Aborted revolutions in Modena, Parma, and Papal States	1830
King Charles Albert of Piedmont	1831–1849
Revolutions in Italy	1848
Charles Albert attacks Austrians	1848
Austrians reestablish control in Lombardy and Venetia	1849
Russia	
Tsar Paul I	1796–1801
Tsar Alexander I	1801–1825
Decembrist Revolt	1825
Tsar Nicholas I	1825–1855
Polish uprising	1830
Suppression of Polish revolt	1831

cane during the day and a saber at night, underscoring the fact that they made up a civilian, not a military, body. Initially, there were not many of the new police officers. Paris had 85 by August of 1829 and only 500 in 1850. Before the end of the century, their number had increased to 4,000.

The British, fearful of the powers exercised by military or secret police in authoritarian continental European states, had long resisted the creation of a professional police force. Instead, Britain depended upon a system of unpaid constables recruited by local author-

ities. Often these local constables were incapable of keeping order, preventing crimes, or apprehending criminals. Such jobs could also be dangerous and involve incidents like the one reported by a man passing by a local pub in 1827:

> I saw Thomas Franklin [constable of the village of Leighton Buzzard] coming out backwards. John Brandon . . . was opposite and close to the constable. I saw the said John Brandon strike the said constable twice "bang full in the face" the blows knocked the constable down on his back. John Brandon fell down with him. Sarah Adams . . . got on

top of the constable and jostled his head against the ground. . . . The constable appeared very much hurt and his face was all over blood.[10]

The failure of the local constables led to a new approach. Between September 1829 and May 1830, 3,000 uniformed police officers appeared on the streets of London. They came to be known as bobbies after Sir Robert Peel, who had introduced the legislation that created the force. By 1856, the new police had become obligatory for all local authorities.

As is evident from the first instruction book for the new British police, their primary goal was to prevent crime: "Officers and police constables should endeavour to distinguish themselves by such vigilance and activity as may render it impossible for any one to commit a crime within that portion of the town under their charge."[11] The municipal authorities soon found, however, that the police were also useful for imposing order on working-class urban inhabitants. On Sundays they were called upon to clean up after Saturday night's drinking bouts. As demands for better pay and treatment led to improved working conditions, British police began to develop a sense of professionalism (see the box on p. 635).

Police systems were reorganized throughout the Western world during the nineteenth century. Reformers followed first the French and then the British model, but local traditions were often important in shaping a nation's system. After the revolutions of 1848 in Germany, a state-financed police force called the *Schutzmannschaft*, modeled after the London police, was established for the city of Berlin. The *Schutzmannschaft* began as a civilian body, but already by 1851 the force had become organized more along military lines and was used for political purposes. Their military nature was reinforced by their weaponry, which included swords, pistols, and brass knuckles. One observer noted that "A German policeman on patrol is armed as if for war."[12]

Although the new police alleviated some of the fears about the increase in crime, contemporary reformers approached the problem in other ways. Some of them believed that the increase in crime was related to the dramatic increase in poverty. As one commented in 1816: "Poverty, misery are the parents of crime." Strongly influenced by the middle-class belief that unemployment was the result of sheer laziness, European states passed poor laws that attempted to force paupers to find work on their own or enter workhouses designed to make people so utterly uncomfortable they would choose to reenter the labor market.

Meanwhile, another group of reformers was arguing that poor laws failed to address the real problem, which was that poverty was a result of the moral degeneracy of the lower classes, increasingly labeled the "dangerous classes" because of the threat they posed to middle-class society. This belief led one group of secular reformers to form institutes to instruct the working classes in the applied sciences in order to make them more productive members of society. The London Mechanics' Institute, established in Britain, and the Society for the Diffusion of Useful Knowledge in the Field of Natural Sciences, Technical Science, and Political Economy, founded in Germany, are but two examples of this approach to the "dangerous classes."

Organized religion took a different approach. British evangelicals set up Sunday Schools to improve the morals of working children, and in Germany evangelical Protestants established nurseries for orphans and homeless children, women's societies to care for the sick and poor, and prison societies that prepared women to work in prisons. The Catholic church attempted the same kind of work through a revival of its religious orders; dedicated priests and nuns used spiritual instruction and recreation to turn young male workers away from the moral vices of gambling and drinking and female workers from lives of prostitution.

THE LONDON POLICE. One response to the revolutionary upheavals of the late eighteenth and early nineteenth centuries was the development of civilian police forces that would be responsible for preserving property, arresting criminals, and maintaining domestic order. This early photograph shows a group of London policemen who came to be known as bobbies after Sir Robert Peel, the man who was responsible for introducing the legislation that initiated the London police force.

The New British Police: "We Are Not Treated as Men"

The new British police forces, organized first in London in 1829, were generally well established throughout a good part of Britain by the 1840s. As professionalism arose in the ranks of the forces, so too did demands for better pay and treatment. In these two selections, police constables make clear their demands and complaints.

❋ Petition for Higher Pay by a Group of Third-Class Constables (1848)

Men joining the Police service as 3rd Class Constables and having a wife and 3 children to support on joining, are not able properly to do so on the pay of 16/8d. Most of the married men on joining are somewhat in debt, and are unable to extricate themselves on account of rent to pay and articles to buy which are necessary for support of wife and children. We beg leave to state that a married man having a wife and 2 children to support on joining, that it is as much as he can do upon 16/8d per week, and having to remain upon that sum for the first 12 to 18 months.

❋ Complaints from Constables of D Division of the London Metropolitan Police

We are not treated as men but as slaves we englishmen do not like to be terrorized by a set of Irish Sergeants who are only lenient to their own countrymen we the D division of Paddington are nearly all ruled by these Irish Sergeants after we have done our night-Duty may we not have the privilege of going to Church or staying at home to Suit our own inclination when we are ordered by the Superintendent to go to church in our uniform on wednesday we do not object to the going to church we like to go but we do not like to be ordered there and when we go on Sunday nights we are asked like so many schoolboys have we been to church should we say no let reason be what it may it does not matter we are forthwith ordered from Paddington to Marylebone lane the next night—about 2 hours before we go to Duty that is 2 miles from many of our homes being tired with our walk there and back we must either loiter about the streets or in some public house and there we do not want to go for we cannot spare our trifling wages to spend them there but there is no other choice left—for us to make our time out to go on Duty at proper time on Day we are ordered there for that offense another Man may faultlessly commit—the crime of sitting 4 minutes during the night—then we must be ordered there another to Shew his old clothes before they are given in even we must go to the expense of having them put in repair we have indeed for all these frightful crimes to walk 3 or 4 miles and then be wasting our time that makes our night 3 hours longer than they ought to be another thing we want to know who has the money that is deducted out of our wages for fines and many of us will be obliged to give up the duty unless we can have fair play as to the stationing of us on our beats why cannot we follow round that may all and each of us go over every beat and not for the Sergeants to put their favorites on the good beats and the others kept back their favorites are not the best policemen but those that will spend the most with them at the public house there are a great many of these things to try our temper.

❋ The Reform of Prisons

The increase in crime led to a rise in arrests. By the 1820s, in most countries the indiscriminate use of capital punishment, even for crimes against property, was increasingly being viewed as ineffective and was replaced by imprisonment. Although the British had shipped people convicted of serious offenses to their colonial territory of Australia, that practice began to slow down in the late 1830s when the colonists loudly objected. Incarceration, then, was the only alternative. Prisons served to isolate criminals from society, but a growing number of reformers questioned their purpose and effectiveness, especially when prisoners were subjected to harsh and even humiliating work as punishment. By the 1830s, European governments were seeking ways to reform their penal systems. Motivated by the desire not just to punish, but to rehabilitate and transform criminals into new persons, the British and French sent missions to the United States in the early 1830s to examine how the two different systems then used in American prisons accomplished this goal. At the Auburn Prison in New York, for example, prisoners were separated at night but worked together in the same workshop during the day. At Walnut Street Prison in Philadelphia, prisoners were separated into individual cells.

After examining the American prisons, both the French and British constructed prisons on the Walnut Street model with separate cells that isolated prisoners from one another. At Petite Roquette in France and Pentonville in Britain, prisoners wore leather masks while they exercised and sat in separate stalls when in chapel. Solitary confinement, it was believed, forced prisoners back on their own consciences, led to greater remorse, and increased the possibility that they would change their evil ways. One supporter of the separate-cell system noted how:

> a few months in the solitary cell renders a prisoner strangely impressible. The chaplain can then make the brawny navvy cry like a child; he can work on his feelings in almost any way he pleases; he can, so to speak,

photograph his thoughts, wishes and opinions on his patient's mind, and fill his mouth with his own phrases and language.[13]

As prison populations increased, however, solitary confinement proved expensive and less feasible. The French even returned to their custom of sending prisoners to French Guiana to handle the overload.

Prison reform and police forces were geared toward one primary end, the creation of a more disciplined society. Disturbed by the upheavals associated with revolutions and the social discontent wrought by industrialization and urbanization, the ruling elites sought to impose some order upon society. Even many radical working-class activists, who were often the object of police activity, welcomed the domestication and discipline that the new system imposed.

◆ Culture in an Age of Reaction and Revolution: The Mood of Romanticism

At the end of the eighteenth century, a new intellectual movement known as Romanticism was developing as a reaction against the Enlightenment's preoccupation with reason in discovering truth. Though the Romantics, especially the early Romantics, by no means disparaged reason, they tried to balance its use by stressing the importance of intuition, feeling, emotion, and imagination as sources of knowing. As one German Romantic put it: "It was my heart that counseled me to do it, and my heart cannot err."

❋ The Characteristics of Romanticism

Romanticism had its beginnings in Germany when a group of German poets began to emphasize emotion, sentiment, and the importance of inner feelings in their works. An important model for Romantics was the tragic figure in *The Sorrows of the Young Werther,* a novel by the great German writer, Johann Wolfgang von Goethe (1749–1832), who later rejected Romanticism in favor of Classicism. Werther was a Romantic figure who sought freedom in order to fulfill himself. Misunderstood and rejected by society, he continued to believe in his own worth through his inner feelings, but his deep love for a girl who did not love him finally led him to commit suicide. After Goethe's *Sorrows of the Young Werther,* numerous novels and plays appeared whose plots revolved around young maidens tragically carried off at an early age (twenty-three was most common) by disease (usually tuberculosis, at that time a protracted disease that was usually fatal) to the sorrow and sadness of their male lovers.

Another important characteristic of Romanticism was individualism or an interest in the unique traits of each person. The Romantics' desire to follow their inner drives led them to rebel against middle-class conventions. Long hair, beards, and outrageous clothes served to reinforce the individualism that young Romantics were trying to express. Many Romantic novels focused on the theme of the individual's conflict with society.

Sentiment and individualism came together in the Romantics' stress on the heroic. The Romantic hero was a solitary genius who was ready to defy the world and sacrifice his life for a great cause. In the hands of the British writer, Thomas Carlyle (1795–1881), however, the Romantic hero did not destroy himself in ineffective protests against society, but transformed society instead. In his historical works, Carlyle stressed that historical events were largely determined by the deeds of such heroes.

Many Romantics believed that states and societies, like individual organisms, evolved through time, and that each people had a *Geist* or spirit that made that people unique. This perspective inspired Romantics to study history because they saw it as a way to understand how a nationality came to be what it was. They singled out one period of history—the Middle Ages—for special attention because the European states had first emerged during that time. The medieval period was also seen as an age of faith and religious emotion rather than reason. No doubt, the Romantic reverence for history contributed to the nineteenth century's fascination with nationalism.

This historical mindedness was manifested in many ways. In Germany, the Grimm brothers collected and published local fairy tales, as did Hans Christian Andersen in Denmark. The revival of medieval Gothic architecture left European countrysides adorned with pseudo-medieval castles and cities bedecked with grandiose neo-Gothic cathedrals, city halls, parliamentary buildings, and even railway stations. Literature, too, reflected this historical consciousness. The novels of Walter Scott (1771–1832) became European best-sellers in the first half of the nineteenth century. *Ivanhoe,* in which Scott tried to evoke the clash between Saxon and Norman knights in medieval England, became one of his most popular works.

To the historical mindedness of the Romantics could be added an attraction to the bizarre and unusual. In an exaggerated form, this preoccupation gave rise to so-called Gothic literature (see the box on p. 638), chillingly evident in the short stories of horror by the American Edgar Allan Poe (1808–1849) and in *Frankenstein* by Mary Shelley (1797–1851). Her novel was the story of a mad scientist who brings into being a humanlike monster who goes berserk. Some Romantics even sought the unusual in their own lives by pursuing extraordinary states of experience in dreams, nightmares, frenzies, and suicidal depression or by experimenting with cocaine, opium, and hashish to produce drug-induced, altered states of consciousness.

NEO-GOTHIC REVIVAL (BRITISH HOUSES OF PARLIAMENT). The Romantic movement of the first half of the nineteenth century led, among other things, to a revival of medieval Gothic architecture that left European cities bedecked with neo-Gothic buildings. After the Houses of Parliament in London burned down in 1834, they were replaced with the new buildings of neo-Gothic design seen in this photograph.

❉ Romantic Poets and the Love of Nature

To the Romantics, poetry ranked above all other literary forms because they believed it was the direct expression of one's soul. The Romantic poets were viewed as seers who could reveal the invisible world to others. Their incredible sense of drama made some of them the most colorful figures of their era, living intense but short lives. Percy Bysshe Shelley (1792–1822), expelled from school for advocating atheism, set out to reform the world. His *Prometheus Unbound*, completed in 1820, is a portrait of the revolt of human beings against the laws and customs that oppress them. He drowned in a storm in the Mediterranean. Lord Byron (1788–1824) dramatized himself as the melancholy Romantic hero that he had described in his work, *Childe Harold's Pilgrimage*. He participated in the movement for Greek independence and died in Greece fighting the Ottomans.

Romantic poetry gave full expression to one of the most important characteristics of Romanticism: love of nature, especially evident in the works of William Wordsworth (1770–1850). His experience of nature was almost mystical as he claimed to receive "authentic tidings of invisible things":

> One impulse from a vernal wood
> May teach you more of man,
> Of Moral Evil and of good,
> Than all the sages can.[14]

To Wordsworth, nature contained a mysterious force that the poet could perceive and learn from. Nature served as a mirror into which humans could look to learn about themselves. Nature was, in fact, alive and sacred:

> To every natural form, rock, fruit or flower,
> Even the loose stones that cover the high-way,

> I gave a moral life, I saw them feel,
> Or link'd them to some feeling: the great mass
> Lay bedded in a quickening soul, and all
> That I beheld, respired with inward meaning.[15]

Other Romantics carried this worship of nature further into pantheism by identifying the great force in nature with God. The Romantics would have nothing to do with the deist God of the Enlightenment, the remote creator of the world-machine. As the German Romantic poet Friedrich Novalis said: "Anyone seeking God will find him anywhere."

The worship of nature also led Wordsworth and other Romantic poets to a critique of the mechanistic materialism of eighteenth-century science, which, they believed, had reduced nature to a cold object of study. Against that view of the natural world, Wordsworth offered his own vivid and concrete experience. To him the scientists' dry, mathematical approach left no room for the imagination or for the human soul. The poet who left to the world "one single moral precept, one single affecting sentiment," Wordsworth said, did more for the world than scientists who were soon forgotten. The monster created by Frankenstein in Mary Shelley's Gothic novel symbolized well the danger of science when it tries to conquer nature. Many Romantics were convinced that the emerging industrialization would cause people to become alienated from their inner selves and the natural world around them.

❉ Romanticism in Art and Music

Like the literary arts, the visual arts were also deeply affected by Romanticism. Although their works varied widely, Romantic artists shared at least two fundamental

Gothic Literature: Edgar Allan Poe

American writers and poets made significant contributions to the movement of Romanticism. Although Edgar Allan Poe (1809–1849) was influenced by the German Romantic school of mystery and horror, many literary historians give him the credit for pioneering the modern short story. This selection from the conclusion of "The Fall of the House of Usher" gives a sense of the nature of so-called Gothic literature.

❀ Edgar Allan Poe, *"The Fall of the House of Usher"*

No sooner had these syllables passed my lips, than—as if a shield of brass had indeed, at the moment, fallen heavily upon a floor of silver—I became aware of a distinct, hollow, metallic, and clangorous, yet apparently muffled, reverberation. Complete unnerved, I leaped to my feet; but the measured rocking movement of Usher was undisturbed. I rushed to the chair in which he sat. His eyes were bent fixedly before him, and throughout his whole countenance there reigned a stony rigidity. But, as I placed my hand upon his shoulder, there came a strong shudder over his whole person; a sickly smile quivered about his lips and I saw that he spoke in a low, hurried, and gibbering murmur, as if unconscious of my presence. Bending closely over him, I at length drank in the hideous import of his words.

"Not hear it?—yes, I hear it, and *have* heard it. Long-long-long-many minutes, many hours, many days, have I heard it—yet I dared not—oh, pity me, miserable wretch that I am!—I dared not—I *dared* not speak! We have put her living in the tomb! Said I not that my senses were acute? I *now* tell you that I heard her first feeble movements in the hollow coffin. I heard them—many, many days ago—yet I dared not—I *dared not speak!* And now—to-night—. . . the rending of her coffin, and the grating of the iron hinges of her prison, and her struggles within the coppered archway of the vault! Oh whither shall I fly? Will she not be here anon? Is she not hurrying to upbraid me for my haste? Have I not heard her footstep on the stair? Do I not distinguish that heavy and horrible beating of her heart? MADMAN!"—here he sprang furiously to his feet, and shrieked out his syllables, as if in the effort he were giving up his soul—"MADMAN! I TELL YOU THAT SHE NOW STANDS WITHOUT THE DOOR!"

As if in the superhuman energy of his utterance there had been found the potency of a spell, the huge antique panels to which the speaker pointed threw slowly back, upon the instant, their ponderous and ebony jaws. It was the work of the rushing gust—but then without those doors there DID stand the lofty and enshrouded figure of the lady Madeline of Usher. There was blood upon her white robes, and the evidence of some bitter struggle upon every portion of her emaciated frame. For a moment she remained trembling and reeling to and fro upon the threshold, then, with a low moaning cry, fell heavily inward upon the person of her brother, and in her violent and now final death-agonies, bore him to the floor a corpse, and a victim to the terrors he had anticipated.

characteristics. All artistic expression to them was a reflection of the artist's inner feelings; a painting should mirror the artist's vision of the world and be the instrument of his own imagination. Moreover, Romantic artists deliberately rejected the principles of Classicism. Beauty was not a timeless thing; its expression depended on one's culture and one's age. The Romantics abandoned classical restraint for warmth, emotion, and movement. Through an examination of three painters, we can see how Romanticism influenced the visual arts.

The early life experiences of Caspar David Friedrich (1774–1840) left him with a lifelong preoccupation with God and nature. Friedrich painted many landscapes but with an interest that transcended the mere presentation of natural details. His portrayal of mountains shrouded in mist, gnarled trees bathed in moonlight, and the stark ruins of monasteries surrounded by withered trees all conveyed a feeling of mystery and mysticism. For Friedrich, nature was a manifestation of divine life. As in *Man and Woman Gazing at the Moon,* he liked to depict one or two solitary figures gazing upon the grandeur of a natural scene with their backs to the viewer. Not only were his human figures dwarfed by the overwhelming presence of nature, but they expressed the human yearning for infinity, the desire to lose oneself in the universe. To Friedrich, the artistic process depended upon one's inner vision. He advised artists: "Shut your physical eye and look first at your picture with your spiritual eye, then bring to the light of day what you have seen in the darkness."

Another artist who dwelled on nature and made landscape his major subject was the Englishman Joseph Malford William Turner (1775–1851). Turner was an incredibly prolific artist who produced over 20,000 paintings, drawings, and watercolors. Turner's concern with nature manifested itself in innumerable landscapes and seascapes, sunrises and sunsets. He did not idealize nature or reproduce it with realistic accuracy, however. He sought instead to convey its moods by using a skilled interplay of light and color to suggest natural effects. In allowing his objects to melt into their surroundings, he anticipated the Impressionist painters of the last half of the nineteenth century (see Chapter 24). John Consta-

CASPAR DAVID FRIEDRICH, *MAN AND WOMAN GAZING AT THE MOON.* **The German artist Caspar David Friedrich sought to express in painting his own mystical view of nature. "The divine is everywhere," he once wrote, "even in a grain of sand." In this painting, two solitary wanderers are shown from the back gazing at the moon. Overwhelmed by the all-pervasive presence of nature, the two figures express the human longing for infinity.**

ble, a contemporary English Romantic painter, described Turner's paintings as "airy visions, painted with tinted steam."

Eugène Delacroix (1798–1863) was the most famous French Romantic artist. Largely self-taught, he was fascinated by the exotic and had a passion for color. Both characteristics are visible in his *The Death of Sardanapalus*. Significant for its use of light and its patches of interrelated color, this portrayal of the world of the last Assyrian king was criticized at the time for its

brilliant color. In Delacroix, theatricality and movement combined with a daring use of color. Many of his works reflect his own belief that "a painting should be a feast to the eye."

To many Romantics, music was the most Romantic of the arts because it enabled the composer to probe deeply into human emotions. One Romantic writer noted: "It has been rightly said that the object of music is the awakening of emotion. No other art can so sublimely arouse human sentiments in the innermost heart of

J. M. W. TURNER, *RAIN, STEAM, AND SPEED—THE GREAT WESTERN RAILWAY.* **Although Turner began his artistic career by painting accurate representations of the natural world, he increasingly sought to depict an atmosphere by a skillful use of light and color. In this painting, Turner eliminates specific details and uses general fields of color to portray the image of a locomotive rushing toward the spectator.**

EUGÈNE DELACROIX, *THE DEATH OF SARDANAPALUS*. Delacroix's *The Death of Sardanapalus* was based on Lord Byron's verse account of the last dramatic moments of the decadent Assyrian king. Besieged by enemy troops and with little hope of survival, Sardanapalus orders that his harem women and prize horses go to their death with him. At the right, a guard stabs one of the women as the king looks on.

man."[16] Although music historians have called the eighteenth century an age of Classicism and the nineteenth the era of Romanticism, there was much carryover of classical forms from one century to the next. One of the greatest composers of all time, Ludwig van Beethoven, served as a bridge between Classicism and Romanticism.

Beethoven (1770–1827) is one of the few composers who was able singlehandedly to transform the art of music. Set ablaze by the events in France, a revolutionary mood burned brightly across Europe, and Beethoven, like other creative personalities, yearned to communicate his cherished beliefs. He said, "I *must* write, for what weighs on my heart, I *must* express." For Beethoven, music had to reflect his deepest inner feelings.

Born in Bonn, Beethoven came from a family of musicians who worked for the electors of Cologne and became assistant organist at the court by the age of thirteen. He soon made his way to Vienna, then the musical capital of Europe, where he studied briefly under Haydn. Beginning in 1792, this city became his permanent residence although his unruly manner and offensive appearance made him barely tolerable to Viennese society.

During his first major period of composing, which extended from 1792 to 1800, his work was still largely within the classical framework of the eighteenth century, and the influences of Haydn and Mozart are paramount. During the next period of his creative life, which began in 1800, Beethoven declared, "I am making a fresh start." With the composition of the Third Symphony (1804), also called the *Eroica*, which was originally intended for Napoleon, Beethoven broke through to the elements of Romanticism in his use of uncontrolled rhythms to create dramatic struggle and uplifted resolutions. E. T. A. Hoffman, a contemporary composer and writer, said,

"Beethoven's music opens the flood gates of fear, of terror, of horror, of pain, and arouses that longing for the eternal which is the essence of Romanticism. He is thus a pure Romantic composer."[17] Beethoven went on to write a vast quantity of works including symphonies, piano and violin sonatas, concerti, masses, an opera, and a cycle of songs. In the midst of this productivity and growing fame, Beethoven was more and more burdened by his growing deafness, which intensified noticeably after 1800. One of the most moving pieces of music of all time, the chorale finale of his Ninth Symphony, was composed when Beethoven was totally deaf.

Beethoven served as a bridge from the classical era to Romanticism; after him came a number of musical geniuses who composed in the Romantic style. The Frenchman Hector Berlioz (1803–1869) was one of the most outstanding. His father, a doctor in Grenoble, intended that his son should also study medicine. The young Berlioz eventually rebelled, however, maintaining to his father's disgust that he would be "no doctor or apothecary but a great composer." Berlioz managed to fulfill his own expectations, achieving fame in Germany, Russia, and Britain, although the originality of his work kept him from receiving any real recognition in his native France.

Berlioz was one of the founders of program music, which was an attempt to use the moods and sound effects of instrumental music to depict the actions and emotions inherent in a story, event, or even a personal experience. This development of program music was evident in his concert overtures to Shakespeare's plays and, above all, in his most famous piece, the first complete program symphony, known as the *Symphonie fantastique*. In this work, Berlioz used music to evoke the passionate emotions of a tortured love affair, including a fifth movement in which he musically creates an opium-induced nightmare of a witches' gathering.

✳ *The Revival of Religion in the Age of Romanticism*

After 1815, Catholicism experienced a revival. In the eighteenth century, Catholicism had lost its attraction for many of the educated elite as even the European nobility flirted with the ideas of the Enlightenment. The restoration of the nobility brought a new appreciation for the Catholic faith as a force for order in society. This appreciation was greatly reinforced by the Romantic movement. The attraction of Romantics to the Middle Ages and their emphasis on emotion led them to their own widespread revival of Christianity.

Catholicism, in particular, benefited from this Romantic enthusiasm for religion. Especially among German Romantics, there were many conversions to the Catholic faith. One of the most popular expressions of this Romantic revival of Catholicism was found in the work of the Frenchman François-René de Chateaubriand (1768–1848). His book, *Genius of Christianity*, published in 1802, was soon labeled the "Bible of Romanticism." His defense of Catholicism was based not upon historical, theological, or even rational grounds, but largely upon Romantic sentiment. As a faith, Catholicism echoed the harmony of all things. Its cathedrals brought one into the very presence of God; according to Chateaubriand: "You could not enter a Gothic church without feeling a kind of awe and a vague sentiment of the Divinity . . . every thing in a Gothic church reminds you of the labyrinths of a wood; every thing excites a feeling of religious awe, of mystery, and of the Divinity."[18]

Protestantism also experienced a revival. That revival, or Awakening as it was called, had already begun in the eighteenth century with the enthusiastic emotional experiences of Methodism in Britain and Pietism in Germany (see Chapter 17). Methodist missionaries from England and Scotland carried their messages of sin and redemption to liberal Protestant churches in France and Switzerland, winning converts to their strongly evangelical message. Germany, too, witnessed a Protestant Awakening as enthusiastic evangelical preachers found that their messages of hellfire and their methods of emotional conversion evoked a ready response among people alienated by the highly educated establishment clergy of the state churches.

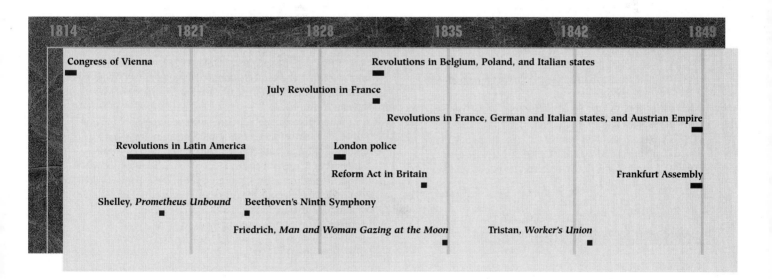

CONCLUSION ▨▨▨▨▨▨▨▨▨▨▨

In 1815, a conservative order was reestablished throughout Europe, and the cooperation of the great powers, embodied in the Concert of Europe, tried to ensure its durability. But the revolutionary waves of the early 1820s and the early 1830s made it clear that the ideologies of liberalism and nationalism, unleashed by the French Revolution and now reinforced by the spread of the Industrial Revolution, were still alive and active. They faced enormous difficulties, however,

as failed revolutions in Poland, Russia, Italy, and Germany all testify. At the same time, reform legislation in Britain and successful revolutions in Greece, France, and Belgium demonstrated the continuing strength of these forces of change. In 1848, they erupted once more all across Europe. And once more they failed. But not all was lost. Both liberalism and nationalism would succeed in the second half of the nineteenth century but in ways not foreseen by the idealistic liberals and nationalists who were utterly convinced that their time had come when they manned the barricades in 1848.

NOTES

1. Quoted in Charles Breunig, *The Age of Revolution and Reaction, 1789–1850* (New York, 1970), p. 119.
2. Quoted in M. S. Anderson, *The Ascendancy of Europe, 1815–1914*, 2d ed. (London, 1985), p. 1.
3. Quotations from Burke can be found in Peter Viereck, *Conservatism* (Princeton, N.J., 1956), pp. 27, 114.
4. Quoted in René Albrecht-Carrié, *The Concert of Europe* (New York, 1968), p. 48.
5. Quoted in G. de Berthier de Sauvigny, *Metternich and His Times* (London, 1962), p. 105.
6. Quoted in Donald E. Emerson, *Metternich and the Political Police* (The Hague, 1968), p. 110.
7. Quoted in S. Joan Moon, "Feminism and Socialism: The Utopian Synthesis of Flora Tristan," in Marilyn J. Boxer and Jean H. Quataert, eds., *Socialist Women* (New York, 1978), p. 38.
8. Quoted in Stanley Z. Pech, *The Czech Revolution of 1848* (Chapel Hill, N.C., 1969), p. 82.
9. Quoted in Clive Emsley, *Policing and Its Context, 1750–1870* (New York, 1984), p. 58.
10. Quoted in Clive Emsley, *Crime and Society in England, 1750–1900* (London, 1987), p. 173.
11. Quoted in Emsley, *Policing and Its Context, 1750–1870*, p. 66.
12. Quoted in ibid., p. 102.
13. Quoted in Emsley, *Crime and Society in England, 1750–1900*, p. 226.
14. William Wordsworth, "The Tables Turned," *Poems of Wordsworth*, ed. Matthew Arnold (London, 1963), p. 138.
15. William Wordsworth, *The Prelude* (Harmondsworth, 1971), p. 109.
16. Quoted in H. G. Schenk, *The Mind of the European Romantics* (Garden City, N.Y., 1969), p. 205.
17. Quoted in Siegbert Prawer, ed., *The Romantic Period in Germany* (London, 1970), p. 285.
18. Quoted in John B. Halsted, ed., *Romanticism* (New York, 1969), p. 156.

SUGGESTIONS FOR FURTHER READING

For a good survey of the entire nineteenth century, see R. Gildea, *Barricades and Borders: Europe 1800–1914*, 2d ed. (Oxford, 1996) in the Short Oxford History of the Modern World series. Also valuable is M. S. Anderson, *The Ascendancy of Europe, 1815–1914*, 2d ed. (London, 1985). For surveys of the period covered in this chapter, see M. Broers, *Europe after Napoleon: Revolution, Reaction, and Romanticism, 1814–1848* (New York, 1996); and C. Breunig, *The Age of Revolution and Reaction, 1789–1850*, 2d ed. (New York, 1979). There are also some useful books on individual countries that cover more than the subject of this chapter. These include R. Magraw, *France, 1815–1914: The Bourgeois Century* (London, 1983); D. Saunders, *Russia in the Age of Reaction and Reform, 1801–1881* (London, 1992); J. J. Sheehan, *German History, 1770–1866* (New York, 1989); C. A. Macartney, *The Habsburg Empire, 1790–1918* (London, 1971); S. J. Woolf, *A History of Italy, 1700–1860* (London, 1979); R. Carr, *Spain, 1808–1939* (Oxford, 1991); and N. McCord, *British History, 1815–1906* (New York, 1991).

On the peace settlement of 1814–1815, there is the older work by H. Nicolson, *The Congress of Vienna, 1814–15* (New York, 1946). A concise summary of the international events of the entire nineteenth century can be found in R. Bullen and F. R. Bridge, *The Great Powers and the European States System, 1815–1914* (London, 1980). See also N. Rich, *Great Power Diplomacy, 1814–1914* (New York, 1992). On the man whose conservative policies dominated this era, see the brief but good biography by A. Palmer, *Metternich* (New York, 1972). On the revolutions in Europe in 1830, see C. Church, *Europe in 1830: Revolution and Political Change* (Chapel Hill, N.C., 1983). The standard work on the revolution of 1830 in France is D. Pinkney, *The French Revolution of 1830* (Princeton, N.J., 1972). On Great Britain's reform legislation, see M. Brock, *Great Reform Act* (London, 1973); and D. C. Moore, *The Politics of Deference: A Study of the Mid-Nineteenth Century English Political System* (New York, 1976). The Greek revolt is examined in detail in D. Dakin, *The Greek Struggle for Independence, 1821–33* (Berkeley, 1973).

The best introduction to the revolutions of 1848 is J. Sperber, *The European Revolutions, 1848–1851* (New York, 1994). See also P. Stearns, *1848: The Revolutionary Tide in Europe* (New York, 1974). Good accounts of the revolutions in individual countries include G. Duveau, *1848: The Making of a Revolution* (New York, 1967); R. J. Rath, *The Viennese Revolution of 1848* (Austin, Tex., 1957); I. Déak, *The Lawful Revolution: Louis Kossuth and the Hungarians, 1848–49* (New York, 1979); P. Brock, *The Slovak National Awakening* (Toronto, 1976); R. Stadelmann, *Social and Political History of the German 1848 Revolution* (Athens, Ohio, 1975); and P. Ginsborg, *Daniele Manin and the Venetian Revolution of 1848–49* (New York, 1979). On Mazzini, see D. M. Smith, *Mazzini* (New Haven, Conn., 1994).

Good introductions to the major ideologies of the first half of the nineteenth century including both analysis and readings from the major figures can be found in H. Kohn, *Nationalism* (Princeton, N.J., 1955); J. S. Schapiro, *Liberalism: Its Meaning and History* (Princeton, N.J., 1958); and P. Viereck, *Conservatism* (Princeton, N.J., 1956). For a more detailed examination of liberalism, see J. Gray, *Liberalism* (Minneapolis, Minn., 1995). An excellent work on French utopian socialism is F. Manuel, *The Prophets of Paris* (New York, 1962).

On changes in the treatment of crime and punishment, see M. Foucault, *Discipline and Punish: The Birth of the Prison* (New York, 1977). The new police forces are examined in C. Emsley, *Policing and Its Context, 1750–1870* (New York, 1984). Also useful on crime, police, and prisons are M. Ignatieff, *A Just Measure of Pain: The Penitentiary in the Industrial Revolution, 1750–1850* (New York, 1978); and C. Emsley, *Crime and Society in England, 1750–1900* (London, 1987).

On the ideas of the Romantics, see H. G. Schenk, *The Mind of the European Romantics* (Garden City, N.Y., 1969); and M. Cranston, *The Romantic Movement* (Oxford, 1994). There is an excellent collection of writings by Romantics in J. B. Halsted, ed., *Romanticism* (New York, 1969). On Wordsworth and English Romanticism, see J. Wordsworth, *William Wordsworth and the Age of English Romanticism* (New Brunswick, N.J.,

1987). For an introduction to the arts, see W. Vaughan, *Romanticism and Art* (New York, 1994). A briefer survey (with illustrations) can be found in D. M. Reynolds, *Cambridge Introduction to the History of Art: The Nineteenth Century* (Cambridge, 1985).

For additional reading, go to InfoTrac College Edition, your online research library at http://web1.infotrac-college.com

Enter the search term *Romanticism* using the Subject Guide.

Enter the search term *Habsburg* and also the term *Hapsburg* using Key Terms.

Enter the search terms *John Stuart Mill* using Key Terms.

Enter the search term *Goethe* using Key Terms.

CHAPTER

22

An Age of Nationalism and Realism, 1850–1871

CHAPTER OUTLINE

- The France of Napoleon III
- National Unification: Italy and Germany
- Nation Building and Reform: The National State in Mid-Century
- Industrialization and the Marxist Response
- Science and Culture in an Age of Realism
- Conclusion

FOCUS QUESTIONS

- What were the characteristics of Napoleon III's government, and how did his foreign policy contribute to the unification of Italy and Germany?
- What actions did Cavour and Bismarck take to bring about unification in Italy and Germany, respectively, and what role did war play in their efforts?
- What efforts for reform occurred in the Austrian Empire and in Russia between 1850 and 1870, and how successful were they in alleviating each nation's problems?
- What were the main ideas of Karl Marx?
- How did the belief that the world should be viewed realistically manifest itself in science, art, and literature in the second half of the nineteenth century?

ACROSS THE EUROPEAN CONTINENT, *the revolutions of 1848 had failed. The forces of liberalism and nationalism appeared to have been decisively defeated as authoritarian governments reestablished their control almost everywhere in Europe by 1850. And yet within twenty-five years, many of the goals sought by the liberals and nationalists during the first half of the nineteenth century seemed to have been achieved. National unity became a reality in Italy and Germany, and many European states were governed by constitutional monarchies, even though the constitutional-parliamentary features were frequently facades.*

All the same, these goals were not achieved by liberal and nationalist leaders but by a new generation of conservative leaders who were proud of being practitioners of Realpolitik, *the "politics of reality." One* reaction to the failure of the revolutions of 1848 had been a new toughness of mind in which people prided themselves on being realistic in their handling of power. The new conservative leaders used armies and power politics to achieve their foreign policy goals. And they did not hesitate to manipulate liberal means to achieve conservative ends at home. Nationalism had failed as a revolutionary movement in 1848–1849, but between 1850 and 1871, these new leaders found a variety of ways to pursue nation building. One of the most successful was the Prussian Otto von Bismarck who used both astute diplomacy and war to achieve the unification of Germany. On January 18, 1871, Bismarck and 600 German princes, nobles, and generals filled the Hall of Mirrors in the palace of Versailles, twelve miles outside Paris. The Prussian army had defeated the French, and the assembled notables were gathered for the proclamation of the Prussian king as the new emperor of a united German state. When the words "Long live His Imperial Majesty, the Emperor William!" rang out, the assembled guests took up the cry. One participant wrote, "A thundering cheer, repeated at least six times, thrilled through the room while the flags and standards waved over the head of the new emperor of Germany." European rulers who feared the power of the new German state were not so cheerful. "The balance of power has been entirely destroyed," declared the British prime minister.

◆ The France of Napoleon III

After 1850 a new generation of conservative leaders came to power in Europe. Foremost among them was Napoleon III (1852–1870) of France who taught his contemporaries how authoritarian governments could use liberal and nationalistic forces to bolster their own power. It was a lesson others quickly learned.

✳ Louis Napoleon: Toward the Second Empire

Even after his election as the president of the French Republic, many of his contemporaries dismissed Napoleon "the Small" as a nonentity whose success was due only to his name. But physical appearances can be deceiving. Louis Napoleon was a clever politician who was especially astute at understanding the popular forces of his day. Some historians think that as a Bonaparte, Louis Napoleon believed he was destined to govern France. After his election, he was at least clear about his desire to have personal power. He wrote: "I shall never submit to any attempt to influence me . . . . I follow only the promptings of my mind and heart. . . . Nothing, nothing shall trou-

ble the clear vision of my judgment or the strength of my resolution."[1]

Louis Napoleon was a patient man. For three years he persevered in winning the support of the French people while using governmental favors to gain the loyalty of the army and the Catholic church. He faced considerable opposition from the National Assembly, which had a conservative-monarchist majority after elections in May of 1849. When the assembly voted to deprive three million men of the right to vote, Louis Napoleon achieved even more popular favor by posing as the savior of universal male suffrage. When the assembly rejected his proposal to revise the constitution and allow him to stand for reelection, Louis resorted to a coup d'etat. On December 1, 1851, troops loyal to the president seized the major administrative buildings and arrested opposition leaders. After restoring universal male suffrage, Louis Napoleon asked the French people to restructure the government by electing him president for ten years (see the box on p. 646). By an overwhelming majority, 7.5 million "yes" votes to 640,000 "no" votes, they agreed. A year later, on November 21, 1852, Louis Napoleon returned to the people to ask for the restoration of the Empire. This time 97 percent responded affirmatively, and on December 2, 1852, Louis Napoleon assumed the title of Napoleon III (the first Napoleon had abdicated in favor of his son, Napoleon II, on April 6, 1814). The Second Empire had begun.

✳ The Second Napoleonic Empire

The government of Napoleon III was clearly authoritarian in a Bonapartist sense. Louis Napoleon had asked, "Since France has carried on for fifty years only by virtue of the administrative, military, judicial, religious and financial organization of the Consulate and Empire, why should she not also adopt the political institutions of that period?"[2] As chief of state, Napoleon III controlled the armed forces, police, and civil service. Only he could introduce legislation and declare war. His ministers had no collective responsibility and were answerable only to the emperor. The Legislative Corps gave an appearance of representative government since its members were elected by universal male suffrage for six-year terms. But they could neither initiate legislation nor affect the budget. Moreover, only government candidates were allowed to campaign freely. Candidates were supposedly selected from "men enjoying public esteem, concerned more with the interests of the country than with the strife of parties, sympathetic towards the suffering of the laboring classes."[3]

The first five years of Napoleon III's reign were a spectacular success as he reaped the benefits of worldwide economic prosperity as well as of some of his own economic policies. In light of the loss of political freedom, Napoleon realized the importance of diverting "the attention of the French from politics to economics." He believed in using the resources of government to stimulate the national economy and took many steps to encourage industrial growth. He promoted the expansion of credit by

Louis Napoleon Appeals to the People

After his coup d'etat on December 1, 1851, Louis Napoleon asked the French people to approve his actions. By making this appeal, the clever politician was demonstrating how universal male suffrage, considered a democratic and hence revolutionary device, could be used to bolster a basically authoritarian regime. It was a lesson eagerly learned by other conservative rulers in the second half of the nineteenth century. This selection is from Louis Napoleon's proclamation to the French people in 1851.

❈ Louis Napoleon, *Proclamation to the People (1851)*

Frenchmen! The present situation cannot last much longer. Each passing day increases the danger to the country. The [National] Assembly, which ought to be the firmest supporter of order, has become a center of conspiracies . . . it attacks the authority that I hold directly from the people; it encourages all evil passions; it jeopardizes the peace of France: I have dissolved it and I make the whole people judge between it and me. . . .

I therefore make a loyal appeal to the whole nation, and I say to you: If you wish to continue this state of uneasiness which degrades us and makes our future uncertain, choose another in my place, for I no longer wish an authority which is powerless to do good, makes me responsible for acts I cannot prevent, and chains me to the helm when I see the vessel speeding toward the abyss.

If, on the contrary, you still have confidence in me, give me the means to accomplish the great mission that I hold from you. This mission consists in bringing to a close the era of revolutions by satisfying the legitimate wants of the people and by protecting them against subversive passions. It consists, especially, in creating institutions that may survive men and that may be at length foundations on which something durable can be established.

Persuaded that the instability of authority and the preponderance of a single Assembly are permanent causes of trouble and discord, I submit to you the following fundamental bases of a constitution which the Assemblies will develop later.

1. A responsible chief elected for ten years.
2. Ministers dependent upon the executive power alone.
3. A Council of State composed of the most distinguished men to prepare the laws and discuss them before the legislative body.
4. A legislative body to discuss and vote the laws, elected by universal [male] suffrage. . . .

This system, created by the First Consul [Napoleon I] at the beginning of the century, has already given France calm and prosperity; it will guarantee them to her again.

Such is my profound conviction. If you share it, declare that fact by your votes. If, on the contrary, you prefer a government without force, monarchical or republican, borrowed from I know not what past or from which chimerical future, reply in the negative. . . .

If I do not obtain a majority of your votes, I shall then convoke a new assembly, and I shall resign to it the mandate that I received from you. But if you believe that the cause of which my name is the symbol, that is, France regenerated by the revolution of 1789 and organized by the Emperor, is forever yours, proclaim it by sanctioning the powers that I ask from you. Then France and Europe will be saved from anarchy, obstacles will be removed, rivalries will disappear, for all will respect the decree of Providence in the decision of the people.

---

backing the formation of new investment banks, which provided long-term loans for industrial, commercial, and agricultural expansion. Government subsidies were used to foster the rapid construction of railroads as well as harbors, roads, and canals. The major French railway lines were completed during Napoleon's reign, and industrial expansion was evident in the tripling of iron production. In his concern to reduce tensions and improve the social welfare of the nation, Napoleon provided hospitals and free medicine for the workers and advocated better housing for the working class.

In the midst of this economic expansion, Napoleon III undertook a vast reconstruction of the city of Paris. Under the direction of Baron Haussmann, the medieval Paris of narrow streets and old city walls was destroyed and replaced by a modern Paris of broad boulevards, spacious buildings, circular plazas, public squares, an underground sewage system, a new public water supply, and gaslights. The new Paris served a military as well as an aesthetic purpose. Broad streets made it more difficult for would-be insurrectionists to throw up barricades and easier for troops to move rapidly through the city in the event of revolts.

Napoleon III took a great interest in public opinion. Freedom of speech was, of course, not permitted in the authoritarian empire. Freedom of assembly was limited and newspapers were regularly censored. Nevertheless, Napoleon's desire to know the mood of his people led him to request regular reports on public opinion from his subordinates. In the 1860s, as opposition to some of

EMPEROR NAPOLEON III. On December 2, 1852, Louis Napoleon took the title of Napoleon III and then proceeded to create an authoritarian monarchy. As opposition to his policies intensified in the 1860s, Napoleon III began to liberalize his government. However, a disastrous military defeat at the hands of Prussia in 1870–1871 brought the collapse of his regime.

Napoleon's policies began to mount, his sensitivity to the change in the public mood led him to undertake new policies liberalizing his regime. As a result, historians speak of the "liberal empire" for the latter part of the 1860s.

Opposition to Napoleon came from a variety of sources. His attempt to move toward free trade by lowering tariffs on foreign goods, especially those of the British, angered French manufacturers. Then, too, the financial crash of 1857, a silkworm disease, and the devastation of French vineyards by plant lice caused severe damage to the French economy. Retrenchment in government spending proved unpopular as well. To shore up his regime, Napoleon III reached out to the working class by legalizing trade unions and granting them the right to strike. He also began to liberalize the political process.

The Legislative Corps had been closely controlled during the 1850s. In the 1860s, opposition candidates were allowed greater freedom to campaign, and the Legislative Corps was permitted more say in affairs of state, including debate over the budget. Historians do not agree about the ultimate aim and potential of Napoleon's liberalization, although it did initially strengthen the hands of the government. In another plebiscite in May 1870, on whether to accept a new constitution that might have inaugurated a parliamentary regime, the French people gave Napoleon another resounding victory. This triumph was short-lived, however. Foreign policy failures led to growing criticism, and war with Prussia in 1870 turned out to be the death blow for Napoleon III's regime (see The Franco-Prussian War, 1870–1871 later in this chapter).

FLORENCE NIGHTINGALE AND THE NURSING PROFESSION. By her efforts in the Crimean War, the British nurse Florence Nightingale helped to make nursing a modern profession for middle-class women. She is shown here supervising her hospital at Scutari. Her attention to strict hygiene greatly reduced the death rate for wounded British soldiers.

✤ *Foreign Policy: The Crimean War*

As heir to the Napoleonic Empire, Napoleon III was motivated by the desire to free France from the restrictions of the peace settlements of 1814–1815 and to make France the chief arbiter of Europe. Although his foreign policy ultimately led to disaster and his own undoing, Napoleon had an initial success in the Crimean War (1854–1856).

The Crimean War was another chapter in the story of the Eastern Question, or who would be the chief beneficiaries of the disintegration of the Turkish or Ottoman Empire. The Ottoman Empire had long been in control of much of southeastern Europe, but by the beginning of the nineteenth century, it had begun to decline. As Ottoman authority over the outlying territories in southeastern Europe waned, European governments began to take an active interest in the empire's apparent demise. Russia's proximity to the Ottoman Empire and the religious bonds between the Russians and the Greek Orthodox Christians in Ottoman-dominated southeastern Europe naturally gave it special opportunities to enlarge its sphere of influence. Other European powers not only feared Russian ambitions but had ambitions of their own in the area. Austria craved more land in the Balkans, a desire that inevitably meant conflict with Russia, and France and Britain were interested in commercial opportunities and naval bases in the eastern Mediterranean.

War erupted between Russia and the Ottoman Empire in 1853 when the Russians demanded the right to protect Christian shrines in Palestine, a privilege that had already been extended to the French. When the Ottomans refused, the Russians invaded Ottoman Moldavia and Walachia. Failure to resolve the dispute by negotiations led the Ottoman Empire to declare war on Russia on October 4, 1853. In the following year, on March 28, Great Britain and France declared war on Russia.

Why did Britain and France take such a step? Concern over the prospect of an upset in the balance of power was clearly one reason. The British in particular feared that an aggressive Russia would try to profit from the obvious weakness of the Ottoman government by seizing Ottoman territory or the long-coveted Dardanelles. Such a move would make Russia the major power in eastern Europe and would enable the Russians to challenge British naval control of the eastern Mediterranean. Napoleon III believed the Russians had insulted France, first at the Congress of Vienna and now by their insistence on replacing the French as the protectors of Christians living in the Ottoman Empire. The Russians assumed that they could count on support from the Austrians (since Russian troops had saved the Austrian government in 1849). However, the Austrian prime minister blithely explained, "We will astonish the world by our ingratitude," and Austria remained neutral. Since the Austrians had perceived that it was not in their best interest to intervene, Russia had to fight alone.

The Crimean War was poorly planned and poorly fought. Britain and France decided to attack Russia's Crimean peninsula in the Black Sea. After a long siege and at a terrible cost in manpower for both sides, the main Russian fortress of Sevastopol fell in September 1855, six months after the death of Tsar Nicholas I. His successor, Alexander II, soon sued for peace. By the Treaty of Paris, signed in March 1856, Russia was forced to give up Bessarabia at the mouth of the Danube and accept the neutrality of the Black Sea. In addition, the Danubian principalities of Moldavia and Walachia were placed under the protection of all the great powers.

The Crimean War proved costly to both sides. More than 250,000 soldiers died in the war, 60 percent of the deaths coming from disease (especially cholera). Even more would have died on the British side if it had not been for the efforts of Florence Nightingale (1820–1910). Her insistence on strict sanitary conditions saved many lives and helped to make nursing a profession of trained, middle-class women.

The Crimean War broke up long-standing European power relationships and effectively destroyed the Concert of Europe. Austria and Russia, the two chief powers maintaining the status quo in the first half of the nineteenth century, were now enemies because of Austria's unwillingness to support Russia in the war. Russia, defeated, humiliated, and weakened by the obvious failure of its serf-armies, withdrew from European affairs for the next two decades to set its house in order and await a better opportunity to undo the Treaty of Paris. Great Britain, disillusioned by its role in the war, also pulled back from continental affairs. Austria, paying the price for its neutrality, was now without friends among the great powers. Not until the 1870s were new combinations formed to replace those that had disappeared, and in the meantime the European international situation remained fluid. Those willing to pursue the "politics of reality" found themselves in a situation rife with opportunity. It was this new international situation that made possible the unification of Italy and Germany.

Only Louis Napoleon seemed to have gained in prestige from the Crimean War. His experiences in the war had taught him that he was not the military genius his uncle had been, but he became well aware of the explosive power of the forces of nationalism and determined to pursue a foreign policy that would champion national movements. Some historians have argued that Napoleon believed ardently in the cause of national liberation. Be that as it may, as the liberator of national peoples, Napoleon III envisioned France as the natural leader of free European states. His policy proved to be a disaster as we can observe by examining the movements for unification in Italy and Germany.

◆ National Unification: Italy and Germany

The breakdown of the Concert of Europe opened the way for the Italians and the Germans to establish national states. Their successful unifications transformed the power structure of the European continent. Well into the twentieth century, Europe would still be dealing with the consequences.

❈ The Unification of Italy

The Italians were the first people to benefit from the breakdown of the Concert of Europe. In 1850, Austria was still the dominant power on the Italian peninsula. Austria controlled Lombardy and Venetia, and Modena and Tuscany were ruled by members of Austria's house of Habsburg. Moreover, the Papal States governed by the pope, the other petty Italian states, and even the Bourbon kingdom of the Two Sicilies looked to the Austrians to maintain the status quo.

Although a minority, Italian liberals and nationalists had tried earnestly to achieve unification in the first half of the nineteenth century. Some had favored the *risorgimento* movement led by Giuseppe Mazzini, which favored a republican Italy; others looked to a confederation of Italian states under the direction of the pope. Neither of those alternatives was feasible after the defeats of 1849. A growing number of advocates of Italian unification now focused on the northern Italian state of Piedmont as their best hope to achieve their goal. As one observed: "To defeat cannons and soldiers, cannons and soldiers are needed. Arms are needed, and not Mazzinian pratings. Piedmont has soldiers and cannons. Therefore I am Piedmontese. By ancient custom, inclination and duty, Piedmont these days is a monarchy. Therefore I am not a republican."[4]

The royal house of Savoy ruled the kingdom of Piedmont, which also included the island of Sardinia. Although soundly defeated by the Austrians in 1848–1849, Piedmont under King Charles Albert had made a valiant effort; it seemed reasonable that Piedmont would now assume the leading role in the cause of national unity. The little state seemed unlikely to supply the needed leadership, however, until the new king, Victor Emmanuel II (1849–1878), named Count Camillo di Cavour (1810–1861) as his prime minister in 1852.

Cavour was a liberal-minded nobleman who had made a fortune in agriculture and went on to make even more money in banking, railroads, and shipping. He admired the British, especially their parliamentary system, industrial techniques, and economic liberalism. Cavour was a moderate who favored constitutional government. Though he might have wanted Italian unification, he had no preconceived notions about how to obtain it. He was a consummate politician with the ability to persuade others of the rightness of his own convictions. After becoming prime minister in 1852, he pursued a policy of economic expansion, encouraging the building of roads, canals, and railroads and fostering business enterprise by expanding credit and stimulating investment in new industries. The growth in the Piedmontese economy and the subsequent increase in government revenues enabled Cavour to pour money into equipping a large army.

Cavour had no illusions about Piedmont's military strength and was only too well aware that he could not challenge Austria directly. He would need the French. In 1858, Cavour came to an agreement with Napoleon III. The emperor agreed to ally with Piedmont in driving the Austrians out of Italy provided that the war could be justified "in the eyes of the public opinion of France and Europe." Once the Austrians were driven out, Italy would be reorganized. Piedmont would be extended into the kingdom of Upper Italy by adding Lombardy, Venetia, Parma, Modena, and part of the Papal States to its territory. In compensation for its efforts, France would receive the Piedmontese provinces of Nice and Savoy. A kingdom of Central Italy would be created for Napoleon III's cousin, Prince Napoleon, who would be married to the younger daughter of King Victor Emmanuel. This agreement between Napoleon and Cavour seemed to assure the French ruler of the opportunity to control Italy. Confident that the plan would work, Cavour provoked the Austrians into invading Piedmont in April 1859, thus fulfilling Napoleon's demand that the war be justified "in the eyes of the public opinion of France and Europe."

In the initial stages of fighting, it was the French who were largely responsible for defeating the Austrians in two major battles at Magenta and Solferino. It was also the French who made peace with Austria on July 11, 1859, without informing their Italian ally. Why did Napoleon withdraw so hastily? For one thing, he realized that, despite two losses, the Austrian army had not yet been defeated; the struggle might be longer and more costly than he had anticipated. Moreover, the Prussians were mobilizing in support of Austria, and Napoleon III had no desire to take on two enemies at once. As a result of Napoleon's peace with Austria, Piedmont received only Lombardy; Venetia remained under Austrian control. Cavour was furious at the French perfidy, but events in northern Italy now turned in his favor. Soon after the war with Austria had begun, some northern Italian states, namely, Parma, Modena, Tuscany, and part of the Papal States, had been taken over by nationalists. In plebiscites held in 1860, these states agreed to join Piedmont. Napoleon, in return for Nice and Savoy, agreed to the annexations.

Italian unification might have stopped here as there is little indication that Cavour envisioned uniting all of Italy in the spring of 1860. But the forces of Romantic republican nationalism forced Cavour to act. Giuseppe Garibaldi (1807–1882) was a dedicated Italian patriot who had supported Mazzini and the republican cause of Young Italy. While in exile in Latin America, he had gained much experience in guerrilla warfare, which he put to good use in the Italian revolutionary struggles of 1848–1849. In 1859, he became involved in the fighting against Austria. Cavour regarded Garibaldi as a nuisance and encouraged him to move on to southern Italy where a revolt had broken out against the Bourbon king of the Two Sicilies. With

MAP 22.1 **The Unification of Italy.**

GARIBALDI ARRIVES IN SICILY. **The dream of Italian nationalists for a united Italian state finally became a reality by 1870. An important figure in the cause of unification was Giuseppe Garibaldi, a determined Italian patriot. Garibaldi is shown here arriving in Sicily on May 11, 1860, with his band of Red Shirts.**

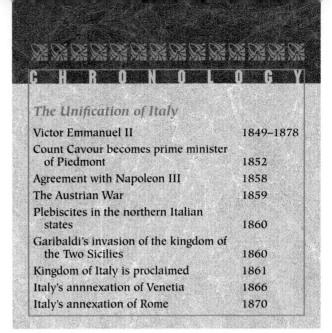
his 1,000 Red Shirts, as his volunteers were called because of their distinctive dress, Garibaldi landed in Sicily on May 11, 1860.

Although his forces were greatly outnumbered, Garibaldi's daring tactics won the day (see the box on p. 652). By the end of July 1860, most of Sicily had been pacified under Garibaldi's control. In August Garibaldi and his forces crossed over to the mainland and began a victorious march up the Italian peninsula. Naples and the kingdom of the Two Sicilies fell in early September. At this point Cavour reentered the scene. Aware that Garibaldi planned to march on Rome, Cavour feared that such a move would bring war with France as the defender of papal interests. Moreover, Garibaldi and his men favored a democratic republicanism; Cavour did not and acted quickly to preempt Garibaldi. The Piedmontese army invaded the Papal States and, bypassing Rome, moved into the kingdom of Naples. Ever the patriot, Garibaldi chose to yield to Cavour's fait accompli rather than provoke a civil war so he retired to his farm. Plebiscites in the Papal States and the kingdom of the Two Sicilies resulted

in overwhelming support for union with Piedmont. On March 17, 1861, a new kingdom of Italy was proclaimed under a centralized government subordinated to the control of Piedmont and King Victor Emmanuel II (1861–1878) of the house of Savoy. Worn out by his efforts, Cavour died three months later.

Despite the proclamation of a new kingdom, the task of unification was not yet complete since Venetia in the north was still held by Austria and Rome was under papal control, supported by French troops. To attack either one meant war with a major European state, which the Italian army was not prepared to handle. It was the Prussian army that indirectly completed the task of Italian unification. In the Austro-Prussian War of 1866 (see The Austro-Prussian War (1866) later in this chapter), the new Italian state became an ally of Prussia. Although the Italian army was defeated by the Austrians, Prussia's victory left the Italians with Venetia. In 1870, the Franco-Prussian War (see The Franco-Prussian War (1870–1871) later in this chapter) resulted in the withdrawal of French troops from Rome. The Italian army then annexed the city on September 20, 1870, and Rome became the new capital of the united Italian state.

❋ The Unification of Germany

After the failure of the Frankfurt Assembly to achieve German unification in 1848–1849, German nationalists focused on Austria and Prussia as the only two states powerful enough to dominate German affairs. Austria had long controlled the existing Germanic Confederation, but Prussian power had grown, strongly reinforced by economic expansion in the 1850s. Prussia had formed the *Zollverein*, a German customs union, in 1834. By eliminating tolls on rivers and roads among member states, the *Zollverein* had stimulated trade and added to the prosperity of its member states. By 1853, all the German states except Austria

Garibaldi and Romantic Nationalism

Giuseppe Garibaldi was one of the more colorful figures involved in the unification of Italy. Accompanied by only 1,000 of his famous "Red Shirts," the Italian soldier of fortune left Genoa on the night of May 5, 1860, for an invasion of the kingdom of the Two Sicilies. The ragged band entered Palermo, the chief city on the island of Sicily, on May 31. This selection is taken from an account by a correspondent for The Times *of London, the Hungarian-born Nandor Eber.*

✤ The Times, June 13, 1860

Palermo, May 31—Anyone in search of violent emotions cannot do better than set off at once for Palermo. However blasé he may be, or however milk-and-water his blood, I promise it will be stirred up. He will be carried away by the tide of popular feeling. . . .

In the afternoon Garibaldi made a tour of inspection round the town. I was there, but find it really impossible to give you a faint idea of the manner in which he was received everywhere. It was one of those triumphs which seem to be almost too much for a man. . . . The popular idol, Garibaldi, in his red flannel shirt, with a loose colored handkerchief around his neck, and his worn "wide-awake," [a soft-brimmed felt hat] was walking on foot among those cheering, laughing, crying, mad thousands; and all his few followers could do was to prevent him from being bodily carried off the ground. The people threw themselves forward to kiss his hands, or, at least, to touch the hem of his garment, as if it contained the panacea for all their past and perhaps coming suffering. Children were brought up, and mothers asked on their knees for his blessing; and all this while the object of this idolatry was calm and smiling as when in the deadliest fire, taking up the children and kissing them, trying to quiet the crowd, stopping at every moment to hear a long complaint of houses burned and property sacked by the retreating soldiers, giving good advice, comforting, and promising that all damages should be paid for. . . .

One might write volumes of horrors on the vandalism already committed, for every one of the hundred ruins has its story of brutality and inhumanity. . . . In these small houses a dense population is crowded together even in ordinary times. A shell falling on one, and crushing and burying the inmates, was sufficient to make people abandon the neighboring one and take refuge a little further on, shutting themselves up in the cellars. When the Royalists retired they set fire to those of the houses which had escaped the shells, and numbers were thus burned alive in their hiding places. . . .

If you can stand the exhalation, try and go inside the ruins, for it is only there that you will see what the thing means and you will not have to search long before you stumble over the remains of a human body, a leg sticking out here, an arm there, a black face staring at you a little further on. You are startled by a rustle. You look round and see half a dozen gorged rats scampering off in all directions, or you see a dog trying to make his escape over the ruins. . . . I only wonder that the sight of these scenes does not convert every man in the town into a tiger and every woman into a fury. But these people have been so long ground down and demoralized that their nature seems to have lost the power of reaction.

---

had joined the Prussian-dominated customs union. A number of middle-class liberals now began to see Prussia in a new light; some even looked openly to Prussia to bring about the unification of Germany.

In 1848, Prussia had framed a constitution that at least had the appearance of constitutional monarchy in that it had established a bicameral legislature with the lower house elected by universal male suffrage. However, the voting population was divided into three classes determined by the amount of taxes they paid, a system that allowed the biggest taxpayers to gain the most seats. Unintentionally, by 1859 this system had allowed control of the lower house to fall largely into the hands of the rising middle classes, whose numbers were growing as a result of continuing industrialization. Their desire was to have a real parliamentary system, but the king's executive power remained too strong; royal ministers answered for their actions only to the king, not the parliament. Nevertheless, the parliament had been granted important legislative and taxation powers upon which it could build.

In 1861, King Frederick William IV died and was succeeded by his brother. King William I (1861–1888) had definite ideas about the Prussian army because of his own military training. He and his advisers believed that the army was in dire need of change if Prussia was to remain a great power. Working closely with Albrecht von Roon as minister for war and Helmuth von Moltke as chief of the army general staff, the king planned to double the size of the army, diminish the role of the *Landwehr,* the popular militia reserves that had first been formed to fight Napoleon in 1806, and institute three years of compulsory military service for all young men.

Middle-class liberals in the parliament, while willing to have reform, feared compulsory military service because they believed the government would use it to inculcate obedience to the monarchy and strengthen the influence of the conservative-military clique in Prussia. The liberals were powerful enough to reject the new military budget submitted to parliament in March 1862. Though frustrated, William I was unwilling to use the army to seize control and instead appointed a new prime minister, Count Otto von Bismarck (1815–1898). Bismarck, regarded even by the king as too conservative, came to determine the course of modern German history. Until 1890, he dominated both German and European politics.

Otto von Bismarck was born into the Junker class, the traditional, landowning aristocracy of Prussia, and remained loyal to it throughout his life. "I was born and raised as an aristocrat," he once said. As a university student, Bismarck indulged heartily in wine, women, and song, yet managed to read widely in German history. After earning a law degree, he embarked upon a career in the Prussian civil service but soon tired of bureaucratic, administrative routine and retired to manage his country estates. Comparing the civil servant to a musician in an orchestra, he responded, "But I want to play the tune the way it sounds good to me or not at all. . . . My pride bids me command rather than obey."[5] In 1847, desirous of more excitement and power than he could find in the country, he reentered public life. Four years later, he began to build a base of diplomatic experience as the Prussian delegate to the diet (parliament) of the Germanic Confederation. This, combined with his experience as Prussian ambassador to Russia and later to France, gave him opportunities to acquire a wide knowledge of European affairs and to learn how to assess the character of rulers.

Because Bismarck succeeded in guiding Prussia's unification of Germany, it is often assumed that he had determined upon a course of action that led precisely to that goal. That is hardly the case. Bismarck was a consummate politician and opportunist. He had a clear idea of his goals, but was willing to show great flexibility in how he reached them. He was not a political gambler, but a moderate who waged war only when all other diplomatic alternatives had been exhausted and when he was reasonably sure that all the military and diplomatic advantages were on his side. Nor was he doctrinaire. Although loyal to the Junkers, the Prussian king, and Lutheranism, he was capable of transcending them all in favor of a broader perspective, although there is no doubt that he came to see the German Empire, which he had helped to create, as the primary focus of his efforts. Bismarck has often been portrayed as the ultimate realist, the foremost nineteenth-century practitioner of *Realpolitik*—the "politics of reality." His ability to manipulate people and power makes that claim justified, but Bismarck also recognized the limitations of power. When he perceived that the advantages to be won from war "no longer justified the risks involved," he could become an ardent defender of peace.

In 1862, the immediate problem facing Bismarck was domestic Prussian politics. Bismarck resubmitted the army appropriations bill to parliament along with a passionate appeal to his liberal opponents: "Germany does not look to Prussia's liberalism but to her power. . . . Not by speeches and majorities will the great questions of the day be decided—that was the mistake of 1848–1849—but by iron and blood."[6] His opponents were not impressed and rejected the bill once again. Bismarck went ahead, collected the taxes, and reorganized the army anyway, blaming the liberals for causing the breakdown of constitutional government. From 1862 to 1866, Bismarck governed Prussia by largely ignoring parliament. Unwilling to revolt, parliament did nothing. In the meantime, opposition to his domestic policy determined Bismarck upon an active foreign policy, which in 1864 led to his first war.

THE DANISH WAR (1864)

In the three wars that he waged, Bismarck's victories were as much diplomatic and political as they were military. Before war was declared, Bismarck always saw to it that Prussia would be fighting only one power and that that opponent was isolated diplomatically. He knew enough Prussian history to realize that Frederick the Great had almost been crushed by a mighty coalition in the eighteenth century (see Chapter 18).

The Danish War arose over the duchies of Schleswig and Holstein. In 1863, contrary to international treaty, the Danish government moved to incorporate the two duchies into Denmark. German nationalists were outraged since both duchies had large German populations and were regarded as German states. The diet of the Germanic Confederation urged its member states to send troops against Denmark, but Bismarck did not care to subject Prussian policy to the Austrian-dominated German diet. Instead, he persuaded the Austrians to join Prussia in declaring war on Denmark on February 1, 1864. The Danes were quickly defeated and surrendered Schleswig and Holstein to the victors. Austria and Prussia then agreed to divide the administration of the two duchies; Prussia took Schleswig while Austria administered Holstein. The plan was Bismarck's. By this time Bismarck had come to the realization that for Prussia to expand its power by dominating the northern, largely Protestant part of the Germanic Confederation, Austria would have to be excluded from German affairs or, less likely, be willing to accept Prussian domination of Germany. The joint administration of the two duchies offered plenty of opportunities to create friction with Austria and provide a reason for war if it came to that. While he pursued negotiations with Austria, he also laid the foundations for the isolation of Austria.

THE AUSTRO-PRUSSIAN WAR (1866)

Bismarck had no problem gaining Russia's agreement to remain neutral in the event of an Austro-Prussian war because Prussia had been the only great power to support Russia's repression of a Polish revolt in 1863. Napoleon III was a thornier problem, but Bismarck was able to buy his neutrality with vague promises of territory in the Rhineland. Finally, Bismarck made an alliance with the new Italian state and promised it Venetia in the event of Austrian defeat.

With the Austrians isolated, Bismarck used the joint occupation of Schleswig-Holstein to goad the Austrians into a war on June 14, 1866. Many Europeans, including Napoleon III, expected a quick Austrian victory, but they overlooked the effectiveness of the Prussian military reforms of the 1860s. The Prussian breech-loading needle gun had a much faster rate of fire than the Austrian muzzle-loader, and a superior network of railroads enabled the Prussians to mass troops quickly. At König-grätz (or Sadowa) on July 3, the Austrian army was decisively defeated. Looking ahead, Bismarck refused to create a hostile enemy by burdening Austria with a harsh peace as the Prussian king wanted. Austria lost no territory except Venetia to Italy but was excluded from German affairs. The German states north of the Main River were organized into a North German Confederation controlled by Prussia. The south German states, largely Catholic, remained independent but were coerced into signing military agreements with Prussia. In addition to Schleswig and Holstein, Prussia annexed Hanover,

Hesse-Cassel, and the free city of Frankfurt because they had openly sided with Austria.

The Austrian War was a rather decisive turning point in Prussian domestic affairs. After the war, Bismarck asked the Prussian parliament to pass a bill of indemnity, retroactively legalizing the taxes he had collected illegally since 1862. Even most of the liberals voted in favor of the bill because they had been won over by Bismarck's successful use of military power. With his victory over Austria and the creation of the North German Confederation, Bismarck had proved Napoleon III's dictum that nationalism and authoritarian government could be combined. In using nationalism to win support from liberals and prevent governmental reform, Bismarck showed that liberalism and nationalism, the two major forces of change in the early nineteenth century, could be separated.

He showed the same flexibility in the creation of a new constitution for the North German Confederation. Each German state kept its own local government, but the king of Prussia was head of the confederation while the

MAP 22.2 The Unification of Germany.

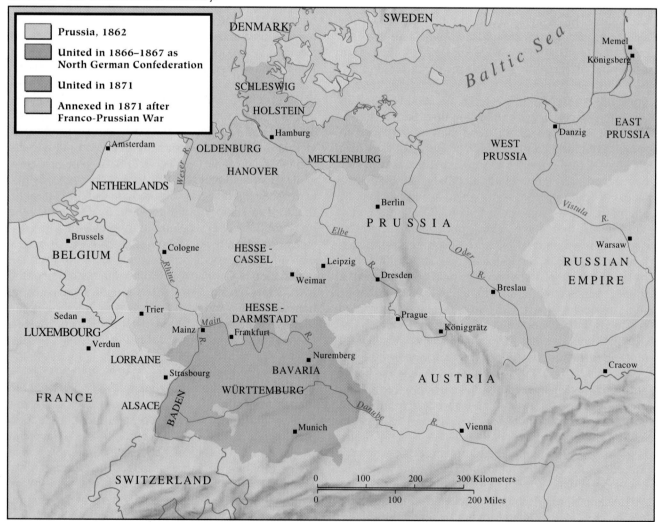

THE UNIFICATION OF GERMANY. Under Prussian leadership, a new German Empire was proclaimed on January 18, 1871, in the Hall of Mirrors in the palace at Versailles. King William of Prussia became Emperor William I of the Second German Empire. In this painting by Anton von Werner, Otto von Bismarck, the man who had been so instrumental in creating the new German state, is shown, resplendently attired in his white uniform, standing at the foot of the throne.

chancellor (Bismarck) was responsible directly to the king. Both the army and foreign policy remained in the hands of the king and his chancellor. Parliament consisted of two bodies: a Bundesrat, or federal council composed of delegates nominated by the states, and a lower house, the Reichstag, elected by universal male suffrage. Like Napoleon, Bismarck believed that the peasants and artisans who made up most of the population were conservative at heart and could be used to overcome the advantages of the liberals. He had not counted on the industrial proletariat whose growth in the years ahead would provide him with some of his most vehement opposition (see Chapter 23).

THE FRANCO-PRUSSIAN WAR (1870–1871)

Bismarck and William I had achieved a major goal by 1866. Prussia now dominated all of northern Germany, and Austria had been excluded from any significant role in German affairs. Nevertheless, unsettled business led to new international complications and further change. Bismarck realized that France would never be content with a strong German state to its east because of the potential threat to French security. At the same time, after a series of setbacks, Napoleon III needed a diplomatic triumph to offset his serious domestic problems. The French were not happy with the turn of events in Germany and looked for opportunities to humiliate the Prussians.

After a successful revolution had deposed Queen Isabella II, the throne of Spain was offered to Prince Leopold of Hohenzollern-Sigmaringen, a distant relative of the Hohenzollern king of Prussia. Bismarck welcomed this possibility for the same reason that the French objected to it. If Leopold were placed on the throne of Spain, France would be virtually encircled by members of the Hohenzollern dynasty. French objections caused King William I to force his relative to withdraw his candidacy. Bismarck was disappointed with the king's actions, but at this point the French overreached themselves. Not con-

tent with their diplomatic victory, they pushed William I to make a formal apology to France and promise never to allow Leopold to be a candidate again. When Bismarck received a telegraph from the king informing him of the French request, Bismarck edited it to make it appear even more insulting to the French, knowing that the French would be angry and declare war (see the box on p. 656). Through diplomacy, Bismarck had already made it virtually certain that no other European power would interfere in a war between France and Prussia. The French reacted as Bismarck expected they would and declared war on Prussia on July 15, 1870. The French prime minister remarked, "We go to war with a light heart."

Unfortunately for the French, a "light heart" was not enough. They had barely started their military reorganization and proved no match for the better led and organized Prussian forces. The south German states honored their military alliances with Prussia and joined the war effort against the French. The Prussian armies advanced into France, and at Sedan, on September 2, 1870, an entire French army and Napoleon III himself were captured. Although the Second French Empire collapsed, the war was not yet over. After four months of bitter resistance, Paris finally capitulated on January 28, 1871, and an official peace treaty was signed in May. France had to pay an indemnity of five billion francs (about one billion dollars), which Bismarck thought would cripple the French for years and keep them out of European affairs. The French responded by paying it off in three years. Even worse, however, the French had to give up the provinces of Alsace and

Bismarck "Goads" France into War

After his meeting with the French ambassador at Ems, King William I of Prussia sent a telegraph to Bismarck with a report of their discussions. By editing the telegraph from King William I before releasing it to the press, Bismarck made it sound as if the Prussian king had treated the ambassador in a demeaning fashion. Six days later, France declared war on Prussia.

❋ The Abeken [Privy Councillor] Text, Ems, July 13, 1870

To the Federal Chancellor, Count Bismarck. His Majesty the King writes to me:

"M. Benedetti intercepted me on the Promenade in order to demand of me most insistently that I should authorize him to telegraph immediately to Paris that I shall obligate myself for all future time never again to give my approval to the candidacy of the Hohenzollerns should it be renewed. I refused to agree to this, the last time somewhat severely, informing him that one dare not and cannot assume such obligations *à tout jamais* [forever]. Naturally, I informed him that I had received no news as yet, and since he had been informed earlier than I by way of Paris and Madrid, he could easily understand why my government was once again out of the matter."

Since then His Majesty has received a dispatch from the Prince [father of the Hohenzollern candidate for the Spanish throne]. As His Majesty has informed Count Benedetti that he was expecting news from the Prince, His Majesty himself, in view of the above-mentioned demand and in consonance with the advice of Count Eulenburg and myself, decided not to receive the French envoy again but to inform him through an adjutant that His Majesty had now received from the Prince confirmation of the news which Benedetti had already received from Paris, and that he had nothing further to say to the Ambassador. His Majesty leaves it to the judgment of Your Excellency whether or not to communicate at once the new demand by Benedetti and its rejection to our ambassadors and to the press.

❋ Bismarck's Edited Version

After the reports of the renunciation by the hereditary Prince of Hohenzollern had been officially transmitted by the Royal Government of Spain to the Imperial Government of France, the French Ambassador presented to His Majesty the King at Ems the demand to authorize him to telegraph to Paris that His Majesty the King would obligate himself for all future time never again to give his approval to the candidacy of the Hohenzollerns should it be renewed.

His Majesty the King thereupon refused to receive the French envoy again and informed him through an adjutant that His Majesty had nothing further to say to the Ambassador.

Lorraine to the new German state, a loss that angered the French and left them burning for revenge.

Even before the war had ended, the south German states had agreed to enter the North German Confederation. On January 18, 1871, in the Hall of Mirrors in Louis XIV's palace at Versailles, William I was proclaimed kaiser or emperor of the Second German Empire (the first was the medieval Holy Roman Empire). German unity had been achieved by the Prussian monarchy and the Prussian army. In a real sense, Germany had been merged into Prussia, not Prussia into Germany. German liberals also rejoiced. They had dreamed of unity and freedom, but the achievement of unity now seemed much more important. One old liberal proclaimed:

> I cannot shake off the impression of this hour. I am no devotee of Mars; I feel more attached to the goddess of beauty and the mother of graces than to the powerful god of war, but the trophies of war exercise a magic charm even upon the child of peace. One's view is involuntarily chained and one's spirit goes along with the boundless row of men who acclaim the god of the moment—success.[7]

The Prussian leadership of German unification meant the triumph of authoritarian, militaristic values over liberal, constitutional sentiments in the development of the new German state. With its industrial resources and military might, the new state had become the strongest power on the Continent. A new European balance of power was at hand.

◆ Nation Building and Reform: The National State in Mid-Century

Though European affairs were dominated by the unification of Italy and Germany, other states were also undergoing transformations. War, civil war, and changing political alignments served as catalysts for domestic reforms.

The Austrian Empire: Toward a Dual Monarchy

After the Habsburgs had crushed the revolutions of 1848–1849, they restored centralized, autocratic government to the empire. What seemed to be the only lasting result of the revolution of 1848 was the act of emancipation of September 7, 1848, that freed the serfs and eliminated all compulsory labor services. Nevertheless, the development of industrialization after 1850, especially in Vienna and the provinces of Bohemia and Galicia, served to bring some economic and social change to the empire in the form of an urban proletariat, labor unrest, and a new industrial middle class.

In 1851, the revolutionary constitutions were abolished, and a system of centralized autocracy was imposed on the empire. Under the leadership of Alexander von Bach (1813–1893), local privileges were subordinated to a unified system of administration, law, and taxation implemented by German-speaking officials. Hungary was subjected to the rule of military officers, and the Catholic church was declared the state church and given control of education. The Bach regime, according to one critic, was composed of "a standing army of soldiers, a sitting army of officials, a kneeling army of priests, and a creeping army of denunciators." Economic troubles and war soon brought change. Failure in war usually had severe internal consequences for European states after 1789, and Austria was no exception. After Austria's defeat in the Italian war in 1859, the Emperor Francis Joseph (1848–1916) attempted to establish an imperial parliament (*Reichsrat*) with a nominated upper house and an elected lower house of representatives. Although the system was supposed to provide representation for the nationalities of the empire, the complicated formula used for elections ensured the election of a German-speaking majority, serving once again to alienate the ethnic minorities, particularly the Hungarians.

Only when military disaster struck again did the Austrians deal with the fiercely nationalistic Hungarians. The result was the negotiated *Ausgleich*, or Compromise, of 1867, which created the dual monarchy of Austria-Hungary. Each part of the empire now had its constitution, its own

MAP 22.3 Ethnic Groups in the Dual Monarchy, 1867.

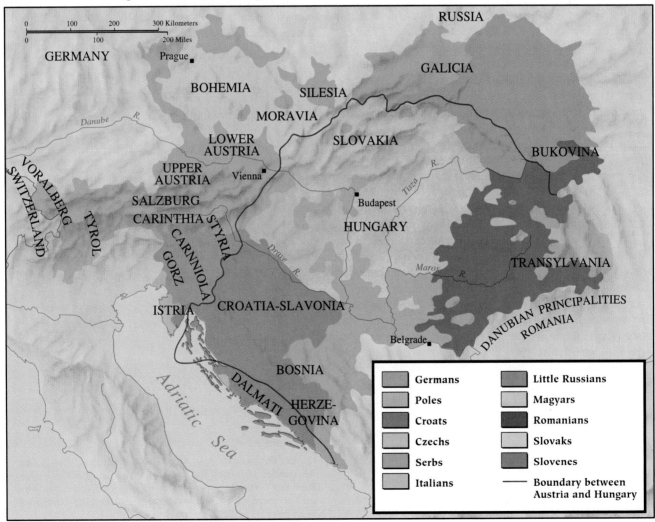

bicameral legislature, its own governmental machinery for domestic affairs, and its own capital (Vienna for Austria and Budapest for Hungary). Holding the two states together were a single monarch (Francis Joseph was emperor of Austria and king of Hungary) and a common army, foreign policy, and system of finances. In domestic affairs, the Hungarians had become an independent nation. The *Ausgleich* did not, however, satisfy the other nationalities that made up the multinational Austro-Hungarian Empire. The dual monarchy simply enabled the German-speaking Austrians and Hungarian Magyars to dominate the minorities, especially the Slavic peoples (Poles, Croats, Czechs, Serbs, Slovaks, Slovenes, Little Russians), in their respective states. As the Hungarian nationalist Louis Kossuth remarked: "Dualism is the alliance of the conservative, reactionary and any apparently liberal elements in Hungary with those of the Austrian Germans who despise liberty, for the oppression of the other nationalities and races."[8] The nationalities problem persisted until the demise of the empire at the end of World War I.

❋ *Imperial Russia*

The Russian imperial autocracy, based on soldiers, secret police, repression, and censorship, had withstood the revolutionary fervor of 1848 and even served as the "arsenal of autocracy" in crushing revolutions elsewhere in Europe. The defeat in the Crimean War at the hands of the British and French revealed the blatant deficiencies behind the facade of absolute power and made it clear even to staunch conservatives that Russia was falling hopelessly behind the western European powers. Tsar Alexander II (1855–1881), who came to power in the midst of the Crimean War, turned his energies to a serious overhaul of the Russian system. Though called the Liberator because of his great reforms, Alexander II was no liberal but a thoughtful realist who knew reforms could not be postponed. Following the autocratic procedures of his predecessors, he attempted to impose those reforms upon the Russian people.

Serfdom was the most burdensome problem in tsarist Russia. The continuing subjugation of millions of peasants to the land and their landlords was an obviously corrupt and failing system. Reduced to antiquated methods of production based on serf labor, Russian landowners were economically pressed and unable to compete with foreign agriculture. The serfs, who formed the backbone of the Russian infantry, were uneducated and consequently increasingly unable to deal with the more complex machines and weapons of war. It was, after all, the failure of the serf-armies in the Crimean War that created the need for change in the first place. Then, too, peasant dissatisfaction still led to local peasant revolts that disrupted the countryside. Alexander II seemed to recognize the inevitable: "The existing order of serfdom," he told a group of Moscow nobles, "cannot remain unchanged. It is better to abolish serfdom from above than to wait until it is abolished from below."

On March 3, 1861, Alexander issued his emancipation edict (see the box on p. 659). Peasants could now own property, marry as they chose, and bring suits in the law courts. Nevertheless, the benefits of emancipation were limited. The government provided land for the peasants by purchasing it from the landowners, but the landowners often chose to keep the best lands. The Russian peasants soon found that they had inadequate amounts of good arable land to support themselves, a situation that worsened as the peasant population increased rapidly in the second half of the nineteenth century.

Nor were the peasants completely free. The state compensated the landowners for the land given to the peasants, but the peasants, in turn, were expected to repay the state in long-term installments. To ensure that the payments were made, peasants were subjected to the authority of their *mir*, or village commune, which was collectively responsible for the land payments to the government. In a very real sense, then, the village commune, not the individual peasants, owned the land the peasants were purchasing. And since the village communes were responsible for the payments, they were reluctant to allow peasants to leave their land. Emancipation, then, led not to a free, landowning peasantry along the Western model, but to an unhappy, land-starved peasantry that largely followed the old ways of farming. Comprehensive reforms that would have freed the peasants completely and given them access

EMANCIPATION OF THE SERFS. On March 3, 1861, Tsar Alexander II issued his emancipation edict for the Russian serfs. This photograph shows a Russian noble on the steps of his country house reading the edict to a gathering of his serfs.

Emancipation: Serfs and Slaves

Although overall their histories have been quite different, Russia and the United States shared a common feature in the 1860s. They were the only states in the Western world that still had large enslaved populations (the Russian serfs were virtually slaves). The leaders of both countries issued emancipation proclamations within two years of each other. The first excerpt is taken from the Imperial Decree of March 3, 1861, which freed the Russian serfs. The second excerpt is from Abraham Lincoln's Emancipation Proclamation, issued on January 1, 1863.

❈ The Imperial Decree, March 3, 1861

By the grace of God, we, Alexander II, Emperor and Autocrat of all the Russias, King of Poland, Grand Duke of Finland, etc., to all our faithful subjects, make known:

Called by Divine Providence and by the sacred right of inheritance to the throne of our ancestors, we took a vow in our innermost heart to respond to the mission which is intrusted to us as to surround with our affection and our Imperial solicitude all our faithful subjects of every rank and of every condition, from the warrior, who nobly bears arms for the defense of the country to the humble artisan devoted to the works of industry; from the official in the career of the high offices of the State to the laborer whose plow furrows the soil. . . .

We thus came to the conviction that the work of a serious improvement of the condition of the peasants was a sacred inheritance bequeathed to us by our ancestors, a mission which, in the course of events, Divine providence called upon us to fulfill. . . .

In virtue of the new dispositions above mentioned, the peasants attached to the soil will be invested within a term fixed by the law with all the rights of free cultivators. . . .

At the same time, they are granted the right of purchasing their close, and, with the consent of the proprietors, they may acquire in full property the arable lands and other appurtenances which are allotted to them as a permanent holding. By the acquisition in full property of the quantity of land fixed, the peasants are free from their obligations toward the proprietors for land thus purchased, and they enter definitely into the condition of free peasants—landholders.

❈ The Emancipation Proclamation, January 1, 1863

Now therefore, I, Abraham Lincoln, President of the United States, by virtue of the power in me vested as Commander-in-Chief of the Army and Navy of the United States in time of actual armed rebellion against the authority and government of the United States, and as a fit and necessary war measure for suppressing such rebellion, do, on this 1st day of January, A.D. 1863, and in accordance with my purpose to do so, . . . order and designate as the States and parts of States wherein the people thereof, respectively, are this day in rebellion against the United States the following, to wit:

Arkansas, Texas, Louisiana, . . . Mississippi, Alabama, Florida, Georgia, South Carolina, North Carolina, and Virginia. . . .

And by virtue of the power for the purpose aforesaid, I do order and declare that all persons held as slaves within said designated States and parts of States are, and henceforward shall be free; and that the Executive Government of the United States, including the military and naval authorities thereof, will recognize and maintain the freedom of said persons.

---

to their own land were unfortunately left until the early twentieth century.

Alexander II also attempted other reforms. In 1864, he instituted a system of zemstvos, or local assemblies, that provided a moderate degree of self-government. Representatives to the zemstvos were to be elected from the noble landowners, townspeople, and peasants, but the property-based system of voting gave a distinct advantage to the nobles. Zemstvos were given a limited power to provide public services, such as education, famine relief, and road and bridge maintenance. They could levy taxes to pay for these services, but their efforts were frequently disrupted by bureaucrats who feared any hint of self-government. As one official noted: "In Russia reform can be carried out only by authority. We have too much disturbance and too much divergence of interests to expect anything good from the representation of those interests."[9] The hope of liberal nobles and other social reformers that the zemstvos would be expanded into a national parliament remained unfulfilled. The legal reforms of 1864, which created a regular system of local and provincial courts and a judicial code that accepted the principle of equality before the law, proved successful, however.

Even the autocratic tsar was unable to control the forces he unleashed by his reform program. Reformers wanted more and rapid change; conservatives opposed what they perceived as the tsar's attempts to undermine the basic institutions of Russian society. By 1870, Russia was witnessing an increasing number of reform movements. One of the most popular stemmed from the radical writings of Alexander Herzen (1812–1870), a Russian exile living in

QUEEN VICTORIA AND HER FAMILY.
Queen Victoria, who ruled Britain
from 1837 to 1901, married Prince
Albert of Saxe-Coburg and Gotha in
1840 and subsequently gave birth to
four sons and five daughters, who
married into a number of European
royal families. Queen Victoria is
seated at the center of this 1881
photograph, surrounded by members
of her family.

London, whose slogan of "land and freedom" epitomized his belief that the Russian peasant must be the chief instrument for social reform. Herzen believed that the peasant village commune could serve as an independent, self-governing body that would form the basis of a new Russia. Russian students and intellectuals who followed Herzen's ideas formed a movement called populism, whose aim was to create a new society through the revolutionary acts of the peasants. The peasants' lack of interest in these revolutionary ideas, however, led some of the populists to resort to violent means to overthrow tsarist autocracy. One such group of radicals, known as the People's Will, succeeded in assassinating Alexander II in 1881. His son and successor, Alexander III (1881–1894), turned against reform and returned to the traditional methods of repression.

❋ Great Britain: The Victorian Age

Like Russia, Britain was not troubled by revolutionary disturbances during 1848, although for quite different reasons. The Reform Act of 1832 had opened the door to political representation for the industrial middle class, and in the 1860s Britain's liberal parliamentary system demonstrated once more its ability to make both social and political reforms that enabled the country to remain stable and prosperous.

One of the reasons for Britain's stability was its continuing economic growth. The British had flaunted their wealth and satisfaction with their achievements to the world in the great Industrial Exhibition in 1851. Now middle-class prosperity was at last coupled with some improvements for the working classes as well. Real wages for laborers increased over 25 percent between 1850 and 1870. The British sense of national pride was well reflected in Queen Victoria (1837–1901), whose self-contentment and sense of moral respectability mirrored the attitudes of her age. The Victorian Age, as Britain during the reign of Queen Victoria has ever since been known, was characterized by a pious complacency.

Politically, this was an era of uneasy stability as the aristocratic and upper-middle-class representatives who dominated Parliament blurred party lines by their internal strife and shifting positions. One political figure who stood out was Henry John Temple, Lord Palmerston (1784–1865), who was prime minister for most of the period from 1855 to 1865. Although a Whig, Palmerston was without strong party loyalty and found it easy to make political compromises. His primary interest was foreign policy, and his chauvinistic defense of British interests worldwide made him a popular figure with the British public. He was not a reformer, however, and opposed expanding the franchise. By extending representation from one class to another, he said, "We should by such an arrangement increase the number of Bribeable Electors and overpower Intelligence and Property by Ignorance and Poverty."

After Palmerston's death in 1865, the movement for the extension of the franchise only intensified. One mass meeting even led to a riot in London's Hyde Park. Although the Whigs (now called the Liberals), who had been responsible for the Reform Act of 1832, talked about passing additional reform legislation, it was actually the Tories (now called the Conservatives) who carried it through. The Tory leader in Parliament, Benjamin Disraeli (1804–1881), was apparently motivated by the desire to win over the newly enfranchised groups to the Conservative Party. He believed that the uneducated classes would defer to their social superiors when they voted. He knew that the Liberals, viewed as the party of reform, would not dare to oppose the reform bill. The Reform Act of 1867 was an important step toward the democratization of Britain. By lowering the monetary requirements for voting (taxes paid or income earned), it by and large enfranchised many male urban workers. The number of voters increased from about one million to slightly over two million. Although Disraeli believed this would benefit the Conservatives, industrial workers helped to produce a huge Liberal victory in 1868.

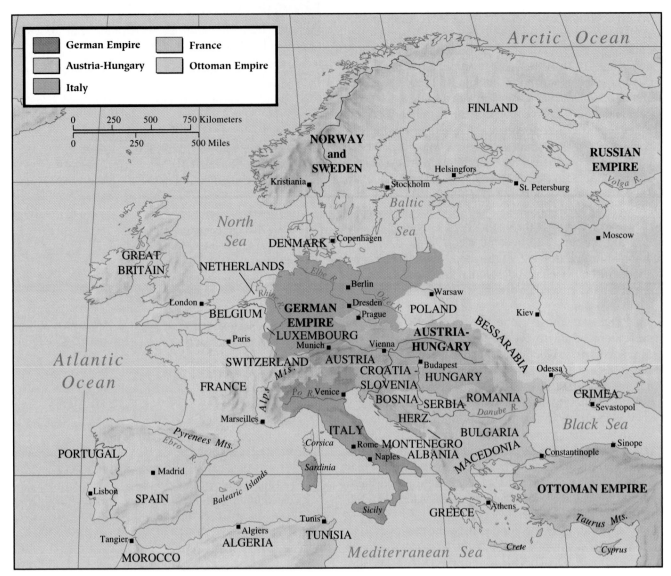

MAP 22.4 **Europe in 1871.**

The extension of the right to vote had an important by-product as it forced the Liberal and Conservative Parties to organize carefully in order to manipulate the electorate. Party discipline intensified, and the rivalry between two well-established political parties, the Liberals and Conservatives, became a regular feature of parliamentary life. In large part this was due to the personal and political opposition of the two leaders of these parties, William Gladstone (1809–1898) and Disraeli.

The first Liberal administration of William Gladstone from 1868 to 1874 was responsible for a series of impressive reforms. In fact, historians have called the first Gladstone ministry the apex of "classical British liberalism." Legislation and government orders opened civil service positions to competitive exams rather than patronage, dropped religious requirements for degrees at Oxford and Cambridge, introduced the secret ballot for voting, and abolished the practice of purchasing military commissions. The Education Act of 1870 attempted to make elementary schools available for all children (see Chapter 24). These reforms were typically liberal. By eliminating abuses and enabling people with talent to compete fairly, they sought to strengthen the nation and its institutions.

✺ The United States: Civil War and Reunion

While the Germans and Italians were fighting Austria and France to achieve national unity, some Americans were hoping to dissolve theirs. During the early existence of the United States, the young republic had shown a remarkable ability to resolve peacefully many issues that might have disrupted national unity. Slavery, however, proved to be an issue beyond compromise.

Like the North, the South had experienced dramatic population growth during the first half of the nineteenth century. But its development was quite different. Its cotton economy and social structure were based on the exploitation of enslaved black Africans and their descendants. The importance of cotton is evident from production figures. In 1810, the South produced a raw cotton crop of 178,000 bales worth $10 million. By 1860, it was generating 4.5 million bales of cotton with a value of $249 million. Ninety-three percent of southern cotton in 1850 was produced by a slave population that had grown dramatically in fifty years. Although new slave imports had been barred in 1808, there were four million Afro-American slaves in the South by 1860 compared to one million in 1800. The cotton economy and a plantation-based slavery were intimately related, and the attempt to maintain them in the course of the first half of the nineteenth century led the South to become increasingly defensive, monolithic, and isolated. At the same time, the rise of an abolitionist movement in the North challenged the southern order and created an "emotional chain reaction" that led to civil war.

The issue arose in the 1810s when the westward movement began to produce new states west of the Appalachians. A balance between slave states and free states was carefully maintained until Missouri applied for admission to the Union in 1819 as a slave state and there was no free state to maintain the balance. The ensuing crisis was settled with the Missouri Compromise of 1820, which separated Maine from Massachusetts in order to maintain the balance. To prevent future crises, the remainder of the territory acquired by the Louisiana Purchase was to be divided at the latitude 36°30′. States formed south of the line would be slave states, and states formed north of the line would be free.

Unfortunately, the line drawn by the Missouri Compromise did not legally extend to the vast new territories acquired by the United States during the 1840s. The Mexican Cession acquired at the close of the Mexican War posed a particular problem because some of its lands were south of 36°30′. By 1850, the country was again facing a crisis over the balance of slave states and free states. This time the problem was caused by California's application for admission as a free state.

The Compromise of 1850, which admitted California as a free state, was really an armistice, not a compromise. It had not solved this divisive issue, but merely postponed it. By the 1850s, the slavery question had caused the Whig Party to become defunct while the Democrats were splitting along North-South lines. The Kansas-Nebraska Act of 1854, which effectively repealed the Missouri Compromise by allowing slavery in the Kansas-Nebraska territories to be determined by popular sovereignty, created a firestorm in the North and led to the creation of a new sectional party. The Republicans were united by antislavery principles and were especially driven by the fear that the "slave power" of the South would attempt to spread the slave system throughout the country.

As polarization over the issue of slavery intensified, compromise became less feasible. When Abraham Lin-

CHRONOLOGY

The National State

France

Louis Napoleon is elected president	1848
Coup d'etat by Louis Napoleon	1851
Creation of the Second Empire	1852
Emperor Napoleon III	1852–1870
The "authoritarian empire"	1852–1860
Crimean War	1854–1856
Treaty of Paris	1856
The "liberal empire"	1860–1870

The Austrian Empire

Establishment of imperial parliament	1859
Ausgleich: the dual monarchy	1867

Russia

Tsar Alexander II	1855–1881
Emancipation edict	1861 (March 3)
Creation of zemstvos and legal reforms	1864

Great Britain

Queen Victoria	1837–1901
Ministry of Palmerston	1855–1865
Reform Act	1867
First Liberal ministry of William Gladstone	1868–1874

The United States

Missouri Compromise	1820
Mexican War	1846–1848
Compromise of 1850	1850
Kansas-Nebraska Act	1854
Election of Lincoln and secession of South Carolina	1860
Outbreak of Civil War	1861
Surrender of Lee	1865 (April 9)

Canada

Formation of the Dominion of Canada	1867

coln, the man who had said in a speech in Illinois in 1858 that "this government cannot endure permanently half slave and half free," was elected president in November 1860, the die was cast. Lincoln carried only 2 of the 1,109 counties in the South; the Republicans were not even on the ballot in ten southern states. On December 20, 1860, a South Carolina convention voted to repeal the state's ratification of the U.S. Constitution. In February 1861, six more southern states did the same, and a rival nation—the Confederate States of America—was formed. In April fighting erupted between North and South.

The American Civil War (1861–1865) was an extraordinarily bloody struggle, a clear foretaste of the total war to come in the twentieth century. More than 360,000 soldiers died, either in battle or from deadly infectious diseases spawned by filthy camp conditions. Over a period of four years, the Union states mobilized their superior assets and gradually wore down the South. As the war dragged on, it had the effect of radicalizing public opinion in the North. What began as a war to save the Union became a war against slavery. On January 1, 1863, Lincoln's Emancipation Proclamation made most of the nation's slaves "forever free" (see the box on p. 659). The increasingly effective Union blockade of the South combined with a shortage of fighting men made the Confederate cause desperate by the end of 1864. The final push of Union troops under General Ulysses S. Grant forced General Robert E. Lee's army to surrender on April 9, 1865. Although the problems of reconstruction were ahead, the Union victory confirmed that the United States would be "one nation, indivisible."

✴ The Emergence of a Canadian Nation

To the north of the United States, the process of nation building was also making progress. By the Treaty of Paris in 1763, Canada—or New France as it was called—passed into the hands of the British. By 1800, most Canadians favored more autonomy, although the colonists disagreed on the form this autonomy should take. Upper Canada (now Ontario) was predominantly English-speaking, whereas Lower Canada (now Quebec) was dominated by French Canadians. Increased immigration to Canada after 1815 also fueled the desire for self-government.

Fearful of American designs on Canada during the American Civil War and eager to reduce the costs of maintaining the colonies, the British government finally capitulated to Canadian demands. In 1867, Parliament established a Canadian nation—the Dominion of Canada—with its own constitution. Canada now possessed a parliamentary system and ruled itself, although foreign affairs still remained under the control of the British government.

◆ Industrialization and the Marxist Response

Between 1850 and 1871, continental industrialization came of age. The innovations of the British Industrial Revolution—mechanized factory production, the use of coal, the steam engine, and the transportation revolution—all

MAP 22.5 The United States: The West and Civil War.

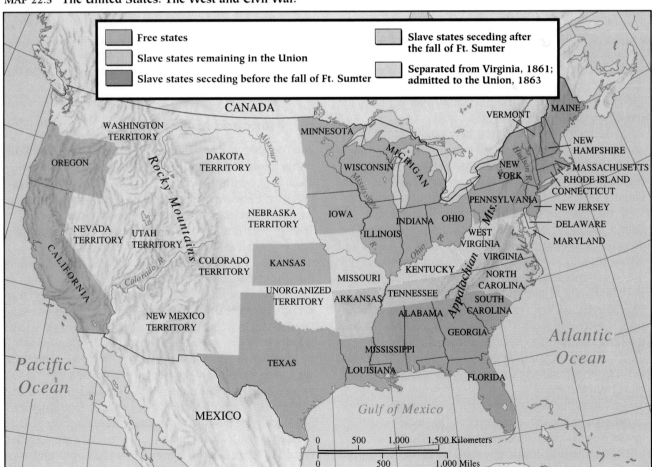

became regular features of economic expansion. Although marred periodically by economic depression (1857–1858) or recession (1866–1867), this was an age of considerable economic prosperity, particularly evident in the growth of domestic and foreign markets.

❊ *Industrialization on the Continent*

The transformation of textile production from hand looms to power looms had largely been completed in Britain by the 1850s (for cotton) and 1860s (for wool). On the Continent, the period from 1850 to 1870 witnessed increased mechanization of the cotton and textile industries, although continental countries still remained behind Britain. By 1870, hand looms had virtually disappeared in Britain whereas in France there were still 200,000 of them compared to 80,000 power looms. However, this period of industrial expansion on the Continent was fueled not so much by textiles as by the growth of railroads. Between 1850 and 1870, European railroad track mileage increased from 14,500 to almost 70,000. The railroads, in turn, stimulated growth in both the iron and coal industries.

Between 1850 and 1870, continental iron industries made the transition from charcoal iron smelting to coke-blast smelting. In Prussia, for example, the portion of the iron output produced with charcoal declined from 82 percent in 1842 to 60 percent in 1852, and to only 12.3 percent by 1862. Despite the dramatic increases in the production of pig iron, the continental countries had not yet come close to surpassing British iron production. In 1870, the British iron industry produced one-half of the world's pig iron, four times as much as Germany and five times as much as France. In the middle decades of the nineteenth century, the textile, mining, and metallurgical industries on the Continent also rapidly converted to the use of the steam engine.

Although policies varied from country to country, continental governments took a more or less active role in passing laws and initiating actions that were favorable to the expansion of industry and commerce. While some countries exercised direct control over nationalized industries, such as Prussia's development of coal mines in the Saar region, others provided financial assistance to private companies to develop mines, ironworks, dockyards, and railways.

An important factor in the expansion of markets was the elimination of barriers to international trade. Essential international waterways were opened up by the elimination of restrictive tolls. The Danube River in 1857 and the Rhine in 1861, for example, were declared freeways for all ships. The negotiation of trade treaties in the 1860s reduced or eliminated protective tariffs throughout much of western Europe.

Governments also played a role in first allowing and then encouraging the formation of joint-stock investment banks (see Chapter 20). These banks were crucial to continental industrial development because they mobilized enormous capital resources for investment. In the 1850s and 1860s, they were very important in the promotion of railway construction, although they were not always a safe investment. During a trip to Spain to examine possibilities for railroad construction, the locomotive manufacturer George Stephenson reported: "I have been a month in the country, but have not seen during the whole of that time enough people of the right sort to fill a single train."[10] His misgivings proved to be well-founded. In 1864, the Spanish banking system, which depended largely on investments in railway shares, collapsed.

During this ongoing process of industrialization between 1850 and 1870, capitalist factory owners remained largely free to hire labor on their own terms based on market forces. Increased mechanization of industry meant further displacement of skilled artisans by semiskilled workers. The working classes needed organizations that would fight for improved working conditions and reasonable wages, but the liberal bourgeoisie condemned such associations as criminal agencies that threatened private property through the use of strikes and pickets. This did not stop the gradual organization of trade unions in the 1860s, however, as conservative regimes sanctioned the formation of trade unions in order to gain popular support against liberals. Bismarck did so in Prussia in 1863, and Napoleon III did likewise in France in 1864. Even where they did form, however, trade unions tended to represent only a small part of the industrial working class, usually such select groups as engineers, shipbuilders, miners, and printers. Real change for the industrial proletariat would only come with the development of socialist parties and socialist trade unions. These emerged after 1870, but the theory that made them possible had already been developed by mid-century in the work of Karl Marx.

❊ *Marx and Marxism*

The beginnings of Marxism can be found in 1848 with the publication of a short treatise entitled *The Communist Manifesto*, written by two Germans, Karl Marx (1818–1883) and Friedrich Engels (1820–1895). Karl Marx was born into a relatively prosperous middle-class family in Trier in western Germany. He descended from a long line of Jewish rabbis although his father, a lawyer, had become a Protestant to keep his job. Marx enrolled at the University of Bonn in 1835, but a year later his carefree student ways led his father to send him to the more serious-minded University of Berlin, where he encountered the ideas of the German philosopher Georg Wilhelm Friedrich Hegel. After receiving a Ph.D. in philosophy, he planned to teach at a university. Unable to obtain a position because of his professed atheism, Marx decided upon a career in journalism and eventually became the editor of a liberal bourgeois newspaper in Cologne in 1842. After the newspaper was suppressed because of his radical views, Marx moved to Paris. There he met Friedrich Engels, who became his lifelong friend and financial patron.

OPENING OF THE SUEZ CANAL. Between 1850 and 1871, continental Europeans built railways, bridges, and canals as part of the ever-spreading process of industrialization. A French diplomat, Ferdinand de Lesseps, was the guiding force behind the construction of the Suez Canal, which provided a link between the Mediterranean and Red Seas. Work on the canal began in 1859 and was completed ten years later. As seen here, an elaborate ceremony marked the opening of the canal. A French vessel led the first convoy of ships through the canal.

Engels, the son of a wealthy German cotton manufacturer, had worked in Britain at one of his father's factories in Manchester. There he had acquired a first-hand knowledge of what he came to call the "wage slavery" of the British working classes, which he detailed in a damning indictment of industrial life entitled *The Conditions of the Working Class in England,* written in 1844. Engels would contribute his knowledge of actual working conditions as well as monetary assistance to the financially strapped Marx.

In 1847, Marx and Engels joined a tiny group of primarily German socialist revolutionaries known as the Communist League. By this time, both Marx and Engels were enthusiastic advocates of the radical working-class movement and agreed to draft a statement of their ideas for the league. The resulting *Communist Manifesto,* published in German in January 1848, appeared on the eve of the revolutions of 1848. One would think from its opening lines that the pamphlet alone had caused this revolutionary upheaval: "A spectre is haunting Europe—the spectre of Communism. All the Powers of Old Europe have entered into a holy alliance to exorcize this spectre: Pope and Czar, Metternich and Guizot, French Radicals and German police spies."[11] In fact, *The Communist Manifesto* was known to only a few of Marx's friends. Although its closing words—"The proletarians have nothing to lose but their chains. They have a world to win. WORKING MEN OF ALL COUNTRIES, UNITE!"—were clearly intended to rouse the working classes to action, they passed unnoticed in 1848. The work, however, became one of the most influential political treatises in modern European history.

According to Engels, Marx's ideas were partly a synthesis of French and German thought. The French provided Marx with ample documentation for his assertion that a revolution could totally restructure society. They also provided him with several examples of socialism. From the German idealistic philosophers such as Hegel, Marx took the idea of dialectic: everything evolves, and all change in history is the result of clashes between antagonistic elements. Marx was particularly impressed by Hegel, but he disagreed with Hegel's belief that history is determined by ideas manifesting themselves in historical forces. Instead, said Marx, the course of history is determined by material forces.

Marx and Engels began the *Manifesto* with the statement, "the history of all hitherto existing society is the history of class struggles." Throughout history, oppressed and oppressor have "stood in constant opposition to one another." In an earlier struggle, the feudal classes of the Middle Ages were forced to accede to the emerging middle class or bourgeoisie. As the bourgeoisie took control in turn, their ideas became the dominant views of the era, and government became their instrument. Marx and Engels declared: "The executive of the modern State is but a committee for managing the common affairs of the whole bourgeoisie."[12] In other words, the government of the state reflected and defended the interests of the industrial middle class and its allies.

Although bourgeois society had emerged victorious out of the ruins of feudal society, Marx and Engels insisted that it had not triumphed completely. Now once again the bourgeoisie were antagonists in an emerging class struggle, but this time they faced the proletariat, or the industrial working class. The struggle would be fierce; in fact, Marx and Engels predicted that the workers would eventually overthrow their bourgeois masters. After their victory, the proletariat would form a dictatorship to reorganize the means of production. Then, a classless society would emerge, and the state—itself an instrument of the bourgeoisie—would wither away since it no longer represented

KARL MARX. Karl Marx was a radical journalist who joined with Friedrich Engels to write *The Communist Manifesto*, which proclaimed the ideas of a revolutionary socialism. After the failure of the 1848 revolution in Germany, Marx fled to Britain, where he continued to write and became involved in the work of the first International Working Men's Association.

the interests of a particular class. Class struggles would then be over (see the box on p. 667). Marx believed that the emergence of a classless society would lead to progress in science, technology, and industry and to greater wealth for all.

After the outbreak of revolution in 1848, Marx returned to Germany where he edited a new newspaper in Cologne, optimistic that the ideas of *The Communist Manifesto* were beginning to be fulfilled in a "colossal eruption of the revolutionary crater." The counterrevolution ended his hopes, and in August 1849, Marx was forced to return to Britain, where he spent the rest of his life in exile. At first life was not easy for Marx, whose income from Engels and newspaper articles was never sufficient for him and his family. After 1869, however, Engels provided an annuity that made Marx's later years quite comfortable. Marx continued his writing on political economy, especially his famous work, *Das Kapital (Capital)*. He only completed one volume. After his death, the remaining volumes were edited by his friend Engels.

One of the reasons *Capital* was not finished was Marx's own preoccupation with organizing the working-class movement. In *The Communist Manifesto*, Marx had defined the communists as "the most advanced and resolute section of the working-class parties of every country." Their advantage was their ability to understand "the line of march, the conditions, and the ultimate general results of the proletarian movement." Marx saw his role in this light and participated enthusiastically in the activities of the International Working Men's Association. Formed in 1864 by British and French trade unionists, this "First International" served as an umbrella organization for working-class interests. Marx was the dominant personality on the organization's General Council and devoted much time to its activities. He wrote in 1865: "Compared with my work on the book [*Capital*] the International Association takes up an enormous amount of time, because I am in fact in charge of the whole business."[13] Internal dissension within the ranks soon damaged the organization. In 1871, Marx supported the Paris Commune as a genuine

The Classless Society

In The Communist Manifesto, *Karl Marx and Friedrich Engels projected the creation of a classless society as the final end product of the struggle between the bourgeoisie and the proletariat. In this selection, they discuss the steps by which that classless society would be reached. Although Marx had criticized the utopian socialists for their failure to approach the labor problem scientifically, his solution sounds equally utopian.*

❊ Karl Marx and Friedrich Engels, *The Communist Manifesto*

We have seen above, that the first step in the revolution by the working class, is to raise the proletariat to the position of ruling class. . . . The proletariat will use its political supremacy to wrest, by degrees, all capital from the bourgeoisie, to centralize all instruments of production in the hands of the State, i.e., of the proletariat organized as the ruling class; and to increase the total of productive forces as rapidly as possible.

Of course, in the beginning, this cannot be effected except by means of despotic inroads on the rights of property, and on the conditions of bourgeois production; by means of measures, therefore, which appear economically insufficient and untenable, but which, in the course of the movement, outstrip themselves, necessitate further inroads upon the old social order, and are unavoidable as a means of entirely revolutionizing the mode of production.

These measures will of course be different in different countries.

Nevertheless, in the most advanced countries, the following will be pretty generally applicable:

1. Abolition of property in land and application of all rents of land to public purposes.
2. A heavy progressive or graduated income tax.
3. Abolition of all right of inheritance. . . .
5. Centralization of credit in the hands of the State, by means of a national bank with State capital and an exclusive monopoly.
6. Centralization of the means of communication and transport in the hands of the State.
7. Extension of factories and instruments of production owned by the State. . . .
8. Equal liability of all to labor. Establishment of industrial armies, especially for agriculture.
9. Combination of agriculture with manufacturing industries; gradual abolition of the distinction between town and country, by a more equable distribution of the population over the country.
10. Free education for all children in public schools. Abolition of children's factory labor in its present form. . . .

When, in the course of development, class distinctions have disappeared, and all production has been concentrated in the whole nation, the public power will lose its political character. Political power, properly so called, is merely the organized power of one class for oppressing another. If the proletariat during its contest with the bourgeoisie is compelled, by the force of circumstances, to organize itself as a class, if, by means of a revolution, it makes itself the ruling class, and, as such, sweeps away by force the old conditions of production, then it will, along with these conditions, have swept away the conditions for the existence of class antagonisms and of classes generally, and will thereby have abolished its own supremacy as a class.

In place of the old bourgeois society, with its classes and class antagonisms, we shall have an association, in which the free development of each is the condition for the free development of all.

---

proletarian uprising (see Chapter 23), but British trade unionists did not want to be identified with the crimes of the Parisians. In 1872, Marx essentially ended the association by moving its headquarters to the United States. The First International had failed. Although it would be revived in 1889, the fate of socialism by that time was in the hands of national socialist parties.

◆ Science and Culture in an Age of Realism

Between 1850 and 1870, two major intellectual developments are evident: the growth of scientific knowledge with its rapidly increasing impact on the Western worldview,

and the shift from Romanticism with its emphasis on the inner world of reality to Realism with its focus on the outer, material world.

❊ A New Age of Science

By the mid-nineteenth century, science was having a greater and greater impact on European life. The Scientific Revolution of the sixteenth and seventeenth centuries had fundamentally transformed the Western worldview and created a modern, rational approach to the study of the natural world. Even in the eighteenth century, however, these intellectual developments had remained the preserve of an educated elite and resulted in few practical benefits. Moreover, the technical advances of the early Industrial Revolution had depended little on pure science and much more on the practical experiments of technologically oriented amateur inventors. Advances in industrial technology, however, fed an interest in basic scientific research, which, in turn, in the 1830s and afterward resulted in a rash of basic scientific discoveries that were soon converted into technological improvements that affected everybody.

The development of the steam engine was important in encouraging scientists to work out its theoretical foundations, a preoccupation that led to thermodynamics, the science of the relationship between heat and mechanical energy. The laws of thermodynamics were at the core of nineteenth-century physics. In biology, the Frenchman Louis Pasteur formulated the germ theory of disease, which had enormous practical applications in the development of modern, scientific medical practices (see A Revolution in Health Care later in this chapter). In chemistry, in the 1860s the Russian Dmitri Mendeleyev classified all the material elements then known on the basis of their atomic weights and provided the systematic foundation for the periodic law. The Englishman Michael Faraday discovered the phenomenon of electromagnetic induction and put together a primitive generator that laid the foundation for the use of electricity, although economically efficient generators were not built until the 1870s.

The steadily increasing and often dramatic material gains generated by science and technology led to a growing faith in the benefits of science. Even ordinary people who did not understand the theoretical concepts of science were impressed by its accomplishments. The popularity of scientific and technological achievement led to the widespread acceptance of the scientific method, based on observation, experiment, and logical analysis, as the only path to objective truth and objective reality. This, in turn, undermined the faith of many people in religious revelation and truth. It is no accident that the nineteenth century was an age of increasing secularization, particularly evident in the growth of materialism or the belief that everything mental, spiritual, or ideal was simply an outgrowth of physical forces. Truth was to be found in the concrete material existence of human beings, not as Romanticists imagined in revelations gained by feeling or intuitive flashes. The importance of materialism was strikingly evident in the most important scientific event of the nineteenth century, the development of the theory of organic evolution according to natural selection. On the theories of Charles Darwin could be built a picture of humans as material beings that were simply part of the natural world.

✷ *Charles Darwin and the Theory of Organic Evolution*

The concept of evolution was not new when Darwin first postulated his theory in 1859. Until the early nineteenth century, most European intellectuals still believed that a divine power had created the world and its species. Humans, of course, occupied a special superior position because the Book of Genesis in the Bible stated: "Let us make man in our image and likeness and let him have dominion over all other things." By the beginning of the nineteenth century, however, people were questioning the biblical account; some had already posited an evolutionary theory. In 1809, the Frenchman Jean-Baptiste Lamarck had presented a theory of evolution that argued that various types of plants and animals exist because of their efforts to adjust to different environments. His assumption that they subsequently passed on their acquired characteristics was later rejected. Geologists had also been busy demonstrating that the earth underwent constant change and was far older than had been believed. They argued that it had evolved slowly over millions of years rather than the thousands of years postulated by theological analysis of the biblical account of creation. Despite the growth in evolutionary ideas, however, even by the mid-nineteenth century there was no widely accepted theory of evolution that explained things satisfactorily.

Charles Darwin (1809–1882), like many of the great scientists of the nineteenth century, was a scientific amateur. Born into an upper-middle-class family, he studied theology at Cambridge University while pursuing an intense side interest in geology and biology. In 1831, at the age of twenty-two, his hobby became his vocation when he accepted an appointment as a naturalist to study animals and plants on an official Royal Navy scientific expedition aboard the H.M.S. *Beagle*. Its purpose was to survey and study the landmasses of South America and the South Pacific. Darwin's specific job was to study the structure of various forms of plant and animal life. He was able to observe animals on islands virtually untouched by external influence and compare them to animals on the mainland. As a result, Darwin came to discard the notion of a special creation and to believe that animals evolved over time and in response to their environment. When he returned to Britain, he eventually formulated an explanation for evolution in the principle of natural selection, a theory that he presented in 1859 in his celebrated book, *On the Origin of Species by Means of Natural Selection*.

The basic idea of this book was that all plants and animals had evolved over a long period of time from earlier and simpler forms of life, a principle known as organic evolution. Darwin was important in explaining how this natural process worked. He took the first step from Thomas Malthus's theory of population: in every species, "many more individuals of each species are born than can possibly survive." This results in a "struggle for existence." Darwin believed that "as more individuals are produced than can possibly survive, there must in every case be a struggle for existence, either one individual with another of the same species, or with the individuals of distinct species, or with the physical conditions of life." Those who succeeded in this struggle for existence had adapted bet-

Darwin and the Descent of Man

Although Darwin published his theory of organic evolution in 1859, his book, The Descent of Man, did not appear until 1871. In it, Darwin argued that human beings have also evolved from lower forms of life. The theory encountered a firestorm of criticism, especially from the clergy. One described Darwin's theory as a "brutal philosophy—to wit, there is no God, and the ape is our Adam."

❋ Charles Darwin, *The Descent of Man*

The main conclusion here arrived at, and now held by many naturalists, who are well competent to form a sound judgment, is that man is descended from some less highly organized form. The grounds upon which this conclusion rests will never be shaken, for the close similarity between man and the lower animals in embryonic development, as well as in innumerable points of structure and constitution, both of high and of the most trifling importance,—the rudiments which he retains, and the abnormal reversions to which he is occasionally liable,—are facts which cannot be disputed. They have long been known, but until recently they told us nothing with respect to the origin of man. Now when viewed by the light of our knowledge of the whole organic world, their meaning is unmistakable. The great principle of evolution stands up clear and firm, when these groups of facts are considered in connection with others, such as the mutual affinities of the members of the same group, their geographical distribution in past and present times, and their geological succession. It is incredible that all

these facts should speak falsely. He who is not content to look, like a savage, at the phenomena of nature as disconnected, cannot any longer believe that man is the work of a separate act of creation. He will be forced to admit that the close resemblance of the embryo of man to that, for instance, of a dog—the construction of his skull, limbs and whole frame on the same plan with that of other mammals, independently of the uses to which the parts may be put—the occasional reappearance of various structures, for instance of several muscles, which man does not normally possess . . . —and a crowd of analogous facts—all point in the plainest manner to the conclusion that man is the co-descendant with other mammals of a common progenitor. . . .

Man may be excused for feeling some pride at having risen, though not through his own exertions, to the very summit of the organic scale; and the fact of his having thus risen, instead of having been aboriginally placed there, may give him hope for a still higher destiny in the distant future. But we are not here concerned with hopes or fears, only with the truth as far as our reason permits us to discover it; and I have given the evidence to the best of my ability. We must, however, acknowledge, as it seems to me, that man with all his noble qualities, with sympathy which feels for the most debased, with benevolence which extends not only to other men but to the humblest living creature, with his god-like intellect which has penetrated into the movements and constitution of the solar system—with all these exalted powers—Man still bears in his bodily frame the indelible stamp of his lowly origin.

---

ter to their environment, a process made possible by the appearance of "variants." Chance variations that occurred in the process of inheritance enabled some organisms to be more adaptable to the environment than others, a process that Darwin called natural selection:

> Owing to this struggle [for existence], variations, however slight . . . , if they be in any degree profitable to the individuals of a species, in their infinitely complex relations to other organic beings and to their physical conditions of life, will tend to the preservation of such individuals, and will generally be inherited by the offspring.[14]

Those that were naturally selected for survival ("survival of the fit") survived. The unfit did not and became extinct. The fit who survived, in turn, propagated and passed on the variations that enabled them to survive until, from Darwin's point of view, a new separate species emerged. Darwin was not able to explain how variants first occurred and did not arrive at the modern explanation of mutations.

In *On the Origin of Species,* Darwin discussed plant and animal species only. He was not concerned with humans themselves and only later applied his theory of natural selection to humans. In *The Descent of Man,* published in 1871, he argued for the animal origins of human beings: "man is the co-descendant with other mammals of a common progenitor." Humans were not an exception to the rule governing other species (see the box above).

Although Darwin's ideas were eventually accepted, initially they were highly controversial. Some people objected to what they considered Darwin's debasement of humans; his theory, they claimed, made human beings ordinary products of nature rather than unique beings. The acceptance of Darwinism, one professor of geology at Cambridge declared, would "sink the human race into a lower grade of degradation than any into which it has fallen since its written records tell of its history." Others were disturbed by the implications of life as a struggle for survival, of "nature red in tooth and claw." Was there a place in the Darwinian world for moral values? For those who believed in a rational order in the world, Darwin's theory seemed to eliminate purpose and design from the universe. Gradually, however, Darwin's theory was accepted by scientists and other intellectuals although Darwin was somewhat overly optimistic when he wrote in 1872 that "almost every scientist admits the principle of evolution." In the process of accepting Darwin's ideas, some people even tried to apply them to society, yet another example of science's increasing prestige.

❈ A Revolution in Health Care

The application of natural science to the field of medicine in the nineteenth century led to revolutionary break-throughs in health care. The first steps toward a more scientific basis for medicine were taken in Paris hospitals during the first half of the nineteenth century. Clinical observation, consisting of an active physical examination of patients, was combined with the knowledge gained from detailed autopsies to create a new clinical medicine. Nevertheless, the major breakthrough toward a scientific medicine occurred with the discovery of microorganisms, or germs, as the agents causing disease. The germ theory of disease was largely the work of Louis Pasteur (1822–1895). Pasteur was not a doctor but a chemist who approached medical problems in a scientific fashion. In 1857, Pasteur went to Paris as director of scientific studies at the École Normale. Through his experiments on fermentations, he soon proved that various microorganisms were responsible for the process of fermentation, thus launching the science of bacteriology.

Government and private industry soon perceived the inherent practical value of Pasteur's work. His examination of a disease threatening the wine industry led to the development in 1863 of a process—subsequently known as pasteurization—for heating a product to destroy the organisms causing spoilage. In 1877, Pasteur turned his attention to human diseases. His desire to do more than simply identify disease-producing organisms led him in 1885 to a preventive vaccination against rabies. In the 1890s, the principle of vaccination was extended to diphtheria, typhoid fever, cholera, and plague, creating a modern immunological science.

The work of Pasteur and the many others who followed him in isolating the specific bacteriological causes of numerous diseases had a far-reaching impact. By providing a rational means of treating and preventing infectious diseases, they transformed the medical world. Both the practice of surgery and public health experienced a renaissance.

Surgeons had already experienced a new professionalism by the end of the eighteenth century (see Chapter 17), but the discovery of germs and the introduction of anesthesia created a new environment for surgical operations. Traditionally, surgeons had mainly set broken bones, treated wounds, and amputated limbs, usually shattered in war. One major obstacle to more successful

THOMAS EAKINS, *THE GROSS CLINIC*.   This painting, completed in 1875, shows Dr. Samuel Gross, one of the foremost surgeons in the United States, scalpel in hand, pausing midway in surgery on a young man's leg to discuss the operation with his students in the amphitheater of the Jefferson Medical College. Various tasks are performed by assistant doctors, including the anesthetist who holds his cloth over the youth's face. Eakins's painting is a realistic portrayal of the new medical science at work.

surgery was the inevitable postoperative infection, which was especially rampant in hospitals.

Joseph Lister (1827–1912), who developed the antiseptic principle, was one of the first people to deal with this problem. Following the work of Pasteur, Lister perceived that bacteria might enter a wound and cause infection. His use of carbolic acid, a newly discovered disinfectant, proved remarkably effective in eliminating infections during surgery. Lister's discoveries dramatically transformed surgery wards as patients no longer succumbed regularly to what was called "hospital gangrene."

The second great barrier to large-scale surgery stemmed from the inability to lessen the pain of the patient. Alcohol and opiates had been used for centuries during surgical operations, but even their use did not allow unhurried operative maneuvers. After experiments with numerous agents, sulfuric ether was first used successfully in an operation at the Massachusetts General Hospital in 1846 (see the box on p. 671). Within a year chloroform began to rival ether as an anesthetic agent.

Although the great discoveries of bacteriology came after the emergence of the first public health movement, they significantly furthered its development. Based on the principle of preventive, rather than curative, medicine, the urban public health movement of the 1840s and 1850s was largely a response to the cholera epidemic (see Chap-

Anesthesia and Modern Surgery

Modern scientific medicine became established in the nineteenth century. Important to the emergence of modern surgery was the development of anesthetic agents that would block the patient's pain and enable surgeons to complete their surgery without the haste that had characterized earlier operations. This document is an eyewitness account of the first successful use of ether anesthesia, which took place at the Massachusetts General Hospital in 1846.

❧ The First Public Demonstration of Ether Anesthesia, October 16, 1846

The day arrived; the time appointed was noted on the dial, when the patient was led into the operating-room, and Dr. Warren and a board of the most eminent surgeons in the State were gathered around the sufferer. "All is ready—the stillness oppressive." It had been announced "that a test of some preparation was to be made for which the astonishing claim had been made that it would render the person operated upon free from pain." These are the words of Dr. Warren that broke the stillness.

Those present were incredulous, and, as Dr. Morton had not arrived at the time appointed and fifteen minutes had passed, Dr. Warren said, with significant meaning, "I presume he is otherwise engaged." This was followed with a "derisive laugh," and Dr. Warren grasped his knife and was about to proceed with the operation. At that moment Dr. Morton entered a side door, when Dr. Warren turned to him and in a strong voice said, "Well, sir, your patient is ready." In a few minutes he was ready for the surgeon's knife, when Dr. Morton said, "Your patient is ready, sir."

Here the most sublime scene ever witnessed in the operating-room was presented, when the patient placed himself voluntarily upon the table, which was to become the altar of future fame. Not that he did so for the purpose of advancing the science of medicine, nor for the good of his fellow-men, for the act itself was purely a personal and selfish one. He was about to assist in solving a new and important problem of therapeutics, whose benefits were to be given to the whole civilized world, yet wholly unconscious of the sublimity of the occasion or the art he was taking.

That was a supreme moment for a most wonderful discovery, and, had the patient died upon the operation, science would have waited long to discover the hypnotic effects of some other remedy of equal potency and safety, and it may be properly questioned whether chloroform would have come into use as it has at the present time.

The heroic bravery of the man who voluntarily placed himself upon the table, a subject for the surgeon's knife, should be recorded and his name enrolled upon parchment, which should be hung upon the walls of the surgical amphitheater in which the operation was performed. His name was Gilbert Abbott.

The operation was for a congenital tumor on the left side of the neck, extending along the jaw to the maxillary gland and into the mouth, embracing a margin of the tongue. The operation was successful; and when the patient recovered he declared he had suffered no pain. Dr. Warren turned to those present and said, "Gentlemen, this is no humbug."

---

ter 23). One medical man, in fact, called cholera "our best ally" in furthering public hygiene. The prebacteriological hygiene movement focused on providing clean water, adequate sewage disposal, and less crowded housing conditions. Bacterial discoveries led to greater emphasis on preventive measures, such as the pasteurization of milk, improved purification of water supplies, immunization against disease, and control of waterborne diseases. The public health movement also resulted in the government hiring medical doctors not just to treat people but to deal with issues of public health.

The new scientific developments also had an important impact on the training of doctors for professional careers in health care. Although there were a few medical schools at the beginning of the nineteenth century, most medical instruction was still done by a system of apprenticeship. In the course of the nineteenth century, virtually every Western country founded new medical schools, but attempts to impose uniform standards on them through certifying bodies met considerable resistance. Entrance requirements were virtually nonexistent, and degrees were granted after several months of lectures. Professional organizations founded around the mid-century, such as the British Medical Association in 1832, the American Medical Association in 1847, and the German Doctors' Society in 1872, attempted to elevate professional standards but achieved little until the end of the century. The establishment of the Johns Hopkins University School of Medicine in 1893, with its four-year graded curriculum, clinical training for advanced students, and use of laboratories for teaching purposes, provided a new model for medical training that finally became standard practice in the twentieth century.

During most of the nineteenth century, medical schools in Europe and the United States were closed to female students. When Harriet Hunt applied to Harvard

Medical School, the male students drew up resolutions that prevented her admission:

> Resolved, that no woman of true delicacy would be willing in the presence of men to listen to the discussion of subjects that necessarily come under consideration of the students of medicine.
>   Resolved, that we object to having the company of any female forced upon us, who is disposed to unsex herself, and to sacrifice her modesty by appearing with men in the lecture room.[15]

Elizabeth Blackwell (1821–1910) achieved the first major breakthrough for women in medicine. Although she had been admitted to the Geneva College of Medicine in New York by a mistake, Blackwell's perseverance and intelligence won her the respect of her fellow male students. She received her M.D. degree in 1849 and eventually established a clinic in New York City.

European women experienced difficulties similar to those of Elizabeth Blackwell. In Britain, Elizabeth Garret and Sophia Jex-Blake had to struggle for years before they were finally admitted to the practice of medicine. The unwillingness of medical schools to open their doors to women led to the formation of separate medical schools for women. The Female Medical College of Pennsylvania, established in 1850, was the first in the United States, and the London School of Medicine for women was founded in 1874. But even after graduation from such institutions, women faced obstacles when they tried to practice as doctors. Many were denied licenses and hospitals often closed their doors to them. In Britain, Parliament finally capitulated to pressure and passed a bill in 1876 allowing women the right to take qualifying examinations. Soon women were entering medical schools in ever-larger numbers. By the 1890s, universities in Great Britain, Sweden, Denmark, Norway, Finland, Russia, and Belgium were admitting women to medical training and practice. Germany and Austria did not do so until after 1900. Even then, medical associations refused to accept women as equals in the medical profession. Women were not given full membership in the American Medical Association until 1915.

Science and the Study of Society

The importance of science in the nineteenth century perhaps made it inevitable that a scientific approach would be applied to the realm of human activity. Marx himself presented his view of history as a class struggle grounded in the material conditions of life as a "scientific" work of analysis. The attempt to apply the methods of science systematically to the study of society was perhaps most evident in the work of the Frenchman Auguste Comte (1798–1857). His major work, entitled *System of Positive Philosophy*, was published between 1837 and 1842, but had its real impact after 1850.

Comte created a system of "positive knowledge" based upon a hierarchy of all the sciences. Mathematics was the foundation on which the physical sciences, earth sciences, and biological sciences were built. At the top was sociology, the science of human society, which for Comte incorporated economics, anthropology, history, and social psychology. Comte saw sociology's task as a difficult one. The discovery of the general laws of society would have to be based upon the collection and analysis of data on humans and their social environment. Although his schemes were often complex and dense, Comte played an important role in the growing popularity of science and materialism in the mid-nineteenth century.

Realism in Literature and Art

The belief that the world should be viewed realistically, frequently expressed after 1850, was closely related to the materialistic outlook. Evident in the "politics of reality" of a Bismarck or Cavour, Realism became a movement in the literary and visual arts as well. The word *Realism* was first employed in 1850 to describe a new style of painting and soon spread to literature.

THE REALISTIC NOVEL

Realism has been more or less a component of literature throughout time, although the literary Realists of the mid-nineteenth century were distinguished by their deliberate rejection of Romanticism. The literary Realists wanted to deal with ordinary characters from actual life rather than Romantic heroes in unusual settings. They also sought to avoid flowery and sentimental language by using careful observation and accurate description, an approach that led them to eschew poetry in favor of prose and the novel. Realists often combined their interest in everyday life with a searching examination of social questions. Even then they tried not to preach but to allow their characters to speak for themselves. Although the French were preeminent in literary Realism, it proved to be international in scope.

The leading novelist of the 1850s and 1860s, the Frenchman Gustave Flaubert (1821–1880), perfected the Realist novel. His *Madame Bovary* (1857) was a straightforward description of barren and sordid provincial life in France. Emma Bovary, a woman of some vitality, is trapped in a marriage to a drab provincial doctor. Impelled by the images of romantic love she has read about in novels, she seeks the same thing for herself in adulterous love affairs. Unfulfilled, she is ultimately driven to suicide, unrepentant to the end for her lifestyle. Flaubert's hatred of bourgeois society was evident in his portrayal of middle-class hypocrisy and smugness. *Madame Bovary* so offended French middle-class sensibilities that the author was prosecuted—unsuccessfully—for public obscenity.

William Thackeray (1811–1863) wrote the opening manifesto of the Realist novel in Britain with his *Vanity Fair* in 1848. Subtitled *A Novel without a Hero*, Thackeray deliberately flaunted the Romantic conventions. A novel, Thackeray said, should "convey as strongly as possible the sentiment of reality as opposed to a tragedy or poem, which may be heroical." Perhaps the greatest of the Vic-

of recreation and fun, and new forms of mass transportation—railroads and streetcars—enabled even workers to make brief excursions to amusement parks. Coney Island was only eight miles from central New York City; Blackpool in England was a short train ride from nearby industrial towns. With their Ferris wheels and other daring rides that threw young men and women together, amusement parks offered a whole new world of entertainment. Thanks to the railroad, seaside resorts, once the preserve of the wealthy, also became accessible to more people for weekend visits, much to the disgust of one upper-class regular who complained about the new "day-trippers": "They swarm upon the beach, wandering listlessly about with apparently no other aim than to get a mouthful of fresh air." Enterprising entrepreneurs in resorts like Blackpool welcomed the masses of new visitors, however, and built piers laden with food, drink, and entertainment to serve them.

The coming of mass society also created new roles for the governments of European nation-states, which now fostered national loyalty, created mass armies by conscription, and took more responsibility for public health and housing measures in their cities. By 1871, the national state had become the focus of Europeans' lives. Within many of these nation-states, the growth of the middle class had led to the triumph of liberal practices: constitutional governments, parliaments, and principles of equality. The period after 1871 also witnessed the growth of political democracy as the right to vote was extended to all adult males; women, though, would still have to fight for the same political rights. With political democracy came a new mass politics and a new mass press. Both would become regular features of the twentieth century.

◆ The Growth of Industrial Prosperity

At the heart of Europeans' belief in progress after 1871 was the stunning material growth produced by what historians have called the Second Industrial Revolution. The First Industrial Revolution had given rise to textiles, railroads, iron, and coal. In the second revolution, steel, chemicals, electricity, and petroleum led the way to new industrial frontiers.

❈ New Products and New Markets

The first major change in industrial development after 1870 was the substitution of steel for iron. New methods of rolling and shaping steel made it useful in the construction of lighter, smaller, and faster machines and

engines, as well as railways, ships, and armaments. In 1860, Great Britain, France, Germany, and Belgium together produced 125,000 tons of steel; by 1913, the total was 32 million tons. Whereas in the early 1870s Britain had produced twice as much steel as Germany, by 1910, German production was double that of Great Britain. Both had been surpassed by the United States in 1890.

Great Britain also fell behind in the new chemical industry. A change in the method of making soda enabled France and Germany to take the lead in producing the alkalies used in the textile, soap, and paper industries. German laboratories soon overtook the British in the development of new organic chemical compounds, such as artificial dyes. By 1900, German firms had cornered 90 percent of the market for dye stuffs and also led in the development of photographic plates and film.

Electricity was a major new form of energy that proved to be of great value since it could be easily converted into other forms of energy, such as heat, light, and motion, and moved relatively effortlessly through space by means of transmitting wires. In the 1870s, the first commercially practical generators of electrical current were developed. By 1881, Britain had its first public power station. By 1910, hydroelectric power stations and coal-fired steam-generating plants enabled entire districts to be tied into a single power distribution system that provided a common source of power for homes, shops, and industrial enterprises.

Electricity spawned a whole new series of inventions. The invention of the lightbulb by the American Thomas Edison (1847–1931) and the Briton Joseph Swan opened homes and cities to illumination by electric lights. A revolution in communications was fostered when Alexander Graham Bell (1847–1922) invented the telephone in 1876 and Guglielmo Marconi (1874–1937) sent the first radio waves across the Atlantic in 1901. Although most electricity was initially used for lighting, it was eventually put to use in transportation. The first electric railway was installed in Berlin in 1879. By the 1880s, streetcars and subways had appeared in major European cities and had begun to replace horse-drawn buses. Electricity also transformed the factory. Conveyor belts, cranes, machines, and machine tools could all be powered by electricity and located anywhere. In the First Industrial Revolution, coal had been the major source of energy. Countries without adequate coal supplies lagged behind in industrialization. Thanks to electricity, they could now enter the industrial age.

The development of the internal combustion engine had a similar effect. The first internal combustion engine, fired by gas and air, was produced in 1878. It proved unsuitable for widespread use as a source of power in transportation until the development of liquid fuels, namely, petroleum and its distilled derivatives. An oil-fired engine was made in 1897, and by 1902, the Hamburg-Amerika Line had switched from coal to oil on its new ocean liners. By the end of the nineteenth century, some naval fleets had been converted to oil burners as well.

AN AGE OF PROGRESS. Between 1871 and 1914, a Second Industrial Revolution led many Europeans to believe that they were living in an age of progress when most human problems would be solved by scientific achievements. This illustration is taken from a special issue of *The Illustrated London News* celebrating the Diamond Jubilee of Queen Victoria in 1897. On the left are scenes from 1837, when Victoria came to the British throne; on the right are scenes from 1897. The vivid contrast underscored the magazine's conclusion: "The most striking . . . evidence of progress during the reign is the ever increasing speed which the discoveries of physical science have forced into everyday life. Steam and electricity have conquered time and space to a greater extent during the last sixty years than all the preceding six hundred years witnessed."

The development of the internal combustion engine gave rise to the automobile and airplane. Gottlieb Daimler's invention of a light engine in 1886 was the key to the development of the automobile. In 1900, world production stood at 9,000 cars; by 1906, Americans had overtaken the initial lead of the French. It was an American, Henry Ford (1863–1947), who revolutionized the car industry with the mass production of the Model T. By 1916, Ford's factories were producing 735,000 cars a year. In the meantime an age of air transportation began with the Zeppelin airship in 1900. In 1903, at Kitty Hawk, North Carolina, the Wright brothers made the first flight in a fixed-wing plane powered by a gasoline engine. It took World War I to stimulate the aircraft industry, however, and the first regular passenger air service was not established until 1919.

The growth of industrial production depended upon the development of markets for the sale of manufactured goods. After 1870, the best foreign markets were already heavily saturated, forcing Europeans to take a renewed look at their domestic markets. As Europeans were the richest consumers in the world, those markets offered abundant possibilities. The dramatic population increases after 1870 (see Population Growth later in this chapter) were accompanied by a steady rise in national incomes. The leading industrialized nations, Britain and Germany, doubled or tripled their national incomes. Between 1850 and 1900, real wages increased by two-thirds in Britain and by one-third in Germany. As the prices of both food and manufactured goods declined due to lower transportation costs, Europeans could spend more on consumer products. Businesses soon perceived the value of using new techniques of mass marketing to sell the consumer goods made possible by the development of the steel and electrical industries. By bringing together a vast array of new products in one place, they created the department store (see the box on p. 681). The desire to own sewing machines, clocks, bicycles, electric lights, and typewriters rapidly created a new consumer ethic that became a crucial part of the modern economy.

The Department Store and the Beginnings of Mass Consumerism

Domestic markets were especially important for the sale of the goods being turned out by Europe's increasing number of industrial plants. New techniques of mass marketing were developed to encourage people to purchase the new consumer goods. The Parisians pioneered the department store, and this selection is taken from a contemporary's account of the growth of these stores in the French capital city.

❈ E. Lavasseur, On Parisian Department Stores, 1907

It was in the reign of Louis-Philippe that department stores for fashion goods and dresses, extending to material and other clothing began to be distinguished. The type was already one of the notable developments of the Second Empire; it became one of the most important ones of the Third Republic. These stores have increased in number and several of them have become extremely large. Combining in their different departments all articles of clothing, toilet articles, furniture and many other ranges of goods, it is their special object so to combine all commodities as to attract and satisfy customers who will find conveniently together an assortment of a mass of articles corresponding to all their various needs. They attract customers by permanent display, by free entry into the shops, by periodic exhibitions, by special sales, by fixed prices, and by their ability to deliver the goods purchased to customers' homes, in Paris and to the provinces. Turning themselves into direct intermediaries between the producer and the consumer, even producing sometimes some of their articles in their own workshops, buying at lowest prices because of their large orders and because they are in a position to profit from bargains, working with large sums, and selling to most of their customers for cash only, they can transmit these benefits in lowered selling prices. They can even decide to sell at a loss, as an advertisement or to get rid of out-of-date fashions. Taking 5–6 percent on 100 million brings them in more than 20 percent would bring to a firm doing a turnover of 50,000 francs.

The success of these department stores is only possible thanks to the volume of their business and this volume needs considerable capital and a very large turnover. Now capital, having become abundant, is freely combined nowadays in large enterprises, although French capital has the reputation of being more wary of the risks of industry than of State or railway securities. On the other hand, the large urban agglomerations, the ease with which goods can be transported by the railways, the diffusion of some comforts to strata below the middle classes, have all favored these developments.

As example we may cite some figures relating to these stores, since they were brought to the notice of the public in the *Revue des Deux-Mondes*. . . .

Le Louvre, dating to the time of the extension of the rue de Rivoli under the Second Empire, did in 1893 a business of 120 million at a profit of 6.4 percent. *Le Bon-Marché*, which was a small shop when Mr. Boucicaut entered it in 1852, already did a business of 20 million at the end of the Empire. During the republic its new buildings were erected; Mme. Boucicaut turned it by her will into a kind of cooperative society, with shares and an ingenious organization; turnover reached 150 million in 1893, leaving a profit of 5 percent. . . .

According to the tax records of 1891, these stores in Paris, numbering 12, employed 1,708 persons and were rated on their site values at 2,159,000 francs; the largest had then 542 employees. These same stores had, in 1901, 9,784 employees; one of them over 2,000 and another over 1,600; their site value has doubled (4,089,000 francs).

Meanwhile, increased competition for foreign markets and the growing importance of domestic demand led to a reaction against free trade. To many industrial and political leaders, protective tariffs guaranteed domestic markets for the products of their own industries. Thus, after a decade of experimentation with free trade in the 1860s, Europeans returned to tariff protection. The Austro-Hungarian Empire was the first in 1874, followed by Russia in 1877, Germany in 1879, Italy in 1887, the United States in 1890, and France in 1892. Only Britain, Denmark, and the Netherlands refused to follow suit.

During this same period, cartels were being formed to decrease competition internally. In a cartel, independent enterprises worked together to control prices and fix production quotas, thereby restraining the kind of competition that led to reduced prices. Cartels were especially strong in Germany, where banks moved to protect their investments by eliminating the "anarchy of competition." German businesses established cartels in potash, coal, steel, and chemicals. Founded in 1893, the Rhenish-Westphalian Coal Syndicate controlled 98 percent of Germany's coal production by 1904.

The formation of cartels was paralleled by a move toward ever-larger manufacturing plants, especially in the iron and steel, machinery, heavy electrical equipment, and chemical industries. Although evident in Britain, France, and Belgium, the trend was most pronounced in Germany. Between 1882 and 1907, the number of people working in German factories with over 1,000 employees rose from 205,000 to 879,000. This growth in the size of industrial plants led to pressure for greater efficiency in factory production at the same time that competition led to demands for greater economy. The result was a desire to streamline or rationalize production as much as possible. One way to accomplish this was by cutting labor costs through the mechanization of transport within plants, such as using electric cranes to move materials. More importantly, the development of precision tools enabled manufacturers to produce interchangeable parts, which, in turn, led to the creation of the assembly line for production. First used in the United States for small arms and clocks, the assembly line had moved to Europe by 1850. In the last half of the nineteenth century, it was primarily used in manufacturing nonmilitary goods, such as sewing machines, typewriters, bicycles, and finally the automobile. Principles of scientific management were also introduced by 1900 to maximize workers' efficiency.

The emergence of protective tariffs and cartels was clearly a response to the growth of the multinational industrial system. Economic competition intensified the political rivalries of the age. The growth of the national state, which had seemed to be the answer to old problems in the mid-nineteenth century, now seemed to be creating new ones.

❋ *New Patterns in an Industrial Economy*

The Second Industrial Revolution played a role in the emergence of basic economic patterns that have characterized much of modern European economic life. Although we have described the period after 1871 as an age of material prosperity, recessions and crises were still very much a part of economic life. Although some historians have questioned the appropriateness of the title Great Depression for the period from 1873 to 1895, Europeans did experience a series of economic crises during those years. Prices, especially those of agricultural products, fell dramatically. Slumps in the business cycle reduced profits although economic recession occurred at different times in different countries. France and Britain, for example, sank into depression in the 1880s while Germany and the United States were recovering from their depression of the 1870s. After 1895, however, until World War I, Europe overall experienced an economic boom and achieved a level of prosperity that encouraged people later to look back to that era as *la belle époque*—a golden age in European civilization.

After 1870, Germany replaced Great Britain as the industrial leader of Europe. Already in the 1890s, Germany's superiority was evident in new areas of manufacturing, such as organic chemicals and electrical equipment, and increasingly apparent in its ever-greater share of worldwide trade. Why had industrial leadership passed from Britain to Germany?

Britain's early lead in industrialization gave it an established industrial plant and made it more difficult to shift to the new techniques of the Second Industrial Revolution. As later entrants to the industrial age, the Germans could build the latest and most efficient industrial plant. British entrepreneurs made the situation worse by their tendency to be suspicious of innovations and their reluctance to invest in new plants and industries. As one manufacturer remarked: "One wants to be thoroughly convinced of the superiority of a new method before condemning as useless a large plant that has hitherto done good service."[1] German managers, on the other hand, were accustomed to change, and the formation of large cartels encouraged German banks to provide enormous sums for investment. Then, too, unlike the Germans, the British were not willing to encourage formal scientific and technical education.

After 1870, the relationship of science and technology grew closer. Newer fields of industrial activity, such as organic chemistry and electrical engineering, required more scientific knowledge than the commonsense tinkering once employed by amateur inventors. Companies began to invest capital in laboratory equipment for their own research or hired scientific consultants for advice. Nowhere was the relationship between science and technology more apparent than in Germany. In 1899, German technical schools were allowed to award doctorate degrees, and by 1900, they were turning out 3,000 to 4,000 graduates a year. Many of these graduates made their way into industrial firms.

The struggle for economic (and political) supremacy between Great Britain and Germany should not cause us to overlook the other great polarization of the age. By 1900, Europe was divided into two economic zones. Great Britain, Belgium, France, the Netherlands, Germany, the western part of the Austro-Hungarian Empire, and northern Italy constituted an advanced industrialized core that had a high standard of living, decent systems of transportation, and relatively healthy and educated peoples. Another part of Europe, the backward and little industrialized area to the south and east, consisting of southern Italy, most of Austria-Hungary, Spain, Portugal, the Balkan kingdoms, and Russia, was still largely agricultural and relegated by the industrial countries to the function of providing food and raw materials. The presence of Romanian oil, Greek olive oil, and Serbian pigs and prunes in western Europe served as reminders of an economic division of Europe that continued well into the twentieth century.

The growth of an industrial economy also led to new patterns for European agriculture. An abundance of grain and lower transportation costs caused the prices of farm commodities to plummet. Some countries responded with tariff barriers against lower priced foodstuffs. Where agricultural labor was scarce and hence expensive, as in Britain and Germany, landowners introduced machines for threshing and harvesting. The slump in grain prices also led some countries to specialize in other food products. Denmark, for example, exported eggs, butter, and cheese; sugar beets predominated in Bohemia and north-

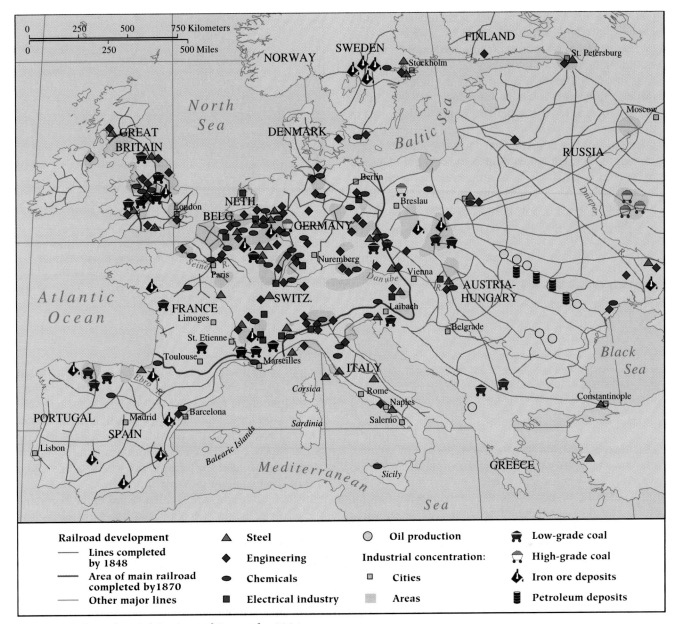

Railroad development
— Lines completed by 1848
— Area of main railroad completed by 1870
— Other major lines

▲ Steel
◆ Engineering
⬭ Chemicals
■ Electrical industry

○ Oil production

Industrial concentration:
▫ Cities
▨ Areas

🛒 Low-grade coal
🛒 High-grade coal
🔨 Iron ore deposits
🔋 Petroleum deposits

MAP 23.1 The Industrial Regions of Europe by 1914.

ern France; fruit in Mediterranean countries; and wine in Spain and Italy. This age also witnessed the introduction of chemical fertilizers. Large estates could make these adjustments easily, but individual small farmers could not afford them and formed farm cooperatives that provided capital for making improvements and purchasing equipment and fertilizer.

The economic developments of the late nineteenth century, combined with the transportation revolution that saw the growth of marine transport and railroads, also fostered a true world economy. By 1900, Europeans were importing beef and wool from Argentina and Australia, coffee from Brazil, nitrates from Chile, iron ore from Algeria, and sugar from Java. European capital was also invested abroad to develop railways, mines, electrical power plants, and banks. High rates of return, such as 11.3 percent on

Latin American banking shares that were floated in London, provided plenty of incentive. Of course, foreign countries also provided markets for the surplus manufactured goods of Europe. With its capital, industries, and military might, Europe dominated the world economy by the end of the nineteenth century.

✳ Women and Work: New Job Opportunities

The Second Industrial Revolution had an enormous impact on the position of women in the labor market. During the course of the nineteenth century, considerable controversy erupted over a woman's "right to work." Working-class organizations tended to reinforce the underlying ideology of domesticity: women should remain at home to bear and nurture children and should not be allowed in the industrial workforce. Working-class men argued that keeping women out of industrial work would ensure the moral and physical well-being of families. In reality, keeping women out of the industrial workforce simply made it easier to exploit them when they needed income to supplement their husbands' wages or to support their families when their husbands were unemployed. The desperate need to work at times forced women to do marginal work at home or labor as pieceworkers in sweatshops. "Sweating" referred to the subcontracting of piecework usually, but not exclusively, in the tailoring trades; it was done at home since it required few skills or equipment. Pieceworkers were poorly paid and worked long hours. The poorest paid jobs for the cheapest goods were called "slop work." In this description of the room of a London slopper, we see how precarious her position was:

> I then directed my steps to the neighborhood of Drury-lane, to see a poor woman who lived in an attic on one of the closest courts in that quarter. On the table was a quarter of an ounce of tea. Observing my eye to rest upon it, she told me it was all she took. "Sugar," she said, "I broke myself of long ago; I couldn't afford it. A cup of tea, a piece of bread, and an onion is generally all I have for my dinner, and sometimes I haven't even an onion, and then I sops my bread."[2]

Often excluded from factories and in need of income, many women had no choice but to work for the pitiful wages of the sweated industries.

After 1870, however, new job opportunities for women became available. Although the growth of heavy industry in the mining, metallurgy, engineering, chemicals, and electrical sectors meant fewer jobs for women in manufacturing, the development of larger industrial plants and the expansion of government services created a large number of service or white-collar jobs. The increased demand for white-collar workers at relatively low wages coupled with a shortage of male workers led employers to hire women. Big businesses and retail shops needed clerks, typists, secretaries, file clerks, and sales clerks. The expansion of government services created opportunities for women to be secretaries and telephone operators and to take jobs in health and social services. Compulsory education necessitated more teachers, and the development of modern hospital services opened the way for an increase in nurses.

Many of the new white-collar jobs were by no means exciting. The work was routine and, except for teaching and nursing, required few skills beyond basic literacy. Although there was little hope for advancement, these jobs had distinct advantages for the daughters of the middle classes and especially the upward-aspiring working classes. For some middle-class women, the new jobs offered freedom from the domestic patterns expected of them. Nevertheless, because middle-class women did not receive an education comparable to men, the careers they could pursue were limited. Thus, they found it easier to fill

NEW JOBS FOR WOMEN: THE TELEPHONE EXCHANGE. The invention of the telephone in 1876 soon led to its widespread use. As is evident from this illustration of a telephone exchange in Paris in 1904, most of the telephone operators were women. This was but one of a number of new job opportunities for women created by the Second Industrial Revolution.

the jobs at the lower end of middle-class occupations, such as teaching and civil service jobs, especially the post office.

Most of the new white-collar jobs, however, were filled by working-class women who saw them as an opportunity to escape from the "dirty" work of the lower-class world. Studies in France and Britain indicate that the increase in white-collar jobs did not lead to a rise in the size of the female labor force, but only to a shift from industrial jobs to the white-collar sector of the economy.

Despite the new job opportunities, many lower-class women were forced to become prostitutes to survive. The rural, working-class girls who flocked into the cities in search of new opportunities often were highly vulnerable. Employment was unstable and wages were low. No longer protected by family or village community and church, some girls faced only one grim alternative—prostitution. In Paris, London, and many other large cities with transient populations, thousands of prostitutes plied their trade. One journalist estimated that there were 60,000 prostitutes in London in 1885. Most prostitutes were active for a short time, usually from late teens through early twenties. Many eventually rejoined the regular workforce or married when they could.

In most European countries, prostitution was licensed and regulated by government and municipal authorities. Although the British government provided minimal regulation of prostitution, it did attempt to enforce the Contagious Diseases Acts in the 1870s and 1880s by giving authorities the right to examine prostitutes for venereal disease. Prostitutes with the disease were confined for some time to special institutions called lock hospitals, where they were given moral instruction. But opposition to the Contagious Diseases Acts soon arose from middle-class female reformers. Their leader was Josephine Butler (1828–1906), who objected to laws that punished women but not men who suffered from venereal disease.

Known as the "shrieking sisters" because they discussed sexual matters in public, Butler and her fellow reformers were successful in gaining the repeal of the acts in 1886.

✳ *Organizing the Working Classes*

The desire to improve their working and living conditions led many industrial workers to form political parties and labor unions. One of the most important of the working-class or socialist parties was formed in Germany in 1875. Under the direction of its two Marxist leaders, Wilhelm Liebknecht and August Bebel, the German Social Democratic Party (SPD) espoused revolutionary Marxist rhetoric while organizing itself as a mass political party competing in elections for the Reichstag (the German parliament). Once in the Reichstag, SPD delegates worked to enact legislation to improve the condition of the working class. As August Bebel explained: "Pure negation would not be accepted by the voters. The masses demand that something should be done for today irrespective of what will happen on the morrow."[3] Despite government efforts to destroy it (see Central and Eastern Europe: Persistence of the Old Order later in this chapter), the German Social Democratic Party continued to grow. In 1890, it received 1.5 million votes and thirty-five seats in the Reichstag. When it received 4 million votes in the 1912 elections, it became the largest single party in Germany.

Socialist parties also emerged in other European states, although none proved as successful as the German Social Democrats. France had a variety of socialist parties, including a Marxist one. The leader of French socialism, Jean Jaurès (1859–1914), was an independent socialist who looked to the French revolutionary tradition rather than Marxism to justify revolutionary socialism. In 1905, the French socialist parties succeeded in unifying themselves into a single mostly Marxist-oriented socialist party. Social Democratic Parties on the German model were founded in Belgium, Austria, Hungary, Bulgaria, Poland, Romania, and the Netherlands before 1900. A Marxist Social Democratic Labor Party had also been organized in Russia by 1898.

As the socialist parties grew, agitation for an international organization that would strengthen their position against international capitalism also grew. In 1889, leaders of the various socialist parties formed the Second International, which was organized as a loose association of national groups. Although the Second International took some coordinated actions—May Day (May 1), for example, was made an international labor day to be marked by strikes and mass labor demonstrations—differences often wreaked havoc at the congresses of the organization. Two issues proved particularly divisive: revisionism and nationalism.

✵ REVISIONISM AND NATIONALISM

Some Marxists believed in a pure Marxism that accepted the imminent collapse of capitalism and the need for socialist ownership of the means of production. The guid-

ing light of the German Social Democrats, August Bebel, confided to another socialist that "every night I go to sleep with the thought that the last hour of bourgeois society strikes soon." Earlier, Bebel had said, "I am convinced that the fulfillment of our aims is so close, that there are few in this hall who will not live to see the day."[4] But a severe challenge to this orthodox Marxist position arose in the form of revisionism.

Most prominent among the revisionists was Eduard Bernstein (1850–1932), a member of the German Social Democratic Party who had spent years in exile in Britain where he had been influenced by moderate English socialism and the British parliamentary system. In 1899, Bernstein challenged Marxist orthodoxy with a book entitled *Evolutionary Socialism* in which he argued that some of Marx's ideas had turned out to be quite wrong (see the box on p. 686). The capitalist system had not broken down, said Bernstein, nor did its demise seem near. Contrary to Marx's assertion, the middle class was actually expanding, not declining. At the same time, the proletariat was

"PROLETARIANS OF THE WORLD, UNITE." **To improve their working and living conditions, many industrial workers, inspired by the ideas of Karl Marx, joined working-class or socialist parties. Pictured here is a socialist-sponsored poster that proclaims in German the closing words of *The Communist Manifesto*: "Proletarians of the World, Unite!"**

The Voice of Evolutionary Socialism: Eduard Bernstein

The German Marxist Eduard Bernstein was regarded as the foremost late nineteenth-century theorist of Marxist revisionism. In his book, Evolutionary Socialism, *Bernstein argued that Marx had made some fundamental mistakes and that socialists needed to stress cooperation and evolution rather than class conflict and revolution.*

❈ Eduard Bernstein, *Evolutionary Socialism*

It has been maintained in a certain quarter that the practical deductions from my treatises would be the abandonment of the conquest of political power by the proletariat organized politically and economically. That is quite an arbitrary deduction, the accuracy of which I altogether deny.

I set myself against the notion that we have to expect shortly a collapse of the bourgeois economy, and that social democracy should be induced by the prospect of such an imminent, great, social catastrophe to adapt its tactics to that assumption. That I maintain most emphatically.

The adherents of this theory of a catastrophe base it especially on the conclusions of the *Communist Manifesto*. This is a mistake in every respect.

The theory which the *Communist Manifesto* sets forth of the evolution of modern society was correct as far as it characterized the general tendencies of that evolution. But it was mistaken in several special deductions, above all in the estimate of the time the evolution would take. . . . But it is evident that if social evolution takes a much greater period of time than was assumed, it must also take upon itself forms and lead to forms that were not foreseen and could not be foreseen then.

Social conditions have not developed to such an acute opposition of things and classes as is depicted in the *Manifesto*. It is not only useless, it is the greatest folly to attempt to conceal this from ourselves. The number of members of the possessing classes is today not smaller but larger. The enormous increase of social wealth is not accompanied by a decreasing number of large capitalists but by an increasing number of capitalists of all degrees. The middle classes change their character but they do not disappear from the social scale. . . .

In all advanced countries we see the privileges of the capitalist bourgeoisie yielding step by step to democratic organizations. Under the influence of this, and driven by the movement of the working classes which is daily becoming stronger, a social reaction has set in against the exploiting tendencies of capital, a counteraction which, although it still proceeds timidly and feebly, yet does exist, and is always drawing more departments of economic life under its influence. Factory legislation, the democratizing of local government, and the extension of its area of work, the freeing of trade unions and systems of cooperative trading from legal restrictions, the consideration of standard conditions of labor in the work undertaken by public authorities—all these characterize this phase of the evolution.

But the more the political organizations of modern nations are democratized the more the needs and opportunities of great political catastrophes are diminished. . . . But is the conquest of political power by the proletariat simply to be by a political catastrophe? Is it to be the appropriation and utilization of the power of the State by the proletariat exclusively against the whole non-proletarian world? . . .

No one has questioned the necessity for the working classes to gain the control of government. The point at issue is between the theory of a social cataclysm and the question whether, with the given social development in Germany and the present advanced state of its working classes in the towns and the country, a sudden catastrophe would be desirable in the interest of the social democracy. I have denied it and deny it again, because in my judgment a greater security for lasting success lies in a steady advance than in the possibilities offered by a catastrophic crash.

not sinking further down; instead, its position was improving as workers experienced a higher standard of living. In the face of this reality, Bernstein discarded Marx's emphasis on class struggle and revolution. The workers, he asserted, must continue to organize in mass political parties and even work together with the other advanced elements in a nation to bring about change. With the extension of the right to vote, workers were in a better position than ever to achieve their aims by democratic channels. Evolution by democratic means, not revolution, would achieve the desired goal of socialism. German and French socialist leaders, as well as the Second International, condemned revisionism as heresy and opportunism. But many socialist parties, including the German Social Democrats, while spouting revolutionary slogans, continued to practice Bernstein's revisionist, gradualist approach.

A second divisive issue for international socialism was nationalism. Marx and Engels had said that "the working men have no country" and that "national differences and antagonisms between peoples are daily more and more vanishing, owing to the development of the bourgeoisie."[5] They proved drastically wrong. Congresses of the Second International passed resolutions in 1907 and 1910 advocating joint action by workers of different countries to avert war, but provided no real machinery to implement the resolutions. In truth, socialist parties varied from country to country and remained tied to national concerns and issues. Socialist leaders always worried that in the end national loyalties might outweigh class loyalties among the masses. When World War I came in 1914, not only the working-class masses, but even many of their socialist party leaders, supported the war efforts of their national governments. Nationalism had proved a much more powerful force than socialism.

❧ THE ROLE OF TRADE UNIONS

Workers also formed trade unions to improve their working conditions. Attempts to organize the workers did not come until the last two decades of the nineteenth century after unions had won the right to strike in the 1870s. Strikes proved necessary to achieve the workers' goals. A walkout by female workers in the match industry in 1888 and by dock workers in London the following year led to the establishment of trade union organizations for both groups. By 1900, two million workers were enrolled in British trade unions, and by the outbreak of World War I, this number had risen to between three and four million, although this was still less than one-fifth of the total workforce.

Trade unions failed to develop as quickly on the Continent as they had in Britain. In France, the trade union movement was from the beginning closely tied to the socialist ideology. As there were a number of French socialist parties, the socialist trade unions remained badly splintered. Not until 1895 did French unions create a national organization called the General Confederation of Labor. Its decentralization and failure to include some of the more important individual unions, however, left it a weak and ineffective movement.

German trade unions, also closely attached to political parties, were first formed in the 1860s. Although there were liberal trade unions comprised of skilled artisans and Catholic or Christian trade unions, the largest German trade unions were those of the socialists. By 1899, even the latter had accepted the practice of collective bargaining with employers. As strikes and collective bargaining achieved successes, German workers were increasingly inclined to forgo revolution for gradual improvements. By 1914, its three million members made the German trade union movement the second largest in Europe after Great Britain's. Almost 85 percent of these three million belonged to socialist unions. Trade unions in the rest of Europe had varying degrees of success, but by the beginning of World War I, they had made considerable progress in bettering both the living and the working conditions of the laboring classes.

❧ THE ANARCHIST ALTERNATIVE

Despite the revolutionary rhetoric, socialist parties and trade unions gradually became less radical in pursuing their goals. Indeed, this lack of revolutionary fervor drove some people from Marxian socialism into anarchism, a movement that was especially prominent in less industrialized and less democratic countries. The growth of universal male suffrage in Great Britain, France, and Germany had led workers there to believe that they could acquire tangible benefits by elections, not by revolution. These democratic channels were not open in other countries where revolutionary violence seemed the only alternative.

Initially, anarchism was not a violent movement. Early anarchists believed that people were inherently good but had been corrupted by the state and society. True freedom could only be achieved by abolishing the state and all existing social institutions. In the second half of the nineteenth century, however, anarchists in Spain, Portugal, Italy, and Russia began to advocate using radical means to accomplish this goal. The Russian Michael Bakunin, for example, believed that small groups of well-trained, fanatical revolutionaries could perpetrate so much violence that the state and all its institutions would disintegrate. To revolutionary anarchists, that would usher in the anarchist golden age. The Russian anarchist Lev Aleshker wrote shortly before his execution:

> Slavery, poverty, weakness, and ignorance—the external fetters of man—will be broken. Man will be at the center of nature. The earth and its products will serve everyone dutifully. Weapons will cease to be a measure of strength and gold a measure of wealth; the strong will be those who are bold and daring in the conquest of nature, and riches will be the things that are useful. Such a world is called "Anarchy." It will have no castles, no place for masters and slaves. Life will be open to all. Everyone will take what he needs—this is the anarchist ideal. And when it comes about, men will live wisely and well. The masses must take part in the construction of this paradise on earth.[6]

After Bakunin's death in 1876, anarchist revolutionaries used assassinations as their primary instrument of terror. The list of victims of anarchist assassins at the turn of the century included a Russian tsar (1881), a president of the French Republic (1894), the king of Italy (1900), and a president of the United States (1901). Despite anarchist hopes, these states did not collapse.

◆ The Emergence of Mass Society

The new patterns of industrial production, mass consumption, and working-class organization that we identify with the Second Industrial Revolution were only one aspect of the new mass society that emerged in Europe after 1870. A larger and vastly improved urban environment, new patterns of social structure, gender issues, mass education, and mass leisure were also important features of Europe's mass society.

Table 23.1 European Populations, 1851–1911

	1851	1881	1911
England and Wales	17,928,000	25,974,000	36,070,000
Scotland	2,889,000	3,736,000	4,761,000
Ireland	6,552,000	5,175,000	4,390,000
France	35,783,000	37,406,000	39,192,000
Germany	33,413,000	45,234,000	64,926,000
Belgium	4,530,000	5,520,000	7,424,000
Netherlands	3,309,000	4,013,000	5,858,000
Denmark	1,415,000	1,969,000	2,757,000
Norway	1,490,000	1,819,000	2,392,000
Sweden	3,471,000	4,169,000	5,522,000
Spain	15,455,000	16,622,000	19,927,000
Portugal	3,844,000	4,551,000	5,958,000
Italy	24,351,000	28,460,000	34,671,000
Switzerland	2,393,000	2,846,000	3,753,000
Austria	17,535,000	22,144,000	28,572,000
Hungary	18,192,000	15,739,000	20,886,000
Russia	68,500,000	97,700,000	160,700,000
Romania		4,600,000	7,000,000
Bulgaria		2,800,000	4,338,000
Greece		1,679,000	2,632,000
Serbia		1,700,000	2,912,000

SOURCE: B.R. Mitchell, *European Historical Statistics, 1750–1970* (1975).

❈ Population Growth

The European population increased dramatically between 1850 and 1910, rising from 270 million to over 460 million by 1910 (see Table 23.1). Between 1850 and 1880, the main cause of the population increase was a rising birthrate, in least in western Europe, but after 1880, a noticeable decline in death rates largely explains the increase in population. Although the causes of this decline have been debated, two major factors—medical discoveries and environmental conditions—stand out. Some historians have stressed the importance of developments in medical science. Smallpox vaccinations, for example, were compulsory in many European countries by the mid-1850s. More important were improvements in the urban environment in the last half of the nineteenth century that greatly reduced fatalities from such infectious diseases as diarrhea, dysentery, typhoid fever, and cholera, which had been spread through contaminated water supplies and improper elimination of sewage. Improved nutrition also made a significant difference in the health of the population. The increase in agricultural productivity combined with improvements in transportation facilitated the shipment of food supplies from areas of surplus to regions with poor harvests. Better nutrition and food hygiene were especially instrumental in the decline in infant mortality by 1900. The pasteurization of milk reduced intestinal disorders that had been a major cause of infant deaths. Although growing agricultural and industrial prosperity

supported an increase in European population, it could not do so indefinitely, especially in areas that had little industrialization and a severe problem of rural overpopulation. Some of the excess labor from underdeveloped areas migrated to the industrial regions of Europe. By 1913, more than 400,000 Poles were working in the heavily industrialized Ruhr region of western Germany, and thousands of Italian laborers had migrated to France. The industrialized regions of Europe, however, were not able to absorb the entire surplus population of heavily agricultural regions like southern Italy, Spain, Hungary, and Romania, where the land could not support the growing numbers of people. The booming economies of North America after 1898 and cheap shipping fares after 1900 led to mass emigration from southern and eastern Europe to North America at the beginning of the twentieth century. In 1880, about 500,000 people left Europe each year on average; between 1906 and 1910, annual departures increased to 1.3 million, many of them from southern and eastern Europe. Altogether, between 1846 and 1932, probably 60 million Europeans left Europe, half of them bound for the United States and most of the rest for Canada or Latin America (see Table 23.2).

It was not only economic motives that caused people to leave eastern Europe. Migrants from Austria and Hungary, for example, were not the dominant nationalities, the Germans and Magyars, but mostly their oppressed minorities, such as Poles, Slovaks, Serbs, Croats, Romanians, and Jews. Between 1880 and 1914, 3.5 million Poles from Russia, Austria, and Germany went to the United States. Jews, who were severely persecuted, constituted 40 percent of the Russian emigrants to the United States between 1900 and 1913 and almost 12 percent of all emigrants to the United States during the first five years of the twentieth century.

❈ Transformation of the Urban Environment

One of the most important consequences of industrialization and the population explosion of the nineteenth century was urbanization. In the course of the nineteenth century, urban dwellers came to make up an ever-increasing percentage of the European population. In 1800, they constituted 40 percent of the population in Britain, 25 percent in France and Germany, and only 10 percent in eastern Europe. By 1914, urban inhabitants had increased to 80 percent of the population in Britain, 45 percent in France, 60 percent in Germany, and 30 percent in eastern Europe. The size of cities also expanded dramatically, especially in industrialized countries. In 1800, there were 21 European cities with populations over 100,000; by 1900, there were 147. Between 1800 and 1900, London's population grew from 960,000 to 6.5 million and Berlin's from 172,000 to 2.7 million.

Urban populations grew faster than the general population primarily because of the vast migration from rural

Table 23.2 *European Emigration, 1876–1910 (Average Annual Emigration to Non-European Countries per 100,000 Population)*

	1876–80	1881–85	1886–90	1891–95	1896–1900	1901–05	1906–10
Europe	94	196	213	185	147	271	322
Ireland	650	1,422	1,322	988	759	743	662
Great Britain	102	174	162	119	88	127	172
Denmark	157	380	401	338	117	292	275
Norway	432	1,105	819	597	312	903	746
Sweden	301	705	759	587	249	496	347
Germany	108	379	207	163	47	50	44
Belgium			86	50	23	57	69
Netherlands	32	136	111	76	25	45	58
France	8	14	49	14	13	12	12
Spain		280	437	434	446	391	758
Portugal	258	356	423	609	417	464	694
Italy	396	542	754	842	974	1,706	1,938
Austria	48	90	114	182	182	355	469
Hungary		92	156	134	205	437	616
Russia	6	13	42	47	32	63	67

SOURCE: Robert Gildea, *Barricades and Borders: Europe, 1800–1914* (Oxford, 1987), p. 283.

areas to cities. People were driven from the countryside to the cities by sheer economic necessity—unemployment, land hunger, and physical want. Urban centers offered something positive as well, usually mass employment in factories and later in service trades and professions. But cities also grew faster in the second half of the nineteenth century because health and living conditions in them were improving.

✄ IMPROVING LIVING CONDITIONS

In the 1840s, a number of urban reformers, such as Edwin Chadwick in Britain (see Chapter 20) and Rudolf Virchow and Solomon Neumann in Germany, had pointed to filthy living conditions as the primary cause of epidemic disease and urged sanitary reforms to correct the problem. Soon, legislative acts created boards of health that brought governmental action to bear on public heath issues. Urban medical officers and building inspectors were authorized to inspect dwellings for public health hazards. New building regulations made it more difficult for private contractors to build shoddy housing. The Public Health Act of 1875 in Britain, for example, prohibited the construction of new buildings without running water and an internal drainage system. For the first time in Western history, the role of municipal governments had been expanded to include detailed regulations for the improvement of the living conditions of urban dwellers.

Essential to the public health of the modern European city was the ability to bring clean water into the city and to expel sewage from it. The accomplishment of those two tasks was a major engineering feat in the last half of the nineteenth century. The problem of fresh water was solved by a system of dams and reservoirs that stored the water and aqueducts and tunnels that carried it from the countryside to the city and into individual dwellings. By the second half of the nineteenth century, regular private baths became accessible to more people as gas heaters in the 1860s and later electric heaters made hot baths possible. Even the shower had appeared by the 1880s. The treatment of sewage was also improved by building mammoth underground pipes that carried raw sewage far from the city for disposal. In the late 1860s, a number of German cities began to construct sewer systems. Frankfurt began its program after a lengthy public campaign enlivened by the slogan "from the toilet to the river in half an hour." London devised a system of five enormous sewers that discharged their loads twelve miles from the city where the waste was chemically treated. Unfortunately, in many places new underground sewers simply continued to discharge their raw sewage into what soon became highly polluted lakes and rivers. Nevertheless, the development of pure water and sewerage systems dramatically improved the public health of European cities by 1914.

Middle-class reformers who denounced the unsanitary living conditions of the working class also focused on their housing needs. Overcrowded, disease-ridden slums were viewed as dangerous not only to physical health, but to the political and moral health of the entire nation. V. A. Huber, the foremost early German housing reformer, wrote in 1861: "Certainly it would not be too much to say that the home is the communal embodiment of family life. Thus the purity of the dwelling is almost as important for the family as is the cleanliness of the body for the individual."[7] To Huber, good housing was a

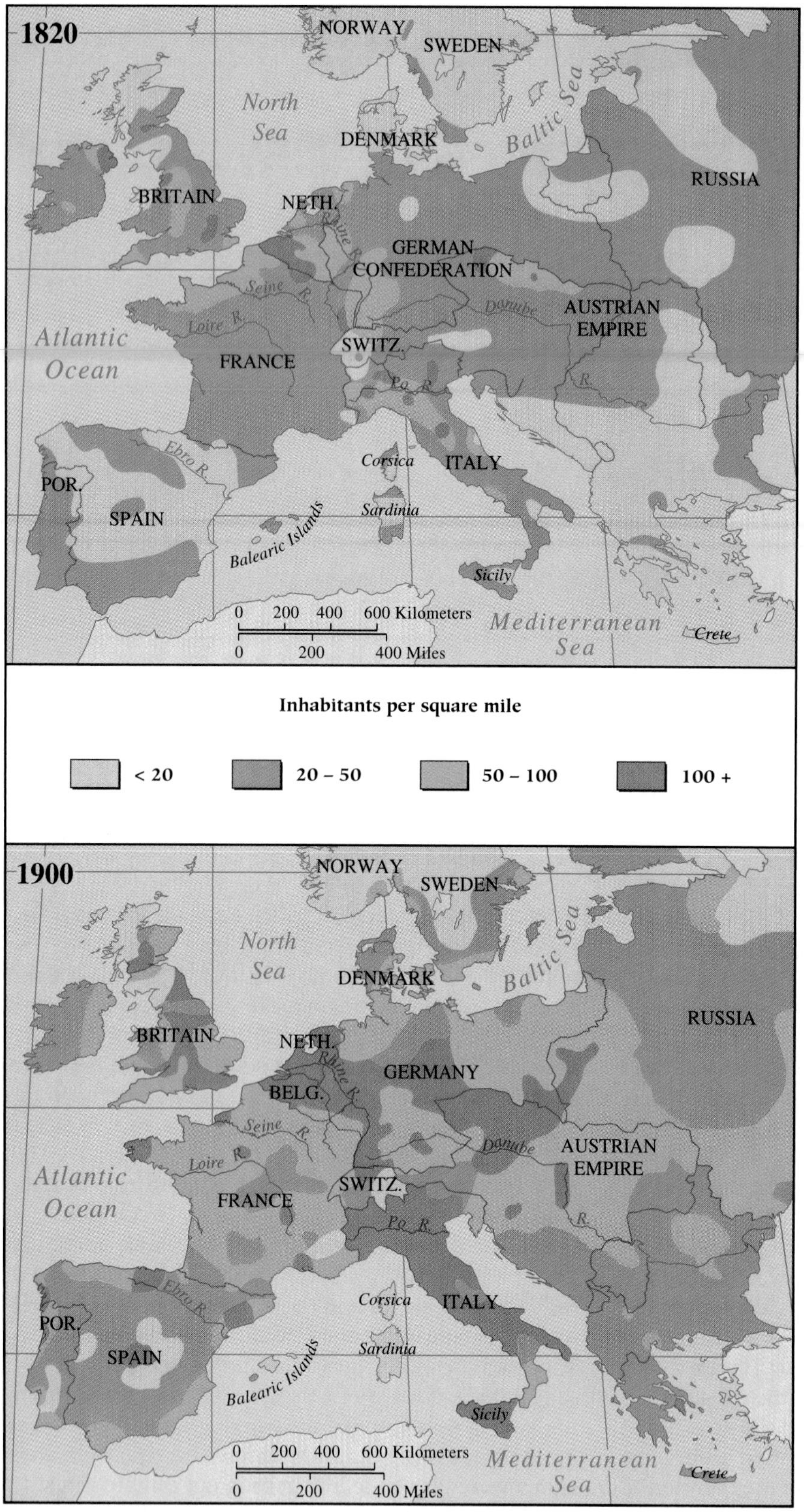

MAP 23.2   **Population Growth in Europe, 1820–1900.**

Inhabitants per square mile

< 20	20 – 50	50 – 100	100 +

prerequisite for stable family life, and without stable family life one of the "stabilizing elements of society" would be dissolved, much to society's detriment.

Early efforts to attack the housing problem emphasized the middle-class, liberal belief in the efficacy of private enterprise. Reformers such as Huber believed that the construction of model dwellings renting at a reasonable price would force other private landlords to elevate their housing standards. A fine example of this approach was the work of Octavia Hill, granddaughter of a cele-

The Housing Venture of Octavia Hill

Octavia Hill was a practical-minded British housing reformer who believed that workers and their families were entitled to happy homes. At the same time, she was convinced that the poor needed guidance and encouragement, not charity. In this selection, she describes her housing venture.

❋ Octavia Hill, *Homes of the London Poor*

About four years ago I was put in possession of three houses in one of the worst courts of Marylebone. Six other houses were bought subsequently. All were crowded with inmates.

The first thing to be done was to put them in decent tenantable order. The set last purchased was a row of cottages facing a bit of desolate ground, occupied with wretched, dilapidated cow-sheds, manure heaps, old timber, and rubbish of every description. The houses were in a most deplorable condition—the plaster was dropping from the walls; on one staircase a pail was placed to catch the rain that fell through the roof. All the staircases were perfectly dark; the banisters were gone, having been burnt as firewood by tenants. The grates, with large holes in them, were falling forward into the rooms. The washhouse, full of lumber belonging to the landlord, was locked up; thus the inhabitants had to wash clothes, as well as to cook, eat and sleep in their small rooms. The dustbin, standing in the front part of the houses, was accessible to the whole neighborhood, and boys often dragged from it quantities of unseemly objects and spread them over the court. The state of the drainage was in keeping with everything else. The pavement of the backyard was all broken up, and great puddles stood in it, so that the damp crept up the outer walls. . . .

As soon as I entered into possession, each family had an opportunity of doing better: those who would not pay, or who led clearly immoral lives, were ejected. The rooms they vacated were cleansed; the tenants who showed signs of improvement moved into them, and thus, in turn, an opportunity was obtained for having each room distempered and papered. The drains were put in order, a large slate cistern was fixed, the washhouse was cleared of its lumber, and thrown open on stated days to each tenant in turn. The roof, the plaster, the woodwork were repaired; the staircase walls were distempered; new grates were fixed; the layers of paper and rag (black with age) were torn from the windows, and glass put in; out of 192 panes only eight were found unbroken. The yard and footpath were paved.

The rooms, as a rule, were re-let at the same prices at which they had been let before; but tenants with large families were counseled to take two rooms, and for these much less was charged than if let singly: this plan I continue to pursue. In-coming tenants are not allowed to take a decidedly insufficient quantity of room, and no sub-letting is permitted. . . .

The pecuniary result has been very satisfactory. Five percent has been paid on all the capital invested. A fund for the repayment of capital is accumulating. A liberal allowance has been made for repairs. . . .

My tenants are mostly of a class far below that of mechanics. They are, indeed, of the very poor. And yet, although the gifts they have received have been next to nothing, none of the families who have passed under my care during the whole four years have continued in what is called "distress," except such as have been unwilling to exert themselves. Those who will not exert the necessary self-control cannot avail themselves of the means of livelihood held out to them. But, for those who are willing, some small assistance in the form of work has, from time to time, been provided—not much, but sufficient to keep them from want or despair.

---

brated social reformer (see the box above). With the financial assistance of a friend, she rehabilitated some old dwellings and constructed new ones to create housing for 3,500 tenants.

Other wealthy reformer-philanthropists took a different approach to the housing problem. In 1887, Lord Leverhulme began construction of a model village called Port Sunlight outside Liverpool for the workers at his soap factory. Port Sunlight offered pleasant living conditions in the belief that good housing would ensure a healthy and happy workforce. Yet another approach was the garden city. At the end of the nineteenth century, Ebenezer Howard founded the British garden city movement, which advocated the construction of new towns separated from each other by open country that would provide the recreational areas, fresh air, and sense of community that would encourage healthy family life. Letchward Garden City, started in 1903, was the first concrete result of Howard's theory.

As the number and size of cities continued to mushroom, governments by the 1880s came to the conclusion—although reluctantly—that private enterprise could not solve the housing crisis. In 1890, a British Housing Act empowered local town councils to collect new taxes and construct cheap housing for the working classes. London and Liverpool were the first communities to take advantage of their new powers. Similar activity had been set in motion in Germany by 1900. In 1894, the French government took a lesser step by providing easy credit for private contractors to build working-class housing.

Everywhere, however, these lukewarm measures failed to do much to meet the real housing needs of the working classes. In Britain, for example, only 5 percent of all dwellings erected between 1890 and 1914 were constructed by municipalities under the Housing Act of 1890. Nevertheless, by the start of World War I, the need for planning had been recognized, and after the war municipal governments moved into housing construction on a large scale. In housing, as in so many other areas of life in the late nineteenth century, the liberal principle that the government that governs least governs best had simply proved untrue. More and more, governments were stepping into areas of activity that they would never have touched earlier.

❧ REDESIGNING THE CITIES

Housing was but one area of urban reconstruction after 1870. As urban populations expanded in the nineteenth century, the older layout in which the city was confined to a compact area enclosed by defensive walls seemed restrictive and utterly useless. In the second half of the nineteenth century, many of the old defensive walls—worthless anyway from a military standpoint—were pulled down, and the areas converted into parks and boulevards. In Vienna, for example, the great boulevards of the Ringstrasse replaced the old medieval walls. While the broad streets served a military purpose—the rapid deployment of troops to crush civil disturbances—they also offered magnificent views of the city hall, the university, and the parliament building, all powerful symbols of middle-class social values.

Like Vienna, many European urban centers were redesigned during the second half of the nineteenth century. The reconstruction of Paris after 1850 by Emperor Napoleon III was perhaps the most famous project and provided a model for other urban centers. The old residential districts in the central city, many of them working-class slums, were pulled down and replaced with town halls, government office buildings, retail stores, including the new department stores, museums, cafes, and theaters, all of which provided for the shopping and recreational pleasures of the middle classes.

As cities expanded and entire groups of people were displaced from urban centers by reconstruction, city populations spilled over into the neighboring villages and countrysides, which were soon incorporated into the cities.

THE CITY AT NIGHT. **Industrialization and the population explosion of the nineteenth century fostered the growth of cities. At the same time, technological innovations dramatically improved living conditions in** **European cities. Gas lighting and later electricity also transformed the nighttime environment of Europe's cities, as is evident in this painting of Liverpool.**

The construction of streetcars and commuter trains by the turn of the century enabled both working-class and middle-class populations to live in their own suburban neighborhoods far removed from their places of work. Cheap, modern transportation essentially separated home and work for many Europeans.

❋ The Social Structure of Mass Society

Historians generally agree that after 1871 the average person enjoyed an improving standard of living. The real wages of British workers, for example, probably doubled between 1871 and 1910. We should not allow this increase in the standard of living to mislead us, however. Great poverty did remain in Western society, and the gap between rich and poor was enormous. In the western and central European countries most affected by industrialization, the richest 20 percent of the populations received between 50 and 60 percent of the national income. This meant that while the upper and middle classes received almost three-fifths of the wealth, the remaining 80 percent of the population received only two-fifths. It would, however, be equally misleading to portray European society as split simply into rich and poor. Between the small group of the elite at the top and the large number of very poor at the bottom, there were many different groups of varying wealth.

✗ THE ELITE

At the top of European society stood a wealthy elite, constituting only 5 percent of the population but controlling between 30 and 40 percent of its wealth. This nineteenth-century elite was an amalgamation of the traditional landed aristocracy that had dominated European society for centuries and the wealthy upper middle class. In the course of the nineteenth century, aristocrats coalesced with the most successful industrialists, bankers, and merchants to form a new elite. The growth of big business had created this group of wealthy plutocrats while aristocrats, whose income from landed estates declined, invested in railway shares, public utilities, government bonds, and even businesses, sometimes on their own estates. Gradually, the greatest fortunes shifted into the hands of the upper middle class. In Great Britain, for example, landed aristocrats constituted 73 percent of the country's millionaires in mid-century while the commercial and financial magnates made up 14 percent. By the period 1900–1914, landowners had declined to 27 percent. The wealthiest person in Germany was not an aristocrat, but Bertha Krupp, granddaughter of Alfred Krupp and heiress to the business dynasty left by her father Friedrich, who committed suicide in 1902 over a homosexual scandal.

Increasingly, aristocrats and plutocrats fused as the wealthy upper middle class purchased landed estates to join the aristocrats in the pleasures of country living and the aristocrats bought lavish town houses for part-time urban life. Common bonds were also forged when the sons of wealthy middle-class families were admitted to the elite schools dominated by the children of the aristocracy. At Oxford, the landed upper class made up 40 percent of the student body in 1870, but only 15 percent in 1910, while undergraduates from business families went from 7 to 21 percent during the same period. This educated elite, whether aristocratic or middle class in background, assumed leadership roles in government bureaucracies and military hierarchies. Marriage also served to unite the two groups. Daughters of tycoons acquired titles while aristocratic heirs gained new sources of cash. Wealthy American heiresses were in special demand. When Consuelo Vanderbilt married the duke of Marlborough, the new duchess brought £2 million (approximately $10 million) to her husband.

It would be misleading, however, to assume that the alliance of the wealthy business elite and traditional aristocrats was always harmonious. In Germany class lines were sometimes well drawn, especially if they were complicated by anti-Semitism. Albert Ballin, the wealthy director of the Hamburg-Amerika luxury liners, may have been close to Emperor William II, who entertained him on a regular basis, but the Prussian aristocracy snubbed Ballin because of his Jewish origins. Although the upper middle class was allowed into the bureaucracy of the German Empire, the diplomatic corps remained an aristocratic preserve.

✗ THE MIDDLE CLASSES

The middle classes consisted of a variety of groups. Below the upper middle class was a middle level that included such traditional groups as professionals in law, medicine, and the civil service as well as moderately well-to-do industrialists and merchants. The industrial expansion of the nineteenth century also added new groups to this segment of the middle class. These included business managers and new professionals, such as the engineers, architects, accountants, and chemists who formed professional associations as the symbols of their newfound importance. A lower middle class of small shopkeepers, traders, manufacturers, and prosperous peasants provided goods and services for the classes above them.

Standing between the lower middle class and the lower classes were new groups of white-collar workers who were the product of the Second Industrial Revolution. They were the traveling sales representatives, bookkeepers, bank tellers, telephone operators, department store sales clerks, and secretaries. Although largely propertyless and often little better paid than skilled laborers, these white-collar workers were often committed to middle-class ideals and optimistic about improving their status. Some even achieved professional standing and middle-class status.

The moderately prosperous and successful middle classes shared a common lifestyle, one whose values tended to dominate much of nineteenth-century society. The members of the middle class were especially active in preaching their worldview to their children and to the upper and lower classes of their society. This was particularly evident in Victorian Britain, often considered a model of middle-class society. It was the European middle classes who accepted and promulgated the importance of progress and science. They believed in hard work, which they viewed as the primary human good, open to everyone and guaranteed to have positive results. Knowledge was important as an instrument for personal gain. They were also regular churchgoers who believed in the good conduct associated with traditional Christian morality. The middle class was concerned with propriety, the right way of doing things, which gave rise to an incessant number of books aimed at the middle-class market with such titles as *The Habits of Good Society* or *Don't: A Manual of Mistakes and Improprieties More or Less Prevalent in Conduct and Speech.*

THE LOWER CLASSES

The lower classes of European society constituted almost 80 percent of the European population. Many of them were landholding peasants, agricultural laborers, and sharecroppers, especially in eastern Europe. This was less true, however, in western and central Europe. About 10 percent of the British population worked in agriculture; in Germany the figure was 25 percent. Many prosperous, landowning peasants shared the values of the middle class. Military conscription brought peasants into contact with the other groups of mass society, and state-run elementary schools forced the children of peasants to speak the national dialect and accept national loyalties.

There was no such thing as a single urban working class. The elite of the working class included, first of all, skilled artisans in such traditional handicraft trades as cabinetmaking, printing, and jewelry making. As the production of more items was mechanized in the course of the nineteenth century, these highly skilled workers found their economic security threatened. Printers, for example, were replaced by automatic typesetting machines operated by semiskilled workers. The Second Industrial Revolution, however, also brought new entrants into the group of highly skilled workers, such as machine-tool specialists, shipbuilders, and metal workers. Many of the skilled workers attempted to pattern themselves after the middle class by seeking good housing and educating their children.

Semiskilled laborers, who included such people as carpenters, bricklayers, and many factory workers, earned wages that were about two-thirds of those of highly skilled workers. At the bottom of the working-class hierarchy stood the largest group of workers, the unskilled laborers. They included day laborers, who worked irregularly for very low wages, and large numbers of domestic servants. One out of every seven employed persons in Great Britain in 1900 was a domestic servant. Most of them were women.

Urban workers did experience a real improvement in the material conditions of their lives after 1871. For one thing, urban improvements meant better living conditions. A rise in real wages, accompanied by a decline in many consumer costs, especially in the 1880s and 1890s, made it possible for workers to buy more than just food and housing. French workers in 1900, for example, spent 60 percent of their income on food, down from 75 percent in 1870. Workers' budgets now provided money for more clothes and even leisure at the same time that strikes and labor agitation were providing ten-hour days and Saturday afternoons off.

The "Woman Question": The Role of Women

The "woman question" was the term used to refer to the debate over the role of women in society. In the nineteenth century, women remained legally inferior, economically dependent, and largely defined by family and household roles. Many women still aspired to the ideal of femininity popularized by writers and poets. Alfred Lord Tennyson's *The Princess* expressed it well:

> *Man for the field and woman for the hearth:*
> *Man for the sword and for the needle she:*
> *Man with the head and woman with the heart:*
> *Man to command and woman to obey;*
> *All else confusion.*

Historians have pointed out that this traditional characterization of the sexes, based on gender-defined social roles, was virtually elevated to the status of universal male and female attributes in the nineteenth century, largely due to the impact of the Industrial Revolution on the family. As the chief family wage earners, men worked outside the home while women were left with the care of the family for which they were paid nothing. Of course, the ideal did not always match reality, especially for the lower classes, where the need for supplemental income drove women to do "sweated" work.

Throughout most of the nineteenth century, marriage was viewed as the only honorable and available career for most women. Though the middle class glorified the ideal of domesticity (see the box on p. 696), for most women marriage was a matter of economic necessity. The lack of meaningful work and the lower wages paid to women made it difficult for single women to earn a living. Since retiring to convents as in the past was no longer an option, many spinsters who could not find sufficiently remunerative work entered domestic service as live-in servants. Most women chose instead to marry, which was reflected in an increase in marriage rates and a decline in illegitimacy rates in the course of the nineteenth century.

Birthrates also dropped significantly at this time. A very important factor in the evolution of the modern family was the decline in the number of offspring born to the average woman. The change was not necessarily due to new technological products. Although the invention of vulcanized rubber in the 1840s made possible the production

WORKING-CLASS HOUSING IN LONDON. Although urban workers experienced some improvements in the material conditions of their lives after 1871, working-class housing remained drab and depressing. This 1912 photograph of working-class housing in the East End of London shows rows of similar-looking buildings on treeless streets. Most often, these buildings had no gardens or green areas.

of condoms and diaphragms, they were not widely used as effective contraceptive devices until the era of World War I. Some historians maintain that the change in attitude that led parents to deliberately limit the number of offspring was more important than the method used. Although some historians attribute increased birth control to more widespread use of coitus interruptus, or male withdrawal before ejaculation, others have emphasized the ability of women to restrict family size through abortion and even infanticide or abandonment. That a change in attitude occurred was apparent in the emergence of a movement to increase awareness of birth control methods. Authorities prosecuted those who spread information about contraception for "depraving public morals," but were unable to stop them. In 1882 in Amsterdam, Dr. Aletta Jacob founded Europe's first birth control clinic. Initially, "family planning" was the suggestion of reformers who thought that the problem of poverty could be solved by reducing the number of children among the lower classes. In fact, the practice spread quickly among the propertied classes, rather than among the impover-

ished, a good reminder that considerable differences still remained between middle-class and working-class families.

THE MIDDLE-CLASS FAMILY

The family was the central institution of middle-class life. Men provided the family income while women focused on household and child care. The use of domestic servants in many middle-class homes, made possible by an abundant supply of cheap labor, reduced the amount of time middle-class women had to spend on household work. At the same time, by reducing the number of children in the family, mothers could devote more time to child care and domestic leisure. The idea that leisure should be used for constructive purposes supported and encouraged the cult of middle-class domesticity.

The middle-class family fostered an ideal of togetherness. The Victorians created the family Christmas with its yule log, Christmas tree, songs, and exchange of gifts. In the United States, Fourth of July celebrations changed from drunken revels to family picnics by the 1850s. The

Advice to Women: Be Dependent

Industrialization had a strong impact on middle-class women as gender-based social roles became the norm. Men worked outside the home to support the family while women provided for the needs of their children and husband at home. In this selection, one woman gives advice to middle-class women on their proper role and behavior.

❊ Elizabeth Poole Sanford, *Woman in Her Social and Domestic Character*

The changes wrought by Time are many. It influences the opinions of men as familiarity does their feelings; it has a tendency to do away with superstition, and to reduce every thing to its real worth.

It is thus that the sentiment for woman has undergone a change. The romantic passion which once almost deified her is on the decline; and it is by intrinsic qualities that she must now inspire respect. She is no longer the queen of song and the star of chivalry. But if there is less of enthusiasm entertained for her, the sentiment is more rational, and, perhaps, equally sincere; for it is in relation to happiness that she is chiefly appreciated.

And in this respect it is, we must confess, that she is most useful and most important. Domestic life is the chief source of her influence; and the greatest debt society can owe to her is domestic comfort; for happiness is almost an element of virtue; and nothing conduces more to improve the character of men than domestic peace. A woman may make a man's home delightful, and may thus increase his motives for virtuous exertion. She may refine and tranquilize his mind,—may turn away his anger or allay his grief. Her smile may be the happy influence to gladden his heart, and to disperse the cloud that gathers on his brow. And in proportion to her endeavors to make those around her happy, she will be esteemed and loved. She will secure by her excellence that interest and that regard which she might formerly claim as the privilege of her sex, and will really merit the deference which was then conceded to her as a matter of course. . . .

Perhaps one of the first secrets of her influence is adaptation to the tastes, and sympathy in the feelings, of those around her. This holds true in lesser as well as in graver points. It is in the former, indeed, that the absence of interest in a companion is frequently most disappointing. Where want of congeniality impairs domestic comfort, the fault is generally chargeable on the female side. It is for woman, not for man, to make the sacrifice, especially in indifferent matters. She must, in a certain degree, be plastic herself if she would mold others. . . .

Nothing is so likely to conciliate the affections of the other sex as a feeling that woman looks to them for support and guidance. In proportion as men are themselves superior, they are accessible to this appeal. On the contrary, they never feel interested in one who seems disposed rather to offer than to ask assistance. There is, indeed, something unfeminine in independence. It is contrary to nature, and therefore it offends. We do not like to see a woman affecting tremors, but still less do we like to see her acting the amazon. A really sensible woman feels her dependence. She does what she can; but she is conscious of inferiority, and therefore grateful for support. She knows that she is the weaker vessel, and that as such she should receive honor. In this view, her weakness is an attraction, not a blemish.

In every thing, therefore, that women attempt, they should show their consciousness of dependence. If they are learners, let them evince a teachable spirit; if they give an opinion, let them do it in an unassuming manner. There is something so unpleasant in female self-sufficiency that it not unfrequently deters instead of persuading, and prevents the adoption of advice which the judgment even approves.

---

education of middle-class females in domestic crafts, singing, and piano playing prepared them for their function of providing a proper environment for home recreation.

The new domestic ideal had an impact on child raising and children's play. Late eighteenth-century thought, beginning with Rousseau, had encouraged a new view of children as unique beings, not small adults, which had carried over into the nineteenth century. They were entitled to a long childhood involved in activities with other children their own age. The early environment in which they were raised, it was thought, would determine how they turned out. And mothers were seen as the most important force in protecting children from the harmful influences of the adult world. New children's games and toys, including mass-produced dolls for girls, appeared in middle-class homes. The middle-class emphasis on the functional value of knowledge was also evident in these games. One advice manual maintained that young children should learn checkers because it "calls forth the resources of the mind in the most gentle, as well as the most successful manner."

Since the sons of the middle-class family were expected to follow careers like their father's, they were sent to schools where they were kept separate from the rest of society until the age of sixteen or seventeen. Sport was used in the schools to "toughen" boys up while their leisure activities centered around both national military concerns and character building. This combination was

A MIDDLE-CLASS FAMILY. Nineteenth-century middle-class moralists considered the family the fundamental pillar of a healthy society. The family was a crucial institution in middle-class life, and togetherness constituted one of the important ideals of the middle-class family. This painting by William P. Frith, entitled *Many Happy Returns of the Day,* shows a family birthday celebration for a little girl in which grandparents, parents, and children take part. The servant at the left holds the presents for the little girl.

especially evident in the establishment of the Boy Scouts in Britain in 1908. Boy Scouts provided organized recreation for boys between twelve and eighteen; adventure was combined with the discipline of earning merit badges and ranks in such a way as to instill ideals of patriotism and self-sacrifice. Many men viewed such activities as a corrective to the possible dangers that female domination of the home posed for male development. As one scout leader wrote: "The REAL Boy Scout is not a sissy. [He] adores his mother [but] is not hitched to [her] apron strings." There was little organized recreational activity of this type for girls, although Robert Baden-Powell, the founder of the Boy Scouts, did encourage his sister to establish a girls' division as an afterthought. Its goal is evident from Agnes Baden-Powell's comment that "you do not want to make tomboys of refined girls, yet you want to attract, and thus raise, the slum girl from the gutter. The main object is to give them all the ability to be better mothers and Guides to the next generation."[8] Despite her comment, most organizations of this kind were for middle-class children, although some reformers tried to establish boys' clubs for working-class youths to reform them.

The new ideal of the middle-class woman as nurturing mother and wife who "determined the atmosphere of the household" through her character, not her work, frequently did not correspond to reality. Recent research indicates that in France, Germany, and even mid-Victorian Britain, relatively few families could actually afford to hire a host of servants. More often, middle-class families had one servant, usually a young working-class or country girl not used to middle-class lifestyles. Women, then, were often forced to work quite hard to maintain the expected appearance of the well-ordered household. A German housekeeping manual makes this evident:

It often happens that even high-ranking ladies help at home with housework, and particularly with kitchen chores, scrubbing, etc., so that, above all the hands have good cause to become very rough, hard, and calloused. When these ladies appear in society, they are extremely upset at having such rough-looking hands. In order to perform the hardest and most ordinary chores . . . and, at the same time, to keep a soft hand like those fine ladies who have no heavier work to do than embroidering and sewing, always keep a piece of fresh bacon, rub your hands with it just before bedtime, and you will fully achieve your goal. You will, as a result, have the inconvenience of having to sleep with gloves on, in order not to soil the bed.[9]

Many middle-class wives, then, were caught in a no-win situation. Often for the sake of the advancement of her husband's career, she was expected to maintain in public the image of the "idle" wife, freed from demeaning physical labor and able to pass her days in ornamental pursuits. In truth, it was frequently the middle-class woman who paid the price for this facade in a life of unpaid work, carefully managing the family budget and participating in housework that could never be done by only one servant girl. As one historian has argued, the reality of many middle-class women's lives was that "what appears at first glance to be idleness is revealed, on closer examination, to be difficult and tiresome work."

THE WORKING-CLASS FAMILY

Hard work was, of course, standard fare for women in working-class families. Daughters in working-class families were expected to work until they married; even after marriage, they often did piecework at home to help support the family. For the children of the working classes, childhood was over by the age of nine or ten when they became apprentices or were employed in odd jobs.

Between 1890 and 1914, however, family patterns among the working class began to change. High-paying jobs in heavy industry and improvements in the standard of living made it possible for working-class families to depend on the income of husbands and the wages of grown children. By the early twentieth century, some working-class mothers could afford to stay at home, following the pattern of middle-class women. At the same time, new consumer products, such as sewing machines, clocks, bicycles, and cast-iron stoves, created a new mass consumer society whose focus was on higher levels of consumption.

These working-class families also followed the middle classes in limiting the size of their families. Children began to be viewed as dependents rather than wage earners as child labor laws and compulsory education took children out of the workforce and into schools. Improvements in public health as well as advances in medicine and a better diet resulted in a decline in infant mortality rates for the lower classes, especially noticeable in the cities after 1890, and made it easier for working-class families to choose to have fewer children. At the same time, strikes and labor agitation led to laws that reduced work hours to ten per day by 1900 and eliminated work on Saturday afternoons, which enabled working-class parents to devote more attention to their children and develop more emotional ties with them. Even working-class fathers became involved in their children's lives. One observer in the French town of Belleville in the 1890s noted that "the workingman's love for his children borders on being an obsession."[10] Interest in educating children as a way to improve their future also grew.

※ Education and Leisure in an Age of Mass Society

Mass education was a product of the mass society of the late nineteenth century. Being "educated" in the early nineteenth century meant attending a secondary school or possibly even a university. Secondary schools, such as the *Gymnasien* in Germany and the public schools (which were really private boarding schools) in Britain, mostly emphasized a classical education based on the study of Greek and Latin. Secondary and university education were primarily for the elite, the sons of government officials, nobles, or wealthier middle-class families. After 1850, secondary education was expanded as more middle-class families sought employment in public service and the professions or entry into elite scientific and technical schools. Existing secondary schools also placed more emphasis on practical and scientific education by adding foreign languages and natural sciences to their curriculum.

At the beginning of the nineteenth century, European states showed little interest in primary education. Only in the German states was there a state-run system of elementary education. In 1833, the French government created a system of state-run, secular schools by instructing local government to establish an elementary school for both boys and girls. None of these primary schools required attendance, however, and it tended to be irregular at best. In rural society, children were still expected to work in the fields. In industrializing countries like Britain and France, both employers and parents were eager to maintain the practice of child labor.

In the decades after 1870, the functions of the state were extended to include the development of mass education in state-run systems. Between 1870 and 1914, most Western governments began to offer at least primary education to both boys and girls between the ages of six and twelve. In most countries it was not optional. Austria had established free, compulsory elementary education in 1869. In France, a law of March 29, 1882, made primary education compulsory for all children between six and thirteen. In 1880, elementary education was made compulsory in Britain, but it was not until 1902 that an act of Parliament brought all elementary schools under county and town control. States also assumed responsibility for the quality of teachers by establishing teacher-training schools. By 1900, many European states, especially in northern and western Europe, were providing state-financed primary schools, salaried and trained teachers, and free, compulsory mass elementary education.

Why did European states make this commitment to mass education? Liberals believed that education was important to personal and social improvement and also sought, as in France, to supplant Catholic education with moral and civic training based on secular values. Even conservatives were attracted to mass education as a means of improving the quality of military recruits and training people in social discipline. In 1875, a German military journal stated: "We in Germany consider education to be one of the principal ways of promoting the strength of the nation and above all military strength."[11]

Another incentive for mass education came from industrialization. In the early Industrial Revolution, unskilled labor was sufficient to meet factory needs, but the new firms of the Second Industrial Revolution demanded skilled labor. Both boys and girls with an elementary education had new possibilities of jobs beyond their villages or small towns, including white-collar jobs in railways, new metro stations, post offices, banking and shipping firms, teaching, and nursing. To industrialists, then, mass education furnished the trained workers they needed.

Nevertheless, the chief motive for mass education was political. For one thing, the expansion of voting rights necessitated a more educated electorate. Even more important, however, mass compulsory education instilled patriotism and nationalized the masses, providing an opportunity for even greater national integration. As people lost their ties to local regions and even to religion, nationalism supplied a new faith. The use of a single national language created greater national unity than did loyalty to a ruler.

A nation's motives for universal elementary education largely determined what was taught in the elementary schools. Obviously, indoctrination in national values took on great importance. At the core of the academic curriculum were reading, writing, arithmetic, national history, especially geared to a patriotic view, geography, literature, and some singing and drawing. The education of boys and girls varied, however. Where possible, the sexes were separated. Girls did less math and no science but concentrated on such domestic skills as sewing, washing, ironing, and cooking, all prerequisites for providing a good home for husband and children. Boys were taught some practical skills, such as carpentry, and even some military drill. Most of the elementary schools also inculcated the middle-class virtues of hard work, thrift, sobriety, cleanliness, and respect for the family. For most students, elementary education led to apprenticeship and a job.

The development of compulsory elementary education created a demand for teachers, and most of them were female. In the United States, for example, women constituted two-thirds of all teachers by the 1880s. Many men viewed the teaching of children as an extension of women's "natural role" as nurturers of children. Moreover, females were paid lower salaries, in itself a considerable incentive for governments to encourage the establishment of teacher-training institutes for women. The first female colleges were really teacher-training schools. In Britain, the women's colleges of Queen's and Bedford were established in the 1840s to provide teacher training for middle-class spinsters who needed to work. A pioneer in the development of female education was Barbara Bodichon (1827–1891), who established her own school where girls were trained for economic independence as well as domesticity. It was not until the beginning of the twentieth century that women were permitted to enter the male-dominated universities. In France, 3 percent of university students in 1902 were women; by 1914, their number had increased to 10 percent of the total.

The most immediate result of mass education was an increase in literacy. Compulsory elementary education and the growth of literacy were directly related. In Germany, Great Britain, France, and the Scandinavian countries, adult illiteracy was virtually eliminated by 1900. Where there was less schooling, the story is very different. Adult illiteracy rates were 79 percent in Serbia, 78 percent in Romania, 72 percent in Bulgaria, and 79 percent in Russia. All of these countries had made only a minimal investment in compulsory mass education.

A WOMEN'S COLLEGE. Women were largely excluded from male-dominated universities before 1900. Consequently, the demand of women for higher education led to the foundation of women's colleges, most of which were primarily teacher-training schools. This photograph shows a group of women in an astronomy class at Vassar College in the United States in 1878. Maria Mitchell, a famous female astronomer, was head of the department.

With the dramatic increase in literacy after 1871 came the rise of mass newspapers, such as the *Evening News* (1881) and *Daily Mail* (1896) in London, which sold millions of copies a day. Known as the "yellow press" in the United States, these newspapers shared some common characteristics. They were written in an easily understood style and tended to be extremely sensational. Unlike eighteenth-century newspapers, which were full of serious editorials and lengthy political analysis, these tabloids provided lurid details of crimes, jingoistic diatribes, gossip, and sports news. There were other forms of cheap literature as well. Specialty magazines, such as the *Family Herald* for the entire family, and women's magazines began in the 1860s. Pulp fiction for adults included the extremely popular westerns with their innumerable variations on conflicts between cowboys and Indians. Literature for the masses was but one feature of a new mass culture; another was the emergence of new forms of mass leisure.

✵ MASS LEISURE

In the preindustrial centuries, play or leisure activities had been closely connected to work patterns based on the seasonal or daily cycles typical of the life of peasants and artisans. The process of industrialization in the nineteenth century had an enormous impact upon those traditional patterns. The factory imposed new work patterns that were determined by the rhythms of machines and clocks and removed work time completely from the family environment of farms and workshops. Work and leisure became opposites as leisure came to be viewed as what people do for fun after work. In fact, the new leisure hours created by the industrial system—evening hours after work, weekends, and later a week or two in the summer—largely determined the contours of the new mass leisure.

At the same time, the influx of rural people into industrial towns eventually caused the demise of traditional village culture, especially the fairs and festivals that had formed such an important part of that culture. Industrial progress, of course, demanded that such traditional celebrations as Whitsuntide, which had occasioned thirteen days of games and drinking, be eliminated or reduced. In fact, by the 1870s Whitsuntide had been reduced to a single one-day holiday.

New technology and business practices also determined the forms of the new mass leisure. The new technology created novel experiences for leisure, such as the Ferris wheel at amusement parks. The mechanized urban transportation systems of the 1880s meant that even the working classes were no longer dependent on neighborhood bars, but could make their way to athletic events, amusement parks, and dance halls. Likewise, railroads could take people to the beaches on weekends.

Music and dance halls appeared in the last half of the nineteenth century. The first music hall in London was constructed in 1849 for a lower-class audience. As is evident from one Londoner's observation, music halls were primarily for males:

> [They were a] popular place of Saturday night resort with working men, as at them they can combine the drinking of the Saturday night glass and smoking of the Saturday night pipe, with the seeing and hearing of a variety of entertainments, ranging from magnificent ballets and marvelous scenic illusions to inferior tumbling, and from well-given operatic selections to the most idiotic of the so-called comic songs of the Jolly Dogs Class.[12]

By the 1880s, there were 500 music halls in London. Promoters gradually made them more respectable and broadened their fare to entice both women and children to attend the programs. The new dance halls, which were all the rage by 1900, were more strictly oriented toward adults. Contemporaries were often shocked by the sight of young people engaged in sexually suggestive dancing.

The upper and middle classes had created the first market for tourism, but as wages increased and workers were given paid vacations, tourism, too, became another form of mass leisure. Thomas Cook (1808–1892) was a British pioneer of mass tourism. Secretary to a British temperance group, Cook had been responsible for organizing a railroad trip to temperance gatherings in 1841. This experience led him to offer trips on a regular basis after he

MIDDLE CLASSES AT THE BEACH. By the beginning of the twentieth century, changing work and leisure patterns had created a new mass leisure. The upper and middle classes created the first market for tourism, although it too became another form of mass leisure as wages increased and workers received paid vacations. This photograph shows middle-class Britons enjoying a beach at the beginning of the twentieth century.

The Fight Song: Sports in the English Public School

In the second half of the nineteenth century, organized sports were often placed at the center of the curriculum in English public schools. These sports were not just for leisure but were intended to instill character, strength, and teamwork. This "fight song" was written by H. B. Tristam for the soccer team at Loretto School.

✳ H. B. Tristam, *Going Strong*

Sing Football the grandest of sports in the world,
And you know it yourself if your pluck's never curled,
If you've gritted your teeth and gone hard to the last,
And sworn that you'll never let anyone past.

Chorus
Keeping close upon the ball—we drive it through them all,

And again we go rushing along, along, along;
O the tackle and the run, and the matches we have won,
From the start to the finish going strong, strong, strong, going strong!

If you live to be a hundred you'll never forget
How they hacked in the scrum, how you payed back the debt;
The joy of the swing when you tackled your man,
The lust of the fray when the battle began.

Long hence when you look with a quivering eye
On the little white tassel you value so high;
You'll think of the matches you've played in and won,
And you'll long for the days that are over and done.

---

found that he could make substantial profits by renting special trains, lowering prices, and increasing the number of passengers. In 1867, he offered tours to Paris and by the 1880s to Switzerland. Of course, overseas tours were for the industrial and commercial middle classes, but through their savings clubs even British factory workers were able to take weekend excursions by the turn of the century.

By the late nineteenth century, team sports had also developed into yet another form of mass leisure. Sports were by no means a new activity. Unlike the old rural games, however, they were no longer chaotic and spontaneous activities, but became strictly organized with sets of rules and officials to enforce them. These rules were the products of organized athletic groups, such as the English Football Association (1863) and the American Bowling Congress (1895).

The new sports were not just for leisure or fun, but like other forms of middle-class recreation, they were intended to provide excellent training for people, especially youth. Not only could the participants develop individual skills, but they could also acquire a sense of teamwork useful for military service. These characteristics were already evident in the British public schools in the 1850s and 1860s when such schools as Harrow, Uppingham, and Loretto placed organized sports at the center of the curriculum (see the box above). At Loretto, for example, education was supposed to instill "First—Character. Second—Physique. Third—Intelligence. Fourth—Manners. Fifth—Information."

The new team sports rapidly became professionalized. In Britain, soccer had its Football Association in 1863 and rugby its Rugby Football Union in 1871. In the United States, the first National Association to recognize professional baseball players was formed in 1863. By 1900, the National League and American League had a complete monopoly over professional baseball. The development of urban transportation systems made possible the construction of stadiums where thousands could attend, making mass spectator sports a big business. In 1872, 2,000 people watched the British Soccer Cup finals. By 1885, the crowd had increased to 10,000 and by 1901 to 100,000. Professional teams became objects of mass adulation by crowds of urbanites who compensated for their lost sense of identity in mass urban areas by developing these new loyalties. Spectator sports even reflected class differences. Upper-class soccer teams in Britain viewed working-class teams as vicious and prone to "money-grubbing, tricks, sensational displays, and utter rottenness."

The sports cult of the late nineteenth century was mostly male oriented. Many men believed that females were not particularly suited for "vigorous physical activity," although it was permissible for middle-class women to indulge in less active sports such as croquet and lawn tennis. Eventually, some athletics crept into women's colleges and girls' public schools in England.

The new forms of popular leisure were standardized forms of amusement that drew mass audiences. Although some argued that the new amusements were important for improving people, in truth, they mostly served to provide entertainment and distract people from the realities of their work lives. Much of mass leisure was secular. Churches found that they had to compete with popular amusements for people's attention on Sundays. The new mass leisure also represented a significant change from earlier forms of popular culture. Festivals and fairs had been based on an ethos of active community participation, whereas the new forms of mass leisure were standardized for largely passive mass audiences. Amusement parks and professional sports teams were, after all, big businesses organized to make profits.

◆ The National State

Within the major European states, considerable progress was made in achieving liberal practices (constitutions, parliaments, and individual liberties) and reforms that encouraged the expansion of political democracy through voting rights for men and the creation of mass political parties. At the same time, however, these developments were strongly resisted in parts of Europe where the old political forces remained strong.

❖ Western Europe: The Growth of Political Democracy

In general, parliamentary government was most firmly rooted in the western European states. Both Britain and France saw an expansion of the franchise, but liberal reforms proved less successful in Spain and Italy.

REFORM IN BRITAIN

The growth of political democracy was one of the preoccupations of British politics after 1871, and its cause was pushed along by the expansion of suffrage. Much advanced by the Reform Act of 1867 (see Chapter 22), the right to vote was further extended during the second ministry of William Gladstone (1880–1885) with the passage of the Reform Act of 1884. It gave the vote to all men who paid regular rents or taxes, thus largely enfranchising the agricultural workers, a group previously excluded. The following year, a Redistribution Act eliminated historic boroughs and counties and established constituencies with approximately equal populations and one representative each. The payment of salaries to members of the House of Commons beginning in 1911 further democratized that institution by at least opening the door to people other than the wealthy. The British system of gradual reform through parliamentary institutions had become the way of British political life.

Gradual reform failed to solve the problem of Ireland, however. The Irish had long been subject to British rule, and an Act of Union in 1801 had united the English and Irish parliaments. Like other unfree ethnic groups in Europe, the Irish developed a sense of national self-consciousness. They detested the absentee British landlords and their burdensome rents.

WILLIAM GLADSTONE IN HIS LATER YEARS.
The first Liberal ministry of William Gladstone had been responsible for a series of significant liberal reforms. During his second ministry, Gladstone and the Liberals expanded the right to vote by enfranchising agricultural workers.

A Leader of the Paris Commune

Louise Michel was a schoolteacher in Paris who took an interest in radical ideas. She became active among revolutionary groups in Paris in 1870 and then emerged as a leader of the Paris Commune in 1871. Exiled to New Caledonia after the crushing of the Commune, she was allowed to return to France in 1880, where she became a heroic figure among radical groups. Later, she spent three years in prison and then lived much of the time in England in self-imposed exile. In her memoirs, Michel discusses what happened on March 18, 1871, when the National Assembly sent troops to seize cannon that had been moved earlier to the hills of Montmartre. She also reflected on her activities in the Commune.

❖ Louise Michel, *Memoirs*

Learning that the Versailles soldiers [troops of the National Assembly] were trying to seize the cannon, men and women of Montmartre swarmed up the Butte in a surprise maneuver. Those people who were climbing believed they would die, but they were prepared to pay the price.

The Butte of Montmartre was bathed in the first light of day, through which things were glimpsed as if they were hidden behind a thin veil of water. Gradually the crowd increased. The other districts of Paris, hearing of the events taking place on the Butte of Montmartre, came to our assistance.

The women of Paris covered the cannon with their bodies. When their officers ordered the soldiers to fire, the men refused. The same army that would be used to crush Paris two months later decided now that it did not want to be an accomplice of the reaction. They gave up their attempt to seize the cannon from the National Guard. They understood that the people were defending the Republic by defending the arms that the royalists and imperialists would have turned on Paris in agreement with the Prussians. When we had won our victory, I looked around and noticed my poor mother, who had followed me to the Butte of Montmartre, believing that I was going to die.

On this day, the eighteenth of March, the people awakened. If they had not, it would have been the triumph of some king; instead it was a triumph of the people. The eighteenth of March could have belonged to the allies of kings, or to foreigners, or to the people. It was the people's. . . .

During the entire time of the Commune, I only spent one night at my poor mother's. I never really went to bed during that time. I just napped a little whenever there was nothing better to do, and many other people lived the same way. Everybody who wanted deliverance gave himself totally to the cause. . . . During the Commune I went unhurt except for a bullet that grazed my wrist, although my hat was literally riddled with bullet holes.

In 1870, William Gladstone attempted to alleviate Irish discontent by enacting limited land reform, but as Irish tenants continued to be evicted in the 1870s, the Irish peasants responded with terrorist acts. When the government reacted in turn with more force, Irish Catholics began to demand independence. Although the Liberals introduced home rule bills that would have given Ireland self-government in 1886 and 1893, the bills failed to win a majority vote. When the Liberals finally enacted a Home Rule Act in 1914, an explosive situation in Ireland itself created more problems. Irish Protestants in northern Ireland, especially in the province of Ulster, wanted no part of an Irish Catholic state. The outbreak of World War I enabled the British government to sidestep the potentially explosive issue and to suspend Irish home rule for the duration of the war.

THE THIRD REPUBLIC IN FRANCE

The defeat of France by the Prussian army in 1870 brought the downfall of Louis Napoleon's Second Empire. French republicans initially set up a provisional government, but the victorious Otto von Bismarck intervened and forced the French to choose a government by universal male suffrage. The French people rejected the republicans and overwhelmingly favored the monarchists, who won 400 of the 630 seats in the new National Assembly. In response, on March 26, 1871, radical republicans formed an independent republican government in Paris known as the Commune.

But the National Assembly refused to give up its power and decided to crush the revolutionary Commune. Vicious fighting broke out in April. Many working-class men and women stepped forth to defend the Commune. At first, women's activities were the traditional ones: caring for the wounded soldiers and feeding the troops. Gradually, however, women expanded their activities to include taking care of weapons, working as scouts, and even setting up their own fighting brigades. Louise Michel (1830–1905), a schoolteacher, emerged as one of the leaders of the Paris Commune (see the box above). She proved tireless in forming committees for the defense of the revolutionary Commune.

All of these efforts were in vain, however. In the last week of May, government troops massacred thousands of the Commune's defenders. Estimates are that 20,000 were shot; another 10,000 (including Louise Michel) were shipped overseas to the French penal colony of New Caledonia. The brutal repression of the Commune bequeathed a legacy of hatred that continued to plague French politics for decades. The split between the middle and working classes, begun in the revolutionary hostilities of 1848–1849, had widened immensely. The harsh punishment of women who participated in the revolutionary activity also served to discourage any future efforts by working-class women to improve their conditions.

Although a majority of the members of the monarchist-dominated National Assembly wished to restore a monarchy to France, inability to agree on who should be king caused the monarchists to miss their opportunity and led in 1875 to an improvised constitution that established a republican form of government as the least divisive compromise. This constitution established a bicameral legislature with an upper house, or Senate, elected indirectly and a lower house, or Chamber of Deputies, chosen by universal male suffrage; a president, selected by the legislature for a term of seven years, served as executive of the government. The Constitution of 1875, intended only as a stopgap measure, solidified the republic—the Third Republic—which lasted sixty-five years. New elections in 1876 and 1877 strengthened the hands of the republicans who managed by 1879 to institute ministerial responsibility and establish the power of the Chamber of Deputies. The prime minister or premier and his ministers were now responsible not to the president, but to the Chamber of Deputies.

Although the government's moderation gradually encouraged more and more middle-class and peasant support, the position of the Third Republic remained precarious because monarchists, Catholic clergy, and professional army officers were still its enemies.

A major crisis in the 1880s, however, actually served to strengthen the republican government. General Georges Boulanger (1837–1891) was a popular military officer who attracted the public attention of all those discontented with the Third Republic: the monarchists, Bonapartists, aristocrats, and nationalists who favored a war of revenge against Germany. Boulanger appeared as the strong man on horseback, the savior of France. By 1889, just when his strength had grown to the point where many expected a coup d'etat, he lost his nerve and fled France, a completely discredited man. In the long run, the Boulanger crisis served to rally support for the resilient republic.

SPAIN AND ITALY

In Spain, a new constitution, created in 1875 under King Alfonso XII (1874–1885), established a parliamentary government dominated by two political groups, the Conservatives and Liberals, whose members stemmed from the same small social group of great landowners allied with a few wealthy industrialists. Because suffrage was limited to the propertied classes, Liberals and Conservatives alternated in power but followed basically the same conservative policies. Spain's defeat in the Spanish-American War in 1898 and the loss of Cuba and the Philippines to the United States increased the discontent with the status

quo. When a group of young intellectuals known as the Generation of 1898 called for political and social reforms, both Liberals and Conservatives attempted to enlarge the electorate and win the masses' support for their policies. The attempted reforms did little to allay the unrest, however, and the growth of industrialization in some areas resulted in more workers being attracted to the radical solutions of socialism and anarchism. When violence erupted in Barcelona in July 1909, the military forces brutally suppressed the rebels. The revolt and its repression made clear that reform would not be easily accomplished because the Catholic church, large landowners, and the army remained tied to a conservative social order.

By 1870, Italy had emerged as a geographically united state with pretensions to great power status. Its internal weaknesses, however, gave that claim a particularly hollow ring. Sectional differences—a poverty-stricken south and an industrializing north—weakened any sense of community. Chronic turmoil between workers and industrialists undermined the social fabric. The Italian government was unable to deal effectively with these problems because of the extensive corruption among government officials and the lack of stability created by ever-changing government coalitions. The granting of universal male suffrage in 1912 did little to correct the extensive corruption and weak government. Even Italy's pretensions to great power status proved hollow when Italy became the first European power to lose to an African state—Ethiopia.

✻ Central and Eastern Europe: Persistence of the Old Order

Germany, Austria-Hungary, and Russia pursued political policies that were quite different from those of the western European nations. The central European states (Germany and Austria-Hungary) had the trappings of parliamentary government including legislative bodies and elections by universal male suffrage, but authoritarian forces, especially powerful monarchies and conservative social groups, remained strong. In eastern Europe, especially Russia, the old system of autocracy was barely touched by the winds of change.

❧ GERMANY

Despite unification, important divisions remained in German society that could not simply be papered over by the force of nationalism. These divisions were already evident in the new German constitution that provided for a federal system with a bicameral legislature. The Bundesrat, or upper house, represented the twenty-five states that made up Germany. Individual states, such as Bavaria and Prussia, kept their own kings, their own post offices, and even their own armies in peacetime. The lower house of the German parliament, known as the Reichstag, was elected on the basis of universal male suffrage, but it did not have ministerial responsibility. Ministers of government, the most important of which was the chancellor, were responsible not to the parliament, but to the emperor. The emperor also commanded the armed forces and controlled foreign policy and internal administration. Though the creation of a parliament elected by universal male suffrage presented opportunities for the growth of a real political democracy, it failed to develop in Germany before World War I. The army and Bismarck were two major reasons why it did not.

The German (largely Prussian) army viewed itself as the defender of monarchy and aristocracy and sought to escape any control by the Reichstag by operating under a general staff responsible only to the emperor. Prussian military tradition was strong, and military officers took steps to ensure the loyalty of their subordinates to the emperor, which was easy as long as Junker landowners were officers. As the growth of the army made it necessary to turn to the middle class for officers, extreme care was taken to choose only sons "of honorable bourgeois families in whom the love for King and Fatherland, a warm heart for the soldier's calling, and Christian morality are planted and nurtured."

The policies of Bismarck, who served as chancellor of the new German state until 1890, often served to prevent the growth of more democratic institutions. At first, Bismarck worked with the liberals to achieve greater cen-

tralization of Germany through common codes of criminal and commercial law. The liberals also joined Bismarck in his attack on the Catholic church, the so-called *Kulturkampf* or "struggle for civilization." Like Bismarck, middle-class liberals distrusted Catholic loyalty to the new Germany. Bismarck's strong-arm tactics against Catholic clergy and Catholic institutions proved counterproductive, however, and Bismarck welcomed an opportunity in 1878 to abandon the attack on Catholicism by making an abrupt shift in policy.

In 1878, Bismarck abandoned the liberals and began to persecute the socialists. When the Social Democratic Party elected twelve deputies to the Reichstag in 1877, Bismarck grew alarmed. He genuinely believed that the socialists' antinationalistic, anticapitalistic, and antimonarchical stance represented a danger to the empire. In 1878, Bismarck got parliament to pass a stringent antisocialist law that outlawed the Social Democratic Party and limited socialist meetings and publications, although socialist candidates were still permitted to run for the Reichstag. In addition to repressive measures, Bismarck also attempted to woo workers away from socialism by enacting social welfare legislation (see the box on p. 706). Between 1883 and 1889, the Reichstag passed laws that created sickness, accident, and disability benefits as well as old age pensions financed by compulsory contributions from workers, employers, and the state. Bismarck's social

BISMARCK AND WILLIAM II. In 1890, Bismarck sought to undertake new repressive measures against the Social Democrats. Disagreeing with this policy, Emperor William II forced him to resign. This political cartoon shows William II reclining on a throne made of artillery and cannonballs and holding a doll labeled "socialism." Bismarck bids farewell as Germany, personified as a woman, looks on with grave concern.

Bismarck and the Welfare of the Workers

In his attempt to win workers away from socialism, Bismarck favored an extensive program of social welfare benefits, including old age pensions as well as compensation for absence from work due to sickness, accident, and disability. This selection is taken from Bismarck's address to the Reichstag on March 10, 1884, in which he explained his motives for social welfare legislation.

❈ Bismarck, Address to the Reichstag

The positive efforts began really only in the year . . . 1881 . . . with the imperial message . . . in which His Majesty William I said: "Already in February of this year, we have expressed our conviction that the healing of social ills is not to be sought exclusively by means of repression of Social Democratic excesses, but equally in the positive promotion of the welfare of the workers."

In consequence of this, first of all the insurance law against accidents was submitted. . . . And it reads . . . "But those who have, through age or disability, become incapable of working have a confirmed claim on all for a higher degree of state care than could have been their share heretofore. . . ."

The workers' real sore point is the insecurity of his existence. He is not always sure he will always have work. He is not sure he will always be healthy, and he foresees some day he will be old and incapable of work. But also if he falls into poverty as a result of long illness, he is completely helpless with his own powers, and society hitherto does not recognize relief, even when he has worked ever so faithfully and diligently before. But ordinary poor relief leaves much to be desired, especially in the great cities where it is extraordinarily much worse than in the country. . . . We read in Berlin newspapers of suicide because of difficulty in making both ends meet, of people who died from direct hunger and have hanged themselves because they have nothing to eat, of people who announce in the paper they were tossed out homeless and have no income. . . . For the worker it is always a fact that falling into poverty and onto poor relief in a great city is synonymous with misery, and this insecurity makes him hostile and mistrustful of society. That is humanly not unnatural, and as long as the state does not meet him halfway, just as long will this trust in the state's honesty be taken from him by accusations against the government, which he will find where he wills; always running back again to the socialist quacks . . . and, without great reflection, letting himself be promised things, which will not be fulfilled. On this account, I believe that accident insurance, with which we show the way, . . . will still work on the anxieties and ill-feeling of the working class.

---

security system was the most progressive the world had yet seen, although even his system left much to be desired as the Social Democrats pointed out. A full pension, for example, was payable only at age seventy after forty-eight years of contributions. In the event of a male worker's death, no benefits were paid to his widow or children.

Both the repressive and the social welfare measures failed to stop the growth of socialism, however. The Social Democratic Party continued to grow. In his frustration, Bismarck planned still more repressive measures in 1890, but before he could carry them out, the new emperor, William II (1888–1918), eager to pursue his own policies, cashiered the aged chancellor.

❧ AUSTRIA-HUNGARY

After the creation of the dual monarchy of Austria-Hungary in 1867, the Austrian part received a constitution that established a parliamentary system with the principle of ministerial responsibility. But Emperor Francis Joseph largely ignored ministerial responsibility and proceeded to personally appoint and dismiss his ministers and rule by decree when parliament was not in session.

The problem of the minorities continued to trouble the empire. The ethnic Germans, who made up only one-third of Austria's population, governed Austria but felt increasingly threatened by the Czechs, Poles, and other Slavic groups within the empire. The difficulties in dealing with this problem were especially evident from 1879 to 1893 when Count Edward von Taaffe served as prime minister. Taaffe attempted to "muddle through" by relying on a coalition of German conservatives, Czechs, and Poles to maintain a majority in parliament. But his concessions to national minorities, such as allowing the Slavic languages as well as German to be used in education and administration, served to antagonize the German-speaking Austrian bureaucracy and aristocracy, two of the basic pillars of the empire. Opposition to Taaffe's policies brought his downfall in 1893, but did not solve the nationalities problem. While the dissatisfied non-German groups demanded concessions, the ruling Austrian Germans resisted change. The granting of universal male suffrage in 1907 served only to make the problem worse as nationalities that had played no role in the government now agitated in the parliament for autonomy. This led prime ministers after 1900 to ignore the parliament and rely increasingly on imperial emergency decrees to govern.

Unlike Austria, Hungary had a working parliamentary system, but one controlled by the great Magyar landowners who dominated both the Hungarian peasantry and the other ethnic groups in Hungary. The Hungarians attempted to solve their nationalities problem by systematic Magyarization. The Magyar language was imposed upon all schools and was the only language that could be used by government and military officials.

RUSSIA

In Russia, the government made no concession whatever to liberal and democratic reforms. The assassination of Alexander II in 1881 convinced his son and successor, Alexander III (1881–1894), that reform had been a mistake, and he quickly instituted what he said were "exceptional measures." The powers of the secret police were expanded. Advocates of constitutional monarchy and social reform, along with revolutionary groups, were persecuted. Entire districts of Russia were placed under martial law if the government suspected the inhabitants of treason. The powers of the zemstvos, created by the reforms of Alexander II, were sharply curtailed. When Alexander III died, his weak son and successor, Nicholas II (1894–1917), began his rule with his father's conviction that the absolute power of the tsars should be preserved: "I shall maintain the principle of autocracy just as firmly and unflinchingly as did my unforgettable father."[13] But conditions were changing, especially with the growth of industrialization, and the tsar's approach was not realistic in view of the new circumstances he faced.

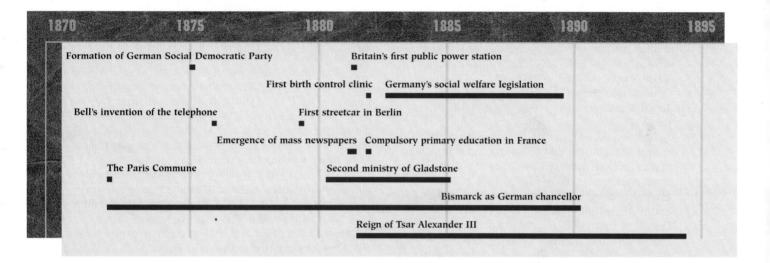

CONCLUSION

The Second Industrial Revolution helped create a new material prosperity that led Europeans to believe they had ushered in a new "age of progress." A major feature of this age was the emergence of a mass society. The lower classes in particular benefited from the right to vote, a higher standard of living, and new schools that provided them with a modicum of education. New forms of mass transportation, combined with new work patterns, enabled large numbers of people to enjoy weekend excursions to amusement parks and seaside resorts and to participate in new mass leisure activities.

By 1871, the national state had become the focus of people's lives. Liberal and democratic reforms brought new possibilities for greater participation in the political process, although women were still largely excluded from political rights. After 1871, the national state also began to expand its functions beyond all previous limits. Fearful of the growth of socialism and trade unions, governments attempted to appease the working masses by adopting such social insurance measures as protection against accidents, illness, and old age. These social welfare measures were narrow in scope and limited in benefits, but they signaled a new direction for state action to benefit the mass of its citizens. The enactment of public health and housing measures, designed to curb the worst ills of urban living, were yet another indication of how state power could be used to benefit the people.

This extension of state functions took place in an atmosphere of increased national loyalty. After 1871, nation-states increasingly sought to solidify the social order and win the active loyalty and support of their citizens by deliberately cultivating national feelings. Yet this policy contained potentially great dangers. As we shall see in the next chapter, nations had discovered once again that imperialistic adventures and military successes could arouse nationalistic passions and smother domestic political unrest. But they also found that nationalistic feelings could also lead to intense international rivalries that made war almost inevitable.

NOTES 🪶🪶🪶🪶🪶🪶🪶🪶🪶🪶🪶🪶🪶

1. Quoted in David Landes, *The Unbound Prometheus: Technological Change and Industrial Development in Western Europe from 1750 to the Present* (Cambridge, 1969), p. 353.
2. Quoted in Barbara Franzoi, ". . . with the wolf always at the door. . . . Women's Work in Domestic Industry in Britain and Germany," in Marilyn J. Boxer and Jean H. Quataert, eds., *Connecting Spheres: Women in the Western World, 1500 to the Present* (New York, 1987), p. 151.
3. Quoted in W. L. Guttsman, *The German Social Democratic Party, 1875–1933* (London, 1981), p. 63.
4. Quoted in Leslie Derfler, *Socialism since Marx: A Century of the European Left* (New York, 1973), p. 58.
5. Karl Marx and Friedrich Engels, *The Communist Manifesto* (Harmondsworth, 1967), p. 102.
6. Quoted in Paul Avrich, *The Russian Anarchists* (Princeton, N.J., 1971), p. 67.
7. Quoted in Nicholas Bullock and James Read, *The Movement for Housing Reform in Germany and France, 1840–1914* (Cambridge, 1985), p. 42.
8. Quoted in Gary Cross, *A Social History of Leisure since 1600* (State College, Pa., 1990), pp. (in order of quotations) 116, 119.
9. Quoted in Sibylle Meyer, "The Tiresome Work of Conspicuous Leisure: On the Domestic Duties of the Wives of Civil Servants in the German Empire (1871–1918)," in Boxer and Quataert, *Connecting Spheres*, p. 161.
10. Quoted in Lenard R. Berlanstein, *The Working People of Paris, 1871–1914* (Baltimore, 1984), p. 141.
11. Quoted in Robert Gildea, *Barricades and Borders: Europe, 1800–1914*, 2d ed. (Oxford, 1996), pp. 240–241.
12. Quoted in Cross, *A Social History of Leisure since 1600*, p. 130.
13. Quoted in Shmuel Galai, *The Liberation Movement in Russia, 1900–1905* (Cambridge, 1973), p. 26.

SUGGESTIONS FOR FURTHER READING 🪶🪶🪶🪶

In addition to the general works on the nineteenth century and individual European countries cited in Chapters 21 and 22, two more specialized works on the subject matter of this chapter are available in N. Stone, *Europe Transformed, 1878–1919* (London, 1983); and F. Gilbert, *The End of the European Era, 1890 to the Present*, 4th ed. (New York, 1991).

The subject of the Second Industrial Revolution is well covered in D. Landes, *The Unbound Prometheus*, cited in Chapter 20. For a fundamental survey of European industrialization, see A. S. Milward and S. B. Saul, *The Development of the Economies of Continental Europe, 1850–1914* (Cambridge, Mass., 1977). For an introduction to the development of mass consumerism in Britain, see W. H. Fraser, *The Coming of the Mass Market, 1850–1914* (Hamden, Conn., 1981). The impact of the new technology on European thought is imaginatively discussed in S. Kern, *The Culture of Time and Space, 1880–1918* (Cambridge, Mass., 1983).

For an introduction to international socialism, see A. Lindemann, *A History of European Socialism* (New Haven, Conn., 1983); and L. Derfler, *Socialism since Marx: A Century of the European Left* (New York, 1973). On the emergence of German social democracy, see W. L. Guttsman, *The German Social Democratic Party, 1875–1933* (London, 1981); and V. Lidtke, *The Outlawed Party: Social Democracy in Germany, 1878–1890* (Princeton, N.J., 1966). There is a good introduction to anarchism in R. D. Sonn, *Anarchism* (New York, 1992).

Demographic problems are examined in T. McKeown, *The Modern Rise of Population* (New York, 1976). On European emigration, see C. Erickson, *Emigration from Europe, 1815–1914* (Cambridge, 1976); and L. P. Moch, *Moving Europeans: Migration in Western Europe since 1650* (Bloomington, Ind., 1993).

For a good introduction to housing reform on the Continent, see N. Bullock and J. Read, *The Movement for Housing Reform in Germany and France, 1840–1914* (Cambridge, 1985). Working-class housing in Paris during its reconstruction is the subject of A. L. Shapiro, *Housing the Poor of Paris, 1850–1902* (Madison, Wis., 1985). The reconstruction of Paris is discussed in D. Pinkney, *Napoleon III and the Rebuilding of Paris* (Princeton, N.J., 1958).

An interesting work on aristocratic life is D. Cannadine, *The Decline and Fall of the British Aristocracy* (New Haven, Conn., 1990). On the middle classes, see P. Pilbeam, *The Middle Classes in Europe, 1789–1914* (Basingstoke, 1990). On the working classes, see L. Berlanstein, *The Working People of Paris, 1871–1914* (Baltimore, 1984); and R. Magraw, *A History of the French Working Class* (Cambridge, Mass., 1992).

There are good overviews of women's experiences in the nineteenth century in B. Smith, *Changing Lives: Women in European History since 1700* (Lexington, Mass., 1989); and M. J. Boxer and J. H. Quataert, eds., *Connecting Spheres: Women in the Western World, 1500 to the Present* (New York, 1987). The world of women's work is examined in L. A. Tilly and J. W. Scott, *Women, Work, and Family* (New York, 1978). Important studies of women include M. J. Peterson, *Family, Love and Work in the Lives of Victorian Gentlewomen* (Bloomington, Ind., 1989); B. G. Smith, *Ladies of the Leisure Class: The Bourgeoises of Northern France in the Nineteenth Century* (Princeton, N.J., 1981); P. Robertson, *An Experience of Women: Pattern and Change in Nineteenth-Century Europe* (Philadelphia, 1982); and B. Franzoi, *At the Very Least She Pays the Rent: Women and German Industrialization, 1871–1914* (Westport, Conn., 1985). Prostitution is discussed in J. R. Walkowitz, *Prostitution and Victorian Society: Women, Class, and the State* (Cambridge, 1980). On the family and children, see M. Mitterauer and R. Sieder, *The European Family* (Chicago, 1982). The treatment of children is examined in G. Behlmer, *Child Abuse and Moral Reform in England, 1870–1908* (Stanford, 1982).

On various aspects of education, see M. J. Maynes, *Schooling in Western Europe: A Social History* (Albany, N.Y., 1985); and J. S. Hurt, *Elementary Schooling and the Working Classes, 1860–1918* (London, 1979). A concise and well-presented survey of leisure patterns is G. Cross, *A Social History of Leisure since 1600* (State College, Pa., 1990).

The domestic politics of the period can be examined in the general works on individual countries listed in the bibliographies for Chapters 21 and 22. There are also specialized works on aspects of each country's history. On Britain, see D. Read, *The Age of Urban Democracy: England, 1868–1914* (New York, 1994). The Irish problem is covered in O. MacDonagh, *States of Mind: A Study of Anglo-Irish Conflict, 1780–1980*

(London, 1983). For a detailed examination of French history from 1871 to 1914, see J. M. Mayeur and M. Reberioux, *The Third Republic from Its Origins to the Great War, 1871–1914* (Cambridge, 1984). On the Paris Commune, see R. Tombs, *The War against Paris, 1871* (Cambridge, 1981). On Italy, see C. Seton-Watson, *Italy from Liberalism to Fascism* (London, 1967). An important aspect of Spanish history is examined in S. G. Payne, *Politics and the Military in Modern Spain* (Stanford, 1967). On Germany, see W. J. Mommsen, *Imperial Germany, 1867–1918* (New York, 1995); and V. R. Berghahn, *Imperial Germany, 1871–1914* (Providence, R.I., 1995). On the nationalities problem in the Austro-Hungarian Empire, see R. Kann, *The Multinational Empire, Nationalism and National Reform in the Habsburg Monarchy, 1848–1918*, 2 vols. (New York, 1950). On aspects of Russian history, see H. Rogger, *Russia in the Age of Modernization and Revolution, 1881–1917* (London, 1983).

For additional reading, go to InfoTrac College Edition, your online research library at http://web1.infotrac-college.com

Enter the search term *Marxism* using Key Terms.

Enter the search term *anarchism* using Key Terms.

Enter the search terms *family nineteenth century* using Key Terms.

Enter the search terms *socialism history* using Key Terms.

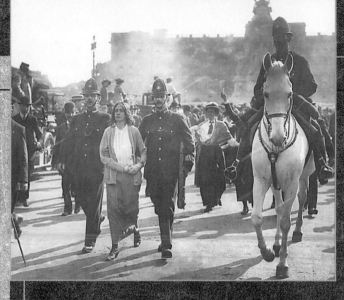

24

An Age of Modernity and Anxiety, 1894–1914

CHAPTER OUTLINE

- Toward the Modern Consciousness: Intellectual and Cultural Developments
- Politics: New Directions and New Uncertainties
- The New Imperialism
- International Rivalry and the Coming of War
- Conclusion

FOCUS QUESTIONS

- What developments in science, intellectual affairs, and the arts in the late nineteenth and early twentieth centuries "opened the way to a modern consciousness," and how did this consciousness differ from earlier worldviews?
- What difficulties did women, Jews, and the working classes face in the late nineteenth and early twentieth centuries, and how successful were they in achieving their goals?
- What were the causes of the new imperialism that took place after 1880, and what effects did the European quest for colonies have on Africa and Asia?
- What was the Bismarckian system of alliances, and how successful was it at keeping the peace?
- What issues lay behind the international crises that Europe faced in the late nineteenth and early twentieth centuries?

MANY EUROPEANS AFTER 1894 *continued to believe they lived in an era of material and human progress. For some, however, progress entailed much struggle. Emmeline Pankhurst, who became the leader of the women's suffrage movement in Britain, said that her determination to fight for women's rights stemmed from a childhood memory: "My father bent over me, shielding the candle flame with his big hand and I heard him say, somewhat sadly, 'What a pity she wasn't born a lad.'" Eventually, Emmeline Pankhurst and her daughters marched and fought for women's right to vote. The struggle was often violent: "They came in bruised, hatless, faces scratched, eyes* swollen, noses bleeding," one of the Pankhurst daughters recalled. Arrested and jailed in 1908, Pankhurst informed her judges: "If you had the power to send us to prison, not for six months, but for six years, or for our lives, the Government must not think they could stop this agitation. It would go on!" It did go on, and women in Britain did eventually receive the right to vote; to some, this was yet another confirmation of Europe's progress.

But the period after 1894 was not just a time of progress; it was also a time of great tension as imperialist adventures, international rivalries, and cultural uncertainties disturbed the apparent calm. After 1880, Europeans engaged in a great race for colonies around the world. This competition for lands abroad greatly intensified existing antagonisms among European states.

Ultimately, Europeans proved incapable of finding constructive ways to cope with their international rivalries. The development of two large alliance systems—the Triple Alliance and the Triple Entente—may have helped preserve peace for a time, but eventually the alliances made it easier for the European nations to be drawn into World War I. The alliances helped maintain a balance of power, but also led to the creation of large armies, enormous military establishments, and immense arsenals. The alliances also helped create tensions that were unleashed when Europeans rushed into the catastrophic carnage of World War I.

The cultural life of Europe in the decades before 1914 reflected similar dynamic tensions. The advent of mass education produced more well-informed citizens, but also made it easier for governments to stir up the masses by nationalistic appeals through the new mass journalism. At the same time, despite the appearance of progress, European philosophers, writers, and artists were creating modern cultural expressions that questioned traditional ideas and values and increasingly provoked a crisis of confidence. Before 1914, many intellectuals had a sense of unease about the direction society was heading, accompanied by a feeling of imminent catastrophe. They proved remarkably prophetic.

◆ Toward the Modern Consciousness: Intellectual and Cultural Developments

Before 1914, most Europeans continued to believe in the values and ideals that had been generated by the Scientific Revolution and the Enlightenment. Reason, science, and progress were still important words in the European vocabulary. The ability of human beings to improve themselves and achieve a better society seemed to be well demonstrated by a rising standard of living, urban improvements, and mass education. Such products of modern technology as electric lights, phonographs, and automobiles reinforced the popular prestige of science and the belief in the ability of the human mind to comprehend the universe through the use of reason. Near the end of the nineteenth century, however, a dramatic transformation in the realm of ideas and culture challenged many of these assumptions. A new view of the physical universe, an appeal to the irrational, alternative views of human nature, and radically innovative forms of literary and artistic expression shattered old beliefs and opened the way to a modern consciousness. Although the real impact of many of these ideas was not felt until after World War I, they served to provoke a sense of confusion and anxiety before 1914 that would become even more pronounced after the war.

✿ Developments in the Sciences: The Emergence of a New Physics

Science was one of the chief pillars underlying the optimistic and rationalistic view of the world that many Westerners shared in the nineteenth century. Supposedly based on hard facts and cold reason, science offered a certainty of belief in the orderliness of nature that was comforting to many people for whom traditional religious beliefs no longer had much meaning. This faith in science's ability to explain the world was reflected in an introductory paragraph in the University of Chicago's catalog in 1893: "It seems probable that most of the grand underlying principles in the physical sciences have been firmly established and that further advances are to be sought chiefly in the rigorous application of these principles to all the phenomena which come under our notice." Many naively believed that the application of already known scientific laws would give humanity a complete understanding of the physical world and an accurate picture of reality. The new physics dramatically altered that perspective.

Throughout much of the nineteenth century, Westerners adhered to the mechanical conception of the universe postulated by the classical physics of Isaac Newton. In this perspective, the universe was viewed as a giant machine in which time, space, and matter were objective realities that existed independently of those observing them. Matter was thought to be composed of indivisible and solid material bodies called atoms.

These views were first seriously questioned at the end of the nineteenth century. The French scientist Marie Curie (1867–1934) and her husband Pierre (1859–1906) discovered that an element called radium gave off rays of radiation that apparently came from within the atom itself. Atoms were not simply hard, material bodies but small worlds containing such subatomic particles as electrons and protons that behaved in seemingly random and inexplicable fashion. Inquiry into the disintegrative process within atoms became a central theme of the new physics.

MARIE CURIE. Marie Curie was born in Warsaw, Poland, but studied at the University of Paris where she received degrees in both physics and mathematics. She was the first woman to win two Nobel Prizes, one in 1903 in physics and another in chemistry in 1911. She is shown here in her Paris laboratory in 1921.

Building upon this work, in 1900 a Berlin physicist, Max Planck (1858–1947), disclosed a discovery that he believed was "as important as that of Newton." Planck rejected the belief that a heated body radiates energy in a steady stream, but maintained instead that energy is radiated discontinuously, in irregular packets that he called "quanta." The quantum theory raised fundamental questions about the subatomic realm of the atom. By 1900, the old view of atoms as the basic building blocks of the material world was being seriously questioned, and the world of Newtonian physics was in trouble.

Albert Einstein (1879–1955), a German-born patent officer working in Switzerland, pushed these new theories of thermodynamics into new terrain. In 1905, Einstein published a paper, entitled "The Electro-dynamics of Moving Bodies," that contained his special theory of relativity. According to relativity theory, space and time are not absolute, but relative to the observer, and both are interwoven into what Einstein called a four-dimensional space-time continuum. Neither space nor time had an existence independent of human experience. As Einstein later explained simply to a journalist: "It was formerly believed that if all material things disappeared out of the universe, time and space would be left. According to the relativity theory, however, time and space disappear together with the things."[1] Moreover, matter and energy reflected the relativity of time and space. Einstein concluded that matter was nothing but another form of energy. His epochal formula $E = mc^2$—that each particle of matter is equivalent to its mass times the square of the velocity of light—was the key theory explaining the vast energies contained within the atom. It led to the atomic age.

Like many geniuses throughout the ages, Einstein soon learned that new ideas are not readily accepted by people accustomed to old patterns. His work threatened the long-accepted Newtonian celestial mechanics and was not well received initially. When Einstein applied for a position at the University of Bern in 1907, he was immediately rejected. Many scientists were also unable to comprehend Einstein's ideas. During a total eclipse of the sun in May 1919, however, scientists were able to demonstrate that light was deflected in the gravitational field of the sun, just as Einstein had predicted. This confirmed Einstein's general theory of relativity and opened the scientific and intellectual world to his ideas. The 1920s would become the "heroic age" of physics.

❊ Toward a New Understanding of the Irrational

Intellectually, the decades before 1914 witnessed a combination of contradictory developments. Thanks to the influence of science, confidence in human reason and progress still remained a dominant thread. At the same time, however, a small group of intellectuals attacked the idea of optimistic progress, dethroned reason, and glorified the irrational. Although these thinkers and writers were a distinct minority, the destructiveness of World War I made their ideas even more appealing after 1918 when it seemed that they had been proved right.

Friedrich Nietzsche (1844–1900) was one of the intellectuals who glorified the irrational. According to Nietzsche, Western bourgeois society was decadent and incapable of any real cultural creativity, primarily because of its excessive emphasis on the rational faculty at the expense of emotions, passions, and instincts. Reason, claimed Nietzsche, actually played little role in human life because humans were at the mercy of irrational life forces.

Nietzsche believed that Christianity should shoulder much of the blame for Western civilization's enfeeblement. The "slave morality" of Christianity, he believed, had obliterated the human impulse for life and had crushed the human will:

> I call Christianity the one great curse, the one enormous and innermost perversion. . . . I call it the one immortal blemish of mankind. . . . Christianity has taken the side of everything weak, base, ill-constituted, it has made an ideal out of opposition to the preservative instincts of strong life.

. . . Christianity is called the religion of pity.—Pity stands in antithesis to the basic emotions which enhance the energy of the feeling of life: it has a depressive effect. One loses force when one pities.[2]

According to Nietzsche, Christianity had crushed spontaneous human instincts and inculcated weakness and humility.

How, then, could Western society be renewed? First, said Nietzsche, one must recognize that "God is dead." Europeans had killed God, he said, and it was no longer possible to believe in some kind of cosmic order. Eliminating God and hence Christian morality had liberated human beings and made it possible to create a higher kind of being Nietzsche called the superman: "I teach you the Superman. Man is something that is to be surpassed."[3] Superior intellectuals must free themselves from the ordinary thinking of the masses, "the slaves, or the populace, or the herd, or whatever name you care to give them." Beyond good and evil, the supermen would create their own values and lead the masses: "It is necessary for higher man to declare war upon the masses." Nietzsche rejected and condemned political democracy, social reform, and universal suffrage.

Another popular revolutionary against reason in the 1890s was Henri Bergson (1859–1941), a French Jewish philosopher whose lectures at the University of Paris made him one of the most important influences in French thought in the early twentieth century. Bergson accepted rational, scientific thought as a practical instrument for providing useful knowledge, but maintained that it was incapable of arriving at truth or ultimate reality. To him, reality was the "life force" that suffused all things; it could not be divided into analyzable parts. Reality was a whole that could only be grasped intuitively and experienced directly. When we analyze it, we have merely a description, no longer the reality we have experienced.

Georges Sorel (1847–1922), a French political theorist, combined Bergson's and Nietzsche's ideas on the limits of rational thinking with his own passionate interest in revolutionary socialism. Sorel understood the political potential of the nonrational and advocated violent action as the only sure way to achieve the aims of socialism. To destroy capitalist society, he recommended the use of the general strike, envisioning it as a mythic image that had the power to inspire workers to take violent, heroic action against the capitalist order. Sorel also came to believe that the new socialist society would have to be governed by a small elite ruling body because the masses were incapable of ruling themselves.

✳ *Sigmund Freud and the Emergence of Psychoanalysis*

Although poets and mystics had revealed a world of unconscious and irrational behavior, many scientifically oriented intellectuals under the impact of Enlightenment thought continued to believe that human beings responded to conscious motives in a rational fashion. At the end of the nineteenth century and beginning of the twentieth, the Viennese doctor Sigmund Freud (1856–1939) put forth a series of theories that undermined optimism about the rational nature of the human mind. Freud's thought, like the new physics and the irrationalism of Nietzsche, added to the uncertainties of the age. His major ideas were published in 1900 in *The Interpretation of Dreams*, which contained the basic foundation of what came to be known as psychoanalysis.

According to Freud, human behavior was strongly determined by the unconscious, by former experiences and inner drives of which people were largely oblivious. To explore the contents of the unconscious, Freud relied not only on hypnosis but also on dreams, but the latter were dressed in an elaborate code that had to be deciphered if the contents were to be properly understood.

But why did some experiences whose influence persisted in controlling an individual's life remain unconscious? According to Freud, the answer was repression (see the box on p. 714), a process by which unsettling experiences were blotted from conscious awareness but still continued to influence behavior because they had become part of the unconscious. To explain how repression worked, Freud elaborated an intricate theory of the inner life of human beings.

According to Freud, a human being's inner life was a battleground of three contending forces: the id, ego, and superego. The id was the center of unconscious drives and was ruled by what Freud termed the pleasure principle. As creatures of desire, human beings directed their energy toward pleasure and away from pain. The id contained all kinds of lustful drives and desires, crude appetites and impulses, loves and hates. The ego was the seat of reason and hence the coordinator of the inner life. It was governed by the reality principle. Although humans were dominated by the pleasure principle, a true pursuit of pleasure was not feasible. The reality principle meant that people rejected pleasure so that they might live together in society. The superego was the locus of conscience and represented the inhibitions and moral values that society in general and parents in particular imposed upon people. The superego served to force the ego to curb the unsatisfactory drives of the id.

The human being was thus a battleground between id, ego, and superego. Ego and superego exerted restraining influences on the unconscious id and repressed or kept out of consciousness what they wanted to. The most important repressions, according to Freud, were sexual, and he went on to develop a theory of infantile sexual drives embodied in the Oedipus complex (Electra complex for females), or the infant's craving for exclusive possession of the parent of the opposite sex. Repression began in childhood, and psychoanalysis was accomplished through a dialogue between psychotherapist and patient in which the therapist probed deeply into memory in order to retrace the chain of repression all the way back to its

Freud and the Concept of Repression

Freud's psychoanalytical theories resulted from his attempt to understand the world of the unconscious. This excerpt is taken from a lecture given in 1909 in which Freud describes how he arrived at his theory of the role of repression. Although Freud valued science and reason, his theories of the unconscious produced a new image of the human being as governed less by reason than by irrational forces.

❀ Sigmund Freud, *Five Lectures on Psychoanalysis*

I did not abandon it [his technique of encouraging patients to reveal forgotten experiences], however, before the observations I made during my use of it afforded me decisive evidence. I found confirmation of the fact that the forgotten memories were not lost. They were in the patient's possession and were ready to emerge in association to what was still known by him; but there was some force that prevented them from becoming conscious and compelled them to remain unconscious. The existence of this force could be assumed with certainty, since one became aware of an effort corresponding to it if, in opposition to it, one tried to introduce the unconscious memories into the patient's consciousness. The force which was maintaining the pathological condition became apparent in the form of resistance on the part of the patient.

It was on this idea of resistance, then, that I based my view of the course of physical events in hysteria. In order to effect a recovery, it had proved necessary to remove these resistances. Starting out from the mechanism of cure, it now became possible to construct quite definite ideas of the origin of the illness. The same forces which, in the form of resistance, were now offering opposition to the forgotten material's being made conscious, must formerly have brought about the forgetting and must have pushed the pathogenic experiences in question out of consciousness. I gave the name of "repression" to this hypothetical process, and I considered that it was proved by the undeniable existence of resistance.

The further question could then be raised as to what these forces were and what the determinants were of the repression in which we now recognized the pathogenic mechanism of hysteria. A comparative study of the pathogenic situations which we had come to know through the cathartic procedure made it possible to answer this question. All these experiences had involved the emergence of a wishful impulse which was in sharp contrast to the subject's other wishes and which proved incompatible with the ethical and aesthetic standards of his personality. There had been a short conflict, and the end of this internal struggle was that the idea which had appeared before consciousness as the vehicle of this irreconcilable wish fell a victim to repression, was pushed out of consciousness with all its attached memories, and was forgotten. Thus the incompatibility of the wish in question with the patient's ego was the motive for the repression; the subject's ethical and other standards were the repressing forces. An acceptance of the incompatible wishful impulse or a prolongation of the conflict would have produced a high degree of unpleasure; this unpleasure was avoided by means of repression, which was thus revealed as one of the devices serving to protect the mental personality.

---

childhood origins. By making the conscious mind aware of the unconscious and its repressed contents, the patient's psychic conflict was resolved.

Freud, Marx, and Darwin have often been linked together as the three intellectual giants of the nineteenth century. Although many of Freud's ideas have been shown to be wrong in many details, he is still regarded as an important figure because of the impact his theories have had. Many historians still accept Freud's judgment of himself: "I have the distinct feeling that I have touched on one of the great secrets of nature."

❀ The Impact of Darwin: Social Darwinism and Racism

In the second half of the nineteenth century, scientific theories were sometimes wrongly applied to achieve other ends. The application of Darwin's principle of organic evolution to the social order came to be known as Social Dar-winism. The most popular exponent of Social Darwinism was the British philosopher Herbert Spencer (1820–1903). Using Darwin's terminology, Spencer argued that societies were organisms that evolved through time from a struggle with their environment. Progress came from "the struggle for survival," as the "fit"—the strong—advanced while the weak declined. As Spencer expressed it in 1896 in his book *Social Statics*:

Pervading all Nature we may see at work a stern discipline which is a little cruel that it may be very kind. . . . Meanwhile, the well-being of existing humanity and the unfolding of it into this ultimate perfection, are both secured by the same beneficial though severe discipline to which the animate creation at large is subject. It seems hard that an unskillfulness, which with all his efforts he cannot overcome, should entail hunger upon the artisan. It seems hard that a laborer, incapacitated by sickness from competing with his stronger fellows, should have to bear the resulting privations. It seems hard that widows and orphans should be left to struggle for life or death. Nevertheless, when

CLAUDE MONET, *IMPRESSION, SUNRISE.*
Impressionists rejected "rules and principles" and sought to paint what they observed and felt in order "not to lose the first impression." As is evident in *Impression, Sunrise*, Monet sought to capture his impression of the fleeting moments of sunrise through the simple interplay of light, water, and atmosphere.

BERTHE MORISOT, *YOUNG GIRL BY THE WINDOW.* Berthe Morisot came from a wealthy French family that settled in Paris when she was seven. The first female painter to join the Impressionists, she developed her own unique Impressionist style. Her gentle colors and strong use of pastels are especially evident in *Young Girl by the Window*, painted in 1878. Many of her paintings focus on women and domestic scenes.

By the 1880s, a new movement known as Post-Impressionism arose in France but soon spread to other European countries. Post-Impressionism retained the Impressionist emphasis upon light and color but revolutionized it even further by paying more attention to structure and form. Post-Impressionists sought to use both color and line to express inner feelings and produce a personal statement of reality rather than an imitation of objects. Impressionist paintings had retained a sense of realism, but the Post-Impressionists shifted from objective reality to subjective reality and, in so doing, began to withdraw from the artist's traditional task of depicting the external world. Post-Impressionism was the real beginning of modern art.

Paul Cézanne (1839–1906) was one of the most important Post-Impressionists. Initially, he was influenced by the Impressionists but soon rejected their work. In his paintings, such as *Woman with Coffee Pot*, Cézanne sought to express visually the underlying structure and form of everything he painted. The geometric shapes (cylinders and triangles) of the human form are related to the geometric shapes (cylinders and rectangles) of the other objects in the picture. As Cézanne explained to one young painter: "You must see in nature the cylinder, the sphere, and the cone."

Another famous Post-Impressionist was the tortured and tragic figure, Vincent van Gogh (1853–1890). For van Gogh, art was a spiritual experience. He was especially interested in color and believed that it could act as its own form of language. Van Gogh maintained that artists should paint what they feel. In his *Starry Night*, he painted a sky alive with whirling stars that overwhelm the buildings huddled in the village below.

By the beginning of the twentieth century, the belief that the task of art was to represent "reality" had lost much of its meaning. By that time, the new psychology and the new physics had made it evident that many people were not sure what constituted reality anyway. Then, too, the development of photography gave artists another reason to reject visual realism. First invented in the 1830s, photography became popular and widespread after George Eastman produced the first Kodak camera for the mass market in 1888. What was the point of an artist doing what the camera did better? Unlike the camera, which could only mirror reality, artists could create reality. As in literature, so also in modern art, individual consciousness became the source of meaning. As one artist expressed it: "Each [artist] should follow where the pulse of his own heart leads. . . . Our pounding heart drives us down, deep down to the source of all. What springs from this source, whether it may be called dream, idea or phantasy—must be taken seriously."[11] Between 1905 and 1914, this search for individual expression produced a wide variety of schools of painting, all of which had their greatest impact after World War I.

By 1905, one of the most important figures in modern art was just beginning his career. Pablo Picasso

PAUL CÉZANNE, *WOMAN WITH COFFEE POT*. Post-Impressionists sought above all to express their inner feelings and capture on canvas their own vision of reality. In *Woman with Coffee Pot*, Paul Cézanne tried to relate the geometric shapes of his central female figure to the geometric shapes of the coffee pot and the rectangles of the door panels.

(1881–1973) was from Spain but settled in Paris in 1904. Picasso was extremely flexible and painted in a remarkable variety of styles. He was instrumental in the development of a new style called Cubism that used geometric designs as visual stimuli to re-create reality in the viewer's mind. Picasso's 1907 work *Les Demoiselles d'Avignon* has been called the first Cubist painting.

The modern artist's flight from "visual reality" reached a high point in 1910 with the beginning of abstract painting. A Russian who worked in Germany, Vasily Kandinsky (1866–1944), was one of the founders of Abstract Expressionism. As is evident in his *Painting with White Border*, Kandinsky sought to avoid representation altogether. He believed that art should speak directly to the soul. To do so, it must avoid any reference to visual reality and concentrate on color.

MODERNISM IN MUSIC

In the first half of the nineteenth century, the Romantics' attraction to exotic and primitive cultures had sparked a fascination with folk music, which became increasingly important as musicians began to look for ways to express

VINCENT VAN GOGH, *THE STARRY NIGHT* (1889).
The Dutch painter Vincent van Gogh was a major figure
among the Post-Impressionists. His originality and power
of expression made a strong impact upon his artistic
successors.

In *The Starry Night*, van Gogh's subjective vision was
given full play as the dynamic swirling forms of the
heavens above overwhelmed the village below. The
heavens seem alive with a mysterious spiritual force.

their national identities. In the second half of the century, new flames of nationalistic spirit were fanned in both literary and musical circles. Nationalistic feelings were expressed in a variety of ways, from the employment of national themes for operas to the incorporation of folk songs and dances in new compositions.

One example of this new nationalistic spirit may be found in the Scandinavian composer Edvard Grieg (1843–1907), who remained a dedicated supporter of Norwegian nationalism throughout his life. Grieg's nationalism expressed itself in the lyric melodies found in the folk music of his homeland. These simple melodies were far better suited to smaller compositional forms, so he tended not to write in the grand symphonic style. Among his best-known works is the *Peer Gynt Suite* (1876), incidental music to Henrik Ibsen's play. Grieg's music paved the way for the creation of a national music style in Norway.

The Impressionist movement in music followed its artistic counterpart by some thirty years. Impressionist music stressed elusive moods and haunting sensations and is distinct in its delicate beauty and elegance of sound. The composer most tangibly linked to the Impressionist movement was Claude Debussy (1862–1918), whose musical compositions were often inspired by the visual arts. The titles that Debussy often assigned to his works, such as *Sketches*, *Images*, and *Prints*, are indicative of this close association between painters and musicians.

One of Debussy's most famous works, *Prelude to the Afternoon of a Faun* (1894), was actually inspired by a poem, "Afternoon of a Faun," composed by his friend, the Symbolist poet Stéphane Mallarmé. But Debussy did not tell a story in music, as was the goal of the Romantic tone poems. Rather, *Prelude to the Afternoon of a Faun* re-created in sound the overall feeling of the poem. Said

PABLO PICASSO, *LES DEMOISELLES D'AVIGNON* (1907). Pablo Picasso, a major pioneer and activist of modern art, experimented with a remarkable variety of modern styles. His *Les Demoiselles d'Avignon* was the first great example of Cubism, which one art historian has called "the first style of this century to break radically with the past." Geometric shapes replace traditional forms, forcing the viewer to re-create reality in his or her own mind.

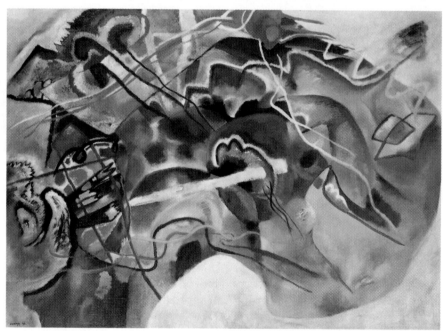

VASILY KANDINSKY, *COMPOSITION VIII, NO. 2 (PAINTING WITH WHITE BORDER).* One of the founders of Abstract Expressionism was the Russian Vasily Kandinsky, who sought to eliminate representation altogether by focusing on color and avoiding any resemblance to visual reality. In *Painting with White Border,* Kandinsky used color "to send light into the darkness of men's hearts." He believed that color, like music, could fulfill a spiritual goal of appealing directly to the human being.

Mallarmé upon listening to Debussy's piece, "I was not expecting anything like this. This music prolongs the emotion of my poem, and evokes the scene more vividly than color."[12]

Other composers adopted stylistic idioms that imitated presumably primitive forms in an attempt to express less refined, and therefore more genuine, feelings. A chief exponent of musical primitivism was Igor Stravinsky (1882–1971), one of the twentieth century's most important composers, both for his compositions and for his impact on other composers. He gained international fame as a ballet composer and together with the Ballet Russe, under the direction of Sergei Diaghilev (1872–1929), rev-

olutionized the world of music with a series of ballets. The three most significant ballets Stravinsky composed for Diaghilev's company were *The Firebird* (1910), *Petrushka* (1911), and *The Rite of Spring* (1913). All three were based on Russian folk tales. *The Rite of Spring* proved to be a revolutionary piece in the development of music. At the premiere on May 29, 1913, the pulsating rhythms, sharp dissonances, and unusual dancing overwhelmed the Paris audience and caused a riot at the theater. Like the intellectuals of his time, Stravinsky sought a new understanding of irrational forces in his music, which became an important force in inaugurating a modern musical movement.

◆ Politics: New Directions and New Uncertainties

The uncertainties in European intellectual and cultural life were paralleled by growing anxieties in European political life. The seemingly steady progress in the growth of liberal principles and political democracy after 1871 was soon slowed or even halted altogether after 1894. The new mass politics had opened the door to changes that many nineteenth-century liberals found unacceptable, and liberals themselves were forced to move in new directions. The appearance of a new right-wing politics based on racism added an ugly note to the already existing anxieties. With their newfound voting rights, workers elected socialists who demanded new reforms when they took their places in legislative bodies. Women, too, made new demands, insisting on the right to vote and using new tactics to gain it. In central and eastern Europe, tensions grew as authoritarian governments refused to meet the demands of reformers. And outside Europe, a new giant appeared in the Western world as the United States emerged as a great industrial power with immense potential.

✺ *The Movement for Women's Rights*

In the 1830s, a number of women in the United States and Europe, who worked together in several reform movements, became frustrated by the apparent prejudices against females. They sought improvements for women by focusing on specific goals. Family and marriage laws were especially singled out since it was difficult for women to secure divorces and property laws gave husbands almost complete control over the property of their wives. These early efforts were not overly successful, however. For example, women did not gain the right to their own property until 1870 in Britain, 1900 in Germany, and 1907 in France. Although the British legalized divorce in 1857, the French state permitted only a limited degree of divorce in 1884. In Catholic countries such as Spain and Italy, women had no success at all in achieving the right to divorce their husbands.

Custody and property rights were only a beginning for the women's movement, however. Some middle- and upper-middle-class women gained access to higher education, and others sought entry into occupations dominated by men. The first to fall was teaching. As medical training was largely closed to women, they sought alternatives in the development of nursing. One nursing pioneer was Amalie Sieveking (1794–1859), who founded the Female Association for the Care of the Poor and Sick in Hamburg, Germany. As she explained: "To me, at least as important were the benefits which [work with the poor] seemed to promise for those of my sisters who would join me in such a work of charity. The higher interests of my sex were close to my heart."[13] Sieveking's work was followed by the more famous British nurse, Florence Nightingale (1820–1910), whose efforts during the Crimean War, along with those of Clara Barton (1821–1912) in the American Civil War, transformed nursing into a profession of trained, middle-class "women in white."

By the 1840s and 1850s, the movement for women's rights had entered the political arena with the call for equal political rights. Many feminists believed that the right to vote was the key to all other reforms to improve the position of women. This movement was most vibrant in Great Britain and the United States, both countries that had been influenced by the natural rights tradition of the Enlightenment. It was not as strong in Germany because of that country's authoritarian makeup nor in France where feminists were unable to organize mass rallies in support of women's rights.

The British women's movement was the most vocal and active in Europe, but divided over tactics. The liberal Millicent Fawcett (1847–1929) organized a moderate group who believed that women must demonstrate that they would use political power responsibly if they wanted Parliament to grant them the right to vote. Another group, however, favored a more radical approach. Emmeline Pankhurst (1858–1928) and her daughters, Christabel and Sylvia, founded the Women's Social and Political Union in 1903, which enrolled mostly middle- and upper-class women. Pankhurst's organization realized the value of the media and used unusual publicity stunts to call attention to its demands. Derisively labeled suffragettes by male politicians, they pelted government officials with eggs, chained themselves to lampposts, smashed the windows of department stores on fashionable shopping

THE ARREST OF SUFFRAGISTS. **The nineteenth century witnessed the development of a strong movement for women's rights. For many feminists, the right to vote came to represent the key to other reforms that would benefit women. In Britain, suffragists attracted attention to their cause by unusual publicity stunts. This photograph shows the arrest of suffragists after a demonstration near Buckingham Palace, the London residence of the royal family.**

streets, burned railroad cars, and went on hunger strikes in jail. In 1913, Emily Davison accepted martyrdom for the cause when she threw herself in front of the king's horse at the Epsom Derby horse race. Suffragists had one fundamental aim, the right of women to full citizenship in the nation-state.

Although few women elsewhere in Europe used the Pankhursts' confrontational methods, demands for women's rights were heard throughout Europe and the United States before World War I. Nevertheless, only in Finland, Norway, and some American states did women actually receive the right to vote before 1914. It would take the dramatic upheaval of World War I before male-dominated governments capitulated on this basic issue (see Chapter 25).

Women reformers took on other issues besides suffrage. In many countries, women supported peace movements. Bertha von Suttner (1843–1914) became the head of the Austrian Peace Society and protested against the growing arms race of the1890s. Her novel *Lay Down Your Arms* became a best-seller and brought her the Nobel Peace Prize in 1905. Lower-class women also took up the cause of peace. In 1911, a group of female workers marched in Vienna and demanded: "We want an end to armaments, to the means of murder and we want these millions to be spent on the needs of the people."[14]

THE NEW WOMAN

Bertha von Suttner was only one of the "new women" who were becoming more prominent at the turn of the century. These women renounced traditional feminine roles (see the box on p. 725). Although some of them supported political ideologies such as socialism that flew in the face of the ruling classes, others simply sought new freedom outside the household and new roles other than those of wives and mothers.

Maria Montessori (1870–1952) was a good example of the "new woman." Breaking with tradition, she attended medical school at the University of Rome. Although often isolated by the male students, she persisted and in 1896 became the first Italian woman to receive a medical degree. Three years later she undertook a lecture tour in Italy on the subject of "The New Woman," whom she characterized as a woman who followed a rational, scientific perspective. In keeping with this ideal, Montessori put her medical background to work in a school for mentally retarded children. She devised new teaching materials that enabled these children to read and write and became convinced, as she later wrote, "that similar methods applied to normal students would develop or set free their personality in a marvelous and surprising way." Subsequently, she established a system of childhood education based on natural and spontaneous activities in which students learned at their own pace. By the 1930s, hundreds of Montessori schools had been established in Europe and the United States. As a professional woman and an unwed mother, Montessori also embodied some of the freedoms of the "new woman."

✻ Jews within the European Nation-State

Near the end of the nineteenth century, a revival of racism combined with extreme nationalism to produce a new right-wing politics aimed primarily at the Jews. Of course, anti-Semitism was not new to European civilization. Since the Middle Ages, Jews had been portrayed as the murderers of Jesus and subjected to mob violence; their rights had been restricted, and they had been physically separated from Christians in quarters known as ghettos.

In the nineteenth century, as a result of the ideals of the Enlightenment and the French Revolution, Jews were increasingly granted legal equality in many European countries. The French revolutionary decrees of 1790 and 1791 emancipated the Jews and admitted them to full citizenship. They were not completely accepted, however, and anti-Semitism remained a fact of French life. In 1805, Napoleon consolidated their position as citizens, but followed this in 1808 with an "Infamous Decree" that placed restrictions on Jewish moneylending and on the movement of Jews within France.

This ambivalence toward the Jews was apparent throughout Europe. In Prussia, for example, Jews were emancipated in 1812 but still restricted. They could not hold government offices or take advanced degrees in universities. After the revolutions of 1848, emancipation became a fact of life for Jews throughout western and central Europe. For many Jews, emancipation enabled them to leave the ghetto and become assimilated as hundreds of thousands of Jews entered what had been the closed worlds of parliaments and universities. In 1880, for example, Jews made up 10 percent of the population of the city of Vienna, Austria, but 39 percent of its medical students and 23 percent of its law students. "A Jew could leave his Jewishness" behind as the career of Benjamin Disraeli, who became prime minister of Great Britain, demonstrated. Many other Jews became eminently successful as bankers, lawyers, scientists, scholars, journalists, and stage performers.

These achievements represent only one side of the picture, however, as is evident from the Dreyfus affair in France. Alfred Dreyfus, a Jew, was a captain in the French general staff. Early in 1895, a secret military court found him guilty of selling army secrets and condemned him to life imprisonment on Devil's Island. During his trial, right-wing mobs yelled "Death to the Jews." Soon after the trial, however, evidence emerged that pointed to Dreyfus's innocence. The government pardoned Dreyfus in 1899, and in 1906, he was finally fully exonerated.

In Austrian politics, the Christian Socialists combined agitation for workers with a virulent anti-Semitism. They were most powerful in Vienna where they were led by Karl Lueger, mayor of Vienna from 1897 to 1910. Imperial Vienna at the turn of the century was a brilliant center of European culture, but it was also the home of an insidious German nationalism that blamed Jews for the corruption of German culture. It was in Vienna between 1907 and 1913 that Adolf Hitler later claimed to have

Advice to Women: Be Independent

Although a majority of women probably followed the nineteenth-century middle-class ideal of women as keepers of the household and nurturers of husband and children, an increasing number of women fought for the rights of women. This selection is taken from Act III of Henrik Ibsen's A Doll's House *(1879), in which the character Nora Helmer declares her independence from her husband's control.*

❋ Henrik Ibsen, *A Doll's House*

NORA (*Pause*): Does anything strike you as we sit here?

HELMER: What should strike me?

NORA: We've been married eight years; does it not strike you that this is the first time we two, you and I, man and wife, have talked together seriously?

HELMER: Seriously? What do you mean, *seriously*?

NORA: For eight whole years, and more—ever since the day we first met—we have never exchanged one serious word about serious things. . . .

HELMER: Why, my dearest Nora, what have you to do with serious things?

NORA: There we have it! You have never understood me. I've had great injustice done to me, Torvald; first by father, then by you.

HELMER: What! Your father *and* me? We, who have loved you more than all the world!

NORA (*Shaking her head*): You have never loved me. You just found it amusing to think you were in love with me.

HELMER: Nora! What a thing to say!

NORA: Yes, it's true, Torvald. When I was living at home with father, he told me his opinions and mine were the same. If I had different opinions, I said nothing about them, because he would not have liked it. He used to call me his doll-child and played with me as I played with my dolls. Then I came to live in your house.

HELMER: What a way to speak of our marriage!

NORA (*Undisturbed*): I mean that I passed from father's hands into yours. You arranged everything to your taste and I got the same tastes as you; or pretended to—I don't know which—both, perhaps; sometimes one, sometimes the other. When I look back on it now, I seem to have been living here like a beggar, on handouts. I lived by performing tricks for you, Torvald. But that was how you wanted it. You and father have done me a great wrong. It is your fault that my life has come to naught.

HELMER: Why, Nora, how unreasonable and ungrateful! Haven't you been happy here?

NORA: No, never. I thought I was, but I never was.

HELMER: Not—not happy! . . .

NORA: I must stand quite alone if I am ever to know myself and my surroundings; so I cannot stay with you.

HELMER: Nora! Nora!

NORA: I am going at once. I daresay [my friend] Christina will take me in for tonight.

HELMER: You are mad! I shall not allow it! I forbid it!

NORA: It's no use your forbidding me anything now. I shall take with me only what belongs to me; from you I will accept nothing, either now or later.

HELMER: This is madness!

NORA: Tomorrow I shall go home—I mean to what was my home. It will be easier for me to find a job there.

HELMER: On, in your blind inexperience—

NORA: I must try to gain experience, Torvald.

HELMER: Forsake your home, your husband, your children! And you don't consider what the world will say.

NORA: I can't pay attention to that. I only know that I must do it.

HELMER: This is monstrous! Can you forsake your holiest duties?

NORA: What do you consider my holiest duties?

HELMER: Need I tell you that? Your duties to your husband and children.

NORA: I have other duties equally sacred.

HELMER: Impossible! What do you mean?

NORA: My duties toward myself.

HELMER: Before all else you are a wife and a mother.

NORA: That I no longer believe. Before all else I believe I am a human being just as much as you are—or at least that I should try to become one. I know that most people agree with you, Torvald, and that they say so in books. But I can no longer be satisfied with what most people say and what is in books. I must think things out for myself and try to get clear about them.

---

found his worldview, one that was largely based on a violent German nationalism and a rabid anti-Semitism.

Germany, too, had its right-wing anti-Semitic parties, such as Adolf Stocker's Christian Social Workers. These parties used anti-Semitism to win the votes of traditional lower-middle-class groups who felt threatened by the new economic forces of the times. These German anti-Semitic parties were based on race. In medieval times Jews could convert to Christianity and escape from their religion. To modern racial anti-Semites, Jews were racially stained; this could not be altered by conversion. One could not be both German and Jew. Hermann Ahlwardt, an anti-Semitic member of the German Reichstag, made this clear in a speech to that body: "The Jew is no German. . . . A Jew who was born in Germany does not thereby become a German; he is still a Jew. Therefore it is imperative that we

THEODOR HERZL. A journalist for a Viennese newspaper, Herzl became an ardent advocate of political Zionism. In *The Jewish State*, he argued for the creation of a Jewish state in Palestine. He is seen here in Basel, Switzerland, where he was attending an international Zionist congress that he had helped to organize.

realize that Jewish racial characteristics differ so greatly from ours that a common life of Jews and Germans under the same laws is quite impossible because the Germans will perish."[15] After 1898, the political strength of the German anti-Semitic parties began to decline.

The worst treatment of Jews in the last two decades of the nineteenth century and the first decade of the twentieth occurred in eastern Europe where 72 percent of the entire world Jewish population lived. Russian Jews were admitted to secondary schools and universities only under a quota system and were forced to live in certain regions of the country. Persecutions and pogroms were widespread. Between 1903 and 1906, pogroms took place in almost 700 Russian towns and villages, mostly in Ukraine. Hundreds of thousands of Jews decided to emigrate to escape the persecution. Between 1881 and 1899, an average of 23,000 Jews left Russia each year. Many of them went to the United States and Canada, although some (probably about 25,000) moved to Palestine, which soon became the focus for a Jewish nationalist movement called Zionism.

The emancipation of the nineteenth century had presented vast opportunities for some Jews, but dilemmas for others. What was the price of citizenship? Did emanci-

pation mean full assimilation, and did assimilation mean the disruption of traditional Jewish life? Many paid the price willingly, but others questioned its value and advocated a different answer, a return to Palestine. For many Jews, Palestine, the land of ancient Israel, had long been the land of their dreams. During the nineteenth century, as nationalist ideas spread and Italians, Poles, Irish, Greeks, and others sought national emancipation so too did the idea of national independence capture the imagination of some Jews. A key figure in the growth of political Zionism was Theodor Herzl (1860–1904). Herzl had received a law degree in Vienna where he became a journalist for a Viennese newspaper. He was shocked into action on behalf of Jews when he covered the Dreyfus trial as a correspondent for his newspaper in Paris. In 1896, he published a book called *The Jewish State* (see the box on p. 727) in which he straightforwardly advocated that "the Jews who wish it will have their state." Financial support for the development of yishuvs, or settlements in Palestine, came from wealthy Jewish banking families who wanted a refuge in Palestine for persecuted Jews, not a political Jewish state. Even settlements were difficult because Palestine was then part of the Ottoman Empire and Ottoman authorities were opposed to Jewish immi-

The Voice of Zionism: Theodor Herzl and the Jewish State

The Austrian Jewish journalist Theodor Herzl wrote The Jewish State *in the summer of 1895 in Paris while he was covering the Dreyfus case for his Vienna newspaper. During several weeks of feverish composition, he set out to analyze the fundamental causes of anti-Semitism and devise a solution to the "Jewish problem." In this selection, he discusses two of his major conclusions.*

✻ Theodor Herzl, *The Jewish State*

I do not intend to arouse sympathetic emotions on our behalf. That would be a foolish, futile, and undignified proceeding. I shall content myself with putting the following questions to the Jews: Is it true that, in countries where we live in perceptible numbers, the position of Jewish lawyers, doctors, technicians, teachers, and employees of all descriptions becomes daily more intolerable? True, that the Jewish middle classes are seriously threatened? True, that the passions of the mob are incited against our wealthy people? True, that our poor endure greater sufferings than any other proletariat?

I think that this external pressure makes itself felt everywhere. In our economically upper classes it causes discomfort, in our middle classes continual and grave anxieties, in our lower classes absolute despair.

Everything tends, in fact, to one and the same conclusion, which is clearly enunciated in that classic Berlin phrase: "Juden 'raus!" (Out with the Jews!)

I shall now put the Jewish Question in the curtest possible form: Are we to "get out" now? And if so, to what place?

Or, may we yet remain? And if so, how long?

Let us first settle the point of staying where we are. Can we hope for better days, can we possess our souls in patience, can we wait in pious resignation till the princes and peoples of this earth are more mercifully disposed toward us? I say that we cannot hope for a change in the current of feeling. And why not? Were we

as near to the hearts of princes as are their other subjects, even so they could not protect us. They would only feed popular hatred of Jews by showing us too much favor. By "too much," I really mean less than is claimed as a right by every ordinary citizen, or by every race. The nations in whose midst Jews live are all, either covertly or openly, Anti-Semitic. . . .

The whole plan is in its essence perfectly simple, as it must necessarily be if it is to come within the comprehension of all.

Let the sovereignty be granted us over a portion of the globe large enough to satisfy the rightful requirements of a nation; the rest we shall manage for ourselves.

The creation of a new State is neither ridiculous nor impossible. We have in our day witnessed the process in connection with nations which were not in the bulk of the middle class, but poorer, less educated, and consequently weaker than ourselves. The Governments of all countries scourged by Anti-Semitism will be keenly interested in assisting us to obtain the sovereignty we want. . . .

Palestine is our ever-memorable historic home. The very name of Palestine would attract our people with a force of marvelous potency. Supposing his Majesty the Sultan were to give us Palestine, we could in return undertake to regulate the whole finances of Turkey. We should there form a portion of the rampart of Europe against Asia, an outpost of civilization as opposed to barbarism. We should as a neutral State remain in contact with all Europe, which would have to guarantee our existence. The sanctuaries of Christendom would be safeguarded by assigning to them an extra-territorial status such as is well known to the law of nations. We should form a guard of honor about these sanctuaries, answering for the fulfillment of this duty with our existence. This guard of honor would be the great symbol of the solution of the Jewish Question after eighteen centuries of Jewish suffering.

---

gration. In 1891, one Jewish essayist pointed to the problems this would create:

> We abroad are accustomed to believe that Erez Israel [the land of Israel] is almost totally desolate at present . . . but in reality it is not so. . . . Arabs, especially those in towns, see and understand our activities and aims in the country but keep quiet and pretend as if they did not know, . . . and they try to exploit us, too, and profit from the new guests while laughing at us in their hearts. But if the time comes and our people make such progress as to displace the people of the country . . . they will not lightly surrender the place.[16]

Despite the warnings, however, the First Zionist Congress, which met in Switzerland in 1897, proclaimed as its aim

the creation of a "home in Palestine secured by public law" for the Jewish people. In 1900, 1,000 Jews migrated to Palestine. Although 3,000 Jews went annually to Palestine between 1904 and 1914, the Zionist dream remained just that on the eve of World War I.

✻ The Transformation of Liberalism: Great Britain and Italy

In dealing with the problems created by the new mass politics, liberal governments often followed policies that undermined the basic tenets of liberalism. This was certainly true in Great Britain, where the demands of the working-class movement caused Liberals to move away from their ideals. Although workers were enjoying better wages and living standards, those improvements were relative to the miseries of the first half of the nineteenth century. Considerable suffering still remained. Neither Liberals nor Conservatives were moved to accommodate the working class with significant social reforms until they were forced to do so by the pressure of two new working-class organizations: trade unions and the Labour Party.

Trade unions began to advocate more radical change of the economic system, calling for "collective ownership and control over production, distribution and exchange." At the same time, a movement for laborers emerged among a group of intellectuals known as the Fabian Socialists who stressed the need for the workers to use their right to vote to capture the House of Commons and pass legislation that would benefit the laboring class. Neither the Fabian Socialists nor the British trade unions were Marxist oriented. They did not advocate class struggle and revolution but evolution toward a socialist state by democratic means. In 1900, representatives of the trade unions and Fabian Socialists coalesced to form the Labour Party. Initially, they were not too successful, but by 1906 they had managed to elect twenty-nine members to the House of Commons.

The Liberals, who gained control of the House of Commons in that year and held the government from 1906 to 1914, perceived that they would have to enact a program of social welfare or lose the support of the workers. The policy of reform was especially advanced by David Lloyd George (1863–1945), a brilliant young orator from Wales who had been deeply moved by the misery of Welsh coal miners. The Liberals abandoned the classical principles of laissez-faire and voted for a series of social reforms. The National Insurance Act of 1911 provided benefits for workers in case of sickness and unemployment, to be financed by compulsory contributions from workers, employers, and the state. Additional legislation provided a small pension for those over seventy and compensation for those injured in accidents while at work. To pay for the new program, Lloyd George increased the tax burden on the wealthy classes. Though both the benefits of the program and the tax increases were modest, they were the first hesitant steps toward the future British welfare state. Liberalism, which had been based on the principle that the government that governs least governs best, had been transformed.

Liberals had even greater problems in Italy. A certain amount of stability was achieved from 1903 to 1914 when the liberal leader Giovanni Giolitti served intermittently as prime minister. Giolitti was a master of using *trasformismo* or transformism, a system in which old political groups were transformed into new government coalitions by political and economic bribery. In the long run, however, Giolitti's devious methods made Italian politics even more corrupt and unmanageable. When urban workers turned to violence to protest their living and working conditions, Giolitti tried to appease them with social welfare legisla-

tion and universal male suffrage in 1912. To strengthen his popularity, he also aroused nationalistic passions by conquering Libya. Despite his efforts, however, worker unrest continued, and in 1914 government troops had to be used to crush rioting workers.

❀ *Growing Tensions in Germany*

The new imperial Germany begun by Bismarck in 1871 continued as an "authoritarian, conservative, military-bureaucratic power state" during the reign of Emperor William II (1888–1918). Unstable and aggressive, the emperor was inclined to tactless remarks, as when he told the soldiers of a Berlin regiment that they must be prepared to shoot their fathers and mothers if he ordered them to do so. A small group of about twenty powerful men joined William in setting government policy.

By 1914, Germany had become the strongest military and industrial power on the Continent. New social configurations had emerged as over 50 percent of German workers had jobs in industry while only 30 percent of the workforce was still in agriculture. Urban centers had mushroomed in number and size. The rapid changes in William's Germany helped to produce a society torn between modernization and traditionalism.

The growth of industrialization led to even greater expansion for the Social Democratic Party. Despite the enactment of new welfare legislation to favor the working classes, William II was no more successful than Bismarck at slowing the growth of the Social Democrats. By 1912, it had become the largest single party in the Reichstag. At the same time, the party increasingly became less revolutionary and more revisionist in its outlook. Nevertheless, its growth frightened the middle and upper classes who blamed labor for their own problems.

With the expansion of industry and cities came demands for more political participation and growing sentiment for reforms that would produce greater democratization. Conservative forces, especially the landowning nobility and representatives of heavy industry, two of the powerful ruling groups in Germany, tried to block it by supporting William II's activist foreign policy (see New Directions and New Crises later in this chapter). Expansionism, they believed, would divert people from further democratization.

The tensions in German society created by the conflict between modernization and traditionalism were also manifested in a new, radicalized, right-wing politics. A number of nationalist pressure groups arose to support nationalistic goals. Antisocialist and antiliberal, such groups as the Pan-German League stressed strong German nationalism and advocated imperialism as a tool to overcome social divisions and unite all classes. They were also anti-Semitic and denounced Jews as the destroyers of the national community. Traditional conservatives, frightened by the growth of the socialists, often made common cause with these radical right-wing groups, giving them respectability.

Industrialization and Revolution in Imperial Russia

Starting in the 1890s, Russia experienced a massive surge of state-sponsored industrialism under the guiding hand of Sergei Witte (1849–1915), the minister for finance from 1892 to 1903. Count Witte saw industrial growth as crucial to Russia's national strength. Believing that railroads were a very powerful weapon in economic development, Witte pushed the government toward a program of massive railroad construction. By 1900, 35,000 miles of railroads, including large parts of the 5,000-mile trans-Siberian line between Moscow and Vladivostok on the Pacific Ocean, had been built. Witte also encouraged a system of protective tariffs to help Russian industry and persuaded Tsar Nicholas II (1894–1917) that foreign capital was essential for rapid industrial development. Witte's program made possible the rapid growth of a modern steel and coal industry in Ukraine, making Russia by 1900 the fourth largest producer of steel behind the United States, Germany, and Great Britain.

With industrialization came factories, an industrial working class, industrial suburbs around St. Petersburg and Moscow, and the pitiful working and living conditions that accompanied the beginnings of industrialization everywhere. Socialist thought and socialist parties developed, although repression in Russia soon forced them to go underground and become revolutionary. The Marxist Social Democratic Party, for example, held its first congress in Minsk in 1898, but the arrest of its leaders caused the next one to be held in Brussels in 1903, attended by Russian émigrés. The Social Revolutionaries worked to overthrow the tsarist autocracy and establish peasant socialism. Having no other outlet for their opposition to the regime, they advocated political terrorism and attempted to assassinate government officials and members of the ruling dynasty. The growing opposition to the tsarist regime finally exploded into revolution in 1905.

THE REVOLUTION OF 1905

As had happened elsewhere in Europe in the nineteenth century, defeat in war led to political upheaval at home. Russia's territorial expansion to the south and east, especially its designs on northern Korea, led to a confrontation with Japan. Japan made a surprise attack on the Russian eastern fleet at Port Arthur on February 8, 1904. In turn, Russia sent its Baltic fleet halfway around the world to the East, only to be defeated by the new Japanese navy at Tsushima Strait off the coast of Japan. Much to the astonishment of many Europeans who could not believe that an Asian state was militarily superior to a great European power, the Russians admitted defeat and sued for peace in 1905.

In the midst of the war, the growing discontent of increased numbers of Russians rapidly led to upheaval. A middle class of business and professional people longed for liberal institutions and a liberal political system. Nationalities were dissatisfied with their domination by an ethnic Russian population that constituted only 45 percent of the empire's total population. Peasants were still suffering from lack of land, and laborers felt oppressed by their working and living conditions in Russia's large cities. The breakdown of the transport system caused by the Russo-Japanese War led to food shortages in the major cities of Russia. As a result, on January 9, 1905, a massive procession of workers went to the Winter Palace in St. Petersburg to present a petition of grievances to the tsar (see the box on p. 730). Troops foolishly opened fire on the peaceful demonstration, killing hundreds and launching a revolution. This "Bloody Sunday" incited workers to call strikes and form unions; meanwhile zemstvos demanded the formation of parliamentary government, ethnic groups revolted, and peasants burned the houses of landowners. After a general strike in October 1905, the government capitulated. Count Witte had advised the tsar to divide his opponents: "It is not on the extremists that the existence

NICHOLAS II. **The last tsar of Russia hoped to preserve the traditional autocratic ways of his predecessors. In this photograph, Nicholas II and his wife Alexandra are shown returning from a church at Tsarskoe-Selo.**

Russian Workers Appeal to the Tsar

On January 9, 1905, a massive procession of workers led by a Russian Orthodox priest loyal to the tsar, Father George Gapon, carried a petition to present to the tsar at his imperial palace in St. Petersburg. Although the tsar was not even there, government officials ordered troops to fire on the crowd. "Bloody Sunday," as it was called, precipitated the Revolution of 1905. This selection is an excerpt from the petition that was never presented.

❈ George Gapon and Ivan Vasimov, Petition to the Tsar

Sovereign!

We, the workers and the inhabitants of various social strata of the city of St. Petersburg, our wives, children, and helpless old parents, have come to you, Sovereign, to seek justice and protection. We are impoverished; our employers oppress us, overburden us with work, insult us, consider us inhuman, and treat us as slaves who must suffer a bitter fate in silence. Though we have suffered, they push us deeper and deeper into a gulf of misery, disfranchisement, and ignorance. Despotism and arbitrariness strangle us and we are gasping for breath. Sovereign, we have no strength left. We have reached the limit of endurance. We have reached that terrible moment when death is preferable to the continuance of unbearable sufferings.

And so we left our work and informed our employers that we shall not resume work until they meet our demands. We do not demand much; we only want what is indispensable to life and without which life is nothing but hard labor and eternal suffering. Our first request was that our employers discuss our needs jointly with us. But they refused to do this; they even denied us the right to speak about our needs, saying that the law does not give us such a right. Also unlawful were our requests to reduce the working day to eight hours, to set wages jointly with us; to examine our disputes with lower echelons of factory administration; to increase the wages of unskilled workers and women to one ruble [about $1.00] per day; to abolish overtime work; to provide medical care without insult. . . .

Sovereign, there are thousands of us here; outwardly we resemble human beings, but in reality neither we nor the Russian people as a whole enjoy any human right, have any right to speak, to think, to assemble, to discuss our needs, or to take measures to improve our conditions. They have enslaved us and they did it under the protection of your officials, with their aid and with their cooperation. They imprison and send into exile any one of us who has the courage to speak on behalf of the interests of the working class and of the people. . . . All the workers and the peasants are at the mercy of bureaucratic administrators consisting of embezzlers of public funds and thieves who not only disregard the interests of the people but also scorn these interests. . . . The people are deprived of the opportunity to express their wishes and their demands and to participate in determining taxes and expenditures. The workers are deprived of the opportunity to organize themselves in unions to protect their interests.

Sovereign! Is all this compatible with God's laws, by the grace of which you reign? And is it possible to live under such laws? Wouldn't it be better for all of us if we, the toiling people of all Russia, died? . . . Sovereign, these are the problems that we face and these are the reasons that we have gathered before the walls of your palace. Here we seek our last salvation. Do not refuse to come to the aid of your people.

---

and integrity of the state depend. As long as the government has support in the broad strata of society, a peaceful solution to the crisis is still possible."[17] Nicholas II issued the October Manifesto, in which he granted civil liberties and agreed to create a Duma, or legislative assembly, elected directly by a broad franchise. This satisfied the middle-class moderates who now supported the government's repression of a workers' uprising in Moscow at the end of 1905.

But real constitutional monarchy proved short-lived. Under Peter Stolypin, who served as the tsar's chief adviser from late 1906 until his assassination in 1911, important agrarian reforms dissolved the village ownership of land and opened the door to private ownership by enterprising peasants. Nicholas II, however, was no friend of reform. Already by 1907, the tsar had curtailed the power of the Duma, and after Stolypin's murder he fell back on the army and bureaucracy to rule Russia. World War I would give revolutionary forces another chance to undo the tsarist regime, and this time they would not fail.

❈ The Rise of the United States

Between 1860 and 1914, the United States made the shift from an agrarian to a mighty industrial nation. American heavy industry stood unchallenged in 1900. In that year, the Carnegie Steel Company alone produced more steel than Great Britain's entire steel industry. Industrialization also led to urbanization. While established cities, such as New York, Philadelphia, and Boston, grew even larger, other moderate-size cities, such as Pittsburgh, grew by leaps and bounds because of industrialization. Whereas 20 percent of Americans lived in cities in 1860, over 40 percent did in 1900. Four-fifths of the population growth in cities came from migration. Eight to 10 million Americans moved from rural areas into the cities, and 14 million foreigners came from abroad.

By 1900, the United States had become the world's richest nation and greatest industrial power. Yet serious questions remained about the quality of American life. In 1890, the richest 9 percent of Americans owned an incredible 71 percent of all the wealth. Labor unrest over unsafe working conditions, strict work discipline, and periodic cycles of devastating unemployment led workers to organize. By the turn of the century, one national organization, the American Federation of Labor, emerged as labor's dominant voice. Its lack of real power, however, is reflected in its membership figures. In 1900, it included only 8.4 percent of the American industrial labor force.

During the so-called Progressive Era after 1900, an age of reform swept through the United States. At the state level, reforming governors sought to achieve clean government by introducing elements of direct democracy, such as direct primaries for selecting nominees for public office. State governments also enacted economic and social legislation, such as laws that governed hours, wages, and working conditions, especially for women and children. The realization that state laws were ineffective in dealing with nationwide problems, however, led to a Progressive movement at the national level. The Meat Inspection Act and Pure Food and Drug Act provided for a limited degree of federal regulation of corrupt industrial practices. The presidency of Woodrow Wilson (1913–1921)

witnessed the creation of a graduated federal income tax and the establishment of the Federal Reserve System, which permitted the federal government to play a role in important economic decisions formerly made by bankers. Like European nations, the United States was slowly adopting policies that extended the functions of the state.

❈ The Growth of Canada

Canada faced problems of national unity at the end of the nineteenth century. At the beginning of 1870, the Dominion of Canada had four provinces: Quebec, Ontario, Nova Scotia, and New Brunswick. With the addition of two more provinces in 1871—Manitoba and Briish Columbia—the Dominion of Canada extended from the Atlantic to the Pacific.

Real unity was difficult to achieve, however, because of the distrust between the English-speaking and French-speaking peoples of Canada. Wilfred Laurier, who became the first French-Canadian prime minister in 1896, was able to reconcile Canada's two major groups. During his administration, industrialization boomed and immigrants from Europe helped to populate Canada's vast territories.

◆ The New Imperialism

Beginning in the 1880s, European states engaged in an intense scramble for overseas territory. This revival of imperialism, or the "new imperialism" as some have called it, led Europeans to carve up Asia and Africa. But why did Europeans begin their mad scramble for colonies after 1880?

❈ Causes of the New Imperialism

The existence of competitive nation-states after 1870 was undoubtedly a major determinant in the growth of this new imperialism. As European affairs grew tense, heightened competition led European states to acquire colonies abroad that provided ports and coaling stations for their navies. Colonies were also a source of international prestige. Once the scramble for colonies began, failure to enter the race was perceived as a sign of weakness, totally unacceptable to an aspiring great power.

Late nineteenth-century imperialism, then, was closely tied to nationalism. After the unification of Italy and Germany in 1871, nationalism entered a new stage of development. In the first half of the nineteenth century, nationalism had been closely identified with liberals who had pursued both individual rights and national unification and independence. Liberal nationalists maintained that unified, independent nation-states could best preserve individual rights. The new nationalism of the late nineteenth century, tied to conservatism, was loud and chauvinistic. As one exponent expressed it: "A true nationalist places his country above everything"; he believes in the "exclusive pursuit of national policies" and "the steady increase in national power—for a nation declines when it loses military might."

Then, too, imperialism was tied to Social Darwinism and racism. Social Darwinists believed that in the struggle between nations, the fit are victorious and survive. Superior races must dominate inferior races by military force to show how strong and virile they are. As British professor of mathematics Karl Pearson arrogantly argued in 1900: "The path of progress is strewn with the wrecks of nations; traces are everywhere to be seen of the [slaughtered remains] of inferior races. . . . Yet these dead people are, in very truth, the stepping stones on which mankind has arisen to the higher intellectual and deeper emotional life of today."[18] Others were equally blunt. One Englishman wrote: "To the development of the White Man, the Black Man and the Yellow must ever remain inferior, and as the former raised itself higher and yet higher, so did these latter seem to shrink out of humanity and appear nearer and nearer to the brutes."[19]

A more religious-humanitarian approach to imperialism was taken by some Europeans when they argued that Europeans had a moral responsibility to civilize ignorant peoples. This notion of the "white man's burden" (see the box on p. 734) helped at least the more idealistic individuals to rationalize imperialism in their own minds. Nevertheless, the belief that the superiority of their civilization obligated them to impose modern cities and new medicines on supposedly primitive nonwhites was yet another form of racism.

Some historians have emphasized an economic motivation for imperialism. There was a great demand for natural resources and products not found in Western countries, such as rubber, oil, and tin. Instead of just trading for these products, European investors advocated direct control of the areas where the raw materials were found. The large surpluses of capital that bankers and industrialists were accumulating often encouraged them to seek higher rates of profit in underdeveloped areas. All of these factors combined to create an economic imperialism whereby European finance dominated the economic activity of a large part of the world. This economic imperialism, however, was not necessarily the same thing as colonial expansion. Businesses invested where it was most profitable, not necessarily where their own countries had colonial empires. For example, less than 10 percent of French foreign investments before 1914 went to French colonies; most of the rest went to Latin American and European countries. It should also be remembered that much of the colonial territory that was acquired was mere wasteland from the point of view of industrialized Europe and cost more to administer than it produced economically. Only the search for national prestige could justify such losses.

Followers of Karl Marx were especially eager to argue that imperialism was economically motivated because they associated imperialism with the ultimate demise of the capitalist system. Marx had hinted at this argument, but it was one of his followers, the Russian Vladimir Lenin (see Chapter 25), who in *Imperialism, the Highest Stage*

The first step towards lightening

The White Man's Burden

is through teaching the virtues of cleanliness.

Pears' Soap

is a potent factor in brightening the dark corners of the earth as civilization advances, while amongst the cultured of all nations it holds the highest place—it is the ideal toilet soap.

SOAP AND THE WHITE MAN'S BURDEN. The concept of the "white man's burden" included the belief that the superiority of their civilization obligated Europeans to impose their practices on supposedly primitive nonwhites. This advertisement for Pears' Soap clearly communicates the Europeans' view of their responsibility toward other peoples.

of World Capitalism developed the idea that capitalism leads to imperialism. According to Lenin, as the capitalist system concentrates more wealth in ever-fewer hands, the possibility for investment at home is exhausted, and capitalists are forced to invest abroad, establish colonies, and exploit small, weak nations. In his view, then, the only cure for imperialism was the destruction of capitalism.

✳ The Creation of Empires

Whatever the reasons for the new imperialism, it had a dramatic effect on Africa and Asia as European powers competed for control of these two continents.

✥ THE SCRAMBLE FOR AFRICA

Europeans controlled relatively little of the African continent before 1880. During the Napoleonic wars, the British had established themselves in South Africa by taking con-

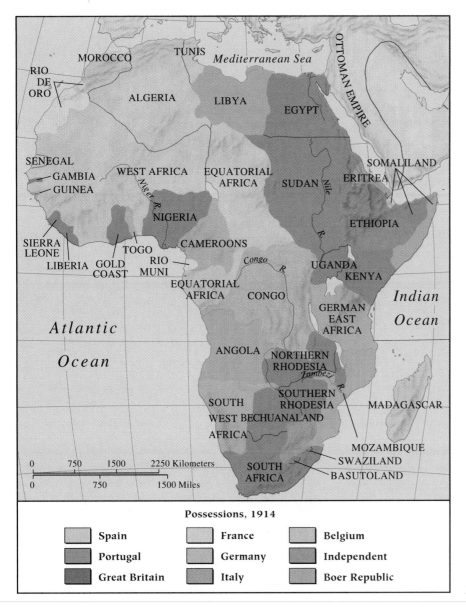

MAP 24.1 **Africa in 1914.**

trol of Capetown, originally founded by the Dutch. After the wars, the British encouraged settlers to come to what they called Cape Colony. British policies disgusted the Boers or Afrikaners, as the descendants of the Dutch colonists were called, and led them in 1835 to migrate north on the Great Trek to the region between the Orange and Vaal Rivers (later known as the Orange Free State) and north of the Vaal River (the Transvaal). Hostilities between the British and the Boers continued, however. In 1877, the British governor of Cape Colony seized the Transvaal, but a Boer revolt led the British government to recognize Transvaal as the independent South African Republic. These struggles between the British and the Boers did not prevent either white group from massacring and subjugating the Zulu and Xhosa peoples of South Africa.

In the 1880s, British policy in South Africa was largely determined by Cecil Rhodes (1853–1902). Rhodes founded both diamond and gold companies that monopolized production of these precious commodities and enabled him to gain control of a territory north of Transvaal that he named Rhodesia after himself. Rhodes was a great champion of British expansion. One of his goals was to create a series of British colonies "from the Cape to Cairo"—all linked by a railroad. His imperialist ambitions led to his downfall in 1896, however, when the British government forced him to resign as prime minister of Cape Colony after he conspired to overthrow the Boer government of the South African Republic without British approval. Although the British government had hoped to avoid war with the Boers, it could not stop extremists on both sides from precipitating a conflict. The Boer War dragged on from 1899 to 1902 when the Boers were overwhelmed by the larger British army. British policy toward the defeated Boers was remarkably conciliatory. Transvaal and the Orange Free State had representative governments by 1907, and in 1910, a Union of South Africa was created. Like Canada, Australia, and New Zealand, it became a fully self-governing dominion within the British Empire.

The White Man's Burden

One of the justifications for European imperialism was the notion that superior white peoples had the moral responsibility to raise ignorant native peoples to a higher level of civilization. The British poet Rudyard Kipling (1865–1936) captured this notion in his poem, The White Man's Burden.

✸ Rudyard Kipling, *The White Man's Burden*

Take up the White Man's burden—
Send forth the best ye breed—
Go bind your sons to exile
to serve your captives' needs;
To wait in heavy harness,
On fluttered folk and wild—
Your new-caught sullen peoples,
Half-devil and half-child.

Take up the White Man's burden—
In patience to abide,
To veil the threat of terror
And check the show of pride;
By open speech and simple,
An hundred times made plain
To seek another's profit,
And work another's gain.

Take up the White Man's burden—
The savage wars of peace—
Fill full the mouth of Famine
And bid the sickness cease;
And when your goal is nearest
The end for others sought,
Watch sloth and heathen Folly
Bring all your hopes to nought.

Take up the White Man's burden—
No tawdry rule of kings,
But toil of serf and sweeper—
The tale of common things.
The ports ye shall not enter,
The roads ye shall not tread,
Go mark them with your living,
And mark them with your dead.

Take up the White Man's burden—
And reap his old reward:
The blame of those ye better,
The hate of those ye guard—
The cry of hosts ye humour
(Ah, slowly;) toward the light—
'Why brought he us from bondage,
Our loved Egyptian night?'

Take up the White Man's burden—
Ye dare not stoop to less—
Nor call too loud on Freedom
To cloke your weariness;
By all ye cry or whisper,
By all you leave or do,
The silent, sullen peoples
Shall weigh your gods and you.

Take up the White Man's burden—
Have done with childish days—
The lightly proferred laurel,
The easy, ungrudged praise.
Comes now, to search your manhood
Through all the thankless years,
Cold, edged with dear-bought wisdom,
The judgment of your peers!

Before 1880, the only other European settlements in Africa had been made by the French and Portuguese. The Portuguese had held on to their settlements in Angola on the west coast and Mozambique on the east coast. The French had started the conquest of Algeria in Muslim North Africa in 1830, although it was not until 1879 that French civilian rule was established there. The next year, 1880, the European scramble for possession of Africa began in earnest. Before 1900, the French had added the huge area of French West Africa and Tunisia to their African empire. In 1912, they established a protectorate over much of Morocco; the rest was left to Spain.

The British took an active interest in Egypt after the Suez Canal was opened by the French in 1869. Believing that the canal was essential to their lifeline to India, the British sought to control the canal area. Egypt was a well-established state with an autonomous Muslim government, but that did not stop the British from landing an expeditionary force there in 1882. Although they asserted that their occupation was only temporary, they soon established a protectorate over Egypt. From Egypt, the British moved south into Sudan and seized it after narrowly averting a war with France. Not to be outdone, Italy joined in the imperialist scramble. Their humiliating defeat by the Ethiopians in 1896 only led the Italians to try again in 1911 when they invaded and seized Ottoman Tripoli, which they renamed Libya.

Central Africa was also added to the list of European colonies. Popular interest in the forbiddingly dense tropical jungles of central Africa was first aroused in the 1860s and 1870s by explorers, such as the Scottish missionary David Livingstone and the British-American journalist Henry M. Stanley. But the real driving force for the colonization of central Africa was King Leopold II

The Black Man's Burden

The Western justification of imperialism that was based on a sense of moral responsibility, evident in Rudyard Kipling's poem, was often hypocritical. Edward Morel, a British journalist who spent time in the Congo, pointed out the destructive effects of Western imperialism on Africans in his book, The Black Man's Burden.

✳ Edward Morel, *The Black Man's Burden*

It is [the Africans] who carry the "Black man's burden." They have not withered away before the white man's occupation. Indeed . . . Africa has ultimately absorbed within itself every Caucasian and, for that matter, every Semitic invader, too. In hewing out for himself a fixed abode in Africa, the white man has massacred the African in heaps. The African has survived, and it is well for the white settlers that he has. . . .

What the partial occupation of his soil by the white man has failed to do; what the mapping out of European political "spheres of influence" has failed to do; what the Maxim [machine gun] and the rifle, the slave gang, labor in the bowels of the earth and the lash, have failed to do; what imported measles, smallpox and syphilis have failed to do; whatever the overseas slave trade failed to do; the power of modern capitalistic exploitation, assisted by modern engines of destruction, may yet succeed in accomplishing.

For from the evils of the latter, scientifically applied and enforced, there is no escape for the African. Its destructive effects are not spasmodic: they are permanent. In its permanence resides its fatal consequences. It kills not the body merely, but the soul. It breaks the spirit. It attacks the African at every turn, from every point of vantage. It wrecks his polity, uproots him from the land, invades his family life, destroys his natural pursuits and occupations, claims his whole time, enslaves him in his own home. . . .

In Africa, especially in tropical Africa, which a capitalistic imperialism threatens and has, in part, already devastated, man is incapable of reacting against unnatural conditions. In those regions man is engaged in a perpetual struggle against disease and an exhausting climate, which tells heavily upon childbearing; and there is no scientific machinery for saving the weaker members of the community. The African of the tropics is capable of tremendous physical labors. But he cannot accommodate himself to the European system of monotonous, uninterrupted labor, with its long and regular hours, involving, moreover, as it frequently does, severance from natural surroundings and nostalgia, the condition of melancholy resulting from separation from home, a malady to which the African is specially prone. Climatic conditions forbid it. When the system is forced upon him, the tropical African droops and dies.

Nor is violent physical opposition to abuse and injustice henceforth possible for the African in any part of Africa. His chances of effective resistance have been steadily dwindling with the increasing perfectibility in the killing power of modern armament. . . .

Thus the African is really helpless against the material gods of the white man, as embodied in the trinity of imperialism, capitalistic exploitation, and militarism. . . .

To reduce all the varied and picturesque and stimulating episodes in savage life to a dull routine of endless toil for uncomprehended ends, to dislocate social ties and disrupt social institutions; to stifle nascent desires and crush mental development; to graft upon primitive passions the annihilating evils of scientific slavery, and the bestial imaginings of civilized man, unrestrained by convention or law; in fine, to kill the soul in a people—this is a crime which transcends physical murder.

(1865–1909) of Belgium, who had rushed enthusiastically into the pursuit of empire in Africa: "To open to civilization," he said, "the only part of our globe where it has not yet penetrated, to pierce the darkness which envelops whole populations, is a crusade, if I may say so, a crusade worthy of this century of progress." Profit, however, was far more important to Leopold than progress; his treatment of the Africans was so brutal that even other Europeans condemned his actions. In 1876, Leopold created the International Association for the Exploration and Civilization of Central Africa and engaged Henry Stanley to establish Belgian settlements in the Congo. Alarmed by Leopold's actions, the French also moved into the territory north of the Congo River.

Between 1884 and 1900, most of the rest of Africa was carved up by the European powers. Germany also entered the ranks of the imperialist powers at this time. Initially, Bismarck had downplayed the significance of colonies, but as domestic political pressures for a German empire intensified, Bismarck became a political convert to colonialism. As he expressed it: "All this colonial business is a sham, but we need it for the elections." The Germans established colonies in South-west Africa, the Cameroons, Togoland, and East Africa.

By 1914, Britain, France, Germany, Belgium, Spain, and Portugal had divided Africa. Only Liberia, founded by emancipated American slaves, and Ethiopia remained free states. Despite the humanitarian rationalizations about the "white man's burden," Africa had been conquered by European states determined to create colonial empires (see the box on p. 735). Any peoples who dared to resist (with the exception of the Ethiopians, who defeated the Italians) were simply devastated by the superior military force of the Europeans. In 1898, Sudanese tribesmen attempted to defend their independence and stop a British expedition armed with the recently developed machine gun. In the ensuing Battle of Omdurman, the Sudanese were massacred. One observer noted: "It was not a battle but an execution. . . . The bodies were not in heaps—bodies hardly ever are; but they spread evenly over acres and acres. Some lay very composedly with their slippers placed under their heads for a last pillow; some knelt, cut short in the middle of a last prayer. Others were torn to pieces."[20] The battle casualties at Omdurman tell the story of the one-sided conflicts between Europeans and Africans: 28 British deaths to 11,000 Sudanese. Military superiority was frequently accompanied by brutal treatment of blacks. Nor did Europeans hesitate to deceive the Africans to gain their way. One South African king, Lo Bengula, informed Queen Victoria about how he had been cheated:

> Some time ago a party of men came to my country, the principal one appearing to be a man called Rudd. They asked me for a place to dig for gold, and said they would give me certain things for the right to do so. I told them to bring what they could give and I would show them what I would give. A document was written and presented to me for signature. I asked what it contained, and was told that in it were my words and the words of those men. I put my hand to it. About three months afterwards I heard from other sources that I had given by that document the right to all the minerals of my country.[21]

ASIA IN AN AGE OF IMPERIALISM

Although Asia had been open to Western influence since the sixteenth century, not much of its immense territory had fallen under direct European control. The Dutch were established in the East Indies, the Spanish were in the Philippines, and the French and Portuguese had trading posts on the Indian coast. China, Japan, Korea, and Southeast Asia had largely managed to exclude Westerners. The British and the Russians, however, had acquired the most Asian territory.

It was not until the explorations of Australia by Captain James Cook between 1768 and 1771 that Britain took an active interest in the East. The availability of land for grazing sheep and the discovery of gold in Australia led to an influx of free settlers who slaughtered many of the indigenous inhabitants. In 1850, the British government granted the various Australian colonies virtually complete self-government, and fifty years later, on January 1, 1901, all the colonies were unified into a Commonwealth of Australia. Nearby New Zealand, which the British had declared a colony in 1840, was also granted dominion status in 1907.

A private trading company known as the British East India Company had been responsible for subjugating much of India. In 1858, however, after a revolt of the sepoys, or Indian troops of the East India Company's army had been crushed, the British Parliament transferred the company's powers directly to the government in London. In 1876, the title Empress of India was bestowed upon Queen Victoria; Indians were now her colonial subjects.

Russian expansion in Asia was a logical outgrowth of its traditional territorial aggrandizement. Russian explorers had penetrated the wilderness of Siberia in the seventeenth century and reached the Pacific coast in 1637. In the eighteenth century, Russians established a claim on Alaska, which was later sold to the United States in 1867. Gradually, Russian settlers moved into cold and forbidding Siberia. Altogether seven million Russians settled in Siberia between 1800 and 1914; by 1914, 90 percent of the Siberian population were Slavs, not Asiatics.

The Russians also moved south, attracted by warmer climates and the crumbling Ottoman Empire. By 1830, the Russians had established control over the entire northern coast of the Black Sea and then pressed on into central Asia, securing the trans-Caspian area by 1881 and Turkestan in 1885. These advances brought the Russians to the borders of Persia and Afghanistan where the British also had interests because of their desire to protect their holdings in India. In 1907, the Russians and British agreed to make Afghanistan a buffer state between Russian Turkestan and British India and to divide Persia into two spheres of influence. Halted by the British in their expansion to the south, the Russians moved east in Asia. The Russian occupation of Manchuria and their attempt to move into Korea brought war with the new imperialist power, Japan. After losing the Russo-Japanese War in 1905, the Russians agreed to a Japanese protectorate in

Korea, and their Asian expansion was brought to a temporary halt.

The thrust of imperialism after 1880 led Westerners to move into new areas of Asia hitherto largely free of Western influence. By the nineteenth century, the ruling Manchu dynasty of the Chinese Empire was showing signs of decline. In 1842, the British had obtained (through war) the island of Hong Kong and trading rights in a number of Chinese cities. Other Western nations soon rushed in to gain similar trading privileges. Chinese attempts to resist this encroachment of foreigners led to military defeats and new demands. Only rivalry among the great powers themselves prevented the complete dismemberment of the Chinese Empire. Instead, Britain, France, Germany, Russia, the United States, and Japan established spheres of influence and long-term leases of Chinese territory. In 1899, urged along by the American secretary of state John Hay, they agreed to an "Open Door" policy in which one country would not restrict the commerce of the other countries in its sphere of influence.

Japan avoided Western intrusion until 1853–1854 when American naval forces under Commodore Matthew Perry forced the Japanese to grant the United States trading and diplomatic privileges. Japan, however, managed to avoid China's fate. Korea had also largely excluded Westerners. The fate of Korea was determined by the struggle first between China and Japan in 1894–1895 and later between Japan and Russia in 1904–1905. Japan's victories gave it a clear superiority, and in 1910 Japan formally annexed Korea.

In Southeast Asia, Britain established control over Burma and the Malay States, and France played an active role in subjugating Indochina. The city of Saigon was occupied in 1858, and four years later Cochin China was taken. In the 1880s, the French extended "protection" over Cambodia, Annam, Tonkin, and Laos and organized them into a Union of French Indochina. Only Siam (Thailand) remained free as a buffer state because of British-French rivalry.

The Pacific islands were also the scene of great power competition and witnessed the entry of the United States onto the imperialist stage. The Samoan Islands became the first important American colony; the Hawaiian Islands were the next to fall. Soon after Americans had made Pearl Harbor into a naval station in 1887, American settlers gained control of the sugar industry on the islands. When Hawaiian natives tried to reassert their authority, the U.S. Marines were brought in to "protect" American lives. Hawaii was annexed by the United States in 1898 during the era of American nationalistic fervor generated by the Spanish-American War. The American defeat of Spain encouraged Americans to extend their empire by acquiring Cuba, Puerto Rico, Guam, and the Philippine Islands. Although the Filipinos hoped for independence, the Americans refused to grant it. As President William McKinley said, the United States had the duty "to educate the Filipinos and uplift and Christianize them," a remark-

able statement in view of the fact that most of them had been Roman Catholics for centuries. It took three years and 60,000 troops to pacify the Philippines and establish American control. Not until 1946 did the Filipinos receive complete independence.

❉ Asian Responses to Imperialism

When Europeans imposed their culture upon peoples they considered inferior, how did the conquered peoples respond? Initial attempts to expel the foreigners only led to devastating defeats at the hands of Westerners, whose industrial technology gave them modern weapons of war with which to crush the indigenous peoples. Accustomed to rule by small elites, most people simply accepted their new governors, making Western rule relatively easy. The conquered peoples subsequently adjusted to foreign rule in different ways. Traditionalists sought to maintain their cultural traditions, but modernizers believed that adoption of Western ways would enable them to reform their societies and eventually challenge Western rule. Most people probably stood somewhere between these two extremes. Three eventually powerful Asian nations—China, Japan, and India—present different approaches to the question of how Asian populations responded to foreign rule.

❧ CHINA

The humiliation of China by the Western powers led to much antiforeign violence, but the Westerners only used this lawlessness as an excuse to extort further concessions from the Chinese. A major outburst of violence against foreigners occurred in the Boxer Rebellion in 1900–1901. Boxers was the popular name given to Chinese who belonged to a secret organization called the Society of Harmonious Fists, whose aim was to push the foreigners out of China. The Boxers murdered foreign missionaries, Chinese who had converted to Christianity, railroad workers, foreign businessmen, and even the German envoy to Beijing. Response to the killings was immediate and overwhelming. An allied army consisting of British, French, German, Russian, American, and Japanese troops attacked Beijing, restored order, and demanded more concessions from the Chinese government. The imperial government was so weakened that the forces of the revolutionary leader Sun Yat-sen (1866–1925), who adopted a program of "nationalism, democracy, and socialism," overthrew the Manchu dynasty in 1912. The new Republic of China remained weak and ineffective, and China's travails were far from over.

❧ JAPAN

In the late 1850s and early 1860s, it looked as if Japan would follow China's fate and be carved up into spheres of influence by aggressive Western powers. A remarkably rapid transformation, however, produced a very different result. Before 1868, the shogun, a powerful hereditary

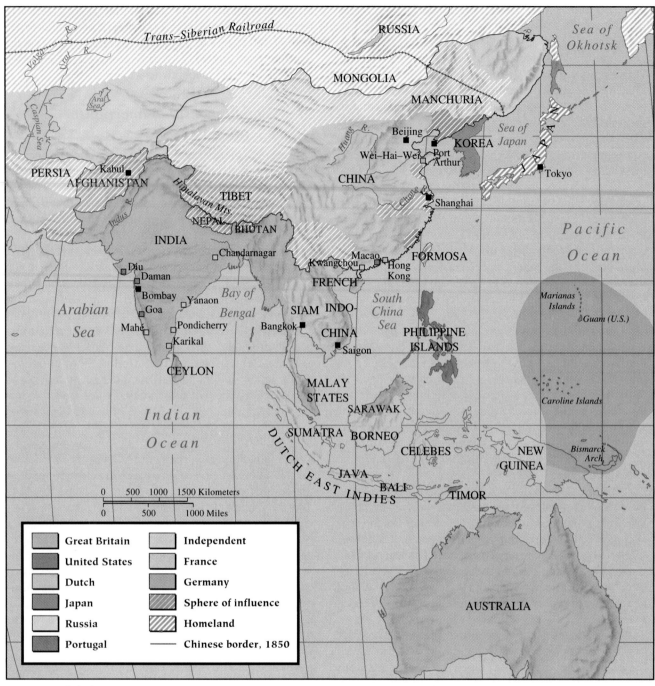

MAP 24.2 Asia in 1914.

military governor assisted by a warrior nobility known as the samurai, exercised real power in Japan. The emperor's functions had become primarily religious. After the shogun's concessions to the Western nations, antiforeign sentiment led to a samurai revolt in 1867 and the restoration of the emperor as the rightful head of the government. The new emperor was the astute, dynamic, young Mutsuhito (1867–1912), who called his reign the Meiji (Enlightened Government). The new leaders who controlled the emperor now inaugurated a remarkable transformation of Japan that has since been known as the Meiji Restoration.

Recognizing the obvious military and industrial superiority of the West, the new leaders decided to modernize Japan by absorbing and adopting Western methods. Thousands of young Japanese were sent abroad to receive Western educations, especially in the social and natural sciences. A German-style army and a British-style navy were established. The Japanese copied the industrial and financial methods of the United States and developed a modern commercial and industrial system. A highly centralized administrative system copied from the French replaced the old feudal system. Initially, the Japanese adopted the French principles of social and legal equality,

The New Imperialism: Asia

Britain obtains Hong Kong and trading rights from Chinese government	1842
Australian colonies receive self-government	1850
Mission of Commodore Perry to Japan	1853–1854
Rebellion of sepoys in India	1857–1858
French occupy Saigon	1858
Overthrow of the shogun in Japan	1867
Emperor Mutsuhito and the Meiji Restoration	1867–1912
Queen Victoria is made Empress of India	1876
Russians in central Asia (trans-Caspian area)	1881
Formation of Indian National Congress	1883
Russians in Turkestan	1885
Japanese defeat of China	1894–1895
Spanish-American War; United States annexes Philippines	1898
"Open Door" policy in China	1899
Boxer Rebellion in China	1900–1901
Commonwealth of Australia	1901
Commonwealth of New Zealand	1907
Russian-British agreement over Afghanistan and Persia	1907
Japan annexes Korea	1910
Overthrow of Manchu dynasty in China	1912

but by 1890 they had created a political system that was democratic in form but authoritarian in practice.

In imitating the West, Japan also developed a powerful military state. Universal military conscription was introduced in 1872, and a modern peacetime army of 240,000 was eventually established. The Japanese avidly pursued the Western imperialistic model. They defeated China in 1894–1895, annexed some Chinese territory, and established their own sphere of influence in China. After they had defeated the Russians in 1905, the Japanese made Korea a colony under harsh rule. The Japanese had proved that an Asian power could play the "white man's" imperialistic game and provided a potent example to peoples in other regions of Asia and Africa.

INDIA

The British government had been in control of India since the mid-nineteenth century. After crushing a major revolt in 1858, the British ruled India directly. Under Parliament's supervision, a small group of British civil servants directed the affairs of India's almost 300 million people.

The British brought order to a society that had been divided by civil wars for some time and created a relatively honest and efficient government. They also brought Western technology—railroads, banks, mines, industry, medical knowledge, and hospitals. The British introduced Western-style secondary schools and colleges where the Indian upper and middle classes and professional classes were educated so that they could serve as trained subordinates in the government and army.

But the Indian people paid a high price for the peace and stability brought by British rule. Due to population growth in the nineteenth century, extreme poverty was a way of life for most Indians; almost two-thirds of the population were malnourished in 1901. British industrialization brought little improvement for the masses. British manufactured goods destroyed local industries, and Indian wealth was used to pay British officials and a large army. The system of education served only the elite, upper-class Indians, and it was conducted only in the rulers' English language while 90 percent of the population remained illiterate. Even for the Indians who benefited the most from their Western educations, British rule was degrading. The best jobs and the best housing were reserved for Britons. Despite their education, the Indians were never considered equals of the British whose racial attitudes were made quite clear by Lord Kitchener, one of Britain's foremost military commanders in India, when he said: "It is this consciousness of the inherent superiority of the European which has won for us India. However well educated and clever a native may be, and however brave he may prove himself, I believe that no rank we can bestow on him would cause him to be considered an equal of the British officer."[22] Such smug racial attitudes made it difficult for British rule, no matter how beneficent, ever to be ultimately accepted and led to the rise of an Indian nationalist movement. By 1883, when the Indian National Congress was formed, moderate, educated Indians were beginning to seek self-government. By 1919, in response to British violence and British insensitivity in trying to divide Bengal, Indians were demanding complete independence.

◆ International Rivalry and the Coming of War

Before 1914, Europeans had experienced almost fifty years of peace. There had been wars (including wars of conquest in the non-Western world), but none had involved the great powers. A series of crises had occurred, however, that might easily have led to general war. One reason they did not is that until 1890 Bismarck of Germany exercised a restraining influence on the Europeans.

The Bismarckian System

Bismarck knew that the emergence of a unified Germany in 1871 had upset the balance of power established at Vienna in 1815. By keeping the peace, he could best maintain the new status quo and preserve the new German state. Fearing the French desire for revenge over their loss of Alsace-Lorraine in the Franco-Prussian War, Bismarck made an alliance in 1873 with the traditionally conservative powers Austria-Hungary and Russia. The Three Emperors' League, as it was called, failed to work very well, however, primarily because of Russian-Austrian rivalry in eastern Europe, specifically, in the Balkans.

The problem in the Balkans was yet another chapter in the story of the disintegration of the Ottoman Empire. Subject peoples in the Balkans clamored for independence, while corruption and inefficiency weakened the Ottoman government. Only the interference of the great European powers, who were fearful of each other's designs on its territories, kept the Ottoman Empire alive. Complicating the situation was the rivalry between Russia and Austria, which both had designs on the Balkans. For Russia, the Balkans provided the shortest overland route to Constantinople and the Straits. Austria viewed the Balkans as fertile ground for Austrian expansion. Both Britain and France feared the extension of Russian power into the Mediterranean and Middle East. Although Germany had no real interests in the Balkans, Bismarck was fearful of the consequences of a war between Russia and Austria over the Balkans and served as a restraining influence on both powers. Events in the Balkans, however, precipitated a new crisis.

In 1876, the Balkan states of Serbia and Montenegro declared war on the Ottoman Empire. Both were defeated, but Russia, with Austrian approval, attacked and defeated the Ottomans. By the Treaty of San Stefano in 1878, a large Bulgarian state, extending from the Danube in the north to the Aegean Sea in the south, was created. As Bulgaria was viewed as a Russian satellite, this Russian success caused the other great powers to call for a congress of European powers to discuss a revision of the treaty.

The Congress of Berlin, which met in the summer of 1878, was dominated by Bismarck. The congress effectively demolished the Treaty of San Stefano, much to Russia's humiliation. The new Bulgarian state was considerably reduced, and the rest of the territory was returned to Ottoman control. The three Balkan states of Serbia, Montenegro, and Romania, until then nominally under Ottoman control, were recognized as independent. The other Balkan territories of Bosnia and Herzegovina were placed under Austrian protection; Austria could occupy but not annex them. Although the Germans received no territory, they believed they had at least preserved the peace among the great powers.

After the Congress of Berlin, the European powers sought new alliances to safeguard their security. Angered by the Germans' actions at the congress, the Russians had terminated the Three Emperors' League. Bismarck then made an alliance with Austria in 1879 that was joined by a third party—Italy—in 1882. The Triple Alliance of 1882 committed Germany, Austria, and Italy to support the existing political order while providing a defensive alliance against France or "two or more great powers not members

of the alliance." At the same time, Bismarck sought to remain on friendly terms with the Russians and made a Reinsurance Treaty with Russia in 1887, hoping to prevent a French-Russian alliance that would threaten Germany with the possibility of a two-front war. The Bismarckian system of alliances, geared to preserving peace and the status quo, had worked, but in 1890 Emperor William II dismissed Bismarck and began to chart a new direction for Germany's foreign policy.

❁ New Directions and New Crises

Bismarck's alliances had served to bring the European powers into an interlocking system in which no one state could be certain of much support if it chose to initiate a war of aggression. After 1890, a new European diplomacy unfolded in which Europe became divided into two opposing camps that became more and more inflexible and unwilling to compromise.

After Bismarck's dismissal, Emperor William II embarked upon an activist foreign policy dedicated to enhancing German power by finding, as he put it, Germany's rightful "place in the sun." One of his changes in Bismarck's foreign policy was to drop the Reinsurance Treaty with Russia, which he viewed as being at odds with Germany's alliance with Austria. Although William II tried to remain friendly with Russia, the ending of the alliance achieved what Bismarck had feared: it brought France and Russia together. Long isolated by Bismarck's policies, republican France leaped at the chance to draw closer to tsarist Russia, and in 1894 the two powers concluded a military alliance.

The attitude of the British now became crucial. Secure in their vast empire, the British had long pursued a policy of "splendid isolation" toward the Continent. The British were startled, however, when many Europeans condemned their activity in the Boer War (1899–1902) in South Africa. Fearful of an anti-British continental alliance, they saw the weakness of "splendid isolation" and sought an alliance with a continental power. Initially, neither France nor Russia seemed a logical choice. Britain's traditional enmity with France had only intensified because of their imperialistic rivalries in Africa and Asia. Likewise, British and Russian imperialistic interests had frequently collided.

Germany, therefore, seemed the most likely potential ally. Certainly, some people in both Britain and Germany believed that their common German heritage (Anglo-Saxons from Germany had settled in Britain in the Early Middle Ages) made them "natural allies." But Britain was not particularly popular in Germany, nor did the British especially like the Germans. Industrial and commercial rivalry had created much ill feeling, and William II's imperial posturing and grabbing for colonies made the British suspicious of Germany's ultimate aims (see the box on p. 742). Especially worrisome to the British was the Germans' construction of a large navy, including a number of battleships advocated by the persistent Admiral von Tirpitz, secretary of the German navy. The British now turned to their traditional enemy, France, and

in 1904 concluded the Entente Cordiale by which the two settled all of their outstanding colonial disputes.

German response to the Entente was swift, creating what has been called the First Moroccan Crisis in 1905. The Germans chose to oppose French designs on Morocco in order to humiliate them and drive a wedge between the two new allies—Britain and France. Refusing to compromise, the Germans insisted upon an international conference to settle the problem. Germany's foolish saber rattling had the opposite effect of what had been intended and succeeded only in uniting Russia, France, Great Britain, and even the United States against Germany. The conference at Algeciras, Spain, in January 1906 awarded control of Morocco to France. Germany came out of the conference with nothing.

The First Moroccan Crisis of 1905–1906 had important repercussions. France and Britain drew closer together as both began to view Germany as a real threat to European peace. German leaders, on the other hand, began to speak of sinister plots to encircle Germany and hinder its emergence as a world power. Russia, too, grew more and more suspicious of the Germans and signed an agreement in 1907 with Great Britain. By that year, Europe's division into two major blocs—the Triple Alliance of Germany, Austria-Hungary, and Italy and the Triple Entente, as the loose confederation of Russia, France, and Great Britain was called—grew increasingly rigid at the same time that the problems in the Balkans were heating up.

MAP 24.3   The Balkans in 1878.

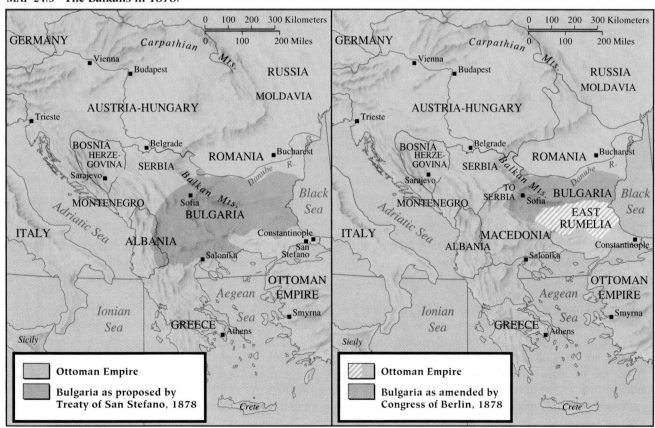

The Emperor's "Big Mouth"

Emperor William II's world policy, which was aimed at finding Germany's "place in the sun," created considerable ill will and unrest among other European states, especially Britain. Moreover, the emperor had the unfortunate tendency to stir up trouble by his often tactless public remarks. In this 1908 interview, for example, William II intended to strengthen Germany's ties with Britain. His words had just the opposite effect and raised a storm of protest in both Britain and Germany.

❋ *Daily Telegraph* Interview, October 28, 1908

As I have said, his Majesty honored me with a long conversation, and spoke with impulsive and unusual frankness. "You English," he said, "are mad, mad, mad as March hares. What has come over you that you are so completely given over to suspicions quite unworthy of a great nation? What more can I do than I have done? I declared with all the emphasis at my command, in my speech at Guildhall, that my heart is set upon peace, and that it is one of my dearest wishes to live on the best of terms with England. Have I ever been false to my word? Falsehoods and prevarication are alien to my nature. My actions ought to speak for themselves, but you listen not to them but to those who misinterpret and distort them. That is a personal insult which I feel and resent. To be forever misjudged, to have my repeated offers of friendship weighed and scrutinized with jealous, mistrustful eyes, taxes my patience severely. I have said time after time that I am a friend of England, and your Press—or, at least, a considerable section of it—bids the people of England to refuse my proffered hand, and insinuates that the other holds a dagger. How can I convince a nation against its will?"

"I repeat," continued his Majesty, "that I am a friend of England, but you make things difficult for me. My task is not of the easiest. The prevailing sentiment among large sections of the middle and lower classes of my own people is not friendly to England. I am, therefore, so to speak, in a minority in my own land, but it is a minority of the best elements as it is in England with respect to Germany. That is another reason why I resent your refusal to accept my pledged word that I am the friend of England. I strive without ceasing to improve relations, and you retort that I am your arch-enemy. You make it hard for me. Why is it? . . ."

"But, you will say, what of the German Navy? Surely, that is a menace to England! Against whom but England are my squadrons being prepared? If England is not in the minds of those Germans who are bent on creating a powerful fleet, why is Germany asked to consent to such new and heavy burdens of taxation? My answer is clear. Germany is a young and growing Empire. She has a world-wide commerce, which is rapidly expanding, and to which the legitimate ambition of patriotic Germans refuses to assign any bounds. Germany must have a powerful fleet to protect that commerce, and her manifold interests in even the most distant seas. She expects those interests to go on growing, and she must be able to champion them manfully in any quarter of the globe. Germany looks ahead. Her horizons stretch far away. She must be prepared for any eventualities in the Far East. Who can foresee what may take place in the Pacific in the days to come, days not so distant as some believe, but days, at any rate, for which all European Powers with Far Eastern interests ought steadily to prepare? Look at the accomplished rise of Japan; think of the possible national awakening of China; and then judge of the vast problems of the Pacific. Only those Powers which have great navies will be listened to with respect, when the future of the Pacific comes to be solved; and, if for that reason only, Germany must have a powerful fleet. It may even be that England herself will be glad that Germany has a fleet when they speak together on the same side in the great debates of the future."

Between 1908 and 1913, a new series of crises over the control of the remnants of the Ottoman Empire in the Balkans set the stage for World War I.

✄ CRISES IN THE BALKANS (1908–1913)

The Bosnian Crisis of 1908–1909 initiated a chain of events that eventually went out of control. Since 1878, Bosnia and Herzegovina had been under the protection of Austria, but in 1908, Austria took the drastic step of annexing these two Slavic-speaking territories. Serbia became outraged at this action because it dashed the Serbs' hopes of creating a large Serbian kingdom that would include most of the south Slavs. This was why the Austrians had annexed Bosnia and Herzegovina. To the Austrians, a large Serbia would be a threat to the unity of the Austro-Hungarian Empire with its large Slavic population. The Russians, as protectors of their fellow Slavs and with their own desire to increase their authority in the Balkans, supported the Serbs and opposed the Austrian action. Backed by the Russians, the Serbs prepared for war against Austria. At this point William II intervened and demanded that the Russians accept Austria's annexation of Bosnia and Herzegovina or face war with Germany. Weakened from their defeat in the Russo-Japanese War in 1904–1905, the

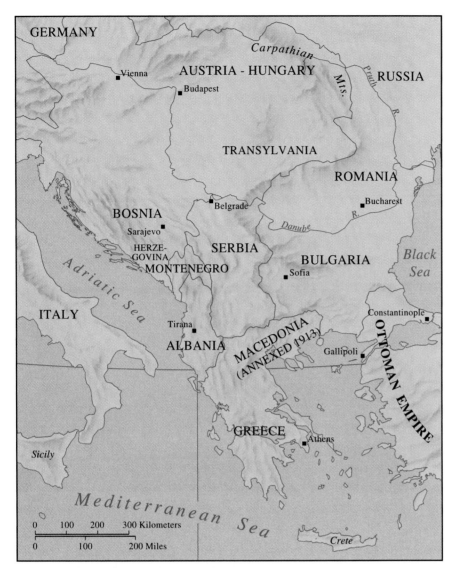

MAP 24.4 The Balkans in 1913.

Russians were afraid to risk war and backed down. Humiliated, the Russians vowed revenge.

European attention returned to the Balkans in 1912 when Serbia, Bulgaria, Montenegro, and Greece organized a Balkan League and defeated the Ottomans in the First Balkan War. When the victorious allies were unable to agree on how to divide the conquered Ottoman provinces of Macedonia and Albania, the Second Balkan War erupted in 1913. Greece, Serbia, Romania, and the Ottoman Empire attacked and defeated Bulgaria. As a result, Bulgaria obtained only a small part of Macedonia, and most of the rest was divided between Serbia and Greece. Yet Serbia's aspirations remained unfulfilled. The two Balkan wars left the inhabitants embittered and created more tensions among the great powers.

One of Serbia's major ambitions had been to acquire Albanian territory that would give it a port on the Adriatic. At the London Conference arranged by Austria at the end of the two Balkan wars, the Austrians had blocked Serbia's wishes by creating an independent Albania. The Germans, as Austrian allies, had supported this move. In their frustration, Serbian nationalists increasingly portrayed the Austrians as evil monsters who were keeping the Serbs from becoming a great nation. As Serbia's chief supporters, the Russians were also upset by the turn of events in the Balkans. A feeling had grown among Russian leaders that they could not back down again in the event of a confrontation with Austria or Germany in the Balkans. One Russian military journal even stated early in 1914: "We are preparing for a war in the west. The whole nation must accustom itself to the idea that we arm ourselves for a war of annihilation against the Germans."

Austria-Hungary had achieved another of its aims, but it was still convinced that Serbia was a mortal threat to its empire and must at some point be crushed. Meanwhile, the French and Russian governments renewed their

OTTOMAN ARMY IN RETREAT.
In 1912, a coalition of Serbia, Bulgaria, Montenegro, and Greece defeated the Ottomans and took possession of the Ottoman provinces of Macedonia and Albania. This picture shows the Ottoman army in retreat, pursued by Bulgarian forces.

alliance and promised each other that they would not back down at the next crisis. Britain drew closer to France. By the beginning of 1914, two armed camps viewed each other with suspicion. An American in Europe observed, "The whole of Germany is charged with electricity. Every-body's nerves are tense. It only needs a spark to set the whole thing off." The German ambassador to France noted at the same time that "peace remains at the mercy of an accident." The European "age of progress" was about to come to an inglorious and bloody end.

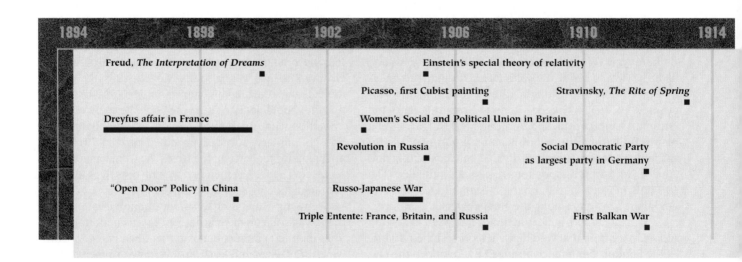

1894	1898	1902	1906	1910	1914

Freud, *The Interpretation of Dreams* ■

Einstein's special theory of relativity ■

Picasso, first Cubist painting ■

Stravinsky, *The Rite of Spring* ■

Dreyfus affair in France ▬▬▬

Women's Social and Political Union in Britain ■

Revolution in Russia ■

Social Democratic Party as largest party in Germany ■

"Open Door" Policy in China ■

Russo-Japanese War ▬▬

Triple Entente: France, Britain, and Russia ■

First Balkan War ■

CONCLUSION ░▓░▓░▓░▓░▓░▓

What many Europeans liked to call their "age of progress" in the decades before 1914 was also an era of anxiety. Frenzied imperialist expansion had created vast European empires and spheres of influence around the globe. This feverish competition for colonies, however, had markedly increased the existing antagonisms among the European states. At the same time, the Western treatment of non-Western peoples as racial inferiors caused educated, non-Western elites in these colonies to initiate movements for national independence. Before these movements could be successful, however, the power that Europeans had achieved through their mass armies and technological superiority had to be weakened. The Europeans inadvertently accomplished this task for their colonial subjects by demolishing their own civilization on the battlegrounds of Europe in World War I and World War II.

The cultural revolutions before 1914 had also produced anxiety and a crisis of confidence in European civilization. A brilliant minority of intellectuals had created a modern consciousness that questioned most Europeans' optimistic faith in reason, the rational structure of nature, and the certainty of progress. The devastating experiences of World War I turned this culture of uncertainty into a way of life after 1918.

NOTES ░▓░▓░▓░▓░▓░▓░▓░▓

1. Quoted in Arthur E. E. McKenzie, *The Major Achievements of Science* (New York, 1960), 1:310.
2. Friedrich Nietzsche, *Twilight of the Idols and The Anti-Christ*, trans. R. J. Hollingdale (New York, 1972), pp. 117–118.
3. Friedrich Nietzsche, *Thus Spake Zarathustra*, in *The Philosophy of Nietzsche* (New York, 1954), p. 6.
4. Herbert Spencer, *Social Statics* (New York, 1896), pp. 146–150.
5. Friedrich von Bernhardi, *Germany and the Next War*, trans. Allen H. Powles (New York, 1914), pp. 18–19.
6. Quoted in Edward R. Tannenbaum, *1900: The Generation before the Great War* (Garden City, N.Y., 1976), p. 337.
7. Quoted in Owen Chadwick, *The Secularization of the European Mind in the Nineteenth Century* (Cambridge, 1975), p. 125.
8. William Booth, *In Darkest England and the Way Out* (London, 1890), p. 45.
9. Quoted in John Rewald, *The History of Impressionism* (New York, 1961), pp. 456–458.
10. Quoted in Anne Higonnet, *Berthe Morisot's Images of Women* (Cambridge, Mass., 1992), p. 19.
11. Paul Klee, *On Modern Art*, trans. Paul Findlay (London, 1948), p. 51.
12. Quoted in Craig Wright, *Listening to Music* (St. Paul, Minn., 1992), p. 327.
13. Quoted in Catherine M. Prelinger, "Prelude to Consciousness: Amalie Sieveking and the Female Association for the Care of the Poor and the Sick," in John C. Fout, ed., *German Women in the Nineteenth Century: A Social History* (New York, 1984), p. 119.
14. Quoted in Bonnie Smith, *Changing Lives: Women in European History since 1700* (Lexington, Mass., 1989), p. 379.
15. Quoted in Paul Massing, *Rehearsal for Destruction: A Study of Political Anti-Semitism in Imperial Germany* (New York, 1949), p. 147.
16. Quoted in Abba Eban, *Heritage: Civilization and the Jews* (New York, 1984), p. 249.
17. Quoted in Geoffrey A. Hosking, *The Russian Constitutional Experiment, 1907–1914* (Cambridge, 1973), p. 5.
18. Karl Pearson, *National Life from the Standpoint of Science* (London, 1905), p. 184.
19. Quoted in John Ellis, *The Social History of the Machine Gun* (New York, 1975), p. 80.
20. Quoted in ibid., p. 86.
21. Quoted in Louis L. Snyder, ed., *The Imperialism Reader* (Princeton, N.J., 1962), p. 220.
22. Quoted in K. M. Panikkar, *Asia and Western Dominance* (London, 1959), p. 116.

SUGGESTIONS FOR FURTHER READING ░▓░▓░▓

A well-regarded study of Freud is P. Gay, *Freud: A Life for Our Time* (New York, 1988). Also, see J. Neu, ed., *The Cambridge Companion to Freud* (New York, 1991). Nietzsche is examined in R. C. Holub, *Friedrich Nietzsche* (New York, 1995). On the impact of Nietzsche, see R. H. Thomas, *Nietzsche in German Politics and Society, 1890–1918* (Dover, N.H., 1983). On Bergson, see A. E. Pilkington, *Henri Bergson and His Influence* (Cambridge, 1976). The basic study on Sorel is J. J. Roth, *The Cult of Violence: Sorel and the Sorelians* (Berkeley, 1980). A useful study on the impact of Darwinian thought on religion is J. Moore, *The Post-Darwinian Controversies: A Study of the Protestant Struggle to Come to Terms with Darwin in Great Britain and America, 1870–1900* (Cambridge, 1979). Studies of the popular religion of the period include T. A. Kselman, *Miracles and Prophesies in Nineteenth-Century France* (New Brunswick, N.J., 1983); and J. Sperber, *Popular Catholicism in Nineteenth-Century Germany* (Princeton, N.J., 1984). Very valuable on modern art are M. Powell-Jones, *Impressionism* (London, 1994); B. Denvir, *Post-Impressionism* (New York, 1992); and T. Parsons, *Post-Impressionism: The Rise of Modern Art* (London, 1992). On literature, see R. Pascal, *From Naturalism to Expressionism: German Literature and Society, 1880–1918* (New York, 1973). The intellectual climate of Vienna is examined in C. E. Schorske, *Fin de Siècle Vienna: Politics and Culture* (New York, 1980).

The rise of feminism is examined in J. Rendall, *The Origins of Modern Feminism: Women in Britain, France and the United States* (London, 1985). The subject of modern anti-Semitism is covered in J. Katz, *From Prejudice to Destruction* (Cambridge, Mass., 1980); and A. S. Lindemann, *Esau's Tears: Modern Anti-Semitism and the Rise of the Jews* (New York,

1997). European racism is analyzed in G. L. Mosse, *Toward the Final Solution* (New York, 1980); German anti-Semitism as a political force is examined in P. J. Pulzer, *The Rise of Political Anti-Semitism in Germany and Austria* (New York, 1964). Anti-Semitism in France is the subject of E. Cahm, *The Dreyfus Affair in French Society and Politics* (New York, 1996). The problems of Jews in Russia are examined in J. Frankel, *Prophecy and Politics: Socialism, Nationalism and the Russian Jews, 1862–1917* (Cambridge, 1981). For a recent biography of Theodor Herzl, see J. Kornberg, *Theodor Herzl: From Assimilation to Zionism* (Bloomington, Ind., 1993). The beginnings of the Labour Party are examined in H. Pelling, *The Origins of the Labour Party*, 2d ed. (Oxford, 1965). There are good introductions to the political world of William II's Germany in T. A. Kohut, *Wilhelm II and the Germans: A Study in Leadership* (New York, 1991); and J. C. G. Röhl, *The Kaiser and His Court: Wilhelm II and the Government of Germany* (New York, 1994). An important study on right-wing German politics is G. Eley, *Reshaping the German Right: Radical Nationalism and Political Change after Bismarck* (New Haven, Conn., 1980). On Russia, see T. H. Von Laue, *Sergei Witte and the Industrialization of Russia* (New York, 1963); and A. Ascher, *The Revolution of 1905: Russia in Disarray*, 2 vols. (Stanford, 1988–1992).

For broad perspectives on imperialism, see the works by T. Smith, *The Pattern of Imperialism* (Cambridge, 1981); M. W. Doyle, *Empires* (Ithaca, N.Y., 1986); and P. Darby, *Three Faces of Imperialism: British and American Approaches to Asia and Africa, 1870–1970* (New Haven, Conn., 1987). Different aspects of imperialism are covered in R. Robinson and J. Gallagher, *Africa and the Victorians*, 2d ed. (New York,

1981); A. Burton, *Burdens of History: British Feminists, Indian Women, and Imperial Culture, 1865–1915* (Chapel Hill, N.C., 1994); M. Strobel, *European Women and the Second British Empire* (Bloomington, Ind., 1991); P. J. Marshall, ed., *The Cambridge Illustrated History of the British Empire* (Cambridge, 1996); and T. Pakhenham, *The Scramble for Africa* (New York, 1991).

Two fundamental works on the diplomatic history of the period are W. L. Langer, *European Alliances and Alignments*, 2d ed. (New York, 1966); and *The Diplomacy of Imperialism*, 2d ed. (New York, 1965). Also valuable are G. Kennan, *The Decline of Bismarck's European Order: Franco-Prussian Relations, 1875–1890* (Princeton, N.J., 1979); and the masterful study by P. Kennedy, *The Rise of Anglo-German Antagonism, 1860–1914* (London, 1982).

For additional reading, go to InfoTrac College Edition, your online research library at http://web1.infotrac-college.com

Enter the search term *Nietzsche* using Key Terms.

Enter the search terms *Sigmund Freud* using Key Terms.

Enter the search terms *Social Darwinism* using Key Terms.

Enter the search term *imperialism* using Subject Guide.

25

The Beginning of the Twentieth-Century Crisis: War and Revolution

CHAPTER OUTLINE

- The Road to World War I
- The War
- War and Revolution
- The Peace Settlement
- Conclusion

FOCUS QUESTIONS

- What where the long-range and immediate causes of World War I?
- What did the belligerents expect at the beginning of World War I, and why did the course of the war turn out to be so different from their expectations?
- How did World War I affect the belligerents' governmental and political institutions, economic affairs, and social life?
- What were the causes of the Russian Revolution of 1917, and why did the Bolsheviks prevail in the civil war and gain control of Russia?
- What were the objectives of the chief participants at the Paris Peace Conference of 1919, and how closely did the final settlement reflect these objectives?

O N JULY 1, 1916, *British and French infantry forces attacked German defensive lines along a twenty-five-mile front near the Somme River in France. Each soldier carried almost seventy pounds of equipment, making it "impossible to move much quicker than a slow walk." German machine guns soon opened fire: "We were able to see our comrades move forward in an attempt to cross No-Man's Land, only to be mown down like meadow grass," recalled one British soldier. "I felt sick at the sight of this carnage and remember weeping." In one day more than 21,000 British soldiers died. After six months of fighting, the British had advanced five miles; one million British, French, and German soldiers had been killed or wounded.*

World War I (1914–1918) was the defining event of the twentieth century. It devastated the prewar economic, social, and political order of Europe, and its uncertain outcome served to prepare the way for an even more destructive war. Overwhelmed by the size of its battles, the number of its casualties, and the extent of its impact on all facets of

European life, contemporaries referred to it simply as the "Great War."

The Great War was all the more disturbing to Europeans because it came after a period that many believed to have been an age of progress. There had been international crises before 1914, but somehow Europeans had managed to avoid serious and prolonged military confrontations. When smaller European states had gone to war, as in the Balkans in 1912 and 1913, the great European powers had shown the ability to keep the conflict localized. Material prosperity and a fervid belief in scientific and technological progress had convinced many people that Europe stood on the verge of creating the utopia that humans had dreamed of for centuries. The historian Arnold Toynbee expressed what the pre–World War I era had meant to his generation:

> *[it was expected] that life throughout the World would become more rational, more humane, and more democratic and that, slowly, but surely, political democracy would produce greater social justice. We had also expected that the progress of science and technology would make mankind richer, and that this increasing wealth would gradually spread from a minority to a majority. We had expected that all this would happen peacefully. In fact we thought that mankind's course was set for an earthly paradise.[1]*

After 1918, it was no longer possible to maintain naive illusions about the progress of Western civilization. As World War I was followed by the destructiveness of World War II and the mass murder machines of totalitarian regimes, it became all too apparent that instead of a utopia, European civilization had become a nightmare. The Great War resulted not only in great loss of life and property, but also in the annihilation of one of the basic intellectual precepts upon which Western civilization had been thought to have been founded—the belief in progress. A sense of hopelessness and despair soon replaced an almost blind faith in progress. World War I and the revolutions it spawned can properly be seen as the first stage in the crisis of the twentieth century.

◆ The Road to World War I

On June 28, 1914, the heir to the Austrian throne, the Archduke Francis Ferdinand, was assassinated in the Bosnian city of Sarajevo. Although this event precipitated the confrontation between Austria and Serbia that led to World War I, war was not inevitable. Previous assassinations of European leaders usually had not led to war,

and European statesmen had managed to localize such conflicts on a number of occasions. Although the decisions that European statesmen made during this crisis were crucial in leading to war, there were also long-range, underlying forces that were propelling Europeans toward armed conflict.

✳ Nationalism and Internal Dissent

In the first half of the nineteenth century, liberals had maintained that the organization of European states along national lines would lead to a peaceful Europe based on a sense of international fraternity. They had been very wrong. The system of nation-states that had emerged in Europe in the last half of the nineteenth century led not to cooperation but to competition. Rivalries over colonial and commercial interests intensified during an era of frenzied imperialist expansion, and the division of Europe's great powers into two loose alliances (Germany, Austria, and Italy and France, Great Britain, and Russia) only added to the tensions. The series of crises that tested these alliances in the 1900s and early 1910s had taught European states a dangerous lesson. Those governments that had exercised restraint in order to avoid war wound up being publicly humiliated, whereas those that went to the brink of war to maintain their national interests had often been praised for having preserved national honor. In either case, by 1914, the major European states had come to believe that their allies were important and that their security depended on supporting those allies, even when they took foolish risks.

Diplomacy based on brinkmanship was especially frightening in view of the nature of the European state system. Each nation-state regarded itself as sovereign, subject to no higher interest or authority. Each state was motivated by its own self-interest and success. As Emperor William II of Germany remarked: "In questions of honor and vital interests, you don't consult others." Such attitudes made war an ever-present possibility, particularly since most statesmen considered war an acceptable way to preserve the power of their national states.

The growth of nationalism in the nineteenth century had yet another serious consequence. Not all ethnic groups had achieved the goal of nationhood. Slavic minorities in the Balkans and the Austrian Empire, for example, still dreamed of creating their own national states. So did the Irish in the British Empire and the Poles in the Russian Empire.

National aspirations, however, were not the only source of internal strife at the beginning of the twentieth century. Socialist labor movements had grown more powerful and were increasingly inclined to use strikes, even violent ones, to achieve their goals. Some conservative leaders, alarmed at the increase in labor strife and class division, even feared that European nations were on the verge of revolution. Did these statesmen opt for war in

1914 because they believed that "prosecuting an active foreign policy," as one leader expressed it, would smother "internal troubles"? Some historians have argued that the desire to suppress internal disorder may have encouraged some leaders to take the plunge into war in 1914.

❋ Militarism

The growth of large mass armies after 1900 not only heightened the existing tensions in Europe, but made it inevitable that if war did come it would be highly destructive. Conscription had been established as a regular practice in most Western countries before 1914 (the United States and Britain were major exceptions). European military machines had doubled in size between 1890 and 1914. With its 1.3 million men, the Russian army had grown to be the largest, but the French and Germans were not far behind with 900,000 each. The British, Italian, and Austrian armies numbered between 250,000 and 500,000 soldiers. Most European land armies were filled with peasants, since many young, urban working-class males were unable to pass the physical examinations required for military service.

Militarism, however, involved more than just large armies. As armies grew, so too did the influence of military leaders who drew up vast and complex plans for quickly mobilizing millions of men and enormous quantities of supplies in the event of war. Fearful that changes in these plans would cause chaos in the armed forces, military leaders insisted that their plans could not be altered. In the crises during the summer of 1914, the generals' lack of flexibility forced European political leaders to make decisions for military instead of political reasons.

❋ The Outbreak of War: The Summer of 1914

Militarism, nationalism, and the desire to stifle internal dissent may all have played a role in the coming of World War I, but the decisions made by European leaders in the summer of 1914 directly precipitated the conflict. It was another crisis in the Balkans that forced this predicament upon European statesmen.

As we have seen, states in southeastern Europe had struggled to free themselves from Ottoman rule in the course of the nineteenth and early twentieth centuries. But the rivalry between Austria-Hungary and Russia for domination of these new states created serious tensions in the region. The crises between 1908 and 1913 had only intensified the antagonisms. By 1914, Serbia, supported by Russia, was determined to create a large, independent Slavic state in the Balkans, but Austria, which had its own Slavic minorities to contend with, was equally set on preventing that possibility. Many Europeans perceived the inherent dangers in this combination of Serbian ambition bolstered by Russian hatred of Austria and Austrian

conviction that Serbia's success would mean the end of its empire. The British ambassador to Vienna wrote in 1913:

> Serbia will some day set Europe by the ears, and bring about a universal war on the Continent. . . . I cannot tell you how exasperated people are getting here at the continual worry which that little country causes to Austria under encouragement from Russia. . . . It will be lucky if Europe succeeds in avoiding war as a result of the present crisis. The next time a Serbian crisis arises . . . , I feel sure that Austria-Hungary will refuse to admit of any Russian interference in the dispute and that she will proceed to settle her differences with her little neighbor by herself.[2]

It was against this backdrop of mutual distrust and hatred between Austria-Hungary and Russia, on the one hand, and Austria-Hungary and Serbia, on the other, that the events of the summer of 1914 were played out.

The assassination of the Austrian Archduke Francis Ferdinand and his wife Sophia on June 28, 1914, was carried out by a Bosnian activist who worked for the Black Hand, a Serbian terrorist organization dedicated to the creation of a pan-Slavic kingdom. Although the Austrian government did not know whether the Serbian government had been directly involved in the archduke's assassination, it saw an opportunity to "render Serbia impotent once and for all by a display of force," as the Austrian foreign minister put it. Fearful of Russian intervention on Serbia's behalf, Austrian leaders sought the backing of their German allies. Emperor William II and his chancellor, Theobald von Bethmann-Hollweg, responded with the infamous "blank check," their assurance that Austria-Hungary could rely on Germany's "full support," even if "matters went to the length of a war between Austria-Hungary and Russia." Much historical debate has focused on this "blank check" extended to the Austrians. Did the Germans realize that an Austrian-Serbian war could lead to a wider war? If so, did they actually want one? Historians are still seriously divided on the answers to these questions.

APPREHENSION OF AN ASSASSIN. World War I was precipitated by the assassination of the Archduke Francis Ferdinand, heir to the Austrian throne, on June 28, 1914. His assassin was Gavrillo Princip, an eighteen-year-old Bosnian activist and student who favored the creation of a pan-Slavic kingdom at Austria's expense. As shown here, he was arrested soon after killing Francis Ferdinand and his wife.

Strengthened by German support, Austrian leaders issued an ultimatum to Serbia on July 23. Austrian leaders made their demands so extreme that Serbia had little choice but to reject some of them in order to preserve its sovereignty. Austria then declared war on Serbia on July 28. Although both Germany and Austria had hoped to keep the war limited to Serbia and Austria in order to ensure Austria's success in the Balkans, these hopes soon vanished.

Still smarting from its humiliation in the Bosnian crisis of 1908, Russia was determined to support Serbia's cause. On July 28, Tsar Nicholas II ordered partial mobilization of the Russian army against Austria. At this point, the rigidity of the military war plans played havoc with diplomatic and political decisions. The Russian General Staff informed the tsar that their mobilization plans were based on a war against both Germany and Austria simultaneously. They could not execute partial mobilization without creating chaos in the army. Consequently, the Russian government ordered full mobilization of the Russian army on July 29, knowing that the Germans would consider this an act of war against them (see the box on p. 751). Germany responded to Russian mobilization with its own ultimatum that the Russians must halt their mobilization within twelve hours. When the Russians ignored it, Germany declared war on Russia on August 1.

At this stage of the conflict, German war plans determined whether France would become involved in the war. Under the guidance of General Alfred von Schlieffen, chief of staff from 1891 to 1905, the German General Staff had devised a military plan based on the assumption of a two-front war with France and Russia, since the two powers had formed a military alliance in 1894. The Schlieffen Plan called for a minimal troop deployment against Russia while most of the German army would make a rapid invasion of western France by way of neutral Belgium. After the planned quick defeat of the French, the German army expected to redeploy to the east against Russia. Under the Schlieffen Plan, Germany could not mobilize its troops solely against Russia and therefore declared war on France on August 3 after issuing an ultimatum to Belgium on August 2 demanding the right of German troops to pass through Belgian territory. On August 4, Great Britain declared war on Germany, officially over this violation of Belgian neutrality, but in fact over the British desire to maintain their world power. As one British diplomat argued, if Germany and Austria were to win the war, "what would be the position of a friendless England?" By August 4, all the great powers of Europe were at war. Through all the maneuvering of the last few days before the war, one fact stands out—all the great powers seemed willing to risk the Great War. They were not disappointed.

"You Have to Bear the responsibility for War or Peace"

After Austria declared war on Serbia on July 28, 1914, Russian support of Serbia and German support of Austria threatened to escalate the conflict in the Balkans into a wider war. As we can see in these last-minute telegrams between the Russians and Germans, neither side was able to accept the other's line of reasoning.

Communications between Berlin and St. Petersburg on the Eve of World War I

❋ Emperor William II to Tsar Nicholas II, July 28, 10:45 P.M.

I have heard with the greatest anxiety of the impression which is caused by the action of Austria-Hungary against Servia [Serbia]. The inscrupulous agitation which has been going on for years in Servia, has led to the revolting crime of which Archduke Franz Ferdinand has become a victim. The spirit which made the Servians murder their own King and his consort still dominates that country. Doubtless You will agree with me that both of us, You as well as I, and all other sovereigns, have a common interest to insist that all those who are responsible for this horrible murder shall suffer their deserved punishment. . . .

Your most sincere and devoted friend and cousin

(Signed)
Wilhelm

❋ Tsar Nicholas II to Emperor William II, July 29, 1:00 P.M.

I am glad that you are back in Germany. In this serious moment I ask You earnestly to help me. An ignominious war has been declared against a weak country and in Russia the indignation which I full share is tremendous. I fear that very soon I shall be unable to resist the pressure exercised upon me and that I shall be forced to take measures which will lead to war. To prevent a calamity as a European war would be, I urge You in the name of our old friendship to do all in Your power to restrain Your ally from going too far.

(Signed)
Nicolas

❋ Emperor William II to Tsar Nicholas II, July 29, 6:30 P.M.

I have received Your telegram and I share Your desire for the conservation of peace. However: I cannot—as I told You in my first telegram—consider the action of Austria-Hungary as an "ignominious war." Austria-Hungary knows from experience that the promises of Servia as long as they are merely on paper are entirely unreliable. . . . I believe that a direct understanding is possible and desirable between Your Government and Vienna, an understanding which I—as I have already telegraphed You—my Government endeavors to aid with all possible effort. Naturally military measures by Russia, which might be construed as a menace by Austria-Hungary, would accelerate a calamity which both of us desire to avoid and would undermine my position as mediator which—upon Your appeal to my friendship and aid—I willingly accepted.

(Signed)
Wilhelm

❋ Emperor William II to Tsar Nicholas II, July 30, 1:00 A.M.

My Ambassador has instructions to direct the attention of Your Government to the dangers and serious consequences of a mobilization. I have told You the same in my last telegram. Austria-Hungary has mobilized only against Servia, and only a part of her army. If Russia, as seems to be the case, according to Your advice and that of Your Government, mobilizes against Austria-Hungary, the part of the mediator with which You have entrusted me in such friendly manner and which I have accepted upon Your express desire, is threatened if not made impossible. The entire weight of decision now rests upon Your shoulders, You have to bear the responsibility for war or peace.

(Signed)
Wilhelm

❋ German Chancellor to German Ambassador at St. Petersburg, July 31, URGENT

In spite of negotiations still pending and although we have up to this hour made no preparations for mobilization, Russia has mobilized her entire army and navy, hence also against us. On account of these Russian measures, we have been forced, for the safety of the country, to proclaim the threatening state of war, which does not yet imply mobilization. Mobilization, however, is bound to follow if Russia does not stop every measure of war against us and against Austria-Hungary within 12 hours, and notifies us definitely to this effect. Please to communicate this at once to M. Sasonof and wire hour of communication.

MAP 25.1 Europe in 1914.

◆ The War

Before 1914, many political leaders had become convinced that war involved so many political and economic risks that it was not worth fighting. Others had believed that "rational" diplomats could control any situation and prevent the outbreak of war. At the beginning of August 1914, both of these prewar illusions were shattered, but the new illusions that replaced them soon proved to be equally foolish.

※ *1914–1915: Illusions and Stalemate*

Europeans went to war in 1914 with remarkable enthusiasm (see the box on p. 753). Government propaganda had been successful in stirring up national antagonisms before the war. Now in August of 1914, the urgent pleas of governments for defense against aggressors fell on receptive ears in every belligerent nation. Most people seemed genuinely convinced that their nation's cause was just. Even domestic differences were temporarily shelved in the midst of war fever. Socialists had long derided "imperialist war" as a blow against the common interests that united the working classes of all countries. Nationalism, however,

proved more powerful than working-class solidarity in the summer of 1914 as socialist parties everywhere dropped plans for strikes and workers expressed their readiness to fight for their country. The German Social Democrats, for example, decided that it was imperative to "safeguard the culture and independence of our own country."

A new set of illusions fed the enthusiasm for war. Almost everyone in August 1914 believed that the war would be over in a few weeks. People were reminded that all European wars since 1815 had, in fact, ended in a matter of weeks, conveniently overlooking the American Civil War (1861–1865), which was the "real prototype" for World War I. The illusion of a short war was also bolstered by another illusion, the belief that in an age of modern industry war could not be conducted for more than a few months without destroying a nation's economy. Both the soldiers who exuberantly boarded the trains for the war front in August 1914 and the jubilant citizens who bombarded them with flowers when they departed believed that the warriors would be home by Christmas.

Then, too, war held a fatal attraction for many people. To some, war was an exhilarating release from humdrum bourgeois existence, from a "world grown old and cold and weary," as one poet wrote. To some, war meant a glorious adventure, as a young German student wrote

The Excitement of War

The incredible outpouring of patriotic enthusiasm that greeted the declaration of war at the beginning of August 1914 demonstrated the power that nationalistic feeling had attained at the beginning of the twentieth century. Many Europeans seemingly believed that the war had given them a higher purpose, a renewed dedication to the greatness of their nation. This selection is taken from the autobiography of Stefan Zweig, an Austrian writer who captured well the orgiastic celebration of war in Vienna in 1914.

✳ Stefan Zweig, *The World of Yesterday*

The next morning I was in Austria. In every station placards had been put up announcing general mobilization. The trains were filled with fresh recruits, banners were flying, music sounded, and in Vienna I found the entire city in a tumult.... There were parades in the street, flags, ribbons, and music burst forth everywhere, young recruits were marching triumphantly, their faces lighting up at the cheering....

And to be truthful, I must acknowledge that there was a majestic, rapturous, and even seductive something in this first outbreak of the people from which one could escape only with difficulty. And in spite of all my hatred and aversion for war, I should not like to have missed the memory of those days. As never before, thousands and hundreds of thousands felt what they should have felt in peace time, that they belonged together. A city of two million, a country of nearly fifty million, in that hour felt that they were participating in world history, in a moment which would never recur, and that each one was called upon to cast his infinitesimal self into the glowing mass, there to be purified of all selfishness. All differences of class, rank, and language were flooded over at that moment by the rushing feeling of fraternity. Strangers spoke to one another in the streets, people who had avoided each other for years shook hands, everywhere one saw excited faces. Each individual experienced an exaltation of his ego, he was no longer the isolated person of former times, he had been incorporated into the mass, he was part of the people, and his person, his hitherto unnoticed person, had been given meaning....

What did the great mass know of war in 1914, after nearly half a century of peace? They did not know war, they had hardly given it a thought. It had become legendary, and distance had made it seem romantic and heroic. They still saw it in the perspective of their school readers and of paintings in museums; brilliant cavalry attacks in glittering uniforms, the fatal shot always straight through the heart, the entire campaign a resounding march of victory—"We'll be home at Christmas," the recruits shouted laughingly to their mothers in August of 1914.... A rapid excursion into the romantic, a wild, manly adventure—that is how the war of 1914 was painted in the imagination of the simple man, and the younger people were honestly afraid that they might miss this most wonderful and exciting experience of their lives; that is why they hurried and thronged to the colors, and that is why they shouted and sang in the trains that carried them to the slaughter; wildly and feverishly the red wave of blood coursed through the veins of the entire nation.

---

to his parents: "My dear ones, be proud that you live in such a time and in such a nation and that you . . . have the privilege of sending those you love into so glorious a battle."[3] And finally some believed that the war would have a redemptive effect, that millions would abandon their petty preoccupations with material life, ridding the nation of selfishness and sparking a national rebirth based on self-sacrifice, heroism, and nobility. All of these illusions about war died painful deaths on the battlefields of World War I.

German hopes for a quick end to the war rested upon a military gamble. The Schlieffen Plan had called for the German army to make a vast encircling movement through Belgium into northern France that would sweep around Paris and encircle most of the French army. German troops crossed into Belgium on August 4 and by the first week of September had reached the Marne River, only twenty miles from Paris. The Germans seemed on the verge of success, but had underestimated the speed with which the British would be able to mobilize and put troops into battle in France. An unexpected counterattack by British and French forces under the French commander General Joseph Joffre stopped the Germans at the First Battle of the Marne (September 6–10). The German troops fell back, but the exhausted French army was unable to pursue its advantage. The war quickly turned into a stalemate as neither the Germans nor the French could dislodge the other from the trenches they had begun to dig for shelter. Two lines of trenches soon extended from the English Channel to the frontiers of Switzerland. The Western Front had become bogged down in a trench warfare that kept both sides immobilized in virtually the same positions for four years.

In contrast to the west, the war in the east was marked by much more mobility, although the cost in lives was equally enormous. At the beginning of the war, the Russian army moved into eastern Germany but was decisively defeated at the Battles of Tannenberg on August 30

THE EXCITEMENT OF WAR. World War I was greeted with incredible enthusiasm. Each of the major belligerents was convinced of the rightness of its cause. Everywhere in Europe, jubilant civilians sent their troops off to war with joyous fervor. Their belief that the soldiers would be home by Christmas proved to be a pathetic illusion.

and the Masurian Lakes on September 15. These battles established the military reputations of the commanding general, Paul von Hindenburg, and his chief of staff, General Erich Ludendorff. The Russians were no longer a threat to German territory.

The Austrians, Germany's allies, fared less well initially. They had been defeated by the Russians in Galicia and thrown out of Serbia as well. To make matters worse, the Italians betrayed the Germans and Austrians and entered the war on the Allied side by attacking Austria in May 1915. By this time, the Germans had come to the aid of the Austrians. A German-Austrian army defeated and routed the Russian army in Galicia and pushed the Russians back 300 miles into their own territory. Russian casualties stood at 2.5 million killed, captured, or wounded; the Russians had almost been knocked out of the war. Buoyed by their success, the Germans and Austrians, joined by the Bulgarians in September 1915, attacked and eliminated Serbia from the war.

✻ 1916–1917: *The Great Slaughter*

The successes in the east enabled the Germans to move back to the offensive in the west. The early trenches dug in 1914 had by now become elaborate systems of defense. Both lines of trenches were protected by barbed wire entanglements three to five feet high and thirty yards wide, concrete machine-gun nests, and mortar batteries,

supported further back by heavy artillery. Troops lived in holes in the ground, separated from each other by a "no man's land."

The unexpected development of trench warfare baffled military leaders who had been trained to fight wars of movement and maneuver. But public outcries for action put them under heavy pressure. The only plan generals could devise was to attempt a breakthrough by throwing masses of men against enemy lines that had first been battered by artillery barrages. Once the decisive breakthrough had been achieved, they thought, they could then return to the war of movement that they knew best. Periodically, the high command on either side would order an offensive that would begin with an artillery barrage to flatten the enemy's barbed wire and leave the enemy in a state of shock. After "softening up" the enemy in this fashion, a mass of soldiers would climb out of their trenches with fixed bayonets and try to work their way toward the enemy trenches. The attacks rarely worked, since the machine gun put hordes of men advancing unprotected across open fields at a severe disadvantage. In 1916 and 1917, millions of young men were sacrificed in the search for the elusive breakthrough. In the German offensive at Verdun in 1916, the British campaign on the Somme in 1916, and the French attack in the Champagne in 1917, the senselessness of trench warfare became all too obvious. In ten months at Verdun, 700,000 men lost their lives over a few miles of terrain.

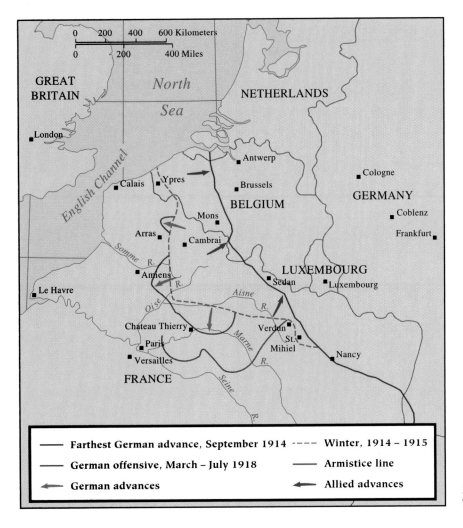

MAP 25.2
The Western Front, 1914–1918.

Legend:
— Farthest German advance, September 1914
— German offensive, March – July 1918
← German advances
---- Winter, 1914 – 1915
— Armistice line
← Allied advances

THE HORRORS OF WAR.   The slaughter of millions of men in the trenches of World War I created unimaginable horrors for the participants. For the sake of survival, many soldiers learned to harden themselves against the stench of decomposing bodies and the sight of bodies horribly dismembered by artillery barrages.

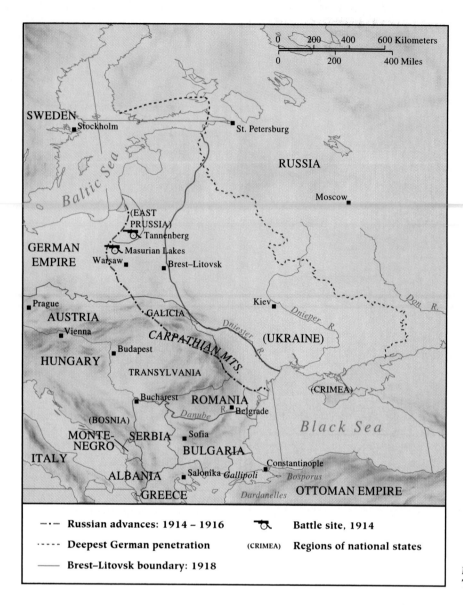

MAP 25.3
The Eastern Front, 1914–1918.

Legend:
- —·— Russian advances: 1914–1916
- ----- Deepest German penetration
- ——— Brest–Litovsk boundary: 1918
- Battle site, 1914
- (CRIMEA) Regions of national states

DAILY LIFE IN THE TRENCHES

Warfare in the trenches of the Western Front produced unimaginable horrors (see the box on p. 757). Many participants commented on the cloud of confusion that covered the battlefields. When attacking soldiers entered "no man's land," the noise, machine-gun fire, and exploding artillery shells often caused them to panic and lose their sense of direction; they went forward only because they were carried on by the momentum of the soldiers beside them. Rarely were battles as orderly as they were portrayed on military maps and in civilian newspapers.

Battlefields were hellish landscapes of barbed wire, shell holes, mud, and injured and dying men. The introduction of poison gas in 1915 produced new forms of injuries, as one British writer described:

> I wish those people who write so glibly about this being a holy war could see a case of mustard gas . . . could see the poor things burnt and blistered all over with great mustard-colored suppurating blisters with blind eyes all sticky . . .

and stuck together, and always fighting for breath, with voices a mere whisper, saying that their throats are closing and they know they will choke.[4]

Soldiers in the trenches also lived with the persistent presence of death. Since combat went on for months, they had to carry on in the midst of countless bodies of dead men or the remains of men dismembered by artillery barrages. Many soldiers remembered the stench of decomposing bodies and the swarms of rats that grew fat in the trenches.

Soldiers on the Western Front did not spend all of their time on the front line or in combat when they were on the front line. An infantryman spent one week out of every month in the front-line trenches, one week in the reserve lines, and the remaining two weeks somewhere behind the lines. Daily life in the trenches was predictable. Thirty minutes before sunrise, troops had to "stand to" or be combat ready to repel any attack. If no attack were forthcoming that day, the day's routine consisted of break-

The Reality of War: Trench Warfare

The romantic illusions about the excitement and adventure of war that filled the minds of so many young men who marched off to battle (see the box on p. 753) quickly disintegrated after a short time in the trenches on the Western Front. This description of trench warfare is taken from the most famous novel that emerged from World War I, Erich Maria Remarque's All Quiet on the Western Front, *written in 1929. Remarque had fought in the trenches in France.*

❊ Erich Maria Remarque, *All Quiet on the Western Front*

We wake up in the middle of the night. The earth booms. Heavy fire is falling on us. We crouch into corners. We distinguish shells of every caliber.

Each man lays hold of his things and looks again every minute to reassure himself that they are still there. The dug-out heaves, the night roars and flashes. We look at each other in the momentary flashes of light, and with pale faces and pressed lips shake our heads.

Every man is aware of the heavy shells tearing down the parapet, rooting up the embankment and demolishing the upper layers of concrete. . . . Already by morning a few of the recruits are green and vomiting. They are too inexperienced. . . .

The bombardment does not diminish. It is falling in the rear too. As far as one can see it spouts fountains of mud and iron. A wide belt is being raked.

The attack does not come, but the bombardment continues. Slowly we become mute. Hardly a man speaks. We cannot make ourselves understood.

Our trench is almost gone. At many places it is only eighteen inches high, it is broken by holes, and craters, and mountains of earth. A shell lands square in front of our post. At once it is dark. We are buried and must dig ourselves out. . . .

Towards morning, while it is still dark, there is some excitement. Through the entrance rushes in a swarm of fleeing rats that try to storm the walls. Torches light up the confusion. Everyone yells and curses and slaughters. The madness and despair of many hours unloads itself in this outburst. Faces are distorted, arms strike out, the beasts scream; we just stop in time to avoid attacking one another. . . .

Suddenly it howls and flashes terrifically, the dugout cracks in all its joints under a direct hit, fortunately only a light one that the concrete blocks are able to withstand. It rings metallically, the walls reel, rifles, helmets, earth, mud, and dust fly everywhere. Sulphur fumes pour in. . . . The recruit starts to rave again and two others follow suit. One jumps up and rushes out, we have trouble with the other two. I start after the one who escapes and wonder whether to shoot him in the leg— then it shrieks again, I fling myself down and when I stand up the wall of the trench is plastered with smoking splinters, lumps of flesh, and bits of uniform. I scramble back.

The first recruit seems actually to have gone insane. He butts his head against the wall like a goat. We must try tonight to take him to the rear. Meanwhile we bind him, but so that in case of attack he can be released.

Suddenly the nearer explosions cease. The shelling continues but it has lifted and falls behind us, our trench is free. We seize the hand-grenades, pitch them out in front of the dug-out and jump after them. The bombardment has stopped and a heavy barrage now falls behind us. The attack has come.

No one would believe that in this howling waste there could still be men; but steel helmets now appear on all sides out of the trench, and fifty yards from us a machine-gun is already in position and barking.

The wire-entanglements are torn to pieces. Yet they offer some obstacle. We see the storm-troops coming. Our artillery opens fire. Machine-guns rattle, rifles crack. The charge works its way across. Haie and Kropp begin with the hand-grenades. They throw as fast as they can, others pass them, the handles with the strings already pulled. Haie throws seventy-five yards, Kropp sixty, it has been measured, the distance is important. The enemy as they run cannot do much before they are within forty yards.

We recognize the distorted faces, the smooth helmets: they are French. They have already suffered heavily when they reach the remnants of the barbed-wire entanglements. A whole line has gone down before our machine-guns; then we have a lot of stoppages and they come nearer.

I see one of them, his face upturned, fall into a wire cradle. His body collapses, his hands remain suspended as though he were praying. Then his body drops clean away and only his hands with the stumps of his arms, shot off, now hang in the wire.

---

fast followed by inspection, sentry duty, restoration of the trenches, care of personal items, or whiling away the time as best they could. Soldiers often recalled the boredom of life in the dreary, lice-ridden, muddy or dusty trenches.

At many places along the opposing lines of trenches, a "live and let live" system evolved based on the realization that neither side was going to drive out the other anyway. The "live and let live" system resulted in such arrangements as not shelling the latrines or attacking

THE DESTRUCTION OF VERDUN.   In 1916, the German
high command decided to take the offensive against the
French fortifications at Verdun, which was 125 miles east
of Paris. The ferocious Battle of Verdun cost 700,000
lives and resulted in an exchange of only a few miles of
land. The city of Verdun was subjected to massive
artillery shelling and, as this photograph shows, was
severely damaged. The population of Verdun dropped
from 15,000 to 3,000 in the course of the battle.

IMPACT OF THE MACHINE GUN:
THE GUNNERS.   The development of trench warfare on the
Western Front stymied military
leaders who had expected to
fight a war based on movement
and maneuver. Their efforts to
effect a breakthrough by sending masses of men against
enemy lines were the height of
folly in view of the machine
gun. This photograph shows a
group of German soldiers in
their machine gun nest.

during breakfast. Some parties even worked out agreements to make noise before lesser raids so that the opposing soldiers could retreat to their bunkers.

On both sides, troops produced their own humorous magazines to help pass the time and fulfill the need to laugh in the midst of their daily madness. The British trench magazine, the B.E.F. Times, devoted one of its issues to defining military terms. A typical definition "DUDS—These are of two kinds. A shell on impact failing to explode is called a dud. They are unhappily not as plentiful as the other kind, which often draws a big salary and explodes for no reason. These are plentiful away from the fighting areas."[5] Soldiers' songs also captured a mixture of the sentimental and the frivolous (see the box on p. 760).

❊ *The Widening of the War*

As another response to the stalemate on the Western Front, both sides sought to gain new allies who might provide a winning advantage. The Turkish or Ottoman Empire had already come into the war on Germany's side in August 1914. Russia, Great Britain, and France declared war on the Ottoman Empire in November. Although the forces of the British Empire attempted to open a Balkan front by landing forces at Gallipoli, southwest of Constantinople, in April 1915, the entry of Bulgaria into the war on the side of the Central Powers (as Germany, Austria-Hungary, and the Ottoman Empire were called) and a disastrous campaign at Gallipoli caused them to withdraw. The Italians, as we have seen, also entered the war on the Allied side after France and Britain promised to further their acquisition of Austrian territory. In the long run, however, Italian military incompetence forced the Allies to come to the assistance of Italy.

By 1917, the war that had begun in Europe was having an increasing impact on other parts of the world. In the Middle East, a British officer who came to be known as Lawrence of Arabia incited Arab princes to revolt against their Ottoman overlords. In 1918, British forces from Egypt destroyed the rest of the Ottoman Empire in the Middle East. For their Middle East campaigns, the British mobilized forces from India, Australia, and New Zealand. The Allies also took advantage of Germany's preoccupations in Europe and lack of naval strength to seize German colonies in the rest of the world.

☙ ENTRY OF THE UNITED STATES

At first, the United States tried to remain neutral in the Great War, but found it more difficult to do so as the war dragged on. Although there was considerable sentiment for the British side in the conflict, the immediate cause of American involvement grew out of the naval conflict between Germany and Great Britain. Only once did the German and British naval forces engage in direct battle—at the Battle of Jutland on May 31, 1916, when the Germans won an inconclusive victory.

Britain used its superior naval power to maximum effect, however, by imposing a naval blockade on Germany. Germany retaliated with a counterblockade enforced by the use of unrestricted submarine warfare. At the beginning of 1915, the German government declared the area around the British Isles a war zone and threatened to torpedo any ship caught in it. Strong American protests over the German sinking of passenger liners, especially the British ship *Lusitania* on May 7, 1915, when more than 100 Americans lost their lives,

IMPACT OF THE MACHINE GUN: THE VICTIMS. Masses of men weighed down with equipment and advancing slowly across open land made magnificent targets for opponents armed with the machine gun. This photograph shows French soldiers moving across a rocky terrain, all open targets for their enemies manning the new weapons.

The Songs of World War I

On the march, in bars, in trains, and even in the trenches, the soldiers of World War I spent time singing. The songs sung by soldiers of different nationalities varied considerably. A German favorite, The Watch on the Rhine, focused on heroism and patriotism. British war songs often partook of black humor, as in The Old Barbed Wire. An American favorite was the rousing Over There, written by the professional songwriter George M. Cohan.

✳ From *The Watch on the Rhine*

> There sounds a call like thunder's roar,
> Like the crash of swords, like the surge of waves.
> To the Rhine, the Rhine, the German Rhine!
> Who will the stream's defender be?
> > Dear Fatherland, rest quietly
> > Sure stands and true the Watch,
> > The Watch on the Rhine.
>
> To heaven he gazes.
> Spirits of heroes look down.
> He vows with proud battle-desire:
> O Rhine! You will stay as German as my breast!
> > Dear Fatherland, [etc.]
> Even if my heart breaks in death,
> You will never be French.
> As you are rich in water
> Germany is rich in hero's blood.
> > Dear Fatherland, [etc.]
>
> So long as a drop of blood still glows,
> So long a hand the dagger can draw,
> So long an arm the rifle can hold—
> Never will an enemy touch your shore.
> > Dear Fatherland, [etc.]

✳ From *The Old Barbed Wire*

> If you want to find the old battalion,
> I know where they are,
> I know where they are.
> If you want to find a battalion,

> I know where they are,
> They're hanging on the old barbed wire.
> I've seen 'em, I've seen 'em,
> Hanging on the old barbed wire,
> I've seen 'em,
> Hanging on the old barbed wire.

✳ George M. Cohan, *Over There*

> Over There
> Over There
> Send the word
> Send the word
> Over There
> That the boys are coming
> The drums rum-tuming everywhere.
> Over There
> Say a prayer
> Send the word
> Send the word
> To Beware.
> It will be over.
> We're coming over
> And we won't come back
> Till it's over
> Over There.
>
> Johnnie get your gun
> > get your gun
> > get your gun
> Back in town to run
> Home to run
> Home to run
> Hear them calling you and me
> Every son of liberty
> Hurry right away
> Don't delay go today
> Make your Daddy glad
> To have had such a lad
> Tell your sweetheart not to pine
> To be proud their boy's in line.

forced the German government to modify its policy of unrestricted submarine warfare starting in September 1915 and to briefly suspend unrestricted submarine warfare a year later.

In January 1917, however, eager to break the deadlock in the war, the Germans decided on another military gamble by returning to unrestricted submarine warfare. German naval officers convinced Emperor William II that the use of unrestricted submarine warfare could starve the British into submission within five months. When the emperor expressed concern about the Americans, he was told not to worry. The Americans, the chief of the German Naval Staff said, were "disorganized and undisciplined." The British would starve before the Americans could act. And even if the Americans did intervene, Admiral Holtzendorff assured the emperor, "I give your Majesty my word as an officer, that not one American will land on the continent."

The return to unrestricted submarine warfare brought the United States into the war on April 6, 1917.

Although American troops did not arrive in large numbers in Europe until 1918, the entry of the United States into the war in 1917 gave the Allied powers a psychological boost when they needed it. The year 1917 was not a good year for them. Allied offensives on the Western Front were disastrously defeated. The Italian armies were smashed in October, and in November 1917 the Bolshevik Revolution in Russia led to Russia's withdrawal from the war (see The Russian Revolution later in this chapter). The cause of the Central Powers looked favorable, although war weariness in the Ottoman Empire, Bulgaria, Austria-Hungary, and Germany was beginning to take its toll. The home front was rapidly becoming a cause for as much concern as the war front.

✻ *The Home Front: The Impact of Total War*

The prolongation of World War I made it a total war that affected the lives of all citizens, however remote they might be from the battlefields. World War I transformed the governments, economies, and societies of the European belligerents in fundamental ways. The need to organize masses of men and matériel for years of combat (Germany alone had 5.5 million men in active units in 1916) led to increased centralization of government powers, economic regimentation, and manipulation of public opinion to keep the war effort going.

✣ TOTAL WAR: POLITICAL CENTRALIZATION AND ECONOMIC REGIMENTATION

As we have seen, the outbreak of World War I was greeted with a rush of patriotism; even socialists joined enthusiastically into the fray. As the war dragged on, governments realized, however, that more than patriotism would be needed. Since the war was expected to be short, little thought had been given to economic problems and long-term wartime needs. Governments had to respond quickly, however, when the war machines failed to achieve their knockout blows and made ever-greater demands for men and matériel.

The extension of government power was a logical outgrowth of these needs. Most European countries had already devised some system of mass conscription or military draft. It was now carried to unprecedented heights as countries mobilized tens of millions of young men for that elusive breakthrough to victory. Even countries that traditionally relied on volunteers (Great Britain had the largest volunteer army in modern history—one million men—in 1914 and 1915) were forced to resort to conscription, especially to ensure that skilled workers did not enlist but remained in factories that were crucial to the production of munitions. In 1916, despite widespread resistance to this extension of government power, compulsory military service was introduced in Great Britain.

Throughout Europe, wartime governments expanded their powers over their economies. Free-market capitalistic systems were temporarily shelved as governments experimented with price, wage, and rent controls, the rationing of food supplies and materials, the regulation of imports and exports, and the nationalization of transportation systems and industries. Some governments even moved toward compulsory labor employment. In effect, in order to mobilize the entire resources of their nations for the war effort, European nations had moved toward planned economies directed by government agencies. Under total war mobilization, the distinction between soldiers at war and civilians at home was narrowed. In the view of political leaders, all citizens constituted a national army dedicated to victory. As the American president Woodrow Wilson expressed it, the men and women "who remain to till the soil and man the factories are no less a part of the army than the men beneath the battle flags."

Not all European nations made the shift to total war equally well. Germany had the most success in developing a planned economy. At the beginning of the war, the government asked Walter Rathenau, head of the German General Electric Company, to use his business methods to organize a War Raw Materials Board that would allocate strategic raw materials to produce the goods that were most needed. Rathenau made it possible for the German war machine to be effectively supplied. The Germans were much less successful with the rationing of food, however. Even before the war, Germany had had to import about 20 percent of its food supply. The British blockade of Germany and a decline in farm labor made food shortages inevitable. Daily food rations in Germany were cut from 1,350 calories in 1916 to 1,000 by 1917, barely adequate for survival. As a result of a poor potato harvest in the winter of 1916–1917, turnips became the basic staple for the poor. An estimated 750,000 German civilians died of hunger during World War I.

The German war government was eventually consolidated under military authority. The two popular military heroes of the war, General Paul von Hindenburg, chief of the General Staff, and Erich Ludendorff, deputy chief of staff, came to control the government by 1916 and virtually became the military dictators of Germany. In 1916, Hindenburg and Ludendorff decreed a system of complete mobilization for total war. In the Auxiliary Service Law of December 2, 1916, they required all male noncombatants between the ages of seventeen and sixty to work only in jobs deemed crucial for the war effort.

Germany, of course, had already possessed a rather authoritarian political system before the war began. France and Britain did not, but even in those countries the power of the central government was dramatically increased. At first, Great Britain tried to fight the war by continuing its liberal tradition of limited government interference in the economy. The pressure of circumstances, however, forced the British government to take a more active role in economic matters. The need to ensure an adequate production of munitions led to the creation in July 1915 of a Ministry of Munitions under the dynamic leader, David Lloyd George. The Ministry of Munitions took numerous steps to ensure that private industry would produce war matériel

THE LEADERS OF GERMANY. Over the course of the war, the power of central governments was greatly enlarged in order to meet the demands of total war. In Germany, the two military heroes of the war, Paul von Hindenburg and Erich Ludendorf, became virtual military dictators by 1916. The two are shown here (Hindenburg on the left) with Emperor William II, whose power declined as the war dragged on.

at limited profits. It developed a vast bureaucracy, which expanded from 20 to 65,000 clerks to oversee munitions plants. Beginning in 1915, it was given the power to take over plants manufacturing war goods that did not cooperate with the government. The British government also rationed food supplies and imposed rent controls.

The French were less successful than the British and Germans in establishing a strong war government during much of the war. For one thing, the French faced a difficult obstacle in organizing a total war economy. German occupation of northeastern France cost the nation 75 percent of its coal production and almost 80 percent of its steel-making capacity. Then, too, the relationship between civil and military authorities in France was extraordinarily strained. For the first three years of the war, military and civil authorities struggled over who would oversee the conduct of the war. Not until the end of 1917 did the French war government find a strong leader in Georges Clemenceau. Declaring that "war is too important to be left to generals," Clemenceau established clear civilian control of a total war government.

The three other major belligerents—Russia, Austria-Hungary, and Italy—had much less success than Great Britain, Germany, and France in mobilizing for total war.

The autocratic empires of Russia and Austria-Hungary had backward economies that proved incapable of turning out the quantity of war matériel needed to fight a modern war. The Russians, for example, conscripted millions of men but could arm only one-fourth of them. Unarmed Russian soldiers were sent into battle anyway and advised to pick up rifles from their dead colleagues. With their numerous minorities, both the Russian and Austro-Hungarian Empires found it difficult to achieve the kind of internal cohesion needed to fight a prolonged total war. Italy, too, lacked both the public enthusiasm and the industrial resources needed to wage a successful total war.

PUBLIC ORDER AND PUBLIC OPINION

As the Great War dragged on and both casualties and privations worsened, internal dissatisfaction replaced the patriotic enthusiasm that had marked the early stages of the war. By 1916, there were numerous signs that civilian morale was beginning to crack under the pressure of total war.

The first two years of the war witnessed only a few scattered strikes, but by 1916 strike activity had increased dramatically. In 1916, 50,000 German workers carried out a three-day work stoppage in Berlin to protest the arrest of a radical socialist leader. In both France and Britain, the number of strikes increased significantly. Even worse was the violence that erupted in Ireland when members of the Irish Republican Brotherhood and Citizens Army occupied government buildings in Dublin on Easter Sunday (April 24), 1916. British forces crushed the Easter Rebellion and then condemned its leaders to death.

Internal opposition to the war came from two major sources in 1916 and 1917, liberals and socialists. Liberals in both Germany and Britain sponsored peace resolutions calling for a negotiated peace without any territorial acquisitions. They were largely ignored. Socialists in Germany and Austria also called for negotiated settlements. By 1917, war morale had so deteriorated that more dramatic protests took place. Mutinies in the Italian and French armies were put down with difficulty. Czech leaders in the Austrian Empire openly called for an independent democratic Czech state. In April 1917, 200,000 workers in Berlin went out on strike for a week to protest the reduction of bread rations. Only the threat of military force and prison brought them back to their jobs. Despite the strains, all of the belligerent countries except Russia survived the stresses of 1917 and fought on.

War governments also fought back against the growing opposition to the war. Authoritarian regimes, such as those of Germany, Russia, and Austria-Hungary, had always relied on force to subdue their populations. Under the pressures of the war, however, even parliamentary regimes resorted to an expansion of police powers to stifle internal dissent. The British Parliament passed a Defence of the Realm Act (DORA) at the very beginning of the war that allowed the public authorities to arrest dissenters as traitors. The act was later extended to authorize public officials to censor newspapers by deleting objectionable material and even to suspend newspaper publication. In France, government authorities had initially been lenient about public opposition to the war. But by 1917, they began to fear that open opposition to the war might weaken the French will to fight. When Georges Clemenceau became premier near the end of 1917, the lenient French policies came to an end, and basic civil liberties were suppressed for the duration of the war. The editor of an antiwar newspaper was even executed on a charge of treason. Clemenceau also punished journalists who wrote negative war reports by having them drafted.

Wartime governments made active use of propaganda to arouse enthusiasm for the war. At the beginning, public officials needed to do little to achieve this goal. The British and French, for example, exaggerated German atrocities in Belgium and found that their citizens were only too willing to believe these accounts. But as the war progressed and morale sagged, governments were forced to devise new techniques to stimulate declining enthusiasm. In one British recruiting poster, for example, a small daughter asked her father, "Daddy, what did YOU do in the Great War?" while her younger brother played with toy soldiers and cannon.

BRITISH RECRUITING POSTER. As the conflict persisted month after month, governments resorted to active propaganda campaigns to generate enthusiasm for the war. In this British recruiting poster, the government tried to pressure men into volunteering for military service. By 1916, the British were forced to adopt compulsory military service.

THE SOCIAL IMPACT OF TOTAL WAR

Total war made a significant impact on European society, most visibly by bringing an end to unemployment. The withdrawal of millions of men from the labor market to fight, combined with the heightened demand for wartime products, led to jobs for everyone able to work.

The cause of labor also benefited from the war. The enthusiastic patriotism of workers was soon rewarded with a greater acceptance of trade unions. To ensure that labor problems would not disrupt production, war governments in Britain, France, and Germany not only sought union cooperation but also for the first time allowed trade unions to participate in making important government decisions on labor matters. In return, unions cooperated on wage limits and production schedules. Labor gained two benefits from this cooperation. It opened the way to the collective bargaining practices that became more widespread after World War I and increased the prestige of trade unions, enabling them to attract more members.

World War I also created new roles for women. With so many men off fighting at the front, women were called

Women in the Factories

During World War I, women were called upon to assume new job responsibilities, including factory work. In this selection, Naomi Loughnan, a young, upper-middle-class woman, describes the experiences in a munitions plant that considerably broadened her perspective on life.

✤ Naomi Loughnan, "Munition Work"

We little thought when we first put on our overalls and caps and enlisted in the Munition Army how much more inspiring our life was to be than we had dared to hope. Though we munition workers sacrifice our ease we gain a life worth living. Our long days are filled with interest, and with the zest of doing work for our country in the grand cause of Freedom. As we handle the weapons of war we are learning great lessons of life. In the busy, noisy workshops we come face to face with every kind of class, and each one of these classes has something to learn from the others. . . .

Engineering mankind is possessed of the unshakable opinion that no woman can have the mechanical sense. If one of us asks humbly why such and such an alteration is not made to prevent this or that drawback to a machine, she is told, with a superior smile, that a man has worked her machine before her for years, and that therefore if there were any improvement possible it would have been made. As long as we do exactly what we are told and do not attempt to use our brains, we give entire satisfaction, and are treated as nice, good children. Any swerving from the easy path prepared for

us by our males arouses the most scathing contempt in their manly bosoms. . . . Women have, however, proved that their entry into the munition world has increased the output. Employers who forget things personal in their patriotic desire for large results are enthusiastic over the success of women in the shops. But their workmen have to be handled with the utmost tenderness and caution lest they should actually imagine it was being suggested that women could do their work equally well, given equal conditions of training—at least where muscle is not the driving force. . . .

The coming of the mixed classes of women into the factory is slowly but surely having an educative effect upon the men. "Language" is almost unconsciously becoming subdued. There are fiery exceptions who make our hair stand up on end under our close-fitting caps, but a sharp rebuke or a look of horror will often straighten out the most savage. . . . It is grievous to hear the girls also swearing and using disgusting language. Shoulder to shoulder with the children of the slums, the upper classes are having their eyes opened at last to the awful conditions among which their sisters have dwelt. Foul language, immorality, and many other evils are but the natural outcome of overcrowding and bitter poverty. . . . Sometimes disgust will overcome us, but we are learning with painful clarity that the fault is not theirs whose actions disgust us, but must be placed to the discredit of those other classes who have allowed the continued existence of conditions which generate the things from which we shrink appalled.

---

upon to take over jobs and responsibilities that had not been open to them before. These included certain clerical jobs that only small numbers of women had held earlier. In Britain, for example, the number of women who worked in banking rose from 9,500 to almost 64,000 in the course of the war, while the number of women in commerce rose from a half million to almost one million. Overall, 1,345,000 women in Britain obtained new jobs or replaced men during the war. Women were also now employed in jobs that had been considered beyond the "capacity of women." These included such occupations as chimney sweeps, truck drivers, farm laborers, and, above all, factory workers in heavy industry (see the box above). In France, 684,000 women worked in armaments plants for the first time; in Britain, the figure was 920,000. Thirty-eight percent of the workers in the Krupp Armaments works in Germany in 1918 were women.

Male resistance, however, often made it difficult for women to enter these new jobs, especially in heavy industry. One Englishwoman who worked in a munitions factory recalled her experience: "I could quite see it was hard on the men to have women coming into all their pet jobs and in some cases doing them a good deal better. I sympathized with the way they were torn between not wanting the women to undercut them, and yet hating them to earn as much."[6] While male workers expressed concern that the employment of females at lower wages would depress their own wages, women began to demand equal pay legislation. The French government passed a law in July 1915 that established a minimum wage for women homeworkers in textiles, an industry that had grown dramatically because of the need for military uniforms. Later in 1917, the government decreed that men and women should receive equal rates for piecework. Despite the noticeable increase in women's wages that resulted from government regulations, women's industrial wages still were not equal to men's wages by the end of the war.

Even worse, women had achieved little real security about their place in the workforce. Both men and women seemed to think that many of the new jobs for women were only temporary, an expectation quite evident in the British poem, "War Girls," written in 1916:

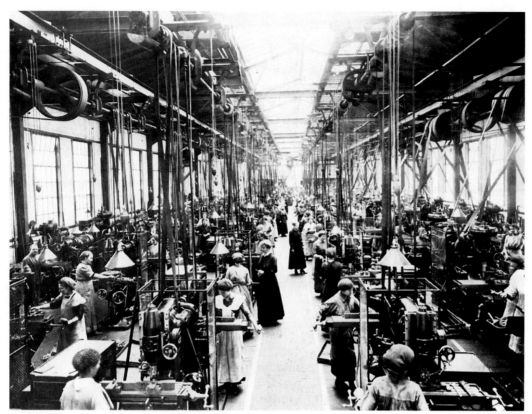

WOMEN WORKERS IN A GERMAN MUNITIONS FACTORY.
World War I created new job opportunities for women.
They were now employed in jobs that had earlier been
considered beyond their capacity. As seen in this picture,
this included factory work in heavy industry. These German women are performing a variety of tasks in a shell
factory. Between 1913 and 1917, female metalworkers
increased from 5 to 28 percent of the total labor force.

There's the girl who clips your ticket for the train,
And the girl who speeds the lift from floor to floor,
There's the girl who does a milk-round in the rain,
And the girl who calls for orders at your door.
Strong, sensible, and fit,
They're out to show their grit,
And tackle jobs with energy and knack.
No longer caged and penned up,
They're going to keep their end up
Till the khaki soldier boys come marching back.[7]

At the end of the war, governments moved quickly to
remove women from the jobs they had encouraged them
to take earlier. By 1919, there were 650,000 unemployed
women in Britain, and wages for women who were still
employed were also lowered. The work benefits for women
from World War I seemed to be short-lived.

Nevertheless, in some countries the role played by
women in the wartime economies did have a positive
impact on the women's movement for social and political emancipation. The most obvious gain was the right
to vote that was given to women in Germany and Austria
immediately after the war (in Britain already in January

1918). The Nineteenth Amendment to the Constitution
gave women in the United States the right to vote in 1919.
Contemporary media, however, tended to focus on the
more noticeable, yet in some ways more superficial, social
emancipation of upper- and middle-class women. In ever-
larger numbers, these young women took jobs, had their
own apartments, and showed their new independence
by smoking in public and wearing shorter dresses, cos-
metics, and new hair styles.

In one sense, World War I had been a great social
leveler. Death in battle did not distinguish between classes.
Although all social classes suffered casualties in battle, two
groups were especially hard-hit. Junior officers who led the
charges across the "no man's land" that separated the lines
of trenches experienced death rates that were three times
higher than regular casualty rates. Many of these junior
officers were members of the aristocracy (see the box on
p. 766). The unskilled workers and peasants who made up
the masses of soldiers mowed down by machine guns also
suffered heavy casualties. The fortunate ones were the
skilled laborers who gained exemptions from military service because they were needed at home to train workers
in the war industries.

The Reality of War: War and the Family

John Mott was a captain in the British army. He came from an aristocratic family with a strong military tradition. He married Muriel Backhouse in 1907, and they had three sons before he was called up for service in World War I. These excerpts are taken from four of Mott's letters to his wife and a letter informing her of her husband's death during the Gallipoli campaign. The human experience of World War I was made up of millions of stories like that of John Mott and his family.

❄ One Family's War

1 July [1915]

My darling Childie,

I hope you got home safely. I have been promised that I shall know the ship we go on tomorrow. But it will be no good writing to Gibraltar as we should get there before the letter. Try Malta as that goes over land. If you get overdrawn go and see Cox. Goodbye Darling. Don't worry I shall come back alright. Your devoted husband John F. Mott

13 July

Mediterranean field force, Mudros

My darling Childie,

This island is very hot indeed but beastly windy. We have absolutely no news from the Front. Troops are pouring out now and I expect we shall be in it next week.

We have all gone through our little bout of diarrhea. I was not too bad and only had pains in my stomach otherwise I am very well indeed.

Everyone is standing the heat very well. The Brigadier has a tent but everybody else is out in the blazing sun.

31 July

My darling Childie,

I got more letters from you today dated 5th, 6th, 7th. I had no idea till I read the letter that they could do all that about writs. I would never have left things in such a muddle, I only hope you can get straight.

Yesterday I left here at 5:30 AM to go to the trenches with the Brigadier. We had an awful day, and I am not at all keen to go into that lot at all events. We sailed over in a trawler and had a long walk in the open under shrapnel fire. It was not very pleasant. Then we got to the communications trenches and had a mile and a half

of them to go up. When we got to the fire trenches the stink was awful. Arms and legs of Turks sticking out of the trench parapets and lying dead all round. In one place the bottom of the trench was made up by dead Turks, but this has been abandoned as the place was too poisonous.

Our battle ships have been shelling very heavily so there may be an attack on. I must write to my mother tonight. All my love and kisses for ever Your loving husband John F. Mott

6 August

My darling Childie,

We are off today just as we stand up, with four days rations. I can't say where we are going but we shall see spots. I shall not get a chance to write again for a bit as we shall be on the move. I expect you have got a map of the place by now and perhaps you will hear where we have gone.

Very good to get away. All my love and kisses for ever Your loving husband John F. Mott

Best love to all kids and baby

Pte A Thompson
6 Batt Y and L Red Cross Hospital

We landed on the 6th of Aug and took 2 hills and at daybreak on the 7th advanced across an open plain to the left of Salt Lake and got an awful shelling. We came to a small hill which was flat on top and it was about 2 hundred yards further on where the Capt was hit. They gave us it worse than ever when we got on there and I might have been happen 50 yds away when I saw the Capt and about 5 men fall badly hit. I could not say whether it was shrapnel or common shell but I think it was most probably shrapnel as they use that mostly. It was that thick that no one could get to the Capt at the time and I don't think he lived very long, well he could not the way they were hit and was afterwards buried when things had quietened down in the evening and a cross was put on his grave with an inscription and he got as good a burial as could be given out there. Well I think I have told you all I know about Capt Mott. I only wishe I could have given you better news, so I will close with Kind Regards
Yours Obediently,
Pte Thompson

The burst of patriotic enthusiasm that marked the beginning of the war deceived many into believing that the war was creating a new sense of community that meant the end of the class conflict that had marked European society at the end of the nineteenth and beginning of the twentieth centuries. David Lloyd George, who became the British prime minister in 1916, wrote in September 1914 that "all classes, high and low, are shedding themselves of selfishness. . . . It is bringing a new outlook to all classes. . . . We can see for the first time the fundamental things that matter in life, and that have been obscured from our vision by the . . . growth of prosperity."[8] Lloyd George's optimistic opinion proved to be quite misguided, however. The Great War did not eliminate the class conflict that had characterized pre-1914 Europe, and this became increasingly apparent as the war progressed.

Certainly, the economic impact of the war was felt unevenly. One group of people who especially benefited were the owners of the large industries manufacturing the weapons of war. Despite public outrage, governments rarely limited the enormous profits made by the industrial barons. In fact, in the name of efficiency, wartime governments tended to favor large industries when scarce raw materials were allocated. Small firms considered less essential to the war effort even had to shut down because of a lack of resources.

Growing inflation also caused inequities. The combination of full employment and high demand for scarce consumer goods caused prices to climb. Many skilled workers were able to earn wages that enabled them to keep up with the inflation, but this was not true for unskilled workers and for those in nonessential industries. Only in Great Britain did the wages of workers outstrip prices. Everywhere else in Europe, people experienced a loss of purchasing power.

Many middle-class people were especially hard-hit by inflation. They included both those who lived on fixed incomes, such as retired people on pensions, and professional people, such as clerks, lesser civil servants, teachers, small shopkeepers, and members of the clergy, whose incomes remained stable at a time when prices were rising. By the end of the war, many of these people were actually doing less well economically than skilled workers. Their discontent would find expression after the war.

◆ War and Revolution

By 1917, total war was creating serious domestic turmoil in all of the European belligerent states. Most countries were able to prop up their regimes and convince their peoples to continue the war for another year, but others were coming close to collapse. In Austria, for example, a government minister warned that "if the monarchs of the Central Powers cannot make peace in the coming months, it will be made for them by their peoples." Russia, however, was the only belligerent that actually experienced the kind of complete collapse in 1917 that others were predicting might happen throughout Europe. Out of Russia's collapse came the Russian Revolution, whose impact would be widely felt in Europe for decades to come.

❀ *The Russian Revolution*

After the Revolution of 1905 had failed to bring any substantial changes to Russia, Tsar Nicholas II fell back on the army and bureaucracy as the basic props for his autocratic regime. Perhaps Russia could have survived this way, as some have argued, but World War I magnified Russia's problems and severely challenged the tsarist government.

Russia was unprepared both militarily and technologically for the total war of World War I. Competent military leadership was lacking. Even worse, the tsar, alone of all European monarchs, insisted upon taking personal charge of the armed forces despite his obvious lack of ability and training for such an awesome burden. Russian industry was unable to produce the weapons needed for the army. Ill-led and ill-armed, Russian armies suffered incredible losses. Between 1914 and 1916, two million soldiers were killed while another four to six million were wounded or captured. By 1917, the Russian will to fight had vanished.

The tsarist government was totally inadequate for the tasks that it faced in 1914. The surge of patriotic enthusiasm that greeted the outbreak of war was soon dissipated by a government that distrusted its own people. When leading industrialists formed committees to improve factory production, a government suspicious of their motives undermined their efforts. Although the middle classes and liberal aristocrats still hoped for a constitutional monarchy, they were sullen over the tsar's revocation of the political concessions made during the Revolution of 1905. Peasant discontent flourished as conditions worsened. The concentration of Russian industry in a few large cities made workers' frustrations all the more evident and dangerous. Even conservative aristocrats were appalled by the incompetent and inefficient bureaucracy that controlled the political and military system. In the meantime, Tsar Nicholas II was increasingly insulated from events by his wife Alexandra.

This German-born princess was a stubborn, willful, and ignorant woman who had fallen under the influence of Rasputin, a Siberian peasant who belonged to a religious sect that indulged in sexual orgies. To the tsarina, Rasputin was a holy man for he alone seemed able to stop the bleeding of her hemophiliac son Alexis. Rasputin's influence made him an important power behind the throne, and he did not hesitate to interfere in government affairs. As the leadership at the top stumbled its way through a series of military and economic disasters, the middle class, aristocrats, peasants, soldiers, and workers grew more and more disenchanted with the tsarist regime. Even conservative aristocrats who supported the monarchy felt the need to do something to reverse the deteriorating situation. For a start, they assassinated Rasputin in December 1916. By then it was too late to save the monarchy, and its fall came quickly at the beginning of March 1917.

⚛ THE MARCH REVOLUTION
At the beginning of March, a series of strikes broke out in the capital city of Petrograd (formerly St. Petersburg). Here the actions of working-class women helped to change the course of Russian history. In February of 1917,

the government had introduced bread rationing in the capital city after the price of bread had skyrocketed. Many of the women who stood in the lines waiting for bread were also factory workers who had put in twelve-hour days. The number of women working in Petrograd factories had doubled since 1914. The Russian government had become aware of the volatile situation in the capital from a police report:

> Mothers of families, exhausted by endless standing in line at stores, distraught over their half-starving and sick children, are today perhaps closer to revolution than [the liberal opposition leaders] and of course they are a great deal more dangerous because they are the combustible material for which only a single spark is needed to burst into flame.[9]

On March 8, a day celebrated since 1910 as International Women's Day, about 10,000 Petrograd women marched through the city demanding "Peace and Bread" and "Down with Autocracy." Soon the women were joined by other workers, and together they called for a general strike that succeeded in shutting down all the factories in the city on March 10. The tsarina wrote to Nicholas II at the battlefront that "this is a hooligan movement. If the weather were very cold they would all probably stay at home." Nicholas ordered the troops to disperse the crowds by shooting them if necessary. Initially, the troops did so, but soon significant numbers of the soldiers joined the demonstrators. The situation was out of the tsar's control. The Duma or legislative body, which the tsar had tried to dissolve, met anyway and on March 12 established a Provisional Government that urged the tsar to abdicate. He did so on March 15.

In just one week, the tsarist regime had fallen apart. It was not really overthrown since there had been no deliberate revolution. Even those who were conscious revolutionaries were caught by surprise at the rapidity of the monarchy's disintegration. Although no particular group had been responsible for the outburst, the moderate Constitutional Democrats were responsible for establishing the Provisional Government. They represented primarily a middle-class and liberal aristocratic minority. Their program consisted of a nineteenth-century liberal agenda: freedom of speech, religion, assembly, and civil liberties. Their determination to carry on the war to preserve Russia's honor was a major blunder since it satisfied neither the workers nor the peasants who above all wanted an end to the war.

The Provisional Government was also faced with another authority, the soviets, or councils of workers' and soldiers' deputies. The soviet of Petrograd had been formed in March 1917; at the same time soviets sprang up spontaneously in army units, factory towns, and rural areas. The soviets represented the more radical interests of the lower classes and were largely composed of socialists of various kinds. Most numerous were the Socialist Revolutionaries, who wished to establish peasant socialism by seizing the great landed estates and creating a rural democracy. Since the beginning of the twentieth century, the Socialist Revolutionaries had come to rely on the use of political terrorism to accomplish their goals. Since 1893, Russia had also had a Marxist Social Democratic Party, which had divided in 1903 into two factions known as the Mensheviks and Bolsheviks. The Mensheviks wanted the Social Democrats to be a mass electoral socialist party

THE WOMEN'S MARCH IN PETROGRAD. After the introduction of bread rationing in Petrograd, 10,000 women engaged in mass demonstrations and demanded "Peace and Bread" for the families of soldiers. This photograph shows the women marching through the streets of Petrograd on March 8, 1917.

based on a Western model. Like the Social Democrats of Germany, they were willing to cooperate temporarily in a parliamentary democracy while working toward the ultimate achievement of the socialist state.

The Bolsheviks were a small faction of Russian Social Democrats who had come under the leadership of Vladimir Ulianov, known to the world as V. I. Lenin (1870–1924). Born in 1870 to a middle-class family, Lenin received a legal education and became a lawyer. In 1887, he turned into a dedicated enemy of tsarist Russia when his older brother was executed for planning to assassinate the tsar. Lenin's search for a revolutionary faith led him to Marxism, and in 1894 he moved to St. Petersburg where he organized an illegal group known as the Union for the Liberation of the Working Class. Arrested for this activity, Lenin was shipped to Siberia. After his release, he chose to go into exile in Switzerland and eventually assumed the leadership of the Bolshevik wing of the Russian Social Democratic Party.

Under Lenin's direction, the Bolsheviks became a party dedicated to violent revolution. He believed that only a violent revolution could destroy the capitalist system and that a "vanguard" of activists must form a small party of well-disciplined professional revolutionaries to accomplish the task. Between 1900 and 1917, Lenin spent most of his time in Switzerland. When the Provisional Government was formed in March 1917, he believed that an opportunity for the Bolsheviks to seize power had come. In April 1917, with the connivance of the German High Command, who hoped to create disorder in Russia, Lenin, his wife, and a small group of his followers were shipped to Russia in a "sealed train" by way of Finland.

Lenin's arrival in Russia opened a new stage of the Russian Revolution. In his "April Theses," issued on April 20, Lenin presented a blueprint for revolutionary action based on his own version of Marxist theory. According to Lenin, it was not necessary for Russia to experience a bourgeois revolution before it could move toward socialism, as orthodox Marxists had argued. Instead, Russia could move directly into socialism. In the "April Theses," Lenin maintained that the soviets of soldiers, workers, and peasants were ready-made instruments of power. The Bolsheviks must work to gain control of these groups and then use them to overthrow the Provisional Government. At the same time, Bolshevik propaganda must seek mass support through promises geared to the needs of the people: an end to the war; the redistribution of all land to the peasants; the transfer of factories and industries from capitalists to committees of workers; and the relegation of government power from the Provisional Government to the soviets. Three simple slogans summed up the Bolshevik program: "Peace, Land, Bread," "Worker Control of Production," and "All Power to the Soviets."

In late spring and early summer, while the Bolsheviks set about winning over the masses to their program and gaining a majority in the Petrograd and Moscow soviets, the Provisional Government struggled to gain control of Russia against almost overwhelming obstacles. Although the Provisional Government promised that a constitutional convention called for the fall of 1917 would confiscate and redistribute royal and monastic lands, the offer was meaningless since many peasants had already started seizing lands on their own in March. The military situation was also deteriorating. The Petrograd soviet had issued its Army Order No. 1 in March to all Russian military forces, encouraging them to remove their officers and replace them with committees composed of "the elected representatives of the lower ranks" of the army. Army Order No. 1 led to the collapse of all discipline and created military chaos. When the Provisional Government

LENIN ADDRESSES A CROWD. V. I. Lenin was the driving force behind the success of the Bolsheviks in seizing power in Russia and creating the Union of Soviet Socialist Republics. Here Lenin is seen addressing a rally in Moscow in 1917.

attempted to initiate a new military offensive in July, the army simply dissolved as masses of peasant soldiers turned their backs on their officers and returned home to join their families in seizing lands.

✣ THE BOLSHEVIK REVOLUTION

In July 1917, Lenin and the Bolsheviks were falsely accused of inciting an attempt to overthrow the Provisional Government, and Lenin was forced to flee to Finland. But the days of the Provisional Government were numbered. In July 1917, Alexander Kerensky, a Socialist Revolutionary, had become prime minister in the Provisional Government. In September, when General Lavr Kornilov attempted to march on Petrograd and seize power, Kerensky released Bolsheviks from prison and turned to the Petrograd soviet for help. Although General Kornilov's forces never reached Petrograd, Kerensky's action had strengthened the hands of the Petrograd soviet and had shown Lenin how weak the Provisional Government really was.

By the end of October, the Bolsheviks had achieved a slight majority in the Petrograd and Moscow soviets. The number of party members had also grown from 50,000 to 240,000. Reports of unrest abroad had convinced Lenin that "we are on the threshold of a world proletarian revolution," and he tried to persuade his fellow Bolsheviks that the time was ripe for the overthrow of the Provisional Government. Although he faced formidable opposition within the Bolshevik ranks, he managed to gain support for his policy. He was especially fortunate to have the close cooperation of Leon Trotsky (1877–1940), a former Menshevik turned fervid revolutionary. Lenin and Trotsky organized a Military Revolutionary Committee within the Petrograd soviet to plot the overthrow of the government. On the night of November 6–7, Bolshevik forces seized the Winter Palace, seat of the Provisional Government. The Provisional Government collapsed quickly with little bloodshed.

This coup d'etat had been timed to coincide with a meeting in Petrograd of the all-Russian Congress of Soviets representing local soviets from all over the country. Lenin nominally turned over the sovereignty of the Provisional Government to this Congress of Soviets. Real power, however, passed to a Council of People's Commissars, headed by Lenin (see the box on p. 771). One immediate problem faced by the Bolsheviks was the Constituent Assembly, which had been initiated by the Provisional Government and was scheduled to meet in January 1918. Elections to the assembly by universal male suffrage had resulted in a defeat for the Bolsheviks, who had only 225 delegates compared to the 420 garnered by the Socialist Revolutionaries. But no matter. Lenin simply broke the Constituent Assembly by force. "To hand over power," he said, "to the Constituent Assembly would again be compromising with malignant bourgeoisie." The Bolsheviks did not want majority rule, but rather the rule of the proletariat, exercised for them, of course, by the Bolsheviks.

But the Bolsheviks (soon renamed the Communists) still had a long way to go. Lenin, ever the opportunist, realized the importance of winning mass support as quickly as possible by fulfilling Bolshevik promises. In his first law, Lenin declared the land nationalized and turned it over to local rural soviets. In effect, this action merely ratified the peasants' seizure of the land and assured the Bolsheviks of peasant support, especially against any attempt by the old landlords to restore their power. Lenin also met the demands of urban workers by turning over control of the factories to committees of workers. To Lenin, however, this was merely a temporary expedient.

The new government also introduced a number of social changes. Alexandra Kollontai (1872–1952), who had become a supporter of revolutionary socialism while in exile in Switzerland, took the lead in pushing a Bolshevik program for women's rights and social welfare reforms. As minister of social welfare, she tried to provide health care for women and children by establishing Palaces for the Protection of Maternity and Children. Between 1918 and 1920, the new regime enacted a series of reforms that made marriage a civil act, legalized divorce, decreed the equality of men and women, and permitted abortions. Kollontai was also instrumental in establishing a Women's Bureau within the Communist Party known as Zhenotdel. This organization sent men and women to all

Ten Days That Shook the World: Lenin and the Bolshevik Seizure of Power

John Reed was an American journalist who helped to found the American Communist Labor Party. Accused of sedition, he fled the United States and went to Russia. In Ten Days That Shook the World, *Reed left an impassioned eyewitness account of the Russian Revolution. It is apparent from his comments that Reed considered Lenin the indispensable hero of the Bolshevik success.*

❋ John Reed, *Ten Days That Shook the World*

It was just 8:40 when a thundering wave of cheers announced the entrance of the presidium, with Lenin—great Lenin—among them. A short, stocky figure, with a big head set down in his shoulders, bald and bulging. Little eyes, a snubbish nose, wide, generous mouth, and heavy chin; clean-shaven now, but already beginning to bristle with the well-known beard of his past and future. Dressed in shabby clothes, his trousers much too long for him. Unimpressive, to be the idol of a mob, loved and revered as perhaps few leaders in history have been. A strange popular leader—a leader purely by virtue of intellect; colorless, humorless, uncompromising and detached; without picturesque idiosyncrasies—but with the power of explaining profound ideas in simple terms, of analyzing a concrete situation. And combined with shrewdness, the greatest intellectual audacity. . . .

Now Lenin, gripping the edge of the reading stand, letting his little winking eyes travel over the crowd as he stood there waiting, apparently oblivious to the long-rolling ovation, which lasted several minutes. When it finished, he said simply, "We shall now proceed to construct the Socialist order!" Again that overwhelming human roar.

"The first thing is the adoption of practical measures to realize peace. . . . We shall offer peace to the peoples of all the belligerent countries upon the basis of the Soviet terms—no annexations, no indemnities, and the right of self-determination of peoples. At the same time, according to our promise, we shall publish and repudiate the secret treaties. . . . The question of War and Peace is so clear that I think that I may, without preamble, read the project of a Proclamation to the Peoples of All the Belligerent Countries. . . ."

His great mouth, seeming to smile, opened wide as he spoke; his voice was hoarse—not unpleasantly so, but as if it had hardened that way after years and years of speaking—and went on monotonously, with the effect of being able to go forever. . . . For emphasis he bent forward slightly. No gestures. And before him, a thousand simple faces looking up in intent adoration.

[Reed then reproduces the full text of the Proclamation.]

When the grave thunder of applause had died away, Lenin spoke again: "We propose to the Congress to ratify this declaration. . . . This proposal of peace will meet with resistance on the part of the imperialist governments—we don't fool ourselves on that score. But we hope that revolution will soon break out in all the belligerent countries; that is why we address ourselves especially to the workers of France, England and Germany. . . ."

"The revolution of November 6th and 7th," he ended, "has opened the era of the Social Revolution. . . . The labor movement, in the name of peace and Socialism, shall win, and fulfill its destiny. . . ."

There was something quiet and powerful in all this, which stirred the souls of men. It was understandable why people believed when Lenin spoke.

parts of the Russian Empire to explain the new social order. Members of Zhenotdel were especially eager to help women with matters of divorce and women's rights. In the eastern provinces, several Zhenotdel members were brutally murdered by angry males who objected to any kind of liberation for their wives and daughters. Much to Kollontai's disappointment, many of these Communist social reforms were later undone as the Communists came to face more pressing matters, including the survival of the new regime.

Lenin had also promised peace and that, he realized, was not an easy task because of the humiliating losses of Russian territory that it would entail. There was no real choice, however. On March 3, 1918, the new Communist government signed the Treaty of Brest-Litovsk with Germany and gave up eastern Poland, Ukraine, Finland, and the Baltic provinces. To his critics, Lenin argued that it made no difference since the spread of socialist revolution throughout Europe would make the treaty largely irrelevant. In any case, he had promised peace to the Russian people, but real peace did not come for the country soon lapsed into civil war.

⚔ CIVIL WAR

There was great opposition to the new Bolshevik or Communist regime, not only from groups loyal to the tsar but also from bourgeois and aristocratic liberals and anti-Leninist socialists, including Mensheviks and Socialist

Revolutionaries. In addition, thousands of Allied troops were eventually sent to different parts of Russia in the hope of bringing Russia back into the war.

Between 1918 and 1921, the Bolshevik (or Red) Army was forced to fight on many fronts. The first serious threat to the Bolsheviks came from Siberia where a White (anti-Bolshevik) force under Admiral Alexander Kolchak pushed westward and advanced almost to the Volga River before being stopped. Attacks also came from the Ukrainians in the southeast and from the Baltic regions. In mid-1919, White forces under General Anton Denikin, probably the most effective of the White generals, swept through Ukraine and advanced almost to Moscow. At one point in late 1919, three separate White armies seemed to be closing in on the Bolsheviks, but were eventually pushed back. By 1920, the major White forces had been defeated, and Ukraine retaken. The next year, the Communist regime regained control over the independent nationalist governments in the Caucasus: Georgia, Russian Armenia, and Azerbaijan.

How had Lenin and the Bolsheviks triumphed over what seemed at one time to be overwhelming forces? For one thing, the Red Army became a well-disciplined and formidable fighting force, largely due to the organizational genius of Leon Trotsky. As commissar of war, Trotsky reinstated the draft and even recruited and gave commands to former tsarist army officers. Trotsky insisted on rigid discipline; soldiers who deserted or refused to obey orders were summarily executed. The Red Army also had the advantage of interior lines of defense and was able to move its troops rapidly from one battlefront to the other.

The disunity of the anti-Communist forces seriously weakened the efforts of the Whites. Political differences created distrust among the Whites and prevented them from cooperating effectively with each other. Some Whites, such as Admiral Kolchak, insisted on restoring the tsarist regime, but others understood that only a more liberal and democratic program had any chance of success. Since the White forces were forced to operate on the exterior fringes of the Russian Empire, it was difficult enough to achieve military cooperation. Political differences made it virtually impossible.

The Whites' inability to agree on a common goal contrasted sharply with the Communists' single-minded

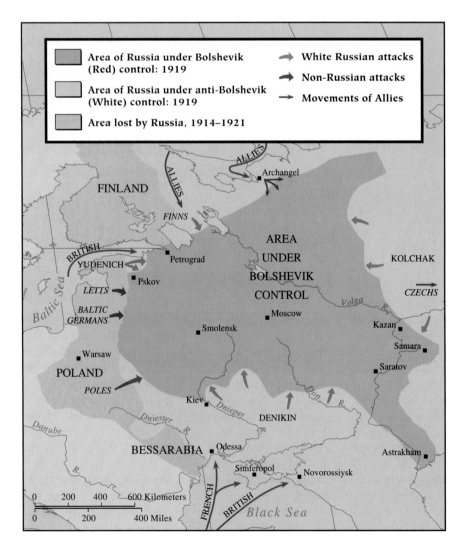

MAP 25.4
The Russian Revolution and Civil War.

sense of purpose. Inspired by their vision of a new socialist order, the Communists had the advantage of possessing the determination that comes from revolutionary fervor and revolutionary convictions.

The Communists also succeeded in translating their revolutionary faith into practical instruments of power. A policy of "war communism," for example, was used to ensure regular supplies for the Red Army. "War communism" included the nationalization of banks and most industries, the forcible requisition of grain from peasants, and the centralization of state administration under Bolshevik control. Another Bolshevik instrument was "revolutionary terror." Although the old tsarist secret police had been abolished, a new Red secret police—known as the Cheka—replaced it. The Red Terror instituted by the Cheka aimed at nothing less than the destruction of all those who opposed the new regime. "Class enemies"—the bourgeoisie—were especially singled out, at least according to a Cheka officer: "The first questions you should put to the accused person are: To what class does he belong, what is his origin, what was his education, and what is his profession? These should determine the fate of the accused." In practice, however, the Cheka promulgated terror against all classes, including the proletariat, if they opposed the new regime. The Red Terror added an element of fear to the Bolshevik regime.

Finally, the intervention of foreign armies enabled the Communists to appeal to the powerful force of Russian patriotism. Although the Allied powers had initially intervened in Russia to encourage the Russians to remain in the war, the end of the war on November 11, 1918, had made that purpose inconsequential. Nevertheless, Allied troops remained, and more were even sent as Allied countries did not hide their anti-Bolshevik feelings. At one point, over 100,000 foreign troops, mostly Japanese, British, American, and French, were stationed on Russian soil. These forces rarely engaged in pitched battles, however, nor did they pursue a common strategy, although they did give material assistance to anti-Bolshevik forces. This intervention by the Allies enabled the Communist government to appeal to patriotic Russians to fight the attempts of foreigners to control their country. Allied interference was never substantial enough to make a military difference in the civil war, but it did serve indirectly to help the Bolshevik cause.

By 1921, the Communists had succeeded in retaining control of Russia. In the course of the civil war, the Bolshevik regime had also transformed Russia into a bureaucratically centralized state dominated by a single party. It was also a state that was largely hostile to the Allied powers that had sought to assist the Bolsheviks' enemies in the civil war. To most historians, the Russian Revolution is unthinkable without the total war of World War I, for only the collapse of Russia made it possible for a radical minority like the Bolsheviks to seize the reins of power. In turn, the Russian Revolution had an impact on the course of World War I.

✳ *The Last Year of the War*

For Germany, the withdrawal of the Russians from the war in March 1918 offered renewed hope for a favorable end to the war. The victory over Russia persuaded Ludendorff and most German leaders to make one final military gamble—a grand offensive in the west to break the military stalemate. The German attack was launched in March and lasted into July. The German forces succeeded in advancing forty miles to the Marne River, within thirty-five miles of Paris. But an Allied counterattack, led by the French General Ferdinand Foch and supported by the arrival of 140,000 fresh American troops, defeated the Germans at the Second Battle of the Marne on July 18. Ludendorff's gamble had failed. Having used up his reserves, Ludendorff knew that defeat was now inevitable. With the arrival of two million more American troops on the Continent, Allied forces began making a steady advance toward Germany.

On September 29, 1918, General Ludendorff informed German leaders that the war was lost. Unwilling to place the burden of defeat on the army, Ludendorff demanded that the government sue for peace at once. When German officials discovered that the Allies were unwilling to make peace with the autocratic imperial government, they instituted reforms to create a liberal government. But these constitutional reforms came too late for the exhausted and angry German people. On November 3, naval units in Kiel mutinied, and within days councils of workers and soldiers, German versions of the Russian soviets, were forming throughout northern Germany and taking over the supervision of civilian and military administrations. William II capitulated to public pressure and left the country on November 9, while the Socialists under Friedrich Ebert announced the establishment of a republic. Two days later, on November 11, 1918, an armistice agreed to by the new German government went into effect. The war was over, but the revolutionary forces set in motion by the war were not yet exhausted.

✳ *Revolutionary Upheavals in Germany and Austria-Hungary*

Like Russia, Germany and Austria-Hungary experienced political revolution as a result of military defeat. In November 1918, when Germany began to disintegrate in a convulsion of mutinies and mass demonstrations (known as the November Revolution), only the Social Democrats were numerous and well organized enough to pick up the pieces. But the German socialists had divided into two groups during the war. A majority of the Social Democrats still favored parliamentary democracy as a gradual approach to social democracy and the elimination of the capitalist system. A minority of German socialists, however, disgusted with the Social Democrats' support of the war, had formed an Independent Social

in Berlin in January 1919, Friedrich Ebert and the moderate socialists called on the regular army and groups of antirevolutionary volunteers known as Free Corps to crush the rebels. The victorious forces brutally murdered Liebknecht and Luxemburg. A similar attempt at Communist revolution in the city of Munich in southern Germany was also crushed by the Free Corps and the regular army. The German republic had been saved, but only because the moderate socialists had relied on the traditional army—in effect, the same conservatives who had dominated the old imperial regime. Moreover, this "second revolution" of January 1919, bloodily crushed by the republican government, created a deep fear of communism among the German middle classes. All too soon, this fear would be cleverly manipulated by a politician named Adolf Hitler.

Austria-Hungary, too, experienced disintegration and revolution. In 1914, when it attacked Serbia, the imperial regime had tried to crush the nationalistic forces that it believed were destroying the empire. By 1918, those same nationalistic forces had brought the complete breakup of the Austro-Hungarian Empire. As war weariness took hold of the empire, ethnic minorities increasingly sought to achieve national independence. This desire was further encouraged by Allied war aims that included calls for the independence of the subject peoples. By the time the war ended, the Austro-Hungarian Empire had been replaced by the independent republics of Austria, Hungary, and Czechoslovakia and the large south Slav monarchical state called Yugoslavia. Other regions clamored to join Italy, Romania, and a reconstituted Poland. Rivalries among the nations that succeeded Austria-Hungary would weaken eastern Europe for the next eighty years. Ethnic pride and national statehood proved far more important to these states than class differences. Only in Hungary was there an attempt at social revolution when Béla Kun established a communist state. It was crushed after a brief five-month existence.

Democratic Party in 1916. In 1918, the more radical members of the Independent Socialists favored an immediate social revolution carried out by the councils of soldiers, sailors, and workers. Led by Karl Liebknecht and Rosa Luxemburg, these radical, left-wing socialists formed the German Communist Party in December 1918. In effect, two parallel governments were established in Germany: the parliamentary republic proclaimed by the majority Social Democrats and the revolutionary socialist republic declared by the radicals.

Unlike Russia's Bolsheviks, Germany's radicals failed to achieve control of the government. By ending the war on November 11, the moderate socialists had removed a major source of dissatisfaction. When the radical socialists (now known as Communists) attempted to seize power

◆ The Peace Settlement

In January 1919, the delegations of twenty-seven victorious Allied nations gathered in Paris to conclude a final settlement of the Great War. Some delegates believed that this conference would avoid the mistakes made at Vienna in 1815 (see Chapter 21) when aristocrats rearranged the map of Europe to meet the selfish desires of the great powers. Harold Nicolson, one of the British delegates, expressed what he believed this conference would achieve instead: "We were journeying to Paris not merely to liquidate the war, but to found a New Order in Europe. We were preparing not Peace only, but Eternal Peace. There was about us the halo of some divine mission. . . . For we were bent on doing great, permanent and noble things."[10]

Two Voices of Peacemaking: Woodrow Wilson and Georges Clemenceau

When the Allied powers met at Paris in January 1919, it soon became apparent that the victors had different opinions on the kind of peace they expected. The first excerpt is from a speech of Woodrow Wilson in which the American president presented his idealistic goals for a peace based on justice and reconciliation. The French wanted revenge and security. In the second selection, from Georges Clemenceau's Grandeur and Misery of Victory, *the French premier revealed his fundamental dislike and distrust of Germany.*

❊ Woodrow Wilson, May 26, 1917

We are fighting for the liberty, the self-government, and the undictated development of all peoples, and every feature of the settlement that concludes this war must be conceived and executed for that purpose. Wrongs must first be righted and then adequate safeguards must be created to prevent their being committed again. . . .

No people must be forced under sovereignty under which it does not wish to live. No territory must change hands except for the purpose of securing those who inhabit it a fair chance of life and liberty. No indemnities must be insisted on except those that constitute payment for manifest wrongs done. No readjustments of power must be made except such as will tend to secure the future peace of the world and the future welfare and happiness of its peoples.

And then the free peoples of the world must draw together in some common covenant, some genuine and practical cooperation that will in effect combine their force to secure peace and justice in the dealings of nations with one another.

❊ Georges Clemenceau, *Grandeur and Misery of Victory*

War and peace, with their strong contrasts, alternate against a common background. For the catastrophe of 1914 the Germans are responsible. Only a professional liar would deny this. . . .

I have sometimes penetrated into the sacred cave of the Germanic cult, which is, as every one knows, the *Bierhaus* [beer hall]. A great aisle of massive humanity where there accumulate, amid the fumes of tobacco and beer, the popular rumblings of a nationalism upheld by the sonorous brasses blaring to the heavens the supreme voice of Germany, *Deutschland über alles! Germany above everything!* Men, women, and children, all petrified in reverence before the divine stoneware pot, brows furrowed with irrepressible power, eyes lost in a dream of infinity, mouths twisted by the intensity of willpower, drink in long draughts the celestial hope of vague expectations. These only remain to be realized presently when the chief marked out by Destiny shall have given the word. There you have the ultimate framework of an old but childish race.

National expectations, however, made Nicolson's quest for "eternal peace" a difficult one. Over the years, the reasons for fighting World War I had been transformed from selfish national interests to idealistic principles. At the end of 1917, after they had taken over the Russian government, Lenin and the Bolsheviks had publicly revealed the contents of secret wartime treaties found in the archives of the Russian foreign ministry. The documents made it clear that European nations had gone to war primarily to achieve territorial gains. But the American president Woodrow Wilson attempted at the beginning of 1918 to shift the discussion of war aims to a higher ground. Wilson outlined "Fourteen Points" to the American Congress that he believed justified the enormous military struggle then being waged. Later, Wilson spelled out additional steps for a truly just and lasting peace. Wilson's proposals included "open covenants of peace, openly arrived at" instead of secret diplomacy; the reduction of national armaments to a "point consistent with domestic safety"; and the self-determination of people so that "all well-defined national aspirations shall be accorded the utmost satisfaction." Wilson characterized World War I as a people's war waged against "absolutism and militarism," two scourges of liberty that could only be eliminated by creating democratic governments and a "general association of nations" that would guarantee the "political independence and territorial integrity to great and small states alike" (see the box above). As the spokesman for a new world order based on democracy and international cooperation, Wilson was enthusiastically cheered by many Europeans when he arrived in Europe for the peace conference.

Wilson soon found, however, that other states at the Paris Peace Conference were guided by considerably more pragmatic motives. The secret treaties and agreements, for example, that had been made before the war could not be totally ignored, even if they did conflict with the principle of self-determination enunciated by Wilson.

National interests also complicated the deliberations of the Paris Peace Conference. David Lloyd George, prime minister of Great Britain, had won a decisive electoral victory in December of 1918 on a platform of making the

THE BIG FOUR AT PARIS. Shown here are the Big Four at the Paris Peace Conference: Lloyd George of Britain, Orlando of Italy, Clemenceau of France, and Wilson of the United States. Although Italy was considered one of the Big Four powers, Britain, France, and the United States (the Big Three) made the major decisions at the peace conference.

Germans pay for this dreadful war. Public opinion had been inflamed during the war by a government propaganda campaign that portrayed the Germans as beasts. With the war over, the influence of that propaganda continued to be felt as many British believed that only a total victory over Germany could ever compensate for the terrible losses of the war.

France's approach to peace was primarily determined by considerations of national security. Georges Clemenceau, the feisty premier of France who had led his country to victory, believed the French people had borne the brunt of German aggression. They deserved revenge and security against future German aggression (see the box on p. 775). The French knew that Germany's larger population (60 million to 40 million) posed a long-term threat to France. Clemenceau wanted a demilitarized Germany, vast German reparations to pay for the costs of the war, and a separate Rhineland as a buffer state between France and Germany—demands that Wilson viewed as vindictive and contrary to the principle of national self-determination.

Yet another consideration affected the negotiations at Paris, namely, the fear that Bolshevik revolution would spread from Russia to other European countries. This concern led the Allies to enlarge and strengthen such eastern European states as Poland, Czechoslovakia, and Romania at the expense of both Germany and Bolshevik Russia.

Although twenty-seven nations were represented at the Paris Peace Conference, the most important decisions were made by Woodrow Wilson, Georges Clemenceau, and David Lloyd George. Italy was considered one of the so-called Big Four powers, but played a much less important role than the other three countries. Germany, of

course, was not invited to attend and Russia could not because of its civil war.

In view of the many conflicting demands at Versailles, it was inevitable that the Big Three would quarrel. Wilson was determined to create a League of Nations to prevent future wars. Clemenceau and Lloyd George were equally determined to punish Germany. In the end, only compromise made it possible to achieve a peace settlement. Wilson's wish that the creation of an international peacekeeping organization be the first order of business was granted, and already on January 25, 1919, the conference adopted the principle of a League of Nations. The details of its structure were left for later sessions, and Wilson willingly agreed to make compromises on territorial arrangements to guarantee the establishment of the league, believing that a functioning league could later rectify bad arrangements. Clemenceau also compromised to obtain some guarantees for French security. He renounced France's desire for a separate Rhineland and instead accepted a defensive alliance with Great Britain and the United States. Both states pledged to help France if it were attacked by Germany.

The final peace settlement of Paris consisted of five separate treaties with the defeated nations—Germany, Austria, Hungary, Bulgaria, and the Ottoman Empire. The Treaty of Versailles with Germany, signed on June 28, 1919, was by far the most important. The Germans considered it a harsh peace, conveniently overlooking that the Treaty of Brest-Litovsk, which they had imposed on Bolshevik Russia, was even more severe. The Germans were particularly unhappy with Article 231, the so-called War Guilt Clause, which declared Germany (and Austria) responsible for starting the war and ordered Germany to

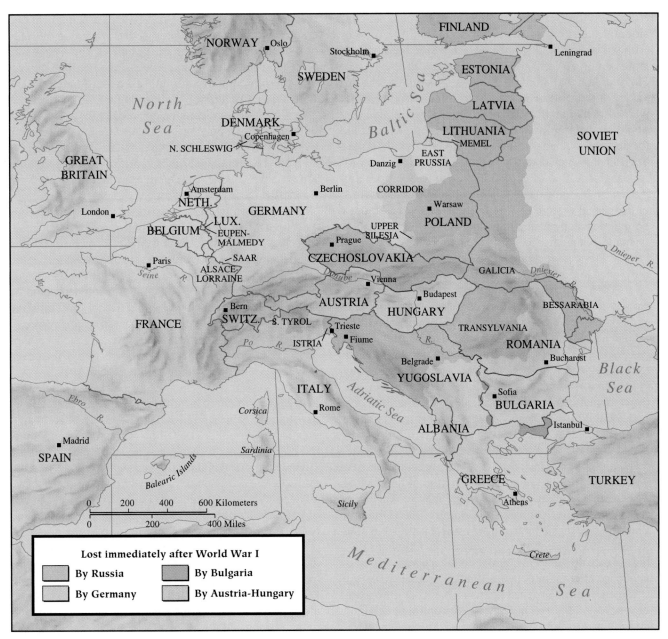

MAP 25.5 Europe in 1919.

pay reparations for all the damage to which the Allied governments and their people were subjected as a result of the war "imposed upon them by the aggression of Germany and her allies." Reparations were a logical consequence of the wartime promises that Allied leaders had made to their people that the Germans would pay for the war effort. The treaty did not establish the amount to be paid, but left that to be determined later by a reparations commission (see Chapter 26).

The military and territorial provisions of the treaty also rankled the Germans, although they were by no means as harsh as the Germans claimed. Germany had to reduce its army to 100,000 men, cut back its navy, and eliminate its air force. German territorial losses included the cession of Alsace and Lorraine to France and sections of Prussia to the new Polish state. German land west and

as far as thirty miles east of the Rhine was established as a demilitarized zone and stripped of all armaments or fortifications to serve as a barrier to any future German military moves westward against France. Outraged by the "dictated peace," the new German government vowed to resist rather than accept the treaty, but it had no real alternative. Rejection meant a renewal of the war, and as the army pointed out, that was no longer possible.

The separate peace treaties made with the other Central Powers (Austria, Hungary, Bulgaria, and the Ottoman Empire) extensively redrew the map of eastern Europe. Many of these changes merely ratified what the war had already accomplished. The empires that had controlled eastern Europe for centuries had been destroyed or weakened, and a number of new states appeared on the map of Europe.

Both the German and Russian Empires lost considerable territory in eastern Europe, and the Austro-Hungarian Empire disappeared altogether. New nation-states emerged from the lands of these three empires: Finland, Latvia, Estonia, Lithuania, Poland, Czechoslovakia, Austria, and Hungary. Territorial rearrangements were also made in the Balkans. Romania acquired additional lands from Russia, Hungary, and Bulgaria. Serbia formed the nucleus of a new south Slav state, called Yugoslavia, which combined Serbs, Croats, and Slovenes. Although the Paris Peace Conference was supposedly guided by the principle of self-determination, the mixtures of peoples in eastern Europe made it impossible to draw boundaries along neat ethnic lines. Compromises had to be made, sometimes to satisfy the national interest of the victors. France, for example, had lost Russia as its major ally on Germany's eastern border and wanted to strengthen and expand Poland, Czechoslovakia, Yugoslavia, and Romania as much as possible so that those states could serve as barriers against Germany and Communist Russia. As a result of compromises, virtually every eastern European state was left with a minorities problem that could lead to future conflicts. Germans in Poland, Hungarians, Poles, and Germans in Czechoslovakia, and the combination of Serbs, Croats, Slovenes, Macedonians, and Albanians in Yugoslavia all became sources of later conflict. Moreover, the new map of eastern Europe was based upon the temporary collapse of power in both Germany and Russia. Since neither country accepted the new eastern frontiers, it seemed only a matter of time before a resurgent Germany or Russia would make changes.

Yet another centuries-old empire—the Ottoman Empire—was dismembered by the peace settlement after the war. To gain Arab support against the Ottomans during the war, the Allies had promised to recognize the independence of Arab states in the Middle Eastern lands of the Ottoman Empire. But the imperialist habits of Europeans died hard. After the war, France took control of Lebanon and Syria, and Britain received Iraq and Palestine. Officially, both acquisitions were called mandates. Since Woodrow Wilson had opposed the outright annexation of

colonial territories by the Allies, the peace settlement had created a system of mandates whereby a nation officially administered a territory on behalf of the League of Nations. The system of mandates could not hide the fact that the principle of national self-determination at the Paris Peace Conference was largely for Europeans.

The peace settlement negotiated at Paris soon came under attack, not only by the defeated Central Powers, but by others who felt that the peacemakers had been shortsighted. The famous British economist John Maynard Keynes, for example, condemned the preoccupation with frontiers at the expense of economic issues that left Europe "inefficient, unemployed, disorganized." Other people, however, thought the peace settlement was the best that could be achieved under the circumstances. They believed that self-determination had served reasonably well as a central organizing principle, and the establishment of the League of Nations gave some hope that future conflicts could be resolved peacefully. And yet, within twenty years after the signing of the peace treaties, Europe was again engaged in deadly conflict. As some historians have suggested, perhaps lack of enforcement rather than the structure of the peace may have caused the failure of the peace of 1919.

Successful enforcement of the peace necessitated the active involvement of its principal architects, especially in assisting the new German state to develop a peaceful and democratic republic. The failure of the American Senate to ratify the Treaty of Versailles, however, meant that the United States never joined the League of Nations. In addition, the American Senate also rejected Wilson's defensive alliance with Great Britain and France. Already by the end of 1919, the United States was pursuing policies intended to limit its direct involvement in future European wars.

This retreat had dire consequences. American withdrawal from the defensive alliance with Britain and France led Britain to withdraw as well. By removing itself from European affairs, the United States forced France to stand alone facing its old enemy, leading the embittered nation to take strong actions against Germany that only intensified German resentment. By the end of 1919, it appeared that the peace of 1919 was already beginning to unravel.

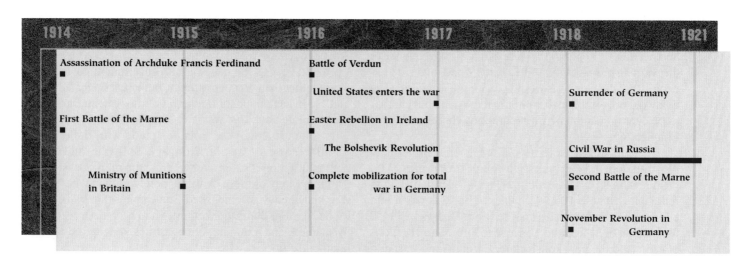

1914   1915   1916   1917   1918   1921

Assassination of Archduke Francis Ferdinand

First Battle of the Marne

Ministry of Munitions in Britain

Battle of Verdun

United States enters the war

Easter Rebellion in Ireland

The Bolshevik Revolution

Complete mobilization for total war in Germany

Surrender of Germany

Civil War in Russia

Second Battle of the Marne

November Revolution in Germany

CONCLUSION ✕✕✕✕✕✕✕✕✕✕✕

World War I shattered the liberal and rational assumptions of late nineteenth- and early twentieth-century European society. The incredible destruction and the death of almost 10 million people undermined the whole idea of progress. New propaganda techniques had manipulated entire populations into sustaining their involvement in a meaningless slaughter.

World War I was a total war and involved a mobilization of resources and populations and increased government centralization of power over the lives of its citizens. Civil liberties, such as freedom of the press, speech, assembly, and movement, were circumscribed in the name of national security. Governments' need to plan the production and distribution of goods and to ration consumer goods restricted economic freedom. Although the late nineteenth and early twentieth centuries had witnessed the extension of government authority into such areas as mass education, social welfare legislation, and mass conscription, World War I made the practice of strong central authority a way of life.

Finally, World War I ended the age of European hegemony over world affairs. In 1917, the Russian Revolution laid the foundation for the creation of a new Soviet power, and the United States entered the war. The termination of the European age was not evident to all, however, for it was clouded by two developments— American isolationism and the withdrawal of the Soviets from world affairs while they nurtured the growth of their own socialist system. Although these developments were only temporary, they created a political vacuum in Europe that all too soon was filled by the revival of German power.

NOTES ✕✕✕✕✕✕✕✕✕✕✕✕✕✕

1. Arnold Toynbee, *Surviving the Future* (New York, 1971), pp. 106–107.
2. Quoted in Joachim Remak, "1914—The Third Balkan War: Origins Reconsidered," *Journal of Modern History* 43 (1971): 364–365.
3. Quoted in Robert G. L. Waite, *Vanguard of Nazism* (New York, 1969), p. 22.
4. Quoted in J. M. Winter, *The Experience of World War I* (New York, 1989), p. 142.
5. Quoted in ibid., p. 137.
6. Quoted in Gail Braybon, *Women Workers in the First World War: The British Experience* (London, 1981), p. 79.
7. Quoted in Catherine W. Reilly, ed., *Scars upon My Heart: Women's Poetry and Verse of the First World War* (London, 1981), p. 90.
8. Quoted in Robert Paxton, *Europe in the Twentieth Century*, 2d ed. (New York, 1985), p. 110.
9. Quoted in William M. Mandel, *Soviet Women* (Garden City, N.Y., 1975), p. 43.
10. Harold Nicolson, *Peacemaking, 1919* (Boston and New York, 1933), pp. 31–32.

SUGGESTIONS FOR FURTHER READING ✕✕✕✕

The historical literature on the causes of World War I is enormous. Good starting points are J. Joll, *The Origins of the First World War*, 2d ed. (London, 1992); and J. Remak, *The Origins of World War I, 1871–1914*, 2d ed. (Fort Worth, Tex., 1995). The belief that Germany was primarily responsible for the war was argued vigorously by the German scholar F. Fischer, *Germany's Aims in the First World War* (New York, 1967); *World Power or Decline: The Controversy over Germany's Aims in World War I* (New York, 1974); and *War of Illusions: German Policies from 1911 to 1914* (New York, 1975). The role of each great power has been reassessed in a series of books on the causes of World War I. They include V. R. Berghahn, *Germany and the Approach of War in 1914*, 2d ed. (London, 1993); Z. S. Steiner, *Britain and the Origins of the First World War* (New York, 1977); R. Bosworth, *Italy and the Approach of the First World War* (New York, 1983); J. F. Keiger, *France and the Origins of the First World War* (New York, 1984); and D. C. B. Lieven, *Russia and the Origins of the First World War* (New York, 1984). On the role of militarism, see D. Hermann, *The Arming of Europe and the Making of the First World War* (New York, 1997).

There are two good recent accounts of World War I in M. Gilbert, *The First World War* (New York, 1994); and the lavishly illustrated book by J. M. Winter, *The Experience of World War I* (New York, 1989). See also the brief work by N. Heyman, *World War I* (Westport, Conn., 1997). There is an excellent collection of articles in H. Strachan, *The Oxford Illustrated History of the First World War* (New York, 1998). For an account of the military operations of the war, see the classic work by B. H. Liddell Hart, *History of the First World War* (Boston, 1970). The nature of trench warfare is examined in T. Ashworth, *Trench Warfare, 1914–1918: The Live and Let-Live System* (London, 1980). The use of poison gas is examined in L. F. Haber, *The Poisonous Cloud: Chemical Warfare in the First World War* (Oxford, 1985). On the morale of soldiers in World War I, see J. Keegan, *The Face of Battle* (London, 1975). The war at sea is examined in R. Hough, *The Great War at Sea, 1914–18* (Oxford, 1983). In *The Great War and Modern Memory* (London, 1975), Paul Fussell attempted to show how British writers described their war experiences. Although scholars do not always agree with her conclusions, B. Tuchman's *The Guns of August* (New York, 1962) is a magnificently written account of the opening days of the war. For an interesting perspective on World War I and the beginnings of the modern world, see M. Eksteins, *Rites of Spring, The Great War and the Birth of the Modern Age* (Boston, 1989).

On the role of women in World War I, see G. Braybon, *Women Workers in the First World War: The British Experience* (London, 1981); J. M. Winter and R. M. Wall, eds., *The Upheaval of War: Family, Work and Welfare in Europe, 1914–1918* (Cambridge, 1988); G. Braybon and P. Summerfield, *Women's Experiences in Two World Wars* (London, 1987); and M. R. Higonnet, J. Jensen, S. Michel, and M. C. Weitz, *Behind the Lines: Gender and the Two World Wars* (New Haven, Conn., 1987).

A good introduction to the Russian Revolution can be found in S. Fitzpatrick, *The Russian Revolution, 1917–1932*, 2d ed. (New York, 1994). See also R. Pipes, *The Russian Revolution* (New York, 1990). On Lenin, see R. W. Clark, *Lenin* (New York, 1988); and the valuable work by A. B. Ulam, *The Bolsheviks* (New York, 1965). On social reforms, see W. Goldman, *Women, the State, and Revolution* (Cambridge, 1993). There is now a comprehensive study of the Russian civil war in W. B. Lincoln, *Red Victory: A History of the Russian Civil War* (New York, 1989). On the revolutions in Germany and Austria-Hungary, see F. L. Carsten, *Revolution in Central Europe* (Berkeley, 1972); and A. J. Ryder, *The German Revolution of 1918* (Cambridge, 1967).

The role of war aims in shaping the peace settlement is examined in V. H. Rothwell, *British War Aims and Peace Diplomacy, 1914–1918* (Oxford, 1971); and D. R. Stevenson, *French War Aims against Germany, 1914–1919* (New York, 1982).

World War I and the Russian Revolution are also well covered in two good general surveys of European history in the twentieth century, R. Paxton, *Europe in the Twentieth Century*, 2d ed. (New York, 1985); and A. Rudhart, *Twentieth Century Europe* (Englewood Cliffs, N.J., 1986).

For additional reading, go to InfoTrac College Edition, your online research library at http://web1.infotrac-college.com

Enter the search terms *World War, 1914–1918* using the Subject Guide.

Enter the search terms *Russia Revolution* using Key Terms.

Enter the search term *Bolshevik* using Key Terms.

Enter the search terms *Versailles Treaty* using Key Terms.

26

The Futile Search for a New Stability: Europe Between the Wars, 1919–1939

CHAPTER OUTLINE

- An Uncertain Peace: The Search for Security
- The Democratic States
- The Retreat from Democracy: The Authoritarian and Totalitarian States
- The Expansion of Mass Culture and Mass Leisure
- Cultural and Intellectual Trends in the Interwar Years
- Conclusion

FOCUS QUESTIONS

- How did France, Great Britain, and the United States respond to the various crises, including the Great Depression, that they faced in the interwar years?
- What conditions led to the emergence of Fascists in Italy and Nazis in Germany, and how did each group attain power?
- What are the characteristics of totalitarian states, and to what degree were these characteristics present in Fascist Italy, Nazi Germany, and Stalinist Russia?
- What new dimensions in mass culture and mass leisure emerged during the interwar years, and what role did these activities play in totalitarian states?
- What were the main cultural and intellectual trends in the interwar years?

*O*NLY TWENTY YEARS AFTER the Treaty of Versailles, Europeans were again at war. And yet in the 1920s, many people assumed that Europe and the world were about to enter a new era of international peace, economic growth, and political democracy. In all of these areas, the optimistic hopes of the 1920s failed to be realized. After 1919, most people wanted peace but were unsure how to maintain it. The League of Nations, conceived as a new instrument to provide for collective security, failed to work well. New treaties that renounced the use of war looked good on paper but had no means of enforcement. Then, too, virtually everyone favored disarmament, but few could agree on how to achieve it.

At home, Europe was faced with severe economic problems after World War I. The European economy did not begin to recover from the war until 1922, and even then it was beset by financial problems left over from the war and, most devastating of all, the Great Depression that began at the end of 1929. The Great Depression brought untold misery to millions of people. Begging for food on the streets became widespread, especially when soup kitchens were unable to keep up with the demand. Larger and larger numbers of people were homeless and moved from place to place looking for work and shelter. In the United States, the homeless set up shantytowns they named "Hoovervilles" after the American president, Herbert Hoover. In their misery, some people saw but one solution; as one unemployed person expressed it: "Today, when I am experiencing this for the first time, I think that I should prefer to do away with myself, to take gas, to jump into the river, or leap from some high place. . . . would I really come to such a decision? I do not know. Animals die, plants wither, but men always go on living." Social unrest spread rapidly, and some unemployed staged hunger marches to get attention. In democratic countries, more and more people began to listen to and vote for radical voices calling for extreme measures.

According to Woodrow Wilson, World War I had been fought to make the world safe for democracy, and for a while after 1919, political democracy seemed well established. But the hopes for democracy, too, soon faded as authoritarian regimes spread into Italy and Germany and across eastern Europe.

◆ An Uncertain Peace: The Search for Security

The peace settlement at the end of World War I had tried to fulfill the nineteenth-century dream of nationalism by redrawing boundaries and creating new states. From its inception, however, this peace settlement had left nations unhappy. Conflicts over disputed border regions between Germany and Poland, Poland and Lithuania, Poland and Czechoslovakia, Austria and Hungary, and Italy and Yugoslavia poisoned mutual relations in eastern Europe for years. Many Germans viewed the Peace of Versailles as a dictated peace and vowed to seek its revision.

The American president Woodrow Wilson had recognized that the peace treaties contained unwise provisions that could serve as new causes for conflicts and had placed many of his hopes for the future in the League of Nations. The league, however, was not particularly effective in maintaining the peace. The failure of the United States to join the league and the subsequent American determination to be less involved in European affairs undermined the effectiveness of the league from its beginning. Moreover, the league could only use economic sanctions to halt aggression. The French attempt to strengthen the league's effectiveness as an instrument of collective security by creating some kind of international army was rejected by nations that feared giving up any of their sovereignty to a larger international body.

The weakness of the League of Nations and the failure of both the United States and Great Britain to honor their promises to form defensive military alliances with France left France embittered and alone. Before World War I, France's alliance with Russia had served to threaten Germany with the possibility of a two-front war. But Communist Russia was now a hostile power. To compensate, France built a network of alliances in eastern Europe with Poland and the members of the so-called Little Entente (Czechoslovakia, Romania, Yugoslavia). Although these alliances looked good on paper as a way to contain Germany and maintain the new status quo, they overlooked the fundamental military weaknesses of those nations. Poland and the Little Entente states were no real substitutes for Russia.

❈ *The French Policy of Coercion (1919–1924)*

France's search for security between 1919 and 1924 was founded primarily upon a strict enforcement of the Treaty of Versailles. This tough policy toward Germany began with the issue of reparations, or the payments that the Germans were supposed to make to compensate for the "damage done to the civilian population of the Allied and Associated Powers and to their property," as the treaty asserted. In April 1921, the Allied Reparations Commission settled on a sum of 132 billion marks ($33 billion) for German reparations, payable in annual installments of 2.5 billion (gold) marks. Allied threats to occupy the Ruhr valley, Germany's chief industrial and mining center, led the new German republic to accept the reparations settlement and make its first payment in 1921. By the following year, however, faced with rising inflation, domestic turmoil, and lack of revenues due to low tax rates, the German government announced that it was unable to pay more. Outraged by what they considered to be Germany's violation of one aspect of the peace settlement, the French government sent troops to occupy the Ruhr valley. Since the Germans would not pay reparations, the French would collect reparations in kind by operating and using the Ruhr mines and factories.

Both Germany and France suffered from the French occupation of the Ruhr. The German government adopted a policy of passive resistance that was largely financed by printing more paper money, but this only intensified the inflationary pressures that had already appeared in Germany by the end of the war. The German mark soon became worthless. In 1914, 4.2 marks equaled one dollar; by November 1, 1923, the ratio had reached 130 billion to

THE EFFECTS OF INFLATION. Germany experienced a number of serious economic problems after World War I. The inflationary pressures that had begun in Germany at the end of the war intensified during the French occupation of the Ruhr. By the early 1920s, the value of the German mark had fallen precipitously. This photograph shows a German housewife using the worthless currency to light a fire in her cooking stove.

one; by the end of November, it had increased to an incredible 4.2 trillion. Economic disaster fueled political upheavals as Communists staged uprisings in October 1923, and Adolf Hitler's band of Nazis attempted to seize power in Munich in November (see Hitler and Nazi Germany later in this chapter). But the French were hardly victorious. The cost of the French occupation was not offset by the gains. Meanwhile, pressure from the United States and Great Britain against the French policy forced the French to agree to a new conference of experts to reassess the reparations problem. By the time the conference did its work in 1924, both France and Germany were opting to pursue a more conciliatory approach toward each other.

✳ *The Hopeful Years (1924–1929)*

The formation of liberal-socialist governments in both Great Britain and France opened the door to conciliatory approaches to Germany and the reparations problem. At the same time, a new German government led by Gustav Stresemann (1878–1929) ended the policy of passive resis-

tance and committed Germany to carry out most of the provisions of the Treaty of Versailles while seeking a new settlement of the reparations question.

In August 1924, an international commission produced a new plan for reparations. Named the Dawes Plan after the American banker who chaired the commission, it reduced reparations and stabilized Germany's payments on the basis of its ability to pay. The Dawes Plan also granted an initial $200 million loan for German recovery, which opened the door to heavy American investments in Europe that helped create a new era of European prosperity between 1924 and 1929.

A new era of European diplomacy accompanied the new economic stability. A spirit of international cooperation was fostered by the foreign ministers of Germany and France, Gustav Stresemann and Aristide Briand (1862–1932), who concluded the Treaty of Locarno in 1925. This guaranteed Germany's new western borders with France and Belgium. Although Germany's new eastern borders with Poland were conspicuously absent from the agreement, a clear indication that Germany did not accept those borders as permanent, the Locarno pact was viewed by many as the beginning of a new era of European peace. On the day after the pact was concluded, the headline in the *New York Times* ran "France and Germany Ban War Forever," while the London Times declared, "Peace at Last."[1]

Germany's entry into the League of Nations in March 1926 soon reinforced the new spirit of conciliation engendered at Locarno. Two years later, similar optimistic attitudes prevailed in the Kellogg-Briand pact, drafted by the American secretary of state Frank B. Kellogg and the French foreign minister Aristide Briand. Sixty-three nations eventually agreed to the pact, in which they pledged "to renounce war as an instrument of national policy." Nothing was said, however, about what would be done if anyone violated the treaty.

The spirit of Locarno was based on little real substance. Germany lacked the military power to alter its western borders even if it wanted to. Pious promises to renounce war without mechanisms to enforce them were virtually worthless. And the issue of disarmament soon proved that even the spirit of Locarno could not induce nations to cut back on their weapons. The League of Nations Covenant had suggested the "reduction of national armaments to the lowest point consistent with national safety." Germany, of course, had been disarmed with the expectation that other states would do likewise. Numerous disarmament conferences, however, failed to achieve anything substantial as states proved unwilling to trust their security to anyone but their own military forces. When a World Disarmament Conference finally met in Geneva in 1932, the issue was already dead.

One other hopeful sign in the years between 1924 and 1929 was the new coexistence of the West with Soviet Russia. By the beginning of 1924, Soviet hopes for communist revolutions in Western states had largely dissipated. In turn, these states had realized by then that the

Bolshevik regime could not be ousted. By 1924, Germany, Britain, France, and Italy, as well as several smaller European countries, had established full diplomatic relations with Soviet Russia. Nevertheless, Western powers remained highly suspicious of Soviet intentions, especially when the Soviet Union continued to support the propaganda activities of the Comintern, or Communist International, a worldwide organization of pro-Soviet Marxist parties originally formed in 1919 by Lenin to foster world revolution.

❈ *The Great Depression*

After World War I, most European states hoped to return to the liberal ideal of a market economy based on private enterprise and largely free of state intervention. But the war had vastly strengthened business cartels and labor unions, making some government regulation of these powerful organizations appear necessary. At the same time, reparations and war debts had severely damaged the postwar international economy, making the prosperity that did occur between 1924 and 1929 at best a fragile one and the dream of returning to the liberal ideal of a self-regulating market economy merely an illusion. What destroyed the dream altogether was the Great Depression.

Two factors played an important role in the coming of the Great Depression: a downturn in domestic economies and an international financial crisis created by the collapse of the American stock market in 1929. Already in the mid-1920s, prices for agricultural goods were beginning to decline rapidly due to overproduction of basic commodities, such as wheat. In 1925, states in central and eastern Europe began to impose tariffs to close their markets to other countries' goods. An increase in the use of oil and hydroelectricity led to a slump in the coal industry even before 1929.

In addition to these domestic economic troubles, much of the European prosperity between 1924 and 1929 had been built upon American bank loans to Germany. Twenty-three billion marks had been invested in German municipal bonds and German industries since 1924. Already in 1928 and 1929, American investors had begun to pull money out of Germany in order to invest in the booming New York stock market. The crash of the American stock market in October 1929 led panicky American investors to withdraw even more of their funds from Germany and other European markets. The withdrawal of funds seriously weakened the banks of Germany and other central European states. The Credit-Anstalt, Vienna's most prestigious bank, collapsed on May 31, 1931. By that time, trade was slowing down, industrialists were cutting back production, and unemployment was increasing as the ripple effects of international bank failures had a devastating impact on domestic economies.

THE GREAT DEPRESSION: BREAD LINES IN PARIS. The Great Depression devastated the European economy and had serious political repercussions. Because of its more balanced economy, France did not feel the effects of the depression as quickly as other European countries. By 1931, however, even France was experiencing lines of unemployed people at free-food centers.

The Great Depression: Unemployed and Homeless in Germany

In 1932, Germany had six million unemployed workers, many of them wandering aimlessly through the country, begging for food and seeking shelter in city lodging houses for the homeless. The Great Depression was an important factor in the rise to power of Adolf Hitler and the Nazis. This selection presents a description of unemployed homeless in 1932.

❋ Heinrich Hauser, "With Germany's Unemployed"

An almost unbroken chain of homeless men extends the whole length of the great Hamburg-Berlin highway. . . . All the highways in Germany over which I have traveled this year presented the same aspect. . . .

Most of the hikers paid no attention to me. They walked separately or in small groups, with their eyes on the ground. And they had the queer, stumbling gait of barefooted people, for their shoes were slung over their shoulders. Some of them were guild members,—carpenters . . . milkmen . . . and bricklayers . . . but they were in a minority. Far more numerous were those whom one could assign to no special profession or craft—unskilled young people, for the most part, who had been unable to find a place for themselves in any city or town in Germany, and who had never had a job and never expected to have one. There was something else that had never been seen before—whole families that had piled all their goods into baby carriages and wheelbarrows that they were pushing along as they plodded forward in dumb despair. It was a whole nation on the march.

I saw them—and this was the strongest impression that the year 1932 left with me—I saw them, gathered into groups of fifty or a hundred men, attacking fields of potatoes. I saw them digging up the potatoes and throwing them into sacks while the farmer who owned the field watched them in despair and the local policeman looked on gloomily from the distance. I saw them staggering toward the lights of the city as night fell, with their sacks on their backs. What did it remind me of? Of the War, of the worst periods of starvation in 1917 and 1918, but even then people paid for the potatoes. . . .

I saw that the individual can know what is happening only by personal experience. I know what it is to be a tramp. I know what cold and hunger are. . . . But there are two things that I have only recently experienced—begging and spending the night in a municipal lodging house.

I entered the huge Berlin municipal lodging house in a northern quarter of the city. . . .

Distribution of spoons, distribution of enameled-ware bowls with the words "Property of the City of Berlin" written on their sides. Then the meal itself. A big kettle is carried. Men with yellow smocks have brought it in and men with yellow smocks ladle out the food. These men, too, are homeless and they have been expressly picked by the establishment and given free food and lodging and a little pocket money in exchange for their work about the house.

Where have I seen this kind of food distribution before? In a prison that I once helped to guard in the winter of 1919 during the German civil war. There was the same hunger then, the same trembling, anxious expectation of rations. Now the men are standing in a long row, dressed in their plain nightshirts that reach to the ground, and the noise of their shuffling feet is like the noise of big wild animals walking up and down the stone floor of their cages before feeding time. The men lean far over the kettle so that the warm steam from the food envelops them and they hold out their bowls as if begging and whisper to the attendant, "Give me a real helping. Give me a little more." A piece of bread is handed out with every bowl.

My next recollection is sitting at a table in another room on a crowded bench that is like a seat in a fourth-class railway carriage. Hundreds of hungry mouths make an enormous noise eating their food. The men sit bent over their food like animals who feel that someone is going to take it away from them. They hold their bowl with their left arm part way around it, so that nobody can take it away, and they also protect it with their other elbow and with their head and mouth, while they move the spoon as fast as they can between their mouth and the bowl.

Economic depression was by no means a new phenomenon in European history. But the depth of the economic downturn after 1929 fully justifies the label Great Depression. During 1932, the worst year of the depression, one British worker in four was unemployed, and six million or 40 percent of the German labor force were out of work. Between 1929 and 1932, industrial production plummeted almost 50 percent in the United States and over 40 percent in Germany. The unemployed and homeless filled the streets of the cities throughout the advanced industrial countries (see the box above).

The economic crisis also had unexpected social repercussions. Women were often able to secure low-paying jobs as servants, housecleaners, or laundresses while many men remained unemployed, either begging on the streets or staying at home to do household tasks. Many unemployed men, resenting this reversal of traditional gender roles, were open to the shrill cries of demagogues with simple solutions to the economic crisis. High unemployment rates among young males often led them to join gangs that gathered in parks or other public places, arousing fear among local residents.

Governments seemed powerless to deal with the crisis. The classical liberal remedy for depression, a deflationary policy of balanced budgets, which involved cutting costs by lowering wages and raising tariffs to exclude other countries' goods from home markets, only served to worsen the economic crisis and create even greater mass discontent. This, in turn, led to serious political repercussions. Increased government activity in the economy was one reaction, even in countries like the United States that had a strong laissez-faire tradition. Another effect was a renewed interest in Marxist doctrines since Marx had predicted that capitalism would destroy itself through overproduction. Communism took on new popularity, especially with workers and intellectuals. Finally, the Great Depression increased the attractiveness of simplistic dictatorial solutions, especially from a new movement known as fascism. Everywhere in Europe, democracy seemed on the defensive in the 1930s. We can best understand the full impact of the depression on Europe by examining the domestic scene in the Western states between the two world wars.

◆ The Democratic States

According to Woodrow Wilson, World War I had been fought to make the world safe for democracy. In 1919, there seemed to be some justification for his claim. Four major European states and a host of minor ones had functioning political democracies. In a number of states, universal male suffrage had even been replaced by universal suffrage as male politicians rewarded women for their contributions to World War I by granting them the right to vote (except in Italy, France, and Spain where women had to wait until the end of World War II). Women also began to enter political life as deputies to parliamentary bodies. In the new German republic, for example, almost 10 percent of the deputies elected to the Reichstag in 1919 were women, although the number dropped to 6 percent by 1926.

❋ *Great Britain*

After World War I, Great Britain went through a period of painful readjustment and serious economic difficulties. During the war, Britain had lost many of its markets for industrial products, especially to the United States and Japan. The postwar decline of such staple industries as coal, steel, and textiles led to a rise in unemployment, which reached the two million mark in 1921. The Liberal government of David Lloyd George proved unable either to change this situation or to meet the demands of the working class for better housing and an improved standard of living.

By 1923, British politics experienced a major transformation when the Labour Party surged ahead of the Liberals as the second most powerful party in Britain after the Conservatives. In fact, after the elections of November 1923, a Labour-Liberal coalition enabled Ramsay MacDonald (1866–1937) to become the first Labour prime minister of Britain. Dependent on Liberal support, MacDonald rejected any extreme social or economic experimentation. His government lasted only ten months, however, as the Conservative Party's charge that his administration was friendly toward communism proved to be a highly successful campaign tactic.

Under the direction of Stanley Baldwin (1867–1947) as prime minister, the Conservatives guided Britain during an era of renewed prosperity from 1925 to 1929. This prosperity, however, was relatively superficial. British exports in the 1920s never compensated for the overseas investments lost during the war, and even in these so-called prosperous years, unemployment remained at a startling 10 percent level. Coal miners were especially affected by the decline of the antiquated and inefficient British coal mines, which also suffered from a world glut of coal. Attempts by mine owners to lower coal miners' wages only led to a national strike (the General Strike of 1926) by miners and sympathetic trade unions. A compromise settled the strike, but many miners refused to accept the settlement and were eventually forced back to work at lower wages for longer hours.

In 1929, just as the Great Depression was beginning, a second Labour government came into power, but its failure to solve the nation's economic problems caused it to fall in 1931. A National Government (a coalition of all three parties) claimed credit for bringing Britain out of the worst stages of the depression, primarily by using the traditional policies of balanced budgets and protective tariffs. By 1936, unemployment had dropped to 1.6 million after reaching a depression high of 3 million in 1932 (see the box on p. 787).

British politicians largely ignored the new ideas of a Cambridge economist, John Maynard Keynes (1883–1946). In 1936, Keynes published his *General Theory of Employment, Interest, and Money*. Contrary to the traditional view that depressions should be left to work themselves out through the self-regulatory mechanisms of a free economy, Keynes argued that unemployment stemmed not from overproduction but from a decline in demand, and that demand could be increased by public works, financed, if necessary, through deficit spending to stimulate production. These policies, however, could only be accomplished by government intervention in the economy, and Britain's political leaders were unwilling to go that far in the 1930s.

The Struggles of a Democracy: Unemployment and Slums in Great Britain

During the 1920s and 1930s, Britain struggled with the problems of economic depression. Unemployment was widespread, especially after the onset of the Great Depression. Even after Britain began to recover in the late 1930s, many Britons still lived in wretched conditions. These selections reflect Britain's economic and social problems.

❈ Men without Work: A Report Made to the Pilgrim Trust, 1938

A week's notice may end half a lifetime's service, with no prospects, if he is elderly, but the dole, followed by a still further reduction in his means of livelihood when the old age pension comes. We take as an example a shoe laster from Leicester, who had worked thirty-seven years with one firm. "When I heard the new manager going through and saying: 'The whole of this side of this room, this room, and this room is to be stopped, I knew it would be uphill work to get something.'" He went on to describe to us how he had not been able to bring himself to tell his wife the bad news when he got home, how she had noticed that something was wrong, how confident she had been that he would get work elsewhere, but how he had known that the chances were heavily against him. For months and indeed often for years such men go on looking for work, and the same is true of many casual laborers. There were in the sample old men who have not a remote chance of working again but yet make it a practice to stand every morning at six o'clock at the works gates in the hope that perhaps they may catch the foreman's eye.

❈ George Orwell, "A Woman in the Slums" from *The Road to Wigan Pier,* 1937

As we moved slowly through the outskirts of the town we passed row after row of little grey slum houses. . . . At the back of one of the houses a young woman was kneeling on the stones, poking a stick up the leaden wastepipe which ran from the sink inside, and which I suppose was blocked. . . . She had a round pale face, the usual exhausted face of the slum girl who is twenty-five and looks forty, thanks to miscarriages and drudgery; and it wore, for the second in which I saw it, the most desolate, hopeless expression I have ever seen. It struck me then that we are mistaken when we say that "It isn't the same for them as it would be for us," and that people bred in the slums can imagine nothing but the slums. For what I saw in her face was not the ignorant suffering of an animal. She knew well enough what was happening to her—understood as well as I did how dreadful a destiny it was to be kneeling there in the bitter cold, on the slimy stones of a slum backyard, poking a stick up a foul drain-pipe.

❈ France

After the defeat of Germany and the demobilization of the German army, France had become the strongest power on the European continent. Its biggest problem involved the reconstruction of the devastated areas of northern and eastern France. The conservative National Bloc government, led by Raymond Poincaré (1860–1934), sought to use German reparations for this purpose. Tying French economic stability to German reparations resulted in Poincaré's hard-line policy toward Germany and the Ruhr invasion. When Poincaré's conservative government was forced to raise taxes in 1924 to pay for the cost of the Ruhr fiasco, his National Bloc was voted out of power and replaced by the so-called Cartel of the Left.

The Cartel of the Left was a coalition government formed by two French parties of the left, the Radicals and Socialists. These two leftist parties shared beliefs in antimilitarism, anticlericalism, and the importance of education. But despite their name, the Radicals were a democratic party of small property owners whereas the Socialists were nominally committed to Marxist socialism. Although they cooperated to win elections, their differences on economic and financial issues made their efforts to solve France's financial problems between 1924 and 1926 largely futile. The failure of the Cartel of the Left led to the return of Raymond Poincaré, whose government from 1926 to 1929 stabilized the French economy during a period of relative prosperity.

France did not feel the effects of the depression as soon as other countries because of its more balanced economy. The French population was almost evenly divided between urban and agricultural pursuits, and a slight majority of industrial plants were small enterprises employing five workers or less. Even large industrialists tended to be conservative and invested little in foreign goods. Not until 1932 did France begin to feel the full effects of the Great Depression, but then economic instability soon had political repercussions. During a nineteen-month period in 1932 and 1933, six different cabinets were formed as France faced political chaos. During the same time, French Fascist groups, adhering to far-right policies similar to those of the Fascists in Italy and the Nazis in Germany (see Fascist Italy and Hitler and Nazi Germany later in this chapter), marched through French streets in a number of demonstrations. The February riots of 1934, caused by a number of French Fascist leagues, frightened many into believing that the Fascists intended to seize

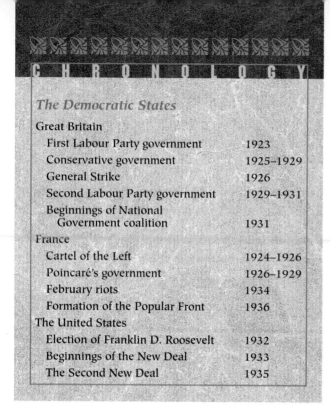

power. These fears began to drive the leftist parties together despite their other differences and led in 1936 to the formation of the Popular Front.

The first Popular Front government was formed in June 1936 and was a coalition of the Communists, Socialists, and Radicals. The Socialist leader, Léon Blum (1872–1950), served as prime minister. The Popular Front succeeded in initiating a program for workers that some have called the French New Deal. It established the right of collective bargaining, a forty-hour work week, two-week paid vacations, and minimum wages. The Popular Front's policies failed to solve the problems of the depression, however. In 1938, French industrial production was still below the levels of 1929. Although the Popular Front survived in name until 1938, it was for all intents and purposes dead before then. By 1938, the French were experiencing a serious decline of confidence in their political system that left them unprepared to deal with their aggressive Nazi enemy to the east.

❖ The Scandinavian Example

The Scandinavian states were particularly successful in coping with the Great Depression. Socialist parties had grown steadily in the late nineteenth and early twentieth centuries and between the wars came to head the governments of Sweden, Denmark, Norway, and Finland. These Social Democratic governments encouraged the development of rural and industrial cooperative enterprises. Ninety percent of the Danish milk industry, for example, was organized on a cooperative basis by 1933. Privately owned and managed, Scandinavian cooperatives

seemed to avoid the pitfalls of either communist or purely capitalist economic systems.

Social Democratic governments also greatly expanded social services. Not only did Scandinavian governments increase old age pensions and unemployment insurance, but they also provided such novel forms of assistance as subsidized housing, free prenatal care, maternity allowances, and annual paid vacations for workers. To achieve their social welfare states, the Scandinavian governments required high taxes and large bureaucracies, but these did not prevent both private and cooperative enterprises from prospering. Indeed, between 1900 and 1939, Sweden experienced a greater rise in real wages than any other European country.

❖ The United States

After Germany, no Western nation was more affected by the Great Depression than the United States. Industrial production began to decline in the summer of 1929, but after the stock market crash in October, it plummeted. Between 1929 and the end of 1932, industrial production fell almost 50 percent. By 1933, there were 15 million unemployed. With no national unemployment payments or system of poor relief, state and local communities were overwhelmed by the needs of the dramatically increasing numbers of poor and homeless. When the administration of President Herbert Hoover seemed unable to halt the economic downswing, the Democrat Franklin Delano Roosevelt (1882–1945) won the 1932 presidential election by an electoral landslide.

During his first 100 days in office, the new president pushed for the rapid enactment of major new legislation to combat the worst effects of the depression. This policy of active government intervention in the economy came to be known as the New Deal. The first New Deal created a variety of new agencies designed to bring relief, recovery, and reform. To support the nation's banks, the Federal Deposit Insurance Corporation was established; it insured the safety of bank deposits up to $5,000. The Securities and Exchange Commission was created to provide closer supervision of the stock market. The Federal Emergency Relief Administration provided funds to help states and local communities meet the needs of the destitute and homeless. The Civilian Conservation Corps employed over two million people on reforestation projects. To deal with industrial problems, Roosevelt had Congress establish the National Recovery Administration (NRA), which was intended to provide an element of government planning in industrial output. The NRA was ineffective and accomplished little; in any case, the Supreme Court declared it unconstitutional in 1935.

By that time it was becoming apparent that the initial efforts of Roosevelt's administration had produced only a slow recovery at best. As his policies came under more and more criticism by people who advocated more radical change, Roosevelt inaugurated new efforts that collectively became known as the Second New Deal. These included a stepped-up program of public works, such as the Works Progress Administration (WPA) established in 1935. This government organization employed between two and three million people who worked at building bridges, roads, post offices, and airports. The Roosevelt administration was also responsible for social legislation that launched the American welfare state. In 1935, the Social Security Act created a system of old age pensions and unemployment insurance. Moreover, the National Labor Relations Act of 1935 encouraged the rapid growth of labor unions.

No doubt, the New Deal provided some social reform measures that perhaps averted the possibility of social revolution in the United States. It did not, however, solve the unemployment problems of the Great Depression. During the winter of 1937–1938, the economy experienced another downturn after the partial recovery between 1933 and 1937. In May 1937, American unemployment still stood at 7 million; by the following year, it had increased to 11 million. Only World War II and the subsequent growth of armaments industries brought American workers back to full employment.

◆ The Retreat from Democracy: The Authoritarian and Totalitarian States

The apparent triumph of liberal democracy in 1919 proved extremely short-lived. By 1939, only two major states, France and Great Britain, and a host of minor ones, the Low Countries, the Scandinavian states, Switzerland, and Czechoslovakia, remained democratic. Italy and Germany had succumbed to the political movement called fascism, and Soviet Russia under Stalin moved toward a repressive totalitarian state. A host of other European states, especially in eastern Europe, adopted authoritarian structures of various kinds. The crisis of European civilization, inaugurated in the total war of World War I, seemed only to be worsening with new assaults on individual liberties.

The dictatorial regimes between the wars assumed both old and new forms. Dictatorship was by no means a new phenomenon, but the modern totalitarian state was. The totalitarian regimes, whose best examples can be found in Stalinist Russia and Nazi Germany, extended the functions and power of the central state far beyond what they had been in the past. The immediate origins of totalitarianism can be found in the total warfare of World War I when governments, even in the democratic states, exercised controls over economic, political, and personal freedom in order to achieve victory.

The modern totalitarian state might have begun as an old-fashioned political dictatorship, but it soon moved beyond the ideal of passive obedience expected in a tra-

ditional dictatorship or authoritarian monarchy. The new "total states" expected the active loyalty and commitment of citizens to the regime's goals. They used modern mass propaganda techniques and high-speed modern communications to conquer the minds and hearts of their subjects. The total state aimed to control not only the economic, political, and social aspects of life, but the intellectual and cultural as well. But that control also had a purpose: the active involvement of the masses in the achievement of the regime's goals, whether they be war, a socialist state, or a 1,000 year Reich.

The modern totalitarian state was to be led by a single leader and a single party. It ruthlessly rejected the liberal ideal of limited government power and constitutional guarantees of individual freedoms. Indeed, individual freedom was to be subordinated to the collective will of the masses, organized and determined for them by a leader or leaders. Modern technology also gave total states unprecedented police controls to enforce their wishes on their subjects.

Totalitarianism is an abstract term, and no state followed all its theoretical implications. The fascist states—Italy and Nazi Germany—as well as Stalin's Communist Russia have all been labeled totalitarian, although their regimes exhibited significant differences and met with varying degrees of success. Totalitarianism transcended traditional political labels. Fascism in Italy and Nazism in Germany grew out of extreme rightist preoccupations with nationalism and, in the case of Germany, with racism. Communism in Soviet Russia emerged out of Marxian socialism, a radical leftist program. Thus, totalitarianism could and did exist in what were perceived as extreme right-wing and left-wing regimes. This fact helped bring about a new concept of the political spectrum in which the extremes were no longer seen as opposites on a linear scale, but came to be viewed as being similar to each other in at least some respects.

❋ Fascist Italy

In the early 1920s, in the wake of economic turmoil, political disorder, and the general insecurity and fear stemming from World War I, Benito Mussolini burst upon the Italian scene with a movement that he called the *Fascio di Combattimento* (League of Combat). It was the beginning of the first fascist movement in Europe.

❧ THE BIRTH OF FASCISM
As a new European state after 1870, Italy faced a number of serious problems that were only magnified when it became a belligerent in World War I. The war's cost in lives and money was enormous. An estimated 700,000 Italian soldiers died, and the treasury reckoned the cost of the war at 148 billion lire, twice the sum of all government expenditures between 1861 and 1913. Italy did gain some territory, namely, Trieste, and a new northern border that included the formerly Austrian South Tyrol area. Italy's demands for Fiume and Dalmatia on the Adriatic coast

were rejected, however, which gave rise to the myth that Italy had been cheated of its just rewards by the other victors. The war created untold domestic confusion. Inflation undermined middle-class security. Demobilization of the troops created high unemployment and huge groups of dissatisfied veterans. The government, which continued to be characterized by parliamentary paralysis due to the politicians' reliance on tactical and often unprincipled maneuvering to maintain their grip on power, was unable to deal effectively with these problems.

Benito Mussolini (1883–1945) was an unruly and rebellious child who ultimately received a diploma as an elementary school teacher. After an unsuccessful stint as a teacher, Mussolini became a socialist and gradually became well known in Italian socialist circles. In 1912, he obtained the important position of editor of *Avanti* (*Forward*), the official socialist daily newspaper. After editorially switching his position from ardent neutrality, the socialist position, to intervention in World War I, he was expelled from the socialist party.

In 1919, Mussolini laid the foundations for a new political movement that came to be called fascism after the name of his group, the *Fascio di Combattimento*. Mussolini's small group received little attention and were themselves unclear about their beliefs. In elections held in November 1919, the Fascists won no delegates, and Mussolini reflected bitterly that fascism had "come to a dead end." But political stalemate in Italy's parliamentary system and strong nationalist sentiment saved Mussolini and the Fascists.

The new parliament elected in November quickly proved to be incapable of governing Italy. Three major parties, the socialists, liberals, and popolari (or Christian Democrats, a new Catholic party formed in January 1919), and numerous small ones were unable to form an effective governmental coalition. The socialists, who had now become the largest party, spoke theoretically of the need for revolution, which alarmed conservatives who quickly associated them with Bolsheviks or Communists. The success of the Communists in Russia had frightened the propertied classes, who were concerned about what a Communist takeover would mean. Thousands of industrial and agricultural strikes in 1919 and 1920 created a climate of class warfare and continual violence. Mussolini realized the advantages of capitalizing on the fear aroused by these conditions and shifted quickly from leftist to rightist politics. The rewards were immediate as Mussolini's Fascist movement began to gain support from middle-class industrialists fearful of working-class agitation and large landowners who objected to the agricultural strikes. Mussolini also perceived that Italians were angry over Italy's failure to receive more fruits of victory in the form of territorial acquisitions after World War I. He realized then that anticommunism, antistrike activity, and nationalist rhetoric combined with the use of brute force might help him obtain what he had been unable to achieve in free elections.

In 1920 and 1921, bands of armed Fascists called *squadristi* were formed and turned loose in attacks on socialist offices and newspapers. Strikes by trade unionists and socialist workers and peasant leagues were broken up by force. At the same time, Mussolini entered into a political alliance with the liberals under then Prime Minister Giovanni Giolitti. No doubt, Giolitti and the liberals believed that the Fascists could be used to crush socialism temporarily and then be dropped. In this game of mutual deceit, Mussolini soon proved to be the more skillful player. By allying with the government coalition, he gained respectability and a free hand for his *squadristi* violence. Mussolini's efforts were rewarded when the Fascists won thirty-five parliamentary seats, or 7 percent of the total, in the election of May 1921. Mussolini's Fascist movement had gained a new lease on life.

Crucial to Mussolini's plans was the use of violence. By 1921, the black-shirted Fascist squads numbered 200,000 and had become a regular feature of Italian life. World War I veterans and students were especially attracted to the *squadristi* and relished the opportunity to use unrestrained violence. Administering large doses of castor oil to unwilling victims became one of their favorite tactics.

Mussolini and the Fascists believed that these terrorist tactics would eventually achieve political victory. They deliberately created conditions of disorder knowing that fascism would flourish in such an environment. Fascists construed themselves as the party of order and drew the bulk of their support from the middle and upper classes; white-collar workers, professionals and civil servants, landowners, merchants and artisans, and students made up almost 60 percent of the membership of the Fascist Party. The middle-class fear of socialism, communist revolution, and disorder made the Fascists attractive.

With the further deterioration of the Italian political situation, Mussolini and the Fascists were emboldened to plan a march on Rome in order to seize power. In a speech in Naples to Fascist blackshirts on October 24, 1922, Mussolini exclaimed: "Either we are allowed to govern, or we will seize power by marching on Rome" to "take by the throat the miserable political class that governs us."[2] Bold words, but in truth the planned march on Rome was really a calculated bluff to frighten the government into giving them power. The bluff worked, and the government capitulated even before the march occurred. On October 29, 1922, King Victor Emmanuel III (1900–1946) made Mussolini prime minister of Italy. Twenty-four hours later, the Fascist blackshirts were allowed to march into Rome in order to create the "myth" that they had gained power by an armed insurrection after a civil war.

MUSSOLINI AND THE ITALIAN FASCIST STATE

Since the Fascists constituted but a small minority in parliament, the new prime minister was forced to move slowly. Mussolini also had to balance two conflicting interests. The rural Fascists were eager to assume complete power, but the traditional institutions, such as the industrialists, the landowners, the Catholic church, and the military, wanted a period of domestic tranquillity. In the summer of 1923, Mussolini began to prepare for a national election

MUSSOLINI—THE IRON DUCE. One of Mussolini's favorite images of himself was that of the iron Duce—the strong leader who is always right. Consequently, he was often seen in military-style uniforms and military poses. This photograph shows Mussolini in one of his numerous uniforms with his Black Shirt bodyguards giving the Fascist salute.

that would consolidate the power of his Fascist government and give him a more secure base from which to govern. In July 1923, parliament enacted the Acerbo Law, which stipulated that any party winning at least 25 percent of the votes in the next national election would automatically be allotted two-thirds of the seats in parliament. The national elections that were subsequently held on April 6, 1924, resulted in an enormous victory for the Fascists. They won 65 percent of the votes and garnered 374 seats out of a total of 535 in parliament. Although the elections were conducted in an atmosphere of Fascist fraud, force, and intimidation, the size of the victory indicated the growing popularity of Mussolini and his Fascists.

With this victory, Mussolini moved faster to consolidate his power. A campaign of intimidation of opposition deputies reached its high point with the assassination of the socialist deputy Giacomo Matteotti in June of 1924. Mussolini was severely challenged for his assumed complicity in the murder of Matteotti. The public outcry even caused numerous Italian political leaders to predict in December 1924 that Mussolini would have to resign. At the beginning of 1925, yielding to extremists within his own Fascist Party who demanded decisive action and a "second wave" of Fascist change, Mussolini counterattacked.

To save himself, Mussolini now pushed to establish a full dictatorship. This may have been his ultimate intention anyway, but the Matteotti crisis forced him to make his move at this time. In a speech to parliament on January 3, Mussolini accepted responsibility for all Fascist violence and vowed to establish a new order: "Italy wants peace, tranquility, calm in which to work; we will give it to her, by means of love if possible, by force if necessary."

By 1926, Mussolini had established the institutional framework for his Fascist dictatorship. Press laws gave the government the right to suspend any publications that fostered disrespect for the Catholic church, monarchy, or the state. The prime minister was made "Head of Government" with the power to legislate by decree. A police law empowered the police to arrest and confine anybody for both nonpolitical and political crimes without due process of law. The government was given the power to dissolve political and cultural associations. In 1926, all anti-Fascist parties were outlawed. A secret police, known as the OVRA, was also established. By the end of 1926, Mussolini ruled Italy as *Il Duce*, the leader.

Mussolini conceived of the Fascist state as totalitarian: "Fascism is totalitarian, and the Fascist State, the synthesis and unity of all values, interprets, develops and

The Voice of Italian Fascism

In 1932, an article on fascism appeared in the Italian Encyclopedia. Supposedly authored by Mussolini, it was largely written by the philosopher Giovanni Gentile. Mussolini had always argued that fascism was based only on the need for action, not on doctrines, but after its success he felt the need to summarize the basic political and social ideas of fascism. These excerpts are taken from Mussolini's article.

✤ Benito Mussolini, *The Political and Social Doctrine of Fascism*

Above all, Fascism . . . believes neither in the possibility nor the utility of perpetual peace. It thus repudiates the doctrine of Pacifism—born of a renunciation of struggle and an act of cowardice in the face of sacrifice. War alone brings up to its highest tension all human energy and puts the stamp of nobility upon the peoples who have the courage to meet it. All other trials are substitutes, which never really put men into the position where they have to make the great decision—the alternative of life or death. Thus a doctrine which is founded upon this harmful postulate of peace is hostile to Fascism. . . . Thus the Fascist accepts life and loves it, knowing nothing of and despising suicide: he rather conceives of life as duty and struggle and conquest. . . .

Fascism is the complete opposite of Marxian socialism, the materialist conception of history; according to which the history of human civilization can be explained simply through the conflict of interests among the various social groups and by the change and development in the means and instruments of production. That the changes in the economic field have their importance no one can deny; but that these factors are sufficient to explain the history of humanity excluding all others is an absurd delusion. Fascism, now and always, believes in holiness and in heroism; that is to say, in actions influenced by no economic motive, direct or indirect. . . .

After Socialism, Fascism combats the whole complex system of democratic ideology, and repudiates it, whether in its theoretical premises or in its practical application. Fascism denies that the majority, by the simple fact that it is a majority, can direct human society; it denies that numbers alone can govern by means of a periodical consultation, and it affirms the immutable, beneficial, and fruitful inequality of mankind, which can never be permanently leveled through the mere operation of a mechanical process such as universal suffrage.

The foundation of Fascism is the conception of the State, its character, its duty and its aim. Fascism conceives of the State as an absolute, in comparison with which all individuals or groups are relative, only to be conceived of in their relation to the State. . . . The Fascist state organizes the nation, but leaves a sufficient margin of liberty to the individual; the latter is deprived of all useless and possibly harmful freedom, but retains what is essential; the deciding power in the question cannot be the individual, but the State alone. . . .

For Fascism, the growth of empire, that is to say the expansion of the nation, is an essential manifestation of vitality, and its opposite a sign of decadence. Peoples which are rising, or rising again after a period of decadence, are always imperialist; any renunciation is a sign of decay and of death. Fascism is the doctrine best adapted to represent the tendencies and the aspirations of a people, like the people of Italy, who are rising again after many centuries of abasement and foreign servitude. But Empire demands discipline, the coordination of all forces and a deeply felt sense of duty and sacrifice.

---

gives strength to the whole life of the people"[3] (see the box above). Mussolini did try to create a totalitarian apparatus for police surveillance and for controlling mass communications, but this machinery was not all that effective. Police activities in Italy were never as repressive, efficient, or savage as those of Nazi Germany. Likewise, the Italian Fascists' attempt to exercise control over all forms of mass media, including newspapers, radio, and cinema, in order to use propaganda as an instrument to integrate the masses into the state failed to achieve its major goals. Most commonly, Fascist propaganda was disseminated through simple slogans, such as "Mussolini is always right," plastered on walls all over Italy.

Mussolini and the Fascists also attempted to mold Italians into a single-minded community by pursuing a Fascist educational policy and developing Fascist organizations. In 1939, Giuseppe Bottai, minister of education, proposed a new School Charter whose basic aim was "the will to substitute, both in principle and practice, for the bourgeois schools a people's school, which will really be for everyone and which will really meet the needs of everyone, that is the needs of the State."[4] Bottai hoped to make the educational system an instrument to create the "new Fascist man," but his reforms were never implemented, primarily because the middle class resisted any alterations in the traditional paths of upward mobility.

Since the secondary schools maintained considerable freedom from Fascist control, the regime relied more and more on the activities of Fascist youth organizations, known as the Young Fascists, to indoctrinate the young people of the nation in Fascist ideals. By 1939, about 6.8 million children, teenagers, and young adults of both sexes, or 66 percent of the population between eight and eighteen, were enrolled in some kind of Fascist youth group. Activities for these groups included unpopular Saturday afternoon marching drills and calisthenics, seaside and mountain summer camps, and youth contests. An underlying motif for all of these activities was the Fascist insistence on militarization. Beginning in the 1930s, all male groups were given some kind of premilitary exercises to develop discipline and provide training for war. Results were mixed. Italian teenagers, who liked neither military training nor routine discipline of any kind, simply refused to attend Fascist youth meetings on a regular basis.

The Fascist organizations hoped to create a new Italian, who would be hard-working, physically fit, disciplined, intellectually sharp, and martially inclined; this ideal was symbolized by the phrase, "book and musket—the perfect Fascist." In practice, the Fascists largely reinforced traditional social attitudes in Italy, as is evident in their policies regarding women. The Fascists portrayed the family as the pillar of the state and women as the basic foundation of the family. "Woman into the home" became the Fascist slogan. Women were to be homemakers and baby producers, "their natural and fundamental mission in life," according to Mussolini, who viewed population growth as an indicator of national strength. To Mussolini, female emancipation was "unfascist." Employment outside the home was an impediment distracting women from conception. "It forms an independence and consequent physical and moral habits contrary to child bearing."[5] A practical consideration also underlay the Fascist attitude toward women. Working women would compete with males for jobs in the depression economy of the 1930s. Eliminating women from the market reduced male unemployment figures.

In the 1930s, the Fascists translated their attitude toward women into law by a series of enactments that aimed at encouraging larger families by offering supplementary pay, loans, prizes, and subsidies for families with many offspring. Gold medals were given to mothers of many children. A national holiday of "the Mother and the Child" was held on December 24 with prizes awarded for fertility. Also in the 1930s, decrees were passed that set quotas on the employment of women, but they were not overly successful in accomplishing their goal.

Despite the instruments of repression, the use of propaganda, and the creation of numerous Fascist organizations, Mussolini failed to achieve the degree of totalitarian control accomplished in Hitler's Germany or Stalin's Soviet Union. Mussolini and the Fascist Party never really destroyed the old power structure. Some institutions, including the armed forces and monarchy, were never absorbed into the Fascist state and mostly managed to maintain their independence. Mussolini had boasted that he would help workers and peasants, but instead he generally allied himself with the interests of the industrialists and large landowners at the expense of the lower classes.

CHRONOLOGY

Fascist Italy

Creation of *Fascio di Combattimento*	1919
Squadristi violence	1920–1921
Fascists win thirty-five seats in Parliament	1921
Mussolini is made prime minister	1922 (October 29)
Acerbo Law	1923
Electoral victory for Fascists	1924
Establishment of Fascist dictatorship	1925–1926
Lateran Accords with Catholic church	1929
Fascist School Charter	1939

Even more indicative of Mussolini's compromise with the traditional institutions of Italy was his attempt to gain the support of the Catholic church. In the Lateran Accords of February 1929, Mussolini's regime recognized the sovereign independence of a small enclave of 109 acres within Rome, known as Vatican City, which had remained in the church's possession since the unification of Italy in 1870; in return, the papacy recognized the Italian state. The Lateran Accords also guaranteed the church a large grant of money and recognized Catholicism as the "sole religion of the state." In return, the Catholic church urged Italians to support the Fascist regime.

In all areas of Italian life under Mussolini and the Fascists, there was a noticeable dichotomy between Fascist ideals and practice. The Italian Fascists promised much but delivered considerably less, and they were soon overshadowed by a much more powerful fascist movement to the north. Adolf Hitler was a great admirer of Benito Mussolini, but the German pupil soon proved to be far more adept in the use of power than his Italian teacher.

❋ *Hitler and Nazi Germany*

In 1923, a small, south German rightist party, known as the Nazis, led by an obscure Austrian rabble-rouser named Adolf Hitler, created a stir when it tried to seize power in southern Germany in conscious imitation of Mussolini's march on Rome in 1922. Although the attempt failed, Adolf Hitler and the Nazis achieved sudden national prominence. Within ten years, Hitler and the Nazis had taken over complete power.

WEIMAR GERMANY AND THE RISE OF THE NAZIS After the Imperial Germany of William II had come to an end with Germany's defeat in World War I, a German democratic state known as the Weimar Republic had been established. From its beginnings, the Weimar Republic was plagued by a series of problems. The Republic had no truly outstanding political leaders. Even its more able leaders, such as Friedrich Ebert, who served as president, and Gustav Stresemann, the foreign minister and chancellor, died in the 1920s. When Ebert died in 1925, Paul von Hindenburg, the World War I military hero, was elected president. Hindenburg was a traditional military man, monarchist in sentiment, who at heart was not in favor of the Republic. The young Republic also suffered politically from attempted uprisings and attacks from both the left and the right.

Another of the Republic's problems was its inability to change the basic structure of Germany. The government never really controlled the army, which operated as a state within a state. This independence was true of other institutions as well. Hostile judges, teachers, and bureaucrats remained in office and used their positions to undermine democracy from within. At the same time, important groups of landed aristocrats and leaders of powerful business cartels refused to accept the overthrow of the imperial regime and remained hostile to the Weimar Republic.

The Weimar Republic also faced serious economic difficulties. Germany experienced runaway inflation in 1922 and 1923 with serious social effects. Widows, orphans, the retired elderly, army officers, teachers, civil servants, and others who lived on fixed incomes all watched their monthly stipends become worthless or their lifetime savings disappear. Their economic losses increasingly pushed the middle class to the rightist parties that were hostile to the Republic. To make matters worse, after a period of prosperity from 1924 to 1929, Germany faced the Great Depression. Unemployment increased to 3 million in March 1930 and 4.38 million by December of the same year. The depression paved the way for social discontent, fear, and extremist parties. The political, economic, and social problems of the Weimar Republic provided an environment in which Adolf Hitler and the Nazis were able to rise to power.

Born on April 20, 1889, Adolf Hitler was the son of an Austrian customs official. He was a total failure in secondary school and eventually made his way to Vienna to become an artist. Rejected by the Vienna Academy of Fine Arts and supported by an inheritance and orphan's pension, Hitler stayed on in Vienna to live the bohemian lifestyle of an artist. In his autobiography, *Mein Kampf*, Hitler characterized his years in Vienna from 1908 to 1913 as an important formative period in his life: "In this period there took shape within me a world picture and a philosophy which became the granite foundation of all my acts. In addition to what I then created, I have had to learn little, and I have had to alter nothing."[6]

Hitler experienced four major influences in Vienna. Georg von Schönerer, the leader of the Austrian Pan-German movement, was an extreme German nationalist who urged the union of all Germans in one national state. Karl Lueger was mayor of Vienna and leader of the anti-Semitic Christian Social Party. Hitler called him "the greatest German mayor of all time" and especially admired his demagogic methods and leadership of a mass party that was formed with the aid of emotional slogans. Much of Hitler's early anti-Semitism was imbibed from an ex-Catholic monk named Adolf Lanz who called himself Lanz von Liebenfels. Hitler was an avid reader of *Ostara*, a periodical published by Liebenfels in which he propagated his racial beliefs that the German Aryans were exalted beings destined to rule the earth. Liebenfels characterized the Jews and other allegedly inferior races as "animal-men" who must someday be eliminated by sterilization, deportation, forced labor, and even "direct liquidation." Finally, Hitler was also strongly influenced by Richard Wagner's operas, which he attended frequently in Vienna. Hitler absorbed Wagner's ideal of the true artist as a social outcast from the bourgeois world who is subject to his own rhythms. Wagner's music also spoke of a boundless will to power and a need to dominate.

In Vienna, then, Hitler established the basic ideas of an ideology from which he never deviated for the rest of his life. At the core of Hitler's ideas was racism, especially anti-Semitism (see the box on p. 795). His hatred of the Jews lasted to the very end of his life. Hitler had also become an extreme German nationalist who had learned from the mass politics of Vienna how political parties could effectively use propaganda and terror. Finally, in his Viennese years, Hitler also came to a firm belief in the need for struggle, which he saw as the "granite foundation of the world." Hitler emphasized a crude Social Darwinism (see Chapter 24); the world was a brutal place filled with constant struggle in which only the fit survived.

In 1913, Hitler moved to Munich, still without purpose and with no real future in sight. World War I saved him: "Overpowered by stormy enthusiasm, I fell down on my knees and thanked Heaven from an overflowing heart for granting me the good fortune of being permitted to live at this time."[7] As a dispatch runner on the Western Front, Hitler distinguished himself by his brave acts. At the end of the war, finding again that his life had no purpose or meaning, he returned to Munich and decided to enter politics and found, at last, his true profession.

As a Munich politician from 1919 to 1923, Hitler accomplished a great deal. He joined the obscure German Workers' Party, one of a number of right-wing extreme nationalist parties in Munich. By the summer of 1921, Hitler had assumed total control over the party, which he renamed the National Socialist German Workers' Party (NSDAP), or Nazi for short. His idea was that the party's name would distinguish the Nazis from the socialist parties while gaining support from both working-class and nationalist circles. Hitler worked assiduously to develop the party into a mass political movement with flags, party badges, uniforms, its own newspaper, and its own police force or party militia known as the SA, the *Sturmabteilung*,

Adolf Hitler's Hatred of the Jews

A believer in Aryan racial supremacy, Adolf Hitler viewed the Jews as the archenemies of the Aryans. He believed that the first task of a true Aryan state would be the elimination of the Jewish threat. This is why Hitler's political career both began and ended with a warning against the Jews. In this excerpt from his autobiography, Mein Kampf, *Hitler describes how he came to be an anti-Semite when he lived in Vienna in his early twenties.*

❈ Adolf Hitler, *Mein Kampf*

My views with regard to anti-Semitism thus succumbed to the passage of time, and this was my greatest transformation of all. . . .

Once, as I was strolling through the Inner City [of Vienna], I suddenly encountered an apparition in a black caftan and black hair locks. Is this a Jew? was my first thought.

For, to be sure, they had not looked like that in Linz. I observed the man furtively and cautiously, but the longer I stared at this foreign face, scrutinizing feature for feature, the more my first question assumed a new form:

Is this a German?

As always in such cases, I now began to try to relieve my doubts by books. For a few pennies I bought the first anti-Semitic pamphlets of my life. . . .

Yet I could no longer very well doubt that the objects of my study were not Germans of a special religion, but a people in themselves; for since I had begun to concern myself with this question and to take cognizance of the Jews, Vienna appeared to me in a different light than before. Wherever I went, I began to see Jews, and the more I saw, the more sharply they became distinguished in my eyes from the rest of humanity. . . .

In a short time I was made more thoughtful than ever by my slowly rising insight into the type of activity carried on by the Jews in certain fields.

Was there any form of filth or profligacy, particularly in cultural life, without at least one Jew involved in it? . . .

Sometimes I stood there thunderstruck.

I didn't know what to be more amazed at: the agility of their tongues or their virtuosity at lying.

Gradually I began to hate them.

---

or Storm Troops. The SA was used to defend the party in meeting halls and to break up the meetings of other parties. It added an element of force and terror to the growing Nazi movement. Hitler's own oratorical skills were largely responsible for attracting an increasing number of followers. By 1923, the party had grown from its early hundreds into a membership of 55,000 with 15,000 SA members.

In its early years, the Nazi Party had been only one of many radical right-wing political groups in southern Germany. By 1923, it had become the strongest. When it appeared that the Weimar Republic was on the verge of collapse in the fall of 1923, the Nazis and other right-wing leaders in the south German state of Bavaria decided to march on Berlin to overthrow the Weimar government. When his fellow conspirators reneged, Hitler and the Nazis decided to act on their own by staging an armed uprising in Munich on November 8. The so-called Beer Hall Putsch was quickly crushed. Hitler was arrested, put on trial for treason, and sentenced to prison for five years, a lenient sentence indeed from sympathetic right-wing judges.

❧ THE NAZI SEIZURE OF POWER

The Beer Hall Putsch proved to be a major turning point in Hitler's career. Rather than discouraging him, his trial and imprisonment reinforced his faith in himself and in his mission. He now saw clearly the need for a change in tactics. The Nazis could not overthrow the Weimar Republic by force, but would have to use constitutional means

to gain power. This implied the formation of a mass political party that would actively compete for votes with the other political parties.

Hitler occupied himself in prison with the writing of *Mein Kampf* (*My Struggle*), an autobiographical account of his movement and its underlying ideology. Extreme German nationalism, virulent anti-Semitism, and vicious anticommunism are linked together by a Social Darwinian theory of struggle that stresses the right of superior nations to *Lebensraum* (living space) through expansion and the right of superior individuals to secure authoritarian leadership over the masses. The only originality in *Mein Kampf*, as historians have pointed out, is in Hitler's analysis of mass propaganda, mass psychology, and the mass organization of peoples. What is perhaps most remarkable about *Mein Kampf* is its elaboration of a series of ideas that directed Hitler's actions once he took power. That others refused to take Hitler and his ideas seriously was one of his greatest advantages.

When Hitler was released, the Nazi Party was in shambles, and he set about to reestablish his sole control over the party and organize it for the lawful takeover of power. Hitler's position on leadership in the party was quite clear. There was to be no discussion of ideas in the party, and the party was to follow the *Führerprinzip*, the leadership principle, which entailed nothing less than a single-minded party under one leader. As Hitler expressed it: "A good National Socialist is one who would let himself be killed for his Führer at any time."[8]

The late 1920s were a period of building and waiting. These were years of relative prosperity for Germany, and, as Hitler perceived, they were not conducive to the growth of extremist parties. He declared, however, that the prosperity would not last and that his time would come. In the meantime, Hitler worked to establish a highly structured party that could compete in elections and attract new recruits when another time of troubles arose. He reorganized the Nazi Party on a regional basis and expanded it to all parts of Germany. By 1929, the Nazi Party had a national party organization. It also grew from 27,000 members in 1925 to 178,000 by the end of 1929. Especially noticeable was the youthfulness of the regional, district, and branch leaders of the Nazi organization. Many were between the ages of twenty-five and thirty and were fiercely committed to Hitler because he gave them the kind of active politics they sought. Rather than democratic debate, they wanted brawls in beer halls, enthusiastic speeches, and comradeship in the building of a new Germany. One new, young Nazi member expressed his excitement about the party:

> For me this was the start of a completely new life. There was only one thing in the world for me and that was service in the movement. All my thoughts were centered on the movement. I could talk only politics. I was no longer aware of anything else. At the time I was a promising athlete; I was very keen on sport, and it was going to be my career. But I had to give this up too. My only interest was agitation and propaganda.[9]

Such youthful enthusiasm gave the Nazi movement an aura of a "young man's movement" and a sense of dynamism that the other parties could not match. In 1931, almost 40 percent of Nazi Party members were under thirty.

By 1929, the Nazi Party had also made a significant shift in strategy. Between 1925 and 1927, Hitler and the Nazis had pursued an urban strategy geared toward winning workers from the Socialists and Communists. But failure in the 1928 elections, when the Nazis gained only 2.6 percent of the vote and twelve seats in the Reichstag or German parliament, convinced Hitler of the need for a change. By 1929, the party began to pursue middle-class and lower-middle-class votes in small towns and rural areas, especially in northern, central, and eastern Germany. By the end of 1929, the Nazis had successfully made their shift to the new strategy. The end of 1929 was the beginning of the depression and the beginning of Hitler's real success.

Germany's economic difficulties made possible the Nazi rise to power. Unemployment rose dramatically, from 4.35 million in 1931 to 6 million by the winter of 1932. The economic and psychological impact of the Great Depression made the extremist parties more attractive. Already in the Reichstag elections of September 1930, the Nazis polled 18 percent of the vote and gained 107 seats in the Reichstag, making the Nazi Party one of the largest parties.

By 1930, Chancellor Heinrich Brüning (1885–1970) had found it impossible to form a working parliamentary majority in the Reichstag and relied on the use of emergency decrees by President Hindenburg to rule. In a real sense, then, parliamentary democracy was already dying in 1930, three years before Hitler destroyed it.

Hitler's quest for power from late 1930 to early 1933 depended on the political maneuvering around President Hindenburg. Nevertheless, the elections from 1930 through 1932 were indirectly responsible for the Nazi rise to power since they showed the importance of the Nazi Party. The party itself grew dramatically during this period, from 289,000 members in September 1930 to 800,000 by 1932. The SA also rose to 500,000 members.

The Nazis proved very effective in developing modern electioneering techniques. They crossed Germany in whirlwind campaigns by car, train, and airplane. His "Hitler Over Germany" campaign by airplane saw Hitler speaking in fifty cities in fifteen days. The Nazis were successful in presenting two fundamentally different approaches to the German voters. In their election campaigns, party members pitched their themes to the needs and fears of different social groups. In working-class districts, for example, the Nazis attacked international high finance, but in middle-class neighborhoods, they exploited fears of a Communist revolution and its threat to private property. At the same time that the Nazis made blatant appeals to class interests, they were denouncing conflicts of interest and maintaining that they stood above classes and parties. Hitler, in particular, claimed to stand above all differences and promised to create a new Germany free of class differences and party infighting. His appeal to national pride, national honor, and traditional militarism struck chords of emotion in his listeners.

Elections, however, proved to have their limits. In the elections of July 1932, the Nazis won 230 seats, making them the largest party in the Reichstag. But four months later, in November, they declined to 196 seats. It became apparent to many Nazis that they would not gain power simply by the ballot box. Hitler saw clearly, however, that the Reichstag after 1930 was not all that important, since the government ruled by decree with the support of President Hindenburg. Increasingly, the right-wing elites of Germany, the industrial magnates, landed aristocrats, military establishment, and higher bureaucrats, came to see Hitler as the man who had the mass support to establish a right-wing, authoritarian regime that would save Germany and their privileged positions from a Communist takeover. These people almost certainly thought that they could control Hitler and, like many others, may well have underestimated his abilities. Under pressure from these elites, President Hindenburg agreed to allow Hitler to become chancellor (on January 30, 1933) and to form a new government, but with supposed safeguards. There would be only three Nazis in

HITLER AND THE BLOOD FLAG RITUAL. In developing his mass political movement, Adolf Hitler used ritualistic ceremonies as a means of binding party members to his own person. Hitler is shown here touching the "blood flag," which had supposedly been stained with the blood of Nazis killed during the Beer Hall Putsch, to an SS banner while the SS standard-bearer makes a "blood oath" of allegiance: "I vow to remain true to my Führer, Adolf Hitler. I bind myself to carry out all orders conscientiously and without reluctance. Standards and flags shall be sacred to me."

the cabinet, and Franz von Papen (1878–1969), who had served as chancellor and done so much to win over Hindenburg to the arrangements, would serve as vice-chancellor. When some reproached von Papen for giving power to Hitler, he responded: "What do you want? I have Hindenburg's trust. Within two months, we will have pushed Hitler so far into a corner that he will squeak."[10]

Within those two months, Hitler basically laid the foundations for the Nazis' complete control over Germany. One of Hitler's important cohorts, Hermann Göring (1893–1946), had been made minister of the interior and hence head of the police of the Prussian state, the largest of the federal states in Germany. He used his power to purge the police of non-Nazis and to establish an auxiliary police force composed of SA members. This action legitimized Nazi terror. On the day after a fire broke out in the Reichstag building (February 27), supposedly set by the Communists, but possibly by the Nazis themselves, Hitler was also able to convince President Hindenburg to issue a decree that gave the government emergency powers. It suspended all basic rights of citizens for the full duration of the emergency, thus enabling the Nazis to

arrest and imprison anyone without redress. Although Hitler promised to return to the "normal order of things" when the Communist danger was past, in reality this decree provided the legal basis for the creation of a police state.

The crowning step of Hitler's "legal seizure" of power came after the Nazis had gained 288 Reichstag seats in the elections of March 5, 1933. Since they still did not possess an absolute majority, on March 23 the Nazis sought the passage of an Enabling Act, which would empower the government to dispense with constitutional forms for four years while it issued laws that would deal with the country's problems. Since the act was to be an amendment to the Weimar constitution, the Nazis needed and obtained a two-thirds vote to pass it. Only the Social Democrats had the courage to oppose Hitler. The Enabling Act provided the legal basis for Hitler's subsequent acts. He no longer needed either the Reichstag or President Hindenburg. In effect, Hitler became a dictator appointed by the parliamentary body itself.

With their new source of power, the Nazis acted quickly to enforce *Gleichschaltung*, or the coordination of all institutions under Nazi control. The civil service was

Propaganda and Mass Meetings in Nazi Germany

Propaganda and mass rallies were two of the chief instruments that Hitler used to prepare the German people for the tasks he set before them. In the first selection, taken from Mein Kampf, Hitler explains the psychological importance of mass meetings in creating support for a political movement. In the second excerpt, taken from his speech to a crowd at Nuremberg, he describes the kind of mystical bond he hoped to create through his mass rallies.

❋ Adolf Hitler, *Mein Kampf*

The mass meeting is also necessary for the reason that in it the individual, who at first, while becoming a supporter of a young movement, feels lonely and easily succumbs to the fear of being alone, for the first time gets the picture of a larger community, which in most people has a strengthening, encouraging effect. . . . When from his little workshop or big factory, in which he feels very small, he steps for the first time into a mass meeting and has thousands and thousands of people of the same opinions around him, when, as a seeker, he is swept away by three or four thousand others into the mighty effect of suggestive intoxication and enthusiasm, when the visible success and agreement of thousands confirm to him the rightness of the new doctrine and for the first time arouse doubt in the truth of his previous conviction—then he himself has succumbed to the magic influence of what we designate as "mass suggestion." The will, the longing, and also the power of thousands are accumulated in every individual. The man who enters such a meeting doubting and wavering leaves it inwardly reinforced: he has become a link in the community.

❋ Adolf Hitler, *Speech at the Nuremberg Party Rally, 1936*

Do we not feel once again in this hour the miracle that brought us together? Once you heard the voice of a man, and it struck deep into your hearts; it awakened you, and you followed this voice. Year after year you went after it, though him who had spoken you never even saw. You heard only a voice, and you followed it. When we meet each other here, the wonder of our coming together fills us all. Not everyone of you sees me, and I do not see everyone of you. But I feel you, and you feel me. It is the belief in our people that has made us small men great, that has made us poor men rich, that has made brave and courageous men out of us wavering, spiritless, timid folk; this belief made us see our road when we were astray; it joined us together into one whole! . . . You come, that . . . you may, once in a while, gain the feeling that now we are together; we are with him and he with us, and we are now Germany!

purged of Jews and democratic elements, concentration camps were established for opponents of the new regime, the autonomy of the federal states was eliminated, trade unions were dissolved and swallowed up by a gigantic Labor Front, and all political parties except the Nazis were abolished. By the end of the summer of 1933, within seven months of being appointed chancellor, Hitler and the Nazis had established the foundations for a totalitarian state.

Why had this seizure of power been so quick and easy? The Nazis were not only ruthless in their use of force, but had also been ready to seize power. The depression had weakened what little faith the Germans had in their democratic state. But negative factors alone cannot explain the Nazi success. To many Germans, the Nazis offered a national awakening. "Germany Awake," one of the many Nazi slogans, had a powerful appeal to a people psychologically crushed by their defeat in World War I. The Nazis presented a strong image of a dynamic new Germany that was above parties and above classes.

By the end of 1933, there were only two sources of potential danger to Hitler's authority: the armed forces and the SA within his own party. The SA, under the leadership of Ernst Röhm, openly criticized Hitler and spoke of the need for a "second revolution" and the replacement of the regular army by the SA. Neither the army nor Hitler favored such a possibility. Hitler solved both problems simultaneously on June 30, 1934, by having Ernst Röhm and a number of other SA leaders killed in return for the army's support in allowing Hitler to succeed Hindenburg when the president died. When Hindenburg died on August 2, 1934, the office of Reich president was abolished, and Hitler became sole ruler of Germany. Public officials and soldiers were all required to take a personal oath of loyalty to Hitler as the "Führer of the German Reich and people." On August 19, 1934, Hitler held a plebiscite in which 85 percent of the German people indicated their approval of the new order. The Third Reich had begun.

❧ THE NAZI STATE (1933–1939)

Having smashed the parliamentary state, Hitler now felt the real task was at hand: to develop the "total state." Hitler's aims had not been simply power for power's sake or a tyranny based on personal power. He had larger ideological goals. The development of an Aryan racial state that would dominate Europe and possibly the world for generations to come required a massive movement in which the German people would be actively involved, not passively cowed by force. Hitler stated:

THE NAZI MASS SPECTACLE. Hitler and the Nazis made clever use of mass spectacles to rally the German people behind the Nazi regime. These mass demonstrations evoked intense enthusiasm, as is evident in this photograph of Hitler arriving at the Bückeberg near Hamelin for the Harvest Festival in 1937. Almost one million people were present for the celebration.

We must develop organizations in which an individual's entire life can take place. Then every activity and every need of every individual will be regulated by the collectivity represented by the party. There is no longer any arbitrary will, there are no longer any free realms in which the individual belongs to himself. . . . The time of personal happiness is over.[11]

The Nazis pursued the creation of this totalitarian state in a variety of ways.

Mass demonstrations and spectacles were employed to integrate the German nation into a collective fellowship and to mobilize it as an instrument for Hitler's policies (see the box on p. 798). These mass demonstrations, especially the Nuremberg party rallies that were held every September and the Harvest Festivals celebrated at the Bückeberg near Hamelin every fall, combined the symbolism of a religious service with the merriment of a popular amusement. They had great appeal and usually evoked mass enthusiasm and excitement. Even foreigners were frequently affected by the passions aroused by these mass demonstrations.

Some features of the state apparatus of Hitler's "total state" seem contradictory. One usually thinks of Nazi Germany as having an all-powerful government that maintained absolute control and order. In truth, Nazi Germany was the scene of almost constant personal and institutional conflict, which resulted in administrative chaos.

In matters such as foreign policy, education, and economics, parallel government and party bureaucracies competed with each other over spheres of influence. Incessant struggle characterized relationships within the party, within the state, and between party and state. Why this "authoritarian anarchy," as one observer called it, existed is a source of much controversy. One group of historians has assumed that Hitler's aversion to making decisions resulted in the chaos that subverted his own authority and made him a "weak dictator." Another group believes that Hitler's style of leadership led to his regime's administrative chaos, but maintains that Hitler deliberately created this institutional confusion. By fostering rivalry within the party and between party and state, he would be the final decision maker and absolute ruler.

In the economic sphere, Hitler and the Nazis also established control, but industry was not nationalized as the left wing of the Nazi Party wanted. Hitler felt that it was irrelevant who owned the means of production so long as the owners recognized their master. Although the regime pursued the use of public works projects and "pump-priming" grants to private construction firms to foster employment and end the depression, there is little doubt that rearmament was a far more important contributor to solving the unemployment problem. Unemployment, which had stood at 6 million in 1932, dropped to 2.6 million in 1934 and less than 500,000 in 1937. The regime claimed full credit for solving Germany's economic woes, and this was an important factor in leading many Germans to accept the new regime, despite its excesses.

The German Labor Front under Robert Ley regulated the world of labor. The Labor Front was a single, state-controlled union. To control all laborers, it used the workbook. Every salaried worker had to have one in order to hold a job. Only by submitting to the policies of the Nazi-controlled Labor Front could a worker obtain and retain a workbook. The Labor Front also sponsored activities to keep the workers happy (see Mass Leisure later in this chapter).

For those who needed coercion, the Nazi total state had its instruments of terror and repression. Until 1934, the SA had been most visible in terrorizing the people, but after the June 30 purge, the SS took over that function in a much more systematic fashion. Originally created as Hitler's personal bodyguard, the SS, under the direction of Heinrich Himmler (1900–1945), came to control all of the regular and secret police forces. Himmler and the SS functioned on the basis of two principles: terror and ideology. Terror included the instruments of repression and murder: the secret police, criminal police, concentration camps, and later the execution squads and death camps for the extermination of the Jews (see Chapter 27). For Himmler, the SS was a crusading order whose primary goal was to further the Aryan master race. SS members, who constituted a carefully chosen elite, were thoroughly indoctrinated in racial ideology.

Other institutions, such as the Catholic and Protestant churches, primary and secondary schools, and universities, were also brought under the control of the Nazi totalitarian state. Nazi professional organizations and leagues were formed for civil servants, teachers, women, farmers, doctors, and lawyers. These groups were inspired by a sound principle perverted to other ends. Common flags, uniforms, meetings, and indoctrination gave individuals a sense of identity, a sense of belonging and human warmth, but one that was cultivated to produce inhuman brutality.

Since the early indoctrination of the nation's youth would create the foundation for a strong totalitarian state for the future, youth organizations, the *Hitler Jugend* (Hitler Youth) and its female counterpart, the *Bund deutscher Mädel* (League of German Maidens), were given special attention. The oath required of Hitler Youth members demonstrates the degree of dedication expected of youth in the Nazi state: "In the presence of this blood banner, which represents our Führer, I swear to devote all my energies and my strength to the savior of our country, Adolf Hitler. I am willing and ready to give up my life for him, so help me God."

The Nazi total state was intended to be an Aryan racial state. From its beginning, the Nazi Party reflected the strong anti-Semitic beliefs of Adolf Hitler. Once in power, it did not take long for the Nazis to translate anti-Semitic ideas into anti-Semitic policies. Already on April

Nazi Germany	
Hitler as Munich politician	1919–1923
Beer Hall Putsch	1923
Election of Hindenburg as president	1925
Nazis win 107 seats in Reichstag	1930 (September)
Hitler is made chancellor	1933 (January 30)
Reichstag fire	1933 (February 27)
Enabling Act	1933 (March 23)
Purge of the SA	1934 (June 30)
Hindenburg dies; Hitler as sole ruler	1934 (August 2)
Nuremberg laws	1935
Kristallnacht	1938 (November 9–10)

1, 1933, the new Nazi government initiated a two-day boycott of Jewish businesses. A series of laws soon followed that excluded "non-Aryans" (defined as anyone "descended from non-Aryans, especially Jewish parents or grandparents") from the legal profession, civil service, judgeships, the medical profession, teaching positions, cultural and entertainment enterprises, and the press.

In 1935, the Nazis unleashed another stage of anti-Jewish activity when new racial laws were announced in September at the annual party rally in Nuremberg. These "Nuremberg laws" excluded German Jews from German citizenship and forbade marriages and extramarital relations between Jews and German citizens. The "Nuremberg laws" essentially separated Jews from the Germans politically, socially, and legally and were the natural extension of Hitler's stress upon the creation of a pure Aryan race.

Another, considerably more violent phase of anti-Jewish activity took place in 1938 and 1939; it was initiated on November 9–10, 1938, the infamous *Kristallnacht*, or night of shattered glass. The assassination of a third secretary in the German embassy in Paris by a young Polish Jew became the occasion for a Nazi-led destructive rampage against the Jews in which synagogues were burned, 7,000 Jewish businesses were destroyed, and at least 100 Jews were killed. Moreover, 30,000 Jewish males were rounded up and sent to concentration camps. *Kristallnacht* also led to further drastic steps. Jews were barred from all public buildings and prohibited from owning, managing, or working in any retail store. Finally, under the direction of the SS, Jews were encouraged to "emigrate from Germany." After the outbreak of World War II, the policy of emigration was replaced by a more gruesome one.

The creation of the Nazi total state also had an impact on women. The Nazi attitude toward women was

ANTI-SEMITISM IN NAZI GERMANY. **At the core of Hitler's ideology was an intense anti-Semitism. Soon after seizing power, Hitler and the Nazis began to translate their anti-Semitic ideas into anti-Semitic policies. This photograph shows one example of Nazi action against the Jews. Two women clean up some of the debris the morning after *Kristallnacht*, the night of shattered glass.**

largely determined by ideological considerations. Women played a crucial role in the Aryan racial state as bearers of the children who would bring about the triumph of the Aryan race. To the Nazis, the differences between men and women were quite natural. Men were warriors and political leaders whereas women were destined to be wives and mothers. By maintaining this clear distinction, each could best serve to "maintain the whole community."

Nazi ideas determined employment opportunities for women. The Nazis hoped to drive women out of certain areas of the labor market. These included heavy industry or other jobs that might hinder women from bearing healthy children, as well as certain professions, including university teaching, medicine, and law, which were considered inappropriate for women, especially married women. The Nazis encouraged women to pursue professional occupations that had direct practical application, such as social work and nursing. In addition to restrictive legislation against females, the Nazi regime pursued its campaign against working women with such poster slogans as "Get ahold of pots and pans and broom and you'll sooner find a groom!" Nazi policy toward female workers remained inconsistent, however. Especially after the rearmament boom and increased conscription of males for military service resulted in a labor shortage, the government

encouraged women to work, even in areas previously dominated by males.

✳ *Soviet Russia*

Yet another example of totalitarianism was to be found in Soviet Russia. The civil war in Russia had come to an end by the beginning of 1921. It had taken an enormous toll of life, but the Red Terror and the victories of the Red Army had guaranteed the survival of the Communist regime. During the civil war, Lenin had pursued a policy of "war communism." Under this policy of expedience, the government had nationalized transportation and communication facilities as well as banks, mines, factories, and businesses that employed more than ten workers. The government had also assumed the right to requisition the produce of peasants. War communism worked during the civil war, but once the war was over, peasants began to sabotage the program by hoarding food. Added to this problem was drought, which caused a great famine between 1920 and 1922 that claimed as many as five million lives. Industrial collapse paralleled the agricultural disaster. By 1921, industrial output was only 20 percent of its 1913 levels. Russia was exhausted. As Leon Trotsky said: "The collapse of the productive forces surpassed anything of the kind that history had ever seen. The country, and the government with it, were at the very edge of the abyss."[12]

THE NEW ECONOMIC POLICY

In March 1921, Lenin pulled Russia back from the abyss by aborting war communism in favor of his New Economic Policy (NEP). Lenin's New Economic Policy was a modified version of the old capitalist system. Forced requisitioning of food from the peasants was halted as peasants were now allowed to sell their produce openly. Retail stores as well as small industries that employed fewer than twenty employees could now operate under private ownership, although heavy industry, banking, and mines remained in the hands of the government. Already by 1922, a revived market and good harvest had brought an end to famine; Soviet agriculture climbed to 75 percent of its prewar level. Industry, especially state-owned heavy industry, fared less well and continued to stagnate. Only coal production had reached prewar levels by 1926. Overall, the NEP had saved Communist Russia from complete economic disaster even though Lenin and other leading Communists intended it to be only a temporary, tactical retreat from the goals of communism.

Between 1922 and 1924, Lenin suffered a series of strokes that finally led to his death on January 21, 1924. Although Communist Party rule theoretically rested on a principle of collective leadership, in fact, Lenin had provided an example of one-man rule. His death inaugurated a struggle for power among the members of the Politburo, the institution that had become the leading organ of the party.

In 1924, the Politburo of seven members was severely divided over the future direction of Soviet Russia. The Left, led by Leon Trotsky, wanted to end the NEP and launch Russia on the path of rapid industrialization, primarily at the expense of the peasantry. This same group wanted to carry the revolution on, believing that the survival of the Russian Revolution ultimately depended on the spread of communism abroad. Another group in the Politburo, called the Right, rejected the cause of world revolution and wanted instead to concentrate on constructing a socialist state in Russia. Believing that too rapid industrialization would worsen the living standards of the Soviet peasantry, this group also favored a continuation of Lenin's NEP.

These ideological divisions were underscored by an intense personal rivalry between Leon Trotsky and Joseph Stalin. Trotsky had been a key figure in the success of the Bolshevik Revolution and the Red Army. In 1924, he held the post of commissar of war and was the leading spokesman for the Left in the Politburo. Joseph Stalin (1879–1953) had joined the Bolsheviks in 1903 and had come to Lenin's attention after staging a daring bank robbery to obtain funds for the Bolshevik cause. Stalin, who was neither a dynamic speaker nor a forceful writer, was content to hold the dull bureaucratic job of party general secretary while other Politburo members held party positions that enabled them to display their brilliant oratorical abilities. He was a good organizer (his fellow Bolsheviks called him "Comrade Card-Index"), and the other members of the Politburo soon found that the position of party secretary was really the most important in the party hierarchy. The general secretary appointed the regional, district, city, and town party secretaries. In 1922, for example, Stalin had made some 10,000 appointments, many of them trusted followers whose holding of key positions proved valuable in the struggle for power. Although Stalin at first refused to support either the Left or Right in the Politburo, he finally came to favor the goal of "socialism in one country" rather than world revolution.

Stalin used his post as party general secretary to gain complete control of the Communist Party. Trotsky was expelled from the party in 1927. Eventually, he made his way to Mexico where he was murdered in 1940, no doubt on Stalin's orders. By 1929, Stalin had succeeded in eliminating the Old Bolsheviks of the revolutionary era from the Politburo and establishing a dictatorship so powerful that the Russian tsars of old would have been envious.

THE STALIN ERA (1929–1939)

The Stalinist era marked the beginning of an economic, social, and political revolution that was more sweeping in its results than the revolutions of 1917. Stalin made a significant shift in economic policy in 1928 when he launched his first five-year plan. Its real goal was nothing less than the transformation of Russia from an agricultural country into an industrial state virtually overnight. Instead of consumer goods, the first five-year plan emphasized maximum production of capital goods and armaments and succeeded in quadrupling the production of heavy machinery and doubling oil production. Europe's largest electrical power station was also built during this period. Between 1928 and 1937, during the first two five-year plans, steel production increased from 4 to 18 million tons per year, and hard coal output went from 36 to 128 million tons. The annual growth rate of the Soviet Union was between 14 and 20 percent a year, a phenomenal accomplishment. At the same time, new industrial cities, located near iron ore and coal deposits, sprang up overnight in the Urals and Siberia.

The social and political costs of industrialization were enormous. Little provision was made for absorbing the expanded labor force into the cities. Though the industrial labor force increased by millions between 1932 and 1940, total investment in housing actually declined after 1929; as a result, millions of workers and their families lived in pitiful conditions. Real wages in industry also declined by 43 percent between 1928 and 1940, and strict laws limited workers' freedom of movement. To inspire and pacify the workers, government propaganda stressed the need for sacrifice to create the new socialist state. Soviet labor policy stressed high levels of achievement, typified by the Stakhanov cult. Alexei Stakhanov was a coal miner

The Formation of Collective Farms

Accompanying the rapid industrialization of the Soviet Union was the collectivization of agriculture, a feat that involved nothing less than transforming Russia's 26 million family farms into 250,000 collective farms (kolkhozes). This selection provides a firsthand account of how the process worked.

❊ Max Belov, *The History of a Collective Farm*

General collectivization in our village was brought about in the following manner: Two representatives of the [Communist] Party arrived in the village. All the inhabitants were summoned by the ringing of the church bell to a meeting at which the policy of general collectivization was announced. . . . The upshot was that although the meeting lasted two days, from the viewpoint of the Party representatives nothing was accomplished.

After this setback the Party representatives divided the village into two sections and worked each one separately. Two more officials were sent to reinforce the first two. A meeting of our section of the village was held in a stable which had previously belonged to a kulak. The meeting dragged on until dark. Suddenly someone threw a brick at the lamp, and in the dark the peasants began to beat the Party representatives who jumped out the window and escaped from the village barely alive. The following day seven people were arrested. The militia was called in and stayed in the village until the peasants, realizing their helplessness, calmed down. . . .

By the end of 1930 there were two kolkhozes in our village. Though at first these collectives embraced at most only 70 percent of the peasant households, in the months that followed they gradually absorbed more and more of them.

In these kolkhozes the great bulk of the land was held and worked communally, but each peasant household owned a house of some sort, a small plot of ground and perhaps some livestock. All the members of the kolkhoz were required to work on the kolkhoz a certain number of days each month; the rest of the time they were allowed to work on their own holdings. They derived their income partly from what they grew on their garden strips and partly from their work in the kolkhoz.

When the harvest was over, and after the farm had met its obligations to the state and to various special funds (for instance, seed, etc.) and had sold on the market whatever undesignated produce was left, the remaining produce and the farm's monetary income were divided among the kolkhoz members according to the number of "labor days" each one had contributed to the farm's work. . . . It was in 1930 that the kolkhoz members first received their portions out of the "communal kettle." After they had received their earnings, at the rate of 1 kilogram of grain and 55 kopecks per labor day, one of them remarked, "You will live, but you will be very, very thin."

In the spring of 1931 a tractor worked the fields of the kolkhoz for the first time. The tractor was "capable of plowing every kind of hard soil and virgin soil," as Party representatives told us at the meeting in celebration of its arrival. The peasants did not then know that these "steel horses" would carry away a good part of the harvest in return for their work. . . .

By late 1932 more than 80 percent of the peasant households . . . had been collectivized. . . . That year the peasants harvested a good crop and had hopes that the calculations would work out to their advantage and would help strengthen them economically. These hopes were in vain. The kolkhoz workers received only 200 grams of flour per labor day for the first half of the year; the remaining grain, including the seed fund, was taken by the government. The peasants were told that industrialization of the country, then in full swing, demanded grain and sacrifices from them.

---

who mined 102 tons of coal in one shift, exceeding the norm by 1,300 percent. He was held up as an example to others.

Rapid industrialization was accompanied by an equally rapid collectivization of agriculture. Almost all of the Bolsheviks had been appalled by one result of Lenin's New Economic Policy, the growth of a class of well-to-do peasant proprietors known as kulaks who employed wage labor. Of the 26 million peasant households in 1929, 2 million were kulaks. It seemed an anomaly to have this capitalist group in the midst of a communist society. To rectify this, Stalin inaugurated a policy of collectivization of agriculture even before he initiated the first five-year plan. Its goal was to eliminate private farms and push people into collective farms (see the box above). One of its major aims was to stimulate industrial growth through profits from the rural economy.

Initially, Stalin planned to collectivize only the wealthier kulaks, but strong resistance from peasants who hoarded crops and killed livestock led him to step up the program. By 1930, 10 million peasant households had been collectivized; by 1934, Russia's 26 million family farms had been collectivized into 250,000 units. This was done at tremendous cost, since the hoarding of food and the slaughter of livestock produced widespread famine. Stalin himself is supposed to have told Winston Churchill during World War II that 10 million peasants died in the artificially created famines of 1932 and 1933. The only

Disturbed by a rapidly declining birthrate, Stalin also reversed much of the permissive social legislation of the early 1920s. Advocating complete equality of rights for women, the Communists had made divorce and abortion easy to obtain while also encouraging women to work outside the home and liberate themselves sexually. After Stalin came to power, the family was praised as a miniature collective in which parents were responsible for inculcating values of duty, discipline, and hard work. Abortion was outlawed, and divorced fathers who did not support their children were fined heavily. The new divorce law of June 1936 imposed fines for repeated divorces, and homosexuality was declared a criminal activity. The regime now praised motherhood and urged women to have large families as a patriotic duty. But by this time many Soviet women worked in factories and spent many additional hours waiting in line to purchase increasingly scarce consumer goods. There was no dramatic increase in the birthrate.

❄ *Authoritarianism in Eastern Europe*

A number of other states in Europe were not totalitarian but did possess conservative authoritarian governments. These states adopted some of the trappings of totalitarian states, especially wide police powers, but their greatest concern was not the creation of a mass movement aimed at the establishment of a new kind of society, but rather the defense of the existing social order. Consequently, the authoritarian states tended to limit the participation of the masses and were content with passive obedience rather than active involvement in the goals of the regime. A number of states in eastern Europe adopted this kind of authoritarian government.

concession Stalin made to the peasants was to allow each household to have one tiny, privately owned garden plot.

Stalin's program of rapid industrialization entailed additional costs as well. To achieve his goals, Stalin strengthened the party bureaucracy under his control. Those who resisted were sent into forced labor camps in Siberia. Stalin's desire for sole control of decision making also led to purges of the Old Bolsheviks. Between 1936 and 1938, the most prominent Old Bolsheviks were put on trial and condemned to death. During this same time, Stalin undertook a purge of army officers, diplomats, union officials, party members, intellectuals, and numerous ordinary citizens. Estimates are that eight million Russians were arrested; millions were sent to Siberian forced labor camps, from which they never returned. The Stalinist blood bath made what some Western intellectuals had hailed as the "New Civilization" much less attractive by the late 1930s.

STALIN SIGNS A DEATH WARRANT. Terror played an important role in the authoritarian system created by Joseph Stalin. Here, Stalin is shown signing what is supposedly a death warrant in 1933. As the terror increased in the late 1930s, Stalin signed such lists every day.

Nowhere had the map of Europe been more drastically altered by World War I than in eastern Europe. The new states of Austria, Poland, Czechoslovakia, and Yugoslavia (known as the kingdom of the Serbs, Croats, and Slovenes until 1929) adopted parliamentary systems, and the preexisting kingdoms of Romania and Bulgaria gained new parliamentary constitutions in 1920. Greece became a republic in 1924. Hungary's government was parliamentary in form, but controlled by its landed aristocrats. At the beginning of the 1920s, political democracy seemed well established, but almost everywhere in eastern Europe, parliamentary governments soon gave way to authoritarian regimes.

Several problems helped to create this situation. Eastern European states had little tradition of liberalism or parliamentary politics and no substantial middle class to support them. Then, too, these states were largely rural and agrarian in character. Not only were many of the peasants largely illiterate, but much of the land was still dominated by large landowners who feared the growth of agrarian peasant parties with their schemes for land redistribution. Ethnic conflicts also threatened to tear these countries apart. Fearful of land reform, communist agrarian upheaval, and ethnic conflict, powerful landowners, the churches, and even some members of the small middle class looked to authoritarian governments to maintain the old system.

Already in the 1920s, some eastern European states began to move away from political democracy toward authoritarian structures. Poland established an authoritarian regime in 1926 when Marshal Joseph Pilsudski created a military dictatorship. King Alexander I (1921–1934) abolished the constitution and imposed a royal dictatorship on Yugoslavia in 1929. King Boris III (1918–1943) established an authoritarian regime in Bulgaria in 1923.

During the 1930s, all of the remaining parliamentary regimes (except Czechoslovakia) succumbed to authoritarianism. No doubt, the Great Depression was a crucial factor in this development. The collapse of farm prices worldwide in the late 1920s adversely affected a region so agrarian as eastern Europe. Eastern European states were increasingly attracted to the authoritarian examples of Fascist Italy and Nazi Germany.

Although Admiral Miklós Horthy had ruled Hungary as "regent" since 1919, the appointment of Julius Gömbös as prime minister in 1932 brought Hungary even closer to Italy and Germany. In Austria, the Christian Socialist chancellor Engelbert Dollfuss used the armed forces to crush the Social Democrats and create his own brand of authoritarian state, a Christian Corporate State. Romania witnessed the development of a strong fascist movement led by Corneliu Codreanu. Known as the Legion of the Archangel Michael, it possessed its own paramilitary squad called the Iron Guard. As Codreanu's fascist movement grew and became Romania's third largest political party, King Carol II (1930–1940) responded in 1938 by ending parliamentary rule, crushing the leadership of the legion, and imposing authoritarian

rule. At the beginning of World War II, General Ian Antonescu seized power and established his own military dictatorship in Romania. In Greece, General John Metaxas imposed a dictatorship in 1936. The new Baltic republics of Lithuania, Latvia, and Estonia also succumbed to dictatorial governments after brief experiments with democracy.

Only Czechoslovakia, with its substantial middle class, liberal tradition, and strong industrial base, maintained its political democracy. Thomas Masaryk, an able and fair leader who served as president from 1918 to 1935, was able to maintain an uneasy but stable alliance of reformist socialists, agrarians, and Catholics.

❋ Dictatorship in the Iberian Peninsula

Parliamentary regimes also failed to survive in both Spain and Portugal. Both countries were largely agrarian, illiterate, and dominated by powerful landlords and Catholic clergy.

Spain's parliamentary monarchy was unable to deal with the social tensions generated by the industrial boom and inflation that accompanied World War I. Supported by King Alfonso XIII (1886–1931), General Miguel Primo de Rivera led a successful military coup in September 1923 and created a personal dictatorship that lasted until 1930. But a faltering economy because of the Great Depression led to the collapse of Primo de Rivera's regime in January 1930 as well as to a widespread lack of support for the monarchy. King Alfonso XIII left Spain in 1931, and a new Spanish Republic was instituted, governed by a coalition of democrats and reformist socialists. Political turmoil ensued as control of the government passed from leftists to rightists until a Popular Front, an antifascist coalition composed of democrats, socialists, and the revolutionary left, took over in 1936. The Popular Front was unacceptable, however, to senior army officers. Led by General Francisco Franco (1892–1975), Spanish military forces revolted against the government and inaugurated a brutal and bloody civil war that lasted three years.

Foreign intervention complicated the Spanish Civil War. The Popular Front was assisted by trucks, planes, tanks, and military advisers from the Soviet Union and 40,000 volunteers from other countries; Franco's forces were aided by arms, money, and men from the fascist regimes of Italy and Germany. Hitler used the Spanish Civil War as an opportunity to test the new weaponry of his revived air force. Gradually, Franco's forces wore down the Popular Front, and after the capture of Madrid on March 28, 1939, the Spanish Civil War finally came to an end.

General Francisco Franco soon established a dictatorship that lasted until his death in 1975. It was not a fascist government, although it was unlikely to oppose the Fascists in Italy or the Nazis in Germany. The fascist movement in Spain, known as the Falange and led by José Antonio Primo de Rivera, son of the former dictator, contributed little to Franco's success and played a minor role in the new regime. Franco's government, which favored large landowners, business, and the Catholic clergy, was yet another example of a traditional, conservative, authoritarian regime.

In 1910, the Portuguese had overthrown their monarchy and established a republic. Severe inflation after World War I, however, undermined support for the republic and helped to intensify political instability. In 1926, a group of army officers seized power, and by the early 1930s, the military junta's finance minister, Antonio Salazar (1889–1970), had become the strong man of the regime. Salazar controlled the Portuguese government for the next forty years.

◆ The Expansion of Mass Culture and Mass Leisure

Technological innovations continued to have profound effects upon European society. Nowhere is this more evident than in mass culture and mass leisure. The mass distribution of commercialized popular forms of entertainment had a profound effect on European society.

❋ Radio and Movies

A series of technological inventions in the late nineteenth century had prepared the way for a revolution in mass communications. Especially important was Marconi's discovery of "wireless" radio waves. But it was not until June 16, 1920, that a radio broadcast (of a concert by soprano Nellie Melba from London) for a mass audience was attempted. Permanent broadcasting facilities were then constructed in the United States, Europe, and Japan during 1921 and 1922, while mass production of radios (receiving sets) also began. In 1926, when the British Broadcasting Corporation (BBC) was made into a public corporation, there were 2.2 million radios in Great Britain. By the end of the 1930s, there were 9 million. Although broadcasting networks in the United States were privately owned and financed by advertising, those in Europe were usually controlled by the government.

The technical foundation for motion pictures had already been developed in the 1890s when short moving pictures were produced as novelties for music halls. Shortly before World War I, full-length features, such as the Italian film *Quo Vadis* and the American film *Birth of a Nation*, became available and made it apparent that cinema had created a new form of mass entertainment. By 1939, about 40 percent of adults in the more advanced industrial countries were attending a movie once a week. That figure increased to 60 percent by the end of World War II.

Mass forms of communication and entertainment were, of course, not new. But the increased size of audiences and the ability of radio and cinema, unlike the printed word, to provide an immediate mass experience did add new dimensions to mass culture. Favorite film actors and actresses became stars, whose lives then became subject to public adoration and scrutiny. Sensuous actresses such as Marlene Dietrich, whose appearance in the early sound film *The Blue Angel* catapulted her to fame, created new images of women's sexuality.

Of course, radio and movies could also be used for political purposes. Hitler had said that "without motor cars, sound films, and wireless, no victory of National Socialism." Radio seemed to offer great opportunities for reaching the masses, especially when it became apparent that the emotional harangues of an Adolf Hitler had just as much impact on people when heard on radio as in person. The Nazi regime encouraged radio listening by urging manufacturers to produce cheap radios that could be bought on installment plans. The Nazis also erected loudspeaker pillars in the streets to encourage communal radio listening, especially to broadcasts of mass meetings.

Film, too, had propaganda potential, a possibility not lost on Joseph Goebbels (1897–1945), the propaganda minister of Nazi Germany. Believing that film constituted one of the "most modern and scientific means of influencing the masses," Goebbels created a special film section in his Propaganda Ministry and encouraged the production of both documentaries and popular feature films that carried the Nazi message. *The Triumph of the Will*, for example, was a documentary of the 1934 Nuremberg party rally that forcefully conveyed the power of National Socialism to viewers. Both Fascist Italy and Nazi Germany controlled and exploited the content of newsreels.

❊ *Mass Leisure*

Mass leisure activities had developed at the turn of the century, but new work patterns after World War I dramatically expanded the amount of free time available to take advantage of them. By 1920, the eight-hour day had become the norm for many office and factory workers in northern and western Europe.

Professional sporting events for mass audiences became an especially important aspect of mass leisure. Attendance at association football (soccer) games increased dramatically, and the inauguration of the World Cup contest in 1930 added to the nationalistic rivalries that began to surround such mass sporting events. Increased attendance also made the 1920s and 1930s a great era of stadium building. For the 1936 Olympics, the Germans built a stadium in Berlin that seated 140,000 people. Strahav Stadium in Prague held 240,000 spectators for gymnastics and track meets. As the popularity of mass spectator sports grew, so too did the amount of money spent on betting.

Travel opportunities also added new dimensions to mass leisure activities. The military use of aircraft during World War I helped to improve planes and make civilian air travel a reality. The first regular international air mail service began in 1919, and regular passenger service soon followed. Although air travel remained the preserve of the wealthy or the adventurous, trains, buses, and private cars made excursions to beaches or holiday resorts more and more popular and affordable. Beaches, such as the one at Brighton in Great Britain, were increasingly mobbed by crowds of people from all social classes.

Mass leisure provided totalitarian regimes with new ways to control their populations. Mussolini's Italy created the *Dopolavoro* (Afterwork) as a vast national recreation agency. The *Dopolavoro* was responsible for establishing clubhouses with libraries, radios, and athletic facilities in virtually every town and village. In some places, they included auditoriums for plays and films and travel agencies that arranged tours, cruises, and resort vacations on the Adriatic at reduced rates. *Dopolavoro* groups introduced many Italians to various facets of mass culture and mass leisure with activities such as band concerts, movies, choral groups, roller skating, and ballroom dancing. Essentially, the *Dopolavoro* enabled the Italian government to provide recreational activities and supervise them as well.

NEW PATTERNS OF RECREATION: THE FORD MODEL T. **Mass leisure activities expanded between the wars as new work patterns increased the free time available to members of the working class. For the middle classes, mass-produced automobiles, such as the American Ford Model T, made possible a new freedom of movement.**

Mass Leisure: Strength through Joy

In November 1933, the German Labor Front established an organization called Kraft durch Freude (Strength through Joy), whose purpose was to organize the leisure time of workers in the interests of the Nazi regime. These excerpts are taken from the reports of the Social Democratic Party's contact men in Germany and give a fairly accurate account of the attitudes of the German workers toward the Kraft durch Freude (KdF) program.

The SOPADE [Social Democratic Party in Exile] Reports

❈ Central Germany, April 1939

While Beauty of Labor [another Labor Front organization] makes no impressions whatsoever . . . Strength through Joy is not without impact. However, workers' wages are only barely sufficient for essentials and nobody can afford a trip to Madeira, 150 Reichsmarks per person—300 RM with the wife. Even the shorter trips produce so many additional expenses that they often double the cost. But some people like them nonetheless. Anybody who has never made a trip in his life and sees the sea for the first time is much impressed. The effect is: "The Nazis have done some good things after all." The enthusiasm is, however, greater on the first trip. On the second, many are put off by the crowds.

❈ Berlin, February 1938

Strength through Joy is very popular. The events appeal to the yearning of the little man who wants an opportunity to get out and about himself and to take part in the pleasures of the "top people." It is a clever appeal to the petty bourgeois inclinations of the unpolitical workers. For such a man it really means something to have been on a trip to Scandinavia, or even if he only went to the Black Forest or the Harz Mountains, he imagines that he has thereby climbed up a rung on the social ladder.

❈ Bavaria, April 1939

On the group tours there is a sharp social differentiation. The "top people" only go on big trips where there will be a more select clientele. The big mass trips are for the proletariat. People now look for places where there are no KdF visitors. "Not visited by KdF" is now a particular asset for summer vacations. A landlord in a mountain village in Upper Bavaria wrote in his prospects: "Not visited by KdF tourists." The Labor Front, which was sent the prospectus by someone, took the landlord to court. He had to withdraw the prospectus and was not allowed to receive summer guests. Nevertheless, information about summer Pensions [boardinghouses] which are not used by KdF is becoming more and more widespread.

By doing so, the state imposed new rules and regulations on previously spontaneous activities, thus breaking down old group solidarities and enabling these groups to be guided by the goals of the state.

The Nazi regime adopted a program similar to the *Dopolavoro* in its *Kraft durch Freude* (Strength through Joy). The purpose of the *Kraft durch Freude* was to coordinate the free time of the working class by offering a variety of leisure time activities, including concerts, operas, films, guided tours, and sporting events (see the box above). Especially popular were the inexpensive vacations, essentially the modern package tour. This could be a cruise to Scandinavia or the Mediterranean or, more likely for workers, a shorter trip to various sites in Germany. Only 130,000 workers took cruises in 1938, compared with the seven million who took short trips.

More and more, mass culture and mass leisure had the effect of expanding the homogeneity of national populations, a process that had begun in the nineteenth century with the development of the national state. Local popular culture was increasingly replaced by national and even international culture as new forms of mass production and consumption brought similar styles of clothing and fashion to people throughout Europe.

◆ Cultural and Intellectual Trends in the Interwar Years

The artistic and intellectual innovations of the pre-World War I period, which had shocked many Europeans, had been the preserve primarily of a small group of avant-garde artists and intellectuals. In the 1920s and 1930s, they became more widespread as artists and intellectuals continued to work out the implications of the ideas developed before 1914. But what made the prewar avant-garde culture acceptable in the 1920s and the 1930s? Perhaps the most important factor was the impact of World War I.

The optimistic liberal-rationalist clichés that many Europeans had taken for granted before 1914 seemed hopelessly outdated in 1918. Four years of devastating war left many Europeans with a profound sense of despair and disillusionment. World War I indicated to many people that something was dreadfully wrong with Western values. In his *Decline of the West*, the German writer Oswald Spengler (1880–1936) reflected the disillusionment when he emphasized the decadence of Western civilization and posited its collapse. To many people, the experiences of World War I seemed to confirm the prewar avant-garde

Hitler's Foreign Policy Goals

Adolf Hitler was a firm believer in the geopolitical doctrine of Lebensraum, which advocated that nations must find sufficient living space to be strong. This idea was evident in Mein Kampf, but it was explained in even more detail in a treatise that Hitler wrote in 1928. It was not published in his lifetime.

❋ Hitler's Secret Book, 1928

I have already dealt with Germany's various foreign policy possibilities in this book. Nevertheless I shall once more briefly present the possible foreign policy goals so that they may yield a basis for the critical examination of the relations of these individual foreign policy aims to those of other European states.

1. Germany can renounce setting a foreign policy goal altogether. This means that in reality she can decide for anything and need be committed to nothing at all. . . . [Hitler rejects this alternative.]

2. Germany desires to effect the sustenance of the German people by peaceful economic means, as up to now. Accordingly even in the future she will participate most decisively in world industry, export and trade. . . . From a folkish standpoint setting this foreign policy aim is calamitous, and it is madness from the point of view of power politics.

3. Germany establishes the restoration of the borders of the year 1914 as her foreign policy aim. This goal is insufficient from a national standpoint, unsatisfactory from a military point of view, impossible from a folkish standpoint with its eye on the future, and mad from the viewpoint of its consequences. . . .

4. Germany decides to go over to [her future aim] a clear, far-seeing territorial policy. Thereby she abandons all attempts at world-industry and world-trade and instead concentrates all her strength in order, through the allotment of sufficient living space for the next hundred years to our people, also to prescribe a path of life. Since this territory can be only in the East, the obligation to be a naval power also recedes into the background. Germany tries anew to champion her interests through the formation of a decisive power on land.

This aim is equally in keeping with the highest national as well as folkish requirements. It likewise presupposes great military power means for its execution, but does not necessarily bring Germany into conflict with all European great powers. As surely as France here will remain Germany's enemy, just as little does the nature of such a political aim contain a reason for England, and especially for Italy, to maintain the enmity of the World War.

---

these goals, and his fears for his health pushed him to fulfill his mission as quickly as possible. His impatience would become a major cause of his own undoing.

❋ The "Diplomatic Revolution" (1933–1936)

Between 1933 and 1936, Hitler and Nazi Germany achieved a "diplomatic revolution" in Europe. When Hitler became chancellor of Germany on January 30, 1933, Germany's position in Europe seemed weak. The Versailles treaty had created a demilitarized zone on Germany's western border that would allow the French to move into the heavily industrialized parts of Germany in the event of war. To Germany's east, the smaller states, such as Poland and Czechoslovakia, had defensive treaties with France. The Versailles treaty had also limited Germany's army to 100,000 troops with no air and limited naval forces.

The Germans were not without advantages, however. Germany was the second most populous European state after the Soviet Union and still possessed a great industrial capacity. Hitler was also well aware that Great Britain and France, dismayed by the costs and losses of World War I, wanted to avoid another war. Hitler knew that France posed a threat to an unarmed Germany, but he believed that if he could keep the French from acting against Germany in his first years, he could remove the restrictions imposed on Germany by Versailles and restore its strength.

Hitler's ability to rearm Germany and fulfill his expansionist policies depended initially upon whether he could convince others that his intentions were peaceful. Posing as the man of peace in his public speeches, Hitler emphasized that Germany wished only to revise the unfair provisions of Versailles by peaceful means and achieve Germany's rightful place among the European states. During his first two years in office, Hitler pursued a prudent foreign policy without unnecessary risks. His dramatic action in October 1933, when he withdrew Germany from the Geneva Disarmament Conference and the League of Nations, was done primarily for domestic political reasons, to give the Germans the feeling that their country was no longer dominated by other European states.

By the beginning of 1935, Hitler had become convinced that Germany could break some of the provisions of the Treaty of Versailles without serious British and French opposition. Hitler had come to believe, based on their responses to his early actions, that both states wanted to maintain the international status quo, but without using force. Consequently, he decided to announce publicly what had been going on secretly for some time—Germany's military rearmament. On March 9, 1935, Hitler announced the creation of a new air force and, one week later, the introduction of a military draft that would expand Germany's army from 100,000 to 550,000 troops.

Hitler's unilateral repudiation of the disarmament clauses of the Versailles treaty brought a swift reaction as France, Great Britain, and Italy condemned Germany's action and warned against future aggressive steps. But nothing concrete was done. Even worse, Britain subsequently moved toward an open acceptance of Germany's right to rearm when it agreed to the Anglo-German Naval Pact on June 18, 1935. This treaty allowed Germany to build a navy that would be 35 percent of the size of the British navy, with equality in submarines. The British were starting a policy of appeasement, based on the belief that if European states satisfied the reasonable demands of dissatisfied powers, the latter would be content, and stability and peace would be achieved in Europe. British appeasement was grounded in large part upon Britain's desire to avoid another war, but it was also fostered by those British statesmen who believed that Nazi Germany offered a powerful bulwark against Soviet communism.

On March 7, 1936, buoyed by his conviction that the Western democracies had no intention of using force to maintain all aspects of the Treaty of Versailles, Hitler sent German troops into the demilitarized Rhineland. According to the Versailles treaty, the French had the right to use force against any violation of the demilitarized Rhineland. But France would not act without British support, and the British viewed the occupation of German territory by German troops as another reasonable action by a dissatisfied power. The London *Times* noted that the Germans were only "going into their own back garden." The French and British response only reinforced Hitler's growing conviction that they were weak nations unwilling to use force to defend the old order. At the same time, since the German generals had opposed his plan, Hitler became even more convinced of his own superior abilities. Many Germans expressed fresh enthusiasm for a leader who was restoring German honor.

Meanwhile, Hitler gained new allies. In October 1935, Benito Mussolini had committed Fascist Italy to imperial expansion by invading Ethiopia. Angered by French and British opposition to his invasion, Mussolini welcomed Hitler's support and began to draw closer to the German dictator he had once called a buffoon. The joint intervention of Germany and Italy on behalf of General Francisco Franco in the Spanish Civil War in 1936 also drew the two nations closer together. In October 1936,

Mussolini and Hitler concluded an agreement that recognized their common political and economic interests, and one month later, Mussolini referred publicly to the new Rome-Berlin Axis. Also in November 1936, Germany and Japan (the rising military power in the East) concluded the Anti-Comintern Pact and agreed to maintain a common front against communism.

By the end of 1936, Hitler and Nazi Germany had achieved a "diplomatic revolution" in Europe. The Treaty of Versailles had been virtually scrapped and Germany was once more a "World Power," as Hitler proclaimed. Hitler had demonstrated a great deal of diplomatic skill in taking advantage of Europeans' burning desire for peace. He had used the tactic of peaceful revision as skillfully as he had used the tactic of legality in his pursuit of power in Germany. By the end of 1936, Nazi power had increased enough that Hitler could initiate an even more daring foreign policy. As Hitler perceived, if the Western states were so afraid of war that they resisted its use when they were strong and Germany was weak, then they would be even more reluctant to do so now that Germany was strong. Although many Europeans still wanted to believe that Hitler desired peace, his moves had actually made war more possible.

❋ The Path to War (1937–1939)

On November 5, 1937, at a secret conference with his military leaders in Berlin, Adolf Hitler revealed his future aims. Germany's ultimate goal, he assured his audience, must be the conquest of living space in the east. Although this might mean war with France and Great Britain, Germany had no alternative if the basic needs of the German people were to be met. First, however, Germany must deal with Austria and Czechoslovakia and secure its eastern and southern flanks.

By the end of 1937, Hitler was convinced that neither the French nor the British would provide much opposition to his plans. Neville Chamberlain (1869–1940), who had become prime minister of Britain in May 1936, was a strong advocate of appeasement and believed that the survival of the British Empire depended upon an accommodation with Germany. Chamberlain had made it known to Hitler in November 1937 that he would not oppose changes in central Europe, provided that they were executed peacefully.

Hitler decided to move first on Austria. By threatening Austria with invasion, Hitler coerced the Austrian chancellor, Kurt von Schuschnigg (1897–1977), into putting Austrian Nazis in charge of the government. The new government promptly invited German troops to enter Austria and assist in maintaining law and order. One day later, on March 13, 1938, after his triumphal return to his native land, Hitler formally annexed Austria to Germany. Great Britain's ready acknowledgment of Hitler's action and France's inability to respond due to a political crisis

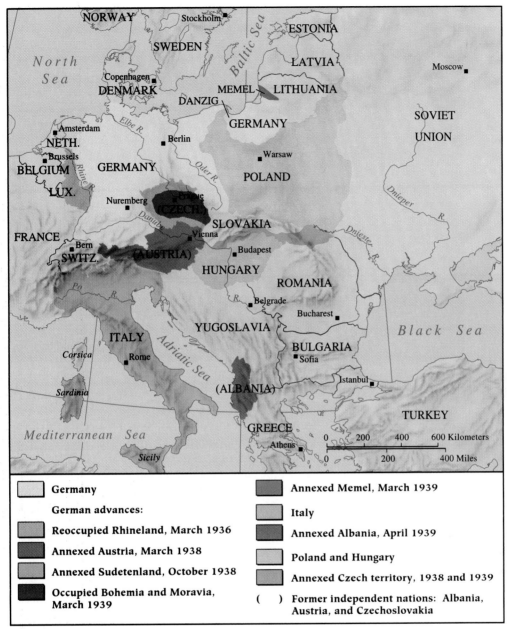

MAP 27.1 Changes in Central Europe, 1936–Summer 1939.

only increased the German dictator's contempt for Western weakness.

The annexation of Austria improved Germany's strategic position in central Europe and put Germany in position for Hitler's next objective—the destruction of Czechoslovakia. On May 30, 1938, Hitler had already told his generals that it was his "unalterable decision to smash Czechoslovakia by military action in the near future."[2] This goal might have seemed unrealistic since democratic Czechoslovakia was quite prepared to defend itself and was well supported by pacts with France and Soviet Russia. Nevertheless, Hitler believed that France and Britain would not use force to defend Czechoslovakia.

In the meantime, Hitler had stepped up his demands on the Czechs. Initially, the Germans had asked for autonomy for the Sudetenland, the mountainous northwestern border area of Czechoslovakia that was home to three million ethnic Germans. As Hitler knew, the Sudetenland also contained Czechoslovakia's most important frontier defenses and considerable industrial resources as well. But on September 15, 1938, Hitler demanded the cession of the Sudetenland to Germany and expressed his willingness to risk "world war" to achieve his objective. War was not necessary, however, as appeasement triumphed once again. On September 29, at the hastily arranged Munich Conference, the British, French, Germans, and Italians

HITLER ENTERS THE SUDETENLAND. The Sudetenland was an area of Czechoslovakia inhabited by 3.5 million Germans. The Munich Conference allowed the Germans to occupy the Sudetenland. This picture shows Hitler and his entourage arriving at Eger (now Cheb) in October 1938 to the cheers of an enthusiastic crowd.

(neither the Czechs nor the Russians were invited) reached an agreement that essentially met all of Hitler's demands. German troops were allowed to occupy the Sudetenland as the Czechs, abandoned by their Western allies, stood by helplessly. The Munich Conference was the high point of Western appeasement of Hitler. When Chamberlain returned to England from Munich, he boasted that the Munich agreement meant "peace for our time." Hitler had promised Chamberlain that he had made his last demand; all other European problems could be settled by negotiation. Like many German politicians, Chamberlain had believed Hitler's assurances (see the box on p. 821).

In fact, Munich confirmed Hitler's perception that the Western democracies were weak and would not fight. Increasingly, Hitler was convinced of his own infallibility, and he had by no means been satisfied at Munich. Already at the end of October 1938, Hitler told his generals to prepare for the final liquidation of the Czechoslovakian state. Using the internal disorder that he had deliberately fostered as a pretext, Hitler occupied the Czech lands (Bohemia and Moravia) while the Slovaks, with Hitler's encouragement, declared their independence of the Czechs and became a puppet state (Slovakia) of Nazi Germany. On the evening of March 15, 1939, Hitler triumphantly declared in Prague that he would be known as the greatest German of them all.

At last, the Western states reacted vigorously to Hitler's threat. After all, the Czechs were not Germans crying for reunion with Germany. Hitler's naked aggression made clear that his promises were utterly worthless. When Hitler began to demand the return of Danzig (which had been made a free city by the Treaty of Versailles to serve as a seaport for Poland) to Germany, Britain recognized the danger and offered to protect Poland in the event of war. At the same time, both France and Britain realized that only the Soviet Union was powerful enough to help contain Nazi aggression and began political and military negotiations with Joseph Stalin and the Soviets. The West's distrust of Soviet communism, however, made an alliance unlikely.

Meanwhile, Hitler pressed on in the belief that the West would not really fight over Poland. He ordered his generals to prepare for the invasion of Poland on September 1, 1939. To preclude an alliance between the West and the Soviet Union, which would create the danger of a two-front war, Hitler, ever the opportunist, negotiated his own nonaggression pact with Stalin and shocked the world with its announcement on August 23, 1939. A secret protocol to the treaty created German and Soviet spheres of influence in eastern Europe: Finland, the Baltic states (Estonia, Latvia, and Lithuania), and eastern Poland would go to the Soviet Union while Germany would acquire western Poland. The treaty with the Soviet Union gave Hitler the freedom to attack Poland. He told his generals: "Now Poland is in the position in which I wanted her . . . I am only afraid that at the last moment some swine or other will yet submit to me a plan for mediation."[3] He need not have worried. On September 1, German forces invaded Poland; two days later, Britain and France declared war on Germany. Two weeks later, on September 17, Germany's newfound ally, the Soviet Union, sent its troops into eastern Poland. Europe was again at war.

The Munich Conference

At the Munich Conference, the leaders of France and Great Britain capitulated to Hitler's demands on Czechoslovakia. While the British prime minister, Neville Chamberlain, defended his actions at Munich as necessary for peace, another British statesman, Winston Churchill, characterized the settlement at Munich as "a disaster of the first magnitude."

✿ Winston Churchill, Speech to the House of Commons, October 5, 1938

I will begin by saying what everybody would like to ignore or forget but which must nevertheless be stated, namely, that we have sustained a total and unmitigated defeat, and that France has suffered even more than we have. . . . The utmost my right honorable Friend the Prime Minister . . . has been able to gain for Czechoslovakia and in the matters which were in dispute has been that the German dictator, instead of snatching his victuals from the table, has been content to have them served to him course by course. . . . And I will say this, that I believe the Czechs, left to themselves and told they were going to get no help from the Western Powers, would have been able to make better terms than they have got. . . .

We are in the presence of a disaster of the first magnitude which has befallen Great Britain and France. Do not let us blind ourselves to that. . . .

And do not suppose that this is the end. This is only the beginning of the reckoning. This is only the first sip, the first foretaste of a bitter cup which will be proffered to us year by year unless by a supreme recovery of moral health and martial vigor, we arise again and take our stand for freedom as in the olden time.

✿ Neville Chamberlain, Speech to the House of Commons, October 6, 1938

That is my answer to those who say that we should have told Germany weeks ago that, if her army crossed the border of Czechoslovakia, we should be at war with her. We had no treaty obligations and no legal obligations to Czechoslovakia. . . . When we were convinced, as we became convinced, that nothing any longer would keep the Sudetenland within the Czechoslovakian State, we urged the Czech Government as strongly as we could to agree to the cession of territory, and to agree promptly. . . . It was a hard decision for anyone who loved his country to take, but to accuse us of having by that advice betrayed the Czechoslovakian State is simply preposterous. What we did was to save her from annihilation and give her a chance of new life as a new State, which involves the loss of territory and fortifications, but may perhaps enable her to enjoy in the future and develop a national existence under a neutrality and security comparable to that which we see in Switzerland today. Therefore, I think the Government deserve the approval of this House for their conduct of affairs in this recent crisis which has saved Czechoslovakia from destruction and Europe from Armageddon.

◆ The Course of World War II

Nine days before he attacked Poland, Hitler made clear to his generals what was expected of them: "When starting and waging a war it is not right that matters, but victory. Close your hearts to pity. Act brutally. Eighty million people must obtain what is their right . . . . The wholesale destruction of Poland is the military objective. Speed is the main thing. Pursuit until complete annihilation."[4] Hitler's remarks set the tone for what became the most destructive war in human history.

✿ Victory and Stalemate

Using *Blitzkrieg*, or "lightning war," Hitler stunned Europe with the speed and efficiency of the German attack. Armored columns or panzer divisions (a panzer division was a strike force of about 300 tanks and accompanying forces and supplies) supported by airplanes broke quickly through Polish lines and encircled the overwhelmed Polish troops. Regular infantry units then moved in to hold the newly conquered territory. Within four weeks, Poland had surrendered. On September 28, 1939, Germany and the Soviet Union officially divided Poland between them.

Although Hitler's hopes of avoiding a war with the West were dashed when France and Britain declared war on September 3, he was confident that he could control the situation. Expecting another war of attrition and economic blockade, Britain and France refused to go on the offensive. Between 1930 and 1935, France had built a series of concrete and steel fortifications armed with heavy artillery—known as the Maginot Line—along its border with Germany. Now France was quite happy to remain in its defensive shell. After a winter of waiting (called the "phony war"), Hitler resumed the war on April 9, 1940, with another *Blitzkrieg*, this time against Denmark and Norway. One month later, on May 10, the Germans launched their attack on the Netherlands, Belgium, and France. The main assault through Luxembourg and the

Ardennes forest was completely unexpected by the French and British forces. German panzer divisions broke through the weak French defensive positions there, outflanking the Maginot Line, and raced across northern France. The maneuver split the Allied armies and trapped French troops and the entire British army on the beaches of Dunkirk. A heroic rescue effort ensued with hundreds of ships and small boats ferrying troops from the French port to Britain. The British succeeded in evacuating an army of 330,000 Allied (mostly British) troops that would fight another day.

On June 5, the Germans launched another offensive into southern France. Five days later, Mussolini, believing that the war was over and eager to grab some of the spoils, declared war on France and invaded from the south. Dazed by the speed of the German offensive, the French were never able to mount an adequate resistance and surrendered on June 22. German armies occupied about three-fifths of France while the French hero of World War I, Marshal Henri Pétain (1856–1951), established an authoritarian regime (known as Vichy France) over the remainder. The Allies regarded the Pétain government as a Nazi puppet state, and a French government-in-exile took up residence in Britain. Germany was now in control of western and central Europe, but Britain still had not been defeated.

German victories in Denmark and Norway coincided with a change of government in Great Britain. On May 10, 1940, Winston Churchill (1874–1965), a longtime advocate for a hard-line policy toward Nazi Germany, replaced the apostle of appeasement, Neville Chamberlain. Churchill was confident that he could guide Britain to ultimate victory. "I thought I knew a great deal about it all," he later wrote, "and I was sure I should not fail." Churchill proved to be an inspiring leader who rallied the British people with stirring speeches. Hitler hoped that the British could be persuaded to make peace so that he could fulfill his long-awaited opportunity to gain living space in the east. Led by the stubbornly determined Churchill, the British refused, and Hitler was forced to prepare for an invasion of Britain, a prospect that he faced with little confidence.

As Hitler realized, an amphibious invasion of Britain would only be possible if Germany gained control of the air. At the beginning of August 1940, the *Luftwaffe* (the German air force) launched a major offensive against British air and naval bases, harbors, communication centers, and war industries. The British fought back doggedly, supported by an effective radar system that gave them early warning of German attacks. Moreover, the Ultra intelligence operation, which had broken German military codes, gave the British air force information about the specific targets of German air attacks. Nevertheless, the British air force suffered critical losses by the end of August and was probably saved by Hitler's change of strategy. In September, in retaliation for a British attack on Berlin, Hitler ordered a shift from military targets to massive bombing of cities to break British morale. The British rebuilt their air strength quickly and were soon inflicting major losses on *Luftwaffe* bombers. By the end of September, Germany had lost the Battle of Britain, and the invasion of Britain had to be postponed.

At this point, Hitler pursued the possibility of a Mediterranean strategy, which would involve capturing Egypt and the Suez Canal and closing the Mediterranean to British ships, thereby shutting off Britain's supply of oil. Hitler's commitment to the Mediterranean was never wholehearted, however. His initial plan was to let the Italians, whose role was to secure the Balkan and Mediterranean flanks, defeat the British in North Africa, but this strategy failed when the British routed the Italian army. Although Hitler then sent German troops to the North African theater of war, his primary concern lay elsewhere: he had already reached the decision to fulfill his lifetime obsession with the acquisition of living space in the east.

Already at the end of July 1940, Hitler had told his army leaders to begin preparations for the invasion of the Soviet Union. Although he had no desire for a two-front war, Hitler became convinced that Britain was remaining

in the war only because it expected Soviet support. If the Soviet Union were smashed, Britain's last hope would be eliminated. Moreover, Hitler had convinced himself that the Soviet Union, with its Jewish-Bolshevik leadership and a pitiful army, could be defeated quickly and decisively. Although the invasion of the Soviet Union was scheduled for spring 1941, the attack was delayed because of problems in the Balkans. Hitler had already obtained the political cooperation of Hungary, Bulgaria, and Romania. Mussolini's disastrous invasion of Greece in October 1940 exposed Hitler's southern flank to British air bases in Greece. To secure his Balkan flank, German troops seized both Yugoslavia and Greece in April. Now reassured, Hitler turned to the east and invaded the Soviet Union on June 22, 1941, in the belief that the Soviets could still be decisively defeated before winter set in.

The massive attack stretched out along an 1,800-mile front. German troops advanced rapidly, capturing two million Soviet soldiers. By November, one German army group had swept through Ukraine, while a second was besieging Leningrad; a third approached within twenty-five miles of Moscow, the Soviet capital. An early winter and unexpected Soviet resistance, however, brought a halt to

the German advance. For the first time in the war, German armies had been stopped. Moreover, after the Japanese bombed Pearl Harbor on December 7, 1941, Stalin concluded that the Japanese would not strike at the Soviet Union and transferred troops from eastern Siberia to the Moscow front. A counterattack in December 1941 by a Soviet army supposedly exhausted by Nazi victories brought an ominous ending to the year for the Germans. By that time, another of Hitler's decisions—the declaration of war on the United States—had probably made his defeat inevitable and turned another European conflict into a global war.

THE WAR IN ASIA

The war in Asia arose from the ambitions of Japan, whose rise to the status of world power had been swift. Japan had defeated China in 1895 and Russia in 1905 and had taken over many of Germany's eastern and Pacific colonies in World War I. By 1933, the Japanese Empire included Korea, Formosa (now Taiwan), Manchuria, and the Marshall, Caroline, and Mariana Islands in the Pacific.

By the early 1930s, Japan was experiencing severe internal tensions. Its population had exploded from 30

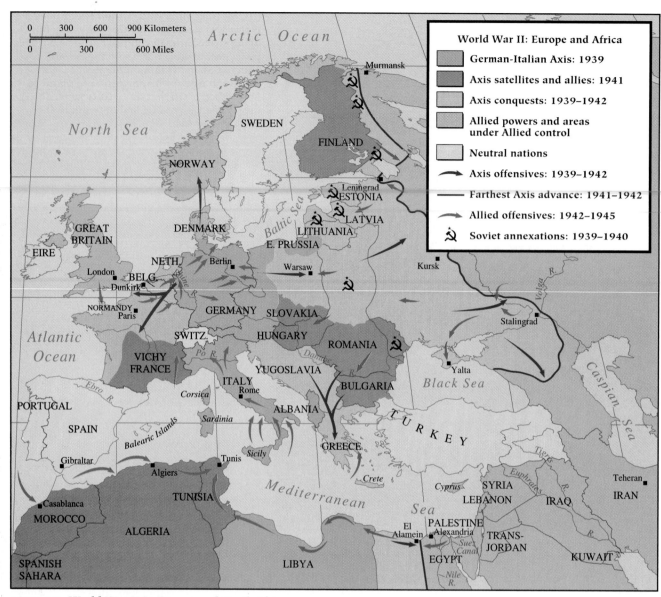

MAP 27.2 **World War II in Europe and North Africa.**

GERMAN PANZER TROOPS IN THE SOVIET UNION. At first, the German attack on the Soviet Union was enormously successful, leading one German general to remark in his diary, "It is probably no overstatement to say that the Russian campaign has been won in the space of two weeks." This picture shows German panzer troops jumping from their armored troop carriers to attack Red Army snipers who had taken refuge in a farmhouse.

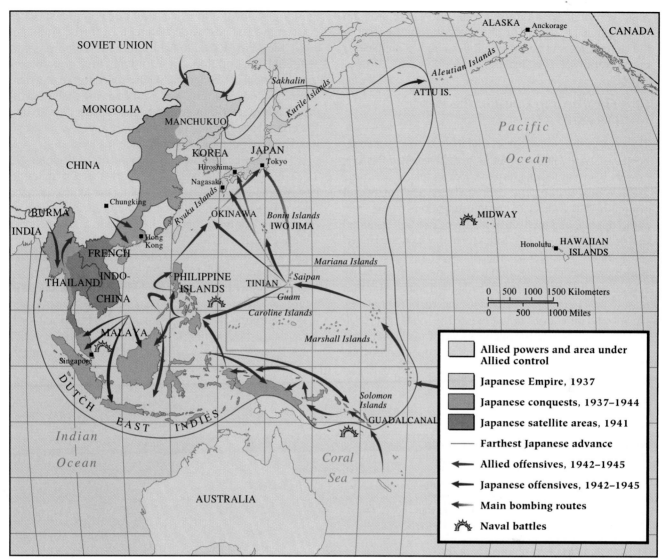

MAP 27.3 **World War II in Asia and the Pacific.**

million in 1870 to 80 million by 1937. Much of Japan's ability to feed its population and to pay for industrial raw materials depended upon the manufacture of heavy industrial goods (especially ships) and textiles. But in the 1930s, Western nations established tariff barriers to protect their own economies from the effects of the depression. Japan was devastated, both economically and politically.

Although political power had been concentrated in the hands of the emperor and his cabinet, Japan had also experienced a slow growth of political democracy with universal male suffrage in 1924 and the emergence of mass political parties. The economic crises of the 1930s stifled this democratic growth. Right-wing patriotic societies allied themselves with the army and navy to push a program of expansion at the expense of China and the Soviet Union, while the navy hoped to make Japan self-sufficient in raw materials by conquering British Malaya and the Dutch East Indies. In 1935, Japan began to construct a modern naval fleet, and after 1936 the armed forces exercised much influence over the government.

The war in Asia began in July 1937 when Japanese troops invaded northern China. Moreover, Japanese naval expansion brought the Japanese into conflict with the European imperial powers—Britain (in India, Burma, Malaya), France (in Indochina), and the Netherlands (in Indonesia)—as well as with the other rising power in the Pacific, the United States. When the Japanese occupied Indochina in July 1941, the Americans responded by cutting off sales of vital scrap iron and oil to Japan. Japan's military leaders decided to preempt any further American response by attacking the American naval fleet at Pearl Harbor on December 7, 1941. The United States declared war on Japan the next day. Three days later, Hitler declared war on the United States, although he was by no means required to do so by his loose alliance with Japan. This action enabled President Roosevelt to overcome strong American isolationist sentiment and to bring the United States into the European conflict. Actually, the United States had made no pretense of neutrality from the beginning of World War II and had been supplying the

Allies with military aid through its Lend-Lease program since March 11, 1941. The simultaneous involvement of the United States in both the European and Asian theaters made World War II a single, truly world war.

✸ The Turning Point of the War (1942–1943)

The entry of the United States into the war created a coalition (the Grand Alliance) that ultimately defeated the Axis powers (Germany, Italy, Japan). Nevertheless, the three major Allies, Britain, the United States, and the Soviet Union, had to overcome mutual suspicions before they could operate as an effective alliance. Two factors aided that process. First, Hitler's declaration of war on the United States made it easier for the Americans to accept the British and Soviet contention that the defeat of Germany should be the first priority of the United States. For that reason, the United States increased the quantity of trucks, planes, and other arms that it sent to the British and Soviets. Also important to the alliance was the tacit agreement of the three chief Allies to stress military operations while ignoring political differences and larger strategic issues concerning any postwar settlement. At the beginning of 1943, the Allies agreed to fight until the Axis powers surrendered unconditionally. Although this principle of unconditional surrender might have discouraged dissident Germans and Japanese from overthrowing their governments in order to arrange a negotiated peace, it also had the effect of cementing the Grand Alliance by making it nearly impossible for Hitler to divide his foes.

Defeat was far from Hitler's mind at the beginning of 1942, however. As Japanese forces advanced into Southeast Asia and the Pacific after crippling the American naval fleet at Pearl Harbor, Hitler and his European allies continued the war in Europe against Britain and the Soviet Union. Until the fall of 1942, it appeared that the Germans might still prevail on the battlefield. Reinforcements in North Africa enabled the Afrika Korps under General Erwin Rommel to break through the British defenses in Egypt and advance toward Alexandria. The Germans were also continuing their success in the Battle of the North Atlantic as their submarines continued to attack Allied ships carrying supplies to Great Britain. In the spring of

THE AIR WAR. **Air power played a major role in the battles of World War II. Because his supply lines in North Africa were extended, the German general Erwin Rommel was forced to rely heavily on transport aircraft to keep his forces supplied. This photograph shows a group of German aircraft at an airfield in Libya during the summer of 1941. In the background are the three-engined Junkers Ju-52s used for transporting reinforcements and supplies. Two Messerschmidt fighter planes are in the foreground.**

A German Soldier at Stalingrad

The Soviet victory at Stalingrad was a major turning point in World War II. This excerpt comes from the diary of a German soldier who fought and died in the Battle of Stalingrad. His dreams of victory and a return home with medals were soon dashed by the realities of Soviet resistance.

✸ Diary of a German Soldier

Today, after we'd had a bath, the company commander told us that if our future operations are as successful, we'll soon reach the Volga, take Stalingrad and then the war will inevitably soon be over. Perhaps we'll be home by Christmas.

July 29. The company commander says the Russian troops are completely broken, and cannot hold out any longer. To reach the Volga and take Stalingrad is not so difficult for us. The Führer knows where the Russians' weak point is. Victory is not far away. . . .

August 10. The Führer's orders were read out to us. He expects victory of us. We are all convinced that they can't stop us.

August 12. This morning outstanding soldiers were presented with decorations. . . . Will I really go back to Elsa without a decoration? I believe that for Stalingrad the Führer will decorate even me. . . .

September 4. We are being sent northward along the front toward Stalingrad. We marched all night and by dawn had reached Voroponovo Station. We can already see the smoking town. It's a happy thought that the end of the war is getting nearer. That's what everyone is saying. . . .

September 8. Two days of non-stop fighting. The Russians are defending themselves with insane stubbornness. Our regiment has lost many men. . . .

September 16. Our battalion, plus tanks, is attacking the [grain storage] elevator, from which smoke is pouring—the grain in it is burning, the Russians seem to have set light to it themselves. Barbarism. The battalion is suffering heavy losses. . . .

October 10. The Russians are so close to us that our planes cannot bomb them. We are preparing for a decisive attack. The Führer has ordered the whole of Stalingrad to be taken as rapidly as possible. . . .

October 22. Our regiment has failed to break into the factory. We have lost many men; every time you move you have to jump over bodies. . . .

November 10. A letter from Elsa today. Everyone expects us home for Christmas. In Germany everyone believes we already hold Stalingrad. How wrong they are. If they could only see what Stalingrad has done to our army. . . .

November 21. The Russians have gone over to the offensive along the whole front. Fierce fighting is going on. So, there it is—the Volga, victory and soon home to our families! We shall obviously be seeing them next in the other world.

November 29. We are encircled. It was announced this morning that the Führer has said: "The army can trust me to do everything necessary to ensure supplies and rapidly break the encirclement."

December 3. We are on hunger rations and waiting for the rescue that the Führer promised. . . .

December 14. Everybody is racked with hunger. Frozen potatoes are the best meal, but to get them out of the ice-covered ground under fire from Russian bullets is not so easy. . . .

December 26. The horses have already been eaten. I would eat a cat; they say its meat is also tasty. The soldiers look like corpses or lunatics, looking for something to put in their mouths. They no longer take cover from Russian shells; they haven't the strength to walk, run away and hide. A curse on this war!

1942, a renewed German offensive in the Soviet Union led to the capture of the entire Crimea, causing Hitler to boast in August 1942:

> As the next step, we are going to advance south of the Caucasus and then help the rebels in Iran and Iraq against the English. Another thrust will be directed along the Caspian Sea toward Afghanistan and India. Then the English will run out of oil. In two years we'll be on the borders of India. Twenty to thirty elite German divisions will do. Then the British Empire will collapse.[5]

But this would be Hitler's last optimistic outburst. By the fall of 1942, the war had turned against the Germans.

In North Africa, British forces had stopped Rommel's troops at El Alamein in the summer of 1942 and then forced them back across the desert. In November 1942, British and American forces invaded French North Africa and forced the German and Italian troops to surrender in May 1943. By that time, new detection devices had enabled the Allies to destroy increasing numbers of German submarines in the shipping war in the Atlantic. On the Eastern Front, the turning point of the war occurred at Stalingrad. After the capture of the Crimea, Hitler's generals wanted him to concentrate on the Caucasus and its oil fields, but Hitler decided that Stalingrad, a major industrial center on the Volga, should be taken first. Between November 1942 and February 1943, German troops were stopped, then encircled, and finally forced to surrender on February 2, 1943 (see the box above). The entire

German Sixth Army of 300,000 men was lost. By February 1943, German forces in the Soviet Union were back to their positions of June 1942. By the spring of 1943, even Hitler knew that the Germans would not defeat the Soviet Union.

The tide of battle in Asia also turned dramatically in 1942. In the Battle of the Coral Sea on May 7–8, 1942, American naval forces stopped the Japanese advance and temporarily relieved Australia of the threat of invasion. On June 4, at the Battle of Midway Island, American planes destroyed all four of the attacking Japanese aircraft carriers and established American naval superiority in the Pacific. After a series of bitter engagements in the waters near the Solomon Islands from August to November, Japanese fortunes began to fade.

❀ The Last Years of the War

By the beginning of 1943, the tide of battle had turned against Germany, Italy, and Japan, but it would take a long time to achieve the goal of unconditional surrender of the three Axis powers. After the Axis forces had surrendered in Tunisia on May 13, 1943, the Allies crossed the Mediterranean and carried the war to Italy, an area that Winston Churchill had called the "soft underbelly" of Europe. After taking Sicily, Allied troops began the invasion of mainland Italy in September. In the meantime, after the ouster and arrest of Benito Mussolini, a new Italian government offered to surrender to Allied forces. But Mussolini was liberated by the Germans in a daring raid and then set up as the head of a puppet German state in northern Italy while German troops moved in and occupied much of Italy. The new defensive lines established by the Germans in the hills south of Rome were so effective that the Allied advance up the Italian peninsula was a painstaking affair accompanied by heavy casualties. Rome did not fall to the Allies until June 4, 1944. By that time, the Italian war had assumed a secondary role anyway as the Allies opened their long-awaited "second front" in western Europe two days later.

Since the autumn of 1943, the Allies had been planning a cross-channel invasion of France from Britain. A series of Allied deceptions managed to trick the Germans into believing that the invasion would come on the flat plains of northern France. Instead, the Allies, under the direction of the American general, Dwight D. Eisenhower (1890–1969), landed five assault divisions on the Normandy beaches on June 6 in history's greatest naval invasion. An initially indecisive German response enabled the Allied forces to establish a beachhead. Within three months, they had landed two million men and a half-million vehicles that pushed inland and broke through German defensive lines.

After the breakout, Allied troops moved south and east and liberated Paris by the end of August. Supply problems as well as a last-minute, desperate (and unsuccessful) offensive by German troops in the Battle of the Bulge

CHRONOLOGY

The Course of World War II

Germany and the Soviet Union divide Poland	September 1939
Blitzkrieg against Denmark and Norway	April 1940
Blitzkrieg against Belgium, Netherlands, and France	May 1940
Churchill becomes British prime minister	May 10, 1940
France surrenders	June 22, 1940
Battle of Britain	Fall 1940
Nazi seizure of Yugoslavia and Greece	April 1941
Germany invades the Soviet Union	June 22, 1941
Japanese attack on Pearl Harbor	December 7, 1941
Battle of the Coral Sea	May 7–8, 1942
Battle of Midway Island	June 4, 1942
Allied invasion of North Africa	November 1942
German surrender at Stalingrad	February 2, 1943
Axis forces surrender in North Africa	May 1943
Battle of Kursk	July 5–12, 1943
Invasion of mainland Italy	September 1943
Allied invasion of France	June 6, 1944
Hitler commits suicide	April 30, 1945
Surrender of Germany	May 7, 1945
Atomic bomb dropped on Hiroshima	August 6, 1945
Japan surrenders	August 14, 1945

slowed the Allied advance. Nevertheless, by March 1945, Allied armies had crossed the Rhine River and advanced further into Germany. At the end of April, Allied forces in northern Germany moved toward the Elbe River where they finally linked up with the Soviets.

The Soviets had come a long way since the Battle of Stalingrad in 1943. In the summer of 1943, Hitler's generals had urged him to build an East Wall based on river barriers to halt the Soviets. Instead, Hitler gambled on taking the offensive by making use of newly developed heavy tanks. German forces were soundly defeated by the Soviets at the Battle of Kursk (July 5–12), the greatest tank battle of World War II. The Germans lost eighteen of their best panzer divisions. Soviet forces now began a relentless advance westward. The Soviets had reoccupied Ukraine by the end of 1943 and lifted the siege of Leningrad and moved into the Baltic states by the beginning of 1944. Advancing along a northern front, Soviet troops occupied

CROSSING THE RHINE. After landing at Normandy, Allied forces liberated France and prepared to move into Germany. Makeshift bridges enabled the Allies to cross the Rhine in some areas and advance deeper into Germany. Units of the 7th U.S. Army of General Patch are shown here crossing the Rhine at Worms on a pontoon bridge constructed by battalions of engineers alongside the ruins of the old bridge.

Warsaw in January 1945 and entered Berlin in April. Meanwhile, Soviet troops swept along a southern front through Hungary, Romania, and Bulgaria.

In January 1945, Adolf Hitler had moved into a bunker fifty-five feet under Berlin to direct the final stages of the war. Hitler continued to arrange his armies on worn-out battle maps as if it still made a difference. In his final political testament, Hitler, consistent to the end in his rabid anti-Semitism, blamed the Jews for the war: "Above all I charge the leaders of the nation and those under them to scrupulous observance of the laws of race and to merciless opposition to the universal poisoner of all peoples, international Jewry."[6] Hitler committed suicide on April 30, two days after Mussolini had been shot by partisan Italian forces. On May 7, German commanders surrendered. The war in Europe was over.

The war in Asia continued. Beginning in 1943, American forces had gone on the offensive and advanced their way, slowly at times, across the Pacific. American forces took an increasing toll of enemy resources, especially at sea and in the air. When President Harry Truman (Roosevelt had died on April 12, 1945) and his advisers became convinced that American troops might suffer heavy casualties in the invasion of the Japanese homeland, they made the decision to drop the newly developed atomic bomb on Hiroshima and Nagasaki. The Japanese surrendered unconditionally on August 14. World War II, in which 17 million died in battle and perhaps 18 million civilians perished as well (some estimate total losses at 50 million), was finally over.

◆ The Nazi New Order

After the German victories in Europe between 1939 and 1941, Nazi propagandists painted glowing images of a new European order based on "equal chances" for all nations and an integrated economic community. This was not Hitler's conception of a European New Order. He saw the Europe he had conquered simply as subject to German domination. Only the Germans, he once said, "can really organize Europe."

❋ The Nazi Empire

The Nazi empire stretched across continental Europe from the English Channel in the west to the outskirts of Moscow in the east. In no way was this empire organized systematically or governed efficiently. Some states—Spain, Portugal, Switzerland, Sweden, and Turkey—remained neutral and outside the empire. Germany's allies—Italy, Romania, Bulgaria, Hungary, and Finland—kept their independence, but found themselves increasingly restricted by the Germans as the war progressed. The remainder of Europe was largely organized in one of two ways. Some areas, such as western Poland, were directly annexed by Nazi Germany and made into German provinces. Most of occupied Europe was administered by German military or civilian officials, combined with varying degrees of indirect control from collaborationist regimes. Competing lines of authority by different offices in occupied Europe made German occupation inefficient.

Hitler's Plans for a New Order in the East

Hitler's nightly monologues to his postdinner guests, which were recorded by the Führer's private secretary, Martin Bormann, reveal much about the New Order he wished to create. On the evening of October 17, 1941, he expressed his views on what the Germans would do with their newly conquered territories in the east.

❋ Hitler's Secret Conversations, October 17, 1941

In comparison with the beauties accumulated in Central Germany, the new territories in the East seem to us like a desert. . . . This Russian desert, we shall populate it. . . . We'll take away its character of an Asiatic steppe, we'll Europeanize it. With this object, we have undertaken the construction of roads that will lead to the southernmost point of the Crimea and to the Caucasus. These roads will be studded along their whole length with German towns, and around these towns our colonists will settle.

As for the two or three million men whom we need to accomplish this task, we'll find them quicker than we think. They'll come from Germany, Scandinavia, the Western countries and America. I shall no longer be here to see all that, but in twenty years the Ukraine will already be a home for twenty million inhabitants besides the natives. In three hundred years, the country will be one of the loveliest gardens in the world.

As for the natives, we'll have to screen them carefully. The Jew, that destroyer, we shall drive out. . . . We shan't settle in the Russian towns, and we'll let them fall to pieces without intervening. And, above all, no remorse on this subject! We're not going to play at children's nurses; we're absolutely without obligations as far as these people are concerned. To struggle against the hovels, chase away the fleas, provide German teachers, bring out newspapers—very little of that for us! We'll confine ourselves, perhaps, to setting up a radio transmitter, under our control. For the rest, let them know just enough to understand our highway signs, so that they won't get themselves run over by our vehicles. . . . There's only one duty: to Germanize this country by the immigration of Germans, and to look upon the natives as Redskins. If these people had defeated us, Heaven have mercy! But we don't hate them. That sentiment is unknown to us. We are guided only by reason. . . .

All those who have the feeling for Europe can join in our work.

In this business I shall go straight ahead, cold-bloodedly. What they may think about me, at this juncture, is to me a matter of complete indifference. I don't see why a German who eats a piece of bread should torment himself with the idea that the soil that produces this bread has been won by the sword.

Racial considerations played an important role in how conquered peoples were treated. German civil administrations were established in Norway, Denmark, and the Netherlands because the Nazis considered their peoples to be Aryan or racially akin to the Germans and hence worthy of more lenient treatment. "Inferior" Latin peoples, such as the occupied French, were given military administrations. By 1943, however, as Nazi losses continued to multiply, all the occupied territories of northern and western Europe were ruthlessly exploited for material goods and workers for Germany's war needs.

Because the conquered lands in the east contained the living space for German expansion and were populated in Nazi eyes by racially inferior Slavic peoples, Nazi administration there was considerably more ruthless. Hitler's racial ideology and his plans for an Aryan racial empire were so important to him that he and the Nazis began to implement their racial program soon after the conquest of Poland. Heinrich Himmler, a strong believer in Nazi racial ideology and the leader of the SS, was put in charge of German resettlement plans in the east. Himmler's task was to evacuate the inferior Slavic peoples and replace them with Germans, a policy first applied to the new German provinces created from the lands of western Poland. One million Poles were uprooted and dumped in southern Poland. Hundreds of thousands of ethnic Germans (descendants of Germans who had migrated years earlier from Germany to various parts of southern and eastern Europe) were encouraged to colonize the designated areas in Poland. By 1942, two million ethnic Germans had been settled in Poland.

The invasion of the Soviet Union inflated Nazi visions of German colonization in the east. Hitler spoke to his intimate circle of a colossal project of social engineering after the war, in which Poles, Ukrainians, and Soviets would become slave labor and German peasants would settle on the abandoned lands and Germanize them (see the box above). Nazis involved in this kind of planning were well aware of the human costs. Himmler told a gathering of SS officers that although the destruction of 30 million Slavs was a prerequisite for German plans in the east, "Whether nations live in prosperity or starve to death interests me only insofar as we need them as slaves for our culture. Otherwise it is of no interest."[7]

Economically, the Nazi New Order meant the ruthless exploitation of conquered Europe's resources. In eastern Europe, economic exploitation was direct and severe. The Germans seized raw materials, machines, and food, leaving only enough to maintain local peoples at a bare subsistence level. Although the Germans adopted legal formalities in their economic exploitation of western Europe, military supplies and important raw materials were taken outright. As Nazi policies created drastic shortages of food, clothing, and shelter, many Europeans suffered severely.

Labor shortages in Germany led to a policy of ruthless mobilization of foreign labor for Germany. After the invasion of the Soviet Union, the four million Soviet prisoners of war captured by the Germans became a major source of heavy labor, but it was wasted by allowing three million of them to die from neglect. In 1942, a special office was created to recruit labor for German farms and industries. By the summer of 1944, seven million foreign workers were laboring in Germany and constituted 20 percent of Germany's labor force. At the same time, another seven million workers were supplying forced labor in their own countries on farms, in industries, and even in military camps. Forced labor often proved counterproductive, however, because it created economic chaos in occupied countries and disrupted industrial production that could have helped Germany. Even worse for the Germans, the brutal character of Germany's recruitment policies often led more and more people to resist the Nazi occupation forces.

❈ Resistance Movements

German policies toward conquered peoples quickly led to the emergence of resistance movements throughout Europe, especially in the east, where brutality toward the native peoples produced a strong reaction. In Ukraine and the Baltic states, for example, the Germans were initially hailed as liberators from Communist rule, but Hitler's policies of treating Slavic peoples as subhumans only drove those peoples to support and join guerrilla forces.

Resistance movements were formed throughout Europe. Active resisters committed acts of sabotage against German installations, assassinated German officials, spread anti-German newspapers, wrote anti-German sentiments on walls, and spied on German military positions for the Allies. Some anti-Nazi groups from occupied countries, such as the Free French movement under Charles de Gaulle, created governments-in-exile in London. In some countries, resistance groups even grew strong enough to take on the Germans in pitched battles. In Yugoslavia, for example, Josip Broz, known as Tito (1892–1980), led a band of guerrillas against German occupation forces. By 1944, his partisan army numbered 250,000, including 100,000 women.

After the invasion of the Soviet Union in 1941, Communists throughout Europe assumed leadership roles in underground resistance movements. This sometimes led to conflict with other local resistance groups who feared the postwar consequences of Communist power. Charles de Gaulle's Free French movement, for example, thwarted the attempt of French Communists to dominate the major French resistance groups.

Women, too, joined resistance movements in large numbers throughout Nazi-occupied Europe. Women served as message carriers, planted bombs in Nazi headquarters, assassinated Nazi officers, published and spread anti-German underground newspapers, spied on German military movements and positions, and used shopping baskets to carry weapons, medicines, and money to help their causes. In Norway, women smuggled Jews into neutral Sweden. In Greece, wives dressed their husbands as women to save them when the Nazis sought to stop acts of sabotage by vicious reprisals in which all the males of a village were executed.

Germany, too, had its resistance movements, although the increased control of the SS over everyday life made resistance both dangerous and ineffectual. The White Rose movement involved an attempt by a small group of students and one professor at the University of Munich to distribute pamphlets denouncing the Nazi regime as lawless, criminal, and godless. Its members were caught, arrested, and promptly executed. Likewise, Communist resistance groups were mostly crushed by the Gestapo.

Only one plot against Hitler and the Nazi regime came remotely close to success. It was the work primarily of a group of military officers and conservative politicians who were appalled at Hitler's warmongering and sickened by the wartime atrocities he had encouraged. One of their number, Colonel Count Claus von Stauffenberg (1907–1944), believed that only the elimination of Hitler would bring the overthrow of the Nazi regime. On July 20, 1944, a bomb planted by Stauffenberg in Hitler's East Prussian headquarters exploded, but failed to kill the dictator. The plot was then quickly uncovered and crushed. Five thousand people were executed, and Hitler remained in control of Germany.

❈ The Holocaust

There was no more terrifying aspect of the Nazi New Order than the deliberate attempt to exterminate the Jewish people of Europe. Racial struggle was a key element in Hitler's ideology and meant to him a clearly defined conflict of opposites: the Aryans, creators of human cultural development, against the Jews, parasites who were trying to destroy the Aryans. At a meeting of the Nazi Party in 1922, Hitler proclaimed: "There can be no compromise—there are only two possibilities: either victory of the Aryan or annihilation of the Aryan and the victory of the Jew."[8] Although Hitler later toned down his anti-Semitic message when his party sought mass electoral victories, anti-Semitism was a recurring theme in Nazism and resulted in a wave of legislative acts against the Jews between 1933 and 1939.

By the beginning of 1939, Nazi policy focused on promoting the "emigration" of German Jews from Germany. At the same time, Hitler had given ominous warnings about the future of European Jewry. When he addressed the German Reichstag on January 30, 1939, he stated:

> I have often been a prophet in life and was generally laughed at. During my struggle for power, the Jews primarily received with laughter my prophecies that I would someday assume the leadership of the state and thereby of the entire Volk and then, among many other things, achieve a solution of the Jewish problem. . . . Today I will be a prophet again: if international finance Jewry within Europe and abroad should succeed once more in plunging the peoples into a world war, then the consequence will be not the Bolshevization of the world and therewith a victory of Jewry, but on the contrary, the destruction of the Jewish race in Europe.[9]

At the time, emigration was still the favored policy. Once the war began in September 1939, the so-called Jewish problem took on new dimensions. For a while there was discussion of the Madagascar Plan, which aspired to the mass shipment of Jews to the African island of Madagascar. When war contingencies made this plan impractical, an even more drastic policy was conceived.

Heinrich Himmler and the SS organization closely shared Adolf Hitler's racial ideology. The SS was given responsibility for what the Nazis called their Final Solution to the Jewish problem, that is, the annihilation of the Jewish people. Reinhard Heydrich (1904–1942), head of the SS's Security Service, was given administrative responsibility for the Final Solution. After the defeat of Poland, Heydrich ordered the special strike forces (*Einsatzgruppen*) that he had created to round up all Polish Jews and concentrate them in ghettos established in a number of Polish cities.

In June 1941, the *Einsatzgruppen* were given new responsibilities as mobile killing units. These SS death squads followed the regular army's advance into the Soviet Union. Their job was to round up Jews in their villages and execute and bury them in mass graves, often giant pits dug by the victims themselves before they were shot. The leader of one of these death squads described the mode of operation:

> The unit selected for this task would enter a village or city and order the prominent Jewish citizens to call together all Jews for the purpose of resettlement. They were requested to hand over their valuables to the leaders of the unit, and shortly before the execution to surrender their outer clothing. The men, women, and children were led to a place of execution which in most cases was located next to a more deeply excavated anti-tank ditch. Then they were shot, kneeling or standing, and the corpses thrown into the ditch.[10]

Such regular killing created morale problems among the SS executioners. During a visit to Minsk in the Soviet Union, SS leader Himmler tried to build morale by pointing out that "he would not like it if Germans did such a thing gladly. But their conscience was in no way impaired, for they were soldiers who had to carry out every order unconditionally. He alone had responsibility before God and Hitler for everything that was happening, . . . and he was acting from a deep understanding of the necessity for this operation."[11]

Although it has been estimated that as many as one million Jews were killed by the *Einsatzgruppen*, this approach to solving the Jewish problem was soon perceived as inadequate. Instead, the Nazis opted for the systematic annihilation of the European Jewish population in specially built death camps. The plan was basically simple. Jews from countries occupied by Germany (or sympathetic to Germany) would be rounded up, packed like cattle into freight trains, and shipped to Poland, where six extermination centers were built for this purpose. The largest and most infamous was Auschwitz-Birkenau. Technical assistance for the construction of the camps was provided by experts from the T-4 program, which had been

THE HOLOCAUST: ACTIVITIES OF THE *EINSATZGRUPPEN*. The activities of the mobile killing units known as the *Einsatzgruppen* were the first stage in the mass killings of the Holocaust. This picture shows the execution of a Jew by a member of one of these SS killing squads. Onlookers include members of the German army, the German Labor Service, and even Hitler Youth. When it became apparent that this method of killing was inefficient, it was replaced by the death camps.

responsible for the extermination of 80,000 alleged racially unfit, mental and physical defectives in Germany between 1938 and 1941. Based on their experiences, medical technicians chose Zyklon B (the commercial name for hydrogen cyanide) as the most effective gas for quickly killing large numbers of people in gas chambers designed to look like shower rooms to facilitate the cooperation of the victims. After gassing, the corpses would be burned in specially built crematoria.

To inform party and state officials of the general procedures for the Final Solution, a conference was held at Wannsee, outside Berlin, on January 20, 1942. Reinhard Heydrich outlined the steps that would now be taken to "solve the Jewish question." He explained how "in the course of the practical implementation of the final solution Europe is to be combed through from west to east" for Jews, who would then be brought "group by group, into so-called transit ghettos, to be transported from there farther to the east." The conference then worked out all of the bureaucratic details so that party and state officials would cooperate fully in the final elimination of the Jews.

By the spring of 1942, the death camps were in operation. Although initial priority was given to the elimination of the ghettos in Poland, by the summer of 1942, Jews were also being shipped from France, Belgium, and Holland. In 1943, there were shipments of Jews from the capital cities of Berlin, Vienna, and Prague and from Greece, southern France, Italy, and Denmark. Even as the Allies were making important advances in 1944, Jews were being shipped from Greece and Hungary. These shipments depended on the cooperation of Germany's Transport Ministry, and despite desperate military needs, the Final Solution had priority in using railroad cars for the transportation of Jews to death camps. Even the military argument that Jews could be used to produce armaments was overridden by the demands of extermination.

A harrowing experience awaited the Jews when they arrived at one of the six death camps. Rudolf Höss, commandant at Auschwitz-Birkenau, described it:

THE HOLOCAUST: THE EXTERMINATION CAMP AT AUSCHWITZ. After his initial successes in the east, Hitler set in motion the machinery for the physical annihilation of Europe's Jews. Shown here is a group of Hungarian Jews who have just arrived at Auschwitz. Hungarian Jews were not rounded up and shipped to the death camps until 1944, at a time when the Allies were making significant advances in the war.

The Holocaust: The Camp Commandant and the Camp Victims

The systematic annihilation of millions of men, women, and children in extermination camps makes the Holocaust one of the most horrifying events in history. The first document is taken from an account by Rudolf Höss, commandant of the extermination camp at Auschwitz-Birkenau. In the second document, a French doctor explains what happened to the victims at one of the crematoria described by Höss.

❋ Commandant Höss Describes the Equipment

The two large crematoria, Nos. I and II, were built during the winter of 1942–43. . . . They each . . . could cremate c. 2,000 corpses within twenty-four hours. . . . Crematoria I and II both had underground undressing and gassing rooms which could be completely ventilated. The corpses were brought up to the ovens on the floor above by lift. The gas chambers could hold c. 3,000 people.

The firm of Topf had calculated that the two smaller crematoria, III and IV, would each be able to cremate 1,500 corpses within twenty-four hours. However, owing to the wartime shortage of materials, the builders were obliged to economize and so the undressing rooms and gassing rooms were built above ground and the ovens were of a less solid construction. But it soon became apparent that the flimsy construction of these two four-retort ovens was not up to the demands made on it. No. III ceased operating altogether after a short time and later was no longer used. No. IV had to be repeat-edly shut down since after a short period in operation of 4–6 weeks, the ovens and chimneys had burnt out. The victims of the gassing were mainly burnt in pits behind crematorium IV.

The largest number of people gassed and cremated within twenty-four hours was somewhat over 9,000.

❋ A French Doctor Describes the Victims

It is mid-day, when a long line of women, children, and old people enter the yard. The senior official in charge . . . climbs on a bench to tell them that they are going to have a bath and that afterward they will get a drink of hot coffee. They all undress in the yard. . . . The doors are opened and an indescribable jostling begins. The first people to enter the gas chamber begin to draw back. They sense the death which awaits them. The SS men put an end to this pushing and shoving with blows from their rifle butts beating the heads of the horrified women who are desperately hugging their children. The massive oak double doors are shut. For two endless minutes one can hear banging on the walls and screams which are no longer human. And then— not a sound. Five minutes later the doors are opened. The corpses, squashed together and distorted, fall out like a waterfall. . . . The bodies which are still warm pass through the hands of the hairdresser who cuts their hair and the dentist who pulls out their gold teeth. . . . One more transport has just been processed through No. IV crematorium.

We had two SS doctors on duty at Auschwitz to examine the incoming transports of prisoners. The prisoners would be marched by one of the doctors who would make spot decisions as they walked by. Those who were fit for work were sent into the camp. Others were sent immediately to the extermination plants. Children of tender years were invariably exterminated since by reason of their youth they were unable to work. . . . at Auschwitz we endeavored to fool the victims into thinking that they were to go through a delousing process. Of course, frequently they realized our true intentions and we sometimes had riots and difficulties due to that fact.[12]

About 30 percent of the arrivals at Auschwitz were sent to a labor camp; the remainder went to the gas chambers (see the box above). After they had been gassed, the bodies were burned in the crematoria. The victims' goods and even their bodies were used for economic gain. Female hair was cut off, collected, and turned into mattresses or cloth. Some inmates were also subjected to cruel and painful "medical" experiments. The Germans killed between five and six million Jews, over three million of them in the death camps. Virtually 90 percent of the Jewish populations of Poland, the Baltic countries, and Germany were exterminated. Overall, the Holocaust was responsible for the death of nearly two out of every three European Jews.

The Nazis were also responsible for the deliberate death by shooting, starvation, or overwork of at least another 9 to 10 million people. Because the Nazis also considered the Gypsies of Europe (like the Jews) a race containing alien blood, they were systematically rounded up for extermination. About 40 percent of Europe's one million Gypsies were killed in the death camps. The leading elements of the "subhuman" Slavic peoples—the clergy, intelligentsia, civil leaders, judges, and lawyers—were arrested and deliberately killed. Probably, an additional four million Poles, Ukrainians, and Belorussians lost their lives as slave laborers for Nazi Germany, and at least three to four million Soviet prisoners of war were killed in captivity. The Nazis also singled out homosexuals for persecution, and thousands lost their lives in concentration camps.

MAP 27.4 The Holocaust.

Legend:
- Dachau — Concentration camp
- Treblinka — Extermination camp
- 277,000 — Estimated Jewish death toll (per country)

◆ The Home Front

World War II was even more of a total war than World War I. Fighting was much more widespread and covered most of the world. Economic mobilization was more extensive; so too was the mobilization of women. The number of civilians killed was far higher; almost 20 million died as a result of bombing raids, mass extermination policies, and attacks by invading armies.

❋ *The Mobilization of Peoples: Four Examples*

The home fronts of the major Western countries varied considerably, based on national circumstances.

❧ GREAT BRITAIN

The British mobilized their resources more thoroughly than their allies or even Germany. By the summer of 1944, 55

percent of the British people were in the armed forces or civilian "war work." The British were especially determined to make use of women. Most women under forty years of age were called upon to do war work of some kind. By 1944, women held almost 50 percent of the civil service positions, and the number of women in agriculture doubled as "Land Girls" performed agricultural labor usually undertaken by men.

The government encouraged a "Dig for Victory" campaign to increase food production. Fields normally reserved for athletic events were turned over to citizens to plant gardens in "Grow Your Own Food" campaigns. Even with 1.4 million new gardens in 1943, Britain still faced a shortage of food as German submarines continued to sink hundreds of British merchant vessels. Food rationing, with its weekly allotments of bacon, sugar, fats, and eggs, intensified during the war as the British became accustomed to a diet dominated by bread and potatoes. For many British people, hours after work were spent in such wartime activities as "Dig for Victory," the Civil Defence, or Home

WOMEN IN THE FACTORIES. Although only the Soviet Union used women in combat positions, the number of women working in industry increased dramatically in most belligerent countries. British women are shown here preparing artillery shells that will be filled with explosives.

Guard. The latter had been founded in 1940 to fight off German invaders. Even elderly people were expected to help manufacture airplane parts in their homes.

During the war, the British placed much emphasis on a planned economy. In 1942, the government created a ministry for fuel and power to control the coal industry and a ministry for production to oversee supplies for the armed forces. Although controls and bureaucratic "red tape" became unpopular, especially with businesspeople, most British citizens seemed to accept that total war required unusual governmental interference in people's lives. The British did make substantial gains in manufacturing war materials. Tank production quadrupled between 1940 and 1942, and the production of aircraft grew from 8,000 in 1939 to 26,000 in 1943 and 1944.

THE SOVIET UNION

World War II had an enormous impact on the Soviet Union. Known to the Soviets as the Great Patriotic War, the German-Soviet war witnessed the greatest land battles in history as well as incredible ruthlessness. To Nazi Germany, it was a war of oppression and annihilation that called for merciless measures. Two out of every five persons killed in World War II were Soviet citizens.

The shift to a war footing necessitated only limited administrative change in the Soviet Union. As the central authority, the dictator Joseph Stalin simply created a system of "super-centralization," by which he directed military and political affairs. All civil and military organizations were subjected to the control of the Communist Party and Soviet police.

The initial defeats of the Soviet Union led to drastic emergency mobilization measures that affected the civilian population. Leningrad, for example, experienced 900 days of siege, during which its inhabitants became so desperate for food that they ate dogs, cats, and mice. As the German army made its rapid advance into Soviet territory, the factories in the western part of the Soviet Union were dismantled and shipped to the interior—to the Urals, western Siberia, and the Volga region. Machines were placed on the bare ground, and walls went up around them as workers began their work. The Kharkov Tank Factory produced its first 25 T-34 tanks only ten weeks after the plant had been rebuilt.

This widespread military, industrial, and economic mobilization created yet another Industrial Revolution for the Soviet Union. Stalin labeled it a "battle of machines," and the Soviets won, producing 78,000 tanks and 98,000 artillery pieces. Fifty-five percent of Soviet national income went for war matériel compared to 15 percent in 1940. As a result of the emphasis on military goods, Soviet citizens experienced incredible shortages of both food and housing. Civilian food consumption fell by 40 percent during the war; in the Volga area, the Urals, and Siberia, workers lived in dugouts or dilapidated barracks.

Soviet women played a major role in the war effort. Women and girls worked in industries, mines, and railroads. Women constituted between 26 and 35 percent of the laborers in mines and 48 percent in the oil industry. Overall, the number of women working in industry increased almost 60 percent. Soviet women were also expected to dig anti-tank ditches and work as air-raid wardens. In addition, the Soviet Union was the only country in World War II to use women as combatants. Soviet women functioned as snipers and also as aircrews in bomber squadrons. The female pilots who helped to defeat the Germans at Stalingrad were known as the "Night Witches."

Soviet peasants were asked to bear enormous burdens. Not only did the peasants furnish 60 percent of the military forces, but at the same time, they were expected to feed the Red Army and the Soviet people under very trying conditions. The German occupation in the early months of the war resulted in the loss of 47 percent of the country's grain-producing regions. Although new land was opened in the Urals, Siberia, and Soviet Asia, a shortage of labor and equipment hindered the effort to expand agricultural production. Because farm tractors and trucks were requisitioned to carry guns for the military, women and children were literally harnessed to do the plowing, and everywhere peasants worked long hours on collective farms for no pay. In 1943, the Soviet harvest was only 60 percent of its 1940 figure, a shortfall that meant extreme hardship for many people.

Total mobilization produced victory for the Soviet Union. Stalin and the Communist Party had quickly realized after the start of the German invasion that the Soviet people would not fight for communist ideology, but would do battle to preserve "Mother Russia." Government propaganda played on patriotic feelings. In a speech on the anniversary of the Bolshevik Revolution in November 1941, Stalin rallied the Soviet people by speaking of the country's past heroes, including the famous tsars of Imperial Russia.

THE UNITED STATES

The home front in the United States was quite different from those of its two chief wartime allies, largely because the United States faced no threat of war in its own territory. Although the economy and labor force were slow to mobilize, eventually the United States became the arsenal of the Allied powers, producing the military equipment they needed. The mobilization of the United States also had a great impact on American social and economic developments.

The American economy was never completely mobilized. In 1941, industries were hesitant to change over to full-time war operations because they feared too much production would inundate postwar markets and create another depression. Unemployment did not decrease significantly in the United States until mid-1943, a situation that affected the use of women in industrial jobs. Seventy-one percent of American women over eighteen years of age remained at home, in part due to male attitudes concerning women's traditional place in the home, but also because the services of women were not really necessary. During the high point of war production in the United States in November 1943, the nation was constructing six ships a day and $6 billion worth of other military equipment a month. Within a year many small factories were being shut down because of overproduction.

Even this partial mobilization of the American economy produced social problems. The construction of new factories created boomtowns where thousands came to work but then faced a shortage of houses, health facilities, and schools. The dramatic expansion of small towns into large cities often brought a breakdown in traditional social mores, especially evident in the growth of teenage prostitution. Economic mobilization also led to a widespread movement of people, which in turn created new social tensions. Sixteen million men and women were enrolled in the military, and another 16 million, mostly wives and sweethearts of the servicemen or workers looking for jobs, also relocated. Over one million African Americans migrated from the rural South to the industrial cities of the North and West, looking for jobs in industry. The presence of African Americans in areas where they had not lived before led to racial tensions and sometimes even racial riots. In Detroit in June 1943, white mobs roamed the streets attacking African Americans. Many of the one million African Americans who enlisted in the military, only to be segregated in their own battle units, were angered by the way they were treated. Some became militant and prepared to fight for their civil rights.

Japanese Americans were treated even more shabbily. On the West Coast, 110,000 Japanese Americans, 65 percent of whom had been born in the United States, were removed to camps encircled by barbed wire and required to take loyalty oaths. Although public officials claimed this policy was necessary for security reasons, no similar treatment of German Americans or Italian Americans ever took place. The racism inherent in this treatment of Japanese Americans was evident when the California governor, Culbert Olson, said: "You know, when I look out at a group of Americans of German or Italian descent, I can tell whether they're loyal or not. I can tell how they think and even perhaps what they are thinking. But it is impossible for me to do this with inscrutable orientals, and particularly the Japanese."[13]

GERMANY

In August 1914, Germans had enthusiastically cheered their soldiers marching off to war. In September 1939, the streets were quiet. Many Germans were apathetic or, even worse for the Nazi regime, had a foreboding of disaster. Hitler was very aware of the importance of the home front. He believed that the collapse of the home front in World War I had caused Germany's defeat, and in his determination to avoid a repetition of that experience, he adopted economic policies that may indeed have cost Germany the war.

To maintain the morale of the home front during the first two years of the war, Hitler refused to convert production from consumer goods to armaments. *Blitzkrieg* allowed the Germans to win quick victories, after which they could plunder the food and raw materials of conquered countries in order to avoid diverting resources away from the civilian economy. After the German defeats on the Soviet front and the American entry into the war, the economic situation changed. Early in 1942, Hitler finally ordered a massive increase in armaments production and the size of the army. Hitler's personal architect, Albert Speer, was made minister for armaments and munitions in 1942. By eliminating waste and rationalizing procedures, Speer was able to triple the production of armaments between 1942 and 1943 despite the intense Allied air raids. Speer's urgent plea for a total mobilization of resources for the war effort went unheeded, however. Hitler, fearful of civilian morale problems that would undermine the home front, refused any dramatic cuts in the production of consumer goods. A total mobilization of the economy was not implemented until 1944, when schools, theaters, and cafes were closed and Speer was finally permitted to use all remaining resources for the production of a few basic military items. By that time, it was in vain. Total war mobilization was too little and too late in July 1944 to save Germany from defeat.

The war produced a reversal in Nazi attitudes toward women. Nazi resistance to female employment declined as the war progressed and more and more men were called up for military service. Nazi magazines now proclaimed: "We see the woman as the eternal mother of our people, but also as the working and fighting comrade of the man."[14] But the number of women working in industry, agriculture, commerce, and domestic service increased only slightly. The total number of employed women in September 1944 was 14.9 million compared to 14.6 in May 1939. Many women, especially those of the middle class, resisted regular employment, particularly in factories. Even the introduction of labor conscription for women in January 1943 failed to achieve much as women found ingenious ways to avoid the regulations.

❋ The Frontline Civilians: The Bombing of Cities

Bombing was used in World War II in a variety of ways: against nonhuman military targets, against enemy troops, and against civilian populations. The latter made World War II as devastating for civilians as for frontline soldiers (see the box on p. 839). A small number of bombing raids in the last year of World War I had given rise to the argument, expressed in 1930 by the Italian general Giulio Douhet, that the public outcry generated by the bombing of civilian populations would be an effective way to coerce governments into making peace. Consequently, European air forces began to develop long-range bombers in the 1930s.

The first sustained use of civilian bombing contradicted Douhet's theory. Beginning in early September 1940, the German *Luftwaffe* subjected London and many other British cities and towns to nightly air raids, making the Blitz (as the British called the German air raids) a national experience. Londoners took the first heavy blows and set the standard for the rest of the British population by refusing to panic. One British woman expressed well what many others apparently felt:

> It was a beautiful summer night, so warm it was incredible, and made more beautiful than ever by the red glow from the East, where the docks were burning. We stood and stared for a minute, and I tried to fix the scene in my mind, because one day this will be history, and I shall be one of those who actually saw it. I wasn't frightened any more.[15]

But London morale was helped by the fact that German raids were widely scattered over a very large city. Smaller communities were more directly affected by the devastation. On November 14, 1940, for example, the *Luftwaffe* destroyed hundreds of shops and 100 acres of the city center of Coventry. The destruction of smaller cities did produce morale problems as wild rumors of heavy casualties spread quickly in these communities. Nevertheless, morale was soon restored. In any case, war production in these areas seems to have been little affected by the raids.

The British failed to learn from their own experience, however, and soon proceeded to bomb German cities. Churchill and his advisers believed that destroying German communities would break civilian morale and bring victory. Major bombing raids began in 1942 under the direction of Arthur Harris, the wartime leader of the British air force's Bomber Command, which was rearmed with four-engine heavy bombers capable of taking the war into the center of occupied Europe. On May 31, 1942, Cologne became the first German city to be subjected to an attack by 1,000 bombers.

With the entry of the Americans into the war, the bombing strategy changed. American planes flew daytime missions aimed at the precision bombing of transportation facilities and war industries, while the British Bomber Command continued nighttime saturation bombing of all German cities with populations over 100,000. Bombing raids added an element of terror to circumstances already made difficult by growing shortages of food, clothing, and fuel. Germans especially feared the incendiary bombs that created firestorms that swept destructive paths through the cities. Four raids on Hamburg in August 1943 produced temperatures of 1,800 degrees Fahrenheit, obliterated half the city's buildings, and killed 50,000 civilians. The ferocious bombing of Dresden from February 13 to 15, 1945,

The Bombing of Civilians

The home front became a battle front when civilian populations became the targets of mass bombing raids. Many people believed that mass bombing could effectively weaken the morale of the people and shorten the war. Rarely did it achieve its goal. In these selections, British, German, and Japanese civilians relate their experiences during bombing raids.

❋ London, 1940

Early last evening, the noise was terrible. My husband and Mr. P. were trying to play chess in the kitchen. I was playing draughts with Kenneth in the cupboard. . . . Presently I heard a stifled voice "Mummy! I don't know what's become of my glasses." "I should think they are tied up in my wool." My knitting had disappeared and wool seemed to be everywhere! We heard a whistle, a bang which shook the house, and an explosion. . . . Well, we straightened out, decided draughts and chess were no use under the circumstances, and waited for a lull so we could have a pot of tea.

❋ Hamburg, 1943

As the many fires broke through the roofs of the burning buildings, a column of heated air rose more than two and a half miles high and one and a half miles in diameter. . . . This column was turbulent, and it was fed from its base by in-rushing cooler ground-surface air. One and one half miles from the fires this draught increased the wind velocity from eleven to thirty-three miles per hour. At the edge of the area the velocities must have been appreciably greater, as trees three feet in diameter were uprooted. In a short time the temperature reached ignition point for all combustibles, and the entire area was ablaze. In such fires complete burn-out occurred; that is, no trace of combustible material remained, and only after two days were the areas cool enough to approach.

❋ Hiroshima, August 6, 1945

I heard the airplane; I looked up at the sky, it was a sunny day, the sky was blue. . . . Then I saw something drop—and pow!—a big explosion knocked me down. Then I was unconscious—I don't know for how long. Then I was conscious but I couldn't see anything. . . . Then I see people moving away and I just follow them. It is not light like it was before, it is more like evening. I look around; houses are all flat! . . . I follow the people to the river. I couldn't hear anything, my ears are blocked up. I am thinking a bomb has dropped! . . . I didn't know my hands were burned, nor my face. . . . My eyes were swollen and felt closed up.

THE DESTRUCTION OF CLYDEBANK. The bombing of an enemy's cities brought the war home to civilian populations. This picture shows a street in Clydebank, near Glasgow in Scotland, the day after the city was bombed by the Germans in March 1941. Only 7 of the city's 12,000 houses were left undamaged; 35,000 of the 47,000 inhabitants became homeless overnight. Clydebank was Scotland's only severe bombing experience.

created a firestorm that may have killed as many as 100,000 inhabitants and refugees. Even some Allied leaders began to criticize what they saw as the unnecessary terror bombing of German cities. Urban dwellers became accustomed to living in air-raid shelters, usually cellars in businesses or houses. Occupants of shelters could be crushed to death if the shelters were hit directly or die by suffocation from the effects of high-explosive bombs. Not until 1943 did Nazi leaders begin to evacuate women and children to rural areas. This evacuation policy, however, created its own problems since people in country villages were often hostile to the urban newcomers.

Germany suffered enormously from the Allied bombing raids. Millions of buildings were destroyed, and possibly half a million civilians died from the raids. Nevertheless, it is highly unlikely that Allied bombing sapped the morale of the German people. Instead, Germans, whether pro-Nazi or anti-Nazi, fought on stubbornly, often driven simply by a desire to live. Nor did the bombing destroy Germany's industrial capacity. The Allied Strategic Bombing survey revealed that the production of war matériel actually increased between 1942 and 1944. Even in 1944 and 1945, Allied raids cut German production of armaments by only 7 percent. Nevertheless, the widespread destruction of transportation systems and fuel supplies made it extremely difficult for the new matériel to reach the German military. The destruction of German cities from the air did accomplish one major goal. There would be no stab-in-the-back myth after World War II as there had been after World War I. The loss of the war could not be blamed on the collapse of

the home front. Many Germans understood that the home front had been a battlefront, and they had fought bravely on their front just as the soldiers had on theirs.

The bombing of civilians eventually reached a new level with the dropping of the first atomic bomb on Japan. Fearful of German attempts to create a superbomb through the use of uranium, the American government pursued a dual strategy. While sabotaging German efforts, the United States and Britain recruited scientists, including many who had fled from Germany, to develop an atomic bomb. Working under the direction of J. Robert Oppenheimer at a secret laboratory in Los Alamos, New Mexico, Allied scientists built and tested the first atomic bomb by the summer of 1945. A new era in warfare was about to begin.

Japan was especially vulnerable to air raids because its air force had been virtually destroyed in the course of the war, and its crowded cities were built of flimsy materials. Attacks on Japanese cities by the new American B-29 Superfortresses, the biggest bombers of the war, had begun on November 24, 1944. By the summer of 1945, many of Japan's factories had been destroyed along with one-fourth of its dwellings. After the Japanese government decreed the mobilization of all people between the ages of thirteen and sixty into a People's Volunteer Corps, President Truman and his advisers feared that Japanese fanaticism might mean a million American casualties. This concern led them to drop the atomic bomb on Hiroshima (August 6) and Nagasaki (August 9). The destruction was incredible. Of 76,000 buildings near the hypocenter of the explosion in Hiroshima, 70,000 were flattened; 140,000 of

HIROSHIMA. The most devastating destruction of civilians came near the end of World War II when the United States dropped atomic bombs on the Japanese cities of Hiroshima and Nagasaki. This panoramic view of Hiroshima after the bombing shows the incredible devastation produced by the atomic bomb.

the city's 400,000 inhabitants died by the end of 1945. By the end of 1950, another 50,000 had perished from the effects of radiation.

◆ The Aftermath of the War: The Emergence of the Cold War

The total victory of the Allies in World War II was not followed by a real peace, but by the beginnings of a new conflict known as the Cold War that dominated European and world politics until the end of the 1980s. The origins of the Cold War stemmed from the military, political, and ideological differences, especially between the Soviet Union and the United States, that became apparent at the Allied war conferences held in the last years of the war. Although Allied leaders were mostly preoccupied with how to end the war, they also were strongly motivated by differing, and often conflicting, visions of postwar Europe.

❊ The Conferences at Teheran, Yalta, and Potsdam

Stalin, Roosevelt, and Churchill, the leaders of the Big Three of the Grand Alliance, met at Teheran (the capital of Iran) in November 1943 to decide the future course of the war. Their major tactical decision concerned the final assault on Germany. Churchill had wanted British and American forces to follow up their North African and Italian campaigns by an indirect attack on Germany through the Balkans. Although an extremely difficult route, this would give the Western Allies a better position in postwar central Europe. Stalin and Roosevelt, however, overruled Churchill and argued successfully for an American-British invasion of the Continent through France, which they scheduled for the spring of 1944. The acceptance of this plan had important consequences. It meant that Soviet and British-American forces would meet in defeated Germany along a north-south dividing line and that, most likely, Eastern Europe would be liberated by Soviet forces. The Allies also agreed to a partition of postwar Germany, but differences over questions like the frontiers of Poland were carefully set aside. Roosevelt was pleased with the accord with Stalin. Harry Hopkins, one of Roosevelt's advisers at the conference, remarked:

> We really believed in our hearts that this was the dawn of the new day. . . . We were absolutely certain that we had won the first great victory of the peace—and by "we," I mean all of us, the whole civilized human race. The Russians had proved that they could be reasonable and far-seeing and there wasn't any doubt in the minds of the President or any of us that we could live with them and get along with them peacefully for as far into the future as any of us could imagine.[16]

Winston Churchill was more cautious about future relations with the Soviets. Although overruled at the Teheran Conference, in October of 1944, Churchill met with Stalin in Moscow and was able to pin him down to a more specific determination of postwar spheres of influence. The agreement between Churchill and Stalin, written on a scrap of paper, assigned the various Allies a certain percentage of political influence in a given area on the basis of past historical roles. The Soviet Union received 90 percent influence in Romania and 75 percent in Bulgaria, whereas Britain obtained 90 percent influence in Greece. Eastern European countries that had a strong tradition of Western ties, such as Yugoslavia and Hungary, were divided "fifty-fifty." Churchill perceived how callous this division of sovereign countries might seem from a distance. He remarked to Stalin, "Might it not be thought rather cynical if it seemed we had disposed of these issues, so fateful to millions of people, in such an offhand manner? Let us burn the paper." Stalin, not worried about what others might think, simply replied, "No, you keep it."[17]

By the time of the conference at Yalta in southern Ukraine in February 1945, the defeat of Germany was a foregone conclusion. The Western powers, which had earlier believed that the Soviets were in a weak position, were now faced with the reality of 11 million Red Army soldiers taking possession of Eastern and much of central Europe. Stalin was still operating under the notion of spheres of influence. He was deeply suspicious of the Western powers and desired a buffer to protect the Soviet Union from possible future Western aggression. At the same time, however, Stalin was eager to obtain economically important resources and strategic military positions. Roosevelt by this time was moving away from the notion of spheres of influence to the ideal of self-determination. He called for "the end of the system of unilateral action, exclusive alliances, and spheres of influence." The Grand Alliance approved a "Declaration on Liberated Europe." This was a pledge to assist liberated European nations in the creation of "democratic institutions of their own choice." Liberated countries were to hold free elections to determine their political systems.

At Yalta, Roosevelt sought Soviet military help against Japan. The atomic bomb was not yet assured, and American military planners feared the possible loss of as many as one million men in amphibious assaults on the Japanese home islands. Roosevelt therefore agreed to Stalin's price for military assistance against Japan: possession of Sakhalin and the Kurile Islands as well as two warm water ports and railroad rights in Manchuria.

The creation of the United Nations was a major American concern at Yalta. Roosevelt hoped to ensure the participation of the Big Three powers in a postwar international organization before difficult issues divided them into hostile camps. After a number of compromises, both Churchill and Stalin accepted Roosevelt's plans for a United Nations organization and set the first meeting for San Francisco in April of 1945.

THE VICTORIOUS ALLIED LEADERS AT YALTA. Even before World War II ended, the leaders of the Big Three of the Grand Alliance, Churchill, Roosevelt, and Stalin (shown from left to right), met in wartime conferences to plan the final assault on Germany and negotiate the outlines of the postwar settlement. At the Yalta meeting (February 5–11, 1945), the three leaders concentrated on postwar issues. The American president, who died two months later, was already a worn-out man at Yalta.

The issues of Germany and Eastern Europe were treated less decisively. The Big Three reaffirmed that Germany must surrender unconditionally and created four occupation zones. Churchill, over the objections of the Soviets and Americans, insisted that the French be given one occupation zone, carved out of the British and American zones. German reparations were set at $20 billion. A compromise was also worked out in regard to Poland. It was agreed that a provisional government would be established with members of both the Lublin Poles, who were Polish Communists living in exile in the Soviet Union, and the London Poles, who were non-Communists exiled in Britain. Stalin also agreed to free elections in the future to determine a new government. But the issue of free elections in Eastern Europe caused a serious rift between the Soviets and the Americans. The principle was that Eastern European governments would be freely elected, but they were also supposed to be pro-Soviet. As Churchill expressed it: "The Poles will have their future in their own hands, with the single limitation that they must honestly follow in harmony with their allies, a policy friendly to Russia."[18] This attempt to reconcile two irreconcilable goals was doomed to failure, as soon became evident at the next conference of the Big Three powers.

Even before the conference at Potsdam took place in July 1945, Western relations with the Soviets were deteriorating rapidly. The Grand Alliance had been one of necessity in which disagreements had been subordinated to the pragmatic concerns of the war. The Allied powers' only common aim was the defeat of Nazism. Once this aim had all but been accomplished, the many differences that troubled East-West relations came to the surface. Each side committed acts that the other viewed as unbecoming of "allies."

From the perspective of the Soviets, the United States' termination of Lend-Lease aid before the war was over and its failure to respond to the Soviet request for a $6 billion loan for reconstruction exposed the Western desire to keep the Soviet state weak. On the American side, the Soviet Union's failure to fulfill its Yalta pledge on the "Declaration on Liberated Europe" as applied to Eastern Europe set a dangerous precedent. This was evident in Romania as early as February 1945, when the Soviets engineered a coup and installed a new government under the Communist Petra Groza, called the "Little Stalin." One month later, the Soviets sabotaged the Polish settlement by arresting the London Poles and their sympathizers and placing the Soviet-backed Lublin Poles in power. To the Americans, the Soviets seemed to be asserting control of Eastern European countries under puppet Communist regimes.

The Potsdam Conference of July 1945 consequently began under a cloud of mistrust. Roosevelt had died on April 12 and had been succeeded by Harry Truman. During the conference, Truman received word that the atomic bomb had been successfully tested. Some historians have argued that this knowledge resulted in Truman's stiffened resolve against the Soviets. Whatever the reasons, there was a new coldness in the relations between the Soviets and Americans. At Potsdam, Truman demanded free elections throughout Eastern Europe. Stalin responded: "A freely elected government in any of these East European countries would be anti-Soviet, and that we cannot allow."[19] After a bitterly fought and devastating war, Stalin sought absolute military security. To him, it could only be gained by the presence of Communist states in Eastern Europe. Free elections might result in governments hostile to the Soviets. By the middle of 1945, only an invasion by Western

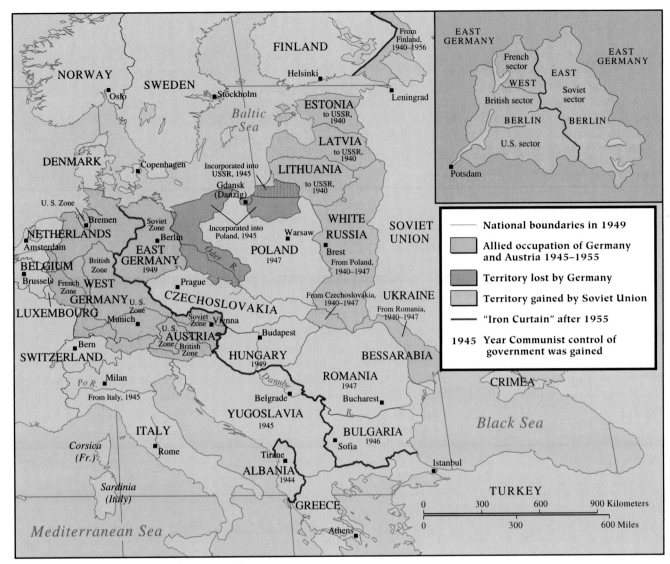

MAP 27.5 Territorial Changes after World War II.

forces could undo developments in Eastern Europe, and after the world's most destructive conflict had ended, few people favored such a policy.

The Soviets did not view their actions as dangerous expansionism but as legitimate security maneuvers. Was it not the West that had attacked the East? When Stalin sought help against the Nazis in the 1930s, had not the West turned a deaf ear? But there was little sympathy in the West for Soviet fears and even less trust in Stalin. When the American secretary of state James Byrnes proposed a twenty-five-year disarmament of Germany, the Soviet Union rejected it. In the West, many saw this as proof of Stalin's plans to expand in central Europe and create a Communist East German state. When Byrnes responded by announcing that American troops would be needed in Europe for an indefinite time and made moves that foreshadowed the creation of an independent West Germany, the Soviets saw this as a direct threat to Soviet security in Europe.

As the war slowly receded into the past, the reality of conflicting ideologies had reappeared. Many in the West interpreted Soviet policy as part of a worldwide Communist conspiracy. The Soviets, for their part, viewed Western, especially American, policy as nothing less than global capitalist expansionism or, in Leninist terms, as nothing less than economic imperialism. Vyacheslav Molotov, the Russian foreign minister, referred to the Americans as "insatiable imperialists" and "war-mongering groups of adventurers."[20] In March 1946, in a speech to an American audience, the former British prime minister, Winston Churchill, declared that "an iron curtain" had "descended across the continent," dividing Germany and Europe into two hostile camps. Stalin branded Churchill's speech a "call to war with the Soviet Union" (see the box on p. 844). Only months after the world's most devastating conflict had ended, the world seemed once again bitterly divided. Would the twentieth-century crisis of Western civilization never end?

Emergence of the Cold War: Churchill and Stalin

Less than a year after the end of World War II, the major Allies that had fought together to destroy Hitler's Germany had divided into two hostile camps. These excerpts, taken from Winston Churchill's speech to an American audience on March 5, 1946, and Joseph Stalin's reply to Churchill only nine days later, reveal the divisions in the Western world that marked the beginning of the Cold War.

❀ Churchill's Speech at Fulton, Missouri, March 5, 1946

From Stettin in the Baltic to Trieste in the Adriatic, an iron curtain has descended across the continent. Behind that line lie all the capitals of the ancient states of central and eastern Europe. Warsaw, Berlin, Prague, Vienna, Budapest, Belgrade, Bucharest, and Sofia, all these famous cities and the populations around them lie in the Soviet sphere and all are subject, in one form or another, not only to Soviet influence but to a very high and increasing measure of control from Moscow. . . .

The Russian-dominated Polish Government has been encouraged to make enormous and wrongful inroads upon Germany, and mass expulsions of millions of Germans on a scale grievous and undreamed of are now taking place. The Communist parties, which were very small in all these eastern states of Europe, have been raised to preeminence and power far beyond their numbers and are seeking everywhere to obtain totalitarian control. Police governments are prevailing in nearly every case, and so far, except in Czechoslovakia, there is no true democracy. . . . Whatever conclusions may be drawn from these facts—and facts they are—this is certainly not the liberated Europe we fought to build up. Nor is it one which contains the essentials of permanent peace.

❀ Stalin's Reply to Churchill, March 14, 1946

In substance, Mr. Churchill now stands in the position of a firebrand of war. And Mr. Churchill is not alone here. He has friends not only in England but also in the United States of America.

In this respect, one is reminded remarkably of Hitler and his friends. Hitler began to set war loose by announcing his racial theory, declaring that only people speaking the German language represent a fully valuable nation. Mr. Churchill begins to set war loose, also by a racial theory, maintaining that only nations speaking the English language are fully valuable nations, called upon to decide the destinies of the entire world.

The German racial theory brought Hitler and his friends to the conclusion that the Germans, as the only fully valuable nation, must rule over other nations. The English racial theory brings Mr. Churchill and his friends to the conclusion that nations speaking the English language, being the only fully valuable nations, should rule over the remaining nations of the world.

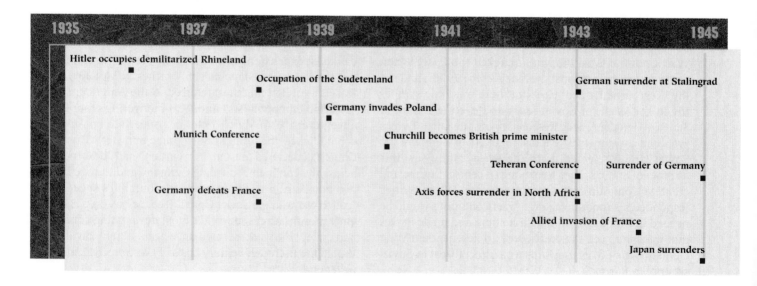

Timeline (1935–1945):
- Hitler occupies demilitarized Rhineland
- Occupation of the Sudetenland
- German surrender at Stalingrad
- Germany invades Poland
- Munich Conference
- Churchill becomes British prime minister
- Teheran Conference
- Surrender of Germany
- Germany defeats France
- Axis forces surrender in North Africa
- Allied invasion of France
- Japan surrenders

CONCLUSION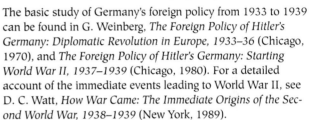

Between 1933 and 1939, Europeans watched as Adolf Hitler rebuilt Germany into a great military power. For Hitler, military power was an absolute prerequisite for the creation of a German racial empire that would dominate Europe and the world for generations to come. If Hitler had been successful, the Nazi New Order, built upon authoritarianism, racial extermination, and the brutal oppression of peoples, would have meant a triumph of barbarism and the end of freedom and equality, which, however imperfectly realized, had become important ideals in Western civilization.

The Nazis lost, but only after tremendous sacrifices and costs. Much of European civilization lay in ruins, and the old Europe had disappeared forever. Europeans, who had been accustomed to dominating the world at the beginning of the twentieth century, now watched helplessly at mid-century as the two new superpowers created by the two world wars took control of their destinies. Even before the last battles had been fought, the United States and the Soviet Union had arrived at different visions of the postwar European world. No sooner had the war ended than their differences created a new and potentially even more devastating conflict known as the Cold War. Yet even though Europeans seemed merely pawns in the struggle between the two superpowers, they managed to stage a remarkable recovery of their own civilization.

NOTES

1. Adolf Hitler, *Mein Kampf*, trans. Ralph Manheim (Boston, 1971), p. 654.
2. *Documents on German Foreign Policy* (London, 1956), Series D, 2:358.
3. Ibid., 7:204.
4. Quoted in Norman Rich, *Hitler's War Aims* (New York, 1973), 1:129.
5. Albert Speer, *Spandau*, trans. Richard and Clara Winston (New York, 1976), p. 50.
6. *Nazi Conspiracy and Aggression* (Washington, D.C., 1946), 6:262.
7. International Military Tribunal, *Trial of the Major War Criminals* (Nuremberg, 1947–49), 22:480.
8. Adolf Hitler, *My New Order*, ed. Raoul de Roussy de Sales (New York, 1941), pp. 21–22.
9. Quoted in Lucy Dawidowicz, *The War against the Jews* (New York, 1975), p. 106.
10. *Nazi Conspiracy and Aggression*, 5:341–42.
11. Quoted in Raul Hilberg, *The Destruction of the European Jews*, rev. ed. (New York, 1985), 1:332–333.
12. *Nazi Conspiracy and Aggression*, 6:789.
13. Quoted in John Campbell, *The Experience of World War II* (New York, 1989), p. 170.
14. Quoted in Claudia Koonz, "Mothers in the Fatherland: Women in Nazi Germany," in Renate Bridenthal and Claudia Koonz, eds., *Becoming Visible: Women in European History* (Boston, 1977), p. 466.
15. Quoted in Campbell, *The Experience of World War II*, p. 177.
16. Quoted in Robert E. Sherwood, *Roosevelt and Hopkins: An Intimate History* (New York, 1948), p. 870.
17. Quoted in Walter Laqueur, *Europe since Hitler*, rev. ed. (New York, 1982), p. 102.
18. Quoted in Norman Graebner, *Cold War Diplomacy, 1945–1960* (Princeton, N.J., 1962), p. 117.
19. Quoted in ibid.
20. Quoted in Wilfried Loth, *The Division of the World, 1941–1955* (New York, 1988), p. 81.

SUGGESTIONS FOR FURTHER READING

The basic study of Germany's foreign policy from 1933 to 1939 can be found in G. Weinberg, *The Foreign Policy of Hitler's Germany: Diplomatic Revolution in Europe, 1933–36* (Chicago, 1970), and *The Foreign Policy of Hitler's Germany: Starting World War II, 1937–1939* (Chicago, 1980). For a detailed account of the immediate events leading to World War II, see D. C. Watt, *How War Came: The Immediate Origins of the Second World War, 1938–1939* (New York, 1989).

Hitler's war aims and the importance of ideology to those aims are examined in N. Rich, *Hitler's War Aims*, vol. 1, *Ideology, the Nazi State and the Course of Expansion* (New York, 1973), and vol. 2, *The Establishment of the New Order* (New York, 1974). On the origins of the war in the Pacific, see A. Iriye, *The Origins of the Second World War in Asia and the Pacific* (London, 1987). General works on World War II include the comprehensive work by G. Weinberg, *A World at Arms: A Global History of World War II* (Cambridge, 1994); M. K. Dziewanowski, *War at Any Price: World War II in Europe, 1939–1945*, 2d ed. (Englewood Cliffs, N.J., 1991); P. Calvocoressi and G. Wint, *Total War: Causes and Courses of the Second World War* (New York, 1979); J. Campbell, *The Experience of World War II* (New York, 1989); and G. Wright, *The Ordeal of Total War, 1939–1945* (New York, 1968). On Hitler as a military leader, see R. Lewin, *Hitler's Mistakes* (New York, 1986). The Eastern Front is covered in J. Erickson, *Stalin's War with Germany*, vol. 1, *The Road to Stalingrad*; vol. 2, *The Road to Berlin* (London, 1973, 1985); and O. Bartov, *The Eastern Front, 1941–45: German Troops and the Barbarisation of Warfare* (London, 1986). The second front in Europe is examined in C. D'Este, *Decision in Normandy* (London, 1983).

A standard work on the German New Order in Russia is A. Dallin, *German Rule in Russia, 1941–1945*, rev. ed. (London, 1981). On Poland, see J. T. Gross, *Polish Society under German Occupation* (Princeton, N.J., 1981). On foreign labor, see E. Homze, *Foreign Labor in Nazi Germany* (Princeton, N.J., 1967). Resistance movements in Europe are covered in M. R. D. Foot, *Resistance: An Analysis of European Resistance to Nazism* (London, 1976). A fundamental study on resistance in Germany is P. Hoffmann, *The History of the German Resistance, 1933–1945*, trans. R. Barry (Cambridge, Mass., 1977). There is a good collection of articles in W. Benz and W. H. Pehle, eds., *Encyclopedia of German Resistance to the Nazi Movement* (New

York, 1997). On women in resistance movements, see M. Rossiter, *Women in the Resistance* (New York, 1986); and M. C. Weitz, *Sisters in the Resistance: How Women Fought to Free France, 1940–1945* (New York, 1995).

The best studies of the Holocaust include R. Hilberg, *The Destruction of the European Jews*, rev. ed., 3 vols. (New York, 1985); L. Dawidowicz, *The War against the Jews* (New York, 1975); L. Yahil, *The Holocaust* (Oxford, 1990); and M. Gilbert, *The Holocaust: The History of the Jews of Europe during the Second World War* (New York, 1985). For brief studies, see J. Fischel, *The Holocaust* (Westport, Conn., 1998); and R. S. Botwinick, *A History of the Holocaust* (Upper Saddle River, N.J., 1996). There is a good overview of the scholarship on the Holocaust in M. Marrus, *The Holocaust in History* (New York, 1987). The role of Hitler in the Holocaust has been well examined in G. Fleming, *Hitler and the Final Solution* (Berkeley, 1984). On the extermination camps, see K. G. Feig, *Hitler's Death Camps: The Sanity of Madness* (New York, 1981). Other Nazi atrocities are examined in R. C. Lukas, *Forgotten Holocaust: The Poles under German Occupation, 1939–44* (Lexington, Ky., 1986); and B. Wytwycky, *The Other Holocaust* (Washington, D.C., 1980).

General studies on the impact of total war include J. Costello, *Love, Sex and War: Changing Values, 1939–1945* (London, 1985); A. Marwick, *War and Social Change in the Twentieth Century: A Comparative Study of Britain, France, Germany, Russia and the United States* (London, 1974); P. Summerfield, *Women Workers in the Second World War: Production and Patriarchy in Conflict* (London, 1984); and M. R. Marrus, *The Unwanted: European Refugees in the Twentieth Century* (New York, 1985). On the home front in Germany, see E. R. Beck, *Under the Bombs: The German Home Front, 1942–1945* (Lexington, Ky., 1986); M. Kitchen, *Nazi Germany at War* (New York, 1995); J. Stephenson, *The Nazi Organisation of Women* (London, 1981); and L. J. Rupp, *Mobilizing Women for War: German and American Propaganda, 1939–1945* (Princeton, N.J., 1978). On the home front in

Britain, see A. Marwick, *The Home Front* (London, 1976). The Soviet Union during the war is examined in M. Harrison, *Soviet Planning in Peace and War, 1938–1945* (Cambridge, 1985). On the American home front, see the collection of essays in K. P. O'Brien and L. H. Parsons, *The Home-Front War: World War II and American Society* (Westport, Conn., 1995).

On the destruction of Germany by bombing raids, see H. Rumpf, *The Bombing of Germany* (London, 1963). The German bombing of Britain is covered in T. Harrisson, *Living through the Blitz* (London, 1985). On Hiroshima, see A. Chisholm, *Faces of Hiroshima* (London, 1985).

On the emergence of the Cold War, see W. Loth, *The Division of the World, 1941–1955* (New York, 1988), and the more extensive list of references at the end of Chapter 28. On the wartime summit conferences, see H. Feis, *Churchill, Roosevelt, Stalin: The War They Waged and the Peace They Sought*, 2d ed. (Princeton, N.J., 1967). The impact of the atomic bomb on Truman's relationship to Stalin is discussed in M. Sherwin, *A World Destroyed: The Atomic Bomb and the Grand Alliance* (New York, 1975).

For additional reading, go to InfoTrac College Edition, your online research library at http://web1.infotrac-college.com

Enter the search terms *World War, 1939–1945* using Key Terms.

Enter the search terms *socialism history* using Key Terms.

Enter the search term *Holocaust* using the Subject Guide.

Enter the search term *Hitler* using Key Terms.

28

Cold War and a New Western World, 1945–1970

CHAPTER OUTLINE

- The Development of the Cold War
- Recovery and Renewal in Europe
- The United States and Canada: A New Era
- The Emergence of a New Society
- Conclusion

FOCUS QUESTIONS

- Why were the United States and the Soviet Union suspicious of each other after World War II, and what events between 1945 and 1949 heightened the tensions between the two nations?
- What role did the Cuban Missile Crisis and the Vietnam War play in the Cold War?
- What were the main developments in the Soviet Union and Eastern Europe between 1945 and 1970?
- What were the main political developments in the nations of Western Europe and North America between 1945 and 1970?
- What major changes occurred in Western society between 1945 and 1970?

*T*HE END OF World War II in Europe had been met with great joy. One visitor to Moscow reported: "I looked out of the window [at 2 A.M.], almost everywhere there were lights in the window—people were staying awake. Everyone embraced everyone else, someone sobbed aloud." But after the victory parades and celebrations, Europeans awoke to a devastating realization: their civilization was in ruins. Some wondered if Europe would ever regain its former prosperity and importance. Winston Churchill wrote: "What is Europe now? A rubble heap, a charnel house, a breeding ground of pestilence and hate." There was ample reason for his pessimism. Almost 40 million people (both soldiers and civilians) had been killed during the preceding six years. Massive air raids and artillery bombardments had reduced many of the great cities of Europe to heaps of rubble. The Polish capital of Warsaw had been almost completely obliterated. An American general described Berlin: "Wherever we looked we saw desolation. It was like a city of the dead. Suffering and shock were visible in every face. Dead bodies still remained in canals and lakes and were being dug out from under bomb debris." Millions of Europeans faced starvation as grain harvests were only half of what they had been in 1939. Millions were also homeless. In the parts of the Soviet Union that had been occupied by the Germans, almost 25 million people were without homes. The destruction of bridges, roads, and railroads had left transportation systems paralyzed. Untold millions of people had been uprooted by the war; now they became "displaced persons," trying to find food and then their way home. Eleven million prisoners of war had to be returned to their native countries while 15 million Germans and East Europeans were driven out of countries where they were no longer wanted. Yet, despite the chaos, Europe was soon on the road to a remarkable recovery. Already by 1950, Europe's industrial and agricultural output was 30 percent above prewar levels.

World War II had cost Europe more than physical destruction, however. European supremacy in world affairs had also been destroyed. After 1945, the colonial empires of the European nations rapidly disintegrated, and Europe's place in the world changed radically. As the Cold War conflict between the world's two superpowers—the United States and the Soviet Union—intensified, the European nations were divided into two armed camps dependent upon one or the other of these two major powers. The United States and the Soviet Union, whose rivalry raised the specter of nuclear war, seemed to hold the survival of Europe and the world in their hands.

◆ The Development of the Cold War

Even before World War II had ended, the two major Allied powers—the United States and the Soviet Union—had begun to disagree on the nature of the postwar European world. Unity had been maintained during the war because of the urgent need to defeat the Axis powers, but once they were defeated, the differences between the Americans and Soviets again surged to the front.

❋ The Confrontation of the Superpowers

There has been considerable historical debate about who was most responsible for the beginning of the Cold War. No doubt, both the United States and the Soviet Union took steps at the end of the war that were unwise or might have been avoided. Both nations, however, were working within a framework conditioned by the past. Ultimately,

the rivalry between the two superpowers stemmed from their different historical perspectives and their irreconcilable political ambitions. Intense competition for political and military supremacy had long been a regular feature of Western civilization. The United States and the Soviet Union were the heirs of that European tradition of power politics, and it should not surprise us that two such different systems would seek to extend their way of life to the rest of the world. Because of its need to feel secure on its western border, the Soviet Union was not prepared to give up the advantages it had gained in Eastern Europe from Germany's defeat. But neither were American leaders willing to give up the power and prestige the United States had gained throughout the world. Suspicious of each other's motives, the United States and the Soviet Union soon raised their mutual fears to a level of intense competition. Between 1945 and 1949, a number of events entangled the two countries in continual conflict.

Eastern Europe was the first area of disagreement. The United States and Great Britain had championed self-determination and democratic freedom for the liberated nations of Eastern Europe. Stalin, however, fearful that the Eastern European nations would return to traditional anti-Soviet attitudes if they were permitted free elections, opposed the West's plans. Having liberated Eastern Europe from the Nazis, the Red Army proceeded to install pro-Soviet governing regimes in Poland, Romania, Bulgaria, and Hungary. These pro-Soviet governments satisfied Stalin's desire for a buffer zone against the West, but the local populations and their sympathizers in the West saw the regimes as an expansion of Stalin's empire. Only another war could change this situation, and few people wanted another armed conflict.

A civil war in Greece created another arena for confrontation between the superpowers. In 1946, the Communist People's Liberation Army and the anti-Communist forces supported by the British were fighting each other for control of Greece. But continued postwar economic problems caused the British to withdraw from the active role they had been playing in both Greece and Turkey. President Harry S Truman of the United States, alarmed by British weakness and the possibility of Soviet expansion into the eastern Mediterranean, responded with the Truman Doctrine (see the box on p. 849). According to the president, "It must be the policy of the United States to support free peoples who are resisting attempted subjugation by armed minorities or by outside pressures." This statement was made to the U.S. Congress in March 1947 when Truman requested $400 million in economic and military aid for Greece and Turkey. The Truman Doctrine said in essence that the United States would provide money to countries that claimed they were threatened by Communist expansion. If the Soviets were not stopped in Greece, the Truman argument ran, then the United States would have to face the spread of communism throughout the free world. As Dean Acheson, the American secretary of state explained: "Like apples in a barrel

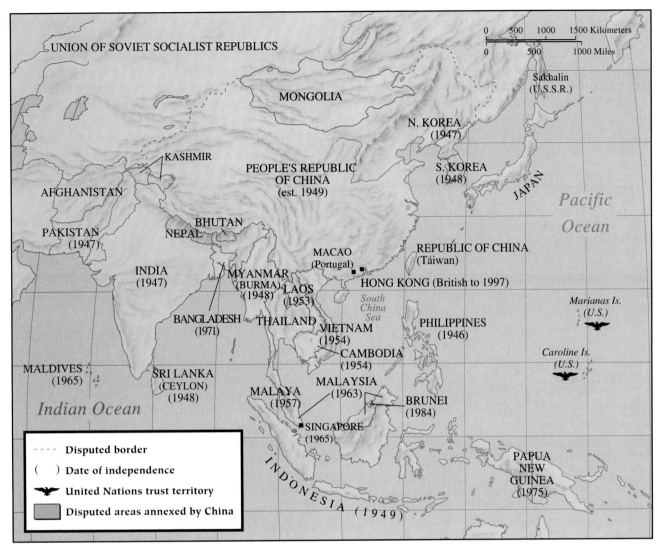

MAP 28.2 **Decolonization in Asia.**

many and Italy, economic revival brought a renewed growth to European society, although major differences remained between Western and Eastern Europe. Moreover, many Europeans, who had feared that European states would suffer tremendously from the loss of their colonies, found that they could even adjust to decolonization.

✳ *The End of European Colonies*

Not only did World War II leave Europe in ruins, but it also cost Europe its supremacy in world affairs. World War I had initiated nationalistic movements against colonial rule, and World War II greatly accelerated this process. The Japanese had already humiliated the Western states by overrunning their colonial empires during the war. In addition, colonial soldiers who had fought on behalf of the Allies were well aware that Allied war aims included the principle of self-determination for the peoples of the world. Equally important to the process of decolonization after the war, the power of the European states had been de-

stroyed by the exhaustive struggles of World War II. The greatest colonial empire builder, Great Britain, no longer had the energy or wealth to maintain its colonial empire after the war and quickly sought to let its colonies go. Given the combination of circumstances, a rush of decolonization swept through the world. Between 1947 and 1962, virtually every colony achieved independence and attained statehood. Although some colonial powers willingly relinquished their control, others, especially the French, had to be driven out by national wars of liberation (see the box on p. 856). Decolonization was a difficult and even bitter process, but it created a new world as the non-Western states ended the long-held ascendancy of the Western nations.

In Asia, the United States initiated the process of decolonization in 1946 when it granted independence to the Philippines. Britain soon followed suit with its oldest and largest nonwhite possession—India. The conflict between India's Hindu and Muslim populations was solved by forming two states, a mostly Hindu India and a predominantly Muslim Pakistan in 1947. In 1948, Britain

Frantz Fanon and the Wretched of the Earth

Born in French Martinique, Frantz Fanon (1925–1961) studied psychiatry in France. His work as head of a psychiatric hospital in Algeria led him to favor violence as a necessary instrument to overthrow Western imperialism, which to Fanon was itself rooted in violence. The Wretched of the Earth, published in 1961, provided an argument for national liberation movements in the Third World. In the last part of the book, Fanon discussed the problem of mental disorders that arose from Algeria's war of national liberation.

❋ The Wretched of the Earth
Colonial War and Mental Disorders, Series B

We have here brought together certain cases or groups of cases in which the event giving rise to the illness is in the first place the atmosphere of total war which reigns in Algeria.

Case No. 1: The murder by two young Algerians, thirteen and fourteen years old respectively, of their European playmate.

We had been asked to give expert medical advice in a legal matter. Two young Algerians thirteen and fourteen years old, pupils in a secondary school, were accused of having killed one of their European schoolmates. They admitted having done it. The crime was reconstructed, and photos were added to the record. Here one of the children could be seen holding the victim while the other struck at him with a knife. The little defendants did not go back on their declarations. We had long conversations with them. We here reproduce the most characteristic of their remarks:

The boy fourteen years old:

This young defendant was in marked contrast to his school fellow. He was already almost a man, and an adult in his muscular control, his appearance, and the content of his replies. He did not deny having killed

either. Why had he killed! He did not reply to the question but asked me had I ever seen a European in prison. Had there ever been a European arrested and sent to prison after the murder of an Algerian? I replied that in fact I had never seen any Europeans in prison.

"And yet there are Algerians killed every day, aren't there?"

"Yes."

"So why are only Algerians found in the prisons? Can you explain that to me?"

"No. But tell me why you killed this boy who was your friend."

"I'll tell you why. You've heard tell of the Rivet business?" [Rivet was a village near Algiers where in 1956 the French militia dragged forty men from their own beds and afterward murdered them.]

"Yes."

"Two of my family were killed then. At home, they said that the French had sworn to kill us all, one after the other. And did they arrest a single Frenchman for all those Algerians who were killed?"

"I don't know."

"Well, nobody at all was arrested. I wanted to take to the mountains, but I was too young. So [my friend] and I said we'd kill a European."

"Why?"

"In your opinion, what should we have done?"

"I don't know. But you are a child and what is happening concerns grown-up people."

"But they kill children too."

"That is no reason for killing your friend."

"Well, kill him I did. Now you can do what you like."

"Had your friend done anything to harm you?"

"Not a thing."

"Well?"

"Well, there you are."

---

granted independence to Ceylon (modern Sri Lanka) and Burma (modern Myanmar). When the Dutch failed to reestablish control over the Dutch East Indies, Indonesia emerged as an independent nation in 1949. The French effort to remain in Indochina led to a bloody struggle with the Vietminh, Vietnamese nationalist guerrillas, led by Ho Chi Minh, the Communist and nationalist leader of the Vietnamese. After their defeat in 1954, the French granted independence to Laos and Cambodia, and Vietnam was temporarily divided in anticipation of elections in 1956 that would decide its fate. But the elections were never held, and the division of Vietnam by Communist and pro-Western regimes eventually led to the Vietnam War.

In the midst of the decolonization of Asia, the Nationalist Chinese under Chiang Kai-Shek (1887–1975)

and the Communists under Mao Zedong were fighting a bloody civil war. Mao's victory in 1949 led to the creation of a powerful Communist state in Asia.

In the Middle East and North Africa, Arab nationalism was a powerful factor in ending colonial empires. Some Arab states had already become independent before the end of World War II. Now they were joined by other free Arab states, but not without considerable bloodshed and complications. When the British left Palestine in 1947, the United Nations voted to create both an Arab state and a Jewish state. When the Arabs attempted to destroy the new Israeli state, Israel's victories secured its existence. But the problem of the Palestinian refugees, supported by existing Arab states, created an Arab-Israeli conflict that has lasted to this day.

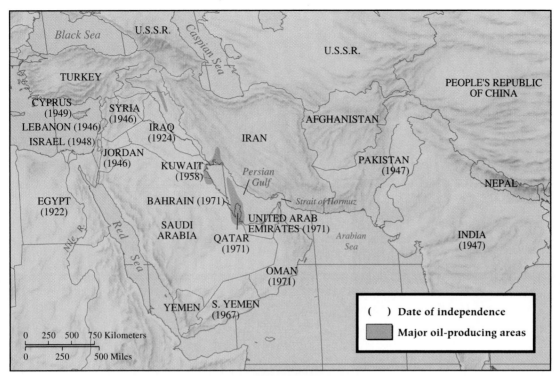

MAP 28.3 Decolonization in the Middle East and South Asia.

ALGERIAN INDEPENDENCE. Although the French wanted to retain control of their Algerian colony, a bloody war of liberation finally led to Algeria's freedom. This photograph shows a group of Algerians celebrating the announcement of independence on July 3, 1962.

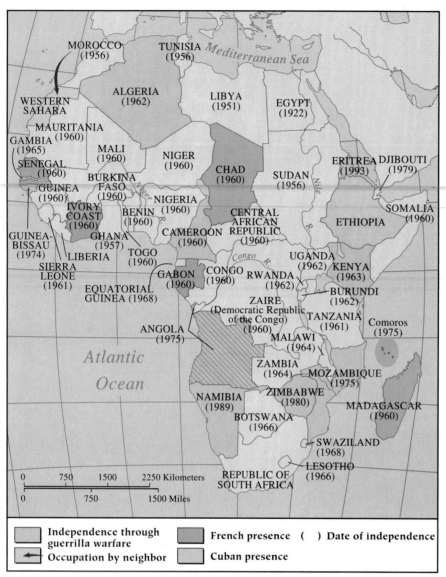

MAP 28.4   Decolonization in Africa.

In North Africa, the French, who were simply not strong enough to maintain control of their far-flung colonial empire, granted full independence to Morocco and Tunisia in 1956. Since Algeria was home to two million French settlers, however, France chose to retain its dominion there. But a group of Algerian nationalists organized the National Liberation Front (FLN) and in 1954 initiated a guerrilla war to liberate their homeland. The French people became so divided over this war that the French leader, Charles de Gaulle, accepted the inevitable and granted Algerian independence in 1962.

Decolonization in Africa south of the Sahara took place less turbulently. Ghana proclaimed its independence in 1957, and by 1960, almost all French and British possessions in Africa had gained their freedom. In 1960, the Belgians freed the Congo (the modern Democratic Republic of the Congo, formerly Zaire). The Portuguese held on stubbornly but were also driven out of Africa by 1975.

Nevertheless, the continuing European economic presence in sub-Saharan Africa led radicals to accuse Europeans of "neocolonial" attitudes.

Although expectations ran high in the new states, they soon found themselves beset with problems of extreme poverty and antagonistic tribal groups that felt little loyalty to the new nations. These states come to be known collectively as the "Third World" (the "First World" consisted of the advanced industrial countries—Japan and the states of Western Europe and North America—and the "Second World" comprised the Soviet Union and its satellites). Their status as "backward" nations led many Third World countries to modernize by pursuing Western technology and industrialization. In many instances, this has basically meant that these peoples have had to adjust to the continuing imposition of Western institutions and values upon their societies.

The Soviet Union: From Stalin to Khrushchev

World War II devastated the Soviet Union. To create a new industrial base, Stalin returned to the method that he had used in the 1930s—the acquisition of development capital from Soviet labor. Working hard for little pay, poor housing, and precious few consumer goods, Soviet laborers were expected to produce goods for export with little in return for themselves. The incoming capital from abroad could then be used to purchase machinery and Western technology. The loss of millions of men in the war meant that much of this tremendous workload fell upon Soviet women. Almost 40 percent of heavy manual labor was performed by women.

Economic recovery in the Soviet Union was nothing less than spectacular. By 1947, Russian industrial production had attained prewar levels; three years later, it had surpassed them by 40 percent. New power plants, canals, and giant factories were built, and new industries and oil fields were established in Siberia and Soviet central Asia. Stalin's newly announced five-year plan of 1946 reached its goals in less than five years.

Although Stalin's economic policy was successful in promoting growth in heavy industry, primarily for the benefit of the military, consumer goods were scarce. While the development of thermonuclear weapons in 1953, MIG fighters from 1950 to 1953, and the first space satellite (*Sputnik*) in 1957 elevated the Soviet state's reputation as a world power abroad, the Soviet people were shortchanged domestically. Heavy industry grew at a rate three times that of personal consumption. Moreover, the housing shortage was acute. A British military attaché in Moscow reported that "all houses, practically without exception, show lights from every window after dark. This seems to indicate that every room is both a living room by day and a bedroom by night. There is no place in overcrowded Moscow for the luxury of eating and sleeping in separate rooms."[6]

To sustain the war effort against the Germans, Stalin had fostered superpatriotism among all Soviets, but found that contact with Western ways during the war had shaken many people's belief in the superiority of the Soviet system. Returning Soviet soldiers brought back stories of the prosperity of the West, and the obvious disparity between the Western and Soviet systems led to a "crisis of faith" for many young Communists. Partly for this reason, Stalin imprisoned many soldiers, who were simply shipped from German concentration camps to Soviet concentration camps. In Stalin's view, Western influence was a threat to Communist ideals.

When World War II ended in 1945, Stalin had been in power for more than fifteen years. During that time, he had removed all opposition to his rule and remained the undisputed master of the Soviet Union. Other leading members of the Communist Party were completely obedient to his will. Increasingly distrustful of competitors, Stalin exercised sole authority and pitted his subordinates against one another.

Stalin's morbid suspicions fueled the constantly increasing repression that was a characteristic of his regime. In 1946, the government decreed that all literary and scientific works must conform to the political needs of the state. Along with this anti-intellectual campaign came political terror. A new series of purges seemed imminent in 1953 when a number of Jewish doctors were implicated in a spurious plot to kill high-level party officials. Only Stalin's death on March 5, 1953, prevented more bloodletting.

A new collective leadership succeeded Stalin until Nikita Khrushchev emerged as the chief Soviet policymaker. Khrushchev had been responsible for ending the system of forced-labor camps, a regular feature of Soviet life under Stalin. At the Twentieth Congress of the Communist Party in 1956, Khrushchev condemned Stalin for his "administrative violence, mass repression, and terror" (see the box on p. 860).

Once in power, Khrushchev took steps to undo some of the worst features of Stalin's repressive regime. A certain degree of intellectual freedom was now permitted; Khrushchev said that "readers should be given the chance to make their own judgments" regarding the acceptability of controversial literature and that "police measures shouldn't be used."[7] In 1962, he allowed the publication of Alexander Solzhenitsyn's *A Day in the Life of Ivan Denisovich*, a grim portrayal of the horrors of the forced-labor camps. Most importantly, Khrushchev extended the process of destalinization by reducing the powers of the secret police, freeing a number of political prisoners, and closing some of the Siberian prison camps. Nevertheless, when Khrushchev's revelations about Stalin at the Twentieth Congress created turmoil in Communist ranks everywhere and encouraged a spirit of rebellion in Soviet satellite countries in Eastern Europe, there was a reaction. Soviet troops crushed an uprising in Hungary in 1956 (see the next section on Eastern Europe), and Khrushchev and the Soviet leaders, fearful of further undermining the basic foundations of the regime, downplayed their campaign of destalinization.

Economically, Khrushchev tried to place more emphasis on light industry and consumer goods. Likewise, he encouraged the decentralization of agriculture by allowing more local decision making with less interference from Moscow. Khrushchev's attempts to increase agricultural output by growing corn and cultivating vast lands east of the Ural Mountains proved less successful and damaged his reputation within the party. These failures, combined with increased military spending, hurt the Soviet economy. The industrial growth rate, which had soared in the early 1950s, now declined dramatically from 13 percent in 1953 to 7.5 percent in 1964.

Khrushchev's personality also did not endear him to the higher Soviet officials who frowned at his tendency to crack jokes and play the clown. Nor were the higher members of the party bureaucracy pleased when Khrushchev tried to curb their privileges. Foreign policy failures caused additional damage to Khrushchev's

Khrushchev Denounces Stalin

Three years after the death of Stalin, the new Soviet premier, Nikita Khrushchev, addressed the Twentieth Congress of the Communist Party and denounced the former Soviet dictator for his crimes. This denunciation was the beginning of a policy of destalinization.

❄ Nikita Khrushchev Addresses the Twentieth Party Congress, February 1956

Comrades, . . . quite a lot has been said about the cult of the individual and about its harmful consequences. . . . The cult of the person of Stalin . . . became at a certain specific stage the source of a whole series of exceedingly serious and grave perversions of Party principles, of Party democracy, of revolutionary legality.

Stalin absolutely did not tolerate collegiality in leadership and in work and . . . practiced brutal violence, not only toward everything which opposed him, but also toward that which seemed to his capricious and despotic character, contrary to his concepts.

Stalin abandoned the method of ideological struggle for that of administrative violence, mass repressions and terror. . . . Arbitrary behavior by one person encouraged and permitted arbitrariness in others. Mass arrests and deportations of many thousands of people, execution without trial and without normal investigation created conditions of insecurity, fear and even desperation.

Stalin showed in a whole series of cases his intolerance, his brutality and his abuse of power. . . . He often chose the path of repression and annihilation, not only against actual enemies, but also against individuals who had not committed any crimes against the Party and the Soviet government. . . .

Many Party, Soviet and economic activists who were branded in 1937—8 as "enemies" were actually never enemies, spies, wreckers and so on, but were always honest communists; they were only so stigmatized, and often, no longer able to bear barbaric tortures, they charged themselves (at the order of the investigative judges-falsifiers) with all kinds of grave and unlikely crimes.

This was the result of the abuse of power by Stalin, who began to use mass terror against the Party cadres. . . . Stalin put the Party and the NKVD [the secret police] up to the use of mass terror when the exploiting classes had been liquidated in our country and when there were no serious reasons for the use of extraordinary mass terror. The terror was directed . . . against the honest workers of the Party and the Soviet state. . . .

Stalin was a very distrustful man, sickly suspicious. . . . Everywhere and in everything he saw "enemies," "two-facers" and "spies." Possessing unlimited power, he indulged in great willfulness and choked a person morally and physically. A situation was created where one could not express one's own will. When Stalin said that one or another would be arrested, it was necessary to accept on faith that he was an "enemy of the people." What proofs were offered? The confession of the arrested. . . . How is it possible that a person confesses to crimes that he had not committed? Only in one way —because of application of physical methods of pressuring him, tortures, bringing him to a state of unconsciousness, deprivation of his judgment, taking away of his human dignity.

---

reputation among his colleagues. His rash plan to place missiles in Cuba was the final straw. While he was away on vacation in 1964, a special meeting of the Soviet Politburo voted him out of office (because of "deteriorating health") and forced him into retirement. Although a group of leaders succeeded him, real power came into the hands of Leonid Brezhnev (1906–1982), the "trusted" supporter of Khrushchev who had engineered his downfall.

❄ *Eastern Europe: Behind the Iron Curtain*

At the end of World War II, Soviet military forces had occupied all of Eastern Europe and the Balkans (except Greece, Albania, and Yugoslavia). All of the occupied states came to be part of the Soviet sphere of influence and, after 1945, experienced similar political developments. Coalitions of all political parties (except fascist or right-wing parties) were formed to run the government, but within a year or two, the Communist parties in these coalitions had assumed the lion's share of power. The next step was the creation of one-party Communist governments. The timetables in these takeovers varied from country to country, but between 1945 and 1947, Communist governments became firmly entrenched in East Germany, Bulgaria, Romania, Poland, and Hungary. In Czechoslovakia, which had a strong tradition of democratic institutions, the Communists did not achieve their goals until 1948. In the elections of 1946, the Communist Party of Czechoslovakia had become the largest party. But it was not all-powerful and shared control of the government with the non-Communist parties. When it appeared that the latter might win new elections early in 1948, the Communists seized control of the government on February 25. All other parties were dissolved, and Klement Gottwald, the leader of the Communists, became the new president of Czechoslovakia.

KHRUSHCHEV'S VISIT TO YUGOSLAVIA. The leadership of Nikita Khrushchev appeared for a while to open the door to more flexible Soviet policies. In 1955, he visited Yugoslavia in an attempt to improve relations with a Communist state that had deviated from Soviet policies. Khrushchev is shown here making a conciliatory speech with Marshall Tito, the leader of Yugoslavia, looking on.

Albania and Yugoslavia were notable exceptions to this progression of Soviet dominance in Eastern Europe. Both had had strong Communist resistance movements during the war, and in both countries, the Communist Party simply took over power when the war ended. In Albania, local Communists established a rigidly Stalinist regime, but one that grew increasingly independent of the Soviet Union.

In Yugoslavia, Josip Broz, known as Tito (1892–1980), leader of the Communist resistance movement, seemed to be a loyal Stalinist. After the war, however, he moved toward the establishment of an independent Communist state in Yugoslavia. Stalin hoped to take control of Yugoslavia, just as he had done in other Eastern European countries, but Tito refused to capitulate to Stalin's demands and gained the support of the people by portraying the struggle as one of Yugoslav national freedom. In 1958, the Yugoslav party congress asserted that Yugoslav Communists did not see themselves as deviating from communism, only Stalinism. They considered their way closer to the Marxist-Leninist ideal. This included a more decentralized economic and political system in which workers could manage themselves and local communes could exercise some political power.

Between 1948 and Stalin's death in 1953, the Eastern European satellite states followed a policy of Stalinization. They instituted Soviet-type five-year plans with emphasis on heavy industry rather than consumer goods. They began to collectivize agriculture. They eliminated all non-Communist parties and established the institutions of repression—secret police and military forces. But communism—a foreign product—had not developed deep roots among the peoples of Eastern Europe. Moreover, Soviet economic exploitation of Eastern Europe made living conditions harsh for most people. The Soviets demanded reparations from their defeated wartime enemies Bulgaria, Romania, and Hungary—often in the form of confiscated plants and factories removed to the Soviet Union—and forced all of the Eastern European states to trade with the Soviet Union to the latter's advantage.

After Stalin's death, many Eastern European states began to pursue a new, more nationalistically oriented course, as the new Soviet leaders, including Khrushchev, interfered less in the internal affairs of their satellites. But in the late 1950s and 1960s, the Soviet Union also made it clear, particularly in Poland, Hungary, and Czechoslovakia, that it would not allow its Eastern European satellites to become independent of Soviet control.

In 1956, after the circulation of Khrushchev's denunciation of Stalin, protests—especially by workers—erupted in Poland. In response, the Polish Communist Party adopted a series of reforms in October 1956 and elected Wladyslaw Gomulka (1905–1982) as first secretary. Gomulka declared that Poland had the right to follow its own socialist path. Fearful of Soviet armed response, however, the Poles compromised. Poland pledged to remain loyal to the Warsaw Pact, and the Soviets agreed to allow Poland to follow its own path to

socialism. The Catholic church, an extremely important institution to many Poles, was also permitted to administer its own affairs.

The developments in Poland in 1956 inspired national Communists in Hungary to seek the same kinds of reforms and independence. Intense debates eventually resulted in the ouster of the ruling Stalinist and the selection of Imry Nagy (1896–1958) as the new Hungarian leader. Internal dissent, however, was not directed simply against the Soviets, but against communism in general, which was viewed as a creation of the Soviets, not the Hungarians. The Stalinist secret police had also bred much terror and hatred. This dissatisfaction, combined with economic difficulties, created a situation ripe for revolt. In order to quell the rising rebellion, Nagy declared Hungary a free nation on November 1, 1956. He promised free elections, and the mood of the country made it clear that this could mean the end of Communist rule in Hungary. But Khrushchev was in no position at home to allow a member of the Communist flock to leave. Just three days after Nagy's declaration, the Red Army attacked the capital city of Budapest (see the box on p. 863). The Soviets reestablished control over the country, and János Kádár (1912–1989), a reform-minded cabinet minister, replaced Nagy and worked with the Soviets to squash the revolt. By collaborating with the Soviet invaders, Kádár saved many of Nagy's economic reforms.

The developments in Poland and Hungary in 1956 did not generate similar revolts in Czechoslovakia. The "Little Stalin," Antonin Novotny (1904–1975), placed in power in 1952 by Stalin himself, remained firmly in control. By the late 1960s, however, Novotny had alienated many members of his own party and was particularly resented by Czechoslovakia's writers, such as the playwright Vaclav Havel (b. 1936). A writers' rebellion late in 1967, in fact, led to Novotny's resignation. In January 1968, Alexander Dubcek (1921–1992) was elected first secretary of the Communist Party and soon introduced a number of reforms, including freedom of speech and press, freedom to travel abroad, and a relaxation of secret police activities. Dubcek hoped to create "communism with a human face." A period of euphoria erupted that came to be known as the "Prague Spring."

It proved to be short-lived. This euphoria had led many to call for more far-reaching reforms, including neutrality and withdrawal from the Soviet bloc. To forestall the spreading of this "spring" fever, the Red Army invaded Czechoslovakia in August of 1968 and crushed the reform movement. Gustav Husák (b. 1913), a committed nonreformist, replaced Dubcek, crushed his reforms, and maintained the old order until the end of 1987.

❊ Western Europe: The Revival of Democracy and the Economy

All the countries of Western Europe faced similar kinds of problems at the end of World War II. They needed to rebuild their economies, recreate their democratic institutions, and face the growth of Communist parties.

The important role that Communists had played in the resistance movements against the Nazis gained them a new respectability and strength once the war was over. Communist parties did well in elections in Italy and France in 1946 and 1947 and even showed strength in some countries, such as Belgium and the Netherlands, where they had not been much of a political factor before the war. But Communist success was short-lived. After the hardening of the divisions in the Cold War, their advocacy of Soviet policies hurt the Communist parties at home, and their support began to dwindle. The Communist Party in Belgium, for example, received 14 percent of the vote in 1946, but only 4 percent in the 1960s. Only in France and Italy, where social inequities remained their focus, did Communist parties still garner significant support—about 25 percent of the vote.

As part of their electoral strategy, Communist parties had often joined forces with other left-wing parties, such as the Social Democrats. The Socialist parties had also fared well immediately after the war as the desire to overthrow the old order led to the abandonment of conservative parties. But support for the Socialists soon waned. In France, for example, Socialists won 23 percent of the vote in 1945, but 18 percent in 1946 and only 12.6 percent in 1962. The Cold War also hurt the cause of socialism. Socialist parties had originally been formed in the late nineteenth century as Marxist parties, and their identification with Communist parties in postwar coalitions cost them dearly. In the late 1950s, many Socialist parties on the Continent perceived the need to eliminate their old doctrinal emphasis on class struggle and began to call for social justice and liberty. Although they advocated economic and social planning, they no longer demanded the elimination of the capitalist system.

By 1950, moderate political parties had made a remarkable comeback in Western Europe. Especially important was the rise of Christian Democratic parties. The new Christian Democrats were not connected to the pre-

Soviet Repression in Eastern Europe: Hungary, 1956

Developments in Poland in 1956 inspired the Communist leaders of Hungary to begin to remove their country from Soviet control. But there were limits to Khrushchev's tolerance, and he sent Soviet troops to crush Hungary's movement for independence. The first selection is a statement by the Soviet government justifying the use of Soviet troops; the second is a brief and tragic final statement from Imry Nagy, the Hungarian leader.

✤ Statement of the Soviet Government, October 30, 1956

The Soviet Government regards it as indispensable to make a statement in connection with the events in Hungary.

The course of the events has shown that the working people of Hungary, who have achieved great progress on the basis of their people's democratic order, correctly raise the question of the necessity of eliminating serious shortcomings in the field of economic building, the further raising of the material well-being of the population, and the struggle against bureaucratic excesses in the state apparatus.

However, this just and progressive movement of the working people was soon joined by forces of black reaction and counterrevolution, which are trying to take advantage of the discontent of part of the working people to undermine the foundations of the people's democratic order in Hungary and to restore the old landlord and capitalist order.

The Soviet Government and all the Soviet people deeply regret that the development of events in Hungary has led to bloodshed. On the request of the Hungarian People's Government the Soviet Government consented to the entry into Budapest of the Soviet Army units to assist the Hungarian People's Army and the Hungarian authorities to establish order in the town.

✤ The Last Message of Imry Nagy, November 4, 1956

This fight is the fight for freedom by the Hungarian people against the Russian intervention, and it is possible that I shall only be able to stay at my post for one or two hours. The whole world will see how the Russian armed forces, contrary to all treaties and conventions, are crushing the resistance of the Hungarian people. They will also see how they are kidnapping the Prime Minister of a country which is a Member of the United Nations, taking him from the capital, and therefore it cannot be doubted at all that this is the most brutal form of intervention. I should like in these last moments to ask the leaders of the revolution, if they can, to leave the country. I ask that all that I have said in my broadcast, and what we have agreed on with the revolutionary leaders during meetings in Parliament, should be put in a memorandum, and the leaders should turn to all the peoples of the world for help and explain that today it is Hungary and tomorrow, or the day after tomorrow, it will be the turn of other countries because the imperialism of Moscow does not know borders, and is only trying to play for time.

---

war church-based parties that had been advocates of church interests and had crusaded against both liberal and socialist causes. The new Christian Democrats were sincerely interested in democracy and in significant economic reforms. They were especially strong in Italy and Germany and played a particularly important role in achieving Europe's economic restoration.

Western European countries recovered relatively rapidly from the devastation of World War II. No doubt, the Marshall Plan played a significant role in this process. Between 1947 and 1950, European countries received $9.4 billion to be used for new equipment and raw materials. By 1950, industrial output in Europe was 30 percent above prewar levels. Between 1947 and 1950, steel production alone expanded by 70 percent. And this economic recovery continued well into the 1950s and 1960s. The decades of the 1950s and 1960s were periods of dramatic economic growth and prosperity in Western Europe. Indeed, Western Europe experienced virtually full employment during these decades.

SOVIET INVASION OF CZECHOSLOVAKIA, 1968. The attempt of Alexander Dubcek, the new first secretary of the Communist Party, to liberalize Communist rule in Czechoslovakia failed when Soviet troops invaded and crushed the reform movement. This photograph shows a confrontation between Soviet tanks and Czechs in Prague. The tanks won.

The history of France for nearly a quarter century after the war was dominated by one man—Charles de Gaulle (1890–1970)—who possessed an unshakable faith that he had a historical mission to reestablish the greatness of the French nation. During the war, de Gaulle had assumed leadership of some resistance groups and played an important role in ensuring the establishment of a French provisional government after the war. The creation of the Fourth Republic, with a return to a parliamentary system based on parties that de Gaulle considered weak, led him to withdraw from politics. Eventually, he formed the "French Popular Movement," a decidedly rightist organization. It blamed the parties for France's political mess and called for an even stronger presidency, a goal that de Gaulle finally achieved in 1958.

The fragile political stability of the Fourth Republic had been badly shaken by the Algerian crisis. The French army had suffered defeat in Indochina in 1954 and was determined to resist Algerian demands for independence. But a strong antiwar movement among French intellectuals and church leaders led to bitter divisions within France. The army's unwillingness to accept anything but complete victory in Algeria led some French army officers to instigate a revolt against their own government and open the door to the possibility of civil war in France. The panic-stricken leaders of the Fourth Republic offered to let de Gaulle take over the government and revise the constitution.

In 1958, de Gaulle immediately drafted a new constitution for the Fifth Republic that greatly enhanced the power of the president, who now had the right to choose the prime minister, dissolve parliament, and supervise both defense and foreign policy. DeGaulle had always believed in strong leadership, and the new Fifth Republic was by no means a democratic system. As the new president, de Gaulle sought to return France to the position of a great power. He believed that playing a pivotal role in the Cold War might enhance France's stature. For that reason, he pulled France out of the NATO high command. He increased French prestige among the Third World countries by consenting to Algerian independence despite strenuous opposition from the army. With an eye toward achieving the status of a world power, de Gaulle invested heavily in the nuclear arms race. France exploded its first nuclear bomb in 1960. Despite his successes, de Gaulle did not really achieve his ambitious goals of world power. Although his successors maintained that France was the "third nuclear power" after the United States and the Soviet Union, in truth France was too small for such global ambitions.

Although the cost of the nuclear program increased the defense budget, de Gaulle did not neglect the French economy. Economic decision making was centralized, a reflection of the overall centralization undertaken by the Gaullist government. Between 1958 and 1968, the French gross national product increased by 5.5 percent annually,

CHARLES DE GAULLE. As president, Charles de Gaulle sought to revive the greatness of the French nation. He is shown here dressed in his military uniform participating in a formal state ceremony.

faster than the U.S. economy was growing. By the end of de Gaulle's era, France was a major industrial producer and exporter, particularly in such areas as automobiles and armaments. Nevertheless, problems remained. France failed to build the hospitals, houses, and schools that it needed. Moreover, the expansion of traditional industries, such as coal, steel, and railroads, which had all been nationalized (put under government ownership), led to large government deficits. The cost of living increased faster than in the rest of Europe. Consumer prices were 45 percent higher in 1968 than they had been ten years earlier.

Increased dissatisfaction with the inability of de Gaulle's government to deal with these problems soon led to more violent action. In May 1968, a series of student protests, followed by a general strike by the labor unions, shook the government. Although de Gaulle managed to restore order, the events of May 1968 had seriously undermined the French people's respect for their aloof and imperious president. Tired and discouraged, de Gaulle resigned from office in April 1969 and died within a year.

⚜ WEST GERMANY: A NEW NATION?

Already by the end of 1945, the Western powers (the United States, Britain, and France) occupying Germany had allowed the reemergence of political parties in their zones. Three major parties came forth: the Social Democrats (SPD), the Christian Democrats (CDU), and the Free Democrats (FDP). Over the next three years, the

Affordable health care for all people was another goal of the welfare state, although the methods of achieving this goal varied. In Britain, Italy, and Germany, for example, medical care was free to all people with some kind of insurance, but in France, the Scandinavian countries, Belgium, and Switzerland, people had to contribute toward the cost of their medical care. The amount ranged from 10 to 25 percent of the total cost.

Two other features of welfare states were family allowances and new educational policies. Family allowances were instituted in some countries to provide a minimum level of material care for children. Most family allowance programs provided a fixed amount per child. In 1964, for example, France granted $60 per month per child, Italy $24, and Britain only $10. Welfare states also sought to remove class barriers to opportunity by expanding the number of universities and providing scholarship aid to allow everyone to attend these institutions of higher learning. Overall, European states moved toward free tuition or modest fees for university attendance. These policies did not always achieve their goals, however. In the early 1960s, most students in Western European universities still came from privileged backgrounds. In Britain, 25 percent of university students came from working-class backgrounds; in France, the figure was only 17.6 percent.

The welfare state dramatically increased the amount of money states expended on social services. In 1967, such spending constituted 17 percent of the gross national product of the major European countries; by the 1980s, it absorbed 40 to 50 percent. To some critics, these figures proved that the welfare state had produced a new generation of citizens overly dependent on the state. But most people favored the benefits, and most leaders were well aware that it was political suicide to advocate curtailing or seriously lowering those benefits.

Gender issues also influenced the form that the welfare state took in different countries. One general question dominated the debate: Should women be recognized in a special category as mothers, or should they be regarded as individuals? William Beveridge, the economist who drafted the report that formed the basis for the British welfare state, said that women had "vital work to do in ensuring the adequate continuance of the British race." "During marriage," he said, "most women will not be gainfully employed. The small minority of women who undertake paid employment or other gainful employment or other gainful occupations after marriage require special treatment differing from that of single women."[8] Accordingly, the British welfare system was based on the belief that women should stay home with their children: women received subsidies for children, but married women who worked were given few or no benefits. Employers were also encouraged to pay women lower wages to discourage them from joining the workforce. Thus, the British welfare system encouraged the dependence of wives on their husbands. So, too, did the West German system. The West German government passed laws that discouraged women from working. In keeping its women at home, West Germany sought to differentiate itself from neighboring Communist countries in Eastern Europe and the Soviet Union, where women were encouraged to work outside the home. At the same time, to help women who worked to have children, Communist governments also provided day-care facilities as well as family subsidies and maternity benefits.

France sought to maintain the individual rights of women in its welfare system. The French government recognized women as equal to men and thus as entitled to the same welfare benefits as men for working outside the home. At the same time, wanting to encourage population growth, the government provided incentives for women to stay home and bear children as well as day care and after-school programs for working mothers.

❋ New (and Old) Patterns: Women in the Postwar Western World

Despite their enormous contributions to the war effort, women were removed from the workforce at the end of World War II to provide jobs for the soldiers returning home. After the horrors of war, people seemed willing for a while to return to traditional family practices. Female participation in the workforce declined, and birthrates began to rise, creating a "baby boom." This increase in the birthrate did not last, however, and birthrates, and thus the size of families, began to decline by the end of the 1950s. Largely responsible for this decline was the widespread practice of birth control. Invented in the nineteenth century, the condom was already in wide use, but the development in the 1960s of oral contraceptives, known as birth control pills, provided a reliable means of birth control that quickly spread to all Western countries.

No doubt, the trend toward smaller families contributed to the change in the character of women's employment in both Europe and the United States as women experienced considerably more years when they were not involved in rearing children. The most important development was the increased number of married women in the workforce. At the beginning of the twentieth century, even working-class wives tended to stay at home if they could afford to do so. In the postwar period, this was no longer the case. In the United States, for example, in 1900, married women made up about 15 percent of the female labor force; by 1970, their number had increased to 62 percent. The percentage of married women in the female labor force in Sweden increased from 47 to 66 percent between 1963 and 1975. Figures for the Soviet Union and its satellites were even higher. In 1970, 92.5 percent of all women in the Soviet Union held jobs compared to around 50 percent in France and West Germany. The industrial development of the Soviet Union relied on female labor.

But the increased number of women in the workforce did not change some old patterns. Working-class women in particular still earned salaries lower than those of men for equal work. In the 1960s, women earned only 60 percent of men's wages in Britain, 50 percent in France, and 63 percent in West Germany. In addition, women still tended to enter traditionally female jobs. As one Swedish female guidance counselor remarked in 1975: "Every girl now thinks in terms of a job. This is progress. They want children, but they don't pin their hopes on marriage. They don't intend to be housewives for some future husband. But there has been no change in their vocational choices."[9] Many European women also still faced the double burden of earning income on the one hand and raising a family and maintaining the household on the other. Such inequalities led increasing numbers of women to rebel.

THE FEMINIST MOVEMENT: THE SEARCH FOR LIBERATION

The participation of women in World War I and II helped them achieve one of the major aims of the nineteenth-century women's movement—the right to vote. Already after World War I, many governments acknowledged the contributions of women to the war effort by granting them the right to vote. Sweden, Great Britain, Germany, Poland, Hungary, Austria, and Czechoslovakia did so in 1918, followed by the United States in 1920. Women in France and Italy did not obtain the right to vote until 1945. After World War II, European women tended to fall back into the traditional roles expected of them, and little was heard of feminist concerns. But by the late 1960s, women began to assert their rights again and speak as feminists. Along with the student upheavals of the late 1960s came renewed interest in feminism, or the women's liberation movement, as it was now called. Increasingly, women protested that the acquisition of political and legal equality had not brought true equality with men:

> We are economically oppressed: in jobs we do full work for half pay, in the home we do unpaid work full time. We are commercially exploited by advertisement, television, and the press; legally, we often have only the status of children. We are brought up to feel inadequate, educated to narrower horizons than men. This is our specific oppression as women. It is as women that we are, therefore, organizing.[10]

These were the words of a British Women's Liberation Workshop in 1969.

Of great importance to the emergence of the postwar women's liberation movement was the work of Simone de Beauvoir (1908–1986). Born into a Catholic middle-class family and educated at the Sorbonne in Paris, she supported herself as a teacher and later as a novelist and writer. She maintained a lifelong relationship (but not marriage) with Jean-Paul Sartre. Her involvement in the existentialist movement—the leading intellectual movement of the time—led to her involvement in political causes. De Beauvoir believed that she lived a "liberated" life for a twentieth-century European woman, but for all her freedom, she still came to perceive that as a woman she faced limits that men did not. In 1949, she published her highly influential work, *The Second Sex*, in which she argued that as a result of male-dominated societies, women had been defined by their differences from men and consequently received second-class status: "What peculiarly signalizes the situation of woman is that she—a free and autonomous being like all human creatures—nevertheless finds herself living in a world where men compel her to assume the status of the Other."[11] De Beauvoir took an active role in the French women's movement of the 1970s, and her book was a major influence on both the American and European women's movements (see the box on p. 873)

Another important contributor to the growth of a women's movement in the 1960s was Betty Friedan (b. 1921). A journalist and the mother of three children, Friedan grew increasingly uneasy with her attempt to fulfill the traditional role of the "ideal housewife and mother." In 1963, she published *The Feminine Mystique*, in which she analyzed the problems of middle-class American women in the 1950s and argued that women were being denied equality with men. She wrote: "The problem that has no name—which is simply the fact that American women are kept from growing to their full human capacities—is taking a far greater toll on the physical and mental health of our country than any known disease."[12]

WOMEN'S LIBERATION MOVEMENT. In the late 1960s, as women began once again to assert their rights, a revived women's liberation movement emerged. Feminists in the movement maintained that women themselves must alter the conditions of their lives. During this women's liberation rally, some women climbed the statue of Admiral Farragut in Washington, D.C., to exhibit their signs.

The Voice of the Women's Liberation Movement

Simone de Beauvoir was an important figure in the emergence of the postwar women's liberation movement. This excerpt is taken from her influential book, The Second Sex, *in which she argued that women have been forced into a position subordinate to men.*

✺ Simone de Beauvoir, *The Second Sex*

Now, woman has always been man's dependent, if not his slave; the two sexes have never shared the world in equality. And even today woman is heavily handicapped, though her situation is beginning to change. Almost nowhere is her legal status the same as man's and frequently it is much to her disadvantage. Even when her rights are legally recognized in the abstract, long-standing custom prevents their full expression in the mores. In the economic sphere men and women can almost be said to make up two castes; other things being equal, the former hold the better jobs, get higher wages, and have more opportunity for success than their new competitors. In industry and politics men have a great many more positions and they monopolize the most important posts. In addition to all this they enjoy a traditional prestige that the education of children tends in every way to support, for the present enshrines the past—and in the past all history has been made by men. At the present time, when women are beginning to take part in the affairs of the world, it is still a world that belongs to men—they have no doubt of it at all and

women have scarcely any. To decline to be the Other, to refuse to be a party to a deal—this would be for women to renounce all the advantages conferred upon them by their alliance with the superior caste. Man-the-sovereign will provide woman-the-liege with material protection and will undertake the moral justification of her existence; thus she can evade at once both economic risk and the metaphysical risk of a liberty in which ends and aims must be contrived without assistance. Indeed, along with the ethical urge of each individual to affirm his subjective existence, there is also the temptation to forgo liberty and become a thing. This is an inauspicious road, for he who takes it—passive, lost, ruined— becomes henceforth the creature of another's will, frustrated in his transcendence and deprived of every value. But it is an easy road; on it one avoids the strain involved in undertaking an authentic existence. When man makes of woman the *Other* he may, then, expect her to manifest deep-seated tendencies toward complicity. Thus woman may fail to lay claim to the status of subject because she lacks definite resources, because she feels the necessary bond that ties her to man regardless of reciprocity, and because she is often very well pleased with her role as the *Other*.

Now, what peculiarly signalizes the situation of woman is that she—a free and autonomous being like all human creatures—nevertheless finds herself living in a world where men compel her to assume the status of the Other.

The Feminine Mystique became a best-seller and propelled Friedan into a newfound celebrity. In 1966, she founded the National Organization of Women (NOW), whose stated goal was to take "action to bring women into full participation in the mainstream of American society *now*, exercising all the privileges and responsibilities thereof in truly equal partnership with men." Friedan's voice was also prominent in calling for the addition to the U.S. Constitution of an equal rights amendment for women.

✺ *The Permissive Society*

The "permissive society" was yet another term used by critics to describe the new society of postwar Europe. World War I had seen the first significant crack in the rigid code of manners and morals of the nineteenth century. Subsequently, the 1920s had witnessed experimentation with drugs, the appearance of hard-core pornography, and a new sexual freedom (police in Berlin, for example, issued cards that permitted female and male homosexual prostitutes to practice their trade). But these indications of a

new attitude appeared mostly in major cities and touched only small numbers of people. After World War II, changes in manners and morals were far more extensive and far more noticeable.

Sweden took the lead in the propagation of the so-called sexual revolution of the 1960s, and the rest of Europe and the United States soon followed. Sex education in the schools and the decriminalization of homosexuality were but two aspects of Sweden's liberal legislation. The introduction of the birth control pill, which became widely available by the mid-1960s, gave people more freedom in sexual behavior. Meanwhile, sexually explicit movies, plays, and books broke new ground in the treatment of once-hidden subjects. Cities like Amsterdam, which allowed open prostitution and the public sale of hard-core pornography, attracted thousands of curious tourists.

The new standards were evident in the breakdown of the traditional family. Divorce rates increased dramatically, especially in the 1960s, and premarital and extramarital sexual experiences also rose substantially. A survey in the Netherlands in 1968 revealed that 78

THE "LOVE-IN." In the 1960s, a number of outdoor public festivals for young people combined music, drugs, and sex. Flamboyant dress, facial painting, free-form dancing, and drugs were vital ingredients in creating an atmosphere dedicated to "love and peace." Shown here is a "love-in" that was held on the grounds of an English country estate in the Summer of Love, 1967.

percent of men and 86 percent of women had engaged in extramarital sex. The appearance of *Playboy* magazine in the 1950s also added a new dimension to the sexual revolution for adult males. Along with photographs of nude women, *Playboy* offered well-written articles on various aspects of masculinity. *Playboy*'s message was clear: men were encouraged to seek sexual gratification outside marriage.

The decade of the 1960s also saw the emergence of a drug culture. Marijuana was widely used among college and university students as the recreational drug of choice. For young people more interested in mind expansion into higher levels of consciousness, Timothy Leary, who had done psychedelic research at Harvard on the effects of LSD (lysergic acid diethylamide), became the high priest of hallucinogenic experiences.

New attitudes toward sex and the use of drugs were only two manifestations of a growing youth movement in the 1960s that questioned authority and fostered rebellion against the older generation. Spurred on by the Vietnam War and a growing political consciousness, the youth rebellion became a youth protest movement by the second half of the 1960s (see the box on p. 875).

❋ *Education and Student Revolt*

Before World War II, higher education had largely remained the preserve of Europe's wealthier classes. Even in 1950, for example, only 3 or 4 percent of West European young people were enrolled in a university. In addition, European higher education remained largely centered on the liberal arts, pure science, and preparation for the professions of law and medicine.

Much of this changed after World War II. European states began to foster greater equality of opportunity in higher education by reducing or eliminating fees, and universities experienced an influx of students from the middle and lower classes. Enrollments grew dramatically; in France, 4.5 percent of young people attended a university in 1950. By 1965, the figure had increased to 14.5 percent. Enrollments in European universities more than tripled between 1940 and 1960.

But there were problems. Classrooms with too many students, professors who paid little attention to their students, and administrators who acted in an authoritarian fashion led to student resentment. In addition, despite changes in the curriculum, students often felt that the universities were not providing an education relevant to the realities of the modern age. This discontent led to an outburst of student revolts in the late 1960s (see the box on p. 876). In part, these protests were an extension of the spontaneous disruptions in American universities in the mid-1960s, which were often sparked by student opposition to the Vietnam War. Perhaps the most famous student revolt occurred in France in 1968. It erupted at the University of Nanterre outside Paris but soon spread to the Sorbonne, the main campus of the University of Paris. French students demanded a greater voice in the administration of the university, took over buildings, and then expanded the scale of their protests by inviting workers to support them. Half of France's workforce went on strike in May 1968. After the Gaullist government instituted a hefty wage hike, the workers returned to work and the police repressed the remaining student protesters.

The French revolt spurred student protests elsewhere in Europe, although none of them succeeded in becoming

"The Times They Are a-Changin'": The Music of Youthful Protest

In the 1960s, the lyrics of rock music reflected the rebellious mood of many young people. Bob Dylan (b. 1941), a well-known recording artist, expressed the feelings of the younger generation. His song, "The Times They Are a-Changin'," released in 1964, has been called an "anthem for the protest movement."

✻ Bob Dylan, *The Times They Are a-Changin'*

Come gather round people
Wherever you roam
And admit that the waters
Around you have grown
And accept it that soon
You'll be drenched to the bone
If your time to you
Is worth savin'
Then you better start swimmin'
Or you'll sink like a stone
For the times they are a-changin'

Come writers and critics
Who prophesize with your pen
And keep your eyes wide
The chance won't come again
And don't speak too soon
For the wheel's still in spin
And there's no tellin' who
That it's namin'
For the loser now
Will be later to win
For the times they are a-changin'

Come senators, congressmen
please heed the call

Don't stand in the doorway
Don't block up the hall
For he that gets hurt
Will be he who has stalled
There's a battle outside
And it is ragin'
It'll soon shake your windows
And rattle your walls
For the times they are a-changin'

Come mothers and fathers
Throughout the land
And don't criticize
What you can't understand
Your sons and your daughters
Are beyond your command
Your old road
Is rapidly agin'
Please get out of the new one
If you can't lend your hand
For the times they are a-changin'

The line it is drawn
The curse it is cast
The slow one now
Will later be fast
As the present now
Will later be past
The order is
Rapidly fadin'
And the first one now
Will later be last
For the times they are a-changin'

---

mass movements. In West Berlin, university students led a protest against Axel Springer, leader of Germany's largest newspaper establishment. Many German students were motivated by a desire to destroy what they considered to be the corrupt old order and were especially influenced by the ideas of the German-American social philosopher, Herbert Marcuse. In *One-Dimensional Man*, published in 1964, Marcuse argued that capitalism had undermined the dissatisfaction of the oppressed masses by encouraging the consumption of material things. He proposed that a small cadre of unindoctrinated students could liberate the masses from the control of the capitalist ruling class. But the German students' attempt at revolutionary violence backfired as angry Berliners supported police repression of the students.

The student protest movement reached its high point in 1968, although scattered incidents lasted into the early 1970s. There were several reasons for the student radicalism. Some students were genuinely motivated by the desire to reform the university. Others were protesting the Vietnam War, which they viewed as a product of Western imperialism. They also attacked other aspects of Western society, such as its materialism, and expressed concern about becoming cogs in the large and impersonal bureaucratic jungles of the modern world. For many students, the calls for democratic decision making within the universities were a reflection of their deeper concerns about the direction of Western society. Although student revolts fizzled out in the 1970s, the larger issues they raised were increasingly revived in the 1990s.

1968: The Year of Student Revolts

The outburst of student upheavals in the late 1960s reached its high point in 1968. These two very different selections illustrate some of the issues that prompted university students to occupy campus buildings and demand reforms.

❋ A Student Manifesto in Search of a Real and Human Educational Alternative (University of British Columbia), June 1968

Today we as students are witnessing a deepening crisis within our society. We are intensely aware, in a way perhaps not possible for the older generation, that humanity stands on the edge of a new era. Because we are young, we have insights into the present and visions of the future that our parents do not have. Tasks of an immense gravity wait solution in our generation. We have inherited these tasks from our parents. We do not blame them so much for that . . . but we do blame them for being unwilling to admit that there are problems or for saying that it is we who have visited these problems on ourselves because of our perversity, ungratefulness and unwillingness to listen to "reason."

Much of the burden of solving the problems of the new era rests on the university. We have been taught to look to it for leadership. While we know that part of the reason for the university is to render direct services to the community, we are alarmed at its servility to industry and government as to what and how it teaches. We are scandalized that the university fails to realize its role in renewing and vivifying those intellectual and moral energies necessary to create a new society—one in which a sense of personal dignity and human community can be preserved.

❋ Student Inscriptions on the Walls of Paris, May and June 1968

The dream is the reality.
May 1968. World revolution is the order of the day.
I decree a state of permanent happiness.
To be free in 1968 is to take part.
Take the trip every day of your life.
Make love, not war.
No exams.
The mind travels farther than the heart but it doesn't go as far.
Run, comrade, the old are behind you!
Don't make a revolution in the image of your confused and hide-bound university.
Exam = servility, social promotion, hierarchic society.
Love each other.
SEX. It's good, said Mao, but not too often.
Alcohol kills. Take LSD.
Are you consumers or participants?
Professors, you are as old as your culture; your modernism is only the modernization of the police.
Live in the present.
Revolution, I love you.
    Long live direct democracy!

STUDENT REVOLT IN PARIS, 1968. The discontent of university students exploded in the late 1960s in a series of student revolts. Perhaps best known was the movement in Paris in 1968. This photograph shows the barricades erected on a Parisian street on the morning of May 11 during the height of the revolt.

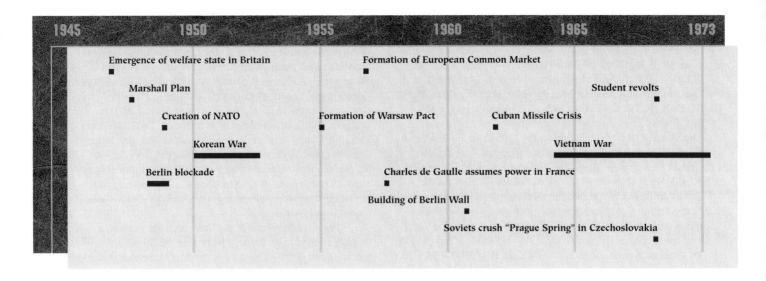

| 1945 | 1950 | 1955 | 1960 | 1965 | 1973 |

Emergence of welfare state in Britain

Formation of European Common Market

Marshall Plan

Student revolts

Creation of NATO

Formation of Warsaw Pact

Cuban Missile Crisis

Korean War

Vietnam War

Berlin blockade

Charles de Gaulle assumes power in France

Building of Berlin Wall

Soviets crush "Prague Spring" in Czechoslovakia

CONCLUSION

At the end of World War II, a new conflict erupted in the Western world as the two new superpowers, the United States and the Soviet Union, competed for political domination. Europeans, whether they wanted to or not, were forced to become supporters of one side or the other. But this ideological division also spread to the rest of the world as the United States fought in Korea and Vietnam to prevent the spread of communism, and the Soviet Union used its armies to prop up pro-Soviet regimes in Eastern Europe.

In addition to the Cold War conflict, the postwar era was characterized by decolonization and the creation of a new Europe. After World War II, the colonial empires of the European states were largely dissolved, and the liberated territories of Africa, Asia, and the Middle East emerged as sovereign states. By the late 1980s, the approximately 160 sovereign states of the world would become an emerging global community.

Western Europe also became a new community in the 1950s and the 1960s. Although Western Europeans staged a remarkable economic recovery, the Cuban Missile Crisis made it clear that their future still depended on the conflict between the two superpowers. At the same time, the student protests of the late 1960s caused many to rethink some of their basic assumptions. And yet, looking back, the student upheavals were not a "turning point in the history of postwar Europe," as some people thought at the time. In the 1970s and 1980s, student rebels would become middle-class professionals, and the vision of a revolutionary politics would remain mostly a memory.

NOTES

1. Quoted in Joseph M. Jones, *The Fifteen Weeks (February 21–June 5, 1947)*, 2d ed. (New York, 1964), pp. 140–141.
2. Quoted in Walter Laqueur, *Europe in Our Time* (New York, 1992), p. 111.
3. Quoted in Wilfried Loth, *The Division of the World, 1941–1955* (New York, 1988), pp. 160–161.
4. Quoted in Peter Lane, *Europe since 1945: An Introduction* (Totowa, N.J., 1985), p. 248.
5. Quoted in Robert F. Kennedy, *Thirteen Days: A Memoir of the Cuban Missile Crisis* (New York, 1969), pp. 89–90.
6. R. Hilton, *Military Attaché in Moscow* (London, 1949), p. 41.
7. Nikita Khrushchev, *Khrushchev Remembers*, trans. Strobe Talbott (Boston, 1970), p. 77.
8. Quoted in Bonnie G. Smith, *Changing Lives: Women in European History since 1700* (Lexington, Mass., 1989), p. 513.
9. Quoted in Hilda Scott, *Sweden's 'Right to be Human'—Sex-Role Equality: The Goal and the Reality* (London, 1982), p. 125.
10. Quoted in Marsha Rowe et al., *Spare Rib Reader* (Harmondsworth, 1982), p. 574.
11. Simone de Beauvoir, *The Second Sex*, trans. H. M. Parshley (New York, 1961), p. xxviii.
12. Betty Friedan, *The Feminine Mystique*, (New York, 1963), p. 10.

SUGGESTIONS FOR FURTHER READING

Three introductory surveys on postwar Europe are P. Lane, *Europe since 1945: An Introduction* (Totowa, N.J., 1985); J. R. Wegs, *Europe since 1945: A Concise History*, 2d ed. (New York, 1984); and W. Laqueur, *Europe in Our Time* (New York, 1992). There is a detailed literature on the Cold War. A general account is J. W. Langdon, *A Hard and Bitter Peace: A Global*

History of the Cold War (Englewood Cliffs, N.J., 1995). Two brief works on the entire Cold War are J. H. Mason, *The Cold War* (New York, 1996); and J. Smith, *The Cold War, 1945–1991* (Oxford, 1998). For an illustrated history, see J. Isaacs and T. Downing, *Cold War: An Illustrated History, 1945–1991* (Boston, 1998). There is a brief survey of the early Cold War in M. Dockrill, *The Cold War 1945–1963* (Atlantic Highlands, N.J., 1988). The following works maintain that the Soviet Union was chiefly responsible for the Cold War: H. Feis, *From Trust to Terror: The Onset of the Cold War, 1945–1950* (New York, 1970); and A. Ulam, *The Rivals: America and Russia since World War II* (New York, 1971). Revisionist studies on the Cold War have emphasized the responsibility of the United States for the Cold War, especially its global aspects. These works include J. and G. Kolko, *The Limits of Power: The World and United States Foreign Policy, 1945–1954* (New York, 1972); W. LaFeber, *America, Russia and the Cold War, 1945–1966*, 2d ed. (New York, 1972); and M. Sherwin, *A World Destroyed: The Atomic Bomb and the Grand Alliance* (New York, 1975). For a critique of the revisionist studies, see R. L. Maddox, *The New Left and the Origins of the Cold War* (Princeton, N.J., 1973). For a study of Soviet foreign policy, see J. L. Nogee, *Soviet Foreign Policy since World War I*, 4th ed. (New York, 1992). The effects of the Cold War on Germany are examined in J. H. Backer, *The Decision to Divide Germany: American Foreign Policy in Transition* (Durham, N.C., 1978). For a good introduction to the arms race, see E. M. Bottome, *The Balance of Terror: A Guide to the Arms Race*, rev. ed. (Boston, 1986). On the Cuban Missile Crisis, see R. A. Chayes, *The Cuban Missile Crisis* (New York, 1974). On decolonization after World War II, see R. F. Betts, *Decolonization* (London, 1998).

For a general view of Soviet society, see D. K. Shipler, *Russia: Broken Idols, Solemn Dreams* (New York, 1983). On the Khrushchev years, see C. A. Linden, *Khrushchev and the Soviet Leadership* (Baltimore, 1990). For a general study of the Soviet satellites in Eastern Europe, see A. Brown and J. Gary, *Culture and Political Changes in Communist States* (London, 1977). On the Soviet Union's actions against Czechoslovakia in 1968, see J. Valenta, *Intervention in Czechoslovakia in 1968* (Baltimore, 1991). The unique path of Yugoslavia is examined in L. J. Cohen and P. Warwick, *Political Cohesion in a Fragile Mosaic: The Yugoslav Experience* (Boulder, Colo., 1983). On Romania, see L. S. Graham, *Rumania: A Developing Socialist State* (Boulder, Colo., 1978). On Hungary, see B. Kovrig, *The Hungarian People's Republic* (Baltimore, 1970). On East Germany, see C. B. Scharf, *Politics and Change in East Germany* (Boulder, Colo., 1984).

The rebuilding of postwar Europe is examined in A. S. Milward, *The Reconstruction of Western Europe, 1945–51* (Berkeley, 1984); and M. Hogan, *The Marshall Plan: America,* *Britain, and the Reconstruction of Western Europe, 1947–1952* (New York, 1987). On the building of common institutions in Western Europe, see S. Henig, *The Uniting of Europe: From Discord to Concord* (London, 1997). For surveys of West Germany, see H. A. Turner, *Germany from Partition to Reunification* (New Haven, Conn., 1992); and T. G. Ash, *In Europe's Name: Germany and the Enduring Balance* (New York, 1993). France under de Gaulle is examined in A. Shennen, *De Gaulle* (New York, 1993); and D. J. Mahoney, *De Gaulle: Statesmanship, Grandeur, and Modern Democracy* (Westport, Conn., 1996). On Britain, see K. O. Morgan, *The People's Peace: British History 1945–1990* (Oxford, 1992). On Italy, see P. Ginsbourg, *A History of Contemporary Italy: Society and Politics, 1943–1988* (New York, 1990).

The student revolts of the late 1960s are put into a broader context in D. Caute, *The Year of the Barricades: A Journey through 1968* (New York, 1988). On the welfare state, see A. de Swann, *In Care of the State: Health Care, Education, and Welfare in Europe and the United States in the Modern Era* (New York, 1988). On women and the welfare state, see E. Wilson, *Women and the Welfare State* (London, 1977); and D. Sainsbury, ed., *Gendering Welfare States* (London, 1994). On the women's liberation movement, see D. Bouchier, *The Feminist Challenge: The Movement for Women's Liberation in Britain and the United States* (New York, 1983); D. Meyer, *Sex and Power: The Rise of Women in America, Russia, Sweden, and Italy* (Middletown, Conn., 1987); T. Keefe, *Simone de Beauvoir* (New York, 1998); and C. Duchen, *Women's Rights and Women's Lives in France, 1944–1968* (New York, 1994). More general works that include much information on the contemporary period are B. G. Smith, *Changing Lives: Women in European History since 1700* (Lexington, Mass., 1989); and F. Thebuad, ed., *A History of Women in the West*, vol. 5: *Toward a Cultural Identity in the Twentieth Century* (Cambridge, Mass., 1994).

For additional reading, go to InfoTrac College Edition, your online research library at http://web1.infotrac-college.com

Enter the search terms *Cold War* using the Subject Guide.

Enter the search terms *Soviet Union relations with the United States* using the Subject Guide.

Enter the search term *decolonization* using Key Terms.

Enter the search term *Khrushchev* using Key Terms.

CHAPTER

29

The Contemporary Western World (since 1970)

CHAPTER OUTLINE

- From Cold War to Post–Cold War: Toward a New World Order?
- Toward a New Western Order
- New Directions and New Problems in Western Society
- The World of Western Culture
- Toward a Global Civilization?

FOCUS QUESTIONS

- How and why did the Cold War end?
- What reforms did Gorbachev institute in the Soviet Union, and what role did he play in the Soviet Union's demise?
- What changes have occurred in Eastern Europe as a result of the revolutions of 1989?
- What are the major political and social developments in Western Europe and North America since 1970?
- What major cultural and intellectual trends have emerged since 1970?

*B*ETWEEN 1945 AND 1970, Europe not only recovered from the devastating effects of World War II, but also experienced an economic recovery that seemed nothing less than miraculous to many people. Some historians have even labeled the years from 1950 to 1973 "the golden age of the European economy." Economic growth and virtually full employment continued so long that the first postwar recession in 1973 came as a shock to Western Europe.

By that time, too, after more than two decades of the Cold War, Europeans had become accustomed to a new division of Europe between West and East. A prosperous Western Europe allied to the United States stood opposed to a still-struggling Eastern Europe that remained largely subject to the Soviet Union. The division of Germany symbolized the new order that seemed so well established. And yet, within two decades, a revolutionary upheaval in the Soviet Union and Eastern Europe brought an end to the Cold War and ended the long-standing division of postwar Europe. Even the Soviet Union ceased to exist as a single nation. On August 19, 1991, a group of Soviet leaders opposed to reform arrested Mikhail Gorbachev, the president of the Soviet Union, and tried to seize control of the government. Hundreds of thousands of

Russians, led by Boris Yeltsin, poured into the streets of Moscow and Leningrad to resist the attempted coup. Some army units, sent out to enforce the wishes of the rebels, defected to Yeltsin's side, and within days, the rebels were forced to surrender. This failed attempt to seize power had unexpected results as Russia and a host of other Soviet states declared their independence. By the end of 1991, the Soviet Union—one of the largest empires in world history—had come to an end, and a new era of cooperation between the successor states in the old Soviet Union and the nations of the West had begun.

In the midst of the transformation from Cold War to post–Cold War, other changes also shaped a new Western world. New artistic and intellectual currents, the growth of science and technology, a religious revival, new threats from terrorists, the realization of environmental problems, the surge of a women's liberation movement—all of these spoke of a vibrant, ever-changing, and yet challenging new world.

◆ From Cold War to Post–Cold War: Toward a New World Order?

By the 1970s, American-Soviet relations had entered a new phase known as détente, which was marked by a reduction of tensions between the two superpowers. In the late 1970s, however, the apparent collapse of détente initiated a new period of East-West confrontation. But after the accession of Mikhail Gorbachev in 1985, the Soviet Union began to make changes in its foreign policy, and the Cold War came rapidly to an end.

An appropriate symbol of détente was the Antiballistic Missiles (ABM) Treaty in 1972. Despite some lessening of tensions after the Cuban Missile Crisis, both the Soviet Union and the United States had continued to expand their nuclear arsenals. In the 1960s, both nations sought to extend the destructive power of their missiles by arming them with multiple warheads. By 1970, Americans had developed the capacity to arm their intercontinental ballistic missiles (ICBMs) with "multiple independently targeted re-entry vehicles" (MIRVs) that enabled one missile to hit ten different targets. The Soviet Union soon followed suit. Between 1968 and 1972, both sides had also developed antiballistic missiles (ABMs), whose purpose was to hit and destroy incoming missiles. In the 1972 ABM Treaty, the two nations agreed to limit their antiballistic missile systems.

In 1975, the Helsinki Agreements provided yet another example of reduced tensions between the superpowers. Signed by the United States, Canada, and all European nations, these accords recognized all borders in central and eastern Europe that had been established since the end of World War II, thereby acknowledging the Soviet sphere of influence in Eastern Europe. The Helsinki Agreements also committed the signatory powers to recognize and protect the human rights of their citizens.

This protection of human rights became one of the major foreign policy goals of the next American president, Jimmy Carter (b. 1924). Although hopes ran high for the continuation of détente, the Soviet invasion of Afghanistan in 1979, undertaken to restore a pro-Soviet regime, hardened relations between the United States and the Soviet Union. President Carter canceled American participation in the 1980 Olympic Games held in Moscow and placed an embargo on the shipment of American grain to the Soviet Union.

The early administration of President Ronald Reagan (b. 1911) witnessed a return to the harsh rhetoric, if not all of the harsh practices, of the Cold War. Calling the Soviet Union an "evil empire," Reagan began a military buildup that stimulated a renewed arms race. In 1982, the Reagan administration introduced the nuclear-tipped cruise missile, whose ability to fly at low altitudes made it difficult to detect. President Reagan also became an ardent proponent of the Strategic Defense Initiative (SDI), nicknamed "Star Wars." Its purpose was to create a space shield that could destroy incoming missiles. By providing military support to the Afghan insurgents, the Reagan administration helped to maintain a Vietnam-like war in Afghanistan that the Soviet Union could not win. Like the Vietnam War, the war in Afghanistan demonstrated that the power of a superpower was actually limited in the face of strong nationalist, guerrilla-type opposition.

✻ The End of the Cold War

The accession of Mikhail Gorbachev (b. 1931) to power in the Soviet Union (see The Gorbachev Era later in this chapter) in 1985 eventually brought a dramatic end to the Cold War. Gorbachev was willing to rethink many of the fundamental assumptions underlying Soviet foreign policy, and his "New Thinking," as it was called, opened the door to a series of stunning changes. For one, Gorbachev initiated a plan for arms limitation that led in 1987 to an agreement with the United States to eliminate intermediate-range nuclear weapons (the INF Treaty). Both sides had incentives to dampen the expensive arms race. Gorbachev hoped to make extensive economic and internal reforms, and the United States had serious deficit problems. During the Reagan years, the United States had moved from being a creditor nation to being the world's biggest debtor nation. By 1990, both countries were becoming aware that their large military budgets made it difficult for them to solve their serious social problems.

The years 1989 and 1990 were a crucial period in the ending of the Cold War. The postwar settlements that had become the norm in central and eastern Europe came unstuck as a mostly peaceful revolutionary upheaval swept through Eastern Europe. Gorbachev's policy of

REAGAN AND GORBACHEV. The willingness of Mikhail Gorbachev and Ronald Reagan to dampen the arms race was a significant factor in ending the Cold War confrontation between the United States and the Soviet Union. Reagan and Gorbachev are shown here standing before St. Basil's Cathedral during Reagan's visit to Moscow in 1988.

allowing greater autonomy for the Communist regimes of Eastern Europe meant that the Soviet Union would no longer militarily support Communist governments that were faced with internal revolt. The unwillingness of the Soviet regime to use force to maintain the status quo, as it had in Hungary in 1956 and in Czechoslovakia in 1968, opened the door to the overthrow of the Communist regimes (see Eastern Europe: The Collapse of the Communist Order later in this chapter). On October 3, 1990, the reunification of Germany destroyed one of the most prominent symbols of the Cold War era.

The Gulf War provided the first major opportunity for testing the new relationship between the United States and the Soviet Union in the post–Cold War era. In early August 1990, Iraqi military forces suddenly moved across the border and occupied the small neighboring country of Kuwait in the northeastern corner of the Arabian peninsula at the head of the Persian Gulf. The immediate pretext was Iraq's claim that Kuwait was pumping oil from fields inside Iraqi territory, but the deeper reason was the former's contention that Kuwait was legally a part of Iraq. The Iraqi invasion of Kuwait sparked an international outcry and the creation of an international force led by the United States that liberated Kuwait and destroyed a substantial part of Iraq's armed forces in the early months of 1991.

The Gulf War was the first important military conflict in the post–Cold War period. Although Mikhail Gorbachev made some attempt to persuade Iraq to withdraw its forces from Kuwait before the war began, overall the Soviets played a minor role in the crisis and supported the American action. By the end of 1991, the Soviet Union had disintegrated, making any renewal of global rivalry between two competing superpowers impossible. Although the United States emerged as the world's leading military power by 1992, its role in the creation of the "New World Order" that President George Bush advocated at the time of the Gulf War was not clear. After some hesitation, President

Bill Clinton (b. 1946) began to reassert American power in the world. He sent American troops to Haiti in September 1994 to restore that country's fragile democratic system. In December 1995, the United States took the lead in bringing a negotiated end to the war in Bosnia. As part of the agreement signed by the warring parties, 20,000 American troops were sent to the region as part of a NATO military presence intended to enforce the peace. In 1999, the United States tried to arrange a settlement between Yugoslavia and the Kosovo Liberation Army. When Slobodan Milošević, the Yugoslavian president, refused to accept a peace plan, the United States and its NATO allies began a bombing campaign against Yugoslavia to force it to cooperate (see The War in Kosovo later in this chapter).

◆ Toward a New Western Order

Between 1945 and 1970, economic recovery had brought renewed growth to Europe. Nevertheless, the political divisions between Western and Eastern Europe remained; so, too, did the disparity in levels of prosperity. But in the late 1980s and early 1990s, the Soviet Union and its Eastern European satellite states underwent a revolutionary upheaval that dramatically altered the European scene and left many Europeans with both new hopes and new fears.

❋ The Revolutionary Era in the Soviet Union

Between 1964 and 1982, revolutionary change in the Soviet Union appeared highly unlikely. The man in charge—Leonid Brezhnev (1906–1982)—had as his slogan "no experimentation." Brezhnev had entered the ranks of the party leadership under Stalin and, after the overthrow of Khrushchev in 1964, had become head of both party and state. He was always optimistic, yet reluctant to reform. Overall, the Brezhnev years were relatively calm, although the Brezhnev doctrine—the right of the Soviet Union to intervene if socialism was threatened in another "socialist state"—became an article of faith and led to the use of Soviet troops in Czechoslovakia in 1968.

Brezhnev benefited from the more relaxed atmosphere associated with détente. The Soviets had reached a rough parity with the United States in nuclear arms and enjoyed a sense of external security that seemed to allow for a relaxation of authoritarian rule. The regime permitted more access to Western styles of music, dress, and art, although dissenters were still punished. Andrei Sakharov, for example, who had played an important role in the development of the Soviet hydrogen bomb, was placed under house arrest for his defense of human rights.

In his economic policies, Brezhnev continued to emphasize heavy industry. Overall industrial growth declined, although the Soviet production of iron, steel, coal, and cement surpassed that of the United States. Two problems bedeviled the Soviet economy. The government's insistence on vigorous central planning led to a huge, complex bureaucracy that discouraged efficiency and reduced productivity. Moreover, the Soviet system, based on guaranteed employment and a lack of incentives, bred apathy, complacency, absenteeism, and drunkenness.

Agricultural problems added to Soviet economic woes. Collective farmers lacked incentives. Many preferred working their own small private plots to laboring in the collective work brigades. To make matters worse, bad harvests in the mid-1970s, caused by a series of droughts, heavy rains, and early frosts, forced the Soviet government to buy grain from the West, particularly the United States. To their chagrin, the Soviets were increasingly dependent on capitalist countries.

By the 1970s, the Soviet Union had developed a ruling system that depended on patronage as a major avenue of advancement. Those who aspired to rise in the party and the state bureaucracy needed the support of successful party leaders. At the same time, party and state leaders—as well as leaders of the army and the secret police (KGB)—received awards and numerous material privileges. Brezhnev was unwilling to tamper with the party leadership and state bureaucracy despite the inefficiency and corruption that the system encouraged. Increasingly, the lack of vigorous leadership in the Soviet Union was becoming all too apparent and difficult to rectify.

By 1980, the Soviet Union was seriously ailing. A declining economy, a rise in infant mortality rates, a dramatic surge in alcoholism, and a deterioration in working conditions all gave impetus to a decline in morale and a growing perception that the system was foundering. Within the party, a small group of reformers emerged who understood the real condition of the Soviet Union. One member of this group was Yuri Andropov (1914–1985), head of the KGB and successor to Brezhnev after the latter's death in November 1982. But Andropov was already old and in poor health when he came to power, and he was unable to make any substantive changes. His most significant move may have been his support for a young reformer—Mikhail Gorbachev—who was climbing the rungs of the party ladder. Finally, after a brief interlude under Konstantin Chernenko (1911–1985)—another old and ailing member of the Soviet leadership—a new era began when party leaders chose Gorbachev to succeed Chernenko in March 1985.

❧ THE GORBACHEV ERA

Born into a peasant family in 1931, Mikhail Gorbachev combined farm work with school and received the Order of the Red Banner for his agricultural efforts. This award and his good school record enabled him to study law at the University of Moscow. After receiving his law degree in 1955, he returned to his native southern Russia, where he eventually became first secretary of the Communist Party in the city of Stavropol (he had joined the Communist Party in 1952) and then first secretary of the regional party committee. In 1978, Gorbachev was made a member of the party's Central Committee in Moscow. Two years later, he became a full member of the ruling Politburo and secretary of the Central Committee. In March 1985, party leaders elected him general secretary of the party, and he became the new leader of the Soviet Union.

Educated during the reform years of Khrushchev, Gorbachev seemed intent on taking earlier reforms to their logical conclusions. By the 1980s, Soviet economic problems were obvious. Rigid, centralized planning led to mismanagement and stifled innovation. Although the Soviets still excelled in space exploration, they fell behind the West in high technology, especially in the development and production of computers for private and public use. Most noticeable to the Soviet people was the actual decline in the standard of living. In February 1986, at the Twenty-Seventh Congress of the Communist Party, Gorbachev made clear the need for changes in Soviet society: "The practical actions of the Party and state agencies lag behind the demands of the times and of life itself. . . . Problems grow faster than they are solved. Sluggishness, ossification in the forms, and methods of management decrease the dynamism of work. . . . Stagnation begins to

show up in the life of society."[1] Thus, from the start, Gorbachev preached the need for radical reforms.

The cornerstone of Gorbachev's radical reforms was *perestroika* or "restructuring" (see the box on p. 884). At first this meant only a reordering of economic policy as Gorbachev called for the beginning of a market economy with limited free enterprise and some private property. His initial economic reforms proved difficult to implement, however. Radicals demanded decisive measures; conservatives feared that rapid changes would be too painful. In his attempt to compromise, Gorbachev often pursued partial liberalization, which satisfied neither faction and also failed to work, producing only more discontent.

Gorbachev soon perceived that in the Soviet system, the economic sphere was intimately tied to the social and political spheres. Attempts to reform the economy without political or social reform would be doomed to failure. One of the most important instruments of *perestroika* was *glasnost* or "openness." Soviet citizens and officials were encouraged to discuss openly the strengths and weaknesses of the Soviet Union. *Pravda*, the official newspaper

MAP 29.1   The New Europe.

Gorbachev and Perestroika

After assuming the leadership of the Soviet Union in 1985, Mikhail Gorbachev worked to liberalize and restructure the country. His policies opened the door to rapid changes in Eastern Europe and in Soviet-American relations at the end of the 1980s. In his book Perestroika, *Gorbachev explained some of his "New Thinking."*

✳ Mikhail Gorbachev, *Perestroika*

The fundamental principle of the new political outlook is very simple: *nuclear war cannot be a means of achieving political, economic, ideological or any other goals.* This conclusion is truly revolutionary, for it means discarding the traditional notions of war and peace. It is the political function of war that has always been a justification for war, a "rational" explanation. Nuclear war is senseless; it is irrational. There would be neither winners nor losers in a global nuclear conflict: world Civilization would inevitably perish. . . .

But military technology has developed to such an extent that even a non-nuclear war would now be comparable with a nuclear war in its destructive effect. That is why it is logical to include in our category of nuclear wars this "variant" of an armed clash between major powers as well.

Thereby, an altogether different situation has emerged. A way of thinking and a way of acting, based on the use of force in world politics, have formed over centuries, even millennia. It seems they have taken root as something unshakable. Today, they have lost all reasonable grounds . . . . For the first time in history, basing international politics on moral and ethical norms that are common to all humankind, as well as humanizing interstate relations, has become a vital requirement. . . .

There is a great thirst for mutual understanding and mutual communication in the world. It is felt among politicians, it is gaining momentum among the intelligentsia, representatives of culture, and the public at large. And if the Russian word "perestroika" has easily entered the international lexicon, this is due to more than just interest in what is going on in the Soviet Union. Now the whole world needs restructuring, i.e., progressive development, a fundamental change.

People feel this and understand this. They have to find their bearings, to understand the problems besetting mankind, to realize how they should live in the future. The restructuring is a must for a world overflowing with nuclear weapons; for a world ridden with serious economic and ecological problems; for a world laden with poverty, backwardness and disease; for a human race now facing the urgent need of ensuring its own survival.

We are all students, and our teacher is life and time. I believe that more and more people will come to realize that through RESTRUCTURING in the broad sense of the word, the integrity of the world will be enhanced. Having earned good marks from our main teacher—life—we shall enter the twenty-first century well prepared and sure that there will be further progress.

---

of the Communist Party, began to include reports of official corruption, sloppy factory work, and protests against government policy. The arts also benefited from the new policy as previously banned works were now published, and motion pictures began to show negative aspects of Soviet life. Music based on Western styles, such as jazz and rock, began to be performed openly.

Political reforms were equally revolutionary. In June 1987, the principle of two-candidate elections was introduced; previously, voters had been presented with only one candidate. Most dissidents, including Andrei Sakharov, who had spent years in internal exile, were released. At the Communist Party conference in 1988, Gorbachev called for the creation of a new Soviet parliament, the Congress of People's Deputies, whose members were to be chosen in competitive elections. It convened in 1989, the first such meeting in Russia since 1918. Early in 1990, Gorbachev legalized the formation of other political parties and struck Article 6, which had guaranteed the "leading role" of the Communist Party, from the Soviet constitution. At the same time, Gorbachev attempted to consolidate his power by creating a new state presidency. The new position was a consequence of the separation of the state from the Communist Party. Hitherto, the position of first secretary of the party had been the most important post in the Soviet Union, but as the Communist Party became less closely associated with the state, the powers of this office diminished correspondingly. In March 1990, Gorbachev became the Soviet Union's first president.

One of Gorbachev's most serious problems stemmed from the character of the Soviet Union. The Union of Soviet Socialist Republics was a truly multiethnic country, containing 92 nationalities and 112 recognized languages. Previously, the iron hand of the Communist Party, centered in Moscow, had kept a lid on the centuries-old ethnic tensions that had periodically erupted. As Gorbachev released this iron grip, tensions resurfaced, a by-product of *glasnost* that Gorbachev had not anticipated. Ethnic groups took advantage of the new openness to protest what they perceived to be ethnically motivated slights. As violence erupted, the Soviet army, in disrepair since Afghanistan, had difficulty controlling the situation.

The period 1988 to 1990 also witnessed the appearance of nationalist movements throughout the republics of the Soviet Union. Many were motivated by ethnic concerns, with calls for sovereignty of the republics and

A ROMANIAN REVOLUTIONARY. The revolt against Communist rule in Eastern Europe in 1989 came last to Romania. It was also more violent as the government at first tried to stem the revolt by massacring demonstrators. This picture shows a young Romanian rebel waving the national flag with the Communist emblem cut out of the center.

AND THE WALL CAME TUMBLING DOWN. The Berlin Wall, long a symbol of Europe's Cold War divisions, became the site of massive celebrations after the East German government opened its border with the West. The activities included spontaneous acts of demolition as Germans used sledgehammers and crowbars to tear down parts of the wall.

ties had emerged, and on March 18, 1990, in East Germany's first free elections ever, the Christian Democrats won almost 50 percent of the vote.

The Christian Democrats supported rapid monetary unification followed shortly by political unification with West Germany. On July 1, 1990, the economies of West and East Germany were united with the West German deutsche mark becoming the official currency of the two countries. Political reunification was achieved on October 3, 1990. What had seemed almost impossible at the beginning of 1989 had become a reality by the end of 1990—the country of East Germany had ceased to exist.

THE WAR IN BOSNIA. By mid-1993, irregular Serb forces had overrun much of Bosnia-Herzegovina amid scenes of untold suffering. This photograph shows two brothers in Sarajevo, the Bosnian capital, holding each other and weeping during the funeral of a third brother.

❊ *The Disintegration of Yugoslavia*

From its beginning in 1919, Yugoslavia had been an artificial creation. After World War II, the dictatorial Tito had managed to hold the six republics and two autonomous provinces that constituted Yugoslavia together. After his death in 1980, no strong leader emerged, and his responsibilities passed to a collective state presidency and the League of Communists of Yugoslavia. At the end of the 1980s, Yugoslavia was caught up in the reform movements sweeping through Eastern Europe. On January 20, 1990, the League of Communists called for the creation of a pluralistic political system with freedom of speech, other civil liberties, and free elections. But divisions between Slovenes who wanted a loose federation and Serbians who wanted to retain the centralized system caused the collapse of the party congress, and hence the Communist Party. New parties quickly emerged.

The Yugoslav political scene was complicated by the development of separatist movements that brought the disintegration of Yugoslavia in the 1990s. When new non-Communist parties won elections in 1990 in the republics of Slovenia, Croatia, Bosnia-Herzegovina, and the Former Yugoslav Republic of Macedonia, they began to lobby for a new federal structure of Yugoslavia that would fulfill their separatist desires. Slobodan Milošević, who had become the leader of the Serbian Communist Party in 1987 and had managed to stay in power by emphasizing his Serbian nationalism, rejected these efforts. He maintained that these republics could only be independent if new border arrangements were made to accommodate the Serb minorities in those republics who did not want to live outside the boundaries of a Greater Serbian state. Serbs constituted 11.6 percent of Croatia's population and 32 percent of Bosnia-Herzegovina's population in 1981.

After negotiations among the six republics failed, Slovenia and Croatia declared their independence in June 1991. Milošević's government sent the Yugoslavian army, which it controlled, into Slovenia, but without much success. In September 1991, it began a full assault against Croatia. Increasingly, the Yugoslavian army was becoming the Serbian army, while Serbian irregular forces played a growing role in military operations. Before a cease-fire was arranged, the Serbian forces had captured one-third of Croatia's territory in brutal and destructive fighting.

The recognition of Slovenia, Croatia, and Bosnia-Herzegovina by many European states and the United States early in 1992 did not stop the Serbs from turning their guns on Bosnia-Herzegovina. By mid-1993, Serbian forces had acquired 70 percent of Bosnian territory (see the box on p. 893. The Serbian policy of "ethnic cleansing"—killing or forcibly removing Bosnian Muslims from their lands—revived memories of Nazi atrocities in World War II. Nevertheless, despite worldwide outrage, European governments failed to take a decisive and forceful stand against these Serbian activities. By 1995, 250,000 Bosnians (mostly civilians) had been killed, and two million others were left homeless, often driven from their homes by "ethnic cleansing."

The Bosnian Serbs seemed well in control of Bosnia until 1995 when a sudden turn of events occurred. New offensives by mostly Muslim Bosnian government army forces and by the Croatian army regained considerable territory that had been lost to Serbian forces. Air strikes by NATO bombers, strongly advocated by President Bill Clinton, were launched in retaliation for Serb attacks on civilians and weakened the Serb military positions. All sides were now encouraged by the United States to end the war and met in Dayton, Ohio, in November 1995 for negotiations. A formal peace treaty, based on the Dayton accords, was signed in Paris on December 14. The

THE WAR IN KOSOVO. In 1999, war erupted in Yugoslavia as Slobodan Milošević pursued a ruthless policy of ethnic cleansing in the province of Kosovo. Serbian troops forced hundreds of thousands of ethnic Albanians to flee their homeland in terror. This photograph shows ethnic Albanian refugees moving into a temporary relief camp after crossing the border into Macedonia on April 24, 1999.

agreement split Bosnia into a loose union of a Serb republic (with 49 percent of the land) and a Muslim-Croat federation (with 51 percent of the land). NATO agreed to send a force of 60,000 troops (20,000 American troops made up the largest single contingent) that would monitor the frontier between the new political entities. It remained to be seen whether the agreement would bring a lasting peace to war-torn Bosnia.

THE WAR IN KOSOVO

Peace in Bosnia, however, did not bring peace to the lands of former Yugoslavia. A new war erupted in 1999 over Kosovo, which had been made an autonomous province within Yugoslavia by Marshall Tito in 1974. Kosovo's inhabitants were mainly ethnic Albanians who were allowed to keep their Albanian language. But Kosovo also contained a Serbian minority who considered Kosovo a sacred territory because it contained the site where Serbian forces had been defeated by the Ottoman Turks in the fourteenth century in a battle that became a defining moment in Serbian history.

In 1989, Slobodan Milošević, the Yugoslav president, who had become an ardent Serbian nationalist to remain in power, stripped Kosovo of its autonomous status and outlawed any official use of the Albanian language. Many Kosovo Albanians favored forming an independent

republic, a move that was strongly opposed by Milošević. In 1993, some groups of ethnic Albanians founded a Kosovo Liberation Army (KLA) and began a campaign against Serbian rule in Kosovo. When Serb forces began to massacre ethnic Albanians in an effort to crush the KLA, the United States and its NATO allies sought to arrange a settlement. After months of negotiations, the Kosovo Albanians agreed to a peace plan that would have given the ethnic Albanians in Kosovo broad autonomy for a three-year interim period. When Milošević refused to sign the agreement, the United States and its NATO allies began a bombing campaign to force the Yugoslavian government to cooperate. Instead, Serb forces in Kosovo began a ruthless campaign of ethnic cleansing, forcing hundreds of thousands of ethnic Albanians to flee their homeland.

✳ After the Fall

The fall of Communist governments in Eastern Europe during the revolutions of 1989 brought a wave of euphoria to Europe. The new structures meant an end to a postwar European order that had been imposed on unwilling peoples by the victorious forces of the Soviet Union. In 1989 and 1990, new governments throughout Eastern

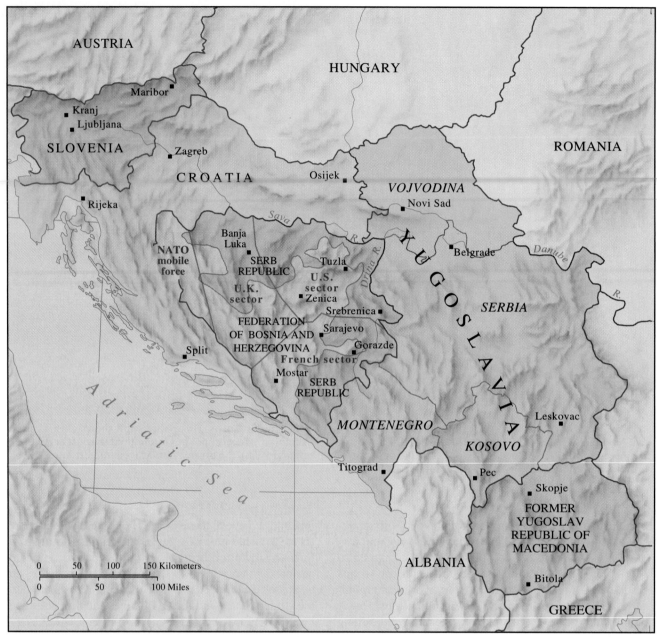

MAP 29.2   **The Lands of Former Yugoslavia.**

Europe worked diligently to scrap the remnants of the old system and introduce the democratic procedures and market systems that they believed would revitalize their scarred lands. But this process proved to be neither simple nor easy, and the mood of euphoria had largely faded by the mid-1990s.

Most Eastern European countries had little or virtually no experience with democratic systems. Moreover, most people had had little or no chance under Communist rule to participate in public life in general and in democratic debate in particular. Then, too, ethnic divisions, which had troubled these areas before World War II and had been forcibly submerged under Communist rule, reemerged with a vengeance, making political unity almost impossible. Though Czechoslovakia resolved its differ-

ences peacefully, Yugoslavia descended into the kind of brutal warfare that had not been seen in Europe since World War II. In the lands of the former Soviet Union, ethnic and nationalist problems threatened to tear some of the new states apart.

The rapid conversion to market economies also proved painful. The adoption of "shock-therapy" austerity measures produced much suffering and uncertainty. Unemployment climbed to over 15 percent in the former East Germany and 13 percent in Poland in 1992. Wages remained low while prices skyrocketed. Russia experienced a 2,000 percent inflation rate in 1992. At the same time, in many countries former Communists were able to retain important positions of power or become the new owners of private property. Resentment against former

Bosnia: Two Faces of War

In April 1993, Serbian forces surrounded the Muslim town of Srebrenica in eastern Bosnia. After ferocious shelling by the Serbs, the town appeared ready to surrender. On April 17, 1993, newspapers in Sarajevo (the capital of Bosnia-Herzegovina) and Belgrade (the capital of Serbia) gave their readers very different versions of what was happening in Srebrenica.

❋ *Olsobodjenje (Sarajevo)*

Tomorrow, a Canadian battalion serving with the United Nations Protection Force should enter Srebrenica as a result of negotiations between Lieut. Gen. Lars-Eric Wahlgren, commander of the U.N. force, and the war criminal Karadzic [Radovan Karadzic, leader of the Bosnian Serbs]. A Golgotha continues for the citizens of Srebrenica. . . . Zlatko Lagumdzija, the Deputy Prime Minister of Bosnia and Herzegovina, has told the world that Mladic's army [General Ratko Mladic, commander of the Bosnian Serb forces], that is Milošević's army [President Slobodan Milošević of Serbia], has to be stopped, that the only thing that the aggressor army understands is force, and that the only way it can be stopped is by confronting it with a greater force. . . . The aggressor forces continued their offensive at Srebrenica throughout the day yesterday with undiminished intensity, and the people of the town continued to give a heroic account of themselves in resisting the attempt by the more numerous and better-armed attackers to penetrate the town's outskirts. Besides their push across the front lines, the Chetniks [Serbian forces] continued to use their heavy artillery to shell the center of Srebrenica, massacring civilians. During the morning hours alone, the Chetnik artillery killed six people and injured 15, including several children. In Tuzla . . . local and foreign reporters were presented with a transcript of an intercepted radio-telephone conversation between war crimi-

nal Mladic and the Chetnik commanders in the area . . . in which he ordered them to press the attacks so as to enter Srebrenica before he began his negotiations on a cease-fire.

❋ *Politika (Belgrade)*

In spite of the fact that the Muslim armed forces are facing a total military defeat, they again launched attacks this morning from various directions from the territory of Srebrenica. According to Tanjug [Yugoslav news agency] reporting from this region, the Muslim units are using all their artillery and firing equipment. The Serbian sources say that Serbian defenders had tens of dead and wounded following attacks by Muslim forces which lasted for days. The army of the Republika Srpska [the name Serb nationalists gave to their self-proclaimed government in Bosnia] was forced to respond strongly in a counterattack and it has reached strategically important peaks around Srebrenica. The Serbian lines are only about one kilometer by air from Srebrenica. Using the fact that the Serbian side is not undertaking any action against Srebrenica itself, the Muslim extremists continued to attack. During the morning the most severe attacks of the Muslims were launched on Ratkovic, Zeleni Jadar, Podravanje and Milici. According to Tanjug, the Serbian sources are reporting that Muslim soldiers have started surrendering arms yesterday. There were such individual cases in the region of Skelani, Bratunac, Derventa and Podravanje. The Muslim extremists are in a hopeless situation from the military point of view. They are still reluctant to surrender because they were the ones to destroy 56 Serbian villages near Srebrenica, Bratunac and Skelani and on several occasions have killed in a most brutal way more than 1,300 Serbs, mostly women, children and aged people.

Communists created yet another source of social instability. For both political and economic reasons, the new non-Communist states of Eastern Europe faced dangerous and uncertain futures. Nevertheless, by the end of the twentieth century, some of these states, especially Poland and the Czech Republic, were making a successful transition to both free markets and democracy.

❋ *Western Europe: The Winds of Change*

After two decades of incredible economic growth, Europe experienced severe economic recessions in the mid-1970s and early 1980s (specifically, 1973–1974 and 1979–1983). Both inflation and unemployment rose dramatically. No doubt, the substantial increase in the price of oil that fol-

lowed the Arab-Israeli conflict in 1973 was a major cause for the first downturn. But other factors were present as well. A worldwide recession had led to a decline in demand for European goods, and in Europe itself the reconstruction of many European cities after their devastation in World War II had largely been completed. The economies of the Western European states recovered in the course of the 1980s, although problems remained. Unemployment was still high, even after almost a decade of growth. France had a 10.6 unemployment rate in 1993; it reached 11.7 percent by the end of 1995. Nevertheless, despite their economic woes, Western Europeans were full participants in the technological growth of the age and seemed quite capable of standing up to American and Japanese economic competition.

Europeans also moved toward further integration of their economies after 1970. The European Economic Community expanded in 1973 when Great Britain, Ireland, and Denmark joined what its members now began to call the European Community (EC). By 1986, three additional members—Spain, Portugal, and Greece—had been added. The economic integration of the members of the European Community led to cooperative efforts in international and political affairs as well. The foreign ministers of the twelve members consulted frequently and provided a common front for negotiations on important issues.

Nevertheless, the European Community was still primarily an economic union, not a political one. By 1992, the European Community comprised 344 million people and constituted the world's largest single trading entity, transacting almost one-fourth of the world's commerce. In the 1980s and 1990s, the European Community moved toward even greater economic integration. The Treaty on European Union (also called the Maastricht Treaty after the city in the Netherlands where the agreement was reached) represented an attempt to create a true economic and monetary union of all European Community members. The treaty did not go into effect until all members agreed. Finally, on January 1, 1994, the European Community became the European Union. One of its first goals was to introduce a common currency, called the "euro," a goal that was met for eleven of the European Union nations early in 1999.

Politically, Western Europe had also become accustomed to democracy. Even Spain and Portugal, which had maintained their prewar dictatorial regimes until the mid-1970s, established democratic systems in the late 1970s. Western European Communist Parties also declined drastically. During the mid-1970s, a new variety of Communism called Eurocommunism briefly emerged as Communist Parties tried to work within the democratic system as mass movements committed to better government. But by the 1980s, internal political developments in Western Europe and events within the Communist world itself had combined to undermine the Eurocommunist experiment.

✄ FROM WEST GERMANY TO GERMANY

After the Adenauer era, German voters moved politically from the center-right politics of the Christian Democrats to center-left politics, and in 1969, the Social Democrats became the leading party. By forming a ruling coalition with the small Free Democratic Party (FPD), the Social Democrats remained in power until 1982. The first Social Democratic chancellor was Willy Brandt (1913–1992). Brandt was especially successful with his "opening toward the east" (known as *Ostpolitik*), for which he received the Nobel Peace Prize in 1972. In the same year, Brandt made a Basic Treaty with East Germany that called for "good neighborly" relations, which soon led to greater cultural, personal, and economic contacts between West and East Germany. Despite this success, the discovery of an East German spy among Brandt's advisers caused his resignation in 1974.

His successor, Helmut Schmidt (b. 1918), was more of a technocrat than a reform-minded socialist and concentrated primarily on the economic problems largely brought about by high oil prices between 1973 and 1975. Schmidt was successful in eliminating a deficit of 10 billion marks in three years. In 1982, when the coalition of Schmidt's Social Democrats with the Free Democrats fell apart over the reduction of social welfare expenditures, the Free Democrats joined with the Christian Democratic Union of Helmut Kohl (b. 1930) to form a new government.

Helmut Kohl was a clever politician who benefited greatly from an economic boom in the mid-1980s. Gradually, however, discontent with the Christian Democrats increased, and, by 1988, their political prospects seemed diminished. But unexpectedly, the 1989 revolution in East Germany led to the reunification of the two Germanies, leaving the new Germany with its 79 million people the leading power in Europe. Reunification, accomplished during Kohl's administration, brought rich political dividends to the Christian Democrats. In the first all-German federal election, Kohl's Christian Democrats won 44 percent of the vote, while their coalition partners—the Free Democrats—received 11 percent.

But the excitement over reunification soon dissipated as new problems arose. All too soon, the realization set in that the revitalization of eastern Germany would take far more money than was originally thought, and Kohl's government was soon forced to face the politically undesirable task of raising taxes substantially. Moreover, the virtual collapse of the economy in eastern Germany led to extremely high levels of unemployment and severe discontent. One of the responses was a return to power for the Social Democrats as a result of elections in 1998.

✄ GREAT BRITAIN: THATCHER AND THATCHERISM

Between 1964 and 1979, Conservatives and Labour alternated in power in Britain. Both parties had to deal with bitter conflict between Catholics and Protestants in Northern Ireland. Violence increased as the Irish Republican Army (IRA) staged a series of dramatic terrorist acts in response to the suspension of Northern Ireland's parliament in 1972 and the establishment of direct rule by London. The problems in Northern Ireland have not yet been solved. Nor was either party able to deal with Britain's ailing economy. Failure to modernize made British industry less and less competitive. Moreover, Britain was hampered by frequent labor strikes, many of them caused by conflicts between rival labor unions.

In 1979, after Britain's economic problems had seemed to worsen during five years under a Labour government, the Conservatives returned to power under Margaret Thatcher (b. 1925). She became the first woman to serve as prime minister in British history (see the box on p. 895). Thatcher pledged to lower taxes, reduce government bureaucracy, limit social welfare, restrict union power, and end inflation. The "Iron Lady," as she was

Margaret Thatcher: Entering a Man's World

In 1979, Margaret Thatcher became the first woman to serve as Britain's prime minster. In this excerpt from her autobiography, Thatcher describes how she was interviewed by Conservative Party officials when they first considered her as a possible candidate for Parliament. Thatcher ran for Parliament for the first time in 1950; she lost, but increased the Conservative vote total in the district by 50 percent over the previous election.

❀ Margaret Thatcher, *The Path to Power*

And, as always with me, there was politics. I immediately joined the Conservative Association and threw myself into the usual round of Party activities. In particular, I thoroughly enjoyed what was called the "39–'45" discussion group, where Conservatives of the war generation met to exchange views and argue about the political topics of the day. . . . It was as a representative of the Oxford University Graduate Conservative Association (OUGCA) that I went to the Llandudno Conservative Party Conference in October 1948.

It had originally been intended that I should speak at the Conference, seconding an OUGCA motion deploring the abolition of university seats. At that time universities had separate representation in Parliament, and graduates had the right to vote in their universities as well as in the constituency where they lived. (I supported separate university representation, but not the principle that graduates should have more than one vote . . . .) It would have been my first Conference speech, but in the end the seconder chosen was a City man, because the City seats were also to be abolished.

My disappointment at this was, however, very quickly overcome and in a most unexpected way. After one of the debates, I found myself engaged in one of those speculative conversations which young people have about their future prospects. An Oxford friend, John Grant, said he supposed that one day I would like to be a Member of Parliament. "Well, yes," I replied, "but there's not much hope of that. The chances of my being selected are just nil at the moment." I might have added that with no private income of my own there was no way I could have afforded to be an MP on the salary then

called, did break the power of the labor unions. Although she did not eliminate the basic components of the social welfare system, she did use austerity measures to control inflation. "Thatcherism," as her economic policy was termed, improved the British economic situation but at a price. The south of England, for example, prospered, but the old industrial areas of the Midlands and north declined and were beset by high unemployment, poverty, and even

available. I had not even tried to get on the Party's list of approved candidates.

Later in the day, John Grant happened to be sitting next to the Chairman of the Dartford Conservative Association, John Miller. The Association was in search of a candidate. I learned afterwards that the conversation went something like this: "I understand that you're still looking for a candidate at Dartford?" . . .

"That's right. Any suggestions?"

"Well, there's a young woman, Margaret Roberts, that you might look at. She's very good."

"Oh, but Dartford is a real industrial stronghold. I don't think a woman would do at all."

"Well, you know best of course. But why not just look at her?"

And they did. I was invited to have lunch with John Miller and his wife, Phee, and the Dartford Woman's Chairman, Mrs. Fletcher, on the Saturday on Llandudno Pier. Presumably, and in spite of any reservations about the suitability of a woman candidate for their seat, they liked what they saw. I certainly got on well with them. . . .

I did not hear from Dartford until December, when I was asked to attend an interview at Palace Chambers, Bridge Street . . . . Very few outside the political arena know just how nerve-racking such occasions are. The interviewee who is not nervous and tense is very likely to perform badly: for, as any chemist will tell you, the adrenaline needs to flow if one is to perform at one's best. . . .

I found myself short-listed, and was asked to go to Dartford itself for a further interview. . . . As one of five would-be candidates, I had to give a fifteen-minute speech and answer questions for a further ten minutes.

It was the questions which were more likely to cause me trouble. There was a good deal of suspicion of woman candidates, particularly in what was regarded as a tough industrial seat like Dartford. This was quite definitely a man's world into which not just angels feared to tread. . . .

The most reliable sign that a political occasion has gone well is that you have enjoyed it. I enjoyed that evening at Dartford, and the outcome justified my confidence. I was selected.

violence. Cutbacks in education seriously undermined the quality of British education, long regarded as among the world's finest.

In the area of foreign policy, Thatcher, like Ronald Reagan in the United States, took a hard-line approach toward communism. She oversaw a large military buildup aimed at replacing older technology and reestablishing Britain as a world police officer. In 1982, when Argentina

MARGARET THATCHER. Great Britain's first female prime minister, Margaret Thatcher was a strong leader who dominated British politics in the 1980s. This picture of Thatcher was taken at the Chelsea Flower Show in May 1990. Six months later, a revolt within her own party caused her to resign as prime minister.

attempted to take control of the Falkland Islands (one of Britain's few remaining colonial outposts) 300 miles off its coast, the British successfully rebuked the Argentines, although at great economic cost and the loss of 255 lives. The Falklands War, however, did generate much popular patriotic support for Thatcher.

Margaret Thatcher dominated British politics in the 1980s. The Labour Party, beset by divisions between its moderate and radical wings, offered little effective opposition. Only in 1990 did Labour's fortunes seem to revive when Thatcher's government attempted to replace local property taxes with a flat-rate tax payable by every adult to his or her local authority. Though Thatcher maintained that this would make local government more responsive to its electors, many argued that this was nothing more than a poll tax that would enable the rich to pay the same rate as the poor. In 1990, after antitax riots broke out, Thatcher's once remarkable popularity fell to all-time lows. At the end of November, a revolt within her own party caused Thatcher to resign as prime minister. She was replaced by John Major, whose Conservative Party won a narrow victory in the general elections held in April 1992. His government, however, failed to capture the imagination of most Britons, and in new elections on May 1, 1997, the Labour Party led by Tony Blair won a landslide victory.

UNCERTAINTIES IN FRANCE

The worsening of France's economic situation in the 1970s brought a shift to the left politically. By 1981, the Socialists had become the dominant party in the National Assembly, and the Socialist leader, François Mitterrand

(1916–1995), was elected president. His first concern was with France's economic difficulties. In 1982, Mitterrand froze prices and wages in the hope of reducing the huge budget deficit and high inflation. He also passed a number of liberal measures to aid workers: an increased minimum wage, expanded social benefits, a mandatory fifth week of paid vacation for salaried workers, a thirty-nine-hour workweek, and higher taxes for the rich. Mitterrand's administrative reforms included both centralization (nationalization of banks and industry) and decentralization (granting local governments greater powers). Their victory had convinced the Socialists that they could enact some of their more radical reforms. Consequently, the government nationalized the steel industry, major banks, the space and electronics industries, and important insurance firms.

The Socialist policies largely failed to work, however, and within three years, a decline in support for the Socialists caused the Mitterrand government to pursue what it called "modernization," basically a return of some of the economy to private enterprise and a narrowing of bureaucratic powers. Some economic improvement in the late 1980s enabled Mitterrand to win a second seven-year term in the 1988 presidential elections. But France's economic decline continued. In 1993, French unemployment stood at 10.6 percent, and in the elections in March of that year, the Socialists won only 28 percent of the vote as a coalition of conservative parties gained 80 percent of the seats in the National Assembly. The move to the right in France was strengthened when the conservative mayor of Paris, Jacques Chirac, was elected president in May 1995.

CONFUSION IN ITALY

In the 1970s and 1980s, Italy continued to practice the politics of coalitions that had characterized much of its history. Italy witnessed the installation of its fiftieth postwar government in 1991, and its new prime minister, Giulio Andreotti, had already served six times in that office. Italian governments continued to consist of coalitions mostly led by the Christian Democrats.

In the 1980s, even the Communists had been included briefly in the government. The Italian Communists had become advocates of Eurocommunism, basically an attempt to broaden communism's support by dropping its Marxist ideology. Although its vote declined in the 1980s, even in 1987, the Communist Party still garnered 26 percent of the vote. The Communists also won a number of local elections and took charge of municipal governments in several cities, including Rome and Naples for a brief time.

In the 1970s, Italy suffered from a severe economic recession. The Italian economy, which depended on imported oil as its chief source of energy, was especially vulnerable to the steep increase in oil prices in 1973. Parallel to the economic problems was a host of political and social problems: student unrest, mass strikes, and terror-

ist attacks. In 1978, a former prime minister, Aldo Moro, was kidnapped and killed by the Red Brigades, a terrorist organization. Then, too, there was the all-pervasive and corrupting influence of the Mafia, which had always been an important factor in southern Italy, but spread to northern Italy as well in the 1980s.

Italy survived the crises of the 1970s and in the decade of the 1980s began to experience remarkable economic growth. But severe problems remained. Corruption continued to trouble Italian politics. In 1993, hundreds of politicians and business leaders were under investigation for their involvement in a widespread scheme to use political bribes to secure public contracts. Public disgust with political corruption became so intense that in April 1996 Italian voters took the unusual step of giving control of the government to a center-left coalition that included the Communists.

The United States: Domestic Turmoil

With the election of Richard Nixon as president in 1968, American politics made a shift to the right. Nixon ended American involvement in Vietnam by gradually withdrawing American troops. Politically, he pursued a "southern strategy," carefully calculating that "law and order" issues and a slowdown in racial desegregation would appeal to southern whites. The South, which had once been a Democratic stronghold, began to form a new allegiance to the Republican Party. The Republican strategy also gained support among white Democrats in northern cities, where court-mandated busing to achieve racial integration had led to a white backlash.

As president, Nixon was paranoid about conspiracies and began to use illegal methods to gather political intelligence on his political opponents. One of the president's advisers explained that their intention was to "use the available Federal machinery to screw our political enemies." Nixon's zeal led to the Watergate scandal—the attempted bugging of Democratic National Headquarters, located in the Watergate Hotel in Washington, D.C. Although Nixon repeatedly lied to the American public about his involvement in the affair, secret tapes of his own conversations in the White House revealed the truth. On August 9, 1974, Nixon resigned the presidency rather than face possible impeachment and trial by the U.S. Congress.

After Watergate, American domestic politics focused on economic issues. Vice President Gerald Ford (b. 1913) became president when Nixon resigned, only to lose in the 1976 election to the former governor of Georgia, Jimmy Carter (b. 1924). Both Ford and Carter faced severe economic problems. The period from 1973 to the mid-1980s was one of economic stagnation, which came to be known as stagflation—a combination of high inflation and high unemployment. In part, the economic downturn stemmed from a dramatic change in oil prices. Oil was considered a cheap and abundant source of energy in the 1950s, and Americans had grown dependent on imported oil from the

Middle East. But an oil embargo and price increases by the Organization of Petroleum Exporting Countries (OPEC) as a result of the Arab-Israeli War in 1973 quadrupled oil prices. Additional price hikes increased oil prices twentyfold by the end of the 1970s, no doubt encouraging inflationary tendencies throughout the entire economy.

By 1980, the Carter administration was faced with two devastating problems. High inflation and a noticeable decline in average weekly earnings were causing a drop in American living standards. At the same time, a crisis abroad had erupted when fifty-three Americans were taken hostage by the Iranian government of Ayatollah Khomeini. Carter's inability to gain the release of the hostages led to perceptions at home that he was a weak president. His overwhelming loss to Ronald Reagan (b. 1911) in the election of 1980 enabled the chief exponent of right-wing Republican policies to assume the presidency and initiate a new political order.

The Reagan Revolution, as it has been called, involved a number of new policies. Reversing decades of increased spending on social welfare, Reagan cut back on the welfare state by reducing spending on food stamps, school lunch programs, and job programs. At the same time, his administration fostered the largest peacetime military buildup in American history. Total federal spending rose from $631 billion in 1981 to over $1 trillion by 1986. But instead of raising taxes to pay for the new expenditures, which far outweighed the budget cuts in social areas, Reagan convinced Congress to support supply-side economics. Massive tax cuts would supposedly stimulate rapid economic growth and produce new revenues. Much of the tax cut went to the wealthy. Reagan's policies seemed to work in the short run as the United States experienced an economic upturn that lasted until the end of the 1980s. The spending policies of the Reagan administration, however, also produced record government deficits, which loomed as an obstacle to long-term growth. In the 1970s, the total deficit was $420 billion. Between 1981 and 1987, Reagan's budget deficits were three times that amount.

The inability of George Bush (b. 1924), Reagan's successor, to deal with the deficit problem as well as an economic downturn, enabled a Democrat, William Clinton, to become president in November 1992. The new president was a southern Democrat who claimed to be a new Democrat—one who favored a number of the Republican policies of the 1980s. This was a clear indication that the Democratic victory had by no means halted the rightward drift in American politics. In fact, Clinton's reelection in 1996 was partially due to his adoption of Republican ideas and policies. Much of Clinton's second term, however, was overshadowed by charges of presidential misconduct stemming from the president's sexual affair with Monica Lewinsky, a White House intern. After a bitter partisan struggle, the U.S. Senate acquitted the president on two articles of impeachment brought by the House of Representatives.

❋ The Development of Canada

In 1963, during a major economic recession, the Liberals had been returned to power in Canada. The most prominent Liberal government was that of Pierre Trudeau (b. 1919), who came to power in 1968. Although French in background, Trudeau was dedicated to Canada's federal union, and in 1968 his government passed the Official Languages Act that allowed both English and French to be used in the federal civil service. Although Trudeau's government vigorously pushed an industrialization program, high inflation and Trudeau's efforts to impose the will of the federal government on the powerful provincial governments alienated voters and weakened his government. Economic recession in the early 1980s brought Brian Mulroney (b. 1939), leader of the Progressive Conservative Party to power in 1984. Mulroney's government sought greater privatization of Canada's state-run corporations and negotiated a free trade agreement with the United States. Bitterly resented by many Canadians, the agreement cost Mulroney's government much of its popularity. In 1993, the ruling Conservatives were overwhelmingly defeated, and the Liberal leader, Jean Chrétien, became prime minister.

Mulroney's government was also unable to settle the ongoing crisis over the French-speaking province of Quebec. In the late 1960s, the Parti Québécois, headed by René Lévesque, ran on a platform of Quebec's secession from the Canadian union. To pursue their dream of separation, some underground separatist groups even used terrorist bombings. In 1976, the Parti Québécois won Quebec's provincial elections and in 1980 called for a referendum that would enable the provincial government to negotiate Quebec's independence from the rest of Canada. Quebec voters narrowly rejected the plan in 1995, however, and debate over the province's status continues to divide Canada at the end of the twentieth century.

◆ New Directions and New Problems in Western Society

Dramatic social developments have accompanied political and economic changes since 1970. New opportunities for women emerged, and a reinvigorated women's movement sought to bring new meaning to the principle of equality with men. New problems for Western society also arose with the advent of terrorism, a reaction against foreign workers and immigrants, and a growing awareness of environmental dangers.

❋ Transformation in Women's Lives

It is estimated that women need to average 2.1 children to ensure a natural replacement of a country's population. In many European countries, the population stopped grow-

AN ANTINUCLEAR PROTEST. Women were active participants in the antinuclear movement of the 1980s. Shown here are some of the 10,000 antinuclear protesters who linked hands to form a human chain around the nine-mile perimeter of the U.S. Air Force base at Greenham Common, England, on December 13, 1982. They were protesting the planned siting of ninety-six U.S. cruise missiles at the base.

ing in the 1960s, and the trend has continued since then. By the 1990s, birthrates had declined drastically; among the nations of the European Union, the average number of children per mother was 1.4. Italy's rate of 1.2 was the lowest in the world in 1997.

At the same time, the number of women in the workforce continued to rise. In Britain, for example, women made up 44 percent of the labor force in 1990, up from 32 percent in 1970. Moreover, women were entering new employment areas. Greater access to universities and professional schools enabled women to take jobs in law, medicine, government, business, and education. In the Soviet Union, for example, about 70 percent of doctors and teachers were women. Nevertheless, economic inequality still often prevailed; women received lower wages than men for comparable work and found fewer opportunities for advancement to management positions.

✴ THE WOMEN'S MOVEMENT

Feminists in the women's liberation movement came to believe that women themselves must transform the fundamental conditions of their lives. They did so in a variety of ways after 1970. First, they formed numerous "consciousness raising" groups to heighten awareness of women's issues. Women met together to share their personal experiences and become aware of the many ways that male dominance affected their lives. This "consciousness raising" helped many women to become activists.

Women sought and gained a measure of control over their own bodies by insisting that they had a right to both contraception and abortion. In the 1960s and 1970s, hundreds of thousands of European women worked, often successfully, to repeal the laws that outlawed contraception and abortion. In 1968, a French law permitted the sale

of contraceptive devices, and in the 1970s French feminists began to call for the legalization of abortion. One group of 343 prominent French women even signed a manifesto declaring that they had had abortions. In 1979, abortion became legal in France. Even in Catholic countries, where the church remained adamantly opposed to abortion, legislation allowing contraception and abortion was passed in the 1970s and 1980s.

As more women became activists, they also became involved in new issues. In the 1980s and 1990s, women faculty in universities concentrated on developing new cultural attitudes through the new academic field of women's studies. Courses in women's studies, which stressed the role and contributions of women in history, mushroomed in both American and European colleges and universities.

Other women began to try to affect the political environment by allying with the antinuclear movement. In 1982, a group of women protested American nuclear missiles in Britain by chaining themselves to the fence of an American military base. Thousands more joined in creating a peace camp around the military compound. Enthusiasm ran high; one participant said: "I'll never forget that feeling; it'll live with me forever . . . as we walked round, and we clasped hands . . . it was for women; it was for peace; it was for the world."[2]

Some women joined the ecological movement. As one German writer who was concerned with environmental issues said, it is women "who must give birth to children, willingly or unwillingly, in this polluted world of ours." Especially prominent were the female members of the Green Party in Germany (see The Environment and the Green Movements later in this chapter), which supported environmental issues and elected forty-two delegates to the West German parliament in 1987. Among the delegates was Petra Kelly (b. 1947), one of the founders of the German Green Party and a tireless campaigner for the preservation of the environment as well as human rights and equality.

Women in the West have also reached out to work with women from the rest of the world in international conferences to change the conditions of their lives. Between 1975 and 1995, the United Nations held conferences in Mexico City, Copenhagen, Nairobi, and Beijing. These meetings made clear that women from Western and non-Western countries had different priorities. Whereas women from Western countries spoke about political, economic, cultural, and sexual rights, women from developing countries in Latin America, Africa, and Asia focused their attention on bringing an end to the violence, hunger, and disease that haunt their lives. Despite these differences, the meetings were an indication of how women in both developed and developing nations were organizing to make people aware of women's issues.

The Growth of Terrorism

Acts of terror by those opposed to governments became a frightening aspect of modern Western society. During the late 1970s and early 1980s in particular, concern about terrorism was often at the top of foreign policy agendas in the United States and many European countries. Small bands of terrorists used assassination, indiscriminate killing of civilians, especially by bombing, the taking of hostages, and the hijacking of airplanes to draw attention to their demands or to destabilize governments in the hope of achieving their political goals. Terrorist acts garnered considerable media attention. When Palestinian terrorists kidnapped and killed eleven Israeli athletes at the Munich Olympic Games in 1972, hundreds of millions of people watched the drama unfold on television. Indeed, some observers believe that media exposure has been an important catalyst for some terrorist groups.

Motivations for terrorist acts varied considerably. Left- and right-wing terrorist groups flourished in the late 1970s and early 1980s. Left-wing groups, such as the Baader-Meinhof gang (also known as the Red Army Faction) in Germany and the Red Brigades in Italy, consisted chiefly of affluent middle-class young people who denounced the injustices of capitalism and supported acts of revolutionary terrorism in an attempt to bring down the system. Right-wing terrorist groups, such as the New Order in Italy and the Charles Martel Club in France, used bombings to foment disorder and bring about authoritarian regimes. These groups received little or no public support, and authorities were able to crush them fairly quickly.

But terrorist acts also stemmed from militant nationalists who wished to create separatist states. Because they received considerable support from local populations sympathetic to their cause, these terrorist groups could maintain their activities over a long period of time. Most prominent was the Irish Republican Army (IRA), which resorted to vicious attacks against the ruling government and innocent civilians in Northern Ireland. Over a period of twenty years, IRA terrorists were responsible for the death of 2,000 people in Northern Ireland; three-fourths of the victims were civilians.

Although left- and right-wing terrorist activities declined in Europe in the 1980s, international terrorism remained rather commonplace. Angered over the loss of their territory to Israel by 1967, some militant Palestinians responded with a policy of terrorist attacks against Israel's supporters. Palestinian terrorists operated throughout European countries, attacking both Europeans and American tourists; vacationers at airports in Rome and Vienna were massacred by Palestinian terrorists in 1985. State-sponsored terrorism was often an integral part of international terrorism. Militant governments, especially in Iran, Libya, and Syria, assisted terrorist organizations that made attacks on Europeans and Americans. On December 21, 1988, Pan American flight 103 from Frankfurt to New York exploded over Lockerbie, Scotland, killing all 259 passengers and crew members. A massive investigation finally revealed that the bomb responsible for the explosion had been planted by two Libyan terrorists who were connected to terrorist groups based in both Iran and Syria.

Governments fought back by creating special antiterrorist units that became extremely effective in responding to terrorist acts. In 1977, for example, the German special antiterrorist unit, known as GSG, rescued ninety-one hostages from a Lufthansa airplane that had been hijacked to Mogadishu in Somalia. Counterterrorism, or a calculated policy of direct retaliation against terrorists, also made states that sponsored terrorism more cautious. In 1986, the Reagan administration responded to the terrorist bombing of a West German disco club popular with American soldiers by an air attack on Libya, long suspected as a major sponsor of terrorist organizations. Some observers attribute the overall decline in terrorist attacks in the late 1980s to the American action. In the 1990s, however, acts of terrorism have continued to be a disturbing element in Western life.

Guest Workers and Immigrants

As the economies of the Western European countries revived in the 1950s and 1960s, a severe labor shortage forced them to rely on foreign workers. Scores of Turks and eastern and southern Europeans came to Germany, North Africans to France, and people from the Caribbean, India, and Pakistan to Great Britain. Overall, there were probably 15 million guest workers in Europe in the 1980s. They constituted 17 percent of the labor force in Switzerland and 10 percent in Germany.

Although these workers were necessary for economic reasons, socially and politically their presence created problems for their host countries. Many foreign workers complained that they received lower wages and inferior social benefits. Moreover, their concentration in certain

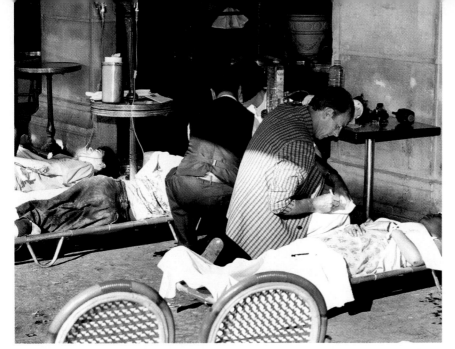

TERRORISM IN EUROPE. Terrorist acts became a regular feature of European life beginning in the 1970s. This photograph shows some of the victims of a bomb set off in a subway during rush hour in Paris in July 1995. Fifty people were injured by the explosion.

cities and even certain sections of those cities often created tensions with the local native populations. Foreign workers, many of them nonwhites, constituted almost one-fifth of the population in the German cities of Frankfurt, Munich, and Stuttgart. Having become settled in their new countries, many were unwilling to leave, even after the end of the postwar boom in the early 1970s led to mass unemployment. Moreover, as guest workers settled permanently in their host countries, additional family members migrated to join them. Although they had little success in getting guest workers already there to leave, some European countries passed legislation or took other measures to restrict new immigration. In 1991, thousands of Albanians fled their homeland after its Communist government began to fall apart, but when they arrived in Italy, the Italian authorities forcibly evicted them and sent them back to Albania.

In the 1980s, the problem of foreign workers was intensified by an influx of other refugees, especially to West Germany, which had liberal immigration laws that permitted people seeking asylum for political persecution to enter the country. During the 1970s and 1980s, West Germany absorbed over a million refugees from Eastern Europe and East Germany. In 1986 alone, 200,000 political refugees from Pakistan, Bangladesh, and Sri Lanka entered the country.

This great influx of foreigners, many of them non-white, strained not only the social services of European countries, but the patience of many native residents who opposed making their countries ethnically diverse. Anti-foreign sentiment, especially in a time of growing unemployment, increased and was encouraged by new right-wing political parties that catered to people's complaints. Thus, the National Front in France, organized by Jean-Marie Le Pen, and the Republican Party in Germany, led by Franz Schönhuber, a former SS officer, advocated restricting all new immigration and limiting the assimilation of settled immigrants. Although these parties have had only limited success in elections so far, even that modest

accomplishment has encouraged traditional conservative and even moderately conservative parties to adopt more nationalistic policies. Even more frightening, however, have been the organized campaigns of violence, especially against African and Asian immigrants, by radical, right-wing groups (see the box on p. 902).

❉ The Environment and the Green Movements

Beginning in the 1970s, environmentalism became an important item on the European political agenda. By that time, serious ecological problems had become all too apparent. Air pollution, produced by nitrogen oxide and sulfur dioxide emissions from road vehicles, power plants, and industrial factories, was causing respiratory illnesses and having corrosive effects on buildings and monuments. Many rivers, lakes, and seas had become so polluted that they posed serious health risks. Dying forests and disappearing wildlife alarmed more and more people. The opening of Eastern Europe after the revolutions of 1989 brought to the world's attention the incredible environmental destruction of that region caused by unfettered industrial pollution. Communist governments had obviously operated under the assumption that production quotas were much more significant than protection of the environment.

Environmental concerns forced the major political parties in Europe to advocate new regulations for the protection of the environment. The Soviet nuclear power disaster at Chernobyl in 1986 made Europeans even more aware of potential environmental hazards, and 1987 was touted as the "year of the environment." Many European states also established government ministries to oversee environmental issues.

Growing ecological awareness also gave rise to the Green movements and Green parties that emerged throughout Europe in the 1970s. The origins of these

Violence against Foreigners in Germany

As the number of foreign guest workers and immigrants increased in Europe, violent attacks against them also escalated. Especially in the former East Germany where unemployment rose dramatically after reunification, gangs of neo-Nazi youth have perpetrated violent attacks on foreigners. This document is taken from a German press account of an attack on guest workers from Vietnam and Mozambique who had originally been recruited by the East German government

✵ Knud Pries, "East Germans Have Yet to Learn Tolerance"

The police headquarters in Dresden, the capital of Saxony, announced that "a political situation" had developed in the town of Hoyerswerda. Political leaders and the police needed to examine the problem and corresponding measures should be taken: "In the near future the residents of the asylum hostel will be moved."

The people of Hoyerswerda prefer to be more direct, referring to the problem of *Neger* (niggers) and *Fidschis* (a term for Asian foreigners). The loudmouths of the neo-fascist gangs make the message clear: "Niggers Go Home!"

It looks as if some Germans have had enough of bureaucratic officialese. What is more, they will soon make sure that no more foreign voices are heard in Hoyerswerda.

The municipality in northern Saxony has a population of just under 70,000, including 70 people from Mozambique and Vietnam who live in a hostel for foreigners and about 240 asylum-seekers in a hostel at the other end of town.

The "political situation" was triggered by an attack by a neo-Nazi gang on Vietnamese traders selling their goods on the market square on 17 September. After being dispersed by the police the Faschos carried out their first attack on the hostel for foreigners.

The attacks then turned into a regular evening "hunt" by a growing group of right-wing radicals, some of them minors, who presented their idea of a clean Germany by roaming the streets armed with truncheons, stones, steel balls, bottles and Molotov cocktails. Seventeen people were injured, some seriously.

After the police stepped in on a larger scale the extremists moved across the town to the asylum hostel.

To begin with, only the gang itself and onlookers were outside the building, but on the evening of 22 September members of the "Human Rights League" and about 100 members of "autonomous" groups turned up to help the foreigners who had sought refuge in the already heavily damaged block of flats.

A large police contingent, reinforced by men from Dresden and the Border Guard, prevented the situation from becoming even more critical. Two people were seriously injured. The mob was disbanded with the help of dogs, tear gas and water-cannons.

Thirty-two people were arrested, and blank cartridge guns, knives, slings and clubs were seized. On 23 September, a police spokesman announced that the situation was under control. It seems doubtful whether things will stay this way, since the pogroms have become an evening ritual. Politicians and officials are racking their brains about how to grapple with the current crisis and the basic problem. One thing is clear: without a massive intervention by the police the problem cannot even be contained. But what then?

Saxony's Interior Minister, Rudolf Krause, initially recommended that the hostels concerned should be "fenced in," but then admitted that this was "not the final solution." Providing the Defense Ministry approves, the "provisional solution" will be to move the foreigners to a barracks in Kamenz.

Even if this operation is completed without violence it would represent a shameful success for the right-wing radicals. Although the Africans and Asians still living in Hoyerswerda will have to leave at the end of November anyway once the employment contracts drawn up in the former [East Germany] expire, they are unwilling to endure the terror that long. "Even if we're going anyway—they want all foreigners to go now," says the 29-year-old Martinho from Mozambique.

His impression is that the gangs of thugs are doing something for which others are grateful: "The neighbors are glad when the skinheads arrive."

Interior Minister Krause feels that the abuse of asylum laws, the social problems in East Germany and an historically rooted deficit explain this situation: "The problem is that we were unable in the past to practice the tolerance needed to accept alien cultures."

---

movements were by no means uniform. Some came from the antinuclear movement; others arose out of such causes as women's liberation and concerns for foreign workers. Most started at the local level and then gradually expanded to include activities at the national level, where they became formally organized as political parties. Most visible was the Green Party in Germany, which was officially organized in 1979 and, by 1987, had elected forty-two delegates to the West German parliament. Green parties also competed successfully in Sweden, Austria, and Switzerland.

Despite their repressive policies, Communist countries in Eastern Europe also witnessed the formation of ecologically conscious groups. In the 1980s, environmental groups emerged in East Germany and Czechoslovakia, two especially environmentally devastated countries, as well as in Poland and Hungary. The Czech dissident group, Charter 77, emphasized environmental damage as one of the chief crimes of its Communist government.

Although the Green movements and parties have played an important role in making people aware of ecological problems, they have by no means replaced the traditional political parties, as some political analysts in the mid-1980s forecast. For one thing, the coalitions that made up the Greens found it difficult to agree on all issues and tended to splinter into different cliques. Then, too, many of the founders of these movements, who often expressed a willingness to work with the traditional political parties, were ousted from leadership positions by fundamentalists unwilling to compromise their principles in any way. Finally, traditional political parties have co-opted the environmental issues of the Greens. By the 1990s, more and more European governments were beginning to sponsor projects to safeguard the environment and clean up the worst sources of pollution.

◆ The World of Western Culture

Intellectually and culturally, the Western world during the last half of the twentieth century has been marked by much diversity. Although many trends represent a continuation of prewar modern developments, new directions in the last two decades have led some to speak of a postmodern cultural world.

❊ *Recent Trends in Art, Music, and Literature*

Modern art continued to prevail at exhibitions and museums. For the most part, the United States dominated the art world, much as it did the world of popular culture (see Popular Culture and the Americanization of the World later in this chapter). American art, often vibrantly colored and filled with activity, reflected the energy and exuberance of the postwar United States. After 1945, New York City became the artistic center of the Western world. The Guggenheim Museum, the Museum of Modern Art, and the Whitney Museum of American art, together with New York's numerous art galleries, promoted modern art and helped determine artistic tastes not only in New York and the United States, but throughout much of the world.

Abstractionism, especially Abstract Expressionism, emerged as the artistic mainstream (see Chapters 24 and 26). American exuberance in Abstract Expressionism is evident in the enormous canvases of Jackson Pollock (1912–1956). In such works as *Lavender Mist* (1950), paint seems to explode, assaulting the viewer with emotion and movement. Pollock's swirling forms and seemingly chaotic patterns broke all conventions of form and structure. His drip paintings, with their total abstraction, were extremely

JACKSON POLLOCK DOES A PAINTING. One of the best-known practitioners of Abstract Expressionism, which remained at the center of the artistic mainstream after World War II, was the American Jackson Pollock, who achieved his ideal of total abstraction in his drip paintings. He is shown here at work in his Long Island studio. Pollock found it easier to cover his large canvases with exploding patterns of color when he put them on the floor.

influential with other artists, although the public was initially quite hostile to his work. Pollock also introduced the technique of painting with the canvas laid on the floor. He said: "On the floor I am more at ease. I feel nearer, more a part of the painting, since this way I can walk around in, work from four sides and be literally *in* the painting. When I am in the painting I am not aware of what I am doing. There is pure harmony."

The early 1960s saw the emergence of Pop Art, which took images of popular culture and transformed them into works of fine art. Andy Warhol (1930–1987), who began as an advertising illustrator, was the most famous of the pop artists. Warhol adapted images from commercial art, such as the Campbell soup cans, and photographs of such celebrities as Marilyn Monroe. Derived from mass culture, these works were mass produced and

ANSELM KIEFER, *DEPARTURE FOR EGYPT.* Although Western artists experimented with a variety of modern and even postmodern styles in the 1970s and 1980s, Abstract Expressionism continued to be popular. The German artist Anselm Kiefer used the tradition of Abstract Expressionism to create haunting images that reflect the horrors of Germany's Nazi past.

deliberately "of the moment," expressing the fleeting whims of popular culture.

In the 1980s, styles emerged that some have referred to as Postmodern. Although as yet ill-defined, Postmodernism tends to move away from the futurism or "cutting edge" qualities of Modernism. Instead it favors "utilizing tradition," whether that includes more styles of painting or elevating traditional crafts to the level of fine art. Weavers, potters, glassmakers, metalsmiths, and furniture makers have gained respect as artists.

Another response to Modernism can be seen in a return to realism in the arts. Some extreme realists paint or sculpt with such minute attention to realistic detail that their paintings appear to be photographs and their sculptures living human beings. Their subjects are often ordinary individuals, stuck in ordinary lives. These works are often pessimistic and cynical.

Abstract Expressionism, however, continues to proliferate. Anselm Kiefer, born in Germany in 1945, combines aspects of Abstract Expressionism, collage, and German Expressionism to create works that are stark and haunting. His *Departure from Egypt* (1984) is a meditation on Jewish history and its descent into the horrors of Nazism. Kiefer hoped that a portrayal of Germany's atrocities could free Germans from their past and bring some good out of evil. His international stature reflects a movement away from American dominance in the fine arts, a trend that gained momentum in the 1980s.

Like modern art, modern music has focused on variety and radical experimentation. Also, like modern art, modern classical music witnessed a continuation of prewar developments. Some composers, the neoclassicists, remained closely tied to nineteenth-century Romantic music, although they occasionally incorporated some twentieth-century developments, such as atonality and dissonance. Their style was strongly reminiscent of Stravinsky (see Chapter 24).

The major musical trend since the war, however, has been serialism. Inspired mostly by the twelve-tone music of Schönberg (see Chapter 26), serialism is a compositional procedure where an order of succession is set for specific values: pitch (for tones of the tempered scale); loudness (for dynamic levels); and units of time (for rhythm). By predetermining the order of succession, the composer restricts his or her intuitive freedom as the work to some extent creates itself. However, the mechanism the composer initially establishes could generate unanticipated musical events, thereby creating new and exciting compositions. Serialist composition diminishes the role of intuition and emotion in favor of intellect and mathematical precision. The first recognized serialist was the Frenchman Olivier Messiaen (b. 1908). Significantly, Messiaen was influenced in part by Indian and Greek music, plain chant, folk music, and birdsongs. Most critics have respected serialism, although the public has been largely indifferent, if not hostile, to it.

An offshoot of serialism that has won popular support, but not the same critical favor, is minimalism. Like serialism, this style uses repeated patterns and series and steady pulsation with gradual changes occurring over time. But whereas serialism is often atonal, minimalism is usually tonal and more harmonic. Perhaps the most successful minimalist composer is Philip Glass (b. 1937), who demonstrated in *Einstein on the Beach* that minimalist music could be adapted to full-scale opera. Like other modern American composers, Glass found no contradiction in moving between the worlds of classical music and popular music. His *Koyaanisqatsi* was used as background music to a documentary film on the disintegrative forces in Western society.

The most significant new trend in postwar literature has been called the "Theater of the Absurd." This new convention in drama began in France in the 1950s, although its most famous proponent was the Irishman Samuel

Beckett (1906–1990), who lived in France. In Beckett's *Waiting for Godot* (1952), it is readily apparent that the action on stage is not realistic. Two men wait incessantly for the appearance of someone, with whom they may or may not have an appointment. No background information on the two men is provided. During the course of the play, nothing seems to be happening. The audience is never told if the action in front of them is real or unreal. Unlike traditional theater, suspense is maintained not by having the audience wonder, "what is going to happen next?" but by having them ask simply, "what is happening now?"

The Theater of the Absurd reflected its time. The postwar period was a time of disillusionment with fixed ideological beliefs in politics or religion. A sense of the world's meaninglessness underscored the desolate worldview of absurdist drama and literature. This can be seen in Günter Grass's *Tin Drum*, published in 1959, which reflected postwar Germany's preoccupation with the seeming incomprehensibility of Nazi Germany.

The Theater of the Absurd also questioned the ability of language to reflect reality accurately. Beckett's play *Act without Words* contains no dialogue. In another play, Beckett used a beam of light and a buzzing sound as "words" of the discourse. The Czech playwright Vaclav Havel, in his *Memorandum* (1966), examined the language and mechanics of bureaucracy. The plot revolved around the introduction of an artificial language that is imposed on people in the hope of fostering more efficient communication. Because no one can understand the new language, communication breaks down and, therefore, so do human relationships. The artificial language is finally eliminated, only to be replaced by an equally incomprehensible language imposed from above. The overt critique of Communist bureaucracy and the absurdity of imposing artificial systems in the hope of re-creating society along ideological lines did little for Havel's position in Communist Czechoslovakia.

✻ *The Philosophical Dilemma: Existentialism*

The sense of meaninglessness that inspired the Theater of the Absurd also underscored the philosophy of existentialism. It was largely born of the desperation caused by two world wars and the breakdown of traditional values. Existentialism reflected the anxieties of the twentieth century and became especially well known after World War II through the works of two Frenchmen, Jean-Paul Sartre (1905–1980) and Albert Camus (1913–1960).

The beginning point of the existentialism of Sartre and Camus was the absence of God in the universe (see the box on p. 906). Though the death of God was tragic, it meant that humans had no preordained destiny and were utterly alone in the universe with no future and no hope. As Camus expressed it:

A world that can be explained even with bad reasons is a familiar world. But, on the other hand, in a universe suddenly divested of illusions and lights, man feels an alien, a stranger. His exile is without remedy since he is deprived of the memory of a lost home or the hope of a promised land. This divorce between man and his life, the actor and his setting, is properly the feeling of absurdity.[3]

According to Camus, then, the world was absurd and without meaning; humans, too, are without meaning and purpose. Reduced to despair and depression, humans have but one ground of hope—themselves.

Though the world might be absurd, Camus argued, it could not be absurd unless people judged it to be so. People are unique in the world, and their kind of being is quite different from that of all others. In the words of Sartre, human "existence precedes essence." Humans are beings who first exist and then afterward define themselves. They determine what they will be. According to Sartre: "Man is nothing else but what he makes of himself. Such is the first principle of existentialism." People then must take full responsibility for what they are. They create their values and give their lives meaning. And this can only be done by their involvement in life. Only through a person's acts can one determine his or her values. According to Sartre: "I may say that I like so-and-so well enough to sacrifice a certain amount of money for him, but I may say so only if I've done it."

SARTRE AND DE BEAUVOIR. Jean-Paul Sartre and Simone de Beauvoir were two of the leading intellectuals in twentieth-century Europe. Sartre and de Beauvoir had a lifelong relationship that lasted until his death in 1980. Both were actively involved in the existentialist movement. De Beauvoir also played a crucial role in the emergence of the postwar women's liberation movement.

The Voice of Existentialism

Jean-Paul Sartre, a famous French intellectual of the early postwar years, became identified with the existentialist movement. He himself had been a student of German philosophy and was especially affected by the ideas of Martin Heidegger, whose Being and Time *is considered an influential existentialist work. This selection is taken from* Existentialism, *written by Sartre in 1946 to provide a general description of existentialism. In this passage, he discusses atheistic existentialism.*

✸ Jean-Paul Sartre, *Existentialism*

Dostoievsky said, "If God didn't exist, everything would be possible." That is the very starting point of existentialism. Indeed, everything is permissible if God does not exist, and as a result man is forlorn, because neither within him nor without does he find anything to cling to. He can't start making excuses for himself.

If existence really does precede essence, there is no explaining things away by reference to a fixed and given human nature. In other words, there is no determinism, man is free, man is freedom. On the other hand, if God does not exist, we find no values or commands to turn to which legitimize our conduct. So, in the bright realm of values, we have no excuse behind us, nor justification before us. We are alone with no excuses.

That is the idea I shall try to convey when I say that man is condemned to be free. Condemned, because he did not create himself, yet, in other respects is free; because, once thrown into the world, he is responsible for everything he does. The existentialist does not believe in the power of passion. He will never agree that a sweeping passion is a ravaging torrent which fatally leads a man to certain acts and is therefore an excuse. He thinks that man is responsible for his passion.

The existentialist does not think that man is going to help himself by finding in the world some omen by which to orient himself. Because he thinks that man will interpret the omen to suit himself. Therefore, he thinks that man, with no support and no aid, is condemned every moment to invent man. . . .

There can be no other truth to take off from than this: *I think; therefore, I exist.* There we have the absolute truth of consciousness becoming aware of itself. Every theory which takes man out of the moment in which he becomes aware of himself is, at its very beginning, a theory which confounds truth, for outside the Cartesian *cogito,* all views are only probable, and a doctrine of probability which is not bound to a truth dissolves into thin air. In order to describe the probable, you must have a firm hold on the true. Therefore, before there can be any truth whatsoever, there must be an absolute truth; and this one is simple and easily arrived at; it's on everyone's doorstep; it's a matter of grasping it directly.

Secondly, this theory is the only one which gives man dignity, the only one which does not reduce him to an object. The effect of all materialism is to treat all men, including the one philosophizing, as objects, that is, as an ensemble of determined reactions in no way distinguished from the ensemble of qualities and phenomena which constitute a table or a chair or a stone. We definitely wish to establish the human realm as an ensemble of values distinct from the material realm. . . .

Moreover, to say that we invent values means nothing else but this: life has no meaning a priori. Before you come alive, life is nothing; it's up to you to give it a meaning, and value is nothing else but the meaning that you choose. In that way, you see, there is a possibility of creating a human community.

Existentialism, therefore, involved an ethics of action, of involvement in life. But people could not define themselves without their involvement with others. Thus, existentialism's ethical message was just as important as its philosophy of being. Essentially, the message of existentialism was one of authenticity. Individuals true to themselves refused to be depersonalized by their society. As one author noted: "Existentialism is the struggle to discover the human person in a depersonalized age."

✸ *The Revival of Religion*

Existentialism was one response to the despair generated by the apparent collapse of civilized values in the twentieth century. The revival of religion has been another. Ever since the Enlightenment of the eighteenth century, Christianity and religion had been on the defensive. But

a number of religious thinkers and leaders attempted to bring new life to Christianity in the twentieth century. Despite the attempts of the Communist world to build an atheistic society and the West to build a secular society, religion continued to play an important role in the lives of many people.

One expression of this religious revival was the attempt by such theologians as the Protestant Karl Barth (1886–1968) and the Catholic Karl Rahner (1904–1984) to infuse traditional Christian teachings with new life. In his numerous writings, Barth attempted to reinterpret the religious insights of the Reformation era for the modern world. To Barth, the sinful and hence imperfect nature of human beings meant that humans could know religious truth not through reason, but only through the grace of God. Karl Rahner attempted to revitalize traditional Catholic theology by incorporating aspects of modern

Pope John Paul II: An Appeal for Peace

Pope John Paul II became the spiritual leader of the Catholic church in 1978. He has made numerous trips to all parts of the globe, advocating a variety of spiritual and social issues. He has made a point of speaking directly to as many lay groups as possible, often focusing on one of his chief themes—the desire for peace.

❋ Pope John Paul II, Speeches

Today peace has become, throughout the world, a preoccupation not only for those responsible for the destiny of nations but even more so for broad sections of the population and innumerable individuals who generously and tenaciously dedicate themselves to creating an outlook of peace and to establishing genuine peace between peoples and nations. This is comforting. But there is no hiding the fact that in spite of the efforts of all men and women of good will, there are still serious threats to peace in the world. Some of these threats take the form of divisions within various nations; others stem from deep-rooted and acute tensions between opposing nations and blocs within the world community. In reality, the confrontations that we witness today are distinguished from those of past history by certain new characteristics. In the first place they are worldwide: even a local conflict is often an expression of tensions originating elsewhere in the world. In the same way, it often happens that a conflict has profound effects far from where it broke out. Another characteristic is totality: present day tensions mobilize all the forces of

the nations involved; moreover, selfish monopolization and even hostility are to be found today as much in the way economic life is run and in the technological application of science as in the way that the mass media or military resources are utilized . . . .

Elsewhere, fear of a precarious peace, military and political imperatives, and economic and commercial interests lead to the establishment of arms stockpiles or to the sale of weapons capable of appalling destruction. The arms race, then, prevails over the great tasks of peace, which ought to unite peoples in new solidarity; it fosters sporadic but murderous conflicts and builds up the gravest threats. It is true that at first sight the cause of peace seems to be handicapped to a crippling extent.

But we must reach peace. Peace, as I said earlier, is threatened when uncertainty, doubt, and suspicion reign, and violence makes good use of this. Do we really want peace? Then we must dig deep within ourselves, and going beyond the divisions we find within us and between us, we must find the areas in which we can strengthen our conviction that human beings' basic driving forces and the recognition of their real nature carry them toward openness to others, mutual respect, community, and peace. The course of this laborious search for the objective and universal truth about humanity, and the result of the search, will develop men and women of peace and dialogue, people who draw both strength and humility from a truth that they realize they must serve and not make use of for partisan interests.

---

thought. He was careful, however, to emphasize the continuity between ancient and modern interpretations of Catholic doctrine.

In the Catholic church, attempts at religious renewal also came from two charismatic popes—John XXIII and John Paul II. Pope John XXIII (1881–1963) reigned as pope for only a short time (1958–1963), but sparked a dramatic revival of Catholicism when he summoned the twenty-first ecumenical council of the Catholic church. Known as Vatican Council II, it liberalized a number of Catholic practices. New avenues of communication with other Christian faiths were also opened for the first time since the Reformation.

John Paul II (b. 1920), who had been the archbishop of Cracow in Poland before his elevation to the papacy in 1978, was the first non-Italian to be elected pope since the sixteenth century. Although he alienated a number of people by reasserting traditional Catholic teaching on such issues as birth control, women in the priesthood, and clerical celibacy, John Paul's numerous travels around the world helped strengthen the Catholic church throughout the non-Western world. A strong believer in social justice,

John Paul II has been a powerful figure in reminding Europeans of their spiritual heritage and the need to temper the pursuit of materialism with spiritual concerns. He has also condemned nuclear weapons and constantly reminded leaders and laity of their obligations to prevent war (see the box above).

❉ The New World of Science and Technology

Since the Scientific Revolution of the seventeenth century and the Industrial Revolution of the nineteenth century, science and technology have played increasingly important roles in Western civilization. Many of the scientific and technological achievements since World War II have revolutionized people's lives. When American astronauts walked on the moon, millions watched the event on their televisions in the privacy of their living rooms.

Before World War II, theoretical science and technology were largely separated. Pure science was the domain of university professors who were far removed from the practical technological concerns of technicians and engineers. But during World War II, university scientists were recruited to work for their governments and develop new weapons and practical instruments of war. British physicists played a crucial role in the development of an improved radar system in 1940 that helped to defeat the German air force in the Battle of Britain. German scientists converted coal to gasoline to keep the German war machine moving and created self-propelled rockets as well as jet airplanes to keep Hitler's hopes alive for a miraculous turnaround in the war. The computer, too, was a wartime creation. The British mathematician Alan Turing designed a primitive computer to assist British intelligence in breaking the secret codes of German ciphering machines. The most famous product of wartime scientific research was the atomic bomb, created by a team of American and European scientists under the guidance of the physicist J. Robert Oppenheimer. Obviously, most wartime devices were created for destructive purposes, but merely to mention computers and jet airplanes demonstrates that they could easily be adapted for peacetime uses.

The sponsorship of research by governments and the military during World War II created a new scientific model. Science had become very complex, and only large organizations with teams of scientists, huge laboratories, and complex equipment could undertake such large-scale projects. Such facilities were so expensive, however, that they could only be provided by governments and large corporations. Because of its postwar prosperity, the United States was able to lead in the development of the new science. Almost 75 percent of all scientific research funds in the United States came from the government in 1965. Unwilling to lag behind, especially in military developments, the Soviet Union was also forced to provide large outlays for scientific and technological research. In fact, the defense establishments of the United States and the Soviet Union generated much of postwar scientific research. One-fourth of the trained scientists and engineers after 1945 were utilized in the creation of new weapons systems. Universities found their research agendas increasingly determined by government funding for military-related projects. In his farewell address to the American people in 1961, President Dwight Eisenhower coined the phrase "military-industrial complex" and warned of the danger inherent in the new mutual relationship between industrial corporations and the military services: "In the councils of government, we must guard against the acquisition of unwarranted influence, whether sought or unsought, by the military-industrial complex. The potential for the disastrous rise of misplaced power exists and will persist."

There was no more stunning example of how the new scientific establishment operated than the space race of the 1960s. The announcement by the Soviets in 1957 that they had sent the first space satellite—*Sputnik I*—into orbit around the earth caused the United States to launch a gigantic project to place a manned spacecraft on the moon within a decade. Massive government funds financed the scientific research and technological advances that attained this goal in 1969.

The postwar alliance of science and technology led to an accelerated rate of change that became a fact of life in Western society. One product of this alliance—the computer—may yet prove to be the most revolutionary of all the technological inventions of the twentieth century. Early computers, which required thousands of vacuum tubes to function, were large and took up considerable space. An important figure in the development of the early computer was Grace Hopper (1906–1992), a career Navy officer. Hopper was instrumental in inventing COBOL, a computer

ON THE MOON. The first landing on the moon in 1969 was one of the great technological achievements of the twentieth century. This picture shows astronaut James Irwin shortly after he erected the American flag during a moonwalk in 1971. The lunar module and lunar rover are also visible in the picture.

Small Is Beautiful: The Limits of Modern Technology

Although science and technology have produced an amazing array of achievements in the postwar world, some voices have been raised in criticism of their sometimes destructive aspects. In 1975, in his book Small Is Beautiful, *the British economist E. F. Schumacher examined the effects modern industrial technology has had on the earth's resources.*

❄ E. F. Schumacher, *Small Is Beautiful*

Is it not evident that our current methods of production are already eating into the very substance of industrial man? To many people this is not at all evident. Now that we have solved the problem of production, they say, have we ever had it so good? Are we not better fed, better clothed, and better housed than ever before—and better educated? Of course we are: most, but by no means all, of us: in the rich countries. But this is not what I mean by "substance." The substance of man cannot be measured by Gross National Product. Perhaps it cannot be measured at all, except for certain symptoms of loss. However, this is not the place to go into the statistics of these symptoms, such as crime, drug addiction, vandalism, mental breakdown, rebellion, and so forth. Statistics never prove anything.

I started by saying that one of the most fateful errors of our age is the belief that the problem of production has been solved. This illusion, I suggested, is mainly due to our inability to recognize that the modern industrial system, with all its intellectual sophistication, consumes the very basis on which it has been erected. To use the language of the economist, it lives on irreplaceable capital which it cheerfully treats as income. I specified three categories of such capital: fossil fuels, the tolerance margins of nature, and the human substance. Even if some readers should refuse to accept all three parts of my argument, I suggest that any one of them suffices to make my case.

And what is my case? Simply that our most important task is to get off our present collision course. And who is there to tackle such a task? I think every one of us. . . . To talk about the future is useful only if it leads to action *now*. And what can we do *now*, while we are still in the position of "never having had it so good"? To say the least . . . we must thoroughly understand the problem and begin to see the possibility of evolving a new life-style, with new methods of production and new patterns of consumption: a life-style designed for permanence. To give only three preliminary examples: in agriculture and horticulture, we can interest ourselves in the perfection of production methods which are biologically sound, build up soil fertility, and produce health, beauty and permanence. Productivity will then look after itself. In industry, we can interest ourselves in the evolution of small-scale technology, relatively nonviolent technology, "technology with a human face," so that people have a chance to enjoy themselves while they are working, instead of working solely for their pay packet and hoping, usually forlornly, for enjoyment solely during their leisure time.

---

language that enabled computers to respond to words as well as numbers.

The development of the transistor and then the silicon chip produced a revolutionary new approach to computers. In 1971, the invention of the microprocessor, a machine that combines the equivalent of thousands of transistors on a single, tiny silicon chip, opened the road for the development of the personal computer.

The computer is a new kind of machine whose chief function is to store and produce information, now considered an essential element of our fast-paced civilization. By the 1990s, the personal computer had become a regular fixture in businesses, schools, and homes. It not only makes a whole host of tasks much easier, but it has also become an important tool in virtually every area of modern life. Indeed, other tools and machines now depend for their functioning on computers. Many of the minute-by-minute decisions involved in flying an airplane, for example, are made by a computer.

Despite the marvels that were produced by the alliance of science and technology, some people came to question the underlying assumption of this alliance—that

scientific knowledge gave human beings the ability to manipulate the environment for their benefit. They maintained that some technological advances had far-reaching side effects damaging to the environment. The chemical fertilizers, for example, that were touted for producing larger crops wreaked havoc with the ecological balance of streams, rivers, and woodlands. *Small Is Beautiful*, written by the British economist E. F. Schumacher (1911–1977), was a fundamental critique of the dangers of the new science and technology (see the box above). The widespread proliferation of fouled beaches and dying forests and lakes made environmentalism one of the important issues of the 1990s.

After World War II, a number of physicists continued to explore the implications of Einstein's revolution in physics and raised fundamental questions about the nature of reality. To some physicists, quantum and relativity theory described the universe as a complicated web of relations in which there were no isolated building blocks. Thus, the universe was not a "collection of physical objects," but a complicated web of relations between "various parts of a unified whole." Moreover, this web of relations that is the universe also included the human observer. Human beings could not be objective observers of objects detached from themselves because the very act of observation made them participants in the process itself. These speculations implied that the old Newtonian conception of the universe as a machine was an outdated tool for understanding the nature of the universe.

The Explosion of Popular Culture

Since World War II, popular culture has played an increasingly important role in helping Western people define themselves. At one level popular culture is but the history of the ever-changing whims of mass taste, but on another level "it is a history of how modern society has created images of itself and expressed its fantasies, its fears, its ambitions."[4]

The history of popular culture is also the history of the economic system that supports it, for this system manufactures, distributes, and sells the images that people consume as popular culture. As popular culture and its economic support system become increasingly intertwined, industries of leisure emerge. As one historian of popular culture has argued: "Industrial societies turn the provision of leisure into a commercial activity, in which their citizens are sold entertainment, recreation, pleasure, and appearance as commodities that differ from the goods at the drugstore only in the way they are used."[5] Modern popular culture therefore is an integral part of the mass consumer society in which it has emerged, making it quite different from the folk culture of preceding centuries. Folk culture is something people make whereas popular culture is something people buy.

POPULAR CULTURE AND THE AMERICANIZATION OF THE WORLD

The United States has been the most influential force in shaping popular culture in the West and, to a lesser degree, the entire world. Through movies, music, advertising, and television, the United States has spread its particular form of consumerism and the American Dream to millions around the world. Already in 1923 the New York *Morning Post* noted that "the film is to America what the flag was once to Britain. By its means Uncle Sam may hope some day . . . to Americanize the world."[6] In movies, television, and popular music, the impact of American popular culture on the Western world is apparent.

Motion pictures were the primary vehicle for the diffusion of American popular culture in the years immediately following the war and continued to dominate both European and American markets in the next decades (40 percent of Hollywood's income in the 1960s came from the European market). Nevertheless, the existence of a profitable art-house circuit in America and Europe enabled European filmmakers to make films whose themes and avant-garde methods were quite different from those of Hollywood. Italy and Sweden, for example, developed a tradition of "national cinema" that reflected "specific cultural traits in a mode in which they could be successfully exported." The 1957 film *The Seventh Seal*, by the Swedish director Ingmar Bergman, was a good example of the successful European art film. Bergman's films caused him to be viewed as "an artist of comparable stature to a novelist or playwright." So too were François Truffaut in France and Federico Fellini in Italy; such directors gloried in experimenting with subject matter and technique and produced films dealing with more complex and daring themes than Hollywood would attempt.

Although developed in the 1930s, television did not become readily available until the late 1940s. By 1954, there were 32 million sets in the United States as television became the centerpiece of middle-class life. It has been said that television was perfect for the suburban home, the "nuclear family's bunker," as it was "a piece of furniture that did something."

In the 1960s, as television spread around the world, American networks unloaded their products on Europe and the Third World at extraordinarily low prices. For instance, the British Broadcasting Corporation (BBC) could buy American programs for one-tenth the cost per viewer of producing its own. Only the establishment of quota systems prevented American television from completely inundating these countries. Nevertheless, American shows have remained popular in Europe. *Baywatch* was the most popular show in Italy in 1996.

Unlike the United States, television and radio in Europe have largely been controlled by the state. The BBC model strongly influenced German broadcasting after the war. In France, de Gaulle saw state control of television as an important counterbalance to the opposition French press. The 1980s, however, saw an increasing trend toward commercial television in Western Europe. In the Communist countries of Eastern Europe and the Soviet Union, state control was even more pervasive, but as communism lost its grip in Eastern Europe in the revolutions of 1989, calls for freedom of speech and press were extended to mass media. In 1990, independent television and radio productions were allowed in the Soviet Union for the first time.

The United States has dominated popular music since the end of World War II. Jazz, blues, rhythm and blues, rap, and rock and roll have been by far the most popular music forms in the Western world—and much of the non-Western world—during this time. All of them originated in the United States, and all are rooted in African American musical innovations. These forms later spread to the rest of the world, inspiring local artists who then transformed the music in their own way. Often these transformed models then returned to the United States to inspire American artists. This was certainly the case with rock and roll. Through the 1950s, American figures such as Chuck Berry, Little Richard, and Elvis Presley inspired the Beatles and other British performers, who then led an "invasion" of the United States in the 1960s, creating a sensation and in part sparking new rockers in America. Rock music itself developed in the 1950s. In 1952, white disc jockeys began playing rhythm and blues and tradi-

THE BEATLES IN CONCERT. Although rock and roll originated in the United States, it also inspired musical groups in Europe. This was certainly true of Britain's Beatles, who created a sensation among young people when they came to the United States in the 1960s. Here the Beatles are shown during a performance on *The Ed Sullivan Show.*

tional blues music performed by African Americans to young white audiences. The music was popular with this audience, and record companies began recording watered-down white cover versions of this music. It was not until performers such as Elvis Presley mixed white "folkabilly" with rhythm and blues that rock and roll became popular with the larger white audience.

The period from 1967 to 1973 was probably the true golden age of rock. During this brief period, much experimentation in rock music took place, as it did in society in general. Straightfoward rock and roll competed with a new hybrid blues rock, created in part by British performers such as the Rolling Stones, who were in turn inspired by African American blues artists. Many musicians also experimented with non-Western musical sounds, such as Indian sitars. Some of the popular music of the 1960s also focused on social issues. It was against the Vietnam War and materialism and promoted "peace and love" as alternatives to the prevailing "establishment" culture.

The same migration of a musical form from the United States to Britain and back to the United States occurred when the early punk movement in New York spread to Britain in the mid-1970s after failing to make an immediate impact in the United States. The more influential British punk movement of 1976–1979 was also fueled by an economic crisis that had resulted in large numbers of unemployed and undereducated young people. However, punk was not simply a proletarian movement. Many of its supporters, performers, and promoters were British art school graduates who applied avant-garde experimentation to the movement. Punk rockers rejected most social conventions and preached anarchy and rebellion. They often wore tattered clothes and clothespins in their cheeks, symbolizing their rejection of a materialistic and degenerate culture. Musically, punk was extremely primitive in structure and performance, with noise and distortion elevated to art. Pure punk was short-lived, partly because its intense energy quickly burned out (as did many of its performers) and partly because, as ex-punk Mick Hucknall said, "the biggest mistake of the punks was that they rejected music." Offshoots of punk proliferated through the 1980s, however, and continue to influence the rock and roll scene.

THE GROWTH OF MASS SPORTS

In the postwar years, sports have become a major product of both popular culture and the leisure industry. The development of satellite television and various electronic breakthroughs helped make sports a global phenomenon. Olympic Games could now be broadcast across the globe from anywhere in the world. Sports became a cheap form of entertainment for the consumer as fans did not have to leave their homes to enjoy athletic competitions. In fact, some sports organizations initially resisted television fearing that it would hurt ticket sales. Soon, however, the tremendous revenues possible from television contracts overcame this hesitation. As sports television revenue escalated, many sports came to receive the bulk of their yearly revenue from television contracts. The Olympics, for example, are now funded primarily by American television. These contracts are paid for by advertising sponsors, mostly for products to be consumed along with the sport: beer, soda, and snack foods.

Sports have become big politics as well as big business. The politicization of sports has been one of the most significant trends in sports during the second half of the twentieth century. Football (soccer) remains the dominant world sport and more than ever has become a vehicle for nationalist sentiment and expression. The World Cup is the most watched event on television. Although the sport can be a positive outlet for national and local pride, all too often it has been marred by violence as nationalistic energies have overcome rational behavior. Events in Britain in particular have been marred by fan violence as extreme hooligans have rioted at matches.

The most telling example of the potent mix of politics and sport continues to be the Olympic Games. When the Soviets entered Olympic competition in 1952, the Olympics began to take on Cold War implications and became known as the "war without weapons." The Soviets saw the Olympics as a way to stimulate nationalist spirit, as well as to promote the Communist system as the best path for social progress. The Soviets led the Olympics in terms of total medals won between 1956 and 1988. The nature of the Olympics, with their daily medal count by nation and elaborate ceremonies and rituals such as the playing of the national anthem of the winning athletes and the parade of nations, virtually ensured the politicization of the games originally intended to foster international cooperation through friendly competition.

The political nature of the games found expression in other ways as well. In 1956, six nations withdrew from the games to protest the Soviet crushing of the Hungarian uprising. In 1972, twenty-seven African nations threatened to pull out of the Munich Olympics because of apartheid in South Africa. Also at the Munich Games, the Palestinian terrorist group Black September seized eleven Israeli athletes as hostages, all of whom died in a confrontation at an airport. The United States led a boycott of the 1980 Moscow Games to protest the Soviet invasion of Afghanistan, and the Soviets responded by boycotting the Los Angeles Games in 1984.

POPULAR CULTURE: TOWARD A NEW GLOBALISM
Media critic and theorist Marshall McLuhan predicted in the 1960s that advances in mass communications technology, such as satellites and electronics, would eventually lead to a shrinking of the world, a lessening of cultural distinctions, and a breaking down of cultural barriers, all of which would in time transform the world into a single "global village." McLuhan was quite optimistic about these developments, and his ideas became quite popular at the time. Many critics have since argued that McLuhan was too utopian about the benefits of technological progress and maintain that the mass media that these technological breakthroughs created are still controlled by a small number of multinational corporations that "colonize the rest of the world, sometimes benignly, sometimes not." They argue that this has allowed Western popular culture to disrupt the traditional cultures of less developed countries and inculcate new patterns of behavior as well as new desires and new dissatisfactions.

Cultural contacts, however, often move in two directions. While the world has been "Americanized" to a great extent, formerly unfamiliar ways of life and styles of music have also come into the world of the West. This has expanded the horizons of Westerners and led to the creation of new cultural hybrids in music, philosophy, and religion. This emergence of a global culture has become part of the new globalism at the beginning of the twenty-first century.

◆ Toward a Global Civilization?

Increasingly, more and more people are becoming aware of the political and economic interdependence of the world's nations as well as the global nature of our contemporary problems. On the threshold of the twenty-first century, human beings are coming to understand that destructive forces generated in one part of the world soon affect the entire world. Nuclear proliferation makes nuclear war an ever-present possibility; nuclear war would mean radioactive fallout for the entire planet. Smokestack pollution in one nation can produce acid rain in another. Oil spills and dumping of wastes in the ocean have an impact on the shores of many nations. The consumption of drugs in the world's wealthy nations affects the stability of both wealthy and less developed nations. As food, water, energy, and natural resources crises proliferate, one nation's solutions often become other nations' problems. The new globalism includes the recognition that the challenges that seem to threaten human existence at the beginning of the twenty-first century are global. As a Soviet physicist and an American engineer jointly concluded in 1988: "The emergence of global problems and the recognition of their importance is perhaps the greatest accomplishment of contemporary thought."[7]

As the heirs of Western civilization have become aware that the problems humans face are global—not only national—they have responded to this challenge in different ways. One approach has been to develop grass-roots social movements, including environmental, women's and men's liberation, human potential, appropriate-technology, and nonviolence movements. "Think globally, act locally" is frequently the slogan of these grass-roots groups. Related to the emergence of these social movements is the growth of nongovernmental organizations (NGOs).

According to one analyst, NGOs are an important instrument in the cultivation of global perspectives: "Since NGOs by definition are identified with interests that transcend national boundaries, we expect all NGOs to define problems in global terms, to take account of human interests and needs as they are found in all parts of the planet."[8] NGOs are often represented at the United Nations and include professional, business, and cooperative organizations; foundations; religious, peace, and disarmament groups; youth and women's organizations; environmental and human rights groups; and research institutes. The number of international NGOs increased from 176 in 1910 to 18,000 in 1988.

And yet, hopes for global approaches to global problems have also been hindered by political, ethnic, and religious disputes. Pollution of the Rhine River by factories along its banks provokes angry disputes among European nations, and the United States and Canada have argued about the effects of acid rain on Canadian forests. The collapse of the Soviet Union and its satellite system between 1989 and 1991 seemed to provide an enormous boost to the potential for international cooperation on global issues. In fact, the collapse of the Soviet empire has had almost the opposite effect, as the disintegration of the Soviet Union has led to the emergence of squabbling new nations and an atmosphere of conflict and tension throughout much of Eastern Europe. The bloody conflict in the lands of the former Yugoslavia clearly indicates the dangers inherent in the rise of nationalist sentiment among various ethnic and religious groups in Eastern Europe.

Thus, even as the world becomes more global in culture and interdependent in its mutual relations, centrifugal forces are still at work attempting to redefine the political, cultural, and ethnic ways in which the world is divided. Such efforts are often disruptive and can sometimes work against measures to enhance our human destiny.

Many lessons can be learned from the history of Western civilization, but one of them is especially clear.

THE EARTH.   For many people in the West as in the rest of the world, the view of earth from outer space fostered an important image of global unity. The American astronaut Russell Schweickart wrote: "From where you see it, the thing is a whole, and it is so beautiful." In a similar reaction, Yuri Gagarin, a Soviet cosmonaut, remarked: "What strikes me, is not only the beauty of the continents . . . but their closeness to one another . . . their essential unity."

Lack of involvement in the affairs of one's society can lead to a sense of powerlessness. In an age that is often crisis-laden and chaotic, an understanding of our Western heritage and its lessons can be instrumental in helping us create new models for the future. For we are all creators of history and upon us depends the future of Western and indeed world civilization.

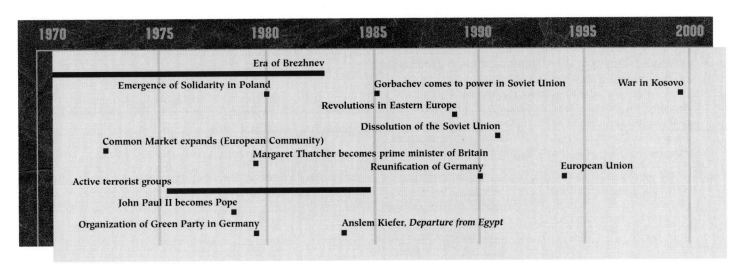

| 1970 | 1975 | 1980 | 1985 | 1990 | 1995 | 2000 |

Era of Brezhnev

Emergence of Solidarity in Poland

Gorbachev comes to power in Soviet Union

War in Kosovo

Revolutions in Eastern Europe

Dissolution of the Soviet Union

Common Market expands (European Community)

Margaret Thatcher becomes prime minister of Britain

Reunification of Germany

European Union

Active terrorist groups

John Paul II becomes Pope

Organization of Green Party in Germany

Anslem Kiefer, *Departure from Egypt*

NOTES

1. Mikhail Gorbachev, "Report to the 27th Party Congress," February 25, 1986, in *Current Soviet Policies 9* (1986): 10.
2. Quoted in Renate Bridenthal, "Women in the New Europe," in Renate Bridenthal, Susan Mosher Stuard, and Merry E. Weisner, eds., *Becoming Visible: Women in European History*, 3d ed. (Boston, 1998), pp. 564–565.
3. Quoted in Henry Grosshans, *The Search for Modern Europe* (Boston, 1970), p. 421.
4. Richard Maltby, ed., *Passing Parade: A History of Popular Culture in the Twentieth Century* (Oxford, 1989), p. 8.
5. Ibid.
6. Quoted in ibid., p. 11.
7. Sergei Kapitza and Martin Hellman, "A Message to the Scientific Community," in Anatoly Gromyko and Martin Hellman, eds., *Breakthrough—Emerging New Thinking: Soviet and Western Scholars Issue a Challenge to Build a World beyond War* (New York, 1988), p. xii.
8. Elise Boulding, *Women in the Twentieth Century World* (New York, 1977), pp. 186–187.

SUGGESTIONS FOR FURTHER READING

For general surveys of contemporary European history, see the references in Chapter 28. General studies on the Cold War are also listed in Chapter 28. There is a detailed analysis of American-Soviet relations in the 1970s and 1980s in R. Garthoff, *Détente and Confrontation: American-Soviet Relations from Nixon to Reagan* (Washington, D.C., 1985). On the end of the Cold War, see B. Denitch, *The End of the Cold War* (Minneapolis, 1990); W. G. Hyland, *The Cold War Is Over* (New York, 1990); and W. Laqueur, *Soviet Union 2000: Reform or Revolution?* (New York, 1990).

Recent problems in the Soviet Union are analyzed in M. Lewin, *The Gorbachev Phenomenon* (Berkeley, 1988); G. Hosking, *The Awakening of the Soviet Union* (London, 1990); and S. White, *Gorbachev and After* (Cambridge, 1991). For general studies of the Soviet satellites in Eastern Europe, see S. Fischer-Galati, *Eastern Europe in the 1980s* (London, 1981); and the references in Chapter 28. Additional studies on the recent history of these countries include T. G. Ash, *The Polish Revolution: Solidarity* (New York, 1984); T. G. Ash, *The Magic Lantern: The Revolution of '89 Witnessed in Warsaw, Budapest, Berlin and Prague* (New York, 1990); M. Shafir, *Romania: Politics, Economics and Society* (London, 1985); C. S. Maier, *Dissolution: The Crisis of Communism and the End of East Germany* (Princeton, N.J., 1997); and S. Ramet, *Nationalism and Federalism in Yugoslavia* (Bloomington, Ind., 1992).

For general works on Western Europe and individual countries, see the references in Chapter 28. On the recent history of these countries, see E. J. Evans, *Thatcher and Thatcherism* (New York, 1997); P. A. Hall, *Governing the Economy: The Politics of State Intervention in Britain and France* (New York, 1986); S. Baumann-Reynolds, *François Mitterand* (Westport, Conn., 1995); R. J. Dalton, *Politics in West Germany* (Glenview, Ill., 1989); and K. Jarausch, *The Rush to German Unity* (New York, 1994).

The changing role of women is examined in C. Duchen, *Feminism in France* (London, 1986). On terrorism, see the works by W. Laqueur, *Terrorism*, 2d ed. (New York and London, 1988); and R. Rubenstein, *Alchemists of Revolution: Terrorism in the Modern World* (London, 1987). The problems of guest workers and immigrants are examined in J. Miller, *Foreign Workers in Western Europe* (London, 1981); and S. Castles, *Here for Good: Western Europe's New Ethnic Minorities* (London, 1984). On the development of the Green parties, see M. O'Neill, *Green Parties and Political Change in Contemporary Europe* (Aldershot, 1997); and D. Richardson and C. Rootes, eds., *The Green Challenge: The Development of the Green Parties in Europe* (London, 1995).

For a general view of postwar thought, see R. N. Stromberg, *European Intellectual History since 1789*, 5th ed. (Englewood Cliffs, N.J., 1990). On contemporary art, see R. Lambert, *Cambridge Introduction to the History of Art: The Twentieth Century* (Cambridge, 1981); and the general work by B. Cole and A. Gealt, *Art of the Western World* (New York, 1989). A physicist's view of science is contained in J. Ziman, *The Force of Knowledge: The Scientific Dimension of Society* (Cambridge, 1976). A physicist's view of a new conception of reality is D. Bohm, *Wholeness and the Implicate Order* (Boston, 1980). The space race is examined in W. A. McDougall, *The Heavens and the Earth: A Political History of the Space Age* (New York, 1984). A classic work on existentialism is W. Barrett, *Irrational Man* (Garden City, N.Y., 1962). There is an excellent survey of twentieth-century popular culture in R. Maltby, ed., *Passing Parade: A History of Popular Culture in the Twentieth Century* (Oxford, 1989). On film and the media, see L. May, *Screening Out the Past: The Birth of Mass Culture and the Motion Picture Industry* (New York, 1980); and F. Wheen, *Television* (London, 1985). On popular music, see P. Eberly, *Music in the Air* (New York, 1982). Sport is examined in A. Guttmann, *From Ritual to Record: The Nature of Modern Sports* (New York, 1978); and R. Mandell, *Sport: A Cultural History* (New York, 1984). On the "global village" idea, see M. McLuhan, *Understanding Media: The Extensions of Man* (London, 1964).

For additional reading, go to InfoTrac College Edition, your online research library at http://web1.infotrac-college.com

Enter the search terms *Single European Market* using the Subject Guide.

Enter the search terms *Europe Communism* using Key Terms.

Enter the search term *perestroika* using the Subject Guide.

Enter the search terms *Green Parties* using Key Terms.

Glossary

absolutism a form of government where the sovereign power or ultimate authority rested in the hands of a monarch who claimed to rule by divine right and was therefore responsible only to God.

Agricultural (Neolithic) Revolution the shift from hunting animals and gathering plants for sustenance to producing food by systematic agriculture that occurred gradually between 10,000 and 4000 B.C. (the Neolithic or "New Stone" Age).

agricultural revolution the application of new agricultural techniques that allowed for a large increase in productivity in the eighteenth century.

anarchism a political theory that holds that all governments and existing social institutions are unnecessary and advocates a society based on voluntary cooperation.

anti-Semitism hostility toward or discrimination against Jews.

appeasement the policy, followed by the European nations in the 1930s, of accepting Hitler's annexation of Austria and Czechoslovakia in the belief that meeting his demands would assure peace and stability.

Arianism a Christian heresy that taught that Jesus was inferior to God. Though condemned by the Council of Nicaea in 325, Arianism was adopted by many of the Germanic peoples who entered the Roman Empire over the next centuries.

aristocracy a class of hereditary nobility in medieval Europe; a warrior class who shared a distinctive lifestyle based on the institution of knighthood, although there were social divisions within the group based on extremes of wealth.

Ausgleich the "Compromise" of 1867 that created the dual monarchy of Austria-Hungary. Austria and Hungary each had its own capital, constitution, and legislative assembly, but were united under one monarch.

authoritarian state a state that has a dictatorial government and some other trappings of a totalitarian state, but does not demand that the masses be actively involved in the regime's goals as totalitarian states do.

auxiliaries troops enlisted from the subject peoples of the Roman Empire to supplement the regular legions composed of Roman citizens.

balance of power a distribution of power among several states such that no single nation can dominate or interfere with the interests of another.

benefice in the Christian church, a position, such as a bishopric, that consisted of both a sacred office and the right of the holder to the annual revenues from the position.

bicameral legislature a legislature with two houses.

Black Death the outbreak of plague (mostly bubonic) in the mid-fourteenth century that killed from 25 to 50 percent of Europe's population.

Blitzkrieg "lightning war." A war conducted with great speed and force, as in Germany's advance at the beginning of World War II.

Bolsheviks a small faction of the Russian Social Democratic Party who were led by Lenin and dedicated to violent revolution; seized power in Russia in 1917 and were subsequently renamed the Communists.

boyars the Russian nobility.

Brezhnev Doctrine the doctrine, enunciated by Leonid Brezhnev, that the Soviet Union had a right to intervene if socialism was threatened in another socialist state; used to justify the use of Soviet troops in Czechoslovakia in 1968.

caliph the secular leader of the Islamic community.

capital material wealth used or available for use in the production of more wealth.

cartel a combination of independent commercial enterprises that work together to control prices and limit competition.

Cartesian dualism Descartes's principle of the separation of mind and matter (and mind and body) that enabled scientists to view matter as something separate from themselves that could be investigated by reason.

chansons de geste a form of vernacular literature in the High Middle Ages that consisted of heroic epics focusing on the deeds of warriors.

chivalry the ideal of civilized behavior that emerged among the nobility in the eleventh and twelfth centuries under the influence of the church; a code of ethics knights were expected to uphold.

Christian (northern) humanism an intellectual movement in northern Europe in the late fifteenth and early sixteenth centuries that combined the interest in the classics of the Italian Renaissance with an interest in the sources of early Christianity, including the New Testament and the writings of the church fathers.

civic humanism an intellectual movement of the Italian Renaissance that saw Cicero, who was both an intellectual and a statesman, as the ideal and held that humanists should be involved in government and use their rhetorical training in the service of the state.

civil rights the basic rights of citizens including equality before the law, freedom of speech and press, and freedom from arbitrary arrest.

Cold War the ideological conflict between the Soviet Union and the United States after World War II.

collective farms large farms created in the Soviet Union by Stalin by combining many small holdings into one large farm worked by the peasants under government supervision.

collective security the use of an international army raised by an association of nations to deter aggression and keep the peace.

coloni free tenant farmers who worked as sharecroppers on the large estates of the Roman Empire (singular: *colonus*).

common law law common to the entire kingdom of England; imposed by the king's courts beginning in the twelfth century to replace the customary law used in county and feudal courts that varied from place to place.

commune in medieval Europe, an association of townspeople bound together by a sworn oath for the purpose of obtaining basic liberties from the lord of the territory in which the town was located; also, the self-governing town after receiving its liberties.

conciliarism a movement in fourteenth- and fifteenth-century Europe that held that final authority in spiritual matters resided with a general church council, not the pope; emerged in response to the Avignon papacy and the Great Schism and used to justify the summoning of the Council of Constance (1414–1418).

condottieri leaders of bands of mercenary soldiers in Renaissance Italy who sold their services to the highest bidder.

conquistadors "conquerors." Leaders in the Spanish conquests in the Americas, especially Mexico and Peru, in the sixteenth century.

conscription a military draft.

conservatism an ideology based on tradition and social stability that favored the maintenance of established institutions, organized religion, and obedience to authority and resisted change, especially abrupt change.

consuls the chief executive officers of the Roman Republic. Two were chosen annually to administer the government and lead the army in battle.

consumer society a term applied to Western society after World War II as the working classes adopted the consumption patterns of the middle class and installment plans, credit cards, and easy credit made consumer goods such as appliances and automobiles widely available.

Continental System Napoleon's effort to bar British goods from the Continent in the hope of weakening Britain's economy and destroying its capacity to wage war.

cosmopolitanism the quality of being sophisticated and having wide international experience.

cottage industry a system of textile manufacturing in which spinners and weavers worked at home in their cottages using raw materials supplied to them by capitalist entrepreneurs.

cultural relativism the belief that no culture is superior to another because culture is a matter of custom, not reason, and derives its meaning from the group holding it.

cuneiform "wedge-shaped." A system of writing developed by the Sumerians that consisted of wedge-shaped impressions made by a reed stylus on clay tablets.

decolonization the process of becoming free of colonial status and achieving statehood; occurred in most of the world's colonies between 1947 and 1962.

deism belief in God as the creator of the universe who, after setting it in motion, ceased to have any direct involvement in it and allowed it to run according to its own natural laws.

demesne the part of a manor retained under the direct control of the lord and worked by the serfs as part of their labor services.

depression a very severe, protracted economic downturn with high levels of unemployment.

destalinization the policy of denouncing and undoing the most repressive aspects of Stalin's regime; begun by Nikita Khrushchev in 1956.

détente the relaxation of tension between the Soviet Union and the United States that occurred in the 1970s.

dialectic logic, one of the seven liberal arts that made up the medieval curriculum. In Marxist thought, the process by which all change occurs through the clash of antagonistic elements.

Diaspora the scattering of Jews throughout the ancient world after the Babylonian captivity in the sixth century B.C.

dictator in the Roman Republic, an official granted unlimited power to run the state for a short period of time, usually six months, during an emergency.

diocese the area under the jurisdiction of a Christian bishop; based originally on Roman administrative districts.

direct representation a system of choosing delegates to a representative assembly in which citizens vote directly for the delegates who will represent them.

divination the practice of seeking to foretell future events by interpreting divine signs, which could appear in various forms, such as in entrails of animals, in patterns in smoke, or in dreams.

divine-right monarchy a monarchy based on the belief that monarchs receive their power directly from God and are responsible to no one except God.

domino theory the belief that if the Communists succeeded in Vietnam, other countries in Southeast and East Asia would also fall (like dominoes) to communism; a justification for the U.S. intervention in Vietnam.

dualism the belief that the universe is dominated by two opposing forces, one good and the other evil.

dynastic state a state where the maintenance and expansion of the interests of the ruling family is the primary consideration.

economic imperialism the process in which banks and corporations from developed nations invest in underdeveloped regions and establish a major presence there in the hope of making high profits; not necessarily the same as colonial expansion in that businesses invest where they can make a profit, which may not be in their own nation's colonies.

empiricism the practice of relying on observation and experiment.

enclosure movement   in the eighteenth century, the fencing in of the old open fields, combining many small holdings into larger units that could be farmed more efficiently.

encyclical   a letter from the pope to all the bishops of the Roman Catholic church.

enlightened absolutism   an absolute monarchy where the ruler follows the principles of the Enlightenment by introducing reforms for the improvement of society, allowing freedom of speech and the press, permitting religious toleration, expanding education, and ruling in accordance with the laws.

Enlightenment   an eighteenth-century intellectual movement, led by the philosophes, that stressed the application of reason and the scientific method to all aspects of life.

entrepreneur   one who organizes, operates, and assumes the risk in a business venture in the expectation of making a profit.

Epicureanism   a philosophy founded by Epicurus in the fourth century B.C. that taught that happiness (freedom from emotional turmoil) could be achieved through the pursuit of pleasure (intellectual rather than sensual pleasure).

equestrians   a group of extremely wealthy men in the late Roman Republic who were effectively barred from high office, but sought political power commensurate with their wealth; called equestrians because many had gotten their start as cavalry officers (*equites*).

ethnic cleansing   the policy of killing or forcibly removing people of another ethnic group; used by the Serbs against Bosnian Muslims in the 1990s.

eucharist   a Christian sacrament in which consecrated bread and wine are consumed in celebration of Jesus' Last Supper; also called the Lord's Supper or communion.

evolutionary socialism   a socialist doctrine espoused by Eduard Bernstein who argued that socialists should stress cooperation and evolution to attain power by democratic means rather than by conflict and revolution.

fascism   an ideology or movement that exalts the nation above the individual and calls for a centralized government with a dictatorial leader, economic and social regimentation, and forcible suppression of opposition; in particular, the ideology of Mussolini's Fascist regime in Italy.

feminism   the belief in the social, political, and economic equality of the sexes; also, organized activity to advance women's rights.

fief   a landed estate granted to a vassal in exchange for military services.

Final Solution   the physical extermination of the Jewish people by the Nazis during World War II.

folk culture   the traditional arts and crafts, literature, music, and other customs of the people; something that people make, as opposed to modern popular culture, which is something people buy.

free trade   the unrestricted international exchange of goods with low or no tariffs.

general strike   a strike by all or most workers in an economy; espoused by Georges Sorel as the heroic action that could be used to inspire the workers to destroy capitalist society.

gentry   well-to-do English landowners below the level of the nobility; played an important role in the English Civil War of the seventeenth century.

geocentric theory   the idea that the earth is at the center of the universe and that the sun and other celestial objects revolve around the earth.

glasnost   "openness." Mikhail Gorbachev's policy of encouraging Soviet citizens to openly discuss the strengths and weaknesses of the Soviet Union.

good emperors   the five emperors who ruled from 96 to 180 (Nerva, Trajan, Hadrian, Antoninus Pius, and Marcus Aurelius), a period of peace and prosperity for the Roman Empire.

Great Schism   the crisis in the late medieval church when there were first two and then three popes; ended by the Council of Constance (1414–1418).

guest workers   foreign workers working temporarily in European countries.

guild   an association of people with common interests and concerns, especially people working in the same craft. In medieval Europe, guilds came to control much of the production process and to restrict entry into various trades.

gymnasium   in classical Greece, a place for athletics; in the Hellenistic Age, a secondary school with a curriculum centered on music, physical exercise, and literature.

heliocentric theory   the idea that the sun (not the earth) is at the center of the universe.

Hellenistic   literally, "to imitate the Greeks"; the era after the death of Alexander the Great when Greek culture spread into the Near East and blended with the culture of that region.

helots   serfs in ancient Sparta, who were permanently bound to the land that they worked for their Spartan masters.

heresy   the holding of religious doctrines different from the official teachings of the church.

Hermeticism   an intellectual movement beginning in the fifteenth century that taught that divinity is embodied in all aspects of nature; included works on alchemy and magic as well as theology and philosophy. The tradition continued into the seventeenth century and influenced many of the leading figures of the Scientific Revolution.

hetairai   highly sophisticated courtesans in ancient Athens who offered intellectual and musical entertainment as well as sex.

hieroglyphics   a highly pictorial system of writing used in ancient Egypt.

high culture   the literary and artistic culture of the educated and wealthy ruling classes.

Holocaust   the mass slaughter of European Jews by the Nazis during World War II.

hoplites   heavily armed infantry soldiers used in ancient Greece in a phalanx formation.

Huguenots   French Calvinists.

humanism   an intellectual movement in Renaissance Italy based upon the study of the Greek and Roman classics.

iconoclasm   an eighth-century Byzantine movement against the use of icons (pictures of sacred figures), which was condemned as idolatry.

ideology   a political philosophy such as conservatism or liberalism.

imperium   "the right to command." In the Roman Republic, the chief executive officers (consuls and praetors) possessed the *imperium*; a military commander was an *imperator*. In the Roman Empire, the title *imperator*, or emperor, came to be used for the ruler.

indirect representation   a system of choosing delegates to a representative assembly in which citizens do not choose the delegates directly but instead vote for electors who choose the delegates.

individualism   emphasis on and interest in the unique traits of each person.

indulgence   the remission of part or all of the temporal punishment in purgatory due to sin; granted for charitable contributions and other good deeds. Indulgences became a regular practice of the Christian church in the High Middle Ages, and their abuse was instrumental in sparking Luther's reform movement in the sixteenth century.

infanticide   the practice of killing infants.

inflation   a sustained rise in the price level.

intendants   royal officials in seventeenth-century France who were sent into the provinces to execute the orders of the central government.

intervention, principle of   the idea, after the Congress of Vienna, that the great powers of Europe had the right to send armies into countries experiencing revolution to restore legitimate monarchs to their thrones.

isolationism   a foreign policy in which a nation refrains from making alliances or engaging actively in international affairs.

jihad   "striving in the way of the Lord." In Islam, the practice of conducting raids against neighboring peoples, which was an expansion of the Arab tradition of tribal raids against their persecutors.

joint-stock company   a company or association that raises capital by selling shares to individuals who receive dividends on their investment while a board of directors runs the company.

joint-stock investment bank   a bank created by selling shares of stock to investors. Such banks potentially have access to much more capital than do private banks owned by one or a few individuals.

justification of faith   the primary doctrine of the Protestant Reformation; taught that humans are saved not through good works, but by the grace of God, bestowed freely through the sacrifice of Jesus.

laissez-faire   "to let alone." An economic doctrine that holds that an economy is best served when the government does not interfere but allows the economy to self-regulate according to the forces of supply and demand.

latifundia   large landed estates in the Roman Empire (singular: *latifundium*).

lay investiture   the practice in which a layperson chose a bishop and invested him with the symbols of both his temporal office and his spiritual office; led to the Investiture Controversy, which was ended by compromise in the Concordat of Worms in 1122.

Lebensraum   "living space." The doctrine, adopted by Hitler, that a nation's power depends on the amount of land it occupies; thus, a nation must expand to be strong.

legitimacy, principle of   the idea that after the Napoleonic wars peace could best be reestablished in Europe by restoring legitimate monarchs who would preserve traditional institutions; guided Metternich at the Congress of Vienna.

Leninism   Lenin's revision of Marxism that held that Russia need not experience a bourgeois revolution before it could move toward socialism.

liberal arts   the seven areas of study that formed the basis of education in medieval and early modern Europe. Following Boethius and other late Roman authors, they consisted of grammar, rhetoric, and dialectic or logic (the *trivium*) and arithmetic, geometry, astronomy, and music (the *quadrivium*).

liberalism   an ideology based on the belief that people should be as free from restraint as possible. Economic liberalism is the idea that the government should not interfere in the workings of the economy. Political liberalism is the idea that there should be restraints on the exercise of power so that people can enjoy basic civil rights in a constitutional state with a representative assembly.

limited liability   the principle that shareholders in a joint-stock corporation can be held responsible for the corporation's debts only up to the amount they have invested.

limited (constitutional) monarchy   a system of government in which the monarch is limited by a representative assembly and by the duty to rule in accordance with the laws of the land.

mandates   a system established after World War I whereby a nation officially administered a territory (mandate) on behalf of the League of Nations. Thus, France administered Lebanon and Syria as mandates, and Britain administered Iraq and Palestine.

manor   an agricultural estate operated by a lord and worked by peasants who performed labor services and paid various rents and fees to the lord in exchange for protection and sustenance.

Marshall Plan   the European Recovery Program, under which the United States provided financial aid to European countries to help them rebuild after World War II.

Marxism   the political, economic, and social theories of Karl Marx, which included the idea that history is the story of class struggle and that ultimately the proletariat will overthrow the bourgeoisie and establish a dictatorship en route to a classless society.

mass education   a state-run educational system, usually free and compulsory, that aims to ensure that all children in society have at least a basic education.

mass leisure forms of leisure that appeal to large numbers of people in a society including the working classes; emerged at the end of the nineteenth century to provide workers with amusements after work and on weekends; used during the twentieth century by totalitarian states to control their populations.

mass politics a political order characterized by mass political parties and universal male and (eventually) female suffrage.

mass society a society in which the concerns of the majority—the lower classes—play a prominent role; characterized by extension of voting rights, an improved standard of living for the lower classes, and mass education.

materialism the belief that everything mental, spiritual, or ideal is an outgrowth of physical forces and that truth is found in concrete material existence, not through feeling or intuition.

mercantilism an economic theory that held that a nation's prosperity depended on its supply of gold and silver and that the total volume of trade is unchangeable; therefore, advocated that the government play an active role in the economy by encouraging exports and discouraging imports, especially through the use of tariffs.

Mesolithic Age the period from 10,000 to 7000 B.C., characterized by a gradual transition from a food-gathering/hunting economy to a food-producing economy.

metics resident foreigners in ancient Athens; not permitted full rights of citizenship but did receive the protection of the laws.

militarism a policy of aggressive military preparedness; in particular, the large armies based on mass conscription and complex, inflexible plans for mobilization that most European nations had before World War I.

ministerial responsibility a tenet of nineteenth-century liberalism that held that ministers of the monarch should be responsible to the legislative assembly rather than to the monarch.

Modernism the new artistic and literary styles that emerged in the decades before 1914 as artists rebelled against traditional efforts to portray reality as accurately as possible (leading to Impressionism and Cubism) and writers explored new forms.

monotheistic/monotheism having only one god; the doctrine or belief that there is only one god.

mutual deterrence the belief that nuclear war could best be prevented if both the United States and the Soviet Union had sufficient nuclear weapons so that even if one nation launched a preemptive first strike, the other could respond and devastate the attacker.

mystery religions religions that involve initiation into secret rites that promise intense emotional involvement with spiritual forces and a greater chance of individual immortality.

nationalism a sense of national consciousness based on awareness of being part of a community—a "nation"—that has common institutions, traditions, language, and customs and that becomes the focus of the individual's primary political loyalty.

nationalities problem the dilemma faced by the Austro-Hungarian Empire in trying to unite a wide variety of ethnic groups including, among others, Austrians, Hungarians, Poles, Croats, Czechs, Serbs, Slovaks, and Slovenes in an era when nationalism and calls for self-determination were coming to the fore.

nationalization the process of converting a business or industry from private ownership to government control and ownership.

nation in arms the people's army raised by universal mobilization to repel the foreign enemies of the French Revolution.

nation-state a form of political organization in which a relatively homogeneous people inhabits a sovereign state, as opposed to a state containing people of several nationalities.

NATO the North Atlantic Treaty Organization; a military allianced formed in 1949 in which the signatories (Belgium, Canada, Denmark, France, Great Britain, Iceland, Italy, Luxembourg, the Netherlands, Norway, Portugal, and the United States) agreed to provide mutual assistance if any one of them was attacked; later expanded to include other nations.

natural laws a body of laws or specific principles held to be derived from nature and binding upon all human society even in the absence of positive laws.

natural rights certain inalienable rights to which all people are entitled; include the right to life, liberty, and property, freedom of speech and religion, and equality before the law.

natural selection Darwin's idea that organisms that are most adaptable to their environment survive and pass on the variations that enabled them to survive, while other, less adaptable organisms become extinct; "survival of the fittest."

Nazi New Order the Nazis' plan for their conquered territories; included the extermination of Jews and others considered inferior, ruthless exploitation of resources, German colonization in the east, and the use of Poles, Russians, and Ukrainians as slave labor.

Neoplatonism a revival of Platonic philosophy. In the third century A.D., a revival associated with Plotinus; in the Italian Renaissance, a revival associated with Marsilio Ficino who attempted to synthesize Christianity and Platonism.

New Economic Policy a modified version of the old capitalist system introduced in the Soviet Union by Lenin in 1921 to revive the economy after the ravages of the civil war and war communism.

new imperialism the revival of imperialism after 1880 in which European nations established colonies throughout much of Asia and Africa.

new monarchies the governments of France, England, and Spain at the end of the fifteenth century, where the rulers were successful in reestablishing or extending centralized royal authority, suppressing the nobility, controlling the church, and insisting upon the loyalty of all peoples living in their territories.

nobiles "nobles." The small group of families from both patrician and plebeian origins who produced most of the men who were elected to office in the late Roman Republic.

nominalism a school of thought in medieval Europe that, following Aristotle, held that only individual objects are real and that universals are only names created by humans.

nuclear family a family group consisting only of father, mother, and children.

old regime/old order the political and social system of France in the eighteenth century before the Revolution.

oligarchy rule by a few.

optimates "best men." Aristocratic leaders in the late Roman Republic who generally came from senatorial families and wished to retain their oligarchical privileges.

orders/estates the traditional tripartite division of European society based on heredity and quality rather than wealth or economic standing, first established in the Middle Ages and continuing into the eighteenth century; traditionally consisted of those who pray (the clergy), those who fight (the nobility), and those who work (all the rest).

organic evolution Darwin's principle that all plants and animals have evolved over a long period of time from earlier and simpler forms of life.

Paleolithic Age the period of human history when humans used simple stone tools (c. 2,500,000–10,000 B.C.).

pantheism a doctrine that equates God with the universe and all that is in it.

paterfamilias the dominant male in a Roman family whose powers over his wife and children were theoretically unlimited, though they were sometimes circumvented in practice.

patriarchal/patriarchy a society in which the father is supreme in the clan or family; more generally, a society dominated by men.

patriarchal family a family in which the husband/father dominates his wife and children.

patricians great landowners who became the ruling class in the Roman Republic.

patronage the practice of awarding titles and making appointments to government and other positions to gain political support.

Pax Romana "Roman peace." A term used to refer to the stability and prosperity that Roman rule brought to the Mediterranean world and much of western Europe during the first and second centuries A.D.

Pentateuch the first five books of the Hebrew Bible (Genesis, Exodus, Leviticus, Numbers, and Deuteronomy).

perestroika "restructuring." A term applied to Mikhail Gorbachev's economic, political, and social reforms in the Soviet Union.

permissive society a term applied to Western society after World War II to reflect the new sexual freedom and the emergence of a drug culture.

Petrine supremacy the doctrine that the bishop of Rome—the pope—as the successor of Saint Peter (traditionally considered the first bishop of Rome) should hold a preeminent position in the church.

phalanx a rectangular formation of tightly massed infantry soldiers.

philosophes intellectuals of the eighteenth-century Enlightenment who believed in applying a spirit of rational criticism to all things, including religion and politics, and who focused on improving and enjoying this world, rather than on the afterlife.

plebeians the class of Roman citizens who included nonpatrician landowners, craftspeople, merchants, and small farmers in the Roman Republic. Their struggle for equal rights with the patricians dominated much of the Republic's history.

pluralism the practice in which one person holds several church offices simultaneously; a problem of the late medieval church.

pogroms organized massacres of Jews.

polis an ancient Greek city-state encompassing both an urban area and its surrounding countryside; a small but autonomous political unit where all major political and social activities were carried out in a central location.

political democracy a form of government characterized by universal suffrage and mass political parties.

politiques a group who emerged during the French Wars of Religion in the sixteenth century; placed politics above religion and believed that no religious truth was worth the ravages of civil war.

polytheistic/polytheism having many gods; belief in or the worship of more than one god.

popular culture as opposed to high culture, the unofficial, written and unwritten culture of the masses, much of which was passed down orally; centers on public and group activities such as festivals. In the twentieth century, refers to the entertainment, recreation, and pleasures that people purchase as part of mass consumer society.

populares "favoring the people." Aristocratic leaders in the late Roman Republic who tended to use the people's assemblies in an effort to break the stranglehold of the *nobiles* on political offices.

popular sovereignty the doctrine that government is created by and subject to the will of the people, who are the source of all political power.

praetorian guard the military unit that served as the personal bodyguard of the Roman emperors.

predestination the belief, associated with Calvinism, that God, as a consequence of his foreknowledge of all events, has predetermined those who will be saved (the elect) and those who will be damned.

price revolution the dramatic rise in prices (inflation) that occurred throughout Europe in the sixteenth and early seventeenth centuries.

primogeniture an inheritance practice in which the eldest son receives all or the largest share of the parents' estate.

principate the form of government established by Augustus for the Roman Empire; continued the constitutional forms of the Republic and consisted of the *princeps* ("first citizen") and the senate, although the *princeps* was clearly the dominant partner.

proletariat the industrial working class. In Marxism, the class who will ultimately overthrow the bourgeoisie.

Puritans English Protestants inspired by Calvinist theology who wished to remove all traces of Catholicism from the Church of England.

querelles des femmes "arguments about women." A centuries-old debate about the nature of women that continued during the Scientific Revolution as those who argued for the inferiority of women found additional support in the new anatomy and medicine.

rationalism a system of thought based on the belief that human reason and experience are the chief sources of knowledge.

realism in medieval Europe, the school of thought that, following Plato, held that the individual objects we perceive are not real but merely manifestations of universal ideas existing in the mind of God. In the nineteenth century, a school of painting that emphasized the everyday life of ordinary people, depicted with photographic realism.

Realpolitik "politics of reality." Politics based on practical concerns rather than theory or ethics.

real wages/income/prices wages/income/prices that have been adjusted for inflation.

reason of state the principle that a nation should act on the basis of its long-term interests and not merely to further the dynastic interests of its ruling family.

relativity theory Einstein's theory that holds, among other things, that (1) space and time are not absolute but are relative to the observer and interwoven into a four-dimensional space-time continuum and (2) matter is a form of energy ($E = mc^2$).

relics the bones of Christian saints or objects intimately associated with saints that were considered worthy of veneration.

Renaissance the "rebirth" of classical culture that occurred in Italy between c. 1350 and c. 1550; also, the earlier revivals of classical culture that occurred under Charlemagne and in the twelfth century.

rentier a person who lives on income from property and is not personally involved in its operation.

reparations payments made by a defeated nation after a war to compensate another nation for damage sustained as a result of the war; required from Germany after World War I.

revisionism a socialist doctrine that rejected Marx's emphasis on class struggle and revolution and argued instead that workers should work through political parties to bring about gradual change.

revolution a fundamental change in the political and social organization of a state.

revolutionary socialism the socialist doctrine espoused by Georges Sorel who held that violent action was the only way to achieve the goals of socialism.

rhetoric the art of persuasive speaking; in the Middle Ages, one of the seven liberal arts.

sacraments rites considered imperative for a Christian's salvation. By the thirteenth century consisted of the eucharist or Lord's Supper, baptism, marriage, penance, extreme unction, holy orders, and confirmation of children; Protestant reformers of the sixteenth century generally recognized only two—baptism and communion (the Lord's Supper).

salons gatherings of philosophes and other notables to discuss the ideas of the Enlightenment; so-called from the elegant drawing rooms (salons) where they met.

sans-culottes the common people who did not wear the fine clothes of the upper classes (sans-culottes means "without breeches") and played an important role in the radical phase of the French Revolution.

satrap/satrapy a governor with both civil and military duties in the ancient Persian Empire, which was divided into satrapies, or provinces, each administered by a satrap.

scholasticism the philosophical and theological system of the medieval schools, which emphasized rigorous analysis of contradictory authorities; often used to try to reconcile faith and reason.

scientific method a method of seeking knowledge through inductive principles; uses experiments and observations to develop generalizations.

Scientific Revolution the transition from the medieval worldview to a largely secular, rational, and materialistic perspective; began in the seventeenth century and was popularized in the eighteenth.

secularization the process of becoming more concerned with material, worldly, temporal things and less with spiritual and religious things.

self-determination the doctrine that the people of a given territory or a particular nationality should have the right to determine their own government and political future.

senate/senators the leading council of the Roman Republic; composed of about 300 men (senators) who served for life and dominated much of the political life of the Republic.

serf a peasant who is bound to the land and obliged to provide labor services and pay various rents and fees to the lord; considered unfree but not a slave because serfs could not be bought and sold.

skepticism a doubtful or questioning attitude, especially about religion.

Social Darwinism the application of Darwin's principle of organic evolution to the social order; led to the belief that progress comes from the struggle for survival as the fittest advance and the weak decline.

socialism an ideology that calls for collective or government ownership of the means of production and the distribution of goods.

social security/social insurance government programs that provide social welfare measures such as old age pensions and sickness, accident, and disability insurance.

Socratic method a form of teaching that uses a question-and-answer format to enable students to reach conclusions by using their own reasoning.

Sophists wandering scholars and professional teachers in ancient Greece who stressed the importance of rhetoric and tended toward skepticism and relativism.

soviets councils of workers' and soldiers' deputies formed throughout Russia in 1917; played an important role in the Bolshevik Revolution.

sphere of influence a territory or region over which an outside nation exercises political or economic influence.

Stoicism a philosophy founded by Zeno in the fourth century B.C. that taught that happiness could be obtained by accepting one's lot and living in harmony with the will of God, thereby achieving inner peace.

subinfeudation the practice in which a lord's greatest vassals subdivided their fiefs and had vassals of their own, and those vassals, in turn, subdivided their fiefs and so on down to simple knights whose fiefs were too small to subdivide.

suffrage the right to vote.

suffragists those who advocate the extension of the right to vote (suffrage), especially to women.

surplus value in Marxism, the difference between a product's real value and the wages of the worker who produced the product.

syncretism the combining of different forms of belief or practice, as, for example, when two gods are regarded as different forms of the same underlying divine force and are fused together.

tariffs duties (taxes) imposed on imported goods; usually imposed both to raise revenue and to discourage imports and protect domestic industries.

tetrarchy rule by four; the system of government established by Diocletian (284–305) in which the Roman Empire was divided into two parts, each ruled by an "Augustus" assisted by a "Caesar."

theocracy a government ruled by a divine authority.

three-field system in medieval agriculture, the practice of dividing the arable land into three fields so that one could lie fallow while the others were planted in winter grains and spring crops.

tithe a tenth of one's harvest or income; paid by medieval peasants to the village church.

Torah the body of law in Hebrew Scripture, contained in the Pentateuch (the first five books of the Hebrew Bible).

totalitarian state a state characterized by government control over all aspects of economic, social, political, cultural, and intellectual life, the subordination of the individual to the state, and insistence that the masses be actively involved in the regime's goals.

total war warfare in which all of a nation's resources, including civilians at home as well as soldiers in the field, are mobilized for the war effort.

trade union an association of workers in the same trade, formed to help members secure better wages, benefits, and working conditions.

transubstantiation a doctrine of the Roman Catholic church that teaches that during the eucharist the substance of the bread and wine is miraculously transformed into the body and blood of Jesus.

trench warfare warfare in which the opposing forces attack and counterattack from a relatively permanent system of trenches protected by barbed wire; characteristic of World War I.

trivium and quadrivium together formed the seven liberal arts that were the basis of medieval and early modern education. Grammar, rhetoric, and dialectic or logic made up the *trivium*; arithmetic, geometry, astronomy, and music made up the *quadrivium*.

Truman Doctrine the doctrine, enunciated by Harry Truman in 1947, that the United States would provide economic aid to countries that said they were threatened by Communist expansion.

tyrant/tyranny in an ancient Greek *polis* (or an Italian city-state during the Renaissance), a ruler who came to power in an unconstitutional way and ruled without being subject to the law.

uncertainty principle a principle in quantum mechanics, posited by Heisenberg, that holds that one cannot determine the path of an electron because the very act of observing the electron would affect its location.

unconditional surrender complete, unqualified surrender of a belligerent nation.

utopian socialists intellectuals and theorists in the early nineteenth century who favored equality in social and economic conditions and wished to replace private property and competition with collective ownership and cooperation; deemed impractical and "utopian" by later socialists.

vassal a person granted a fief, or landed estate, in exchange for providing military services to the lord and fulfilling certain other obligations such as appearing at the lord's court when summoned and making a payment on the knighting of the lord's eldest son.

vernacular the everyday language of a region, as distinguished from a language used for special purposes. For example, in medieval Paris, French was the vernacular, but Latin was used for academic writing and for classes at the University of Paris.

volkish thought the belief that German culture is superior and that the German people have a universal mission to save Western civilization from inferior races.

war communism Lenin's policy of nationalizing industrial and other facilities and requisitioning the peasants' produce during the civil war in Russia.

War Guilt Clause the clause in the Treaty of Versailles that declared that Germany (and Austria) were responsible for starting World War I and ordered Germany to pay reparations for the damage the Allies had suffered as a result of the war.

Warsaw Pact a military alliance, formed in 1955, in which Albania, Bulgaria, Czechoslovakia, East Germany, Hungary, Poland, Romania, and the Soviet Union agreed to provide mutual assistance.

welfare state a social/political system in which the government assumes the primary responsibility for the social welfare of its citizens by providing such things as social security, unemployment benefits, and health care.

wergeld "money for a man." In early Germanic law, a person's value in monetary terms, which was paid by a wrongdoer to the family of the person who had been injured or killed.

world-machine Newton's conception of the universe as one huge, regulated, and uniform machine that operated according to natural laws in absolute time, space, and motion.

ziggurat a massive stepped tower upon which a temple dedicated to the chief god or goddess of a Sumerian city was built.

Zionism an international movement that called for the establishment of a Jewish state or a refuge for Jews in Palestine.

Zoroastrianism a religion founded by the Persian Zoroaster in the seventh century B.C.; characterized by worship of a supreme god Ahuramazda who represents the good against the evil spirit, identified as Ahriman.

al-Abbas, Abu   al-AH-bus, AH-boo

Abbasid   AB-uh-sid *or* a-BA-sid

Adenauer, Konrad   AD-n'our-er

aediles   EE-diles

Aeolians   ee-OH-lee-uns

Aeschylus   ESS-kuh-lus

Afrikaners   a-fri-KAH-ners

Agincourt   AJ-in-kor

Ahuramazda   ah-HOOR-ah-MAHZ-duh

Akhenaton   ah-kuh-NAH-tun

Akkadians   a-KAY-dee-uns

Albigensians   al-bi-GEN-see-uns

d'Albret, Jeanne   dahl-BRAy, ZHAHN

Albuquerque, Afonso de   AL-buh-kur-kee, ah-FON-soh d'

Alcibiades   al-suh-BY-uh-deez

Alcuin   AL-kwin

Aliz, Ramiz   AL-ee-uh, ra-MEEZ

Allah   AH-luh *or* AL-uh

Amenhotep   ah-mun-HOE-tep

Andreotti, Giulio   ahn-dray-AH-tee, JOOL-yoh

Andropov, Yuri   an-DROP-ov, YOOR-ee

Anjou   AN-joo

Antigonid   an-TIG-oh-nid

Antigonus Gonatus   an-TIG-oh-nus goh-NAH-tus

Antiochus   an-TIE-uh-kus

Antonescu, Ion   An-tuh-NES-koo, YON

Antoninus Pius   an-toh-NIGH-nus PIE-us

apella   a-PELL-uh

Apollonius   ap-uh-LOH-nee-us

Aquinas, Thomas   uh-KWIGH-nus

aratrum   a-RA-trum

Archimedes   are-kuh-MEE-deez

Argonautica   ARE-guh-NOT-i-kuh

Aristarchus   ar-is-TAR-kus

Aristotle   ar-i-STAH-tul

Arsinoë   ar-SIN-oh-ee

artium baccalarius   are-TEE-um back-uh-LAR-ee-us

artium magister   are-TEE-um ma-GIS-ter

Ashkenazic   ash-kuh-NAH-zic

Ashurnasirpal   ah-shoor-NAH-suh-pul

asiento   a-SEE-en-toh

assignat   as-seen-YAH *or* AS-sig-nat

Assyrians   uh-SEER-ee-uns

Atahualpa   ah-tuh-WALL-puh

Attalid   AT-a-lid

audiencias   ah-DEE-en-CEE-ahs

Augustine   AW-gus-STEEN

Avicenna   av-i-SEN-uh

Avignon   ah-veen-YONE

Auschwitz-Birkenau   OUSH-vitz-BUR-kuh-now

Ausgleich   OUS-glike

Babeuf, Gracchus   bah-BUHF, GRAK-us

Bach, Johann Sebastian   BAHK, yoh-HAHN suh-BASS-chen

Bakunin, Michael   ba-KOO-nin

Balboa, Vasco Nuñez de   bal-BOH-uh, VASH-koh NOON-yez duh

Ballin, Albert   BAHLL-een

Barbarossa   bar-buh-ROH-suh

Bastille   ba-STEEL

Bayle, Pierre   BAYL, PYER

Beauvoir, Simone de   boh-VWAH, see-MOAN duh

Bebel, August   BAY-bul

Beccaria, Cesare   bek-KAH-ree-uh, CHAY-zahr-ay

Beguines   bi-GEENS

Belisarius   bell-i-SAR-ee-us

benefice   BEN-uh-fiss

Bergson, Henri   BERG-son, AWN-ree

Bernini, Gian Lorenzo   bur-NEE-nee, JAHN loh-RENT-soh

Bernstein, Eduard   BURN-stine, AY-doo-art

Blitzkrieg   BLITZ-kreeg

Blum, Léon   BLOOM, LAY-OHN

Boccaccio, Giovanni   boh-KAH-chee-oh, joe-VAHN-nee

Bodichon, Barbara   BOH-duh-chon

Boer   BOHR

Boethius   boh-EETH-ee-us

Boleyn, Anne   BUH-lin

Bólivar, Simón   BOH-luh-VAR, see-MOAN

Bologna   buh-LOHN-yuh

Bossuet, Jacques   baw-SWAY, ZHAHK

Bottai, Giuseppe   BOT-tah, joo-ZEP-pay

Boticelli, Sandro   BOT-i-CHELL-ee, SAHN-droh

Boulanger, Georges   boo-lahn-ZHAY, ZHORZH

Bracciolini, Poggio   braht-choh-LEE-nee, POD-joh

Brahe, Tycho   BRAH, TIE-koh

Bramante, Donato   brah-MAHN-tee, doe-NAY-toe

Brandt, Willy   BRAHNT, VIL-ee

Brétigny bray-tee-NYEE

Brezhnev, Leonid BREZH-nef, lyi-on-YEET

Briand, Aristide bree-AHN, a-ree-STEED

Brunelleschi, Filippo BROO-nuh-LES-kee, fee-LEEP-poe

Brüning, Heinrich BROO-ning, HINE-rik

Bulganin, Nilolai bul-GAN-in, nyik-uh-LYE

Bund deutscher Mädel BUNT DOICHer MAIR-del

Burschenschaften BOOR-shen-shaft-un

Calais ka-LAY

Caligula ka-LIG-yuh-luh

caliph/caliphate KAY-lif/KAY-li-FATE

Calonne, Charles de kah-LAWN, SHARL duh

Cambyses kam-BY-seez

Camus, Albert kuh-MOO, al-BEAR

Canaanites KAY-nuh-nites

Capet/Capetian ka-PAY *or* KAY-put/kuh-PEE-shun

Caraffa, Gian Pietro kah-RAH-fuh, JAHN PYEE-troh

carbonari kar-buh-NAH-ree

Carolingian kar-oh-LIN-jun

carruca ca-ruh-kuh

Carthage/Carthaginian KAR-thij/KAR-thuh-JIN-ee-un

Cassiodorus kass-ee-oh-DOR-us

Castlereagh, Viscount KAS-ul-RAY

Catharism KA-tha-ri-zem

Catullus ka-TULL-us

Cavendish, Margaret KAV-un-dish

Cavour, Camillo di ka-VOOR, kah-MIL-oh

Ceausescu, Nicolai chow-SHES-koo, nee-koh-LYE

cenobitic sen-oh-BIT-ik

Cèzanne, Paul say-ZAN

Chaeronea ker-oh-NEE-uh

Chaldean kal-DEE-un

chanson de geste shahn-SAWN duh ZHEST

Charlemagne SHAR-luh-mane

Chateaubriand, François-René de shah-TOH-bree-AHN, FRAN-swah-ruh-NAY duh

Chernenko, Konstantin cher-NYEN-koh, kon-stunTEEN

Chiang Kai-Shek CHANG KIGH-shek

Chrétien de Troyes KRAY-tee-ahn duh TRWAH

Cicero SIS-uh-roh

ciompi CHOM-pee

Cistercians si-STIR-shuns

Claudius KLAW-dee-us

Cleisthenes KLISE-thuh-neez

Clemenceau, Georges klem-un-SOH, ZHORZH

Clovis KLOH-vis

Codreanu, Corneliu kaw-dree-AH-noo, kor-NELL-yoo

colonus kuh-LOH-nus

Columbanus kol-um-BAHN-us

comitia centuriata kuh-MISH-ee-uh sen-TYOO-ree-ah-tuh

Commodus KOM-uh-dus

Comnenus kom-NEE-nus

Comte, Auguste KOHNT

concilium plebis con-CIL-ee-um PLE-bis

Concordat of Worms kon-KOR-dat of WURMZ *or* VAWRMZ

Condorcet, Marie-Jean de kawn-dar-SAY, mur-REE-ZHAHN duh

condottieri kon-dah-TEE-AIR-ee

consul KON-sul

Contarini, Gasparo kahn-tuh-REE-nee, GAHS-pah-roh

conversos kon-VAIR-sohs

Copernicus, Nicolaus koh-PURR-nuh-kus, nee-koh-LAH-us

Corinth KOR-inth

corregidores kor-REG-uh-DOR-ays

Cortés, Hernán kor-TEZ, er-NAHN

Corvinus, Matthias kor-VIE-nus, muh-THIGH-us

Courbet, Gustave koor-BAY, guh-STAWV

Crassus KRASS-us

Crécy kray-SEE

Crédit Mobilier kred-EE mohb-eel-YAY

Croesus KREE-sus

Danton, Georges dahn-TAWN, ZHORZH

Darius duh-RYE-us

dauphin DAW-fin

David, Jacques-Louis dah-VEED, ZHAHK-LWEE

Debussy, Claude de-BYOO-see, KLODE

Decameron di-KAM-uh-run

Deffand, marquise du di-FAHN, mar-KEEZ doo

de Gaulle, Charles duh GOLL, SHARL

Delacroix, Eugène del-uh-KWAW, yoo-ZHAHN

Demosthenes di-MOSS-thuh-neez

Denikin, Anton dyi-NYEE-kin, an-TAWN

Descartes, René day-KART, ruh-NAY

Diaghilev, Sergei dee-AHG-uh-lef, syir-GYAY

Dias, Bartholomeu DEE-us, bar-too-loo-MAY

Diaspora die-AS-pur-uh

Diderot, Denis DEE-duh-roh, duh-NEE

Diocletian die-uh-KLEE-shun

Disraeli, Benjamin diz-RAY-lee

Dollfuss, Engelbert DOLL-foos

Domesday Book DOOMZ-day

Domitian doh-MISH-un

Donatus/Donatist doh-NAY-tus/DOH-nuh-tist

Dorians DOR-ee-uns

Dostoevsky, Fyodor DOS-tuh-YEF-skee, FYOD-ur

Douhet, Giulio doo-EE, JOOL-yoh

Dreyfus, Alfred DRY-fus

Dubcek, Alexander DOOB-chek

Duma DOO-muh

Dürer, Albrecht DOO-er, AWL-brekt

ecclesia eh-KLEE-zee-uh

Eckhart, Meister EK-hart, MY-ster

encomienda en-koh-mee-EN-dah

Engels, Friedrich ENG-ulz, FREE-drik

Entente Cordiale ahn-TAHNT kor-DYALL

Epaminondas i-PAM-uh-NAHN-dus

ephor EF-or

Epicurus/Epicureanism EP-i-KYOOR-us/EP-i-kyoo-REE-uh-ni-zem

equestrians i-KWES-tree-uns

equites EK-wuh-tays

Erasistratus er-uh-SIS-truh-tus

Erasmus, Desiderius i-RAZZ-mus, des-i-DIR-ee-us

Eratosthenes er-uh-TOSS-thuh-neez

eremitical air-uh-MITT-i-cul

d'Este, Isabella ES-tay

Erhard, Ludwig AIR-hart

Etruscans i-TRUSS-kuhns

Euclid YOO-klid

Euripides yoo-RIP-i-deez

exchequer EX-chek-ur

fasces FASS-eez

Fascio di Combattimento FASH-ee-oh di com-BATT-ee-men-toh

Fatimid FAT-i-mid

Fedele, Cassandra FAY-del-ee

Feltre, Vittorino da FELL-tree, vee-tor-EE-noh dah

Ficino, Marsilio fee-CHEE-noh, mar-SIL-ee-oh

Flaubert, Gustave floh-BEAR, guh-STAWV

Fleury, Cardinal floe-REE

Fontainebleau FAWN-tin-BLOW

Fontenelle, Bernard de fawnt-NELL, BER-nar duh

Fouquet, Nicolas foo-KAY, nee-KOH-lah

Frequens FREE-kwens

Friedan, Betty fri-DAN

Frimaire free-MARE

Fronde FROND

Führerprinzip FYOOR-ur-PRIN-tseep

gabelle gah-BELL

Gama, Vasco da GAM-uh, VASH-koh duh

Gamond, Zoé Gatti de gah-MAHN, zaw-ay GAHT-tee duh

Garibaldi, Giuseppe gar-uh-BAWL-dee, joo-ZEP-pay

Gasperi, Alcide de GAHS-pe-ree, awl-CHEE-day de

Gaugamela gaw-guh-MEE-luh

Gentileschi, Artemisia jen-tul-ESS-kee, are-tee-MISS-ee-uh

gerousia juh-ROO-see-uh

Gierek, Edward GYER-ek

Gilgamesh GILL-guh-mesh

Giolitti, Giovanni joh-LEET-tee, joe-VAHN-nee

Giotto JAW-toh

Girondins juh-RAHN-dins

glasnost GLAZ-nohst

Gleichschaltung GLIKE-shalt-ung

Goebbels, Joseph GUHR-bulz

Gomulka, Wladyslaw goh-MOOL-kuh, vla-DIS-lawf

gonfaloniere gon-fa-loh-NEE-ree

Gorbachev, Mikhail GOR-buh-chof, meek-HALE

Gracchus, Tiberius and Gaius GRAK-us, tie-BIR-ee-us and GAY-us *or* GUY-us

grandi GRAHN-dee

Grieg, Edvard GREEG, ED-vart

Groote, Gerard GROH-tuh

Gropius, Walter GROH-pee-us, VAHL-ter

Grossdeutsch gross-DOICH

Guicciardini, Francesco gwee-char-DEE-nee, frahn-CHASE-koh

Guizot, François gee-ZOH, FRAN-swah

Gustavus Adolphus gus-STAY-vus a-DOLF-us

Guzman, Gaspar de goos-MAHN, gahs-PAR day

Habsburg HAPS-burg

Hadrian HAY-dree-un

Hagia Sophia HAG-ee-uh soh-FEE-uh

hajj HAJ

Hammurabi ham-uh-RAH-bee

Handel, George Friedrich HAN-dul

Hannibal HAN-uh-bul

Hanukkah HAH-nuh-kuh

Hardenberg, Karl von HAR-d'n-burg

Harun al-Rashid huh-ROON al-ra-SHEED

Hatshepsut hat-SHEP-soot

Haussmann, Baron HOUS-mun

Havel, Vaclav HAH-vuhl, VAHT-slaf

Haydn, Franz Joseph HIDE-n, FRAHNTS

hegemon HEJ-uh-mon

Heisenberg, Werner HIGH-zun-burg, VUR-nur

Hellenistic hell-uh-NIS-tik

helots HELL-uts

hermandades er-mahn-DAHDH-ays

Herodotus hi-ROD-oh-tus

Herophilus hi-ROF-uh-lus

Herzen, Alexander HER-tsun

Herzl, Theodor HERT-sul, TAY-oh-dor

Hesiod HEE-see-ud

Heydrich, Reinhard HIGH-drik, RINE-hart

hieroglyph HIGH-ur-oh-glif

Hildegard of Bingen HILL-duh-gard of BING-en

Hitler Jugend JOO-gunt

Ho Chi Minh HOE CHEE MIN

Höch, Hannah HOKH

Hohenstaufen HOE-un-SHTAU-fun

Hohenzollern HOE-un-ZAHL-lurn

d'Holbach, Paul awl-BAHK

Honecker, Erich HOE-nuh-ker

hoplites HOP-lites

Horace HOR-us

Horthy, Miklós HOR-tee, MIK-lohsh

Hoxha, Enver HAW-jah

Huguenots HYOO-guh-nots

Husák, Gustav HOO-sahk, guh-STAHV

Ibn Sina ib-en SEE-nuh

Ignatius of Loyola ig-NAY-shus of loi-OH-luh
Il Duce eel DOO-chay
imperator im-puh-RAH-tor
imperium im-PIER-ee-um
intendant in-TEN-duhnt
Isis EYE-sis
Issus ISS-us
ius gentium YOOS GEN-tee-um
Jacobin JAK-uh-bin
Jacquerie zhah-KREE
Jagiello yah-GYELL-oh
Jahn, Friedrich Ludwig YAHN, FREE-drik
Jaruzelski, Wojciech yahr-uh-ZEL-skee, VOI-chek
Jaurés, Jean zhaw-RESS, ZHAHN
jihad ji-HAHD
Judaea joo-DEE-uh
Judas Maccabaeus JOO-dus mak-uh-BEE-us
Jung, Carl YOONG
Junkers YOONG-kers
Jupiter Optimus Maximus JOO-pi-ter OPP-tuh-mus
  MAK-suh-mus
Justinian juh-STIN-ee-un
Juvenal JOO-vuh-nul
Kádár, János KAY-dahr, YAHN-us
Kadinsky, Vasily kan-DIN-skee, vus-YEEL-yee
Karlowitz KARL-oh-vitz
Kaunitz, Wenzel von KOU-nits, VENT-sul
Kerensky, Alexander kuh-REN-skee
Keynes, John Maynard KAYNZ
Khrushchev, Nikita KROOSH-chef, nuh-KEE-tuh
Kleindeutsch kline-DOICH
Kohl, Helmut KOLE, HELL-mut
koiné koi-NAY
Kolchak, Alexander KAWL-chok
Kollantai, Alexandra kawl-un-TIE
Kosciuszko, Thaddeus kos-ee-US-koh, tah-DE-us
Kossuth, Louis KOSS-ooth
kouros KOO-raws
Kraft durch Freude CRAFT durch FROI-duh
Kristallnacht KRIS-tal-NAHCHT
Krupp, Alfred KROOP
Kuchuk-Kainarji koo-CHOOK-kigh-NAR-jee
kulaks koo-LAKS
kulturkampf kool-TOOR-kahmf
Kun, Béla KOON, BAY-luh
Lafayette, marquis de lah-fee-ETTE, mar-KEE duh
laissez-faire les-ay-FAIR
Lamarck, Jean-Baptiste luh-MAHRK, ZHAHN-buh-
  TEEST
Lancaster LAN-kas-ter
latifundia lat-uh-FUN-dee-uh
Latium LAY-shee-um
Laurier, Wilfred LAWR-ee-ay
Lebensraum LAY-benz-roum

Lespinasse, Julie de les-peen-AHS
Le Tellier, François Michel luh tel-YAY, FRAN-swah-
  mee-SHELL
Lévesque, René luh-VEK, ruh-NAY
Leyster, Judith LE-ster
Liebenfels, Lanz von LEE-bun-felz, LAHNZ
Liebknecht, Karl LEEP-knekt
Liebknecht, Wilhelm LEEP-knekt, VIL-helm
Lionne, Hugues de LYAWN, UGH
List, Friedrich LIST, FREE-drik
Liszt, Franz LIST, FRAHNZ
Livy LIV-ee
Lucretius loo-KREE-shus
Luddites LUD-ites
Ludendorff, Erich LOOD-un-dorf
Lueger, Karl LOO-ger
Luftwaffe LUFT-vaf-uh
Luxemburg, Rosa LUK-sum-burg
Machiavelli, Niccolò mak-ee-uh-VELL-ee, nee-koh-LOH
Magna Graecia MAG-nuh GREE-shuh
Magyars MAG-yars
Maistre, Joseph de MES-truh
Malleus Maleficarum mall-EE-us mal-uh-FIK-ar-um
al-Ma'mun al-MAH-moon
Manetho MAN-uh-THOH
Mao Zedong mau zee-DONG
Marcus Aurelius MAR-kus au-REE-lee-us
Marcuse, Herbert mar-KOO-zuh
Marie Antoinette muh-REE an-twuh-NET
Marius MAR-ee-us
Marsiglio of Padua mar-SIL-ee-oh of PA-juh-wuh
Masaryk, Thomas MAS-uh-rik
Matteotti, Giacomo mat-ee-OH-tee, JAHK-oh-moh
Mazarin maz-uh-RAN
Mazzini, Giuseppe maht-SEE-nee, joo-ZEP-pay
Meiji MAY-jee
Mein Kampf mine KAHMF
Melanchthon, Philip muh-LANGK-thun
Menander me-NAN-der
Mendeleyev, Dmitri men-duh-LAY-ef, di-MEE-tri
Merian, Maria Sibylla MARE-ee-un
Mesopotamia mess-oh-poh-TAME-ee-uh
Messiaen, Olivier me-SYAHN, 0-LEEV-yay
Metaxas, John me-TAK-sus
Metternich, Klemens von MET-er-nik, KLAY-mens
Michel, Louise mee-SHELL
Michelangelo my-kell-AN-juh-loh
Mieszko MYESH-koh
Millet, Jean-François mi-LAY, ZHAHN-FRAN-swah
Milošević, Slobodan mi-LOH-suh-vik, SLOW-buh-dan
Miltiades mil-TIE-uh-deez
Mirandola, Pico della muh-RAN-duh-luh, PEE-koh
  DELL-uh
missi dominici MISS-ee doe-MIN-ee-chee

Moctezuma   mahk-tuh-ZOO-muh
Mohács   MOH-hach
Moldavia   mahl-DAY-vee-uh
Molière, Jean-Baptiste   mole-YAIR, ZHAHN-buh-TEEST
Moltke, Helmuth von   MOLT-kuh, HELL-mut fahn
Monet, Claude   moh-NAY, KLODE
Montaigne, Michel de   mahn-TANE, mee-SHELL duh
Montefeltro, Federigo da   mahn-tuh-FELL-troh, fay-day-REE-goh dah
Montesquieu   MONT-ess-skyoo
Montessori, Maria   mon-ti-SOR-ee
Morisot, Berthe   mor-ee-ZOH, BERT
Muawiyah   moo-AH-wee-yah
Mühlberg   mool-BERK
Muhammad   moe-HA-mud
Müntzer, Thomas   MOON-tsur
Muslim   MUZ-lum
Mutsuhito   moo-tsoo-HEE-toe
Mycenaean   my-suh-NEE-un
Nabonidas   na-bun-EYE-dus
Nagy, Imry   NAHJD, IM-re
Navarre   nuh-VARR
Nebuchadnezzar   neb-uh-kad-NWZZ-ar
Nero   NEE-roh
Nerva   NUR-vuh
Neumann, Balthasar   NOI-mahn, BAHL-tah-zar
Neumann, Solomon   NOI-mahn
Nevsky, Alexander   NEW-skee
Newcomen, Thomas   new-KUH-mun
Ngo Dinh Diem   NGOH din dee-EM
Nietzsche, Friedrich   NEE-chuh, FREE-drik
Nimwegen   NIM-vay-gun
Ninhursaga   nin-HUR-sah-guh
Nogaret, William de   noh-guh-RAY
Nogarola, Isotta   NOH-guh-roll-uh, eye-SOT-tuh
Novalis, Friedrich   noh-VAH-lis, FREE-drik
Novotny, Antonin   noh-VOT-nee, AN-ton-yeen
Nystadt   nee-STAHD
Octavian   ok-TAY-vee-un
Odoacer   oh-doh-AY-ser
optimates   opp-tuh-MAH-tays
Osiris   oh-SIGH-ris
Ovid   OV-id
Paleologus   pay-lee-OHL-uh-gus
papal curia   PAY-pul KOOR-ee-uh
Papen, Franz von   PAH-pun, FRAHNTZ fahn
Paracelsus   par-uh-SELL-sus
Parlement   par-luh-MAHN
Pascal, Blaise   pass-KAL, BLEZ
paterfamilias   pay-ter-fuh-MILL-ee-us
Pentateuch   PEN-tuh-tuke
Pepin   PEP-in
perestroika   pair-ess-TROY-kuh
Pergamum   PURR-guh-mum

Pericles   PER-i-kleez
perioeci   per-ee-EE-sie
Pétain, Henri   pay-TAN, AHN-ree
Petrarch   PE-trark
Petronius   pi-TROH-nee-us
philosophe   fee-luh-ZAWF
Phoenicians   fi-NISH-uns
Photius   FOH-shus
Picasso, Pablo   pi-KAW-soh
Pilsudski, Joseph   peel-SOOT-skee
Pisistratus   pi-SIS-truh-tus
Pissaro, Camille   pi-SARR-oh, kah-MEEYL
Pizarro, Francesco   pi-ZARR-oh, frahn-CHASE-koh
Planck, Max   PLAHNK
Plantagenet   plan-TA-juh-net
Plato   PLAY-toe
Plautus   PLAW-tus
Poincaré, Raymond   pwan-kah-RAY, re-MOAN
polis   POE-lis
politiques   puh-lee-TEEKS
Polybius   poe-LIB-ee-us
Pombal, marquis de   pom-BAHL, mar-KEE duh
Pompadour, madame de   POM-puh-door, muh-DAM duh
Pompey   POM-pee
pontifex maximus   PON-ti-feks MAK-suh-mus
populares   POP-yoo-lar-ays
populo grasso   POP-uh-loh GRAH-soh
Poussin, Nicholas   poo-SAN, NEE-kaw-lah
Praecepter Germaniae   PREE-sep-ter ger-MAN-ee-eye
praetor   PREE-ter
princeps   PRIN-seps
Procopius   proh-KOH-pee-us
procurator   PROK-yuh-ray-ter
Ptolemy/Ptolemaic   TOL-uh-mee/TOL-uh-MAY-ik
Pugachev, Emelyan   POO-guh-choff, yim-yil-YAHN
Punic   PYOO-nik
Pyrrhus/Pyrrhic   PIR-us/PIR-ik
quaestors   KWES-ters
Quetzelcoatl   ket-SAHL-koh-ATE-ul
Quran   kuh-RAN
Racine, Jean-Baptiste   ra-SEEN, ZHAHN-buh-TEEST
al-Rahman, Abd   al-RAH-mun, abd
Ramesses   RAM-i-seez
Raphael   RAFF-ee-ul
Rasputin   rass-PYOO-tin
Realpolitik   ray-AHL-poe-li-teek
Reichsrat   RIKES-raht
Rembrandt van Rijn   REM-brant vahn RINE
Renan, Ernst   re-NAHN
Ricci, Matteo   REECH-ee, mah-TAY-oh
Richelieu   RISH-uh-loo
Rilke, Rainer Maria   RILL-kuh, RYE-ner
risorgimento   ree-SOR-jee-men-toe

Robespierre, Maximilien   ROHBZ-pee-air, mak-SEE-meel-yahn

Rococo   ro-KOH-koh

Röhm, Ernst   RURM

Roon, Albrecht von   ROHN AHL-brekt

Rousseau, Jean-Jacques   roo-SOH ZHAHN-ZHAHK

Rurik   ROOR-ik

Ryswick   RIZ-wik

Sacrosancta   sak-roh-SANK-tuh

Saint-Just   san-ZHOOST

Saint-Simon, Henri de   san-see-MOAN, AHN-ree duh

Sakharov, Andrei   SAH-kuh-rof, ahn-DRAY

Saladin   SAL-uh-din

Sallust   SALL-ust

Samnites   SAM-nites

San Martín, José de   san mar-TEEN, hoe-SAY day

Sartre, Jean-Paul   SAR-truh, ZHAHN-PAUL

satrap/satrapy   SAY-trap/SAY-truh-pee

Satyricon   SAY-tir-ee-kon

Schaumburg-Lippe   SHAHM-berkh-LI-puh

Schleswig-Holstein   SCHLES-vig-HOLE-stine

Schlieffen, Alfred von   SHLEE-fun

Schmidt, Helmut   SHMIT, HELL-mut

Schönberg, Arnold   SHURN-burg, ARR-nawlt

Schönerer, George von   SHURN-er-er, ZHORSH

Schuschnigg, Karl von   SHOOSH-nik

Schutzmannschaft   SHOOTS-mun-shaft

Scipio Africanus   SI-pee-oh af-ri-KAY-nus

Scipio Aemilianus   SI-pee-oh i-mill-ee-AY-nus

scriptoria   skrip-TOR-ee-uh

Sejm   SAME

Seleucus/Seleucid   si-LOO-kus/si-LOO-sid

Seljuk Turks   SELL-juke

Seneca   SEN-i-kuh

Sephardic   suh-FAR-dik

Septimius Severus   sep-TIM-ee-us se-VIR-us

Sforza, Ludovico   SFORT-zuh, loo-doe-VEE-koh

Sieveking, Amalie   SEEVE-king

Sieyès, Abbé   sye-YES, a-BAY

signoria   seen-YOOR-ee-uh

Socrates   SOK-ruh-teez

Solon   SOH-lun

Solzhenitsyn, Alexander   SOLE-zhuh-NEET-sin

Sophocles   SOF-uh-kleez

Sorel, Georges   sah-RELL, ZHORZH

Spartacus   SPAR-tuh-kus

Speer, Albert   SHPIER

Speransky, Michael   spyuh-RAHN-skee

Spinoza, Benedict de   spi-NOH-zuh

squadristi   sqah-DREES-tee

Staël, Germaine de   STAWL, ZHER-men duh

Stein, Heinrich von   STINE, HINE-rik

Stoicism   STOH-i-siz-um

Stolypin, Peter   stuh-LEE-pyin

Stravinsky, Igor   struh-VIN-skee, EE-gor

Stresemann, Gustav   SHTRAY-zuh-mahn, GUS-tahf

Struensee, John Frederick   SHTROO-un-zay

Sulla   SULL-uh

Sumerians   soo-MER-ee-uns

Suppiluliumas   suh-pil-oo-LEE-uh-mus

Suttner, Bertha von   ZOOT-ner

Taafe, Edward von   TAH-fuh

Tacitus   TASS-i-tus

taille   TAH-yuh *or* TIE

Talleyrand, Prince   TAL-ee-ran

Tauler, Johannes   TOU-ler, yoh-HAHN-us

Tenochtitlán   tay-NAWCH-teet-LAWN

Tertullian   tur-TULL-yun

Theocritus   thee-OCK-ri-tus

Theodora   thee-uh-DOR-uh

Theognis   thee-OGG-nus

Thermidor   ter-mee-DOR

Thermopylae   thur-MOP-uh-lee

Thiers, Adolphe   tee-ER, a-DOLF

Thucydides   thoo-SID-uh-deez

Thutmosis   thoot-MOH-sus

Tiberius   tie-BIR-ee-us

Tiepolo, Giovanni Battista   tee-AY-puh-loh, joe-VAHN-ee baht-TEES-tah

Tiglath-pileser   TIG-lath-puh-LEE-zur

Tirpitz, Admiral von   TUR-puts

Tito   TEE-toh

Tlaxcala   tlah-SKAHL-uh

Torah   TOR-uh

Tordesillas   tor-duh-SEE-yus

Trajan   TRAY-jun

Trevithick, Richard   TREV-uh-thik

Tristan, Flora   TRIS-tun

Tyche   TIE-kee

Ulbricht, Walter   UL-brikt, VAHL-ter

Umayyads   oo-MY-ads

Unam Sanctam   OON-ahm   SANK-tahm

universitas   yoo-ni-VER-si-tahs

Valois   VAL-wah

van Eyck, Jan   van IKE

van Gogh, Vincent   van GOE

Vasa, Gustavus   VAH-suh, gus-STAY-vus

Vega, Lope de   VAY-guh, LOH-pay day

Vendée   vahn-DAY

Venetia   vuh-NEE-shee-uh

Vesalius, Andreas   vi-SAY-lee-us, ahn-DRAY-us

Vespasian   ves-PAY-zhun

Vespucci, Amerigo   ves-POO-chee, ahm-ay-REE-goe

Vichy   VISH-ee

Vierzenheiligen   feer-tsun-HILE-i-gun

Virchow, Rudolf   FEER-koh, roo-DOLF

Virgil   VUR-jul

Volkschulen   FOLK-shool-un

Voltaire   vole-TAIR

von Bora, Katherina   BOR-uh

Wagner, Richard   VAHG-ner, RIK-art

Walesa, Lech   va-WENZ-uh, LEK

Wallachia   wah-lay-KEE-uh

Wallenstein, Albrecht von   WOLL-un-stine, AWL-brekt

Watteau, Antoine   wah-TOE, AHN-twahn

Wannsee   VAHN-say

Weizsäcker, Richard von   VITS-zek-er, RIK-art

wergeld   wur-GELD

Windischgrätz, Alfred   vin-dish-GRETS

Winkelmann, Maria   VING-kul-mun

Witte, Sergei   VIT-uh, syir-GYAY

Worms, Edict of   WURMZ *or* VAWRMZ

Wyclif, John   WIK-lif

Xavier, Francis   ZAY-vee-ur

Xerxes   ZURK-seez

Xhosa   KOH-suh

Ximenes   hee-MAY-nus

Yahweh   YAH-wah

Yeats, William Butler   YATES

Yeltsin, Boris   YELT-sun

yishuv   YISH-uv

Zemsky Sobor   ZEM-skee SOH-bur

zemstvos   ZEMPST-voh

Zeno   ZEE-noh

Zeus   ZOOS

Zhivkov, Todor   ZHEV-kof, toh-DOR

ziggurat   ZIG-guh-rat

Zimmermann, Domenikus   TSIM-ur-mahn, doe-MEE-nee-kus

Zinzendorf, Nikolaus von   ZIN-zun-dorf, nee-koh-LAH-us

Zola, Emile   ZOH-luh, ay-MEEL

zollverein   TSOL-fuh-rine

Zoroaster   ZOR-oh-as-ter

Index

Note: Page references in italics indicate map or figure.

Continental Congress, American, 552
Continental System of Napoleon I, 577, 578, 590
Contraception (birth control)
    in 18th century, 535
    in late 19th century, 694–95
    in 20th century, 871, 899
Cook, James, 736
Cook, Thomas, 700–701
Copernicus, 461, 463–64
    heliocentric universe of, *465, 466, 468–70*
Coral Sea, Battle of (1942), 828
Corn Laws (British), 616, 626, 627
Cortés, Hernán (Spanish explorer), 394, 397–99
Corvinus, Matthias (king of Hungary), 356–67
Cossacks, revolt of Russian, in 1767, 526
Cotton
    production of, in American South, 662
    textile manufacturing and, 538, 584–85, 586, *590,* 593, 599
    working conditions in mills, 601, 602
Council for Mutual Economic Assistance (COMECON), 851
Council of Constance (1414-1418), 315, 358
Council of Pisa (1409), 315
Council of Trent (1542), 388–90, 438
Counter Reformation, 386–90
Counterterrorism, 900
Courbet, Gustave, 673, *674,* 675
Courtly society of Italian Renaissance, 329–31
Courts
    Consistory, in Geneva, 383–84
    in 18th century, 506–7
Craftspeople and artisans
    contemporary art and, 904
    of Dutch republic, 466–67
    French, at time of French Revolution, 556
    Luddites, 605
    as 19th-century urban workers, 600, 694
    women and Scientific Revolution linked to, 474
Cranmer, Thomas, 381
Creation of Adam (Michelangelo), *349*
Crécy, Battle of (1346), 305, *306*
Crime
    control of, in 19th century, 631–35
    Nazi war crime trials, 865
    prison reform in 19th century, 635–36
    punishment of criminals in 18th century, 506–7
    in Renaissance Italy, 332
Crimean War (1854-1856), 648–49
Crisis of confidence in early 20th century, 711
Croatia and Croats, 631, 658, 778
    disintegration of Yugoslavia and, 890, 891
Crompton, Samuel, 584
Cromwell, Oliver
    English civil wars and Commonwealth and, 448–49
    New Model Army of, 415, 448
Cromwell, Thomas, 381, 407
Crystal Palace, 589
Cuban missile crisis (1962), 852–54
Cubism, 720, *722*
Culture. *See also* Intellectual life

European, in mid-16th to mid-17th centuries, 418–23
European, in 17th century, 455–58
high, in 18th century, 504–6
history (*see* Historiography)
in Late Middle Ages (14th century), 317–20
in late 19th and early 20th century, 711–22
in late 20th century, 903–12
popular (*see* Popular culture)
radio and movies in mass culture of 20th century, 806
Romanticism and, in 19th century, 636–41
between world wars of 20th century, 808–12
Curie, Marie, 711, *712*
Curie, Pierre, 711
Cut with the Kitchen Knife. (Höch), *809*
Cyprus, 404
Czechoslovakia
    Communist control of post-World War II, 860, 862
    democracy in, 887
    formation of, 774, 778
    Nazi German annexation of, 819–20
    participation of, in Little Entente, 782
    Prague Spring and revolt of 1968 in, 862, 863, 882
    between world wars, 805
Czech Republic, 887
Czechs, 356, 658
    Hussitism in, 358
    uprising of, in Austrian empire, 629–30
    in World War I, 763

D

Dada art, 809
Daily life. *See also* Family life; Society and social structures
    at court of Louis XIV, 431–33
    in World War I trenches, 756–59
Daimler, Gottlieb, 680
Dali, Salvador, 810
Danish War (1864), 653
Dante, *Divine Comedy* of, 317–18
Danton, Georges, 565, 566
Darwin, Charles, theory of evolution by, 668–70, 716
Darwinism, social, 714–16
David (Donatello), 346, *347*
David (Michelangelo), 348, *349*
David, Jacques-Louis (artist), 502, *558*
Da Vinci, Leonardo, 345, 347–48, 350, 462
Dawes Plan, 783
Dayton Accords (1995), 890
Death camps, Nazi, 832–35
Death of Sardanapolis, The (Delacroix), 639, *640*
Debussy, Claude, 721–22
Decameron, The (Boccaccio), 299, 300, 319
Declaration of Independence, American, 517, 552, 553, 561
Declaration of the Rights of Man and the Citizen, French, 555, 561, 562, 620
Declaration of the Rights of Woman and the Female Citizen, French, 562, 563

Decline and Fall of the Roman Empire (Gibbon), 504, 505
Decline of the West (Spengler), 808
Defender of the Peace (Marsiglio of Padua), 315
Defense of the Realm Act (DORA, British), 763
Defoe, Daniel, 584
De Gaulle, Charles, 831, 858, 864
Deism, 491
Delacroix, Eugène, *615, 639, 640*
Demian (Hesse), 811, 812
Democracy and democratic states
    growth of, in 19th-century western Europe, 702–5
    growth of, in 20th-century eastern Europe, 886–87
    between world wars, 786–89, 805
Demoiselles d'Avignon (Picasso), 720, *722*
Denmark
    Danish War of 1864 with Prussia, 653
    Lutheranism in, 375–76
    monarchy in 17th-century, 441
    monarchy in 18th-century, 528
    Thirty Years' War and, 412–13
    World War II and, 821, 822
    between world wars, 788
Department store, growth of mass consumerism and, 680, 681
Departure for Egypt (Kiefer), *904*
Descartes, René, 476–77, 478
Descent of Man, The (Darwin), 669
D'Este, Isabella, 335
    letters of, 337
Diaghilev, Sergei, 722
Dialogue on the Two Chief World Systems: Ptolemaic and Copernican (Galileo), 469, 470
Dias, Bartholomeu, 395
Dickens, Charles, 673
Diderot, Denis, 491–92, *493,* 517
    on Christian sexual standards, 494
    on 18th-century Paris hospitals, 508
    on Jews, 511
    on women, 497
Diefenbaker, John, 869
Diet. *See* Food and diet
Diet of Augsburg (1530), 373, 374
Diplomacy
    balance of power, 335–36, 529, 611, 645
    birth of modern, in Italian Renaissance, 336–37
    Bismarck's alliance system in 19th century and, 739–40
    of brinksmanship, World War I and, 748–51
    late 19th-century alliances and creation of two opposing camps, 711, 740–44
Directory, French, 572
Discourse on Method (Descartes), 476, 477, 478
Discovery, age of expansionism and (16th and 17th centuries)
    impact of, 400–401
    motives for, 393–95
    Portuguese maritime empire, 395–96
    Spanish empire in New World, 397–400
    voyages to New World, 396–97
Disraeli, Benjamin, 660, 661, 724

European Atomic Energy Commission (EURATOM), 866
European Coal and Steel Community (ECSC), 866
European Community (EC), 894
European Economic Community (Common Market), 866–67
European Recovery Program (Marshall Plan), 849, 863, 866
European Union, 894
Evolution, Charles Darwin and theory of, 668–70, 716
Evolutionary Socialism (Bernstein), 685, 686
Existentialism, 905–6
Expansionism. *See* Discovery, age of expansionism and (16th and 17th centuries); Imperialism
Explorers, 393, 395–97, 736
Eyeglasses, invention of, 323

F

Fabian Socialists (British political party), 728
Facetiae (Poggio Bracciolini), 341–42
Factory Acts (British), 602, 605
Factory system
    automation in, 682
    development of, in Industrial Revolution, 588–89
    women in, during World War I, 764, *765*
    working conditions in, in 19th century, 600–603
Falklands War (1982), 896
Fall of the House of Usher, The (Poe), 638
Family life
    breakdown of traditional, in late 20th century, 873–74
    European, in 18th century, 533–36
    in Fascist Italy, 793
    impact of World War I on, 766
    in late 19th century, 694–98
    Protestant Reformation and idea of, 384
    in Renaissance Italy, 332–34
Famine and malnutrition
    in Ireland, in 19th century, 596
    in Soviet Union, in 20th century, 801, 803
    in 13th and 14th centuries, 297
Fanon, Frantz, 856
Farady, Michael, 668
Fascio di Combattimento, 789, 790
Fascism
    birth of, 789–90
    in France, 787–88
    in Italy, 789–93
    Mussolini on, 792
    in Nazi Germany, 794, 795–801 (*see also* Germany, Nazi)
    in Spain, 805–6
Fawcett, Millicent, 723
Fedele, Cassandra, 344
Federalist Party (United States), 627
Feltre, Vittorino da, 342
Feminine Mystique, The (Friedan), 872–73
Feminism. *See also* Women's rights
    alignment of, with other social issues in late 20th century, 899–900
    voting rights, 710–11, 723–24
    M. Wollstonecraft as founder of, 497–98
    women's rights movement in late 19th and early 20th centuries, 723–24

women's rights movement in post-World War II era, 872–73
    utopianism and, 623
Ferdinand (Holy Roman emperor), 412
Ferdinand I (emperor of Austria), 629
Ferdinand I (king of Naples and Sicily), 613
Ferdinand VII (king of Spain), 613, 616–17
Ferdinand of Aragon, 336, 354–55
Feudalism, political instability with breakdown of, 309
Ficino, Marsilio, 342
Fielden, Joshua, 599
Fielding, Henry, 504
Film and motion picture, 806, 910
Finance in 18th century, 537–38. *See also* Banking industry
Finland, 778, 820
Flagellants movement, 299, *300*
Flanders
    manufacturing in, 328
    Renaissance art in, 351
    workers' revolts in, 304, 305
Flaubert, Gustave, 672
Florence (Italy), 312
    artists of, 320, 345
    Black Death in, 298, 299, 300, 320
    economic recovery of, 328
    humanism in Renaissance, 340–42
    Renaissance in, 334, *334*
    rule of medieval, by patrician class, 304
    workers' revolts in medieval, 304
Foch, Ferdinand, 773
Fontenelle, Bernard de, 487–88
Food and diet
    18th-century peasant, 542
    Renaissance banquet, 330
Food crops from Americas, 536–37
Food supply
    contamination of, in 19th-century cities, 598
    increase in, in 18th-century Europe, 536, 583
    Irish famine of 19th century, 596
    legislation for protection of, 598, 731
    pasteurization and, 670
    shortages in France at time of French Revolution, 557
Ford, Gerald (U. S. president), 897
Ford, Henry, 680
Fourier, Charles, 622
France
    absolute monarchy in, in 17th century, 427–35
    anti-Semitism in, in 19th century, 724
    appeasement of Hitler by, 817–21
    Austro-Prussian War (1866) and, 651, 653–55
    Black Death in, 298, *299*
    colonies of, 734, 737, 854
    Crimean War and, 648–49
    decolonization of, 855–56, *857*, 858
    C. de Gaulle as leader of (Fourth Republic), 864
    Franco-Prussian War and, 647, 651, 655–56
    Great Depression in, 784, 787–88
    growth of democracy in Third Republic of late 19th century, 703–4
    growth of monarchy in, during Renaissance, 353–54

guest workers and refugees in, 901
    Habsburg-Valois wars between Germany and, 372–73
    Hundred Years' War between England and, 304–9
    industrialization in, 591–92, 593
    involvement of, in Italian city-states, 336
    July Revolution in, in 19th century, 623–24
    monarchy of, in 18th century, 518, 519
    under Napoleon I, 572–79
    under Napoleon III, 645–49
    Nazi occupation of, 821–22
    parliament (Estates-General) of, 310, 557
    peasant revolts in medieval, 301–2, 303
    police force in, in 19th century, 632–33
    politics and economy of, in late 20th century, 896
    problems of monarchy of, in 14th century, 309–10
    restoration of Bourbon monarchy in (1815), 616
    revolution in (*see* French Revolution (1789-1799))
    revolution of 1848 and Second Republic of, 627–28
    Seven Years' War and, 530–32
    social unrest in (1968), 864, 874, *876*
    Thirty Years' War and role of, 411, 413
    tough enforcement of World War I peace treaty by, 782–83
    Triple Entente including, 711, 741
    Vichy government in, 822
    Wars of Religion in (1562-1598), 401–3
    World War I and, 750, 752–67
    World War II and, 821–22, 828
    World War II resistance movements in, 831
    between world wars, 787–88
Franciscan order, 386
Francis I (emperor of Austria), 609
Francis I (king of France), 336, *373*, 382, 401
Francis Ferdinand, Archduke, assassination of, 748
Francis Joseph I (emperor of Austria), 629–30, 657, 706
Francis of Assisi, Saint, 386
Francken, Frans, the Young, *416*
Franco, Francisco, dictatorship of, 805–6
Franco-Prussian War (1870-1871), 647, 651, 655–56
Frankenstein (Shelley), 636
Frederick I (king of Denmark), 375
Frederick II (king of Denmark), 465
Frederick II the Great (king of Prussia), 509, 517, 518, 521, 523, 530
Frederick III (Holy Roman emperor), 356
Frederick III of Brandenburg-Prussia, 437
Frederick IV (Elector of Palatinate), 412
Frederick V (Elector of Palatinate), 412
Frederick William II (king of Prussia), 564
Frederick William III (king of Prussia), 617
Frederick William IV (king of Prussia), 628, 652
Frederick William of Brandenburg-Prussia (the Great Elector), 436–37, 521–22
Free Democrat political party, 864, 894
Freemasons, 500
French and Indian War (Seven Years' War), 530–32, 551

786, 865–66, 894–96
impact of World War I "total war" on, 761–62
in Italy in 19th century, 728
in Italy in 20th century, 790–93, 866, 897
in Japan, 738–39
Montesquieu on three kinds of, 490
Polish, in 18th century, 526–28
in Portugal in 20th century, 806
Russian, in 17th century, 439–40
Russian, in 18th century, 525–26
Russian, in 19th century, 618–19, 659, 707, 729
Russian, in 20th century, 762, 768–71, 801–4
separation of powers in, 490
A. Smith on basic functions of, 493
in Soviet Union, 802–4, 859–60, 882–85
in Spain in 20th century, 805–6
support for industrialization from, 583–84, 591
of United States, foundation of, 553–54
of United States in 20th century, 788–89, 868
of West Germany, 864–65, 887–89
of Yugoslavia, disintegration of, 890–93
Granada, kingdom of, 354
Grand Alliance (Britain, United States, Soviet Union), 841–44
Grandeur and Misery of Victory (Clemenceau), 775
Grand National Consolidated Trades Union, 605
Grand Tour, 544–45
Gravitation, I. Newton's studies on, 470, 471
Great Britain. *See also* England; Scotland
agricultural revolution in, in 18th century, 536–37
appeasement of Hitler by Chamberlain of, 818–21
aristocratic life in, in 18th century, 543–45
in Boer War, 733, 741
W. Churchill as wartime leader of, 822–23, 838
colonial empire of, 539–41, 732–34, 736, 737, 739
conservative order in control of (1815-1830), 615–16
Crimean War and, 648–49
decolonization of, 855–56, 865
democracy and reform in, in late 19th century, 702–3
in 18th century, 518–21, 543–45
emergence of Cold War between Soviet Union and, 841–44
formation of (1707), 518
Great Depression in, 786, 787
industrial revolution in, 583–90
Parliament in (*see* Parliament, English/British)
police force in, in 19th century, 633–35
reformism in, in 19th century, 599, 605, 625–27, 660–61, 690–92
revolution of American colonies and, 551–55
Seven Years' War and, 530–32
Thatcher era in, 894–96
Triple Entente including, 711, 741

Victorian age in, 660–61
war against Napoleon I and, 576, 577, 578, 579
welfare state in post-World War II, 865–66
women's movement in, 723–24
World War I and, 750, 752–67
World War II home front and, 835–36, 838–39
World War II military actions and, 821–22, 826–28
between world wars, 786, 787
Great Depression (1929), 782, 784–86, 809
democratic states' response to, 787–89
Great Exhibition (Great Britain in 1851), 589–90
Great Northern War (1701-1721), 440–41
Great Schism, 314–15
Greco-Roman culture
Enlightenment as heir to, 487
humanism based on, 338–45, 363–66
Renaissance of 15th century in Italy and, 327
Greece
Balkan League including, 743–44
civil war in post-World War II, 848
revolution against Ottoman Turks, 614–15, 637
World War II and, 823, 841
between world wars, 805
Green movements, 901–3
Green Party (Germany), 899–900, 901, 902
Gregory XI, 314
Grieg, Edvard, 721
Grimm Brothers, 636
Grimmelshausen, Jakob von, on warfare in 17th century, 414
Groote, Gerard, 316
Gropius, Walter, 810, *811*
Guest workers, 900, 901
violence against, in Germany, 902
Guicciardini, Francesco, 344
Guilds, craft and merchant, 600
Guise family, French Wars of Religion and, 402–3
Gulf War (1990), 881
Gunpowder, invention of, 323–24
Gustavus III (king of Sweden), 528
Gustavus Adolphus (king of Sweden), 413, 415, 441
Gutenberg, Johannes, 344
Gymnasium, Protestant, 385–86
Gypsies, Nazi Holocaust and, 834

H

Habsburg dynasty, 336, 355–56, 372–74
in early 19th century, 617–18
emergence of Austria in 17th century under, 437–38
Thirty Years' War and, 411
War of Austrian Succession and, 523, 529
Habsburg-Valois Wars (mid-16th century), 373, 374
Haiti, 540–41
Hamburg, Germany, World War II bombing of, 838, 839
Hamilton, Alexander, 627
Handbook of the Christian Knight, The (Erasmus), 364

Handel, George Frederick, 502–3
Hanover dyansty (Great Britain), 519
Hanseatic League, 328
Hargreaves, James, 584
Harkort, Fritz, 591
Harvey, William
anatomical studies of, 473
on human reproduction, 475
Hauser, Heinrich, 785
Havel, Vaclav, 862, 887
call for new politics by, 888
Hawaiian Islands, 737
Haydn, Franz Joseph, 503
Health. *See also* Medicine
public, in Late Middle Ages, 320, 323
public, in 19th-century industrialized cities, 597–99
revolution in health care in 19th century, 670–72
Hebrew people. *See* Jews and Judaism
Heisenberg, Werner, 812
Hellenistic civilization. *See* Greco-Roman culture
Helsinki Agreements (1975), 880
Henry II (king of France), 374, 401
Henry III (king of England), 304–5
Henry III (king of France), 403
Henry IV (king of England), 309
Henry V (king of England), 307
Henry VII (king of England), 354
Henry VIII (king of England), 397, 406
Reformation and, 380–81
Henry of Navarre, 403
Henry the Navigator (prince of Portugal), 394, 395
Heresy, Christian
Inquisition and (*see* Inquisition)
Lollardy and Hussitism in Renaissance, 358–59, 380
Martin Luther and charges of, 362–63
papal-state conflicts and, 313
Hermeticism, 342, 462, 470, 471, 483
Herzegovina. *See* Bosnia-Herzegovina
Herzen, Alexander, 659–60
Herzl, Theodor, 726, 727
Hesse, Hermann, 811, 812
Heydrich, Reinhard, 832
Hill, Octavia (housing reformer), 690, 691
Himmler, Heinrich, 800, 830, 832
Hindenburg, Paul von, 754, 761, 762, 794, 796
Historical and Critical Dictionary (Bayle), 488
Historiography
Enlightenment and philosophes' work in, 504
Middle Ages, 302, 303, 306
Renaissance humanism and, 344
History of a Collective Farm (Belov), 803
History of the Cotton Manufacture in Great Britain (Baines), 585
Hitler, Adolf, 724–25, 774, 793–801. *See also* Germany, Nazi
anti-Semitism of, 794, 795, 829, 831, 832
on art, 811
death of, 829
"diplomatic revolution" of (1933-1936), 817–18
formation of Nazi party by, 794–95
Holocaust and "final solution" of, 831–34

famine and emigration from, in 19th century, 596
nationalism and home rule in, 702–3
Irish Republican Army (IRA), 894, 900
Iron industry, 586–87
Irrational, modern understanding of the, 712–13
Isabella II (queen of Spain), 655
Isabella of Castile (queen of Spain), 354–55
Islam, 355
Israel, 856, 900
Italy, fascism in, in 20th century, 789–90. *See also* Italy/Italian states
alliance with Germany and conquest of Ethiopia by, 818
birth of, 789–90
declaration of war against France by, 822
invasion of Greece by, 723
invasion of Italy by Allied troops, 828
mass leisure (*Dopolavoro*) in, 807–8
Mussolini and Fascist Italian state, 790–93
Italy/Italian states
Black Death in, 298, 299, 300, 304
city-states of medieval, 311–12
colonies of, 734
Congress of Vienna intervention in, 616
in 18th century, 528
fascism in (*see* Italy, fascism in, in 20th century)
guest workers and refugees in, 901
in late 19th century, 704–5, 728
nationalist uprising in, in 19th century, 625
national unification of, in 19th century, 649–51, 652
politics and economy of, in post-war 20th century, 866, 897
Renaissance in (*see* Renaissance)
revolts in, in 19th century, 613, 625, 630, 631
Spanish and Austrian rule of, in 17th century, 438
trading cities of medieval northern, 298
Triple Alliance of 1882 including, 711, 740, 741
in World War I, 754, 759
in World War II, 818, 822, 823, 828
Ivan III of Russia, 357
Ivan IV of Russia, 438

J

Jackson, Andrew, 627
Jacobins, 564
Jacquerie peasants' revolt, 301–2, 303
Jamaica, 540
James I (king of England), 447, 468
James II (king of England), 449, 450
Janissaries, 443
Japan
atomic bomb dropped on (1945), 829, 839, 840, 841
Meiji Restoration in, 738
Russo-Japanese War (1904-1905), 729, 736
United States imperialism in, and responses of, 737–39
in World War II, 816, 823–26, 839–41, 855
Japanese-Americans, 837

Jaruzelski, Wojciech, 886
Jefferson, Thomas, 552, 553, 627
Jesuits, 386, 387–89
state attempts to control, 511
Jewish State, The (Herzl), 726, 727
Jews and Judaism
Enlightenment and attitudes toward, 511–12
in nation-states of late 19th and early 20th centuries, 724–27
persecution of Jews by Nazi Germany (Holocaust), 800–801, 831–35
persecution of Jews in Middle Ages, 300–301, 302, 355
as religious minority in unified Spain, 355
Zionism and, 726–27
Jex-Blake, Sophia, 672
Joan of Arc, 307–8
John II (king of France), 306
John IV (king of Portugal), 435
John XXIII (pope), 907
John of Leiden, 379
John Paul II (pope), 907
Johnson, Lyndon B. (U. S. president), 854, 867, 868
Johnson, Samuel, 545
Joint-stock investment banks, 592, 664
Joint-stock trading companies, 409–10, 587
Joseph II (emperor of Austria), 511–12, 518, 524–25, 528
Joyce, James, 811
Judaism. *See* Jews and Judaism
Judith Beheading Holofernes, 420, *421*
Julius II (pope), 326–27, 359
July Revolution (France), 624
Jung, Carl, 812
Junkers (German class), 436, 522, 653
Justification through faith doctrine, 367–68, 382
Jutland, Battle of (1916), 759

K

Kádár, János, 862, 886
Kandinsky, Vasily, 720, *722*
Kansas-Nebraska Act of 1854, 662
Kant, Immanuel, 487
Kapital, Das (Marx), 666
Karlsbad Decrees of 1819 (Germany), 617
Kay-Shuttleworth, James, 598
Kellogg-Briand pact, 783
Kelly, Petra, 899–900
Kempis, Thomas à, 367
Kennan, George, 850
Kennedy, John F. (U. S. president), 852, 867, 868
Cuban missile crisis and, 852–54
Kepler, Johannes, 465–66, *468*, 481
laws of planetary motion by, 466
letters of, to other scientists, 467
Keymer, John, on Dutch economics, 446
Keynes, John Maynard, 470, 778, 786
Khrushchev, Nikita, 852
on Cuban missile crisis, 853
denunciation of Stalin by, 859, 860
government of, 859–60, 861
Kiefer, Anselm, 904
Kingship, 353–58. *See also* Monarchies; Queenship
Kipling, Rudyard, 734
Kirch, Gottfried, 474

Knighton, Henry, 296–97
Knights, 305
Knox, John (Calvinist reformer), 384, 406
Knox, John (historian), 531
Kohl, Helmut, 894
Kollontai, Alexandra, 770–71
Königshofen, Jacob von, 302
Korea, 729, 737
post-World War II division of, 851–52, 868
Korean War (1950-1953), 852, 865
Kosovo, war in Yugoslavian province of, 891
Kossuth, Louis, 658
Krämer, Heinrich, 416
Kristallnacht (Nazi Germany), 800, *801*
Krupp, Bertha, 693
Kulaks (Soviet Union), 803
Kursk, Battle of (1943), 828
Kuwait, 881

L

Labor, 588–89, 594, 600–603. *See also* Workers; Working class
children and women in industrial, 601, 602, 603
efforts to organize and improve conditions in, 604–6
guest workers and migrants in late 20th century, 900–901, 902
impact of World War I on, 763–65
Solidarity movement in Poland, 886
unions (*see* Trade unions)
in United States, 731
Labour Party (British political party), 728, 786, 865, 896
Lafayette, marquis de, 554–55, 560
Laissez-faire economics, 493, 619
Lamarck, Jean-Baptiste, 668
Landing of Marie de' Medici at Marsailles (Rubens), *420*
Landscape with the Burial of Phocian (Poussin), *455*
Languages
distribution of, in 19th-century Europe, *622*
English, 422
Greek, 341
Latin, 341
Laocöon (El Greco), *419*
Las Casas, Bartolomé de, 400
Last Conquest of Ireland, The (Mitchell), 596
Last Supper, The (Leonardo da Vinci), *347*
Lateran Accords (1929), 793
Latin America
European colonial empires in, 396–400, 540
nationalist revolutions in, in 19th century, 613–14
Latin Christian Church. *See* Roman Catholic Church
Latvia, 778, 820
Lavasseur, E., on Parisian department stores, 681
Law
labor, 602, 603, 604, 605
Napoleon I and codification of French, 575
reduced legal rights for women in 14th century, 321
Russian, Catherine the Great's proposals for new, 525

Yeltsin, Boris, 880, 885
Young, Arthur, on 18th-century agricultural revolution, 537
Young Girl by the Window (Morisot), *719*
Young Italy movement in 19th century, 630, 631
Yugoslavia
    disintegration of, in late 20th century, 890–93
    formation of, 778
    participation of, in Little Entente, 782
    post-World War II communist government of, 861
    Tito as leader of, 831, *861*
    war in Bosnia and, *890*, 893
    war in Kosovo and, 891
    World War II and, 823, 831, 841
    between world wars, 805

Z

Zell, Katherine, 385
Zemstvos, 659

Zhivkov, Todor, 887
Zimmermann, Domenikus, 501–2
Zinzendorf, Nikolaus von, 512
Zionism, 726–27
Zola, Émile, 717
Zürich, Switzerland, 378
    Zwinglian reformation in, *376*, 377
Zweig, Stefan, 753
Zwingli, Ulrich, 376–78
Zwinglian reformation, 376–78